The American
DEMOCRACY

The American
DEMOCRACY
Ninth Edition

Thomas E. Patterson

Bradlee Professor of Government and the Press
John F. Kennedy School of Government
Harvard University

 **Higher Education**

Boston   Burr Ridge, IL   Dubuque, IA   Madison, WI   New York   San Francisco   St. Louis
Bangkok   Bogotá   Caracas   Kuala Lumpur   Lisbon   London   Madrid   Mexico City
Milan   Montreal   New Delhi   Santiago   Seoul   Singapore   Sydney   Taipei   Toronto

Higher Education

THE AMERICAN DEMOCRACY

Published by McGraw-Hill, an imprint of The McGraw-Hill Companies, Inc., 1221 Avenue of the Americas, New York, NY 10020. Copyright © 2009, 2008, 2005, 2003, 2001, 1999, 1997, 1993, 1990. All rights reserved. No part of this publication may be reproduced or distributed in any form or by any means, or stored in a database or retrieval system, without the prior written consent of The McGraw-Hill Companies, Inc., including, but not limited to, in any network or other electronic storage or transmission, or broadcast for distance learning.

This book is printed on acid-free paper.

1 2 3 4 5 6 7 8 9 0 CCI/CCI 0 9 8

ISBN: 978-0-07-340387-8
MHID: 0-07-340387-3

Editor in Chief: *Michael Ryan*
Director, Editorial: *Beth Mejia*
Sponsoring Editor: *Mark Georgiev*
Marketing Manager: *Bill Minick*
Director of Development: *Nancy Crochiere*
Developmental Editor: *Erin K. Grelak*
Production Editor: *David Blatty*
Manuscript Editor: *Thomas L. Briggs*

Design Manager: *Ashley Bedell*
Text Designer: *Elise Lansdon*
Cover Designer: *Irene Morris*
Lead Photo Editor: *Alexandra Ambrose*
Photo Research: *Toni Michaels/PhotoFind*
Production Supervisor: *Rich DeVitto*
Composition: *10/12 Palatino by Aptara®, Inc.*
Printing: *45# Publishers Matte Plus, Courier*

Cover Photos: All photos royalty-free except the following. Barack Obama: © Chip Somodevilla/Getty Images; John McCain: © David McNew/Getty Images; Jon Stewart: © Duffy-Marie Arnoult/WireImage/Getty Images; Nancy Pelosi: © SAUL LOEB/AFP/Getty Images; Hillary Clinton: © MANDEL NGAN/AFP/Getty Images; Cesar Chavez: © Arthur Schatz/Time Life Pictures/Getty Images; Rosa Parks: © Angel Franco/New York Times Co./Getty Images; Martin Luther King, Jr.: Library of Congress; Ronald Reagan: Library of Congress; John F. Kennedy: Library of Congress, Prints and Photographs Division [LC-USZ62-117124]; Jacqueline Kennedy Onassis: Library of Congress, Prints & Photographs Division [LC-USZ62-21796; Abraham Lincoln: Library of Congress, Prints and Photographs Division [LC-USZ62-13016]; George Washington: Library of Congress, Prints and Photographs Division [LC-USZ62-7265]; Eleanor Roosevelt: Library of Congress, Prints & Photographs Division [LC-USZ62-25812]; Franklin D. Roosevelt: Library of Congress.

Credits: The credits section for this book begins on page 545 and is considered an extension of the copyright page

Library of Congress Cataloging-in-Publication Data

Patterson, Thomas E.
    The American democracy / Thomas Patterson. — 9th ed.
        p. cm.
    Includes index.
    ISBN-13: 978-0-07-340387-8 (alk. paper)
    ISBN-10: 0-07-340387-3 (alk. paper)
    1. United States—Politics and government—Textbooks.   I. Title.
JK276.P37 2008c
320.473—dc22   2008045659

The Internet addresses listed in the text were accurate at the time of publication. The inclusion of a Web site does not indicate an endorsement by the authors or McGraw-Hill, and McGraw-Hill does not guarantee the accuracy of the information presented at these sites.

www.mhhe.com

About the Author

THOMAS E. PATTERSON is Bradlee Professor of Government and the Press in the John F. Kennedy School of Government at Harvard University. He was previously Distinguished Professor of Political Science in the Maxwell School of Citizenship at Syracuse University. Raised in a small Minnesota town near the Iowa and South Dakota borders, he attended South Dakota State University as an undergraduate and served in the military in Vietnam before enrolling at the University of Minnesota, where he received his Ph.D. in 1971.

He is the author of numerous books and articles, which focus mainly on elections and the media. His book *The Vanishing Voter* (2002) describes and explains the long-term decline in Americans' electoral participation. An earlier book, *Out of Order* (1994), received national attention when President Clinton said every politician and journalist should be required to read it. In 2002, *Out of Order* received the American Political Science Association's Graber Award for the best book of the past decade in political communication. Another of Patterson's books, *The Mass Media Election* (1980), received a *Choice* award as Outstanding Academic Book, 1980–1981. Patterson's first book, *The Unseeing Eye* (1976), was selected by the American Association for Public Opinion Research as one of the fifty most influential books of the past half-century in the field of public opinion.

His research has been funded by major grants from the National Science Foundation, the Markle Foundation, the Smith-Richardson Foundation, the Ford Foundation, the Knight Foundation, The Carnegie Corporation, and the Pew Charitable Trusts.

Contents in Brief

Preface xviii | Supplements Package xxii | Acknowledgments xxiii

PART 1 Foundations

1 American Political Culture: Seeking a More
Perfect Union   3

2 Constitutional Democracy: Promoting Liberty
and Self-Government   27

3 Federalism: Forging a Nation   57

4 Civil Liberties: Protecting Individual Rights   85

5 Equal Rights: Struggling Toward Fairness   117

PART 2 Mass Politics

6 Public Opinion and Political Socialization: Shaping
the People's Voice   147

7 Political Participation and Voting: Activating the
Popular Will   171

8 Political Parties, Candidates, and Campaigns: Defining
the Voters' Choice   191

9 Interest Groups: Organizing for Influence   221

10 The News Media: Communicating Political Images   247

PART 3 Governing Institutions

11 Congress: Balancing National Goals
and Local Interests   275

12 The Presidency: Leading the Nation   307

13 The Federal Bureaucracy: Administering
the Government   339

14 The Federal Judicial System: Applying the Law   365

PART 4 Public Policy

15 Economic and Environmental Policy: Contributing to Prosperity 393

16 Welfare and Education Policy: Providing for Personal Security and Need 425

17 Foreign and Defense Policy: Protecting
the American Way 449

18 State and Local Politics: Maintaining Our Differences 473

Appendixes 502

Glossary 524

Notes 533

Credits 545

Index 546

Contents

Preface xviii | Supplements Package xxii | Acknowledgments xxiii

PART 1 Foundations

1 American Political Culture: Seeking a More Perfect Union   3

Political Culture: The Core Principles of American Government   4

America's Core Values   5

   Liberty, Equality, and Self-Government   6

   The Power and Limits of Americans' Ideals   8

Politics: The Resolution of Conflict   12

   The Social Contract   14

   The Rules of American Politics   15

Political Power and Authority: The Control of Policy   18

   Theories of Power   19

   Who Governs?   21

The Concept of a Political System and This Book's Organization   22

Summary   24

Study Corner   24

2 Constitutional Democracy: Promoting Liberty and Self-Government   27

Before the Constitution: The Colonial and Revolutionary Experiences   29

   "The Rights of Englishmen"   29

   The Declaration of Independence   30

   The Articles of Confederation   30

   Shays's Rebellion: A Nation Dissolving   32

Negotiating Toward a Constitution   33

   The Great Compromise: A Two-Chamber Congress   33

   The North-South Compromise: The Issue of Slavery   34

   A Strategy for Ratification   36

   The Ratification Debate   36

   The Framers' Goals   37

Protecting Liberty: Limited Government   38
  Grants and Denials of Power   39
  Using Power to Offset Power   40
  *Separated Institutions Sharing Power:
    Checks and Balances   41*
  The Bill of Rights   43
  Judicial Review   44
Providing for Self-Government   46
  Democracy Versus Republic   46
  Limited Popular Rule   47
  Altering the Constitution: More Power to the People   48
Constitutional Democracy Today   52
Summary   53
Study Corner   53

3 Federalism: Forging a Nation   57

Federalism: National and State Sovereignty   58
  The Argument for Federalism   60
  The Powers of the Nation   63
  The Powers of the States   64
Federalism in Historical Perspective   64
  An Indestructible Union (1789–1865)   64
  Dual Federalism and Laissez-Faire Capitalism (1865–1937)   67
  Toward National Citizenship   72
Federalism Today   72
  Interdependency and Intergovernmental Relations   72
  Government Revenues and Intergovernmental Relations   73
  Devolution   76
The Public's Influence: Setting the Boundaries of
  Federal–State Power   79
Summary   80
Study Corner   81

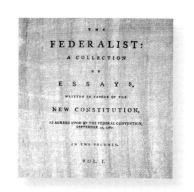

4 Civil Liberties: Protecting Individual Rights   85

Freedom of Expression   87
  *The Early Period: The Uncertain Status of the
    Right of Free Expression   88*
  The Modern Period: Protecting Free Expression   88
  Free Expression and State Governments   90
  Libel and Slander   93
  Obscenity   93

Freedom of Religion   95
  The Establishment Clause   96
  The Free-Exercise Clause   97
The Right to Bear Arms   98
The Right of Privacy   99
  Abortion   100
  Sexual Relations Among Consenting Adults   101
Rights of Persons Accused of Crimes   102
  Selective Incorporation of Procedural Rights   103
  Limits on Defendants' Rights   104
  Crime, Punishment, and Police Practices   107
Rights and the War on Terrorism   110
  Detention of Enemy Combatants   111
  Surveillance of Suspected Terrorists   112
The Courts and a Free Society   113
Summary   113
Study Corner   114

5   Equal Rights: Struggling Toward Fairness   117
The Struggle for Equality   118
  African Americans   118
  Women   120
  Native Americans   124
  Hispanic Americans   126
  Asian Americans   129
  Other Groups and Their Rights   130
Equality Under the Law   134
  *Equal Protection: The Fourteenth
    Amendment   134*
  *Equal Access: The Civil Rights Acts of 1964
    and 1968   135*
  *Equal Ballots: The Voting Rights Act of 1965,
    as Amended   136*
Equality of Result   137
  Affirmative Action: Workplace Integration   138
  Affirmative Action in the Law   139
  Busing: School Integration   140
Persistent Discrimination: Superficial Differences,
  Deep Divisions   142
Summary   143
Study Corner   143

PART 2 Mass Politics

6 Public Opinion and Political Socialization: Shaping the People's Voice 147

The Nature of Public Opinion 148

How Informed Is Public Opinion? 148

The Measurement of Public Opinion 150

Political Socialization: How Americans Learn Their Politics 154

The Process of Political Socialization 154

The Agents of Political Socialization 154

Frames of Reference: How Americans Think Politically 157

Cultural Thinking: Common Ideas 158

Ideological Thinking: The Outlook of Some 158

Group Thinking: The Outlook of Many 159

Partisan Thinking: The Line That Divides 162

The Influence of Public Opinion on Policy 164

Summary 167

Study Corner 167

7 Political Participation and Voting: Activating the Popular Will 171

Voter Participation 172

Factors in Voter Turnout: The United States in Comparative Perspective 173

Why Some Americans Vote and Others Do Not 179

Conventional Forms of Participation Other Than Voting 181

Campaign and Lobbying Activities 182

Virtual Participation 182

Community Activities 184

Unconventional Activism: Social Movements and Protest Politics 184

Participation and the Potential for Influence 186

Summary 187

Study Corner 188

8 Political Parties, Candidates, and Campaigns: Defining the Voters' Choice 191

Party Competition and Majority Rule: The History of U.S. Parties 192

The First Parties 193

Andrew Jackson and Grassroots Parties 194

*Republicans Versus Democrats: Realignments and the
    Enduring Party System 194*

Today's Party Alignment and Its Origins 196

Parties and the Vote 197

Electoral and Party Systems 199

The Single-Member-District System of Election 199

Politics and Coalitions in the Two-Party System 200

Minor (Third) Parties 202

Party Organizations 204

The Weakening of Party Organizations 205

The Structure and Role of Party Organizations 206

The Candidate-Centered Campaign 211

Campaign Funds: The Money Chase 211

Organization and Strategy: Hired Guns 211

Voter Contacts: Pitched Battle 214

Parties, Candidates, and the Public's Influence 215

Summary 217

Study Corner 218

9 Interest Groups: Organizing for Influence 221

The Interest-Group System 223

Economic Groups 223

Citizens' Groups 227

A Special Category of Interest Group: Governments 230

Inside Lobbying: Seeking Influence Through Official Contacts 230

Acquiring Access to Officials 231

Webs of Influence: Groups in the Policy Process 233

Outside Lobbying: Seeking Influence Through Public Pressure 235

Constituency Advocacy: Grassroots Lobbying 236

Electoral Action: Votes and PAC Money 236

The Group System: Indispensable but Biased 239

The Contribution of Groups to Self-Government: Pluralism 240

Flaws in Pluralism: Interest-Group Liberalism and Economic Bias 240

A Madisonian Dilemma 242

Summary 243

Study Corner 243

10 The News Media: Communicating Political Images   247

Historical Development: From the Nation's Founding to Today   249

The Objective Journalism Era   250

The Rise of the "New" News   251

The Politics of News   252

The Signaling Function   252

The Watchdog Function   256

The Common-Carrier Function   260

The Partisan Function   261

Attention to News   267

The Shrinking Audience for News   267

Age and Attention to News   268

Media and Public in the Internet Age   269

Summary   271

Study Corner   271

PART 3 Governing Institutions

11 Congress: Balancing National Goals and Local Interests   275

Congress as a Career: Election to Congress   277

Using Incumbency to Stay in Congress   277

Pitfalls of Incumbency   280

Safe Incumbency and Representation   283

Who Are the Winners in Congressional Elections?   283

Party Leadership in Congress   285

House Leadership   285

Senate Leadership   286

The Power of Party Leaders   286

The Committee System   288

Committee Jurisdiction   289

Committee Membership   290

Committee Chairs   291

Committees and Parties: Who Is in Control?   291

How a Bill Becomes Law   292

Committee Hearings and Decisions   292

From Committee to the Floor   294

Leadership and Floor Action   294

Conference Committees and the President   295

Congress's Policymaking Role 296

    The Lawmaking Function of Congress 296

    The Representation Function of Congress 299

    The Oversight Function of Congress 301

Congress: Too Much Pluralism? 302

Summary 303

Study Corner 304

12 The Presidency: Leading the Nation   307

Foundations of the Modern Presidency 309

    Asserting a Claim to National Leadership 311

    The Need for Presidential Leadership of an Activist Government 311

Choosing the President 313

    The Primary Elections 315

    The National Party Conventions 317

    The Campaign for Election 317

Staffing the Presidency 323

    Presidential Appointees 323

    The Problem of Control 325

Factors in Presidential Leadership 326

    The Force of Circumstance 327

    The Stage of the President's Term 327

    The Nature of the Issue: Foreign or Domestic 328

    Relations with Congress 329

    Public Support 332

Summary 335

Study Corner 336

13 The Federal Bureaucracy: Administering the Government   339

Federal Administration: Form, Personnel, and Activities 340

    The Structure of the Federal Bureaucracy 342

    Federal Employment 345

    The Federal Bureaucracy's Policy Responsibilities 345

Development of the Federal Bureaucracy: Politics and Administration 346

    Small Government and the Patronage System 346

    Growth in Government and the Merit System 347

    Big Government and the Executive Leadership System 348

The Bureaucracy's Power Imperative   350
   The Agency Point of View   350
   Sources of Bureaucratic Power   351
Bureaucratic Accountability   353
   Accountability Through the Presidency   354
   Accountability Through Congress   357
   Accountability Through the Courts   358
   Accountability Within the Bureaucracy Itself   359
Reinventing Government?   360
Summary   361
Study Corner   362

14 The Federal Judicial System: Applying the Law   365

The Federal Judicial System   367
   The Supreme Court of the United States   367
   Other Federal Courts   370
   The State Courts   372
Federal Court Appointees   374
   The Selection of Supreme Court Justices and Federal Judges   375
   Justices and Judges as Political Officials   376
The Nature of Judicial Decision Making   378
   The Constraints of the Facts   378
   The Constraints of the Law   378
Political Influences on Judicial Decisions   381
   Outside Influences on Court Decisions   382
   Inside Influences: The Justices' Own Political Beliefs   383
Judicial Power and Democratic Government   385
   The Limits of Judicial Power   385
   Debating the Judiciary's Proper Role   386
Summary   389
Study Corner   389

PART 4 Public Policy

15 Economic and Environmental Policy: Contributing to Prosperity   393

The Public Policy Process   394
   Problem Recognition   394
   Policy Formation   395
   Policy Implementation   396

Government as Regulator of the Economy   397

  Efficiency Through Government Intervention   398

  Equity Through Government Intervention   401

  The Politics of Regulatory Policy   401

Government as Protector of the Environment   402

  Conservationism: The Older Wave   403

  Environmentalism: The Newer Wave   404

Government as Promoter of Economic Interests   408

  Promoting Business   408

  Promoting Labor   408

  Promoting Agriculture   409

Fiscal Policy: Government as Manager of Economy, I   409

  Taxing and Spending Policy and Politics   410

  The Budgetary Process   414

Monetary Policy: Government as Manager of
  Economy, II   417

  The Fed   418

  The Politics of the Fed   420

Summary   420

Study Corner   421

**16 Welfare and Education Policy: Providing for
Personal Security and Need   425**

Poverty in America: The Nature of the Problem   427

  The Poor: Who and How Many?   427

  Living in Poverty: By Choice or Chance?   428

The Politics and Policies of Social Welfare   429

  Social Insurance Programs   431

  Public Assistance Programs   433

  Culture, Welfare, and Income   436

Education and Equality of Opportunity   439

  Public Education: Leveling Through the Schools   440

  Public School Issues   441

  *The Federal Role in Education: Political
    Differences   442*

The American Way of Promoting the
  General Welfare   444

Summary   445

Study Corner   446

17 Foreign and Defense Policy: Protecting the American Way   449

The Roots of U.S. Foreign and Defense Policy   450

  The Cold War Era   451

  A New World Order   452

  The War on Terrorism   453

  The Iraq War   454

The Military Dimension of National Security Policy   457

  Military Power, Uses, and Capabilities   457

  The Politics of National Defense   460

The Economic Dimension of National Security Policy   461

  Promoting Global Trade   463

  Access to Oil and Other Natural Resources   466

  Assistance to Developing Nations   467

A Challenging World   468

Summary   469

Study Corner   469

18 State and Local Politics: Maintaining Our Differences   473

The Structure of State Government   475

  The State Constitutions   475

  Branches of Government   477

  Citizen Politics: Elections, Parties, and Interest Groups   482

The Structure of Local Government   485

  Types of Local Government   486

  Local Elections and Participation   490

State and Local Finance   491

  Sources of State Revenue   492

  Sources of Local Revenue   494

State and Local Policy   494

  Policy Priorities   494

  Public Policy Patterns   495

The Great Balancing Act: Localism in a Large Nation   499

Summary   500

Study Corner   500

Appendixes   502

Glossary   524

Notes   533

Credits   545

Index   546

Preface

I have tried to write a text that expands students' horizons as well as informs their thinking, a text that they will *want* to read as opposed to one they are simply required to read. Four features of the text support this aim.

Narrative Style

This is a narrative-based text. Unlike a text that piles fact upon fact and in the process squeezes the life out of its subject, the narrative style brings the subject to life. The details reinforce the main points rather than burying them. Studies have shown that students read more attentively and for a longer period of time when a text is narrative in form. The narrative draws students into the material, rousing their interest. And of all the social sciences, political science should be the liveliest subject. Politics has all the elements of high drama while affecting the lives of real people.

Critical Thinking

A key goal of this text is to help students think critically. Students cannot learn to think critically by engaging in rote memorization; they develop the capacity for critical thinking by reflecting on what they have read, resolving challenges to their assumptions, and confronting inconvenient truths. In the first chapter, for example, I discuss the inexact meanings and unfinished promise of Americans' most cherished ideals, including liberty and equality. The discussion includes the "Chinese Exclusion," a grotesque and not widely known chapter in our history that forces students to consider what it means to be an American.

In addition, two of the book's boxed features, "How the United States Compares" and "States in the Nation," are designed to promote critical thinking; these features help students gain a better understanding of their nation or state through an increased awareness of how it differs from others.

Citizen Involvement

All Americans share a role—that of citizen—that is both a right and a duty. Young Americans recognize this fact but do not always know how to act on it. To address this concern, each chapter of this text includes a specific suggestion for student participation, ranging from everything from voter registration to a legislative internship to getting involved in campus organizations.

Politics as Discipline and Practice

I have attempted in this book to present American government through the analytical lens of political science but in a way that captures the vivid world of real-life politics. In writing this text, I regularly reminded myself that only a tiny percentage of introductory students intend to pursue an academic political science career. Most students take the course because they are required to do so or because they like politics. I have sought to write a book that will kindle political interest in the first type of student and deepen it in the second type.

My hope is that the readers of this text will learn, as I did as an undergraduate, to value what political science offers, and to relish "politics"—the ongoing struggle of Americans to find agreeable ways to govern themselves. This struggle fills many pages of the text, most pointedly in the "Debating the Issues" boxes that appear in each chapter. These boxes present opposing opinions on current issues, including immigration, global warming, warrantless wiretaps, same-sex marriage, and the Iraq conflict.

Political Culture and Other Dimensions of American Politics

Political scientists have identified several tendencies that are critical to a systematic understanding of the U.S. political system. These tendencies are introduced in the first chapter of this text and developed in subsequent ones. Even if students forget many of the points made in this book, they may at least retain an understanding of the regularities of American politics:

- Enduring ideals that are the basis of Americans' political identity and culture and a source of many of their beliefs, aspirations, and conflicts.

- Extreme fragmentation of governing authority that is based on an elaborate system of checks and balances. These checks and balances protect against abuses of political power, but also make it difficult for political majorities to assert power when confronting an entrenched or intense political minority.

- Many competing groups—the result of the nation's great size, population diversity, and economic complexity—that exercise considerable influence on public policy, sometimes to society's benefit and sometimes to its detriment.

- Strong emphasis on individual rights, which results in substantial benefits to the individual and places substantial restrictions on majorities.

- Preference for the marketplace as a means of allocating resources, which has the effect of placing many economic issues beyond the reach of political majorities.

All these regularities figure prominently in this book, but the first one on the list has a special place. As Tocqueville, Bryce, Hartz, Rossiter, and other observers have stressed, Americans' deep-rooted political beliefs are the basis of their national identity. Americans are a diverse people with origins in many lands. Their nation was founded on a set of principles—including liberty, self-government, equality, and individualism—that became the people's unifying bond. When an American confronts an everyday situation and responds by saying "It's my right," he or she is acting in a way that is distinctly if not uniquely American. And when all such patterned behaviors are taken into account, they constitute a unique political perspective—an American political perspective.

Although this text's primary focus is the workings of political institutions and processes, these occur within the context of the nation's political culture. Why, for example, is the United States the only affluent democracy without government-provided medical care for all? Or why do Americans, though deeply divided over America's involvement in Iraq, universally believe the Iraqi people would be better off if they lived in a democracy? Why are issues such as stem-cell research and biological evolution larger controversies in the United States than in other Western democracies? Why do lobbying groups have more political clout in the United States than elsewhere?

No analysis of American institutions or processes can fully answer such questions. Americans' cultural beliefs must also be taken into account. Government-provided health care for all, as an example, is at odds with American individualism, which emphasizes self-reliance—a reason why Presidents Roosevelt and Johnson backed away from proposing universal health care and why Presidents Truman and Clinton failed when they did so. Americans govern themselves differently than do other people because they have different beliefs about the purposes of government. Indeed, each of the other regularities on the list above is a prominent feature of U.S. politics because it stems from Americans' cultural beliefs. The prominence in American politics of the marketplace, of interest groups, of individual rights, and of checks and balances owes in significant part to Americans' deep-seated ideas about the proper way to govern.

The significance of political culture in this text is apparent in the "Political Culture" boxes it contains. They challenge students to think about the encompassing nature of America's political culture. The box in the opening chapter, for example, explores the connection between Americans' political ideals and their religious traditions.

New to This Edition

The chapters have been thoroughly updated to include recent scholarship and the latest developments at home and abroad. The largest changes were occasioned by the 2008 presidential election, which in both its candidates and its consequences has altered American politics far more than anyone would have predicted two years ago, when the previous edition was published.

A key change to this edition is the complete revision and reorganization of Chapter 10: The News Media. This front to back revision addresses the extraordinary changes taking place in the media, not only in regard to Internet-based communication but also in regard to traditional news media (for example, the decline in the newspaper). The chapter reflects the mix of messages—informational, critical, and partisan—that Americans encounter through the media. New to the chapter is a section on how Americans use the media—exposure to different amounts and kinds of information, as well as increased interactivity. A main point in the revised version of the chapter is how today's media system fosters political polarization and a widening information gap between America's best informed and least informed citizens.

Other important changes:

Chapter 1: Political Culture The discussion of the limits and power of America's cultural ideals and the discussion of the theoretical underpinnings of the U.S. political system have been tightened and sharpened to help students see more clearly their connection to American politics.

Chapter 3: Federalism No Child Left Behind (NCLB) and policies relating to the war on terrorism are explored for their effect on federalism.

Chapter 4: Civil Liberties This chapter includes the most important cases from the 2006–2008 Supreme Court terms.

Chapter 5: Civil Rights The sections on Native Americans and Hispanics have been expanded, as has the discussion of the immigration issue. The Louisville and Seattle school busing decisions are discussed at length. They are important symbolically and substantively, as well as for what they say about the Supreme Court's positioning. The justices' sharp division over the application of the equal-protection clause—and the legal reasoning of the two sides—is a topic that will engage students.

Chapter 6: Public Opinion The section on "Problems with Polls" has been expanded. Telephone-based polling is becoming increasingly problematic as a result of rising refusal rates and the spread of cell-phone usage. As well, the emergence of Barack Obama as a top presidential candidate resurrected an earlier survey issue that is discussed in the chapter—namely, whether respondents are truthful when it comes to expressing opinions that relate to race and similar subjects. The section on ideology has been reworked to reflect the latest research and to frame the section in the context of how ordinary citizens understand and apply ideological labels.

Chapter 7: Political Participation The turnout increase in the 2008 election is discussed. The Internet as a medium of political participation is given additional attention, including its role in the 2008 primaries. A new topic is the move by several state legislatures to impose a photo-ID requirement on registration and voting. This topic is also the basis for the chapter's "Debating the Issues" box.

Chapter 8: Parties, Candidates, and Campaigns This chapter has been substantially reworked to include,

wherever sensible, material on the 2008 presidential campaign. The section on third parties has been reworked to sharpen the argument about their role in the American party system. Campaign finance receives additional attention, as does the Internet's role in the modern campaign. The chapter includes an expanded discussion of candidate-centered campaigns, including, as an example, the political history of Barack Obama.

Chapter 11: Congress The revised chapter more fully separates the discussion of the party and committee systems within Congress, so that students can see more clearly the contribution of each system to the functioning of the institution. Results of the 2008 congressional elections have been included.

Chapter 12: Presidency The 2008 Democratic and Republican presidential nominating races and the 2008 general election campaign receive considerable attention in the new edition, as does the final phase of the Bush presidency.

Chapter 14: Judiciary In addition to picking up the significance of Alito's appointment to the Court, the revised chapter includes an expanded discussion of the judiciary's role in a democracy. This discussion now includes, in addition to a discussion of judicial review and judicial activism, a discussion of the difference between and implications of the originalism school of thought represented by, for example, Justice Scalia and the "living Constitution" school reflected in the opinions of, for example, Justice Breyer.

Chapter 15: Economic and Environmental Policy The section on environmental policy has been expanded, and oil and gas policy have been added. The country's current economic woes are addressed in the context of fiscal and monetary policy.

Chapter 16: Welfare and Education Policy The No Child Left Behind Act and the controversy surrounding it get more attention in this edition, as do the pending problems of out-year expenditures on social security, Medicare, and Medicaid. The health care issue as it played out in the 2008 presidential campaign is also addressed.

Chapter 17: Foreign and Defense Policy The chapter's revisions include, among other things, the evolving situation in Iraq and in the Afghanistan-Pakistan theater, the rising tide of trade protectionism, and the implications for America's place in the world of the weakening dollar.

Features

The ninth edition of the text retains the following popular features:

- **States in the Nation** features are included in each chapter and illustrate differences and similarities among states. Each box includes a color-coded U.S. map that allows readers to see at a glance how their state compares with other states on specific topics addressed.

- **How the U.S. Compares** features, also found in each chapter, indicate how the U.S. system differs from other democracies on key dimensions such as their political party systems.

- **Debating the Issues** introduces a current controversy and includes opposing opinions on the issue, covering current topics such as the war in Iraq.

- **Get Involved** boxes provide suggestions for how students can get involved in civic and political activity.

- **Leaders** features highlight the contributions of exemplary Americans.

- **Study Corner** is a built-in study guide at the end of each chapter including key terms, a self-quiz, a critical-thinking exercise, and resources for further study.

- **Historical background icons** in the book's margin highlight the inclusion of important historical discussions that are seamlessly woven throughout the narrative.

Finally, in response to suggestions from instructors who have found that many of today's students are less than voracious readers, I have shortened this edition of the text, not by cutting content but by tightening the discussion and eliminating a few frills. In doing this, I acquired a deeper appreciation of what Thomas Jefferson said in a letter to John Adams. Wrote Jefferson: "I didn't have time to write a short letter, so I wrote a long one instead." Streamlining does take more time, but the resulting prose is clearer and more vigorous.

Your Suggestions Are Invited

The American Democracy has been in use in college classrooms for nearly twenty years. During that time, the text (including its concise edition, *We the People*) has been adopted at roughly a thousand colleges and universities. I am extremely grateful to all who have used it. I am particularly indebted to the many instructors and students who have sent me corrections or recommendations. Professor Paul David in the University of Nevada system, for example, pointed out a mistaken entry on Nevada state politics. Joe Sheeler, a student at the University of Maryland, caught an error in a date in one of the chapters. You can contact me at the John F. Kennedy School, Harvard University, Cambridge, MA 02138, or by e-mail: thomas_patterson@harvard.edu.

Thomas E. Patterson

Supplements Package

This text is accompanied by supplementary materials. Please contact your local McGraw-Hill representative or McGraw-Hill Customer Service (800-338-3987) for details concerning policies, prices, and availability, as some restrictions may apply.

For Students and Instructors
OnLine Learning Center

www.mhhe.com/pattersontad9e
The book's website includes separate instructor and student areas. The instructor area contains the instructor's manual, test bank, and PowerPoints, while the student area hosts a wealth of study materials such as chapter outlines, chapter objectives, multiple choice and essay quizzes, flashcards, and weblinks. All chapter-by-chapter material has been updated for the new edition.

CourseSmart E-Textbooks

CourseSmart is a new way for faculty to find and review eTextbooks. It's also a great option for students who are interested in accessing their course materials digitally and saving money. CourseSmart offers thousands of the most commonly adopted textbooks across hundreds of courses from a wide variety of higher education publishers. It is the only place for faculty to review and compare the full text of a textbook online, providing immediate access without the environmental impact of requesting a print exam copy. At CourseSmart, students can save up to 50% off the cost of a print book, reduce their impact on the environment, and gain access to powerful web tools for learning including full text search, notes and highlighting, and e-mail tools for sharing notes between classmates.

For Instructors
Instructor's Manual/Test Bank

Available online, the instructor's manual includes the following for each chapter: learning objectives, focus points and main points, a chapter summary, a list of major concepts, and suggestions for complementary lecture topics. The test bank consists of approximately fifty multiple-choice questions and five suggested essay topics per chapter, with page references given alongside the answers.

PowerPoints and CPS questions are also available to instructors.

McGraw-Hill American Government Lecture Launchers

Lecture Launchers provide approximately two to three minutes of chapter-specific video to help instructors "launch" their lecture. Roundtable discussions, famous speeches, and everyday stories are followed by two "Pause and Think" questions per clip aimed at the heart of new debate. These invite students to consider who sets policy and how they can get involved. In addition to reinforcing the basics, these short video clips focus on civic involvement and consider the Framers of the Constitution. Available in VHS and DVD, with selected clips also available on PoliCentral.com.

PRIMIS Online

Instructors can use this text as a whole, or they can select specific chapters and customize the text to suit their specific classroom needs. The customized text can be created as a hardcopy or as an e-book. Also available in this format are custom chapters on "California Government" and "Texas Government."

For Students
Study Materials

Through the book's Online Learning Center, students have free access to the following materials: chapter outlines, chapter objectives, multiple choice and essay quizzes, flashcards, and weblinks. In addition, the site offers a Presidential Timeline, a Spanish-English Glossary, and guidelines for avoiding plagiarism.

Acknowledgments

Nearly two decades ago, when planning the first edition of *The American Democracy*, my editor and I concluded that it would be enormously helpful if a way could be found to bring into each chapter the judgment of those political scientists who teach the introductory course year in and year out. Thus, in addition to soliciting general reviews from a select number of expert scholars, we sent each chapter to a dozen or so faculty members at U.S. colleges and universities of all types—public and private, large and small, two-year and four-year. These political scientists, 213 in all, had well over a thousand years of combined experience in teaching the introductory course, and they provided countless good ideas.

Since then, scores of other political scientists have reviewed subsequent editions. These many reviewers will go unnamed here, but my debt to all of them remains undiminished by time.

For this new, ninth edition, I again received an enormous amount of sound advice. Reviewers are the life-blood of a text, and I was fortunate to have the assistance of a skilled group of scholars. I am deeply grateful to each and all of them for their help:

Brad Best, *Buena Vista University*

Frank Colucci, *Purdue University–Calumet*

Paul B. Davis, *Truckee Meadows Community College*

Dennis S. Driggers, *California State University–Fresno*

Herbert E. Gooch III, *California Lutheran University*

Marilyn K. Howard, *Columbus State Community College*

Stephen E. Medvec, *Holy Family University*

Mark C. Milewicz, *Gordon College*

Luke Perry, *Southern Utah University*

Geoff Peterson, *University of Wisconsin–Eau Claire*

Keith Reeves, *Swarthmore College*

Bruce Snyder, *California State University–Sacramento*

Margaret Tseng, *Marymount University*

James Van Arsdall, *Metropolitan Community College, Omaha*

Robert P. Watson, *Florida Atlantic University*

Gary Wekkin, *University of Central Arkansas*

James White, *Concord University*

David G. Wigg, *St. Louis Community College*

I also want to thank those at McGraw-Hill who contributed to the ninth edition. Mark Georgiev, my editor, assumed that position shortly before we began the revision process and provided a seamless transition to the new edition. Nancy Crochiere, the director of development, was, as always, superb in guiding the revision process. Erin Grelak, the freelance development editor, was my everyday contact on the revisions and was enormously helpful in keeping the revision process moving along smoothly and constructively. Finally, Briana Porco, editorial coordinator, handled the review process and other countless details flawlessly.

I would also like to thank the book's production editor, David Blatty. He carefully oversaw the book's production and schedule. Thomas Briggs, the copyeditor, had a deft touch that strengthened the prose. Toni Michaels was again involved in the photo research, providing a marvelous set of choices.

At Harvard, I had the diligent and cheerful support of my extraordinary faculty assistant, Alyssa Barrett, who helped update the text and copied endless drafts of it. Alex Patterson served as my photo adviser and photo researcher; his keen eye is behind each of the photo selections in this edition. I owe both of them a deep thanks.

Thomas Patterson

TO MY CHILDREN ■ Alex and Leigh

American Political Culture
Seeking a More Perfect Union

Political Culture: The Core Principles of American Government

America's Core Values

Liberty, Equality, and Self-Government

The Power and Limits of Americans' Ideals

Politics: The Resolution of Conflict

The Social Contract

The Rules of American Politics

Political Power and Authority: The Control of Policy

Theories of Power

Who Governs?

The Concept of a Political System and This Book's Organization

One hears people say that it is inherent in the habits and nature of democracies to change feelings and thoughts at every moment. . . . But I have never seen anything like that happening in the great democracy on the other side of the ocean. What struck me most in the United States was the difficulty experienced in getting an idea, once conceived, out of the head of the majority. **Alexis de Tocqueville[1]**

On the night of November 4, 2008, Barack Obama gave his first speech as president-elect of the United States. Earlier that day, more than 100 million Americans had cast their ballots, choosing Obama over his Republican challenger, John McCain. In his victory speech, Obama spoke of renewing the American dream. He called upon Americans to reclaim their sense of citizenship, to move forward in common purpose, and to put aside the divisions that had kept them apart. He said that, as president, he would listen to the American people, using their voices as his guide. He pledged to use his office to reinvigorate the nation's values and to restore Americans' trust in their government.

The ideals that guided Obama's speech would have been familiar to any generation of Americans. These ideals have been invoked when Americans have gone to war, declared peace, celebrated national holidays, launched major policy initiatives, and asserted new rights.[2] The ideals contained in Obama's speech were the same ones that had punctuated the speeches of George Washington and Abraham Lincoln, Susan B. Anthony and Franklin D. Roosevelt, Martin Luther King and Ronald Reagan.

The ideals were also there at the nation's beginning, when they were put into words in the Declaration of Independence and the Constitution. Of course, the practical meaning of these words has changed greatly during the more than two centuries the United States has been a sovereign nation. When the writers of the Constitution began the document with the words "We the People," they did not have all Americans equally in mind. Black slaves, women, and white men without property did not have the same rights as white men with property.

In accepting victory on election night, Barack Obama, as America's leaders have done throughout the nation's history, invoked America's founding ideals. In the background, Obama appears on one of the giant television screens set up to project his image to the large crowd that had gathered in Chicago for his acceptance speech.

Nevertheless, America's ideals have been remarkably enduring. Throughout their history, Americans have embraced the same set of core values. They have quarreled over the meaning and practice of these ideals, but they have never seriously questioned the principles themselves. As historian Clinton Rossiter concluded, "There has been in a doctrinal sense, only one America."[3]

This book is about contemporary American politics, not U.S. history or culture. Yet American politics today cannot be understood apart from the nation's heritage. Government does not begin anew with each generation; it builds on the past. In the case of the United States, the main link between past and present lies in the nation's founding ideals. The Frenchman Alexis de Tocqueville was among the first to see that major tendencies in American politics cannot be understood without taking into account the country's core beliefs. "Habits of the heart" was Tocqueville's description of Americans' ingrained ideals.[4]

This chapter briefly examines the principles that have helped shape American politics since the nation's earliest years. The chapter also explains basic concepts—such as power, pluralism, and constitutionalism—that are important in the study of American politics. The main points made in this chapter are these:

■ *The American political culture centers on a set of core ideals—liberty, equality, and self-government—that serve as the people's common bond.* These mythic principles have a substantial influence on what Americans will regard as reasonable and acceptable and on what they will try to achieve.

■ *Politics is the process that determines whose values will prevail in society.* The play of politics in the United States takes place in the context of democratic procedures, constitutionalism, and capitalism and involves elements of majority, pluralist, bureaucratic, and elitist rule.

■ *Politics in the United States is characterized by a number of major patterns.* These include a division of governing authority, a high degree of pluralism, an extraordinary emphasis on individual rights, and a substantial separation of the political and economic spheres.

Political Culture: The Core Principles of American Government

The people of every nation have a few central ideals that characterize their political life, but, as James Bryce observed, Americans are a special case.[5] Their ideals are the basis of their national identity. Other people take their identity from the common ancestry that led them gradually to gather under one flag. Thus, long before there was a France or a Japan, there were French and Japanese people, each a kinship group united through ancestry. Even today, it is kinship that links them. There is no way to become fully Japanese except to be born of Japanese parents. Not so for Americans. They are a multitude of people from different lands—England, Germany, Ireland, Africa, Italy, Poland, Mexico, and China, to

The United States was founded on a set of ideals that have served to unify its people, whose immigrant origins trace to every corner of the world. America's diversity is evident here, as Los Angeles's Mayor-elect Antonio Villaraigosa leads his supporters to city hall for his inauguration in 2005.

name just a few. Americans are linked not by a shared ancestry but by allegiance to a common set of ideals.

These ideals are habits of mind, a customary way of thinking about the world. They are part of what social scientists call **political culture,** a term that refers to the characteristic and deep-seated beliefs of a particular people about government and politics.[6]

America's core ideals are rooted in the European heritage of the first white settlers. They arrived during the Enlightenment period, when people were awakening to the idea of human progress. These settlers were not trying to invent a wholly new way of life.[7] Their goals were shaped by their European experiences, which included a centuries-old tradition of aristocratic rule. However, their vision of society changed as they discovered the possibilities that America offered. There was in America no hereditary nobility that controlled nearly all the power and land. The opportunities provided by the New World's vast territory and its great distance from European rulers gave ordinary people a level of freedom and opportunity unimaginable in the Old World. In the end, the colonists rejected the European way of governing. The American Revolution was the first successful large-scale rebellion in human history driven largely by an image of an entirely different form of government.[8] In the words of the Declaration of Independence:

> We hold these truths to be self-evident, that all men are created equal; that they are endowed by their Creator with certain unalienable rights; that among these, are life, liberty, and the pursuit of happiness. That, to secure these rights, governments are instituted among men, deriving their just powers from the consent of the governed; that, whenever any form of government becomes destructive of these ends, it is the right of the people to alter or to abolish it, and to institute a new government, laying its foundation on such principles, and organizing its powers in such form, as to them shall seem most likely to effect their safety and happiness.

political culture

The characteristic and deep-seated beliefs of a particular people.

America's Core Values

An understanding of America's ideals begins with the recognition that they are based on the notion that government exists to serve the people. The cornerstone of society is the individual rather than the government.

TABLE 1-1 | America's Core Political Ideals   The United States was founded on a set of political ideals that have served as its people's common bond. Foremost among these ideals are liberty, equality, and self-government.

Ideal	Description	Origin (In Part)
Liberty	The principle that individuals should be free to act and think as they choose, provided they do not infringe unreasonably on the rights and freedoms of others.	Colonial America's vast open lands offered a degree of liberty unattainable in Europe; the American Revolution was fought over liberty.
Equality	The notion that all individuals are equal in their moral worth, in their treatment under the law, and in their political voice.	Colonial America's openness made Europe's aristocratic system unenforceable; greater personal opportunity in America fostered a sense of social equality.
Self-government	The idea that the people are the ultimate source and proper beneficiary of governing authority and must have a voice in how they are governed.	Colonial America had a degree of self-government; Americans' sense of personal freedom and equality led them to want self-determination in public affairs as well.

Liberty, Equality, and Self-Government

liberty

The principle that individuals should be free to act and think as they choose, provided they do not infringe unreasonably on the rights and freedoms of others.

Liberty, equality, and self-government are widely regarded as America's core political ideals (see Table 1-1). **Liberty** is the principle that individuals should be free to act and think as they choose, provided they do not infringe unreasonably on the freedom and well-being of others. The United States, as political scientist Louis Hartz said, was "born free."[9] The Declaration of Independence rings with the proclamation that people are entitled to "life, liberty and the pursuit of happiness." The preamble to the Constitution declares that the U.S. government was founded to secure "the Blessings of Liberty to ourselves and our Posterity." The Statue of Liberty stands in New York harbor as the symbol of the American people, and the "Star-Spangled Banner" rings out with the words "land of the free."

For early Americans, liberty was nearly a birthright. Ordinary people did not have to accept the European system of absolute government and aristocratic privilege when greater personal liberty was as close as the next area of unsettled land. Not surprisingly, these early Americans were determined, when forming their own government, to protect their liberty. The First Amendment of the Constitution prohibits laws that restrict personal freedom: "Congress shall make no law respecting the establishment of religion, or prohibiting the free exercise thereof; or abridging the freedom of speech, or of the press; or the right of the people to peaceably assemble, and to petition the Government for a redress of grievances."

individualism

The idea that people should take the initiative, be self-sufficient, and accumulate the material advantages necessary for their well-being.

Liberty for early Americans meant economic opportunity as well as political freedom. Property ownership was widespread, as was a commitment to self-reliance. Frontier America was marked by a "rugged individualism" that became a key cultural value. **Individualism** is a commitment to personal initiative and self-sufficiency; it rests on the belief that people should be free of undue government restraints as they seek to advance themselves economically.

Americans' demand for political and economic liberty has persisted. Observers from Tocqueville onward have seen fit to note that liberty in America, as in no other country, is ingrained in people's thinking. Americans' chief aim, wrote Tocqueville, "is to remain their own masters."

equality

The notion that all individuals are equal in their moral worth and thereby entitled to equal treatment under the law.

A second American political ideal is **equality**—the notion that all individuals are equal in their moral worth and thereby entitled to equal treatment under the law. America provided its white settlers a new level of equality. Europe's rigid aristocratic system based on land ownership was unenforceable in frontier America. Almost any free citizen who wanted to own land could obtain it. It was this natural sense of personal equality that Thomas Jefferson expressed so

POLITICAL
CULTURE

LIBERTY, EQUALITY, AND SELF-GOVERNMENT: RELIGION AND AMERICAN IDEALS

The United States is a nation established in 1776 on a set of principles—liberty, equality, and self-government. These ideals derived in part from broad lessons of history, the direct experiences of the colonists, and treatises such as those of Locke and Rousseau. Religious beliefs also played a major part.

Many of the early colonists came to America in order to practice their religions freely. Church and state in Europe were joined. Government there sided with a particular religion—Roman Catholicism in France and Spain, Anglicanism in England. Rhode Island's founder, the Reverend Roger Williams, was a Calvinist who left his native England for reasons of religious freedom. Williams was the first to assert that church and state in America ought to be separate. Williams argued that salvation required an acceptance of God, which is meaningful only if it is an act of free will—and this is impossible if religion is imposed on the individual by the state. To Williams and others, religious liberty and political liberty were inseparable. The prevalence of this view is apparent in the First Amendment to the Constitution, which at once provides for freedom of political expression *and* for religious freedom.

Liberty is not the only American ideal with a religious basis. Equality was considered God's work: "all men are created equal." Every individual was a child of God and thus equal in his eyes. (This belief posed a dilemma for slaveholders, who finessed it by claiming that slaves either were soulless or were secondary beings in God's "natural order.") Self-government, too, had a religious foundation, though a Protestant one. Unlike the Catholic Church, which was hierarchical in its organization, with the pope and bishops at its head, many Protestant sects had self-governing congregations. This feature affected their members' views on the proper form of government.

America, said the British writer G. K. Chesterton, is "a nation with the soul of a church" and "the only country founded on a creed." He could have added that America is also a nation that emulated a religious model in its governing document. The first colonists formed religious communities governed by written covenant, a model for the written Constitution drafted and ratified by Americans more than a century later.

forcefully in the Declaration of Independence: "We hold these truths to be self-evident, that all men are created equal."

Equality, however, has always been a less clearly defined concept than liberty. Even Jefferson professed not to know its exact meaning. A slave owner, Jefferson distinguished between free citizens, who were entitled to equal rights, and slaves, who were not. After slavery was abolished, Americans continued to argue over the meaning of equality, and the debate continues today. Does equality require that wealth and opportunity be widely shared? Or does it merely require that artificial barriers to advancement be removed? Despite differing opinions about such questions, an insistence on equality is a distinctive feature of the American experience. Americans, said Bryce, reject "the very notion" that some people might be "better" than others merely because of birth or position.[10]

America's third great political ideal is **self-government**—the principle that the people are the ultimate source of governing authority and should have a voice in their governing. "Governments," the Declaration of Independence proclaims, "deriv[e] their just powers from the consent of the governed." In his Gettysburg Address, Lincoln extolled a government "of the people, by the people, for the people." Etched in a corridor of the nation's Capitol building are the words Alexander Hamilton spoke when asked about the foundation of the nation's government: "Here, sir, the people govern."

Americans' belief in self-government formed in colonial America. The Old World was an ocean away, and European governments had no option but to allow the American colonies a degree of self-determination. Out of this experience came the vision of a self-governing nation. It was an ideal that led tens of thousands of ordinary farmers, merchants, and tradesmen to risk their lives in

self-government
The principle that the people are the ultimate source and proper beneficiary of governing authority; in practice, a government based on majority rule.

the cause of self-government during the American Revolution. The ensuing federal and state constitutions were based on the idea that government is properly founded on the will of the people. The Constitution of the United States opens with the words "We the People."

America's principles hold out the promise of a government of high purpose, in which power is widely shared and used for the common good. The principles are not, however, wholly compatible with each other. They derive from somewhat different experiences and philosophical traditions, and there are points at which they conflict. Self-government, for example, emphasizes majority rule, whereas liberty emphasizes personal freedom and security. Conflict between the two is inevitable at times—for example, the ideal of self-government asserts that the view of the many should prevail over the opinion of the few, whereas the principle of liberty asserts that individuals have inviolate rights. How far should the majority be permitted to go in imposing its will on the individual? To what extent should the individual be allowed to act in ways objectionable to the majority? These are everyday questions of American politics, affecting issues as diverse as taxes, gay marriage, capital punishment, affirmative action, property use, abortion, and national security.

Moreover, America's core ideals are general principles, not fixed rules of conduct. During the writing of the Declaration of Independence, Thomas Jefferson and John Adams argued over the meaning of liberty, with Jefferson contending that its basis was in individual freedom and Adams countering that it rested on the nation's freedom. This debate has been restaged many times in U.S. history. After the terrorist attacks on New York and Washington on September 11, 2001, President George W. Bush secretly ordered the monitoring of Americans' telephone and email communication. When the policy was exposed, Bush claimed he was protecting Americans' liberty from the terrorist threat. Bush said, "Given that choice, I will defend America every time." Critics said Bush's policy was an assault on Americans' liberty. Senator Patrick Leahy (D-Vt.) said the "rights of American citizens are being arrogantly abridged at almost every turn in the name of national security."

LEADERS

THOMAS JEFFERSON
(1743–1826)

Thomas Jefferson was the principal author of the Declaration of Independence. It was Jefferson who at age thirty-three coined the renowned words "Life, Liberty and the Pursuit of Happiness." A man of contradictions, Jefferson owned slaves while arguing for human equality and liberty. Elected to the presidency in 1800, Jefferson was a proponent of states' rights and of a strict interpretation of the national government's constitutional powers. Yet he overlooked the Constitution, which had no authorization for such an act, in purchasing the Louisiana Territory from the French emperor Napoleon in 1803, doubling the area of the United States. A quiet man who was a better writer than public speaker, Jefferson dedicated much of his energy to strengthening his home state of Virginia. He drafted the state's Bill of Rights, which included a provision for religious freedom—a right not guaranteed in all states at the time. After retiring to his Monticello estate following his two terms as president, Jefferson designed and founded the University of Virginia, calling it one of his greatest achievements. To Jefferson, the success of the American experiment in self-government rested ultimately on an educated citizenry.

The Power and Limits of Americans' Ideals

Cultural beliefs originate in a country's political and social practices, but they are not perfect representations of these practices. They are mythic ideas—symbolic positions taken by a people to justify and give meaning to their way of life.[11] Myths contain elements of truth, but they are not the full truth.

Ideals affect people's aspirations, but they exist alongside other impulses. For some people and at some times, politics is purely an issue of self-interest. In *Federalist* No. 10, James Madison deplored the readiness of people "to oppress each other [rather] than to cooperate for their common good." The clearest proof of this tendency in the American case is the human tragedy that began nearly four centuries ago and continues today. In 1619 the first black slaves were brought in chains to America. Slavery lasted 250 years. Slaves worked in the fields from dawn to dark (from "can see, 'til can't"), in both the heat of summer and the cold of winter. The Civil War brought an end to slavery but not to racial oppression. Slavery was followed by the Jim Crow era of legal segregation: black people in the South were forbidden by law to use the same schools, hospitals, restaurants, and restrooms as white people. Those who spoke out against this system were subjected to beatings, firebombings, castrations, rapes, and murder—hundreds of African Americans were lynched in the early 1900s by white vigilantes. Today African Americans have equal rights under the law, but in fact they are far from equal. Compared with whites, blacks are twice as likely to live in poverty, twice as likely to be unable to find a job, and twice as likely to die in infancy.[12] There have always been two Americas, one for whites and one for blacks.

Despite the lofty claim that "all men are created equal," equality has never been an American birthright. In 1882, Congress suspended Chinese immigration on the assumption that the Chinese were an inferior people. Calvin Coolidge in 1923 asked Congress for a permanent ban on Chinese immigration, saying that people "who do not want to be partakers of the American spirit ought not to settle in America."[13] Not until 1965 was discrimination against the Chinese and other Asians eliminated from U.S. immigration laws. Tight limits on Hispanic immigration were also lifted at this time, and since then, most immigrants have come from Latin America and Asia (see Figure 1-1).

The claim that the United States is a gigantic melting pot is a blend of fact and fiction. On the one hand, no other nation has so fully opened its doors to groups from around the world. Even today, Americans are substantially more likely than Europeans to say that recent immigrant groups are having a positive influence on the society (see Figure 1-2). Nevertheless, established groups in America have never fully embraced new arrivals. When Catholics and Jews from Ireland, Italy, and eastern Europe came to this country in large numbers in the nineteenth and early twentieth centuries, many Americans, including some members of Congress, sought to bar them from entry because of their religious beliefs. After the September 11, 2001, terrorist attacks on the World Trade Center and the Pentagon, polls indicated that most Americans wanted Middle East immigration sharply reduced or halted entirely.

America's callous treatment of some groups is not among the stories that the American people like to tell about themselves. A University of Virginia survey found that American adults are far more likely to want children to be taught about the nation's achievements than its shortcomings (see Table 1-2). Selective

HISTORICAL Background

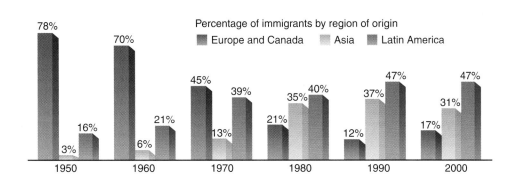

FIGURE 1-1 **The Changing Face of Immigration**
Until 1965, immigration laws were biased in favor of European immigrants. The laws enacted in 1965 increased the proportion of immigrants from Asia and Latin America.
Source: U.S. Immigration and Naturalization Service, 2008. Percentages are totals for each decade, for example, the 2000 figures are for the 1991–2000 period.

Source: The Pew Research Center for the People and the Press, Global Attitudes Survey, 2005. Respondents were asked about immigration from a particular region (the Middle East and North Africa, in the case of the European countries; Mexico and Latin America, in the case of the United States).

FIGURE 1-2 **Opinion of the Influence on Society of Recent Immigrants**
Americans are more likely than most Europeans to believe that recent immigrants have had a positive influence on their society.

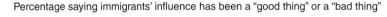
Percentage saying immigrants' influence has been a "good thing" or a "bad thing"

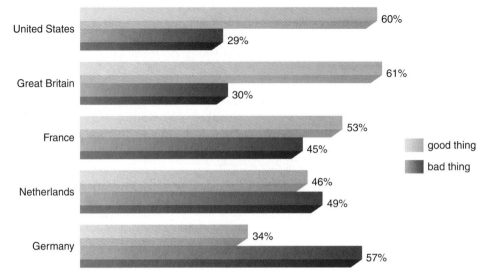

memory can be found among all peoples, but the tendency to recast history is perhaps exaggerated in the American case because Americans' beliefs are so idealistic. How could a nation that claims to be the model of human equality have barred the Chinese, enslaved the blacks, massacred the Indians, and subordinated women?

Although ideals do not determine exactly what people will do, they do affect their hopes and desires. If racial, gender, ethnic, and other forms of intolerance constitute the nation's sorriest legacy, the centuries-old struggle of Americans to build a more equal society is among its finest. Few nations have battled so relentlessly against the insidious discrimination that stems from superficial human differences such as the color of one's skin. The abolition and suffrage movements of the 1800s and the more recent civil rights movements of black Americans, women, Hispanics, and gays testify to Americans' persistent effort to build a more equal society. At the height of the Civil War, which was the bloodiest

TABLE 1-2 | Telling the American Story to Children   Americans' values and myths are reflected in their preferences in teaching children about the nation's history.

In Teaching the American Story to Children, How Important Is the Following Theme?	Essential/Very Important	Somewhat Important	Somewhat Unimportant/ Very Unimportant/Leave It Out of the Story
With hard work and perseverance, anyone can succeed in America.	83%	14%	4%
Our founders limited the power of government so government would not intrude too much into the lives of its citizens.	74	19	8
America is the world's greatest melting pot in which people from different countries are united into one nation.	73	21	5
America's contribution is one of expanding freedom for more and more people.	71	22	6
Our nation betrayed its founding principles by cruel mistreatment of blacks and American Indians.	59	24	17
Our founders were part of a male-dominated culture that gave important roles to men while keeping women in the background.	38	28	35

Used by permission of the Survey of American Political Culture, James Davison Hunter and Carol Bowman, directors, Institute for Advanced Studies in Culture, University of Virginia.

STATES IN THE NATION

A COLLEGE EDUCATION

Reflecting their cultural beliefs of individualism and equality, Americans have developed the world's largest college system. Every state has at least eight colleges within its boundaries. No European democracy has as many colleges as either California or New York—each of which has more than 300 institutions of higher education. The extensive U.S. college system has enabled large numbers of Americans to earn a college degree. Among adults twenty-five years of age and older, roughly one in four is a college graduate. Even the states that rank low on this indicator have a higher percentage of college graduates than do most European countries.

Q: Why do the northeastern and western coastal states have a higher percentage of adults with college degrees?

A: The northeastern and western coastal states are more affluent and urbanized than most states. Accordingly, young people in these states can better afford the costs of college and are more likely to require a college degree for the careers they pursue.

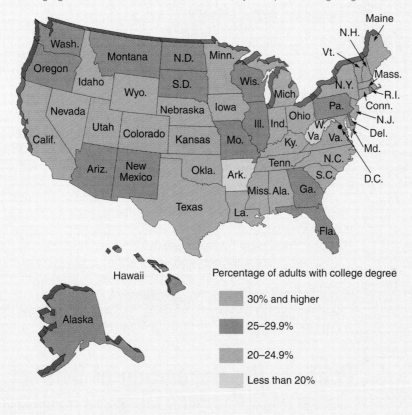

Percentage of adults with college degree

■ 30% and higher

■ 25–29.9%

■ 20–24.9%

■ Less than 20%

Source: U.S. Bureau of the Census, 2008. Based on percentage of adults twenty-five years of age or older with a college degree.

conflict to date in the whole of world history, Abraham Lincoln emancipated the slaves, saying "I never, in my life, felt more certain that I was doing right."[14]

The power of Americans' commitment to equality is today evident in the country's elaborate system of higher education, which includes nearly three thousand two-year and four-year institutions. In many countries, access to a college education is sharply restricted and widely available only to the children of wealthy families. America's higher education system has a different foundation: it is designed to promote equality of opportunity. Although some young Americans do not have a realistic prospect of attending college, the nation's higher education system is an open one compared with those elsewhere. About a fourth of America's adult citizens have a college degree, the world's highest rate. Even West Virginia, the American state with the lowest proportion of college graduates (see "States in

During the era of racial segregation in the South, this sign at the entrance to the Memphis public zoo meant that it was Tuesday—the only day black people were allowed to go to the zoo. On the other six days of the week, the sign excluded black people from entering.

the Nation"), has a higher percentage than do most European countries.

The principles of liberty and self-government have also shaped American society. No country holds as many elections or has as many publicly elected officials as does the United States, which is also nearly the only country to allow voters through primary elections to decide which candidates will be the party nominees in the general election. And few people have as many legally protected individual rights—ranging from free-expression rights to fair-trial protections—as do Americans.

The power of American ideals is perhaps nowhere more evident, however, than in their continuing influence. Their fulfillment is an ongoing quest, not a settled issue. The Great Depression of the 1930s, for example, forced Americans to reconsider the meaning of personal liberty. Until then, freedom had been a matter of freedom *from* government. But this type of freedom was an empty promise for the tens of millions who were jobless, homeless, and hungry as a result of the depression. A fourth of American laborers were unemployed, and another fourth could find only part-time work. Americans turned *to* government for help. In his 1941 State of the Union Address, President Franklin D. Roosevelt spoke to people's hopes when he declared that "freedom from want" was among Americans' fundamental liberties.

Like the Great Depression generation, every generation of Americans has embraced the nation's founding principles and sought ways to update and strengthen them. The writer Theodore H. White aptly described America as a nation relentlessly "in search of itself."[15] *A defining feature of the U.S. political system is Americans' ongoing pursuit of the political ideals upon which the nation was founded.*

Politics: The Resolution of Conflict

Although cultural values affect what people seek through politics, politics is more than shared ideals. It is also a struggle for power and advantage. Commenting on the competitive nature of politics, political scientist Harold Lasswell described politics as the struggle over "who gets what, when, and how."[16] **Politics** is the process through which a society settles its conflicts and decides the policies by which it will be governed.

Political conflict has two primary sources. One is *scarcity*. Even the richest societies do not have enough wealth to satisfy everyone's desires, and conflict over the distribution of resources is the predictable result. Consider, for example, the issue of school quality. Affluent suburban districts have better schools than do poor inner-city districts. Lacking a strong local tax base, inner-city residents have pressured state governments to provide equal funding to all schools. Residents of suburban communities have fought this arrangement, fearing that it would increase their taxes and weaken their local schools.

Differences in values are the other main source of political conflict. People see issues differently as a result of differences in their backgrounds and interests.

politics

The process through which a society settles it conflicts and decides the policies by which it will be governed.

DEBATING THE ISSUES

SHOULD THE UNITED STATES HAVE A TEMPORARY WORKER PROGRAM FOR MEXICAN CITIZENS?

Although the United States is a nation of immigrants, it has not always been welcoming of new immigrant groups. At the turn of the twentieth century, when American industry had a huge shortage of workers, immigration was encouraged—but only for the able-bodied. Strict inspection standards denied entry to the weak and the infirm. Some Americans, the so-called Nativists, wanted to deny admission to all Catholics and Jews arriving from southern and eastern Europe, declaring their beliefs and customs "un-American." Immigration is still a contentious issue, particularly in regard to the illegal entry of Mexicans. Although a source of inexpensive labor, they place a burden on local schools and services. Early in his second term, President George W. Bush proposed legislation that would tighten security on the U.S.-Mexican border while creating a temporary worker program that would enable more than 10 million otherwise illegal immigrants to work in the United States for a period not to exceed six years. The guest worker program would relieve pressures on the Mexican government stemming from high unemployment in Mexico. In turn, the Mexican government would do more to prevent Mexicans from illegally entering the United States.

President Bush's proposal was rejected in Congress, where most of the opposition came from members of Bush's own party. Among the most vocal critics was Tom Tancredo, a U.S. representative from Colorado, who unsuccessfully sought the GOP's 2008 presidential nomination. Below are statements by Bush and Tancredo on the issue of guest workers. Which position do you find more persuasive? Why?

YES
As we enforce our immigration laws, comprehensive immigration reform also requires us to improve those laws by creating a new temporary worker program. This program would create a legal way to match willing foreign workers with willing American employers to fill jobs that Americans will not do. Workers would be able to register for legal status for a fixed period of time, and then be required to go home. This program would help meet the demands of a growing economy, and it would allow honest workers to provide for their families while respecting the law. This plan would also help us relieve pressure on the border. By creating a legal channel for those who enter America to do an honest day's labor, we would reduce the number of workers trying to sneak across the border. . . . The program that I propose would not create an automatic path to citizenship, it wouldn't provide for amnesty—I oppose amnesty. Rewarding those who have broken the law would encourage others to break the law and keep pressure on our border. . . . I support increasing the number of annual green cards that can lead to citizenship [but do not support] amnesty. . . . In this new century, we must continue to welcome immigrants, and to set high standards for those who follow the laws to become a part of our country. Every new citizen of the United States has an obligation to learn our customs and values, including liberty and civic responsibility, equality under God and tolerance for others, and the English language.

—George W. Bush, president of the United States

NO
Let's take the President's first claim: "we will not be able to effectively enforce our immigration laws until we create a temporary worker program." Really? That is, cannot the United States government stop illegal aliens from getting to our soil? The challenge is not catching *every single person*, but stopping enough to make the trip into the U.S. costly and to reverse many of the side effects of massive illegal immigration (cultural bifurcation, social service hemorrhaging, downward wage pressure, etc.). The president's next line: "The program that I propose would not create an automatic path to citizenship, it wouldn't provide for amnesty—I oppose amnesty." . . . What the White House is trying to do is to confuse amnesty with a "path to citizenship," so that when the public hears "no path to citizenship," it thinks "no amnesty." . . . The president's new plan is still amnesty in two respects. First, it protects persons who have broken the law from the punishment prescribed by the law (deportation) while offering them a privilege that few get (living and working in the U.S.). Second, does anyone really think that at the end of six years they'll go home or that Congress will have the political will to make them? Six years from now, after we've secured the border and gotten tough on interior enforcement, there will be tremendous political pressure to go soft on the "guest workers" who have been here for years.

—Tom Tancredo, U.S. representative (R-Colo.)

Social contract theory holds that people agree to be governed in order to protect their rights and interests. Neither the government nor the people always hold up their side of the bargain. Shown here are some of the thousands of New Orleans residents who were abandoned by government as Hurricane Katrina roared in from the Gulf Coast. A much smaller number of New Orleans residents took advantage of the chaos to loot homes and businesses.

Abortion is an issue of freedom of choice for some and an issue of murder for others. People bring to politics a wide range of conflicting standards—about abortion, the environment, crime and punishment, the poor, the economy, and countless other issues.

The Social Contract

Politics operates by "rules" that determine whose voice will prevail when conflict arises over resources and values. Without such rules, people would be constantly at each other's throats, and society would dissolve into anarchy.

For a long period of world history, the rules of politics were stacked against ordinary people. They had no say in their governing and were at the mercy of those in authority. Government was controlled by absolute monarchs, whose word was law. Many of them were tyrants, and others levied onerous taxes in order to build lavish palaces.

Roughly four centuries ago, ideas about the proper form of government began to change. Ironically, one of the theorists who contributed to this development was an advocate of absolute rule. In *Leviathan* (published in 1651), the English philosopher Thomas Hobbes argued that government rests on a **social contract** in which ordinary people surrender the freedom they would have in a state of nature in return for the protection that a sovereign ruler can provide. People give up their freedom, Hobbes said, because life in its natural state is "nasty, brutish, and short"—the strong prey on the weak. For this reason, people seek the protection of rulers whom they are obliged to obey, even if some rulers turn out to be cruel or inept. The alternative—a never-ending "war of all against all"—is far worse.

social contract

A voluntary agreement by individuals to form government, which is then obliged to act within the confines of the agreement.

Four decades later, the English philosopher John Locke used Hobbes's concept of a social contract to argue *against* absolutism. In his *Second Treatise on Civil Government* (1690), Locke claimed that all individuals have certain natural (or inalienable) rights, including those of life, liberty, and property. When people form governments for the purpose of securing their physical safety, they retain these individual rights. The social contract—their agreement to submit to governing authority—is based on the premise that government will protect these rights. If it fails to do so, said Locke, the people can overthrow it and form a new government.

Three-quarters of a century later, the French philosopher Jean-Jacques Rousseau extended the idea of a social contract to include popular sovereignty. Like Locke, Rousseau despised absolute government. "Man was born free, but everywhere he is in chains" are the opening words of Rousseau's *Social Contract* (1762). Rousseau claimed that people in their natural state are innocent and happy. Accordingly, the only legitimate government is one that promotes their interests and governs with their consent. As Rousseau saw it, government is simply the instrument for carrying out the people's will. Sovereignty rests with them, not the government. Rousseau worried, however, that the people would act selfishly and claimed that popular rule also had proper limits. It would be legitimate only if the people acted in the interests of all—what Rousseau called "the general will."

These ideas—that people have individual rights and should have a say in their governing—sparked the American Revolution in 1776. A decade later, the writing of the Constitution formalized the basic principle of social contract theory—that the power of leaders is limited by a prescribed set of rules.

The Rules of American Politics

The major rules of American politics—democracy, constitutionalism, and capitalism—establish a political process that is intended to promote self-government, uphold equality, and defend political and economic rights. The U.S. political system is, at once, a democratic system, a constitutional system, and a capitalist (free-market) system.

Democracy

Democracy is a set of rules intended to give ordinary people a significant voice in government. The word *democracy* comes from the Greek words *demos*, meaning "the people," and *kratis*, meaning "to rule." In simple terms, **democracy** is a form of government in which the people govern, either directly or through elected representatives (see Chapter 2). A democracy thus is different from an **oligarchy** (in which control rests with a small group, such as top-ranking military officers or a few wealthy families) and from an **autocracy** (in which control rests with a single individual, such as a king or dictator).

A *democratic system* reflects the Rousseauist idea that legitimate authority stems from the consent of the governed, which in practice has meant majority rule through voting in elections. More direct forms of democracy exist, such as the town meeting in which citizens vote directly on issues affecting them, but the impracticality of such an arrangement in a large society has made majority rule through elections the basic form of self-government in modern democracies, including the United States.

Unlike some countries, the United States has an unbroken history of free elections as the means of acquiring governmental power. At no time has power been obtained through a military coup or mass uprising. However, America's voters do not control their government as directly as voters in some democracies. The U.S. electoral system was established in a period when the power of

democracy
A form of government in which the people govern, either directly or through elected representatives.

oligarchy
A form of government in which control rests with a few persons.

autocracy
A form of government in which absolute control rests with a single person.

government—whether it rested with a monarch or the majority—was greatly feared. To protect against abuses of power, the writers of the U.S. Constitution devised an elaborate system of checks and balances. Authority was divided among the executive, legislative, and judicial branches so that each branch could act as a check on the power of the others (see Chapter 2). Indeed, *a substantial division of governing authority is a defining characteristic of the American political system.* One result of this constitutional arrangement is that majority rule is less direct in the United States than in many democracies. In most European countries, a majority has the power through its vote in a single election to give full executive and legislative power to the victorious political party. In the United States, however, there are separate elections for the president, U.S. senators, and U.S. representatives, and their terms of office differ in length. Thus, a voting majority in the United States must have the lasting power to dominate a series of elections in order to assert its full influence (see Chapter 2).

Constitutionalism

The concept of democracy implies that the will of the majority should prevail over the wishes of the minority. If unrestrained, this principle would allow a majority to ride roughshod over the minority. The majority would have the power to deprive the minority even of its liberty, a clearly unacceptable outcome. Individuals have rights and freedoms that cannot lawfully be denied by the majority.

constitutionalism

The idea that there are definable limits on the rightful power of a government over its citizens.

Constitutionalism holds that there are limits on the rightful power of government over its citizens. In a *constitutional system,* officials govern according to law, and citizens have basic rights that government cannot deny or abridge.[17] Free speech is an example. The U.S. government is prohibited by the First Amendment from infringing on free speech. No right is absolute, which means that some restrictions are allowed. No student, for example, has a First Amendment right to shout loudly and disrupt a classroom. Nevertheless, free speech is broadly protected by the courts. During the buildup to war with Iraq in 2003, tens of thousands of antiwar demonstrators took to the streets. Those who vocally opposed the government's war policy did so without risk of fine or imprisonment.

The constitutional tradition in the United States is as strong as the democratic tradition.[18] *A defining characteristic of the American political system is its extraordinary emphasis on individual rights.* Americans have a broad set of individual rights, ranging from those surrounding free expression to those guaranteeing due process of law. Moreover, issues that in other democracies would be resolved through elections and in legislative bodies are, in the United States, decided in courts of law as well. Abortion rights, nuclear power, busing, toxic waste disposal, and welfare services are among the scores of issues that in recent years have played out in part as questions of rights to be settled through the courts.

Constitutionalism is not practiced by all governments. Although every country has a constitution that supposedly restricts government's lawful powers, these constitutional

Adolf Hitler's Nazi Germany was a brutal totalitarian regime responsible for the deaths of millions of people.

guarantees are sometimes not worth the paper on which they are written. **Authoritarian governments** openly repress their political opponents as a means of staying in power, although they do so in varying degrees. Some of these regimes are **totalitarian governments,** meaning they assert complete dominance over individuals and the institutions of society. They control the media, direct the economy, dictate what can and cannot be taught in schools, define family relations, and decide which religions—if any—can be practiced openly. In fact, virtually no area of life is beyond their sphere of control, which results in brutal one-party rule. Millions of individuals in Adolf Hitler's Nazi Germany and in Josef Stalin's Soviet Union were imprisoned or murdered by the state. Other authoritarian regimes—including most of those that have taken power in Latin America, Africa, and Asia in recent decades as a result of military coups—are less repressive because those nations have other powerful institutions, such as religious organizations or large corporations, that might actively oppose them if they go too far.

Capitalism

Just as democracy and constitutionalism are sets of rules for allocating power in American society, so too is capitalism. **Capitalism** holds that the government should interfere with the economy as little as possible. In a capitalist system, firms are allowed to operate in a free marketplace, and individuals are expected to rely on their own initiative to establish their economic security. Firms decide what they will produce and how much they will charge for their goods, while consumers decide what they will buy and at what price. Meanwhile, following a Lockean principle, private property rights are vigorously protected through government action.

Alternatives to capitalism include **socialism,** which assigns government a large role in the ownership of the means of production, in economic decision making, and in providing for the economic security of the individual. Under the form of socialism practiced in Sweden and some other democracies, the government does not attempt to manage the overall economy. Under **communism,** which characterized the former Soviet Union and is practiced today in North Korea and a few other countries, the government owns most or all major industries and also takes responsibility for overall management of the economy, including production quotas, supply points, and pricing.

The United States has a largely capitalist (free-market) system. The government does play an economic role through its tax, regulatory, monetary, and spending policies, but the bulk of economic decisions are made by private firms and consumers (see Chapter 15). Like the rules of democracy and constitutionalism, the rules of capitalism are not neutral. Whereas democracy responds to numbers and constitutionalism responds to individual rights, capitalism responds to wealth. "Money talks" in a capitalist system, which means, among other things, that wealthier interests have disproportionate political influence, as well as the lion's share of economic power (see Chapters 7 and 9).

Capitalist systems characterize most Western countries, but the United States relies more heavily on the free market than do the others (see "How the U.S. Compares"). Health care is an example. In Europe and Canada, health care is paid for by the government and is universal—every citizen has access to medical care at government expense. In contrast, health care in the United States is delivered largely through the private sector, and access to it depends in part on the individual's ability to pay. In effect, many of the economic benefits and costs that are allocated through the political process in other countries are allocated through the economic system in the United States. *A major characteristic of the*

authoritarian government

A form of government in which leaders, though they admit to no limits on their powers, are effectively limited by other centers of power in the society.

totalitarian government

A form of government in which the leaders assert complete dominance of all individuals and institutions.

capitalism

An economic system based on the idea that government should interfere with economic transactions as little as possible. Free enterprise and self-reliance are the collective and individual principles that underpin capitalism.

socialism

An economic system in which government owns and controls many of the major industries.

communism

An economic system in which government owns most or all major industries and also takes responsibility for overall management of the economy.

HOW THE U.S. COMPARES

TAX RATES

The United States was labeled "the country of individualism par excellence" by William Watts and Lloyd Free in their book *State of the Nation*. They were referring to the emphasis that Americans place on economic self-reliance and free markets.

In European democracies, such views also prevail but are moderated by a greater acceptance of tax and social policies that redistribute wealth. The differences between American and European culture reflect their differing political traditions. Colonial America was an open country ruled by a foreign power, and its revolution was fought largely over the issue of personal liberty. In the European revolutions, economic and social equality was also at issue, because wealth was held by hereditary aristocracies. Europeans' concern with equality was gradually translated into a willingness to use government as a means of economic redistribution. An example is government-paid medical care for all citizens, which is provided throughout nearly the whole of Europe and Canada, but not in the United States. More than 40 million Americans are without health insurance.

Such differences affect tax rates. Although many Americans complain that their taxes are too high, the tax rate in the United States is lower than in Canada and Europe, reflecting the degree to which the various countries seek through taxes to provide economic security to the less-well-off. According to figures obtained in 2008 from the Organization for Economic Cooperation and Development (OECD), the tax rates—the total amount of individual taxes relative to a country's Gross Domestic Product (GDP)—in the following countries are:

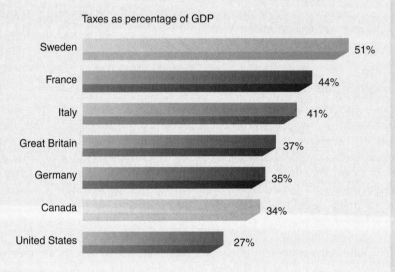

Taxes as percentage of GDP

Sweden	51%
France	44%
Italy	41%
Great Britain	37%
Germany	35%
Canada	34%
United States	27%

American system is a relatively sharp distinction between what is political, and therefore to be decided in the public realm, and what is economic, and therefore to be settled in the private realm.

Political Power and Authority: The Control of Policy

public policy

A decision of government to pursue a particular course of action.

power

The ability of persons or institutions to control policy.

Rules are necessary in politics because the stakes are so high. Politics is a struggle for control of **public policy**—a decision by government to pursue a particular course of action. **Power** refers to the ability of persons, interests, or institutions to control public policy.[19] Americans who have enough power can levy or cut taxes, permit or prohibit abortions, protect or take away private property, provide or refuse health benefits, impose or relax trade barriers, and make war or declare peace. With so much at stake, it is not surprising that Americans, like people elsewhere, seek political power.

Political power resides with private individuals and organizations as well as in the hands of those who occupy government positions. A case in point is the power exercised by the National Rifle Association (NRA) over gun control policy. NRA members oppose restrictions on gun ownership and have used their votes, campaign contributions, and lobbying efforts to block gun control legislation.

Government officials have a special kind of power as a result of the positions they hold. When government officials exercise power, it is called **authority,** defined as the right to make binding decisions. By this definition, government is not the only source of authority. For example, parents have authority over their children, professors have authority over their students, and firms have authority over their employees. However, government is a special case. Government's authority extends to all people within its geographical boundaries and can be used to redefine the authority of the parent, the professor, or the firm.

authority

The recognized right of an individual, organization, or institution to exercise power.

Theories of Power

Who has power in America? Who, in the end, decides the policies that the U.S. government pursues? Do the people themselves hold this power, or does it reside in the hands of a relatively small group of influential individuals, either within or outside of government?

This issue is compelling because the ultimate question of any political system is the question of who governs. Is power widely shared and used for the benefit of the many, or is it narrowly held and used to the advantage of the few? The issue is compelling for a second reason: power is easy to define but hard to pinpoint. Consider, for example, the votes that a member of Congress casts. Are these votes an expression of the member's power, or are they an expression of the power of groups on whom the member depends for reelection?

The pattern of political power in America has been shown to differ substantially across individuals, institutions, and policy areas. There are four broad theories of who holds power in America (see Table 1-3). None of them describes every aspect of American politics, but each applies in some situations.

Majoritarianism: Government by the People

A basic principle of democracy is the idea of majority rule. **Majoritarianism** is the notion that the majority should prevail not only in the counting of votes but also in the determination of public policy.

At times, a majority of the American public in effect decides policy issues. When Congress in 1996 passed a welfare reform bill that required welfare recipients to accept a job or job training after a two-year period or face the loss of their welfare benefits, it was acting in accord with the thinking of most Americans. They had come to believe that too many able-bodied individuals were taking advantage of the welfare system. A fuller assessment of majority power is provided by Benjamin Page and Robert Shapiro's study of the relationship between

majoritarianism

The idea that the majority prevails not only in elections but also in policy determination.

TABLE 1-3 | **Theories of Power: Who Governs America?**   There are four theories of power in America, each of which must be taken into account in any full explanation of the nation's policies.

Theory	Description
Majoritarianism	Holds that numerical majorities determine issues of policy
Pluralism	Holds that policies are effectively decided through power wielded by special interests that dominate particular policy areas
Elitism	Holds that policy is controlled by a small number of well-positioned, highly influential individuals
Bureaucratic rule	Holds that policy is controlled by well-placed administrators within the government bureaucracy

majority opinions and more than three hundred policy issues. On major issues particularly, Page and Shapiro found that when majority opinion shifted, public policy tended to shift in the same direction.[20]

Nevertheless, most policy decisions are not determined by majority opinion. Government makes thousands of policy decisions each year, and the general public is neither aware of nor interested in most of them (see Chapter 6). Other theories of power are required to explain these cases.

Pluralism: Government by Groups

pluralism

A theory of American politics that holds that society's interests are substantially represented through the activities of groups.

One such theory is **pluralism,** which focuses on group activity and holds that many policies are effectively decided through power wielded by diverse (plural) interests. Farm subsidies, for example, are ordinarily determined more by pressure from agricultural groups than by pressure from the general public.

From a pluralist perspective, society's general interest is served if a diverse range of interests have a voice in government policy. Pluralists see society largely as a collection of separate interests. Farmers, broadcasters, truck drivers, and multinational corporations have different needs and, according to the pluralist view, should have the major voice in policies directly affecting them. Thus, as long as numerous groups have influence in their policy area, government is responding to the interests of most Americans. Pluralists such as Robert Dahl have argued that this is in fact the way the American political system operates most of the time.[21]

Critics argue that pluralists wrongly assume that the public interest is somehow represented in a system that allows special interests, each in its own sphere, to set public policy (see Chapter 9). Any such outcome, they say, represents the triumph of minority over majority rule. Critics also say that society's wealthier interests have undue advantage because they have the organization and money to lobby government effectively.

Elitism: Government by a Few

elitism

The view that the United States essentially is run by a tiny elite (composed of wealthy or well-connected individuals) who control public policy through both direct and indirect means.

Elite theory offers a largely pessimistic view of power in America. **Elitism** holds that power is held by a small number of well-positioned, highly influential individuals. A

Free speech is a familiar aspect of constitutionalism. This anti–gun control rally took place in Austin, Texas.

leading proponent of elite theory was sociologist C. Wright Mills, who argued that key policies are decided by an overlapping coalition of select leaders, including corporate executives, top military officers, and centrally placed public officials.[22] Other proponents of elite theory have defined the core group somewhat differently, but their contention is the same: America is governed not by majorities or by a plurality of groups but by a small number of well-placed, privileged individuals.

Proponents of elite theory differ, however, in the extent to which they believe elites control policy for their own purposes. Some observers claim that elites operate behind the scenes in order to manipulate government for largely selfish purposes.[23] Other observers claim that elites, in part to protect their privileged positions and in part from a sense of public duty, pursue policies that serve society's interest as well as their own. One such view holds that competing elites appeal to voters for support and, in the process, adopt policy positions favored by large blocs of voters.[24]

Unquestionably, certain policies are basically decided by a small circle of influential people. When the U.S. financial system went into a tailspin in 2008, for example, the federal government provided billions of dollars in subsidies and loans to troubled banks. Some of the decisions were made in near secrecy by the Federal Reserve Board chairman, the Treasury secretary, and a few others. In announcing the decisions, they claimed to be acting in the public's interest. The most immediate beneficiaries, however, were a select number of America's most powerful financial institutions.

Bureaucratic Rule: Government by Administrators

A fourth theory holds that power resides in the hands of career government bureaucrats. The leading proponent of the theory of **bureaucratic rule** was the German sociologist Max Weber, who argued that all large organizations tend toward the bureaucratic form, with the result that decision-making power devolves to career administrators whose experience and knowledge of policy issues exceed those of elected officials.[25] Another sociologist, Roberto Michels, propounded the "iron law of oligarchy," concluding that power inevitably gravitates toward experienced administrators at the top of large-scale organizations, even in the case of organizations that aim to be governed democratically.[26]

bureaucratic rule
The tendency of large-scale organizations to develop into the bureaucratic form, with the effect that administrators make key policy decisions.

Bureaucratic politics raises the possibility of a large, permanent government run by unaccountable administrators. Elections come and go, but the bureaucrats who staff executive agencies stay on. As public policy issues have become increasingly complex, bureaucrats often are the most knowledgeable on these issues and also are well positioned to influence their resolution. Modern government could not function without career bureaucrats, but in most cases, they are not instruments of the majority. They tend instead to act in ways that will promote their own agency and its programs (see Chapter 13).

Who Governs?

The perspective of this book is that each of these theories—majoritarianism, pluralism, elitism, and bureaucratic rule—must be taken into account in any full explanation of politics and power in America. As subsequent chapters will demonstrate, some policies are decided by majority influence, while others reflect the influence of special interests, bureaucrats, or elites.

One thing is certain. Few countries in the world have more competing interests than does the United States. The nation's settlement by people of different lands and religions, its great size and geographical variation, and its economic complexity have made the United States a diverse nation. *Competition for power among a great many interests of all kinds is a major characteristic of American politics.* Indeed, America's great diversity helps explain why its political life is not a life-and-death struggle. In *Federalist* No. 10, James Madison argued that government is most dangerous when a single group is powerful enough to gain full political control. In such cases, the group will use government to further its interests at the expense of all others in society. Because the United States is so diverse, however, interests normally must work together to exercise power, a process that requires them to accommodate the interests of others.

The Concept of a Political System and This Book's Organization

As the foregoing discussion suggests, American government consists of a great many related parts. It is instructive to view these components as constituting a **political system.** The parts are separate, but they connect with one another, affecting how each performs. Political scientist David Easton, who was a pioneer in this conception of politics, said that it makes little sense to study political relations piecemeal when they are, in reality, "interrelated."[27]

The political-system concept is the basis for this book's organization (see Figure 1-3). The political system operates against the backdrop of a constitutional framework that defines how power is to be obtained and exercised. This structure is the focus of the opening chapters, which examine how the Constitution defines, in theory and practice, the institutions of government and the rights of individuals. Another part of the political system is *inputs:* the demands people and organizations place on government and the support they provide for institutions, leaders, and policies. These inputs are explored in chapters on public opinion, political participation, political parties, interest groups, and the news media. The functioning of governing officials is addressed in chapters on the nation's *political institutions*—Congress, the presidency, the federal bureaucracy, and the federal courts. Some of the discussion in these chapters is devoted simply to describing these institutions, but much of the discussion explores their interrelationships and the way their actions are affected by inputs and by the constitutional system in which they operate. Throughout the book, but particularly in the closing chapters, attention is given to the political system's *outputs*—policy decisions that are binding on

political system

The various components of American government. The parts are separate, but they connect with one another, affecting how each performs.

The structure of U.S. society helps promote the American dream of success—for example, by encouraging young people to attend college. Shown here are New York University students celebrating their commencement.

Constitutional Framework

Includes provisions for limited government (e.g., checks and balances), representative government, civil liberties, and civil rights

Inputs	Political Institutions	Outputs
Include public opinion, voting and other forms of participation, political parties, campaigns, interest groups, and the news media	⟶ Include the major institutions of government: Congress, the presidency, the judiciary, and the bureaucracy	⟶ Include laws, programs, and other actions in areas such as economic policy, social policy, foreign policy, and defense policy

FIGURE 1-3 **The American Political System** This book's chapters are organized within a political-system framework.

society. These decisions, which are made by political institutions in response to inputs, affect American life in many areas, including the economy, the environment, social welfare, education, foreign affairs, and national defense.

The chapters are collectively designed to convey a reliable body of knowledge that will enable the reader to think systematically about the nature of the American political system. This body of knowledge derives from the full range of methodological approaches that political scientists have applied to the study of politics. Political science, unlike some academic disciplines, has been defined more by its subjects of inquiry than by a particular methodology. Normative theory, historical reasoning, legal analysis, and cultural analysis are among the strains, along with political psychology, political sociology, and political economy. Rational choice theory, organizational theory, and institutional analysis are other strains. Each approach can illuminate certain aspects of politics. For example, rational choice theory is based on the assumption that actors pursue their interests rationally and has proved to be a powerful model to describe, for instance, the behavior of elected officials as they seek to position themselves for reelection. As another example, cultural analysis is a powerful lens through which to view the values that motivate political action.

Political scientists have uncovered numerous tendencies in American political behavior, institutions, and processes. Five of these tendencies have been identified in this opening chapter as deserving special attention:

- Enduring cultural ideals that are Americans' common bond and a source of their political goals
- A substantial division of governing authority that is based on an elaborate system of checks and balances
- Many competing interests that are the result of the nation's great size, population diversity, and economic complexity
- A strong emphasis on individual rights, which is a consequence of the nation's political traditions
- A relatively sharp separation of the political and economic spheres that has the effect of placing many economic issues outside the reach of political majorities

As subsequent chapters will reveal, these tendencies are a key to understanding how the American political system operates. They are not the full story, however, nor could they be. The fact is, America's democracy is an unfinished story, one that will be decided in turn by each new generation. The political scientist E. E. Schattschneider said it best: "In the course of centuries, there has come a great deal of agreement about what democracy is, but nobody has a monopoly on it and the last word has not been spoken."[28]

Summary Self-Test www.mhhe.com/pattersontad9e

The United States is a nation that was formed on a set of ideals. Liberty, equality, and self-government are foremost among these ideals, which also include the principles of individualism, diversity, and unity. These ideals became Americans' common bond and today are the basis of their political culture. Although they are mythic, inexact, and conflicting, these ideals have had a powerful effect on what generation after generation of Americans has tried to achieve politically, for themselves and others.

Politics in the United States plays out through rules of the game that include democracy, constitutionalism, and capitalism. Democracy is rule by the people, which in practice refers to a representative system of government in which the people rule through their elected officials. Constitutionalism refers to rules that limit the rightful power of government over citizens. Capitalism is an economic system based on a free-market principle that allows the government only a limited role in determining how economic costs and benefits will be allocated.

Politics is the process by which it is determined whose values will prevail in society. The basis of politics is conflict over scarce resources and competing values. Those who have power win out in this conflict and are able to control governing authority and policy choices. In the United States, no one faction controls all power and policy. Majorities govern on some issues, while groups, elites, and bureaucrats each govern on other issues.

CHAPTER 1

Study Corner

Key Terms

authoritarian government (*p. 17*)
authority (*p. 19*)
autocracy (*p. 15*)
bureaucratic rule (*p. 21*)
capitalism (*p. 17*)
communism (*p. 17*)
constitutionalism (*p. 16*)
democracy (*p. 15*)
elitism (*p. 20*)
equality (*p. 6*)
individualism (*p. 6*)
liberty (*p. 6*)

majoritarianism (*p. 19*)
oligarchy (*p. 15*)
pluralism (*p. 20*)
political culture (*p. 5*)
political system (*p. 22*)
politics (*p. 12*)
power (*p. 18*)
public policy (*p. 18*)
self-government (*p. 7*)
social contract (*p. 14*)
socialism (*p. 17*)
totalitarian government (*p. 17*)

Self-Test

1. American political culture centers on a set of core ideals that includes all **except** which of the following?
   a. socialism
   b. liberty
   c. equality
   d. self-government

2. Compared with citizens in European democracies, Americans:
   a. emphasize individualism.
   b. feel that success in life is determined by forces outside their control.
   c. are willing to use government to redistribute economic resources.
   d. a and b.
   e. all of the above.

3. When people are able to control policy decisions and prevail in political conflicts, they are said to have:
   a. political culture.
   b. political power.
   c. pluralism.
   d. diversity.

4. America's commitment to the principle of constitutionalism means:
   a. the majority can decide all policy issues.
   b. there are limits on the rightful power of government over citizens.
   c. direct democracy will be favored over representative democracy.
   d. a "mixed economy" must be upheld at all costs.

5. Which one of the following is **not** among the four theories of power concerning who governs America mentioned in the text?
   a. majoritarianism
   b. pluralism
   c. aristocratic rule
   d. bureaucratic rule

6. Which of the following statements are true about American ideals?
   a. They do not fully match what happens in reality.
   b. There is inevitable conflict between these ideals.
   c. Americans have no interest in putting the ideals into practice.
   d. only a and b
   e. only b and c

7. Cultural beliefs are mythical in the sense that they are based on wishful thinking and serve no useful purpose for society. (T/F)

8. Historically, America has been relatively free from racial and ethnic discrimination. (T/F)

9. Authority can be defined as the recognized right of an individual, organization, or institution to make binding decisions. (T/F)

10. Americans have the world's most extensive system of college education. (T/F)

Critical Thinking

How are Americans' beliefs about liberty, equality, and self-government related to their preference for constitutionalism? For capitalism? For democracy?

Suggested Readings

Domhoff, G. William. *Who Rules America? Power and Politics,* 5th ed. New York: McGraw-Hill, 2005. A critical assessment of American government by a leading proponent of elite theory.

Ferguson, Robert A. *Reading the Early Republic.* Cambridge, Mass.: Harvard University Press, 2004. Claims that Americans have always been a people striving to live up to their ideals.

Foley, Michael. *American Credo: The Place of Ideas in American Politics.* New York: Oxford University Press, 2007. An analysis of the political influence of Americans' core beliefs.

Katz, Michael B., and Mark J. Stern. *One Nation Divisible: What America Was and What It's Becoming.* New York: Russell Sage Foundation, 2006. A penetrating look at the transformation of American society during the twentieth century.

Lipset, Seymour Martin. *American Exceptionalism: A Double-Edged Sword.* New York: Norton, 1996. Argues that Americans' tendency to view society in idealized terms is a source of both alienation and progress.

Schuck, Peter H. *Diversity in America: Keeping Government at a Safe Distance.* Cambridge, Mass.: Belknap Press of Harvard, 2003. A far-reaching analysis of when diversity does and does not serve America's interests.

Stout, Jeffrey. *Democracy and Tradition.* Princeton, N.J.: Princeton University Press, 2004. An analysis of the moral claims associated with democracy.

White, John Kenneth. *The Values Divide.* Washington, D.C.: CQ Press, 2002. A look at Americans' values in a time of change.

List of Websites

http://www.conginst.org/
A site that provides up-to-date survey data on the American political culture.

http://www.loc.gov/
The Library of Congress website; provides access to over 70 million historical and contemporary U.S. documents.

http://www.stateline.org/
A University of Richmond/Pew Charitable Trusts site dedicated to providing citizens with information on major policy issues.

http://www.tocqueville.org/
Includes biographical and other references to Alexis de Tocqueville and his writings.

Participate!

The American political culture includes a belief in liberty, equality, and self-government. As a prelude to getting involved in public affairs, reflect on what these ideals mean to you. What types of political activity are associated with each of these ideals? Thinking of your own experiences, what have you done to promote these ideals? What might you consider doing in the future to promote them?

Extra Credit

For up-to-the-minute *New York Times* articles, interactive simulations, graphics, study tools, and more links and quizzes, visit the text's Online Learning Center at www.mhhe.com/pattersontad9e.

Self-Test Answers

1. a   2. a   3. b   4. b   5. c   6. d   7. F   8. F   9. T   10. T

Generation 'We'

The Awakened Giant

During the first presidential campaign of the new millennium, Harvard students Erin Ashwell and Trevor Dryer, like their counterparts at colleges across the country, eagerly awaited the thrill of voting in a national election for the first time. Their anticipation was tempered, however, by dismissive talk about the apparent political disaffection of young people and the youth vote's irrelevance in the 2000 elections.

This didn't strike Ashwell and Dryer as the whole story. "In 2000, there was a lot of press about how young people don't vote, don't get involved, don't care about politics," Ashwell recalls. "Trevor and I wanted to know if it was true. It didn't seem right: All of our friends were into community service." Although they were only college sophomores—or perhaps because they were college sophomores—the pair decided to test conventional wisdom. They also sought to shed light on the paradox of a generation of young activists who devoted hours each week to tutoring underprivileged children, volunteering at food banks, and promoting environmental activism—but who couldn't be bothered to register or vote.

Ashwell and Dryer began delving into the attitudes of their fellow collegians via a nationwide survey, a project Harvard continued after they graduated. Over the ensuing years, the poll by the Institute of Politics at the John F. Kennedy School of Government has penetrated more deeply than other surveys, using the Internet and other innovative techniques, such as having undergraduates help formulate the questions.

The survey has drawn a picture of a unique generation. Today's youth are an underrated force in American civic life—difficult to stereotype, with attitudes markedly different from those of their predecessors. College students overwhelmingly favor the partial privatization of Social Security, a conservative Republican position and one at odds with the preferences of older Americans. Yet they are far more supportive of gay marriage, gay adoption, and gays' being allowed to serve openly in the military than any other age

group, views that place them in the vanguard of Democratic liberalism. In many respects, they are available to both major parties and, judging by their weak party affiliation, would be receptive to an independent presidential candidate. The 2006 IOP poll went even further, concluding that the traditional labels of "liberal" and "conservative" don't adequately capture the complexity of college students' attitudes. One in four college students identify themselves as "religious centrists," a stance that indicates deep concern over the moral direction of the country—and that encompasses issues such as environmental protection, universal health care, and free trade.

Today's college students are not isolationist, but they are the furthest thing from unilateralists. The Institute of Politics poll shows that college students are twice as likely as older Americans to favor a United Nations solution to a foreign crisis than a plan conceived in Washington.

These young people are so little understood that many of the 2006 congressional campaigns ignored them utterly, although candidates who did paid a price for their inattention. Social scientists can't even agree on what to call this generation. Some label those ages 18 to 29 "Generation Y," to distinguish them from the Generation X-ers who preceded them. Others call them "Millennials." The Pew Research Center calls them simply "Generation Next." They are certainly not the "Me Generation." Harvard professor David C. King, research director at the Institute of Politics, calls them "Generation We." Is that an exaggeration?

Released in April 2000, "Attitudes Toward Public Service: A National Survey of College Undergraduates" found that although 59.5 percent of the students surveyed had participated in active community service in the previous 12 months, only 16 percent had signed on to a government, political, or issue-oriented organization and only 6.5 percent had volunteered for any kind of political campaign. The students' attitudes toward government ranged from cynicism to antipathy: Almost two-thirds of them said they didn't

trust the federal government to "do the right thing" all or most of the time. Asked about the motivations of politicians, three-fourths of the respondents said that elected officials "seem to be motivated by selfish reasons." More than 70 percent said that America's political institutions were unconcerned with the desires of college students.

A study by the National Association of Secretaries of State, moreover, showed that turnout among young voters in the 1996 presidential election was the lowest on record, and hinted at an even worse performance in 2000. Eight years of Bill Clinton's White House, a contentiously partisan Congress, and a scandal-mongering media had produced nearly the opposite effect that Clinton's boyhood hero JFK had had on the nation's young people. "They were just turned off to politics," pollster John Della Volpe says. "Community service was something they could get their hands on. You could feed a hungry person or teach a struggling high school kid his math problem, and it was tangible. Political success was more ephemeral. We'd get these responses in the focus groups: 'What difference does it make who the president is? It's just some old white guy.' To them, politics wasn't ever cool, and it wasn't very fun."

The dismal forecast for November 2000 came true. According to the Census Bureau's supplemental information (available several months after each election), the turnout among voters ages 18 to 24 stayed at the all-time-low 1996 figure of 36 percent—and turnout among 18-to-21-year-olds fell below 30 percent for the first time.

Then the planes hit.

On September 11, 2001, former Sen. David Pryor of Arkansas was director of the Institute of Politics. Acting on gut instinct, he ginned up the poll again. The results this time couldn't have been more different. "The attacks of 9/11 totally changed the way the Millennial Generation thinks about politics," Della Volpe says today. "Overnight, their attitudes were more like the Greatest Generation."

A stunning 60 percent of college students in the institute's new survey said they had faith in the government to do the right thing all or most of the time, compared with 36 percent in 2000. Fully three-fourths of them expressed "trust" in the military, 69 percent said they trusted the president, and 62 percent said they trusted Congress. Four out of five supported U.S. military action in Afghanistan, and the same number rated terrorism as the top issue facing the United States.

Yet two intriguing elements in the 2001 poll were little noticed at the time. First, the college students' newfound hawkishness did not replace their altruism; it supplemented it. The number participating in community service increased, to 69 percent. The second facet that, in hindsight, seems significant is that in the days just after 9/11, college students' support for a military solution, while quite high, was noticeably lower than that of older voters.

By the spring of 2003, 65 percent of college students supported the war (compared with 78 percent of the entire country), but a trend toward multinationalism—particularly support for the United Nations—was building among the students.

The Millennials were, in Della Volpe's words, "creating a unique political voice of their own." By then, the institute was polling twice a year, and the October survey underscored the point about the students' singular identity. In that poll, college students revealed themselves to be more pro-Bush than their older counterparts but simultaneously more skeptical of the Iraq war. The youth vote in the impending presidential race, it seemed, was up for grabs, and by the time of the April 2004 institute poll, John Kerry had emerged on college campuses as a 10-point favorite.

Inside the Kerry campaign and in groups such as Rock the Vote, the high expectations

Today's youth are an **underrated force in American civic life**—difficult to stereotype, with attitudes markedly different from those of their predecessors.

were palpable: The 18-to-24-year-olds were going to lead Democrats back into the White House. But Election Day brought heartburn to liberals, starting with erroneous early exit polls that seemed to presage a big Kerry win and then compounded by a widely distributed news service article (also based on exit polls) asserting that the youth-vote surge had not materialized.

But this interpretation was mistaken. David King, the Harvard professor, whose specialty is analyzing voting patterns, says that exit polls weren't taken near college campuses. Furthermore, Election Night stories confused turnout with vote share. Months later, after the Census Bureau released its supplemental information, it became apparent that the number of voters younger than 25 had jumped 11 points—compared with an increase of 4 points among those 25 and older. "One of the missed angles of the 2004 election is that college-age people drove the increase in voter turnout nationally," Jeanne Shaheen, the institute's current director, said at the time.

In 2002, David W. Nickerson made a name for himself as a graduate student at Yale by writing a thesis showing that young voters were just as susceptible to the blandishments of politicians as anyone else, but that it was three times as costly for a political campaign

to reach them. If one also considers that young voters are more fickle than older ones—studies have shown that they are more likely to change their preferences in midcampaign—only a very stubborn campaign manager would spend money wooing the young. But five years can be a long time in politics, especially when a nation is at war, and most especially when technology is developing rapidly. "That calculus is wrong now," King said. "This is the stock you want to invest in—the young."

What has happened in the meantime? Well, Iraq, and the online YouTube and Facebook, to name three things.

It's common political wisdom that George Allen of Virginia narrowly lost his Senate seat—and the Republican majority along with it—after he was videotaped calling one of Democrat Webb's volunteers a "macaca." What's often forgotten is that Webb's campaign, not knowing quite what to do with the footage, simply posted it on YouTube. The effect was devastating.

King has just finished work on a study in which 56 campaign managers involved in 2006 congressional races were interviewed about their outreach efforts aimed at young voters. The questions ranged from what technology they employed to how many of their staffers were younger than 30. Did they upload to YouTube, make appeals on MySpace, or set up a Facebook page, and raise money online?

King's and Della Volpe's assessment is not that e-mails and podcasts have replaced political volunteers at the grassroots. It's that the new technology has altered Nickerson's cost-benefit analysis. It is now far less expensive to reach young volunteers and voters. But a candidate still must have charisma and a message, and be able to translate high-technology methods into good, old-fashioned ground organizing.

FOR DISCUSSION: Will Generation We be more involved in politics than previous generations?

Will campaigns increasingly use internet technology to successfully mobilize the youth vote, thereby increasing the participation of future generations of young voters?

What effect will the presidential election of 2008 have on the participation of tomorrow's college students in the political process?

Constitutional Democracy

Promoting Liberty and Self-Government

Before the Constitution:
The Colonial and Revolutionary
Experiences

"The Rights of Englishmen"
The Declaration of Independence
The Articles of Confederation
Shays's Rebellion: A Nation
    Dissolving

Negotiating Toward a Constitution

The Great Compromise:
    A Two-Chamber Congress
The North-South Compromise:
    The Issue of Slavery
A Strategy for Ratification
The Ratification Debate
The Framers' Goals

Protecting Liberty:
Limited Government

Grants and Denials of Power
Using Power to Offset Power
Separated Institutions Sharing
    Power: Checks and Balances
The Bill of Rights
Judicial Review

Providing for Self-Government

Democracy Versus Republic
Limited Popular Rule
Altering the Constitution:
    More Power to the People

Constitutional Democracy Today

The people must be governed by a majority, with whom all power resides. But how is the sense of this majority to be obtained? Fisher Ames (1788)[1]

On the night of June 17, 1972, a security guard at the Watergate apartment–office complex in Washington, D.C., noticed that the latch on the door to the Democratic Party's national headquarters had been taped open. He called the police, who captured the five burglars inside. As it turned out, the men had links to Republican President Richard Nixon's Committee to Re-elect the President. Nixon called the incident "bizarre" and denied that anyone on his staff had a part in the break-in.

The reality was that the Watergate break-in was part of an orchestrated campaign of "dirty tricks" designed to ensure Nixon's reelection. The dirty-tricks campaign included wiretaps, tax audits, and burglaries of Nixon's political opponents (the "enemies list"), who included journalists and antiwar activists in addition to Democrats. Although the Nixon White House managed for a time to hide the truth, the facts of the dirty-tricks campaign gradually became known. During Senate investigative hearings, a White House assistant revealed that Nixon had tape-recorded all his telephone calls and personal conversations in the Oval Office. Nixon at first refused to release the tapes but then made public what he claimed were "all the relevant" ones. Congress demanded additional tapes, as did the special prosecutor who had been appointed to investigate criminal aspects of the Watergate affair. In late July, the U.S. Supreme Court, which included four justices appointed by Nixon, unanimously ordered the president to supply sixty-four additional tapes. The tapes were incriminating, and two weeks later, on August 9, 1974, Richard Nixon resigned from office, becoming the first president in U.S. history to do so.

Nixon's downfall was owed in no small measure to the handiwork two centuries earlier of the writers of the Constitution. They were well aware that power could never be entrusted to the goodwill of leaders. "If angels were to govern men," James Madison wrote in *Federalist* No. 51, "neither external nor internal controls on government would be necessary." Madison's point, of course, was

The Senate Judiciary Committee holds hearings on allegations of illegal acts by President Richard Nixon. The congressional investigation led to Nixon's resignation.

limited government

A government that is subject to strict limits on its lawful uses of power, and hence on its ability to deprive people of their liberty.

self-government

The principle that the people are the ultimate source and proper beneficiary of governing authority; in practice, a government based on majority rule.

that leaders are not angels and can harbor a lust for power—hence the Framers' insistence on constitutional checks on power, as when they gave Congress the authority to impeach and remove the president from office.

The writers of the Constitution were determined through their system of checks and balances to protect liberty from the threat of a too-powerful government. The Framers sought a **limited government:** one that is subject to strict limits on its lawful uses of power. They also had a second and partly conflicting objective. They wanted **self-government:** a government based on the people and subject to their control. Self-government requires that the majority through its representatives have the power to rule. However, limited government requires that majority rule stop at the point where it infringes on the legitimate rights and interests of the minority. This consideration led the Framers to forge a Constitution that provides for majority rule but has built-in restrictions on the majority's power.

This chapter describes how the principles of self-government and limited government are embodied in the Constitution and explains the tension between them. The chapter also indicates how these principles have been modified in practice in the course of American history. The main points of this chapter are these:

- *America during the colonial period developed traditions of limited government and self-government.* These traditions were rooted in governing practices, philosophy, and cultural values.

- *The Constitution provides for limited government mainly by defining lawful powers and by dividing those powers among competing institutions.* The Constitution, with its Bill of Rights, also prohibits government from infringing on individual rights. Judicial review is an additional safeguard of limited government.

- *The Constitution in its original form provided for self-government mainly through indirect systems of popular election of representatives.* The Framers' theory of self-government was based on the notion that political power must be separated from immediate popular influences if sound policies are to result.

- *The idea of popular government—in which the majority's desires have a more direct and immediate impact on governing officials—has gained strength since the nation's beginning.* Originally, the House of Representatives was the only institution subject to direct vote of the people. This mechanism has been extended to other institutions and, through primary elections, even to the nomination of candidates for public office.

Before the Constitution: The Colonial and Revolutionary Experiences

Early Americans' admiration for limited government was based partly on their British heritage. Unlike other European governments of the time, Britain did not have an absolute monarchy. Parliament was an independent body with lawmaking powers, and British subjects had certain rights, including that of jury trial. This tradition carried over to the American colonies. In each colony, there was a right to trial by jury. There was also freedom of expression, although of a limited kind. Not all colonies, for example, granted freedom to all religions. The colonies also had a degree of self-government. Each had an elected representative assembly, which was subject to British oversight but nonetheless had substantial legislative powers.

The colonists also had the example of Native American governments, particularly that of the Iroquois Confederacy. This confederacy was a union of the Mohawk, Oneida, Onondaga, Cayuga, and Seneca tribes, governed by a fifty-member council made up of representatives of the five tribes. To protect each tribe's separate interests, the confederacy's constitution included a system of checks and balances—a feature that would become a hallmark of the U.S. Constitution. Historians disagree over the extent of the influence of the Iroquois Confederacy on colonial thought, but Benjamin Franklin and Thomas Jefferson were among those who admired the confederacy's governing system.

"The Rights of Englishmen"

The Revolutionary War was partly a rebellion against Britain's failure to respect its own tradition of limited government in the colonies. Many of the colonial charters had conferred upon Americans "the rights of Englishmen," but Britain showed progressively less respect for these rights over time. During the French and Indian War (1756–1763), the colonists fought alongside British soldiers to drive the French out of the western territories. At the end of the war, however,

HISTORICAL *Background*

This 1790s colored engraving by William Birch depicts a Philadelphia street scene. Philadelphia's role in the birth of the American nation is rivaled only by Boston's contribution.

Britain for the first time imposed heavy taxes on the colonies. The war with France, which was also waged in Europe, had created a budget crisis in Britain. Taxing the colonies was a way to reduce the debt, so Parliament levied a stamp tax on colonial newspapers and business documents. The colonists were not represented in Parliament, and they responded angrily. "No taxation without representation" became the rallying cry.

Although Parliament backed down and repealed the Stamp Act, it then passed the Townshend Act, which imposed taxes on all glass, paper, tea, and lead. The colonists again objected, and Parliament again backed down, except for the tax on tea, which was kept to demonstrate that Britain was still in charge of colonial affairs. The tea tax sparked an act of defiance that became known as the "Boston Tea Party." In December 1773, under the cover of darkness, a small band of patriots disguised as Native Americans boarded an English ship in Boston Harbor and dumped its cargo of tea overboard.

In 1774, the colonists met in Philadelphia at the First Continental Congress to decide what they would demand from Britain. They asked for their own councils for the imposition of taxes, an end to the British military occupation, and a guarantee of trial by local juries. (British authorities had resorted to shipping "troublemakers" to London for trial.) King George III rejected their demands, and British troops and colonial minutemen clashed at Lexington and Concord on April 19, 1775. Eight colonists died on the Lexington green in what became known as "the shot heard 'round the world." The American Revolution had begun.

The Declaration of Independence

Although grievances against Britain were the immediate cause of the American Revolution, ideas about the proper form of government were also on the colonists' minds.[2] The century-old theory of John Locke was particularly influential. Locke held that people have **inalienable rights** (or **natural rights**)—including those of life, liberty, and property—and can rebel against a ruler who tramples on these rights (see Chapter 1).

Thomas Jefferson declared that Locke "was one of the three greatest men that ever lived, without exception," and Jefferson paraphrased Locke's ideas in passages of the Declaration of Independence, including those asserting that "all men are created equal," that governments derive "their just powers from the consent of the governed," and that "it is the right of the people to alter or abolish" a tyrannical government. The Declaration was a call to revolution rather than a framework for a new form of government, but the ideas it contained—liberty, equality, individual rights, self-government, lawful powers—became the basis, eleven years later, for the Constitution of the United States. (The Declaration of Independence and the Constitution are reprinted in their entirety in the book's appendixes.)

The Articles of Confederation

The first government of the United States was based not on the Constitution but on the Articles of Confederation. The Articles, which were adopted during the Revolutionary War, created a very weak national government that was subordinate to the states. The colonies had always been governed separately, and their people considered themselves Virginians, New Yorkers, Pennsylvanians, and so on as much as they thought of themselves as Americans. Moreover, they were wary of a powerful central government. The American Revolution was sparked

inalienable (natural) rights

Those rights that persons theoretically possessed in the state of nature, prior to the formation of governments. These rights, including those of life, liberty, and property, are considered inherent and, as such, are inalienable. Since government is established by people, government has the responsibility to preserve these rights.

HISTORICAL
Background

This is a portion of Thomas Jefferson's handwritten draft of the Declaration of Independence, a formal expression of America's governing ideals.

by grievances against the arbitrary policies of King George III, and Americans were in no mood to replace him with a strong national authority of their own making.

Under the Articles of Confederation, each state retained its "sovereignty, freedom and independence." There was a national Congress, but its members were appointed and paid by their respective state governments. Each of the thirteen states had one vote in Congress, and the agreement of nine states was required to pass legislation. Moreover, any state could block constitutional change: the Articles of Confederation could be amended only by unanimous approval of the states.

The American union held together out of necessity during the Revolutionary War. If the states had not stayed together, they would have had no choice but to surrender to the British. But once the war ended, the states felt free to go their separate ways. Several states sent representatives abroad to negotiate their own trade agreements with foreign nations. New Hampshire, with its eighteen-mile coastline, even established its own navy. In a melancholy letter to Thomas Jefferson, George Washington wondered whether the United States deserved to be called "a nation."

Congress was expected to provide for the nation's defense and establish the basis for a general economy, but the Articles of Confederation did not give it the powers necessary to achieve these goals. The Articles prohibited Congress from interfering in the states' commerce policies, and the states were soon engaged in ruinous trade wars. The Articles also denied to Congress the power to tax, and as a result, it had no money with which to build a navy or hire an army.

Shays's Rebellion: A Nation Dissolving

By 1784, the new nation was unraveling. Congress was so weak that its members often did not bother to attend its sessions.[3] Then, in late 1786, a revolt in western Massachusetts prompted leading Americans to seek a change in the country's form of government. A ragtag army of two thousand farmers armed with pitchforks marched on county courthouses to prevent foreclosures on their land. Many of the farmers were veterans of the Revolutionary War; their leader, Daniel Shays, had been a captain in the American army. They had been given

County courthouses in Massachusetts in 1786 were the scenes of brawls between angry farmers and citizens who supported the state's attempts to foreclose on farmers' property because of unpaid debts. The violence of Shays's Rebellion convinced many political leaders that anarchy was spreading and that a more powerful national government was required to stop it.

assurances during the Revolution that their land, which sat unploughed because they were away at war, would not be confiscated for unpaid debts and taxes. They were also promised the back pay owed to them for their military service. (Congress had run out of money during the Revolution.) Instead, they received no back pay, and heavy new taxes were levied on their farms. Many farmers faced not only losing their property but being sent to prison for unpaid debts.

Shays's Rebellion frightened wealthy interests, who called on the governor of Massachusetts to put down the revolt. He in turn asked Congress for help, but it had no army to send. The governor finally raised enough money to hire a militia that put down the uprising, but Shays's Rebellion made it clear that Congress and the army were weak and that civil unrest was spreading. The crisis could not be ignored. Five states held an emergency meeting in Annapolis and sent a plea to Congress to authorize a constitutional convention of all the states in Philadelphia. Congress authorized the convention but placed a restriction on it: the delegates were to meet for "the sole and express purpose of revising the Articles of Confederation."

Negotiating Toward a Constitution

The delegates to the Philadelphia constitutional convention ignored the instructions of Congress, instead drafting a plan for an entirely new form of government. Prominent delegates (among them George Washington, Benjamin Franklin, and James Madison) were determined from the outset to establish an American nation built on a strong central government.

The Great Compromise: A Two-Chamber Congress

Debate at the constitutional convention of 1787 began over a plan put forward by the Virginia delegation, which was dominated by strong nationalists. The **Virginia Plan** (also called the **large-state plan**) called for a two-chamber Congress that would have supreme authority in all areas "in which the separate states are incompetent," particularly defense and interstate trade. The Virginia Plan also provided that representation in both chambers would be based on size. Small states such as Delaware and Rhode Island would be allowed only one representative in the lower chamber, while large states such as Massachusetts and Virginia would have more than a dozen.

The Virginia Plan was sharply attacked by delegates from the smaller states. They rallied around a counterproposal made by New Jersey's William Paterson. The **New Jersey Plan** (also called the **small-state plan**) called for a stronger national government with the power to tax and to regulate commerce among the states; in most other respects, however, the Articles would remain in effect. Congress would have a single chamber in which each state, large or small, would have a single vote.

The debate over the two plans dragged on for weeks before the delegates reached what is now known as the **Great Compromise.** It provided for a bicameral (two-chamber) Congress. One chamber, the House of Representatives, would be apportioned among the states on the basis of population. The other chamber, the Senate, would be apportioned on the basis of an equal number of votes (two) for each state. This compromise was critical. The small states would not have agreed to join a union in which their vote was always weaker than that of large states, a fact reflected in Article V of the Constitution: "No state, without its consent, shall be deprived of its equal suffrage in the Senate."

Virginia (large-state) Plan

A constitutional proposal for a strong Congress with two chambers, both of which would be based on numerical representation, thus granting more power to the larger states.

New Jersey (small-state) Plan

A constitutional proposal for a strengthened Congress but one in which each state would have a single vote, thus granting a small state the same legislative power as a large state.

Great Compromise

The agreement at the constitutional convention to create a two-chamber Congress with the House apportioned by population and the Senate apportioned equally by state.

The North-South Compromise: The Issue of Slavery

North-South Compromise

The agreement over economic and slavery issues that enabled northern and southern states to settle differences that threatened to defeat the effort to draft a new constitution. Southern delegates at the constitutional convention sought assurances that Congress would not bar the importation and sale of slaves and that their slave-based agricultural economy would be protected.

The separate interests of the states were also the basis for a second major agreement: the **North-South Compromise** on economic issues. The southern states feared that the states of the North, which were more numerous and had a larger population, would use their numerical majority in Congress to tax them unfairly. If Congress imposed high tariffs on manufactured goods imported from Europe in order to protect domestic manufacturers, the South would be disadvantaged, since U.S. manufacturing was largely based in the North. Then, if Congress also imposed high tariffs on agricultural exports, the South would again be disadvantaged because it was the prime source of agricultural exports, which, if taxed, would be more expensive and therefore of less interest to European buyers. The South's delegates were also concerned that northern representatives in Congress would tax or even bar the importation of slaves.

After extended debate, a compromise was reached. Congress would have the authority to tax imports but would be prohibited from taxing exports. Congress also would be prohibited until 1808 from passing laws to end the slave trade. However, the most controversial trade-off was the so-called Three-Fifths Compromise. For purposes of apportionment of taxes and seats in the U.S. House of Representatives, each slave was to count as less than a full person. Northern delegates had argued against the counting of slaves because they did not have legal rights. Southern delegates wanted to count them as full persons for purposes of apportioning House seats (which would have the effect of increasing the number of southern representatives) and to count them as

The photo shows a Civil War–era building in Atlanta that was a site of slave auctions.

nonpersons for purposes of apportioning taxes (which would have the effect of decreasing the amount of federal taxes levied on the southern states). The delegates finally settled on a compromise that included both taxation and apportionment but counted each slave as three-fifths of a person. Although the southern states did not get all that they wanted, they got the better end of the bargain. If slaves had not been counted at all, the southern states would have had only slightly more than 35 percent of House seats. With the compromise, they held nearly 45 percent of the seats, giving them considerable power over national policy.

These compromises have led critics to claim that the Framers of the Constitution had no objections to slavery. In fact, most of the delegates were deeply troubled by it, recognizing the stark inconsistency between the practice of slavery and a professed belief in liberty and equality. "It is inconsistent with the principles of the Revolution," Maryland's Luther Martin stated. George Mason, a Virginian and a slaveholder, said: "[Slaveholders] bring the judgment of heaven on a country."[4] Benjamin Franklin and Alexander Hamilton were among the delegates who were involved in antislavery organizations.

Yet the southern states' dependence on slavery was a reality that the delegates had to confront if there was to be a union of the states. The northern states had few slaves, whereas the southern economies were based on slavery (see Figure 2-1). John Rutledge of South Carolina asked during the convention debate whether the North regarded southerners as "fools." Southern delegates declared that they would form their own union rather than join one that banned slavery.

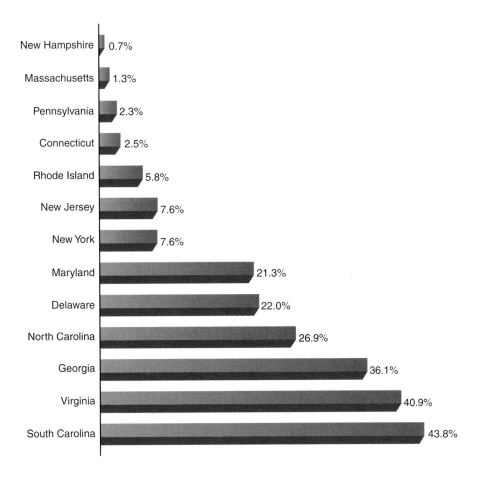

FIGURE 2-1 **African Americans as a Percentage of State Population, 1790**
At the time of the writing of the Constitution, African Americans (most of whom were slaves) were concentrated in the southern states.
Source: U.S. Bureau of the Census.

A Strategy for Ratification

The compromises over slavery and the structure of the Congress took up most of the four months that the convention was in session. Some of the other issues, such as the structure and powers of the federal judiciary, were the subject of surprisingly little debate.

There remained a final issue, however: would those Americans not attending the convention support the proposed Constitution? The delegates realized that ratification was not a sure thing. Congress had not authorized a wholesale restructuring of the federal government. In fact, in authorizing the Philadelphia convention, Congress had stated that any proposed change in the Articles of Confederation would have to be "agreed to in Congress" and then "confirmed by [all of] the states." The delegates recognized that if unanimous consent were required, the Constitution would have no chance of ratification. Rhode Island had refused even to send a delegation to the convention. In a bold move, the delegates established their own ratification process. They instructed Congress to submit the document directly to the states, where it would become law after having been approved by at least nine states in special ratifying conventions of popularly elected delegates. It was a masterful strategy. There was little hope that all thirteen state legislatures would approve the Constitution, but nine states through conventions might be persuaded to ratify it. Indeed, North Carolina and Rhode Island were steadfastly opposed to the new union and did not ratify the Constitution until the other eleven states had ratified it and begun the process of establishing the new government.

The Ratification Debate

Anti-Federalists

A term used to describe opponents of the Constitution during the debate over ratification.

The debate over ratification was contentious. The **Anti-Federalists** (as opponents of the Constitution were labeled) raised arguments that still echo in American politics. They claimed that the national government would be too powerful and would threaten self-government in the separate states and the liberty of the people. Many Americans had an innate distrust of centralized power and worried that the people's liberty could be eclipsed as easily by a distant American government as it had been by the British king. The fact that the Constitution contained no bill of rights heightened this concern. Did its absence indicate that the central government would be free to define for itself what the people's rights would be?

The presidency was another source of contention. No such office had existed under the Articles of Confederation, and some worried that it would lead to the creation of an American monarchy. The fact that the president would be chosen by electors appointed by the states (the electoral college) lessened but did not eliminate this concern.

Even the motives of the men who wrote the Constitution came under attack. They were men of wealth and education who had acted in response to debtors' riots. Would the Constitution become a tool by which the wealthy ruled over those with little or no money? And who would bear the burden of additional taxation? For Americans struggling with local and state tax payments, the thought of paying national taxes as well was not appealing.

Most Anti-Federalists acknowledged a need to strengthen national commerce and defense. What they opposed was the creation of a powerful national government as the mechanism. They favored a revision of the Articles of Confederation, which in their opinion could accomplish these goals without the risk of establishing a government that could threaten their liberties, their livelihoods, and their local interests. (The Anti-Federalist argument is discussed further in Chapter 3.)

Federalists

A term used to describe proponents of the Constitution during the debate over ratification.

The **Federalists** (as the Constitution's supporters called themselves) responded with a persuasive case of their own. Their strongest arguments were set forth by James Madison and Alexander Hamilton, who along with John Jay wrote a series of essays that were published in a New York City newspaper under the pen name Publius. (The essays, collectively referred to as *The Federalist Papers,* are widely acknowledged as a brilliant political treatise.) Madison and Hamilton argued that the government of the Constitution would correct the defects of the Articles; it would have the power necessary to forge a secure and prosperous union. At the same time, because of restrictions on its powers, the new government would endanger neither the states nor personal liberty. In *Federalist* Nos. 47, 48, 49, 50, and 51, for example, Madison explained how the separation of national institutions was designed both to empower and to restrict the federal government. (The Federalist argument is discussed further in Chapter 3.)

Whether the ratification debate changed many minds is unclear. Historical evidence suggests, however, that a majority of ordinary Americans opposed the Constitution's ratification. But their voice in the state ratifying conventions was smaller than that of wealthier interests, which in the main supported the change. The pro-ratification forces were also bolstered by the assumption that George Washington, the country's most trusted and popular leader, would become the first president. In the view of historians, this assumption, and the fact that Washington had presided over the Philadelphia convention, tipped the balance in favor of ratification.

Delaware was the first state to ratify the Constitution, and Connecticut, Georgia, and New Jersey followed, an indication that the Great Compromise had satisfied several of the small states. In the early summer of 1788, New Hampshire became the ninth state to ratify. The Constitution was law. But neither Virginia nor New York had ratified it, and a stable union without these major states was almost unthinkable. As large in area as many European countries, they conceivably could have survived as independent nations. In fact, they nearly did choose a separate course. In both states, the Constitution barely passed, and then only after the Federalists promised to support a bill of rights designed to protect individual liberty from the power of the central government.

LEADERS

ALEXANDER HAMILTON
(1755–1804)

Born an illegitimate child, Alexander Hamilton left his native West Indies in his teens for New York. A brilliant student and essayist, Hamilton joined the revolutionary army, distinguishing himself in early fighting around New York, and became aide to General George Washington—the beginning of a relationship that would serve both men well. After the war, Hamilton pursued a career in law and politics and went to the 1787 Philadelphia convention as a New York delegate. A firm believer in a strong national government, Hamilton contributed to the Constitution's ratification through his *Federalist Papers* essays. Appointed the nation's first secretary of the treasury by President Washington, he fought with Secretary of State Thomas Jefferson over the direction of national policy. In a brilliant political move, Hamilton agreed to locate the nation's capital at the tip of Virginia in exchange for Jefferson's support of the consolidation of state debts at the federal level. This financial system, along with the creation of the First Bank of the United States, enabled Hamilton to establish a national fiscal policy. Creditors at home and abroad henceforth would place their trust in the federal government. His dispute with Jefferson led to the creation of America's first political parties—the Republicans, founded by Jefferson, and the Federalists, founded by Hamilton. When John Adams replaced Washington as president, Hamilton stayed on as secretary of the treasury, a situation that became uncomfortable when several members of Adams's cabinet showed more loyalty to Hamilton than to Adams. In 1804, Hamilton was fatally wounded in a pistol duel with Aaron Burr, a political and personal foe.

The Framers' Goals

The Englishman James Bryce ranked America's Constitution as its greatest contribution to the practice of government. The Constitution offered the world a new model of government in which a written document defining the government's

TABLE 2-1 | Major Goals of the Framers of the Constitution

1. To establish a government strong enough to meet the nation's needs—an objective sought through substantial grants of power to the federal government in areas such as defense and commerce (see Chapter 3)

2. To establish a government that would not threaten the existence of the separate states—an objective sought through federalism (see Chapter 3) and through a Congress connected to the states through elections

3. To establish a government that would not threaten liberty—an objective sought through an elaborate system of checks and balances

4. To establish a government based on popular consent—an objective sought through provisions for the direct and indirect election of public officials

constitution

The fundamental law that defines how a government will legitimately operate.

lawful powers would represent a higher authority than the actions of any political leader or institution.

A **constitution** is the fundamental law that defines how a government will legitimately operate—the method for choosing its leaders, the institutions through which these leaders will work, the procedures they must follow in making policy, and the powers they can lawfully exercise. The U.S. Constitution is exactly such a law; it is the highest law of the land. Its provisions define how power is to be acquired and how it can be used.

The Constitution embodied the Framers' vision of a proper government for the American people (see Table 2-1). One of the Framers' goals was the creation of a national government strong enough to meet the nation's needs, particularly in the areas of defense and commerce. Another goal was to preserve the states as governing entities. Accordingly, the Framers established a system of government (federalism) in which power is divided between the national government and the states. Federalism is discussed at length in Chapter 3, which also explains how the Constitution laid the foundation for a strong national government.

The Framers' other goals were to establish a national government that was restricted in its lawful uses of power (limited government) and that gave the people a voice in their governance (self-government). These two goals and the story of how they were written into the Constitution are the focus of the rest of this chapter.

Protecting Liberty: Limited Government

A challenge facing the Framers of the Constitution was how to control the coercive force of government. Government's unique characteristic is that it alone can legally arrest, imprison, and even kill people who break its rules. Force is not the only basis of effective government, but government must be able to use force to prevent lawless elements from brutalizing innocent people. The dilemma is that government itself can use its force to abuse its opponents. "It is a melancholy reflection," James Madison wrote to Thomas Jefferson shortly after the Constitution's ratification, "that liberty should be equally exposed to danger whether the government has too much or too little power."[5]

The men who wrote the Constitution sought to establish a government strong enough to enforce national interests, including defense and commerce among the states (see Chapter 3), but not so strong as to destroy liberty. Limited government is built into the Constitution through both grants of political power and restrictions on that power (see Table 2-2).

TABLE 2-2 | **Constitutional Provisions for Limited Government**   The U.S. Constitution creates an elaborate governing structure designed to protect against the abusive exercise of power—in short, to create a limited government.

Mechanism	Purpose
Grants of power	Powers granted to the national government; accordingly, powers not granted it are denied it unless they are necessary and proper to the carrying out of the granted powers.
Separated institutions	The division of the national government's power among three power-sharing branches, each of which is to act as a check on the powers of the other two.
Federalism	The division of political authority between the national government and the states, enabling the people to appeal to one authority if their rights and interests are not respected by the other authority.
Denials of power	Powers expressly denied to the national and state governments by the Constitution.
Bill of Rights	The first ten amendments to the Constitution, which specify rights of citizens that the national government must respect.
Judicial review	The power of the courts to declare governmental action null and void when it is found to violate the Constitution.
Elections	The power of the voters to remove officials from office.

Grants and Denials of Power

The Framers chose to limit the national government in part by confining its scope to constitutional **grants of power.** Congress's lawmaking powers are specifically listed in Article I, Section 8 of the Constitution. Seventeen in number, these listed powers include, for example, the powers to tax, to establish an army and navy, to declare war, to regulate commerce among the states, to create a national currency, and to borrow money. Powers *not* granted to the government by the Constitution are in theory denied to it. In a period when other governments had unrestricted powers, this limitation was remarkable.

The Framers also used **denials of power** as a means to limit government, prohibiting certain practices that European rulers had routinely used to intimidate political opponents. The French king, for example, could imprison a subject indefinitely without charge. The U.S. Constitution prohibits such action: citizens have the right to be brought before a court under a writ of habeas corpus for a judgment as to the legality of their confinement. The Constitution also forbids Congress and the states from passing ex post facto laws, under which citizens can be prosecuted for acts that were legal at the time they were committed.

As a further denial of power, the Framers made the Constitution difficult to amend, thereby making it hard for those in power to increase their lawful authority by changing the Constitution. An amendment could be proposed only by a two-thirds majority in both chambers of Congress or by a national constitutional convention called by two-thirds of the state legislatures. Such a proposal would then become law only if ratified by three-fourths of state legislatures or state conventions. In all but one case (the Twenty-first Amendment), state

grants of power

The method of limiting the U.S. government by confining its scope of authority to those powers expressly granted in the Constitution.

denials of power

A constitutional means of limiting government by listing those powers that government is expressly prohibited from using.

legislatures have done the ratifying. The national constitutional convention as a means of proposing amendments has never been used.

Using Power to Offset Power

Although the Framers believed that grants and denials of power could act as controls on government, they had no illusion that written words alone would suffice. As a consequence, they sought to control government by dividing its powers among separate institutions.[6]

separation of powers
The division of the powers of government among separate institutions or branches.

The idea of a **separation of powers** had been proposed decades earlier by the French theorist Montesquieu. His reasoning was widely accepted in America, and when the states drafted new constitutions after the start of the Revolutionary War, they built their governments around this concept. Pennsylvania was an exception, and its experience only seemed to prove the necessity of separated powers. Unrestrained by an independent judiciary or executive, Pennsylvania's all-powerful legislature ignored basic rights and freedoms: Quakers were disenfranchised for their religious beliefs, conscientious objectors to the Revolutionary War were prosecuted, and the right of trial by jury was eliminated.

In *Federalist* No. 10, Madison asked why governments often act according to the interests of overbearing majorities rather than according to principles of justice. He attributed the problem to "the mischiefs of faction." People, he argued, are divided into opposing religious, geographical, ethnic, economic, and other factions. These divisions are natural and desirable in that free people have a right to their personal opinions and interests. Yet factions can themselves be a source of oppressive government. If a faction gains full power, it will use government to advance itself at the expense of all others. (*Federalist* No. 10 is widely regarded as the finest political essay ever written by an American. It is reprinted in an appendix at the back of this book.)

Out of this concern came the Framers' special contribution to the doctrine of the separation of powers. They did not believe that it would be enough, as Montesquieu had suggested, to divide the government's authority strictly along institutional lines, granting all legislative power to the legislature, all judicial power to the courts, and all executive power to the presidency. This total separation would make it too easy for a single faction to exploit a particular area of political power. A faction that controlled the legislature, for example, could enact

The Constitution was written in Philadelphia during the summer of 1787 in the East Room of the Old Pennsylvania State House, where the Declaration of Independence had been signed a decade earlier. George Washington (standing on the right) presided over the constitutional convention. As presiding officer, Washington remained neutral during the deliberations, allowing the other delegates to debate and decide upon the Constitution's provisions.

laws ruinous to other interests. A better system of divided government would be one in which political power could be applied forcibly only when institutions agreed on its use. This system would require separate but overlapping powers. Because no one faction could easily gain control over all institutions, factions would have to work together, a process that would require each of them to respect the interests of the others.[7]

Separated Institutions Sharing Power: Checks and Balances

The Framers' concept of divided powers has been described by political scientist Richard Neustadt as the principle of **separated institutions sharing power**.[8] The separate branches are interlocked in such a way that an elaborate system of **checks and balances** is created (see Figure 2-2). No institution can

separated institutions sharing power

The principle that, as a way to limit government, its powers should be divided among separate branches, each of which also shares in the power of the others as a means of checking and balancing them. The result is that no one branch can exercise power decisively without the support or acquiescence of the others.

checks and balances

The elaborate system of divided spheres of authority provided by the U.S. Constitution as a means of controlling the power of government. The separation of powers among the branches of the national government, federalism, and the different methods of selecting national officers are all part of this system.

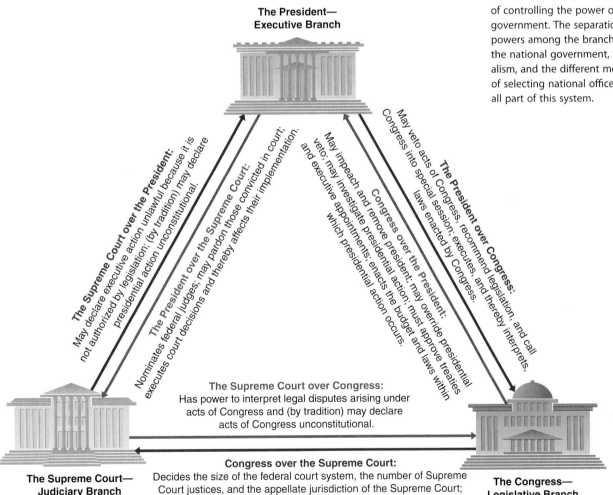

FIGURE 2-2 **The System of Checks and Balances** This elaborate system of divided spheres of authority was provided by the U.S. Constitution as a means of controlling the power of government. The separation of powers among the branches of the national government, federalism, and the different methods of selecting national officers are all part of this system.

HOW THE U.S. COMPARES

CHECKS AND BALANCES

All democracies place constitutional limits on the power of government. The concept of rule by law, for example, is characteristic of democratic governments but not of authoritarian regimes. Democracies differ, however, in the extent to which political power is restrained through constitutional mechanisms. The United States is an extreme case in that its government rests on an elaborate system of constitutional checks and balances. The system employs a separation of powers among the executive, legislative, and judicial branches. It also includes judicial review, the power of the courts to invalidate actions of the legislative or executive branch. These constitutional restrictions on power are not part of the governing structure of all democracies.

Most democracies have parliamentary systems, which invest both executive and legislative leadership in the office of prime minister. Britain is an example of this type of system. Parliament under the leadership of the prime minister is the supreme authority in Britain. Its laws are not subject to override by Britain's high court, which has no power to review the constitutionality of parliamentary acts.

In parliamentary systems, moreover, either there is only one legislative chamber or, if there are two, power resides primarily in one chamber. The British House of Lords, for example, has only a limited ability to check the actions of the British House of Commons, which the prime minister heads. In the United States, the two legislative chambers—the House and the Senate—are coequal bodies. Because legislation can be enacted only with the approval of both houses, each serves as a check on the other.

Country	Separation of Executive & Legislative Powers?	Judicial Review?
Belgium	No	Yes
Canada	No	Yes
France	Yes	No
Germany	No	Yes
Great Britain	No	No
Italy	No	Yes
Japan	No	Yes
Mexico	Yes	Yes
United States	Yes	Yes

act decisively without the support or acquiescence of the other institutions. Legislative, executive, and judicial powers in the American system are divided in such a way that they overlap: each of the three branches of government checks the others' powers and balances those powers with powers of its own.

As natural as this system now might seem to Americans, most democracies are of the parliamentary type, with executive and legislative power combined in a single institution rather than vested in separate ones. In a parliamentary system, the majority in the legislature selects the prime minister, who then serves as both the legislative leader and the chief executive (see "How the U.S. Compares").

Shared Legislative Powers

Under the Constitution, Congress has legislative authority, but that power is partly shared with the other branches and thus checked by them. The president can veto acts of Congress, recommend legislation, and call special sessions of Congress. The president also has the power to execute—and thereby interpret—the laws Congress makes.

The Supreme Court has the power to interpret acts of Congress that are disputed in legal cases. The Court also has the power of judicial review: it can declare laws of Congress void when it finds that they are not in accord with the Constitution.

Within Congress, there is a further check on legislative power: for legislation to be passed, a majority in each chamber of Congress is required. Thus, the Senate and the House of Representatives can block each other from acting.

Shared Executive Powers

Executive power is vested in the president but is constrained by legislative and judicial checks. The president's power to make treaties and appoint high-ranking officials, for example, is subject to Senate approval. Congress also has the power to impeach and remove the president from office. In practical terms, Congress's greatest checks on executive action are its lawmaking and appropriations powers. The executive branch cannot act without laws that authorize its activities or without the money that pays for these activities.

The judiciary's major check on the presidency is its power to declare an action unlawful because it is not authorized by the legislation that the executive claims to be implementing.

Shared Judicial Powers

Judicial power rests with the Supreme Court and with lower federal courts, which are subject to checks by the other branches of the federal government. Congress is empowered to establish the size of the federal court system, to restrict the Supreme Court's appellate jurisdiction in some circumstances, and to impeach and remove federal judges from office. More importantly, Congress can rewrite legislation that the courts have misinterpreted and can initiate amendments when it disagrees with the courts' rulings on constitutional issues.

The president has the power to appoint federal judges with the consent of the Senate and to pardon persons convicted in the courts. The president also is responsible for executing court decisions, a function that provides opportunities to influence the way rulings are carried out.

The Bill of Rights

Although the delegates to the Philadelphia convention discussed the possibility of placing a list of individual rights (such as freedom of speech and the right to a fair trial) in the Constitution, they ultimately decided that such a list was unnecessary because of the doctrine of expressed powers: government could not lawfully engage in actions, such as the suppression of speech, that were not authorized by the Constitution. Moreover, the delegates argued that a bill of rights was undesirable because government might feel free to disregard any right that was inadvertently left off the list or that might emerge in the future.

These arguments did not persuade leading Americans who believed that no possible safeguard of liberty should be omitted. "A bill of rights," Jefferson argued, "is what the people are entitled to against every government on earth, general or particular, and what no just government should refuse or rest on inference." Jefferson had included a bill of rights in the constitution he wrote for Virginia at the outbreak of the Revolutionary War, and all but four states had followed Virginia's example.

Ultimately, the demand for a bill of rights led to its addition to the Constitution. Madison himself introduced a series of amendments during the First Congress, ten of which were soon ratified by the states. These amendments, traditionally called the **Bill of Rights,** include rights such as freedom of speech and religion and due process protections (such as jury trial and legal counsel) for persons accused of crimes. (These rights, termed *civil liberties,* are discussed in Chapter 4.)

Bill of Rights
The first ten amendments to the Constitution. They include rights such as freedom of speech and religion.

The Bill of Rights is a precise expression of the concept of limited government. In consenting to be governed, the people agree to accept the authority of government in certain areas but not in others; the people's constitutional rights cannot lawfully be denied by government officials.

Judicial Review

The writers of the Constitution both empowered and limited government. But who was to decide whether officials were operating within the limits of their constitutionally authorized powers? The Framers did not specifically entrust this power to a particular branch of government, although they did grant the Supreme Court the authority to decide on "all cases arising under this Constitution." Moreover, at the ratifying conventions of at least eight of the thirteen states, it was claimed that the judiciary would have the power to nullify actions that violated the Constitution.[9]

Nevertheless, because the Constitution did not explicitly grant the judiciary this authority, the principle had to be established in practice. The opportunity arose with an incident that occurred after the election of 1800, in which John Adams lost his bid for a second presidential term after a bitter campaign against Jefferson. Between November 1800, when Jefferson was elected, and March 1801, when he was inaugurated, the Federalist-controlled Congress created fifty-nine additional lower-court judgeships, enabling Adams to appoint loyal Federalists to those positions before he left office. However, Adams's term expired before his secretary of state could deliver the judicial commissions to all the appointees. Without this authorization, an appointee could not take office. Knowing this, Jefferson told his secretary of state, James Madison, not to deliver the commissions. William Marbury was one of those who did not receive his commission, and he asked the Supreme Court to issue a writ of mandamus (a court order directing an official to perform a specific act) that would force Madison to deliver it.

Marbury v. Madison (1803) became the foundation for judicial review by the federal courts. Chief Justice John Marshall wrote the *Marbury* opinion, which declared that Marbury had a legal right to his commission. The opinion also said, however, that the Supreme Court could not issue him a writ of mandamus because it lacked the constitutional authority to do so. Congress had passed legislation in 1789 that gave the Court this power, but Marshall noted that the Constitution prohibits Congress from expanding the Supreme Court's authority except through a constitutional amendment. That being the case, Marshall argued, the legislation that provided the authorization was constitutionally invalid.[10] In striking down this act of Congress on constitutional grounds, the Court asserted its power of **judicial review**—that is, the power of the judiciary to decide whether a government official or institution has acted within the limits of the Constitution and, if not, to declare its action null and void.

Marshall's decision was ingenious because it asserted the power of judicial review without creating the possibility of its rejection by either the executive or the legislative branch. In declaring that Marbury had a right to his commission, the Court in effect said that President Jefferson had failed in his constitutional duty to execute the laws faithfully. However, because it did not order Jefferson to deliver the commission, he was deprived of the opportunity to disregard the Court's ruling. At the same time, the Court reprimanded Congress for passing legislation that exceeded its constitutional authority. But Congress also had no way to retaliate. It could not force the Court to accept the power to issue writs of mandamus if the Court itself refused to do so.

HISTORICAL
Background

judicial review

The power of courts to decide whether a governmental institution has acted within its constitutional powers and, if not, to declare its action null and void.

DEBATING THE ISSUES

IS WARRANTLESS DOMESTIC SURVEILLANCE CONSTITUTIONAL WHEN AUTHORIZED ONLY BY THE PRESIDENT?

Based on the principle of checks and balances, the U.S. Constitution is designed to limit the ability of officials to act on their own in ways that infringe on personal liberty. This principle was at issue in the 2006 congressional hearings into whether President George W. Bush had exceeded his constitutional and statutory powers by authorizing warrantless phone taps. After the terrorist attacks of September 11, 2001, Bush authorized the National Security Agency (NSA), without first obtaining a court order, to intercept international phone calls and e-mails placed from or received in the United States. The Foreign Intelligence Surveillance Act (FISA) of 1978 had prohibited such surveillance. Moreover, the Fourth Amendment protects individuals from unjustified searches. Ordinarily, officials are not allowed to spy on U.S. citizens without obtaining a warrant from a judge who has reviewed and approved the proposed surveillance. The Bush administration tried to keep NSA's surveillance program secret. When it became known, the Administration argued that the president was acting within his lawful powers. Members of Congress questioned that claim, and congressional hearings were held.

On the hearings' opening day, Attorney General Alberto Gonzalez defended the surveillance program, while Senator Patrick Leahy, the ranking minority member on the Senate Judiciary Committee, was among the senators who questioned its legality. Which argument do you find more convincing? Where would you draw the line on the limits of presidential power in time of war?

YES The Constitution charges the President with the primary responsibility for protecting the safety of all Americans, and the Constitution gives the President the authority necessary to fulfill this solemn duty. . . . The President authorized the terrorist surveillance program in response to the deadliest foreign attack on American soil, and it is designed solely to prevent the next al Qaeda attack. After all, the goal of our enemy is to blend in with our civilian population in order to plan and carry out future attacks within America. We cannot forget that the September 11th hijackers were in our country, living in our communities. . . .

The President's authority to take military action—including the use of communications intelligence targeted at the enemy—does not come merely from his constitutional powers. It comes directly from Congress as well. Just a few days after the attacks of September 11th, Congress enacted a joint resolution to support and authorize the military response to the attacks on American soil. . . . Some contend that even if the President has constitutional authority to engage in the surveillance of our enemy during an armed conflict, that authority has been constrained by Congress with the passage in 1978 of the Foreign Intelligence Surveillance Act (FISA). It is a serious question whether, consistent with the Constitution, FISA may encroach upon the President's Article II powers during the current armed conflict with al Qaeda by prohibiting the terrorist surveillance program. . . . Many people ask why the President elected not to use FISA's procedures for securing court orders for the terrorist surveillance program. We have to remember that what is at issue is a wartime intelligence program designed to protect our Nation from another attack in the middle of an armed conflict. It is an "early warning system" with only one purpose: to detect and prevent the next attack on the United States from foreign agents hiding in our midst. It is imperative for national security that we can detect reliably, immediately, and without delay whenever communications associated with al Qaeda enter or leave the United States. That may be the only way to alert us to the presence of an al Qaeda agent in our country and to the existence of an unfolding plot. . . . The key question under the Fourth Amendment is not whether there was a warrant, but whether the search was reasonable. Determining the reasonableness of a search for Fourth Amendment purposes requires balancing privacy interests with the Government's interests and ensuring that we maintain appropriate safeguards. Although the terrorist surveillance program may implicate substantial privacy interests, the Government's interest in protecting our Nation is compelling. Because the need for the program is reevaluated every 45 days and because of the safeguards and oversight, the al Qaeda intercepts are reasonable.

—*Alberto Gonzalez, attorney general of the United States*

NO We all agree that we should be wiretapping al Qaeda terrorists—of course we should. Congress has given the President authority to monitor these messages legally, with checks to guard against abuses when Americans' conversations and email are being monitored. But instead, the President has chosen to do it illegally, without those safeguards. . . . The President and the Justice Department have a constitutional duty to faithfully execute the laws. They do not write them. They do not pass them. They do not have unchecked power to decide what laws to follow and what laws to ignore. They cannot violate the law or the rights of ordinary Americans. In America no one, not even the President, is above the law. . . . [FISA] expressly states that it provides the "exclusive" source of authority for wiretapping for intelligence purposes. Wiretapping that is not authorized under that statute is a federal crime. That is what the law says, and that is what the law means. This law was enacted to define how domestic surveillance for intelligence purposes may be conducted while protecting the fundamental liberties of Americans. Two or more generations of Americans are too young to know this from their experience, but there's a reason we have the FISA law. It was enacted after decades of abuses by the Executive, including the wiretapping of Dr. Martin Luther King Jr. and other political opponents of earlier government officials, and the White House "horrors" of the Nixon years, during which another President asserted that whatever he did was legal because he was the President. . . . I have many questions for the Attorney General. But first, I have a message to give him and the President. It is a message that should be unanimous, from every Member of Congress regardless of party and ideology. Under our Constitution, Congress is the co-equal branch of Government that makes the laws. If you believe we need new laws, you can come to us and tell us. If Congress agrees, we will amend the law. If you do not even attempt to persuade Congress to amend the law, you must abide by the law as written. That is as true for this President as it is for any other American. That is the rule of law, on which our Nation was founded, and on which it endures and prospers.

—*Patrick Leahy, U.S. senator (D-Vt.)*

Providing for Self-Government

"We the People" is the opening phrase of the Constitution. It expresses the idea that in the United States the people will have the power to govern themselves. In a sense, there is no contradiction between this idea and the Constitution's provisions for limited government, because individual *liberty* is an essential element of *self-government*. If people cannot express themselves freely, they cannot be self-governing. In another sense, however, the contradiction is clear: restrictions on the power of the majority are a denial of its right to govern society as it sees fit.

tyranny of the majority

The potential of a majority to monopolize power for its own gain to the detriment of minority rights and interests.

The Framers believed that the people deserved and required a voice in their government, but they worried that the people would become inflamed by a passionate issue or fiery demagogue and act rashly. To the Framers, the great risk of popular government was **tyranny of the majority:** the people acting as an irrational mob that tramples on the rights of the minority. Their fear was not without foundation. The history of democracies was filled with examples of majority tyranny, and there were even examples from the nation's brief history. In 1786, for instance, debtors had gained control of Rhode Island's legislature and made paper money a legal means of paying debts, even though existing contracts called for payment in gold. Creditors were then hunted down and held captive in public places so that debtors could come and pay them in full with worthless paper money. A Boston newspaper wrote that Rhode Island should be renamed Rogue Island.

Rhode Island was nicknamed "Rogue Island" for its disregard of property rights. Shown here is the Rhode Island three-dollar bank note, which came to be worth no more than the paper on which it was written and yet was used to pay off gold debts.

Democracy Versus Republic

No form of self-government could eliminate completely the threat to liberty of majority tyranny, but the Framers believed that the danger would be greatly diminished by creating a republican government as opposed to a democratic government.[11] Today, the terms **democracy, republic,** and **representative government** are often used interchangeably to refer to a system of government in which political power rests with the people through their ability to choose representatives in free and fair elections. To the writers of the Constitution, however, a democracy and a republic were different forms of government.

By the term *democracy,* the Framers meant a government in which the power of the majority is unlimited, whether exercised directly (as in the case of town meetings open to all citizens) or through a representative body. The majority's rule is absolute. Should it decide to act tyrannically—to run roughshod over the minority—there is nothing in the law to stop it. By the term *republic,* the Framers meant a government that is based on majority rule but that protects the minority through a guarantee of individual rights and other checks on majority power. The purpose of republican government is to limit the power of the majority, not as a means of preventing the people from governing themselves but as a means of safeguarding minority rights and interests. The majority rules, but it does so within prescribed limits.[12]

The Framers believed that a republican government is superior to a democratic one. They also believed that a republic, to work well in practice, requires virtuous representatives—lawmakers who have an enlightened sense of the public interest. In this respect, their outlook was similar to that of the English theorist Edmund Burke (1729–97). In his *Letter to the Sheriffs of Bristol,* Burke argued that representatives should act as the public's **trustees;** representatives are obliged to serve the interest of those who elect them, but the nature of this interest is for the representatives, not the voters, to decide. Burke was concerned with the ease with which a majority can think like a mob, and he claimed that representatives should not surrender their judgment to irrational majorities.

Limited Popular Rule

The Constitution provided that all power would be exercised through representative institutions. There was no provision for any form of direct popular participation in the making of policy decisions. In view of the fact that the United States was much too large to be governed directly by the people in popular assemblies, a representative system was necessary. The Framers went beyond what was necessary, however, and placed officials at a considerable distance from the people they represented (see Table 2-3).

The House of Representatives was the only institution that would be based on direct popular election—its members would be elected to serve for two years by a vote of the people. Frequent and direct election of House members was intended to make government sensitive to the concerns of popular majorities.

U.S. senators would be appointed by the legislatures of the states they represented. Because state legislators were popularly elected, the people would be

democracy

A form of government in which the people rule, either directly or through elected representatives.

republic

Historically, the form of government in which representative officials met to decide on policy issues. These representatives were expected to serve the public interest but were not subject to the people's immediate control. Today, the term *republic* is used interchangeably with *democracy.*

representative democracy

A system in which the people participate in the decision-making process of government not directly but indirectly, through the election of officials to represent their interests.

trustees

Elected representatives whose obligation is to act in accordance with their own consciences as to what policies are in the best interests of the public.

TABLE 2-3 | **Methods of Choosing National Leaders** Fearing the concentration of political power, the Framers devised alternative methods of selection and terms of service for national officials.

Office	Method of Selection	Term of Service
President	Electoral College	4 years
U.S. senator	State legislature	6 years (one-third of senators' terms expire every 2 years)
U.S. representative	Popular election	2 years
Federal judge	Nominated by president, approved by Senate	Indefinite (subject to "good behavior")

choosing their senators indirectly. Every two years, a third of the senators would be appointed to six-year terms. The Senate was expected to check and balance the House. The Senate, by virtue of the less frequent and indirect election of its members, presumably would be less responsive to popular whim.

Presidential selection was an issue of considerable debate at the Philadelphia convention. Direct election of the president was twice proposed and twice rejected because it would link executive power directly to popular majorities. The Framers finally chose to have the president selected by the votes of electors (the so-called **Electoral College**). Each state would have the same number of **electoral votes** as it had members in Congress and could select its electors by a method of its choosing. The president would serve four years and be eligible for reelection.

The Framers decided that federal judges and justices would be appointed rather than elected. They would be nominated by the president and confirmed through approval by the Senate. Once confirmed, they would "hold their offices during good behavior." In effect, they would be allowed to hold office for life unless they committed a crime. The judiciary was an unelected institution that would uphold the rule of law and serve as a check on the elected branches of government.[13]

These differing methods of selecting national officeholders would not prevent a determined majority from achieving unchecked power, but control could not be attained quickly. Unlike the House of Representatives, institutions such as the Senate, presidency, and judiciary would not yield to an impassioned majority in a single election. The delay would reduce the likelihood that government would degenerate into mob rule driven by momentary passions.

Altering the Constitution: More Power to the People

The Framers' conception of self-government was at odds with what the average American in 1787 had come to expect. Every state but South Carolina held annual legislative elections, and several states also chose their governors through direct annual election. Not long after ratification of the Constitution, Americans began to challenge the Constitution's restrictions on majority rule (see Table 2-4).

Jeffersonian Democracy: A Revolution of the Spirit

Thomas Jefferson, who otherwise admired the Constitution, was among the prominent Americans who questioned its provisions for self-government—and it was Jefferson who may have spared the nation a bloody civil conflict over the issue

Electoral College

An unofficial term that refers to the electors who cast the states' electoral votes.

electoral votes

The method of voting that is used to choose the U.S. president. Each state has the same number of electoral votes as it has members in Congress (House and Senate combined). By tradition, electoral voting is tied to a state's popular voting. The candidate with the most popular votes in a state (or, in a few states, the most votes in a congressional district) receives its electoral votes.

HISTORICAL *Background*

TABLE 2-4 | Measures Taken to Make Government More Responsive to Popular Majorities   The U.S. Constitution created barriers designed to limit direct popular influence on government. Subsequent changes were designed to lower these barriers and increase the power of voting majorities.

Earlier Situation	Subsequent Development
Separation of powers, as a means of dividing authority and blunting passionate majorities	Political parties, as a means of uniting authorities and linking them with popular majorities
Indirect election of all national officials except House members, as a means of buffering officials from popular influence	Direct election of U.S. senators and popular voting for president (linked to electoral votes), as a means of increasing popular control of officials
Nomination of candidates for public office through political party organizations	Primary elections, as a direct means of selecting party nominees

of popular sovereignty. Under John Adams, the second president, the national government increasingly favored the nation's wealthy interests. Adams publicly indicated that the Constitution was designed for a governing elite and hinted that he might use force to suppress dissent.[14] Jefferson asked whether Adams, with the aid of a strong army, intended to deprive ordinary people of their rights. Jefferson challenged Adams in the next presidential election and, upon defeating him, hailed his victory as the "Revolution of 1800."

Although Jefferson was a champion of the common people, he had no clear vision of how a popular government might work in practice. He saw Congress, not the presidency, as the institution better suited to representing majority opinion.[15] He also had no illusions about a largely uneducated population's ability to play a substantial governing role and feared the consequences of inciting the masses to rise against the rich. Jeffersonian democracy was mostly a revolution of the spirit. Jefferson taught Americans to look on national government institutions as belonging to all, not just to the privileged few.[16]

Jacksonian Democracy: Linking the People and the Presidency

Not until the election of Andrew Jackson in 1828 did the nation have a powerful president who was willing and able to involve the public more fully in government. Jackson carried out the constitutional revolution that Jeffersonian democracy had foreshadowed.

Jackson recognized that the president was the only official who could legitimately claim to represent the people as a whole. Unlike the president, members of Congress were elected from separate states and districts rather than from the entire country. Yet the president's claim to popular leadership was weakened by the fact that the president was chosen by electors rather than by the voters. Jackson's ingenious solution was to have each state give its electoral votes to whichever candidate got the most popular votes in the state. This arrangement, still in effect, places the selection of the president in the voters' hands in most elections. The candidate who gets the most popular votes nationally is also likely to finish first in enough states to win a majority of the electoral votes. Since Jackson's time, only three candidates—Rutherford B. Hayes in 1876, Benjamin Harrison in 1888, and George W. Bush in 2000—have won the presidency after losing the popular vote. (The Electoral College is discussed further in Chapter 12.)

Drafting the Declaration of Independence, a painting by J. L. Ferris. Benjamin Franklin, John Adams (seated, center), and Thomas Jefferson (standing) drafted the historic document. Jefferson was the principal author; he inserted the inspirational words about liberty, equality, and self-government. Jealous of the attention that Jefferson received, Adams declared that there wasn't anything in Jefferson's words that others hadn't already said. Later, they became bitter political rivals, with Jefferson defeating Adams in the presidential election of 1800. Still later, they reconciled and corresponded frequently. They died on the same day, July 4, 1826, the fiftieth anniversary of the writing of the Declaration of Independence.

The Progressives: Senate and Primary Elections

The Progressive Era of the early 1900s brought another wave of democratic reforms. The Progressives rejected the Burkean idea of representatives as trustees, instead embracing the idea of representatives as **delegates**—officeholders who are obligated to respond directly to the expressed opinions of the people they represent.

The Progressives sought to place power more directly in the hands of the people.[17] They succeeded in changing the way some state and local governments operate. Progressive reforms at state and local levels included the initiative and

delegates
Elected representatives whose obligation is to act in accordance with the expressed wishes of the people they represent.

Pictured here is the Old Senate Chamber, where the U.S. Senate met until 1859, when a new and larger chamber was constructed. The Old Senate Chamber was the scene of heated debates over slavery. Daniel Webster, Henry Clay, and John C. Calhoun gained national reputations here. After the Senate vacated the chamber, it was occupied by the U.S. Supreme Court until 1935, when the Court's own building across the street from the Capitol was completed. Not until 1914 were U.S. senators chosen by direct vote of the people.

primary election

A form of election in which voters choose a party's nominees for public office. In most states, eligibility to vote in a party's primary election is limited to voters who are registered members of the party.

the referendum, which enable citizens to vote directly on legislative issues (see "States in the Nation"). Another Progressive reform was the recall election, which enables citizens through petition to force an officeholder to submit to reelection before the regular expiration of his or her term. (In 2003, a recall election enabled actor Arnold Schwarzenegger to become California's governor.)

The Progressives also instigated two changes in federal elections. One was the direct election of U.S. senators, who before the Seventeenth Amendment was ratified in 1913 had been chosen by state legislatures and were widely perceived as agents of big business (the Senate was nicknamed the "Millionaires' Club"). Senators who stood to lose their seats in a direct popular vote had blocked earlier attempts to change the Constitution. However, the Senate was persuaded to support an amendment following pressure from the Progressives and revelations that corporate bribes had influenced the selection of several senators. The second change was the **primary election,** which gives rank-and-file voters the power to select party nominees. In the early 1900s, nearly all states adopted the primary election as a means of choosing nominees for at least some federal and state offices. Prior to this change, nominees were selected by party leaders.

The Progressive Era spawned attacks on the Framers. A prominent criticism was laid out in historian Charles S. Beard's *An Economic Interpretation of the Constitution.*[18] Arguing that the Constitution grew out of wealthy Americans' fears of the debtor rebellions, Beard claimed that the Constitution's elaborate systems of power and representation were devices for keeping power in the hands of the rich. As evidence, Beard cited the Constitution's protections of property and referred to Madison's notes on the Philadelphia convention, which showed that property concerns were high on the Framers' agenda. Beard further noted that not one of the delegates was a workingman or farmer. Most of the Framers had large landholdings, controlled substantial interests, or were major credit holders.

Beard's thesis was challenged by other historians, and he later acknowledged that he had not taken the Framers' full array of motives into account. Their

STATES IN THE NATION

DIRECT DEMOCRACY: THE INITIATIVE AND POPULAR REFERENDUM

In some states, by gathering enough signatures on a petition, citizens can directly enact or defeat legislation through their votes in an election. This action can occur through either an *initiative* (where citizens place a legislative proposal of their own choosing on the ballot) or a *popular referendum* (where citizens place an act of the state legislature on the ballot, which the voters can then accept or reject). A popular referendum is different from a *legislative referendum*, where the state legislature itself places a proposal on the ballot for the voters to accept or reject. All states have a form of the legislative referendum, but only some states, as indicated in the map below, have the initiative and the popular referendum.

Q: *Why are southern and northeastern states less likely to have the initiative and popular referendum than states in other areas?*

A: *The initiative and popular referendum were introduced in the early 1900s by the Progressives, who sought to weaken the power of political bosses and give voters a larger voice in their governance. In the Northeast, party machines had enough strength in state legislatures to block their enactment. In the South, these devices were blocked by the white establishment, which feared that blacks and poor whites would make use of them.*

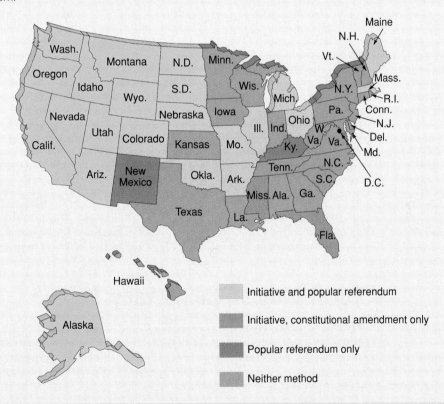

Initiative and popular referendum

Initiative, constitutional amendment only

Popular referendum only

Neither method

Source: Initiative and Referendum Institute at the University of Southern California

conception of separation of powers, for example, was a governing principle that had earlier been incorporated into state constitutions. Nevertheless, Beard held onto his claim that the Constitution was designed to protect the interests of the wealthy rather than to promote self-government.

Beard's claim has some validity, but to say that the Framers were foes of democracy is inaccurate. Although they did not have great trust in popular rule, they were determined to balance the need to create a system of self-government with the need to create a system of limited government. Convinced that unchecked majority rule was likely to devolve into tyranny, the Framers devised institutions that were responsive to majority opinion but not slaves to it.

The Progressive Era declined in the 1920s, after most of its institutional reforms had been achieved. If it had not subsided then, it would surely have done so soon thereafter, when the Western world's trust in majority government was shaken by developments in Europe, particularly in Germany. Germany's Weimar Republic (1918–1933) had been founded on popular institutions; it was about as close as any modern nation had come to establishing a pure democracy. When the Weimar Republic degenerated first into chaos and then into Hitler's Third Reich, its demise seemed to confirm Madison's assertion in *Federalist* No. 10 that unchecked democracies are "spectacles of turbulence and contention. . . . as short in their lives as they have been violent in their deaths."

Nevertheless, the idea of popular government regained strength in the United States after World War II, when changes in communication, technology, and political organization brought the American people and their representatives into an increasingly close relationship. The new mass medium of television began to enable political leaders to communicate more easily with the public. And as televised politics become routine, Americans increasingly came to believe that leaders should deal with the public directly rather than through political parties.

This perspective was evident during the late 1960s, when reform Democrats took action to make the presidential nominating system directly responsive to the voters. In 1968, Democratic Party leaders nominated Hubert Humphrey, who, as Lyndon Johnson's vice president, was associated with the unpopular Vietnam War. Even though several states held presidential primaries, most states did not, enabling state party leaders to pick the state's delegates to the national nominating convention. Humphrey had not competed in any of the primaries, and antiwar Democrats challenged the legitimacy of his nomination, saying that the party elite had ignored the will of Democratic primary voters. When Humphrey then lost the general election to Richard Nixon, reform Democrats engineered a change in the nominating process that required states to select their convention delegates through a primary election or a caucus open to all registered voters of the party. Since then, every presidential nominee, Republican as well as Democrat, has gained nomination by appealing directly to the voters for their support.

Constitutional Democracy Today

The type of government created in the United States in 1787 is today called a **constitutional democracy.** It is *democratic* in its provisions for majority influence through elections and *constitutional* in its requirement that power gained through elections be exercised in accordance with law and with due respect for individual rights.

By some standards, the American system of today is a model of *self-government.*[19] The United States schedules the election of its larger legislative chamber (the House of Representatives) and its chief executive more frequently than does any other democracy. In addition, it is the only major democracy to rely extensively on primary elections rather than party organizations for the selection of party nominees. The principle of popular election to office, which the writers of the Constitution regarded as a prerequisite of popular sovereignty but a method to be used sparingly, has been extended further in the United States than anywhere else.

By other standards, however, the U.S. system is less democratic than some. Popular majorities must work against the barriers to influence devised by the Framers—divided powers, staggered terms of office, and separate constituencies. In fact, the link between an electoral majority and a governing majority is less

constitutional democracy

A government that is democratic in its provisions for majority influence through elections, and constitutional in its provisions for minority rights and rule by law.

direct in the American system than in nearly all other democratic systems. In the European parliamentary democracies, for example, legislative and executive power is not divided, is not subject to close check by the judiciary, and is acquired through the winning of a legislative majority in a single national election. The Framers' vision was a different one, dominated by a concern with liberty and therefore with controls on political power. It was a response to the experiences they brought with them to Philadelphia in the summer of 1787.

Summary Self-Test www.mhhe.com/pattersontad9e

The Constitution of the United States is a reflection of the colonial and revolutionary experiences of the early Americans. Freedom from abusive government was a reason for the colonies' revolt against British rule, but the English tradition also provided ideas about government, power, and freedom that were expressed in the Constitution and, earlier, in the Declaration of Independence.

The Constitution was designed in part to provide for a limited government in which political power would be confined to proper uses. The Framers wanted to ensure that the government they were creating would not itself be a threat to freedom. To this end, they confined the national government to expressly granted powers and also denied it certain specific powers. Other prohibitions on government were later added to the Constitution in the form of stated guarantees of individual liberties in the Bill of Rights. The most significant constitutional provision for limited government, however, was a separation of powers among the three branches. The powers given to each branch enable it to act as a check on the exercise of power by the other two, an arrangement that during the nation's history has in fact served as a barrier to abuses of power.

The Constitution, however, made no mention of how the powers and limits of government were to be judged in practice. In its historic ruling in *Marbury v. Madison,* the Supreme Court assumed the authority to review the constitutionality of legislative and executive actions and to declare them unconstitutional and thus invalid.

The Framers of the Constitution, respecting the idea of self-government but distrusting popular majorities, devised a system of government that they felt would temper popular opinion and slow its momentum so that the public's "true interest" (which includes a regard for the rights and interests of the minority) would guide public policy. Different methods were advanced for selecting the president, the members of the House and Senate, and federal judges as a means of insulating political power against momentary majorities.

Since the adoption of the Constitution, the public gradually has assumed more direct control of its representatives, particularly through measures that affect the way officeholders are chosen. Presidential popular voting (linked to the Electoral College), direct election of senators, and primary elections are among the devices aimed at strengthening the majority's influence. These developments are rooted in the idea, deeply held by ordinary Americans, that the people must have substantial direct influence over their representatives if government is to serve their interests.

CHAPTER 2

Study Corner

Key Terms

Anti-Federalists (*p. 36*)
Bill of Rights (*p. 43*)
checks and balances (*p. 41*)
constitution (*p. 38*)

constitutional democracy (*p. 52*)
delegates (*p. 49*)
democracy (*p. 47*)

denials of power (*p. 39*)
Electoral College (*p. 48*)
electoral votes (*p. 48*)
Federalists (*p. 36*)

grants of power (*p. 39*)
Great Compromise (*p. 33*)
inalienable (natural) rights (*p. 30*)

judicial review (*p. 44*)

limited government (*p. 28*)

New Jersey (small-state)
   Plan (*p. 33*)

North-South Compromise
   (*p. 34*)

primary election (*p. 50*)

representative democracy
   (*p. 47*)

republic (*p. 47*)

self-government (*p. 28*)

separated institutions
   sharing power (*p. 41*)

separation of powers (*p. 40*)

trustees (*p. 47*)

tyranny of the majority (*p. 46*)

Virginia (large-state)
   Plan (*p. 33*)

Self-Test

1. The principle of checks and balances in the U.S. system of government:
   a. requires the federal budget to be a balanced budget.
   b. provides that checks cashed at U.S. banks will be honored as legal tender.
   c. was a principle invented by the Progressives.
   d. allows the majority's will to work through representative institutions but places checks on the power of those institutions.

2. The U.S. Constitution provides for limited government mainly:
   a. through direct election of representatives.
   b. through indirect systems of popular election of representatives.
   c. by defining lawful powers and by dividing those powers among competing institutions.
   d. by making state law superior to national law when the two conflict.

3. The U.S. Constitution provides for self-government mainly:
   a. through direct and indirect systems of popular election of representatives.
   b. by defining the lawful powers of government.
   c. by dividing governing powers among competing institutions.
   d. by giving the majority absolute power to govern as it pleases.

4. Shays's Rebellion called attention to:
   a. the lack of ability of Congress under the Articles of Confederation to put down popular rebellion.
   b. Americans' anger with Britain over "taxation without representation."
   c. the inability of the states under the Articles to bring the American Revolution to a successful conclusion.
   d. the conditions that were leading to mutiny on U.S. naval vessels.

5. The addition of the Bill of Rights to the U.S. Constitution meant that:
   a. a list of individual rights would be protected by law.
   b. the Anti-Federalists no longer had any reason to oppose the adoption of the Constitution.
   c. the national government could infringe on the rights of the states.
   d. the state governments could infringe on the rights of the national government.

6. Of the issues taken up during the constitutional convention, which one consumed the most time and attention?
   a. structure of the presidency
   b. structure of Congress
   c. structure and powers of the federal judiciary
   d. ratification of the new Constitution

7. The Framers of the Constitution feared political apathy more than tyranny of the majority. (T/F)

8. The idea of popular government—in which the majority's desires have a more direct and immediate impact on public policy—has gained strength since the nation's beginning. (T/F)

9. The Supreme Court decision in *Marbury v. Madison* gave courts the power to declare governmental action null and void when it is found to violate the Constitution. (T/F)

10. The Virginia Plan (also known as the large-state plan) called for a Congress with equal representation of each state but with greatly strengthened powers. (T/F)

Critical Thinking

How does the division of power in the U.S. political system contribute to limited government? How do the provisions for representative government (the various methods of choosing national officials) contribute to limited government?

Suggested Readings

Beard, Charles S. *An Economic Interpretation of the Constitution.* New York: Macmillan, 1941. Argues that the Framers had selfish economic interests uppermost in their minds when they wrote the Constitution.

Edling, Max M. *A Revolution in Favor of Government.* New York: Oxford University Press, 2003. Argues that the Framers intended the Constitution to create a strong government.

Ellis, Joseph J. *Founding Brothers: The Revolutionary Generation.* New York: Vintage, 2002. A riveting account of the lives of America's leading Founders.

Federalist Papers. Many editions, including a one-volume paperback version edited by Isaac Kramnick (New York: Penguin, 1987). A series of essays written by Alexander Hamilton, James Madison, and John Jay under the pseudonym Publius; the essays, published in a New York newspaper in 1787–88, explain the Constitution and support its ratification.

Hardin, Russell. *Liberalism, Constitutionalism, and Democracy.* New York: Oxford University Press, 1999. Analysis of the great ideas that underlie the Constitution.

McGerr, Michael. *A Fierce Discontent: The Rise and Fall of the Progressive Movement in America, 1870–1920.* New York: Free Press, 2005. Assessment of the Progressive movement's contribution to American democracy.

Ostrom, Vincent. *The Political Theory of a Compound Republic: Designing the American Experiment.* Lanham, Md.: Lexington Books, 2007. An analysis of the logic of the Constitution as its writers envisioned it.

Tocqueville, Alexis de. *Democracy in America*, vols. 1 and 2, ed. J. P. Mayer. New York: Doubleday/Anchor, 1969. A classic analysis (originally published 1835–40) of American democracy by an insightful French observer.

Wilentz, Sean. *The Rise of American Democracy: Jefferson to Lincoln.* New York: Norton, 2005. An account of how democratic ideas triumphed over aristocratic ones.

List of Websites

http://www.nara.gov/
The National Archives site; includes an in-depth look at the history of the Declaration of Independence.

http://odur.let.rug.nl/~usa/P/aj7/about/bio/jackxx.htm
A site that focuses on Andrew Jackson and his role in shaping U.S. politics.

http://www.yale.edu/lawweb/avalon/constpap.htm
Includes documents on the Constitution, the American Revolution, and the constitutional convention.

http://www.yale.edu/lawweb/avalon/presiden/jeffpap.htm
A site that includes the papers of Thomas Jefferson, as well as his autobiography.

Participate!

The classroom provides an everyday opportunity to develop a skill that is basic to effective citizenship—the ability to speak clearly and persuasively. To the Greek philosopher Aristotle, rhetoric was the defining skill of citizenship. Aristotle did not define rhetoric as it is often used today, as a derisive term for speech that is long on wind and short on reason. Rather, he saw rhetoric as a tool in the search for truth, a form of persuasion that flourishes when people exchange ideas. The college classroom is a good place to develop rhetorical skills. Speak up in the classroom when you have a point to make and can support it. Rhetorical skills are honed only through practice, and few settings offer more opportunities for practice than the classroom.

Extra Credit

For up-to-the-minute *New York Times* articles, interactive simulations, graphics, study tools, and more links and quizzes, visit the text's Online Learning Center at www.mhhe.com/pattersontad9e.

Self-Test Answers

1. d 2. c 3. a 4. a 5. a 6. b 7. F 8. T 9. T 10. F

IS JUDICIAL REVIEW OBSOLETE?

The big Supreme Court decision that the Second Amendment protects an individual right to keep a loaded handgun for self-defense at home is the high-water mark of the "original meaning" approach to constitutional interpretation championed by Justice Antonin Scalia and many other conservatives. At the same time, the decision may show "originalism" to be a false promise.

Scalia's 64-page opinion for the five-justice majority was a tour de force of originalist analysis. Without pausing to ask whether gun rights is good policy, Scalia parsed the Second Amendment's 27 words one by one while consulting 18th-century dictionaries, early American history, the 1689 English Bill of Rights, 19th-century treatises, and other historical material.

And even the lead dissent for the Court's four liberals—who are accustomed to deep-sixing original meaning on issues ranging from the death penalty to abortion, gay rights, and many others—all but conceded that this case should turn mainly on the original meaning of the 217-year-old Second Amendment. They had little choice, given the unusual absence of binding precedent.

But in another sense, the case, *District of Columbia v. Heller* belies the two great advantages that originalism has been touted as having over the liberals' "living Constitution" approach. Originalism is supposed to supply first principles that will prevent justices from merely voting their policy preferences and to foster what Judge Robert Bork once called "deference to democratic choice." But the gun case suggests that originalism does neither.

First, even though all nine justices claimed to be following original meaning, they split angrily along liberal-conservative lines perfectly matching their apparent policy preferences, with the four conservatives (plus swing-voting Anthony Kennedy) voting for gun rights and the four liberals against.

These eight justices cleaved in *exactly* the same way—with Kennedy tipping the balance from case to case—in the decision the same day striking down a campaign finance provision designed to handicap rich, self-funded political candidates; decisions earlier in 2008 barring the death penalty for raping a child and striking down the elected branches' restrictions on judicial review of Guantánamo detainees' petitions for release; and past decisions on abortion, affirmative action, gay rights, religion, and more.

This pattern does not mean that the justices are *insincerely* using legal doctrines as a cover for politically driven votes. Rather, it shows that ascertaining the original meaning of provisions drafted more than 200 years

"A well-regulated militia, being necessary to the security of a free state, the right of the people to keep and bear arms, shall not be infringed."

And even if there is a clear right answer, the voting pattern suggests that conservative and liberal justices will never agree on what it is. More broadly, even when there is no dispute as to original meaning, it is often intolerable to liberals and conservatives alike. For example, no constitutional provision or amendment was ever designed to prohibit the federal government from discriminating based on race (or sex). This has not stopped conservatives from voting to strike down federal racial preferences for minorities (by seeking to extend liberal precedents) any more than

If originalism **does not deliver on its promises** to channel judicial discretion and constrain judicial usurpations of elected officials' power, what good is it?

ago, in a very different society, is often a subjective process on which reasonable people disagree—and often reach conclusions driven consciously or subconsciously by their policy preferences. And some of us have trouble coming to confident conclusions either way.

Scalia's argument for striking down the District of Columbia's gun laws—the strictest in the country—was persuasive. But so were the dissents by liberal Justices John Paul Stevens and Stephen Breyer. Scalia and the two dissenters all made cogent arguments while papering over weaknesses in their positions. Scalia may have won on points. But more study might tip an observer the other way.

The reason is that the justices' exhaustive analyses of the text and relevant history do not definitively resolve the ambiguity inherent in the amendment's curious wording:

it stopped liberals from striking down the federal laws that once discriminated against women.

Second, the notion that originalists would defer more to democratic choices than would the loosey-goosey liberals has come to ring a bit hollow. The originalists began with a compelling critique of the liberals' invention of new constitutional rights to strike down all state abortion and death-penalty laws, among others. But the current conservative justices have hardly been models of judicial restraint.

They have used highly debatable interpretations of original meaning to sweep aside a raft of democratically adopted laws. These include federal laws regulating campaign money and imposing monetary liability on states. And in 2007's 5–4 decision striking down two local school-integration laws, the

conservative majority came close to imposing a "colorblind Constitution" vision of equal protection that may be good policy but which is hard to find in the 14th Amendment's original meaning.

In the gun case, as Justice Breyer argued, "the majority's decision threatens severely to limit the ability of more knowledgeable, democratically elected officials to deal with gun-related problems." (Of course, Breyer's solicitude for elected officials disappears when the issue is whether they should be able to execute rapists of children or ban an especially grisly abortion method.)

If originalism does not deliver on its promises to channel judicial discretion and constrain judicial usurpations of elected officials' power, what good is it?

Indeed, it seems almost perverse to be assessing what gun controls to allow based not on examining how best to save lives but on seeking to read the minds of the men who ratified the Bill of Rights well over 200 years ago.

The originalist approach seems especially odd when it comes down to arguing over such matters as whether 18th-century lawyers agreed (as Scalia contends) that "a prefatory clause does not limit or expand the scope of the operative clause" and whether (as Stevens contends) the phrase "'bear arms' most naturally conveys a military meaning" and "the Second Amendment does not protect a 'right to keep and to bear arms,' but rather 'a right to keep and bear arms'" (emphasis in original). The justices may as well have tried reading the entrails of dead hamsters.

Is the answer to embrace liberals' "living Constitution" jurisprudence, which roughly

> Indeed, not one of the nine justices seems to have a modest understanding of his or her powers to set national policy **in the name of enforcing the Constitution.**

translates to reading into the 18th-century document whichever meaning and values the justices consider most fundamental?

By no means. Rather, in the many cases in which nothing close to consensus about the meaning of the Constitution is attainable, the justices should leave the lawmaking to elected officials.

Now it seems that the originalist view of the Constitution is indeed incapable of telling today's judges what to do—not, at least, with any consistency from one judge to the next. So is judicial review itself obsolete?

Not quite. Judicial review remains valuable, perhaps indispensable, because it helps provide the stability and protection for liberty inherent in our tripartite separation of powers, with the legislative, executive, and judicial branches serving as the three legs of a stool and with each potent enough to check abuses and excesses by the others.

The June 12 decision rebuffing President Bush's (and Congress's) denial of fair hearings to Guantánamo detainees proclaiming their innocence is a case in point. But the

broad wording of Kennedy's majority opinion, joined by the four liberals, went too far by flirting with a hubristic vision of unprecedented judicial power to intrude deeply into the conduct of foreign wars.

Indeed, not one of the nine justices seems to have a modest understanding of his or her powers to set national policy in the name of enforcing the Constitution. But the other branches, and most voters, seem content with raw judicial policy-making—except when they don't like the policies. For better or worse, what Scalia has called "the imperial judiciary"—sometimes liberal, sometimes conservative—seems here to stay.

Given this, the best way to restrain judicial imperialism may be for the president and the Senate to worry less about whether prospective justices are liberal or conservative and more about whether they have a healthy sense of their own fallibility.

FOR DISCUSSION: Do the intentions of the Constitution's framers still matter in considering issues like gun control? When they're ambiguous, how would you attempt to deduce what those intentions were?
Do you think the constitution is a "living document" or are you an "originalist"?
Should the 2nd Amendment be read to mean that every individual has a right to a firearm? Where should that protection begin and end?

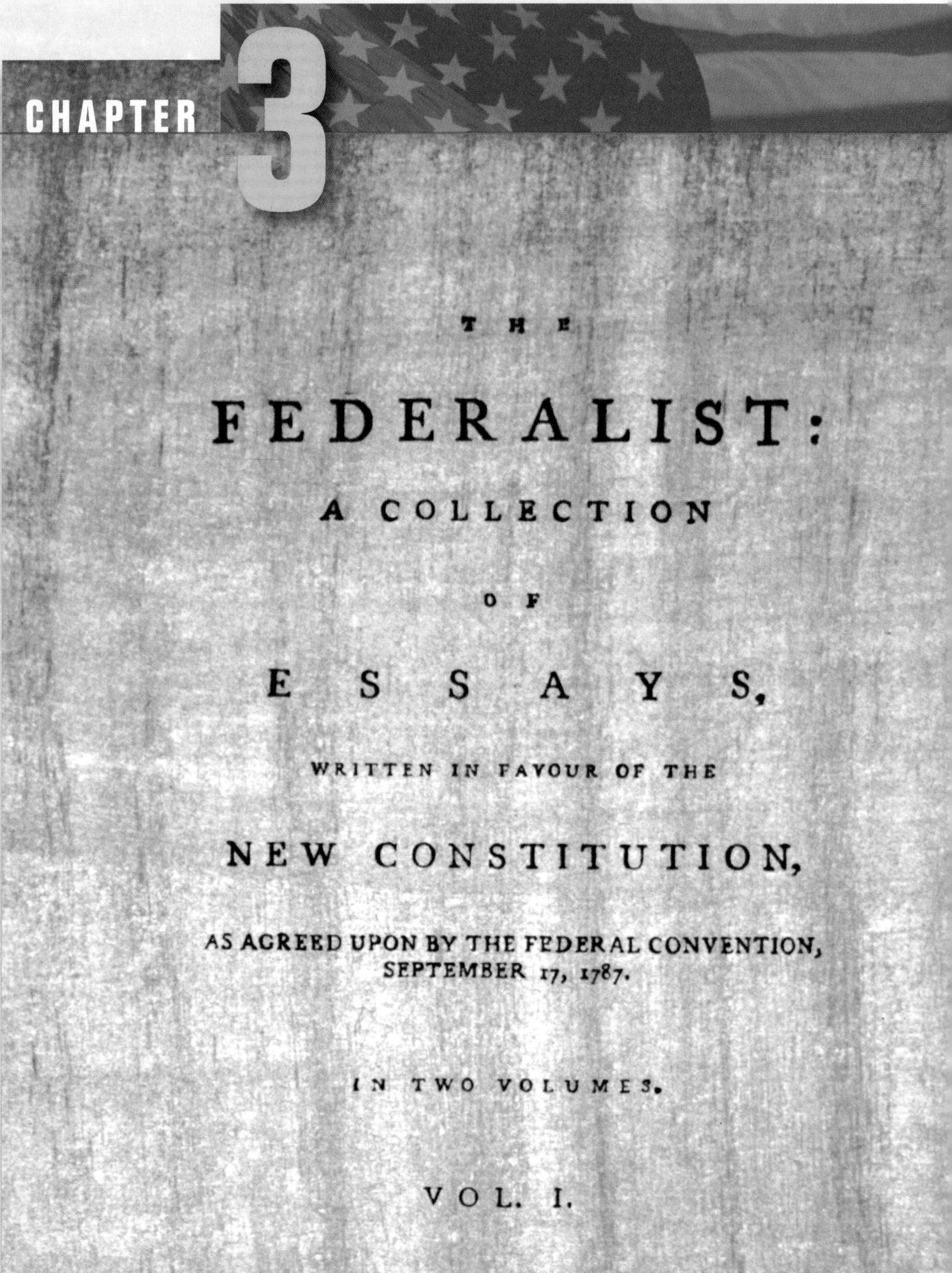

THE

FEDERALIST:

A COLLECTION

OF

ESSAYS,

WRITTEN IN FAVOUR OF THE

NEW CONSTITUTION,

AS AGREED UPON BY THE FEDERAL CONVENTION,
SEPTEMBER 17, 1787.

IN TWO VOLUMES.

VOL. I.

Federalism
Forging a Nation

Federalism: National and State Sovereignty

The Argument for Federalism
The Powers of the Nation
The Powers of the States

Federalism in Historical Perspective

An Indestructible Union (1789–1865)
Dual Federalism and Laissez-Faire
    Capitalism (1865–1937)
Toward National Citizenship

Federalism Today

Interdependency and
    Intergovernmental Relations
Government Revenues and
    Intergovernmental Relations
Devolution

The Public's Influence: Setting the Boundaries of Federal-State Power

The question of the relation of the states to the federal government is the cardinal question of our Constitutional system. It cannot be settled by the opinion of one generation, because it is a question of growth, and each successive stage of our political and economic development gives it a new aspect, makes it a new question. **Woodrow Wilson[1]**

As the reauthorization of the No Child Left Behind (NCLB) Act remained unresolved as Congress headed into 2008, it was unclear whether either side could muster the support necessary to get their way. The legislation had been in effect since 2002 when its most prominent supporter, President George W. Bush, signed it into law. NCLB had required states to test their primary and secondary school students annually and to show improvement in test scores or face a reduction in federal funding.

NCLB was arguably the most intrusive federal initiative yet on how local schools operate. Education has traditionally been the domain of state and local governments. More than 90 percent of the education funding is provided by states and localities, which also set most of the education standards, from teachers' qualifications to the length of the school day. NCLB was a sharp break from that tradition, and opponents said it was destructive of the schools' mission. They claimed that teachers were being forced "to teach to the test," administrators were being swamped with test-related paperwork, and schools were receiving insufficient federal funding to administer the program. Supporters of NCLB did not dismiss these complaints entirely but held to their belief that strict federal testing standards were necessary if America's schools were to be improved.

As the formal deadline for NCLB's reauthorization came and went, the U.S. secretary of education, Margaret Spellings, said: "If Congress doesn't produce a strong bill quickly, I will move forward," adding "we must stay true" to NCLB's goals. Earlier, a bipartisan commission formed by the National Conference of State Legislators had issued a critical assessment of NCLB, saying it had "questionable constitutional underpinnings." Calling the program "overly

The No Child Left Behind Act requires primary and secondary schools to test students' achievement level, and schools can lose their federal funding if test scores are too low. Enacted by Congress, the legislation has had strong supporters but has also faced intense opposition from those who see it as an infringement of state authority. Power struggles between the federal government and the state governments have occurred countless times in American history, a reflection of the U.S. federal system that vests sovereignty in both the national and state governments.

rigid" and "thinly funded," the commission noted that the Tenth Amendment reserves education policy to the states and that the federal government cannot impose a testing program unless it provides adequate funding and does not "coerce" states into participating.[2] Utah and several other states said they would not comply with any NCLB provision that was not properly funded.

The controversy surrounding the No Child Left Behind Act is one of thousands of disagreements over the course of American history that have hinged on whether national or state authority should prevail. Americans possess what amounts to dual citizenship: they are citizens both of the United States and of the state where they reside. The American political system is a *federal system,* in which constitutional authority is divided between a national government and state governments: each government is assumed to derive its powers directly from the people and therefore to have sovereignty (final authority) over the policy responsibilities assigned to it. The federal system consists of nation *and* states, indivisible yet separate.[3]

The relationship between the nation and the states was the most pressing issue when the Constitution was written in 1787. This chapter describes how that issue helped shape the Constitution. The chapter's closing sections discuss how federalism has changed throughout the nation's history and conclude with a brief overview of contemporary federalism. The main points presented in the chapter are these:

■ *The power of government must be equal to its responsibilities.* The Constitution was needed because the nation's preceding system (under the Articles of Confederation) was too weak to accomplish its expected goals, particularly those of a strong defense and an integrated economy.

■ *Federalism—the Constitution's division of governing authority between two levels, nation and states—was the result of political bargaining.* Federalism was not a theoretical principle, but a compromise made necessary in 1787 by the prior existence of the states.

■ *Federalism is not a fixed principle for allocating power between the national and state governments, but a principle that has changed over time in response to new political needs.* Federalism has passed through several distinct stages in the course of the nation's history.

■ *Contemporary federalism tilts toward national authority, reflecting the increased interdependence of American society.* However, there are also efforts to reduce the scope of federal authority.

Federalism: National and State Sovereignty

At the time of the writing of the Constitution, some of America's top leaders were dead set against the creation of a strong national government. When rumors circulated that the delegates to the constitutional convention were planning to

Patrick Henry was a leading figure in the American Revolution ("Give me liberty or give me death!"). He later opposed ratification of the Constitution on grounds that the national government should be a union of states and not also of people.

devise such a government, Patrick Henry, an ardent believer in state-centered government, said that he "smelt a rat." After the convention had adjourned, he realized that his fears were justified. "Who authorized them," he asked, "to speak the language of 'We, the People,' instead of 'We, the States'?"

The question of "people versus states" was precipitated by the failure of the Articles of Confederation. The government under the Articles (see Chapter 2) was a union of states rather than also a union of people. The government had no direct control over citizens. It could not, for example, require them to pay taxes. Congress could pass laws affecting the states, which they were obliged in principle to obey. However, they often ignored national laws that they deemed disagreeable or inconvenient. Georgia and North Carolina, for example, contributed no money at all to the national treasury between 1781 and 1786. The national government could do little more than beg them to pay their allotted share of the costs of defense and other national policies.

The only realistic solution to this problem—if the United States was to be a nation in more than name only—was a government that had direct power over the people. If individuals were ordered to pay taxes, for example, they would ordinarily do so. The alternatives to not paying—imprisonment or confiscation of their property—were too onerous.

Although the writers of the Constitution sought a national government based directly on the people, they also aimed to preserve the states as governing bodies. The states already existed, had their own constitutions, and enjoyed popular support. When Virginia's George Mason said that he would never agree to a union that abolished the states, he was speaking for virtually all the delegates. The Philadelphia convention therefore devised a system of government that came to be known as **federalism.** Federalism is the division of **sovereignty,** or ultimate governing authority, between a national government and regional (that is, state) governments. Each directly governs the people and derives its authority from them.

federalism

A governmental system in which authority is divided between two sovereign levels of government: national and regional.

sovereignty

The ultimate authority to govern within a certain geographical area.

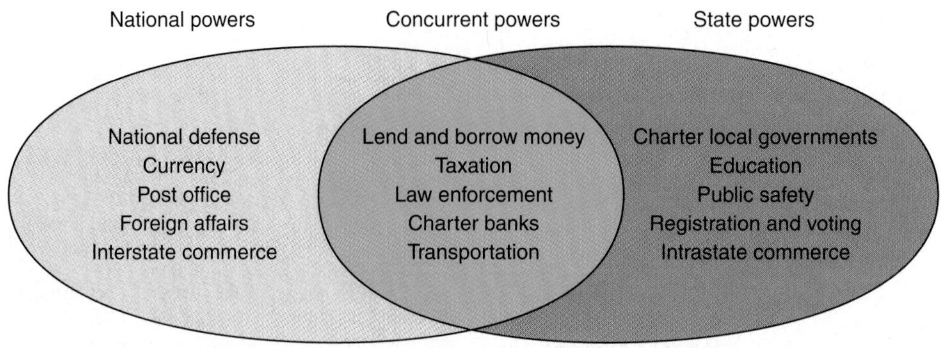

National powers   Concurrent powers   State powers

National powers	Concurrent powers	State powers
National defense	Lend and borrow money	Charter local governments
Currency	Taxation	Education
Post office	Law enforcement	Public safety
Foreign affairs	Charter banks	Registration and voting
Interstate commerce	Transportation	Intrastate commerce

FIGURE 3-1 **Federalism as a Governing System: Examples of National, State, and Concurrent Powers** The American federal system divides sovereignty between a national government and the state governments. Each is constitutionally protected in its existence and authority, although their powers overlap somewhat even in areas granted to one level (for example, the federal government has a role in education policy).

American federalism is basically a system of divided powers (see Figure 3-1). The system gives states the power to address local issues in ways of their choosing. At the same time, federalism gives the national government the power to decide matters of national scope. Although state authority and national authority overlap in some areas, there is also a division of responsibilities. The national government is in charge of national defense and the currency, among other things, while the states have primary responsibility for policy areas such as public education and police protection. The national and state governments also have some concurrent powers (that is, powers exercised over the same policy areas)—for example, the power to raise taxes and borrow money.

A federal system is different from a **confederacy,** the type of government established by the Articles. In a confederacy, the states alone are sovereign. The authority of the central government is derived from them, and they have the power to redefine its authority. Federalism is also different from a **unitary system,** in which sovereignty is vested solely in the national government. Under a unitary system, the people are citizens or subjects only of the national government. Other governments in such a system have only as much authority as it permits. The national government can even abolish them as governing bodies. In contrast, a federal system invests sovereignty—final authority—in both the national and state governments. Each level of government has a permanent existence and authority that is independent of that of the other level.

Federalism was invented in America in 1787. It was different not only from a confederate or a unitary system but also from any other form of government previously known. The ancient Greek city-states and the medieval Hanseatic League were confederacies. The governments of Europe were unitary in form. The United States of America would be the first nation to be governed through federalism.

The Argument for Federalism

Unlike many decisions made at the Philadelphia convention, the choice of federalism had no clear basis in political theory. Federalism was a practical necessity: there was a need for a stronger national government, and yet the states existed and were determined to retain their sovereignty. Nevertheless, the Framers developed arguments for the superiority of federalism. They claimed it would

confederacy

A governmental system in which sovereignty is vested entirely in subnational (state) governments.

unitary system

A governmental system in which the national government alone has sovereign (ultimate) authority.

HOW THE U.S. COMPARES

FEDERAL VERSUS UNITARY GOVERNMENTS

Federalism involves the division of sovereignty between a national government and subnational (such as state) governments. It was invented in 1787 in order to maintain the preexisting American states while establishing an effective central government. Since then, other countries have established a *federal* government, but most countries continue to have a *unitary* government, in which all sovereignty is vested in the national government.

Even within these alternative political systems, differences exist. In Germany's federal system, for example, the states have limited lawmaking powers but exercise broad authority in determining how national laws will be implemented. By comparison, the U.S. federal system grants substantial lawmaking powers to the states except in specified areas such as national defense and currency.

Unitary systems also differ. In Britain, the national government has delegated substantial authority to regions; Scotland, for example, has its own parliament, which exercises lawmaking powers. In France's unitary government, on the other hand, political authority is highly centralized.

In nearly all federal systems, the national legislature has two chambers—one apportioned by population (as in the case of the U.S. House of Representatives) and one apportioned by geographical area (as in the case of the U.S. Senate). The U.S. Senate is a pure federal institution in the sense that each state has the same number of senators. In some federal systems, such as Germany's, the states are not equally represented even in the legislative chamber that is apportioned on the basis of geography rather than population.

Unitary systems typically have but a single national legislative chamber, which is apportioned by population—there is no constitutional justification for a second chamber based on geography.

Country	Form of Government
Canada	Federal
France	Unitary
Germany	Federal
Great Britain	Modified unitary
Italy	Modified unitary
Japan	Unitary
Mexico	Modified federal
Sweden	Unitary
United States	Federal

protect liberty, moderate the power of government, and provide the basis for an effective national government.

Protecting Liberty

Although theorists such as John Locke and Montesquieu had not proposed a division of power between national and local authorities as a means of protecting liberty, the Framers came to view federalism as part of the Constitution's system of checks and balances (see Chapter 2). Alexander Hamilton argued in *Federalist* No. 28 that the American people could shift their loyalties back and forth between the national and state governments in order to keep each under control. "If [the people's] rights are invaded by either," Hamilton wrote, "they can make use of the other as the instrument of redress."

Moderating the Power of Government

To the Anti-Federalists (opponents of the Constitution), the sacrifice of the states' power to the nation was as unwise as it was unnecessary. They claimed that a distant national government could never serve the people's interests as well as the states could. Liberty *and* self-government, they argued, were enhanced by state-centered government. In support of their contention, the Anti-Federalists turned to Montesquieu, who had concluded that a small republic is more likely than a large one to serve the people. When government encompasses a small area, he argued, its leaders are in closer touch with the people and have more concern for their welfare.

In *Federalist* No. 10, James Madison took issue with this claim. He argued that whether a government serves the common good is a function not of its size but of the range of interests that share political power. The problem with a smaller republic, Madison claimed, is that it is likely to have a dominant faction—whether it be landholders, financiers, an impoverished majority, or some other group—that is strong enough to seize control of government and use it for selfish purposes. A large republic is less likely to have such an all-powerful faction. If financiers are strong in one area of a large republic, they are likely to be weaker elsewhere. The same will be true of farmers, merchants, laborers, and other groups. A large republic, Madison concluded, would make it hard for any single group to gain control and would force groups to work together. "Extend the sphere," said Madison, "and you take in a greater variety of parties and interests; you make it less probable that a majority of the whole will have a common motive to invade the rights of other citizens."

Strengthening the Union

The most telling argument in 1787 for a federal system was that it would overcome the deficiencies of the Articles. The Articles had numerous flaws (including a very weak executive and a judiciary subservient to the state courts), and two of them were fatal: the government had neither the power to tax nor the power to regulate commerce.

Under the Articles, Congress was given responsibility for national defense but was not granted the power to tax, so it depended on the states for the money to maintain an army and a navy. During the first six years under the Articles, Congress asked the states for $12 million but received only $3 million—not even enough to pay the interest on Revolutionary War debts. By 1786, the national government had become so desperate for money that it sold the navy's ships and reduced the army to fewer than a thousand soldiers—this at a time when England had an army in Canada and when Spain occupied Florida.

HISTORICAL *Background*

It could take weeks to travel overland or by ship from the most distant points in the American states. The great size of America compared with European countries was used as an argument by both those who favored a strong union and those who opposed it.

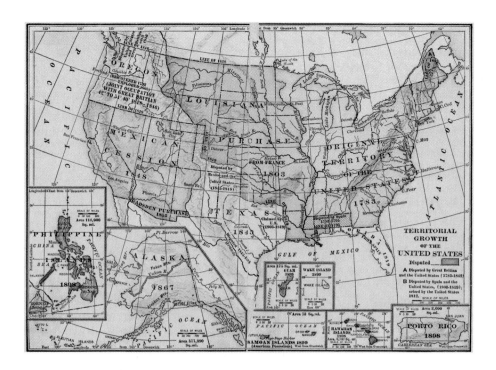

Congress also was expected to shape a national economy, yet it was power-less to do so because the Articles prohibited it from interfering with the states' commerce policies. States, free to do whatever they wanted, exploited the situation by trying to cripple their competitors. Connecticut, for example, placed a higher tariff on manufactured goods from its trading rival Massachusetts than it placed on the same goods shipped from England.

The Articles of Confederation showed the fallacy of the adage "That government is best which governs least." The consequences of an overly weak authority were abundantly clear: public disorder, economic chaos, and inadequate defense.

The Powers of the Nation

The Philadelphia convention met to decide the national government's structure. The delegates had not been sent to determine the form of the state governments. Accordingly, the U.S. Constitution addresses the lawful authority of the national government, which is provided through *enumerated and implied powers.* Authority that is not granted to the national government is left—or "reserved"—to the states. Thus, the states have *reserved powers.*

Enumerated Powers

Article I of the Constitution grants to Congress seventeen **enumerated (expressed) powers.** The Framers intended these powers to be the basis for a government strong enough to forge a union that was secure in its defense and stable in its commerce. Congress's powers to regulate commerce among the states, to create a national currency, and to borrow money, for example, would provide a foundation for a sound national economy. Its power to tax, combined with its authority to establish an army and a navy and to declare war, would enable it to provide for the common defense. In addition, the Constitution prohibits the states from actions that would undermine the national government's lawful powers. Article I, Section 10 prohibits the states from making treaties with other nations, raising armies, waging war, printing money, or entering into commercial agreements with other states without the approval of Congress.

The writers of the Constitution recognized that the lawful exercise of national authority would at times conflict with the actions of the states. In such instances, national law was intended to prevail. Article VI of the Constitution grants this dominance in the so-called **supremacy clause,** which provides that "the laws of the United States . . . shall be the supreme law of the land."

Implied Powers

The Framers of the Constitution worried that a narrow definition of national authority could result in a government incapable of adapting to change. Under the Articles of Confederation, Congress was strictly confined to those powers expressly granted to it, which limited its ability to respond effectively to the country's changing needs after the Revolutionary War. Concerned that the enumerated powers by themselves would be too restrictive of national authority, the Framers added the **"necessary and proper" clause** or, as it later came to be known, the **elastic clause.** Article I, Section 8 gives Congress the power "to make all laws which shall be necessary and proper for carrying into execution the foregoing [enumerated] powers." This grant gave the national government **implied powers:** the authority to take action that is not expressly authorized by the Constitution but that supports actions that are so authorized.

enumerated (expressed) powers
The seventeen powers granted to the national government under Article I, Section 8 of the Constitution. These powers include taxation and the regulation of commerce as well as the authority to provide for the national defense.

supremacy clause
Article VI of the Constitution, which makes national law supreme over state law when the national government is acting within its constitutional limits.

"necessary and proper" (elastic) clause
The authority granted Congress in Article I, Section 8 of the Constitution "to make all laws which shall be necessary and proper" for the implementation of its enumerated powers.

implied powers
The federal government's constitutional authority (through the "necessary and proper" clause) to take action that is not expressly authorized by the Constitution but that supports actions that are so authorized.

The Powers of the States

The Framers' goal of a sovereign national government was not shared in 1787 by all Americans. Although Anti-Federalists recognized a need to strengthen defense and boost interstate commerce, they feared the consequences of a strong central government. The interests of the people of New Hampshire were not identical to those of Georgians or Pennsylvanians, and the Anti-Federalists argued that only state-centered government would protect the differences. Self-government, they claimed, would be weakened if power resided with a distant national government.

The Federalists responded by saying that the national government would have no interest in depriving the states of their liberty or of their right to decide local matters.[4] The national government would take responsibility for establishing a strong defense and for promoting a sound economy, while the states would retain nearly all other governing functions, including public education and safety.

This argument did not persuade the Anti-Federalists that their fear of an overly powerful national government was baseless. The supremacy and "necessary and proper" clauses were particularly worrisome, because they provided a constitutional basis for expansion of national authority. Such concerns led to demands for a constitutional amendment that would protect states' rights and interests. Ratified in 1791 as the Tenth Amendment to the Constitution, it reads: "The powers not delegated to the United States by the Constitution, nor prohibited by it to the States, are reserved to the States." The states' powers under the U.S. Constitution are thus called **reserved powers.**

reserved powers

The powers granted to the states under the Tenth Amendment to the Constitution.

Federalism in Historical Perspective

Since ratification of the Constitution over two centuries ago, no aspect of it has provoked more frequent or bitter conflict than federalism. By establishing two levels of sovereign authority, the Constitution created competing centers of power and ambition, each of which was sure to claim disputed areas as belonging to it.

Conflict between national and state authority was also ensured by the brevity of the Constitution. The Framers deliberately avoided detailed provisions, recognizing that brief phrasing would lend flexibility to the government they were creating. The document does not define, for example, the difference between *inter*state commerce (which the national government is empowered to regulate) and *intra*state commerce (which is reserved for regulation by the states).

Not surprisingly, federalism has been a contentious and dynamic system, its development determined less by constitutional language than by the strength of contending interests and by the country's changing needs. Federalism can be viewed as having progressed through three historical eras, each of which has involved a different relationship between the nation and the states.

An Indestructible Union (1789–1865)

The issue during the first era, which lasted from the Constitution's beginnings in 1789 through the end of the Civil War in 1865, was the Union's survival. Given the state-centered history of America before the Constitution, it was inevitable that the states would dispute national policies that threatened their interests.

The Nationalist View: *McCulloch v. Maryland*

A first dispute over federalism arose when President George Washington's secretary of the treasury, Alexander Hamilton, proposed that Congress establish a national bank. Thomas Jefferson, Washington's secretary of state, opposed the bank on the grounds that its activities would benefit the rich at the expense of ordinary people. Jefferson said the bank was unlawful because the Constitution did not expressly authorize it. Hamilton and his supporters claimed that because the federal government had constitutional authority to regulate currency, it had the "implied power" to establish a national bank.

Hamilton's view prevailed when Congress in 1791 established the First Bank of the United States, granting it a twenty-year charter. Although Congress did not renew the bank's charter when it expired in 1811, Congress decided in 1816 to establish the Second Bank of the United States. State and local banks did not want competition from a national bank and sought help from their state legislatures. Several states, including Maryland, levied taxes on the national bank's operations within their borders, hoping to drive it out of existence by making it unprofitable. Edwin McCulloch, who was in charge of the Maryland branch of the national bank, refused to pay the Maryland tax and the resulting dispute was heard by the Supreme Court.

The chief justice of the Supreme Court, John Marshall, was a strong nationalist, and in *McCulloch v. Maryland* (1819) the Court ruled decisively in favor of national authority. It was reasonable, Marshall concluded, to infer that a government with powers to tax, borrow money, and regulate commerce could establish a bank in order to exercise those powers effectively. Marshall's argument was a clear statement of *implied powers*—the idea that through the "necessary and proper" clause the national government's powers extend beyond a narrow reading of its enumerated powers.

Marshall's ruling also addressed the meaning of the Constitution's supremacy clause. The state of Maryland had argued that, even if the national bank was a legal entity, a state had the sovereign authority to tax it. The Supreme Court rejected Maryland's position, concluding that valid national law prevailed over conflicting state law. Because the national government had the power to create the bank, it also could protect the bank from actions by the states, such as taxation, that might destroy it.[5]

The *McCulloch* decision served as precedent for later rulings in support of national power. In *Gibbons v. Ogden* (1824), for example, the Marshall-led Court rejected a New York law granting a monopoly on a ferry that operated between

HISTORICAL
Background

A first dispute over federalism was whether the Constitution allowed the creation of a Bank of the United States (shown here in an early-nineteenth-century painting). The Constitution had a clause authorizing the printing of currency but not the establishment of a bank itself.

New York and New Jersey, concluding that New York had encroached on Congress's power to regulate commerce among the states. The Court also ruled that Congress's commerce power extended *into* a state when commerce between two or more states was at issue.[6]

Marshall's opinions asserted that legitimate uses of national power took precedence over state authority and that the "necessary and proper" clause and the commerce clause were broad grants of national power. As a nationalist, Marshall provided the U.S. government with the legal justification for expanding its power in ways that fostered the development of the United States as a nation rather than as a collection of states. This constitutional vision was of utmost significance. As Justice Oliver Wendell Holmes Jr. noted a century later, the Union could not have survived if each state had been allowed to determine for itself the extent to which it would accept national authority.[7]

The States'-Rights View: The *Dred Scott* Decision

Although John Marshall's rulings helped strengthen national authority, the issue of slavery posed a growing threat to the Union's survival. Fearing that northern members of Congress might move to abolish slavery, southern leaders did what others have done throughout American history: they devised a constitutional argument to fit their political desires. John C. Calhoun of South Carolina argued that the Constitution had created "a government of states . . . not a government of individuals."[8] This line of reasoning led Calhoun to his famed "doctrine of nullification," which declared that any state had the constitutional right to nullify a national law.

In 1832, South Carolina invoked this doctrine, declaring "null and void" a tariff law that favored northern interests. President Andrew Jackson called South Carolina's action "incompatible with the existence of the Union," a position that was strengthened when Congress authorized Jackson to use military force if necessary against South Carolina. The state backed down when Congress amended the tariff act to soften its impact on the South.

The clash foreshadowed the Civil War, a confrontation of far greater consequence. Although war would not break out for another three decades, conflict over states' rights was intensifying. Westward expansion and immigration into the northern states were tilting power in Congress toward the free states, which increasingly signaled their determination to outlaw slavery in the United States at some future time. Attempts to find a compromise acceptable to both the North and the South were fruitless.

The Supreme Court's infamous *Dred Scott* decision (1857), written by Chief Justice Roger Taney, an ardent states'-rights advocate, exacerbated the conflict. Dred Scott, a slave who had lived in the North for four years, applied for his freedom when his master died, citing a federal law—the Missouri Compromise of 1820—that made slavery illegal in a free state or territory. The

The American Civil War was the bloodiest conflict the world had yet known. Ten percent of fighting-age males died in the four-year war, and uncounted others were wounded. The death toll—618,000 (360,000 from the North, 258,000 from the South)—exceeded that of the American war dead in World War I, World War II, the Korean War, and the Vietnam War combined. This death toll was in a nation with a population only one-tenth the size it is today. Shown here, in one of the earliest war photos ever taken, are the bodies of soldiers killed at the battle of Antietam.

Supreme Court ruled against Scott, claiming that persons of African descent were barred from citizenship and thereby could not sue for their freedom in federal courts. The Court also invalidated the Missouri Compromise. The Court ruled that slaves were property, not people, and as such could be taken into any state or territory. Accordingly, Congress did not have the power to outlaw slavery in any part of the United States.[9]

The Taney Court's decision provoked outrage in the North and contributed to a sectional split in the nation's majority party, the Democrats. In 1860, the Democratic Party's northern and southern wings nominated separate candidates for the presidency, which split the Democratic vote, enabling the Republican candidate, Abraham Lincoln, to win the presidency with only 40 percent of the popular vote. Lincoln had campaigned on a platform that called, not for an immediate end to slavery, but for its gradual abolition through payments to slaveholders. Nevertheless, southern states saw Lincoln's election as a grave threat to their sovereignty. By the time Lincoln assumed office, seven southern states, led by South Carolina, had left the Union. Four more states were to follow. In justifying his decision to wage war on the secessionists, Lincoln said, "The Union is older than the states." In 1865, the superior strength of the Union army settled by force the question of whether national authority is binding on the states.

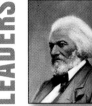

LEADERS

FREDERICK DOUGLASS
(1818–95)

Born a slave, Frederick Douglass never knew his father and rarely saw his mother, who died when he was seven. He spent part of his early childhood in Baltimore, where he was treated decently and learned to read. In his early teens, Douglass was sent to work on a Maryland farm owned by a brutal slaveholder, who whipped Douglass mercilessly. It took Douglass more than two years to escape north to Massachusetts, where he joined the antislavery movement and discovered that he had unusual oratorical skill. As his speaking fame grew, Douglass toured the northern states and Europe, seeking support for abolition. He argued that the Constitution guaranteed freedom for all, not just those of the white race. As much as Douglass despised the slave states, he was dedicated to saving the Union, arguing that abandoning it would mean abandoning those enslaved in the South. After the Civil War ended, Douglass sought constitutional amendments that would give equal rights to former slaves.

Dual Federalism and Laissez-Faire Capitalism (1865–1937)

Although the Civil War preserved the Union, new challenges to federalism were surfacing. Constitutional doctrine held that certain policy areas, such as interstate commerce and defense, belonged exclusively to the national government, whereas other policy areas, such as public health and intrastate commerce, belonged exclusively to the states. This doctrine, known as **dual federalism,** was based on the idea that a precise separation of national and state authority was both possible and desirable. "The power which one possesses," said the Supreme Court, "the other does not."[10]

American society, however, was in the midst of changes that raised questions about the suitability of dual federalism as a governing concept. The Industrial Revolution had given rise to large business firms, which were using their economic power to dominate markets and exploit workers. Government was the logical counterforce to this economic power. Which level of government—state or national—would regulate business?

There was also the issue of the former slaves. The white South had lost the war but was hardly of a mind to share power with newly freed slaves. Would the federal government be allowed to intervene in state affairs to ensure the fair treatment of African Americans?

dual federalism

A doctrine based on the idea that a precise separation of national power and state power is both possible and desirable.

Dual federalism became a barrier to an effective response to these issues. From the 1860s through the 1930s, the Supreme Court held firm to the idea that there was a sharp line between national and state authority and, in both areas, a high wall of separation between government and the economy. The era of dual federalism was characterized by state supremacy in racial policy and business supremacy in commerce policy.

The Fourteenth Amendment and State Discretion

Ratified after the Civil War, the Fourteenth Amendment was intended to protect the newly freed slaves from discriminatory action by state governments. A state was prohibited from depriving "any person of life, liberty, or property without due process of law," from denying "any person within its jurisdiction the equal protection of the laws," and from abridging "the privileges or immunities of citizens of the United States."

Supreme Court rulings in subsequent decades, however, helped to undermine the Fourteenth Amendment's promise of liberty and equality for all. The Court held, for example, that the Fourteenth Amendment did not substantially limit the power of the states to determine the rights to which their residents were entitled.[11] Then, in *Plessy v. Ferguson* (1896), the Court issued its infamous "separate but equal" ruling. A black man, Homer Adolph Plessy, had been convicted of violating a Louisiana law that required white and black citizens to ride in separate railroad cars. The Supreme Court upheld his conviction, concluding that state governments could require blacks to use separate railroad cars and other accommodations as long as those facilities were "equal" in quality to those reserved for use by whites. "If one race be inferior to the other socially," the Court concluded, "the Constitution of the United States cannot put them on the same plane." The lone dissenting justice in the case, John Marshall Harlan, had harsh words for his colleagues: "Our Constitution is color-blind and neither knows nor tolerates classes among citizens. . . . The thin disguise of 'equal' accommodations . . . will not mislead anyone nor atone for the wrong this day done."[12]

HISTORICAL
Background

After the Civil War Reconstruction, the white majority in the South used the power of government to enforce creation of a two-race society in which the public schools and other public facilities for blacks were inferior to those for whites.

POLITICAL CULTURE

LIBERTY, EQUALITY, AND SELF-GOVERNMENT

Federalism

During the debate over ratification of the Constitution, Americans argued over whether liberty, equality, and self-government would be better protected by the states or by the nation. The Anti-Federalists argued that a small republic was closer to the people and therefore would do more to uphold individuals' rights. James Madison, arguing on behalf of the Federalists, countered by saying that a large republic was preferable because its wide diversity of interests would lead groups to find compromise solutions.

Which view—that of the Anti-Federalists or that of the Federalists—is better supported by history? Have America's founding ideals been better nurtured through state governments or through the national government? For a long period in U.S. history, the answer was clear. As political scientist William Riker noted, state-centered government before and

after the Civil War was the tool by which white Americans dominated black Americans, first through slavery and later through institutionalized racism (for example, the separation by law of black and white schoolchildren). As Madison prophesied, a smaller republic makes it easier for a dominant faction to run roughshod over others.

Legal racial discrimination is now a thing of the past, and state governments are less likely to side with one faction against others. How would you judge today's situation? In your view, which level of government—federal or state—is more likely to protect and enhance the ideals of liberty, equality, and self-government? Which level of government is more likely to promote the interests of a particular group at the expense of other groups? In what areas of public policy—taxation, education, public safety, and so on—do you think your opinion is most supported?

With its *Plessy* decision, the Court undercut the Fourteenth Amendment and allowed southern states to segregate the races. Black children were forced into separate schools that seldom had libraries and usually had few teachers. Hospitals for blacks had few doctors and nurses and almost no medical supplies and equipment. Legal challenges to these discriminatory practices were generally unsuccessful. The *Plessy* ruling had become a justification for the separate and *unequal* treatment of black Americans.

Judicial Protection of Business

Through its rulings after the Civil War, the Supreme Court also provided a constitutional basis for unrestricted economic power. Most of the Court's justices believed in laissez-faire capitalism (which holds that business should be "allowed to act" without interference), and they interpreted the Constitution in ways that restricted government's attempts to regulate business activity. In 1886, for example, the Court decided that corporations were "persons" within the meaning of the Fourteenth Amendment, and thereby were protected from substantial regulation by the states.[13] The irony was inescapable. A constitutional amendment that had been enacted to protect the liberty of newly freed slaves was ignored for this purpose but used instead to protect fictitious persons—business corporations.

The Court also weakened the national government's regulatory power by narrowly interpreting its commerce power. The Constitution's **commerce clause** says that Congress shall have the power "to regulate commerce" among the states. However, the clause does not spell out the economic activities included in the grant of power. When the federal government invoked the Sherman Antitrust Act (1890) in an attempt to break up a monopoly on the manufacture of sugar, the Supreme Court blocked the action, claiming that interstate commerce covered only the "transportation" of goods, not their "manufacture."[14] Manufacturing was deemed part of intrastate commerce and thus, according to the

commerce clause

The clause of the Constitution (Article I, Section 8) that empowers the federal government to regulate commerce among the states and with other nations.

Between 1865 and 1937, the Supreme Court's rulings severely restricted national power. Narrowly interpreting Congress's constitutional power to regulate commerce, the Court forbade Congress to regulate child labor and other aspects of manufacturing.

dual federalism doctrine, subject to state regulation only. However, because the Court had previously decided that the states' regulatory powers were limited by the Fourteenth Amendment, the states for the most part were also denied the authority to regulate manufacturing activity in a significant way.

Although some business regulation was allowed, the Supreme Court remained an obstacle to efforts to curb abusive business practices. An example is the case of *Hammer v. Dagenhart* (1918), which arose from a 1916 federal act that prohibited the interstate shipment of goods produced by child labor. The act was popular because factory owners were exploiting children, working them for long hours at low pay. Citing the Tenth Amendment, the Court invalidated the law, ruling that factory practices could be regulated only by the states.[15] However, in an earlier case, *Lochner v. New York* (1905), the Court had prevented a state from regulating labor practices, concluding that such action violated firms' property rights.[16]

In effect, the Court had negated the principle of self-government. Neither the people's representatives in Congress nor their representatives in the state legislatures were allowed to regulate business activity. America's corporations, with the Supreme Court as their protector, were in command.[17]

National Authority Prevails

Judicial supremacy in the economic sphere ended abruptly in 1937. For nearly a decade, the United States had been mired in the Great Depression, which President Franklin D. Roosevelt's New Deal sought to alleviate. However, the Supreme Court had ruled that much of the New Deal's economic recovery legislation was unconstitutional. A constitutional crisis of historic proportions seemed unavoidable until the Court suddenly reversed its position. In the process, American federalism was fundamentally changed.

The Great Depression revealed that Americans had become a national community with national economic needs. More than half the population lived in cities (compared to one-fifth in 1860), and more than 10 million workers were employed by industry (compared to one million in 1860). Urban workers typically were dependent on landlords for their housing, on farmers and grocers for

HISTORICAL
Background

their food, and on corporations for their jobs. Farmers were more independent, but they too were increasingly a part of a larger economic network. Farmers' income depended on market prices and shipping and equipment costs.[18] This economic interdependence meant that, when the depression hit in 1929, its effects could not be contained. At the depths of the Great Depression, one-fourth of the nation's workforce was unemployed and another fourth could find only part-time work.

The states by tradition had responsibility for helping the unemployed, but they were nearly penniless because of declining tax revenues and the huge demand for welfare assistance. Roosevelt's New Deal programs were designed to ease the hardship. The 1933 National Industry Recovery Act (NIRA), for example, established a federal jobs program and enabled major industries to coordinate their production decisions. Economic conservatives strenuously opposed such programs, accusing Roosevelt of leading the country into communism. They found an ally in the Supreme Court. In *Schecter v. United States* (1935), just as it had done in previous New Deal cases, the Supreme Court in a 5-4 ruling declared the NIRA to be unconstitutional.[19]

During the Great Depression, millions of Americans lost their jobs and homes. State and local governments could not cope with the enormous problems created by the Great Depression, so the federal government stepped in with its New Deal programs, greatly changing the nature of federal-state relations.

Frustrated by the Court's opposition, Roosevelt in 1937 proposed that Congress expand the Supreme Court by passing legislation that would allow an additional justice to be appointed whenever a seated member passed the age of seventy. If enacted, the legislation would have enabled Roosevelt to appoint enough new justices to swing the Court to his side. Congress rejected Roosevelt's plan, but the controversy ended with "the switch in time that saved nine." For reasons that have never been fully clear, Justice Owen Roberts switched sides on New Deal cases, giving the president a 5-4 majority on the Court.

Within months, the Court upheld the 1935 National Labor Relations Act, which gave employees the right to organize and bargain collectively.[20] In passing the legislation, Congress claimed that labor–management disputes disrupted the nation's economy and therefore could be regulated through the commerce clause. In upholding the act, the Supreme Court in effect granted Congress the authority to broadly apply its commerce powers.[21] During this same period, the Court also loosened its restrictions on Congress's power to tax and spend.[22] These decisions removed the constitutional barrier to increased federal authority, a change the Court later acknowledged when it said that Congress's commerce power is "as broad as the needs of the nation."[23]

The Supreme Court had finally acknowledged the obvious: that an industrial economy is not confined by state boundaries and must be subject to national regulation. It was a principle that business itself increasingly accepted. The nation's banking industry, for example, was saved in the 1930s from almost complete collapse by the creation of a federal regulatory agency, the Federal Deposit Insurance Corporation (FDIC). By insuring depositors' savings against loss, the FDIC stopped the panic withdrawals that had bankrupted many of the nation's banks.

Toward National Citizenship

The fundamental change in the constitutional doctrine of federalism as applied to economic issues that took place in the 1930s was paralleled by subsequent changes in other areas, including civil rights. In *Brown v. Board of Education* (1954), for example, the Supreme Court held that states could not force black children to attend public schools separate from those for white children (see Chapter 5).[24] National citizenship—the notion that Americans should be equal in their rights and opportunities regardless of the state in which they reside—became a more encompassing idea than it had previously been.

Federalism Today

Since the 1930s, the relation of the nation to the states has changed so fundamentally that dual federalism is no longer even a roughly accurate description of the American situation. An understanding of today's federalism requires a recognition of two countervailing trends. The first trend is a long-term *expansion* of national authority that began in the 1930s and continued for the next half-century. The national government now operates in many policy areas that were once almost exclusively within the control of states and localities. The national government does not dominate in these policy areas, but it does play a significant role. Much of this national influence stems from social welfare policies enacted in the 1960s as part of President Lyndon Johnson's Great Society program, which included initiatives in health care, public housing, nutrition, welfare, urban development, and other areas previously reserved to states and localities.

The second, more recent trend involves a partial contraction of national authority. Known as *devolution,* this trend involves the "passing down" of authority from the national government to the state and local levels in selected areas. Devolution has reversed the decades-long increase in federal authority, but only to a moderate degree.

In short, the national government's policy authority has expanded greatly since the 1930s, even though that authority has been reduced somewhat in recent years. We will explain each trend in more detail.

Interdependency and Intergovernmental Relations

Interdependency is a reason that national authority increased dramatically in the twentieth century. Modern systems of transportation, commerce, and communication transcend local and state boundaries. These systems are national—and even international—in scope, which means that problems affecting Americans living in one part of the country are likely to affect Americans living elsewhere. This situation has required Washington to assume a larger policy role. National problems typically require national solutions.

Interdependency has also encouraged national, state, and local policymakers to work together to solve policy problems. This collaborative effort has been described as **cooperative federalism.**[25] The difference between cooperative federalism and the older dual federalism has been likened to the difference between a marble cake, whose levels flow together, and a layer cake, whose levels are separate.[26]

Cooperative federalism is based on shared policy responsibilities rather than sharply divided ones. An example is the Medicaid program, which was created in 1965 as part of President Johnson's Great Society initiative and provides

cooperative federalism

The situation in which the national, state, and local levels work together to solve problems.

Since the 1930s, the relationship between the federal and state governments has best been described by the term *cooperative federalism*. The two levels, along with the local government level, cooperate in addressing problems of joint concern, such as the wildfires that have erupted with increasing frequency in recent years because of droughts and other factors.

health care for the poor. The Medicaid program is jointly funded by the national and state governments, operates within eligibility standards set by the national government, and gives states some latitude in determining recipients' benefits. The Medicaid program is not an isolated example. Literally hundreds of policy programs today are run jointly by the national and state governments. In many cases, local governments are also involved. These programs have the following characteristics:

- Jointly funded by the national and state governments (and sometimes by local governments)
- Jointly administered, with the states and localities providing most of the direct service to recipients and a national agency providing general administration
- Jointly determined, with both the state and national governments (and sometimes the local governments) having a say in eligibility and benefit levels and with federal regulations, such as those prohibiting discrimination, providing an element of uniformity to the various state and local efforts

Cooperative federalism should not be interpreted to mean that the states are powerless and dependent. States have retained most of their traditional authority in areas such as education, health, public safety, and roadways. Nevertheless, the federal government's involvement in policy areas traditionally reserved for the states has increased its policy influence and diminished state-to-state policy differences. Before the enactment of the federal Medicaid program in 1965, for example, poor people in many states were not entitled to government-paid health care. Now most poor people are eligible for health benefits regardless of where they reside.

Government Revenues and Intergovernmental Relations

The interdependency of American society—the fact that developments in one area affect what happens elsewhere—is one of two major reasons the federal government's policy role has expanded greatly since the early twentieth century.

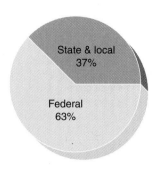

FIGURE 3-2   **Federal, State, and Local Shares of Government Tax Revenue**
The federal government raises more tax revenues than all state and local governments combined.
Source: U.S. Department of Commerce, 2008.

fiscal federalism

A term that refers to the expenditure of federal funds on programs run in part through states and localities.

grants-in-aid

Federal cash payments to states and localities for programs they administer.

FIGURE 3-3   **Federal Grants to State and Local Governments**
Federal aid to states and localities has increased dramatically since the 1950s.
Source: Office of Management and Budget, 2008. Figure is based on constant (2000) dollars in order to control for the effect of inflation.

The other reason is the federal government's superior taxing capacity. States and localities are in a competitive situation with regard to taxation. A state with high taxes will lose firms and people to states with lower taxes. Firms and people are less likely to move to another country in search of lower taxes. The result is that the federal government raises more tax revenues than do all fifty states and the thousands of local governments combined (see Figure 3-2).

Fiscal Federalism

The federal government's revenue-raising advantage has made money a basis for relations between the national government and the states and localities. **Fiscal federalism** refers to the expenditure of federal funds on programs run in part through state and local governments.[27] The federal government provides some or all of the money through **grants-in-aid** (cash payments) to states and localities, which then administer the programs. The pattern of federal assistance to states and localities is shown in Figure 3-3. Federal grants-in-aid have increased dramatically during the past half-century. Roughly one in every five dollars spent by local and state governments in recent decades has been raised not by them, but by the federal government in Washington (see "States in the Nation").

Cash grants to states and localities have increased Washington's policy influence. State and local governments can reject a grant-in-aid, but if they accept it they must spend it in the way specified by Congress. Also, because most grants require states to contribute matching funds, the federal programs in effect determine how states will allocate some of their own tax dollars. Further, federal grants have pressured state and local officials to adopt national goals, such as the elimination of racial and other forms of discrimination. A building constructed with the help of federal funds, for example, must be accessible to persons with disabilities. Nevertheless, federal grants-in-aid also serve the policy interests of state and local officials. While these officials often complain that federal grants contain too many

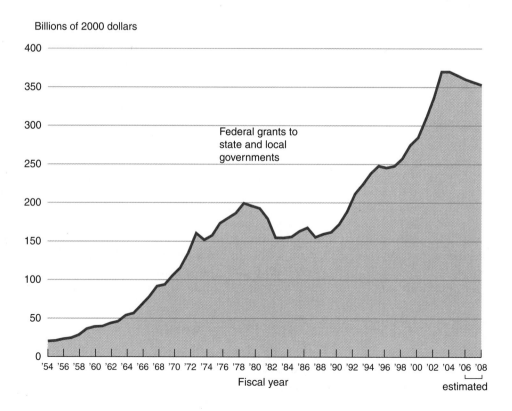

STATES IN THE NATION

FEDERAL GRANTS-IN-AID TO THE STATES

Federal assistance accounts for a significant share of state revenue, but the variation is considerable. New Mexico (with a third of its total revenue coming from federal grants-in-aid) is at one extreme. Nevada (a seventh of its revenue) is at the other.

Q: Why do states in the South, where anti-Washington sentiment is relatively high, get more of their revenue from the federal government than most other states?

A: Many federal grant programs are designed to assist low-income people, and poverty is more widespread in the South. Moreover, southern states traditionally have provided fewer government services, and federal grants accordingly constitute a larger proportion of their budgets.

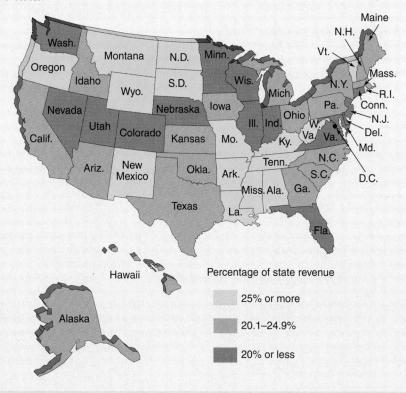

Percentage of state revenue

- 25% or more
- 20.1–24.9%
- 20% or less

Source: U.S. Bureau of the Census, 2008.

restrictions and infringe too much on their authority, they are eager to obtain the money because it permits them to offer services they could not otherwise afford.

Categorical and Block Grants

State and local governments receive two major types of assistance—categorical grants and block grants—which differ in the extent to which Washington defines the conditions of their use. **Categorical grants,** the more restrictive type, can be used only for a designated activity. An example is funds directed for use in school lunch programs. These funds cannot be diverted to other school purposes, such as the purchase of textbooks or the hiring of teachers. **Block grants** are less restrictive. The federal government specifies the general area in which the funds must be used, but state and local officials select the specific projects. A block grant targeted for the health area, for example, might give state and local

categorical grants
Federal grants-in-aid to states and localities that can be used only for designated projects.

block grants
Federal grants-in-aid that permit state and local officials to decide how the money will be spent within a general area, such as education or health.

officials the authority to decide whether to use the money for hospital construction, medical equipment, the training of nurses, or some other health care activity.

State and local officials prefer federal money that comes with fewer strings attached and thus favor block grants. In contrast, members of Congress have at times preferred categorical grants, because this type of assistance gives them greater control over how state and local officials spend federal funds. Recently, however, officials at all levels have looked to block grants as the key to a more workable form of federalism. This tendency is part of a broader trend—devolution.

Devolution

devolution

The passing down of authority from the national government to the state and local governments.

Devolution embodies the idea that American federalism can be strengthened by a partial shift in power from the federal government to the state and local governments.[28] Devolution rests on a belief—held more strongly by Republicans than Democrats—that federal authority has extended too far into areas traditionally governed through state and local governments.

Although lawmakers of both parties had voted for expansions of federal authority, Democrats, led by Presidents Roosevelt and Johnson, had been the strongest advocates of a larger role for the national government, with strong backing from the public. After the 1960s, however, public support for federal domestic spending declined. Some of the programs, particularly those providing welfare benefits to the poor, were widely seen as too costly, too bureaucratic, and too lax—there was a widespread perception that many welfare recipients were getting benefits they neither needed nor deserved. Republican leaders increasingly questioned the effectiveness of the programs. Republican Presidents Richard Nixon and Ronald Reagan proposed versions of a "new federalism" in which some areas of public policy for which the federal government had assumed responsibility would be returned to states and localities.

The Republican Revolution

When the Republican Party scored a decisive victory in the 1994 congressional elections, Speaker of the House Newt Gingrich declared that "1960s-style federalism is dead." Republican lawmakers proposed to cut some federal programs, but, even more, they sought to increase state and local control. Congressional Republicans passed legislation to reduce *unfunded mandates*—federal programs that require action by states or localities but provide no or insufficient funds to pay for it. For example, states and localities are required by federal law to make their buildings accessible to the physically handicapped, but Washington pays only part of the cost of these accommodations. In the Unfunded Mandates Reform Act of 1995, Congress eliminated some of these mandates, although under threat of a veto by Democratic President Bill Clinton, those relating to civil rights were retained. The GOP-controlled Congress also took action to lump additional categorical grants into block grants, thereby giving states more control over how federal money would be spent.

The most significant change occurred in 1996, when Congress enacted the sweeping Welfare Reform Act. Opinion polls at the time revealed that a majority of Americans felt that government was spending too much on welfare and that too many welfare recipients were taking advantage of the system. The Welfare Reform Act tightened spending and eligibility. The legislation's key element, the Temporary Assistance for Needy Families (TANF) block grant, ended the decades-old program that granted cash assistance to every poor family with children. TANF restricts a family's eligibility for federal assistance to five years, and after two years, a family head normally has to go to work for the benefits to continue. Moreover, TANF gives states wide latitude in setting benefit levels, eligibility criteria, and other regulations affecting aid to poor families. TANF also places states in charge of developing training and education programs that will move people off of welfare and into jobs. (TANF and other aspects of the 1996 welfare reform legislation are discussed further in later chapters.)

After passage of the 1996 Welfare Reform Act, congressional efforts to reduce federal authority declined sharply. Welfare had been the main target of Republican lawmakers, and other broad initiatives were politically more difficult to achieve. Devolution had succeeded in rolling back only a small proportion of the federal programs enacted since the 1930s, but it was a significant development nonetheless.

However, the political impulse did not last. One of the first major initiatives of Republican President George W. Bush was the No Child Left Behind Act, which thrust federal authority deeper into local and state education policy. The terrorist attacks of September 11, 2001, led to a further expansion of federal authority when Congress and President Bush established the Department of Homeland Security, a cabinet-level federal agency with policing and emergency-response functions that traditionally have been the responsibility of state and local governments.

As these examples suggest, there are substantial limits on the amount of power that can reasonably be returned to the states. Because of the increased interdependency of American society, the states will never again enjoy the autonomy they had prior to the 1930s.

Devolution, Judicial Style

In the five decades after the 1930s, the Supreme Court granted Congress broad authority in the enactment of policies affecting state and local governments. In *Garcia v. San Antonio Authority* (1985), the Court held that federal minimum wage standards apply even to state and local governments' own employees.[29] The Court noted that the judiciary had experienced great difficulty in drawing a line between "traditional" and "nontraditional" state functions, concluding that the states would have to look to the political process rather than to the courts if they wanted protection from national authority. Reasoning that members of Congress are elected from states and districts within states, the Court said that the states should look to these officials for protection from national actions that "unduly burden the states."[29]

In the 1990s, some policy responsibilities were shifted from the federal government to the states, a process called *devolution*. This trend stalled after 2000 for several reasons, including the terrorist attacks of September 11, 2001, which required a national response. Part of that response was a larger role for the federal government in the area of public safety. Shown here is a scene familiar to air travelers. The screening of airline passengers is the responsibility of federal officers rather than state or local police.

In recent years, however, the Court has restricted to a degree Congress's power to enact laws binding on the states. Newly appointed justices to the Supreme Court since the 1970s have been mainly Republican-appointed conservatives, most of whom believe that Congress has overstepped its constitutional authority in some areas.[30] In *United States v. Lopez* (1995), for example, the Court cited the Tenth Amendment in striking down a federal law that prohibited the possession of guns within 1,000 feet of a school. Congress had invoked the commerce power in passing the bill, but the Court ruled that the ban had "nothing to do with commerce, or any sort of economic activity."[31] Two years later, in *Printz v. United States* (1997), the Court struck down a provision of the federal Handgun Violence Prevention Act (the so-called Brady bill) that required local law enforcement officers to conduct background checks on prospective handgun buyers. The Court said the provision violated the Tenth Amendment because it required state officials—in this case, police officers—to "enforce a federal regulatory program."[32] Congress can require federal officials to take such action, but it cannot order state officials to do so.

DEBATING THE ISSUES

SHOULD THE FEDERAL GOVERNMENT HAVE THE AUTHORITY TO PREVENT STATES FROM LEGALIZING MARIJUANA USE FOR MEDICAL PURPOSES?

Federalism has led to countless disputes between states and the national government. One current dispute is whether the states should have the authority to create medical exceptions to the federal ban on marijuana. In a 1996 ballot initiative, California voters passed a law permitting doctors to prescribe marijuana to relieve pain and other ailments. Nearly a dozen other states enacted similar laws. However, a federal law—the Controlled Substances Act (CSA)—bans marijuana use in all circumstances. In *Gonzales v. Raich* (2005), the Supreme Court upheld the federal ban by a 6-3 vote. Even though the marijuana in question had been raised and consumed locally, the Court concluded that Congress had the power to prohibit it through its authority to regulate commerce among the states. When the ruling was announced, some state and local officials said they would not enforce the ban. Patients then would be at risk of arrest only if their marijuana use came to the attention of federal law enforcement officials.

Justice John Paul Stevens wrote the majority opinion in *Gonzales*. Justice Sandra Day O'Connor wrote a dissenting opinion. Portions of their arguments are provided below. Do you think the commerce clause justifies the outlawing of state laws that permit the local use of medical marijuana? Where do you stand more generally on the issue of medical marijuana? Do you think state and local officials who refuse to enforce the federal ban are acting improperly?

YES Congress' power to regulate purely local activities that are part of an economic "class of activities" that have a substantial effect on interstate commerce is firmly established. If Congress decides that the "total incidence" of a practice poses a threat to a national market, it may regulate the entire class. Of particular relevance here is *Wickard v. Filburn* where, in rejecting the appellee farmer's contention that Congress' admitted power to regulate the production of wheat for commerce did not authorize federal regulation of wheat production intended wholly for the appellee's own consumption, the Court established that Congress can regulate purely intrastate activity that is not itself "commercial," i.e., not produced for sale, if it concludes that failure to regulate that class of activity would undercut the regulation of the interstate market in that commodity. The similarities between this case and *Wickard* are striking. In both cases, the regulation is squarely within Congress' commerce power because production of the commodity meant for home consumption, be it wheat or marijuana, has a substantial effect on supply and demand in the national market for that commodity. In assessing the scope of Congress' Commerce Clause authority, the Court need not determine whether respondents' activities, taken in the aggregate, substantially affect interstate commerce in fact, but only whether a "rational basis" exists for so concluding. Given the enforcement difficulties that attend distinguishing between marijuana cultivated locally and marijuana grown elsewhere, and concerns about diversion into illicit channels, the Court has no difficulty concluding that Congress had a rational basis for believing that failure to regulate the intrastate manufacture and possession of marijuana would leave a gaping hole in the CSA.

—John Paul Stevens, associate justice of the U.S. Supreme Court

NO There is simply no evidence that homegrown medicinal marijuana users constitute, in the aggregate, a sizable enough class to have a discernable, let alone substantial, impact on the national illicit drug market or otherwise to threaten the CSA regime. Explicit evidence is helpful when substantial effect is not visible to the naked eye. And here, in part because common sense suggests that medical marijuana users may be limited in number and that California's Compassionate Use Act and similar state legislation may well isolate activities relating to medicinal marijuana from the illicit market, the effect of those activities on interstate drug traffic is not self-evidently substantial. . . . The Court's [declarations] amount to nothing more than a legislative insistence that the regulation of controlled substances must be absolute. They are asserted without any supporting evidence—descriptive, statistical, or otherwise. . . . [S]imply because Congress may conclude a particular activity substantially affects interstate commerce does not necessarily make it so. Indeed, if declarations like these suffice to justify federal regulation, and if the Court today is right about what passes rationality review before us, then our decision in *Morrison* should have come out the other way. In that case, Congress had supplied numerous findings regarding the impact gender-motivated violence had on the national economy. . . . If, as the Court claims, today's decision does not break with precedent, how can it be that voluminous findings, documenting extensive hearings about the specific topic of violence against women, did not pass constitutional muster in *Morrison*, while the CSA's abstract, unsubstantiated, generalized findings about controlled substances do?

—Sandra Day O'Connor, associate justice of the U.S. Supreme Court

The Eleventh Amendment has also been used to trim Congress's authority over state governments. The Eleventh Amendment protects a state from being sued without its consent in federal court by a private citizen. In *Kimel v. Florida Board of Regents* (2000)[33] and *Board of Trustees of the University of Alabama v. Garrett* (2002),[34] the Supreme Court held that states cannot be sued by their own employees for violations of federal age and disability discrimination laws. The Court said that, unlike race or gender, age and disability are not protected from state action by the Fourteenth Amendment, and so states and localities are free to decide the age and disability policies that will apply to their own workers. In its *Garrett* decision, the Court said: "States are not required by the Fourteenth Amendment to make special accommodations for the disabled, so long as their actions towards such individuals are rational. They could quite hardheadedly—and perhaps hardheartedly—hold to job-qualification requirements which do not make allowance for the disabled. If special accommodations for the disabled are to be required, they have to come [through state law] and not through the Equal Protection Clause [of the Fourteenth Amendment]."

These rulings are significant, but not earthshattering, in that they are limited to state and local government employees and do not apply to other people residing in a state or locality. These individuals are protected by the federal laws in question. Moreover, the Supreme Court in other recent rulings has endorsed congressional authority. In *Gonzales v. Raich* (2005), for example, the Supreme Court upheld Congress's power to regulate marijuana use. Nearly a dozen states, including California, had passed laws enabling patients, with a physician's prescription, to grow and use marijuana. Although the marijuana in question was not shipped across state lines, the Supreme Court held that the commerce clause allows Congress to ban marijuana even for medical purposes.[35]

Most importantly, the Supreme Court has not retreated from the principle established in the 1930s that Congress's taxing, spending, and commerce powers are broad and substantial. This principle has enabled the federal government, through grants-in-aid and regulatory policies, to exercise authority in policy areas once reserved for the states. Even when recent Supreme Court decisions are taken into account, American federalism is a far different governing system today than it was prior to the 1930s.[36] The change can be seen even in the structure of the federal government. Five cabinet departments—Health and Human Services, Housing and Urban Development, Transportation, Education, and Homeland Security—were created to administer federal programs in policy areas traditionally reserved to the states. The states remain powerful governing bodies, but they operate within a system of expanded federal authority.

The Public's Influence: Setting the Boundaries of Federal-State Power

Public opinion has had a decisive influence on the ebb and flow of federal power during the past century. As Americans' attitudes toward the federal government and the states changed, the balance of power between these two levels of government also shifted. Every major change in federalism has been driven by a dramatic shift in public support toward one level of government or the other.

During the Great Depression, when it was clear that the states would be unable to help, Americans turned to Washington for relief. For people without jobs, the fine points of the Constitution were of little consequence. They needed assistance, and would take it from whichever level of government could provide it. President Roosevelt's New Deal programs, which offered both jobs and income security, were a radical departure from the past, but quickly gained public favor.

A 1936 Gallup poll indicated, for example, that 61 percent of Americans supported Roosevelt's social security program, whereas only 27 percent opposed it. This support reflected a new public attitude: the federal government, not the states, was expected to take the lead in protecting Americans from economic hardship.[37]

The second great wave of federal social programs—Lyndon Johnson's Great Society—was also driven by public demands. Income and education levels had risen dramatically after the Second World War, and Americans wanted more and better services from government.[38] When the states were slow to respond, Americans pressured federal officials to act. The Medicare and Medicaid programs, which provide health care for the elderly and the poor, respectively, are examples of the Johnson administration's response. A 1965 Gallup poll indicated that two-thirds of Americans approved of federal involvement in the provision of medical care, despite the fact that health was traditionally the states' responsibility.

Public opinion was also behind the rollback of federal authority in the 1990s. In a 1994 Times Mirror survey, 66 percent of respondents expressed the view that most officials in Washington did not care what people like them were thinking. An even larger proportion felt that the federal government had become too large and intrusive. Americans' dissatisfaction with federal programs and spending provided the springboard for the Republican takeover of Congress in the 1994 midterm election, which led to policies aimed at devolving power to the states, including the widely popular 1996 Welfare Reform Act.[39]

The public's role in determining the boundaries between federal and state power would come as no surprise to the Framers of the Constitution. For them, federalism was a pragmatic issue, one to be decided by the nation's needs rather than by inflexible rules. Alexander Hamilton suggested that Americans would shift their loyalties between the nation and the states according to whichever level seemed more likely to serve their immediate purpose. James Madison said much the same thing in predicting that Americans would look to whichever level of government was more responsive to their interests. Indeed, each succeeding generation of Americans has seen fit to devise a balance of federal and state power suited to its needs. Historian Daniel Boorstin concluded that the true genius of the American people is their political pragmatism—a willingness to try new approaches when the old ones stop working. In few areas of governing has Americans' pragmatism been more apparent than in their approach to federalism.

Summary   Self-Test www.mhhe.com/pattersontad9e

A foremost characteristic of the American political system is its division of authority between a national government and state governments. The first U.S. government, established by the Articles of Confederation, was essentially a union of the states.

In establishing the basis for a stronger national government, the U.S. Constitution also made provision for safeguarding state interests. The result was the creation of a federal system in which sovereignty was vested in both national and state governments. The Constitution enumerates the general powers of the national government and grants it implied powers through the "necessary and proper" clause. Other powers are reserved to the states by the Tenth Amendment.

From 1789 to 1865, the nation's survival was at issue. The states found it convenient at times to argue that their sover-

eignty took precedence over national authority. In the end, it took the Civil War to cement the idea that the United States was a union of people, not of states. From 1865 to 1937, federalism reflected the doctrine that certain policy areas were the exclusive responsibility of the national government, whereas responsibility in other policy areas belonged exclusively to the states. This constitutional position validated the laissez-faire doctrine that big business was largely beyond governmental control. It also allowed the states to discriminate against African Americans in their public policies. Federalism in a form recognizable today began to emerge in the 1930s.

In the areas of commerce, taxation, spending, civil rights, and civil liberties, among others, the federal government now plays an important role, one that is the inevitable consequence of the increasing complexity of American society and the interdependence of its people.

National, state, and local officials now work closely together to solve the nation's problems, a situation known as cooperative federalism. Grants-in-aid from Washington to the states and localities have been the chief instrument of national influence. States and localities have received billions in federal assistance; in accepting federal money, they also have accepted both federal restrictions on its use and the national policy priorities that underlie the granting of the money.

The issue of the relationship between the nation and the states has changed somewhat as a result of devolution—a shift of power downward to the states. This change, like changes throughout U.S. history, sprang from the demands of the American people.

CHAPTER 3

Study Corner

Key Terms

block grants (*p. 75*)
categorical grants (*p. 75*)
commerce clause (*p. 69*)
confederacy (*p. 60*)
cooperative federalism (*p. 72*)
devolution (*p. 76*)
dual federalism (*p. 67*)
enumerated (expressed) powers (*p. 63*)
federalism (*p. 59*)

fiscal federalism (*p. 74*)
grants-in-aid (*p. 74*)
implied powers (*p. 63*)
"necessary and proper" (elastic) clause (*p. 63*)
reserved powers (*p. 64*)
sovereignty (*p. 59*)
supremacy clause (*p. 63*)
unitary system (*p. 60*)

Self-Test

1. Describing the United States as having a federal system of government means that:
   a. the states are not included in the power arrangement.
   b. constitutional authority for governing is divided between a national government on the one hand and the state governments on the other.
   c. the states are not bound by the rules and regulations of the national government.
   d. constitutional authority for governing is placed entirely in the hands of the states rather than the national government.
   e. America set up the exact same type of governing structure as Britain except for the establishment of a monarchy.

2. The significance of the Preamble of the Constitution reading "We the People" rather than "We the States" is that:
   a. there was to be no change in the power relationship between the states and the nation in the new Constitution.

   b. the new Constitution symbolically recognized the people for winning the Revolutionary War.
   c. the states would not have to pay their war debts.
   d. the national government under the Constitution would have direct power over the people, which it did not have under the Articles of Confederation.

3. Which type of power was given to the states under the Constitution?
   a. the power to declare war
   b. supremacy over the national government
   c. reserved power
   d. necessary and proper power

4. The Supreme Court in *McCulloch v. Maryland*:
   a. ruled in favor of state-centered federalism.
   b. affirmed that national law is supreme over conflicting state law.
   c. established the principle of judicial review.
   d. declared the "necessary and proper" clause unconstitutional.

5. All **except** which one of the following describe trends in government revenues and intergovernmental relations in the United States?
   a. The federal government raises more revenues than all state and local governments combined.
   b. Unlike states and localities, the federal government controls the American dollar and has a nearly unlimited ability to borrow money to cover its deficits.
   c. The states possess the organizational resources to make fiscal federalism a workable arrangement.
   d. Financial assistance from the federal government to the states is gradually being eliminated.

6. The concept of devolution is used to explain:
   a. a shift in authority from the federal government to state and local governments.

b. the necessity for keeping federal and state spheres of responsibility absolutely separate from each other.

c. a failed political revolution.

d. increased recognition that the industrial economy is not confined by state boundaries and must be subject to national regulation.

7. Categorical grants allow the states more flexibility and discretion in the expenditure of funds than block grants do. (T/F)

8. The primary goal of the writers of the Constitution was to establish a national government strong enough to forge a union secure in its defense and open in its commerce. (T/F)

9. Dual federalism is the idea that the national and state governments should not interfere in each other's activities. (T/F)

10. Fiscal federalism involves the states raising money for programs and the federal government administering the programs. (T/F)

Critical Thinking

How have interdependency and the federal government's superior taxing power contributed to a larger policy role for the national government? Do you think these factors will increase or decrease in importance in the future? What will this trend mean for the future of American federalism? (You might find it helpful to think about these questions in the context of a specific policy area, such as the terrorist threat facing the country.)

Suggested Readings

Beer, Samuel H. *To Make a Nation: The Rediscovery of American Federalism.* Cambridge, Mass.: Belknap Press of Harvard University, 1993. An innovative interpretive framework for understanding the impact of federalism and nationalism on the nation's development.

Chopra, Pran. *Supreme Court Versus the Constitution: A Challenge to Federalism.* Thousand Oaks, Calif.: Sage Publications, 2006. A look at the Supreme Court's view of federalism.

Cornell, Saul. *The Other Founders: Anti-Federalism and the Dissenting Tradition in America.* Chapel Hill: University of North Carolina Press, 1999. An analysis of Anti-Federalist thought, its origins, and its legacy.

Elkins, Stanley, and Eric McKitrick. *The Age of Federalism: The Early American Republic, 1788–1800.* New York: Oxford University Press, 1993. An award-winning book on the earliest period of American federalism.

Garry, Patrick M. *An Entrenched Legacy: How the New Deal Constitutional Revolution Continues to Shape the Role of the Supreme Court.* State College: Pennsylvania State University Press, 2008. An analysis showing the durability of the constitutional changes in federalism established in the 1930s.

Ross, William G. *A Muted Fury: Populists, Progressives, and Labor Unions Confront the Courts, 1890–1937.* Princeton, N.J.: Princeton University Press, 1993. A valuable study of the political conflict surrounding the judiciary's laissez-faire doctrine in the period 1890–1937.

Teaford, John. *The Rise of the States: Evolution of American State Government.* Baltimore, Md.: Johns Hopkins University Press, 2002. A historical assessment of state government that spans the past century.

Walker, David B. *The Rebirth of Federalism,* 2d ed. Chatham, N.J.: Chatham House, 2000. An optimistic assessment of the state of today's federalism.

List of Websites

http://lcweb2.loc.gov/ammem/amlaw/lawhome.html
A site containing congressional documents and debates from 1774 to 1873.

http://www.csg.org/
The site of the Council of State Governments; includes current news from each of the states and basic information about their governments.

http://www.temple.edu/federalism/
The site of the Center for the Study of Federalism, located at Temple University; offers information and publications on the federal system of government.

http://www.yale.edu/lawweb/avalon/federal/fed.htm
A documentary record of the *Federalist Papers,* the Annapolis convention, the Articles of Confederation, the Madison debates, and the U.S. Constitution.

Participate!

The U.S. federal system of government offers an array of channels for political participation. Vital governing decisions are made at the national, state, and local levels, all of which provide opportunities for citizens to make a difference and also to build skills, such as public speaking and working with others, that will prove valuable in other areas of life. You have a participatory arena close at hand: your college campus. Most colleges and universities support a variety of activities in which students can engage. Student government is one such opportunity; another is the student newspaper. Most colleges and universities offer a wide range of groups and sponsored programs, from debate clubs to fraternal organizations. If you are not now active in campus groups, consider joining one. If you join—or if you already belong to such a group—take full advantage of the participatory opportunities it provides.

Extra Credit

For up-to-the-minute *New York Times* articles, interactive simulations, graphics, study tools, and more links and quizzes, visit the text's Online Learning Center at www.mhhe.com/pattersontad9e.

Self-Test Answers

1. b 2. d 3. c 4. b 5. d 6. a 7. F 8. T 9. T 10. F

IDENTITY PROBLEMS

Sen. Lamar Alexander argues that in the post-9/11 world the United States needs a national identification card to help prevent terrorist attacks. But the Tennessee Republican vehemently opposes Real ID, the leading federal program to create fraud-resistant identification cards for tens of millions of Americans.

Alexander is co-sponsoring legislation to repeal key sections of the Real ID Act of 2005, which requires states to follow federal standards in verifying someone's identity before issuing a driver's license. The senator complained to National Journal that the law turns motor vehicle department workers "into little CIA agents" and burdens states with expensive new unfunded mandates. "If the federal government thinks this is such a good idea, the federal government ought to pay for it," he said.

In theory, at least, beefing up identification requirements for travel, work, and voting is quite popular. In the most recent national poll on the subject, Gallup found in 2005 that two-thirds of Americans support the creation of a national ID card. Many countries already require them. Advocates in the U.S. tout such cards as a way to fight terrorism and more-conventional crime, reduce illegal immigration, prevent election fraud, and curb identity theft.

In practice, however, efforts to outfit virtually all Americans with more-reliable identification have been fraught with headaches and controversy. And Alexander is far from alone in crying foul.

For example, the Real ID Act has spawned a mini-rebellion at the state level. Ten states have enacted statutes declaring that they will not comply with the federal law.

Invariably, the struggle over IDs bumps up against big, even philosophical, questions: How can identity be proved? Can the government ever really be sure that individuals are who they say they are? If so, at what cost—in terms of lost freedom and privacy, not just dollars and cents?

As Sen. George Voinovich, R-Ohio, noted dryly at a congressional hearing earlier this year, improving American ID security is "easier said than done." It's not a new undertaking. Attempts to expand the federal use of Social Security numbers, a system created in 1935 to make it easier to track and distribute federal retirement benefits, have sometimes failed. President Carter opposed the idea of turning Social Security cards into national identification cards; President Reagan opposed the creation of any form of national ID. But in 2001, the September 11 terrorist attacks heightened the intensity of the national ID debate. All but one of the hijackers had carried some form of ID issued by a government agency in this country, such as a Virginia driver's license. Some of the IDs were fraudulently obtained. The 9/11 commission recommended in 2004 that Congress tighten the security of driver's licenses.

Yet even as ID requirements proliferate, the backlash against them has grown. Some experts argue that there are better, more-direct ways to improve security. Others contend that the only way to create truly fraud-proof IDs is to collect DNA or biometrics from all Americans at birth—a Big Brother scenario that smacks of a surveillance society.

Whatever the ideal model in the long run, America's ID policy is at a crossroads. Americans may eventually embrace a national ID card, as Britons have done recently. Or, U.S. citizens may find themselves carrying multiple smart cards with different uses, as privacy experts prefer. In the meantime, ID wars are breaking out on many fronts.

When officials at the Indiana Bureau of Motor Vehicles set out to check the records of the state's 6.4 million licensed drivers last July, the effort began smoothly. The bureau had just upgraded its computer system and could now verify the Social Security numbers of drivers online, as the Real ID Act would soon require.

The records matched for 97 percent of drivers. In most of the other cases, a simple error—such as a typo or the person's failure to alert the Social Security Administration about a name change—caused a mismatch that was easily corrected. But that still left 34,000 Indiana drivers with records that didn't match. The bureau warned them that their licenses would be revoked if they didn't fix the problem within 30 days. When South Bend lawyer Lyn Leone received a notice, she promptly contacted the American Civil Liberties Union. Leone's Social Security card reads "Mary Lyn Leone." But Leone has been known as Lyn all her life, she says, and she maintains that she has a legal right to go by that name on her driver's license.

"They are basically trying to erase my identity," said Leone, 60, now a plaintiff in an ACLU lawsuit challenging the Indiana Bureau of Motor Vehicles. The licenses of thousands of Indiana drivers could be revoked for similar reasons, said Kenneth Falk, legal director of the Indiana ACLU. "If you are named 'William' but you've always used 'Bill,' and your license is in 'Bill,' you will be terminated."

Although few observers disagree with the basic premise of Real ID—before issuing a driver's license, states should obtain the applicant's identifying documents, such as a birth certificate and proof of legal residency, and verify their authenticity—Indiana's experience spotlights the things that can go wrong when a requirement becomes law with no public debate or hearings. Congress initially set out to bring state officials, privacy experts, and other stakeholders together in what's known as a negotiated rule-making. But in 2005, Real ID Act proponents in the House abruptly attached it to a must-pass appropriations bill funding the Iraq war and tsunami relief.

The Homeland Security Department fielded about 21,000 public comments on Real ID before issuing final regulations in January. By then, state governments were in such an uproar that DHS pushed back its deadline for taking the first steps toward full compliance—from May 11, 2008, to December 31, 2009. The final deadlines for states that pass certain benchmarks will be 2014 for drivers under 50 and 2017 for older ones. The extension averted what would have been a public-relations disaster,

Inside Washington

because anyone from a state not issuing Real IDs would have been barred from boarding a plane or entering a federal building.

Both the National Governors Association and the National Conference of State Legislatures have decried Real ID as a massive, unfunded mandate. The law is expected to cost at least $4 billion to implement, according to DHS, but less than $200 million in federal money has been set aside for the changeover. States may use their federal homeland-security money for Real ID, but many governors object.

"It makes our state less homeland-secure," said South Carolina Gov. Mark Sanford, "because while we don't know if we're going to get struck by a terrorist, what we do unquestionably know is that we are going to get struck by another hurricane." In an April 3 letter to members of Congress, the Republican governor called Real ID "the worst piece of legislation I have seen during the 15 years I have been engaged in the political process."

Sen. Daniel Akaka, D-Hawaii, has introduced legislation to repeal Real ID and return to the drawing board by having the negotiations on the issue that were skipped three years ago. Akaka and other critics of Real ID warn that it would create an extraordinary target for hackers and ID thieves: a huge new database loaded with personal information. That's because the states would be forced to link their databases in order to enforce the law's ban on drivers holding licenses from more than one state.

"We believe that this, if ever implemented, is the coming national ID card system," said Tim Sparapani, senior legislative counsel at the ACLU. Bush administration officials strongly disagree. "The notion that there's

Ten states have enacted statutes declaring **that they will not comply** with the federal law.

going to be a national database is just wrong," said Stewart Baker, assistant secretary for policy at DHS. Only "a very narrow" number of state employees will be able to check the databases, and those databases have proven fairly resistant to tampering, he said. Because of the threats posed by terrorism and identity theft, Baker continued, "there's an enthusiasm for good ID that, I think, is going to continue to grow."

Of course, his department's current deadline for final implementation isn't until December 1, 2017, more than 16 years after the 9/11 attacks.

Some experts are convinced that a national, biometric ID card is the answer to the simmering "identity" crisis. "Right now, we are proceeding in hundreds of different ways, for dozens of different IDs, at tremendous expense," said Robert Pastor, co-director of the Center for Democracy and Election Management at American University. It makes more sense to "do it right, once," he maintains.

Pastor's AU colleague Curtis Gans, who heads the university's Center for the Study of the American Electorate, wants to establish a high-level, bipartisan commission to examine the issue of a mandatory biometric government ID. At least theoretically, Americans are receptive, polling shows. Gans is a vigorous advocate: "If we set up this national biometric

ID, we could get rid of identity theft; we could deal with immigration better than the feds; we could provide for success in criminal prosecution and exoneration; we might constructively use it for medical records; we could eliminate the need for physical enumeration in the census. The uses are many and manifold, including the voting process."

But a growing number of scientists and privacy experts insist that requiring a single ID for multiple purposes would actually make Americans less safe. Skeptics liken a national ID to using a skeleton key for one's office, home, and safe deposit box: Lose it—or have it stolen—and you're vulnerable everywhere. The better model, they argue, is using multiple IDs for discrete uses, just as most people carry several keys.

"Uniformity in IDs across the country would create economies of scale" for prying eyes, warns Jim Harper, director of information policy studies at the Cato Institute and author of Identity Crisis: How Identification Is Overused and Misunderstood. "We want to prevent that uniformity. We want to prevent the tools for that surveillance society from being built."

Harper contends, "There's no practical way in a free country to defeat identity fraud." Illegal immigrants, terrorists, and garden-variety criminals forge birth certificates, Social Security cards, and other IDs all too easily, he notes. Reports abound, moreover, of motor vehicle department officials accepting bribes to assist fraud rings.

"Try to prevent it by locking down everybody's ID, and you have to build this cradle-to-grave biometric tracking system," Harper said.

FOR DISCUSSION: Would you support a mandatory biometric ID? Or would you see one as an invasion of your privacy? Would you rather your state or the Federal Government supply your ID? Why? Would a Federal ID be a violation of State sovereignty? What arguments might the Federal Government advance in favor of its right to issue one?

CHAPTER 4

4 ST NW
100
NO GOD
NO GUNS
WHAT NEXT
Armed
Woman
Is A Saf
Woman
Second Amendment Sisters
Sisters

Civil Liberties
Protecting Individual Rights

Freedom of Expression

    The Early Period: The Uncertain
        Status of the Right of Free
        Expression

    The Modern Period: Protecting
        Free Expression

    Free Expression and State
        Governments

    Libel and Slander

    Obscenity

Freedom of Religion

    The Establishment Clause

    The Free-Exercise Clause

The Right to Bear Arms

The Right of Privacy

    Abortion

    Sexual Relations Among
        Consenting Adults

**Rights of Persons Accused
of Crimes**

    Selective Incorporation of
        Procedural Rights

    Limits on Defendants' Rights

    Crime, Punishment, and Police
        Practices

Rights and the War on Terrorism

    Detention of Enemy Combatants

    Surveillance of Suspected Terrorists

The Courts and a Free Society

A bill of rights is what the people are entitled to against every government on earth, general or particular, and what no just government should refuse, or rest on inference.

Thomas Jefferson[1]

Robert and Sarisse Creighton and their three children were asleep when FBI agents and local police broke into their home in the middle of the night. Brandishing guns, the officers searched the house for a relative of the Creightons who was suspected of bank robbery. When asked to show a search warrant, the officers said, "You watch too much TV." The suspect was not there, and the agents and officers left as abruptly as they had entered. The Creightons sued the FBI agent in charge, Russell Anderson, for violating their Fourth Amendment right against unlawful search.

The Creightons won a temporary victory when the U.S. Circuit Court of Appeals for the Eighth Circuit—noting that individuals are constitutionally protected against warrantless searches unless officers have good reason ("probable cause") for a search and unless they have good reason ("exigent circumstances") for conducting that search without a warrant—concluded that Anderson had been derelict in his duty. In the judgment of the appellate court, Anderson should have sought a warrant from a judge, who would have decided whether a search of the Creightons' home was justified.

The Supreme Court of the United States overturned the lower court's ruling. The Court's majority opinion stated: "We have recognized that it is inevitable that law enforcement officials will in some cases reasonably but mistakenly conclude that probable cause is present, and we have indicated that in such cases those officials . . . should not be held personally liable." Justice John Paul Stevens and two other justices sharply dissented. Stevens accused the Court's majority of showing "remarkably little fidelity" to the Fourth Amendment.[2] Civil liberties groups claimed that the Court's decision gave police an open invitation to invade people's homes on the slightest pretext. For their part, law enforcement officials praised the decision, saying that a ruling in the Creightons' favor would have made them hesitant to pursue suspects for fear of a lawsuit whenever the search failed to produce the culprit.

As this case illustrates, issues of individual rights are complex and political. No right is absolute. For example, the Fourth Amendment protects Americans not from *all* searches but from *unreasonable* searches. The public would be unsafe if law officials could never pursue a suspect into a home. Yet the public would also be unsafe if police could invade homes anytime they wanted. The challenge for a civil society is to establish a level of police authority that balances the demands of public safety with those of personal freedom. The balance point, however, is always subject to dispute. Did Agent Anderson have sufficient cause for a warrantless search of the Creightons' home? Or was his evidence so weak that his forcible entry constituted an unreasonable search? Not even the justices of the Supreme Court could agree on these questions. Six justices sided with Anderson, and three backed the Creightons' position.

This chapter examines issues of **civil liberties**—specific individual rights, such as freedom of speech and protection against self-incrimination, that are constitutionally protected against infringement by government. As seen in Chapter 2, the Constitution's failure to enumerate individual freedoms led to demands for the **Bill of Rights** (see Table 4-1). Enacted in 1791, these first ten amendments to the Constitution specify certain rights of life, liberty, and property that the national government is obliged to respect. A later amendment, the Fourteenth, became the basis for protecting these rights from infringement by state and local governments.

Rights have full meaning only as they are protected in law. A constitutional guarantee is not worth the paper on which it is written if authorities can violate it

civil liberties

The fundamental individual rights of a free society, such as freedom of speech and the right to a jury trial, which in the United States are protected by the Bill of Rights.

Bill of Rights

The first ten amendments to the Constitution, which set forth basic protections for individual rights of free expression, fair trial, and property.

TABLE 4-1 | **The Bill of Rights: A Selected List of Constitutional Protections** The Bill of Rights refers to the first ten amendments to the Constitution, which include protections of individual rights.

First Amendment

Speech: You are free to say almost anything except that which is obscene, slanders another person, or has a high probability of inciting others to take imminent lawless action.

Assembly: You are free to assemble, although government may regulate the time and place for reasons of public convenience and safety, provided such regulations are applied evenhandedly to all groups.

Religion: You are protected from having the religious beliefs of others imposed on you, and you are free to believe what you like.

Fourth Amendment

Search and seizure: You are protected from unreasonable searches and seizures, although you forfeit that right if you knowingly waive it.

Arrest: You are protected from arrest unless authorities have probable cause to believe that you have committed a crime.

Fifth Amendment

Self-incrimination: You are protected against self-incrimination, which means that you have the right to remain silent and to be protected against coercion by law enforcement officials.

Double jeopardy: You cannot be tried twice for the same crime if the first trial results in a verdict of innocence.

Due process: You cannot be deprived of life, liberty, or property without proper legal proceedings.

Sixth Amendment

Counsel: You have a right to be represented by an attorney and can demand to speak first with an attorney before responding to questions from law enforcement officials.

Prompt and reasonable proceedings: You have a right to be arraigned promptly, to be informed of the charges, to confront witnesses, and to have a speedy and open trial by an impartial jury.

Eighth Amendment

Bail: You are protected against excessive bail or fines.

Cruel and unusual punishment: You are protected from cruel and unusual punishment, although this provision does not protect you from the death penalty or from a long prison term for a minor offense.

at will. The primary responsibility for seeing that authorities uphold people's rights rests with courts of law. For the most part, they determine what people's rights mean in practice. In some areas, the judiciary devises a specific test to determine whether government action is lawful. A test applied in the area of free speech, for example, is whether general rules (such as restrictions on the time and place of a political rally) are applied fairly. Government officials do not meet this test if they apply one set of rules for groups that they like and a harsher set of rules for those they dislike.

Issues of individual rights have become increasingly complex. The Framers of the Constitution could not possibly have foreseen the United States of the early twenty-first century, with its huge national government, enormous corporations, pervasive mass media, urban crowding, and vulnerability to terrorist acts. These developments are potential threats to personal liberty, and the judiciary in recent decades has seen fit to expand the rights to which individuals are entitled. However, these rights are constantly being balanced against competing rights and society's collective interests. The Bill of Rights operates in an untidy world where people's highest aspirations collide with their worst passions, and it is at this juncture that issues of civil liberties arise. Should an admitted murderer be entitled to recant a confession? Should the press be allowed to print military secrets whose publication might jeopardize national security? Should extremist groups be allowed to publicize their messages of prejudice and hate? Such questions are among the subjects of this chapter, which focuses on these points:

Protest is a constitutionally protected activity. Freedom of expression is widely regarded as the most basic of constitutional rights because other aspects of a free society, such as open and fair elections, are dependent on it.

- *Freedom of expression is the most basic of democratic rights, but like all rights, it is not unlimited.* In recent decades, free expression has been strongly supported by the Supreme Court.

- *"Due process of law" refers to legal protections (primarily procedural safeguards) designed to ensure that individual rights are respected by government.*

- *During the last half-century particularly, the civil liberties of individual Americans have been substantially broadened in law and given greater judicial protection from action by all levels of government.* Of special significance has been the Supreme Court's use of the Fourteenth Amendment to protect individual rights from action by state and local governments.

- *Individual rights are constantly being weighed against the demands of majorities and the collective needs of society.* All political institutions are involved in this process, as is public opinion, but the judiciary plays a central role and is the institution that is most protective of civil liberties.

Freedom of Expression

Freedom of political expression is the most basic of democratic rights. Unless citizens can openly express their political opinions, they cannot properly influence their government or act to protect their other rights. As Justice Harlan Fiske Stone argued in 1938, the right of free expression is the foundation for all other rights. If government can control what people will hear, it can control their thoughts and thereby deprive them of their right to freely decide how they will be governed.[3]

The First Amendment provides the foundation for **freedom of expression**—the right of individual Americans to hold and communicate views of their choosing. For many reasons, such as a desire to conform to social pressure or a fear of harassment, Americans do not always choose to express themselves freely. Moreover, freedom of expression, like other rights, is not absolute. It does not entitle individuals to say or do whatever they want, to whomever they want, whenever they want. Free expression can be denied, for example, if it endangers national security, wrongly damages the reputation of others, or deprives others of their basic rights. Nevertheless, the First Amendment provides for freedom of expression by prohibiting laws that would unreasonably abridge the freedoms of conscience, speech, press, assembly, and petition.

Free expression is vigorously protected by the courts. Today, under most circumstances, Americans can freely express their political views without fear of governmental interference or retribution. In earlier times, however, Americans were less free to express their opinions.

The Early Period: The Uncertain Status of the Right of Free Expression

The first attempt by the U.S. government to restrict free expression was the Sedition Act of 1798, which made it a crime to print harshly critical newspaper stories about the president or other national officials. Thomas Jefferson called the Sedition Act an "alarming infraction" of the Constitution and, upon replacing John Adams as president in 1801, pardoned those who had been convicted under it. Because the Supreme Court did not review the sedition cases, however, the judiciary's position on free expression was an open question. The Court also did not rule on free speech during the Civil War era, when the government severely restricted individual rights.

In 1919, the Court finally ruled on a free-expression case. The defendant had been convicted under the 1917 Espionage Act, which prohibited forms of dissent, including the distribution of antiwar leaflets, that could harm the nation's effort in World War I. In *Schenck v. United States* (1919), the Court unanimously upheld the constitutionality of the Espionage Act. In the opinion written by Justice Oliver Wendell Holmes, the Court said that Congress could restrict speech that was "of such a nature as to create a clear and present danger" to the nation's security. In a famous passage, Holmes argued that not even the First Amendment would permit a person to falsely yell "Fire!" in a crowded theater and create a panic that could kill or injure innocent people.[4]

Although the *Schenck* decision upheld a law that limited free expression, it also established a constitutional standard—the **clear-and-present-danger test**—for determining when government could legally do so. Government could ban speech that posed a clear and present danger, but it could *not* ban speech that posed no such danger. (The clear-and-present-danger test was later replaced by the *imminent lawless action test*, which is discussed later in the chapter.)

The Modern Period: Protecting Free Expression

Until the twentieth century, the tension between national security interests and free expression was not a pressing issue in the United States. The country's great size and ocean barriers provided protection from potential enemies, minimizing

---

freedom of expression

Americans' freedom to communicate their views, the foundation of which is the First Amendment rights of freedom of conscience, speech, press, assembly, and petition.

HISTORICAL
Background

clear-and-present-danger test

A test devised by the Supreme Court in 1919 in order to define the limits of free speech in the context of national security. According to the test, government cannot abridge political expression unless it presents a clear and present danger to the nation's security.

concerns about internal subversion. World War I, however, intruded on America's isolation, and World War II brought it to an abrupt end. Since then, Americans' rights of free expression have been defined largely in the context of national security concerns.

Free Speech

In the period after World War II, many Americans believed that the Soviet Union was bent on destroying the United States, and the Supreme Court allowed government to limit certain types of expression. In 1951, for example, the Court upheld the convictions of eleven members of the U.S. Communist Party who had been prosecuted under a law that made it illegal to voice support for the forceful overthrow of the U.S. government.[5]

By the late 1950s, however, fear of internal communist subversion was subsiding, and the Supreme Court permanently changed its stance.[6] For the past half-century, it has held that national security must be *directly and substantially imperiled* before government can lawfully prohibit citizens from speaking out. During this period, which includes the Vietnam and Iraq wars, not a single individual has been convicted solely for criticizing the government's war policies. (Some dissenters have been found guilty on other grounds, such as inciting a riot or assaulting a police officer.)

The Supreme Court's protection of **symbolic speech** has been less substantial than its protection of verbal speech. For example, the Court in 1968 upheld the conviction of a Vietnam protester who had burned his draft registration card. The Court concluded that the federal law prohibiting the destruction of draft cards was intended primarily to protect the military's need for soldiers, not to prevent people from criticizing government policy.[7] Nevertheless, the Supreme Court has been broadly protective of symbolic speech. In 1989, for example, the Court ruled that the symbolic burning of the American flag is a lawful form of expression. The ruling came in the case of Gregory Lee Johnson, who had set fire to a flag outside the hall in Dallas where the 1984 Republican National Convention was being held. The Supreme Court rejected the state of Texas's argument

symbolic speech
Action (for example, the waving or burning of a flag) for the purpose of expressing a political opinion.

The Supreme Court has ruled that flag burning is a constitutionally protected form of free expression. Shown here is a scene outside California's San Quentin Prison in 2005. The crowd is burning the American flag to protest the execution of convicted murderer Stanley Williams, whose case attracted national attention.

that flag burning is, in every instance, an imminent danger to public safety. "If there is a bedrock principle underlying the First Amendment," the Court ruled in the *Johnson* case, "it is that the Government may not prohibit the expression of an idea simply because society finds the idea itself offensive or disagreeable."[8]

Press Freedom and Prior Restraint

Freedom of the press also receives strong judicial protection. In *New York Times Co. v. United States* (1971), the Court ruled that the *Times*'s publication of the "Pentagon Papers" (secret government documents revealing that officials had deceived the public about aspects of the Vietnam War) could not be blocked by the government, which claimed that publication would hurt the war effort. The documents had been illegally obtained by antiwar activists, who then gave them to the *Times*. The Court ruled that "any system of prior restraints" on the press is unconstitutional unless the government can clearly justify the restriction.[9]

The unacceptability of **prior restraint**—government prohibition of speech or publication before the fact—is basic to the current doctrine of free expression. The Supreme Court has said that any attempt by government to prevent expression carries "a 'heavy presumption' against its constitutionality."[10] News organizations are legally responsible after the fact for what they report or say (for example, they can be sued by an individual whose reputation is wrongly damaged by their words), but government generally cannot stop the media in advance from reporting their views. One exception is the reporting on U.S. military operations during wartime. The courts have allowed the government to censor reports filed by journalists who are granted access to the battlefront. The courts have also upheld the government's authority to ban uncensored publications by certain past and present government employees, such as CIA agents, who have knowledge of classified information and programs.

Free Expression and State Governments

In 1790, Congress rejected a proposed constitutional amendment that would have applied the Bill of Rights to the states. Thus, the freedoms provided in the Bill of Rights initially were protected only from action by the national government.[11] The effect was that the Bill of Rights had limited meaning to the lives of ordinary Americans because state and local governments carry out most of the activities, such as law enforcement, in which people's rights are at issue.

Not until the twentieth century did the Supreme Court begin to protect individual rights from infringement by state and local governments. The instrument for this change was the **due process clause of the Fourteenth Amendment** to the Constitution.

The Fourteenth Amendment and Selective Incorporation

The Fourteenth Amendment, ratified in 1868, includes a clause that forbids a state from depriving any person of life, liberty, or property without due process of law (due process refers to the legal procedures, such as the right to a lawyer, that have been established as a means of protecting individuals' rights).

Although Congress, in passing the Fourteenth Amendment, did not say that it was intended to protect First Amendment rights from infringement by the states, the Supreme Court, six decades later, interpreted it as doing so. In *Gitlow v. New York* (1925), the Supreme Court upheld Benjamin Gitlow's conviction for violating a New York law making it illegal to advocate the violent overthrow of the U.S. government but held that states are not completely free to limit expression.

prior restraint

Government prohibition of speech or publication before the fact, which is presumed by the courts to be unconstitutional unless the justification for it is overwhelming.

HISTORICAL
Background

due process clause (of the Fourteenth Amendment)

The clause of the Constitution that has been used by the judiciary to apply the Bill of Rights to the actions of state governments.

The Court said: "For present purposes we may and do assume that freedom of speech and of the press—which are protected by the First Amendment from abridgement by Congress—are among the fundamental personal rights and "liberties" protected by the due process clause of the Fourteenth Amendment from impairment by the states."[12]

The Supreme Court justified this new interpretation of the Fourteenth Amendment by referring to **selective incorporation**—the process by which certain of the rights contained in the Bill of Rights become applicable through the Fourteenth Amendment to actions by the state governments. The process is selective in the sense that only particular Bill of Rights guarantees, as opposed to all of them, are applied to the states. The process is significant because it enables federal courts to determine whether state governments have acted properly in upholding civil liberties. In the *Gitlow* case, the Court reasoned that the Fourteenth Amendment's due process clause, which says in part that states cannot deprive residents of their personal liberty, would be meaningless if states were allowed to prevent their residents from speaking freely. Thus, through *Gitlow,* the Court selectively incorporated the First Amendment guarantee of free speech into the Fourteenth Amendment, enabling citizens who believe that their free speech rights have been violated by a state to bring suit against the state in federal court.

This interpretation of the Fourteenth Amendment provided the Court with a legal basis for striking down state laws that infringed unreasonably on other forms of free expression. Within a dozen years (see Table 4-2), the Court had issued four rulings that invalidated state laws restricting expression in the areas of speech (*Fiske v. Kansas*), press (*Near v. Minnesota*), religion (*Hamilton v. Regents, University of California*), and assembly and petition (*DeJonge v. Oregon*).[13] The *Near* decision is the best known of these rulings. Jay Near was the publisher of a Minneapolis weekly newspaper that regularly made defamatory statements about blacks, Jews, Catholics, and labor union leaders. His paper was closed down on authority of a state law banning "malicious, scandalous, or defamatory" publications. Near appealed the shutdown on the grounds that it infringed on freedom of the press, and the Supreme Court ruled in his favor, saying that the Minnesota law was "the essence of censorship."[14]

Limiting the Authority of the States to Restrict Expression

Since the 1930s, the Supreme Court has broadly protected freedom of expression from action by the states and by local governments, which derive their authority from the states. The Court has held that the states cannot restrict free expression except when it is almost certain to provoke immediate lawless action such as

selective incorporation

The process by which certain of the rights (for example, freedom of speech) contained in the Bill of Rights become applicable through the Fourteenth Amendment to actions by the state governments.

TABLE 4-2

Selective Incorporation of Rights of Free Expression In the 1920s and 1930s, the Supreme Court selectively incorporated the free-expression provisions of the First Amendment into the Fourteenth Amendment so that these rights would be protected from infringement by the states.

Supreme Court Case	Year	Constitutional Right at Issue
Gitlow v. New York	1925	Fourteenth Amendment protection of free expression
Fiske v. Kansas	1927	Free speech
Near v. Minnesota	1931	Free press
Hamilton v. Regents, U. of California	1934	Religious freedom
DeJonge v. Oregon	1937	Freedom of assembly and of petition

a rampage or riot. A leading free speech case was *Brandenburg v. Ohio* (1969). Clarence Brandenburg was a Ku Klux Klan member who, in a speech delivered at a Klan rally, said that "revenge" might have to be taken if the national government "continues to suppress the white Caucasian race." He was convicted under an Ohio law, but the Supreme Court reversed the conviction, saying a state cannot prohibit speech that advocates the unlawful use of force "except where such advocacy is directed to inciting or producing imminent lawless action, and is likely to produce such action."[15]

imminent lawless action test

A legal test that says government cannot lawfully suppress advocacy that promotes lawless action unless such advocacy is aimed at producing, and is likely to produce, imminent lawless action.

This test—the likelihood of **imminent lawless action**—is a severe limit on the government's power to restrict expression. It is rare for words alone to incite others to immediately take unlawful action. In effect, Americans are free to say almost anything they want on political issues. This protection includes hate speech. In a unanimous 1992 opinion, the Court struck down a St. Paul, Minnesota, ordinance making it a crime to engage in speech likely to arouse "anger or alarm" on the basis of "race, color, creed, religion or gender." The Court said that the First Amendment prohibits government from "silencing speech on the basis of its content."[16] This protection of hate *speech* does not, however, extend to hate *crimes,* such as assault, motivated by racial or other prejudice. A Wisconsin law that provided for increased sentences for hate crimes was challenged as a violation of the First Amendment. In a unanimous 1993 opinion, the Court said that the law was aimed at "conduct unprotected by the First Amendment" rather than the defendant's speech.[17]

In a key case involving freedom of assembly, the U.S. Supreme Court in 1977 upheld a lower-court ruling against local ordinances of Skokie, Illinois, that had been invoked to prevent a parade there by the American Nazi Party.[18] Skokie had a large Jewish population, including many survivors of Nazi Germany's concentration camps. The Supreme Court held that the right of free expression takes precedence over the mere *possibility* that the exercise of that right might have undesirable consequences. Before government can lawfully prevent a speech or rally, it must demonstrate that the event will cause harm and also

Exercising their right of free speech and assembly, antiabortion protesters gather outside a government building. Individuals do not have a constitutional right to demonstrate in any place at any time, but government is required to accommodate requests for marches and other displays of free expression.

must demonstrate the lack of alternative ways (such as assigning police officers to control the crowd) to prevent the harm from happening.

The Supreme Court has recognized that freedom of speech and assembly may conflict with the routines of daily life. Accordingly, individuals do not have the right to hold a public rally at a busy intersection during rush hour, nor do they have the right to immediate access to a public auditorium or the right to turn up the volume on loudspeakers to the point where they can be heard miles away. The Court has held that public officials can regulate the time, place, and conditions of public assembly, provided that these regulations are reasonable and are applied evenhandedly to all groups, including those that hold unpopular views.[19]

In general, the Supreme Court's position is that the First Amendment makes any government effort to regulate the *content* of a message highly suspect. In the flag-burning case, Texas was regulating the content of the message—contempt for the flag and the principles it represents. Texas could not have been regulating the act itself, for the Texas government's own method of disposing of worn-out flags is to burn them. But a content-neutral regulation (no public rally can be held at a busy intersection during rush hour) is acceptable as long as it is reasonable and does not discriminate against certain groups or ideas.

Libel and Slander

The constitutional right of free expression is not a legal license to avoid responsibility for the consequences of what is said or written. If false information that greatly harms a person's reputation is published (**libel**) or spoken (**slander**), the injured party can sue for damages. If it were easy for public officials to claim defamation and win large amounts of money, individuals and organizations would be reluctant to criticize those in power. As it happens, slander and libel laws in the United States are based on the assumption that society has an interest in encouraging citizens and news organizations to express themselves freely. Accordingly, public officials can be criticized nearly at will without fear that the writer or speaker will have to pay them damages for slander or libel. (The courts are less protective of the writer or speaker when allegations are made about a private citizen. What is said about private individuals is considered to be less basic to the democratic process than what is said about public officials.)

The Supreme Court has held that true statements disseminated by the media have "full constitutional protection."[20] In other words, factually accurate statements, no matter how damaging they might be to a public official's career or reputation, are a protected form of expression. Even false or conjectural statements enjoy considerable legal protection. In *New York Times Co. v. Sullivan* (1964), the Supreme Court overruled an Alabama state court that had found the *New York Times* guilty of libel for printing an advertisement that criticized Alabama officials for mistreating student civil rights activists. Even though some of what was alleged was false, the Supreme Court ruled in favor of the *Times*, saying that libel of a public official requires proof of actual malice, which was defined as a knowing or reckless disregard for the truth.[21] It is very difficult to prove that a publication has acted with reckless or deliberate disregard for the truth. In fact, no federal official has won a libel judgment against a news organization in the four decades since the *Sullivan* ruling.

Obscenity

Obscenity is a form of expression that is not protected by the First Amendment and thus can be prohibited by law. However, the Supreme Court has found it

libel
Publication of material that falsely damages a person's reputation.

slander
Spoken words that falsely damage a person's reputation.

DEBATING THE ISSUES

SHOULD FLAG BURNING BE MADE UNCONSTITUTIONAL?

Few Americans believe that the burning of the American flag is an acceptable form of protest. Even fewer would choose to burn the flag as a symbol of their disagreement with U.S. policy. Yet flag burning has been a leading political issue since the Supreme Court in 1989 held that burning the flag is a constitutionally protected form of expression. Since then, Congress has tried several times to initiate a constitutional amendment that would ban flag burning. If such an amendment were ratified, courts would be obliged to uphold it. In 2006, Congress came within one vote in the Senate of obtaining the two-thirds majority in each chamber that is necessary to send a flag-burning amendment to the states for ratification. The congressional debate was heated as proponents of reverence for the flag faced off against proponents of free expression. Below are the statements of two of the senators who took opposite sides on the issue.

Where do you stand on the issue? Is flag burning so disrespectful of a revered national symbol that it should be made a federal crime? Or does the First Amendment's guarantee of free expression take precedence?

YES I was preparing for this debate and thinking about the Lincoln Memorial. What if somebody today, yesterday, or some other time had taken spray paint and sprayed on the Lincoln Memorial: "We want freedom" or "Death to tyrants" or "Down with the flag"? Let's say they wrote that in big spray paint on the Lincoln Memorial and defaced the memorial and then was caught and was brought to trial and claimed: Wait a minute, I have a first amendment right to say what I want to say, and I believe it is important that I say it anywhere, and I want to say it on the Lincoln Memorial. . . . We would all recognize that as being something wrong, violating the law, and something there should be a law against. We don't have a problem with a person standing on the Lincoln Memorial and shouting at the top of his lungs for as long as he wants whatever he wants to say—if it is about the war in Iraq, if it is about the President, if it is about somebody in the Senate, if it is about myself, if it is about the Chair, if it is about anything he wants. We don't have any problem with that. But if he defaces the memorial, we do. It is interesting, that was the dissent Justice Stevens used in the *Texas v. Johnson* case. He made that same point. We have no problem with a person speaking on the Lincoln Memorial. We have a problem with him defacing the Lincoln Memorial. We have no problem with people speaking against the flag. We have a problem with them defacing the flag.

—*Sam Brownback, U.S. senator (R-Kans.)*

NO Let me make one thing clear at the outset. Not a single Senator who opposes the proposed constitutional amendment, as I do, supports burning or otherwise showing disrespect to the flag. Not a single one. None of us think it is "OK" to burn the flag. None of us view the flag as "just a piece of cloth." On those rare occasions when some malcontent defiles or burns our flag, I join everyone in this Chamber in condemning that action. But we must also defend the right of all Americans to express their views about their Government, however hateful or spiteful or disrespectful those views may be, without fear of their Government putting them in jail for those views. America is not simply a Nation of symbols, it is a Nation of principles. And the most important principle of all, the principle that has made this country a beacon of hope and inspiration for oppressed peoples throughout the world, is the right of free expression. This amendment threatens that right, so I must oppose it. We have heard at various times over the years that this amendment has been debated that permitting protestors to burn the American flag sends the wrong message to our children about patriotism and respect for our country. I couldn't disagree more with that argument. We can send no better, no stronger, no more meaningful message to our children about the principles and the values of this country than if we oppose efforts to undermine freedom of expression, even expression that is undeniably offensive. When we uphold First Amendment freedoms despite the efforts of misguided and despicable people who want to provoke our wrath, we explain what America is really about. Our country and our people are far too strong to be threatened by those who burn the flag. That is a lesson we should proudly teach our children.

—*Russell Feingold, U.S. senator (D-Wisc.)*

difficult to define with precision the criteria by which material is to be judged obscene. The Court set forth the first explicit test for obscenity in *Roth v. United States* (1957) by saying that material is obscene if "taken as a whole" it appeals to "prurient interest" and has no "redeeming social value." This assessment was to be made from the standpoint of "the average person, applying contemporary community standards."[22] However, the test proved unworkable in practice. Even the justices of the Supreme Court, when they personally examined allegedly obscene material, argued over whether it appealed to prurient interest and was without redeeming social value. In the end, they usually concluded that the material at issue had at least some social significance.

In *Miller v. California* (1973), the Court narrowed "contemporary community standards" to the local level. The Court said that what might offend residents of "Mississippi might be found tolerable in Las Vegas."[23] But even this test proved too restrictive. The Court subsequently ruled that material cannot be judged obscene simply because the "average" local resident might object to it. "Community standards" were to be judged in the context of a "reasonable person"—someone whose outlook is broad enough to evaluate the material on its overall merit rather than its most objectionable feature. The Court later also modified its content standard, saying that the material must be of a "particularly offensive type."[24] These efforts illustrate the difficulty in defining obscenity and, even more, in establishing a clear legal standard that judges can apply consistently when obscenity cases arise. A basic legal principle is that a person's guilt or innocence should not depend on a judge's uncertainty about the meaning of the law in question.

The Supreme Court has distinguished between obscene materials in public places and those in the home. A unanimous ruling in 1969 held that what adults read and watch in the privacy of their homes cannot be made a crime.[25] The Court created an exception to this rule in 1990 by upholding an Ohio law making it a crime to possess pornographic photographs of children.[26] The Court reasoned that the purchase of such material encourages producers to use children in the making of pornographic materials, which is a crime. In a 2008 decision, the Court extended the ban by upholding a 2003 federal statute that makes it a crime to offer or solicit child pornography, even if the material is based on computer-generated or digitally altered images that merely appear to be those of children. Writing for the majority in the Court's 7-2 decision, Justice Antonin Scalia said: "Offers to provide or requests to obtain child pornography are categorically excluded from the First Amendment."[27]

Children have also been a consideration in court cases involving material transmitted on cable television or over the Internet. On several occasions, Congress has passed legislation (for example, the 1998 Child Online Protection Act) that would restrict the transmission of sexually explicit material that children can access. The Supreme Court has held that the restrictions, though well intentioned, have been so broad that they would ban material adults have a constitutional right to view if they so choose.[28] The Court has directed officials to find less restrictive ways to keep such material from being seen by children. An example is the federal requirement that cable operators must scramble the signal of channels that convey sexually explicit material if a subscriber requests it.

Freedom of Religion

Free religious expression is the precursor of free political expression, at least within the English tradition of limited government. England's Glorious, or Bloodless, Revolution of 1689 centered on the issue of religion and resulted in the Act of Toleration, which gave members of all Protestant sects the right to worship freely and publicly. The English philosopher John Locke (1632–1704) extended this principle, arguing that legitimate government could not inhibit free expression, religious or otherwise. The First Amendment reflects this tradition, providing for freedom of religion along with freedom of speech, press, assembly, and petition.

HISTORICAL
Background

In regard to religion, the First Amendment reads: "Congress shall make no law respecting an establishment of religion, or prohibiting the free exercise thereof." The prohibition on laws aimed at "establishment of religion" (the establishment clause) and its "free exercise" (the free-exercise clause) applies to states and localities through the Fourteenth Amendment.

The Establishment Clause

The **establishment clause** has been interpreted by the courts to mean that government may not favor one religion over another or support religion over no religion. (This position contrasts with that of a country such as England, where Anglicanism is the official, or "established," state religion, though no religion is prohibited.) The Supreme Court's interpretation of the establishment clause has been described as maintaining a "wall of separation" between church and state. The Court held in *Engel v. Vitale* (1962) that the establishment clause prohibits the reciting of prayers in public schools.[29] A year later, the Court struck down Bible readings in public schools.[30]

Religion is a powerful force in American life, and the Supreme Court's ban on religious teaching in public school classrooms has evoked strong opposition. An Alabama law attempted to circumvent the prayer ruling by permitting public schools to set aside one minute each day for silent prayer or meditation. In 1985, the Court declared the law unconstitutional, ruling that "government must pursue a course of complete neutrality toward religion."[31] The Court in 2000 reaffirmed the ban by extending it to include organized student-led prayer at public school football games.[32]

The Supreme Court also has banned religious displays on public property when the purpose of such a display is overtly religious and lacks a historical context. Because of the prominence of religion in American life, many public buildings sport religious symbolism. For instance, a statue of Moses holding the Ten Commandments stands in the rotunda of the Library of Congress building, which opened in 1897. Legal challenges to such displays are unlikely to succeed. In *Van Orden v. Perry* (2005), for example, the Supreme Court rejected a suit asking for the dismantling of a display of the Ten Commandments on a monument on the grounds of the Texas State Capitol. The Court noted that the display had been installed nearly a half-century earlier, had been paid for by a nonreligious group, and had not previously been the subject of dispute.[33] On the other hand, in *McCreary County v. American Civil Liberties Union* (2005), the Supreme Court struck down displays of the Ten Commandments on the walls of two Kentucky courthouses. The displays were recent and had initially hung by themselves on the courtroom walls. Only after county officials were sued did they mount a few historical displays alongside the religious ones. The Supreme Court concluded that the officials had religious purposes in mind when they erected the displays and thus had to remove them.[34]

The Supreme Court generally has taken a pragmatic approach to religious controversies, permitting some establishment activities while disallowing others. For instance, the Court has allowed states to pay for secular textbooks used in church-affiliated schools[35] but has not allowed them to pay part of the salaries of the teachers in such schools.[36] Such distinctions are based on the Court's standard for judging such issues: whether government action involves "*excessive entanglement with religion.*"[37] In allowing public funds to be used by religious schools for secular textbooks but not for teachers' salaries, the courts have indicated that, whereas a math or science text would have little if any religion in it, some teachers might use the classroom as an opportunity to promote religious teachings.[38] Accordingly, public funding of church-affiliated schoolteachers'

The First Amendment's protection of free expression includes religious freedom, which has led the courts to hold that government cannot in most instances promote or interfere with religious practices.

salaries would involve excessive entanglement with religion whereas public funding of secular textbooks would not.

In a key 2002 decision, however, the Supreme Court upheld an Ohio law that allows students in Cleveland's failing public schools to receive a tax-supported voucher to attend private or parochial school. The Court's majority argued in *Zelman v. Simmons-Harris* that the program did not violate the establishment clause because students had a choice between secular and religious education. Four members of the Court dissented sharply with the majority's reasoning. Justice John Paul Stevens said the ruling had removed a "brick from the wall that was once designed to separate religion from government."[39] A piece of the brick was restored in 2004 when the Court in *Locke v. Davey* held that publicly funded scholarships can be denied to students pursuing religious careers. At issue was a state of Washington scholarship program that excluded otherwise eligible students who were studying for the ministry. The state justified the exclusion on grounds that the use of public funds to educate ministers would involve it in the establishment of religion.[40]

The establishment clause is also at issue in the use of faith-based organizations to provide federally funded services, such as drug treatment programs. This use increased with the election of President George W. Bush, who created the White House Office of Faith-Based and Community Initiatives. Although religious organizations are prohibited from promoting their beliefs in the process of providing federally funded services, critics say the prohibition is meaningless because many of these services are provided by religious officials at religious sites, which inevitably serves to promote religion. In *Hein v. Freedom from Religion* (2007), the Supreme Court in a 5-4 ruling held that taxpayers could not sue to stop expenditures by the Office of Faith-Based and Community Initiatives. The Court's majority held that, if money appropriated by Congress is improperly used by the White House for religious purposes, it is up to Congress, not the courts, to fix the problem. In his dissenting opinion, Justice David Souter cited the establishment clause, saying that citizens should have the right to sue in situations where their tax dollars are being used in ways that support religion.[41]

The Free-Exercise Clause

The First and Fourteenth Amendments also prohibit government interference with the free exercise of religion. The idea underlying the **free-exercise clause** is clear: Americans are free to believe what they want. However, they are not always free to act on their beliefs. The courts have allowed government interference in

free-exercise clause

A First Amendment provision that prohibits the government from interfering with the practice of religion or prohibiting the free exercise of religion.

the exercise of religious beliefs when such interference is the secondary result of an overriding social goal. An example is the legal protection of children with life-threatening illnesses whose parents deny them medical treatment on religious grounds. A court may order that such children be given medical assistance because the social good of saving their lives overrides their parents' free-exercise rights.

In a few circumstances, the free-exercise clause has been the basis for allowing certain individuals to disobey otherwise valid laws. The Supreme Court ruled in 1972 that Amish families did not have to abide by a state law requiring children to attend school until they were sixteen years of age because the law conflicted with the age-old Amish religious practice of having children leave school and begin work at an early age.[42] In upholding free exercise in such cases, the Court may be said to have violated the establishment clause by granting preferred treatment to people who hold a particular religious belief. The Court has recognized the potential conflict between the free-exercise and establishment clauses and, in such situations, tries to strike a reasonable balance between them.

When the free-exercise and establishment clauses cannot be balanced, the Supreme Court has been forced to choose. In 1987, the Court overturned a Louisiana law requiring that creationism (the Bible's account of how the world was created) be taught along with the theory of evolution in public school science courses. The Court concluded that creationism is a religious doctrine, not a scientific theory, and that its inclusion in public school curricula violates the establishment clause by promoting a religious belief.[43] In 2005, a federal judge barred a Pennsylvania public school district from requiring that intelligent design (the belief that God has guided evolution) be taught in science classes along with evolution. The judge concluded that the theory of intelligent design is a disguised version of creationism, has no basis in science, and violates the First Amendment's establishment clause. Some religious groups argue that such decisions trample on the free exercise of religion because children are required to study the theory of evolution even though it conflicts with their beliefs about creation.

The Right to Bear Arms

The Second Amendment to the Constitution says: "A well regulated Militia, being necessary to the security of a free State, the right of the people to keep and bear Arms, shall not be infringed." Remarkably, more than two centuries passed before the Supreme Court issued a clear-cut ruling on how the amendment was to be interpreted. It was widely accepted that the amendment blocked the federal government from abolishing state militias, which would have the effect of placing all military power under its full control. What was unclear was whether the amendment also gave individuals the right to possess weapons outside their use in military service. Although some Supreme Court decisions had made reference to the Second Amendment, they had done so only in passing or in an ambiguous way.

In 2008, a sharply divided Supreme Court issued the first ruling to address squarely the meaning of the Second Amendment. In *District of Columbia v. Heller*, the Court ruled that "the Second Amendment protects an individual right to possess a firearm unconnected with service in a militia, and to use that arm for traditionally lawful purposes, such as self-defense within the home." The ruling struck down a District of Columbia law that had banned the possession of handguns but not rifles or shotguns within the district's boundaries. Writing for the 5-4 majority, Justice Antonin Scalia said that the justices were "aware of the problem of handgun violence in this country." But Scalia concluded: "The enshrinement of constitutional rights necessarily takes certain policy choices off the table. These include the absolute prohibition of handguns held and used for self-defense in the home."[44]

In a dissenting opinion, Justice John Paul Stevens said the majority had devised a ruling that fit its partisan aims rather than what the Framers intended when they wrote the Second Amendment. Stevens declared: "When each word in the text is given full effect, the Amendment is most naturally read to secure to the people a right to use and possess arms in conjunction with service in a well-regulated militia. So far as it appears, no more than that was contemplated by its drafters or is encompassed within its terms."

Although the *Heller* decision was a victory for advocates of gun rights, the scope of the ruling was unclear. The District of Columbia is federal territory, and the question remains whether the Supreme Court through selective interpretation will impose the same limitation on the gun laws of state and local governments. The *Heller* decision also leaves open the question of how far government can lawfully go in regulating firearms. The Court's majority was careful to say that some gun restrictions are allowable, such as bans on ownership by former felons. Nevertheless, the Court did not provide strict guidelines on which restrictions are constitutionally permissible and which are not, leaving the issue to be decided by future court cases. Within days of the *Heller* decision, opponents of gun control had filed suit against restrictive gun laws in Chicago, San Francisco, and other cities.

The Right of Privacy

Until the 1960s, Americans' constitutional rights were confined largely to those listed in the Bill of Rights. This situation prevailed despite the Ninth Amendment, which reads, "The enumeration in the Constitution, of certain rights, shall not be construed to deny or disparage others retained by the people." In 1965, however, the Supreme Court added to the list of individual rights, declaring that Americans have "a right of privacy." This judgment arose from the case of *Griswold v. Connecticut*, which challenged a state law prohibiting the use of birth control devices, even by married couples. The Supreme Court struck down the statute, concluding that a state had no business interfering with a married couple's decision regarding contraception. The Court did not invoke the Ninth Amendment but reasoned instead that the freedoms in the Bill of Rights imply an underlying **right of privacy.** The Court held that individuals have a "zone of [personal] privacy" that government cannot lawfully infringe upon.[45]

The right to privacy has not been broadly applied by the courts. For example, the Supreme Court chose not to apply it in a challenge to a state of Washington law that prohibits physician-assisted suicide for terminally ill patients who voluntarily choose it. In denying the petitioner's claim, the Court said that the right of privacy embedded in the U.S. Constitution does not extend to physician-assisted suicide, which has left the issue for each state to decide on its own.[46] In 2008, Washington residents voted to legalize physician-assisted suicide. Such examples notwithstanding, the Supreme Court has invoked a constitutional right to privacy in two major areas—a woman's right to choose an abortion and consensual relations among same-sex adults.

right of privacy
A right implied by the freedoms in the Bill of Rights that grants individuals a degree of personal privacy upon which government cannot lawfully intrude. The right gives individuals a level of free choice in areas such as reproduction and intimate relations.

Abortion rights activists demonstrate outside the Supreme Court while the justices inside hear arguments on Pennsylvania's controversial abortion law. By a 5-4 vote, the Court narrowly reaffirmed the principle that a woman has the right to choose abortion during the early months of pregnancy.

Abortion

The right of privacy was the basis for the Supreme Court's ruling in *Roe v. Wade* (1973), which gave women full freedom to choose abortion during the first three months of pregnancy. In overturning a Texas law banning abortion except to save the life of the mother, the Court said that the right to privacy is "broad enough to encompass a woman's decision whether or not to terminate her pregnancy."[47]

The *Roe* decision was met with praise by some Americans and condemnation by others, provoking a long-lasting debate. Americans are sharply divided over the abortion issue and have been throughout the more than three decades that abortion has been legal (see Figure 4-1). The dispute has included violent

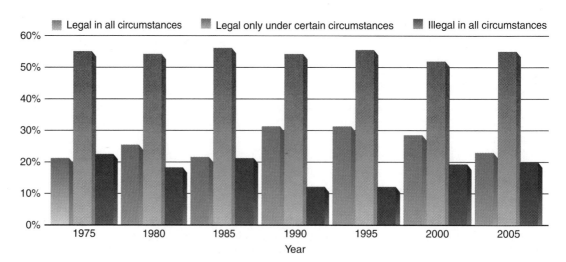

FIGURE 4-1 **Americans' Opinions on Abortion** Since abortion was judged a constitutional right in 1973, public opinion on the issue has not changed greatly.
Source: Gallup polls, various dates.

confrontations at abortion clinics. In 1994, Congress passed a law that makes it illegal to obstruct the entrance to abortion clinics or otherwise prevent people from entering. (The Supreme Court upheld the law, concluding that it regulated abortion protesters' actions as opposed to their words and thus did not violate their right to free speech.[48])

Since *Roe,* antiabortion activists have pursued a variety of strategies in an effort to reverse or limit the scope of the Court's ruling. Attempts at a constitutional amendment that would ban abortions have been unsuccessful, which has prompted abortion foes to seek other ways to restrict the practice. They campaigned successfully to prohibit the use of government funds to pay for abortions for poor women. Then, in *Webster v. Reproductive Health Services* (1989), the Supreme Court upheld a Missouri law that prohibits abortions from being performed in Missouri's public hospitals and by its public employees.[49]

The *Webster* decision was followed in 1992 by the Pennsylvania abortion case *Planned Parenthood v. Casey,* which antiabortion advocates had hoped would reverse the *Roe* precedent. Instead, by a 5-4 margin, the Supreme Court upheld the principle that a woman has a right to abortion in the earliest months of pregnancy. The Court said that "the essential holding of *Roe v. Wade* should be retained and once again reaffirmed."[50] At the same time, however, the Court also said that a state can impose regulations that do not place an "undue burden" on women seeking an abortion. In this vein, the Court upheld a provision of the Pennsylvania law that requires a minor to have parental or judicial consent before obtaining an abortion, saying that it did not constitute an "undue burden." On the other hand, the Court in 2006 struck down by unanimous vote a New Hampshire law that had no medical emergency exception to its parental-consent requirement, concluding that this omission constituted an "undue burden."[51]

In *Gonzales v. Carhart* (2007), the Supreme Court for the first time upheld a ban on the use of a particular method of abortion. At issue was the federal Partial-Birth Abortion Ban Act, passed by Congress in 2003. The law prohibits a form of abortion in which the fetus's life is terminated during delivery even if the mother's life or health is in danger. Any physician who performs such an abortion is subject to a fine and prison term. The Supreme Court in an earlier case, *Stenberg v. Carhart* (2000), had invalidated a Nebraska law that prohibited partial-birth abortion on the grounds that the procedure is sometimes the most appropriate way to protect the mother's health.[52] However, the Nebraska case was decided by a narrow 5-4 margin, with Justice Sandra Day O'Connor providing the swing vote. By the time the 2007 case reached the Supreme Court, she had retired, and her replacement, the more conservative Samuel Alito, voted the opposite way, resulting in a 5-4 vote upholding the congressional ban on partial-birth abortion. Writing for the majority, Justice Anthony Kennedy said that the federal act did not place an "undue burden" on women. In her dissenting opinion, Justice Ruth Bader Ginsburg, the lone woman on the Court, called the decision "alarming," arguing that it ignored established legal precedent.[53]

Sexual Relations Among Consenting Adults

Although it was widely said at the time that the Supreme Court's 1965 *Griswold* ruling on contraceptive use took "government out of people's bedrooms," a clear exception remained. All states prohibited sexual relations between consenting adults of the same sex. A number of states eliminated this prohibition over the next two decades, and others stopped enforcing it. Nevertheless, in a 1986 Georgia case, *Bowers v. Hardwick,* the Supreme Court held that the right of privacy did not extend to homosexual acts among consenting adults.[54]

In 2003, however, the Court reversed itself and in the process struck down the sodomy laws of the thirteen states that still had them. The ruling came in response to a Texas law prohibiting consensual sex between adults of the same sex. In *Lawrence v. Texas,* the Court in a 6-3 vote concluded that the Texas sodomy law violated privacy rights protected by the due process clause of the Fourteenth Amendment. The Court said: "The petitioners are entitled to respect for their private lives. The State cannot demean their existence or control their destiny by making their private sexual conduct a crime."[55] The decision was hailed by gay and lesbian rights groups but condemned by some religious leaders, who said it opened the door to same-sex marriage (see Chapter 5).

Rights of Persons Accused of Crimes

Due process refers to legal protections that have been established to preserve the rights of individuals. The most significant form of these protections is **procedural due process;** the term refers primarily to procedures that authorities must follow before a person can legitimately be punished for an offense. No system of justice is foolproof. Even in the most careful systems, innocent people have been wrongly accused, convicted, and punished with imprisonment or death. But the scrupulous application of procedural safeguards, such as a defendant's right to legal counsel, greatly increases the likelihood that justice will prevail. "The history of liberty has largely been the history of the observance of procedural guarantees," said Justice Felix Frankfurter in *McNabb v. United States* (1943).[56]

The U.S. Constitution provides for several procedures designed to protect a person from wrongful arrest, conviction, and punishment. According to Article I, Section 9, any person taken into police custody is entitled to seek a writ of habeas corpus, which requires law enforcement officials to bring the suspect into court and to specify the legal reason for the detention. The Fifth and Fourteenth Amendments provide generally that no person can be deprived of life, liberty, or property without due process of law. Specific procedural protections for the accused are spelled out in the Fourth, Fifth, Sixth, and Eighth Amendments:

- The Fourth Amendment forbids the police to conduct searches and seizures unless they have probable cause to believe that a crime has been committed.
- The Fifth Amendment protects against double jeopardy (being prosecuted twice for the same offense); self-incrimination (being compelled to testify against oneself); indictment for a crime except through grand jury proceedings; and loss of life, liberty, and property without due process of law.
- The Sixth Amendment provides the right to have legal counsel, to confront witnesses, to receive a speedy trial, and to have a trial by jury in criminal proceedings.
- The Eighth Amendment protects against excessive bail or fines and prohibits the infliction of cruel and unusual punishment on those convicted of crimes.

These protections have been subject to interpretation. The Sixth Amendment, for example, provides the right to have legal counsel. But what if a person cannot afford a lawyer? For most of the nation's history, poor people had virtually no choice but to act as their own attorney. Even though they had a constitutional right to a lawyer, they could not afford to hire one. Today, if a person is accused of a serious crime and cannot afford a lawyer, the government must provide one. This change came about not through a constitutional amendment

procedural due process

The constitutional requirement that government must follow proper legal procedures before a person can be legitimately punished for an alleged offense.

but through Supreme Court rulings that expanded the protection provided by the Sixth Amendment.

Selective Incorporation of Procedural Rights

Early in the nation's history, the procedural protections in the Bill of Rights applied only to the actions of the national government. States in their criminal proceedings were not bound by them. There were limited exceptions, such as a 1932 Supreme Court ruling that a defendant charged in a state court with a crime carrying the death penalty had to be provided with an attorney.[57] Nevertheless, even as the Court was moving to protect free-expression rights from state action in the 1930s, it held back on doing the same for the rights of the accused. The Court claimed that free-expression rights were more deserving of federal protection because they are "the indispensable condition of nearly every other form of freedom."[58]

This view changed abruptly in the 1960s when the Supreme Court required states also to safeguard a broad set of procedural rights. Changes in public education and communication had made Americans more aware of their rights, and the civil rights movement dramatized the fact that rights were administered unequally: the poor and minority group members had many fewer rights in practice than did other Americans. In response, the Supreme Court in the 1960s "incorporated" Bill of Rights protections for the accused by ruling that these rights are protected from state infringement by the Fourteenth Amendment's guarantee of due process of law (see Table 4-3).

The selective incorporation process began with *Mapp v. Ohio* (1961). Police forcibly entered the home of Dollree Mapp, a black woman, saying they had a tip she was harboring a fugitive. After discovering that the fugitive was not there, they handcuffed her and began rummaging through her closets. In the basement, they found a chest that contained obscene photographs. Mapp was arrested and convicted of violating an Ohio law that prohibited the possession of pornography. The Supreme Court overturned her conviction, ruling that police had acted unconstitutionally, citing the Fourth Amendment, which reads, "The right of the people to be secure in their persons, houses, papers, and effects, against unreasonable searches and seizures, shall not be violated . . ." Evidence

TABLE 4-3 | Selective Incorporation of Rights of the Accused   In the 1960s, the Supreme Court selectively incorporated the fair-trial provisions of the Fourth through Eighth Amendments into the Fourteenth Amendment so that these rights would be protected from infringement by the states.

Supreme Court Case	Year	Constitutional Right (Amendment) at Issue
Mapp v. Ohio	1961	Protection against unreasonable search and seizure (Fourth)
Robinson v. California	1962	Protection against cruel and unusual punishment (Eighth)
Gideon v. Wainwright	1963	Right to counsel (Sixth)
Malloy v. Hogan	1964	Protection against self-incrimination (Fifth)
Pointer v. Texas	1965	Right to confront witnesses (Sixth)
Miranda v. Arizona	1966	Protection against self-incrimination and right to counsel (Fifth and Sixth)
Klopfer v. North Carolina	1967	Speedy trial (Sixth)
Duncan v. Louisiana	1968	Jury trial in criminal cases (Sixth)
Benton v. Maryland	1969	Protection against double jeopardy (Fifth)

acquired through such a search, the Court said, cannot be used to obtain a conviction in state courts.[59]

Two years later, the Court's decision in *Gideon v. Wainwright* (1963) required the states to furnish attorneys for poor defendants in all felony cases. Clarence Gideon, an indigent drifter, had been convicted and sentenced to prison in Florida for breaking into a poolroom. The judge had denied his request for counsel, and he was forced to act as his own lawyer. He successfully appealed his conviction on the grounds that he had been denied due process because he did not have proper legal counsel during his trial.[60]

During the 1960s, the Court also ruled that defendants in state criminal proceedings cannot be compelled to testify against themselves,[61] have the right to remain silent and to have legal counsel at the time of arrest,[62] have the right to confront witnesses who testify against them,[63] must be granted a speedy trial,[64] have the right to a jury trial,[65] and cannot be subjected to double jeopardy.[66] The best known of these cases is *Miranda v. Arizona* (1966), which arose when Ernesto Miranda confessed during police interrogation to kidnap and rape. The Supreme Court overturned his conviction on the grounds that he had not been informed of his rights to remain silent and to have legal assistance. This ruling led to the development of the "Miranda warning" that police are now required to read to suspects: "You have the right to remain silent. . . . Anything you say can and will be used against you in a court of law. . . . You have the right to an attorney." (Miranda was subsequently retried and convicted on the basis of evidence other than his confession.)

In a 2000 case, *Dickerson v. United States*, the Supreme Court reaffirmed the *Miranda* decision, saying that it was an established "constitutional rule" that Congress could not abolish by ordinary legislation.[67] The Court further strengthened the Miranda precedent in *Missouri v. Siebert* (2004). This ruling came in response to a police strategy of questioning suspects first and then reading them their Miranda rights, followed by a second round of questioning. In such instances, suspects who admitted wrongdoing in the first round of questioning tended also to do so in the second round. The Court concluded that the strategy was intended "to undermine the Miranda warnings" and was therefore unconstitutional.[68]

Limits on Defendants' Rights

In the courtroom, the rights to have counsel, to confront witnesses, and to remain silent are of paramount importance. Before the courtroom phase in a criminal proceeding, the main protection is the Fourth Amendment's restriction on illegal search and seizure. This restriction holds that police must have suspicion of wrongdoing (and, sometimes, a judge's permission) before they can search your person, your car, or your residence, although involvement in an offense (such as driving faster than the speed limit) can lead to a permissible search that uncovers wrongdoing of another kind (such as drug possession). Without search-and-seizure protection, individuals would be subject to arbitrary police harassment and intimidation, characteristics of a totalitarian state, not a free society.

However, the Fourth Amendment does not provide blanket protection against searches. In 1990, for example, the Supreme Court held that police roadblocks to check drivers for signs of intoxication are legal as long as the action is systematic and not arbitrary (for example, stopping only young drivers would be unconstitutional, whereas stopping all drivers is acceptable). The Court justified its decision by saying that roadblocks serve a public safety purpose.[69] However, the Court does not allow the same types of roadblocks to check for drugs. In *Indianapolis v. Edmund* (2001), the Court held that narcotics roadblocks, because

Surveillance Act (FISA) of 1978. Bush rejected allegations that he had broken the law, saying that he had acted legally under his wartime powers as commander-in-chief and under authority implicitly granted him by the Patriot Act.

The question of governing authority—whether the Bush administration's NSA surveillance activities are within or outside the law—is only now being heard in lower courts. The first such ruling occurred in August 2006; the district judge in that case held that President Bush had exceeded his statutory and constitutional authority in ordering wiretaps without a judicial warrant. Most analysts believe, however, that a definitive judgment on this issue will not come until the Supreme Court itself decides the issue or unless the White House persuades Congress to change the laws governing intelligence-gathering wiretaps.

The Courts and a Free Society

The United States was founded on the idea that individuals have an innate right to liberty—to speak their minds, to worship freely, to be secure in their homes and persons, to be assured of a fair trial. Americans embrace these freedoms in the abstract. In particular situations, however, many Americans would prefer policies that diminish the freedom of those who hold minority views or have a different physical appearance than most Americans. After the September 11 terrorist attacks, for example, a third of Americans in polls said that Arab Americans should be placed under special surveillance and half said that Arab Americans should be required to carry special identification cards. Two-fifths said they would ban college lectures by speakers who argue that aspects of U.S. foreign policy have contributed to terrorist activity.

The judiciary is not isolated from the public mood. Judges inevitably must balance society's need for security and public order against the rights of the individual. Nevertheless, judges can ordinarily be expected to be more protective of individual rights than either elected officials or the general public. How far the courts will go in protecting a person's rights depends on the facts of the case, the existing status of the law, prevailing social needs, and the personal views of the judges. Nevertheless, most judges and justices regard the protection of individual rights as a constitutional imperative, which is the way the Framers saw it. The Bill of Rights was created in order to transform the abstract idea that individuals have inalienable rights to life, liberty, and happiness into a set of specified constitutional rights, thereby bringing them under the protection of courts of law.[103]

Summary Self-Test www.mhhe.com/pattersontad9e

The Bill of Rights was added to the Constitution shortly after its ratification. These amendments guarantee certain political, procedural, and property rights against infringement by the national government.

Freedom of expression is the most basic of democratic rights. People are not free unless they can freely express their views. Nevertheless, free expression may conflict with the nation's security needs during times of war and insurrection. The courts at times have allowed government to limit expression substantially for purposes of national security. In recent decades, however, the courts have protected a wide range of free expression in the areas of speech, press, and

religion. They have also established a right of privacy, which in some areas, such as abortion, remains a source of controversy and judicial action.

The guarantees embodied in the Bill of Rights originally applied only to the national government. Under the principle of selective incorporation of these guarantees into the Fourteenth Amendment, the courts extended them to state governments, though the process was slow and uneven. In the 1920s and 1930s, First Amendment guarantees of freedom of expression were given protection from infringement by the states. The states continued to have wide discretion in criminal proceedings until the early 1960s, when most of the fair-trial rights in the Bill of Rights were given federal protection.

Due process of law refers to legal protections that have been established to preserve individual rights. The most significant form of these protections consists of procedures or methods (for example, the right of an accused person to have an attorney present during police interrogation) designed to ensure that an individual's rights are upheld. A major controversy in this area is the breadth of the exclusionary rule, which bars the use in trials of illegally obtained evidence. The Supreme Court in recent decades has narrowed the rule's application, granting police wider discretion in the search and seizure of suspects.

The war on terrorism that began after the attacks on September 11, 2001, has raised new issues of civil liberties, in-cluding the detention of enemy combatants, the use of harsh interrogation techniques, and warrantless surveillance. The Supreme Court has not ruled on all such issues but has generally held that the president's war-making power does not include the authority to disregard provisions of statutory law, treaties (the Geneva Conventions), and the Constitution.

Civil liberties are not absolute but must be balanced against other considerations (such as national security or public safety) and against one another when different rights conflict. The judicial branch of government, particularly the Supreme Court, has taken on much of the responsibility for protecting and interpreting individual rights. The Court's positions have changed with time and conditions, but the Court is usually more protective of civil liberties than elected officials or popular majorities are.

CHAPTER 4

Study Corner

Key Terms

Bill of Rights (*p. 86*)

civil liberties (*p. 86*)

clear-and-present-danger test (*p. 88*)

due process clause (of the Fourteenth Amendment) (*p. 90*)

establishment clause (*p. 96*)

exclusionary rule (*p. 105*)

freedom of expression (*p. 88*)

free-exercise clause (*p. 97*)

imminent lawless action test (*p. 92*)

libel (*p. 93*)

prior restraint (*p. 90*)

procedural due process (*p. 102*)

right of privacy (*p. 99*)

selective incorporation (*p. 91*)

slander (*p. 93*)

symbolic speech (*p. 89*)

Self-Test

1. Which constitutional amendment, as interpreted by the Supreme Court after 1925, provides protection of individual rights against the actions of state and local governments?
   a. Fourteenth
   b. Tenth
   c. Fifth
   d. Fourth
   e. First

2. The exclusionary rule holds that:
   a. people who are biased against the defendant may be excluded from serving on a jury.
   b. a court can order or constrain an action by an individual.
   c. evidence obtained from an illegal search and seizure cannot be used in a trial.
   d. "fighting words" can be excluded from constitutional protection.

3. The U.S. Bill of Rights as originally approved and interpreted protected individual liberties from violation by:
   a. state governments only.
   b. the national government only.
   c. both national and state governments.
   d. all levels of government in the United States.

4. The establishment clause prohibits government from:
   a. establishing exceptions to the Bill of Rights.
   b. interfering in any matters where the church and the state conflict.
   c. favoring one religion over another or supporting religion over no religion.
   d. interfering with a person's practice of religion.

5. The right to privacy was the basis for the Supreme Court ruling in:
   a. *Roe v. Wade.*
   b. *Mapp v. Ohio.*

c. *Miranda v. Arizona.*
d. *Schenck v. United States.*

6. The term that refers primarily to procedures that authorities must follow before a person can legitimately be punished for an offense is:
   a. the three-point test.
   b. the right to privacy.
   c. procedural due process.
   d. substantive due process.

7. Sexual material that is offensive to any one individual in society is automatically deemed obscene and is not protected under the First Amendment. (T/F)

8. Modern Americans' rights of free expression have been defined largely in the context of national security concerns. (T/F)

9. In order to win a libel suit, public officials must prove that a news organization or journalist acted with knowing or reckless disregard for the truth. (T/F)

10. The Supreme Court supported the effort of the state of Texas to outlaw the burning of the American flag. (T/F)

Suggested Readings

Abraham, Henry J. *Freedom and the Court.* New York: Oxford University Press, 2003. A comprehensive analysis of the Supreme Court's work on civil rights and civil liberties.

Ackerman, Bruce. *Before the Next Attack: Preserving Civil Liberties in an Age of Terrorism.* New Haven, Conn.: Yale University Press, 2007. A thoughtful analysis of how Western democracies should treat civil liberties in the era of global terrorism.

Gup, Ted. *Nation of Secrets: The Threat to Democracy and the American Way of Life.* New York: Doubleday, 2007. An award-winning book that documents government's effort to hide from public view an ever-increasing amount of information on its activities.

Hull, N. E. H., and Peter Charles Hoffer. *Roe v. Wade: The Abortion Rights Controversy in American History.* Lawrence: University Press of Kansas, 2001. A thorough assessment of both sides of the abortion conflict, beginning with the *Roe v. Wade* decision.

Perry, Michael J. *Religion in Politics: Constitutional and Moral Perspectives.* New York: Oxford University Press, 1997. A legal and philosophical analysis of the role of religion in politics.

Schwarz, John E. *Freedom Reclaimed: Rediscovering the American Vision.* Baltimore, Md.: Johns Hopkins University Press, 2005. An impassioned argument for an expansive view of liberty, both from and through government action.

Stone, Geoffrey. *War and Liberty: An American Dilemma: 1790 to the Present.* New York: Norton, 2007. A historical assessment of the tension between civil liberties and national security.

List of Websites

http://www.fepproject.org/
Includes information and opinions on a wide range of free-expression policy issues.

http://www.aclu.org/
The American Civil Liberties Union site; provides information on current civil liberties and civil rights issues, including information on recent and pending Supreme Court cases.

http://www.findlaw.com/casecode/supreme.html
An excellent source of information on Supreme Court and lower-court rulings.

http://www.ncjrs.org/
The site of the National Criminal Justice Reference Service, a federally funded organization that compiles information on a wide range of criminal-justice issues.

Critical Thinking

What is the process of selective incorporation, and why is it important to the rights you have today?

Participate!

Although their right of free expression is protected by law, Americans often choose not to exercise this right for fear of social pressure or official reprisal. Yet constitutional rights tend to wither when people fail to exercise them. The failure of citizens to speak their mind, Alexis de Tocqueville said, reduces them "to being nothing more than a herd of timid and industrious animals of which government is the shepherd." Think of an issue that you care about but that is unpopular on your campus or in your community. Consider writing a letter expressing your opinion to the editor of your college or local newspaper. (Practical advice: keep the letter short and to the point; write a lead sentence that will get readers' attention; provide a convincing and courteous argument for your position; and be sure to sign the letter and provide a return address so the editor can contact you if there are questions.)

Extra Credit

For up-to-the-minute *New York Times* articles, interactive simulations, graphics, study tools, and more links and quizzes, visit the text's Online Learning Center at www.mhhe.com/pattersontad9e.

Self-Test Answers

1. a   2. c   3. b   4. c   5. a   6. c   7. F   8. T   9. T   10. F

SURVEILLANCE STANDOFF

From 1985 to 86 the number of registered mobile-phone subscribers in the United States doubled to 500,000. Within two years after that, the number climbed to 1.6 million. By the end of the decade, the cellphone universe had skyrocketed past 4 million.

Organized crime was an early adopter of the mobile phone. In a communications technique presaging that of Islamic terrorists today, members of the Colombian Cali drug cartel operating in New York would briefly use a phone, toss it, and get a new one. To wiretap a mobile device, technicians had to install listening equipment on an "electronic port." But in most switching stations in New York, there were only half a dozen or so ports available at any one time. Federal prosecutors and agents had to stand in line at phone company offices and fight with each other over whose investigation should take priority. Some prosecutors threatened to haul company employees into court on contempt charges so they could explain to a judge why the phone company was unwilling to execute a wiretap order.

Electronic surveillance, once such a dependable, relatively easy craft, was becoming inordinately difficult. FBI Field Agent Jim Kallstrom may have been the first to alert the FBI and the Justice Department to this new reality. The digital revolution generated a constant tension that exists to this day, a push and pull between the federal government in one camp and technology corporations and civil-liberties activists in the other to control the development of the global communications system, and so the balance of power in the Information Age.

This struggle's latest manifestation is the intensely politicized effort to rewrite the Foreign Intelligence Surveillance Act. At issue is nothing less than the government's authority to broadly monitor communications networks to spot terrorists and other national security threats.

Activists and their allies in the business world have been motivated by different but mutually supportive goals: to extend constitutional safeguards to the digital realm, and to keep the government from suffocating technological development with burdensome surveillance laws. Some in those ranks would have liked, and indeed tried, to make the digital network a wiretap-free zone.

But despite the occasionally extreme positions and deeply held convictions of all of these players, the most important laws governing wiretapping, electronic surveillance, and privacy have been the product of negotiation, of people gathering in a room, sitting at a table, and talking—sometimes screaming—until they reached a settlement. The current debate, however, is missing that crucial spirit. It's not entirely clear where or why minds turned so stubborn. But to understand today's political calcification, it helps to recall a simpler time.

In the summer of 1994, the FBI and the Justice Department made a bold play to force the telecom carriers to help them conduct legal wiretaps. They put forth a proposal that would require the companies to build their networks so that law enforcement agents serving a warrant could access them in real time. The legality of wiretapping was not in question. The government wanted legal assurance that it could tap, at any time, and that the industry had an obligation under law to comply with the government's proper authority.

After months of haggling, the Communications Assistance for Law Enforcement Act passed in November 1994. CALEA would let the industry set its own standards to meet the Justice Department's needs. The department could list its surveillance requirements, but the act let companies decide how to build their equipment. Justice won the right to petition the Federal Communications Commission if its officials felt that the companies weren't fulfilling their obligations. But civil-liberties groups also secured the right to challenge the government's requirements in court.

Had the FBI and the Justice Department stopped there, had the government settled for secure access to phone networks, the history of Internet privacy and civil liberties might have turned out differently.

FBI officials knew in 1994 that they were making a mistake by leaving cyberspace out of CALEA. They understood the Internet's potential as a communications device and an intelligence tool—that is, after all, why CALEA's authors exempted "information services."

In early 1995, the Justice Department issued its list of requirements for wiretapping, known as the punch list. Not surprisingly, many telecom executives and their attorneys viewed the demands as unreasonable. Al Gidari, a lawyer representing the wireless industry, was among the first to see the FBI's requirements, during the initial meeting to develop standards for CALEA, which was held that spring in Vancouver, British Columbia. The Justice Department's wish list, he said, amounted to "the Cadillac of wiretaps."

Over the next few years, the Justice Department continued to seek increasingly sophisticated surveillance capabilities, including real-time geographical tracking of mobile phones; the ability to monitor all parties in a conference call regardless of whether they are on hold or participating; and "dialed digit extraction," a record of any numbers that a subject under surveillance punched in during a call, such as a credit card or bank account number. The government got a lot of what it wanted, but not all.

To be sure, criminals' use of new technologies helped drive the law enforcement demands. But telecom carriers worried that the cost of compliance was too high and that the FBI's technical requirements were illegally broad. CALEA, they argued, had forbidden the government from requiring specific system designs or technologies.

Justice, frustrated by its inability to get all the demands on the punch list, finally asked the Federal Communications Commission to step in. In 1997, the Cellular

Telecommunications Industry Association, which then represented mobile carriers, and the Center for Democracy and Technology complained to the commission that the negotiations had deadlocked because of "unreasonable demands by law enforcement for more surveillance features than either CALEA or the wiretap laws allow." The FCC, however, sided with the Justice Department on a host of requirements that privacy groups found overly broad. The tussle dragged on for two more years and ended up in the U.S. Court of Appeals for the District of Columbia Circuit, which overruled the FCC. After the commission took up matters again, it granted some of the FBI's requests, and the CALEA standards were amended.

The level of government surveillance was so low at that time that some questioned why the FBI wanted such multifaceted access at all. In 1994, federal and state authorities were running 1,154 wiretaps nationwide, mostly for drug investigations, at an average cost of $50,000. The government was asking carriers to "design a nuclear rocket ship" for a rarely used tool, Gidari thought. "In [the FBI's] view, there was no limit to the expense the carrier should spare in order to save a life."

CALEA continued to evolve, shaped by the ongoing arguments over the terms of its birth. Activists and carriers thought that the FBI was reneging on its bargain, asking for more than the law allowed. The FBI believed that carriers were stalling when they failed to meet compliance deadlines. As all sides dug in, the meetings on implementation turned bitter.

The government asked those same questions after September 11, 2001. And this time, telecommunications carriers responded. Outside the normal FISA warrant process, which covers intelligence-gathering, carriers opened access to their networks, their

FBI and Justice officials slammed their hands on tables and screamed at carrier representatives, Gidari recalls. "You're unpatriotic! What do you want to do, help the criminals?"

customer call data, and their valuable transactional information—the kind that CALEA had intended to exclude. President Bush and his administration believed that the extraordinary nature of the terrorist attacks demanded emergency actions that FISA couldn't accommodate, and the carriers answered the call from law enforcement and intelligence agencies. But government officials also seized on the post-9/11 mentality to change other surveillance laws and procedures, which they believed—just as their predecessors did in 1994—were out of step with technology and reality. About three years after 9/11, officials set their sights on rewriting CALEA.

In August 2004, in response to a petition by the Justice Department, the FBI, and the Drug Enforcement Administration, the FCC expanded CALEA to cover Internet communications, including voice calls and instant messages. The Electronic Frontier Foundation sued, along with industry, civil-liberties, and academic groups. In 2005, the Court of Appeals ruled 2–1 to defer to the FCC's reading of the law.

Many of those who had helped craft CALEA believed that the commission had

misread the law and acted on a post-9/11 impulse to give the government more, not less, access to information. But to the FCC, new Internet technologies that operate a lot like telephones blurred the distinction between "information services" and the kinds of technology that CALEA was meant to cover.

After 9/11, law enforcement and intelligence agencies took a variety of measures, apart from wiretaps, to collect and mine potentially valuable information from the Internet. With the cooperation of telecom companies, government accumulated lots of transactional data—including e-mail header information and lists of websites visited by targeted individuals—to support counterterrorism operations. Viewed solely as a reaction to the terrorist attacks of 2001, this kind of collection might seem extraordinary. But through the longer lens of history, the government's steady march into cyberspace is not surprising.

The FISA debate hung on whether companies that assisted warrantless surveillance after 9/11 should have retroactive legal immunity for any laws they may have broken. CALEA has something to say about that, too. The law requires that carriers be able to deliver call identification information to the government remotely. According to Beryl Howell, Sen. Leahy's lead CALEA staffer, that provision was meant to keep government agents from sitting in the phone companies' offices to execute their wiretaps.

It is a basic tenet of wiretapping law, whether for intelligence or law enforcement, that the communications companies act as a buffer between their customers and the government, she says, and that telecom carriers must make their own determination whether official requests

FOR DISCUSSION: Will you support wiretaps, warrantless or otherwise, on new technologies like cell-phone and Internet use? Should telecom companies be responsible for protecting their clients' civil liberties? Will we need to rethink the protection of our civil liberties in the information age?

CHAPTER 5

www.oneunitedmichigan.org
Progress
No Turning Bac
Defend
Affirmativ
Action

Equal Rights
Struggling Toward Fairness

The Struggle for Equality

African Americans
Women
Native Americans
Hispanic Americans
Asian Americans
Other Groups and Their Rights

Equality Under the Law

Equal Protection: The Fourteenth
  Amendment
Equal Access: The Civil Rights Acts
  of 1964 and 1968
Equal Ballots: The Voting Rights Act
  of 1965, as Amended

Equality of Result

Affirmative Action: Workplace
  Integration
Affirmative Action in the Law
Busing: School Integration

Persistent Discrimination: Superficial Differences, Deep Divisions

I have a dream that one day this nation will rise up and live out the true meaning of its creed: "We hold these truths to be self-evident: that all men are created equal."

Martin Luther King Jr.[1]

The producers of ABC television's *Primetime Live* put hidden cameras on two young men, equally well dressed and groomed, and then sent them on different routes to do the same things—search for an apartment, shop for a car, look at albums in a record store. The cameras recorded people's reactions to the two men. One was usually greeted with smiles and quick service, while the other was more often greeted with suspicious looks and was sometimes made to wait. Why the difference? The explanation was straightforward: the young man who was routinely well received was white; the young man who was sometimes treated poorly was black.

The Urban Institute conducted a more substantial experiment. It included pairs of specially trained white and black male college students who were comparable in all respects—education, work experience, speech patterns, physical builds—except for their race. The students responded individually to nearly five hundred classified job advertisements in Chicago and Washington, D.C. The black applicants got fewer interviews and received fewer job offers than did the white applicants. An Urban Institute spokesperson said, "The level of reverse discrimination [favoring blacks over whites] that we found was limited, was certainly far lower than many might have been led to fear, and was swamped by the extent of discrimination against black job applicants."[2]

These two experiments suggest why some Americans are still struggling to achieve equal rights. In theory Americans have equal rights, but in reality they are not now equal nor have they ever been. African Americans, women, Hispanic Americans, the disabled, Jews, Native Americans, Catholics, Asian Americans, gays and lesbians, and members of other minority groups have been victims of discrimination in fact and in law. The nation's creed—"all men are created equal"—has encouraged minorities to demand equal treatment. But inequality is built into almost every aspect of U.S. society. For example, compared with whites, African Americans with correctable health problems are significantly less likely to receive coronary artery bypass surgery, to receive a kidney transplant, or to undergo surgery for early-stage lung cancer.[3]

civil rights, or equal rights
The right of every person to equal protection under the laws and equal access to society's opportunities and public facilities.

This chapter focuses on **equal rights,** or **civil rights**—terms that refer to the right of every person to equal protection under the laws and equal access to society's opportunities and public facilities. As Chapter 4 explained, civil liberties refer to specific *individual* rights, such as freedom of speech, that are protected from infringement by government. Equal rights, or civil rights, have to do with whether individual members of differing *groups*—racial, sexual, and the like—are treated equally by government and, in some areas, by private parties.

Although the law refers to the rights of individuals first and to those of groups in a secondary and derivative way, this chapter concentrates on groups because the history of civil rights has been largely one of group claims to equality. The chapter emphasizes these points:

- *Disadvantaged groups have had to struggle for equal rights.* African Americans, women, Native Americans, Hispanic Americans, Asian Americans, and others have all had to fight for their rights in order to come closer to equality with white males.

- *Americans have attained substantial equality under the law.* They have, in legal terms, equal protection under the laws, equal access to accommodations and housing, and an equal right to vote. Discrimination by law against persons because of race, sex, religion, or ethnicity has been virtually eliminated.

- *Legal equality for all Americans has not resulted in de facto equality.* African Americans, women, Hispanic Americans, and other traditionally disadvantaged groups have a disproportionately small share of America's opportunities and benefits. Existing inequalities, discrimination, and political pressures still are major barriers to their full equality. Affirmative action is a policy designed to help the disadvantaged achieve a fuller degree of equality.

The Struggle for Equality

Equality has always been the least fully developed of America's founding concepts. Not even Thomas Jefferson, who had a deep admiration for the "common man," believed that a precise meaning could be given to the claim of the Declaration of Independence that "all men are created equal."[4]

The history of America shows that disadvantaged groups have rarely achieved a greater measure of justice without a struggle.[5] Their gains have nearly always followed intense and sustained political action, such as the civil rights movement of the 1960s, that forced entrenched interests to relinquish or share their privileged status (see Chapter 7). Although disadvantaged groups have a shared history of political exclusion, each has a distinctive history as well, as is evident in a brief review of the equal rights efforts of African Americans, women, Native Americans, Hispanic Americans, Asian Americans, and other groups.

African Americans

No Americans have faced greater hardship than have black Americans. Their ancestors came to this country as slaves after having been captured in Africa, shipped in chains across the Atlantic, and sold in open markets in Charleston, Boston, and other seaports.

HISTORICAL
Background

Two police dogs attack a black civil rights activist (*center left*) during the 1963 Birmingham demonstrations. Such images of hatred and violence shook many white Americans out of their complacency about the plight of African Americans.

The Civil War ended slavery—but not racism. When federal troops withdrew from the South in 1877, the region's white majority took over the state governments, passing laws that kept blacks from voting. They were also forbidden to use the same public facilities as whites.[6] In *Plessy v. Ferguson* (1896), the Supreme Court endorsed these laws, ruling that "separate" public facilities for the two races did not violate the Constitution as long as the facilities were "equal."[7] The *Plessy* decision became a justification for the separate and *unequal* treatment of African Americans. For example, black children were forced into separate schools that rarely had libraries and had few teachers.

Black Americans challenged these discriminatory practices through legal action, but not until the late 1930s did the Supreme Court begin to respond. The Court began modestly by ruling that where no separate public facilities existed for African Americans, they must be allowed to use those reserved for whites. When Oklahoma, which had no law school for blacks, was ordered to admit Ada Sipuel as a law student in 1949, it created a separate law school for her—she sat alone in a roped-off corridor of the state capitol building. The white students, meanwhile, continued to meet at the University of Oklahoma's law school in Norman, twenty miles away. The Supreme Court then ordered the law school to admit her to regular classes. The law school did so but roped off her seat from the rest of the class and stenciled the word "colored" on it. She was also forced to eat alone in a roped-off area of the law school's cafeteria.[8]

The *Brown* Decision

Substantial judicial intervention on behalf of African Americans finally occurred in 1954 with *Brown v. Board of Education of Topeka*. The case began when Linda Carol Brown, a black child in Topeka, Kansas, was denied admission to an all-white elementary school that she passed every day on her way to her all-black school, which was twelve blocks farther away. In its decision, the Court reversed its *Plessy* doctrine by declaring that racial segregation of public schools "generates [among black children] a feeling of inferiority as to their status in the community that may affect their hearts and minds in a way unlikely ever to be undone. . . . Separate educational facilities are inherently unequal."[9] A 1954 Gallup poll indicated that a substantial majority of southern whites opposed the *Brown* decision. The same poll found that only a narrow majority of whites outside the South agreed with the decision.

The Black Civil Rights Movement

After *Brown*, the struggle of African Americans for their rights became a political movement. Perhaps no single event turned national public opinion so dramatically against segregation as a 1963 march led by Dr. Martin Luther King Jr. in Birmingham, Alabama. As the nation watched on television in disbelief, police officers led by Birmingham's sheriff, Eugene "Bull" Connor, attacked King and his followers with dogs, cattle prods, and fire hoses.

The modern civil rights movement peaked with the triumphant March on Washington for Jobs and Freedom of August 28, 1963. It attracted 250,000 marchers, one of the largest gatherings in the history of the nation's capital. "I have a dream," the Reverend King told the gathering, "that my four little children will one day live in a nation where they will not be judged by the color of their skin but by the content of their character." A year later, after a months-long fight in Congress marked by every parliamentary obstacle that opponents could muster, the Civil Rights Act of 1964 was enacted. The legislation provided African Americans and other minorities with equal access to public facilities and prohibited job discrimination. President Lyndon Johnson, who had been a decisive force in the battle to pass the Civil Rights Act, called for new legislation that would also end racial barriers to voting. Congress answered with the 1965 Voting Rights Act.

The Aftermath of the Civil Rights Movement

Although the most significant progress in history toward the legal equality of all Americans occurred during the 1960s, Dr. King's dream of a color-blind society has remained elusive.[10] Even the legal rights of African Americans do not, in practice, match the promise of the civil rights movement. Studies have found that African Americans accused of crime are more likely to be convicted and to receive stiff sentences than are white Americans on trial for comparable offenses. The U.S. Department of Justice found, for example, that among persons convicted of drug felonies in state courts, half of black defendants received prison sentences compared with a third of white defendants.[11] It should come as no surprise that many African Americans believe that the nation has two standards of justice.

One area in which African Americans have made substantial progress since the 1960s is elective office (see "States in the Nation"). Although the percentage of black elected officials is still far below the proportion of African Americans in the population, it has risen sharply in recent decades.[12] There are now roughly five hundred black mayors and more than forty black members of Congress. The most stunning advance, of course, was the election of Barack Obama in 2008 as the first African American president.

Women

The United States carried over from English common law a political disregard for women, forbidding them to vote, hold public office, or serve on juries.[13] Upon marriage, a woman essentially lost her identity as an individual and could not

STATES IN THE NATION

BLACK AND LATINO REPRESENTATION IN STATE LEGISLATURES

For a long period in U.S. history, there were almost no minorities among the ranks of state legislators. Minorities are still underrepresented relative to their numbers in the population. Although one in every three Americans is a minority-group member, only one in eight state legislators comes from a minority group; of these, about two-thirds are African American.

Q: What accounts for differences between the states in the percentage of minority-group members in their legislatures?

A: States with large populations of minorities tend to have a larger percentage of legislators from minority groups. Alabama and Mississippi have large black populations and have the highest proportion of African American legislators. New Mexico, with its large Hispanic population, has the highest proportion of Latino lawmakers.

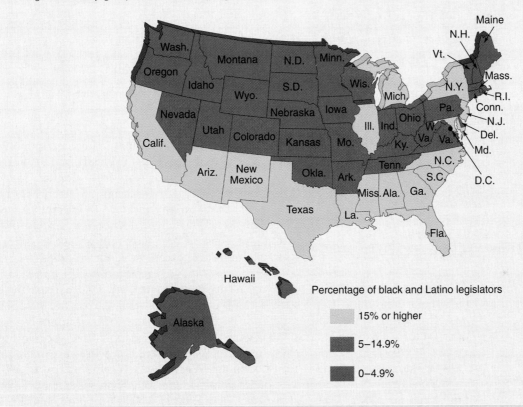

Percentage of black and Latino legislators

- 15% or higher
- 5–14.9%
- 0–4.9%

Source: National Conference of State Legislatures, 2008.

own and dispose of property without her husband's consent. Even a wife's body was not fully hers. A wife's adultery was declared by the Supreme Court in 1904 to be a violation of the husband's property rights![14]

The first women's rights convention in America was held in 1848 in Seneca Falls, New York, after Lucretia Mott and Elizabeth Cady Stanton had been barred from the main floor of an antislavery convention. Thereafter, the struggle for women's rights became closely aligned with the abolitionist movement. However, when the Fifteenth Amendment was ratified after the Civil War, women were not included; the amendment declared that the right to vote could not be abridged on account of race or color but said nothing about sex. Not until passage of the Nineteenth Amendment in 1920 did women gain the right to vote.

HISTORICAL
Background

In 2008, Hillary Clinton nearly captured the Democratic presidential nomination, which would have made her the first woman to be nominated for president by a major U.S. party.

Women's Legal and Political Gains

Ratification of the Nineteenth Amendment encouraged leaders of the women's movement to propose in 1923 a constitutional amendment that would guarantee equal rights for women. Congress rejected that proposal but sixty years later approved the Equal Rights Amendment (ERA) and submitted it to the states for their consideration. The ERA failed by three states to receive the three-fourths majority required for ratification.[15] Other efforts were more successful, however. Among the congressional initiatives were the Equal Pay Act of 1963, which prohibits sex discrimination in salary and wages by some categories of employers; Title IX of the Education Amendment of 1972, which prohibits sex discrimination in education; and the Equal Credit Act of 1974, which prohibits sex discrimination in the granting of financial credit.

Women are also protected by Title VII of the Civil Rights Act of 1964, which bans gender discrimination in employment. This protection extends to sexual harassment. Lewd comments and unwelcome advances are part of the workplace reality for many American women. However, the courts have held, and with increasing firmness, that companies and government agencies can be sued if they do not try hard to prevent this type of behavior.[16] In a 2006 decision, for example, the Supreme Court made it easier for employees to sue an organization that retaliates against them for filing a sexual harassment complaint. The case involved a woman who, after filing such a complaint, was removed from her position as a forklift operator and assigned a less desirable job in the company.[17]

Women have made substantial gains in the area of appointive and elective offices. In 1981, President Ronald Reagan appointed the first woman to serve on the Supreme Court, Sandra Day O'Connor. When the Democratic Party in 1984 chose Geraldine Ferraro as its vice presidential nominee, she became the first woman to run on the national ticket of a major political party. The selection of Sarah Palin as Republican vice-presidential nominee in 2008 marked only the second time a woman has run on a major party's national ticket. In 2008, Hillary Clinton nearly won the Democratic presidential nomination, which would have been the first time that a woman headed the national ticket of a major American political party. Despite such signs of progress, women are still a long way from attaining political equality with men.[18] Women occupy roughly one in six congressional seats and one in five statewide and city council offices (see "How the U. S. Compares").

Although women are underrepresented in political office, their vote is increasingly powerful. Until the 1970s, the political behavior of women and men was nearly identical. Today, there is a substantial **gender gap:** women and men differ in their opinions and their votes.[19] Women are more supportive than men of government programs for the poor, minorities, children, and the elderly. They also have a greater tendency to cast their votes for Democratic candidates (see Figure 5-1). The gender gap is discussed further in Chapter 6.

gender gap

The tendency of women and men to differ in their political attitudes and voting preferences.

HOW THE U.S. COMPARES

WOMEN'S REPRESENTATION IN NATIONAL LEGISLATURES

For a long period in world history, women were largely barred from holding positions of political power. The situation has changed dramatically in recent decades, and women now hold more seats in national legislatures than at any time in history. Yet there are less than a handful of countries where they have nearly reached parity with men. The Scandinavian countries rank highest in terms of the percentage of female lawmakers. Other northern European countries have lower levels, but their levels are higher than in the United States, as the figure below indicates.

The reason the United States ranks relatively low in comparison with other Western democracies has only partly

to do with social biases. In general, women hold more legislative seats in democracies that use a proportional system of election. In such countries, the parties get seats in proportion to the votes they receive in the election, and the parties themselves decide which party members will occupy the seats. In America's system, candidates compete directly for the vote, and the candidate who gets the most votes in a district wins the seat. Further, U.S. incumbents have a very high reelection rate, one that far exceeds the rate in European parliaments. U.S. incumbents are difficult to dislodge, which works against the entry of new members, regardless of sex (see Chapter 11).

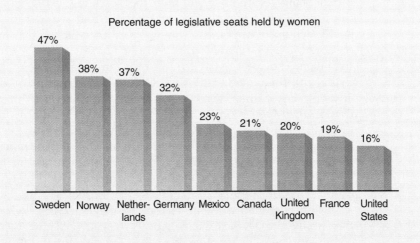

Percentage of legislative seats held by women

Source: Inter-Parliamentary Union, 2008. Based on number of women in the single or lower legislative chamber. In the case of the United States, that chamber is the U.S. House of Representatives.

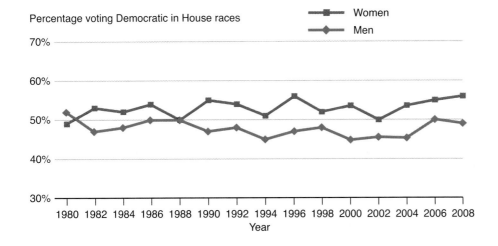

Percentage voting Democratic in House races

FIGURE 5-1   The Gender Gap in Congressional Voting Women and men differ, on average, in their political behavior. For example, women are more likely than men to vote Democratic, as shown by the difference between the women's vote and the men's vote for Democratic candidates in U.S. House races.

Source: National Election Studies (1988–1998); exit polls (2000–2004); 2008 figure based on preliminary data.

Job-Related Issues: Family Leave, Comparable Worth, and Sexual Harassment

In recent decades, increasing numbers of women have sought employment outside the home. Government statistics indicate that employment-age women are six times more likely to work outside the home compared with a half-century ago. Women have made gains in many traditionally male-dominated fields. For example, women now make up nearly half of the new lawyers and physicians who graduate each year. The change in women's work status is also reflected in education statistics. A few decades ago, more white, black, and Hispanic men than women were enrolled in college. Today, the reverse is true, with more women than men of each group enrolled. A U.S. Education Department report issued in 2006 showed that women are ahead of men in more than just college enrollment. Compared with men, they are also more likely to complete their degree, to do it in a shorter period, and to get better grades.[20]

Nevertheless, women have not achieved equality when it comes to jobs. Women increasingly hold managerial positions but, as they rise through the ranks, many of them encounter the so-called *glass ceiling*, which refers to the invisible but nonetheless real barrier that women encounter when firms decide whom to appoint to the top positions. Of the five hundred largest U.S. corporations, less than 5 percent are headed by women. Women also earn less than men. The average pay for full-time female employees is about three-fourths that of full-time male employees. One reason is that many of the jobs traditionally held by women, such as office assistant, pay less than many of the jobs traditionally held by men, such as truck driver. Attempts by women's groups to change this tendency have been largely unsuccessful. Only a tiny percentage of firms and municipalities have instituted a policy of *comparable worth*. Under this policy, wage scales are set such that women and men get equal pay for jobs that involve a similar level of difficulty and that require a similar level of training or education.[21]

Women gained a major victory in the workplace when Congress passed the Family and Medical Leave Act in 1993. It provides for up to twelve weeks of unpaid leave for employees to care for a new baby or a seriously ill family member. Upon return from leave, the employee ordinarily must be given the original or an equivalent job position with equivalent pay, benefits, and other employment terms. These provisions apply to men as well as women, but women were the instigating force behind the legislation and are its primary beneficiaries because they still bear the larger share of responsibility for sick and young family members.

Traditional practices are reflected in Americans' attitudes toward the role of women in society. Roughly two in five adults believe the ideal marriage is one where the wife stays home to take care of the house. This opinion is more prevalent in the United States than in Europe (see Figure 5-2), even though women's legal and employment gains in the United States have been at least as impressive as those in Europe.

Native Americans

When white settlers began arriving in America in large numbers during the seventeenth century, roughly 10 million Native Americans were living in the territory that would become the United States. By 1900, the Native American population had plummeted to less than one million. No people in human history suffered a steeper loss. Diseases brought by white settlers took the largest toll on the various Indian tribes, but wars and massacres contributed. "The only good

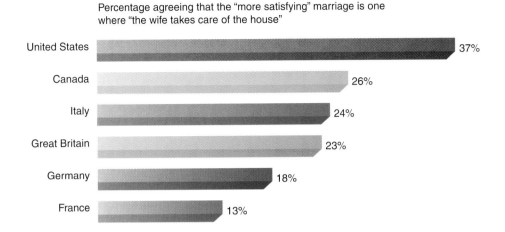

Percentage agreeing that the "more satisfying" marriage is one where "the wife takes care of the house"

United States	37%
Canada	26%
Italy	24%
Great Britain	23%
Germany	18%
France	13%

FIGURE 5-2 **Opinions on Women's Role in Marriage**
Americans are more likely than western Europeans to believe that the "more satisfying" marriage is one where "the wife takes care of the house and children" rather than one where "the husband and wife both have jobs."
Source: Global Attitudes Survey (2002) by the Pew Research Center for the People and the Press.

HISTORICAL
Background

Indian is a dead Indian" is not simply a hackneyed expression from cowboy movies. It was part of a strategy of westward expansion, as settlers and U.S. troops alike mercilessly drove the eastern Indians from their ancestral lands to the Great Plains and later seized most of these lands as well.

In recent years, Native Americans have filed suit to reclaim lost ancestral lands and have won a few settlements. But they stand no realistic chance of getting back even those lands that had been granted to them by federal treaty but later were sold off or seized forcibly by federal authorities. Native Americans were not even official citizens of the United States until passage of an act of Congress in 1924. Their citizenship status came too late to be of much help; their traditional way of life had already largely disappeared. The tragic consequences are still evident. Native Americans are less than half as likely to have completed college as other Americans, their life expectancy is more than ten years lower than the national average, their poverty rate is twice that of the national average, and their infant mortality rate is more than three times higher than that of white Americans.[22]

Today, full-blooded Native Americans, including Alaska Natives, number more than 2 million, about half of whom live on or close to reservations set aside for them by the federal government. Reservations are governed by treaties signed when they were established. State governments have no direct authority over federal reservations, and the federal government's authority is limited by the terms of a particular treaty. Although U.S. policy toward the reservations has varied over time, the current policy is to promote self-government and economic self-sufficiency.[23] Preservation of Native American cultures is also a policy goal. For example, Native American children can now be taught in their own languages; at an earlier time in schools run by the Bureau of Indian Affairs, children were required to use English. Nevertheless, Native American languages have declined sharply in use (see Figure 5-3). Of the larger tribes, the Navajo and Pueblo are the only ones where a majority of the people still speak the native language at home. Ninety percent or more of the Cherokee, Chippewa, Creek, Iroquois, and Lumbee speak only English.

The civil rights movement of the 1960s at first did not include Native Americans. Then, in the early 1970s, militant Native Americans occupied the Bureau of Indian Affairs in Washington, D.C., and later seized control of the village of Wounded Knee on a Sioux reservation in southwestern South Dakota, exchanging gunfire with U.S. marshals. These episodes highlighted the grievances of Native Americans and may have contributed to legislation that in 1974 granted Native Americans living on reservations greater control over

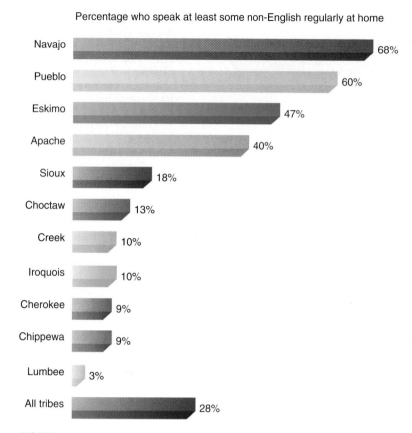

Percentage who speak at least some non-English regularly at home

Navajo — 68%
Pueblo — 60%
Eskimo — 47%
Apache — 40%
Sioux — 18%
Choctaw — 13%
Creek — 10%
Iroquois — 10%
Cherokee — 9%
Chippewa — 9%
Lumbee — 3%
All tribes — 28%

FIGURE 5-3 **Native American Language Use in the Home** The original languages of Native Americans are disappearing from use in their homes. English is now the only language in use by many Native Americans, though there is considerable variation by tribe.

Source: U.S. Census Bureau, 2008.

federal programs that affect them. Native Americans had already benefited from the legislative climate created by the 1960s civil rights movement: in 1968, Congress enacted the Indian Bill of Rights, which gives Native Americans on reservations constitutional guarantees similar to those given to other Americans.

In recent years, some tribes have erected gaming casinos on reservation land. The world's largest casino, Foxwoods, is operated by the Mashantunket Pequots in Connecticut. Casinos have brought opportunities to the Native Americans living on or near the affected reservations. Their employment in these areas has increased by a fourth, and their population has grown by more than 10 percent.[24] However, the casinos have also brought controversy—traditionalists argue that the casinos are creating a gaming culture that, whatever its economic benefits, has a perverse effect on the traditional culture. Ben Nighthorse Campbell, a Native American who served two terms before retiring from the U.S. Senate in 2003, worried that casinos were pitting "tribe against tribe," creating disputes over which tribes would be allowed to have casinos and at what price to tribal traditions. "It becomes much more difficult to find a solution when nobody wants to give," said Campbell.[25]

Hispanic Americans

The fastest-growing minority in the United States is Hispanic Americans, that is, people of Spanish-speaking background. Hispanics recently surpassed African Americans as the nation's largest racial or ethnic minority group. More than 35 million Hispanics live in the United States, an increase of 40 percent over the 1990 census. They have emigrated to the United States primarily from Mexico and the Caribbean islands, mainly Cuba and Puerto Rico. About half of all Hispanics in the United States were born in Mexico or claim a Mexican ancestry. Hispanics are concentrated in their states of entry; thus Florida, New York, and New Jersey have large numbers of Caribbean Hispanics, while California, Texas, Arizona, and New Mexico have many immigrants from Mexico. More than half the population of Los Angeles is of Hispanic—mostly Mexican—descent.

Legal and Political Action

Hispanic Americans have benefited from laws and court rulings aimed primarily at protecting other groups. Although the Civil Rights Act of 1964 was largely a response to the condition of black people, its provisions against discrimination apply broadly to other groups.

Nevertheless, Hispanics had their own civil rights movement. Its hallmark was the farmworkers' strikes of the late 1960s and the 1970s, which sought basic labor rights for migrant workers. Migrants were working long hours for low pay, were living in shacks without electricity or plumbing, and were unwelcome in many local schools as well as in some local hospitals. Farm owners at first refused to bargain with the workers, but a well-organized national boycott of California grapes and lettuce forced that state to pass a law giving migrant workers the right to bargain collectively. The strikes were led in California by Cesar Chavez, who himself grew up in a Mexican American migrant family. Chavez's tactics were copied with less success in other states, including Texas.

The Hispanic civil rights movement also pursued social and political goals. Hispanics had some success, for example, in pressuring federal, state, and local governments to expand bilingual education programs. They also persuaded Congress to require states to provide bilingual ballots in local areas with a sizable number of non-English-speaking residents.

LEADERS

CESAR ESTRADA CHAVEZ
(1927–93)

Cesar Chavez led the first successful farmworkers' strike in U.S. history. Founder of the United Farm Workers of America, Chavez was called "one of the heroic figures of our time" by Robert F. Kennedy and is widely regarded as the most influential Latino leader in modern U.S. history. A migrant worker as a child, Chavez knew firsthand the deprivations suffered by farm laborers. Like Martin Luther King Jr., Chavez was an advocate of nonviolent protest, and he organized food boycotts that eventually caused agricultural firms to improve wages and working conditions for farmworkers. In 1994, Chavez was posthumously awarded the Presidential Medal of Freedom, the highest civilian honor an American can receive.

Hispanics are one of the nation's oldest ethnic groups. Some Hispanics are the descendants of people who helped colonize California, Texas, Florida, New Mexico, and Arizona before those areas were annexed by the United States. However, most Hispanics are recent immigrants or their descendants. A significant number—more than 10 million by some estimates—are in the United States illegally. In past eras, immigration officials could more easily control newcomers because most of them arrived by ship through a port of entry, such as Ellis Island. But most Hispanics have arrived by land, many of them crossing illegally from Mexico. U.S. authorities have had only limited success in stopping this influx. Most of the illegal aliens have come to America seeking jobs, and they now make up an estimated 5 percent of the U.S. workforce. They have had broad support in the Hispanic community, which has sought to ease immigration restrictions and to expand the rights and privileges of illegal aliens—positions that are unpopular with some other Americans.

In 2005, Republican lawmakers pushed a bill through the House of Representatives that would have cracked down sharply on illegal immigrants. The Hispanic community responded with huge protest rallies—ones reminiscent of the 1960s civil rights movement. The rally in Los Angeles drew an estimated half million marchers, reputedly the largest such gathering in the city's history. The scale of the rallies caught even seasoned political observers by surprise. It was by far the largest demonstration ever of Hispanic political solidarity and helped prompt the Senate to kill the legislation.

In 2007, President George W. Bush and a bipartisan congressional coalition, including most of the Senate and House leadership, developed a comprehensive immigration reform bill that contained a provision for guest workers. Under the plan, workers who are in the United States illegally could enroll in the program, which would allow them to work in the country for up to six years. Other noncitizens could enter the United States as guest workers if they had a job waiting for them. The proposal was intended to address the nation's labor needs while simultaneously reducing illegal immigration by increasing border surveillance

When Congress in 2006 seemed on the verge of enacting legislation that would crack down on illegal immigrants, most of whom are from Mexico, pro-immigrant rallies were held in nearly every American city with a sizable Hispanic population. The rally in Los Angeles was the largest in the city's history. Even in locations more distant from Mexico, the rallies were large and enthusiastic. The scene here is of the rally in Lincoln, Nebraska, where the flags of the United States and Mexico were readily visible.

and by raising penalties on employers who hire undocumented aliens. The plan had support from the business community and was backed by most congressional Democrats. However, the plan failed to get the support of most congressional Republicans and was defeated. Opponents insisted, as preconditions for considering any type of guest worker program, that U.S. borders first be secured against illegal entry, that current laws against hiring illegal aliens be enforced rigorously, and that illegal residents be identified and deported.

The split within Congress reflects public opinion on the issue. Polls indicate that most Americans believe stricter restrictions should be placed on immigration, including tightening the borders and penalizing employers who hire illegal immigrants. However, there is no consensus on how to handle the illegal immigrants already in the country. Most Americans favor some path to citizenship for these individuals, provided they meet certain conditions, including holding a job and having no criminal record. A substantial minority, however, want to deport all illegal immigrants and are dead set against any policy that would place them near the front of the line for citizenship. These divisions of opinion have made it difficult to build a congressional majority in support of a specific immigration policy. One thing is certain: the immigration issue is not going away. Each year, an estimated half-million illegal immigrants enter the United States, adding to the pressure on government to act.

Growing Political Power

More than four thousand Hispanic Americans nationwide hold public office. Hispanics have been elected to statewide office in several states, including New Mexico and Arizona. About twenty Hispanic Americans currently serve in the House of Representatives.

Hispanic Americans are a growing political force. By the middle of the century, Hispanics are projected to become the largest racial or ethnic group in California. Their political involvement, like that of other immigrant groups, will increase as they become more firmly rooted in society. At present, about half of all Hispanics are not registered to vote, and only about a third actually vote, limiting the group's political power. Nevertheless, the sheer size of the Hispanic population in states such as Texas and California makes the group a potent force, as was evident in the 2008 election when both the Republicans and the Democrats mounted massive efforts to woo Hispanic voters.

With the exception of the conservative Republican-leaning Cuban Americans of southern Florida, Hispanics lean toward the Democratic Party. This tendency has intensified since congressional Republicans attempted to tighten immigration laws. Hispanics who regard themselves as Democrats outnumber those who consider themselves as Republicans by more than two to one (see Figure 5-4). Polls indicated that nearly 70 percent of Hispanics voted Democratic in the 2006 congressional races, a 10 percent increase from the 2004 level. Democrats also carried the Hispanic vote by a wide margin in the 2008 election. However, compared with African Americans, Hispanics are a less cohesive voting bloc. Whereas blacks of all income levels are solidly Democratic, lower-income Hispanics vote Democratic at substantially higher rates than upper-income Hispanics. Opinion surveys show that Hispanics tend to be relatively liberal on economic issues and relatively conservative on social issues. These tendencies suggest that Hispanics will lean Democratic in the near future but divide more evenly between the parties as their income rises.[26]

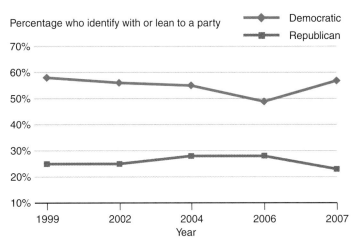

FIGURE 5-4 **Hispanics' Party Identification** Hispanics' party loyalties lean heavily toward the Democratic Party. This tendency increased in 2007 after congressional Republicans attempted to enact tough legislation for dealing with illegal immigrants, most of whom are Hispanic. Source: Pew Hispanic Center, 2002, 2006, 2007; National Survey of Latinos, 2004; Washington Post/Kaiser Family Foundation/Harvard University survey, 1999.

Asian Americans

Chinese and Japanese laborers were brought to the western states during the late 1800s to work in mines and to build railroads. When the need for this labor declined, Congress in 1892 ordered a temporary halt to Asian immigration. Over the next three decades, informal agreements kept all but a few Asians from entering the country. In 1930, Congress completely blocked the entry of Japanese. Japan had protested a California law that prohibited persons of Japanese descent from buying property in the state. Rather than trying to finesse what was called "the California problem," Congress bluntly told Japan that its people were not wanted in the United States.[27]

Discrimination against Asians did not ease substantially until 1965, when Congress enacted legislation that adjusted the immigration quotas to favor those who had previously been assigned very small numbers. This change in the law was a product of the 1960s civil rights movement, which increased public awareness of all forms of discrimination. Asian Americans now number about 12 million, or roughly 4 percent of the total U.S. population. Most Asian Americans live on the West Coast, particularly in California. China, Japan, Korea, India, Vietnam, and the Philippines are the ancestral homes of most Asian Americans.

The rights of Asian Americans have been expanded primarily by court rulings and legislation, such as the Civil Rights Act of 1964, that were initiated in response to pressure from other minority groups. However, in *Lau v. Nichols* (1974), a case initiated by a Chinese American family, the Supreme Court ruled unanimously that placing public school children for whom English is a second language in regular classrooms without special assistance is a violation of the Fourteenth Amendment's equal-protection clause, because it denies them an equal educational opportunity.[28] The Court did not mandate bilingual instruction,

Chinese workers were brought to the United States in the late 1800s to work on the railroads and in the mines, but when the need for their labor diminished, they were discouraged from staying in America. Immigration policies that discriminated against Asians lasted until the 1960s.

but the *Lau* decision prompted many schools to establish bilingual instruction. Since then, some states have restricted its use. For example, California's Proposition 227, enacted in 1998, requires most children for whom English is a second language to take their courses in English after their first year in school.

Asian Americans are an upwardly mobile group. Most Asian cultures emphasize family-based self-reliance, which, in the American context, includes an emphasis on academic achievement. For example, Asians make up a disproportionate share of the students at California's leading public universities, which base admission primarily on high school grades and standardized test scores. However, Asian Americans are still underrepresented in certain areas of the workplace. According to U.S. government figures, Asian Americans account for about 5 percent of professionals and technicians, slightly more than their percentage of the total population. Yet past and present discrimination has kept them from obtaining a proportionate share of top business positions—they hold less than 2 percent of managerial jobs. They are also underrepresented politically, even by comparison with Hispanics and blacks.[29] Not until 1996 was an Asian American elected governor of a state other than Hawaii, and not until 2000 did an Asian American hold a presidential cabinet position.

Other Groups and Their Rights

The 1964 Civil Rights Act (discussed further later in the chapter) prohibits discrimination by sex, race, or national origin. This act classified women and racial and ethnic minorities as legally protected groups, enabling them to pursue their rights in court. As these minority groups gained success, other disadvantaged groups began to press their claims.

Older Americans

Older Americans are one such group. The Age Discrimination Act of 1975 and the Age Discrimination in Employment Act of 1967 prohibit discrimination against older workers in hiring for jobs in which age is not clearly a crucial factor in job performance. More recently, mandatory retirement ages for most jobs have been eliminated by law.

However, forced retirement for reasons of age is permissible if it is justified by the nature of a particular job or by the performance of a particular employee. Commercial airline pilots, for example, are required by law to retire at sixty-five years of age and must pass a rigorous physical examination to continue flying after they reach sixty years of age. As the example suggests, older Americans are not as fully protected by law as women and minority-group members are. Age discrimination is not among the forms of discrimination prohibited by the U.S. Constitution, and the courts have given government and employers leeway in setting their age-based policies.[30]

Disabled Americans

Roughly 40 million Americans have a physical or mental disability, such as difficulty in seeing, hearing, or walking. In an effort to give them greater access to society's opportunities, Congress passed the Americans with Disabilities Act in 1990. The legislation grants employment and other protections to the disabled. Earlier, through the Education for All Handicapped Children Act of 1975, Congress required that schools provide all children, however severe their disability, with a free, appropriate education. Before the legislation, 4 million children with disabilities were getting either no education or an inappropriate one (as in the case of a blind child who is not taught Braille). The Supreme Court has also granted protection to the disabled, ruling, for example, that state governments must take reasonable steps, such as adding access ramps to government buildings, to make public services and facilities available to the disabled.[31]

Although the disabled have substantial legal protections, they, like the elderly, are not a constitutionally protected group. Accordingly, actions that have the effect of discriminating against the disabled are in some cases legal. For example, a business is not required to provide free home delivery when a buyer is disabled and unable to transport a purchased item.

Gays and Lesbians

Gays and lesbians have historically been the object of hostility and discrimination. Until recently, they usually responded by hiding their sexual orientation. Some still do so, but many gays and lesbians now openly pursue a claim to equal protection under the law.[32]

Gays and lesbians gained a significant legal victory when the Supreme Court in *Romer v. Evans* (1996) struck down a Colorado constitutional amendment that nullified all existing and any new legal protections for homosexuals. In a 6-3 ruling, the Court said that the Colorado law violated the Constitution's guarantee of equal protection because it subjected individuals to employment and other discrimination simply because of their sexual preference. The Court concluded that the law had no reasonable purpose but was instead motivated by hostility toward homosexuals.[33] In *Lawrence v. Texas* (2003), the Court handed gays and lesbians another victory by invalidating state laws that prohibited sexual relations between consenting adults of the same sex (see Chapter 4).[34]

These gains have been partially offset by setbacks. In 2000, for example, the Supreme Court held that the Boy Scouts, as a private organization that has a right to free association, can ban gays because the Scout creed forbids homosexuality.[35] Gays and lesbians who are open about their sexual preference are also barred from serving in the military. However, they can serve under the military's

DEBATING THE
ISSUES

SHOULD SAME-SEX MARRIAGE BE LEGALIZED?

Nearly a decade ago, Vermont became the first state to authorize civil unions for same-sex couples, giving them many of the same legal rights of inheritance, spousal benefits, and so on as married couples. The Vermont law generated national controversy, and polls at the time indicated that most Americans opposed civil unions. Since then, a few other states have followed Vermont's example, and polls now show that most Americans favor civil unions.

Same-sex marriage is a different story. Polls indicate that most Americans oppose same-sex marriage, and more than half the states have had ballot initiatives permanently banning such marriages. The issue came to national attention when Massachusetts in 2004 became the first state to allow same-sex marriage. This development occurred through judicial action rather than through legislative action or a ballot initiative. The Massachusetts Supreme Judicial Court declared that the state's constitution requires that same-sex couples be given the same opportunity to marry as opposite-sex couples. The court ordered the state legislature to enact a law to that effect within six months. The ruling produced strong reactions on both sides of the issue throughout the country. Here are two of the ensuing statements, one by a leader in the fight for same-sex marriage and an opposing one by the U.S. Conference of Catholic Bishops. Which position is closest to your own? Do you take a similar position on the issue of civil unions?

YES
The Massachusetts Supreme Judicial Court ruled that the rights, protections, and responsibilities afforded by civil marriage should not be denied to any resident of that state. It is a great victory for the seven couples represented by the Gay & Lesbian Advocates & Defenders, for every gay and lesbian couple in Massachusetts—and for all fair-minded people who believe every American deserves equal treatment under the law. The opening statement of the court's decision says it all: "The exclusive commitment of two individuals to each other nurtures love and mutual support; it brings stability to our society." This decision affirms the inherent value and social benefit that committed, loving relationships between gay and lesbian people bring to society at large—and utterly dismisses the claims made by the anti-gay industry that granting basic protections and rights to same-sex families somehow threatens the fabric of our society. My partner of 22 years and I have experienced firsthand the benefits a loving, mutually supportive relationship has had on our three children. It's gratifying to see the Massachusetts court acknowledge relationships like ours—and we look forward to a day when every state recognizes the benefit of treating relationships like ours equally under the law.

—Joan Garry, executive director, Gay and Lesbian Alliance Against Defamation

NO
Across times, cultures, and very different religious beliefs, marriage is the foundation of the family. The family, in turn, is the basic unit of society. Thus, marriage is a personal relationship with public significance. Marriage is the fundamental pattern for male-female relationships. It contributes to society because it models the way in which women and men live interdependently and commit, for the whole of life, to seek the good of each other. The marital union also provides the best conditions for raising children: namely, the stable, loving relationship of a mother and father present only in marriage. The state rightly recognizes this relationship as a public institution in its laws because the relationship makes a unique and essential contribution to the common good. Laws play an education role insofar as they shape patterns of thought and behavior, particularly about what is socially permissible and acceptable. . . . When marriage is redefined so as to make other relationships equivalent to it, the institution of marriage is devalued and further weakened. The weakening of this basic institution at all levels and by various forces has already exacted too high a social cost.

—U.S. Conference of Catholic Bishops

"don't ask, don't tell" (sometimes called the "don't harass, don't pursue") policy. As long as they do not by words or actions reveal their sexual preference, they are allowed to enlist and stay in the service. In turn, soldiers are instructed not to inquire about other soldiers' sexual orientation, nor are they to try to entrap those they suspect of being gay or lesbian. The courts have upheld the military's ban, citing the unusually close physical proximity with minimal privacy that occurs in the military.

Gay and lesbian couples are currently seeking the same legal status that the law extends to opposite-sex married couples. During the past decade, same-sex couples have succeeded in getting some states, cities, and firms to extend employee benefits, such as health insurance, to their employees' same-sex partners. These arrangements, however, do not extend to things such as inheritance and hospital visitation rights, which are reserved by state law for married couples and their families. In 2000, Vermont became the first state to legalize the civil union of same-sex couples, thereby granting them the same legal rights as those held by opposite-sex married couples. In 2004, upon order of the state's high court, Massachusetts gave same-sex couples the right to marry, becoming the first state to do so. In 2008, California's Supreme Court overturned that state's ban on same-sex marriage, a decision that was challenged by a ballot initiative to amend the state's constitution to prohibit such unions. California voters approved the ban, which led same-sex marriage proponents to file a lawsuit challenging the ballot initiative.

The claim that gay and lesbian couples should have the same legal rights as opposite-sex married couples has been hotly contested. Even before Vermont authorized same-sex unions, Congress passed the Defense of Marriage Act, which defines marriage as "a legal union of one man and one woman as husband and wife." This 1996 law authorizes states to deny marital rights to a same-sex couple that has been granted these rights by another state. Under the U.S. Constitution's "full faith and credit clause," states are required to recognize the laws and contracts of other states, although Congress can create exceptions, as it did with the Defense of Marriage Act.

Social conservatives have sponsored ballot initiatives like the one in California to ban same-sex marriage. In the two dozen or so states where the issue has been on the ballot, the voters in nearly every case have enacted the ban, usually by a wide margin. Americans, perhaps because of their deeper religious beliefs (see Chapter 6), are less supportive of gay and lesbian lifestyles than are Europeans (see Figure 5-5).

Nevertheless, Americans have become more accepting of gay and lesbian relationships. Connecticut and a half dozen other states have recently extended substantial legal rights to same-sex couples, and support for civil unions has increased to the point where a near majority now say they favor them. A 2008 ABC/Washington Post poll, for example, found that Americans were almost evenly split on support for and opposition to civil unions, with only 3 percent undecided about the policy. For its part, Congress has not taken the issue of same-sex unions beyond the Defense of Marriage Act. An attempt by congressional conservatives in 2006 to initiate a constitutional amendment to ban same-sex marriage fell far short of the requisite two-thirds vote in the House

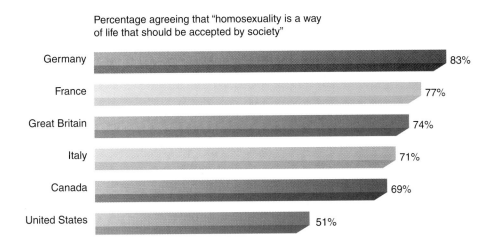

Percentage agreeing that "homosexuality is a way of life that should be accepted by society"

Germany	83%
France	77%
Great Britain	74%
Italy	71%
Canada	69%
United States	51%

FIGURE 5-5   Opinions on Gay and Lesbian Lifestyles
Americans are less likely than western Europeans to believe that society should accept gay and lesbian lifestyles.
Source: Global Attitudes Survey (2002) by the Pew Research Center for the People and the Press.

and Senate. One thing is sure: issues of gay and lesbian rights, including same-sex marriage and civil union, will be sources of political controversy for the foreseeable future.

Equality Under the Law

The catchphrase of nearly every group's claim to a more equal standing in American society has been "equality under the law." When secure in their legal rights, people are positioned to pursue equality in other arenas, such as the economic sector. Americans' claim to legal equality is embodied in a great many laws, a few of which are particularly noteworthy.

Equal Protection: The Fourteenth Amendment

equal-protection clause

A clause of the Fourteenth Amendment that forbids any state to deny equal protection of the laws to any individual within its jurisdiction.

The Fourteenth Amendment, which was ratified in 1868, declares in part that no state shall "deny to any person within its jurisdiction the equal protection of the laws." Through this **equal-protection clause**, the courts have protected groups such as African Americans and women from discrimination by state and local governments.

reasonable-basis test

A test applied by courts to laws that treat individuals unequally. Such a law may be deemed constitutional if its purpose is held to be "reasonably" related to a legitimate government interest.

The Fourteenth Amendment's equal-protection clause does not require government to treat all groups or classes of people the same way in all circumstances. The judiciary allows inequalities that are "reasonably" related to a legitimate government interest. In applying this **reasonable-basis test,** the courts require government only to show that a particular law is reasonable. For example, twenty-one-year-olds can legally drink alcohol but twenty-year-olds cannot. The courts have held that the goal of reducing fatalities from alcohol-related accidents involving young drivers is a valid reason for imposing an age limit on the purchase and consumption of alcohol.

strict-scrutiny test

A test applied by courts to laws that attempt a racial or ethnic classification. In effect, the strict-scrutiny test eliminates race or ethnicity as a legal classification when it places minority-group members at a disadvantage.

The reasonable-basis test does not apply to racial or ethnic classifications (see Table 5-1). Any law that treats people differently because of race or ethnicity is subject to the **strict-scrutiny test,** under which such a law is presumed unconstitutional unless government can provide overwhelming evidence of its necessity. The strict-scrutiny test has virtually eliminated race and ethnicity as permissible classifications when the effect is to place a hardship on members of a racial or ethnic minority. The Supreme Court's position is that race and national origin are **suspect classifications**—in other words, that legal classifications based on race and ethnicity are presumed to have discrimination as their purpose.

suspect classifications

Legal classifications, such as race and national origin, that have invidious discrimination as their purpose and therefore are unconstitutional.

The strict-scrutiny test emerged after the 1954 *Brown v. Board of Education of Topeka* ruling and became a basis for invalidating laws that discriminated against

TABLE 5-1 | Levels of Court Review for Laws That Treat Americans Differently

Test	Applies To	Standard Used
Strict scrutiny	Race, ethnicity	Suspect category—assumed unconstitutional in the absence of an overwhelming justification
Intermediate scrutiny	Gender	Almost suspect category—assumed unconstitutional unless the law serves a clearly compelling and justified purpose
Reasonable basis	Other categories (such as age and income)	Not suspect category—assumed constitutional unless no sound rationale for the law can be provided

black Americans. As other groups, especially women, began to assert their rights more vigorously in the late 1960s and early 1970s, the Supreme Court gave early signs that it might expand the scope of suspect classifications to include gender. In the end, however, the Court announced in *Craig v. Boren* (1976) that sex classifications were permissible if they served "important governmental objectives" and were "substantially" related to the achievement of those objectives.[36] The Court thus placed sex distinctions in an intermediate (or almost suspect) category, to be scrutinized more closely than some other classifications (for example, income or age level) but, unlike racial classifications, justifiable in some instances. In *Rostker v. Goldberg* (1980), for example, the policy of male-only registration for the military draft was upheld on grounds that the exclusion of women from involuntary combat duty serves a legitimate and important purpose.[37]

Although women are excluded by law from having to register for the draft, they are eligible to enlist voluntarily in the U.S. military. Shown here is a U.S. woman soldier controlling the crowd on the streets of Mosul, Iraq. Roughly 2 percent of American military casualties in the Iraq conflict have been women.

Nevertheless, rather than giving the government broad leeway to treat men and women differently, the Supreme Court has struck down most of the laws it has recently reviewed that contain sex classifications. A leading case is *United States v. Virginia* (1996), in which the Supreme Court determined that the male-only admissions policy of Virginia Military Institute (VMI), a 157-year-old state-supported college, was unconstitutional. The state had developed an alternative program for women at another college, but the Court concluded that it was no substitute for VMI's unique educational program. (The VMI decision also had the effect of ending the all-male admissions policy of the Citadel, a state-supported military college in South Carolina.)[38]

Equal Access: The Civil Rights Acts of 1964 and 1968

The Fourteenth Amendment prohibits discrimination by government but not by private parties. As a result, for a long period in American history, owners could legally bar black people from restaurants, hotels, and other accommodations, and employers could freely discriminate in their job-hiring practices. Since the 1960s, however, private parties have had much less freedom to discriminate for reasons of race, sex, ethnicity, or religion.

Accommodations and Jobs

The Civil Rights Act of 1964, which is based on Congress's power to regulate commerce, entitles all persons to equal access to restaurants, bars, theaters, hotels, gasoline stations, and similar establishments serving the general public. The legislation also bars discrimination in the hiring, promotion, and wages of employees of medium-size and large firms. A few forms of job discrimination are still lawful under the Civil Rights Act. For example, an owner-operator of a small business can discriminate in hiring his or her co-workers, and a parochial school can take the religion of a prospective teacher into account.

The Civil Rights Act of 1964 has nearly eliminated the most overt forms of discrimination in the area of public accommodations. Some restaurants and hotels may provide better service to white customers, but outright refusal to serve African Americans or other minority-group members is rare. Such a refusal is a violation of the law and could easily be proved in many instances. It is harder to prove discrimination in job decisions; accordingly, the act has been less effective in rooting out employment discrimination—a subject discussed later in this chapter.

Housing

In 1968, Congress passed civil rights legislation designed to prohibit discrimination in housing. A building owner cannot refuse to sell or rent housing because of a person's race, religion, ethnicity, or sex. An exception is allowed for owners of small multifamily dwellings who reside on the premises.

Despite legal prohibitions on discrimination, housing in America remains highly segregated. Only a third of African Americans live in a neighborhood that is mostly white. One reason is that the annual income of most black families is substantially below that of most white families. Another reason is banking practices. At one time, banks contributed to housing segregation by *redlining*—refusing to grant mortgage loans in certain neighborhoods. This practice drove down the selling prices of homes in these neighborhoods, which led to an influx of African Americans and an exodus of whites. Redlining is prohibited by the 1968 Civil Rights Act, but many of the segregated neighborhoods that it helped create still exist. Studies indicate that minority status is still a factor in the lending practices of some banks. A report of the U.S. Conference of Mayors indicated that, among applicants with average or slightly higher incomes relative to their community, Hispanics and African Americans were about twice as likely as whites to be denied a mortgage.[39]

Equal Ballots: The Voting Rights Act of 1965, as Amended

Free elections are the bedrock of American democracy, yet the right to vote has only recently become a reality for many Americans, particularly African Americans. Although they appeared to have gained that right in 1870 with ratification of the Fifteenth Amendment, southern whites invented a series of devices, including whites-only primaries, poll taxes, and rigged literacy tests, to keep blacks from registering and voting. For example, almost no votes were cast by African Americans in North Carolina between the years 1920 and 1946.[40]

Racial barriers to voting began to crumble in the mid-1940s when the Supreme Court declared that whites-only primary elections were unconstitutional.[41] Two decades later, the Twenty-fourth Amendment outlawed poll taxes. However, the major step toward equal participation by African Americans was passage of the Voting Rights Act of 1965, which forbids discrimination in voting and registration. The legislation empowers federal agents to register voters and to oversee participation in elections. The Voting Rights Act, as interpreted by the courts, also prohibits the use of literacy tests as a registration requirement. The Voting Rights Act had a clear impact on black participation. In the next presidential election, black turnout in the South increased by nearly 20 percent from its previous level.

Congress has renewed the Voting Rights Act several times, most recently in 2006. The act includes a provision that compels states and localities to clear with federal officials any electoral change that has the effect, intended or not, of reducing the voting power of a minority group. One way to reduce the power of a group's votes is to spread members of the group across election districts so that their number in any given district is too small to constitute a voting majority. That situation was at issue in *League of United Latin American Voters v. Perry* (2006), a case involving Texas's 23rd congressional district, the boundaries of which were drawn in a way that deliberately diluted the power of Hispanic voters. In ordering the state of Texas to redraw the district, the Court said, "The troubling blend of politics and race—and the resulting vote dilution of a group that was beginning to [overcome] prior electoral discrimination—cannot be sustained."[42]

On the other hand, the Court has held that an election district cannot be intentionally shaped to allow a minority group to control it. In three separate cases that were each decided by a 5-4 margin, the Supreme Court ruled that the redistricting of several congressional districts in Texas, North Carolina, and Georgia violated the Fourteenth Amendment because race had been the "dominant" consideration in their creation. The Court held that the redistricting violated the equal-protection rights of white voters and ordered the three states to redraw the districts.[43] However, the Court does permit states to create districts that are dominated by a minority group if the district's boundaries were established for partisan reasons rather than racial or ethnic ones. This ruling came in *Easley v. Cromartie* (2001). At issue was a North Carolina district that was drawn with the goal of creating a safe Democratic district, which resulted in a district with a large proportion of black voters. The Court, which has long allowed partisan redistricting, ruled that if such redistricting incidentally creates a minority-dominated district, as in this case, the action does not violate the Fourteenth Amendment.[44]

Equality of Result

America's disadvantaged groups have made significant progress toward equal rights, particularly during the past few decades. Through acts of Congress and rulings of the Supreme Court, most forms of government-sponsored discrimination—from racially segregated public schools to gender-based pension plans—have been banned. Nevertheless, civil rights problems involve deeply rooted conditions, habits, and prejudices and affect whole categories of people. For these reasons, a new civil rights law rarely produces a sudden and dramatic change in society.

Thus, despite their legal gains, America's traditionally disadvantaged groups are still substantially unequal in their daily lives. The average Hispanic or African American family's annual income, for example, is only about 60 percent of the average non-Hispanic white family's income (see Figure 5-6). Such disparities reflect **de facto discrimination,** discrimination that is a consequence of social, economic, and cultural biases and conditions. This type of discrimination is different from **de jure discrimination,** which is discrimination based on law, as in the case of the state laws that forced black and white children to attend separate schools during the pre-*Brown* period. De facto discrimination is the more difficult type to root out because it is embedded in the structure of society.

Equality of result is the aim of policies intended to reduce de facto discriminatory effects. Such policies are inherently controversial because many Americans believe that government's responsibility extends no further than the removal of legal barriers to equality. This attitude reflects the culture's emphasis on personal *liberty*—the freedom to choose one's associates, employees, neighbors, and classmates. Nevertheless, a few policies—notably affirmative action and busing—have addressed the problem of de facto inequality.

de facto discrimination

Discrimination on the basis of race, sex, religion, ethnicity, and the like that results from social, economic, and cultural biases and conditions.

de jure discrimination

Discrimination on the basis of race, sex, religion, ethnicity, and the like that results from a law.

equality of result

The objective of policies intended to reduce or eliminate the effects of discrimination so that members of traditionally disadvantaged groups will have the same benefits of society as do members of advantaged groups.

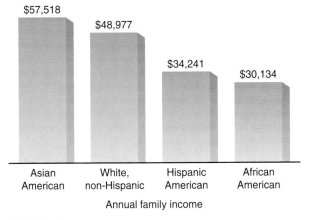

FIGURE 5-6   **U.S. Family Income, by Race and Ethnicity**
The median family income of non-Hispanic whites is substantially higher than that of Hispanics or blacks.
Source: U.S. Bureau of the Census, 2008.

Affirmative Action: Workplace Integration

The difficulty of converting newly acquired legal rights into everyday realities is illustrated by the 1964 Civil Rights Act. Although the legislation prohibited discrimination in employment, women and minorities did not suddenly obtain jobs for which they were qualified. Many employers continued to favor white male employees. Other employers adhered to established employment procedures that kept women and minorities at a disadvantage; membership in many union locals, for example, was handed down from father to son. Moreover, the Civil Rights Act did not require employers to prove that their hiring practices were unbiased. Instead, the burden of proof was on the woman or minority-group member who had been denied a particular job. It was costly and often difficult for individuals to prove in court that their sex or race was the major reason they had not been hired. In addition, a victory in court applied only to the individual in question; it did not help the millions of other women and minorities facing job discrimination.

A broader remedy was obviously required, and the result was the emergence during the late 1960s of affirmative action programs. **Affirmative action** refers to deliberate efforts to provide full and equal opportunities in employment, education, and other areas for members of traditionally disadvantaged groups. Affirmative action requires corporations, universities, and other organizations to establish programs designed to ensure that all applicants are treated fairly. Affirmative action also places a burden of proof on the providers of opportunities, who must demonstrate that any disproportionate granting of opportunities to white males is the result of necessity (such as the nature of the job or the locally available labor pool) and not the result of systematic discrimination against women or minorities.

Few issues in recent decades have sparked more controversy than has affirmative action, a reflection of the public's ambivalence about the policy.[45] The majority of Americans say they *favor* programs that give women and minorities *equal treatment* when applying for jobs, college admission, and the like. The majority also say, however, that they *oppose* programs that would give them *preferential treatment* (see Figure 5-7).

affirmative action

A term that refers to programs designed to ensure that women, minorities, and other traditionally disadvantaged groups have full and equal opportunities in employment, education, and other areas of life.

FIGURE 5-7 Opinions on **Affirmative Action**
Most Americans support affirmative action when it comes to programs that will give women and minorities an equal chance at opportunities but oppose it when it comes to programs that will give them preferential treatment.
Source: The Pew Research Center for the People and the Press, March 22, 2007.

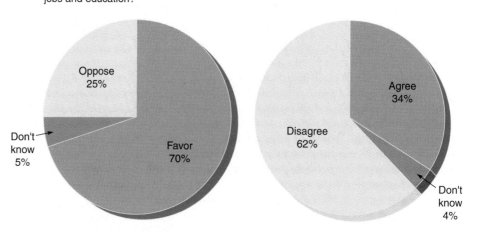

"In order to overcome past discrimination, do you favor or oppose affirmative action programs designed to help blacks, women, and other minorities get better jobs and education?"

Oppose 25%
Don't know 5%
Favor 70%

"We should make every possible effort to improve the position of blacks and other minorities, even if it means giving them preferential treatment."

Agree 34%
Disagree 62%
Don't know 4%

TABLE 5-2 | Key Decisions in the History of Affirmative Action Policy

Year	Action
1969	Nixon administration's Department of Labor initiates affirmative action policy
1978	Supreme Court in *Bakke* invalidates rigid quotas for medical school admissions but does not invalidate affirmative action
1980	Supreme Court in *Fullilove* upholds a quota system for minority-owned firms in granting of federal contracts
1980s	Supreme Court in a series of decisions narrows situations in which preferential treatment of minorities will be permitted
1995	Supreme Court in *Adarand* eliminates fixed quotas in the granting of government contracts, reversing the *Fullilove* (1980) precedent
2003	Supreme Court in *Gratz v. Bollinger* and *Grutter v. Bollinger* upholds affirmative action but invalidates formula-based (quota-like) programs

Affirmative Action in the Law

Issues that pit individuals against each other often end up in the courts, and affirmative action is no exception (see Table 5-2). The policy was first tested before the Supreme Court in *University of California Regents v. Bakke* (1978). Alan Bakke, a white man, was denied admission to a medical school that on the basis of a race-based quota system had admitted several minority-group applicants with lower admission test scores. Bakke sued, and the Supreme Court ruled in his favor without invalidating the principle of affirmative action. The Court held that quotas were unconstitutional but said that race could be among the factors taken into account in schools' efforts to create a diverse student body.[46] The *Bakke* ruling was followed by a decision that affirmed the use of quotas in a different context. In *Fullilove v. Klutznick* (1980), the Court upheld a congressional spending bill that included the requirement that 10 percent of federal funding for building projects be awarded to minority-owned firms.[47]

These rulings strengthened affirmative action as national policy. However, the appointment of more conservative judges to the Supreme Court during the 1980s narrowed the policy's scope. In 1986, for example, the Court held that preferential treatment for minorities could be justified only in cases of severe discrimination and only when the action did not infringe on white workers' employment rights (for example, if a labor contract specified that seniority would detemine which employees to lay off in the case of job cuts, more-senior white workers could not be laid off in order to enable less-senior minority workers to keep their jobs).[48]

A more substantial blow to affirmative action policy was a 1995 decision, *Adarand v. Pena*. The case arose when Adarand Constructors filed suit over a federal contract that was awarded to a Hispanic-owned company even though Adarand had submitted a lower bid. The Court ruled in Adarand's favor, thereby reversing the *Fullilove* precedent. The Court outlawed rules (such as the 10 percent set-aside of government contracts for minority-owned firms) that give firms an advantage simply because the owners' race is that of a people who have been discriminated against historically. The Court also held that, even in situations where a particular firm has been harmed by discrimination, the remedy must be "narrowly tailored" to the situation—that is, the remedy must be in proportion to the harm done to the firm.[49] *Adarand* marked the end of an era. By holding that affirmative action must be designed to rectify specific acts of discrimination, the Court effectively brought a halt to federal contracts that gave preference to

The University of Michigan was the focus of national attention in 2003 as a result of its affirmative action admissions programs. Shown here are demonstrators from both sides of the issue. In its 2003 ruling, the Supreme Court upheld the use of race as a factor in admissions but rejected the use of a "point system" as the method of applying it.

applicants on the basis of race or gender. The Court had earlier halted such contracts at the state and local government levels.

Both advocates and opponents of affirmative action wondered whether race- and gender-based college admission programs would be the next ones struck down by the Supreme Court. In 2003, in what many observers saw as the most important affirmative action ruling since the *Bakke* decision three decades earlier, the Court made its position known. At issue were two University of Michigan affirmative action admission policies: Michigan's point system for undergraduate admission, which granted 20 points (out of a total of 150 possible points) to minority applicants, and its law school admission process, in which race (along with other factors such as work experience and extracurricular activities) was taken into account in admission decisions. The case attracted national attention, including the involvement of major U.S. corporations, which argued that programs such as those at the University of Michigan contributed to their goal of finding well-educated minorities to fill managerial positions.

Opponents of affirmative action hoped that the Court would strike down the Michigan policies, effectively ending the use of race as a factor in college admissions. Indeed, by a 6-3 vote in *Gratz v. Bollinger*, the Supreme Court did strike down Michigan's undergraduate admissions policy because its point system assigned a specific weight to race.[50] However, by a 5-4 vote in *Grutter v. Bollinger*, the Court upheld the law school's program, concluding that it was being applied in a limited and sensible manner and promoted Michigan's "compelling interest in obtaining the educational benefits that flow from a diverse student body." In writing for the majority, Justice Sandra Day O'Connor said further that the law school's policy "promotes 'cross-racial understanding,' helps to break down racial stereotypes, and enables [a] better understand[ing of] persons of different races."[51]

Thus, affirmative action remains a part of national education policy. Both sides of the issue recognize, however, that the Supreme Court's narrow 5-4 majority in the 2003 case means that the controversy is not fully settled. Attempts to address the issue of equal opportunity for people of all backgrounds in unique ways have also provoked controversy. An example is a Texas policy on college admissions. Recognizing the disparity in the quality of its public schools and other factors that result in lower average scores on standardized tests for minorities, the state established a policy that guarantees admission at a University of Texas institution to any Texas high school student who graduates in the top 10 percent of his or her class. This approach initially faced little opposition even from critics of affirmative action, but opposition has increased as a result of growing enrollment pressure at Texas's flagship universities and the widening perception that students at weaker high schools have an unfair advantage. The fact is, almost every conceivable method of allocating society's benefits—whether through the public sector or the private sector, and however fair it might at first appear—inevitably leaves some Americans feeling as if they were unfairly treated. At that point, such policies become political issues.[52]

Busing: School Integration

The 1954 *Brown* ruling ended forced segregation of public schools. Government could no longer require minority children to attend separate schools. However, government was not required by the *Brown* decision to compel minority children and white children to attend school together. Fifteen years after *Brown*, because of neighborhood segregation, fewer than 5 percent of America's black children were attending schools that were predominately white. This situation set the stage for one of the few public policies to bring whites into regular contact with blacks: the forced busing of children out of their neighborhoods for the purpose of achieving racial balance in the schools.

In *Swann v. Charlotte-Mecklenburg County Board of Education* (1971), the Supreme Court ruled that the busing of children was an appropriate way to integrate schools that were segregated because past discrimination had contributed to the creation of racially separate neighborhoods.[53] Unlike *Brown*, which affected mainly the South, *Swann* also applied to northern communities where blacks and whites lived separately in part because of discriminatory housing ordinances and real estate practices. *Swann* triggered protests even larger than those accompanying the *Brown* decision. Angry and sometimes violent demonstrations lasting weeks occurred in Charlotte, Detroit, Boston, and other cities.

Forced busing had mixed results. Studies found that busing improved racial attitudes among schoolchildren and improved the performance of minority children on standardized tests without diminishing the performance of white classmates.[54] However, these achievements came at a price. For many children, forced busing meant long hours riding buses each day to and from school. Moreover, busing contributed to white flight to private schools and to the suburbs, which were protected by a 1974 Supreme Court decision that prohibited busing across school district lines unless those lines had been drawn for the purpose of keeping the races apart.[55] As white students left urban schools, it became harder to achieve racial balance through busing and harder to convince taxpayers to fund these schools adequately.

In the 1990s, the Supreme Court began to allow communities to terminate their busing programs, holding that busing was intended as a temporary rather than a permanent solution to the problem of segregated schools[56] and that communities could devise alternative programs, such as increased spending on neighborhood schools in poorer neighborhoods.[57] Then, in 2007, the Supreme Court took a stand that effectively marks the end of widespread busing. At issue were busing programs that had been established voluntarily (rather than in response to a court order) by the Seattle and Louisville school boards as a means of creating racially diverse student bodies. The programs took race, neighborhood, and student preference into account in assigning students to particular schools. The large majority of students were placed in their school of choice, but some had to attend another school. These arrangements were challenged by several white families whose children did not get their school of choice, and the Supreme Court ruled in their favor, saying they had been denied equal protection under the Fourteenth Amendment.

The Court's opinion was decided by a 5-4 margin with the opposing justices taking starkly different positions. Writing for the majority, Chief Justice John Roberts said, "Before *Brown*, schoolchildren were told where they could and could not go to school based on the color of their skin. The school districts in [Seattle and Louisville] have not carried the heavy burden of demonstrating that we should allow this once again—even for very different reasons." In the dissenting opinion, Justice Stephen Breyer said the ruling is one "the court and the nation will come to regret." Breyer went on to say, "The lesson of history is not that efforts to continue racial segregation are constitutionally indistinguishable from efforts to achieve racial integration. Indeed, it is a cruel distortion of history to compare Topeka, Kansas in the 1950s to Louisville and Seattle in the modern day."[58]

America's public schools have a different makeup than in the pre-Brown era, but the trend in school enrollments is toward increased segregation. As a result

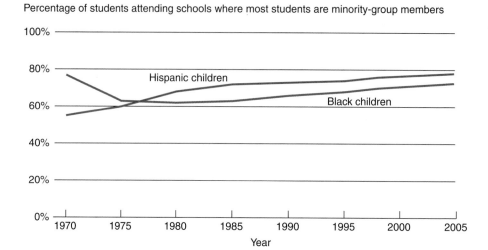

Source: U.S. Department of Education, 2008.

FIGURE 5-8 **Segregation Rates in Public Schools**
In the past two decades, racial and ethnic segregation in America's public schools has increased. More than two-thirds of black and Hispanic children today attend a school in which most of the students are members of a minority group. An increase in the number of non-Hispanic white students attending private schools and a decrease in racial busing are factors in the trend.

of cutbacks in forced busing and white flight to private and suburban schools, America's schools have become less racially diverse (see Figure 5-8). Today, only 30 percent of Hispanic and black children attend a school that is predominately white, compared with 40 percent during the era of widespread busing.

Persistent Discrimination: Superficial Differences, Deep Divisions

In 1944, Swedish sociologist Gunnar Myrdal gained fame for his book *An American Dilemma,* whose title referred to deep-rooted racism in a country that idealized equality.[59] Since then, legal obstacles to the mixing of the races have been nearly eliminated, and public opinion has softened significantly. In the early 1940s, a majority of white Americans believed that black children should not be allowed to go to school with white children; today only a tiny percentage of white Americans hold this opinion. There are also visible signs of racial progress. In the past two decades, increasing numbers of African Americans have attended college, earned undergraduate degrees, obtained jobs as professionals and managers, and moved into suburban neighborhoods.

Nevertheless, true equality for all Americans remains elusive. The realities of everyday American life are still very different for its white and black citizens. For example, a black child born in the United States has more than twice the chance of dying before reaching his or her first birthday than a white child does. The difference in the infant mortality rates of whites and African Americans reflects differences in their nutrition, medical care, and education—in other words, differences in their access to the most basic resources of a modern society.

Equality is a difficult idea in practice because it requires people to shed preconceived notions about how other people think, behave, and feel. Nearly everyone has difficulty seeing beyond superficial differences—whether those differences relate to skin color, national origin, religious preference, sex, or lifestyle—to the shared humanity of people of all backgrounds. Myrdal called discrimination "America's curse." He could have broadened the generalization. Discrimination is civilization's curse, as is clear from the thousands of ethnic, national, and religious conflicts that have marred human history. But America carries a special responsibility because of its high ideals. In the words of Abraham Lincoln, the United States is a nation "dedicated to the proposition that all men are created equal."

Summary Self-Test www.mhhe.com/pattersontad9e

During the past half-century, the United States has undergone a revolution in the legal status of its traditionally disadvantaged groups, including African Americans, women, Native Americans, Hispanic Americans, and Asian Americans. Such groups are now provided equal protection under the law in areas such as education, employment, and voting. Discrimination by race, sex, and ethnicity has not been eliminated from American life, but it is no longer substantially backed by the force of law. This advance was achieved against strong resistance from established interests, which only begrudgingly and slowly responded to demands for equality in law.

Traditionally disadvantaged Americans have achieved fuller equality primarily as a result of their struggle for greater rights. The Supreme Court has been an instrument of change for disadvantaged groups. Its ruling in *Brown v. Board of Education* (1954), in which racial segregation in public schools was declared a violation of the Fourteenth Amendment's equal-protection clause, was a major breakthrough in equal rights. Through its affirmative action and other rulings, such as those providing equal access to the vote, the Court has also mandated the active promotion of social, political, and economic equality. However, because civil rights policy involves large issues concerned with social values and the distribution of society's opportunities and benefits, questions of civil rights are inherently contentious. For this reason, legislatures and executives have been deeply involved in such issues. The history of civil rights includes landmark laws, including the 1964 Civil Rights Act and 1965 Voting Rights Act that were enacted by Congress with the backing of President Lyndon Johnson.

In more recent decades, civil rights issues have receded from the prominence they enjoyed during the 1960s. The scope of affirmative action programs has narrowed, and the use of forced busing to achieve racial integration in America's public schools has been all but eliminated. At the same time, new issues have emerged, including the question of whether same-sex couples will have the same rights as opposite-sex couples and the question of how to treat illegal immigrants, most of whom are Hispanic.

The legal gains of disadvantaged groups over the past half-century have not been matched by material gains. Although progress has been made, it has been slow. Compared with non-Hispanic whites, other Americans lag behind in levels of education, income, and health care. Tradition, prejudice, and the sheer difficulty of social, economic, and political progress stand as formidable obstacles to achieving a more equal America.

CHAPTER 5

Study Corner

Key Terms

affirmative action (*p. 138*)
civil rights (*p. 118*)
de facto discrimination (*p. 137*)
de jure discrimination (*p. 137*)
equality of result (*p. 137*)
equal-protection clause (*p. 134*)
equal rights (*p. 118*)
gender gap (*p. 122*)
reasonable-basis test (*p. 134*)
strict-scrutiny test (*p. 134*)
suspect classifications (*p. 134*)

Self-Test

1. The term *civil rights* refers to:
   a. treating groups equally under the law.
   b. protecting an individual's right to religious belief.
   c. protecting public safety.
   d. permitting marriage by justices of the peace.

2. The Supreme Court of the United States:
   a. has never tolerated discriminating against people on the basis of their race.
   b. outlawed discrimination based on race in the *Plessy* case.
   c. refused to hear the legal case involving school segregation in Topeka, Kansas, because Kansas was not considered part of the South.
   d. in *Brown v. Board of Education* prohibited the practice of separate public schools for the purposes of racial segregation.

3. The legal test that in some cases (such as the legal consumption of alcohol) allows government to treat people

differently based on their characteristics (such as age) is called the:

a. reasonable-basis test.
b. strict-scrutiny test.
c. suspect classification standard.
d. none of the above.

4. Government policies that have been implemented to eliminate discrimination with the goal of achieving "equality of result" include:

a. busing.
b. affirmative action.
c. neither a nor b.
d. both a and b.

5. Regarding job-related issues, women:

a. have made gains in many traditionally male-dominated fields.
b. have achieved gains in the workplace through programs such as day care and parental leave.
c. hold a disproportionate number of the lower-wage jobs and are less likely to hold top-level management positions.
d. all of the above.

6. Regarding affirmative action, Supreme Court decisions in the 1980s and 1990s have:

a. moved to outlaw it entirely.
b. moved to narrow its application to specific past acts of discrimination.
c. asked Congress to clarify the policy.
d. asked the president to clarify the policy.

7. De facto discrimination is much harder to overcome than de jure discrimination. (T/F)

8. The history of discrimination against Hispanics is virtually the same as the history of discrimination against African Americans, which helps account for the similarity of their political and economic situations. (T/F)

9. In recent years, the struggle for equal rights has been extended to the elderly but not to the disabled. (T/F)

10. Asian Americans have made such great progress in overcoming discrimination that the percentage of Asian Americans in top managerial positions and elected political offices is greater than the percentage of Asian Americans in the U.S. population. (T/F)

Critical Thinking

What role have political movements played in securing the legal rights of disadvantaged groups? How has the resulting legislation contributed to a furtherance of these groups' rights?

Suggested Readings

Anderson, Terry H. *The Pursuit of Fairness: A History of Affirmative Action.* New York: Oxford University Press, 2005. A comprehensive look at the affirmative action issue.

Armor, David. *Forced Justice: School Desegregation and the Law.* New York: Oxford University Press, 1996. An evaluation that concludes that the federal courts have overstretched their legal mandate by requiring school integration rather than simply school desegregation.

Blackmon, Douglas A. *Slavery by Another Name: The Re-Enslavement of Black Americans from the Civil War to World War II.* New York: Doubleday, 2008. A historical analysis of the Jim Crow era.

Chang, Gordon H., ed. *Asian Americans and Politics.* Stanford, Calif.: Stanford University Press, 2001. A broad look at the political engagement of Asian Americans.

Garcia, F. Chris, and Gabriel Sanchez. *Hispanics and the U.S. Political System: Moving Into the Mainstream.* Upper Saddle River, N.J.: Prentice-Hall, 2007. A broad examination of Hispanics' growing influence on American politics.

Lawless, Jennifer L., and Richard L. Fox. *It Takes a Candidate: Why Women Don't Run for Office.* New York: Cambridge University Press, 2005. An assessment of why fewer women than men seek public office.

Reeves, Keith. *Voting Hopes or Fears? White Voters, Black Candidates, and Racial Politics in America.* New York: Oxford University Press, 1997. A critical assessment of race and politics in American society.

Rimmerman, Craig A., and Clyde Wilcox. *The Politics of Same-Sex Marriage.* Chicago: University of Chicago Press, 2007. A careful assessment of the political forces surrounding the same-sex marriage issue.

Wilkins, David E. *American Indian Politics and the American Political System.* Lanham, Md.: Rowman & Littlefield, 2006. A comprehensive look at tribal governance and its connection to the American political process.

List of Websites

http://www.airpi.org/
The website of the American Indian Policy Center, which was established by Native Americans in 1992; includes a political and legal history of Native Americans and examines current issues affecting them.

http://www.naacp.org/
The website of the National Association for the Advancement of Colored People (NAACP); includes historical and current information on the struggle of African Americans for equal rights.

http://www.nclr.org/
The website of the National Council of La Raza (NCLR), an organization dedicated to improving the lives of Hispanics; contains information on public policy, immigration, citizenship, and other subjects.

http://www.rci.rutgers.edu/~cawp/
The website of the Center for the American Woman and Politics (CAWP) at Rutgers University's Eagleton Institute of Politics.

Participate!

Think of a disadvantaged group that you would like to assist. It could be one of the federal government's designated groups (such as Native Americans), one of the other groups mentioned in the chapter (such as the disabled), or some other group (such as the homeless). Contact a college, community, national, or international organization that seeks to help this group, and volunteer your assistance. (The Internet provides the names of thousands of organizations, such as Habitat for Humanity, that are involved in helping the disadvantaged.)

Extra Credit

For up-to-the-minute *New York Times* articles, interactive simulations, graphics, study tools, and more links and quizzes, visit the text's Online Learning Center at www.mhhe .com/pattersontad9e.

Self-Test Answers

1. a   2. d   3. a   4. d   5. d   6. b   7. T   8. F   9. F   10. F

National Journal

A Tough Sell Gets Tougher

Black Republicans are already considered a contradiction in terms in the African-American community. And the arrival of Barack Obama as the Democratic presidential nominee made selling black voters on the GOP exponentially more difficult.

That hasn't kept a small group of vociferous conservative blacks from trying. They argue that, historically, the GOP is the true home of African-Americans. They posit an unbroken line of civil-rights victories from Abraham Lincoln's Emancipation Proclamation to George W. Bush's Leave No Child Behind initiative, and they object to the Democratic Party's claim to the mantle.

"The Democrat Party has hijacked the civil-rights record of the Republican Party," said Frances Rice, chairwoman of the National Black Republican Association, which boasts 1,000 members in 48 states. "The Democratic Party is the party of slavery, secession, segregation, and now—socialism."

The nimble historical hopscotch behind that claim irks Democratic activists and historians alike, but there's enough truth in it to keep a parlor argument going late into the night. So far, the African-American community has not bought into the story line. President Bush captured only 11 percent of the black vote in the 2004 election, and no Republican African-American lawmakers are serving in Congress.

"My job is difficult whether Barack Obama is standing there or not," said Michael Steele, chairman of GOPAC, the political action committee charged with electing Republicans to state and local offices. Steele was the first African-American lieutenant governor of Maryland and lost a 2006 U.S. Senate bid to Democrat Ben Cardin. He knows well the challenges facing black Republicans, both as candidates and citizens.

"The reality becomes very difficult when the biases toward all things black-Republican are so stark, so personal," Steele said. "People just don't even give you credit for anything."

Shamed Dogan knows these biases firsthand. He is a black Republican campaigning for state representative in Missouri's 88th district. "I tell people I'm running as a Republican and they give me 'The Look'—like they are seeing a unicorn," Dogan said. "If they talked to me for five minutes, they would realize I'm for the betterment of all people, including African-Americans."

African-American Republicans fondly recall the origins of the Grand Old Party, whose creators were fierce abolitionists.

After the Civil War, Southern Democrats returned to Congress and voted against efforts by the then-majority Republicans to pass the 14th and 15th amendments to the Constitution to grant freed slaves U.S. citizenship and full voting rights, respectively. Historians agree: This was largely a group of sullen Southern sympathizers disdainful of Lincoln's Emancipation Proclamation and the 13th Amendment, which abolished slavery. They did all they could to subjugate blacks during Reconstruction and supported local Jim Crow laws that disenfranchised blacks in the former Confederate states for the next century.

"The Democrats [who were] revived in the wake of the Civil War [belonged to] a largely Southern, white-supremacist party," said Yale history professor David Blight.

Not all of the bigotry came from below the Mason-Dixon line. "The Almighty has made the black man inferior, sir," said Rep. Fernando Wood, D-N.Y., in 1865. "By no legislation, by no military power, can you wipe out this distinction."

The so-called radical Republicans battled Democratic President Andrew Johnson and handed him 15 veto overrides, including the Civil Rights Act of 1866 and the Reconstruction Act of 1867.

Republicans remained staunchly pro-civil rights into the 1870s with the help of GOP President Ulysses S. Grant. Together they saw the adoption of the Force Act of 1871 to provide federal oversight of congressional elections, the Ku Klux Klan Act of 1871 to protect blacks from the racial vigilantes, and the Civil Rights Act of 1875. The latter, never fully enforced and ultimately declared unconstitutional in 1883, called for open access to inns, public transportation, and theaters for all races.

Here the litany of pro-black GOP policies stops until passage of the Civil Rights Act of 1964 with the instrumental support of Sen. Everett Dirksen, R-Ill. Not to be overlooked in the effort was the lobbying of Democratic President Lyndon Johnson and Senate Democrats, who wooed Dirksen relentlessly.

"Dirksen did help make the 1964 act possible," said Senate Associate Historian Donald Ritchie. "LBJ made sure Dirksen was on board, front and center," and he was willing to let the senior Republican senator take a large share of the credit in order to close the deal. It worked. The bill passed, and Dirksen appeared on the cover of Time magazine in June 1964.

Last on the checklist for black Republicans is the creation of affirmative action by Assistant Labor Secretary Art Fletcher in 1970 during the Nixon administration. The program, derived from an earlier Johnson administration plan, helped guarantee equal access for women and minorities to public- and private-sector jobs. "We created it," Steele said, "Democrats bastardized it" by letting it become a quota system.

Critics of the rosy recitation of GOP civil-rights accomplishments say the historical take is selective at best and misleading at worst. "Any use of the 'party of Lincoln' rhetoric by the current Republican Party is, frankly, an egregious twisting of history," Blight said. He explains that the original GOP underwent drastic changes from the 1870s into the early 20th century. "They became the party of Big Business interests, imperial expansionism, and ultimately turned their backs decisively on their more egalitarian origins in the Civil War era," Blight said.

The first turning point came during the Great Depression. Until the economic collapse in 1929, most African-Americans voted Republican—if they could vote at all. But blacks began to shift allegiance as President Roosevelt's progressive New Deal created jobs. FDR won 23 percent of the black vote in 1932, a figure that grew to 71 per-

cent in 1936 and stayed high during World War II. President Truman, who ordered the desegregation of the military and aggressively investigated several high-profile lynchings, won 65 percent of the black vote in 1948.

Presidential candidate John F. Kennedy re-established a strong Democratic relationship with the black community through a phone call to Coretta Scott King in 1960, expressing his concern about the incarceration of her

Sen. Strom Thurmond of South Carolina began the exodus in 1964 by joining the GOP in protest. In 1968, Republican presidential candidate Richard Nixon seized the opportunity to peel off many more disaffected white Democrats with the "Southern strategy" that equated the GOP with "law and order" and "states' rights"—widely regarded as code words for a conservative backlash against civil-rights protections.

capped block grants to states. It also required welfare recipients to enter job-training programs, mandated that states boost child-support enforcement, and limited individual benefits to five years, total. Within three years of enactment, 4.7 million Americans moved off the welfare rolls, and by 2006, caseloads declined 59 percent, according to the Health and Human Services Department.

"We're not against government programs," Steele said. "They need to be suited to the task, not wasteful; and when they've served their purpose, get rid of them."

> "Some Republicans gave up on winning the African-American vote, **looking the other way or trying to benefit from racial polarization**," Mehlman said. "I am here today as the Republican chairman to tell you we were wrong."

husband in the Birmingham, Ala., jail, and subsequent calls for his release. The overture was enough to prompt Martin Luther King Sr., "Daddy King," to publicly renounce the Republican Party and support Kennedy. JFK won the election with the help of 71 percent of black voters.

"What you saw in 1958 to 1964 was more Democratic engagement in the civil-rights movement," said Julianne Malveaux, president of Bennett College for Women in Greensboro, N.C. Although key Republicans ultimately supported the landmark legislation, it was a Democratic Congress and president that made the 1964 Civil Rights Act and the 1965 Voting Rights Act law, Blight said.

President Johnson garnered an estimated 100 percent of the black vote in 1964 but famously remarked at the time that he feared that Democratic support for civil-rights legislation would cause the party to "lose the South for a generation." It was a historic understatement.

The tactic helped both Nixon and Ronald Reagan win the White House, and it became a staple of modern GOP presidential politics. "Republicans have been more likely to use race as a proxy to signal to [white] people— we've got your backs," Malveaux said.

Steele bitterly regrets the move by his party. "It was a dumb strategy," he said. "It alienated a partner. African-Americans and the GOP had been historically linked since day one."

Black Republicans say that a lot in the conservative Goldwater/Reagan doctrine strikes chords within the larger African-American community—particularly the admonition to self-sufficiency and frustrations with the welfare system that evolved from the Johnson administration's War on Poverty.

Black Republicans laud welfare reform, which congressional conservatives pushed in 1994 and President Clinton ultimately signed into law in 1996. The new system dispensed with open-ended entitlements in favor of

While shrinking the government is a staple of conservative thought, the starve-the-beast rallying cry of the GOP may also quietly alienate the black community, Blight says. The federal government ended slavery, gave African-Americans the vote, and promoted civil rights in the 1860s and 1960s. "If you don't believe in government, you're not going to get many black people to vote for you," he said.

In 2005, the Republican National Committee made a concerted effort to woo back at least a small percentage of the black vote. Then-RNC Chairman Ken Mehlman appeared before the NAACP convention in Milwaukee and offered a striking apology for the Southern strategy. "Some Republicans gave up on winning the African-American vote, looking the other way or trying to benefit from racial polarization," Mehlman said. "I am here today as the Republican chairman to tell you we were wrong."

The contrition strategy failed. Blacks voted 89 percent Democratic in the 2006 elections that cost the GOP control of Congress. Distrust of the modern GOP still dominates in the African-American community, and few in it appear willing to countenance black- (or white-) Republican efforts to paint the party in a softer racial light.

FOR DISCUSSION: Who do you think deserves the acclaim for the Civil Rights movement? Can one group really even claim credit? Based on your experience of the two political parties today, which one (if either) is doing more to promote the Civil Rights agenda?

What mistakes do you see politicians making today that they might regret the way Ken Mehlman regrets the GOP's callousness to black voters?

Public Opinion and Political Socialization
Shaping the People's Voice

The Nature of Public Opinion

How Informed Is Public Opinion?
The Measurement of Public Opinion

Political Socialization: How Americans Learn Their Politics

The Process of Political Socialization
The Agents of Political Socialization

Frames of Reference: How Americans Think Politically

Cultural Thinking: Common Ideas
Ideological Thinking: The Outlook of Some
Group Thinking: The Outlook of Many
Partisan Thinking: The Line That Divides

The Influence of Public Opinion on Policy

To speak with precision of public opinion is a task not unlike coming to grips with the Holy Ghost. V. O. Key Jr.[1]

A s the U.S. troop buildup in the Persian Gulf region continued into 2003, Americans were unsure of the best course of action. They had been hearing about Saddam Hussein for years and had concluded that he was a tyrant and a threat. Most Americans expressed a willingness to support a war in Iraq if President George W. Bush deemed it necessary. But Americans had differing opinions on when and whether war should occur. Some wanted to give United Nations inspectors ample time to investigate Iraq's weapons program before a final decision on war was made. Others wanted to delay the decision until the United States could line up international support. Still others supported more immediate action but thought a bombing campaign was preferable to the launching of a ground war that might result in high casualties among U.S. forces. In any case, once the bombs started dropping on Iraq and U.S. ground troops poured into Iraq from their staging base in Kuwait, Americans strongly supported the action. Polls indicated that roughly 70 percent backed President Bush's decision to use military force against Iraq, with 20 percent opposed and 10 percent undecided.

The Iraq war is a telling example of the influence of public opinion on government: public opinion rarely forces officials to take a particular course of action. If President Bush had decided that the Iraq situation could have been resolved through UN weapons inspectors, public opinion would have supported that decision. A majority of Americans would also have supported the president if he had decided that war made sense only if it had broad international support or was limited to an air war.

Although public opinion has a central place in democratic theory, it is seldom an exact guide to policy. As long as the policy seems reasonable, political leaders ordinarily enjoy leeway in choosing a course of action. This chapter discusses public opinion and its influence on U.S. politics. A major theme is that public opinion is a powerful yet inexact force.[2] Government policy cannot be understood apart from public opinion, but it is not a precise determinant of that policy. The main points made in this chapter are these:

- *Public opinion consists of those views held by ordinary citizens that are openly expressed.* Public officials have various means of gauging public opinion but increasingly use public opinion polls for this purpose.

- *The process by which individuals acquire their political opinions is called political socialization.* This process begins during childhood, when, through family and school, Americans acquire many of their basic political values and beliefs. Socialization continues into adulthood, during which peers, political leaders, and the news media are among the major influences.

- *Americans' political opinions are shaped by several frames of reference, including ideology, group attachments, partisanship, and political culture.* These frames of reference are a basis of political consensus in some instances and of political conflict in others.

- *Public opinion has an important influence on government but ordinarily does not directly determine exactly what officials will do.* Public opinion works primarily to place limits on the choices made by officials.

The Nature of Public Opinion

As representative government took root in the 1700s, political philosophers began to theorize about the public's role in such governments. Jeremy Bentham (1748–1832) was the first English-speaking philosopher to write at length on the subject.[3] Originally an advocate of aristocratic government, Bentham came to believe that "public opinion" had a large and rightful place in governing. He contended that public opinion had the power to ensure that government would rule in a way that brought "the greatest happiness" to the greatest number of people.

Although public opinion is now an everyday political term, it is often used sloppily. A common error is the assumption that "the public"—meaning the whole citizenry—actually has an opinion on nearly every issue of politics. In fact, most issues do not attract the attention of anywhere near a majority of citizens. Agricultural conservation programs, for example, are of keen interest to some farmers, hunters, and environmentalists but of little interest to most people. This pattern is so pervasive that opinion analysts have described America as a nation of *many* publics.[4] Accordingly, a precise definition of the term *public opinion* cannot be based on the assumption that all citizens, or even a majority, are actively interested in and actually hold an opinion on every issue. In this text, **public opinion** will be viewed as the politically relevant opinions held by ordinary citizens that they express openly.[5] This expression need not be verbal. It can also take the form, for example, of a protest demonstration or a vote for one candidate rather than another. The crucial point is that people's private opinions on an issue become public opinion when they become publicly visible.

How Informed Is Public Opinion?

An assumption of democratic politics is that public opinion should control what government does. One problem with a simplistic version of this assumption is that people often have conflicting opinions. In responding to one opinion on an issue, the government is compelled to reject other opinions. People's opinions can

public opinion

The politically relevant opinions held by ordinary citizens that they express openly.

also be inconsistent, even contradictory. Polls indicate, for example, that most Americans would like better schools, health care, and other public services while also favoring a reduction in taxes (see Figure 6-1). Which opinion of the people should govern—their desire for more services or their desire for lower taxes?

Another limitation on government by public opinion is that, even on issues of great importance, people's opinions on an issue can be at odds with the reality of that issue. In the buildup to the U.S. invasion of Iraq in 2003, for example, polls revealed that more than half of the American public wrongly believed that Iraq had close ties to the al Qaeda terrorist network and that Iraqis were among the nineteen terrorists who had flown airplanes into the World Trade Center and the Pentagon on September 11, 2001. Moreover, despite widespread opposition to the war on the part of most Europeans, Asians, South Americans, and Africans, one in four Americans believed that world opinion favored the war. Americans who held these mistaken views were more inclined to support an invasion of Iraq than were other Americans.[6]

Even many college-educated Americans are uninformed about public affairs. In 2007, the Intercollegiate Studies Institute surveyed 14,000 first-year and fourth-year college students, giving them a multiple-choice exam to test their "civic literacy." The average college senior had a grade of F, answering only 54 percent of the questions correctly. Only 46 percent of the college seniors could identify the phrase "We hold these truths to be self-evident, that all men are created equal" as being part of the Declaration of Independence. On this and the other questions, college freshmen scored even lower than college seniors.[7] An earlier survey of Ivy League students found that one-third could not identify the British prime minister, half could not name both U.S senators from their state, and three-fourths could not identify Abraham Lincoln as the author of the phrase "a government of the people, by the people, and for the people."[8]

Of course, citizens do not necessarily have to be informed on an issue to have a reasonable opinion about it. Opinions derive mostly from people's values and interests.[9] A person could have a sound opinion on the economy, for example, without a knowledge of the latest economic statistics. Nevertheless, the public's lack of information limits the role that public opinion can play in governing. The choice among policy options sometimes requires an understanding of the causes and consequences of the various options. Citizens frequently lack this type of information.

Dressed in his own clothes and as he requested, the remains (with wax head) of Jeremy Bentham are on display at University College, London. Bentham (1748–1832), who was the first English-speaking theorist to write at length on public opinion, is best known as a founder of utilitarian philosophy. He developed the principle of utility, which holds that action is acceptable if it promotes an increased amount of pleasure and unacceptable if it promotes an increased amount of pain.

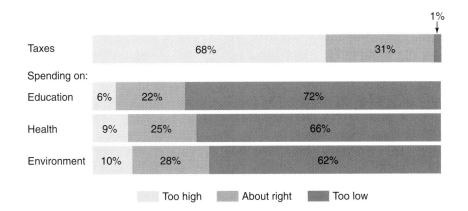

FIGURE 6-1 **Opinions on Taxing and Spending**
People's opinions can be contradictory. Americans say, for example, that taxes are too high and yet also say, when asked about specific policy areas, that government is spending too little.
Source: National Opinion Research Center, University of Chicago.

Public opinion includes contradictory elements. According to surveys, for example, most Americans say they want lower taxes but also say they want more public services. At a Boston rally, this demonstrator expresses anger with tax increases while also demanding that government provide more health benefits.

The Measurement of Public Opinion

Woodrow Wilson once said that he had spent much of his adult life in government and yet had never seen a "government." What Wilson was saying, in effect, was that government is a system of relationships. A government is not a building or a person—it is not tangible in the way that, say, a car or a can of soda is. So it is with public opinion. No one has ever seen a "public opinion," and thus it cannot be measured directly. It must be assessed indirectly.

Election returns are a traditional method of assessing public opinion. Journalists and politicians routinely draw conclusions about what citizens are thinking by how they vote. Letters to the editor in newspapers, e-mail messages to elected officials, and the size of crowds at mass demonstrations are other means of judging public opinion. All these indicators are useful guides for policymakers. None of them, however, is a precise indicator of what the broad public is thinking. Elections offer citizens only a yes-no choice between the candidates, and different voters will have chosen the same candidate for different reasons. As for letter writers and demonstrators, they are nearly always *unrepresentative* of the population as a whole. Fewer than 1 percent of Americans participate each year in a mass demonstration, and fewer than 10 percent write to the president or a member of Congress. Studies have found that the opinions of letter writers and demonstrators are more extreme than those of most citizens.

Public Opinion Polls

In an earlier day, indicators such as elections and letters to the editor were the only means by which public officials could gauge what the public was thinking. Today, they also rely on opinion polls or surveys, which provide a more systematic method of estimating public sentiment.[10]

In a **public opinion poll,** a relatively few individuals—the **sample**—are interviewed in order to estimate the opinions of a whole **population,** such as the residents of a city or country. If a sufficient number of individuals are chosen at random, their views will tend to be representative—that is, roughly the same as the views held by the population as a whole.

How is it possible to measure the thinking of a large population on the basis of a relatively small sample? How can interviews with, say, one thousand Americans provide a reliable estimate of what millions of them are thinking? The answer is found in the laws of probability. Consider the hypothetical example of a huge jar filled with a million marbles, half of them red and half of them blue. If a blindfolded person reaches into the jar, the probability of selecting a marble of a given color is fifty-fifty. And if one thousand marbles are chosen in this random way, it is likely that about half of them will be red and about half will be blue. Opinion sampling works in the same way. If respondents are chosen at random from a population, their opinions will approximate those of the population as a whole.

Random selection is the key to scientific polling, which is based on *probability sampling*—a sample in which each individual in the population has a known probability of being chosen at random for inclusion. A scientific poll is different from the surveys found on many Internet sites; the individuals who respond to such surveys are selecting themselves for the poll rather than being selected randomly

---

public opinion poll

A device for measuring public opinion whereby a relatively small number of individuals (the sample) are interviewed for the purpose of estimating the opinions of a whole community (the population).

sample

In a public opinion poll, the relatively small number of individuals who are interviewed for the purpose of estimating the opinions of an entire population.

population

In a public opinion poll, the people (for example, the citizens of a nation) whose opinions are being estimated through interviews with a sample of these people.

by the pollster. A scientific poll is also different from the "people-in-the-street" interviews that news reporters sometimes conduct. Although a reporter may say that the opinions of those interviewed represent the views of the local population, this claim is clearly faulty. Interviews conducted on a downtown street at the noon hour, for example, will include a disproportionate number of business employees on their lunch break. Housewives, teachers, and factory workers are among the many groups that would be underrepresented in such a sample.

The science of polling is such that the size of the sample, as opposed to the size of the population, is the key to accurate estimates. Although it might be assumed that a much larger sample would be required to poll accurately the people of the United States as opposed to the residents of Georgia or Vermont, the sample requirements are nearly the same. Consider again the example of a huge jar filled with marbles, half of them red and half of them blue. If one thousand marbles were randomly selected, about half would be red and about half would be blue, regardless of whether the jar held one million, 10 million, or 100 million marbles. On the other hand, the size of the sample—the number of marbles selected—does matter. If only ten marbles were drawn, it might happen that five would be of each color but, then again, it would not be unusual for six, seven, or even eight of them to be of the same color. However, if one thousand marbles were drawn, it would be highly unusual for six hundred of the marbles, much less seven or eight hundred of them, to be of the same color.

The accuracy of a poll is expressed in terms of **sampling error**—the degree to which the sample estimates might differ from what the population actually thinks. The larger the sample, the smaller the sampling error, which is usually expressed as a plus-or-minus percentage. For example, a properly drawn sample of one thousand individuals has a sampling error of roughly plus or minus 3 percent. Thus, if 55 percent of a sample of one thousand respondents say they intend to vote for the Republican presidential candidate, then the probability is high that between 52 percent and 58 percent (55 percent plus or minus 3 percent) of all voters actually plan to vote Republican.

The impressive record of the Gallup poll in predicting the outcome of presidential elections indicates that the theoretical accuracy of polls can be matched in practice. The Gallup Organization has polled voters in every presidential election since 1936 (nineteen elections in all) and has erred badly only once: it stopped polling several weeks before the 1948 election and missed a late voter shift that carried Harry Truman to victory.

sampling error

A measure of the accuracy of a public opinion poll. The sampling error is mainly a function of sample size and is usually expressed in percentage terms.

Problems with Polls

Although pollsters assume that their samples are drawn from a particular population, it is seldom the case that everyone in that population has a chance of becoming part of the sample. Only rarely does a pollster have a list of all individuals in a population from which to draw a sample. An expedient alternative is a sample based on telephone numbers. Pollsters use computers to randomly pick telephone numbers, which are then dialed by interviewers to reach households. Within each of these households, a respondent is then randomly selected. Because the computer is as likely to pick one telephone number as any other and because more than 90 percent of U.S. homes have a telephone, a sample selected in this way is assumed to be representative of the population. Nevertheless, some Americans do not have phones, and many of those who are called are not home or refuse to participate. Such factors reduce the accuracy of telephone polling. In fact, although telephone polls continue to provide precise predictions of elections, pollsters are increasingly worried about the future of telephone polling. The percentage of Americans who refuse to participate in telephone surveys has

DEBATING THE ISSUES

SHOULD POLITICIANS BASE THEIR STANDS ON OPINION POLLS?

A fundamental principle of democracy is that public opinion ought to be the foundation of government. However, the role that public opinion should play in specific policy decisions is, and always has been, a subject of dispute. James Madison distinguished between the public's momentary passions and its enduring concerns, arguing that government is obliged to represent only the latter. In contrast, the Jacksonians and Progressives had a strong faith in the judgment of ordinary citizens and a distrust of entrenched elites. With the advent of the public opinion poll, it became possible to measure citizens' policy views more directly. Should policymakers follow the polls in making their decisions?

Some analysts have held that leaders should act in close accord with the polls. Other analysts have argued that polls measure fleeting opinions about topical issues and that leaders are obliged to respond only to the people's enduring beliefs.

YES Sixty-eight percent of Americans think they should have a great deal of influence on the decisions of elected and government officials in Washington, but fewer than one in ten (9%) believe they do. . . . Who instead do Americans think bends the ears of the politicians and officials in the Capitol? According to the public, money talks. Nearly six in ten [say] that politicians pay a great deal of attention to their campaign contributors when making decisions about important issues. . . . Fifty-four percent of Americans expect their officials to follow what the majority wants, even if it goes against the officials' knowledge and judgment. Fewer (42%) want officials to use their own judgment if it goes against the wishes of the majority. . . . If we all lived in small New England towns, then perhaps town hall meetings would be a realistic means of injecting public opinion into the national debate. However, when it takes one western senator a whole year to travel to every single county in his or her home state, it is clear that the limits imposed by geography and time necessitate a continuing place for polling in public policy.

—*Bill McInturff and Lori Weigel, pollsters*

NO True statesmen are not merely mouthpieces for opinion polls. British historian Lord Acton recognized that the will of the majority could be and often is just as tyrannical as the will of a monarch, and in some cases more dangerous because the error has the support of the masses. Thus he observes, "It is bad to be oppressed by a minority, but it is worse to be oppressed by a majority," and "The will of the people cannot make just that which is unjust.". . . In the United States we have compelling historical and contemporary examples of the majority siding with what were, in retrospect, clear-cut cases of injustice. The legalization and promotion of slavery by governments are a prime example, and stand as a stark rebuke to elected officials who think they ought to represent the people without regard to their own conscience. Today, there are a number of hotly contested issues—such as abortion, stem cell research, and, now, marriage—whose partisans often make appeals based on poll data. Our elected officials follow the shifting temper of the electorate with rapt attention. But is this how we ask our elected officials to lead? . . . [T]oo many political leaders have settled on an inadequate answer: the will of the people (and the pollsters).

—*Jordon J. Ballor, Acton Institute*

increased sharply in recent decades, and the use of cell phones—which are not included in most computer-based telephone sampling—has risen significantly.

The accuracy of polling is also diminished when respondents are asked about an issue they have not considered. In such instances, interviewees usually offer a response in order not to appear uninformed or uninterested. Scholars label such responses "nonopinions." Almost always, polls on minor issues overestimate the number of people who truly have an opinion on the issue in question.

Less often, respondents will actually have an opinion but not reveal it. On sensitive topics, some interviewees will give what they regard as the socially correct response rather than say what they actually think. A classic example is voter turnout. Although turnout in presidential elections rarely rises above 60 percent, it is not unusual for 75 percent of respondents in postelection polls to claim that they voted. Some of these respondents are not telling the truth, but they prefer to tell the interviewer that they went to the polls rather than admit that they failed to exercise their right to vote.

President Harry Truman holds up the early edition of the *Chicago Tribune* with the headline "Dewey Defeats Truman." The *Tribune* was responding to analysts' predictions that Dewey would win the 1948 election. A Gallup poll a few weeks before the election had shown Dewey with a seemingly insurmountable lead. The Gallup Organization decided that it did not need to do another poll closer to the election, a mistake that it has not since repeated.

Respondents are also not always truthful when it comes to expressing opinions that relate to race, gender, ethnicity, and the like. Until recently, in high-profile election campaigns pitting a white candidate against a black candidate, the polls regularly overestimated the black candidate's vote. Some white respondents were apparently reluctant to say they planned to vote for the white candidate because they thought they might be regarded as racist if they said so. The most widely known example occurred in Virginia's 1989 gubernatorial race. Doug Wilder, the Democratic nominee and a black man, had a 10-percentage-point lead in the final polls; he won by less than 1 percent. In more recent elections, such as the 2006 gubernatorial race in Massachusetts, which was won by Deval Patrick, a black man, the polls have predicted the outcome of opposite-race contests with about the same accuracy as same-race contests. However, some analysts thought race might have contributed to the inaccuracy of the polls in New Hampshire's 2008 Democratic presidential primary. After Barack Obama won the Iowa caucuses, his momentum carried into New Hampshire, where all the preelection polls showed him with a comfortable lead in that state's primary. However, to the embarassment of the pollsters, he lost the primary to Hillary Clinton. Most pollsters argued that the wrongful prediction was the result of the large number of "undecideds" in the preelection polls and the difficulty of predicting which poll respondents would actually vote in the primary. Nevertheless, a few pollsters suggested Obama's race was a factor, given New Hampshire's overwhelming white electorate. In the November general election, however, the polls accurately predicted the size of Obama's victory, suggesting that race is now a negligible factor in the accuracy of election polls.

Question wording can also affect poll results. The way in which an issue is framed, whether it is accompanied by relevant facts, the ordering in which the alternatives are presented, and the precise alternatives offered can all affect people's responses, and thus how the poll's results are interpreted. Consider, for example, the issue of the death penalty as a sentence for murder. Do Americans favor or oppose its use? As it turns out, the answer to this question depends to some extent on how the issue is worded. Respondents in some Gallup polls have been asked: "Are you in favor of the death penalty for a person convicted of murder?" Respondents in other Gallup polls have been asked a different question: "If you could choose between the following two approaches, which do you think is the better penalty for murder—the death penalty or life imprisonment, with absolutely no possibility of parole?" The two questions produce measurably different results. When asked the first question, Americans by roughly two-to-one say they favor the death penalty. When asked the second question, Americans are almost evenly divided on whether the death sentence is the proper penalty.[11]

Despite these and other issues of polling, the poll or survey is the most relied-upon method of measuring public opinion. More than one hundred organizations are in the business of conducting public opinion polls. Some, like the Gallup Organization, conduct polls that are released to the news media by syndication. Most large news organizations also have their own in-house polls; one of the most prominent of these is the CBS News/New York Times poll. Other polling firms specialize in conducting surveys for candidates and officeholders.

Political Socialization: How Americans Learn Their Politics

political socialization

The learning process by which people acquire their political opinions, beliefs, and values.

Analysts have long been interested in how public opinion originates. The learning process by which people acquire their political opinions, beliefs, and values is called **political socialization.** Just as a language, a religion, or an athletic skill is acquired through a learning process, so too are people's political orientations. For most Americans, the socialization process starts in the family with exposure to the political loyalties and opinions of their parents. The schools later contribute to the process, as do the mass media, friends, work associates, and other agents.

The Process of Political Socialization

The process of political socialization in the United States has two distinguishing characteristics. First, although socialization continues throughout life, most people's political outlook is substantially influenced by their childhood learning. Basic ideas about which political party, the Republicans or the Democrats, is the better one, for example, are often formed uncritically in childhood, in much the same way that beliefs in the superiority of a particular religion—typically, the religion of one's parents—are acquired.

A second characteristic of political socialization is that its effect is cumulative. Early learning affects later learning because people have psychological defenses that protect the beliefs they hold. Many people, for example, remain lifelong Republicans or Democrats even as political conditions or their personal lives change in ways that might logically lead them to identify with the other party. Of course, political change can and does occur. Historically, major shifts in partisan orientation have occurred around major upheavals and have been concentrated among younger adults because their beliefs are less firmly rooted than are those of older adults. For example, President Franklin Roosevelt's New Deal, which sought to alleviate the economic hardship of the Great Depression, prompted many younger Republicans, but not many older ones, to shift their loyalty to the Democratic Party.

The Agents of Political Socialization

agents of socialization

Those agents, such as the family and the media, that have a significant impact on citizens' political socialization.

The socialization process takes place through a variety of **agents of socialization,** including family, schools, mass media, peers, and political leaders and events. It is helpful to consider briefly these agents of socialization and how they affect political learning.

HOW THE U.S. COMPARES

NATIONAL PRIDE

Americans are justifiably proud of their nation. It is the oldest continuous democracy in the world, an economic powerhouse, and a diverse yet harmonious society. What Americans may not recognize, because it is so much a part of everyday life in America, is the degree to which they are bombarded with messages and symbols of their nation's greatness. Political socialization in the United States is not the rigid program of indoctrination that some societies impose on their people. Nevertheless, Americans receive a thorough political education. Their country's values are impressed on them by every medium of communication: newspapers, daily conversations, television, movies, books, magazines, and so on.

The words and symbols that regularly tell Americans of their country's greatness are important to its unity. In the absence of a common ancestral heritage to bind them, Americans need other methods to instill and reinforce the idea that they are one people. As discussed in Chapter 1, America's political ideals have this effect, as do everyday reminders such as the flying of the flag on homes and private buildings, a practice that is almost uniquely American. (Elsewhere, flags are rarely displayed except on public buildings.)

One indicator of Americans' political socialization is the pride they express in their nationality. Americans rank high on this indicator, as shown by the following chart, which is based on polls conducted by the World Values Survey. The percentages are the proportion of respondents in each country that said they were "very proud" or "proud" of their nationality.

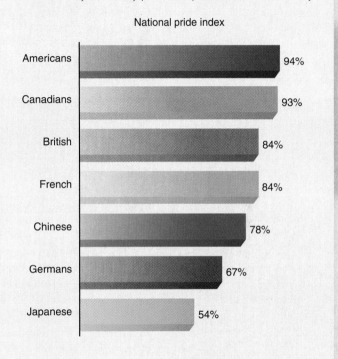

National pride index

Americans	94%
Canadians	93%
British	84%
French	84%
Chinese	78%
Germans	67%
Japanese	54%

Families

The family is a powerful agent of socialization because it has a near-monopoly on the attention of the young child, who places great trust in what a parent says. By the time children reach adulthood, many of the beliefs and values that will stay with them throughout life are firmly in place. Many adults are Republicans or Democrats today because their parents backed that party. They can give all sorts of reasons for preferring their party to the other, but the reasons come later in life. The family also contributes to basic orientations that, while not directly political, have political significance. For example, American families tend to be more egalitarian than families in other nations, and American children often have a voice in family decisions. Basic American values such as equality and individualism have roots in patterns of family interaction.[12]

Schools

The school, like the family, affects children's basic political beliefs. Teachers at the elementary level extol the exploits of national heroes such as George Washington, Abraham Lincoln, and Martin Luther King Jr., and praise the country's economic and political institutions.[13] Although teachers in the middle and high school grades present a more nuanced version of American history, they tend to emphasize the nation's great moments—for example, its decisive role in the two world wars.

Students in a North Carolina school recite the Pledge of Allegiance. Such childhood socialization experiences can have a profound impact on an individual's basic political beliefs.

U.S. schools are more instrumental in building support for the nation than are the schools in most other democracies. The Pledge of Allegiance, which is recited daily in many U.S. schools, has no equivalent in European countries. Their schools do not open the day by asking students to take an oath of loyalty to the nation. American schools also impart a sense of social equality. Most American children, regardless of family income, attend public schools and study a fairly standard curriculum. In many countries, schoolchildren are separated at an early age, with some placed in vocational classes while others are slotted in college preparatory courses.

Mass Media

The mass media are another powerful socializing agent. Public affairs for most Americans is a second-hand affair, something that is observed through the media rather than witnessed directly. The media's images of society affect what people believe is true of society. Repeated exposure to crime on television, for example, can lead people to believe that society itself is more violent than it actually is. Similarly, news stories that routinely portray politics as a fight between Republicans and Democrats can lead people to think that partisan bickering is what politics is all about.

Peers

Peer groups—friends, neighbors, and coworkers—tend to reinforce what a person already believes. Most people trust the opinions of their friends and associates and are unwilling to deviate too far from what they think. In *The Spiral of Silence*, Elisabeth Noelle-Neumann presents evidence indicating that many individuals are reluctant to express opinions contrary to those of the people around them. If nearly everyone in a group appears to believe, for example, that same-sex marriage should be legal, a person who believes otherwise is likely to remain silent rather than to say it should be illegal. One effect, Noelle-Neumann argues, is to make the prevailing opinion in a group appear to be more firmly and widely held than it actually is.[14]

Political Leaders and Institutions

Citizens look to political leaders and institutions, particularly the president and political parties, as guides to opinion.[15] After the terrorist attacks of September 11, 2001, for example, many Americans were confused about who the enemy was and how America should respond. These views changed dramatically a few days later when President George W. Bush in a televised speech identified al Qaeda as the perpetrators and declared that America would attack Afghanistan if its Taliban government continued to provide them sanctuary. Polls indicated that nine of every ten Americans agreed with Bush's view. However, the ability of political leaders to influence public opinion rests on their credibility. After President Bush led America into a costly war in Iraq on the inaccurate claim that it possessed weapons of mass destruction (WMDs), his political support crumbled, as did his ability to persuade Americans that the war in Iraq was worth the price.

Religion is a powerful socializing force in American life. Churches, synagogues, mosques, and temples are places where Americans acquire values and beliefs that can affect their opinions about politics. Shown here are Muslim men gathering at a mosque in the United States. Traditionally, men and women have prayed in different parts of the mosque. Some U.S. mosques have integrated their prayer services, and a few have allowed women to lead prayer sessions—changes that have been sharply criticized by traditionalists.

Churches

Beginning with the Puritans in the seventeenth century, churches have played a substantial role in shaping Americans' social and political opinions. Most Americans say they believe in God, most attend church at least occasionally, and most belong to a religion that includes teachings on social values. Moreover, most Americans say that religion has answers to many of the problems facing society today. In these and other respects, churches and religion are a more powerful force in the United States than in most other Western nations.

Scholars have not studied the influence of churches on political socialization as closely as they have studied the influence of families, schools, peers, or the media.[16] Nevertheless, churches are a significant source of political attitudes, including those related to society's obligations to children, the poor, and the unborn. (The impact of religion is discussed further in a later section of this chapter.)

Frames of Reference: How Americans Think Politically

What are the frames of reference that Americans acquire in the course of their political socialization? The question is an important one. Shared frames of reference enable people to find common cause. The opinions of millions of Americans would mean little if everyone's view was different. But if enough people think the same way, they may decide to work together to promote their shared interest.

Among the frames of reference through which Americans think about politics are cultural values, ideology, group attachments, and partisanship, as the following discussion will explain.

Cultural Thinking: Common Ideas

As was discussed in Chapter 1, Americans embrace a common set of ideals. Principles such as liberty, equality, and individualism have always meant somewhat different things to Americans but nonetheless are a source of agreement. For example, government programs aimed at redistributing wealth from the rich to the poor are more popular among Europeans than among Americans, who have a deeper commitment to individualism.

Ideological Thinking: The Outlook of Some

Analysts sometimes use words such as *liberal* and *conservative* to describe how ordinary Americans think about politics. These are ideological terms, as are terms such as *socialism* and *communism*. An **ideology** is a consistent pattern of political attitudes that stems from a core belief. The core belief of socialism, for example, is that society should ensure that everyone's basic economic needs are met. Accordingly, a socialist would support tax and spending policies that redistribute wealth in ways that help the less-affluent.

By a strict definition of what constitutes a political ideology—a *consistent* pattern of political attitudes—most Americans do not have one. As illustrated by the earlier example of people who favor steep tax cuts while also wanting more spending on government services, many citizens hold incompatible opinions. Other people have opinions that are generally consistent but include a glaring exception. Most Americans say, for example, that they support free trade between nations, but when their particular job or business is threatened by foreign competition, they oppose it. Farmers provide another example. Compared with most groups, farmers are opposed to welfare programs. On the other hand, farmers strongly favor government spending on crop subsidies and other programs that put money in their pockets. Political scientists have concluded that no more than a fourth of Americans have opinions that are consistent enough to meet the definition of a true ideology.[17]

Weaker forms of ideological thinking are more prevalent. Americans differ, for example, in their support of government policies that distribute economic wealth more widely. Those who think government should do more to help the less-well-off are typically described as **economic liberals. Economic conservatives,** in contrast, are people who believe that government should do less in this realm, leaving economic benefits to be distributed to a great extent through the marketplace only.

Opinions on the role of government shift when social issues are involved. Those who think government should do more to promote cultural traditions—for example, by enacting laws that promote certain religious beliefs and practices, such as a ban on abortion or civil unions—are called **social conservatives.** Those who think government should not favor traditional values but should instead leave lifestyle choices to the individual are labeled **social liberals.**

It should be noted that neither conservatives nor liberals hold a consistent view on the power of government. Economic conservatives prefer a smaller role for government than do economic liberals. On the other hand, social conservatives prefer a larger role for government than do social liberals. Each group wants government to be active or inactive, depending on which posture serves their policy goals. It should also be noted that there is no logical reason why an economic conservative must also be a social conservative. Although most economic conservatives are socially conservative as well, some are not. In the Rocky Mountain states particularly, many economic conservatives are social liberals. They oppose big government in both the economic and the social realms.

---

ideology

A consistent pattern of opinion on particular issues that stems from a core belief or set of beliefs.

economic liberals

Those who believe government should do more to assist people who have difficulty meeting their economic needs on their own.

economic conservatives

Those who believe government tries to do too many things that should be left to firms and economic markets.

social conservatives

Those who believe government power should be used to uphold traditional values.

social liberals

Those who believe it is not government's role to buttress traditional values at the expense of unconventional or new values.

POLITICAL CULTURE

LIBERTY, EQUALITY, AND SELF-GOVERNMENT

Americans' Ideologies

Liberty and equality are central beliefs of the American political culture. In practice, however, they sometimes conflict or are applied in contradictory ways. The conflicts between and within them are reflected in America's dominant political ideologies, which center on the extent of government intervention in the economic marketplace and in the maintenance of traditional values. Government intervention in either sphere has implications for liberty and equality—the amount of freedom you should have in deciding your lifestyle and in determining your level of economic security.

You can test your ideology—and thus in a way your conception of liberty and equality—by asking yourself the following questions, which are similar to those used in national surveys:

1. Some people think the government should make greater use of its taxing and spending power to help the less-well-off while other people think government should do less in this realm, leaving economic benefits to be distributed largely through the marketplace. Which position comes closer to your own?

2. Some people think the government should make greater use of its power to promote traditional values in our society while other people think government should do less in this realm, leaving decisions about lifestyle to each individual. Which position comes closer to your own?

If you had been a respondent in a poll that asked these questions, you would have been classified as a *conservative* if you thought government should do less in the economic realm but do more to promote traditional values. You would have been classified as a *liberal* if you would like government to do more to help the less-well-off but to do less in promoting traditional values. You would have been classified a *libertarian* if you would like government to do less in both areas and as a *populist* if you would like government to do more in both realms. Do you ever use one of these labels to describe yourself? Is it the same one that would be assigned to you by this method? If not, how would you explain the difference?

The term **libertarian** is used to characterize this combination of attitudes. It is also the case that some economic liberals are social conservatives. They want to use the power of government to achieve economic redistribution and to uphold traditional values. The term **populist** is used to describe this combination of attitudes.

Thus, although only a minority of Americans can be classified as true ideologues, ideology can be a useful way to talk about opinion tendencies. Ideological terms help to describe the choices that Americans make and the conflicts that divide them. Beginning with the New Deal, for example, liberal attitudes on economic issues—a preference for government action—dominated. Later, Americans became less trusting of government welfare programs and more worried about their financial cost. Economic conservatism gained strength. Other recent disputes—abortion and immigration to name two—have pitted social conservatives against social liberals.

libertarians

Those who believe government tries to do too many things that should be left to firms and markets, and who oppose government as an instrument for upholding traditional values.

populists

Those who believe government should do more to assist people who have difficulty meeting their economic needs and who look to government to uphold traditional values.

Group Thinking: The Outlook of Many

For most citizens, groups are a more important frame of reference than is ideology. Many Americans see politics through the lens of the group or groups that define who they are. Farmers, for example, care a lot more about agricultural issues than do members of other groups. And although farmers are more likely than most Americans to oppose government benefit programs, they favor farm subsidies. Their ideological opposition to "big government" suddenly disappears when their own benefits are at issue.

Because of the country's great size, its settlement by various immigrant groups, and its economic pluralism, Americans are a very diverse people. Later chapters examine group tendencies more fully, but it is useful here to mention a

FRANKLIN D. ROOSEVELT
(1882–1945)

Historians may differ in where they rank Franklin D. Roosevelt among America's great presidents, but all would place him at the top by one indicator: the ability to lead public opinion. He won the presidency in 1932 during the depths of the Great Depression. FDR's job programs put Americans back to work, and his radio talks—the so-called fireside chats—did much to relieve people's anxieties about the economy and to give them hope of a better day ahead. In 1940, Roosevelt broke with tradition and announced that he would seek a third presidential term. Against the backdrop of war in Europe and continuing economic problems at home, he won the election—though by a narrower margin than in his two previous campaigns. Roosevelt was in office when the Japanese attacked Pearl Harbor on December 7, 1941. It was Roosevelt who again calmed the public, while calling them to action, saying that the Japanese attack was "a day that will live in infamy." Roosevelt won a fourth term in 1944 but died in office of a cerebral hemorrhage as the war was concluding. A distant cousin of President Theodore Roosevelt, FDR came to political prominence as secretary of the navy during World War I and was the Democratic Party's vice presidential nominee in 1920. A year later, he contracted polio and lost full use of his legs, a fact that he kept largely hidden from the public, even as he campaigned successfully for governor of New York and later president of the United States.

few major group orientations: religion, class, region, race and ethnicity, gender, and age.

Religion

Religious beliefs have always been a source of solidarity among group members and a source of conflict with outsiders. As Catholics and Jews came to America in large numbers in the nineteenth and early twentieth centuries, they encountered intense hostility from some Protestants. Today, Catholics, Protestants, and Jews have similar opinions on most policy issues.

Nevertheless, important religious differences remain, although the opposing sides shift as the issues shift.[18] Fundamentalist Protestants and Roman Catholics oppose legalized abortion more strongly than do mainline Protestants and Jews. This split reflects different religious teachings about when human life begins, whether at conception or at a later stage in the development of the fetus. Religious doctrine also affects opinions on poverty programs. Catholics and Jews are more supportive of such programs than Protestants are. An obligation to help the poor is a larger theme in Catholic and Jewish teachings; self-reliance is a larger part of Protestant thought.

The most powerful religious force in contemporary American politics is the so-called religious right, which consists primarily of individuals who see themselves as born-again Christians and who view the Bible as infallible truth. Their views on issues such as gay rights, abortion, and school prayer differ significantly from those of the population as a whole. A Time/CNN survey found that born-again Christians are a third more likely than other Americans to agree that "the Supreme Court and the Congress have gone too far in keeping religious and moral values like prayer out of our laws, schools, and many areas of our lives."[19]

Class

Economic class has less influence on political opinion in the United States than in Europe, but it is nevertheless related to opinions on certain economic issues. For example, lower-income Americans are more supportive of social welfare programs, business regulation, and progressive taxation than are Americans in higher-income categories.

An obstacle to class-based politics in the United States is that people with similar incomes but differing occupations do not share the same opinions. Support for collective bargaining, for example, is substantially higher among factory workers than among small farmers, service workers, and workers in the skilled crafts, even though the average income of members of all these groups is similar.

The interplay of class and opinion is examined more closely in Chapter 9, which discusses interest groups.

Region

For a long period, region nearly defined American politics. The North and South were divided over the issue of race, which spilled over into issues such as education and welfare policy. Racial progress has diminished the regional divide, as has the relocation of millions of Americans from the Northeast and Midwest to the South and West. The policy beliefs of these newcomers tend to be less conservative than those of people native to these regions. Nevertheless, regional differences are still evident on policies such as social welfare, civil rights, and national defense. Residents of the southern, mountain, and Great Plains states have more conservative opinions on these issues than do Americans elsewhere—a reflection of long-standing regional attitudes about government. The differences are large enough that when analysts talk about "red states" (Republican bastions) and "blue states" (Democratic bastions), they basically are referring to regions. The red states are concentrated in the South, Great Plains, and Rocky Mountains. The blue states are found mostly in the Northeast, the northern Midwest, and the West Coast.

Economic class as related to jobs and incomes affects Americans' opinions on a range of social and economic issues.

Race and Ethnicity

As Chapter 5 pointed out, race and ethnicity have a significant influence on opinions. White and black Americans, for example, differ on issues of integration: blacks more strongly support affirmative action, busing, and other measures designed to promote racial equality and integration. Racial and ethnic groups also differ on economic issues, largely as a result of differences in their economic situations. Blacks and Hispanics are more supportive of public assistance programs, for example, than are non-Hispanic whites. Law enforcement is another area in which different opinions exist. Opinion polls reveal that blacks and Hispanics are less trusting of police and the judicial system than are non-Hispanic whites.

Gender

Although male-female differences of opinion are small on most issues, gender does affect opinion in some policy areas.[20] Women are somewhat more supportive than men of abortion rights and affirmative action. Gallup polls have found, for example, a consistent difference of about 10 percentage points between women and men on support for affirmative action. The difference is even larger on some social welfare issues, such as poverty and education assistance. Compared with men, women have more liberal opinions on these issues, reflecting their greater economic vulnerability and their traditional responsibility for child care. A Washington Post/ABC News poll found, for example, that women were 20 percent more likely than men to favor increased spending for public education.

Women and men also differ in their opinions on the use of military force. In nearly every case, women are less supportive of military action than men are. The terrorist attacks on the World Trade Center and the Pentagon on September 11, 2001, produced an exception to the normal pattern. Men and women

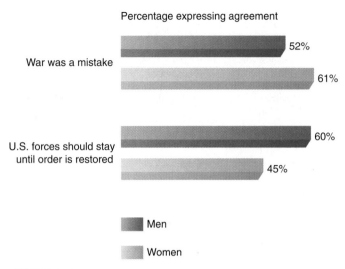

Percentage expressing agreement

War was a mistake
Men: 52%
Women: 61%

U.S. forces should stay until order is restored
Men: 60%
Women: 45%

■ Men
■ Women

FIGURE 6-2 Gender and the Iraq Conflict Compared with men, women are somewhat less inclined to support military force as a means of resolving international conflicts. This difference has been evident in polls on support for the Iraq war, as these examples illustrate.

Source: (In order of questions) Gallup poll, August 2007; ABC News/Washington Post poll, November 2005.

were almost equally likely (90 percent and 88 percent, respectively) to favor a military response. But they differ in expected ways when questioned about the Iraq conflict. Women are less likely than men to think that military intervention in Iraq was worthwhile (see Figure 6-2).

Differences such as these contribute to the gender gap discussed in Chapter 5. Women and men do not differ sharply in their political views, but they differ enough to respond somewhat differently to issues, events, and candidates.

Age

Age has always affected opinions, but the gap between young and old is widening. In her book *Young v. Old*, political scientist Susan MacManus notes that the elderly tend to oppose increases in public school funding while supporting increases in social security spending. MacManus predicts that issues of age will increasingly dominate American politics and that the elderly have the political clout to prevail. They vote at higher rates than do young people, are better organized politically (through groups such as the powerful AARP), and are growing in number as a result of lengthened life spans (the so-called graying of America).[21]

Crosscutting Cleavages

Although group loyalty can have a powerful impact on people's opinions, this influence is diminished when identification with one group is offset by identification with other groups. In a pluralistic society such as the United States, groups tend to be "crosscutting"—that is, each group includes individuals who also belong to other groups, where they encounter different people and opinions. Crosscutting cleavages encourage individuals to appreciate and understand differences, which leads them toward moderate opinions. By comparison, in societies such as Northern Ireland, where group loyalties are reinforcing rather than crosscutting, opinions are intensified by personal interactions. Catholics and Protestants in Northern Ireland live largely apart from each other, differing not only in their religious beliefs but also in their income levels, neighborhoods of residence, ethnicities, and loyalties to the government. The result is widespread mistrust between Northern Ireland's Catholics and Protestants.

Partisan Thinking: The Line That Divides

In the everyday world of politics, no source of opinion more clearly divides Americans than that of their partisanship. Figure 6-3 provides examples, but these show only a few of the differences. On nearly every major political issue, Republicans and Democrats have views that are at least somewhat different. In many cases, such as spending programs for the poor, the differences are substantial.

Party identification refers to a person's ingrained sense of loyalty to a political party. Party identification is not formal membership in a party but rather an emotional attachment to a party—the feeling that "I am a Democrat" or "I am a

party identification

The personal sense of loyalty that an individual may feel toward a particular political party.

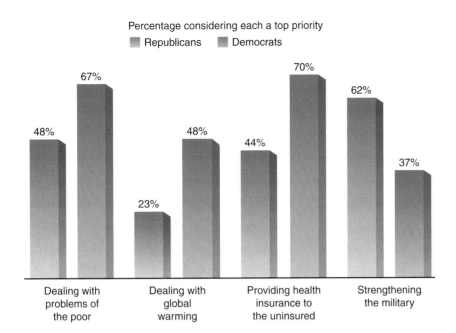

Percentage considering each a top priority

Republicans   Democrats

FIGURE 6-3 **Partisanship and Issue Opinions**
Republicans and Democrats differ significantly in their policy opinions and priorities.
Source: Pew Research Center for the People and the Press, 2008.

Republican." Scholars and pollsters typically have measured party identification with a question of the following type: "Generally speaking, do you think of yourself as a Republican, a Democrat, an Independent, or what?" About two-thirds of adults call themselves Democrats or Republicans. Of the one-third who prefer the label "Independent," most say they lean toward one party or the other and tend to vote primarily for that party's candidates.

Early studies concluded that party loyalties were highly stable and seldom changed over the course of adult life.[22] Subsequent studies have shown that party loyalties are more fluid than originally believed; they can be influenced by the issues and candidates of the moment.[23] Nevertheless, most adults do not switch their party loyalties easily, and a substantial proportion never waver from their initial commitment to a party, which can often be traced to childhood influences.

Once acquired, partisanship affects how people perceive and interpret events. An example is the differing opinions of Republicans and Democrats about U.S. military intervention in Kosovo in 1999 and in Iraq in 2003. Democrats were more supportive of the first war, while Republicans were more supportive of the second. While differences in the nature and purpose of these wars might partially explain this split, partisanship clearly does. The first of these conflicts was initiated by a Democratic president, Bill Clinton, while the second was begun by a Republican president, George W. Bush.

For most people, partisanship is not simply blind faith in the party of their choice. Some Republicans and Democrats know very little about their party's policies and unthinkingly embrace its candidates. However, party loyalties are not randomly distributed across the population, but instead follow a pattern that would be predicted from the parties' histories. The Democratic Party, for example, has been the driving force behind social welfare and workers' rights policies, while the Republican Party has spearheaded probusiness and tax reduction policies. The fact that most union workers are Democrats and most businesspeople are Republicans is not a coincidence. Their partisanship is rooted in their economic self-interest.[24] This and other issues of partisanship are examined in more detail at various points later in this book, particularly in Chapters 7, 8, 11, and 12.

STATES IN THE NATION

PARTY LOYALTIES IN THE STATES

The strength of the major parties varies substantially among the states. One indicator of party dominance is the degree to which the party identification of state residents favors one party or the other. In opinion polls, party identification is measured by a question of the following type: "Generally speaking, do you think of yourself as a Republican, a Democrat, an Independent, or what?" The Gallup Organization, using the results of roughly forty thousand interviews it conducted in 2004, estimated the state-by-state distribution of Republican and Democratic identifiers. For the map below, a state is classified as Republican if Republican identifiers outnumber Democratic identifiers by 7 percentage points or more. It is classified as Democratic if the reverse is true. The remaining states are classified as competitive. By this indicator,

Republican strength is concentrated in the South, the Plains, and the Rockies, while Democratic strength is concentrated in the Northeast and the upper Midwest. Other indicators of party strength, such as control of state elective offices, would result in similar categorizations of the states.

Q: Why is the concentration of Republicans particularly high in some states of the South, the Great Plains, and the Rocky Mountains?

A: The South swung Republican after the Democratic Party took the lead on civil rights in the 1960s. The Great Plains and Rocky Mountain areas have traditionally been Republican, a reflection in part of the rugged individualism that defined their early settlement and contributed to a preference for small government.

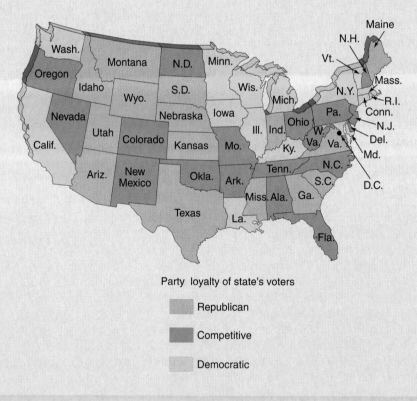

Party loyalty of state's voters

◼ Republican

◼ Competitive

◼ Democratic

Source: Adapted from Gallup Organization report. Alaska and Hawaii are not included; interviews were not conducted in these states.

The Influence of Public Opinion on Policy

As yet unanswered in our discussion is a central question about public opinion: what impact does it have on government? The question does not have a firm or final answer. In any society of appreciable size, self-government takes place through representative institutions. The people themselves do not directly decide issues of policy, but instead entrust them to elected and appointed officials.

Governing decisions are complex, as are the factors that go into them, including the influence of public opinion.

Some observers claim that officials are relatively insensitive to public opinion—that they are so entrenched in their positions that, however much they claim to serve the people, they actually pay little attention to what ordinary citizens think.[25] This assessment undoubtedly applies to some officials and some issues. However, the most comprehensive study ever conducted on the relationship between public opinion and policy concluded that public opinion does in fact sway government. The study, which examined fifty years of polls and policy decisions, found that when public opinion on an issue changed, policy usually changed in the direction of the change in public opinion. In the case of major issues, this pattern was particularly evident—in such cases, policy typically aligned with public opinion. Based on this evidence, the study's authors concluded: "When Americans' policy preferences shift, it is likely that congruent changes in policy will follow."[26]

However, a more recent study by Lawrence Jacobs and Robert Shapiro found a widening gap between public opinion and policy, apparently because elected officials of both parties have tilted toward the more extreme positions favored by powerful groups within their respective parties (such as the Christian right within the Republican Party and lifestyle liberals within the Democratic Party).[27] Jacobs and Shapiro nonetheless conclude that officials remain sensitive to public opinion on many issues, particularly those that could become campaign issues. As the 2008 election approached, for example, a number of congressional Republicans backed away from their earlier strong support for the war in Iraq. They did not necessarily call for a quick withdrawal of U.S. forces, but they offered more qualified support for the Iraq mission than previously. Underlying this repositioning were polls showing that the Iraq conflict was unpopular with most voters, enough so that some of them claimed they would vote against any candidate who advocated a large-scale continuing military presence in Iraq.

If elections heighten officials' attention to public opinion, so do particular issues. Public opinion on some issues is so entrenched or intense that officials have little choice but to accept existing policy. During his first presidential term, Ronald Reagan proposed a major overhaul of the social security system, but he quickly backed down in the face of widespread public opposition, particularly from senior citizens groups. The founder of social security, Franklin D. Roosevelt, understood that public opinion would preserve the program. "No damn politician," he reportedly said, "can ever scrap my social security program." Roosevelt recognized that, by having social security benefits funded by payroll taxes, workers would feel they had rightfully earned their retirement benefits and would fight to maintain them.

Taxation is another example. Politicians will ordinarily go to great lengths—including borrowing huge amounts of money to shift the problem to future generations—to avoid a major tax increase. Elected officials have some latitude when it comes to smaller or selective tax hikes, such as an increase in taxes on

Although public opinion does not always drive government policy, there are times when the impact of public opinion is clearly evident, as in the case of Americans' growing disenchantment with the Iraq conflict as it went beyond the quick ending that President Bush had promised. The public's response encouraged politicians to advocate a scaled-down effort in Iraq. Barack Obama initially centered his 2008 presidential campaign on a withdrawal of troops from Iraq.

alcohol or cigarettes, but they risk political defeat if they take the leadership on a major tax increase, however necessary such action might be. Angry taxpayers are officeholders' worst nightmare.

On some issues, public opinion is so sharply divided that officeholders are unable to satisfy it. The illegal immigration issue is an example. In 2007, President George W. Bush and top congressional leaders of both parties worked out a proposal for comprehensive immigration reform that attempted to accommodate both sides of the issue. In order to reduce illegal immigration, border security would be tightened, as would the monitoring of firms that tend to hire illegal immigrants. At the same time, programs would be established to enable some illegal immigrants to work legally in the United States and over a longer period to gain eligibility for citizenship. The initiative collapsed in Congress due to strong opposition among some constituents to any kind of compromise on the issue.

Ordinarily, public opinion gives politicians room to maneuver, serving only as a guiding force. It establishes a boundary within which officials can act, but does not force a particular action upon them. In some case, inaction is an option. Since the early 1990s, public opinion polls have shown support for reform of America's health care system. Some steps have been taken, but they have been relatively modest ones, such as incremental increases in the number of poor children eligible for government-provided medical care. President Bill Clinton attempted a comprehensive overhaul of the health care system during his first term, but it floundered when middle-class Americans with access to medical care failed to support Clinton's attempt to extend coverage to the uninsured. The failure of Clinton's initiative weakened public support for his presidency, contributing to his party's massive defeat in the 1994 midterm elections. Since then, even though public opinion polls show continuing support for health care reform, elected officials have largely avoided the issue, preferring inaction to the risk of a public backlash.

In other cases, inaction is not an option. When the U.S. economy slumped in 2008, lawmakers knew that they had to respond to the downturn, but had a range of options that would have satisfied the public's demand for action. Among other things, they chose to stimulate the economy through rebates to taxpayers and loans to financial institutions.

Such examples, however, do not provide an answer to the question of whether public officials are *sufficiently* responsive to public opinion. This question is complicated by the fact that it is partly a normative one—the answer rests on beliefs about the proper relationship between people's opinions and government policies. As we discussed in Chapter 2, some theorists hold that representatives should base their policy decisions on what they believe will best serve the people's interests, while others claim that the people themselves are the best judge of their interests and that it is the representative's duty to pay close heed to the people's demands. The question is also complicated by the fact that politics involves attempts to influence public opinion. Citizens' opinions are not fixed. They can be activated, changed, and crystallized through political action. Political leaders invest enormous amounts of money and time in an effort to get citizens to see things their way.

In fact, one of the best indicators of the power of public opinion is the great effort made by political leaders to harness it in support of their goals. In American politics, popular demand for a policy is a powerful argument for that policy. For this reason and others, great effort is made to organize and represent public opinion through elections (Chapter 7), political parties (Chapter 8), interest groups (Chapter 9), the news media (Chapter 10), and political institutions (Chapters 11–14).

Summary Self-Test www.mhhe.com/pattersontad9e

Public opinion can be defined as those opinions held by ordinary citizens that they openly express. Public officials have many ways of assessing public opinion, such as the outcomes of elections, but they have increasingly come to rely on public opinion polls. There are many possible sources of error in polls, and surveys sometimes present a misleading portrayal of the public's views. However, a properly conducted poll can be an accurate indication of what the public is thinking and can dissuade political leaders from thinking that the views of the most vocal citizens (such as demonstrators and letter writers) are shared by the broader public.

The process by which individuals acquire their political opinions is called political socialization. During childhood, the family and schools are important sources of basic political attitudes, such as beliefs about the parties and the nature of the U.S. political and economic systems. Many of the basic orientations that Americans acquire during childhood remain with them in adulthood, but socialization is a continuing process. Major shifts in opinion during adulthood are usually the consequence of changing political conditions; for example, the Great Depression of the 1930s was the catalyst for wholesale changes in Americans' opinions on the government's economic role. Short-term fluctuations in opinion can result from new political issues and problems. Individuals' opinions in these cases are affected by prior beliefs, peers, political leaders, and the news media. Events themselves are also a significant short-term influence on opinions.

The frames of reference that guide Americans' opinions include cultural beliefs, such as individualism, which affect what people will find politically acceptable and desirable. Opinions can also stem from ideology, although most citizens do not have a strong and consistent ideological attachment. In addition, individuals develop opinions as a result of group orientations—notably, religion, income level, occupation, region, race, ethnicity, gender, and age. Partisanship is perhaps the major source of political opinions; Republicans and Democrats differ in their voting behavior and views on many policy issues.

Public opinion has a significant influence on government but seldom determines exactly what government will do in a particular instance. Public opinion serves to constrain the policy choices of officials. Some policy actions are beyond the range of possibility because the public will not accept change in existing policy or will not seriously consider policy that seems clearly at odds with basic American values. Evidence indicates that officials are at least somewhat attentive to public opinion on highly visible and controversial issues of public policy.

CHAPTER 6

Study Corner

Key Terms

agents of socialization (p. 154)
economic conservatives (p. 158)
economic liberals (p. 158)
ideology (p. 158)
libertarians (p. 159)
party identification (p. 162)
political socialization (p. 154)
population (p. 150)
populists (p. 159)
public opinion (p. 148)
public opinion poll (p. 150)
sample (p. 150)
sampling error (p.151)
social conservatives (p. 158)
social liberals (p. 158)

Self-Test

1. The process by which individuals acquire political opinions is called:
   a. public opinion polling.
   b. efficacy.
   c. selective incorporation.
   d. political socialization.
   e. sampling error.

2. Studies on the influence of ideology on public opinion agree that:
   a. it is useless to apply ideological terms to patterns of opinion in America.
   b. most Republicans think of themselves as economic conservatives and social liberals.
   c. most people think of themselves as isolationists.
   d. only a minority of Americans have a true ideology

in the sense of having higher consistent attitudes on public issues.

3. Public officials increasingly rely on which method to assess public opinion?
   a. talk show ratings
   b. election outcomes
   c. public opinion polls
   d. editorials in newspapers
   e. mail received by elected representatives in Washington, D.C.

4. Compared to Europeans, Americans are substantially more likely to form political opinions based on their:
   a. religious beliefs.
   b. economic class.
   c. party identification.
   d. occupation.
   e. age.

5. All of the following factors are associated with differences in political opinions, but all but one of them is today a weaker predictor of opinion differences than it once was. Which factor has become a better predictor of opinions than it was only a few decades ago?
   a. region
   b. gender
   c. economic class
   d. ethnicity

6. The political opinions of males and females differ most significantly on issues of:
   a. the environment.
   b. crime and the judicial system.
   c. the use of military force.
   d. global trade.

7. In general, the larger the size of the sample in a poll, the smaller the sampling error. (T/F)

8. Of the various agents of political socialization, political leaders are by far the most important one. (T/F)

9. People's party identification is measured by asking them to identify the party that they voted for in the most recent presidential election. (T/F)

10. Most Americans pay close attention to and are highly informed about politics and public affairs. (T/F)

Critical Thinking

What factors limit the influence of public opinion on the policy choices of public officials?

Suggested Readings

Alvarez, R. Michael, and John Brehm. *Hard Choices, Easy Answers: Values, Information, and American Public Opinion.* Princeton, N.J.: Princeton University Press, 2002. An analysis arguing that what citizens know about politics is assessed in the context of their values and beliefs.

Asher, Herbert. *Polling and the Public,* 7th ed. Washington, D.C.: Congressional Quarterly Press, 2007. A guide to public opinion poll methods and analysis.

Canes-Wrone, Brandice. *Who Leads Whom? Presidents, Policy, and the Public.* Chicago: University of Chicago Press, 2005. A look at recent presidents and their policies in the context of public opinion.

Green, Donald, Bradley Palmquist, and Eric Schickler. *Partisan Hearts and Minds.* New Haven, Conn.: Yale University Press, 2002. An analysis concluding that partisanship powerfully affects how citizens respond to candidates and issues.

Jacobs, Lawrence, and Robert Shapiro. *Politicians Don't Pander.* Chicago: University of Chicago Press, 2000. An analysis concluding that politicians are not driven by polls.

Stimson, James. *Tides of Consent: How Public Opinion Shapes American Politics.* New York: Cambridge University Press, 2004. An analysis of trends in public opinion and their political impact.

Whitaker, Lois Duke, ed. *Voting the Gender Gap.* Urbana: University of Illinois Press, 2008. An edited volume that explores the voting divide between men and women.

Zaller, John R. *The Nature and Origins of Mass Opinion.* New York: Cambridge University Press, 1992. A superb analysis of the nature of public opinion.

List of Websites

http://www.gallup.com/
The website of the Gallup Organization, America's oldest and best known polling organization.

http://www.people-press.org/
The website of the Pew Research Center for the People and the Press; includes an abundance of recent polling results, including cross-national comparisons.

http://www.realclearpolitics.com/
A site that has numerous up-to-date polls from a variety of organizations and on a variety of topics.

http://www.publicagenda.org/
The nonpartisan Public Agenda's site; provides opinions, analyses, and educational materials on current policy issues.

Participate!

Studies have regularly found that Americans, in relative and in absolute terms, are substantially uninformed about the issues affecting their state, nation, and the world. As a result, Americans' opinions about policy issues and problems are not as informed as they could and should be. Citizenship entails responsibilities, one of which is to stay informed about problems and developments that affect the community, the state, and the nation. As an informed citizen, you will be better able to make judgments about policy issues, to choose wisely when voting during elections, and to recognize situations that call for greater personal involvement. Fortunately, you have access to one of the most substantial news systems in the world. News about public affairs is virtually at your fingertips—through your computer, on television, and in the newspaper. Spending only a small amount of time each day following the news will help you to be a more effective and involved citizen.

Extra Credit

For up-to-the-minute *New York Times* articles, interactive simulations, graphics, study tools, and more links and quizzes, visit the text's Online Learning Center at www.mhhe.com/pattersontad9e.

Self-Test Answers

1. d   2. d   3. c   4. a   5. b   6. c   7. T   8. F   9. F   10. F

National Journal

THE PEOPLE V. WASHINGTON

Alexander Hamilton famously labeled public opinion "a great beast." The notion is that vital matters of state are best left to well-informed professional elites, not to the masses. And if the people don't like an adopted course of action, this reasoning goes, they can always vote out its representatives.

To give the argument its due, it is certainly true that the American public wins no medals for mastery of world geography and the intricacies of foreign politics and culture.

And yet there is a difference between knowledge and judgment. Even in a republic like the United States the unknowledgeable are presumed to possess a capacity, or at least a potential, for good judgment. Otherwise, why permit the average citizen to vote at all?

In early 2007, President Bush informed the nation of his decision to increase the number of U.S. troops in Iraq by about 20,000 as the key element in his new strategy for "a way forward" in the conflict. Bush's plan was based on extensive consultations with foreign-policy and military experts of various stripes, inside and outside the administration. No doubt he received a variety of opinions. But let's consider what "The People" think.

More than five years have passed since the 9/11 attacks, which inaugurated the administration's global war on terrorism and put into play the question of whether to invade Iraq. Over this period, all major polling outfits have been taking the public's pulse at regular intervals on just about every imaginable national security question.

These data indeed tell an interesting story, at odds with certain myths that have taken root about the public's mind-set on Iraq. Perhaps vox populi is a beast. But it is a beast with some fascinating things to say—about its initial attitudes on the Iraq war, about its sentiments as the war has ground on, about what it thinks is "a way forward" on Iraq, and, beyond Iraq, about America's role in the post-9/11 world.

On the eve of the Iraq invasion in March 2003, virtually every major opinion poll showed a solid majority of Americans—64 percent of respondents in the Gallup/CNN/USA Today poll, 59 percent in the Princeton Survey Research Associates/Pew Research Center poll—in favor of taking military action to remove Saddam Hussein from power. From these high numbers, a certain conventional wisdom developed about the public's support for the war.

The saga goes like this: The public backed a war whose rationale was sold, like a product, by the Bush administration and affiliated hucksters and never really challenged by a cowed and gullible news media.

A stream of public opinion surveys suggests . . . that **the federal government is following a misplaced set** of national security priorities.

Team Bush's own pronouncements buttress this story line. In explaining the White House's slow start in the summer of 2002 in putting together a plan to rally the public around the need to confront Saddam, Andy Card, at that point Bush's chief of staff, famously told The New York Times early in September 2002: "From a marketing point of view, you don't introduce new products in August."

According to this plot sequence, public opinion went over to the war camp as a result of the administration's fear-mongering statements about Saddam's weapons of mass destruction capabilities. Just days before the first anniversary of 9/11, on September 8, 2002, then-National Security Adviser Condoleezza Rice said on CNN, "We don't want the smoking gun to be a mushroom cloud."

The problem with this marketing-based account is that it is a myth. In the PSRA/Pew Research Center poll, public support for "military action in Iraq to end Saddam Hussein's rule" was 64 percent in an August 14–25, 2002, survey, before the administration's PR blitz, and at 64 percent in a September 12-14 survey, in the three days following Bush's Ground Zero visit. In the September

26–27 poll, support was 63 percent. Where's the bounce?

In fact, nearly all polls recorded their highest backing for war in the months immediately after the 9/11 attacks, when Washington was not talking much about invading Iraq. In November 2001, public support for military action against Iraq was at 78 percent in the ABC News/Washington Post poll, 77 percent in Fox News/Opinion Dynamics, and 74 percent in Gallup/CNN/USA Today. During the buildup to war that culminated in the invasion 17 months later, those numbers never went higher. This suggests a fierce, if misguided, reaction to the attacks. As everyone now acknowledges, Saddam was not behind 9/11.

Just days after the invasion began on March 20, 2003, 23 percent of respondents said United States had "made a mistake"—that's the key phrase—"in view of the developments since we first sent our troops to Iraq." Because at that starting juncture, virtually no "developments" to speak of had taken place, the 23 percent can be seen as the slice of the people who had already made up their minds about the war. 75 percent said, no, the war was not a mistake. Only 2 percent registered no opinion.

The Gallup consortium kept asking that question. But despite early waves of good news—light casualties, the fall of Baghdad on April 9, Bush's declaration on May 1 of the end of "major combat"—the "mistake" number kept rising. By early October, little more than six months after the invasion, it was already up to 40 percent; and it was 42 percent in the first poll taken after the ballyhooed capture of Saddam in his spider hole in mid-December of that first year of the war. The sensational revelations of the Abu

Ghraib prison torture scandal, in mid-April 2004, did not move the number much.

The "mistake" cohort reached a majority, 54 percent, for the first time in a poll taken on June 21-23, 2004—15 months after the invasion began, and a week after the 9/11 commission found "no credible evidence" of a link between Iraq and Al Qaeda, as the White House had asserted.

In his second inaugural address, Bush declared, "The survival of liberty in our land increasingly depends on the success of liberty in other lands. The best hope for peace in our world is the expansion of freedom in all the world."

In that speech and others, Bush has, in effect, offered both a diagnosis and a prescription for what ails the post-9/11 world. His premise that a freer world is a more placid one may not seem particularly controversial, or even original. Elites generally applauded. The beast, though, was unconvinced.

Eight months later, the Chicago Council on Foreign Relations released a comprehensive poll, "Americans on Promoting Democracy." In that survey, only 26 percent agreed that "when there are more democracies, the world is a safer place." This was not a reaction against democracy per se. Consider this second, more nuanced finding: 68 percent said that "democracy may make life better within a country, but it does not make the world a safer place."

So, broadly speaking, a stream of public opinion surveys suggests, and has been suggesting for several years, that the federal government is following a misplaced set of national security priorities. And while the people are not speaking with a single voice, majorities favor clear positions—and those majorities seem to be not fickle or mercurial but fairly solid.

With respect to Iraq, the balance of opinion, following the logic of accepting the war as a mistake, is clearly in favor of reducing America's involvement in Iraq. In the December 2006 CBS News poll, 57 percent of respondents favored setting a timetable for withdrawing U.S. troops. In the exit poll of midterm election voters, 55 percent said the United States should withdraw some or all troops, and only 17 percent supported "send more." And these beliefs carry some urgency: In Gallup's first poll after the midterms, Republicans, independents, and Democrats, all by very large margins, listed the situation in Iraq as the "top priority" for Washington to address.

These poll numbers are the stuff of front-page news. But they don't tell the whole story. Iraq is the most urgent public priority because it is an active, bleeding mess. But the public does not view Iraq as the key to dealing with America's principal, long-term problems in the world. The people are not saying to Washington, "Disengage from Iraq and then focus on the problems at home."

Americans have said that their No. 1 priority in the war on terrorism is "increasing CIA and FBI efforts to find and capture suspected terrorists," and the second goal was "capturing or killing Osama bin Laden." Even though Washington no longer talks much about getting the devastator of the twin towers, the public has clung to its wrath—and its demand for blood justice.

The Program on International Policy Attitudes posed the broader question, "What kind of foreign policy does the American public want?" In that survey, respondents listed the issues that they believed deserved greater attention from national policy makers. First was "working to reduce U.S. dependence on oil," followed by "port security," and "coordinating with the intelligence and law enforcement agencies of other countries to track and capture members of terrorist groups."

The top priority, reducing U.S. reliance on oil, is a sophisticated choice. Stories about oil dependency are not what lead the evening news, and congressional committee chairmen do not make big splashes with hearings on the subject. "Reducing oil dependency"—a goal that lends itself to quantitative measurement—may sound prosaic compared with "the expansion of freedom in all of the world." No spines tingle at the phrase. But the beast, it seems, is in a mood for prose, not poetry.

The People, to boil things down, think three big things: Washington should disengage from the military conflict in Iraq, take out bin Laden and all other known terrorists who mean America lethal harm, and reduce the nation's dependence on oil.

Two days before the 2006 midterm elections, ABC's George Stephanopoulos noted in an interview with Vice President Dick Cheney, "It seems like the public has turned against" the administration's policy on Iraq. Cheney responded, "It may not be popular with the public. It doesn't matter, in the sense that we have to continue the mission and do what we think is right, and that's exactly what we're doing."

The Iraq debacle is unavoidably calling into question the horse sense of the political establishment. "I would rather be governed by the first 2,000 names in the Boston phone book than by the 2,000 members of the faculty of Harvard University," William F. Buckley Jr. once quipped. Buckley was getting at the idea that ordinary citizens in a democracy can possess a certain collective wisdom. He also once said, less notably, "The best defense against usurpatory government is an assertive citizenry."

◀ FOR DISCUSSION: Has your opinion of the War in Iraq evolved? Did you have a strong opinion when the war was launched? How does it compare to your opinion now?

How much should government listen to polls? Can popular wisdom be trusted to govern something as complex as a war? What are your top three priorities in the War on Terror? How do they compare to the country's?

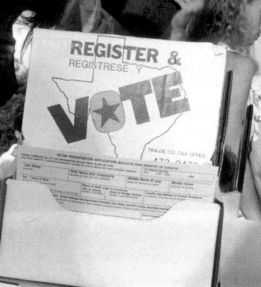

Political Participation
Activating the Popular Will

Voter Participation

Factors in Voter Turnout: The United States in Comparative Perspective
Why Some Americans Vote and Others Do Not

Conventional Forms of Participation Other Than Voting

Campaign and Lobbying Activities
Virtual Participation
Community Activities

Unconventional Activism: Social Movements and Protest Politics

Participation and the Potential for Influence

---

political participation

Involvement in activities intended to influence public policy and leadership, such as voting, joining political groups, writing to elected officials, demonstrating for political causes, and giving money to political candidates.

We are concerned in public affairs, but immersed in our private ones. Walter Lippmann[1]

They seemed to come out of nowhere. In the Iowa Democratic caucuses, their numbers were three times greater than in the previous election. In the New Hampshire Democratic primary, their numbers doubled from the 2004 level. In contest after contest in the 2008 Democratic presidential nominating race, young voters, and older ones, too, expressed their sentiments in numbers not seen since the 1970s. A few analysts had predicted that young adults would vote in higher numbers than usual because of their concern with the war in Iraq, but no one had envisioned anything on the scale that occurred. Young adults mostly supported the candidacy of Illinois senator Barack Obama, but New York senator Hillary Clinton had her supporters, too. When all their votes were counted across all the states, the turnout level in the Democratic primaries was that of an earlier era, when young adults voted at much higher rates than they have in recent elections.

Voting is a form of **political participation**—involvement in activities intended to influence public policy and leadership. Political participation involves other activities in addition to voting, such as joining political groups, writing to elected officials, demonstrating for political causes, and giving money to political candidates. Such activities are basic to a properly functioning democratic society. The concept of self-government is based on the idea that ordinary people have a right and a duty to participate in the affairs of state. As it happens, however, political participation in the United States has a different pattern than in most Western democracies, as this chapter will show. The major points made in this chapter are these:

- *Voter turnout in U.S. elections is low in comparison with that of other democratic nations.* The reasons for this difference include the nature of U.S. election laws, particularly those pertaining to registration requirements and the scheduling of elections.

- *Most citizens do not participate actively in politics in ways other than voting.* Only a minority of Americans can be classified as political activists. Nevertheless, Americans are more likely than citizens of other democracies to contribute time and money to political and community organizations.

■ *Most Americans make a sharp distinction between their personal lives and public life.* This attitude reduces their incentive to participate and contributes to a pattern of participation dominated by citizens of higher income and education.

Voter Participation

suffrage

The right to vote.

HISTORICAL
Background

At the nation's founding, **suffrage**—the right to vote—was limited to property-owning males. Tom Paine ridiculed this restriction in *Common Sense*. Observing that a man whose only item of property was a jackass would lose his right to vote if the jackass died, Paine asked, "Now tell me, which was the voter, the man or the jackass?" It was not until 1840 that all states extended suffrage to property-less white males.

Women did not secure the vote until 1920, with the ratification of the Nineteenth Amendment. Decades earlier, Susan B. Anthony had tried to vote in her hometown of Rochester, New York, asserting that it was her right as a U.S. citizen. She was arrested for "illegal voting" and told that her proper place was in the home. By 1920, men had run out of excuses for denying the vote to women. As Senator Wendell Phillips observed, "One of two things is true: either woman is like man—and if she is, then a ballot based on brains belongs to her as well as to him. Or she is different, and then man does not know how to vote for her as she herself does."[2]

African Americans had to wait nearly fifty years longer than women to secure their right to vote. Blacks seemed to have won that right after the Civil War with passage of the Fifteenth Amendment, but as explained in Chapter 5, they were effectively disenfranchised in the South by a number of electoral tricks, including the poll tax, which was a fee of several dollars that had to be paid before a person could register to vote. Because most blacks in the South were too poor to pay it, the poll tax effectively kept many of them from voting. Not until the ratification of the Twenty-fourth Amendment in 1964 was the poll tax outlawed

After a hard-fought, decades-long campaign, American women finally won the right to vote in 1920.

TABLE 7-1 | Opinions on Obligations of Citizens   Americans rank voting as one of the essential obligations of citizenship.

	Essential Obligation	Very Important Obligation	Somewhat Important	Personal Preference
Treating all people equally regardless of race or ethnic background	57%	33%	6%	4%
Voting in elections	53	29	9	9
Working to reduce inequality and injustice	41	42	12	6
Being civil to others with whom we may disagree	35	45	14	6
Staying informed about news and public affairs	30	42	19	10
Donating blood or organs to help with medical needs	20	37	18	26
Volunteering time to community service	16	42	26	16

Source: Used by permission of the 1996 Survey of American Political Culture, James Davison Hunter and Carol Bowman, Directors, Institute for Advanced Studies in Culture, University of Virginia.

in federal elections. Supreme Court decisions and the Voting Rights Act of 1965 swept away other legal barriers to equal participation by African Americans.

In 1971, the Twenty-sixth Amendment extended voting rights to include citizens eighteen years of age or older. Previously, nearly all states had restricted voting to those twenty-one years of age or older.

Factors in Voter Turnout: The United States in Comparative Perspective

Today nearly any American adult—rich or poor, man or woman, black or white—who is determined to vote can legally and actually do so. Most Americans embrace the symbolism of the vote, saying that they have a duty to vote in elections (see Table 7-1).

Nevertheless, many Americans shirk this duty. Millions choose not to vote regularly, a tendency that sets Americans apart from citizens of most other Western democracies. Since the 1960s, **voter turnout**—the proportion of adult citizens who actually vote in a given election—has averaged about 55 percent in presidential elections (see Figure 7-1). A few presidential elections in this period,

voter turnout

The proportion of persons of voting age who actually vote in a given election.

FIGURE 7-1 **Voter Turnout in Presidential Elections, 1960–2008**
After 1960, as indicated by the proportion of voters in the adult-age population, turnout declined steadily. In the past two decades, turnout has fluctuated, depending on the issues at stake in the particular election.
Source: U.S. Bureau of the Census. Figures based on percent of vote-eligible adults who voted. Figure for 2008 based on preliminary estimates.

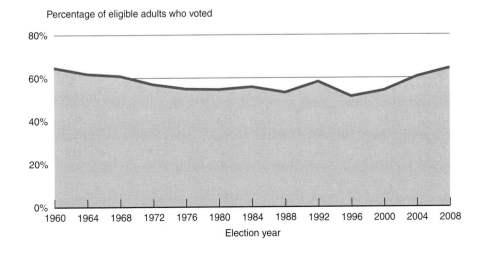

Percentage of eligible adults who voted

HOW THE U.S. COMPARES

VOTER TURNOUT

The United States ranks near the bottom among the world's democracies in the percentage of eligible citizens who participate in national elections. One reason for the low voter turnout is that individual Americans are responsible for registering to vote, whereas in most other democracies voters are automatically registered by government officials. In addition, unlike some other democracies, the United States does not encourage voting by holding elections on the weekend or by imposing penalties, such as fines, on those who do not participate.

Another factor affecting voter turnout rate in the United States is the absence of a major labor or socialist party, which would serve to bring lower-income citizens to the polls. America's individualist culture and its electoral system (see Chapter 8) have inhibited the establishment of a major labor or socialist party. In democracies where such parties exist, the turnout difference between upper- and lower-income groups is relatively small. In the United States, the gap in the turnout level of lower- and upper-income persons is substantial.

Country	Approximate Voter Turnout	Automatic Registration?	Social Democrat, Socialist, or Labor Party?	Election Day a Holiday or Weekend Day?
Belgium	90%	Yes	Yes	Yes
Germany	85	Yes	Yes	Yes
Denmark	85	Yes	Yes	No
Italy	80	Yes	Yes	Yes
Austria	80	Yes	Yes	Yes
France	80	No	Yes	Yes
Great Britain	60	Yes	Yes	No
Canada	60	Yes	Yes	No
Japan	60	Yes	Yes	Yes
United States	55	No	No	No

Source: Developed from multiple sources. Turnout percentages are a rough average of national elections during the past two decades.

including the 2008 election, have resulted in a turnout that is measurably higher than the average, but even in these cases, the nonvoters have outnumbered the voters who backed the winning candidate. Turnout is even lower in the midterm congressional elections that take place between presidential elections. Midterm election turnout has not reached 50 percent since 1920 and, since 1970, has seldom topped the 40 percent mark. After one midterm election, cartoonist Rigby showed an election clerk eagerly asking a stray cat that had wandered into a polling place, "Are you registered?"[3]

Polling places are even lonelier during local elections. In many cities and towns, barely 20 percent show up to vote in local elections, and the trend has been downward for four decades.[4] Even as the voting rate increased in the 2004 and 2008 presidential elections, it slipped in local elections held in 2005 and 2007.

Nonvoting is more prevalent in the United States than in nearly all other democracies (see "How the U.S. Compares"). In recent decades, turnout in major national elections has averaged more than 90 percent in Belgium and more than 80 percent in France, Germany, and Denmark.[5] However, the disparity in turnout between the United States and other nations is not as great as these official voting rates suggest. Some nations calculate turnout solely on the basis of eligible adults, whereas the United States has traditionally based its figures on all adults, including legal aliens and other ineligible groups. Nevertheless, even when such statistical disparities are corrected, turnout in U.S. elections is comparatively low.

Contributing to the relatively low turnout in U.S. elections are registration requirements, the frequency of elections, and the political party system.

Registration Requirements

Before Americans are allowed to vote, they must be registered—that is, their names must appear on an official list of eligible voters. **Registration** began around 1900 as a way of preventing voters from casting more than one ballot on Election Day. Multiple balloting had become a tactic of big-city party machines—"vote early and often" was their motto. Although registration reduced illegal voting, it also placed a burden on honest citizens. Because they could now vote only if they took time beforehand to register, those people who forgot or otherwise failed to do so found themselves unable to participate on election day. Turnout in U.S. elections declined steadily after registration was instituted.

Although other democracies also require registration, they place this responsibility on government. In most European nations, public officials have the duty to enroll citizens on registration lists. When someone moves to a new address, for example, the Postal Service will notify registration officials of the change. The United States—in keeping with its individualistic culture—is one of the few democracies in which registration is the individual's responsibility. Moreover, registration rules have traditionally been set by the state governments, and some states make it somewhat difficult for citizens to qualify. Registration periods and locations usually are not highly publicized.[6] Eligibility can also be a problem. In most states, a citizen must reside at an address for a minimum period, usually thirty days, before becoming eligible to register. Scholars estimate that turnout would be roughly 10 percentage points higher in the United States if it had European-style registration.[7]

States with a tradition of lenient registration laws have a higher average turnout rate than other states. Idaho, Iowa, Maine, Minnesota, Montana,

registration

The practice of placing citizens' names on an official list of voters before they are eligible to exercise their right to vote.

Volunteers at a community event attempt to interest citizens in registering so that they can vote in the next election. Nearly all democracies have automatic voter registration. The United States does not, which makes voter registration efforts an important factor in election turnout.

STATES IN THE NATION

VOTER TURNOUT IN PRESIDENTIAL ELECTIONS

The United States has lower voter turnout than most Western democracies. Within the United States, however, the state-to-state variation is substantial. In a few states, including Minnesota and New Hampshire, nearly seven in ten adults vote in presidential elections. In contrast, there are a few states, including Hawaii and Texas, where barely more than four in ten adults vote.

Q: Why do states in the South and Southwest have relatively low turnout rates?

A: Southern states have more poverty and a tradition of more restrictive registration laws (dating to the Jim Crow era of racial segregation). Both factors are associated with lower voting rates. States with large populations of recent immigrants, including those in the Southwest, also tend to have lower voting rates.

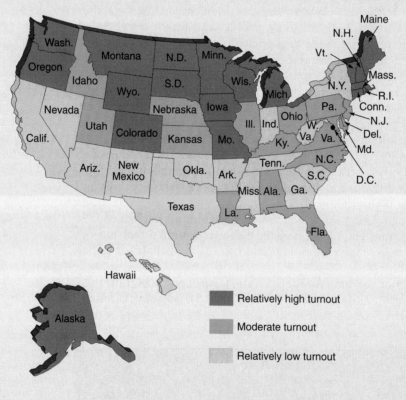

Relatively high turnout

Moderate turnout

Relatively low turnout

Source: Compiled by author from various sources; based on recent midterm and presidential elections.

New Hampshire, Wisconsin, and Wyoming, which are states that allow people to register at their polling place on election day, have high turnout rates. The states that have the most restrictive registration laws are concentrated in the South, continuing a legacy that traces to the time when black people were kept from voting (see "States in the Nation").

In 1993, in an effort to increase registration levels nationwide, Congress enacted a voting registration law known as "motor voter." It requires states to permit people to register to vote when applying for a driver's license or public assistance. Registration is not automatic in these situations; the citizen must voluntarily fill out the registration form. Moreover, the motor voter law does not help citizens who do not drive or do not otherwise have contact with an appropriate state agency. The law has resulted in some new voters but fewer than its proponents envisioned.

A newer device, voter identification cards, will serve to depress voter turnout. Republican-controlled legislatures in several states have enacted laws requiring citizens to have a government-issued photo ID in order to register and vote. These laws are purportedly intended to reduce widespread vote fraud by individual voters, even though scholarly studies have found little evidence to support the claim.[8] Georgia passed such a law, which required citizens without a government-issued photo ID, such as a driver's license or passport, to obtain a voter identification card, which would cost them twenty dollars and expire after five years. To obtain the card, they would need to produce an original birth certificate and other documents and could obtain it only by going to a Department of Motor Vehicles office. Georgia Democrats charged that the law was a blatant attempt to reduce voter turnout among poor people, who are less likely to have a driver's license or passport and less able to afford the fee. After a federal judge invalidated the fee provision, the Georgia legislature eliminated it but retained the photo ID requirement. In 2008, the U.S. Supreme Court ruled on a case involving Indiana's voter identification card law, which is similar to Georgia's. Writing for the Court's 6-3 majority, Justice John Paul Stevens said states have a "valid interest" in improving election procedures and deterring fraud. The Court rejected the argument that the law places an undue burden on the poor. It acknowledged that the law had a partisan element but argued that the law "should not be disregarded simply because partisan interests may have provided one motivation for the votes of individual legislators." In a dissenting opinion, Justice David Souter said the law "threatens to impose nontrivial burdens on the voting rights of tens of thousands of the state's citizens."[9]

Frequency of Elections

Just as America's registration system places a burden on voters, so, too, does its election schedule. The United States holds elections more often than other nations. No other democracy has elections for the lower chamber of its national legislature (the equivalent of the U.S. House of Representatives) as often as every two years, and none schedules elections for chief executive as often as every four years.[10] In addition, most state and local elections in the United States are scheduled separately from federal elections. Over three-fourths of the states elect their governors in nonpresidential election years, and most U.S. cities hold elections of municipal officials in odd-numbered years. Finally, the United States uses primary elections to select the party nominees. In other democracies, party leaders pick them.

Americans are asked to vote two to three times as often as Europeans, which increases the likelihood that they will not participate every time.[11] Moreover, elections in the United States have traditionally been scheduled on Tuesday, forcing most adults to find time before or after work to get to the polls. Many European nations hold their elections on Sunday or declare election day a national holiday, making it easier for working people to vote.

Party Differences

A final contributor to lower voter turnout in the United States is the nation's party system. Most European democracies have three or more significant political parties that have formed along class and social divisions and sometimes along religious and ethnic divisions as well. Labor and social democratic parties abound in Europe, as do middle-class, environmental, and right-wing parties. European voters have a range of choices when they go to the polls and usually can find one that conforms with their views.

SHOULD CITIZENS BE REQUIRED TO HAVE A GOVERNMENT-ISSUED PHOTO IDENTIFICATION CARD IN ORDER TO REGISTER AND VOTE?

On election day, officials unfailingly urge Americans to "get out and vote." Some of these officials are not to be taken seriously. On the whole, U.S. elections are conducted fairly and openly with the support of tens of thousands of public-minded officials and volunteer poll watchers. Lurking in the shadows, however, are policies that serve to depress the vote. The worst abuses, such as whites-only primaries and poll taxes, are in the past. But official obstacles to voting are still part of the electoral system. For example, registration in most states closes two or more weeks in advance of election day. Many officials in these states have no interest in adopting the election-day registration policy that is currently in effect in six states. They prefer a smaller voter turnout because it is more manageable and predictable. Another obstacle is early poll closings. Half the states close the polls before 8 P.M., which disadvantages people who are at work during daylight hours. On the other hand, registration and voting rules are a necessary part of conducting free and fair elections. There is a need, for example, for procedures that restrict the ballot to citizens; they are the only residents eligible to vote in U.S. elections. Moreover, election administration is expensive and time consuming. If the polls or registration offices were open all hours of the day and night, the cost would be prohibitive.

In recent years, several states have enacted laws requiring individuals to have a government-issued photo identification card in order to register and vote. For citizens with a driver's license or passport, this requirement is easily met. Other citizens, in order to vote, must produce an official birth certificate and documentary proof of residency in order to get from the state government a voter identification card that includes their photo. Proponents of these laws—most of whom are Republicans—say government-issued photo ID is needed in order to prevent voter fraud. Critics of these laws—most of whom are Democrats—say the voter ID requirement is a thinly disguised effort to keep lower-income people—many of whom don't have a driver's license or passport—from voting. In every instance, the voter identification card requirement has been enacted by a Republican-controlled state legislature.

Voter identification cards were also addressed by a bipartisan campaign reform commission headed by former President Jimmy Carter and former Secretary of State James Baker. In a narrow vote, the commission recommended a national voter identification card requirement. The following are two responses to that recommendation, one from a commission member who supports the requirement and one who opposes it. Which of the two arguments do you find more persuasive? Do you think your opinion is affected by your identification with one or the other political party?

YES Opponents of a voter photo ID argue that requiring one is unnecessary and discriminatory. Numerous examples of fraud counter the first argument. In 2004, elections in Washington state and Wisconsin were decided by illegal votes. In Washington, this fact was established by a lengthy trial and decision of the court. In Wisconsin, this fact was established by a joint report written by the U.S. attorney, FBI, Chief of Police, senior local election official—both Republican and Democrats. In other states, most notably Ohio and New York, voter rolls were filled with fictional voters like Elmer Fudd and Mary Poppins. Addressing the second concern, the commission recommendation is for states to adopt safeguards that guarantee all Americans an opportunity to obtain an ID required for voting. The safeguards include initiatives to locate those voters without an ID and to provide them one without cost. Under the recommendation, voters can cast a provisional ballot that will be counted if they present their photo ID within 48 hours.

—Susan Molinari, former U.S. representative (R-N.Y.)

NO [A] national ID requirement for voters . . . would inevitably disenfranchise minority voters and the most vulnerable among us—those who live in poverty and the elderly. . . . As the work of this Commission proceeded, I have made no secret of my view that if I thought it had substantial procedural shortcomings. . . . Rather than gathering facts and then developing policy recommendations that follow from those facts, this Commission appeared to have developed its recommendations and simply went through the motions of a fair and deliberative process. . . . If they had spent more time on the issue, they would realize that there are incredibly few documented cases of voter fraud to even respond to via legislation. Essentially, the Commission would have us create a massive and intrusive new bureaucracy, and one that discriminates and disenfranchises, in order to deal with a non-problem. As a whole, the national ID requirement would place steep new hurdles in place for more than ten percent of voters, who currently do not have a photo identification card but are otherwise eligible to vote. Though the Commission's report proposes giving away those cards to voters who cannot afford them for "free," this is an empty promise. The Republican Congress has a consistent record of imposing mandates on the states and then failing to fund the implementation of such mandates. Even if the new cards are cost free, there is little doubt that the ID offices will prove inaccessible or expensive to access for many. As a whole, this type of voter ID requirement has a regressive approach to electoral fairness, and would have the effect of tilting the playing field toward the wealthy and powerful.

—Rep. John Conyers Jr., U.S. representative (D-Mich.)

The United States has only two major parties, the Republicans and the Democrats. Each has its enthusiastic supporters, yet each party, to get the majority support it needs to win, must have broad support. The Republican and Democratic parties normally try to attract a sizable share of votes from nearly all groups in order to gain the 50 percent or more of the vote they need for victory. As a consequence, the parties sometimes take similar positions on leading issues, reducing the voters' choice. From time to time, the parties are fairly far apart. In the 2008 presidential election, for example, which was waged against the backdrop of the Iraq war and a weak economy, the parties were sharply divided in their positions, and Americans believed a lot was at stake in the choice between the Republicans and Democrats. Voter turnout was relatively high in 2008. In most U.S. elections, however, the differences between the parties are not as pronounced, which leads many people to conclude that the election's outcome will not substantially affect their future or that of the nation.[12] In such cases, turnout is lower than in elections where people think the stakes are high. (Chapter 8 has a fuller discussion of the American two-party system and its consequences.)

Why Some Americans Vote and Others Do Not

Even though turnout is lower in the United States than in other major Western democracies, some Americans vote regularly while others seldom or never vote. Among the explanations for these individual differences are civic attitudes, age, and education and income.

Civic Attitudes

Some Americans have a strong sense of **civic duty**—the belief that they are obliged to participate in public affairs. Citizens who hold this belief tend to be regular voters, often turning out for congressional and state elections as well as presidential elections. Other Americans are beset by **apathy**—a lack of interest in politics. Most of them don't bother to vote, whatever the election. Just as some people would not attend the Super Bowl even if it were free and being played across the street, some Americans would not bother to vote even if a ballot were delivered to their door. Still other Americans refrain from voting because of **alienation**—a feeling of powerlessness rooted in the belief that government doesn't care about people like them. Many of these citizens regard voting as a complete waste of time, convinced that government won't respond to their concerns even if they do go to the polls.

Civic duty and apathy are attitudes that are usually acquired from one's parents. When parents vote regularly and take an active interest in politics, their children usually grow up thinking they have a duty to participate. When parents never vote and

civic duty
The belief of an individual that civic and political participation is a responsibility of citizenship.

apathy
A feeling of personal disinterest in or unconcern with politics.

alienation
A feeling of personal powerlessness that includes the notion that government does not care about the opinions of people like oneself.

LEADERS

SUSAN B. ANTHONY
(1820–1906)

Susan B. Anthony's name is synonymous with women's right to vote—and well it should be. She spent much of her adult life fighting for women's suffrage, even at the risk of arrest. When she was in her twenties, she moved to upstate New York and became politically active. Like many of the women who would lead the movement for women's rights, her first crusade was with the temperance movement, which sought to ban the sale of alcohol because of the hardship alcoholism imposed on women and children. She next joined the abolitionist movement, which sought an end to slavery. After the Civil War, Anthony teamed up with an old friend and fellow activist, Elizabeth Cady Stanton, to demand equal pay and voting rights for women. She twice went to the polls in her hometown of Rochester, New York, to assert her right to vote, and she twice was arrested. By then, Anthony had become a national figure who lectured widely on women's suffrage. She died a decade before women gained the right to vote in the United States, but she, as much as any American, made women's suffrage a reality.

show no interest in public affairs, their children are likely to be politically apathetic. Alienation can be traced to childhood socialization, but it often has adult roots. For example, when the Democratic Party took the lead on civil rights issues in the 1960s, some working-class white Democrats felt left out, believing that gains for African Americans would come at their expense. Some of these people switched parties, but a greater number simply stopped voting. Voter turnout among working-class whites dropped sharply in 1968 and in 1972—two presidential elections in which civil rights issues were central.[13]

Age

When viewers tuned into MTV at various times in the 2008 presidential campaign, they might have thought at first that they had selected the wrong channel. Rather than a video of their favorite performer, they saw the presidential candidates urging young people to vote. The candidates had targeted the right audience. Young adults are substantially less likely than middle-aged citizens to vote. Even senior citizens, despite the infirmities of old age, have a far higher turnout rate than do voters under the age of thirty.

In 2004 and again in 2008, turnout among younger voters increased substantially from that of previous recent presidential elections. Underlying this increase was the Iraq war, which mobilized college-educated young adults especially. Most of them opposed the way the Bush administration was conducting the war, and they participated in unusually high numbers. Nevertheless, the voting rate of young adults was still below that of older adults, who are more likely to live in the same residence from one election to the next and thus do not need to reregister in order to vote. Older voters are also more likely to own their homes and to have children, which heightens their sense of having a stake in election outcomes.

Although Americans have voted in relatively low numbers in recent U.S. elections, the turnout rate increased in 2004 and 2008 in response to the issues of the moment. Here, voters stand in a long line waiting to cast their ballot at a polling place in Fort Mill, South Carolina.

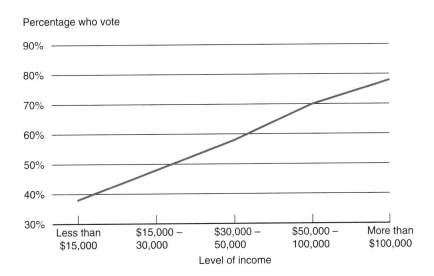

Percentage who vote

FIGURE 7-2 **Voter Turnout and Level of Income, 2008**
Americans of lower income are much less likely to vote than those of higher income. The gap in these voting rates is greater in the United States than in other Western democracies.
Source: U.S. Bureau of the Census.

Education and Income

College-educated and higher-income Americans have above-average voting rates. They have the financial resources and communication skills that encourage participation and make it personally rewarding. Nevertheless, America is unusual in the degree to which education and income are related to voter participation. Europeans with less education and income vote at only slightly lower rates than those with more education and income. In the United States, however, those with a college degree or in the upper-income level are twice as likely to vote in a presidential election as those who did not finish high school or are in the low-income bracket (see Figure 7-2).

Why the huge difference between the United States and Europe? For one thing, Europeans with less income and education are encouraged to participate by the presence of class-based organizations and appeals—strong socialist or labor parties, politically oriented trade unions, and class-based political ideologies. The United States has never had a major socialist or labor party. Although the Democratic Party represents the working class and the poor to a degree, it is more responsive to middle-class voters, who are a larger share of the electorate and hold the balance of power in U.S. elections.[14] In addition, Americans with less income and education are the people most adversely affected by the country's registration system. Many of them do not own cars or homes and are thus less likely to be registered in advance of an election. They are also less familiar with registration locations and requirements.[15]

Conventional Forms of Participation Other Than Voting

Most citizens in most democracies vote in elections. No other active form of political participation is as widespread. Nevertheless, voting is a somewhat limited form of involvement. Citizens have the opportunity to vote only at a particular time and only on the choices listed on the ballot. Other activities, such as working on a campaign or joining a civic group, give citizens fuller opportunities to participate.

FIGURE 7-3

Campaign Activity
Although Americans are less likely to vote in elections than citizens elsewhere, they are more likely to engage in other campaign activities, such as trying to influence the vote choice of others.

Source: Surveys by Comparative Studies of Electoral Systems, 2001–4. Reported in Russell J. Dalton, "The Myth of the Disengaged American," CSES Report, October 25, 2005, web release. Sixteen other countries were included in surveys; none had a higher participation rate than the United States.

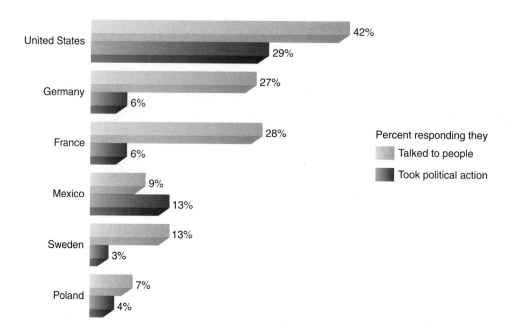

Campaign and Lobbying Activities

Compared with voting, working for a candidate or attending election rallies requires considerably more time. Not surprisingly, the number of citizens who engage in such activities is relatively small. Nevertheless, the number is higher in the United States than in Europe. A recent study of twenty-three countries found that Americans ranked first in terms of making an effort to influence other voters (see Figure 7-3). One reason Americans are more active in campaigns, even though they vote less, is that they have more opportunities to participate. The United States is a federal system with campaigns for national, state, and local offices. A citizen who wants to participate can easily find an opportunity at one level of office or another. Most of the European governments are unitary in form (see Chapter 3), which means that there are fewer elective offices and thus fewer campaigns. (Election campaigns are discussed further in Chapter 8.)

Americans are also more likely than Europeans to lobby elected officials. Although most Americans do not write their member of Congress, state legislator, or city councilor, many do so. And they do so in the expectation of a response, even if it is nothing more than a polite letter thanking them for writing. Americans are also more likely than citizens elsewhere to contribute money to support the activities of lobbying groups, such as Greenpeace, Common Cause, the Christian Moral Government Fund, the American Association of Retired Persons, and the National Conservative Political Action Committee. (Lobbying groups are discussed further in Chapter 9.)

Virtual Participation

The introduction of the World Wide Web in the 1990s opened up an entirely new venue for political participation—the Internet. Through e-mails, chat rooms, like-minded networks, and the like, the Internet has created participation possibilities previously unimaginable. Although the participation is "virtual" rather than face-to-face, much of it is nonetheless personal in that it involves contact with friends, acquaintances, and activists.

Participation through the Internet has been most evident in presidential campaigns, where virtual participation now far outweighs conventional participation

TABLE 7-2 | Online Campaign Activities Substantial numbers of Americans engaged in campaign-related activity online during the nominating phase of the 2008 presidential campaign

	All Adults	Internet Users
Watched video online of candidate speeches/announcement	20%	27%
Read a candidate's position paper on an issue online	16	22
Signed an online petition	10	13
Signed up to receive email from the candidates of campaigns	9	12
Contributed money online to a candidate	6	8
Signed up online for any volunteer activities related to the campaign	2	3

Source: Pew Internet & American Life Project, June 2008.

(see Table 7-2). According to Pew Research Center surveys, huge numbers of Americans send emails to family members, friends, and others in an effort to promote their favorite candidate. Campaign fund-raising through the Internet is also flourishing. In 2004, Howard Dean, though ultimately unsuccessful in his effort to gain the Democratic presidential nomination, raised millions of dollars and attracted thousands of volunteers for his campaign through the Internet. The Internet's potency as a vehicle for citizen-based election politics was even clearer in 2008. Democratic candidate Barack Obama raised more money than his opponents, and most of it was contributed in small amounts through the Internet. He had more than a million contributors and raised more than $300 million online. Never before had a small-donor fund-raising strategy bested the older strategy of raising funds through meetings, dinners, and other contacts with large donors. Obama's personal appeal was a key ingredient; the Internet fund-raising efforts of the other candidates in 2008 were less successful. Internet communication was a key to the Obama campaign's high level of citizen participation—through donations, the emailing of others, and the attending of rallies.

There are other remarkable examples of citizen mobilization through the Internet, few more successful than MoveOn, which claims 2 million "online activists," many of them young people. When MoveOn's organizers make a concerted appeal—whether on behalf of a candidate, a cause, or a bill before Congress—it usually triggers a swift and large response from those in its network.

The full impact of the Web on citizen participation lies in the future. Internet technology will continue to improve, and online use will continue to rise, as will the organizing savvy of Internet operatives.[16] Some analysts believe the Internet will usher in an era of unprecedented citizen involvement and influence. Other analysts are less optimistic, noting that the Internet has hundreds of thousands of websites, most of which have little or nothing to do with public affairs. In the long run, the likely scenario is that the Internet's mobilizing power will ebb and flow, depending less on further advances in technology than

The Internet has vast but as yet unrealized potential as an instrument of mass political participation. Shown here is Markos Moulitsas Zuniga, who aided in the creation of presidential candidate Howard Dean's "meetups"—supporters connected with each other through the Internet. Zuniga runs a political blog called Daily Kos.

on the urgency of the moment. Over the long course of American democracy, citizens have grown more active when issues have intensified and then settled back down as issues have quieted. The Internet Age is unlikely to be different. (The Internet is discussed further in Chapter 10.)

Community Activities

Many Americans participate in public affairs not through election campaigns but through local organizations such as parent-teacher associations, neighborhood groups, business clubs, church-affiliated groups, and hospital auxiliaries. The actual number of citizens who participate actively in community groups is difficult to estimate, but the number is surely in the tens of millions, reflecting in part a tradition of local participation that dates to colonial times. Moreover, compared with cities and towns in Europe, those in the United States have greater authority over local policies, which gives their residents a reason to participate actively. Because of increased mobility and other factors, Americans may be less tied to their local communities than in the past and therefore less involved in community activity. Nevertheless, Americans are more than twice as likely as Europeans to work together in groups on matters of community concern.[17]

In a widely heralded book titled *Bowling Alone*, Harvard's Robert Putnam claims that America has been undergoing a long-term decline in its **social capital** (the sum of the face-to-face civic interactions among citizens in a society).[18] Putnam attributes the decline to television and other factors that draw people inward and away from participation in civic and political groups. Not all scholars accept Putnam's interpretation of the trend in civic involvement (some indicators point toward a rise in certain types of participation), but no one challenges his claims about the value of civic participation. As the theorist John Stuart Mill (1806–73) noted more than a century ago, community involvement brings people together, builds skills that make them more effective citizens, helps them understand the interests of others, and enables them to protect and promote their interests and those of their community.

social capital

The sum of the face-to-face interactions among citizens in a society.

Unconventional Activism: Social Movements and Protest Politics

During the era of absolute monarchies, people resorted to protest as a way of expressing displeasure with their rulers. Tax and food riots occurred with some frequency. When democratic governments came into existence, citizens had a regular and less disruptive way to express themselves—through their votes. Voting is double-edged, however. Although the vote gives citizens a degree of control over government, *the vote also gives government control over citizens.*[19] Elected officials can claim that their policies reflect the will of the electorate and must therefore be respected and obeyed, however much they might hurt certain interests in society.

Social movements, or **political movements** as they are sometimes called, are a way for citizens disenchanted with government policy to express their opposition and work to bring about the change they want.[20] These efforts are sometimes channeled through conventional forms of participation, such as political lobbying, but citizens can also take to the streets in protest against government.

social (political) movements

Active and sustained efforts to achieve social and political change by groups of people who feel that government has not been properly responsive to their concerns.

In 2003, for example, as the Bush administration was preparing for war with Iraq, protest demonstrations were held in many U.S. cities, including Washington and San Francisco. Two percent of adult Americans said they participated in an antiwar demonstration. Many of them were young adults. Participants in social movements are younger on average than nonparticipants, a reversal of the pattern for voting.[21]

Social movements do not always succeed, but they sometimes force government into action. For example, the timing and scope of the landmark 1964 Civil Rights Act and 1965 Voting Rights Act can be explained only as a response by Congress to the pressure created by the civil rights movement. Another effective social movement in the 1960s was that of the farmworkers, whose protests led to improved conditions for migrant workers.

Political protests have taken on new forms in recent years. Protest was traditionally a desperate act that began, often spontaneously, when a group had lost hope of succeeding through more conventional methods. Today, however, protest is usually a calculated act—a means of bringing added attention to a cause.[22] These tactical protests often involve a great deal of planning, including, in some instances, the busing of thousands of people to Washington for a rally staged for television. Civil rights, environmental, agricultural, and pro- and anti-abortion groups are among those that have staged tactical protests in Washington in recent years.

Protest politics has a long history in America. Indeed, the United States was founded on a protest movement that sparked a revolution against Britain. Despite this tradition, however, protest activity is less common today in the United States than in many Western democracies (see Figure 7-4). Spain, France, Germany, Sweden, and Ireland are among the countries that have higher rates of participation in political protests.

Public support for protest activity is also comparatively low in the United States. The Vietnam War protests, which in some cases were accompanied by the burning of draft cards and the American flag, had only marginal public support outside the circle of protesters. When unarmed student protesters at

Protesters demonstrate (in 2003) against the war in Iraq. Although protest movements are an American tradition, they do not routinely receive strong public support.

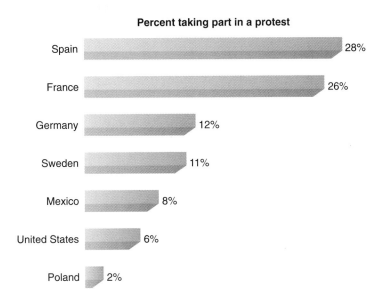

Percent taking part in a protest

Country	Percent
Spain	28%
France	26%
Germany	12%
Sweden	11%
Mexico	8%
United States	6%
Poland	2%

FIGURE 7-4
Protest Activity
Despite the significance of protest activity in U.S. history, Americans are less likely to protest than are citizens of many other democracies. Of twenty-three countries surveyed, the United States ranked eighteenth in level of protest activity. Only selected countries are included in this figure.
Source: Surveys by Comparative Studies of Electoral Systems, 2001–4. Reported in Russell J. Dalton, "The Myth of the Disengaged American," CSES Report, October 25, 2005, web release.

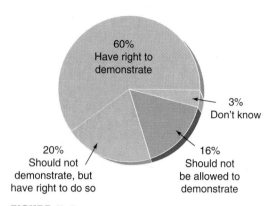

60%
Have right to
demonstrate

3%
Don't know

20%
Should not
demonstrate, but
have right to do so

16%
Should not
be allowed to
demonstrate

FIGURE 7-5 **Americans' Opinions of Iraq War Protests**
A majority supported the right of antiwar protesters to demonstrate, although some Americans felt they should not be allowed to do so.
Source: ABC News/Washington Post Poll, March 23, 2003.

Kent State University and Jackson State University were shot to death in May 1970 by members of the National Guard, many Americans in polls blamed the students, not the guardsmen, for the tragedy. The general public was more accepting of the Iraq war protest in 2003. Even after the fighting had begun, three in every five Americans said they saw the protests as "a sign of a healthy democracy" (see Figure 7-5). Still, almost two in five felt that "opponents of the war should not hold antiwar demonstrations" and half of these said that antiwar demonstrations should be banned entirely. In another poll, about a third of respondents said that protesters were "the kind of people who tend to blame America first."[23] On the other hand, protesters are rarely assaulted by those who disagree with them, and most Americans recognize that protest is part of America's tradition of free expression. In that sense, protest is seen as something to be tolerated, if not admired.

Participation and the Potential for Influence

Although Americans claim that political participation is important, many of them do not practice what they preach. Most citizens show little interest in participation except to vote, and a significant minority cannot even be persuaded that voting is worth their time. However, Americans are not completely apathetic: many millions of them contribute to political causes, and more than 100 million vote in presidential elections.

Yet sustained political activism does not engage a large proportion of the public. Moreover, many of those who do participate are drawn to politics by a habitual sense of civic duty rather than by an intense concern with current issues. The emphasis that American culture places on individualism tends to diminish interest in political participation. "In the United States, the country of individualism *par excellence*," William Watts and Lloyd Free write, "there is a sharp distinction in people's minds between their own personal lives and national life."[24] Although wars and severe recessions can lead Americans to take action on a larger scale than is normal, most people under most conditions expect to solve their problems on their own. This is not to say that Americans have a disdain for collective action. In their communities particularly, citizens frequently take part in collective efforts to support a local hospital, improve the neighborhood, and the like. But most Americans tend not to see their personal well-being as being closely linked to partisan political activity.

This tendency contributes to a class bias in American politics. For one thing, it helps maintain a relatively sharp distinction between that which is properly public (political) and that which is properly private (economic). Americans, as political scientist Robert Lane notes, prefer to see benefits distributed primarily through the economic marketplace rather than through the policies of government.[25] For example, access to medical care in the United States, unlike in Europe where government-provided health care is available to all, is to some degree based on a person's ability to pay for it. Roughly 45 million Americans do not have access to adequate health care because they cannot afford health insurance.

Lower-income Americans are a relatively weak force in the nation's politics. They are less likely to have the financial resources and communication skills that encourage participation in politics and make it personally rewarding. Among citizens who are most active in politics, three times as many have incomes in the top third as in the bottom third.[26] This difference is much greater than in other Western democracies, where poorer citizens are assisted through automatic voter registration and by the presence of class-based political organizations. The poor in the United States must arrange their own registration and must choose between two political parties that are attuned primarily to middle-class interests.

Some writers claim that the country is better off if less interested and less knowledgeable citizens—most of whom are near the bottom of the economic ladder—stay home on election day. In a cover story in *Atlantic Monthly*, Robert Kaplan wrote, "The last thing America needs is more voters—particularly badly educated and alienated ones—with a passion for politics."[27] The gist of this age-old argument is that poorer citizens are prone to backing radical leaders and ideas. The problem with this claim is that there is virtually no historical evidence for it; if anything, poorer Americans have been notable for their aversion to class-based radicalism.[28] On the other hand, low turnout can be a problem. In general, the smaller the electorate, the less representative it is of the public as a whole. Polls indicate that the outcomes of elections would in some instances have changed if the turnout had been substantially higher.

And even if greater voter turnout would not have altered the outcomes, campaign platforms are tailored to those who vote. Studies indicate that representatives are more responsive to the demands of participants than to those of nonparticipants. In *Unequal Democracy*, political scientist Larry Bartels shows that elected officials respond to the concerns of their affluent constituents while largely ignoring those of their poor constituents. He presents recent case after recent case where the interests of the affluent have prevailed.[29] Although high-participation groups do not always pursue their own narrow interests, it would be a mistake to conclude that they regularly support policies that benefit others. For example, a turning point in the defeat of President Bill Clinton's health care reform proposal in 1993, which would have extended health care coverage to nearly all Americans, came when middle- and upper-income groups decided that it might increase the cost and reduce the quality of their own medical care. According to Time/CNN polls, support for the Clinton plan dropped from 57 percent to 37 percent between September 1993 and July 1994. Although this decline reflected a loss of support among all groups, the drop was particularly severe among middle- and higher-income people who already had health insurance, through either an individual policy or an employment-related group policy.

In sum, the pattern of individual political participation in the United States parallels the distribution of influence that prevails in the private sector. Those who have the most power in the marketplace also have the most power in the political arena. However, the issue of individual participation is only one piece of the larger puzzle of who rules America and for what purposes. Subsequent chapters will supply additional pieces.

Summary Self-Test www.mhhe.com/pattersontad9e

Political participation is involvement in activities designed to influence public policy and leadership. A main issue of democratic government is the question of who participates in politics and how fully they participate.

Voting is the most widespread form of active political participation among Americans. Yet voter turnout is significantly lower in the United States than in other democratic nations. The requirement that Americans must personally register in order to establish their eligibility to vote is one reason for lower turnout among Americans; other democracies place the burden of registration on government officials rather than on individual citizens. The fact that the United States holds frequent elections also discourages some citizens from voting regularly. Finally, the major American political parties, unlike many of those in Europe, do not routinely and sharply represent the interests of opposing economic classes; thus, the policy stakes in American elections are lower. Some Americans do not vote because they think that policy will not change greatly regardless of which party holds power.

Only a minority of citizens engage in the more demanding forms of political activity, such as work on community affairs or on behalf of a candidate during a political campaign. Nevertheless, the proportion of Americans who engage in these more demanding forms of activity exceeds the proportion of Europeans who do so. Most political activists are individuals of higher income and education; they have the skills and material resources to participate effectively and tend to take a greater interest in politics. More than in any other Western democracy, political participation in the United States is related to economic status.

Social movements are broad efforts to achieve change by citizens who feel that government is not properly responsive to their interests. These efforts sometimes take place outside established channels; demonstrations, picket lines, and marches are common means of protest. Protesters are younger and more idealistic on average than are other citizens, but they are a very small proportion of the population. Despite America's tradition of free expression, protest activities do not have a high level of public support.

Overall, Americans are only moderately involved in politics. While they are concerned with political affairs, they are mostly immersed in their private pursuits, a reflection in part of a cultural belief in individualism. The lower level of participation among low-income citizens has particular significance in that it works to reduce their influence on public policy and leadership.

CHAPTER 7

Study Corner

Key Terms

alienation (*p. 179*)
apathy (*p. 179*)
civic duty (*p. 179*)
political participation
    (*p. 171*)
registration (*p. 175*)

social capital (*p. 184*)
social (political) movements
    (*p. 184*)
suffrage (*p. 172*)
voter turnout (*p. 173*)

Self-Test

1. Low voter turnout in U.S. elections compared to other democracies is explained by all **except:**

    a. differences in registration requirements.
    b. use of the secret ballot.
    c. frequency of elections.
    d. differences in the political party systems.

2. Unconventional political activism includes all **except:**

    a. participating in a social movement.
    b. taking part in a political demonstration or march.
    c. practicing civil disobedience.
    d. doing volunteer work for a political candidate or party.

3. Which group has the lowest voter turnout level?

    a. high-income Americans
    b. college-educated Americans

    c. young adult Americans
    d. Americans with a strong sense of civic duty

4. In European democracies, voting registration is:

    a. purely an individual's responsibility.
    b. the responsibility of government officials.
    c. taxed, although the tax is only a small amount in most European countries.
    d. open only to citizens thirty years of age and older in most European countries.

5. In comparison with citizens of European democracies, Americans are more likely to:

    a. vote in national elections.
    b. join labor unions.
    c. participate in community activities.
    d. regard protest as the most patriotic form of participation.

6. All of the following statements describe political participation in America **except** which one?

    a. Many people who participate in politics often do so from a sense of civic duty.
    b. America's culture of individualism discourages a reliance on political involvement.
    c. There are more barriers to regular participation in elections in the United States than in Europe.
    d. Americans place more emphasis on the public (political) sphere as a means of attaining their social and economic goals than they place on the private (economic) sphere.

7. More than in other Western democracies, political participation in the United States is related to income level. (T/F)

8. People who participate in social movements tend to be younger than nonparticipants. (T/F)

9. The Internet has increasingly been an important medium of election participation. including as a vehicle for contributing money to candidates' campaigns. (T/F)

10. With regard to election campaigns, Americans are more likely than Europeans to contribute money and to volunteer their time to help a candidate or party. (T/F)

Critical Thinking

Why does economic class—differences in people's incomes—make such a large difference in political participation levels? What are the policy consequences of this difference?

Suggested Readings

Bartels, Larry. *Unequal Democracy*. Princeton, N.J.: Princeton University Press, 2008. An analysis that shows just how fully lower-income Americans are neglected by policymakers because of their low participation rates.

Bimber, Bruce, and Richard Davis. *Campaigning Online: The Internet in U.S. Elections.* New York: Oxford University Press, 2003. A careful study of citizens' use of the Internet in elections.

Burns, Nancy, Kay Lehman Schlozman, and Sidney Verba. *The Private Roots of Public Action: Gender, Equality, and Public Action.* Cambridge, Mass.: Harvard University Press, 2001. An analysis of gender differences in political participation.

Franklin, Mark N. *Voter Turnout and the Dynamics of Electoral Competition in Established Democracies Since 1945.* New York: Cambridge University Press, 2004. A comparison of voter participation and its correlates in advanced democracies.

Leighley, Jan. *Strength in Numbers: The Political Mobilization of Racial and Ethnic Minorities.* Princeton, N.J.: Princeton University Press, 2001. A study of the factors that motivate blacks and Hispanics to participate.

Patterson, Thomas E. *The Vanishing Voter*. New York: Knopf, 2002. A study of the trends in electoral participation and what might be done to encourage higher participation levels.

Putnam, Robert. *Bowling Alone*. New York: Simon & Schuster, 2000. A provocative analysis of the trend in civic participation.

Zukin, Cliff, Scott Keeter, Molly Andolina, Krista Jenkins, and Michael X. Delli Carpini. *A New Engagement: Political Participation, Civic Life, and the Changing American Citizen.* New York: Oxford University Press, 2006. A comprehensive study concluding that young adults are finding ways other than election politics to exercise citizenship.

List of Websites

http://www.rockthevote.org/
The website of Rock the Vote, an organization dedicated to helping young people realize and utilize their power to affect the civic and political life of their communities.

http://www.electionstudies.org/
The University of Michigan's National Election Studies (NES) site; provides survey data on voting, public opinion, and political participation.

http://www.vanishingvoter.org/
Harvard University's election study site; provides information on voter participation.

http://www.vote-smart.org/
The website of Project Vote Smart; includes information on Republican and Democratic candidates and officials, as well as the latest in election news.

Participate!

If you are not currently registered to vote, consider registering. You can obtain a registration form from the election board or clerk in your community of residence. There are several websites that contain state-by-state registration information. One such site is https://electionimpact.votenet.com/declareyourself/voterreg. If you are already registered, consider participating in a registration or voting drive on your campus. Although students typically register and vote at relatively low rates, they will often participate if encouraged by other students to do so.

Extra Credit

For up-to-the-minute *New York Times* articles, interactive simulations, graphics, study tools, and more links and quizzes, visit the text's Online Learning Center at www.mhhe.com/pattersontad9e.

Self-Test Answers

1. b   2. d   3. c   4. b   5. c   6. d   7. T   8. T   9. T   10. T

Pennsylvania: Voter Participation in a Schizophrenic State

Few states resisted Barack Obama more than Pennsylvania during the Democratic primary season. Partly as a result, few states are more critical to his hopes of winning the White House this fall.

Most of Pennsylvania's recent political developments, from the trend in voter registration to the latest statewide results, tilt toward the Democrats, often sharply. But the one exception to that pattern encourages Republicans: Although Democrats have carried the state in the past four presidential elections, their winning margins have dropped from about 9 percentage points under Bill Clinton in 1992 and 1996 to 4 points under Al Gore in 2000 and to just 2.5 points under John Kerry in 2004. And in John McCain, who polls well nationally among independents, Republicans may have a nominee capable of reversing the Democrats' two-decade advance in the affluent, growing, and once reliably Republican suburbs of Philadelphia—the trend most responsible for the Democratic rise in Pennsylvania.

Add to these factors Obama's weak performance in the April primary, and the state's top Democrats are cautioning the party to expect a tough fight in Pennsylvania. "I still think it's a swing state, and all you have to do is look at the trend lines . . . in presidential politics, it has been getting closer and closer," Democratic Gov. Ed Rendell told National Journal. "And McCain is the best Republican candidate they have fielded presidentially since Ronald Reagan, in the sense that his reputation as a maverick and a moderate . . . holds him in very good stead with the independents and [suburban] Republicans who have been tending to vote Democratic in the last four elections."

Yet the very ferocity of the Keystone State's Democratic presidential primary may have strengthened Obama's chances by spurring a registration surge that has swelled the Democratic lead over the GOP on the voter rolls to nearly 1.1 million, almost double the party's 2004 edge. According to Rendell, that's a record voter-registration advantage for the Democrats, and it dramatizes the extent to which Pennsylvania remains a difficult challenge for McCain, especially amid the intense disillusionment with Bush there. The state is "still in play . . . but the idea that it is evenly divided between McCain and Obama, that it is a 50-50 toss-up, I think that is just wrong," says Ruy Teixeira, an electoral analyst at the liberal Brookings Institution who co-authored a recent comprehensive study of the state's demographic and political trends. "It is a purple state leaning blue, and it may be even bluer than it was in 2004. So it is a real uphill climb for McCain in my view."

In its recent political evolution, Pennsylvania has been a tale of two states. It has simultaneously moved sharply toward the Democrats in the southeast, particularly in the comfortable Philadelphia suburbs, and sharply toward the GOP in the southwest, especially in the largely blue-collar suburbs of Pittsburgh. McCain's challenge is to reverse the first trend and reinforce the second, as well as the GOP's more modest gains in presidential races in hardscrabble northeastern counties around Scranton.

"You can play the chess game almost any way, but the Philly 'burbs, southwestern Pennsylvania, and those counties up there [around Scranton] are basically it," says G. Terry Madonna, a longtime Pennsylvania pollster who is now the director of the Center for Politics and Public Affairs at Franklin and Marshall College. "McCain has to win the [blue-collar] Reagan Democrats in the west and the northeast, and he has to win some independents, independent-minded Republicans, and Democrats in the Philly suburbs."

For generations, the Philadelphia suburbs were the home of prosperous "Main Line" moderate Republicans. But like other socially moderate, white-collar suburbs outside the South, these communities began moving toward the Democrats during Clinton's 1992 race. They have shifted even further in that direction under Bush, who has given the GOP a more Southern and more evangelical face.

In the four suburban counties immediately outside Philadelphia, the change has been profound. From 1920 through 1988, no Democratic presidential nominee won Delaware or Montgomery counties, with the exception of Lyndon Johnson in his 1964 landslide. During that period in Bucks County, the only Democratic winners were Johnson and Franklin D. Roosevelt in 1936. As late as 1988, George H.W. Bush won 60 percent of the vote in all three counties.

But starting with Clinton in 1992, Democrats have now carried that trio of counties in four consecutive elections. And their margins in Delaware and Montgomery have increased each time. "The suburbs are a place that really liked Bush 41 but couldn't relate to Bush 43," said Christopher Nicholas, a Harrisburg-based Republican consultant who ran the successful 2004 re-election campaign of Republican Sen. Arlen Specter. "They liked the Connecticut Yankee and had trouble relating to the Texan."

Over the same period, though, the state's southwest corner—the counties surrounding Pittsburgh, such as Beaver, Washington, and Westmoreland—have moved in the opposite direction. Although Pittsburgh itself has remained solidly Democratic, these counties, much less affluent and less white-collar than the Philadelphia suburbs, have responded favorably to George W. Bush's conservative cultural and national security policies.

On balance, this geographic swap has benefited Pennsylvania Democrats, because their new strongholds are bigger and are gaining population, while some of the increasingly Republican areas are shrinking. "Where population is growing, the Democrats are doing better. Where it is declining, Republicans are doing better," says Teixeira,

the co-author of the Brookings analysis with demographer William Frey.

The conversion of the Philadelphia suburbs and exurbs, in addition to the Democrats' continuing dominance of Pittsburgh and heavily African-American Philadelphia, has provided the party a fragile but perceptible advantage in the state. After the 2000 election, Republicans controlled the governorship, both U.S. Senate seats, a majority of U.S. House seats, and both chambers of the state Legislature.

In 2002, Rendell captured the governorship. In 2006, Democrats re-elected Rendell, won a majority of the state House, ousted four GOP lawmakers to gain a majority of the state's U.S. House delegation, and took a U.S. Senate seat as Democrat Bob Casey routed staunchly conservative GOP Sen. Rick Santorum. The 2006 recoil from the GOP was especially powerful in the four Philadelphia suburban counties, where Democrats defeated two Republican House members and Casey annihilated Santorum by more than175,000 votes. Six years earlier, Santorum had swept those counties by nearly 152,000 votes.

In this period of Democratic advance, the one big exception was Specter's successful 2004 campaign. On the day that Bush lost the state to Kerry, Specter won re-election with nearly 53 percent of the vote. Specter, a moderate who supports abortion rights, built a much different coalition from Bush's, actually running behind him in 29 of Pennsylvania's 67 counties. Nearly all of these were culturally conservative counties either near Pittsburgh or in the heavily rural "T" that extends through the state's center. But Specter, a former Philadelphia district attorney, ran far better than Bush through all of the eastern counties, from Philadelphia north to Scranton and beyond to the New York border. Most important, Specter held down his

the very ferocity of the Keystone State's Democratic presidential primary **may have strengthened Obama's chances** by spurring a registration surge

losses in Philadelphia itself and amassed a nearly 150,000-vote lead in the four suburban Philadelphia counties that decisively rejected Bush.

Running against the first African-American presidential nominee of a major party, McCain has little chance of minimizing the Democratic advantage in Philadelphia as much as Specter did. But, apart from that, the Specter map may be "as good a model as McCain can find," Madonna says.

In fact, Republicans hope that McCain can do better than Specter among culturally conservative voters. "Obama's challenge is, how does he win over the working-class white folks that he didn't win [in the primary]?" says consultant Nicholas. "He is just radically different from their lives, and McCain is not. Military, father in the military, grandfather in the military: That's an arc they can understand. The Obama life story, while very unique and interesting, is not something folks in these little railroad towns can relate to."

Rendell, who openly declared during the primary that some Pennsylvania voters might not be willing to vote for a black presidential candidate, says he thinks that economic anxiety may help Obama perform better than Republicans anticipate in the Scranton and Pittsburgh areas. But to hold the state,

Rendell is mostly counting on Obama's energizing new voters and maintaining the Democratic advantage in the Philadelphia suburbs and Lehigh Valley.

Can Obama defend the Democratic beachheads outside Philadelphia? Since 2004, Democrats have posted substantial voter-registration gains in all four suburban counties, as well as across the Lehigh Valley. But in the Democratic primary, Obama did not run as well in these places as he did in white-collar communities elsewhere: Clinton split the four Philadelphia suburbs with him and swept the Lehigh Valley.

Those results worry Rendell, who was Clinton's highest-profile Pennsylvania supporter. "There is a very strong reservoir of support for Clinton among women [in these counties]," he says. "So . . . we have real work to do in the suburbs." Plus, he adds, McCain's reputation for independence will make him a "tough" competitor for moderate suburban voters.

Rendell says that Obama might win the Philadelphia suburbs "by a smaller margin than Kerry did," but he expects the senator from Illinois to run well enough there to hold Pennsylvania. Republicans hope that Rendell is wrong. Both sides agree that no matter how much ground McCain gains elsewhere, he is unlikely to capture the state unless he can run even with or better than Obama immediately outside of Philadelphia. "All roads end up pointing back to those Philly suburbs," one senior McCain campaign aide said.

Madonna agrees. "You can't just give up about 90,000 votes in the Philadelphia suburbs [as Bush did]," he says. "There are so many votes there that making up that kind of deficit elsewhere is really difficult." Such inescapable math ensures the Philadelphia suburbs a spot high on the list of the places picking the next president.

FOR DISCUSSION: Look up the results of the Presidential Election in Pennsylvania. How well did it conform to the pattern *National Journal* observed?

According to the election, how does geography delineate political preference in your own state?

What strategies would you offer candidates looking to maximize their voter turnout in Pennsylvania?

Political Parties, Candidates, and Campaigns
Defining the Voter's Choice

Party Competition and Majority Rule: The History of U.S. Parties

The First Parties

Andrew Jackson and Grassroots Parties

Republicans Versus Democrats: Realignments and the Enduring Party System

Today's Party Alignment and Its Origins

Parties and the Vote

Electoral and Party Systems

The Single-Member-District System of Election

Politics and Coalitions in the Two-Party System

Minor (Third) Parties

Party Organizations

The Weakening of Party Organizations

The Structure and Role of Party Organizations

The Candidate-Centered Campaign

Campaign Funds: The Money Chase

Organization and Strategy: Hired Guns

Voter Contacts: Pitched Battle

Parties, Candidates, and the Public's Influence

political party

An ongoing coalition of interests joined together to try to get their candidates for public office elected under a common label.

> Political parties created democracy and . . . modern democracy is unthinkable save in terms of the parties.
>
> E. E. Schattschneider[1]

Nine hundred miles and a week apart, they faced off, each offering its own plan for a better America.

The Democrats met first, in Denver, Colorado. Their 2008 platform included pledges to draw down U.S. forces in Iraq, bring health coverage to millions of uninsured Americans, combat global warming, and create more jobs and higher wages for working families. The Democrats chose Illinois senator Barack Obama, the first African American ever to be chosen for the position, as their presidential nominee. Their vice presidential nominee was Joe Biden, senator from Delaware.

The Republicans met in Minnesota's capital city, St. Paul. They selected Arizona senator John McCain as their presidential nominee and Sarah Palin, the governor of Alaska, as his running mate. The Republican platform included promises to keep taxes low, limit abortions, expand parental school choice, stimulate the business sector, and provide the Iraq government with the U.S. military support needed for it to succeed.

The political parties, as their nominees and platforms illustrate, are in the business of offering the voting public a choice. Each party seeks to define itself in a way that will attract majority support. Competition between the parties is the mechanism through which the electorate gets its say in governing. A **political party** is an ongoing coalition of interests joined together in an effort to get its candidates for public office elected under a common label.[2] By offering a choice between policies and leaders, parties give voters a chance to influence the direction of government. "It is the competition of [parties] that provides the people with an opportunity to make a choice," political scientist E. E. Schattschneider wrote. "Without this opportunity popular sovereignty amounts to nothing."[3]

This chapter examines political parties and the candidates who run under their banners. U.S. campaigns are **party-centered** politics in the sense that the Republican and Democratic parties compete across the

Republican nominee John McCain is surrounded by party faithful during the 2008 presidential campaign.

party-centered politics

Election campaigns and other political processes in which political parties, not individual candidates, hold most of the initiative and influence.

candidate-centered politics

Election campaigns and other political processes in which candidates, not political parties, have most of the initiative and influence.

party competition

A process in which conflict over society's goals is transformed by political parties into electoral competition in which the winner gains the power to govern.

country election after election. Yet campaigns are also **candidate-centered** politics in the sense that individual candidates devise their own strategies, choose their own issues, and form their own campaign organizations. The following points are emphasized in this chapter:

■ *Political competition in the United States has centered on two parties, a pattern that is explained by the nature of America's electoral system, political institutions, and political culture.* Minor parties exist in the United States but have been unable to compete successfully for governing power.

■ *To win an electoral majority, candidates of the two major parties must appeal to a diverse set of interests.* This necessity has normally led them to advocate moderate and somewhat overlapping policies, although this tendency has weakened in recent years.

■ *U.S. party organizations are decentralized and fragmented.* The national organization is a loose collection of state organizations, which in turn are loose associations of local organizations. This feature of U.S. parties can be traced to federalism and the nation's diversity, which have made it difficult for the parties to act as instruments of national power.

■ *The ability of America's party organizations to control nominations and election to office is weak, which in turn enhances the candidates' role.*

■ *Candidate-centered campaigns are based on money and media and utilize the skills of professional consultants.*

Party Competition and Majority Rule: The History of U.S. Parties

Through their numbers, citizens have the potential for great influence, but that potential cannot be realized unless they act together. Parties give them that capacity. When Americans go to the polls, they have a choice between the Republican and Democratic parties. This **party competition** narrows their options to two and in the process enables people with different backgrounds and opinions to unite behind one of the options. In casting a majority of its votes for one party, the electorate chooses that party's candidates, philosophy, and policies over those of the opposing party.

The history of democratic government is synonymous with the history of parties. When the countries of Eastern Europe gained their freedom from the Soviet Union in the early 1990s, one of their first steps toward democracy was the legalization of parties. When the United States was founded over two centuries ago, the formation of parties was also a first step toward the building of its democracy. The reason is simple: it is the competition among parties that gives popular majorities a choice over how they will be governed.[4] If there were no mechanism like the party to enable citizens to act as one, they would be powerless—each too weak to influence government.

The First Parties

America's early leaders mistrusted parties. George Washington in his farewell address warned the nation of the "baneful effects" of parties, and James Madison likened parties to special interests. However, Madison's misgivings about parties gave way to a grudging admiration. He came to realize that parties enabled like-minded people to work together to achieve their political goals.

America's parties originated in the rivalry within George Washington's administration between Thomas Jefferson, a supporter of states' rights and small landholders, and Alexander Hamilton, a promoter of strong national government and commercial interests (see Figure 8-1). When Hamilton's ideas prevailed in Congress, Jefferson and his followers formed a political party, the Republicans. By adopting this label, which was associated with popular government, the Jeffersonians sought to portray themselves as the rightful heirs to the American Revolution's legacy of self-government.

Hamilton then organized his supporters into a formal party—the Federalists—and in the process created America's first competitive party system. The Federalists took their name from the faction that had supported ratification of the Constitution, thereby implying that they represented America's governing tradition. However, the Federalists' preoccupation with commercial and moneyed interests fueled Jefferson's claim that the Federalists were bent on establishing a government of the rich and wellborn. After Jefferson in the election of 1800 defeated John Adams, who had succeeded Washington as president, the Federalists never again controlled the White House or Congress.

During the so-called Era of Good Feeling, when James Monroe ran unopposed in 1820 for a second presidential term, it appeared as if the political system might operate without parties. Yet by the end of Monroe's second term, policy differences had split the Republicans. The dominant faction, led by Andrew Jackson, retained Jefferson's commitment to the interests of ordinary people. This faction called itself Democratic Republicans, later shortened to Democrats. Thus, the Republican Party of Jefferson is the forerunner of today's Democratic Party rather than of today's Republican Party.

HISTORICAL
Background

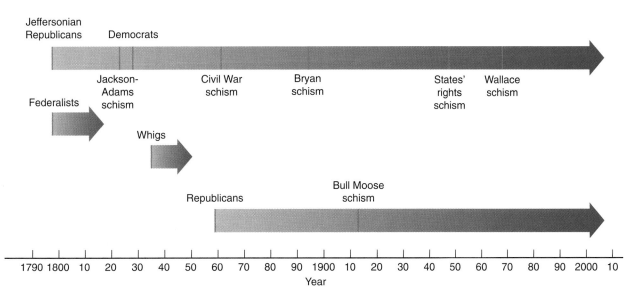

FIGURE 8-1   A Graphic History of America's Major Parties   The U.S. party system has been remarkable for its continuity. Competition between two major parties has been a persistent feature of the system.

Andrew Jackson and Grassroots Parties

Jackson's goal was to wrest political power from the established elite—all the presidents before him had come from old-line Virginia and Massachusetts families. Jackson wanted a government closer to the people, and he saw the party as the instrument for this transformation, recognizing that it could be used to mobilize them behind like-minded candidates. Whereas Jefferson's party had been well organized only at the leadership level, Jackson sought a party that was built from the bottom up. It would be a **grassroots party.** Jackson's Democratic Party consisted of organizations at the local, state, and national levels, with membership open to all eligible voters. These organizations, along with more liberal suffrage laws, contributed to a nearly fourfold rise in voter turnout during the 1830s.[5] At the peak of Jacksonian democracy, Alexis de Tocqueville wrote, "The People reign in the American political world as the Deity does in the universe."[6]

During this period, a new opposition party, the Whigs, emerged to challenge the Democrats. The Whigs were a catchall party whose followers were united not by a coherent philosophy of their own but by their opposition for one reason or another to Jackson and his followers. However, competition between the Whigs and the Democrats was relatively short-lived. During the 1850s, the slavery issue began to tear both parties apart. The Whig Party withered, and a northern-based new party, calling itself Republican, arose as the main challenger to the Democrats. In the 1860 presidential election, the Democratic Party's northern faction nominated Stephen A. Douglas, who held that the question of whether a new territory would permit slavery was for its voters to decide, while the southern faction nominated John C. Breckinridge, who called for legalized slavery in all territories. The Democratic vote split sharply along regional lines between these two candidates—with the result that the Republican nominee, Abraham Lincoln, who had called for the gradual elimination of slavery, was able to win the presidency with only 40 percent of the popular vote. Lincoln's election prompted the southern states to secede from the Union, which led to the Civil War.

The Civil War was the first and only time in the nation's history that the party system failed to peaceably resolve Americans' political conflicts. The issue of slavery was too explosive to be settled through electoral competition. Every time before and since, Americans have worked out their differences by freely electing the political party they thought would better represent them.[7]

Republicans Versus Democrats: Realignments and the Enduring Party System

After the Civil War, the nation settled into the pattern of competition between the Republican and Democratic parties that has lasted till today. The durability of these two parties is due not to their ideological consistency but to their remarkable ability to adapt during periods of crisis. By abandoning at these crucial times their old ways of doing things, the Republican and Democratic parties have repeatedly remade themselves—with new bases of support, new policies, and new public philosophies.

These periods of great political change are known as *realignments*. A **party realignment** involves four basic elements:

1. The disruption of the existing political order because of the emergence of one or more unusually powerful and divisive issues

2. An election contest in which the voters shift their support strongly in favor of one party

---

grassroots party

A political party organized at the level of the voters and dependent on their support for its strength.

party realignment

An election or set of elections in which the electorate responds strongly to an extraordinarily powerful issue that has disrupted the established political order. A realignment has a lasting impact on public policy, popular support for the parties, and the composition of the party coalitions.

3. A major change in policy brought about through the action of the stronger party

4. An enduring change in the party coalitions, which works to the lasting advantage of the dominant party

Realignments are rare. They do not occur simply because one party wrests control of government from the other. They involve deep and lasting changes in the party system that affect not just the most recent election but later ones as well. By this standard, there have been three clear-cut realignments since the 1850s.

The first of these, the Civil War realignment, brought about a thorough change in the party system. The Republicans replaced the Democrats as the nation's majority party. The Republicans dominated the larger and more populous North, while the Democrats were left with a stronghold in what became known as "the Solid South." During the next three decades, the Republicans held the presidency except for Grover Cleveland's two terms in office and had a majority in Congress for all but four years.

The 1896 election resulted in a second realignment of the Republican-Democratic party system. Three years earlier, an economic panic following a bank collapse had resulted in a severe depression. The Democrat Cleveland was president when the crash happened, and people blamed him and his party. In the aftermath, the Republicans made additional gains in the Northeast and Midwest, solidifying their position as the nation's dominant party. During the four decades between the 1890s realignment and the next one in the 1930s, the Republicans held the presidency except for Woodrow Wilson's two terms and had a majority in Congress for all but six years.

The Great Depression of the 1930s triggered yet another realignment of the American party system. The Republican Herbert Hoover was president during the stock market crash of 1929, and many Americans blamed Hoover, his party, and its business allies for the economic catastrophe that followed. The Democrats became the country's majority party. Their political and policy agenda called for an expanded role for the national government. Franklin D. Roosevelt's presidency was characterized by unprecedented policy initiatives in the areas of business regulation and social welfare (see Chapter 3). His election in 1932 began a thirty-six-year period of Democratic presidencies that was interrupted only by Dwight D. Eisenhower's two terms in the 1950s. In this period, the Democrats also dominated Congress, losing control only in 1947–48 and 1953–54.

LEADERS

ABRAHAM LINCOLN
(1809–65)

Abraham Lincoln had been a member of Congress from Illinois before he was elected to the presidency in 1860. Homely and gangly, Lincoln is regarded by many as America's greatest president for his principled leadership during the Civil War. Lincoln's accomplishments are all the more remarkable in that, unlike earlier presidents, he came from a humble background. His father was a frontiersman, his mother died when he was ten, and he was largely self-schooled. His greatest legacy is the preservation of the American Union. The Emancipation Proclamation and the Gettysburg Address are two of his other legacies. He was assassinated at Ford's Theater in the nation's capital shortly after the start of his second term as president. Lincoln was the first Republican elected to the presidency, and his successful pursuit of victory in the Civil War led to a party realignment that solidified the GOP's status as the nation's majority party.

The new order begins: Franklin D. Roosevelt rides to his inauguration with outgoing president Herbert Hoover after the realigning election of 1932.

The reason realignments have such a substantial effect on future elections is that they affect voters' *party identification* (see Chapter 6). Young voters in particular tend to identify with the newly ascendant party and to retain that identity, giving the party a solid base of support for years to come. First-time voters in the 1930s came to identify with the Democratic Party by a two-to-one margin, establishing it as the nation's majority party and enabling it to dominate national politics for the next three decades.[8]

Today's Party Alignment and Its Origins

A party realignment inevitably loses strength over time as the issues that gave rise to it decline in importance. By the late 1960s, with the Democratic Party divided over the Vietnam War and civil rights, it was apparent that the era of New Deal politics was ending.[9]

The change was most dramatic in the South. The region had been solidly Democratic at all levels since the Civil War, but the Democratic Party's leadership on civil rights angered white conservatives. In the 1964 presidential election, five southern states voted Republican, and the South is now a Republican bastion in presidential politics. The Republican Party also made gains, though more gradually, in elections for other offices in the South. Today most top officials in the region are Republicans.

More slowly and less completely, the northeastern states have become more Democratic. The shift is partly attributable to the growing size of minority populations in the Northeast. But it is also due to the declining influence of the Republican Party's moderate wing, which was concentrated in these states. As southern conservatives became Republican in ever larger numbers, the party's stands on social issues such as abortion and affirmative action tilted toward the right, reducing the party's appeal to the Northeast's progressive Republicans, some of whom shifted their loyalty to the Democratic Party.[10]

Party conflict also extended to federal spending on education, health, and economic security programs. The Democrats, who had started nearly all of these programs, defended them, while Republicans attacked them as being too expensive. Taxing and spending became perennial campaign issues, resulting in a further alignment of liberals against conservatives.

The net result of these changes has been a remaking of the party landscape, but the pattern is not that of a classic party realignment. Rather than occurring abruptly in response to a disruptive issue, as was the case in the 1860s, 1890s, and 1930s realignments, the change has taken place gradually and is the product of several issues rather than an overriding disruptive one. But the cumulative result—a reshuffling of the parties' coalitions and platforms—is similar to that of a realignment. In effect, America's parties have realigned without going through the sudden shock of a realigning election.

The GOP (short for "Grand Old Party" and another name for the Republican Party) has gained the most from these changes in party politics. For three decades after the Great Depression, the GOP was decidedly the weaker party. Since 1968, however, Republicans have held the presidency for over twice as many years as the Democrats. The GOP has had less success at the congressional level, but during the past two decades, it has had roughly the same number of Senate seats and only about 5 percent fewer House seats than the Democrats.

On the other hand, the Republican Party has failed to duplicate the success that the advantaged party enjoyed in the realignments of the 1860s, 1890s, and 1930s. Twice it has appeared to be on the verge of becoming the clearly dominant party, only to fall back because of missteps on the part of top leaders. After winning the presidency in 1968 and 1972, Republican Richard Nixon became

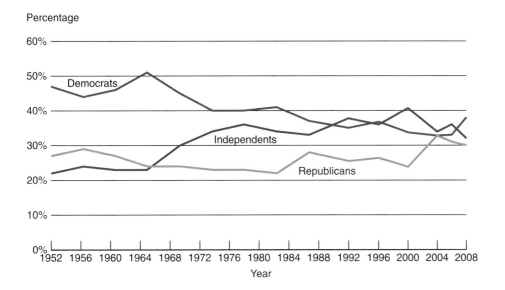

Percentage

FIGURE 8-2 **Partisan Identification** After trailing for decades, Republican identifiers nearly reached parity with Democratic identifiers in 2004, only to fall behind again as Iraq and other issues worked to the Democrats' advantage. Of the roughly one-third of voters who describe themselves as Independents, most also say they "lean" toward one of the two major parties. The leaners divide almost evenly between the two parties.
Source: National Election Studies, 1952–2000; Gallup surveys, after 2000.

embroiled in the Watergate affair and was forced to resign, the first and only president to do so. The Republicans lost a huge number of congressional seats in the 1974 midterm election and did not recover the lost ground until the 1980s. A smaller setback occurred in 1992 when a weak economy enabled Democrat Bill Clinton to defeat incumbent George H. W. Bush in the presidential election. The Republicans won back the presidency in 2000 while also making gains in the 2000 and 2002 congressional elections. However, the Iraq invasion ordered by President George W. Bush in 2003 proved increasingly unpopular, contributing to Republicans' loss of the House and Senate in the 2006 midterm elections and the loss of additional congressional seats and the presidency in the 2008 election.

The Iraq conflict also blunted Republicans' hopes of capturing Americans' partisan loyalties. After trailing the Democrats for years, the Republicans by 2004 had narrowed the partisan gap—Democratic identifiers outnumbered Republican identifiers by only 2 percentage points in the Gallup poll (see Figure 8-2). As discontent with Iraq grew, however, the trend reversed, and the Democrats' lead had widened substantially by the 2008 election.[11]

Analysts differ in their opinions on where the party system is heading in the long run. Some predict a period of Republican dominance after the GOP gets past its current problems and is able to refocus the public's attention on the issues that worked for it before the Iraq war disrupted its momentum.[12] Others foresee a resurgent Democratic Party fueled by the increased voting power of Hispanics and young adults, who lean Democratic.[13] One thing is virtually certain: as they have for over 150 years, Americans will continue to look to the Republican and Democratic parties for political leadership. The enduring strength and appeal of the two major parties is a hallmark of American politics.

Parties and the Vote

The power of party is at no time clearer than when, election after election, Republican and Democratic candidates reap the vote of their party's identifiers. In the 2008 presidential election, John McCain had the support of more than 85 percent of Republican Party identifiers, while Barack Obama garnered the votes of more than 85 percent of self-identified Democrats. Major-party candidates do not always do that well with party loyalists, but it is relatively rare—in congressional races as well as in the presidential race—for a party nominee to get less than 80 percent of the partisan vote.

Even the "independents" are less independent than might be assumed. In polls, when asked whether they are a Republican, a Democrat, or an independent, about a third of Americans say they are independents. However, in the follow-up question that asks whether they lean more toward the Republican Party or more toward the Democratic Party, about two in three independents say they lean toward one of the parties. Moreover, most of these independents vote in the direction they lean. In recent presidential elections, more than eight in ten leaners have backed the candidate of the party to which they feel closer. In other words, the number of true independents is no more than about a sixth of the electorate.

There was a period in the 1970s when the number of true independents was larger. It was a time when many otherwise Democrats were disillusioned with their party over the Vietnam war or civil rights, and many otherwise Republicans were disheartened by the Watergate scandal. During this period, there was a sharp rise in the number of voters in federal elections who cast a **split ticket,** that is, voted for one party's presidential candidate and the other party's congressional candidate. Some analysts described this development as a sign of *dealignment*—a weakening of partisanship.[14] Since 1980, however, this kind of ticket splitting has fallen from slightly under 30 percent of voters to less than 20 percent of voters, which is only somewhat higher than it was in the 1950s (see Figure 8-3).

Nevertheless, some voters in every election are swayed by the issues of the moment. Voters respond to issues both prospectively and retrospectively. **Prospective voting** occurs when the voter chooses a candidate on the basis of what the candidate promises to do if elected. In contrast, **retrospective voting** is based on a judgment about past performance—the situation in which a voter supports the incumbent officeholder or party when pleased with its performance and opposes it when displeased. Retrospective voting is the more common form of issue voting. When things are going poorly with the country, particularly when the economy is bad, voters are inclined to want a change in leadership. In good economic times, incumbents have less to fear. Studies have found, for example, that a weak economy in 1992 contributed to the defeat of incumbent President George H. W. Bush and that a strong economy in 1996 underpinned incumbent President Bill Clinton's successful bid for a second term. The 2008 presidential election was somewhat unusual in that two large problems had developed during the George W. Bush's presidency—a weakened economy and an unsettled Iraq situation. Both issues worked to out-party candidate Barack Obama's advantage.

---

split ticket

The pattern of voting in which the individual voter in a given election casts a ballot for one or more candidates of each major party.

prospective voting

A form of electoral judgment in which voters choose the candidate whose policy positions most closely match their own preferences.

retrospective voting

A form of electoral judgment in which voters support the incumbent candidate or party when its policies are judged to have succeeded and oppose the incumbent party or candidate when its policies are judged to have failed.

FIGURE 8-3 **Split-Ticket Voting in Presidential and Congressional Races** The level of split-ticket voting, as measured by the percentage who backed one party's candidate for president and the other party's candidate for the House of Representatives, has declined in recent elections. The change reflects an increased level of partisanship among America's voters.

Source: National Election Studies. Figure for 2008 based on preliminary polls.

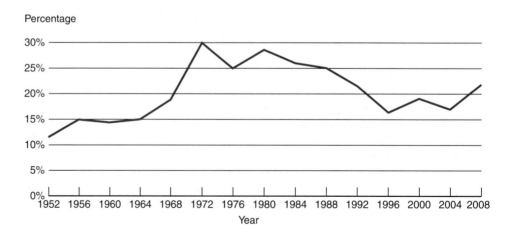

Percentage

PARTY SYSTEMS

For nearly 160 years, electoral competition in the United States has centered on the Republican and Democratic parties. By comparison, most democracies have a multiparty system, in which three or more parties receive substantial support from voters. The difference is significant. In a two-party system, the parties tend to have overlapping coalitions and programs, because each party must appeal to the middle-of-the-road voters who provide the margin of victory. In multiparty systems, particularly those with four or more strong parties, the parties tend to separate themselves as each tries to secure the enduring loyalty of voters who have a particular viewpoint.

Whether a country has a two-party or a multiparty system depends on several factors, but particularly the nature of its electoral system. The United States has a single-member, plurality district system in which only the top vote getter in a district gets elected. This system is biased against smaller parties; even if they have some support in a great many races, they win nothing unless one of their candidates places first in an electoral district. By comparison, proportional representation systems enable smaller parties to compete; each party acquires legislative seats in proportion to its share of the total vote. All the countries in the chart that have four or more parties also have a proportional representation system of election.

NUMBER OF COMPETITIVE PARTIES		
Two	**Three**	**Four or More**
United States	Canada (at times)	Belgium
	Great Britain	Denmark
		France
		Germany
		Italy
		Netherlands
		Sweden

Electoral and Party Systems

The United States traditionally has had a **two-party system:** Federalists versus Jeffersonian Republicans, Whigs versus Democrats, Republicans versus Democrats. These have not been the only American parties, but they have been the only ones with a realistic chance of acquiring political control. A two-party system, however, is the exception rather than the rule (see "How the U.S. Compares"). Most democracies have a **multiparty system,** in which three or more parties have the capacity to gain control of government, separately or in coalition. Why the difference? Why are there three or more major parties in most democracies but only two in the United States?

two-party system
A system in which only two political parties have a real chance of acquiring control of the government.

multiparty system
A system in which three or more political parties have the capacity to gain control of government separately or in coalition.

The Single-Member-District System of Election

America's two-party system is due largely to the fact that the nation chooses its officials through plurality voting in **single-member districts.** Each constituency elects a single member to a particular office, such as U.S. senator or state representative; the candidate with the most votes (a plurality) in a district wins the office. This system discourages minor parties. Assume, for example, that a minor party received exactly 20 percent of the vote in each of the nation's 435 congressional races. Even though one in five voters nationwide backed the minor party, it would not win any seats in Congress because none of its candidates placed first in any of the 435 single-member-district races. The winning candidate in each race would be the major-party candidate who received the bigger share of the remaining 80 percent of the vote.

single-member districts
The form of representation in which only the candidate who gets the most votes in a district wins office.

proportional representation

A form of representation in which seats in the legislature are allocated proportionally according to each political party's share of the popular vote. This system enables smaller parties to compete successfully for seats.

Germany's electoral system allocates legislative seats on the basis of both single-district voting and the overall proportion of votes a party receives. Half the seats go to the candidates who finish first in their respective districts. The other half are allocated to the parties according to the percentage of the votes each receives. This system requires that the German voter cast two ballots in legislative races: one to choose among the candidates in the particular district and one to choose among the parties. Shown here is a ballot from a German election. The left column lists the candidates for the legislative seat in a district, and the right column lists the parties. (Note the relatively large number of parties on the ballot.)

By comparison, most European democracies use some form of **proportional representation,** in which seats in the legislature are allocated according to a party's share of the popular vote. This type of electoral system enables smaller parties to compete for power. In the 2005 German elections, for example, the Green Party received 8 percent of the national vote and thereby won 51 seats in the 603-seat Bundestag, the German parliament. If the Greens had been competing under American electoral rules, they would not have won any seats.

Politics and Coalitions in the Two-Party System

The overriding goal of a major American party is to gain power by getting its candidates elected to office. Because there are only two major parties, however, the Republicans or Democrats can win consistently only by attracting majority support. In Europe's multiparty systems, a party can hope for a share of power if it has the firm backing of a minority faction. In the United States, if either party confines its support to a narrow segment of society, it forfeits its chance of gaining control of government.

Seeking the Center

American parties, Clinton Rossiter said, are "creatures of compromise."[15] The two parties usually take stands that have broad appeal or at least will not alienate significant blocs of voters. Anytime a party makes a pronounced shift toward either extreme, the political center is left open for the opposing party. Barry Goldwater, the Republican presidential nominee in 1964, proposed the elimination of mandatory social security and said he might consider the tactical use of small nuclear weapons in wars such as the Vietnam conflict—extreme positions that cost him many votes. Eight years later, the Democratic nominee, George McGovern, took positions on Vietnam and income security that alarmed many voters; like Goldwater, he was buried in one of the biggest landslides in presidential history.

It is impossible to understand the dynamics of the U.S. party system without recognizing that the true balance of power in American elections rests with the moderate voters in the center rather than with those who hold more extreme positions. When congressional Republicans mistook their 1994 election victory as a mandate to trim assistance programs for the elderly, the poor, and children, they alienated many of the moderate voters who had contributed to their 1994 victory. These voters wanted "less" government but not a government that punished society's most vulnerable citizens. After weak showings in the 1996 and 1998 elections, congressional Republicans shifted course. They unseated Speaker Newt Gingrich, replacing him with a more pragmatic conservative, Dennis Hastert. "We still need to prove that we can be conservative without being mean," was how one Republican member of Congress described the change in strategy.[16] The adjustment reflects a basic truth about U.S. politics: party ideology is acceptable as long as it is tinged with moderation.

Nonetheless, the Republican and Democratic parties do offer somewhat different alternatives and, at times, a clear choice. When Roosevelt was elected president in 1932, Lyndon Johnson in 1964, and Ronald Reagan in 1980, the parties were relatively far apart in their priorities and programs. Roosevelt's New Deal, for example, was an extreme alternative within the American political tradition and caused a decisive split along party lines. A lesson of these periods is that the center of the American political spectrum can be moved. Candidates risk a crushing defeat by straying too far from established ideas during normal times, but they may do so with some chance of success during turbulent times. The

terrorist attacks of September 11, 2001, provided President
George W. Bush with just such an opportunity. During his
first term, Bush pushed major tax cuts through Congress
and also sharply increased defense spending while pursuing an aggressive Middle East policy, backed at every step
by congressional Republicans.

When he sought reelection in 2004, Bush pursued the
unusual strategy, at least in American politics, of mobilizing his conservative base rather than reaching out to
moderates. He won the election, though narrowly. His victory margin was the smallest for a seated president since
Woodrow Wilson's reelection in 1916. But Bush's strategy
haunted his second term when moderates and independents in increasing numbers turned away from his Iraq
policy. When moderates and independents then voted disproportionately Democratic in the 2006 midterm elections,
the Republicans lost control of both the House and the Senate. The Bush presidency is a reminder that parties do not
always govern toward the center, but it is also a reminder
that a party creates trouble for itself by moving too far from
the center.

Party Coalitions

The groups and interests that support a party are collectively referred to as the **party coalition.** In multiparty
systems, each party is supported by a relatively narrow
range of interests. European parties tend to divide along
class lines, with the center and right parties drawing most
of their votes from the middle and upper classes and the
left parties drawing most of theirs from the working class.
By comparison, America's two-party system requires each
party to accommodate a wide range of interests in order
to gain the voting plurality necessary to win elections. The
Republican and Democratic coalitions are therefore relatively broad. Each includes a substantial proportion of voters of nearly every ethnic, religious, regional, and economic
grouping. Only a few groups are tightly aligned with a
party. African Americans are the clearest example; they
vote about 85 percent Democratic in national elections.

Although the Republican and Democratic coalitions overlap, they are hardly
identical (see Figure 8-4). The party coalitions have been forged primarily through
conflict over the federal government's role in solving social and economic problems. Each party has supported government action to promote economic security
and social equality, but the Democrats have favored a greater level of government
involvement. Virtually every major assistance program for the poor, the elderly,
and low-wage workers since the 1930s has been initiated by the Democrats. Accordingly, the Democratic coalition draws support disproportionately from society's
underdogs—blacks, union members, the poor, city dwellers, Hispanics, Jews, and
other "minorities."[17] For a long period, the Democratic Party was also the clear
choice of the nation's elderly as a result of its support for old-age assistance programs and because the basic political loyalties of the elderly were acquired during
the New Deal era, a period favorable to the Democrats. Recently, however, elderly
voters have split their vote about evenly between the parties.

George W. Bush's successful reelection campaign in 2004
illustrates that candidates can sometimes win elections
by positioning themselves away from the political center.
The risk in that strategy became evident, however, in the
2006 midterm elections when Republicans lost control of
Congress due to their loss of support among moderate and
independent voters. Bush is shown here delivering the 2007
State of the Union address. Seated behind him on the right is
Democrat Nancy Pelosi, who became Speaker of the House as
a result of her party's takeover of the House of Representatives
in the 2006 elections.

party coalition
The groups and interests that
support a political party.

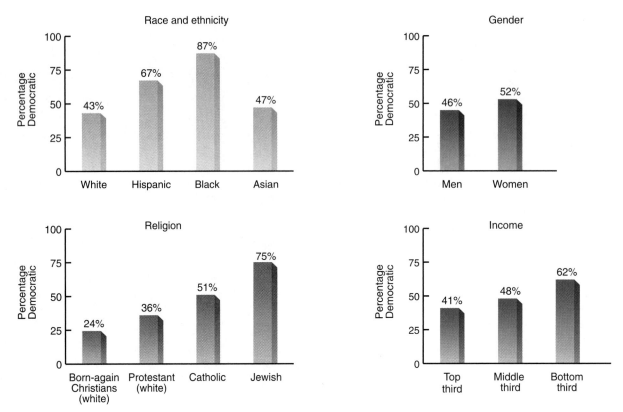

FIGURE 8-4 **The Vote of Selected Demographic Groups in Recent Presidential Elections** Although the Democratic and Republican coalitions overlap substantially, there are important differences, as illustrated by the Democratic Party's percentage of the two-party vote among some major demographic groups in recent elections.

Source: Compiled by author from NES and other surveys.

The Democratic Party's biggest gains recently have been among women, whose voting pattern traditionally was very similar to that of men. Recent elections, however, have revealed a gender gap (see Chapter 6). Women have voted disproportionately for the Democratic Party, apparently as a result of its positions on issues such as abortion rights, education spending, employment policies, and gun control.

The Republican coalition consists mainly of white middle-class Americans. The GOP has historically been the party of tax cuts and business incentives. It has also been more supportive of traditional values, as reflected, for example, in its opposition to abortion and to civil unions. Not surprisingly, the GOP is strongest in the suburbs and in regions, such as the South, the Great Plains, and the Rocky Mountains, where belief in traditional values and low taxes is prevalent.

The Republican Party has made big gains in recent decades among white fundamentalist Christians, who have been drawn to the GOP by its positions on abortion, school prayer, same-sex marriage, stem cell research, and other social issues.[18] In recent presidential elections, the Republican nominee has garnered the votes of roughly three-fourths of fundamentalist Christians.

Minor (Third) Parties

Although the U.S. electoral system discourages the formation of third parties (or, as they are more properly called, minor parties), the nation has always had them—more than a thousand over its history.[19] Most minor parties have been short-lived, and only a few have had a lasting impact. Only one minor party, the Republican Party, has ever achieved majority status.

Minor parties in the United States have formed largely to promote policies that their followers believe are not being adequately represented by either of the two major parties. A major party is always somewhat captive to its past, which is the source of many of its ideas and most of its followers. When conditions change, major parties can be slow to respond, and a minor party can try to capitalize on neglected issues. Whatever success it achieves, however, is usually short-lived. If a minor party gains a following, one or both major parties typically awaken to its issue, at which time the minor party begins to lose support. Nevertheless, the minor party will have served the purpose of making the major parties more responsive to the public's concerns.

Some minor parties have been virtually "antiparties" in the sense that they arose out of a belief that partisan politics is a corrupting influence. The most influential of these **reform parties** was the Progressive Party, which was as much a political movement as a political party. In the early 1900s, it succeeded in achieving its antiparty agenda in many states and localities. Primary elections, recall elections, nonpartisan elections, initiatives, and popular referendums, discussed in Chapter 2, were among the Progressive's contributions. A more recent reform party was titled just that, the Reform Party. It was created by Ross Perot after he ran as an independent and garnered 19 percent of the vote in the 1992 presidential election (second only to Theodore Roosevelt's 27 percent in 1912 among minor-party candidates). Perot's platform was based on middle-class discontent with the major parties' lack of fiscal restraint. Perot ran again in 1996, this time as the Reform Party's nominee, and won 8 percent of the vote. When Perot chose not to run in 2000, a divisive fight ensued over the Reform Party's nomination, which pundit Pat Buchanan received. His reactionary platform attracted only 1 percent of the general election vote and nearly wrecked the Reform Party. Since then, it has been trying without much success to rebuild its base.

Minor parties were at their peak in the nineteenth century, when the party system was still in flux.[20] Many of these parties were **single-issue parties** formed around a lone issue of overriding interest to their followers. The Free Soil Party, which fought the extension of slavery into new territories, and the Greenback Party, which wanted the currency system to be based on paper money rather than gold and silver, are examples. One of these nineteenth-century parties, the Prohibition Party, persisted into the twentieth century and contributed to the ratification in 1919 of the Eighteenth Amendment, which prohibited the manufacture, sale, and transportation of alcoholic beverages (but which was repealed in 1933). Although single-issue parties (for example, the Right to Life Party) exist today, they do not have large followings or much influence. The role that single-issue parties played in the nineteenth century is now played by single-issue interest groups (see Chapter 9).

Other minor parties have been characterized by their ideological commitment to a broad and noncentrist philosophical position, such as redistribution of economic

reform (minor) party

A minor party that bases its appeal on the claim that the major parties are having a corrupting influence on government and policy.

single-issue (minor) party

A minor party formed around a single issue of overriding interest to its followers.

HISTORICAL
Background

Although the United States has long had a two-party system, numerous minor parties have surfaced. A few of them have been influential, including the Free Soil Party, which emerged before the Civil War with a platform that called for the abolition of slavery in new states and territories. Shown here is a Free Soil Party poster from the 1848 election. The party's presidential nominee was Martin Van Buren, who had been president from 1837 to 1841 as a member of the Democratic Party.

ideological (minor) party

A minor party characterized by its ideological commitment to a broad and noncentrist philosophical position.

factional (minor) party

A minor party created when a faction within one of the major parties breaks away to form its own party.

party organizations

The party organizational units at national, state, and local levels; their influence has decreased over time because of many factors.

resources. Modern-day **ideological parties** include the Citizens Party, the Socialist Workers Party, and the Libertarian Party, each of which operates on the fringes of American politics. One of the strongest ideological parties in the nation's history was the Populist Party. Its candidate in the 1892 presidential election, James B. Weaver, gained 8.5 percent of the national vote and won twenty-two electoral votes in six western states. The party began as an agrarian protest movement in response to an economic depression and the anger of small farmers over low commodity prices, tight credit, and the high rates charged by railroad monopolies to transport farm goods. The Populists' ideological platform called for government ownership of the railroads, a graduated income tax, low tariffs on imports, and elimination of the gold standard.[21]

The strongest minor party today is the Green Party, an ideological party that holds liberal positions on the environment, labor, taxation, social welfare, and other issues. Its 2000 presidential nominee, consumer rights advocate Ralph Nader, received 3 percent of the national vote. According to polls, Nader (who ran as an Independent in 2004) got most of his support from voters who otherwise would have backed Democrat Al Gore, thus tipping the election to the more conservative Republican nominee, George W. Bush. In 2004, the Green Party decided to compete in the presidential race, but in a way designed to reduce the chance of tipping the election to the Republicans. The Green Party nominated David Cobb, a little-known Texas lawyer. The low-profile strategy was repeated in 2008. Indeed, the Green Party's 2008 nominee, former congresswoman Cynthia McKinney, attracted many fewer votes than did Ralph Nader, who ran as an independent, and Bob Barr, the Libertarian Party nominee.

The most important minor parties have been **factional parties**, created by a split within one of the major parties. Although the Republican and Democratic parties are normally adept at managing internal divisions, there have been times when internal conflict has led some of its followers to break away and form their own party. The most successful of these factional parties at the polls was Theodore Roosevelt's Bull Moose Party.[22] In 1908, Roosevelt, after having served eight years as president, declined to seek a third term and handpicked William Howard Taft for the Republican nomination. When Taft as president showed neither Roosevelt's enthusiasm for a strong presidency nor his commitment to the goals of the Progressive movement, Roosevelt challenged Taft for the 1912 Republican nomination but lost out. Backed by Progressive Republicans, Roosevelt proceeded to form the Bull Moose Party (a reference to Roosevelt's claim that he was "as strong as a bull moose"). Roosevelt won 27 percent of the presidential vote to Taft's 25 percent, but the split within Republican ranks enabled the Democratic nominee, Woodrow Wilson, to win the 1912 presidential election. The States' Rights Party in 1948 and George Wallace's American Independent Party in 1968 are other examples of strong factional parties. These parties were formed by white southern Democrats angered by northern Democrats' support of civil rights for black Americans. Deep divisions within a party give rise to factionalism and can lead eventually to a change in its coalition. The conflict over civil rights that began within the Democratic Party during the late 1940s continued for the next quarter-century, leading many southern whites to shift their party loyalty to the GOP.

Party Organizations

The Democratic and Republican parties have organizational units at the national, state, and local levels. The main purpose of these **party organizations** is the contesting of elections.

The Weakening of Party Organizations

A century ago, party organizations enjoyed almost complete control of nominations and elections. The party organizations still perform all the activities they formerly engaged in. They recruit candidates, raise money, develop policy positions, and canvass for votes. But they do not control these activities as completely as they once did. For the most part, these activities are now directed by the candidates themselves.[23]

Nomination refers to the selection of the individual who will run as the party's candidate in the general election. Until the early twentieth century, nominees were selected by party organizations. To get a party nomination, an individual had to be loyal to the party organization, a requirement that included, if the candidate was elected, a willingness to share with it the spoils of office—government jobs, benefits, and contracts. The party built its organization by handing out these jobs to followers and helping them obtain government services. Some party leaders also used their positions to extort money from building contractors and service providers. New York City's legendary Boss Tweed once charged the city twenty times what a building had actually cost, amassing a huge personal fortune before eventually winding up in jail. Looking for a way to deprive party bosses of their power, reform-minded Progressives argued that control over nominations should rest with ordinary voters rather than with the party organizations (see Chapter 2).

The result was the introduction of the **primary election** (or **direct primary**), which places nomination in the hands of the voters (see Chapters 2 and 12). The candidate who gets the most votes in a party's primary gets its nomination for the general election. In most states, the nominees are chosen in *closed primaries*, in which participation is limited to voters registered or declared at the polls as members of the party whose primary is being held. A number of other states use *open primaries*, a form that allows independents and voters of either party to choose which primary they will vote in, though they cannot choose to vote in both primaries in a given election. A few states use the blanket primary, where voters get a single ballot listing both the Republican and Democratic candidates by office. Each voter can cast only one vote per office but can select a candidate of either party. The top vote-getter in each party becomes its nominee. Louisiana has a variation on this form in which all candidates are listed on the ballot but are not identified by party; the top two vote-getters, even if of the same party, become the general election candidates.

Primaries hinder the building of strong party organizations. If primaries did not exist, candidates would have to seek nomination through the party organization, and they could be denied renomination if they were disloyal to the party's policy goals. Because of primaries, however, candidates have the option of seeking office on their own, and once elected (with or without the party's help), they can build a personal following that can place them beyond the party's direct control.

In the process of taking control of nominations, candidates also acquired control of most campaign money. At the turn of the twentieth century, when party machines were at their peak, most campaign funds passed through the hands of party leaders. Today, most of the money goes to the candidates directly, without first passing through the parties.

Party organizations were also weakened by the decline of patronage jobs. A century ago, when a party won control of government, it acquired control of nearly all public jobs, which were doled out to loyal party workers. However, as government jobs in the early twentieth century shifted from patronage to the

nomination

The designation of a particular individual to run as a political party's candidate (its "nominee") in the general election.

primary election (direct primary)

A form of election in which voters choose a party's nominees for public office. In most primaries, eligibility to vote is limited to voters who are registered members of the party.

POLITICAL CULTURE

LIBERTY, EQUALITY, AND SELF-GOVERNMENT

Political Parties

Historically, political parties have given weight to the voice of ordinary citizens. Their strength is in their numbers rather than in their wealth or status, and political parties give them a means to express that strength through their votes. It is no accident that the Jacksonian Democrats created the first American grassroots party for the purpose of strengthening self-government.

In backing a party, citizens are choosing more than a single officeholder. They are getting a coalition of officeholders committed to a broad agenda of policies and issues. The old adage "vote the person, not the party" is bad advice. To vote for the person is to assume that the individual officeholder wields singular power. But that's not true even in the case of the president. In selecting one presidential candidate over another, Americans are choosing more than the person who will sit behind the desk in the Oval Office. They are also selecting several hundred other executive officers, including the secretary of state, the attorney general of the United States, and the director of the Central Intelligence Agency. The president also nominates all federal judges and justices. The great majority of these individuals, including the judicial officers, will be of the same party as the president. The election of a senator or a representative is also more than a decision about which individual will occupy a seat in Congress. Rarely does a single member of Congress have a decisive voice in legislation. Congress works through collective action, and power resides with the majority party in each chamber. Dozens of important legislative votes are cast in Congress each term. Typically, most Republican members are on one side of the vote and most Democratic members are on the other side.

Accordingly, a vote based on an issue is usually shortsighted. Once in office, a winning candidate will vote on scores of policy issues, not just the one or two issues that were the cornerstone of the election campaign. And what is the best predictor of how the winning candidate will vote on these issues? In nearly every case, the best predictor is the political party to which the officeholder belongs.

If you've been among the Americans who pride themselves on "voting the person, not the party," give some thought to whether it's the most effective way to make a difference as a voter. If you are a party loyalist already, consider taking your commitment a step further. Party organizations at all levels are looking for volunteers, particularly at election time, when they are engaged in registration, canvassing, and get-out-the-vote efforts.

merit system (see Chapter 13), the party organizations controlled many fewer positions. Today, because of the large size of government, thousands of patronage jobs still exist. These government employees help staff the party organizations (along with volunteers), but most of them are indebted to an individual politician rather than to a party organization. Congressional staff members, for example, are patronage employees, but they owe their jobs and their loyalty to their senator or representative, not to their party.

In Europe, where there are no primary elections, the situation is different. Parties control their nominations, and because of this they also control campaign money and workers. A party's candidates are expected to support the national platform if elected. An officeholder who fails to do so is likely to be denied renomination in the next election.

The Structure and Role of Party Organizations

Although the influence of party organizations has declined, parties are in no danger of dying. Candidates and activists need an organization through which to work, and the party meets that need. Moreover, certain activities, such as get-out-the-vote efforts on election day, affect all of a party's candidates and are more efficiently done through the party organization. Indeed, parties have staged a comeback of sorts.[24] National and state party organizations now assist candidates with fund-raising, polling, research, and media production, all essential ingredients of a successful modern campaign.

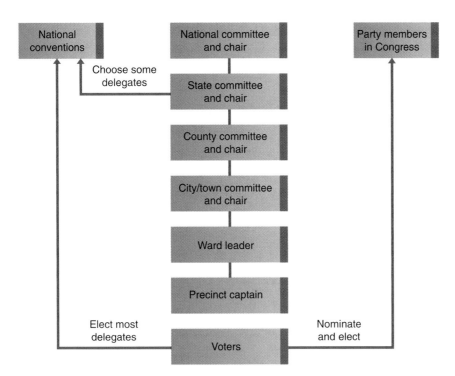

FIGURE 8-5 Formal **Organization of the Political Party** U.S. parties are loosely structured alliances of national, state, and local organizations; most local parties are not as well organized as the chart implies.

Structurally, U.S. parties are loose associations of national, state, and local organizations (see Figure 8-5). The national party organizations cannot dictate the decisions made by the state organizations, which in turn do not control the activities of local organizations. However, there is communication between the levels because they all have a stake in the party's success.[25]

Local Party Organizations

In a sense, U.S. parties are organized from the bottom up, not the top down. Of the roughly five hundred thousand elective offices in the United States, fewer than five hundred are contested statewide and only two—the presidency and vice presidency—are contested nationally. All the rest are local offices; not surprisingly, at least 95 percent of party activists work within local organizations.

It is difficult to generalize about local parties because they vary greatly in their structure and activities. Today only a few local party organizations, including the Democratic organizations in Albany, Philadelphia, and Chicago, bear even a faint resemblance to the fabled old-time party machines that, in return for jobs and even welfare services, were able to deliver the vote on election day. In many urban areas, and in most suburbs and towns, the party organizations today do not have enough activists to do organizing work outside the campaign period, at which time—to the extent their resources allow—they conduct registration drives, send mailings or hand out leaflets, and help get out the vote. These activities are not insignificant. Most local campaigns are not well funded, and the party's efforts can tip the balance in a close race.

Local parties tend to concentrate on elections that coincide with local boundaries, such as races for mayor, city council, state legislature, and county offices. Local parties also take part in congressional, statewide, and presidential contests, but in these instances, their role is typically secondary to that of the candidates' personal campaign organizations, which will be discussed later in this chapter.

State Party Organizations

At the state level, each party is headed by a central committee made up of members of local party organizations and local and state officeholders. State central committees do not meet regularly and provide only general policy guidance for the state organizations. Day-to-day operations are directed by a chairperson, who is a full-time, paid employee of the state party. The central committee appoints the chair, but it often accepts the choice of the party's leading politician, usually the governor or a U.S. senator.

The state party organizations engage in activities, such as fund-raising and voter registration, that can improve their candidates' chances of success. State party organizations concentrate on statewide races, including those for governor and U.S. senator, and also focus on races for the state legislature. They play a smaller role in campaigns for national or local offices, and in most states, they do not endorse candidates in statewide primaries.

National Party Organizations

The national Republican and Democratic Party organizations, which are located in Washington, D.C., are structured much like those at the state level: they have a national committee and a national party chairperson.

The Structure of the National Parties   Although in theory the national parties are run by their committees, neither the Democratic National Committee (DNC) nor the Republican National Committee (RNC) has great power. The RNC (with more than 150 members) and the DNC (with more than 300 members) are too cumbersome and meet too infrequently to oversee party activities. Their power is largely confined to setting organizational policy, such as determining the site of the party's presidential nominating convention and setting the rules governing the selection of convention delegates. They have no power to pick nominees or to dictate candidates' policy positions.

In 2005, the Democratic Party chose Howard Dean as its national party chair. Most party chairs are not widely known, but Dean was familiar to voters as a result of his strong bid for the 2004 Democratic presidential nomination. The Democrats picked Dean as their chair in hopes that he could boost their fund-raising and grassroots efforts.

The national party's day-to-day operations are directed by a national chairperson chosen by the national committee, although the committee defers to the president's choice when the party controls the White House. The national chair directs a large staff operation that seeks to build the party's base and promote its presidential and congressional candidates. The RNC and DNC, among other things, run training programs for candidates and their staffs, raise money, seek media coverage of party positions and activities, conduct issue and group research, and send field representatives to help state and local parties with their operations. In some cases, the national parties also try to recruit potentially strong candidates to run in House and Senate races.

This model of the national party was created in the 1970s when Republican leaders concluded that an expanded and modernized national organization could contribute to the party's electoral success. The DNC has created a similar organization, but it is less substantial than the RNC's. Modern campaigns,

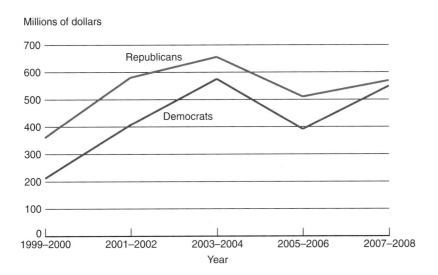

Millions of dollars

FIGURE 8-6   **National Party Fund-Raising, 1999–2008**
Over the years, the Republican Party has raised significantly more money than has the Democratic Party. The figures include fund-raising by the DNC, RNC, DCCC, NRCC, DSCC, and NRSC.
Source: Federal Elections Commission. The 2007–2008 data are based on projections from incomplete cycle.

as David Adamany notes, are based on "cash," and Democrats have less of it.[26] In recent election cycles, the Republican national party has usually outspent its Democratic counterpart by a comfortable margin (see Figure 8-6).

Money and the National Parties   The parties' major role in campaigns is the raising and spending of money. The RNC and the DNC are major sources of campaign funds, but they are not the only national-level party units involved in fund-raising. There are also House and Senate party campaign committees, which raise funds and provide advice to the party's congressional candidates. These committees consist of the Democratic Congressional Campaign Committee (DCCC), the National Republican Congressional Committee (NRCC), the Democratic Senatorial Campaign Committee (DSCC), and the National Republican Senatorial Committee (NRSC).

A party organization can legally give money directly to a House or Senate candidate. The legal limit is greater for Senate candidates than House candidates and, given the enormous cost of today's campaigns, is not particularly high (about $40,000 in the case of Senate candidates). This funding, along with the money a candidate receives from individual contributors and interest groups, which are also subject to strict limits, is termed **hard money**—it goes directly to the candidate and can be spent as he or she chooses.

Limits on party contributions were established when the campaign finance laws were reformed in the 1970s in response to the Watergate scandal. However, a loophole in the laws was exposed when a court ruling allowed the parties to raise and spend unlimited campaign funds provided the funds were not channeled directly to a party's candidates. Thus, whereas a wealthy contributor could legally give a candidate only a limited amount, that same contributor could give an unlimited amount to the candidate's party. These contributions were termed **soft money** in that a party could not hand it over directly to a candidate. But the party could use these contributions to support party activities, such as voter registration efforts, get-out-the-vote drives, and party-centered television ads, that could indirectly benefit its candidates. In some cases, the line between the use of hard and soft money was hard to distinguish. In 1996, for example, the Democratic party ran a $100-million ad campaign that did not directly urge voters to support Clinton but did include pictures of him and references to his accomplishments as president.

In 2002, Congress closed the loophole through enactment of the Bipartisan Campaign Reform Act (BCRA), which prohibits the national parties from raising or spending soft money. BCRA also bans the state parties from spending soft

hard money
Campaign funds given directly to candidates to spend as they choose.

soft money
Campaign contributions that are not subject to legal limits and are given to parties rather than directly to candidates. (These contributions are no longer legal.)

DEBATING THE ISSUES

SHOULD THERE BE LIMITS ON CAMPAIGN CONTRIBUTIONS?

Campaign finance has been a controversial issue in the United States since at least the late nineteenth century. Millionaires literally bought their seats in the U.S. Senate through contributions to state legislators, who prior to ratification of the Seventeenth Amendment in 1913 appointed the Senate's members. Abuses by Richard Nixon's 1972 reelection campaign again put campaign finance in the headlines and prompted Congress to enact legislation that limited campaign contributions. However, big donors found a legal loophole that allowed them to make unrestricted contributions to political parties. More than a billion dollars of so-called soft money was donated to campaigns during the 1990s alone, prompting Congress in 2002 to enact a ban on soft-money contributions. The legislation was upheld by the Supreme Court, but the new law also had a loophole. In the 2004 presidential campaign and again in 2008, tens of millions of dollars in large contributions flowed to so-called 527 groups, which used the money to try to affect the election's outcome.

The regulation of campaign money has always been a contentious issue. Those favoring regulation have focused on the influence of campaign money on policy decisions. Those opposing regulation have focused on the free-speech implications of limiting political contributions.

YES Special interests who give large amounts of soft money to political parties do in fact achieve their objectives. They do get special access. Sitting Senate and House members have limited amounts of time, but they make time available in their schedules to meet with representatives of business and unions and wealthy individuals who gave large sums of money to their parties. These are not idle chit-chats about the philosophy of democracy. In these meetings, these special interests, often accompanied by lobbyists, press elected officials . . . to adopt their position on a matter of interest to them. [Members of Congress] are pressed by their benefactors to introduce legislation, to amend legislation, to block legislation, and to vote on legislation in a certain way. No one says: "We gave money so you should help us with this." No one needs to say it—it is perfectly understood by all participants in every such meeting. . . . Large soft money contributions in fact distort the legislative process. They affect what gets done and how it gets done. They affect whom senators and House members see, whom they spend their time with, what input they get, and—make no mistake about it—this money affects outcomes as well.

—*Warren Rudman, former U.S. senator*

NO This is a sad day for the freedom of speech. Who could have imagined that the same court which, within the past four years, has sternly disapproved of restrictions upon such inconsequential forms of expression as virtual child pornography, tobacco advertising, dissemination of illegally intercepted communications, and sexually explicit cable programming would smile with favor upon a law that cuts to the heart of what the First Amendment is meant to protect: the right to criticize the government. . . . The premise of the First Amendment is that the American people are neither sheep nor fools, and hence fully capable of considering both the substance of the speech presented to them and its proximate and ultimate source. If that premise is wrong, our democracy has a much greater problem to overcome than merely the influence of amassed wealth. Given the premises of democracy, there is no such thing as too much speech. . . . The first instinct of power is the retention of power, and, under a Constitution that requires periodic elections, that is best achieved by the suppression of election-time speech. . . . It is not the proper role of those who govern us to judge which campaign speech has "substance" and "depth" (do you think it might be that which is least damaging to incumbents?) and to abridge the rest.

—*Antonin Scalia, associate justice of the Supreme Court*

money in support of candidates for federal office. The Supreme Court upheld these restrictions in a 2003 decision,[27] but a new loophole soon surfaced. The ban on soft money does not fully apply to so-called 527 groups. (Section 527 of the Internal Revenue Code defines the rules governing not-for-profit political groups.) Much of the money that previously would have been contributed to a party organization now finds its way into the hands of 527 groups. Although they are prohibited from attacking a candidate directly, these groups can legally engage in issue advocacy, which has enabled them to mount thinly veiled candidate attacks. During the 2004 presidential election, 527 groups spent more than $100 million. Several of these groups, including MoveOn and Swift Boat Veterans for Truth, were subsequently fined by the Federal Election Commision (FEC) for crossing the line from issue advocacy to candidate advocacy. Swift Boat Veterans for Truth ran televised ads claiming that Democratic nominee John Kerry's Vietnam combat medals, which included the Silver Star and Purple Heart, were fraudulently acquired. The charges, which were shown to be false, were deliberately designed to hurt Kerry's campaign and thus fell outside the realm of issue advocacy.

Like all previous campaign finance legislation, BCRA has been only partially successful in regulating the flow of campaign money.[28] Just as water always runs downhill, money always seems to find its way into election politics.

The Candidate-Centered Campaign

Party committees have more of a **service relationship** than a power relationship with their party's candidates. Because the party nominees are chosen through primaries, and because many of the potential candidates already have a power base at the local or state level, the national committees are unable to handpick the party nominees. Accordingly, the party organizations tend to back whichever candidate wins the primary. If the candidate then wins the general election, the party at least has denied the office to the opposing party.

Today's campaigns are largely controlled by the candidates, particularly in congressional, statewide, and presidential races. Each candidate has a personal organization, created especially for the campaign and disbanded once it is over. The candidates are entrepreneurs who play what political consultant Joe Napolitan labeled "the election game."[29] The game begins with money—lots of it.

Campaign Funds: The Money Chase

Campaigns for high office are expensive, and the costs keep rising. In 1980, about $250 million was spent on all Senate and House campaigns combined. The figure had jumped to $425 million by 1990. In 2006, the figure easily exceeded $1 billion, more than four times the 1980 level.[30] As might be expected, incumbents have a distinct advantage in fund-raising. They have contributor lists from past campaigns and have the policy influence that donors seek. House and Senate incumbents outspend their challengers by more than two to one.

Because of the high cost of campaigns, candidates spend much of their time raising funds, which come primarily from individual contributors, interest groups (through PACs, discussed in Chapter 9), and political parties. The **money chase** is relentless.[31] A U.S. senator must raise $20,000 a week on average throughout the entire six-year term in order to raise the minimum $6 million it takes to run a competitive Senate campaign in most states. A Senate campaign in a large state can easily exceed that amount. In 2004, despite having a wide lead in the polls over a weak opponent, Barack Obama still spent $10 million on his Senate race in Illinois. House campaigns are less costly, but expenditures of $1 million or more are commonplace. As for presidential elections, even the nominating race is expensive. In 2008, Obama spent more than $200 million during the competitive phase of his campaign for the Democratic nomination. (In presidential races, but not congressional ones, candidates are eligible to receive federal funds, a topic discussed in Chapter 12.)

Organization and Strategy: Hired Guns

The key operatives in today's campaigns are campaign consultants, pollsters, media producers, and fund-raising and get-out-the-vote specialists. They are

service relationship
The situation in which party organizations assist candidates for office but have no power to require them to support the party's main policy positions.

money chase
A term used to describe the fact that U.S. campaigns are very expensive and candidates must spend a great amount of time raising funds in order to compete successfully.

STATES IN THE NATION

PUBLIC FUNDING OF STATE ELECTIONS

About half the states have public funding of election campaigns. Some of them give the money to political parties, which allocate it to candidates or spend it on party activities such as get-out-the-vote efforts. Other states give funds directly to candidates, although this funding typically is limited to candidates for designated offices, such as governor.

Q: What might explain the fact that there is no clear-cut regional pattern to the public funding of state elections?

A: Public funding of elections is relatively new, so additional states may adopt it in the next decade or two, at which time a regional tendency could emerge. (If your state does not have public funding, do you think it is likely to adopt it anytime soon? Why or why not?)

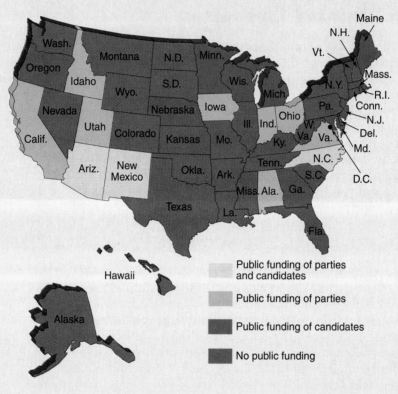

Public funding of parties and candidates
Public funding of parties
Public funding of candidates
No public funding

Source: National Conference of State Legislatures, 2008.

hired guns

A term that refers to the professional consultants who run campaigns for high office.

hired guns who charge hefty fees for their services. "The new king-makers" is the way writer David Chagall characterizes these pros.[32]

These hired guns include campaign strategists who help the candidate to plot and execute a game plan. Over the years, some of these strategists, including James Carville, Dick Morris, and Roger Ailes, developed legendary reputations. Fund-raising specialists are also part of the new politics. They know how to tap into the networks of large donors and interest groups that contribute to election campaigns and are adept at running targeted direct-mail fund-raising campaigns. The hired guns also include experts who conduct polls and focus groups (the latter are small groups of voters brought together to discuss at length their thoughts on the candidates and issues). Polls and focus groups enable candidates to identify issues and messages that will resonate with voters.[33] Media consultants are another staple of the modern campaign. These experts are adept at producing televised political advertising and creating the "photo-ops" and other staged events that attract news coverage.

The hired guns of the modern campaign are skilled at **packaging** a candidate—highlighting those aspects of the candidate's partisanship, policy positions, personal background, and personality that are thought most attractive to voters. Packaging is not new to politics. Andrew Jackson's self-portrayal in the nineteenth century as "the champion of the people" is an image that any modern candidate could appreciate. What is new is the need to fit the image to the requirements of a world of sound bites, thirty-second ads, and televised debates, and to do it in a persuasive way. In the old days, it was sometimes enough for candidates to drive home the point that they were a Republican or a Democrat, playing on the tendency of voters to choose a candidate on that basis. Party appeals are still critical, but today's voters also want to know about a candidate's personality and policy positions. In their quest for the 2008 Democratic nomination, Barack Obama positioned himself as "the candidate of change," while opponent Hillary Clinton claimed to be "the candidate with experience."

Hired consultants have been a driving force for yet another characteristic of modern campaigns—the tearing down of the opponent.[34] In one sense, negative campaigning is as old as American politics. Thomas Jefferson was the subject of a whispering campaign about his sex life, and Abraham Lincoln was ridiculed by opponents as "a baboon" for his hairy, gangly look and his backwoods roots. But today's version of attack politics is unprecedented in its scale, ubiquity, and sophistication. Professional strategists have concluded that they can win more votes by diminishing the opponent than by building up their own candidate. In the past three decades, negative television ads have increased threefold, to the point where they now constitute the large share of political ads.[35] Most campaigns nowadays have a nasty edge, and the attacks can be downright vicious. In 2002, for example, incumbent U.S. Senator Max Cleland lost his bid for reelection when his lead in the polls withered in the face of blistering attacks on his patriotism, including an ad that showed his face alternately with those of Saddam Hussein and Osama bin Laden. Cleland's patriotism would have seemed above reproach; he had lost his legs and right arm in combat in Vietnam. Yet his opponent seized upon Cleland's vote against a Senate bill creating the Department of Homeland Security because it did not include the normal protections for civil service employees. The ad ignored the specifics of Cleland's objection to the bill, portraying him instead as "soft" on terrorism.

packaging
A term of modern campaigning that refers to the process of recasting a candidate's record into an appealing image.

U.S. Senator Hillary Clinton is the only First Lady to seek elective office. She moved to New York to compete in the state's 2000 Senate race, which she won. She ran for reelection in 2006 and then set her sight on the 2008 Democratic presidential nomination, which she lost narrowly to Barack Obama. Clinton is shown here on the campaign trail.

Voter Contacts: Pitched Battle

Today's elections for high office have no historical parallel in their length and penetration. Candidates start their active campaigning much earlier—often a year in advance of election day—than they did in times past. The modern campaign is relentless. Voters are bombarded with messages that arrive by air, by land, and by Web.

Air Wars

The main battleground of the modern campaign is the mass media, particularly television. Television emerged in the 1960s as the major medium of presidential and congressional politics and has remained the dominant medium ever since.

Candidates spend heavily on televised political advertising, which enables them to communicate directly—and on their own terms—with voters. The production and the airing of political ads account for half or more of campaign spending. Indeed, televised ads are the main reason for the high cost of U.S. campaigns. In most democracies, televised campaigning takes place through parties, which receive free air time to make their pitch. Many democracies even prohibit the purchase of televised advertising time by candidates (see Table 8-1).

Air wars is the term that political scientist Darrell West applies to candidates' use of televised ads.[36] Candidates increasingly play off each other's ads, seeking to gain the strategic advantage. Modern production techniques enable well-funded candidates to get new ads on the air within a few hours' time, which allows them to rebut attacks and exploit fast-breaking developments, a tactic known as *rapid response.*

Candidates also use the press to get their message across, although the amount of news coverage they can get varies widely by location and office. Many House candidates are nearly ignored by their local news media. The New York City media market, for example, includes more than a score of House districts in New York, New Jersey, Pennsylvania, and Connecticut, and candidates in these districts get little or no coverage from the New York media. The presidential campaign, in contrast, gets daily coverage from both national and local media. Between these extremes are Senate races, which always get some news coverage and, if hotly contested, may get heavy coverage.

Debates are also part of the modern media campaign. Debates often attract large and attentive audiences, but they can be risky encounters, because they

air wars

A term that refers to the fact that modern campaigns are often a battle of opposing televised advertising campaigns.

TABLE 8-1 | **Television Campaign Practices in Selected Democracies**   In many democracies, free television time is provided to political parties, and candidates are not allowed to buy advertising time. The United States provides no free time to parties and allows candidates to purchase air time. Television debates are also a regular feature of U.S. campaigns.

Country	Paid TV Ads Allowed?	Unrestricted Free TV Time Provided?	TV Debates Held?
Canada	Yes	Yes	Yes
France	No	Yes	Yes
Germany	Yes	Yes	Yes
Great Britain	No	Yes	No
Italy	No	Yes	Yes
Netherlands	No	No	Yes
United States	Yes	No	Yes

give viewers a chance to compare the candidates directly. A weak or bumbling performance can hurt a candidate. Some analysts believe, for example, that Al Gore's performance in the first of the 2000 general election debates, when he grimaced and sighed loudly when George W. Bush was talking, cost him the election. Gore had been slightly ahead in the opinion polls but lost his lead immediately after the debate.

Ground Wars

Candidates' first priority in a close election is "swing voters"—those voters who conceivably could be persuaded to vote for either side. As election day nears, however, candidates concentrate on getting their supporters to the polls.

The get-out-the-vote effort traditionally has been borne by the parties and other organizations, such as labor unions. Although these groups remain the cornerstone of the effort, the candidates are also involved, and increasingly so. As partisanship has intensified in recent years, candidates have found it more difficult to persuade voters to switch sides. It has therefore become important for them to get as many of their supporters as possible to the polls on election day. Some campaign money that formerly would have been spent on televised advertising is now channeled into voter turnout efforts. In the final phase of the 2008 presidential election, millions of potential voters were contacted by phone or in person by the Republican and Democratic campaigns.

Web Wars

New communication technology usually makes its way into campaign politics, and the Internet is no exception. All of the candidates for the 2008 Democratic and Republican nominations, for example, had a website dedicated to providing information, generating public support, attracting volunteers, and raising money. Barack Obama's website was by far the most successful. Through it, he raised tens of millions of dollars and developed a nationwide network of hundreds of thousands of supporters.

Although television is still the principal medium of election politics, some analysts believe that the Internet may eventually overtake it. Email is cheaper than television advertising (and both cheaper and faster than traditional mail). Because it is a targeted medium, the Internet could become the channel through which candidates reach particular voting groups. But the Internet also has some disadvantages relative to television. The most important is that the individual user has greater control over Internet messages. With television, when a political ad appears during a favorite program, most viewers will watch it. An unsolicited message on the Internet is more easily ignored or deleted. Future candidates may conclude that the Internet is the preferred medium for fund-raising and interacting with supporters and that television is the best medium for achieving public recognition and reaching less-interested voters.

Parties, Candidates, and the Public's Influence

Candidate-centered campaigns have some distinct advantages. First, they can infuse new blood into electoral politics. Candidate recruitment is normally a slow process in party-centered systems. Would-be officeholders pay their dues by working in the party and, in the process, tend to adopt the outlook of those already there. By comparison, a candidate-centered system is more open and provides opportunities for newcomers to gain office quickly. Barack Obama is a case in point. He had run unsuccessfully for the U.S. House of Representatives in

John McCain and Sarah Palin campaign during the 2008 presidential election. In America's candidate-centered system, party nominees have considerable latitude in deciding how they will conduct their campaigns. McCain had a nearly free hand in choosing the little-known Palin as his running mate, instantly making her a major political figure, which is a rare occurence in a party-centered system.

2000 before seeking and getting the Democratic nomination, and then winning, the 2004 U.S. Senate race in Illinois. Barely two years later, Obama announced his candidacy for president of the United States, winning his party's 2008 nomination against the more experienced U.S. Senator Hillary Clinton and then beating the even more experienced U.S. Senator John McCain in the general election. Obama's quick rise from political obscurity to the highest office in the country would be almost unthinkable in a party-centered democracy. Nor is he the only example. In 1976, Jimmy Carter went from being an obscure one-term governor of Georgia to winning the presidency two years later.

Candidate-centered campaigns also lend flexibility to electoral politics. When political conditions and issues change, self-directed candidates quickly adjust, bringing new ideas into the political arena. Strong party organizations are rigid by comparison. Until the early 1990s, for example, the British Labour Party was controlled by old-line activists who refused to concede that changes in the British economy called for changes in the party's trade unionist and economic policies. The result was a series of humiliating defeats at the hands of the Conservative Party that ended only after Tony Blair and other proponents of "New Labour" successfully recast the party's image.

Also, candidate-centered campaigns encourage national officeholders to be responsive to local interests. In building personal followings among their state and district constituents, members of Congress respond to local needs. Nearly every significant domestic program enacted by Congress is adjusted to accommodate the interests of states and localities that otherwise would be hurt by the policy. Members of Congress are not obliged to support the legislative position of their party's majority, and they often extract favors for their constituents as the price of their support. Where strong national parties exist, national interests take precedence over local concerns. In both France and Britain, for example, the pleas of representatives of underdeveloped regions have often gone unheeded by their party's majority.

In other respects, however, candidate-centered campaigns have some distinct disadvantages. Often they degenerate into mud-slinging contests, and they are fertile ground for powerful special-interest groups, which contribute much of the money that underwrites candidates' campaigns. Many groups give large sums of money to incumbents of both parties, which enables them to insulate themselves from an election's outcome: whether the Republicans win or the Democrats win, these contributors are assured of having friends in high places.

Candidate-centered campaigns also weaken accountability by making it easier for officeholders to deny personal responsibility for government's actions. If national policy goes awry, an incumbent can always say that he or she is only one vote out of many and that the real problem resides with the president or with "others" in Congress. The problem of accountability in the U.S. system is illustrated by the several trillion dollars that have been added to the national debt since 2000 because of Republican officeholders' insistence on steep tax cuts and huge increases in military spending and Democratic officeholders' refusal to accept significant cuts in domestic spending programs. "Running on empty" is how former cabinet secretary Peter Peterson describes the huge debt being passed along to future generations of Americans that has enabled today's members of Congress to keep their constituents happy enough to vote them back into office.[37] The problem of accountability is also illustrated by surveys that have asked Americans about their confidence in Congress. Although most citizens do not have a high opinion of Congress as a whole, most also say that they have confidence in their local representative in Congress. This paradoxical attitude prevails in so many districts that the net result in most elections is a Congress whose membership is not greatly changed from the previous one (see Chapter 11). In contrast, party-centered campaigns are characterized by collective accountability. When problems occur, voters tend to hold the majority party responsible and invariably vote large numbers of its members out of office.

In sum, candidate-centered campaigns strengthen the relationship between the voters and their individual representative while at the same time weakening the relationship between the full electorate and their representative institutions. Whether this arrangement serves the public's interest is debatable. Nevertheless, it is clear that Americans do not favor party-centered politics. Parties survived the shift to candidate-centered campaigns and will persist, but their organizational heyday has passed. (Congressional and presidential campaigns are discussed further in Chapters 11 and 12, respectively.)

Summary   Self-Test www.mhhe.com/pattersontad9e

Political parties serve to link the public with its elected leaders. In the United States, this linkage is provided by the two-party system; only the Republican and Democratic parties have any chance of winning control of government. The fact that the United States has only two major parties is explained by several factors: an electoral system—characterized by single-member districts—that makes it difficult for third parties to compete for power; each party's willingness to accept differing political views; and a political culture that stresses compromise and negotiation rather than ideological rigidity.

Because the United States has only two major parties, each of which seeks to gain majority support, their candidates normally tend to avoid controversial or extreme political positions. Sometimes, Democratic and Republican candidates do offer sharply contrasting policy alternatives, particularly during times of crisis. Ordinarily, however, Republican and Democratic candidates pursue moderate and somewhat overlapping policies. Each party can count on its party loyalists, but U.S. elections can hinge on swing voters, who respond to the issues of the moment either prospectively, basing their vote on what the candidates promise to do if elected, or retrospectively, basing their vote on their satisfaction or dissatisfaction with what the party in power has already done.

America's parties are decentralized, fragmented organizations. The national party organization does not control the policies and activities of the state organizations, and these in turn do not control the local organizations. Traditionally, the local organizations have controlled most of the party's work force because most elections are contested at the local level. Local parties, however, vary markedly in their vitality. Whatever their level, America's party organizations are relatively weak. They lack control over nominations and elections. Candidates can bypass the party organization and win nomination through primary elections. Individual candidates also control most of the organizational structure and money necessary to win elections. The state and national party organizations have recently expanded their capacity to provide candidates with modern campaign services. Nevertheless, party organizations at all levels have few ways of controlling the candidates who run under their banners. They assist candidates with campaign technology, workers, and funds, but they cannot compel candidates' loyalty to organizational goals.

American political campaigns, particularly those for higher office, are candidate centered. Most candidates are self-starters who become adept at "the election game." They spend much of their time raising campaign funds, and they build their personal organizations around hired guns: pollsters, media producers, fund-raisers, and election consultants. Strategy and image making are key components of the modern campaign,

as is televised political advertising, which accounts for half or more of all spending in presidential and congressional races.

The advantages of candidate-centered politics include a responsiveness to new leadership, new ideas, and local concerns. Yet this form of politics can result in campaigns that are personality-driven, depend on powerful interest groups, and blur responsibility for what government has done.

CHAPTER 8

Study Corner

Key Terms

air wars (*p. 214*)

candidate-centered politics (*p. 192*)

factional (minor) party (*p. 204*)

grassroots party (*p. 194*)

hard money (*p. 209*)

hired guns (*p. 212*)

ideological (minor) party (*p. 204*)

money chase (*p. 211*)

multiparty system (*p. 199*)

nomination (*p. 205*)

packaging (of a candidate) (*p. 213*)

party-centered politics (*p. 192*)

party coalition (*p. 201*)

party competition (*p. 192*)

party organizations (*p. 204*)

party realignment (*p. 194*)

political party (*p. 191*)

primary election (direct primary) (*p. 205*)

proportional representation (*p. 200*)

prospective voting (*p. 198*)

reform (minor) party (*p. 203*)

retrospective voting (*p. 198*)

service relationship (*p. 211*)

single-issue (minor) party (*p. 203*)

single-member districts (*p. 199*)

soft money (*p. 209*)

split ticket (*p. 198*)

two-party system (*p. 198*)

Self-Test

1. The formation of political parties:
   a. acts as a support for an elitist government.
   b. makes it difficult for the public to participate in politics.
   c. can mobilize citizens to collective action to compete for power with those who have wealth and prestige.
   d. can function as an alternative to free and open media.

2. A major change in party activity in the South since the 1960s is:
   a. the emergence of a viable third party.
   b. a sharp decline in voter turnout.

   c. a decline in the level of two-party competition in state and local elections.
   d. a switch to support of Republican candidates in presidential elections.

3. The chief electoral factor supporting a two-party system in the United States is:
   a. proportional representation.
   b. multimember election districts.
   c. single-member districts with proportional voting.
   d. single-member districts with plurality voting.

4. The high cost of campaigns in the United States is largely related to:
   a. running televised ads.
   b. developing a colorful website.
   c. organizing door-to-door canvassing efforts.
   d. paying the legal and accounting expenses related to filing information about campaign donors and expenditures with the Federal Elections Commission.

5. In recent decades, state political party organizations in the United States have:
   a. become weaker and less effective.
   b. taken over control and direction of the national parties.
   c. been hurt by services provided by the national party organizations.
   d. become more professional in staffing and support of statewide races.

6. European and American political parties differ in which of the following ways?
   a. the degree to which they are party-centered as opposed to candidate-centered
   b. the nature of their party organizations: the extent to which they are organized at the local and national levels, and the amount of power that exists at each of these levels

c. the type of electoral system in which they elect their candidates to office
d. all of the above

7. The coalitions of voters that make up the Republican and Democratic parties are virtually identical. (T/F)

8. Primary elections helped strengthen party organizations in the United States. (T/F)

9. U.S. political parties are organized from the bottom up, not the top down. (T/F)

10. Modern-day parties in the United States are described in the text as having more of a service than a power relationship with candidates. (T/F)

Critical Thinking

Why are elections conducted so differently in the United States than in European democracies? Why are the campaigns so much longer, more expensive, and more candidate-centered?

Suggested Readings

Aldrich, John H. *Why Parties? The Origin and Transformation of Political Parties in America.* Chicago: University of Chicago Press, 1995. An insightful analysis of what parties are and how they emerge and develop.

Buell, Emmett H., Jr., and Lee Sigelman. *Attack Politics: Negativity in Presidential Campaigns Since 1960.* Lawrence: University Press of Kansas, 2008. A look at how negative politics has come to pervade campaigns.

Flanigan, William H., and Nancy H. Zingale. *Political Behavior of the American Electorate,* 11th ed. Washington, D.C.: Congressional Quarterly Press, 2005. An overview of Americans' electoral behavior.

Geer, John. *In Defense of Negativity.* Chicago: University of Chicago Press, 2006. A provocative and award-winning analysis of televised political ads.

Greenberg, Stanley B. *The Two Americas: Our Current Political Deadlock and How to Break It.* New York: Thomas Dunne Books, 2004. An assessment of party politics in today's America.

Hershey, Marjorie Randon. *Party Politics in America,* 13th ed. New York: Longman, 2009. A well-written, thorough analysis of U.S. political parties.

Hillygus, D. Sunshine, and Todd G. Shields. *The Persuadable Voter: Wedge Issues in Presidential Campaigns.* Princeton, N.J.: Princeton University Press, 2008. A careful analysis of the use of wedge issues, such as abortion, in campaign strategy.

Patterson, Kelly D. *Political Parties and the Maintenance of Liberal Democracy.* New York: Columbia University Press, 1996. A systematic look at the effects of political parties on American government and politics.

Sifreg, Micah L. *Spoiling for a Fight: Third-Party Politics in America.* New York: Routledge, 2003. An analysis of America's third parties and their impact on the two-party system.

Stonecash, Jeffrey. *Class and Party in American Politics.* Boulder, Colo.: Westview Press, 2001. An insightful analysis that argues that class is still very much a part of America's party politics.

West, Darrell M. *Air Wars: Television Advertising in Election Campaigns, 1952–2004,* 5th ed. Washington, D.C.: Congressional Quarterly Press, 2005. A thorough study of the role of televised advertising in election campaigns.

List of Websites

http://www.democrats.org/
The Democratic National Committee's site; provides information on the party's platform, candidates, officials, and organization.

http://www.greenparties.org/
The Green Party's site; contains information on the party's philosophy and policy goals.

http://www.rnc.org/
Home page of the Republican National Committee; offers information on Republican leaders, policy positions, and organizations.

http://www.jamescarvillesoffice.com/
The website of James Carville, one of the nation's top campaign consultants.

Participate!

Consider becoming a campaign or political party volunteer. The opportunities are numerous. Parties and candidates at every level from the national on down seek volunteers to assist in organizing, canvassing, fund-raising, and other activities. As a college student, you have communication and knowledge skills that would be valuable to a campaign or party organization. You might be pleasantly surprised by the tasks you are assigned.

Extra Credit

For up-to-the-minute *New York Times* articles, interactive simulations, graphics, study tools, and more links and quizzes, visit the text's Online Learning Center at www.mhhe.com/pattersontad9e.

Self-Test Answers

1. c   2. d   3. d   4. a   5. d   6. d   7. F   8. F   9. T   10. T

National Journal

Looking Back: A 'Maverick' Nominee, but Still the Same GOP

John McCain achieved something that no GOP White House hopeful had been able to do in more than half a century—capture the party's nomination without carrying the party's base.

And that's true regardless of whether its "base" is defined as self-identified conservatives or as self-identified Republicans.

Three states were critical to McCain's success—New Hampshire, South Carolina and Florida. McCain won the Republican primaries in all three but, according to the exit polls, he did so without winning a majority or even a plurality of self-identified conservatives. What's more, McCain didn't attract a majority or even a plurality of the self-identified Republicans in any of those three contests.

In Florida, the senator from Arizona and former Massachusetts Gov. Mitt Romney each won 33 percent of the voters in the GOP primary who called themselves Republican. (Even though the primary was open only to registered Republicans, 17 percent of those surveyed said they usually think of themselves as something else, such as independents.) In New Hampshire and South Carolina, McCain's victories came from getting the support of solid pluralities of the independents and self-described moderates who voted in the GOP contest. In Florida, which gave him decisive momentum heading into the bonanza of primaries and caucuses on Super Tuesday, McCain won largely because of independents, moderates, and Latinos.

In the 13 states that held GOP caucuses—where appealing to grassroots conservatives and party regulars is critical to success—McCain came in first only in Hawaii and Washington, yet went on to clinch the GOP nomination.

"It wasn't the normal way to do it, but he did it," says former Republican National Committee Chairman Frank Fahrenkopf.

Most leading Republicans doubt that fundamental change is afoot. Yet, almost universally, they fervently hope that McCain can fundamentally change the way their party is perceived by an electorate that now gives the incumbent Republican president, George W. Bush, abysmal job-approval ratings.

And that's far from the only paradox about McCain's nomination. Many Republicans admit they don't particularly care for McCain or his maverick tendencies, but they readily acknowledge that he had a better chance of holding the presidency for their party than any other 2008 contender they could have nominated.

During the primary season, McCain tried to appeal to the base of a party that, if anything, has grown more conservative because it has bled moderates in recent years. On immigration, tax cuts, and offshore drilling, he shifted his stands to the right. But in doing so, he blurred the very thing that gives him his best chance of winning the independents who this year hold the keys to the White House—his maverick image. So, arguably, McCain has changed more than the party he now heads.

There's not much sense among Republicans that their party's base is shifting beneath them. "I think we are still the conservative political party. And McCain has adapted more to that fact than the party has moved toward some of McCain's more moderate tendencies," said Dick Wadhams, chairman of the Colorado Republican Party.

Conservative Gary Bauer said, "I don't think he's redefining the party ideologically, but I do think because of his persona he is bringing people into the Republican Party that may not have embraced conservative ideas if somebody else was selling them."

Other Republicans note that despite McCain's unconventional path to the nomination, the party base remains much what it has been since Ronald Reagan recast it on his way to winning the presidency in 1980—a coalition of defense and national security hawks, low-tax advocates, and Christian conservatives. "I don't see that any of these groups have dropped out of the party. Hence I don't see the party as having 'moved' anywhere," said California Republican Party Chairman Ron Nehring.

Some Republicans talk of the McCain nomination as though the candidate and his party serendipitously stumbled into something mutually beneficial.

As late as February 7, two days after the Super Tuesday contests gave McCain a huge delegate lead, some conservatives were still plotting to stop him. David Keene, chairman of the American Conservative Union, pulled together some 50 top conservatives during the Conservative Political Action Conference in Washington, in hopes of uniting them behind Romney. But it was too late. Shortly before Keene's group was scheduled to meet, Romney addressed CPAC and shocked the crowd by withdrawing. "It ended up being a goodbye meeting," one attendee recalls.

Not long after Romney spoke, McCain addressed the conservative gathering. Plenty of boos punctuated the applause.

Regardless of whether they supported McCain earlier this year, many Republicans now think that his nomination has thrown them something of a life preserver, given that the public is so hostile to the GOP brand these days. "As much as I liked some of the other candidates, they were in the traditional Republican mold and would probably not be faring as well right now against [Democratic presidential nominee Barack] Obama in this difficult national political environment," Wadhams said. "McCain has the ability to win this election on the strength of his appeal to independent voters, and can help our party across the board. In many ways, I think we lucked out with McCain winning our nomination."

Even though McCain catapulted his way to the top of his party on his strength among moderate Republicans and independents, the GOP remains firmly rooted in conservatism.

One yardstick for measuring conservatives' clout within the party is the composition of the 168-member RNC, which consists of a party chair and a national committeeman and national committeewoman from each state, the District of Columbia, Puerto Rico, and four U.S. territories. Each person was elected by the party leadership or party convention in his or her locale.

"If you look at the RNC elections for national committee folks nationwide, most would argue the party is moving to the right," said Michigan Republican Party Chairman Saul Anuzis, who attributes McCain's triumph to the split among conservatives. Anuzis estimates that one-quarter of the RNC's members are new this year. "The ones that I know have all been elected as more conservative than the people they replaced," he said. Indeed, plenty of evidence backs him up.

Earlier this year, the Kansas Republican State Committee ousted two-term RNC member Alicia Salisbury and replaced her with Helen Van Etten, the president of the Kansas Republican Assembly, an anti-tax, anti-abortion group that described itself as "the Republican wing of the Republican Party" when moderates controlled the state GOP.

But perhaps nowhere was the conservative bloodletting more pronounced than in Iowa, where conservative Mike Huckabee made his dramatic breakout when he won the GOP presidential caucuses on the strength of his support from the born-again and evangelical Christians who swamped the party's precinct meetings. Those conservative Christians also elected delegates to county GOP conventions and then to the July state convention, where they bowled over two pillars of the party establishment, Steve Roberts and state Rep. Sandy Greiner, in elections to the RNC.

A former state party chairman and 20-year RNC member, Roberts was tossed out

Republicans talk of the McCain nomination as though the candidate and his party serendipitously stumbled into something mutually beneficial.

in favor of Steve Scheffler, president of the Iowa Christian Alliance. Roberts, a foe of abortion rights, came under fire for not being more vocal in condemning the Polk County judge who ruled last year that the state's ban on same-sex marriage is unconstitutional. The judge stayed his own decision within 24 hours, but his ruling set off a firestorm among Iowa conservatives.

Roberts' fate is indicative of how the battle for control of the party between hard-right conservatives and somewhat more moderate Republicans is unfolding. "In Iowa, we're in the middle of a real fork in a road, and maybe nationally," Roberts said.

Greiner, an eight-term member of the Iowa House who was endorsed for the RNC post by every one of her state House GOP colleagues, was defeated by Kim Lehman, the president of the Iowa Right to Life Committee. And Greiner is hardly known as a moderate. She was an early Reagan supporter, and in 2008 she served as a state co-chair for the presidential effort of former Sen. Fred Thompson of Tennessee.

"She's as conservative as they come," said retiring state Rep. Carmine Boal. "I've watched the woman vote for 16 years; it's ridiculous."

In Greiner's defeat, Boal sees a troubling aspect of how some conservative Christians and their allies conduct their politics—that is, without regard to whether they alienate many Republicans who agree with them on a host of issues, including social ones. "As far as the future of the party, do we take a sharp right [turn], and that's all we're going to have?" Boal wonders.

For the moment, Boal, like many other conservative Republicans, is prepared to embrace McCain as the GOP nominee, but only out of what she sees as necessity. "As much as I don't like it, in many ways he is the best candidate for us—not in the long term, but he's the best one right now," said Boal, acknowledging that the political environment is anti-Republican these days.

"McCain's got enough of the conservative viewpoints to bring along people, but yet enough of the renegade or independent streak to bring along independents and country-club Republicans," Boal said. "We'd love to have a Reagan Republican. But, at this time, he is the best we can do."

It's hard to predict what direction McCain will go next. "If he becomes the president because he's a safe pair of hands, then there's no new era and you're just reshuffling the deck a little bit," said University of Wisconsin political scientist Byron Shafer, an expert on party coalitions and the presidential nominating process. "Celebrity commercials—they're not a new direction; they don't involve anything that you will do if you win."

If McCain isn't elected, recriminations would likely divide the party: Conservatives would assert that the party should have nominated a true believer, while centrists would argue McCain should have made a sharper break with Bush and the party status quo.

That such a confrontation didn't happen during the nominating contest this year but could happen in a McCain presidency is deeply ironic. Still, maybe it shouldn't be surprising, given that John McCain has never been the first choice of most of his party.

FOR DISCUSSION: How did the unusual nomination of John McCain shape his choice for vice-president? How should political parties balance their imperatives to energize base voters and draw in independents? Would Republicans you know describe themselves as conservatives or moderates? Which way do you see the party moving?

Interest Groups
Organizing for Influence

The Interest-Group System

Economic Groups
Citizens' Groups
A Special Category of Interest
Group: Governments

Inside Lobbying: Seeking Influence Through Official Contacts

Acquiring Access to Officials
Webs of Influence: Groups in the
Policy Process

Outside Lobbying: Seeking Influence Through Public Pressure

Constituency Advocacy: Grassroots
Lobbying
Electoral Action: Votes and PAC
Money

The Group System: Indispensable but Biased

The Contribution of Groups to
Self-Government: Pluralism
Flaws in Pluralism: Interest-Group
Liberalism and Economic Bias
A Madisonian Dilemma

The flaw in the pluralist heaven is that the heavenly chorus sings with a strong upper-class bias. **E. E. Schattschneider[1]**

Senior-citizen groups launched their attack within hours of President George W. Bush's 2005 State of the Union address. Bush had specified for the first time key components of his social security reform plan: workers would be able to funnel a third of their social security taxes into private individual investment accounts, and benefits on the remaining two-thirds would be scaled back. For their part, current retirees and workers fifty-five years of age or older would be exempt from benefit reductions. These reforms, Bush said, would save social security from going "bankrupt" in 2042, the year when benefit payouts were projected to exceed incoming revenue if no change was made in the system.

Led by the American Association of Retired Persons (AARP), the seniors' lobby assailed the plan and orchestrated a campaign involving tens of thousands of angry calls, letters, telegrams, and faxes from retirees to their congressional representatives. The AARP poured nearly $10 million into newspaper advertisements—"If we feel like gambling, we'll play the slots"—attacking Bush's proposal to partially privatize social security. Seniors groups found an ally in congressional Democrats. Senate minority leader Harry Reid (D-Nev.) called Bush's plan "social security roulette." "Democrats are all for giving Americans more of a say and more choices when it comes to their retirement savings," Reid declared. "But that doesn't mean taking Social Security's guarantee and gambling with it. And that's coming from a senator who represents Las Vegas." Within days, opinion polls showed declining support for Bush's plan. Over the next several months, public support for his proposal continued to fall, and by summer the plan had no chance of gaining congressional approval.

The AARP's campaign against Bush's social security initiative suggests why interest groups are both admired and feared. On the one hand, groups have a legitimate right to express their views on public policy issues. It is entirely appropriate for senior citizens or

The American Association of Retired Persons (AARP) has roughly 30 million members and is the largest citizens' group. It regularly encourages its members to contact Congress on issues facing retirees.

other groups—whether farmers, consumers, business firms, or college students—to promote their interests through collective action. In fact, the *pluralist* theory of American politics (see Chapter 1) holds that society's interests are most effectively represented through group action.

On the other hand, groups can wield too much power. If a group gets its way at an unreasonable cost to the rest of society, the public interest is harmed. When Bush announced his intention to reform social security, most Americans felt that some kind of change was needed. Bush did not help his cause by proposing a change—the creation of private retirement accounts—that was more closely aligned with his belief in the marketplace than with his stated goal of protecting social security from bankruptcy. Economists calculated that Bush's plan might actually cost more money than it would save. Nevertheless, the time seemed ripe for a fruitful debate on the future of social security. Did AARP and its group allies, in pursuit of their own agenda, needlessly derail that debate?

Opinions might differ as to the answer to this question, but there is no doubt that groups have considerable influence over public policy. Indeed, most observers believe that group influence has increased in recent decades. The situation has been described as the rise of **single-issue politics**: groups have organized around nearly every conceivable policy issue, with each group pressing its demands to the utmost through lobbying and other forms of political pressure.

An **interest group**—also called a "faction," "pressure group," or "special interest"—has two characteristics: an organized membership and the pursuit of policy goals that stem from its members' shared interest. Thus, a bridge club or an amateur softball team is not an interest group because it does not seek to influence the political process. In contrast, organizations such as the Association of Wheat Growers, the National Organization for Women, the World Wildlife Fund, and the National Rifle Association are interest groups because each is an organized entity and each seeks to further its members' interests through political action.

single-issue politics

The situation in which separate groups are organized around nearly every conceivable policy issue and press their demands and influence to the utmost.

interest group

A set of individuals who are organized to promote a shared political interest.

Interest groups are similar to political parties in some respects, but the two types of organizations differ in important ways.[2] Major political parties address a broad range of issues so as to appeal to diverse blocs of voters. Parties exist to contest elections. They change their policy positions as the voters' preferences change. For the party, the winning of elections is almost everything. Interest groups, in contrast, focus on specific issues of direct concern to their members. A group may involve itself in elections, but its purpose is to influence public policy in its area of interest and on behalf of its members.

This chapter examines the degree to which various interests in American society are represented by organized groups, the process by which interest groups exert influence, and the costs and benefits of group politics with respect to the public good. The main points made in the chapter are these:

- *Although nearly all interests in American society are organized to some degree, those associated with economic activity, particularly business enterprises, are by far the most thoroughly organized.* Their advantage rests on their superior financial resources and on the fact that they offer potential members private goods (such as wages and jobs).

- *Groups that do not have economic activity as their primary function often have organizational difficulties.* These groups pursue public or collective goods (such as a safer environment) that are available even to individuals who are not group members, so individuals may choose not to pay the costs of membership.

- *Lobbying and electioneering are the traditional means by which groups communicate with and influence political leaders.* Recent developments, including grassroots lobbying and PACs, have heightened interest groups' influence.

- *The interest-group system overrepresents business interests and higher-income groups and fosters policies that serve a group's interest more than the public interest.* Thus, although groups are an essential part of the policy process, they also distort that process.

The Interest-Group System

In the 1830s, the Frenchman Alexis de Tocqueville wrote that the "principle of association" was nowhere more evident than in America.[3] It is a description that still holds. Americans are more likely than citizens of other nations to join organized groups (see "How the U.S. Compares"). Nevertheless, Americans are not equals in the group process. Some individuals have the skills, money, contacts, or time to participate in group politics; others do not. Moreover, some groups are inherently more attractive to potential members than others and thus find it easier to organize. Groups also differ in their financial resources and thus in their capacity for political action.

Therefore, a first consideration in regard to group politics in America is the issue of how thoroughly various interests are organized. Interests that are highly organized stand a good chance of having their views heard by policymakers. Those that are poorly organized interests run the risk of being ignored.

Economic Groups

No interests are more fully or effectively organized than those that have economic activity as their primary purpose. Corporations, labor unions, farm groups, and professional associations, among others, exist primarily for economic

HOW THE U.S. COMPARES

GROUPS: "A NATION OF JOINERS"

"A nation of joiners" is how the Frenchman Alexis de Tocqueville described the United States during his visit to this country in the 1830s. Tocqueville was stunned by the group and community activity he saw, suggesting that Europeans would find it hard to comprehend. "The political activity that pervades the United States," said Tocqueville, "must be seen to be understood."

Today, Americans still are more actively involved in groups and community causes than are Europeans. Some observers, including Robert Putnam, believe that group activity in the United States is in decline (*Bowling Alone*, 2000). Even if that is true, Americans are more engaged in groups than citizens elsewhere. Among the reasons are the nation's tradition of free association, the openness of American society, and the prominence of religion and public education. Much of the nation's group life revolves around its churches and its schools.

Another reason is the structure of the U.S. political system. Because of federalism and the separation of powers, the American system offers numerous points at which groups can try to influence public policy. If unsuccessful with legislators, groups can turn to executives or to the courts. If thwarted at the national level, groups can turn to state and local governments. By comparison, the governments of most other democratic nations are not organized in ways that facilitate group access and influence. France's unitary government, for example, concentrates power at the national level.

Such differences are reflected in citizens' participation rates. Americans are more likely to belong to groups than are the French, Italians, British, or Germans, as the accompanying figures from the World Values Survey indicate.

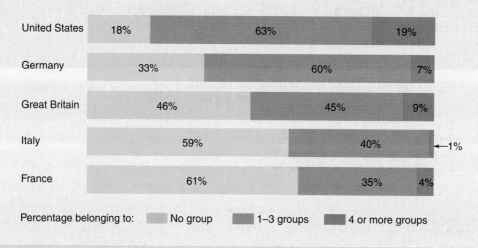

Source: World Values Survey Association, 2008.

economic groups

Interest groups that are organized primarily for economic reasons but that engage in political activity in order to seek favorable policies from government.

purposes—to make profits, provide jobs, improve pay, or protect an occupation. For the sake of discussion, we will call such organizations **economic groups.** Almost all such organizations engage in political activity as a means of promoting and protecting their economic interests. An indicator of this is the fact that Washington lobbyists who represent economic groups outnumber those of all other groups by more than two to one.

The predominance of economic interests was predicted in *Federalist* No. 10, in which James Madison declared that property is "the most common and durable source of factions." Stated differently, nothing seems to matter quite so much to people as their economic self-interest.

Types of Economic Groups

Most economic groups are of four general types: business groups, labor groups, agricultural groups, and professional groups.

Business Groups More than half of all groups formally registered to lobby Congress are business organizations. Virtually all large corporations and many smaller ones are politically active. Business firms are also represented through associations such as the U.S. Chamber of Commerce, which includes nearly 3 million businesses of all sizes. Other business associations, such as the American Petroleum Institute, are confined to a single trade or industry.

Business interests have an advantage that economist Mancur Olson called "the size factor."[4] It might be thought that in a democracy the interests of groups with large memberships would nearly always prevail over the interests of small groups. However, as Olson points out, small groups are ordinarily more united on policy issues and often have more resources, enabling them to win out against large groups. Business groups in a particular industry are usually few in number and tend to work together to influence government on issues of joint interest. In contrast, taxpayers, though they number in the tens of millions and could be powerful if they joined together, have no real interest in paying dues to a taxpayers' group that would lobby on their behalf. In 2008, these differences came together in ways that conceivably hurt taxpayers while helping leading financial institutions. At issue was a government bailout aimed at protecting major investment banks from bankruptcy as a result of their purchase of mortgage-backed securities, which had declined sharply in value as the U.S. housing market weakened. With the backing of policymakers in the Federal Reserve and the Treasury Department, as well as President Bush and some of the top congressional leaders, the banking industry narrowly succeeded in persuading Congress to pass legislation that provided the Treasury Department with $700 billion in taxpayers' money to buy mortgage-related securities from troubled financial institutions in order to keep them afloat, even though it was their purchase of risky high-yield investments that had led them to the point of bankruptcy.

Labor Groups Since the 1930s, organized labor has been politically active on a large scale. Its goal has been to promote policies that benefit workers in general and union members in particular. Although there are some major independent unions, such as the United Mine Workers and the Teamsters, the dominant labor group is the AFL-CIO, which has its national headquarters in Washington, D.C. The AFL-CIO has 9 million members in its roughly fifty affiliated unions, which include the International Brotherhood of Electrical Workers, the Sheet Metal Workers, and the Communications Workers of America.

LEADERS

JAMES MADISON
(1751–1836)

James Madison has been called the "father of the Constitution." Madison himself rejected that label, saying that the Constitution was the work of "many heads and many hands." Nevertheless, of the Framers, Madison was the best political theorist and saw most clearly how government could be structured as a control on the misuse of political power. His *Federalist* No. 10, which deals with the problem of interest groups, is regarded by some as the finest political essay ever penned by an American. Later, Madison assisted Thomas Jefferson in forming a political party that aimed to promote ordinary citizens as opposed to the rich and powerful—the forerunner of today's Democratic Party. He served as secretary of state during Jefferson's presidency and, in 1808, succeeded Jefferson as president. Europe was in the midst of the Napoleonic Wars, and Madison was unsuccessful in maintaining America's neutrality. In 1812, the British invaded Washington, D.C., burning the Capitol and forcing Madison to flee to Maryland. The British withdrew and later were defeated by General Andrew Jackson at New Orleans, leading Americans to claim victory in the War of 1812. Madison completed his second presidential term in 1817. After leaving office, he spoke out often against the growing states'-rights sentiment in the South that eventually would plunge the nation into the Civil War over the issue of slavery. On his deathbed, Madison said he wished for nothing more than preservation of the Union.

Economic groups, which include business firms and labor unions, get the resources for their political activities from their economic activity. This source of support gives them an organizational advantage over citizens' groups, which depend on voluntary contributions to fund their lobbying. Shown here are members of the United Auto Workers (UAW), one of the nation's most powerful labor unions.

At one time, about a third of the U.S. workforce was unionized, but today only about one in eight workers belongs to a union. Skilled and unskilled laborers have historically been the core of organized labor, but their numbers are decreasing while the numbers of professionals, technicians, and service workers are increasing. Professionals have shown little interest in union organization, perhaps because they identify with management or consider themselves economically secure. Service workers and technicians are also difficult for unions to organize because they work closely with managers and, often, in small offices.

Nevertheless, unions have made inroads in their efforts to organize service and public employees. Teachers, hotel workers, police officers, firefighters, social workers, and restaurant employees are among the service and public employee groups that have become increasingly unionized. In fact, the nation's largest unions today are those that represent service and public employees rather than skilled and unskilled laborers (see Table 9-1).

Agricultural Groups Farm organizations represent another large economic lobby. The American Farm Bureau Federation is the largest of the farm groups, with more than 4 million members. The National Farmers Union, the National Grange, and the National Farmers Organization are smaller farm lobbies. Agricultural groups do not always agree on policy issues. For instance, the Farm Bureau sides with agribusiness and owners of large farms, while the Farmers Union promotes the interests of smaller "family" farms.

There are also numerous specialty farm associations, including the Association of Wheat Growers, the American Soybean Association, and Associated Milk Producers. Each association acts as a separate lobby, seeking to obtain policies that will serve its members' particular interest.

TABLE 9-1 **The Largest Labor Unions, 1950 and 2000** The largest labor unions today represent service and public employees; fifty years ago, the largest unions represented skilled and unskilled workers.

1950	2000
1. United Auto Workers	1. National Education Association
2. United Steel Workers	2. International Brotherhood of Teamsters
3. International Brotherhood of Teamsters	3. United Food and Commercial Workers International
4. United Brotherhood of Carpenters & Joiners	4. American Federation of State, County, & Municipal Employees
5. International Association of Machinists	5. Service Employees International

Source: U.S. Department of Labor, 2008.

Professional Groups Most professions have lobbying associations. Among the most powerful of these groups is the American Medical Association (AMA), which, with nearly three hundred thousand members, represents about half the nation's physicians. The AMA has consistently opposed any government policy that would limit physicians' independence. Other professional groups include the American Bar Association (ABA) and the American Association of University Professors (AAUP).

An Organizational Edge

One reason for the abundance of economic groups is their access to financial resources. Political lobbying does not come cheap. If a group is to make its views known, it normally must have a headquarters, an expert staff, and communication facilities. Economic groups pay for these things with money generated by their economic activity. Corporations have the greatest built-in advantage. They do not have to charge membership dues or conduct fundraisers to support their lobbying. Their political money comes from their business profits.

Some economic groups rely on dues rather than profits to support their lobbying, but they have something of economic value to exchange for these dues. Labor unions, for example, offer their members, in return for dues, access to higher-paying jobs. Such groups offer what is called a **private (individual) good**—a benefit, such as a job, that is given directly to a particular individual. An important feature of a private good is that it can be withheld. If an individual is unwilling to pay organizational dues, the group can refuse to provide the benefit it offers.

Citizens' Groups

Economic groups do not have a monopoly on lobbying. There are a great number of other interest groups, which are referred to collectively as **citizens' groups** (or **noneconomic groups**). Group members in this category are joined together not by a material incentive—such as jobs, higher wages, or profits—but by a purposive incentive, the satisfaction of contributing to what they regard as a worthy goal or purpose.[5] Whether a group's purpose is to protect the environment, return prayer to the public schools, or feed the poor at home or abroad, there are citizens who are willing to participate simply because they believe the cause is a worthy one.

However, citizens' groups find it harder than economic groups to raise the money necessary for lobbying. These groups do not generate profits or fees as a result of economic activity. Moreover, the incentives they offer prospective members are not exclusive. As opposed to the private or individual goods provided by many economic groups, most noneconomic groups offer **collective (public) goods** as an incentive for membership. Collective goods are, by definition, benefits that belong to all; they cannot be granted or withheld on an individual basis. The air people breathe and the national forests people visit are examples of collective goods. They are available to one and all, those who do not pay dues to a clean-air group or a wilderness preservation group as well as those who do.

This 1873 lithograph illustrates the benefits of membership in the National Grange, an agricultural interest group.

private (individual) good

Benefits that a group (most often an economic group) can grant directly and exclusively to individual members of the group.

citizens' (noneconomic) groups

Organized interests formed by individuals drawn together by opportunities to promote a cause in which they believe but that does not provide them significant individual economic benefits.

collective (public) goods

Benefits that are offered by groups (usually citizens' groups) as an incentive for membership but that are nondivisible (such as a clean environment) and therefore are available to nonmembers as well as members of the particular group.

The Free-Rider Problem

The shared characteristic of collective goods creates what is called the **free-rider problem**: individuals can receive the good even when they do not contribute to the group's effort. Take the case of National Public Radio (NPR). Although NPR's programs are funded primarily through listeners' donations, those who do not contribute can listen to the programs. These noncontributors are free riders: they receive the benefit without paying for it. About 90 percent of regular listeners to NPR do not contribute to their local station.

In a purely economic sense, as economist Mancur Olson noted, it is not rational for an individual to contribute to a group when its benefit can be obtained for free.[6] Moreover, the dues paid by any single member are too small to affect the group's success one way or another. Why pay dues to an environmental group when any improvements in the air, water, or wildlife from its lobbying efforts are available to everyone and when one's individual contribution is too small to make a real difference? Although many people do join such groups anyway, the free-rider problem is one reason citizens' groups are less fully organized than economic groups.

The free-rider problem has been lessened, but not eliminated, in recent decades by advances in communication that enable citizens' groups to more easily contact prospective members. Computer-assisted direct mail is one of these advances. Group organizers buy mailing lists and flood the mails with computer-typed "personal" letters asking recipients to pay a small annual membership fee. For some individuals, a fee of $25–50 annually represents no great sacrifice and offers the satisfaction of supporting a cause in which they believe. Until the computer era, citizens' groups had great difficulty identifying and contacting potential members, which is one reason the number of such groups was so much smaller in the past than today.

The Internet is also a boon to citizens' groups. Nearly every such group of any size has its own website and email list. MoveOn is an example of the Internet's organizing capacity. MoveOn was started by a handful of liberal activists working out of a garage. By 2004, they had created an Internet network that linked hundreds of thousands of citizens who could be mobilized in support of liberal candidates and causes. MoveOn raised more than $3 million in 2006 for Democratic candidates while also launching a massive get-out-the-vote effort in the election's closing days that helped the Democrats capture control of Congress. In 2008, it used its fund-raising capacity to assist Barack Obama in the Democratic presidential primaries, contributing to his victory over Hillary Clinton.

Despite such examples, the organizational muscle in American politics rests primarily with economic groups. They have an edge on citizens' groups in nearly every respect—money, solidarity, and control (see Table 9-2).

Types of Citizens' Groups

Most citizens' groups are of three general types: public-interest groups, single-issue groups, and ideological groups.

Public-Interest Groups Groups that claim to represent the broad interests of society call themselves public-interest groups. The label is somewhat misleading. The leaders of these groups are not chosen by the public at large, and the issues they target are ones of their own choosing. Moreover, people have different opinions on what constitutes "the public interest." Nevertheless, there is a basis for distinguishing the so-called public-interest groups from economic groups: the latter seek direct material benefits for their members, while the former seek benefits that

TABLE 9-2 | Advantages and Disadvantages Held by Economic and Citizens' Groups   Compared with economic groups, citizens' groups have fewer advantages and more disadvantages.

Economic Groups	Citizens' Groups
Advantages	*Advantages*
Economic activity provides the organization with the resources necessary for political action.	Members are likely to support leaders' political efforts because they joined the group in order to influence policy.
Individuals are encouraged to join the group because of economic benefits they individually receive (such as wages).	*Disadvantages*
	The group has to raise funds, especially for its political activities.
Disadvantages	
Persons within the group may not support leaders' political efforts because they did not join the group for political reasons.	Potential members may choose not to join the group because they get collective benefits even if they do not join (the free-rider problem).

are less tangible and more widely shared. For example, the National Association of Manufacturers, an economic group, seeks policies favorable to large corporations, while the League of Women Voters, a public-interest group, seeks policies—such as simplified voter registration—that benefit the broader public.

More than half of the currently active public-interest groups were established after 1960. Prominent examples are the state-level Public Interest Research Groups (PIRGs), such as NYPIRG (New York), CALPIRG (California), and TexPIRG (Texas). Virtually every state now has a PIRG, which usually has chapters on college campuses. Drawing on their network of researchers, students, and advocates, they lobby on behalf of such issues as product safety and political reform.

Single-Issue Groups   A single-issue group is organized to influence policy in just one area. Notable current examples are the National Rifle Association and the various right-to-life and pro-choice groups that have formed around the issue of abortion. The number of single-issue groups has risen sharply in the past three decades, and these groups now pressure government on almost every conceivable issue, from nuclear arms to day care centers to drug abuse.

Environmental groups are sometimes classified as public-interest groups, but they can also be classified as single-issue organizations in that most of them seek to influence public policy in a specific area, such as pollution reduction, wilderness preservation, or wildlife protection. The Sierra Club, one of the oldest environmental groups, was formed in the 1890s to promote the preservation of scenic areas. Also prominent are the National Audubon Society, the Wilderness Society, the Environmental Defense Fund, Greenpeace U.S.A., and the Izaak Walton League. Since 1960, membership in environmental groups has more than tripled as a result of the public's increased concern about environmental protection.[7]

The Internet has made it easier for citizens' groups to organize and increase their membership. One of the most successful examples is MoveOn. It was founded by a small group of liberal activists.

Ideological Groups　Single-issue groups have an issue-specific policy agenda. In contrast, ideological groups have a broad agenda that derives from a philosophical or moral position. An example is the Christian Coalition of America, which describes itself as "America's leading grassroots organization defending our godly heritage." The group addresses a wide range of issues, including school prayer, abortion, and television programming. Ideological groups on both the left and the right have increased substantially in number since the 1960s.

Some ideological groups are formed squarely around a political philosophy. The American Conservative Union (ACU) is the largest conservative organization and lobbies on issues like taxation and national defense. MoveOn is a liberal counterpart to the ACU, as is Americans for Democratic Action (ADA). One of the oldest ideological groups in the country, the ADA was founded in the 1940s to promote civil rights and working-class interests. Groups such as the National Organization for Women (NOW) and the National Association for the Advancement of Colored People (NAACP) can also be classified generally as ideological groups. Although they represent particular demographic groups, they do so across a wide range of issues. For example, NOW addresses issues ranging from jobs to reproduction to political representation.

A Special Category of Interest Group: Governments

While the vast majority of organized groups represent private interests, some represent governments. Most states and major cities have at least one Washington lobbyist. Intergovernmental lobbying also occurs through groups such as the Council of State Governments, the National Governors Conference, the National Association of Counties, the National League of Cities, and the U.S. Conference of Mayors. These organizations sometimes play a significant role in national policy debates. For example, as Congress was preparing in 2006 to renew and amend the antiterrorism legislation that had gone into effect in 2001, the National Governors Conference and the U.S. Conference of Mayors lobbied heavily to ensure that the changes reflected state and local concerns, including the adequacy of federal funding.

Foreign governments also lobby in Washington. Arms sales, foreign aid, immigration, and trade practices are among the U.S. policies they target.[8] However, foreign governments are prohibited from engaging in certain lobbying activities, including contributions to U.S. election campaigns.

Inside Lobbying: Seeking Influence Through Official Contacts

Modern government is an inviting target for interest groups. Modern government is involved in so many issues—business regulation, income maintenance, urban renewal, cancer research, and energy development, to name only a few—that hardly any interest in society could fail to benefit significantly from having influence over federal policies or programs. Moreover, modern government is action-oriented. Officials are more inclined to solve problems than let them fester. When forest fires in California, Arizona, and other western states destroyed property worth millions in 2008, the federal government granted large sums to meet the clean-up and other costs of the affected states, localities, and residents.

Groups seek government's support through **lobbying,** a term that refers broadly to efforts by groups to influence public policy through contact with

lobbying

The process by which interest-group members or lobbyists attempt to influence public policy through contacts with public officials.

public officials. Lobbying is big business in America. A section of the nation's capital, known as K Street, is populated almost completely by lobbying firms. There are more than twenty thousand Washington lobbyists, and according to official records, they spend more than $1 billion annually on lobbying activities. The actual amount is higher, but no one is quite sure by how much. Lobbying is regulated by the Honest Leadership and Open Government Act of 2007 (which amended the Lobbying Disclosure Act of 1995), which defines who must register as a lobbyist and what lobbying activities and expenditures must be reported. The act was further amended in 2007 to tighten some of its provisions, but it is still the case that some Washington lobbying efforts never become part of the public record.

Interest groups rely on two main lobbying strategies, which have been labeled "inside lobbying" and "outside lobbying."[9] Each strategy involves communication with public officials, but the strategies differ in what is communicated and who does the communicating. This section discusses **inside lobbying,** which is based on group efforts to develop and maintain close ("inside") contacts with policymakers. (Outside lobbying is described in the next section.)

Acquiring Access to Officials

Inside lobbying seeks to give a group direct access to officials in order to influence their decisions. Access is not the same as influence, but it can be a first step in gaining influence. Without access, a group might never have an opportunity to make its position known to policymakers.[10] The importance of access is evident, for example, in the high salaries that former members of Congress can command when they become lobbyists. It is unusual for a seated member of Congress to deny a former member a chance to stop by the congressional office to discuss a group's position on pending legislation. Although former congressional members are prohibited for a period after leaving office from lobbying Congress, they are free to do so thereafter and typically represent groups with which they had close ties while in office.

Lobbying once depended significantly on tangible inducements, sometimes including bribes. This old form of lobbying survives, but modern lobbying generally involves subtler methods than simply slipping a cash-filled envelope to a public official. Lobbyists concentrate on supplying policymakers with information that supports the group's position on pending policy.[11] For the most part, inside lobbying is directed at policymakers who are inclined to support the group rather than at those who have opposed it in the past. This tendency reflects both the difficulty of persuading opponents to change long-held views and the advantage of working through trusted officials. Thus, union lobbyists work mainly with pro-labor officeholders, just as corporate lobbyists work mainly with policymakers who support business interests.

Money is the essential ingredient of inside-lobbying efforts. The American Petroleum Institute, for example, with its abundant

inside lobbying
Direct communication between organized interests and policymakers, which is based on the assumed value of close ("inside") contacts with policymakers.

Inside lobbying offers groups a chance to make their policy views known. Access to public officials is critical to the inside-lobbying strategy.

financial resources, can afford a downtown Washington office staffed by lobby-ists, petroleum experts, and public relations specialists who help the oil com-panies maintain access to and influence with legislative and executive leaders. Many groups spend upward of $1 million annually on lobbying. One of the top spenders, the American Hospital Association (AHA), invested more than $10 million on lobbying in 2008. Other groups get by on much less, but it is hard to lobby effectively on a tiny budget. Given the costs of maintaining a Washington lobby, the domination by corporations and trade associations is understandable. These economic groups have the money to retain high-priced lobbyists, while many other interests do not.

Lobbying Congress

The targets of inside lobbying are officials of all three government branches—leg-islative, executive, and judicial. The benefits of a close relationship with members of Congress are the most obvious. With support in Congress, a group can obtain the legislative help it needs to achieve its policy goals. By the same token, mem-bers of Congress can benefit from working closely with lobbyists. The volume of legislation facing Congress is heavy, and members rely on trusted lobbyists to identify bills that deserve their attention. When Republican lawmakers took con-trol of Congress in 1995, they invited corporate lobbyists to participate directly in drafting legislation affecting business. Congressional Democrats complained loudly, but Republicans said they were merely getting advice from those who best understood business's needs and noted that Democrats had worked closely with organized labor when they were in power.

Lobbyists' effectiveness depends in part on their reputation for fair play. Lob-byists are expected to play it straight. Said one congressman, "If any [lobbyist] gives me false or misleading information, that's it—I'll never see him again."[12] Bullying is also frowned upon. During the debate over the North American Free Trade Agreement in 1993, the AFL-CIO threatened to compaign against congres-sional Democrats who supported the legislation. The backlash from Democrats on both sides of the issue was so intense that the union backed down on its threat. The safe lobbying strategy is the aboveboard approach: provide informa-tion, rely on longtime allies among members of Congress, and push steadily but not too aggressively for legislative goals.

Lobbying Executive Agencies

As the scope of federal policy has widened, lobbying of the executive branch has increased in importance. Bureaucrats make key administrative decisions and develop policy initiatives that the legislative branch later makes into law. By working closely with executive agencies, groups can influence policy decisions at the formulation and implementation stages. In return, groups can help agen-cies by backing them when their programs and budgets are being reviewed for renewal by Congress and the White House.

Nowhere is the link between groups and the bureaucracy more evident than in the regulatory agencies that oversee the nation's business sectors. For example, the Food and Drug Administration (FDA), which regulates the nation's pharmaceutical companies, relies on them for much of the information used in deciding whether new drugs are safe enough to be put on the market. The FDA is sometimes cited as an example of "agency capture." The capture theory sug-gests that regulatory agencies pass through a series of phases that constitute a life cycle. When an agency is first created in response to a marketplace problem, it vigorously regulates the targeted industry to make it more responsive to the public interest, but as the agency gets older, its oversight weakens until at best it protects the status quo and at worst it falls captive to the very industry it is supposed to regulate. The FDA exploded into the news in 2004 when the arthritis drug Vioxx was taken off the market after it was discovered that users had abnormally high rates of stroke and heart attack. The FDA apparently had been lax in reviewing the drug's safety, and some within the agency complained they had been pressured by top officials and drug companies not to find safety problems with drugs.[13] Vioxx was generating $2.5 billion a year in sales for Merck, the pharmaceutical company that had invented and patented it.

Studies indicate that the capture theory describes only some agencies—and then only some of the time. Agencies selectively cooperate with or oppose interest groups, depending on which strategy better suits agency purposes. Agency officials are aware that they can lose support in Congress, which controls agency funding and program authorization, if they show too much favoritism toward an interest group.[14] In response to the Vioxx controversy, as well as similar problems with other new drugs, Congress passed legislation in 2007 that forced the FDA to toughen its pre- and post-marketing drug safety testing.

Lobbying the Courts

Judicial rulings in areas such as education and civil rights have made interest groups recognize that the courts can be a way for them to obtain their policy goals.[15] Interest groups have several judicial lobbying options, including efforts to influence the selection of federal judges. Right-to-life groups have pressured Republican administrations to make opposition to abortion a prerequisite for nomination to the federal bench. Democratic administrations have in turn faced pressure from pro-choice groups in their judicial nominations.[16] Groups also use lawsuits to bring about policy change. For some organizations, such as the American Civil Liberties Union (ACLU), legal action is the primary means of lobbying. The ACLU often takes on unpopular causes, such as the free-speech rights of fringe groups. Such causes have little chance of success in legislative bodies but may prevail in a courtroom.

As interest groups increasingly resort to legal action, they often find themselves facing one another in court. Environmental litigation groups such as the Earthwise Legal Defense Fund and the Environmental Defense Fund have frequently sued oil, timber, and mining corporations.

Webs of Influence: Groups in the Policy Process

To get a fuller picture of how inside lobbying works, it is helpful to consider two policy processes—iron triangles and issue networks—in which many groups are enmeshed.

Iron Triangles

An **iron triangle** consists of a small and informal but relatively stable set of bureaucrats, legislators, and lobbyists who seek to develop policies beneficial to a particular interest. The three "corners" of one such triangle are the Department of Agriculture (bureaucrats), the agriculture committees of Congress (legislators), and farm groups such as the Associated Milk Producers and the Association of Wheat Growers (lobbyists). Together they determine many of the policies affecting farmers. Although the support of other players, including the president and a majority in Congress, is needed to enact new policies, they often defer to the judgment of the agricultural triangle, whose members are most familiar with farmers' needs.

iron triangle

A small and informal but relatively stable group of well-positioned legislators, executives, and lobbyists who seek to promote policies beneficial to a particular interest.

FIGURE 9-1 **How an Iron Triangle Benefits Its Participants**

An iron triangle works to the advantage of each of its participants—an interest group, a congressional subgroup, and a government agency.

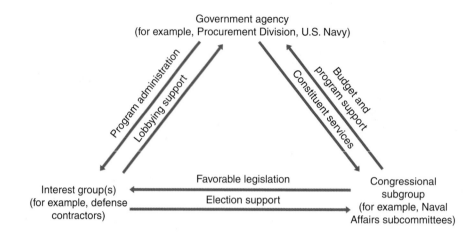

Government agency
(for example, Procurement Division, U.S. Navy)

Program administration
Lobbying support

Budget and program support
Constituent services

Interest group(s)
(for example, defense contractors)

Favorable legislation
Election support

Congressional subgroup
(for example, Naval Affairs subcommittees)

A group in an iron triangle has an inside track to those legislators and bureaucrats who are best positioned to help it. And because the group has something of value to offer in return, the relationships tend to be "ironclad." The group provides lobbying support for the agency's funding and programs and makes campaign contributions to its congressional allies. Agricultural groups, for example, contribute millions of dollars to congressional campaigns, most of which goes to the reelection campaigns of House and Senate agriculture committee members. Figure 9-1 summarizes the benefits that flow to each member of an iron triangle.

Issue Networks

Iron triangles represent the pattern of influence in only certain policy areas and are less common now than in the past. A more frequent pattern of influence today is the **issue network**—an informal grouping of officials, lobbyists, and policy specialists (the "network") who come together *temporarily* around a policy problem (the "issue").

Issue networks are a result of the increasing complexity of policy problems. Participants must have an intimate knowledge of the issue at hand in order to engage it effectively. Thus, unlike iron triangles, where a participant's position is everything, an issue network is built around specialized interests and knowledge. On any given issue, the participants might come from a variety of executive agencies, congressional committees, interest groups, and institutions such as universities or think tanks. Compared to iron triangles, issue networks are less stable. As the issue develops, new participants may join the debate and old ones may drop out. Once the issue is resolved, the network disbands.[17]

An example of an issue network is the set of participants who would come together over the issue of whether a large tract of old forest should be opened to logging. A few decades ago, that issue would have been settled in an iron triangle consisting of the timber companies, the U.S. Forest Service, and relevant members of the House and Senate agriculture committees. But as forestlands have diminished and environmental concerns have grown, such issues can no longer be contained within the cozy confines of an iron triangle. Today, an issue network would form that included logging interests, the U.S. Forest Service, House and Senate agriculture committee members, research scientists, and representatives of environmental groups, the housing industry, and animal-rights groups. Unlike the old iron triangle, which was confined to like-minded interests, this issue network would include opposing interests (for example, the loggers and the environmentalists). And unlike an iron triangle, the issue

issue network

An informal and relatively open network of public officials and lobbyists who have a common interest in a given area and who are brought together by a proposed policy in that area. Unlike an iron triangle, an issue network disbands after the issue is resolved.

U.S. Forest Service rangers start a controlled-burn fire to clear ground for the planting of new-growth trees. The U.S. Forest Service, which is part of the Department of Agriculture, oversees the national forests, as well as their use by logging, mining, and other industries. At an earlier time, decisions about the use of national forests typically would have been made in an iron triangle consisting of Forest Service bureaucrats, Senate and House agricultural committee members, and industry representatives. However, ever since the environmental movement raised awareness of how the national forests are managed, decisions about their use have involved issue networks that include environmentalists, research specialists, community leaders, and others in addition to the traditional decision makers.

network would dissolve once the issue that brought the parties together was resolved.

Issue networks, then, differ substantially from iron triangles. In an iron triangle, a common interest brings the participants together in a long-lasting and mutually beneficial relationship. In an issue network, an immediate issue brings the participants together in a temporary network that is based on their ability to knowledgeably address the issue and where they play out their separate interests before disbanding once the issue is settled.

Despite these differences, iron triangles and issue networks do have one thing in common: they are arenas in which organized groups exercise influence. The interests of the general public may be taken into account in these webs of power, but the interests of the participating groups are foremost.

Outside Lobbying: Seeking Influence Through Public Pressure

Although an interest group may rely solely on inside lobbying, this approach is not likely to be successful unless the group can demonstrate that it represents an important constituency. Accordingly, groups also engage in **outside lobbying,** which involves bringing constituency ("outside") pressure to bear on policymakers (see Table 9-3).[18]

outside lobbying

A form of lobbying in which an interest group seeks to use public pressure as a means of influencing officials.

TABLE 9-3 | Tactics Used in Inside and Outside Lobbying Strategies Inside and outside lobbying are based on different tactics.

Inside Lobbying	Outside Lobbying
Developing contacts with legislators and executives	Encouraging group members to write, phone, or email their representatives in Congress
Providing information and policy proposals to key officials	Seeking favorable coverage by news media
Forming coalitions with other groups	Encouraging members to support particular candidates in elections
	Targeting group resources on key election races
	Making PAC contributions to candidates

Constituency Advocacy: Grassroots Lobbying

grassroots lobbying

A form of lobbying designed to persuade officials that a group's policy position has strong constituent support.

One form of outside pressure is **grassroots lobbying**—that is, pressure designed to convince government officials that a group's policy position has popular support. No group illustrates grassroots lobbying better than the AARP (American Association of Retired Persons). With more than 30 million members and a staff of sixteen hundred, the AARP is a powerful lobby on retirement issues such as social security and Medicare. When major legislation affecting retirees is pending, the AARP swings into action. Congress receives more mail from members of the AARP than it does from members of any other group. The AARP's support was instrumental, for example, in the enactment in 2003 of a controversial prescription drug program for the elderly. Until the AARP's last-minute endorsement, the program seemed headed for a narrow defeat in Congress.

Electoral Action: Votes and PAC Money

An "outside" strategy can also include election activity. "Reward your friends and punish your enemies" is a political adage that loosely describes how interest groups view elections. The possibility of campaign opposition from a powerful group can restrain an officeholder. Opposition from the 3-million-member National Rifle Association, for example, is a major reason the United States has lagged behind other Western societies in its handgun control laws, despite polls indicating that a majority of Americans favor such laws.

Interest groups gain influence by contributing money to candidates' campaigns. As one lobbyist said, "Talking to politicians is fine, but with a little money they hear you better."[19] Members of Congress sometimes get into hot water by listening to lobbyists while also taking contributions from them. When it was alleged in 2005 that lobbyist Jack Abramoff had cheated some of his clients while also lavishing campaign donations

Lobbying in the United States rests on access, information, persuasion, and mutual support. Occasionally, lobbying is also a shadier business where favors are given that skirt the laws governing lobbying. In 2005, news broke that a prominent Washington lobbyist, Jack Abramoff, had engaged in possibly illegal deals with a number of legislative and executive officials. It did not help Abramoff's case that he had lavished expensive trips on some officials. Controversy surrounding his relationship with Abramoff prompted House majority leader Tom DeLay to resign his congressional seat. Abramoff is shown here leaving federal court in Washington in 2006.

on members of Congress in return for favorable legislation, it sent a shock wave through Washington. Several members of Congress quickly returned Abramoff's campaign donations in the hope that doing so would insulate them from the corruption scandal. A casualty of the Abramoff affair was Representative Tom DeLay (R-Tex.), who lost his post as House majority leader when his close relationship with Abramoff became known. Abramoff had funneled hundreds of thousands of dollars, some of it of questionable legality, to DeLay for political purposes.

A group's election contributions are funneled through its **political action committee (PAC).** A group cannot give organizational funds (such as corporate profits or union dues) to candidates, but through its PAC, a group can solicit voluntary contributions from members or employees and then donate this money to candidates. A PAC can back as many candidates as it wants but is legally limited in the amount it can contribute to a single candidate. The ceiling is $10,000 per candidate—$5,000 in the primary campaign and $5,000 in the general election campaign. (These financial limits apply to candidates for federal office. State and local campaigns are regulated by state laws, and some states allow PACs to make unlimited contributions to individual candidates.)

There are more than four thousand PACs, and PAC contributions account for roughly a third of total contributions to congressional campaigns. Their role is less significant in presidential campaigns, which are bigger in scale and depend largely on individual contributors.

More than 60 percent of all PACs are associated with businesses (see Figure 9-2). Most of these are corporate PACs, such as the Ford Motor Company Civic Action Fund, the Sun Oil Company Political Action Committee (Sunpac), and the Coca-Cola PAC. The others are tied to trade associations, such as RPAC (National Association of Realtors). The next-largest set of PACs consists of those linked to citizens' groups (that is, public-interest, single-issue, and ideological groups), such as the liberal People for the American Way and the conservative National Conservative Political Action Committee (NCPAC). Labor unions, once the major source of group contributions, are the source of less than 10 percent of PACs.

PACs contribute roughly eight times as much money to incumbents as to their challengers. PACs recognize that incumbents are likely to win and thus to remain in positions of power. One PAC director, expressing a common view, said, "We always stick with the incumbent when we agree with them both."[20] To some extent, the tendency of PACs to back incumbents has blurred long-standing partisan divisions in campaign funding. Business interests are especially pragmatic. Although they tend to favor Republican candidates, they are reluctant to anger Democratic incumbents. The result is that Democratic incumbents, particularly in House races, have received substantial support over the years from business-related PACs.[21] Other PACs, of course, are less pragmatic. The Christian Moral Government Fund, for example, backs only candidates who take conservative stands on issues such as school prayer and abortion.

political action committee (PAC)
The organization through which an interest group raises and distributes funds for election purposes. By law, the funds must be raised through voluntary contributions.

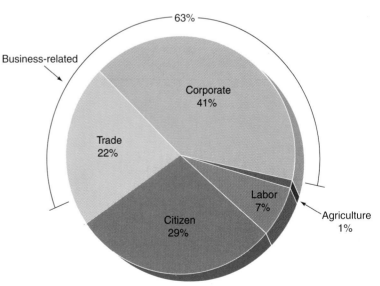

FIGURE 9-2 **Percentage of PACs by Category**   Most PACs represent business. Corporate and trade association PACs make up 63 percent of the total.

Source: Federal Election Commission, 2008.

DEBATING THE
ISSUES

HAVE INTEREST GROUPS HIJACKED THE INITIATIVE PROCESS?

The initiative was pioneered by the Progressives of the early twentieth century, who saw it as a way to wrest power from the political bosses and corporate robber barons and place it in the hands of ordinary citizens. Twenty-four states allow the initiative, which requires the gathering of a sufficient number of citizens' signatures to place a legislative proposal (initiative) on the ballot. If a majority of voters approve it, the initiative becomes law, just as if it had been enacted by the legislature itself. In recent years, however, the initiative process has been used by interest groups to advance their policy agendas. These groups have the money to pay for the signature-gathering process and to conduct a campaign in support of the initiative. To some observers, this development has corrupted the initiative process. Other observers claim that the initiative remains a bulwark of citizen-based politics.

YES The initiative process came to the United States about 100 years ago, imported from Switzerland by populists and progressives worried about the influence of money on legislatures. The purpose was two-fold: one, break the power of interest groups, and two, empower people to write the laws themselves on the ballot. The system worked pretty well [for a time]; it produced a great deal of progressive legislation. . . . [Today, however, the initiative process is] being driven very much by money. With their own political agendas, interest groups of all kinds have latched onto this device as a way of writing the law the way they would like it written without having to go through all the hoops of the normal governmental process. . . . I think it's particularly ironic that a device that was introduced into this country as a way of fighting special interest influence and the power of money now has been largely taken over by those same interest groups and by very wealthy millionaires who have the resources that it now takes to get an initiative on the ballot and to fight these campaigns to get them passed or defeated in the states.

—*David S. Broder, author and* Washington Post *columnist*

NO Many of the concerns about initiatives seem unfounded, and so addressing them in turn seems unfounded as well. Political scientists have found that, whereas 40 percent of all initiatives on the California ballot from 1986 to 1996 passed, only 14 percent of initiatives promoted by special interests passed. Many people are predisposed to believe that money influences elections. But when it comes to initiative campaigns, the proof does not exist. In an era of growing government, the people need a mechanism to check government. Many claim that the people already have that check—elections. But that is a fallacy. Most people who support the initiative process and who use the process use it as a tool for addressing single issues. They want for the most part to keep a particular elected official, and so voting that official out of office for failing to deal with one specific issue is considered an extreme step, far more extreme than allowing the people to make laws occasionally. . . . Representative government and the initiative process are perfect complements to each other—two imperfect systems of government each designed to help the people and both carefully constructed to balance the weaknesses of one with the strengths of the other.

—*M. Dane Waters, president, The Initiative & Referendum Institute*

PAC influence has been hotly debated. Advocates of PACs claim that groups have a right to be heard, including the right to express themselves with money. Advocates also note that PACs raise their money through contributions by small donors and are therefore a better system of campaign finance than one based on wealthy donors. On the other hand, critics complain that PACs give interest groups—economic groups particularly—far too much influence on Congress.[22]

Although members of Congress deny that they are unduly influenced by PACs, there is no question that PACs give interest groups a level of access to lawmakers that ordinary citizens lack. Nevertheless, Congress is unlikely in the foreseeable future to pass legislation that would outlaw PACs. The fact is, most members of Congress are unwilling to eliminate a source of campaign funds that helps them to stay in office.

STATES IN THE NATION

LIMITS ON PAC CONTRIBUTIONS

Elections of state officials (such as governors and state legislators) are regulated by state law rather than by federal law. In federal elections, PACs can contribute to as many candidates as they like, but they cannot contribute more than $10,000 ($5000 in the primary and $5000 in the general election) to a particular candidate. Some states place no limits on how much money a PAC can contribute to a state or local candidate. Of the states that limit PAC contributions, only New York and Nevada allow contributions in excess of $10,000.

Q: Why might states located to the west of the Mississippi River (which runs down the eastern borders of Minnesota, Iowa, Missouri, Arkansas, and Louisiana) place fewer limits on PAC contributions than other states?

A: A possible explanation is that the political cultures of the westernmost states, as a result of their frontier heritage, are less accepting of government regulation of any kind.

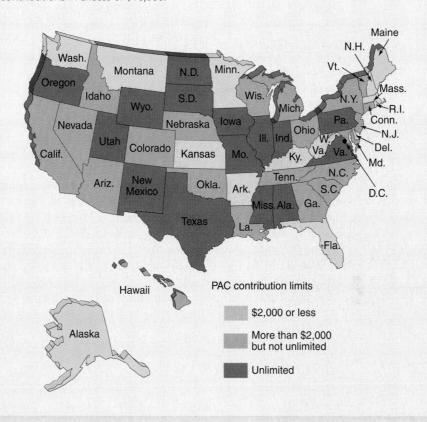

PAC contribution limits

$2,000 or less

More than $2,000 but not unlimited

Unlimited

Source: National Conference of State Legislatures, 2008.

The Group System: Indispensable but Biased

As noted in the chapter's introduction, pluralist theory holds that organized groups are a source of sound governance. On one level, this claim is beyond dispute. Without groups to carry their message, most of society's interests would find it difficult to get government's attention and support. Yet the issue of representation is also a question of whether all interests in society are fairly represented through the group system, and here the pluralist argument is less compelling.

The Contribution of Groups to Self-Government: Pluralism

Group activity is an essential part of self-government. An obstacle to popular sovereignty is the difficulty that public officials have in trying to discover what the people want from government. To discern their wishes, lawmakers consult public opinion polls, meet with constituents, and assess election results. Lobbying activities are also a clue to what people are seeking. Moreover, government does not exist simply to serve majority interests. The fact that most people are not retirees or labor union members or farmers or college students or Hispanics does not mean that the concerns of such "minorities" are unworthy of attention. And what better instrument exists for promoting their interests than lobbying groups working on their behalf?

Some pluralists even question the usefulness of terms such as the *common good* and the *collective interest*. If people disagree on society's goals and priorities, as they always do, how can it be said that people have a "common" or "collective" interest? As an alternative, pluralists contend that the common good ultimately is best served by a process that serves a wide array of separate interests. Thus, if manufacturing interests prevail on one issue, environmentalists on another, farmers on a third, minorities on a fourth, and so on until a great many interests are served, the collective interest of society will have been promoted. Pluralists also note that the promotion of the special interest often works to the benefit of others. Tax incentives for corporations that encourage research and capital investment, for example, can result in better products and additional jobs.

Finally, interest groups often take up issues that are neglected by the political parties. Party leaders typically shy away from issues, such as affirmative action or immigration, on which the party's voters disagree. Such issues would get less notice if not for the groups that promote them. And when groups succeed in drawing attention to these issues, they can sometimes force the parties to address them as well. In this sense, as political scientist Jack Walker noted, the party and group systems together produce a more responsive type of politics than would be the case if the other system somehow did not exist.[23]

Flaws in Pluralism: Interest-Group Liberalism and Economic Bias

Although pluralist theory includes compelling arguments, it also has some questionable aspects. Political scientist Theodore Lowi points out that there is no concept of society's collective interest in a system that gives special interests the ability to determine the policies affecting them.[24] The basis of decision making in such cases is not rule by the majority but rule by a minority—whichever special interest has the most clout in a policy area. Moreover, it cannot be assumed that what a lobbying group wants is what most people would want. Consider the case of the federal law that required auto dealers to list the known defects of used cars on window stickers. The law was repealed after an extensive lobbying campaign financed by contributions of more than $1 million by the National Association of Automobile Dealers to the reelection campaigns of members of Congress.

Lowi uses the term **interest-group liberalism** to describe the tendency of officials to support the policy demands of the interest group or groups that have a special stake in a policy. It is "liberal" in the sense that Republican and Democratic lawmakers alike are in the habit of catering to interest groups. Each party has its favorites—for example, business does better when Republicans are

interest-group liberalism
The tendency of public officials to support the policy demands of self-interested groups (as opposed to judging policy demands according to whether they serve a larger conception of "the public interest").

Because lobbying groups have emerged to represent nearly every dimension of public policy, it is the rare issue that finds groups in agreement. Stem-cell research is no exception. This issue has pitted, among others, religious groups against health advocacy groups. The issue has also divided party leaders. President George W. Bush in 2006 cast the first veto of his presidency when he refused to sign a bill that would expand federal support for stem-cell research. The legislation had the backing of several prominent Republican lawmakers, including Senator Orrin Hatch (R-Utah), who is shown here with actor Michael J. Fox at a news conference to urge passage of the legislation.

in power, and labor does better when Democrats are in power. But neither party is "conservative" in the sense of being reluctant to use the power of government to promote the narrow interests of particular groups. One effect is a weakening of majority rule. Rather than policymaking by the majority acting through its elected representatives, interest-group liberalism involves policymaking by narrow segments of society acting on their own behalf with the help of lawmakers. Another adverse effect is an inefficient use of society's resources: groups get what they want, whether or not their priorities match those of society as a whole.

Another flaw in the pluralist argument resides in its claim that the group system is representative. Although pluralists acknowledge that well-funded interests have more influence, they say that the group process is relatively open and few interests are entirely left out. This claim contains an element of truth, but it is not the full truth. As this chapter has shown, organization is an unequally distributed resource. Economic interests, particularly corporations, are the most highly organized, and studies indicate that group politics works chiefly to the advantage of monied interests.[25] Of course, economic groups do not dominate everything, nor do they operate unchecked. Many of the citizen groups formed since the 1960s were created as checks on the power of corporate lobbies. Environmental groups are an example. Although some of them, including the Sierra Club, have existed for a century or longer, most of them are more recent in origin and work to shield the environment from threats posed by business activity. Activist government has also brought the group system into closer balance; the government's poverty programs have spawned groups that seek to protect these programs. Nevertheless, nearly two-thirds of all lobbying groups in Washington are business-related. The interest-group system is biased toward America's economically oriented groups, particularly its corporations.

The group system is similarly slanted toward the interests of upper-middle-class Americans. Affluent Americans have the money, communication skills, and savvy to participate effectively in special-interest politics. The poor, minorities, women, and the young are greatly underrepresented in the group system. A

POLITICAL CULTURE

LIBERTY, EQUALITY, AND SELF-GOVERNMENT

Interest Groups

Rarely is the tension between liberty and equality more evident than in the activities of interest groups. "Liberty is to faction what air is to fire," wrote James Madison in *Federalist* No. 10. Madison was lamenting the self-interested behavior of factions or, as they are called today, interest groups. Yet Madison recognized that the only way to suppress this behavior was to destroy the liberty that allows people to organize.

Interest groups tend to strengthen the already powerful and thus contribute to political inequality. As political scientist E. E. Schattschneider said, the group system "sings with a strong upper-class bias."

Numerous efforts have been made to harness the power of groups without infringing on Americans' rights of free expression. Laws have been enacted that require lobbyists to register, report their expenditures, and identify the issues on which they are working. Other laws restrict group contributions to candidates for public office. Yet nothing in the end seems to be all that effective in harnessing the self-interested actions of groups.

Do you think there is an answer to "Madison's dilemma"? Or are the excesses of group politics simply one of the costs of living in a free society?

lack of organization does not ensure an interest's failure, just as the existence of organization does not guarantee success. However, organized interests are obviously in a better position to promote their views.

The business and class bias of the group system is especially significant because the most highly organized interests are those least in need of government's help. Corporations and affluent citizens already control the largest share of society's resources. The lobbying system magnifies their advantage.

A Madisonian Dilemma

James Madison recognized the dilemma inherent in group activity. Although he worried that interest groups would have too much political influence, he argued in *Federalist* No. 10 that a free society must allow the pursuit of self-interest. Unless people can promote the separate opinions that stem from differences in their needs, values, and possessions, they are not a free people.

Ironically, Madison's constitutional solution to the problem of factions has become part of the problem. The American system of checks and balances, with a separation of powers at its core, was designed to prevent a majority faction from trampling on the interests of smaller groups. Indeed, throughout the nation's history, majorities have been frustrated in their efforts to exercise power by America's elaborate system of divided government, which makes it relatively easy for a determined minority to block action by the majority.

This same system, however, makes it relatively easy for minority factions—or, as they are called today, special-interest groups—to gain government support. If they can get the backing of even a small number of well-placed policymakers, as in the case of iron triangles, they are likely to get many of the benefits they seek. Because of the system's division of power, they have numerous points at which to exert influence. Often, they need only to find an ally in one place, whether that be a congressional committee or an executive agency or a federal court, to get at least some of what they seek. And once they obtain a government benefit, it is likely to endure. Benefits are hard to eliminate because concerted action by the executive branch and both houses of Congress is usually required. If a group has strong support in even a single institution, it usually can fend off attempts to eliminate a policy or program that serves its interest. Such support ordinarily is easy to acquire, because the group has resources—information, money, and votes—that officeholders want. (Chapters 11 and 13 discuss further the issue of interest-group power.)

Summary Self-Test www.mhhe.com/pattersontad9e

A political interest group is composed of a set of individuals organized to promote a shared concern. Most interest groups owe their existence to factors other than politics. These groups form for economic reasons, such as the pursuit of profit, and maintain themselves by making profits (in the case of corporations) or by providing their members with private goods, such as jobs and wages. Economic groups include corporations, trade associations, labor unions, farm organizations, and professional associations. Collectively, economic groups are by far the largest set of organized interests. The group system tends to favor interests that are already economically and socially advantaged.

Citizens' groups do not have the same organizational advantages as economic groups. They depend on voluntary contributions from potential members, who may lack interest and resources or who recognize that they will get the collective good from a group's activity even if they do not participate (the free-rider problem). Citizens' groups include public-interest, single-issue, and ideological groups. Their numbers have increased dramatically since the 1960s despite their organizational problems.

Organized interests seek influence largely by lobbying public officials and contributing to election campaigns. Using an inside strategy, lobbyists develop direct contacts with legislators, government bureaucrats, and members of the judiciary in order to persuade them to accept the group's perspective on policy. Groups also use an outside strategy, seeking to mobilize public support for their goals. This strategy relies in part on grassroots lobbying—encouraging group members and the public to communicate their policy views to officials. Outside lobbying also includes efforts to elect officeholders who will support group aims. Through political action committees (PACs), organized groups now provide nearly a third of all contributions received by congressional candidates.

The policies that emerge from the group system bring benefits to many of society's interests and often serve the collective interest as well. But when groups can essentially dictate policies, the common good is rarely served. The majority's interest is subordinated to group (minority) interests. In most instances, the minority consists of individuals who already enjoy a substantial share of society's benefits.

CHAPTER 9

Study Corner

Key Terms

citizens' (noneconomic) groups (*p. 227*)
collective (public) goods (*p. 227*)
economic groups (*p. 224*)
free-rider problem (*p. 228*)
grassroots lobbying (*p. 236*)
inside lobbying (*p. 231*)
interest group (*p. 222*)
interest-group liberalism (*p. 240*)

iron triangle (*p. 233*)
issue network (*p. 234*)
lobbying (*p. 230*)
outside lobbying (*p. 235*)
political action committee (PAC) (*p. 237*)
private (individual) goods (*p. 227*)
single-issue politics (*p. 222*)

Self-Test

1. Interest groups tend to do all **except** which one of the following?
   a. try to influence the political process
   b. pursue members' shared policy goals
   c. contribute support to candidates and officials who favor their goals
   d. change policy positions in order to win elections

2. If an interest group wants to influence policy decisions at the implementation stage, efforts should be directed primarily toward the:
   a. judiciary.
   b. bureaucracy.

c. White House.

d. Congress.

3. Interest-group politics is aligned with the political theory of:

a. elitism.

b. inclusion.

c. communitarianism.

d. pluralism.

4. When lobbyists supply policymakers with information and indications of group strength to persuade them to adopt the group's perspective, the activity is called:

a. arm twisting.

b. wrangling.

c. outside lobbying.

d. inside lobbying.

5. Economic interest groups have an advantage over other groups chiefly because of their:

a. ability to muster large numbers of members.

b. emphasis on training people to run for Congress.

c. devotion to promoting the broad public interest.

d. access to financial resources.

6. Political action committees (PACs):

a. raise money for election campaigns by soliciting voluntary contributions from members or employees.

b. have declined rapidly in number since the passage of the recent campaign finance reform legislation.

c. are under no restrictions regarding the amount of money each PAC can give to the election campaign of a single candidate for federal office.

d. are not an important source of funds in congressional campaigns.

7. The free-rider problem results when individuals can benefit from the activities of an interest group even if they do not contribute to the group's activities. (T/F)

8. The key tactic of outside lobbying activity is to put public pressure on officeholders. (T/F)

9. *Interest-group liberalism* is a term used by Theodore Lowi to express the tendency of lawmakers to cater to narrow interests over majority interests. (T/F)

10. Affluent citizens and business groups dominate the interest-group system. (T/F)

Critical Thinking

Why are there so many more organized interests in the United States than elsewhere? Why are so many of these groups organized around economic interests—particularly business interests?

Suggested Readings

Berry, Jeffrey M. *The New Liberalism: The Rising Power of Citizen Groups.* Washington, D.C.: Brookings Institution, 2000. An exploration of the influence that citizen groups exercise.

Browne, William P. *Cultivating Congress: Constituents, Issues, and Interests in Agriculture Policymaking.* Lawrence: University Press of Kansas, 1995. An analysis of the limits of "iron triangles" as a description of congressional policymaking.

Grossman, Gene M., and Elhanan Helpman. *Interest Groups and Trade Policy.* Princeton, N.J.: Princeton University Press, 2002. An examination of the impact of groups' campaign and lobbying activities on trade policy.

Herrnson, Paul S., Ronald G. Shaiko, and Clyde Wilcox, eds. *The Interest Group Connection: Electioneering, Lobbying, and Policymaking in Washington,* 2d ed. Washington, D.C.: CQ Press, 2004. Essays and commentaries on groups and officials and the linkages between them.

Lowery, David, and Holly Brasher. *Organized Interests and American Government.* New York: McGraw-Hill, 2004. An overview of interest-group politics.

Lowi, Theodore J. *The End of Liberalism,* 2d ed. New York: Norton, 1979. A thorough critique of interest groups' influence on American politics.

Olson, Mancur, Jr. *The Logic of Collective Action,* rev. ed. Cambridge, Mass.: Harvard University Press, 1971. A pioneering analysis of why some interests are more fully and easily organized than others.

Rozell, Mark J., Clyde Wilcox, and David Madland. *Interest Groups in American Campaigns,* 2d ed. Washington, D.C.: Congressional Quarterly Press, 2005. An assessment of the election role of interest groups.

List of Websites

http://www.fec.gov/

The Federal Election Commission site; offers information on elections, voting, campaign finance, parties, and PACs; also includes a citizens' guide to campaign contributions.

http://www.pirg.org/

The Public Interest Research Group (PIRG) site; PIRG has chapters on many college campuses, and the site provides state-by-state policy and other information.

http://www.sierraclub.org/

The website of the Sierra Club, one of the oldest environmental protection interest groups, which promotes conservation; provides information on its activities.

http://www.townhall.com/

The website of the American Conservative Union (ACU); includes policy and political information, and has a lively chat room.

Participate!

Consider contributing to a citizens' interest group. Such groups depend on members' donations for operating funds. Citizens' groups cover the political spectrum from right to left and touch on nearly every conceivable public issue. You will not have difficulty locating a group through the Internet that has policy goals consistent with your beliefs and values. If you are interested in contributing your time instead, some citizens' groups (for example, PIRG) have college chapters that might provide opportunities for you to work on issues of personal interest.

Extra Credit

For up-to-the-minute *New York Times* articles, interactive simulations, graphics, study tools, and more links and quizzes, visit the text's Online Learning Center at www.mhhe. com/pattersontad9e.

Self-Test Answers

1. d   2. b   3. d   4. d   5. d   6. a   7. T   8. T   9. T   10. T

National Journal

Why They Lobby

Thank You for Smoking, the 2005 film based on a novel by Christopher Buckley, follows the life of Nick Naylor, a chief spokesman for Big Tobacco with questionable morals, who makes his living defending the rights of smokers and cigarette-makers and then must deal with how his young son, Joey, views him. Naylor may have been a fictitious character, but Washington has its share of lobbyists arguing for the interests of industries with a perceived darker side.

The cynical response is that career decisions and political give-and-take revolve around money: Greenbacks triumph over ethics. But those who represent socially sensitive industries such as tobacco and alcohol have a lot more to say about why, out of all the potential job opportunities, they chose and often "love" what they do.

They all make it a point to note that the First Amendment sanctions lobbying: "the right of the people . . . to petition the government for a redress of grievances."

Tobacco

In the film, Naylor works for the Academy of Tobacco Studies, which Buckley based on the Tobacco Institute, the industry's former trade association. Andrew Zausner, who has lobbied for tobacco for 30 years, feeds off the challenge. "The more unpopular the client, the better you have to be as a lobbyist," he declares. "Believing in your client's position makes you a more forceful advocate." Although Zausner doesn't want his children to use tobacco, he notes that the "product has been continuously used in the United States before the United States existed" and says that the industry has a legitimate point of view and a constitutional right to express it.

Beau Schuyler lobbies for UST Public Affairs, a subsidiary of the holding company that owns U.S. Smokeless Tobacco and Ste. Michelle Wine Estates. A former congressional aide to two Democratic House members from his native state of North Carolina—in the heart of tobacco country—Schuyler says

that the "opportunity to work internally at one of the oldest continually listed companies on the New York Stock Exchange was just too good to pass up."

Gambling

James Reeder, a lobbyist at Patton Boggs, has spent about half his time over the past decade representing the gambling industry. He insists he didn't seek out this niche, adding, "I tell my grandchildren that gambling is a bad habit . . . and to go fishing."

Shortly after Reeder joined Patton Boggs, a client named Showboat called the firm looking for someone who knew about Louisiana because the company was interested in building a casino there. Reeder happened to be from the Pelican State and was put on the case. He reasoned that Louisiana has always been a home to illegal gambling, and "if the culture of the state supports the industry, [the state] might as well make it legal and reap the benefits and get more tax money."

"Whenever you take on one of these vices like booze or gambling and you just pass a law to say it is illegal," Reeder says, "you end up like in Prohibition, when the mob took over the liquor business."

Reeder excelled at lobbying for the gambling industry even though he avoids games of chance. "I don't gamble, because I am not a good card player," he says. "My friends would die laughing because I would go to offices to talk to clients on gambling and I would never go into a casino." If a lawmaker was morally opposed to gambling, Reeder wouldn't argue with him, he says.

John Pappas began working for the industry as a consultant for the Poker Players Alliance while at Dittus Communications.

Pappas calls poker a game of skill that has a rich history in America. He grew up playing cards with family members and friends, and noted during an interview that he would be playing poker with 20 lawmakers that evening at a charity tournament. "Responsibility in all aspects of life is paramount," he says.

Firearms

Richard Feldman's book, *Ricochet: Confessions of a Gun Lobbyist,* has been gaining the former National Rifle Association employee some attention recently. Feldman says that the gun control issue, like most, is not black and white. Working for the NRA, he says, "was the best job I ever had." The "huge power" he was able to wield "in the middle of major political battles" was more attractive to him at the time than the money he earned.

Feldman says he would sometimes play hardball but "didn't hit below the belt" in his pursuit of the gun industry's objectives. "Lobbying an issue that you have some special passion on (guns) is like waking up every day already having consumed a triple espresso," he said in an e-mail to *National Journal.* "On the other hand, if you can empathize with your client's position regardless of the issue, one can be a more convincing advocate, which I've always viewed as the more critical aspect of truly effective lobbying."

Video Games

Because many video games contain a fair share of gunplay and other violence, Entertainment Software Association President Michael Gallagher has had to address complaints that playing violent games causes psychological harm such as increased aggression.

His group lobbies against "efforts to regulate the content of entertainment media in any form, including proposals to criminalize the sale of certain video games to minors; create uniform, government-sanctioned entertainment rating systems; or regulate the marketing practices of industry."

Gallagher, a former assistant Commerce secretary for communications and information in the Bush administration, calls video games a great form of family entertainment. The titles are responsibly rated, he says, and the gaming consoles have easy-to-use parental controls.

"I have been playing video games all my life," Gallagher says, including with his children. He contends that his industry "leads all forms of media when it comes to disclosure on what's in the game" and says that it works with retailers to "make sure minors can't buy games that are inappropriate for them."

Alcohol

Lobbyists who work for the beer, wine, and spirits industries have to deal with a host of negative images, among them drunk-driving accidents, underage drinking, and the effects of alcohol on health.

Mike Johnson, a lobbyist for the National Beer Wholesalers Association, acknowledges that alcohol is a "socially sensitive product" and says that is why the industry operates under strict government guidelines.

"I am blessed. I get to represent some great family-owned and -operated businesses that are very active in their communities and provide some really great jobs," Johnson says. "I am completely comfortable one day having a conversation with my son about who I work for, because I can tell him what a great job that beer distributors do in ensuring a safe marketplace and in protecting consumers from a lot of the problems we see with alcohol in other places in the world."

Craig Wolf, president of the Wine & Spirits Wholesalers, calls alcohol a "great social lubricant" that "creates great environments." Wolf got involved in wine-industry issues when he was counsel for the Senate Judiciary Committee. As his job there was ending, Wolf was offered the post of general counsel at the association; he took over as president in 2006.

"The key to advocating for a socially sensitive product is doing business responsibility," Wolf says. "We spend more time and resources [on the issue of] responsible consumption of alcohol than all other issues combined."

Distilled Spirits Council President Peter Cressy says, "I was interviewed for this position precisely because the Distilled Council wanted to continue and increase its very serious approach to fighting underage drinking." As chancellor of the University of Massachusetts (Dartmouth), Cressy says, he was active in "fighting binge drinking on campuses." The opportunity to join the council, which has lobbyists in 40 states, gave him the chance to have a national audience, he says. After nine years with the council, Cressy notes, he "has not been disappointed."

Snack Foods

Nicholas Pyle stands at the policy divide where junk food meets America's bulging waistlines. "I love my job," says Pyle, a lobbyist for McKee Foods, the makers of Little Debbie, America's leading snack-cake brand.

Many of the brand's affordable treats contain a dose of sugar, along with corn syrup, partially hydrogenated oil, bleached flour, and artificial flavor. Little Debbie "has been the target of a number of folks out there who want to paint people as a victim of the foods they eat," says Pyle, who is also president of the Independent Bakers Association. Little Debbie is a "wonderful food, great product, wholesome," with a wonderful image, he says. Pyle explains that he and his children enjoy the snacks.

"The big question of obesity is all about personal responsibility and people balancing [snacking] with a healthy and active lifestyle," Pyle insists. He contends that McKee, a family-owned business, doesn't target children in its marketing. "We market to the decision makers in the household," he says, adding that the company doesn't advertise on Saturday morning cartoon shows.

Snack Food Association President and CEO Jim McCarthy says that lobbying is one of his many duties as head of the organization. "Our belief is that all foods fit into the diet," McCarthy says, and "we don't like the term 'junk food.'"

The industry has developed healthier products over the years, McCarthy says, but at "certain times consumers haven't bought these products." He attributes the obesity problem to a lack of exercise and shortcomings in educating people about the need for a balanced diet.

Challenging Stereotypes

No matter what industry they represent, lobbyists interviewed for this article said that a good practitioner of their profession knows all sides of an issue, enabling lawmakers and their staffs to make the best-informed decision.

Although many of the lobbyists acknowledge some familiar situations in *Thank You for Smoking*, they insist that the stereotypes are not altogether fair. "I think people don't understand the importance of lobbying to the system. If I don't explain what we do and I am not here to explain it to people, Congress will make uninformed decisions without understanding the consequences to the industry," a former liquor lobbyist says.

For consumers, the message that lobbyists appear to be sending is that the individual is responsible for making the right choices in life. Yet the profusion of advertising, marketing ploys, political rhetoric, and seemingly conflicting studies can be bewildering. And although the financial incentive is ever-present, lobbyists believe they fill a fundamental role in society and deserve some relief from the negative stereotypes.

FOR DISCUSSION: Would you take a job lobbying for a "sin industry"? What about a job lobbying for an industry or cause you believe in but others do not?

Should we regulate the influence of certain lobbies but not others?

Do you feel the positions put forward by the lobbies mentioned in the article have affected the way you think about their industries?

The News Media
Communicating Political Images

Historical Development: From the Nation's Founding to Today
    The Objective-Journalism Era
    The Rise of the "New" News

The Politics of News
    The Signaling Function
    The Watchdog Function
    The Common-Carrier Function
    The Partisan Function

Attention to News
    The Shrinking Audience for News
    Age and Attention to News

Media and the Public in the Internet Age

The press in America . . . determines what people will think and talk about an authority that in other nations is reserved for tyrants, priests, parties, and mandarins. Theodore H. White[1]

The news flashed across America. Eliot Spitzer, governor of New York, had been caught paying for a high-priced call girl. Using the alias George Fox, Spitzer had checked into the Mayflower hotel in Washington, D.C., where he was scheduled to testify at a congressional hearing the next morning on the bond crisis spreading through the financial markets. Unbeknown to Spitzer, the FBI had wiretapped his phone, seeking to account for suspicious money transfers from his New York bank account. In the process, they discovered that Spitzer—known to the prostitution ring as Client No. 9—was wiring the money to pay for a rendezvous with a call girl. After being contacted by the FBI and informed that his calls had been taped, Spitzer called a press conference and, with his wife at his side, apologized for his actions. Two days later, with the story still in the headlines and facing mounting pressure to resign, Spitzer stepped down as New York's governor, saying that he did not want his "private failings to disrupt the public's work." Spitzer concluded his brief resignation speech by noting: "Over the course of my public life, I have insisted—I believe correctly—that people, regardless of their position or power, take responsibility for their conduct. I can and will ask no less of myself."

Spitzer was elected governor in 2006, after having made a reputation for ferreting out Wall Street corruption as state attorney general. Ironically, he had also prosecuted prostitution rings. However, nothing that Spitzer had done previously—not as attorney general, not as gubernatorial candidate, and not as governor—had generated anywhere near the headlines accompanying the revelation that he had paid for the services of a prostitute. It was front-page news throughout the country, the lead story on television newscasts, and the leading topic of conversation on talk shows and Internet blogs. It was also grist for the late-night television shows. On his program, after noting that Spitzer might have used campaign funds to pay for a prostitute, Conan O'Brien quipped: "To be fair, [he] did get her vote."

After getting caught paying for a prostitute, New York governor Eliot Spitzer, with his wife by his side, announces his resignation from office. The scandal generated far more news coverage than anything Spitzer had done in office, including his efforts to weed out Wall Street corruption. The news media, as their coverage of Spitzer illustrates, presents a refracted version of reality, where sensational developments typically get more attention than the day-to-day policy problems that have a larger effect on Americans' lives.

news

The news media's version of reality, usually with an emphasis on timely, dramatic, and compelling events and developments.

press (news media)

Those print and broadcast organizations that are in the news-reporting business.

Although reporters sometimes compare the news to a mirror held up to reality, the news is more accurately described as a refracted version of reality. The **news** is mainly an account of obtruding events, particularly those that are *timely* (new or unfolding developments rather than old or static ones), *dramatic* (striking developments rather than commonplace ones), and *compelling* (developments that arouse people's emotions).[2] These tendencies have their origins in a number of factors, the most significant of which is that news organizations aim to make a profit. Accordingly, they seek news stories that will attract a large audience. Thus, compared with Spitzer's sexual liaison, his work as a top public official was less newsworthy. It was part of the ongoing business of government and did not lend itself to the vivid storytelling of a sex scandal.

News organizations and journalists are referred to collectively as the **press** or the **news media.** The press includes broadcast networks (such as ABC and NPR), cable networks (such as CNN and Fox), newspapers (such as the *Chicago Tribune* and *Dallas Morning News*), news magazines (such as *Time* and *Newsweek*), and Internet sites that provide news and commentary (such as Instapundit and the Drudge Report). The U.S. news system has been undergoing substantial changes. For decades the news system was monopolized by broadcast television and daily newspapers. They are still the dominant players, but over the past quarter-century, they have lost audience and influence to cable news, talk radio, and Internet sites, a point that will be addressed later in the chapter.

This chapter examines the news media's role in the American political system. The chapter will argue that the press is a key intermediary between Americans and their leaders, but it will also argue that the press is a different kind of intermediary than either the political party or the interest group, which seek to represent particular interests in society. Most news organizations do not aim to represent particular interests. They do claim, with some justification, to serve the public interest by keeping people informed about public affairs. Yet their news coverage is driven as much by a need to attract an audience in order to sell advertising, which finances their operations. Accordingly, the news tends to focus on sensational events that will catch people's attention rather than on ordinary developments that are ultimately more important in people's lives. This chapter will explore this and other aspects of the press and its news coverage. The main ideas presented in the chapter are these:

■ *The American press was initially tied to the nation's political party system (the partisan press) but gradually developed an independent position (the objective press).* In the process, the news shifted from a political orientation, which emphasizes political values and ideas, to a journalistic orientation, which stresses newsworthy information and events.

■ *In recent years, traditional news organizations have faced increased competition for people's attention from cable and the Internet, which has contributed to audience fragmentation and the rise of opinionated journalism.*

■ *The news media have several functions—signaling (the press brings relevant events and problems into public view), common-carrier (the press serves as a channel through which leaders and citizens can communicate), watchdog (the press scrutinizes official behavior for evidence of deceitful, careless, or corrupt acts), and partisan (the press promotes particular interests and values).* The traditional media contribute mainly to the first three functions while the "new" news media contribute mainly to the last one.

■ *The news audience has been shifting and fragmenting, partly as a result of new technology and partly because young adults are less likely than older ones to have a daily news habit.* One consequence has been a widening information gap between America's better-informed and less-informed citizens.

Historical Development: From the Nation's Founding to Today

Democracy thrives on a free flow of information.[3] Communication enables a free people to keep in touch with one another and with officials, a fact not lost on America's early leaders. Alexander Hamilton persuaded John Fenno to start a newspaper, the *Gazette of the United States,* as a means of publicizing the policies of George Washington's administration. To finance the paper, Hamilton, as secretary of the treasury, granted it the Treasury Department's printing contracts. Hamilton's political rival, Thomas Jefferson, dismissed the *Gazette*'s reporting as "pure Toryism" and convinced Philip Freneau to start the *National Gazette* as an opposition paper. Jefferson, as secretary of state, gave Freneau the authority to print State Department documents.

Early newspapers were printed a page at a time on flat presses, a process that limited production and kept the cost of each copy beyond the reach of ordinary citizens. Leading papers such as the *Gazette of the United States* had fewer than fifteen hundred readers and could not have survived without party support. Not surprisingly, the "news" they printed was laden with partisanship.[4] In this era of the **partisan press,** publishers openly backed one party or the other.

Technological innovation in the early 1800s helped bring about the gradual decline of the partisan newspaper. With the invention of the telegraph, editors had access to timely information on events outside the local area, which led them to substitute news stories for opinion commentary. Creation of the hand-cranked rotary press was equally important because it enabled publishers to print their newspapers more cheaply and quickly. The *New York Sun* was the first paper to take advantage of the new technology. The *Sun* reduced the price of its daily paper from six cents to a penny, and its daily circulation rose from one thousand to ten thousand in less than a year.[5] Increased circulation meant increased advertising revenue, which helped to free newspapers from their dependence on government printing contracts.

By the late nineteenth century, helped along by the invention of newsprint and power-driven presses, many American newspapers were printing fifty thousand or more copies a day, and their large circulations enabled them to charge high prices for advertising. The period marked the height of newspapers' power and the low point in their sense of public responsibility. A new style of reporting—"yellow journalism"—had emerged as a way of boosting circulation. It was "a shrieking, gaudy, sensation-loving, devil-may-care kind of journalism which lured the reader by any possible means."[6] A circulation battle between William Randolph Hearst's *New York Journal* and Joseph Pulitzer's *New York World* may have contributed to the outbreak of the Spanish-American War through

---

partisan press

Newspapers and other communication media that openly support a political party and whose news in significant part follows the party line.

Yellow journalism was characterized by its sensationalism. William Randolph Hearst's *New York Journal* whipped up public support for a war in Cuba against Spain through inflammatory reporting on the sinking of the battleship *Maine* in Havana Harbor in 1898.

objective journalism

A model of news reporting that is based on the communication of "facts" rather than opinions and that is "fair" in that it presents all sides of partisan debate.

sensational (and largely inaccurate) reports on the cruelty of Spanish rule in Cuba. A young Frederic Remington (who later became a noted painter and sculptor), working as a news artist for Hearst, planned to return home because Cuba appeared calm and safe, but Hearst cabled back: "Please remain. You furnish the pictures and I'll furnish the war."[7]

The Objective-Journalism Era

The excesses of yellow journalism led some publishers to consider ways of reporting the news more responsibly. One step was to separate the newspaper's advertising department from its news department, thus reducing the influence of advertisers on news content. A second development was a new model of reporting called **objective journalism,** which was based on the reporting of "facts" rather than opinions and was "fair" in that it presented both sides of partisan debate. A chief advocate of this new form of journalism was Adolph Ochs of the *New York Times*. Ochs bought the *Times* in 1896, when its circulation was 9,000; four years later, its readership had grown to 82,000. Ochs told his reporters that he "wanted as little partisanship as possible . . . as few judgments as possible."[8] The *Times* gradually acquired a reputation as the country's best newspaper. Objective reporting was also promoted through newly formed journalism schools, such as those at Columbia University and the University of Missouri. Within a few decades, objective journalism was entrenched at most American newspapers.

Until the twentieth century, the print media were the only form of mass communication. By the 1920s, however, hundreds of radio stations were broadcasting throughout the nation. At first the government did not regulate radio broadcasting. The result was chaos. A common problem was that nearby stations often used the same or adjacent radio frequencies, interfering with each other's broadcasts. Finally, in 1934, Congress passed the Communications Act, which regulated broadcasting and created the Federal Communications Commission (FCC) to oversee the process. Broadcasters had to be licensed by the FCC, and because the number of available broadcasting frequencies was limited, licensees had to be evenhanded in their political coverage. Section 315 of the Communications Act imposed on broadcasters an "equal time" restriction, which prohibited them from selling or giving airtime to a political candidate without offering to sell or give an equal amount of airtime to other candidates for the same office. (An exception was later made for election debates; broadcasters can televise them even if third-party candidates are excluded.)

Television followed radio, and by the late 1950s, more than 90 percent of American homes had a TV set. In this period, the FCC imposed a second restriction—the Fairness Doctrine—on broadcasters. The Fairness Doctrine required broadcasters to "afford reasonable opportunity for the discussion of conflicting views of public importance." Broadcasters were prohibited from using their news coverage to promote one party or issue position at the expense of another. In effect, the objective-reporting model practiced voluntarily by the newspapers was imposed by law on broadcasters.

The Rise of the "New" News

During the era of objective journalism, the news was not entirely devoid of partisanship. Although broadcasters were prohibited by law from editorializing, newspapers were not. Most of them backed one political party or the other on their editorial and opinion (op-ed) pages. Nevertheless, it was difficult to tell from their news pages which party they backed editorially. Nearly all of them highlighted the same national stories each day, and if a high-ranking public official got embroiled in a scandal or policy blunder, they played it up, whether the official was a Republican or a Democrat.

The introduction of cable television did not at first change this pattern. Cable television is transmitted by privately owned wire rather than broadcast over the public airways and therefore did not have to comply with the Fairness Doctrine. Nevertheless, when the media mogul Ted Turner started CNN in 1980, he chose to abide by it, instructing his correspondents to pursue a path of partisan neutrality. He sought to attract viewers through round-the-clock news and live on-the-scene reports. Turner's marketing idea worked. CNN's audience and reputation ballooned whenever a major event occurred. In 1991, for example, Americans were riveted to CNN's live coverage from Baghdad as the first American bombs of the Persian Gulf War began falling on that city.

When CNN was launched in 1980, barely more than 10 percent of American homes had cable service. Within a decade, however, the number exceeded 50 percent, which led the FCC to rescind the Fairness Doctrine. The FCC reasoned that the scarcity argument was no longer compelling because cable had greatly increased the number of available channels. Broadcast stations were suddenly free to cover politics in ways of their choosing.

Radio stations were the first to respond to the change. They had previously been required to air a liberal talk show if they aired a conservative one. The reverse was also true. As a consequence, most station owners had chosen not to broadcast political talk shows. After the Fairness Doctrine was eliminated, however, scores of radio stations switched from playing music to airing political talk shows, and today, radio listeners in every market have access to such programming. Cable television, too, provides partisan talk shows, a trend that began when the billionaire media mogul Rupert Murdoch launched Fox News in 1996. He hired Roger Ailes, a Republican political consultant, to run Fox News, instructing him to devise a format appealing to political conservatives. Ailes hired several conservative talk show hosts, including Bill O'Reilly. Within a relatively few years, bouyed by a largely Republican audience, Fox News had surpassed CNN as the most heavily watched cable news network.

In the 1990s, the Internet emerged as yet another source of news and political commentary. Unlike a newspaper, broadcast station, or cable company, where the capital investment can run into the tens or even hundreds of millions of dollars, the Internet has a low cost of entry. Anyone with a computer and technical savvy can create a website or blog devoted to news and public affairs. Thousands of such sites exist. Their sheer number and the stunning success of some of them—the Drudge Report, Instapundit, Daily Kos, and Boing Boing, to name a few—have created an important "new" news media. Such sites resemble political talk radio in that they freely mix news and partisanship.

Elimination of the Fairness Doctrine led to the emergence of Christian broadcasting as a political forum. Although Christian broadcasting, led by Pat Robertson's Christian Broadcasting Network, was widely heard and watched in some parts of the country, it was constrained in its political commentary by the Fairness Doctrine. Once that obstacle was removed, however, Robertson and other conservative Christian broadcasters changed their programming to include political appeals. Robertson even ran for public office himself, entering the 1988 race for the Republican presidential nomination. Robertson is pictured here hosting his television program, *The 700 Club*.

The Politics of News

The news media are Americans' window onto the world of politics. For most people, politics is largely a second-hand experience, something they observe through the media rather than directly. The media are not, however, the main source of citizens' political *opinions*. Party loyalties, group attachments, and social networks are more important sources. On the other hand, people's political *perceptions* derive largely from the media. People's mental pictures of events and policy problems, and even their images of political institutions and leaders, stem primarily from what they see and hear through the news media.

The news media operate as *gatekeepers*. Out of the countless possibilities each day, they determine which events will be covered and which ones will not. These selections, in turn, will influence what citizens are thinking and talking about. What determines these selections? What determines whether something will make the news, and thus become known to the public, or will not make the news, and thus remain largely out of sight except to those directly affected?

As it happens, journalists' selections are channeled by four functions—the signaling, common-carrier, watchdog, and partisan functions—that the media perform. We'll look first at the signaling function.

The Signaling Function

The media's responsibilities include a **signaling function.** The media seek to alert the public to important developments as soon as possible after they happen—a state visit to Washington by a foreign leader, a bill that has just been passed by Congress, a change in the nation's unemployment level, or a terrorist bombing in a foreign capital.

The U.S. media are well equipped to play a signaling role. They are poised to converge on any major news event anywhere in the nation and nearly anywhere in the world. The signaling function is performed largely by the traditional media—the wire services, the daily newspapers, and the television networks. They are staffed and organized to cover events and consequently are the source of most breaking news. Occasionally, an event enters the news stream through the Internet. It was bloggers who first recognized that a racially laden comment by Senate Republican leader Trent Lott in 2002 was big news—big enough that it would eventually force Lott to resign his leadership post. Nevertheless, hundreds of news stories enter the news stream daily, and the great bulk of them are generated by traditional news outlets.

A Common Version of Reality

In their capacity as signalers, the media have the power to focus the public's attention. The term **agenda setting** has been used to describe the media's ability to influence what is on people's minds.[9] By covering the same events, problems, issues, and leaders—simply by giving them space or time in the news—the media place them on the public agenda. The press, as Bernard Cohen notes, "may not be successful much of the time in telling people what to think, but it is stunningly successful in telling them what to think about."[10]

Even when "media reality" does not match "objective reality," it can have a powerful effect on what people think is true. A classic example occurred in the early 1990s when local television newscasts, in an attempt to bolster sagging ratings, upped their crime coverage. "If it bleeds it leads" became the mantra of local TV news. Meanwhile, the national media were playing up several high-profile murder cases, including the arrest of serial killer Joel Rifkin, who murdered eighteen women in New York, and the kidnap-murder of 12-year-old Polly Klaas in California. Crime was the most heavily reported national issue, overshadowing all others, even the timely topics of health care reform and the economy. The effect on public opinion was dramatic. In the previous decade, no more than 5 percent of Americans had believed at any time that crime was the country's biggest problem. By 1994, however, more than 40 percent of Americans said that crime was the top issue facing the nation. Politicians got caught up in the public's anxiety. Lawmakers rushed to enact tough new sentencing policies and spent more money to build new prisons than at any time in the nation's history. The irony was that the actual level of crime in America was *declining* during this period. According to U.S. Justice Department statistics, the rate of violent crime had dropped by 5 percent since 1990.[11]

The press is a powerful agenda setter in part because nearly all major news organizations focus on the same stories and interpret them in pretty much the same way. In view of the freedom and great number of news organizations—there are roughly fifteen hundred daily newspapers and a thousand local television outlets in the United States—it might be expected that Americans would be exposed to widely different versions of national news. The opposite is true. Each day, newspapers and broadcast outlets from coast to coast tend to present the same national news, thus conveying the sense that the news, somehow, *is* reality.

Objective journalism, which inclines news outlets to refrain from using the news as a device for promoting a particular viewpoint, is a reason the national news is everywhere pretty much the same. Unlike some European news systems, where journalism norms allow and even encourage reporters to present the news through a partisan lens, American reporters are expected to treat the political parties and their leaders in a balanced way. They do not always do so, but in their quest for balance, American reporters tend toward a common interpretation of political developments, as opposed to a Republican version or a Democratic version. The difference between the U.S. and European media is evident in a five-country study that asked reporters whether they should remain neutral in reporting on political parties. Compared with their counterparts in Great Britain, Germany, Sweden, and Italy, U.S. journalists were more likely to endorse the principle of partisan neutrality (see Figure 10-1).

Another reason the news everywhere in the United States is pretty much the same is that news outlets rely on the wire services for most of their national coverage. Most U.S. news organizations lack the resources to gather news outside their own location and rely for this coverage on the wire services, particularly the Associated Press (AP), which has three thousand reporters stationed throughout the country and the world to gather news stories and transmit them to

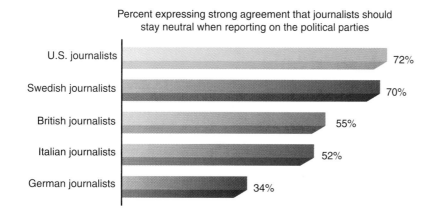

Percent expressing strong agreement that journalists should stay neutral when reporting on the political parties

U.S. journalists — 72%
Swedish journalists — 70%
British journalists — 55%
Italian journalists — 52%
German journalists — 34%

FIGURE 10-1 **Partisan Neutrality as a Journalism Norm** American journalists are more likely than European journalists to think they are obliged to treat political parties equally.
Source: Thomas E. Patterson, Media and Democracy Project, in progress. Published with author's permission.

STATES IN THE NATION

IN THE NEWS, OR OUT?

Most of the news that reaches Americans, no matter where they live, originates with a handful of news outlets, such as NBC News. This coverage, however, concentrates on events in a few places. The map shows the relative frequency with which each of the fifty states was mentioned on NBC News during a one-year period.

Q: Why do some states get more coverage than other states?

A: The heavily covered states are usually the more populous ones, which increases the likelihood that a newsworthy event will occur. In NBC's case, coverage is also heavier in states where one of its news bureaus is located. NBC has bureaus in New York, Washington, Los Angeles, Dallas, Atlanta, Chicago, and Boston.

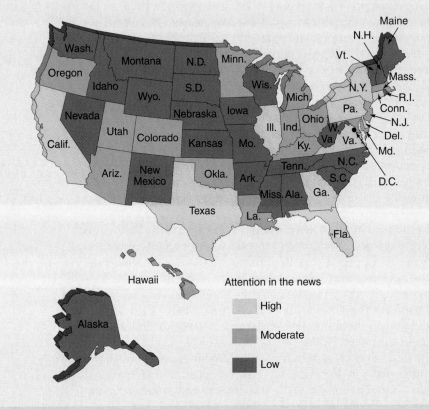

Attention in the news

High

Moderate

Low

Source: Data compiled by the author from Nexis.

subscribing news organizations. More than 95 percent of the nation's dailies (as well as most broadcast stations) subscribe to the AP, which, because it serves the full range of American news outlets, studiously avoids partisanship in preparing its stories. A few U.S. newspapers—including the *New York Times, Wall Street Journal, Los Angeles Times, Washington Post,* and *Chicago Tribune*—have large enough reporting staffs to generate their own national coverage. Nevertheless, these papers, too, give similar coverage to the same top stories each day. They differ mostly in their feature, follow-up, and investigative reports, most of which appear on the inside pages rather the front page.

Local television stations also depend on outside sources for their national news coverage. Television production is hugely expensive, which limits the ability of local stations to produce anything except local news. For their national coverage, they rely on video feeds from the leading television networks—ABC, CBS, NBC, CNN, Fox, and MSNBC. Even the national networks have a similar lineup of stories. Most network newscasts are a half hour in length, with ten minutes devoted to advertising. With so little time for news, the day's top stories tend to dominate the newscasts of all networks. Moreover, network correspondents cover the same beats and rely on many of the same sources, which leads them to report more or less the same things. After filming a congressional hearing, for example, network correspondents are likely to agree on what was most newsworthy about it—often a testy exchange between a witness and one of the committee members.

Informing the Public, or Attracting an Audience?

The signaling function of the press is sometimes called its informing function, but the latter is a much less accurate description of how the media operate. Although news organizations take seriously their responsibility to inform the public, the more pressing concern is a need "to attract and hold a large audience for advertisers."[12] Without ad revenue, nearly all U.S. news organizations would go out of business. Only a few news outlets—an example is National Public Radio, which depends on listener contributions—support themselves through something other than commercial advertising.

The very definition of news—what it is and what it is not—is built around the need to attract an audience.[13] The news is intentionally shortsighted. Each day, journalists must have new stories to tell, ones that are different from yesterday's. The continuing need for fresh stories leads journalists to cover what they call "hard events"—developments that have taken a clear and definable shape within the past twenty-four hours.[14] Without a hard event to lend it form and immediacy, an issue is likely to go unreported. For example, although few developments in the post–World War II era had a bigger impact on U.S. politics than the northward trek of southern blacks, it was rarely mentioned in the news. As African Americans in the late 1940s and 1950s moved into the northern cities by the hundreds each day, white people, pushed by racial fears and pulled by the lure of the suburbs, moved out in equally large numbers. Within a few decades, the political, social, and economic landscape of urban America had been substantially altered—a transformation that was rarely the subject of news coverage. Columnist George Will wryly noted that a ribbon should have been stretched across the Mason-Dixon line as the one-millionth African American crossed it on the way north; the breaking of the ribbon would have given the media a "peg" on which to hang the story of urban America's extraordinary transformation.[15]

At the same time, policy issues and problems do not change much from day to day, and thus are not considered particularly newsworthy. The first time that a top politician talks about a major policy issue, it is likely to be reported, and it may even make the front page. Thereafter, its news value is small; it is "old news." The 2008 presidential nomination contest between Barack Obama and Hillary Clinton, for example, was waged largely in the context of their different levels of experience and their opposing positions on the invasion of Iraq. These differences were not, however, the main focus of the candidates' news coverage. Journalists focused instead on the latest poll results, delegate counts, accusations, gaffes, tactics, and the like. These were the "new" developments in the Democratic race and therefore what journalists saw as "news."[16]

The press's need for novelty also explains why sensational crimes and wayward celebrities get so much attention. In 2008, an ambulance was called to the home of the singer Britney Spears, who was distraught over a child custody dispute with her ex-husband, Kevin Federline. Photos taken by journalists parked outside her residence, along with aerial video provided by television news stations, showed Spears being taken from her home on a stretcher, surrounded by paramedics. The pictures were flashed across the country—the latest episode in the ongoing Spears media saga.

PUBLIC BROADCASTING

Public broadcasting got off to a slow start in the United States. Unlike the case in Europe, where public broadcasting networks (such as Britain's BBC) were created at the start of the radio age, the U.S. government handed control of broadcasting to commercial networks, such as NBC and CBS. By the time Congress decided in the 1960s that public broadcasting was needed, the commercial networks were so powerful that they convinced Congress to assign it second-class status. Public broadcasting was poorly funded and was denied access to the most powerful broadcast frequencies. In fact, most television sets in the 1960s had tuners that could not dial in the stations on which public broadcast programs were aired. Not surprisingly, public broadcasting faltered at the beginning and still operates in the shadow of commercial broadcasting.

Nevertheless, public broadcasting does have a success story—National Public Radio (NPR). Over the past two decades, NPR's audience has quadrupled. Each week, more than 20 million Americans listen to NPR, many of them on a regular basis. NPR's growth is a stark contrast to what has happened to commercial newscasts during the same period. The combined audience of the ABC, CBS, and NBC evening newscasts is now half that of the early 1980s. NPR has built its audience through a strategy opposite to that of the commercial networks. As the news audiences of these networks declined in the face of widening competition from cable television, they

"softened" their newscasts—boosting entertainment content in the hope of luring viewers away from cable programs. Former Federal Communication Commission chairman Newton Minow derided the change as "pretty close to tabloid." In contrast, NPR has held to the notion that news is news and not also entertainment. Although NPR carries features, they are typically tied to news developments. Studies indicate that NPR's audience is more politically interested and informed than any other broadcast news audience. Many of its listeners are refugees from the broadcast network news they used to watch but now find to be lacking in substance.

Despite NPR's success, public broadcasting in the United States is but a small part of the total news system, and the consequences are substantial. In countries like Britain, Germany, and Japan, where public broadcasting is well funded, it sets a standard for high-quality news that conditions the public to prefer it and to expect it from other news providers as well. In the United States, public broadcasting depends on stories reported first by commercial outlets, where the profit motive can lead to news based more on its audience appeal than its social relevance. Accordingly, many Americans have become accustomed to, and even prefer, news produced for its entertainment value. "Amusing ourselves to death" is communication scholar Neil Postman's description of this kind of news.

Of course, serious issues do get some coverage. But the mix of news stories is designed as much to attract an audience as to inform it. Not surprisingly, studies have found that news exposure does not lead to exceptionally high levels of political information.[17] As might be expected, people who pay close attention to the news are better informed on the issues than those who pay little or no attention. Nevertheless, Americans are not exceptionally well informed about public affairs. Some European news systems are less advertising oriented (see "How the U.S. Compares"), and their audiences are somewhat better informed. A study of seven Western countries found, for example, that Americans ranked next to last (ahead of only Spaniards) in their ability to correctly identify prominent world leaders and developments.[18]

The Watchdog Function

watchdog function

The accepted responsibility of the media to protect the public from incompetent or corrupt officials by standing ready to expose any official who violates accepted legal, ethical, or performance standards.

The American press takes responsibility for exposing incompetent, hypocritical, and corrupt officials. In this **watchdog function,** the press stands ready to expose officials who violate accepted legal, ethical, or performance standards. The American news media have rightfully been called a fourth branch of government— part of the political system's checks on abuses of power.

The norms of objective journalism foster watchdog reporting. Although journalists are expected to fairly treat opposing political views, there is no norm that would limit criticism of officials who abuse the public trust. American journalists also operate within a system that provides substantial press freedom. Unlike British journalists who are barred from reporting what the government designates as "official secrets," American journalists operate under the principle of "no prior restraint," which holds that government cannot stop a news story unless it can convince a court that it would gravely harm the nation (see Chapter 4). Thus, it was an American news outlet, the Drudge Report, which reported that Britain's Prince Harry was serving as a British army officer in Afghanistan. Some British journalists were aware of the assignment but had accepted a government ban on reporting it. After the Drudge Report revealed his combat status, he was removed from Afghanistan so that he and his unit would not be targeted by hostile forces there.

The U.S. press is also unusual in the degree to which it is free from libel judgments (see Chapter 4). It is nearly impossible for a U.S. official to win a libel suit against a newspaper, magazine, or broadcast organization even in situations where his or her reputation has been harmed by false allegations. In Britain, where libel judgments are more easily obtained, journalists have to be more judicious in alleging that officials have been guilty of misconduct.

American journalists have not always vigorously fullfilled their watchdog function. One such period was the early phase of the Cold War between the United States and the Soviet Union. When Senator Joseph McCarthy (R-Wisc.) in the early 1950s falsely claimed that hundreds of Americans in the State Department, Hollywood, and the universities were subversive communists, the press served as a megaphone for his wild charges, sometimes with sensational headlines. Only after Republican President Dwight D. Eisenhower and leading members of Congress spoke out against McCarthy did the press flatly reject his trumped-up claims. There were noteworthy exceptions, including CBS's famed Edward R. Murrow, but the press by and large failed in its watchdog role during the McCarthy era.

After the terrorist attacks of September 11, 2001, the news media also stepped back from their watchdog role. Press criticism of political leaders and institutions fell sharply, as journalists sought to contribute to a newfound sense of national unity and purpose. NBC News outfitted its peacock logo with stars and stripes following the World Trade Center and Pentagon attacks, and computer-generated flags festooned the other networks. Although there was some critical reporting during the lead-up to the 2003 invasion of Iraq, news organizations did not vigorously scrutinize the Bush administration's arguments on

LEADERS

IDA TARBELL
(1857–1944)

Watchdog reporting in the United States traces to the Progressive Era of the early 1900s, when the partisan journalism of the nation's early decades began to yield to objective journalism. The objective model obliged journalists to remain neutral on partisan issues but did not prohibit them from aggressively pursuing corruption, favoritism, abuse, and incompetence, whether in the public or the private sector. The early watchdog journalists were known as Muckrakers, and several of them, including Upton Sinclair and Lincoln Steffens, gained fame through their exposés. Sinclair even attacked the newspaper industry itself, claiming in *The Brass Check* that it routinely ignored the corrupt practices of firms that advertised heavily in the newspaper. No muckraker had a bigger impact, however, than Ida Tarbell, who in the two-volume *The History of the Standard Oil Company* (1904) exposed the predatory practices of John D. Rockefeller in building his oil empire. Tarbell's book led the federal government to use the Sherman Anti-Trust Act to break up Rockefeller's firm, Standard Oil of New Jersey. Much of the material in Tarbell's two-volume book appeared earlier in *McClure's*, a widely circulated magazine of the period that also published pieces by other muckrakers. A native Pennsylvanian, Tarbell first gained recognition after moving to Paris where she wrote on Europe for American magazines. She returned to the United States a decade before publication of her book on Rockefeller, taking a job with *McClure's*. During her lifetime, she was one of America's most famous women, though she declined requests that she take a leadership role in the women's suffrage movement. Her best-selling books included biographies of Napoleon Bonaparte and Abraham Lincoln.

the need for war. Moreover, nearly all the major news organizations "embedded" correspondents in U.S. combat units, virtually guaranteeing that the early phase of the war would get favorable coverage.[19]

The Iraq invasion was an exception, however. Journalists are normally skeptical of politicians' motives and actions, an outlook that deepened during the Vietnam War. A turning point was the *New York Times*'s publication in 1970 of the so-called Pentagon Papers—classified documents revealing that government had deceived the public by claiming that the war in Vietnam was going well when in fact it was going badly. The Nixon administration tried to block publication of the documents but was overruled by the Supreme Court (see Chapter 4). The Watergate scandal gave journalists further reason to believe that they should not take politicians at their word. Led by investigative reporting of the *Washington Post*, the press uncovered evidence that high-ranking officials in the Nixon administration had lied about their role in the 1972 burglary of the Democratic National Committee's headquarters and the subsequent cover-up. President Richard Nixon was forced to resign, as was his attorney general, John Mitchell.

Ever since, the press usually has been quick to pounce on any sign of wrongdoing by high-ranking public officials, Democrat or Republican. *Newsweek*'s Meg Greenfield said journalists had previously believed that "the worst thing we could do . . . was [to] falsely accuse someone of wrongdoing" but now thought that "the worst, the most embarrassing, humiliating thing is not that you accuse someone falsely but that you . . . fail to accuse someone of something he ought to be accused of."[20] The list of revelations has ranged from illegal government activity (the Iran-Contra connection) during Republican Ronald Reagan's presidency to illicit personal behavior (the Monica Lewinsky scandal) during Democrat Bill Clinton's presidency.

The list now also includes the Iraq conflict. As the situation in Iraq began to deteriorate in late 2003, the press became more critical. One of its first revelations was that of abuse of prisoners by U.S. soldiers in Iraq. Graphic photos of naked Iraqi prisoners forced into humiliating sexual poses and acts shocked the nation and the world. Allegations of abuse in U.S. military prisons in Iraq had been circulating for months, but publication of the photos brought the issue into the open. High-ranking U.S. officials, including Secretary of Defense Donald Rumsfeld, had learned of the photos months earlier but had not shared the discovery with President Bush or Congress. After the photos were aired on television and published in newspapers and magazines, Congress launched hearings to discover why U.S. troops had violated laws governing the treatment of war prisoners and who should be held responsible.

In late 2005, the press led by the *New York Times* revealed that President George W. Bush, without judicial authorization, had ordered National Security Agency (NSA) wiretapping of communication originating in the United States and connecting to parties overseas. The Bush White House claimed that the story reported in the *Times* had damaged the U.S. government's ability to discover in advance whether terrorist groups were planning attacks on the United States. However, the *Times'* story put the White House on the defensive because a 1978 law expressly prohibits the type of surveillance that NSA was conducting unless authorized by a judge. Even some congressional Republicans called the Bush wiretaps illegal.

Although the value of a watchdog press is beyond question, the press has been criticized for some of its revelations. In 2008, for example, the *New York Times* ran a front-page story alleging that Republican

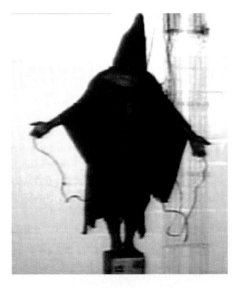

The publication of photos showing the abuse of Iraqi prisoners by U.S. soldiers undermined the U.S. government's claim that allegations about prisoner abuse were exaggerated. The press was acting in its watchdog role when it published the photos and reported on conditions in U.S. military prisons in Iraq. The news coverage led to a congressional investigation.

SHOULD REPORTERS BE PROTECTED AGAINST HAVING TO REVEAL SOURCES OF NATIONAL SECRETS?

Journalists in the nation's capital would have trouble doing their jobs if they were barred from reporting information that is given to them "off the record." Insiders who disagree with what other officials are doing or who are aware of wrongdoing are often reluctant to make that information public through the press unless their identity is shielded. In news stories, they are identified simply as "high-ranking government officials" or "anonymous sources." But what if the information they leak is classified? The leaking of classified information is a federal crime, although the reporting of it ordinarily is not. In cases where the government believes national security has been seriously harmed by a leak, should the reporter involved be required to reveal the source of the information? This question has featured prominently in public debate about two recent controversies involving the *New York Times,* whose reporters were involved in leaks surrounding the outing of a CIA covert agent (Valerie Plame) and the revelation that President George W.

Bush without judicial approval had authorized the wiretapping of overseas messages originating in the United States as part of a top-secret terrorist surveillance program. In each case, the government sought to force *Times* reporters to divulge their sources. Each time, the *Times* resisted, saying that if reporters reveal a confidential source they will not in the future be able to get sources to give them sensitive information the public needs access to.

The following statements are part of the testimony heard by the Senate Judiciary Committee when it was considering the desirability of a law that, in some circumstances, would protect journalists against having to reveal their sources. One statement is an argument in favor of such a law, while the other is in opposition to it. Where do you stand on this issue? Where would you draw the line in terms of when, if ever, journalists should be protected against having to reveal the identity of a source of classified information?

YES

The Justice Department has told you this bill is bad policy and a threat to law enforcement and national security. The implication is that when the press tells its readers, as the *Inquirer* recently did, for example—that nearby refineries are vulnerable to attack and accidents that would imperil hundreds of thousands, it is threatening national security. The threat comes not from inadequate protection of these sites, the Justice Department seems to reason, but from the use of confidential sources to reveal these types of stories. In fact, NOT publishing this material threatens national security. . . . Some of the information needed to tell such stories does indeed come from confidential sources—sources that would not speak out, leak documents, and point the way to change if it were not for the assurance of the *Inquirer's* journalists that they will be protected from reprisals. . . . Last year, in the United States, more than two dozen reporters were subpoenaed or questioned about their confidential sources in federal court cases. Six journalists from across the country were jailed or fined for refusing to disclose a source. That number may seem small to you, but consider that action against these six individuals sent doubt into the minds and spines of whistleblowers and journalists alike. . . . In sum, we can all—each of us—understand why a promise of confidentiality is crucial to disclosure. . . . What is most important here is that the wrongdoing was exposed. Wrongdoers were punished. I could give you a hundred examples. But I don't need to. You read about them every day in the newspaper. You see them on TV and hear about these promises on the radio—but you may not know that what you are hearing about is the promise of confidentiality that one journalist made to a man or woman who had a story to tell. When we hear, as a nation, about Watergate, or the fact that tobacco companies worked to make cigarettes more addictive, or that Enron was a financial nightmare, we are hearing about promises made and kept—about a pact with our forefathers that this nation would respect a free press.

—*Anne Gordon, managing editor,* **Philadelphia Inquirer**

NO

Even in cases involving harm to the national security, [the proposed bill would provide to the government] information about media sources only if it were necessary to prevent imminent and actual harm to the national security. If harm to the national security already had been done, the government would not be able to obtain the information. This may make it difficult, if not impossible, to obtain vital information on how national security information was disclosed and to whom it was disclosed. For instance, in the case of the analysis and assessment of damage to national security, where information revealed through unauthorized disclosure originated can be important in determining what has been put at risk. Not all material "leaked" in a given unauthorized disclosure may be published, but nonetheless [it] may be shared with additional parties, further compounding the damage to national security. Damage also is not always temporally confined to a given point in time; sometimes repeated disclosures magnify the impact by serving as corroboration, especially if they come from different sources. . . . [The bill has] such an expansive definition of "covered person" [i.e., journalist] [that it] could unintentionally offer a safe haven for criminals. As drafted, the definition invites criminals to cloak their activities under the guise of a "covered person," so as to avoid investigation by the Federal government. The overbroad definition of a "covered person" could be read to include any person or corporate entity whose employees or corporate subsidiaries publish a book, newspaper, or magazine; operate a radio or television broadcast station; or operate a news or wire service. Additionally, the definition arguably could include any person who sets up an Internet "blog." . . . More generally, the [Justice] Department does not believe that legislation is necessary because there is no evidence that the subpoena power is being abused by the Department in this context. The Department prides itself on its record of objectivity in reviewing press subpoenas, and any legislation that would impair the discretion of the Attorney General to issue press subpoenas—or to exercise any other investigative options in the exercise of the President's constitutional powers—is unwarranted.

—*Chuck Rosenberg, U.S. attorney on behalf of the Justice Department* presidential nominee John McCain had provided inappropriate favors for a lobbyist and might even have had a sexual relationship with her. The story, which the *Times* claimed was based on careful investigation, was in fact based on circumstantial evidence and allegation. McCain's supporters claimed that it was an attempt to smear their candidate, and the *Times* had few defenders in the mainstream press. Even the *Times'* public editor, Clark Hoyt, openly criticized the story, saying that it did not meet the *Times'* standards for publication.[21]

The Common-Carrier Function

common-carrier function

The media's function as an open channel through which political leaders can communicate with the public.

Although the American press acts as a watchdog on public officials, it also depends on them for much of its news. The press functions as a **common carrier,** serving as a conduit through which political leaders of both parties can communicate with the public. The importance of this role to officials and citizens alike is obvious. Citizens cannot very well support or oppose a leader's plans and actions if they do not know about them, and leaders require news coverage if they are to get the public's attention and support.

Indeed, national news focuses largely on the words and actions of political leaders in Washington. More than half of all national news coverage emanates from the nation's capital, most of it from the White House and Congress. Altogether, more than ten thousand people in Washington work in the news business. The key players are the leading correspondents of the television networks and the major newspapers, the heads of the Washington news bureaus, and a few top editors. The most prestigious news beat is the presidency; more than two hundred reporters are assigned to cover the White House, where they are fed press releases and regularly briefed on presidential actions. The presidency gets almost twice as much coverage in the national press as does Congress, and reporters assigned to the White House are assured of appearing regularly on the front pages, if they work in a newspaper, or at the top of newscasts, if they work in television or radio. Some of their stories are not much more than a summary of what these reporters have been told that day by White House officials.[22]

Although officials often succeed in getting favorable coverage, two things blunt their efforts to manage the news. One is journalists' norm of partisan neutrality. Although reporters depend heavily on official sources, they often present the positions of leaders of both parties—the "he said, she said" style of reporting. If the president, secretary of defense, Senate majority leader, or other high-ranking official says or does something newsworthy, the news report typically includes a contrary statement or action by another official, usually of the opposite party.

Second, although news typically originates in the words and actions of political leaders, they do not monopolize the news, particularly on television. TV news is now more journalist-centered than it is newsmaker-centered.[23] In an effort to keep their viewers tuned in, television newscasts use a fast-paced format in which each story has multiple pieces woven together in story form, with the journalist acting as the storyteller. One indicator of this format is the "shrinking sound bite" in presidential campaigns. In the 1960s, a candidate's sound bite (the length of time within a television story that a candidate speaks without interruption) was more than forty seconds on average.[24] In recent campaigns, the average sound bite has been less than ten seconds, barely enough time for the candidate to utter a long sentence (see Figure 10-2). It is the journalists, not the candidates, who do most of the talking. For every minute that Barack Obama and John McCain spoke on the network evening newscasts during the 2008 presidential campaigns, the journalists who were covering them spoke for more than five minutes.[25] Most of the time that Obama and McCain could be seen on

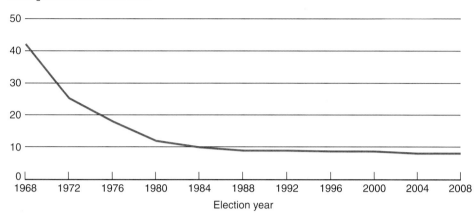

FIGURE 10-2   **The Shrinking Sound Bite of Television Campaign Coverage**   The average length of time that presidential candidates are shown speaking without interruption on broadcast television newscasts has declined sharply in recent elections.

Source: Adapted from Daniel C. Hallin, "Sound Bite News: Television Coverage of Elections 1968–1988." *Journal of Communication* 42 (Spring 1992): 6. The 1992–2008 data are from the Center for Media and Public Affairs.

the evening news with their mouth moving, their voice could not be heard; the journalist's voice was the audible one.

Journalists also say different things than public officials do. Whereas officials talk mainly about policy problems and issues, journalists talk mainly about the "game" of politics. They focus on political strategy and infighting, portraying politics as a struggle for personal power and competitive advantage. Journalists could present politics in the context of policy problems and debates, but they choose instead to present it in the context of its strategic aspects. For the journalist, the strategic context has two advantages over the policy frame. First, the give-and-take among political leaders is more easily observed and reported than are policy positions and conditions. Second, the political game is a reliable source of fresh material. Policy problems and issues do not change much from day to day, but the political game is constantly in motion.[26]

Communication scholars use the term **framing** to describe the way in which events are cast. Framing is a process of selecting certain aspects of reality and making them the most salient part of the communication, thereby conveying a particular interpretation of a situation.[27] Although the strategic game is a natural part of politics, it is an ever larger part of the news about politics because it is the frame through which journalists construct most of their political stories. In effect, the press "depoliticizes" issues, treating them more as objects of competition than as objects of serious debate.[28] The impact of this type of political coverage is substantial. Studies have found that most Americans believe that politicians spend too much time fighting among themselves and that politicians will say almost anything in order to get elected or hold onto power.[29] Although these perceptions are not entirely attributable to journalists' frame of reference, it is a major contributor.

The Partisan Function

Traditionally, the **partisan function**—acting as an advocate for a particular viewpoint or interest—has been the responsibility of political leaders, political institutions, and political organizations. Today, however, the news media—particularly the newer media—also function in that capacity.

framing

The process of selecting certain aspects of reality and making them the most salient part of the communication, thereby conveying a particular interpretation of a situation.

partisan function

Efforts by media actors to influence public response to a particular party, leader, issue, or viewpoint.

Traditional Media: Mostly Neutral

During the era of the partisan press, newspapers sought to guide their readers' opinions. In the presidential election campaign of 1896, for example, the *San Francisco Call*, a Republican newspaper, devoted 1,075 column-inches of photographs to the Republican ticket of McKinley-Hobart and only 11 inches to their Democratic opponents, Bryan and Sewell.[30] San Francisco Democrats had their own bible, the Hearst-owned *Examiner*, which touted William Jennings Bryan as the savior of working men. The emergence of objective journalism brought an end to that style of reporting. Rather than slanting the news to favor the Republican or Democratic side, journalists sought to give their audience both sides, leaving it to them to decide which one was better.

The traditional media—the daily newspapers and broadcast networks—still operate largely in this way. Of course, newspapers have long distinguished their news pages from their editorial pages. Their commitment to two-sided news reporting does not extend to their editorializing. Most newspapers side editorially with the Republican Party, though this tendency varies with national conditions. In the 2000 presidential race, for example, George W. Bush was endorsed by many more daily papers than was his Democratic opponent, Al Gore.[31] In the 2004 race, however, newspaper endorsements split more closely between Bush and the Democratic nominee, John Kerry. Some newspapers that had backed Bush in 2000 deserted him in 2004, citing the deteriorating Iraq situation as the reason.[32]

The traditional broadcast television networks—ABC, CBS, and NBC—do not endorse candidates and say they are unbiased, a claim that is sometimes disputed, particularly by conservatives. In a best-selling recent book, a former network correspondent, Bernard Goldberg, accused the networks of having a liberal agenda.[33] Such allegations are not completely baseless. Until recently, for example, the concerns of evangelical Christians were rarely a subject of broadcast news except in the context of conflict-ridden issues like creationism and abortion. There is also the fact that most broadcast news journalists, as well as most journalists generally, lean Democratic in their personal beliefs.[34]

Scholarly studies indicate, however, that the level of bias in network newscasts is small. In fact, the television-age president with the worst press coverage was a Democrat, Bill Clinton. The Center for Media and Public Affairs found that Clinton's negative coverage exceeded his positive coverage in every quarter of every year of his two-term presidency—a dubious record that no president before or since has equaled.[35]

Instead of a partisan bias, scholars have highlighted a different tendency— the networks' preference for the negative. Michael Robinson concluded that broadcast journalists have a "negativist, contentious" outlook on politics.[36] The networks' preference for "bad news" can be seen, for example, in their coverage of presidential candidates. Virtually every nominee since the 1980s has received mostly negative coverage during the course of the campaign. "Bad news" has characterized network coverage of Democratic and Republican nominees alike. In any given election, one of the nominees gets more favorable coverage than the other, but not by much and not with any partisan regularity.[37]

The news turned negative after Vietnam and Watergate—developments that convinced journalists that politicians could not be trusted—and has largely stayed that way. Studies of news coverage in the 1990s found, for example, that every high-profile agency except the Department of Defense had received more negative than positive coverage. The State Department's coverage was only 13 percent positive, and the Justice Department's coverage was just 10 percent favorable.[38] The legislative branch has fared no better. Press coverage of Congress has been steadily negative since the 1970s, regardless of which party controlled Congress or how much or little was accomplished. "Over the years," concluded scholar Mark Rozell, "press coverage of Congress has moved from healthy skepticism to outright cynicism."[39]

The networks' negativity helps to explain why they are widely perceived as biased. Research has found that negative news is perceived differently by those who support and those who oppose the politician being criticized. Opponents tend to see the criticism as valid while supporters tend to see it as unjustified and therefore biased. This reaction is heightened when people see an attack on television as opposed to reading about it in a newspaper.[40] It is not surprising, then, that Democrats during Bill Clinton's presidency tended to think that the networks favored the Republicans while Republicans during George W. Bush's presidency tended to think that the networks favored the Democrats. Such findings do not mean that the networks are completely unbiased, for they are not. The findings do indicate, however, that much of the perceived bias is in the eye of the beholder.[41]

Scholars have found a correlation between the tone of news coverage and Americans' trust and confidence in political leaders and institutions. The University of Pennsylvania's Joseph Cappella and Kathleen Hall Jamieson demonstrated, for example, that negative messages bring out feelings of mistrust of politicians and political institutions. "The effect," Cappella and Jamieson write, "occurs for broadcast as well as print news."[42] For their part, journalists acknowledge a negative slant but say that Americans are best served when the press errs on the side of criticism, even if that criticism is sometimes unfair or exaggerated. As CNN correspondent Bob Franken put it, "We historically are not supposed to be popular, and it's almost our role to be the bearer of bad news."[43]

Talk Shows: Mostly Conservative

The broadcast networks' partisan bias—real and perceived—has been an issue for conservatives at least since 1970 when Republican Vice President Spiro Agnew called the networks "nattering nabobs of negativism." Nevertheless, Republicans could only pressure the networks to cover politics differently in that there was no realistic alternative. Cable television and the rescinding of the Fairness Doctrine changed that situation by providing a host of new options, including partisan talk shows.

On both radio and television, most of the successful partisan talk shows have been hosted by conservatives. The host with the largest audience is radio's Rush Limbaugh. In the top twenty-five radio markets, Limbaugh's show has more listeners, in all age groups, than the listenership of all the top liberal talk shows combined. Limbaugh built his following in the early 1990s with attacks on Bill Clinton, whom Limbaugh variously characterized as a draft-dodger, womanizer, and wimp. When Republicans in the 1994 midterm elections won control of both the House and Senate for the first time in four decades, Limbaugh's contribution was widely heralded. "Operation Restore Democracy" was Limbaugh's label for his months-long radio campaign to get GOP candidates elected, and political conservatives went to the polls in unusually high numbers, prompting analysts to call Limbaugh the Republicans' "electronic precinct captain."

The success of Limbaugh's radio show led Roger Ailes, a Republican political consultant, to create a television version. However, Limbaugh's television talk show never caught on, and it folded in 1996 after a four-year run. Rubert

Broadcast news dominated television until the advent of cable. Today, the ABC, CBS, and NBC newscasts compete for viewers with those of Fox News, CNN, and MSNBC. Cable news organizations have also developed new models of journalism. For example, CNN specializes in live coverage of events while Fox News pursues a politically conservative news agenda. Shown here is Vice President Dick Cheney appearing on Fox News.

Murdoch then hired Ailes to run a new television network, Fox News. Murdoch reasoned that conservatives, because of discontent with the established networks, would respond to a conservative alternative. Fox's newscasts concentrate on top stories but give them a conservative touch. For example, although Fox did not ignore the postdebate polls in 2004 indicating that most Americans thought John Kerry had outdebated George W. Bush each time, Fox carried fewer debate-related stories than the other networks and was the only network to portray Bush more favorably than Kerry during the debate period.[44] Fox's talk show hosts—including Sean Hannity and Bill O'Reilly, who has the highest-rated political talk show on cable television—tilt toward the conservative side. Like the audience for political talk radio, the Fox News television audience is disproportionately Republican (see Figure 10-3). CNN's audience, which was roughly balanced between Republicans and Democrats until Fox News came along, is now heavily Democratic, as is that of MSNBC, the third-ranked cable network.

CNN and MSNBC have responded to Fox's ratings success by installing talk show hosts who lure their audiences through partisan or hard-edged appeals. MSNBC's lineup is liberal, featuring Keith Olbermann and Rachel Maddow, as well as Chris Matthews, a former Democratic

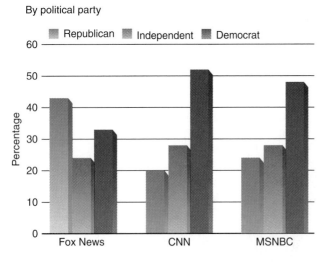

By political party

FIGURE 10-3 Cable Television News Viewers, by Party Identification As indicated by where people say they get most of their cable news, Republicans prefer Fox News while Democrats choose CNN or MSNBC.

Source: Adapted from data in "State of the Media 2008," a report of the Project for Excellence in Journalism. Percentages based only on poll respondents who identified as Republicans, Democrats, or Independents.

congressional staffer who is critical of both parties but aims his sharpest barbs at the Republicans. CNN has a more balanced lineup that includes conservative Glenn Beck, along with the less predictable but no less assertive Lou Dobbs, who has the larger audience of the two. Dobbs is perhaps best described as a populist. He rails against illegal immigrants—which appeals to conservatives—but also rails against wealthy interests and Iraq policy—which appeals to liberals.

The news outlet with the largest liberal following is National Public Radio (NPR). Its weekly audience of 20 million listeners rivals Limbaugh's, although its format is different. NPR's newscasts are based on breaking stories from AP and other news outlets, and they present a balanced view of the two parties. NPR's appeal to liberals is based on its talk shows, which, though neutral in tone, tend to focus on issues of particular concern to liberals, such as global warming.

The most popular of the stridently liberal talk shows rely on political satire to make their point. In fact, the most prominent of these shows —*The Daily Show*, *The Colbert Report*, and *Real Time with Bill Maher*—are televised on entertainment channels (Comedy Central and HBO) rather than news channels. Jon Stewart's *Daily Show*, seen by more than a million viewers each night, has the largest following. Like Limbaugh's radio talk show, which soared in the 1990s when Limbaugh feasted off the actions of Democratic President Bill Clinton, Stewart's show rose in popularity as his attacks on the policies of Republican President George W. Bush became sharper. In a telling episode, Stewart looked blankly at the television screen for seemingly endless seconds before blurting out "Please say, please say, you're kidding me." This comment followed a videotape of Bush's national security advisor, Condoleezza Rice, admitting to Congress that she had read a classified document titled "Bin Laden Determined to Attack Inside the United States" a month before the September 11, 2001, terrorist attacks on the World Trade Center and the Pentagon. Rice had earlier claimed that no one in the Bush administration could possibly have foreseen the attacks.

Unlike talk shows, where conservative viewpoints dominate, Internet blogs and comedy-based shows are bastions of liberal sentiment. Show here is *The Daily Show*'s Jon Stewart, who hosts a left-leaning news and comedy program.

The Internet: Mostly Liberal

Although the First Amendment protects each individual's right to press freedom, this right in practice was once reserved for a tiny few. Journalist A. J. Liebling wrote that freedom of the press belongs to those with the money to own a news organization.[45]

Today, because of the Internet, freedom of the press is enjoyed by a larger number of Americans than ever before. Although access to the Internet is no substitute for owning a newspaper or a television station, it does provide ordinary citizens with an opportunity to be part of the news system. Through their websites, citizens can post news and information about public affairs, harangue officials, argue for public policies, and mobilize the support of others. The Internet has reduced the barriers to public communication to a level not seen since colonial days, when pamphleteers dominated political communication. The most influential pamphleteer was Thomas Paine, whose pamphlet *Common Sense* sold over a hundred thousand copies and mobilized American opposition to British rule. "We have the power to begin the world over again," wrote Paine, who also penned the famous line "These are the times that try men's souls."

The Internet has been a boon to political mobilizers. During the 2008 presidential campaign, Barack Obama used his opposition to the Iraq war, his oratorical skill, and the power of the Internet to go from relative obscurity to the White House. Obama's campaign raised roughly $600 million, much of it through Internet contributions of less than $250. The Internet was also the medium for one of the most successful citizen-led efforts in history—a global movement that succeeded in getting nearly one hundred countries to sign an international treaty banning the use of land mines. Its organizer, Jody Williams, was awarded the Nobel Peace Prize.

The Internet has a capacity that traditional media lack: the ability to interact with its followers. During the 2008 presidential nominating campaigns, Tech-Crunch, which has nearly a half-million unique monthly visitors, polled its readers on their preferences for the Democratic and Republican nominees. TechCrunch then endorsed Barack Obama for the Democratic nomination and John McCain for the Republican nomination, urging its readers to support them with votes and campaign contributions.

When it comes to news, however, the Internet's significance is harder to pinpoint. Because the cost of entry is low, there are literally thousands of websites where news is regularly posted and examined. However, Internet news is characterized by what analysts call "the long tail." When news-based websites are arrayed by the number of visitors to each site, there are a few heavily visited sites on one end and many lightly visited sites on the other end—"the long tail." As it happens, most of the heavily visited sites are those of the traditional media, including CNN.com, nytimes.com, and MSNBC.com. In addition, most of the other heavily visited sites, such as Google News, republish news gathered and reported first by the established media. In other words, most Americans who go to the Internet for news are seeing news generated by the same sources they otherwise rely on for news.

Occasionally, a major story will originate on the Internet. Bloggers were the first to identify as forgeries the government documents CBS's Dan Rather presented during the 2004 campaign as proof that President George W. Bush had shirked his National Guard duties in the early 1970s. Within months, Rather was forced to retire prematurely as anchor of the *CBS Evening News.* Rather's departure was a source of glee for many in the blogging community. Whether liberal or conservative, bloggers tend to share a disdain for the mainstream press, which they accuse of everything from bias to irrelevance.

The special contribution of Internet-based news is that it provides an outlet for opinion, through the news commentary of bloggers and Internet users. Unlike most of the successful talk-radio programs, however, most of the successful blogs have a liberal bias. One of the largest of these sites is the *Huffington Post*, which was started by activist Arianna Huffington. Launched in 2005 as a moderately liberal site, it soon changed into an unabashedly liberal site that made President Bush its primary target. The site has more than 7 million unique visitors each month, which ranks it ahead of the news sites of several major news organizations, including CBS and the *Los Angeles Times.*

The Internet is in its early years as a news medium, so it is hazardous to guess whether initial tendencies will continue. But with Americans increasingly looking to the Internet for information, including news, it is safe to say that the Internet's importance will continue to grow.[46]

Attention to News

The U.S. news system now has more outlets—including newspapers, television stations, talk shows, and bloggers—than at any time in its history. The news system also provides a wider variety of content—everything from straight news to partisan harangues—than ever before. Although it might be assumed, as a result, that Americans are more attentive and more informed about public affairs than ever before, that is not the case. The same media system that makes news available on demand at any time also makes it relatively easy for people without an interest in news to avoid it. America today has many citizens who consume copious amounts of news. It also has many citizens who consume almost none.

The Shrinking Audience for News

The 1980s were the turning point in the shape of the news audience. Until then, and for nearly two centuries, the news audience had been enlarging. Rising literacy rates, increased urbanization, and less-expensive newspapers had widened the audience during the nineteenth century. The introduction of radio news in the early twentieth century, and the emergence of television news a few decades later, further expanded the daily news audience.

The attractiveness of television was critical to the last phase of this expansion. Americans were nearly obsessed with television in its early years and would watch most anything available. In most television markets at the dinner hour, the only choices available to viewers were the ABC newscast, the CBS newscast, and the NBC newscast. Viewers who were intent on watching television in this time slot had no alternative but to sit through the news. They constituted an "inadvertent news audience"—brought to the news less by a strong preference for it than by an addiction to television.[47]

The television news audience at its peak was enormous. At the dinner hour, most television sets in America were turned on, and 85 percent of these sets were tuned to the news. This exposure rubbed off on the children. The evening news was a ritual in many families, and though the children might have preferred something else, they, too, watched it. By the time many of these children finished school, many of them had acquired a television news habit of their own.

Television's capacity to generate an interest in news declined sharply in the 1980s with the rapid spread of cable. Viewers no longer had to sit through the news while waiting for entertainment programming to appear. Television news did not lose most of its regular viewers, but it did lose its ability to develop an interest in news among adults who preferred entertainment programming. And its capacity to generate news interest in children was greatly diminished. Fewer of their parents were watching the dinner-hour news, and even if they were watching, the children, as a Kaiser Family Foundation study revealed, were usually in another room watching entertainment shows.[48]

To be sure, some Americans were getting more news than was possible in earlier times. Round-the-clock news was available to anyone with cable TV. Yet cable also made it possible for people to avoid the news with ease. And large numbers of Americans, mostly younger adults, abandoned news for movies, sitcoms, comedy shows, and other cable programs.[49] The result was a steady decline in the broadcast news audience. Some of the drop was attributable to viewers who shifted to cable news. Even when they are accounted for, however, the absolute proportion of Americans watching television news on a daily basis dropped significantly. Newspaper circulation also declined, partly because cable TV was taking up more and more of people's media time and partly because fewer people had a daily news habit.

Age and Attention to News

Today, the daily audience for news consists disproportionately of older adults. Compared with adults thirty years of age or younger, those over fifty are three times more likely to follow public affairs closely through a newspaper—meaning they read a newspaper nearly every day and pay reasonably close attention to the news pages while doing so. The disparity is not as great with television news, but it is still a substantial one. Older adults are roughly twice as likely as young adults to watch television news almost daily and to sit through most of the newscast while doing so. Age differences shrink for Internet-based news but do not disappear. Even though older adults are somewhat less likely than young adults to access the Web, they make greater use of it as a news source. In fact, roughly half of young adults pay little or no attention on a regular basis to any news source.[50]

A few decades ago, the news habits of younger and older adults were similar. In the late 1950s, for example, 53 percent of those in the 21–29 age group regularly read news coverage of national politics, compared with 61 percent in the 30–44 age group, 60 percent in the 45–60 age group, and 57 percent of those over 60. From this evidence, Martin Wattenberg in his recent book *Is Voting for Young People?* concludes, "Young, middle aged, and old alike took in newspaper coverage at about the same rate." Wattenberg found a similar pattern for television news. Young adults were less likely in the 1960s to watch the nightly news, but not by a wide margin. "There was little variation in news viewing habits by age," Wattenberg writes. "TV news producers could hardly write off young adults, given that two out of three said they had watched such broadcasts every night."[51]

The widening age gap in news consumption has been accompanied by a widening age gap in possession of political information. Wattenberg found that, until the early 1970s, young adults were actually more knowledgeable about current events and leaders than senior citizens, which he attributed largely to differences in education. Most older citizens of that time had not graduated from high school. Since the 1980s, and increasingly so, young adults have been less informed than older ones. In 2004, for example, whereas adults sixty-five years of age and older could answer correctly 55 percent of factual questions about politics contained in the National Election Studies (NES) survey, adults under thirty years of age could answer only 36 percent of the questions accurately. In fact, young adults scored lower than all other age groups on every NES question, whether it was identification of current political leaders, information about the presidential candidates, knowledge of which party controlled Congress, or basic civic facts. The chapter of Wattenberg's book in which these findings are presented is pointedly titled, "Don't Ask Anyone Under 30."[52]

Although some analysts suggest that the Internet will lead young Americans back to the news, there is no evidence to date to support that view. Although, like television, the Internet has its addicts, the sites they choose to visit are largely determined by the interests they bring to the Web. A 2006 Pew Research Center study indicates that the Internet is not even particularly powerful in strengthening the news habit of those who use the Internet as a news source. Compared with the typical newspaper reader or television news viewer, the typical Internet-news user spends many fewer minutes per day attending to the medium's news.

Even the on-demand feature of Internet news can work against the formation of an online news habit because it breaks the link between ritual and habit. Newspaper reading, for example, is a morning ritual for some Americans—the almost unthinking stroll to the door or curb to retrieve the paper, followed by the almost unthinking opening of the paper to the preferred section. As the scholars Maria Len Rios and Clyde Bentley note, online news exposure is less fixed by time, place, and routine—elements that strengthen a habit.

The Internet cannot be faulted for the decline in news interest among young Americans. Other factors, including a weakening of the home as a place where news habits are acquired, underlie this development. Notwithstanding the cartoon father with his nose buried in the paper after a day at work, news exposure in the home was once a family affair. The newspaper sections were shared, as was the space around the radio or in front of the television set. Today, media use is largely a solitary affair, contributing to the tendency of media use to reinforce interests rather than to create new ones, including an interest in news.

Media and the Public in the Internet Age

The news media today are a greatly different political intermediary than they were only a few decades ago, and the political consequences are substantial.

The old media system was dominated by a few powerful news organizations —the broadcast networks in particular. They had a huge daily audience, enabling them to alert Americans of all ages and classes to the same events. They also

The Internet has opened up the media system, allowing citizens, groups, and leaders to communicate more powerfully than was possible during the not-so-distant era when news organizations almost totally controlled the instruments of mass communication. Shown here is a web page of Rock the Vote, an organization dedicated to helping young adults to register and vote.

provided a platform for political leaders who, through a single statement or event, could reach tens of millions of citizens. And because these media reported developments in a largely nonpartisan way, the political translation of these developments rested almost solely with political parties and interest groups, enhancing their political roles.

Today's media system is markedly different. The traditional media are still major players, but their audiences are smaller and their influence is diminished. Moreover, as they have struggled to hold onto their audience, they have "softened" their news—infusing it with more stories about celebrities, crime, and the like. The relentless search for attention-grabbing stories has always blunted the news media's ability to provide the citizens with a clear understanding of what is broadly at issue in politics. Journalist Walter Lippmann put it plainly:

> The press is no substitute for [political] institutions. It is like the beam of a searchlight that moves restlessly about, bringing one episode and then another out of darkness into vision. Men cannot do the work of the world by this light alone. They cannot govern society by episodes, incidents, and interruptions.[53]

Lippmann was writing in a slower media age. Today the "episodes, incidents, and interruptions" occur with remarkable speed, threatening the public's ability to focus on what is truly important politically. The 2008 Democratic presidential nominating race is a case in point. Even though there were major issues in that race—Iraq, the economy, and health care, to name only three—the news of the Obama-Clinton contest was filled with dozens of small controversies, as journalists seized on every misstep by the candidates or their advisers in search of new stories. Everything from Obama's minister to Clinton's trip to the Balkans a decade earlier became headline news, distracting the voters from the real issues separating the candidates.

Partisanship is also a larger part of today's news because the newer media— cable TV and the Internet—rely on it to build their audiences. If Americans were once exposed to a more or less common version of the news, they no longer are. Those citizens who depend for their news on blogs, cable programs, or talk radio get versions laden with partisan arguments. As political scientist Markus Prior shows in *Post-Broadcast Democracy*, today's media system contributes to partisan polarization. Many of the new media outlets play up partisan differences, exhalting their side while tearing down the opposing side. To be sure, the heightened partisan polarization in the electorate (Chapter 8), Congress (Chapter 11), and the presidency (Chapter 12) owes mainly to factors outside the media. Nevertheless, the current media system exacerbates partisan differences, pushing Americans further apart on key issues.

The new media system also contributes to another widening divide—the information gap between America's better-informed and less-informed citizens. The information gap, of course, is not new. At no time in the nation's history have nearly all citizens been well informed about public affairs. However, the gap is widening because today's news system makes it easier for citizens without an intrinsic interest in news to avoid it. When using the media, people can easily bypass the news if it holds little or no appeal. That development might ultimately prove to be the most important consequence of the new media system. For if citizens cannot be prompted to follow news about public affairs, the nation will one day face the larger challenge of how to maintain self-government when huge numbers of citizens know little to nothing about the policy choices their country faces.

Summary Self-Test www.mhhe.com/pattersontad9e

In the nation's first century, the press was allied closely with the political parties and helped the parties mobilize public opinion. Gradually, the press freed itself from this partisan relationship and developed a form of reporting, known as objective journalism, that emphasizes fair and accurate accounts of newsworthy developments. That model still governs the news reporting of the traditional media—daily newspapers and broadcasters—but does not hold for the newer media—radio talk shows, cable TV talk shows, and Internet blogs. Although some of them cover politics in the traditional way, many of them transmit news through a partisan lens.

The press performs four basic functions. First, in their signaling function, journalists communicate information to the public about breaking events and new developments. This information makes citizens aware of developments that impact on their lives. However, because of the media's need to attract an audience, breaking news stories often focus on developments, such as celebrity scandals, that have little to do with issues of politics and government. In a second function, that of watchdog, the press acts to protect the public by exposing deceitful, careless, or corrupt officials. Third, the press functions as a common carrier in that it provides political leaders with a channel for addressing the public. Increasingly, however, the news has centered nearly as much on the journalists themselves as the newsmakers they cover. Finally, the press functions as a partisan advocate. Although the traditional media perform this function to a degree, the newer media—the talk shows and blogs—specialize in it. Their influence has contributed to a rising level of political polarization in the United States.

The news audience has changed substantially in the past few decades. Daily newspapers and broadcast news have lost audience to cable television and the Internet. At the same time, the emergence of cable television and the Internet has made it easier for citizens to avoid news when using the media. Although some citizens today consume more news than was possible at an earlier time, other citizens—young adults in particular—consume less news than was typical at an earlier time. A consequence is that young adults are less informed politically relative to both older adults and to earlier generations of young adults.

CHAPTER 10

Study Corner

Key Terms

agenda setting (p. 252)
common-carrier function (p. 260)
framing (p. 261)
news (p. 248)
objective journalism (p.250)
partisan function (of the press) (p. 261)

partisan press (p. 249)
press (news media) (p. 248)
signaling (signaler) function (p. 252)
watchdog function (p. 256)

Self-Test

1. Recent trends in the news media include:
   a. increased government regulation of news content.
   b. combining the activities of the news and advertising departments.
   c. an increase in partisan news outlets.
   d. an increase in newspaper readership.

2. When the media are playing the role of watchdog, they are primarily:
   a. protecting the public from deceitful, careless, incompetent, or corrupt public officials.
   b. conveying objective information about an event and minimizing reporting bias.
   c. trying to get their audience more interested in world affairs.
   d. trying to help their favorite political party at the expense of the other.

3. The news is said to provide a selective depiction of reality because it:
   a. emphasizes dramatic events rather than the slow and steady social, economic, and political developments that typically have a larger impact on the nation.
   b. is biased in favor of a Democratic point of view.

c. emphasizes the daily lives of ordinary Americans rather than the actions of public officials.

d. places more emphasis on international affairs than these developments deserve.

4. The Internet has revolutionized the American media because:

a. it creates a news habit among millions of young adults who otherwise would care less about the news.

b. it has lowered dramatically the cost of starting a news-based operation, thus opening up the news system to thousands of new outlets.

c. people are willing to devote hours to news on the Internet, whereas they tend to spend only minutes when reading a newspaper or watching television news.

d. all of the above.

5. In its signaling function, the news media are trying to:

a. lure an audience.

b. advance a particular partisan interest.

c. help leaders to communicate effectively with the public.

d. bring important events, developments, and issues to the public's attention.

6. Desire for profit making and an increased share of the audience market encourage the media to:

a. prefer dramatic news stories.

b. keep public policy issues at the top of the news coverage agenda.

c. shun sensational stories.

d. provide the public with a clear understanding of what is broadly at issue in politics.

7. Objective journalism is based on the reporting of opinions in preference to "facts." (T/F)

8. The United States' libel laws strongly favor the press. (T/F)

9. Studies reveal that much of the perceived bias in television news is due to the viewers' partisanship as opposed to slanted news coverage. (T/F)

10. Liberals tend to prefer talk radio while conservatives tend to prefer bloggers. (T/F)

Critical Thinking

Why does almost every U.S. news outlet, despite having the freedom to say nearly anything it wants, cover virtually the same national stories in virtually the same way as other news organizations?

Suggested Readings

Baum, Matthew. *Soft News Goes to War.* Princeton, N.J.: Princeton University Press, 2003. A study of the impact of soft-news coverage of war.

Bennett, W. Lance, Regina G. Lawrence, and Steven Livingston. *When the Press Fails: Political Power and the News Media from Iraq to Katrina.* Chicago: University of Chicago Press, 2008. A revealing account of news coverage, particularly during the buildup to the Iraq conflict.

Bimber, Bruce A., and Richard Davis. *Campaigning Online: The Internet in U.S. Elections.* New York: Oxford University Press, 2003. A careful study of Internet use in election campaigns.

Farnsworth, Stephen J., and S. Robert Lichter. *The Mediated Presidency: Television News and Presidential Governance.* Lanham, Md.: Rowman & Littlefield, 2006. An empirical study of television coverage of the presidency.

Hamilton, James T. *All the News That's Fit to Sell.* Princeton, N.J.: Princeton University Press, 2004. A careful study of the economic influences on news content.

Mindich, David T. Z. *Tuned Out: Why Americans Under 40 Don't Follow the News.* New York: Oxford University Press, 2005. A look at the news habits of young adults.

Overholser, Geneva, and Kathleen Hall Jamieson. *The Press.* New York: Oxford University Press, 2005. A comprehensive survey of U.S. journalism and news.

Patterson, Thomas E. *Out of Order.* New York: Vintage Books, 1994. An analysis of how election news coverage has changed in recent decades.

Prior, Markus. *Post-Broadcast Democracy: How Media Choice Increases Inequality in Political Involvement and Polarizes Elections.* New York: Cambridge University Press, 2007. A thoughtful assessment of how the new media system is widening the information and partisan divides.

List of Websites

http://www.cmpa.com/

The website for the Center for Media and Public Affairs (CMPA), a nonpartisan organization that analyzes news coverage on a continuing basis, provides analyses of news content that are useful to anyone interested in the media's political coverage.

http://www.drudgereport.com/

The website through which Matt Drudge (The Drudge Report) has challenged the traditional media's control of the news.

http://www.fcc.gov/

The Federal Communications Commission (FCC) website; provides information on broadcasting regulation and current issues.

http://www.newslink.org/

A website that provides access to more than a thousand news organizations, including most U.S. daily newspapers.

Participate!

Before the Internet opened new channels of communication, freedom of the press, which is granted by the First Amendment to all Americans, was enjoyed for the most part only by the very few who owned or worked in the news media. With the Internet, the opportunity for citizen communication, though not unlimited, is greater than at any time in the nation's history. Take advantage of the opportunity. Meetup.com is one of literally thousands of Internet sites where you can participate in discussion forums about politics and issues. A more ambitious alternative is to start your own web log. Blogging is time consuming, but it allows you to create an agenda of news, information, and opinion—an activity previously reserved for newspaper editors and broadcast producers. Either of these options will enable you to make your voice heard and also help you to hone your citizenship skills—the ability to communicate, to defend your own views, and to learn what others think.

Extra Credit

For up-to-the-minute *New York Times* articles, interactive simulations, graphics, study tools, and more links and quizzes, visit the text's Online Learning Center at www.mhhe.com/pattersontad9e.

Self-Test Answers

1. c   2. a   3. a   4. b   5. d   6. a   7. F   8. T   9. T   10. F

the very few who owned or worked in the news media. With the Internet, the opportunity for citizen communication, though not unlimited, is greater than at any time in the nation's history. Take advantage of the opportunity. Meetup.com is one of literally thousands of Internet sites where you can participate in discussion forums about politics and issues. A more ambitious alternative is to start your own web log. Blogging is time consuming, but it allows you to create an agenda of news, information, and opinion—an activity previously reserved for newspaper editors and broadcast producers. Either of these options will enable you to make your voice heard and also help you to hone your citizenship skills—the ability to communicate, to defend your own views, and to learn what others think.

Extra Credit

For up-to-the-minute *New York Times* articles, interactive simulations, graphics, study tools, and more links and quizzes, visit the text's Online Learning Center at www.mhhe.com/pattersontad9e.

Self-Test Answers

1. c   2. a   3. a   4. b   5. d   6. a   7. F   8. T   9. T   10. F

NEW MEDIA AS THE MESSAGE

During Super Bowl broadcasts just days before the Super Tuesday primaries, Barack Obama appeared in a 30-second campaign ad that was unremarkable in its presentation save for three words and a number that appeared midway through the footage of the candidate surrounded by excited crowds. As Obama's long arms reached out to grasp outstretched hands, viewers received an invitation: Text HOPE to 62262.

In an around-the-clock media environment fixated on all things political, Obama has experimented with new tools for communication in a media climate so diffuse that it's difficult for any candidate to shape a message let alone hold it for a few hours. He and his team have exploited the elite media's enthusiasms for the history-making features of his campaign, while also making adroit use of technology to push information to supporters using a network that some describe as "off-line."

The people who sent text messages to the campaign that Sunday were greeted with a request to provide some information about themselves: "Welcome to Obama mobile news and updates. Reply with your ZIP code to get local Obama info."

This 2008 twist on political message delivery seized the power of two communications technologies at once: the ability of television to engage a broad audience using emotion, music, and moving images; and the capacity of text messaging to establish social links that can help transform citizen engagement into political support, one person at a time.

Campaigns understand that the quirky electronic new-media platforms can easily spark coverage or help candidates play defense against rivals. Online news aggregators collect establishment reporting but are willing to be guided by what's popular. Many blogs mix opinion with reporting and analysis. And a handful of cliquish, minutia-obsessed political websites follow hour-by-hour developments in polling, horse race predictions, and he-said/she-said sparring among rival candidates.

YouTube and the social-networking sites Facebook and MySpace did not exist as political forces four years ago, and it's anyone's guess how technology will have altered "news" dissemination and voter persuasion by 2012. It's not ridiculous to imagine computer-generated, three-dimensional hologram "candidates" conversing interactively with individual voters in their living rooms.

Obama's Internet savvy and willingness to spend millions of dollars to forge fast new electronic connections with supporters have helped his campaign to set online fundraising records, and enriched his voter-turnout organizations in key states.

Ari Fleischer, a spokesman for candidate George W. Bush during the 2000 election and later his White House press secretary, said that it's possible to get carried away in the midst of a tight, contested race. "The wonderful thing about all these changes is that you can communicate better and faster, but the enduring factor is that you have to have something to communicate," he cautioned. "You have to connect with the voters on something the voters care about. Substance and character come first, and speed comes second."

Dee Dee Myers, who writes a blog for Vanity Fair and appears as a Democratic political analyst on MSNBC, believes that Obama opponent Hillary Clinton's approach to campaign communications reflects what a twice-successful team was familiar with light-years ago. In the 1990s, the media mix was easier to peg; there was a defined news "cycle" during a 24-hour day; and it was possible to pinpoint the power hitters who controlled political information that influenced voter choices.

"A lot of people who are running Hillary Clinton's campaign came of age during Bill Clinton's campaign, so I think a lot of the approaches that they use, the way they see campaigns and the way they see the world, were defined 16, 18, 20 years ago," Myers said. "The Obama campaign culture was created in 2007, not in 1992."

Obama has demonstrated his ease with traditional news outlets and electronic media, but he has also shown his willingness to use alternative outlets. For instance, he posted a written defense of his controversial pastor, the Rev. Jeremiah Wright, on The Huffington Post a political website, before responding to the establishment press. Appearing on the Huffington site showed deference to his younger constituents, who do everything on the Web.

The public's online reactions to the Wright videos were part of the blowback that convinced the Obama campaign that an important speech about race was necessary. And the candidate's March address in Philadelphia got heavy replay of its own on YouTube and was "rebroadcast" as text and video on the mainstream media—seemingly enough exposure to blunt the intense news-industry dissection of Wright's most objectionable video excerpts. After Obama's damage-control speech, public opinion polls indicated that he held his ground with voters, with 10 primary contests left on the calendar.

Obama's approach to media and message complements his personality, his "change" agenda, and his young, educated, and tech-savvy upper-income supporters. "Obama and Clinton have different audiences, and if Hillary Clinton were just as smart about using the new media, it wouldn't do her as much good," analyst Kathleen Hall Jamieson suggested, "because it's not her natural audience. It's not as if the new media alone is able to persuade an audience and bring them in."

If Internet prowess and the swooning of young people were what it took to get to the White House, former Vermont Gov. Howard Dean or Rep. Ron Paul of Texas would have done better against their opponents. Even wealthy Mitt Romney, who tapped a documentary filmmaker, Michael Kolowich, to create a "Mitt TV" video channel for his campaign, could not overcome GOP reservations that he was inauthentic and squishy on core conservative issues.

In a blog post titled "Ten Lessons From Mitt TV," written after the former Massachusetts governor withdrew from the race, Kolowich predicted, "What we're learning from the use of tactical Web video in the 2008 presidential campaign will inform and inspire marketing and communications well beyond politics in 2008." But how a campaign can win more votes with clever videos of a flawed candidate, he did not say.

New forms of information-sharing for election purposes via the Internet, talk radio, and entertainment TV go back at least to the early 1990s, a period when the networks' news programming had already shed millions of viewers and candidates were jostling to find alternatives. Bill Clinton famously appeared on MTV and on Arsenio Hall's late-night talk show, while President George H.W. Bush, seeking a second term, resisted such exposure, believing that it was unpresidential.

Sixteen years later, presidential contenders know they need websites to present themselves. Some have turned to the Internet first to announce their candidacies. And in 2008, no leading presidential candidate would dream of rejecting an opportunity to appear before today's voter-rich talk-show audiences.

The latest research by political scientists is inconclusive about whether candidates' use of new-media technologies and approaches can or will deliver new political outcomes. Did voters turn thumbs-down when some presidential candidates thought that it was silly to answer debate questions posed via citizen-created YouTube videos, one of which featured a talking snowman? Can candidates woo new voters with personalized e-mail? With e-mail carrying videos? Will voters' opinions be shaped more by political attack ads on TV or passed around in cyberspace,

Anyone using the Internet can become a game-changer.

or by the truth-squadding of those same ads by media organizations?

"The big story of this campaign cycle is citizen-generated media," said Diana Owen, a Georgetown University political scientist. Citizen-generated media can be blogs, video, text, recordings, photos, research, pass-around issue papers, Facebook propaganda, text-messaging—virtually anything. Examples this year include the Yes We Can music video that was done for Obama but not by his campaign, and "Obama Girl," the cheeky, scantily clad young woman who appears on BarelyPolitical.com. Owen cautions, however, that these pass-around messages have not yet been transforming; mainly, they've been additives. "What does it take to move the agenda?" she asked. "At this stage, citizen-generated media still has to make it into the mainstream media."

If the diffusion of information and the individualization of political communication on the Internet enlarges participation in the political process, particularly among the 18-to-29-year-olds who year after year always seem to fall short of the turnout forecasts, that expansion could recast the types of candidates and public policies taking center stage.

Keep in mind that social networking on the Web is almost exclusively an interest of young people: 67 percent of those ages 18 to 29 have used the sites, and 27 percent said they used them to get campaign news, Pew has reported.

"This may be an audience in search of a candidacy," Jamieson said. A media era of electronic politics and interactive com-

munications could slice through the establishments of both parties. "It may wipe an entire generation out of politics," Jamieson suggested.

Some 42 percent of adults 29 and younger cite the Internet as a regular source of campaign news for the '08 race. For voters 50 and older, the Internet figure is just 15 percent but even that has doubled since 2004. The people in between also made a big leap in tapping political news on the Internet—up from 16 percent in 2004 to 26 percent now.

Because the coverage surrounding the 2008 race has been especially event-sensitive, anyone using the Internet can become a game-changer. "There's the potential for one blogger, one person with a video camera to have a huge impact," said Amy Mitchell, deputy director of the Project for Excellence in Journalism.

One final thought for 2009: How will the next president be tempted to take advantage of today's communications complexities? Will he use social-networking sites to gin up support for a bill in Congress? Will he stop begging reluctant TV networks to open their prime time to East Room speeches—and instead take every word to YouTube's POTUS channel? Obama pledged in January that if he's elected he will throw open the West Wing to C-SPAN to broadcast his negotiations with "all parties" to get health care legislation.

"We can easily put too much attention on the techniques of delivering a message, rather than focusing on the message itself," warned Martha Joynt Kumar, a Towson University scholar who writes extensively about White House communications. In politics, the new media may have become a message. But in governing, the message is still the message.

FOR DISCUSSION: How did the pervasive use of new media in the 2008 election influence the outcome of the election? How do the ways campaigns have changed their tactics hint at the ways government in general will adapt to the new environment? Will the use of new media ever be more persuasive than the political message itself?

Congress
Balancing National Goals and Local Interests

Congress as a Career:
Election to Congress

Using Incumbency to Stay
   in Congress
Pitfalls of Incumbency
Safe Incumbency and Representation
Who Are the Winners in
   Congressional Elections?

Party Leadership in Congress

House Leadership
Senate Leadership
The Power of Party Leaders

The Committee System

Committee Jurisdiction
Committee Membership
Committee Chairs
Committees and Parties: Who Is
   in Control?

How a Bill Becomes Law

Committee Hearings and Decisions
From Committee to the Floor
Leadership and Floor Action
Conference Committees and the
   President

Congress's Policymaking Role

The Lawmaking Function
   of Congress
The Representation Function
   of Congress
The Oversight Function of Congress

Congress: Too Much Pluralism?

There are two Congresses. . . . The tight-knit complex world of Capitol Hill is a long way from [the member's district], in perspective and outlook as well as in miles.

Roger Davidson and Walter Oleszek[1]

In September 2005, Congress faced the question of how to come up with the billions of dollars that would be required to rebuild New Orleans and the other Gulf Coast communities devastated by hurricane Katrina.

One option was to trim the $286-billion transportation bill that Congress had enacted a little more than a month earlier. In it were hundreds of pork-barrel projects that members of Congress had secured for their home states and districts. One such project was a bridge that came to be known as "the bridge to nowhere." Nearly the length of the Golden Gate Bridge, it would link the town of Ketchikan, Alaska (population 9,000) to Gravina Island (population 50). Its inclusion in the transportation bill was due to the power of its sponsor, Representative Don Young (R-Alaska), who chaired the House Transportation and Infrastructure Committee that oversaw the legislation. Congressman Young's project was only the most salient example. Virtually every member of Congress, House and Senate alike, had put something into the transportation bill that served constituent interests.

When commentators proposed that the projects be canceled and the money spent instead on Katrina relief, the response from Congress was a deafening no. Almost no member stepped forward to say that his or her pet project should be shelved. When a reporter asked Representative Young whether he was willing to cancel the Ketchikan-Gravina bridge, he replied, "They can kiss my ear! That's the dumbest thing I've ever heard." Young later relented, but the money for the bridge, rather than being spent in the Gulf Coast area, was shuttled to Alaska transportation officials to use on other projects in their state.

The story of Katrina and the 2005 transportation bill illustrates the dual nature of Congress. It is both a lawmaking institution for the country and a representative assembly for states and districts.[2] Members of

The U.S. Capitol in Washington, D.C., with the House wing in the foreground. The Senate meets in the wing at the right of the central rotunda (under the dome). The offices of the House and Senate party leaders—Speaker, vice president, majority and minority leaders and whips—are located in the Capitol. Other members of Congress have their offices in nearby buildings.

Congress have a duty to serve both the interests of their constituencies and the interests of the nation as a whole. The nation's needs sometimes come first, but not always. Senators and representatives depend on the voters back home to win reelection, and they seldom miss an opportunity to serve their interests.[3]

The Framers of the Constitution established Congress as the leading branch of the national government. Congress is the first institution defined in the Constitution. Moreover, Article I does not simply give to Congress the lawmaking powers of government. It grants Congress, and Congress alone, this power: "All legislative powers herein granted shall be invested in a Congress, which shall consist of a Senate and House of Representatives." Congress is granted the authority even to decide the form and function of the executive departments and the lower courts. No executive agency or lower court can exist except as authorized by Congress.

The positioning of Congress as the first among equals in a system of divided powers reflected the Framers' trust in representative institutions. Congress was to be the branch where the interests of the people, through the House of Representatives, and the interests of the states, through the Senate, would find their fullest expression, a rejection of the European monarchical model of executive supremacy. Of course, the Framers had an innate mistrust of political power and were not about to give Congress free rein. The president and the courts were granted significant checks on legislative power. Yet the government's lawmaking and representation functions, which are in combination the signature functions of a republic, were granted to Congress.

The Framers' vision of how the federal branches would operate has not withstood fully the test of time, as this chapter and subsequent chapters on the presidency and the judiciary will show. Nevertheless, an accounting of the U.S. political institutions starts naturally with Congress. This chapter examines that institution, beginning with congressional election and organization and concluding with congressional policymaking. The points emphasized in the chapter are these:

■ *Congressional elections tend to have a strong local orientation and to favor incumbents.* Congressional office provides incumbents with substantial resources (free publicity, staff, and legislative influence) that give them (particularly House members) a major advantage in election campaigns. However, incumbency also has some liabilities that contribute to turnover in congressional membership.

- *Leadership in Congress is provided by party leaders, including the Speaker of the House and the Senate majority leader.* Party leaders are in a more powerful position today than a few decades ago because the party caucuses have become more cohesive.

- *The work of Congress is done mainly through its committees and subcommittees, each of which has its separate leadership and policy jurisdiction.* The committee system of Congress allows a broad sharing of power and leadership, which serves the power and reelection needs of Congress's members but fragments the institution.

- *Congress lacks the direction and organization required to provide consistent leadership on major national policies, but it is well organized to handle policies of relatively narrow scope.* At times, Congress takes the lead on broad national issues, but ordinarily it does not do so.

- *Congress's policymaking role is based on three major functions: lawmaking, representation, and oversight.*

Congress as a Career: Election to Congress

In the nation's first century, service in Congress was not a career for most of its members. Before 1900, at least a third of the seats in Congress changed hands at each election. Most members left voluntarily. Because travel was slow and arduous, serving in the nation's capital meant spending months away from one's family. Moreover, the national government was not the center of power that it is today; many politicians preferred to serve in state capitals.

The modern Congress is a different kind of institution. Most of its members are professional politicians, and a seat in the U.S. Senate or House is as high as most of them can expect to rise in politics. The pay (about $170,000 a year) is reasonably good, and the prestige of their office is substantial, particularly if they serve in the Senate. A lengthy career in Congress is the goal of most of its members.

The chances of sustaining a career in Congress are high. Getting elected to Congress is difficult, but staying there is relatively easy. In recent decades, roughly 95 percent of House incumbents and 85 percent of Senate incumbents seeking another term have been reelected (see Figure 11-1). These figures slightly overestimate incumbents' success rate. A few incumbents each term retire from Congress rather than face a challenger they fear will beat them. On balance, however, incumbents have a commanding edge over their opponents. Most of them, particularly those in the House, win reelection by a margin of 20 percentage points or higher.

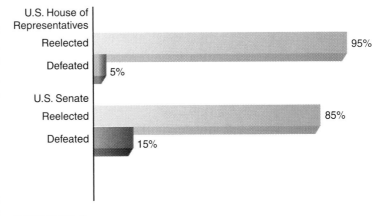

Using Incumbency to Stay in Congress

One reason incumbents run so strongly is that many congressional districts and some states are so lopsidedly Democratic or Republican that candidates of the stronger party seldom lose. In Utah and Kansas, for example, residents who identify themselves as Republicans outnumber

FIGURE 11-1 **Recent Reelection Rates of House and Senate Incumbents** Congressional incumbents have a very good chance of winning another term, as indicated by the reelection rates of U.S. representatives and senators who sought reelection during the five congressional elections from 2000 to 2008.

by a wide margin residents who identify themselves as Democrats. Massachusetts and California are examples of states where the Democrats hold a commanding majority. However, whether their constituency is lopsided or competitive, incumbents have several built-in advantages over their challengers.

The Service Strategy: Taking Care of Constituents

An incumbent promotes his or her reelection prospects by catering to the **constituency:** the body of citizens eligible to vote in the incumbent's state or district. Members of Congress pay attention to constituency opinions when choosing positions on legislation, and they work hard to get their share of **pork-barrel projects** (a term referring to legislation that funds a special project for a particular locale, such as a new highway or hospital). They also respond to their constituents' individual needs, a practice known as the **service strategy.** Whether a constituent is seeking information about a government program, expressing an opinion about pending legislation, or looking for help in obtaining a federal benefit, the representative's staff is ready to assist.

Congressional staffers spend most of their time not on legislative matters but on constituency service and public relations—efforts that pay off on election day.[4] Each House member receives an office allowance of roughly $800,000 a year with which to hire no more than eighteen permanent staff members.[5] Senators receive allowances that range between $2 million and $4 million a year, depending on the population size of the state they represent. Smaller-state senators tend to have staffs in the range of thirty people while larger-state senators have staffs closer in number to fifty people.[6] Each member of Congress is also permitted several free mailings annually to constituent households, a privilege known as the "frank." These mailings, along with press releases and other public relations efforts, help incumbents build name recognition and constituent support—major advantages in their reelection campaigns.

Campaign Fund-Raising: Raking in the Money

Incumbents also have a decided advantage when it comes to raising campaign funds. Congressional elections are expensive because of the high cost of polling, TV advertising, and other modern techniques (see Figure 11-2). Today a successful House campaign in a competitive district costs more than a million dollars. The price of victory in competitive Senate races is much higher, ranging from several million dollars in small states to $20 million or more in larger states. Rarely do incumbents say they had trouble raising enough money to conduct an effective campaign. Challengers, however, usually say their fund-raising fell far short of what they needed.[7] However, challengers, though they still trail incumbents, find it easier to attract funds when they have a chance of winning. In the 2006 midterm election, with political conditions working in their favor, Democratic challengers had a much easier time raising money than they did in the 2002 midterms, when the issues favored the Republicans.

Incumbents' past campaigns and constituent service enable them to develop mailing lists of potential contributors. Individual contributions, most of which are $100 or less, account for about 60 percent of all funds raised by congressional candidates and are obtained mainly through fund-raising events and direct-mail solicitation. Incumbents also have an edge with political action committees (PACs), which are the fund-raising arm of interest groups (see Chapter 9). Most PACs are reluctant to oppose an incumbent unless the candidate clearly is vulnerable. More than 85 percent of PAC contributions in

---

constituency

The individuals who live within the geographical area represented by an elected official. More narrowly, the body of citizens eligible to vote for a particular representative.

pork-barrel projects

Legislation whose tangible benefits are targeted at a particular legislator's constituency.

service strategy

Use of personal staff by members of Congress to perform services for constituents in order to gain their support in future elections.

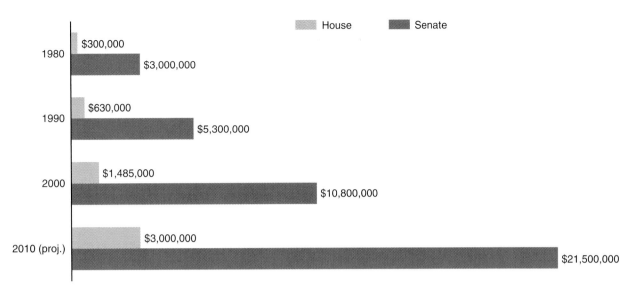

House   Senate

FIGURE 11-2 **Congressional Campaign Expenditures, by Decade** Each decade, the cost of running for congressional office has risen sharply as campaign techniques—TV advertising, opinion polling, and so on—have become more elaborate and sophisticated. The increase in spending can be seen from a comparison of the approximate average spending by both candidates per House or Senate seat at ten-year intervals, beginning in 1980. Roughly speaking, the cost has doubled each decade, which is the basis for the 2010 projection.
Source: Federal Election Commission.

recent elections have been to incumbents; their challengers received less than 15 percent (see Figure 11-3). "Anytime you go against an incumbent, you take a minute and think long and hard about what your rationale is," said Desiree Anderson, director of the Realtors PAC.[8] (A race without an incumbent—called an **open-seat election**—usually brings out a strong candidate from each party and involves heavy spending, especially when the parties are closely matched in the state or district.)

open-seat election

An election in which there is no incumbent in the race.

Redistricting: Favorable Boundaries for House Incumbents

House members, but not senators, have a final advantage in winning reelection. Because incumbents are hard to unseat, they are always a force to be reckoned with, a fact that is blatantly apparent during redistricting. Every ten years, after

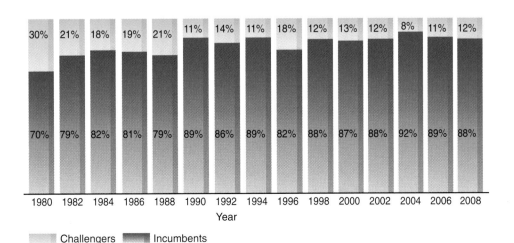

Challengers   Incumbents

FIGURE 11-3 **Allocation of PAC Contributions Between Incumbents and Challengers in Congressional Races That Included an Incumbent, 1980–2008** In allocating campaign contributions, PACs favor incumbent members of Congress over their challengers by a wide margin.
Source: Federal Elections Commission. Figures for 2008 based on preliminary data.

reapportionment

The reallocation of House seats among states after each census as a result of population changes.

redistricting

The process of altering election districts in order to make them as nearly equal in population as possible. Redistricting takes place every ten years, after each population census.

gerrymandering

The process by which the party in power draws election district boundaries in a way that is to the advantage of its candidates.

each population census, the 435 seats in the House of Representatives are reallocated among the states in proportion to their population. This process is called **reapportionment.** States that have gained population since the last census may acquire additional House seats, while those that have lost population may lose seats. New York was among the states that lost one or more House seats as a result of the 2000 census; Arizona was among the states that gained one or more seats. (The Senate is not affected by population change, because each state has two senators regardless of its size.)

The responsibility for redrawing House election districts after a reapportionment—a process called **redistricting**—rests with the state governments. States are required by law to make their districts as nearly equal in population as possible. There are many ways, however, to divide a state into districts of nearly equal size, and the party in power in the state legislature will draw the new district boundaries in ways that favor candidates of its party—a process called **gerrymandering.** The party's incumbents will be given districts packed with enough of the party's voters to ensure their reelection. What about the other party's incumbents? The safest tactic in this case is to place them in districts with overwhelming numbers of voters of their own party, assuring them of an easy victory but also reducing the number of voters of that party in other districts and placing that party at a disadvantage in these other races.

For a small number of House incumbents, redistricting threatens their reelection. When a state loses a congressional seat or seats, there may be fewer seats than there are incumbents who plan to seek another term. In this case, incumbents can end up running against each other. Moreover, the party in control of the state legislature might conclude that a particular incumbent of the opposite party can be beaten and will redraw the boundaries of the incumbent's district to the incumbent's disadvantage. Turnover in House seats typically is higher in the first election after redistricting than in subsequent elections. The newly redrawn districts include some voters who are unfamiliar with the incumbent, diminishing one advantage incumbents ordinarily enjoy over their challengers. By and large, however, incumbents do not suffer greatly from redistricting, and the great majority of them wind up in districts that virtually assure their reelection. After the 2000 census, no more than 60 of the 435 House districts were competitive in the sense that they had a relatively close balance of Republican and Democratic voters. The rest were heavily Republican or heavily Democratic.

When Massachusetts was redistricted in 1812, Governor Elbridge Gerry had the lines of one district redrawn in order to ensure that a candidate of his party would be elected. Cartoonist Elkanah Tinsdale, noting that the strangely shaped district resembled a salamander, called it a "Gerry-mander."

Pitfalls of Incumbency

Incumbency is not without its risks. In addition to the outside possibility that a House member will be placed in an unfavorable district as a result of reapportionment, potential pitfalls for Senate and House members alike include disruptive issues, personal misconduct, and variation in turnout, as well as strong challengers.

Disruptive Issues

Most elections are not waged in the context of disruptive issues, but when they are, incumbents are at greater risk. When voters are angry about existing political conditions, they are more likely to believe that those in power should be

DEBATING THE ISSUES

SHOULD PARTISAN GERRYMANDERING BE ABOLISHED?

The great majority of U.S. House districts are electorally uncompetitive, and partisan gerrymandering is a prime reason. In redrawing election district boundaries after the census, the states tend to draw the lines in ways designed to create safe Democratic or Republican districts. Of the 435 House districts today, roughly 375 are virtually beyond the reach of one party. An issue is whether partisan gerrymandering puts election of House members in the hands of the states rather than in the hands of the voters. A suit to that effect challenged the district boundaries that Pennsylvania established after the 2000 census. Fewer than 10 percent of the state's House districts are competitive. In *Vieth v. Jubelirer* (2004), the Supreme Court by a 5-4 vote refused to overturn Pennsylvania's redistricting arrangement, saying that, although there might be constitutional limits on partisan redistricting, workable standards for the judiciary to apply in determining fairness in redistricting do not exist. Following are excerpts from two amicus curiae briefs (see Chapter 14) filed in the Pennsylvania case.

YES Challengers to incumbents and third-party voters and candidates are disadvantaged when the two political parties create safe seats for themselves. "[Partisan]" gerrymandering violates the Constitution's Equal Protection Clause by intentionally discriminating against identifiable groups and diminishing those groups' political power. Congressional elections are becoming less competitive every year. . . . Over 90 percent of Americans live in congressional districts that are essentially one-party monopolies. The situation is even worse in some states. For example, in California, 50 out of 53 races were decided by margins of greater than 20 percent. In a related phenomenon, incumbents are now more than ever nearly guaranteed reelection. . . . This situation is not mere happenstance, but rather the result of carefully orchestrated political gerrymandering—sometimes by one of the major political parties to the disadvantage of the other, and sometimes by the two parties colluding to protect their seats and their incumbents. . . . [E]ven though most states are close to evenly divided between the two major political parties, the vast majority of districts for the U.S. House of Representatives are drawn so as to prevent any real competition.

—*Center for Voting and Democracy*

NO Fairness in the redistricting process [has evaded] resolution for generations. Scholars cannot even agree on such foundational points as (1) whether there is a problem at all with respect to the ability of Republicans and Democrats to compete for control of the legislature; (2) if there is a problem, whether redistricting is to blame for it; (3) whether creation of safe seats is a bad thing, and, if so, whether it can be avoided; and (4) whether neutral, nonpartisan redistricting standards are either theoretically or practically possible. . . . Justice White [once] cited the work of the late Robert G. Dixon, Jr., "one of the foremost scholars of reapportionment," for the proposition "that there are no neutral lines for legislative districts . . . every line drawn aligns partisans and interest blocs in a particular way different from the alignment that would result from putting the line in some other place." Elsewhere, Professor Dixon rebuked those of his colleagues who aspire to discover universal principles of fair representation: "My own experience tells me that although I may find nonpartisanship in heaven, in the real world, and especially in academia, there are no nonpartisans, although there may be noncombatants."

—*Leadership of the Alabama Senate and House of Representatives*

tossed out of office. In the 1994 midterm elections, when the public was upset over the economy and Democratic President Bill Clinton's leadership, more than 10 percent of congressional incumbents—more than twice the usual percentage and virtually all of them Democrats—were defeated, enabling the Republicans to gain control of the House and Senate. The 2006 midterm election, which was waged in the context of Republican President George W. Bush's leadership of an unpopular war in Iraq, also saw the defeat of more than twice the usual number of incumbents. This time, virtually all of them were Republicans, enabling the Democrats to seize control of both chambers. A prominent victim was Pennsylvania Senator Rick Santorum, who, as chair of the Republican Senate Conference, was the third-ranking member of the Republican Senate leadership. Easily reelected six years earlier, Santorum was defeated by Bob Casey, Pennsylvania's state treasurer.

Former House majority leader Tom DeLay (R-Texas) speaking to reporters. DeLay was known as the "hammer" for his ability to round up the votes necessary to drive home Republican-sponsored legislation. In 2006, months after quitting his House leadership post following accusations of wrongdoing, DeLay resigned his House seat.

Personal Misconduct

Members of Congress can also fall prey to scandal. Life in Washington can be fast-paced, glamorous, and expensive, and some members of Congress get caught up in influence peddling, sex scandals, and other forms of misconduct. Roughly a fourth of House incumbents who lost their bid for reelection in the past two decades were shadowed by ethical questions. "The first thing to being reelected is to stay away from scandal, even minor scandal," says political scientist John Hibbing.[9] Even top congressional leaders are not immune to the effects of scandal, as illustrated by the experience of former House majority leader Tom DeLay. Accused of questionable fund-raising and deal making, DeLay resigned his House seat in 2006. Another House Republican, Florida's Mark Foley, also resigned in 2006. He was discovered to have sent sexually explicit email messages to underage male congressional interns. The Foley scandal was particularly damaging to his party because it occurred within weeks of the November election, placing the GOP on the defensive at an inopportune time.

Turnout Variation: The Midterm Election Problem

Typically, the party holding the presidency loses seats in the midterm congressional elections, particularly in the House of Representatives. In only four of the last twenty-five midterm elections (including those in 1998 and 2002) has the president's party gained seats. The 2006 midterm election, when the Republicans lost seats, fit the typical pattern.

The tendency is attributable partly to the drop-off in turnout that accompanies a midterm election. The electorate in a presidential election is substantially larger than the midterm electorate. People who vote only in the presidential election tend to have weaker party affiliation and to be more responsive to the issues of the moment. These issues are likely to favor one party, which contributes to the success not only of its presidential candidate but also of its congressional candidates. In the subsequent midterm election, many of these voters stay home while those who do go the polls vote largely along party lines. Accordingly, the congressional candidates of the president's party do not get the boost they enjoyed in the previous election, and House seats are lost as a result.[10] The pattern also can be explained by the tendency of voters to frame their view of national politics in terms of their opinion of the president's performance. Presidents usually lose popularity after taking office as a result of tough policy choices or the emergence of new problems. As the president's support declines, so does the voters' inclination to support congressional candidates from the president's party.[11]

Strong Challengers: A Particular Problem for Senators

Incumbents, particularly those in the Senate, are also vulnerable to strong challengers. Except for the presidency, the Senate is the highest rung of the political ladder. Governors and House members are frequent challengers for Senate seats, and they have the electoral base, reputation, and experience to compete effectively. Moreover, the U.S. Senate lures wealthy challengers. Maria Cantwell spent $10 million of her own money to defeat Senator Slade Gorton in the state of Washington's Senate race in 2000. Cantwell made her fortune as an executive with RealNetworks, a high-tech company. Running again in 2006, Cantwell found herself in a tighter-than-expected race, partly because her opponent, Mike McGavick, was himself a millionaire executive.

House incumbents have less reason to fear strong challengers. A House seat often is not attractive enough to induce prominent local politicians, such as mayors or state legislators, to risk their political careers in a challenge to an incumbent.[12] As a result, House incumbents frequently face weak opponents with little or no government or political experience. However, the dynamic changes somewhat when the electorate is angry and wants a change in leadership. Then the party not in power has an easier time convincing potentially strong challengers to run. In 1994, when the political mood favored the Republicans, the GOP fielded a relatively strong slate of challengers, which contributed to its success in unseating Democratic incumbents. In 2006, with the parties' roles reversed, the Democrats fielded an unusually strong group of challengers and picked up House seats.

Safe Incumbency and Representation

Although incumbents can and do lose their reelection bids, they normally win easily. An effect is to reduce Congress's responsiveness to political change. Research indicates that incumbents tend to hold relatively stable policy positions during their time in office.[13] Thus, because few congressional seats normally change hands during an election, Congress normally does not change its direction all that much from election to election.

Safe incumbency weakens the public's influence on Congress. Democracy depends on periodic shifts in power between the parties to bring public policy into closer alignment with public opinion. In European democracies, incumbents tend to win or lose depending on their political party's popularity, which can change markedly from one election to the next; shifts in popularity can produce huge changes in the number of legislative seats controlled by the various parties. In the United States, incumbents often are able to overcome an adverse political climate through constituency service and other advantages of their office. In 1980, for example, the U.S. economy was beset by high levels of inflation and unemployment, but the Democrats nonetheless held onto their majority in the House of Representatives because most of the party's incumbents had enough cushion to win despite the fact that most Americans thought the country was headed in the wrong direction. A similar public mood produced a very different result in Britain's 1997 election. The governing Conservative Party went into the election with a 343-273 seat advantage over the Labour Party in the House of Commons but emerged with only 165 seats compared to Labour's 419.

It is worth noting that national legislators in other democracies do not have the large personal staffs or the travel and publicity budgets that members of Congress have. Nor do national legislators elsewhere enjoy anywhere near the inside track to campaign funding that members of Congress enjoy.

Who Are the Winners in Congressional Elections?

The Constitution places only a few restrictions on who can be elected to Congress. House members must be at least twenty-five years of age and have been a citizen for at least seven years. For senators, the age and citizenship requirements are thirty years and nine years, respectively. Senators and representatives alike must be residents of the state from which they are elected.

But if the formal restrictions are minimal, the informal limits are substantial. Congress is not a microcosm of the population. Although lawyers constitute less than 1 percent of the population, they make up a third of Congress. Attorneys enter

STATES IN THE NATION

WOMEN IN THE STATE LEGISLATURES

Women have had more success in gaining election to state legislatures than to Congress, partly because there is more turn-over and less incumbency advantage at the state level, which creates more opportunities for newcomers to run and to win. More than one in five state legislators are women, a fourfold increase since 1970. The state of Vermont, with more than 35 percent, has the highest proportion of women legislators. South Carolina, with fewer than 10 percent, has the lowest.

Q: Why do the northeastern and western regions have the most women legislators?

A: The northeastern and western regions have a higher propor-tion of college-educated women in the workforce than do other regions. College-educated women are more likely to run for pub-lic office and to actively support those who do run.

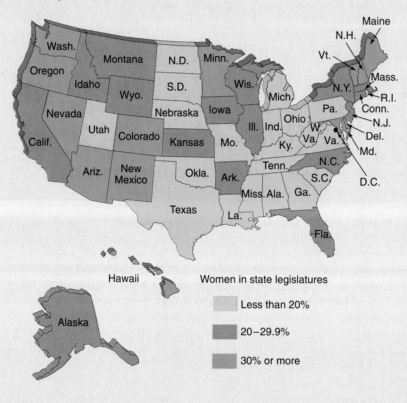

Source: Created from data gathered by the Center for the American Woman and Politics (CAWP); National Information Bank on Women in Public Office; and Eagleton Institute of Politics, Rutgers University, 2008.

politics in large numbers in part because of the central place of law in government and also because seeking elective office is a good way—even if a candidate loses—to build up a law practice. Along with lawyers, professionals such as business executives, educators, bankers, and journalists account for more than 90 percent of congressional membership.[14] Blue-collar workers, clerical employees, and home-makers are seldom elected to Congress. Farmers and ranchers are not as rare; a fair number of House members from rural districts have agricultural backgrounds.

Finally, members of Congress are disproportionately white and male. Although the number of minority-group members and women in Congress is twice that of two decades ago, each of them accounts for only about 15 percent of the members (see Chapter 5). Safe incumbency is a major obstacle to their election to Congress.[15] In open-seat races in which they have run, they have won about half the time. However, they have been no more successful than other challengers in dislodging congressional incumbents. In elections to state and local office, where incumbency is less important, women and minority candidates have made greater inroads (see "States in the Nation").

Party Leadership in Congress

The House and Senate are organized along party lines. (Table 11-1 shows the party composition in Congress during the past two decades.) Members of Congress from each party meet periodically in a **party caucus** to plan strategy and discuss their legislative goals. At the start of each two-year congressional term, the party caucus is also the venue in which party members choose their **party leaders.**

House Leadership

The Constitution specifies that the House of Representatives will be presided over by a Speaker, elected by its members. In practice, this means the Speaker will be a member of the majority party, because it has enough votes to elect one of its own to the post. Thus, when the Democrats took control of the House after the 2006 election, Nancy Pelosi, the Democrats' leader in the chamber, replaced Republican Dennis Hastert as Speaker. Pelosi is the first woman ever to serve as leader of either the House or the Senate.

The Speaker of the House is sometimes said to be the second-most-powerful official in Washington, after the president. The Speaker is active in developing the party's positions on issues and in persuading party members in the House to support these positions. Although the Speaker cannot force party members to support the party's program, they look to the Speaker for leadership. The Speaker also has certain formal powers, including the right to speak first during House debate on legislation and the power to recognize members—that is, give them permission to speak from the floor. Because the House places a time limit on floor debate, not everyone has a chance to speak on a given bill, and the Speaker can sometimes influence legislation simply by exercising the power to decide who will speak and when. The Speaker also chooses the chairperson and the majority-party members of the powerful House Rules Committee, which controls the scheduling of bills for debate. Legislation that the Speaker wants passed is likely to reach the floor under conditions favorable to its enactment; for example, the Speaker may ask the Rules Committee to delay sending a bill to the floor until there is enough support for its

party caucus

A group that consists of a party's members in the House or Senate and that serves to elect the party's leadership, set policy goals, and plan party strategy.

party leaders

Members of the House and Senate who are chosen by the Democratic or Republican caucus in each chamber to represent the party's interests in that chamber and who give some central direction to the chamber's work.

TABLE 11-1 | The Number of Democrats and Republicans in the House of Representatives and Senate, 1999–2010

	1999–2000	2001–2	2003–4	2005–6	2007–8	2009–10
House						
Democrats	212*	213	208	203	235*	256
Republicans	223	222	227	232	200	179
Senate						
Democrats	45*	51*	49	45	51*	57
Republicans	55	49	51	55	49	43

*Chamber not controlled by the president's party. Senate and House members who are independents are included in the total for the party with which they caucused.

passage. The Speaker also has other ways of influencing the work of the House. The Speaker assigns bills to committees, places time limits on the reporting of bills out of committees, and assigns members to conference committees. (The importance of these powers over committee action will become apparent later in this chapter.)

The Speaker is assisted by the House majority leader and the House majority whip, who are also chosen by the majority party's members. The majority leader acts as the party's floor leader, organizing the debate on bills and lining up legislative support. The whip has the job of informing party members when critical votes are scheduled. As voting is getting under way on the House floor, the whip will sometimes stand at a location that is easily seen by party members and let them know where the leadership stands on the bill by giving them a thumbs-up or thumbs-down signal.

The minority party also has its House leaders. The House minority leader heads the party's caucus and its policy committee and plays the leading role in developing the party's legislative positions. The minority leader is assisted by a minority whip.

Senate Leadership

In the Senate, the most important party leadership position is that of the majority leader, who heads the majority-party caucus. The majority leader's role is much like that of the Speaker of the House in that the Senate majority leader formulates the majority party's legislative agenda and encourages party members to support it. Like the Speaker, the Senate majority leader chairs the party's policy committee and acts as the party's voice in the chamber. The majority leader is assisted by the majority whip, who sees to it that members know when important votes are scheduled and ensures that the party's strongest advocates on a legislative measure are present for the debate. The Senate also has a minority leader and a minority whip, whose roles are comparable to those performed by their counterparts in the House.

Unlike the Speaker of the House, the Senate majority leader is not the chamber's presiding officer. The Constitution assigns this responsibility to the vice president of the United States. However, because the vice president is allowed to vote in the Senate only to break a tie, the vice president normally is not in the Senate chamber unless support for a bill is so closely divided that a tie vote appears possible. The Senate has a president pro tempore, who, in the absence of the vice president, has the right to preside over the Senate. President pro tempore is largely an honorary position that by tradition is held by the majority party's senior member. In any case, the presiding official has limited power, because each senator has the right to speak at any length on bills under consideration.

The Senate's tradition of unlimited debate stems mainly from its small size (only 100 members, compared with the House's 435 members). Senators like to view themselves as the equals of all others in their chamber and thus are less inclined than House members to take direction from their leadership. For this reason and others, the Senate majority leader has less influence over what the Senate does than the House Speaker has over the House's actions.

The Power of Party Leaders

Because the reelection of senators and representatives depends largely on their own efforts, they have a considerable degree of independence from their congressional leaders. Although the Speaker of the House and the Senate majority leader, as well as their counterparts in the minority party, wield considerable influence, they cannot, unlike the party leaders in European legislatures, require

HOW THE U.S. COMPARES

LEGISLATIVE LEADERSHIP AND AUTHORITY

The U.S. House and Senate are separate and coequal chambers, each with its own leadership and rules. This type of legislative structure is not found in most democracies. Many democracies, for example, have a single legislative chamber, which is apportioned by population. If the United States had an equivalent legislature, it would consist only of the House of Representatives.

Even democracies that have bicameral (two-chamber) legislatures tend to structure them differently than the U.S. Congress is structured. The U.S. Senate is apportioned strictly by geography: there are two senators from each state. Germany is among the democracies that have a chamber organized along geographical lines, but Germany's upper house (the Bundesrat) differs from the U.S. Senate. Each of the German states (known as Länder) has at least three representatives in the Bundesrat, but the more populous states have more than three representatives.

Moreover, in most bicameral legislatures, one legislative chamber has substantially less power than the other. In the British Parliament, for example, the House of Lords in some instances can slow down legislation that is passed by the House of Commons but cannot stop it from becoming law. In the German Parliament, the Bundesrat has a voice on constitutional policy issues but not on most national policy issues, and its vote can in some cases be overridden by the population-based chamber (the Bundestag). In the United States, the Senate and House are equal in their legislative powers; without their joint agreement, a law cannot be enacted.

The U.S. Congress is fragmented in other ways as well: it has elected leaders with limited formal powers, a network of relatively independent and powerful committees, and members who are free to follow or ignore other members of their party. It is not uncommon for a fourth or more of a party's legislators to vote against their party's position on important legislative issues. In contrast, European legislatures have a centralized power structure: top leaders have substantial authority, the committees are weak, and the parties are unified. European legislators are expected to support their party unless granted permission to vote otherwise on a particular bill. Legislative leadership is much easier to exercise in Europe's hierarchical parliaments than in America's "stratarchical" Congress.

Country	Form of Legislature
Canada	One house dominant
France	One house dominant
Germany	One house dominant (except on certain issues)
Great Britain	One house dominant
Israel	One house only
Japan	One house dominant
Mexico	Two equal houses
Sweden	One house only
United States	Two equal houses

their members to follow their lead (see "How the U.S. Compares"). Accordingly, the power of Senate and House leaders rests heavily on the trust placed in them by the members of their party. If they are adept at promoting ideas and building coalitions, they can exercise considerable power within their chamber. By the same token, their power can evaporate if they make a mistake that hurts their party. In 2002, Republican Senate leader Trent Lott of Mississippi resigned his post after he placed his party at the center of an unwanted controversy by publicly praising the South's segregated past.

Party leaders are in a more powerful position today than a few decades ago as a result of changes in the composition of the congressional parties. The GOP's once substantial progressive faction has been eclipsed by its conservative wing. At the same time, the Democratic Party's conservative wing, represented by its southern lawmakers, has virtually disappeared. As congressional Republicans have become more alike in their thinking and further apart from congressional Democrats, each group has found it easier to band together and stand against the opposing party.[16] Accordingly, the party leaders, working through the party caucuses, have found it easier to bring their party's lawmakers together on legislative issues. This heightened unity is evident in the pattern of *roll-call votes* (votes on which each member's vote is officially recorded, as opposed to voice

FIGURE 11-4 **Percentage of Roll-Call Votes in House and Senate in Which a Majority of Democrats Voted Against a Majority of Republicans**
Democrats and Republicans in Congress are often on opposite sides of issues; party-line voting has been relatively high since the 1980s.
Source: *Congressional Quarterly Weekly,* various dates.

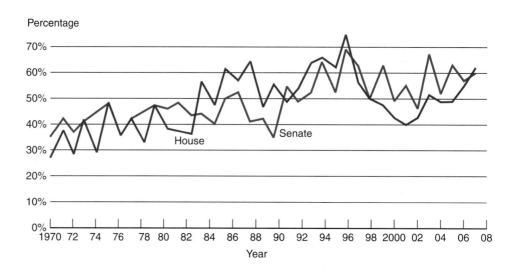

votes, where the members simply say "aye" or "nay" in unison and the presiding officer indicates which side prevails without tallying individual members' positions). Over the past three decades, party-line voting on roll calls has increased considerably (see Figure 11-4). In the 1970s, roll-call votes generally did not pit most Republicans against most Democrats. More recently, most roll-call votes have divided along party lines.

Nevertheless, most party members are secure in their reelection prospects and thus are not compelled to go along with the party leadership. Moreover, members of Congress have their own policy goals, which do not always accord with those of the party leadership. Some members also have close ties to the special interests that back their campaigns and want to help them out, which can put them at odds with the party leadership on particular issues.

The Committee System

standing committees

Permanent congressional committees with responsibility for a particular area of public policy. An example is the Senate Foreign Relations Committee.

Most of the work in Congress is conducted through **standing committees,** which are permanent committees with responsibility for a particular area of public policy. At present there are twenty standing committees in the House and sixteen in the Senate (see Table 11-2). Both the House and the Senate, for example, have a standing committee that handles foreign policy issues. Other important standing committees are those that deal with agriculture, commerce, the interior (natural resources and public lands), defense, government spending, labor, the judiciary, and taxation. House committees, which average about thirty-five to forty members each, are about twice the size of Senate committees. Each standing committee has legislative authority in that it can draft and rewrite proposed legislation and can recommend to the full chamber the passage or defeat of the legislation it considers.

Most of the standing committees have subcommittees, which specialize in some aspect of the committee's work. Altogether there are about two hundred House and Senate subcommittees, each of which has a defined jurisdiction. The House Foreign Affairs Committee, for instance, has seven subcommittees: Africa and Global Health; Asia, the Pacific, and the Global Environment; Europe; International Organizations, Human Rights, and Oversight; Middle East and South Asia; Terrorism, Nonproliferation, and Trade; and Western Hemisphere. Each House and Senate subcommittee has about a dozen members. These few individuals do most of the work and have a leading voice in the disposition of bills in their policy area.

TABLE 11-2 | The Standing Committees of Congress

House of Representatives	Senate
Agriculture	Agriculture, Nutrition, and Forestry
Appropriations	Appropriations
Armed Services	Armed Services
Budget	Banking, Housing, and Urban Affairs
Education and Labor	Budget
Energy and Commerce	Commerce, Science, and Transportation
Financial Services	Energy and Natural Resources
Foreign Affairs	Environment and Public Works
Homeland Security	Finance
House Administration	Foreign Relations
Judiciary	Health, Education, Labor, and Pensions
Natural Resources	Homeland Security and Governmental Affairs
Oversight and Government Reform	Judiciary
Rules	Rules and Administration
Science and Technology	Small Business and Entrepreneurship
Small Business	Veterans' Affairs
Standards of Official Conduct	
Transportation and Infrastructure	
Veterans' Affairs	
Ways and Means	

Congress could not possibly handle its workload without the help of its committee system. About ten thousand bills are introduced during each two-year session of Congress. The sheer volume of legislation would paralyze the institution if it did not divide the work among its various standing committees, each of which has its own staff. Unlike the members' personal staffs, which concentrate on constituency relations, the committee staffs perform an almost entirely legislative function. They help draft legislation, organize hearings, and participate in altering bills within the committee.

In addition to its permanent standing committees, Congress also has a number of *select committees,* which are created for a specific time period and purpose. A current example is the Senate Select Committee on Intelligence, which oversees the work of intelligence agencies, such as the CIA. Congress also has *joint committees,* composed of members of both houses, that perform advisory functions. The Joint Committee on the Library, for example, oversees the Library of Congress, the largest library in the world. Finally, Congress has **conference committees**—joint committees formed temporarily to work out differences in House and Senate versions of a particular bill. The role of conference committees is discussed more fully later in the chapter.

Committee Jurisdiction

The 1946 Legislative Reorganization Act requires that each bill introduced in Congress be referred by the party leaders to the proper committee. An agricultural bill introduced in the Senate must be assigned to the Senate Agriculture Committee, a bill dealing with foreign affairs must be sent to the Senate Foreign

conference committees
Temporary committees formed to bargain over the differences in the House and Senate versions of a bill. A conference committee's members are usually appointed from the House and Senate standing committees that originally worked on the bill.

jurisdiction (of a congressional committee)

The policy area in which a particular congressional committee is authorized to act.

Relations Committee, and so on. This requirement is a major source of each committee's power. Even if its members are known to oppose certain types of legislation, bills clearly within its **jurisdiction**—the policy area in which it is authorized to act—must be sent to it for deliberation.

In some cases, however, jurisdiction is subject to dispute. Which House committee, for example, should handle a major bill addressing the role of financial institutions in global trade? The Financial Services Committee? The Commerce Committee? The International Relations Committee? All committees seek legislative influence, and each is jealous of its jurisdiction, so a bill that overlaps committee boundaries can provoke a "turf war" over which committee will handle it.[17] Party leaders can take advantage of these situations by shuttling a bill to the committee that is most likely to handle it in the way they would like. But because party leaders depend on the committees for support, they cannot regularly ignore a committee that has a strong claim to a bill. At times, party leaders have responded by dividing up a bill, handing over some of its provisions to one committee and other provisions to a second committee.

Committee Membership

Each committee has a fixed number of seats, and the majority party holds most of them. The ratio of Democrats to Republicans on each committee is approximately the same as the ratio in the full House or Senate, but there is no fixed rule on this matter, and the majority party decides what the ratio will be (mindful that at the next election it could become the chamber's minority party). Members of the House typically serve on only two committees. Senators often serve on four, although they can sit on only two major committees, such as Foreign Relations and Finance.

At the start of each new term, the parties decide which of their members will serve on each committee, though reelected members by tradition are allowed to stay on committees on which they have been serving. (An exception occurs when a party loses control of the Senate and House, which will lead it also to lose committee seats, in which case some of its reelected members get bumped.) Because each committee has a fixed number of seats, a committee must have a vacancy before a new member can be appointed. Most vacancies occur after an election as a result of the retirement or defeat of committee members. Each party has a special committee in each chamber that decides who will fill committee vacancies. Several factors influence these decisions, including members' preferences. Most newly elected members of Congress ask for and receive assignment to a committee on which they can serve their constituents' interests and at the same time enhance their reelection prospects. For example, when Amy Klobuchar was elected to the Senate in 2006 from Minnesota, a state that depends heavily on the farm sector, she asked for and received an appointment to the Senate Agriculture Committee, which oversees this sector. Klobuchar's political base was in the Twin Cities area, and her position on the agricultural committee has enabled her to strengthen ties to the state's

Senators Orrin Hatch (R-Utah) and Patrick Leahy (D-Vt.) confer at a Judiciary Committee hearing. Leahy is the senior Democrat on the committee and its chair. Hatch is the committee's senior Republican. Most of the legislative work of Congress is done in committees and their subcommittees.

rural voters. Members of Congress also prefer membership on one of the more prestigious committees, such as the Senate Foreign Relations Committee and the House Ways and Means (taxation) Committee. A seat on these committees is coveted because they deal with vital issues, such as taxes and international affairs. Factors such as members' party loyalty, willingness to work hard on committee business, and length of congressional service weigh heavily in the determination of appointments to these key committees.[18]

Subcommittee assignments are handled differently. The members of each party on a committee decide who among them will serve on each of its subcommittees. The members' preferences and seniority, as well as the interests of their constituencies, are key influences on subcommittee assignments.

Committee Chairs

Each committee (as well as each subcommittee) is headed by a chairperson. The position of committee chair is a powerful one. The chair schedules committee meetings, determines the order in which committee bills are considered, presides over committee discussions, directs the committee's majority staff, and can choose to lead the debate when a committee bill reaches the floor of the chamber for a vote by the full membership.

Committee chairs are always members of the majority party and usually the party member with the most **seniority** (consecutive years of service) on the committee. Seniority is based strictly on time served on a committee, not on time spent in Congress. Thus, if a member switches committees, the years spent on the first committee do not count toward seniority on the second one. The seniority system has advantages: it reduces the number of power struggles that would occur if the chairs were decided each time by open competition, it places committee leadership in the hands of experienced members, and it enables members to look forward to the reward of a position as chair after years of service on the same committee.

The seniority system is not absolute, however, and is less controlling than in the past. There was a period when seniority was a strict rule, which led to abuses. Although most chairs were responsive to the concerns of other members, some were dictatorial. Howard Smith, an arch segregationist, chaired the House Rules Committee from 1955 to 1965 and used his position to keep civil rights legislation from reaching the House floor for a vote. During that era, a committee could not meet unless its chair called it into session, and Smith would leave Washington for his Virginia farm when a civil rights bill came to the Rules Committee, returning only if committee members agreed to withdraw the bill from consideration. Abuses by Smith and other imperious chairs led to reforms in the 1970s that reduced the power of committee chairs. Seniority was no longer an absolute rule, and a committee majority was given the power to call a committee into session if the chair refused to do so.

Committees and Parties: Who Is in Control?

In one sense, committees are an instrument of the majority party, in that it controls most of each committee's seats and appoints its chair. In another sense, each committee is a power in its own right. Committees have been described as "little legislatures," each secure in its jurisdiction, membership, and leadership, and each wielding considerable control over the legislation it handles.

Committees serve to decentralize power in Congress and to meet individual members' power and reelection needs. Less than a dozen members hold a party leadership position, but several hundred serve as committee or subcommittee

seniority
A member of Congress's consecutive years of service on a particular committee.

chairs or are "ranking members," which is the term for the minority party's committee and subcommittee leaders. In these positions, they exercise authority, often in ways that serve local constituencies or personal policy agendas—actions that may or may not be fully consistent with the party leadership's overall goals. The result is an institution very different from European parliaments, where power is concentrated in the top party leadership (an arrangement reflected even in the name for rank-and-file members: "backbenchers").

This characteristic of Congress reflects a fundamental fact. House and Senate members owe their election to their own efforts, as much as to the party's efforts, and consequently have the independence to act somewhat as they please and have an incentive to respond to constituency interests when these run counter to their party's national agenda. In 2007, when Democratic Senate leaders sought to unite their party's members behind comprehensive immigration reform, which would have allowed illegal aliens to remain in the country as guest workers and placed some of them in line for citizenship, nearly every Democratic senator from a state with strong anti-immigrant sentiment voted against the reform bill.

In an effort to strengthen the party's role, Republicans when taking control of Congress in 1995 sought to reduce the power of committees and their chairs. The Republicans passed over some senior party members in selecting the committee chairs and placed term limits on the rest. After six years, a chair or ranking member must relinquish the post. Each chair was to use the position's power to promote the goals of the party as opposed to those of individual committee members. When the Democrats took over Congress in 2007, they left the term limits in place. And in fact, during the past dozen or so years, as will be discussed at length later in the chapter, the political parties have had unusually strong control over the legislative agenda, though less than that of the parties in European legislatures.

The balance between party power and committee power, however, is an ongoing issue. The institution is at once a place for conducting the nation's business and a venue for promoting constituency interests. At times, the balance has tipped toward the committees and their leadership. At other times, it has tipped toward the parties and their leadership. At all times, there has been an attempt to achieve a workable balance of the two. The distinguishing feature of congressional power is its division among the membership, with provision for added power—sometimes more and sometimes less—in the hands of the top party leaders.

How a Bill Becomes Law

Parties, party leaders, and committees are critical actors in the legislative process. Their roles and influence, however, vary with the nature of the legislation under consideration.

Committee Hearings and Decisions

bill

A proposed law (legislative act) within Congress or another legislature.

The formal process by which bills become law is shown in Figure 11-5. A **bill** is a proposed legislative act. Many bills are prepared by executive agencies, interest groups, or other outside parties, but members of Congress also draft bills, and only they can formally submit a bill for consideration by their chamber. Once a bill is introduced by a member of the House or Senate, it is given a number and a title and is then sent to the appropriate committee, which assigns it to one of its subcommittees. Less than 10 percent of the bills that committees consider reach the floor for a vote; the others are "killed" when committees decide that they do not warrant further consideration and table them. The full House or Senate can overrule committee decisions, but this rarely occurs.

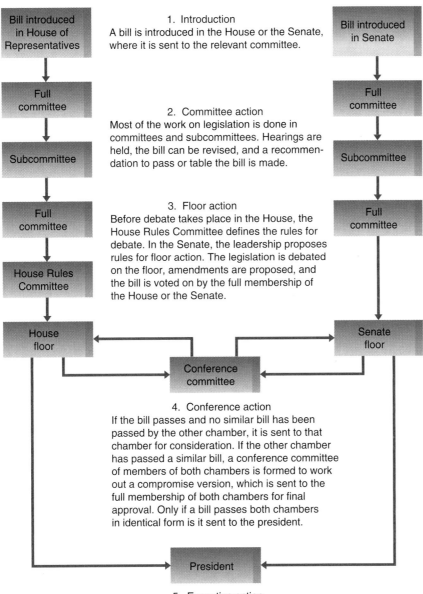

FIGURE 11-5 **How a Bill Becomes Law** Although the legislative process can be short-circuited in many ways, this diagram describes a normal way a bill becomes law.

Bill introduced in House of Representatives

Full committee

Subcommittee

Full committee

House Rules Committee

House floor

1. Introduction
A bill is introduced in the House or the Senate, where it is sent to the relevant committee.

2. Committee action
Most of the work on legislation is done in committees and subcommittees. Hearings are held, the bill can be revised, and a recommendation to pass or table the bill is made.

3. Floor action
Before debate takes place in the House, the House Rules Committee defines the rules for debate. In the Senate, the leadership proposes rules for floor action. The legislation is debated on the floor, amendments are proposed, and the bill is voted on by the full membership of the House or the Senate.

Bill introduced in Senate

Full committee

Subcommittee

Full committee

Senate floor

Conference committee

4. Conference action
If the bill passes and no similar bill has been passed by the other chamber, it is sent to that chamber for consideration. If the other chamber has passed a similar bill, a conference committee of members of both chambers is formed to work out a compromise version, which is sent to the full membership of both chambers for final approval. Only if a bill passes both chambers in identical form is it sent to the president.

President

5. Executive action
If the president signs the bill, it becomes law. A presidential veto can be overridden by a two-thirds majority in each chamber.

The fact that committees kill more than 90 percent of the bills submitted in Congress does not mean that committees exercise 90 percent of the power in Congress. A committee rarely decides fully the fate of legislation that is important to the majority party or its leadership. Most bills die in committee because they are of little interest to anyone other than a few members of Congress or are so poorly conceived that they lack merit. Some bills are not even supported by the members who introduce them. A member may submit a bill to appease a powerful constituent group and then quietly inform the committee to ignore it.

If a bill appears to have merit, the subcommittee will schedule hearings on it. The subcommittee invites testimony on the proposed legislation from lobbyists, administrators, and experts. After the hearings, if the subcommittee still feels that the legislation is needed, members recommend the bill to the full committee, which can hold additional hearings. In the House, both the full committee and a subcommittee can "mark up," or revise, a bill. In the Senate, markup usually is reserved for the full committee.

From Committee to the Floor

If a majority of the committee vote to recommend passage of the bill, it is referred to the full chamber for action. In the House, the Rules Committee has the power to determine when the bill will be voted on, how long the debate on the bill will last, and whether the bill will receive a "closed rule" (no amendments will be permitted), an "open rule" (members can propose amendments relevant to any of the bill's sections), or something in between (for example, only certain sections of the bill will be subject to amendment). The Rules Committee has this scheduling power because the House is too large to operate effectively without strict rules for the handling of legislation by the full chamber. The rules are also a means by which the majority party controls legislation. When they controlled the House in the period before 1995, Democrats employed closed rules to prevent Republicans from proposing amendments to major bills, a tactic House Republicans said they would forgo when they took control in 1995. Once in control, however, the Republicans applied closed rules to a number of major bills. The tactic was too effective to ignore.

On most House bills, only a small number of legislators are granted the opportunity to speak on the floor. In most cases, the decision as to who will speak is delegated to the bill's chief sponsor and one of the bill's leading opponents.

The Senate also has a rules committee, but it has much less power than in the House. In the Senate, the majority leader, usually in consultation with the minority leader, schedules bills. All Senate bills are subject to unlimited debate unless a three-fifths majority of the full Senate votes for **cloture,** which limits debate to thirty hours. Cloture is a way of defeating a Senate **filibuster,** which is a procedural tactic whereby a minority of senators can block a bill by talking until other senators give in and the bill is withdrawn from consideration or altered to fit opponents' demands. In late 2005, for example, Senate Democrats used the filibuster to block a vote on renewal of the USA Patriot Act, saying that they would allow it to come to a vote only if Republicans agreed to add protections of privacy rights. Three months later, Senate Democrats got the changes they wanted, and the bill passed by an overwhelming majority.

In the Senate, members can propose any amendment to any bill. That is not true in the House, where proposed amendments must directly relate to the bill's contents. Senate amendments do not have to be germane to the bill's provisions. For example, a senator may propose an antiabortion amendment to a bill dealing with defense expenditures. Such amendments are called **riders.**

Leadership and Floor Action

Committee action is usually decisive on bills that address small issues. If a majority of committee members favor such a bill, it normally is passed by the full chamber, often without amendment. In a sense, the full chamber merely votes to confirm or modify decisions made previously by committees and subcommittees. Of course, these units do not operate in a vacuum. In making its decisions, a committee takes into account the fact that its action can be reversed by the full chamber, just as a subcommittee recognizes that the full committee can overrule

---

cloture

A parliamentary maneuver that, if a three-fifths majority votes for it, limits Senate debate to thirty hours and has the effect of defeating a filibuster.

filibuster

A procedural tactic in the U.S. Senate whereby a minority of legislators prevent a bill from coming to a vote by holding the floor and talking until the majority gives in and the bill is withdrawn from consideration.

rider

An amendment to a bill that deals with an issue unrelated to the content of the bill. Riders are permitted in the Senate but not in the House.

its decision.[19] Partisanship also serves as a check on committee action. When a committee's vote is sharply divided along party lines, other members may conclude that they need to look more closely at the bill before deciding whether to vote for it.

On major bills, the majority party's leaders (particularly in the House) have increasingly set the agenda.[20] They shape the bill's broad content and work closely with the relevant committee during the bill's committee phase. Once the bill clears the committee, they often assume leadership of the floor debate. In these efforts, they depend on the ongoing support of their party's members. To obtain it, they consult their members informally and through the party caucus. **Party discipline**—the willingness of a party's House or Senate members to act as a unified group—is increasingly important in congressional action and is the key to party leaders' ability to shape major legislation. (The role of parties in Congress is discussed further in the section on Congress's representation function.)

Conference Committees and the President

For a bill to pass, it must have the support of a simple majority (50 percent plus one) of the House or Senate members voting on it. To become law, however, a bill must be passed in identical form by both the House and the Senate. About 10 percent of all bills that pass both chambers—the proportion is larger for major bills—differ in important respects in their House and Senate versions. These bills are referred to conference committees to resolve the differences. Each conference committee is formed temporarily for the sole purpose of handling a particular bill; its members are usually appointed from the House and Senate standing committees that drafted the bill. The conference committee's job is to develop a compromise version, which then goes back to the House and Senate floors for a vote. There it can be passed, defeated, or returned to conference, but not amended.

A bill that is passed in identical form by the House and the Senate is not yet a law. The president also plays a role. If the president signs the bill, it becomes **law.** If the president exercises the **veto,** the bill is sent back to Congress with the president's reasons for rejecting it. Congress can override a veto by a two-thirds vote of each chamber; the bill then becomes law without the president's signature. A bill also becomes law if Congress is in session and the president fails to sign or veto the bill within ten days (Sundays excepted). However, if Congress has concluded its term and the president fails to sign a bill within ten days, the bill does not become law. This last situation, called a *pocket veto,* forces Congress in its next term to start over from the beginning: the bill again must pass both chambers and again is subject to presidential veto.

HENRY CLAY
(1777–1852)

In the 1950s, the Senate appointed a committee to identify its most distinguished former members. Henry Clay was named the best U.S. senator in the country's history. Clay also served in the House, rising to the level of Speaker and holding the post longer than anyone else in the nineteenth century. Clay was a renowned orator, rivaled in the Senate only by Massachusetts's Daniel Webster and South Carolina's John C. Calhoun. The three men were called the "Great Triumvirate," though they were hardly of like mind politically. Clay, the moderate, sought to bridge the widening gulf between North and South. During debate over the Compromise of 1850, which he helped forge in an effort to save the Union, Clay said, "I know no North, no South, no East, no West." A person of contradictions, Clay was a slave owner and yet spoke out against slavery. He eventually emancipated nearly all of his slaves, arguing that gradual emancipation was the only thing that would save the Union. Clay's ambition was to become president of the United States, an office he sought three times, coming closest in 1844, when he lost narrowly to James K. Polk. A native of Kentucky, his influence on his home state was said to be felt even after his death in 1852. Although Kentucky was a slaveholding state, it remained in the Union when other slaveholding states seceded after Abraham Lincoln's election as president in 1860. During his lifetime, Clay had called secession an act of "treason."

party discipline

The willingness of a party's House or Senate members to act as a unified group and thus exert collective control over legislative action.

law (as enacted by Congress)

A legislative proposal, or bill, that is passed by both the House and the Senate and is not vetoed by the president.

veto

The president's rejection of a bill, thereby keeping it from becoming law unless Congress overrides the veto.

Congress's Policymaking Role

The Framers of the Constitution expected that Congress, as the embodiment of representative government, would be the institution to which the people looked for policy leadership. During most of the nineteenth century, Congress had that stature. Aside from a few strong leaders such as Andrew Jackson and Abraham Lincoln, presidents did not play a major legislative role (see Chapter 12). However, as national and international forces combined to place greater leadership and policy demands on the federal government, the president became a vital part of the national legislative process. Today Congress and the president substantially share the legislative effort, although their roles differ greatly.[21]

Congress's policymaking role revolves around its three major functions: lawmaking, representation, and oversight (see Table 11-3). In practice, the three functions overlap, but they are conceptually distinct.

The Lawmaking Function of Congress

lawmaking function

The authority (of a legislature) to make the laws necessary to carry out the government's powers.

Under the Constitution, Congress is granted the **lawmaking function:** the authority to make the laws necessary to carry out the powers granted to the national government. The constitutional powers of Congress are substantial; they include the power to tax, to spend, to regulate commerce, and to declare war. However, whether Congress takes the lead in the making of laws depends heavily on the type of policy at issue.

Broad Issues: Fragmentation as a Limit on Congress's Role

Congress is structured in a way that can make agreement on large issues difficult to obtain. Congress is not one house but two, each with its own authority and constituency base. Neither the House nor the Senate can enact legislation without the other's approval, and the two chambers are hardly two versions of the same thing. California and North Dakota have exactly the same representation in the Senate, but in the House, which is apportioned by population, California has fifty-three seats compared to North Dakota's one.

Congress also includes a lot of lawmakers: 100 members of the Senate and 435 members of the House. They come from different constituencies and represent different and sometimes opposing interests, which leads to disagreements. Nearly every member of Congress, for example, supports the principle of global free trade. Yet when it comes to specific trade provisions, members often disagree. Foreign competition means different things to manufacturers who produce automobiles, computer chips, or underwear; it means different things to farmers who produce corn, sugar, or grapes; and it means different things to firms that deal in international

TABLE 11-3 | The Major Functions of Congress

Function	Basis and Activity
Lawmaking	Through its constitutional grant to enact law, Congress makes the laws authorizing federal programs and appropriating the funds necessary to carry them out.
Representation	Through its elected constitutional officers—U.S. senators and representatives—Congress represents the interests of constituents and the nation in its deliberations and its lawmaking.
Oversight	Through its constitutional responsibility to see that the executive branch carries out the laws faithfully and spends appropriations properly, Congress oversees and sometimes investigates executive action.

finance, home insurance, or student loans. And because it means different things to different people in different parts of the country, members of Congress who represent these areas have conflicting views on when free trade makes sense.

Even when the majority party's members are more or less united, Congress can struggle to take decisive action. The Democrats found themselves in this position after they took control of the House and Senate in the 2006 election. Most of the Democrats had campaigned against the large-scale U.S. military commitment in Iraq, and they joined together on votes to reduce the American presence there. In every case, however, their efforts were blocked either by President Bush's veto, which required a two-thirds vote in each chamber to override, or by the Senate rule requiring sixty votes to invoke cloture. The fact was, the Democrats' congressional majority—which was barely over 50 percent in the Senate and not all that much larger in the House—was far too slim for them to override a presidential veto or secure cloture. Opinion polls indicated growing dissatisfaction with the performance of congressional Democrats, but in truth, they lacked the legislative votes to prevail.

For such reasons, Congress often has difficulty taking the lead on broad issues of national policy. A legislative institution can easily lead on such issues only if it grants this authority to its top leader. But Congress does not have a single leader. The House has its separate leaders, as does the Senate. Moreover, although the rise in party discipline in Congress has strengthened the role of the chambers' leaders, the fact remains that House and Senate members of the same party are still literally free to go their separate ways if they so choose. As a result, Congress sometimes struggles when faced with the task of developing a comprehensive policy response to broad national issues. In 2008, for example, Congress addressed the renewal of legislation pertaining to terrorist surveillance. The Senate backed the bill sought by the White House while the House Democratic leaders objected to a provision granting retroactive immunity to telecom companies that had provided private phone records to the government under the original legislation. This objection proved a big enough obstacle that the existing program expired. Although subsequent negotiations eventually resulted in the program's renewal, the split between the House and Senate and the split within the House among its members produced deadlock, despite wide agreement among lawmakers on the urgency of the legislation.

As an institution, the presidency is better suited to the task of providing leadership on major national issues. First, whereas Congress's authority is divided, executive power is vested constitutionally in the hands of a single individual—the president. Unlike congressional leaders, who must bargain with their members when taking a stand on legislation, the president does not have to negotiate with other executive officials in taking a position. Second, whereas members of Congress tend to see issues mainly from the perspective of their state or district, the president tends to see them from a national perspective.

News coverage also tilts national policy leadership toward the president. On national television news, the presidency gets twice the coverage of Congress, which, when it is covered, is frequently portrayed as simply responding to presidential initiatives. Former House Speaker Thomas P. "Tip" O'Neill once said that if there was only one thing he could accomplish as Speaker it would be to persuade the news media that Congress is a branch of government coequal with the president. Congress established C-SPAN, which carries House and Senate proceedings on cable television, in hopes that it would put the institution more into the national spotlight. Whatever C-SPAN's other effects, it has done little to make Americans look first to Congress for leadership on national policy issues.

Presidential leadership means that Congress normally will pay attention to White House proposals, not that it will adopt them. Congress typically accepts a

Republican Kay Bailey Hutchison was elected to the U.S. Senate from Texas in 1993 to fill the seat vacated by Lloyd Bentsen, who had resigned to become secretary of the treasury. Hutchison is among the growing number of women who sit in the U.S. Congress. Hutchison easily won her race for a third Senate term in 2006.

presidential initiative only as a starting point in its deliberations. It may reject the proposal outright—particularly when the president is from the opposing party— but any such proposal provides Congress with a tangible bill to focus on. If the proposal is at all close to what a congressional majority would regard as acceptable, Congress will use it as a baseline from which to make changes that will bring it in line with the thinking of the congressional majority. (The legislative roles of Congress and the president are discussed further in Chapter 12.)

In its lawmaking activities, Congress has the support of three congressional agencies. One is the Congressional Budget Office (CBO), which was created as part of the Budget Impoundment and Control Act of 1974. Its two hundred fifty employees provide Congress with general economic projections, overall estimates of government expenditures and revenues, and specific estimates of the costs of proposed programs. (The budgetary process is described more fully in later chapters.)

A second congressional agency is the Government Accountability Office (GAO). With three thousand employees, the GAO is the largest congressional agency. Formed in 1921, it has primary responsibility for overseeing executive agencies' spending of money that has been appropriated by Congress. The programs that the executive agencies administer are authorized and funded by Congress. The GAO's responsibility is to ensure that executive agencies operate in the manner prescribed by Congress.

The third and oldest congressional agency is the Congressional Research Service (CRS). It has a staff of one thousand employees and operates as a nonpartisan reference agency. It conducts research and responds to information requests from congressional committees and members.

Congress in the Lead: Fragmentation as a Policymaking Strength

Congress occasionally takes the lead on large issues. Labor legislation, environmental law, federal aid to education, and urban development are policy areas in which Congress has frequently taken the initiating role.[22] Social welfare is not such an area generally, but the Welfare Reform Act of 1996, which dramatically altered the shape of public assistance to the poor, was a congressional initiative (see Chapter 3). Nevertheless, Congress does not routinely develop broad policy programs and carry them through to passage. "Congress remains organized," James Sundquist notes, "to deal with narrow problems but not with broad ones."[23]

Not surprisingly, then, the great majority of the hundreds of bills that Congress considers each session deal with narrow issues. Congress has the leading role in the disposition of these particular bills, which are handled largely through the standing committees. The same fragmentation that makes it difficult for Congress to take the lead on broad issues makes it easy for Congress to tackle scores of narrow issues simultaneously. Most of the legislation passed by Congress is "distributive"—that is, it confers benefits on a particular group while spreading the costs across the taxpaying public. Veterans' benefits are one example. Such legislation, because it directly benefits a particular constituency, is a type of policy that members of Congress prefer to support. The cost of any such policy is spread so widely that taxpayers are unlikely to notice. On the other hand, the benefit is targeted so precisely that the recipients will notice and appreciate the help. Such policies are also the type that Congress, through its committee system, is organizationally best suited to handle. Most committees parallel a major constituent interest, such as agriculture, commerce, labor, or veterans.

The Representation Function of Congress

In the process of making laws, the members of Congress represent various interests within American society, giving them a voice in the national legislature. The proper approach to the **representation function** has been debated since the nation's founding. A recurrent issue has been whether the main concern of a representative should be the interests of the nation as a whole or those of his or her own constituency. These interests overlap to some degree but rarely coincide exactly. Policies that are of benefit to the full society are not always equally advantageous to particular localities and can even cause harm to some constituencies.

representation function
The responsibility of a legislature to represent various interests in society.

Representation of States and Districts

The choice between national and local interests is not a simple one, even for a legislator who is inclined toward either orientation. To be fully effective, members of Congress must be reelected time and again, a necessity that compels them to pay attention to local demands. Yet, as part of the nation's legislative body, no member can easily ignore the nation's needs. In making the choice, most members of Congress, on narrow issues at least, tend toward a local orientation.[24] Opposition to gun control legislation, for example, is much stronger among members of Congress representing rural areas where hunting weapons are commonplace.

Local representation also occurs through the committee system. Although studies indicate that committee members' preferences are not radically different from those of the full House or Senate,[25] representatives and senators typically sit on committees and subcommittees with policy jurisdictions that coincide with their constituents' interests. For example, farm-state legislators dominate the membership of the House and Senate Agriculture Committees, and westerners dominate the Interior Committees (which deal with federal lands and natural resources, most of which are concentrated in the West). Committees are also the site of most of the congressional **logrolling**—the practice of trading one's vote with another member so that both get what they want. It is not uncommon, for example, for Agriculture Committee members from livestock-producing states of the North to trade votes with committee members from the South, where crops such as cotton, tobacco, and peanuts are grown.

logrolling
The trading of votes between legislators so that each gets what he or she most wants.

Nancy Pelosi, House Democratic leader since 2002 and Speaker of the House since 2007, is the first woman in U.S. history to lead a major party in Congress. First elected to Congress in 1987 from a northern California district, Pelosi quickly made a reputation for herself as a diligent legislator and tenacious bargainer. Her father also served in the House of Representatives and later served five terms as mayor of Baltimore, where she grew up. Pelosi is shown here with other Democratic House leaders to announce a bill that had just been passed by the House of Representatives.

Nevertheless, representation of constituency interests has its limits. Constituents have little interest in most issues that come before Congress. Whether Congress should appropriate a few million dollars in foreign aid to Chad or Bolivia is not the sort of issue that local residents know and care about. Moreover, members of Congress often have no choice but to go against the wishes of a significant portion of their constituency. The interests of workers and employers in a district or state, for example, can differ considerably.

Of course, constituent groups are not the only groups that get legislators' support. The nation's capital is filled with powerful lobbies that contribute funds to congressional campaigns. These lobbying groups sometimes have as much influence with a member of Congress as do interest groups in the member's home state or district.

Representation of the Nation Through Parties

When a clear-cut and vital national interest is at stake, members of Congress can be expected to respond to that interest. With the economy showing signs of a recession in early 2008, Congress quickly enacted legislation that provided most taxpayers a rebate of several hundred dollars in the hope that they would spend it, thereby giving the economy a boost. The House voted 380-34 in favor of the tax rebate, while the Senate vote was 81-16.

In most cases, however, members of Congress, though agreeing on a need for national action, disagree on the course of action. Most Americans believe, for example, that the nation's education system requires strengthening. The test scores of American schoolchildren on standardized reading, math, and science examinations are substantially below those of children in many other industrial democracies. This situation creates pressure for political action. But what action is necessary and desirable? Does more money have to be funneled into public schools, and if so, which level of government—federal, state, or local—should provide it? Or does the problem rest with teachers? Should they be subject to higher certification and performance standards? Or is the problem a lack of competition for excellence? Should schools be required to compete for students and the tax dollars they represent? Should private schools be part of any such competition, or would their participation wreck the public school system? There is no general agreement on such issues. The quality of America's schools is of vital national interest, and quality schools would serve the common good. But the means to that end are the subject of endless dispute.

In Congress, debates over national goals occur primarily along party lines. Republicans and Democrats have different perspectives on national issues because their parties differ philosophically and politically. In the end-of-the-year budget negotiations in 1998 and 1999, for example, Republicans and Democrats were deadlocked on the issue of new funding to hire thousands of public school teachers. The initiative had come from President Clinton and was supported by congressional Democrats. But it was opposed by congressional Republicans, who objected to spending federal (as opposed to state and local) funds for that purpose and who also objected to the proposed placement of the new teachers (most of whom would be placed in overcrowded schools, most of which are in Democratic constituencies). Democrats and Republicans alike agreed that more teachers were needed, but they disagreed on how that goal should be reached. In the end, through concessions in other areas, President Bill Clinton and the congressional Democrats obtained federal funding for new teachers, but it was done so through an intensely partisan process.

Partisanship has a large influence on the president's relationship with Congress.[26] Presidents serve as legislative leaders not so much for the whole Congress as for members of their own party. Opposition and support for presidential initiatives usually divides along party lines. Accordingly, the White House's success in getting its initiatives through Congress has depended on which party controls it (see Chapter 12).

In short, any accounting of representation in Congress that minimizes the influence of party is faulty. If constituency interests drive the thinking of many members of Congress, so do partisan values. In fact, constituent and partisan influences are often difficult to separate in practice. In the case of conflicting interests within their constituencies, members of Congress naturally side with those that align with their party. When local business and labor groups take opposing sides on issues before Congress, for example, Republican members tend to back business's position, while Democratic members tend to line up with labor.

The Oversight Function of Congress

Although Congress enacts the nation's laws and appropriates the funds to implement them, the administration of these laws is entrusted to the executive branch. Congress has the responsibility to see that the executive branch carries out the laws faithfully and spends the money properly, a supervisory activity referred to as the **oversight function** of Congress.[27]

Oversight is carried out largely through the committee system of Congress and is facilitated by the parallel structure of the committees and the executive bureaucracy: the House and Senate judiciary committees oversee the work of the Department of Justice, the House and Senate Agriculture Committees monitor the Department of Agriculture, and so on. The Legislative Reorganization Act of 1970 spells out each committee's responsibility for overseeing its parallel agency:

> Each standing committee shall review and study, on a continuing basis, the application, administration, and execution of those laws, or parts of laws, the subject matter of which is within the jurisdiction of that committee.

oversight function
A supervisory activity of Congress that centers on its constitutional responsibility to see that the executive branch carries out the laws faithfully and spends appropriations properly.

Most federal programs must have their funding renewed every year, a requirement that gives Congress leverage in its ongoing oversight function. If an agency has acted improperly, Congress may reduce the agency's appropriation or tighten the restrictions on the way its funds can be spent. A major difficulty is that the House and Senate Appropriations Committees must review nearly the entire federal budget, a task that limits the amount of attention they can give any particular program.

Oversight is a challenging task. The biggest obstacle to effective oversight is the sheer magnitude of the task. With its hundreds of agencies and thousands of programs, the federal bureaucracy is beyond comprehensive scrutiny. If congressional committees were to try to monitor all the bureaucracy's activities, they would have no time to do anything else. Although Congress is required by law to maintain "continuous watchfulness" over programs, oversight normally is not pursued aggressively unless members of Congress are annoyed with an agency, have discovered that a legislative authorization is being grossly abused, or are reviewing a program for possible major changes.

POLITICAL CULTURE

LIBERTY, EQUALITY, AND SELF-GOVERNMENT

Congress and Self-Government

To the Framers of the Constitution, Congress was the first branch of government. It was through their representatives in Congress that the people would have their say on national policy. Congress was expected to be at once the symbol and the instrument of self-government. As Alexander Hamilton expressed it, "Here, sir, the people govern!"

Some analysts wonder whether that claim is as valid today as it has been in the past. The modern Congress is filled with careerists, who have the capacity to hold onto their offices indefinitely. This diminishes the ability of citizens, through their votes, to change the direction of Congress. Moreover, today's election campaigns run more on money than on citizen volunteers. While most congressional campaign money comes from small citizen contributions, significant amounts come from groups that have more access to members of Congress than do ordinary citizens. When in office, members of Congress work closely—some say too closely—with powerful lobbies.

Political scientists have not studied representative-constituency relations closely enough over a long enough time to say whether the public's influence on Congress has been declining. There is observational evidence to suggest that it has declined, but there is also evidence to the contrary, such as the increased use of polls by members of Congress as a means of determining where their constituents stand on issues of policy.

What's your sense of Congress? Do you feel its members are sufficiently in tune with constituent opinion? Regardless of how you feel, can you think of ways to bring members of Congress into closer alignment with the people they serve? How desirable is it to have a close alignment of public sentiment and congressional action? (You might find it helpful to review the distinction made in Chapter 2 between representatives as the public's trustees and representatives as the public's delegates.)

When an agency is suspected of serious abuses, a committee is likely to hold hearings. Except in cases involving *executive privilege* (the right to withhold confidential information affecting national security), executive branch officials must testify at these hearings if asked to do so. If they refuse, they can be cited for contempt of Congress, a criminal offense. Congress's investigative power is not listed in the Constitution, but the judiciary has upheld this power, and Congress uses it routinely.

Congress's zeal for oversight increases substantially when the White House is the target, provided that it's in the opposite party's hands. When hearings were held in 2006 on National Security Agency (NSA) wiretaps that were ordered by President Bush without judicial approval, the Republican-controlled Congress limited the proceedings. Congressional Republicans did not want to stage hearings that day after day would produce headlines damaging to Bush. However, after the Republicans lost control of Congress in 2007, they were powerless to prevent congressional Democrats from holding high-profile hearings. Congressional Democrats held hearing after hearing that pilloried Bush's policy.

Congress: Too Much Pluralism?

Congress is an institution divided between service to the nation and service to the separate constituencies within it. Its members have responsibility for the nation's laws, yet for reelection they depend on the voters of their states and districts and are highly responsive to constituency interests. This latter focus is facilitated by the committee system, which is organized around particular interests. Agriculture, labor, education, banking, and commerce are among the interests represented through this system. It is hard to conceive of a national legislature structured to respond to special interests more closely than is the Congress of the United States.

Pluralists admire this feature of Congress. They argue that the United States has a majoritarian institution in the presidency and that Congress is a place where a *diversity* of interests is represented. Critics reject this view, saying that Congress is sometimes so responsive to particular interests that it neglects the broader national interest. This criticism is blunted from time to time by a strong majoritarian impulse in Congress. The current period is one of those moments. The high level of party discipline in recent years, coupled with the widening ideological gap between the parties, has placed Congress at the center of national debate on Iraq, immigration, health care, and other large issues.

Yet Congress cannot easily be an institution that is highly responsive both to diverse interests and to the national interest. These interests often conflict, as the difficulty of getting agreement on immigration reform illustrates. Although nearly all members of Congress believe illegal immigration is a pressing national issue, a legislative solution has been difficult to achieve because immigration provokes sharply different views in various states and localities, depending on how they are affected by it. Members of Congress from states and districts where anti-immigration sentiment is strong are reluctant, however they might feel personally, to back legislation that runs counter to this sentiment. This inherent tension between congressional members' national role and their local electoral base has been replayed many times in U.S. history. In a real sense, the strengths of Congress are also its weaknesses. Those features of congressional election and organization that make Congress responsive to local constituencies are often the very ones that make it difficult for Congress to act as an instrument of national policy. The perennial challenge for members of Congress is to find a workable balance between what Roger Davidson and Walter Oleszek call the "two Congresses": one embodied by the Capitol in Washington, and the other by the members' separate districts and states.[28]

Summary Self-Test www.mhhe.com/pattersontad9e

Members of Congress, once elected, are likely to be reelected. Members of Congress can use their office to publicize themselves, pursue a service strategy of responding to the needs of individual constituents, and secure pork-barrel projects for their states or districts. House members gain a greater advantage from these activities than do senators, whose larger constituencies make it harder for them to build close personal relations with voters and whose office is more likely to attract strong challengers. Incumbency does have some disadvantages. Members of Congress must take positions on controversial issues, may blunder into political scandal or indiscretion, must deal with changes in the electorate, or may face strong challengers; any of these conditions can reduce members' reelection chances. By and large, however, the advantages of incumbency far outweigh the disadvantages. Incumbents' advantages extend into their reelection campaigns: their influential positions in Congress make it easier for them to raise campaign funds from PACs and individual contributors.

Congress is a fragmented institution. It has no single leader; rather, the House and Senate have separate leaders, neither of whom can presume to speak for the other chamber. The principal party leaders of Congress are the Speaker of the House and the Senate majority leader. They share leadership power with committee and subcommittee chairpersons, who have influence on the policy decisions of their committee or subcommittee.

It is in the committees that most of the day-to-day work of Congress is conducted. Each standing committee of the House or the Senate has jurisdiction over congressional policy in a particular area (such as agriculture or foreign relations), as does each of its subcommittees. In most cases, the full House and Senate accept committee recommendations about the passage of bills, although amendments to bills are quite common and committees are careful to take other members of Congress into account when making legislative decisions. Congress is a legislative system in which influence is widely dispersed, an arrangement that suits the power and reelection needs of its individual members. However, partisanship is a strong and binding force in Congress. It is the basis on which party leaders are able to build support for major legislative initiatives. On this type of legislation, party leaders and caucuses, rather than committees, are the central actors.

The major function of Congress is to enact legislation. Yet the role it plays in developing legislation depends on the type of policy involved. Because of its divided chambers and committee structure, as well as the concern of its members with state and district interests, Congress, through its party leaders and caucuses, only occasionally takes the lead on broad national issues; Congress instead typically looks to the president for this leadership. Nevertheless, presidential initiatives are passed by Congress only if they meet its members' expectations and usually only after a lengthy process of compromise and negotiation. Congress is more adept at handling legislation that deals with problems of narrow interest. Legislation of this sort is decided mainly in congressional committees, where interested legislators, bureaucrats, and groups concentrate their efforts on issues of mutual concern.

A second function of Congress is the representation of various interests. Members of Congress are highly sensitive to the state or district they depend on for reelection. They do respond to overriding national interests, but for most of them local concerns generally come first. National or local representation often operates through party representation, particularly on issues that divide the Democratic and Republican parties and their constituent groups.

Congress's third function is oversight—the supervision and investigation of the way the bureaucracy is implementing legislatively mandated programs. Although oversight is a difficult process, it is an important means of legislative control over the actions of the executive branch.

CHAPTER 11

Study Corner

Key Terms

bill (*p. 292*)
cloture (*p. 294*)
conference committees (*p. 289*)
constituency (*p. 278*)
filibuster (*p. 294*)
gerrymandering (*p. 280*)
jurisdiction (of a congressional committee) (*p. 290*)
law (as enacted by Congress) (*p. 295*)
lawmaking function (*p. 296*)
logrolling (*p. 299*)
open-seat election (*p. 279*)

oversight function (*p. 301*)
party caucus (*p. 285*)
party discipline (*p. 295*)
party leaders (*p. 285*)
pork-barrel projects (*p. 278*)
reapportionment (*p. 280*)
redistricting (*p. 280*)
representation function (*p. 299*)
rider (*p. 294*)
seniority (*p. 291*)
service strategy (*p. 278*)
standing committees (*p. 288*)
veto (*p. 295*)

Self-Test

1. General characteristics of the U.S. Congress include all **except** which one of the following?
   a. Congress is a fragmented institution.
   b. Influence in Congress is widely dispersed.
   c. Congress rather than the president usually takes the lead in addressing broad national issues.
   d. Both the House and the Senate are directly elected by the voters.

2. In Congress, the role of representation of the nation through political parties is illustrated by all **except** which one of the following?
   a. conflicts over national goals occurring primarily along party lines

   b. the emphasis that members of Congress place on pork-barrel legislation
   c. a common division of votes along party lines in committee voting
   d. Republicans aligned against Democrats on roll-call votes

3. Which of the following give(s) the president a policy-making advantage over Congress on broad national issues?
   a. the public's expectation that the president will take the lead on such issues
   b. the fragmented leadership structure of Congress
   c. the president's position as the sole chief executive and thus the authoritative voice of the executive branch
   d. all of the above

4. Which of the following factors usually plays the largest role in the reelection of members of Congress?
   a. incumbency
   b. positions taken on issues
   c. close ties to the president
   d. gender

5. Most bills that are introduced in Congress:
   a. are defeated in committee.
   b. are passed in committee and defeated on the floor.
   c. are passed and become law.
   d. are sent to executive agencies for review.

6. The most important party leadership position in the U.S. Senate is that of:
   a. Speaker.
   b. majority leader.
   c. president pro tempore.
   d. vice president of the United States.

7. Congressional incumbents receive fewer campaign contributions from PACs than their opponents do. (T/F)

8. The Speaker is the only officer of the House of Representatives provided for in the Constitution. (T/F)

9. Most of the work done in Congress is conducted through standing committees. (T/F)

10. A bill must be passed in identical form by both chambers of Congress before it can be sent to the president for approval or veto. (T/F)

Critical Thinking

How does the structure of Congress—for example, its two chambers and its committee system—affect its policymaking role?

Suggested Readings

Burden, Barry C. *Personal Roots of Representation*. Princeton, N.J.: Princeton University Press, 2007. An analysis that reveals how representatives' personal preferences affect their legislative votes.

Dwyre, Diana, and Victoria Farrar-Myers. *Legislative Labyrinth: Congress and Campaign Finance Reform*. Washington, D.C.: Congressional Quarterly Press, 2001. An inside look at the mix of Congress and campaign money.

Herrnson, Paul S. *Congressional Elections: Campaigning at Home and in Washington*, 5th ed. Washington, D.C.: Congressional Quarterly Press, 2008. A study arguing that members of Congress run two campaigns, one at home and one in Washington.

Quirk, Paul J., and Sarah A. Binder, eds. *The Legislative Branch*. New York: Oxford University Press, 2005. A comprehensive set of essays on Congress by many of the best congressional scholars.

Sidlow, Edward. *Challenging the Incumbent: An Underdog's Undertaking*. Washington, D.C.: Congressional Quarterly Press, 2003. A fascinating case study of the difficulties faced by those who dare to challenge an incumbent.

Sinclair, Barbara. *Unorthodox Lawmaking: New Legislative Processes in the U.S. Congress*, 2d ed. Washington, D.C.: Congressional Quarterly Press, 2000. A detailed analysis of the American legislative process.

Smith, Steven S., Jason M. Roberts, and Ryan J. Vander Wielen. *The American Congress*. New York: Cambridge University Press, 2007. An insightful and comprehensive examination of Congress.

Strahan, Randall. *Leading Representatives: The Agency of Leaders in the Politics of the U.S. House*. Baltimore, Md.: Johns Hopkins University Press, 2007. A study arguing that congressional leaders are powerful in their own right.

List of Websites

http://www.usafmc.org/default.asp?pagenumber=8
The website of the United States Association of Former Members of Congress, which has a "Congress to Campus" program that upon request brings former congressional members to campuses for talks.

http://thomas.loc.gov/
The Library of Congress site, named after Thomas Jefferson; provides information about the congressional process, including the status of pending legislation.

http://www.house.gov/
The U.S. House of Representatives' website; has information on party leaders, pending legislation, and committee hearings, as well as links to each House member's office and website.

http://www.senate.gov/
The U.S. Senate's website; is similar to that of the House and provides links to each senator's website.

Participate!

Each year, thousands of college students serve as interns in Congress or a state legislature. Many internships are unpaid, but students can ordinarily receive college credit for the experience. Internships are not always a great adventure. Many legislative interns envision themselves contributing ideas and research that might influence public policy, only to find that they are answering letters, developing mailing lists, or duplicating materials. Nevertheless, few interns conclude that their experience has been a waste of time. Most find it rewarding and, ultimately, memorable. Information about internships can be obtained from the American Political Science Association (www.apsa.org). In addition, there are organizations in Washington that arrange internships in Congress and the executive agencies. These organizations frequently charge a fee for their services, so you might want to contact a legislative office or executive agency directly. It is important to make your request as early as possible in the college year, because some internship programs have deadlines and nearly all offices receive more requests than they can accommodate. You could also check with the student services office at your college or university. Some of these offices have information on internship programs and can be of assistance.

Extra Credit

For up-to-the-minute *New York Times* articles, interactive simulations, graphics, study tools, and more links and quizzes, visit the text's Online Learning Center at www.mhhe.com/pattersontad9e.

Self-Test Answers

1. c 2. b 3. d 4. a 5. a 6. b 7. F 8. T 9. T 10. T

National Journal

A Rookie Congressmen: Savvy, Minus the Seniority

Freshman Rep. Peter Welch, D-Vt., knew immediately who was calling when he picked up the phone in his congressional office a few days before last year's August recess. "Pee-tah," bellowed Sen. Bernie Sanders, I-Vt., "I need your help."

Sanders was asking his successor in the House to perform a daunting task—and with less than 24 hours' notice. He wanted Welch to add to the House version of a sweeping energy bill a Sanders amendment that encouraged universities to support energy-efficiency projects. The Senate had approved the proposal—which was of great interest to environmentally friendly Vermont—but House committees had dropped it. To help Sanders, Welch would have to bump up against Energy and Commerce Committee Chairman John Dingell, D-Mich., the dean of the House who is not accustomed to taking suggestions from the Senate, let alone from a newcomer in his own chamber.

"I had to get Chairman Dingell to be agreeable," Welch recounted in a recent interview. "He agreed that I could call his committee staff, though they objected [to adding Sanders's amendment] because they wanted more leverage in the conference committee with the Senate." Ultimately, Welch used the parliamentary leverage of the Rules Committee, on which he sits, to get the provision inserted into the House-passed package, and it was part of the broader energy bill enacted in December. He explained that the feat was possible because "I had built some relationship at the Rules Committee with Mr. Dingell, who is a very gracious man."

At a time when many freshman House Democrats are worrying about a tough re-election campaign—or are still trying to find their way around the Capitol—Welch acts like a veteran. He has drawn on his background as a lawyer who served two lengthy stretches in the Vermont Senate, including eight years as

president pro tem, to comfortably maneuver through Washington's legislative channels. He has already taken on substantial energy and environmental issues and procurement reforms that Speaker Nancy Pelosi, D-Calif., and committee chairmen have highlighted in their agenda.

"He's very smart, and he takes the initiative," Oversight and Government Reform Committee Chairman Henry Waxman, D-Calif., said of Welch. "He speaks with a great deal of authority. He has a very bright future."

A veteran House Democratic leadership aide added, "It's like [Welch] has been here for years. He is connected in every way. . . .

He's always looking for something to do. He knows that it will help him to be involved."

Involved indeed. When Democrats regained control of Congress, they decided that as an inducement to serve on the Rules Committee, they would permit its members to serve on another prominent House committee as well. Welch used the opportunity to join Waxman's Oversight panel, which has wide-ranging investigative authority. The two have worked together on numerous issues.

Welch's influence was apparent, when the House passed his bill to close a potential loophole on government contracts. He initiated the measure after learning that the Justice Department had published a proposed regulation in November that would have exempted overseas contracts from federal reporting requirements. Even though Bush administration officials later acknowledged and fixed what

they described as an unintentional error, Welch said, "I don't totally trust the administration to get it right, and I'm skeptical of their explanation that this was, quote, a mistake."

Despite the administration's opposition, the House passed Welch's legislation by voice vote. Rep. Tom Davis, R-Va., the ranking member on the Oversight Committee, said he enjoyed working with Welch, and he praised the freshman's handling of the bill, including his willingness to accept some technical changes. "He is thoughtful, nice, and earnest," said a GOP aide who has watched Welch in action. "He clearly wants to learn and has respect for others' views."

At a time when many freshman House Democrats are worrying about a tough re-election campaign— **or are still trying to find their way around the Capitol**—Welch acts like a veteran.

Welch, who recalls with nostalgia the less partisan tone of the Vermont Senate, said, "My goal is to protect taxpayers. And I have more confidence that will happen when there is bipartisan agreement." Although he succeeded a socialist, Sanders, in the House, Welch takes a more pragmatic, middle-of-the-road approach. His score in National Journal's 2007 vote ratings made him the 77th-most-liberal House member, while Sanders was the fourth-most-liberal senator.

Top Democrats took notice of Welch soon after he arrived in Washington. Only a few weeks after he was sworn in, he announced that he had become the first House member to make his congressional office carbon-neutral. By providing financial support for renewable-energy projects in Vermont, he said, he was offsetting the greenhouse-gas emissions generated by his D.C. office.

After Welch discussed his actions with Pelosi aides and with Dan Beard, the House's chief administrative officer, Pelosi and other Democratic leaders announced a "greening the Capitol" initiative last June to make Congress carbon-neutral. "Peter Welch has been a leader on this issue," Pelosi said in unveiling the plan. "The House must lead by example, and Congressman Welch exemplifies this key model."

Welch has been out front on two other major energy and environmental policy initiatives. Working with co-sponsors from California, he took the lead in September in urging the Environmental Protection Agency to grant California a waiver for its stricter tailpipe-emissions standards. That issue has generated significant attention in Vermont and other states that have adopted the California standard; Vermont's attorney general spearheaded a lawsuit against EPA after Administrator Stephen Johnson rejected the application.

More recently, Welch has provided talking points to party leaders to support their call for the president to stop filling the Strategic Petroleum Reserve, because of soaring gasoline prices. With Democratic Caucus Chairman Rahm Emanuel, D-Ill., and Rep. Edward Markey, D-Mass., who chairs the Select Committee on Energy Independence and Global Warming, Welch filed a bill in February to suspend purchases for the reserve. "We should stop paying record prices to top off a reserve that is nearly full," Welch said at the time. History shows that the result will be lower oil and gas prices."

In advocating his energy proposals, Welch has cited the onerous burden of high fuel prices on his home state and what he has called the "Enron loophole" that has allowed energy speculators to "rip off" his constituents who struggle to heat their homes each winter. "My work is all about Vermont," he said.

At the Rules Committee, Welch has managed 17 House rules, which govern floor deliberations on legislation by, for instance, setting the length of debate and the amendments allowed. The panel has long been viewed as a "leadership arm" where politically secure members perform vital housekeeping tasks on behalf of majority-party leaders. Given the leadership's increasingly centralized control, entrepreneurial panel members can be highly productive, as long as their efforts are politically attuned. As the leadership aide noted, the Rules Committee freshmen are "very valuable to the speaker."

While some might find it surprising that a freshman would exert influence at the committee, which was once the bastion of more-senior members, a notable generational shift has taken place on the panel. Rules Chairwoman Louise Slaughter, D-N.Y., is the only Democratic member who served there before the party lost its majority in 1994. Of the panel's eight other Democrats, four are freshmen, two joined the House after 2002, and the two others have served a bit more than a decade.

Republicans started the move toward putting junior lawmakers on Rules when they took control in 1995, although only one GOP member was then a freshman. Perhaps the GOP's most significant internal change at Rules came in 2005, when four veteran members departed to join Ways and Means, Energy and Commerce, and other more-influential House panels. Asked about the exodus from the supposedly prestigious panel, Rep. Deborah Pryce, R-Ohio, said at the time that sitting on the Rules Committee limits members because they "don't get involved as much in the substance" of legislation.

Some committee veterans have viewed these moves with dismay as a downgrading of the panel's influence. "The result is good for individual members, but it distracts from the prestige that the Rules Committee once had," said Don Wolfensberger, a former GOP chief of staff at Rules who is now director of the Congress Project at the Woodrow Wilson International Center for Scholars.

So far, the Rules Committee has clearly been "good" for Welch. But he is modest in refusing to discuss his prospects for advancing in the House. "This is a target-rich environment," he said. "I am philosophical. We work hard, and things will take care of themselves."

He reacted with mock horror to the suggestion that he might be in line to succeed either of his home-state senators, each of whom is several years older than he. "That gets me in trouble," Welch said. "I am very, very friendly with Patrick [Leahy] and Bernie. We have an excellent working relationship. . . . Patrick's seniority has been very helpful to me." In particular, Leahy, who chairs the Judiciary Committee, has told Welch that he enthusiastically supports his contractor-abuse measure and wants to secure Senate passage.

Although Welch noted, "I am old for a freshman," he said his age adds to his comfort level. "I am settled and I don't look at other rungs on the ladder." The death in 2004 of his wife, Joan Smith—who was a dean at the University of Vermont—after a long struggle with cancer "gave me perspective," he added. "She was from Chicago and she loved politics. She would love Congress." Welch appears to be drawing pleasure for the two of them.

FOR DISCUSSION: Will the informal legislative system in which seniority rules and influence are traded back and forth remain an inevitable aspect of Congress?

Will future newcomers to Congress experience similar difficulties in getting things done?

How would you navigate the complicated hierarchy of the House of Representatives to serve your constituents and push your agenda?

CHAPTER 12

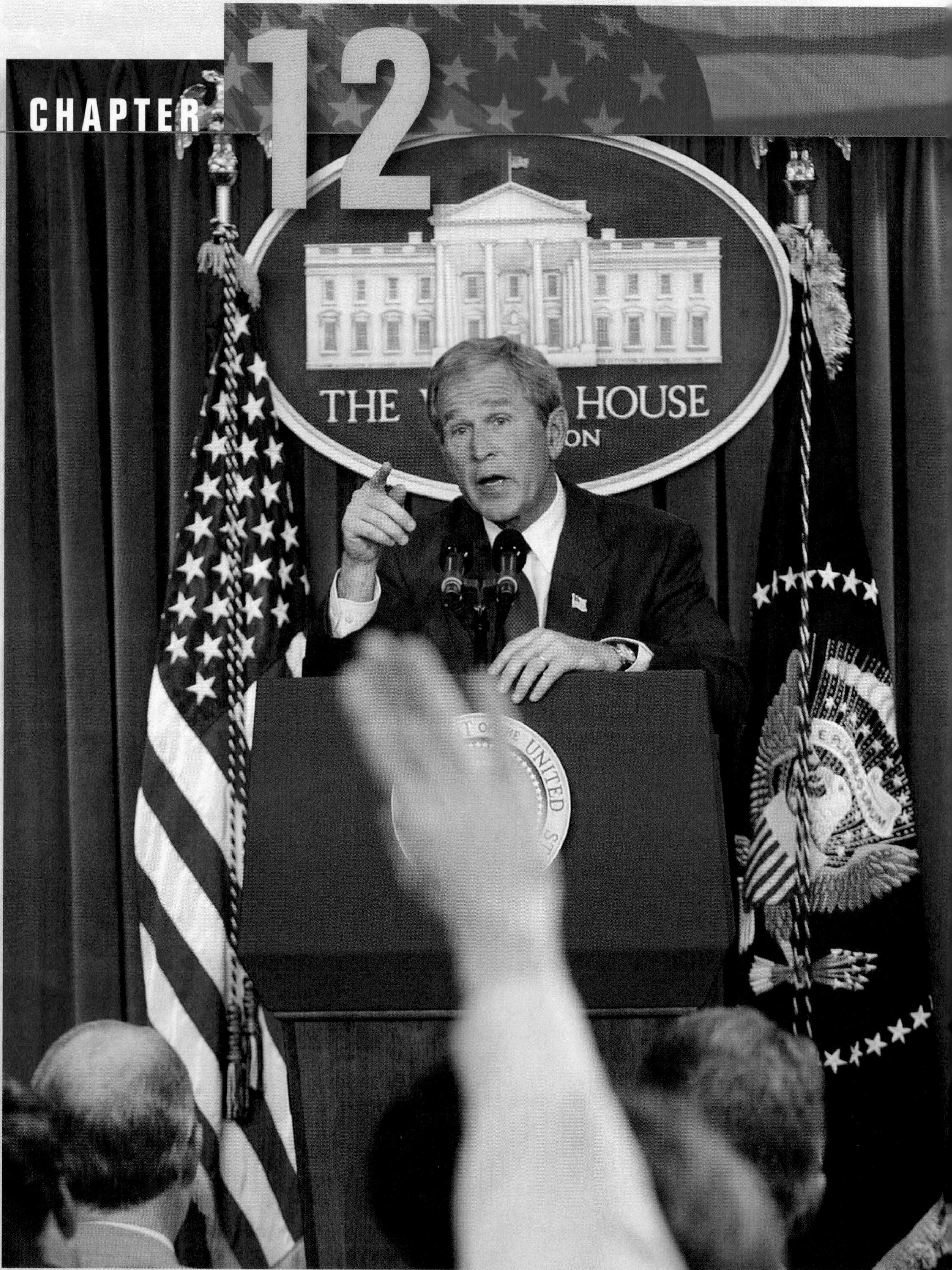

The Presidency
Leading the Nation

Foundations of the Modern Presidency
- Asserting a Claim to National Leadership
- The Need for Presidential Leadership of an Activist Government

Choosing the President
- The Primary Elections
- The National Party Conventions
- The Campaign for Election

Staffing the Presidency
- Presidential Appointees
- The Problem of Control

Factors in Presidential Leadership
- The Force of Circumstance
- The Stage of the President's Term
- The Nature of the Issue: Foreign or Domestic
- Relations with Congress
- Public Support

[The president's] is the only voice in national affairs. Let him once win the admiration and confidence of the people, and no other single voice will easily overpower him.

Woodrow Wilson[1]

George W. Bush was sinking in the polls. The economy was weakening, and the newly elected Bush was being criticized for not doing enough to reverse the downturn. Bush was also getting heat for the defection of Senator James Jeffords of Vermont, which cost Republicans control of the Senate. The news media had given him the honeymoon period traditionally accorded a new president, but they were now turning on him.

Everything changed on September 11, 2001. After the terrorist attacks on the World Trade Center and the Pentagon, Americans rallied around their president. Bush vowed that America would not rest until the terrorists were brought to justice. His presidential approval rating reached 96 percent, the highest level ever recorded. Not even Franklin Roosevelt had received approval ratings that high during the Second World War. During the next two years, buoyed by public support, Bush led the nation into wars in Afghanistan and Iraq as part of his "war on terrorism."

Three years later, everything had changed again for President Bush. The U.S. invasion of Iraq was followed by problems the Bush administration had not anticipated. Ongoing civil strife, continued attacks on U.S. forces, a failure to find weapons of mass destruction, abuses of Iraqi prisoners by U.S. soldiers, and the escalating financial cost of Iraq's reconstruction were eroding his public support. Bush was able to win reelection in 2004, but his victory was by the smallest margin for an incumbent since Harry Truman's victory in 1948. Bush's reelection gave him a boost in the opinion polls, but it was short-lived. By early 2005, his approval rating was dropping again, and it eventually fell below 30 percent, one of the lowest levels ever recorded.

The Bush story is but one in the saga of the ups and downs of the modern presidency. Lyndon Johnson's and Richard Nixon's dogged pursuit of the Vietnam War led to talk of "the imperial presidency," an office so powerful that constitutional checks and balances were no longer an effective constraint on it. Within a few years, because of the undermining effects of Watergate and of changing international conditions during the Ford and Carter presidencies, the watchword became "the imperiled presidency," an office too weak to meet the nation's demands for executive leadership. Ronald Reagan's policy successes prior to 1986 renewed talk heard in the Roosevelt and Kennedy years of "a heroic presidency," an office that is the inspirational center of American politics. After the Iran-Contra scandal in 1986, Reagan was more often called a lame duck. The first George Bush's handling of the Gulf crisis—leading the nation in 1991 into a major war and emerging from it with a stratospheric public approval rating—bolstered the heroic conception of the office. A year later, Bush was defeated in his campaign for a second term. Bill Clinton overcame a fitful start to his presidency to become the first Democrat since Franklin D. Roosevelt in the 1930s to win reelection. As Clinton was launching an aggressive second-term policy agenda, however, he got entangled in an affair with a White House intern, Monica Lewinsky, that led to his impeachment by the House of Representatives and weakened his claim to national leadership.

No other political institution has been subject to such varying characterizations as the modern presidency. One reason is that the formal powers of the office are modest, and so presidential power changes with national conditions, political circumstances, and the personal capacities and policy choices of the office's occupant.[2] The American presidency is always a central office in that its occupant is a focus of national attention. Yet the presidency is not an inherently powerful office, in the sense that presidents routinely get what they want. Presidential power is conditional. It depends on the president's own abilities but even more on circumstances—on whether the situation demands strong leadership and whether the political support for that leadership exists. When conditions are favorable, the president is powerful. When conditions are adverse, the president is vulnerable.

This chapter examines the roots of presidential power, the presidential selection process, the staffing of the presidency, and the factors associated with the success and failure of presidential leadership. The main ideas of this chapter are these:

- *Public expectations, national crises, and changing national and world conditions have required the presidency to become a strong office.* Underlying this development is the public support the president acquires from being nationally elected.

- *The modern presidential election campaign is a marathon affair in which self-selected candidates must plan for a strong start in the nominating contests and center their general-election strategies on media, issues, and a baseline of support.* The lengthy campaign process strengthens the public's belief that the presidency is at the center of the U.S. political system.

- *The modern presidency could not operate without a large staff of assistants, experts, and high-level managers, but the sheer size of this staff makes it impossible for the president to exercise complete control over it.*

- *The president's election by national vote and position as sole chief executive ensure that others will listen to the president's ideas; but to lead effectively, the president must have the help of other officials and, to get their help, must take their interests into account.*

- *Presidential influence on national policy is highly variable.* Whether presidents succeed or fail in getting their policies enacted depends heavily on the force of circumstance, the stage of their presidency, partisan support in Congress, and the foreign or domestic nature of the policy issue.

Foundations of the Modern Presidency

The writers of the Constitution knew what they wanted from a president—national leadership, statesmanship in foreign affairs, command in time of war or insurgency, enforcement of the laws—but they could devise only general phrases to describe the president's constitutional authority. Compared with Article I, which enumerates Congress's specific powers, Article II of the Constitution contains relatively general statements on the president's powers (see Table 12-1).[3]

Over the course of American history, each of the president's constitutional powers has been extended in practice beyond the Framers' intention. For example, the Constitution grants the president command of the nation's military, but only Congress can declare war. In *Federalist* No. 69, Alexander Hamilton wrote that a surprise attack on the United States was the only justification for war by presidential action. Nevertheless, presidents have sent troops into military action abroad more than two hundred times. Of the more than a dozen wars included in that figure, only five were declared by Congress.[4] All of America's most recent wars—the Korean, Vietnam, Persian Gulf, Balkans, Afghanistan, and Iraq conflicts—have been fought by presidential order rather than by a congressional declaration of war.

The Constitution also empowers the president to act as diplomatic leader with the authority to appoint ambassadors and to negotiate treaties with other countries, subject to approval by a two-thirds vote of the Senate. The Framers anticipated that Congress would define the nation's foreign policy objectives, while the president would oversee their implementation. However, the president gradually became the principal architect of U.S. foreign policy and has even acquired the power to make treatylike arrangements with other nations, in the form of executive agreements. In 1937, the Supreme Court ruled that executive agreements, signed and approved only by the president, have the same legal status as treaties, although Congress can cancel

TABLE 12-1 | **The Constitutional Authority for the President's Roles**   Unlike Congress's powers, which are specifically enumerated in the Constitution, the president's powers are provided through relatively general clauses. This openness has facilitated an expansion of presidential power over the course of the nation's history.

Commander in chief: Article II, Section 2: "The President shall be commander in chief of the Army and Navy of the United States, and of the militia of the several states."

Chief executive: Article II, Section 2: "He may require the opinion, in writing, of the principal officer in each of the executive departments, upon any subject relating to the duties of their respective offices, and he shall have power to grant reprieves and pardons for offences against the United States, except in cases of impeachment."

Article II, Section 2: "He shall have power, by and with the advice and consent of the Senate, to make treaties, provided two thirds of the senators present concur; and he shall nominate, and by and with the advice and consent of the Senate, shall appoint ambassadors, other public ministers and consuls, judges of the Supreme Court, and all other officers of the United States, whose appointments are not herein otherwise provided for, and which shall be established by law."

Article II, Section 2: "The President shall have power to fill up all vacancies that may happen during the recess of the Senate, by

granting commissions which shall expire at the end of their next session."

Article II, Section 3: "He shall take care that the laws be faithfully executed, and shall commission all the officers of the United States."

Chief diplomat: Article II, Section 2: "He shall have power, and with the advice and consent of the Senate, to make treaties, provided two thirds of the senators present concur."

Article II, Section 3: "He shall receive ambassadors and other public ministers."

Legislative leader: Article II, Section 3: "He shall from time to time give to the Congress information of the state of the Union, and recommend to their consideration such measures as he shall judge necessary and expedient; he may, on extraordinary occasions, convene both houses, or either of them, and in case of disagreement between them, with respect to the time of adjournment, he may adjourn them to such time as he shall think proper." (Article I, Section 7, which defines the president's veto power, is also part of his legislative authority.)

GEORGE WASHINGTON
(1732–99)

George Washington, the nation's first president and its greatest in the minds of some historians, was born into a Virginia planter family. As a child, he excelled as a horseman, a skill that along with family connections earned him an officer's commission. He was involved in the first major skirmish of the French and Indian War. His daring and bravery under fire—two horses were shot out from under him as he rallied troops who had fled in the face of the enemy—made him a national hero. When the American colonies a decade later declared their independence from Britain, he was the natural choice to lead the Continental Army. Throughout the six-year Revolutionary War, Washington avoided pitched battles, knowing that his poorly equipped soldiers were no match for British regulars. Finally, in 1781, his forces trapped the British army at Yorktown and with the help of French naval vessels scored a decisive victory that ended the war. Some of his countrymen thought Washington should be named king, but he dismissed the idea, saying America was a new type of nation. He retired to his Mount Vernon plantation, only to grow increasingly worried by the growing discord among the states and the inability of Congress to govern effectively.

In 1787, Washington presided over the Philadelphia convention that drafted a constitution that became the basis for a stronger central government. Following ratification of the Constitution, Washington was elected president by unanimous vote of the Electoral College. He recognized that his presidency would define future ones. In a letter to James Madison, Washington wrote, "It is devoutly wished on my part that these precedents may be fixed on true principles." Washington pushed for a strong national government, believing that it could keep the nation from devolving into sectional rivalries. He also kept the United States out of foreign entanglements, believing the new country was too weak militarily to play such a role. Washington could have been elected to a third term, but he stepped down after two terms, stating that the presidency was a citizen's office, not a monarchal one. It was a precedent that all presidents adhered to until Franklin Roosevelt ran for and won a third term in 1940 at a time when the country was confronting the twin threats of economic depression and war. Roosevelt's presidency prompted Congress to initiate the Twenty-second Amendment to the Constitution, which limits a president to two terms in office.

executive agreements with which it disagrees.[5] Since World War II, presidents have negotiated over ten thousand executive agreements—more than ten times the number of treaties ratified by the Senate during the same period.[6]

The Constitution also vests "executive power" in the president. This power includes the responsibility to execute the laws faithfully and to appoint major administrators, such as heads of the various departments of the executive branch. In *Federalist* No. 76, Hamilton indicated that the president's real authority as chief executive was to be found in this appointive capacity. Presidents have indeed exercised substantial power through their appointments, but they have found their administrative authority—the power to execute the laws—to be of greater significance, because it enables them to interpret the meaning of these laws. President Ronald Reagan used his executive power to *prohibit* the use of federal funds by family-planning clinics that offered abortion counseling. President Bill Clinton exerted the same power to *permit* the use of federal funds for this purpose. The same act of Congress was the basis for each of these actions. The act authorizes the use of federal funds for family-planning services, but it neither requires nor prohibits their use for abortion counseling, enabling the president to decide this issue.

Finally, the Constitution provides the president with legislative authority, including use of the veto and the opportunity to recommend proposals to Congress. The Framers expected this authority to be used in a limited way. George Washington acted as the Framers anticipated: he proposed only three legislative measures and vetoed only two acts of Congress. Modern presidents have assumed a more active legislative role. They regularly submit proposals to Congress, and most of them have not hesitated to veto legislation they find disagreeable.

The presidency, for many reasons, is a more powerful office than the Framers envisioned. But two features of the office in particular—*national election* and *singular authority*—have enabled presidents to make use of changing demands on government to claim the position of leader of the American people. It is a claim that no other elected official can routinely make, and it is a key to understanding the role and power of the president.

Asserting a Claim to National Leadership

The first president to forcefully assert a claim to popular leadership was Andrew Jackson, who had been swept into office in 1828 on a tide of public support that broke the hold of the upper classes on the presidency. Jackson used his popular backing to challenge Congress's claim to national policy leadership, contending that he was "the people's tribune."

However, Jackson's view was not shared by most of his successors during the nineteenth century, because national conditions did not routinely call for strong presidential leadership. The prevailing conception was the **Whig theory,** which held that the presidency was a limited or constrained office whose occupant was confined to the exercise of expressly granted constitutional authority. The president had no implicit powers for dealing with national problems but was primarily an administrator, charged with carrying out the will of Congress. "My duty," said President James Buchanan, a Whig adherent, "is to execute the laws . . . and not my individual opinions."[7]

Theodore Roosevelt rejected the Whig tradition upon taking office in 1901. He attacked the business trusts, pursued an aggressive foreign policy, and pressured Congress to adopt progressive domestic policies. Roosevelt embraced the **stewardship theory,** which calls for an assertive presidency that is confined only at points specifically prohibited by law. As "steward of the people," Roosevelt said, he was permitted "to do anything that the needs of the Nation demanded unless such action was forbidden by the Constitution or by the laws."[8]

Roosevelt's image of a strong presidency was shared by Woodrow Wilson, but his other immediate successors reverted to the Whig notion of the limited presidency.[9] Herbert Hoover's restrained conception of the presidency prevented him from acting decisively during the devastation of the Great Depression. Hoover said that he lacked the constitutional authority to establish public relief programs for jobless Americans. However, Hoover's successor, Franklin D. Roosevelt, shared the stewardship theory of his distant cousin Theodore Roosevelt, and FDR's New Deal signaled the end of the limited presidency. As FDR's successor, Harry Truman, wrote in his memoirs, "The power of the President should be used in the interest of the people and in order to do that the President must use whatever power the Constitution does not expressly deny him."[10]

Today the presidency is an inherently strong office. The modern presidency becomes a more substantial office in the hands of a confident individual like George W. Bush, but even a less forceful person like Jimmy Carter is expected to act assertively. This expectation not only is the legacy of former strong presidents but also stems from changes that have occurred in the federal government's national and international policy responsibilities.

The Need for Presidential Leadership of an Activist Government

During most of the nineteenth century (the Civil War being the notable exception), the United States did not need a strong president. The federal government's policymaking role was small, as was its bureaucracy. Moreover, the

HISTORICAL *Background*

Whig theory
A theory that prevailed in the nineteenth century and held that the presidency was a limited or restrained office whose occupant was confined to expressly granted constitutional authority.

stewardship theory
A theory that argues for a strong, assertive presidential role, with presidential authority limited only at points specifically prohibited by law.

nation's major issues were of a sectional nature (especially the North-South split over slavery) and thus were suited to action by Congress, which represented state interests. The U.S. government's role in world affairs was also small. As these conditions changed, however, the presidency also changed.

Foreign Policy Leadership

The president has always been the nation's foreign policy leader, but the role initially was a rather undemanding one. The United States avoided entanglement in the turbulent affairs of Europe and was preoccupied with westward expansion. By the end of the nineteenth century, however, the nation was seeking a world market for its goods. President Theodore Roosevelt advocated an American economic empire and looked south toward Latin America and west toward Hawaii, the Philippines, and China for new markets (the "Open Door" policy). However, the United States' tradition of isolationism remained a powerful influence on national policy. The United States fought in World War I but immediately thereafter demobilized its armed forces. Over President Woodrow Wilson's objections, Congress then voted against the entry of the United States into the League of Nations.

World War II fundamentally changed the nation's international role and the president's role in foreign policy. In 1945 the United States emerged as a global superpower, a giant in world trade, and the recognized leader of the noncommunist world. The United States today has a military presence in nearly every part of the globe and an unprecedented interest in trade balances, energy, and other international issues affecting the nation.

The effect of these developments on America's political institutions has been one-sided.[11] Because of the president's constitutional authority as chief diplomat and military commander and the special demands of foreign policy leadership, the president, not Congress, has taken the lead in addressing the nation's increased responsibilities in the world. Foreign policy requires singleness of purpose and, at times, fast action. Congress—a large, divided, and unwieldy institution—is poorly suited to such a response. In contrast, the president, as sole head of the executive branch, can act quickly and speak authoritatively for the nation as a whole in its relations with other nations. This capacity has rarely been more evident than after the terrorist attacks of September 11, 2001. The initiative in the war on terrorism rested squarely with the White House. President Bush decided on the U.S. response to the attacks and took the lead in obtaining international support for U.S. military, intelligence, and diplomatic initiatives. Congress backed these actions enthusiastically. The joint resolution that endorsed Bush's decision to attack the Taliban government in Afghanistan passed unanimously in the Senate and with only a single dissenting vote in the House. In reality, however, Congress had little choice but to support whatever policies Bush chose. Americans wanted decisive action and were looking to the president, not to Congress, for leadership.

Harry S Truman's presidency was characterized by bold foreign policy initiatives. He authorized the use of nuclear weapons against Japan in 1945, created the Marshall Plan as the basis for the economic reconstruction of postwar Europe, and sent U.S. troops to fight in Korea in 1950. Truman is shown here greeting British Prime Minister Winston Churchill at a Washington airport in early 1952.

In other situations, Congress is less compliant. In recent decades, it has contested presidential positions on issues such as global trade and international human rights. Nevertheless, the president is clearly the leading voice in U.S. foreign policy. (The changing shape of the world and its implications for presidential power and leadership are discussed more fully later in the chapter.)

Domestic Policy Leadership

The change in the president's domestic leadership role has also been substantial. Throughout most of the nineteenth century, Congress jealously guarded its constitutional powers, making it clear that it was in charge of domestic policy. James Bryce wrote in the 1880s that Congress paid no more attention to the president's views on legislation than it did to the editorial positions of newspaper publishers.[12]

By the early twentieth century, however, the national government was taking on regulatory and policy responsibilities imposed by the nation's transition from an agrarian to an industrial society, and the executive branch was growing ever larger. In 1921, Congress conceded that it lacked the centralized authority to coordinate the growing national budget and enacted the Budget and Accounting Act, which provided for an executive budget. Federal departments and agencies would no longer submit their annual budget requests directly to Congress. Instead, the president would develop the various agencies' requests into a comprehensive budgetary proposal, which then would be submitted to Congress as a starting point for its deliberations.

During the Great Depression of the 1930s, Franklin D. Roosevelt's New Deal responded to the public's demand for economic relief with a broad program that required a level of policy planning and coordination beyond the capacity of Congress. In addition to public works projects and social welfare programs, the New Deal made the government a partner in nearly every aspect of the nation's economy. If economic regulation was to work, unified and continuous policy leadership was needed, and only the president could routinely provide it.

Presidential authority has continued to grow since Roosevelt's time. In response to pressures from the public, the national government's role in areas such as education, health, welfare, safety, and protection of the environment has expanded greatly, which in turn has created additional demands for presidential leadership.[13] Large government, with its emphasis on comprehensive planning and program coordination, has favored executive authority at the expense of legislative authority. All democracies have seen a shift in power from their legislature to their executive. In Britain, for example, the prime minister has taken on responsibilities that once belonged to the cabinet or to Parliament.

Choosing the President

As the president's policy and leadership responsibilities changed during the nation's history, so did the process of electing presidents. The changes do not parallel each other exactly, but they are related both politically and philosophically. As the presidency drew ever closer to the people, their role in selecting the president grew ever more direct.[14] The United States in its history has had four systems of presidential selection, each more "democratic" than its predecessor (see Table 12-2).

The delegates to the constitutional convention of 1787 feared that popular election of the president would make the office too powerful and accordingly

HISTORICAL
Background

HISTORICAL
Background

TABLE 12-2 | The Four Systems of Presidential Selection

Selection System	Period	Features
1. Original	1788–1828	Party nominees are chosen in congressional caucuses. Electoral College members act somewhat independently in their presidential voting.
2. Party convention	1832–1900	Party nominees are chosen in national party conventions by delegates selected by state and local party organizations. Electoral College members cast their ballots for the popular-vote winner in their respective states.
3. Party convention, primary	1904–68	As in system 2, except that a *minority* of national convention delegates are chosen through primary elections (the majority still being chosen by party organizations).
4. Party primary, open caucus	1972–present	As in system 2, except that a *majority* of national convention delegates are chosen through primary elections.

devised an electoral vote system (the so-called Electoral College). The president was to be chosen by electors picked by the states, with each state entitled to one elector for each of its members of Congress (House and Senate combined). This system was changed after the election in 1828 of Andrew Jackson, who believed that the people's will had been denied four years earlier when he got the most popular votes but failed to gain an electoral majority. Jackson was unable to persuade Congress to support a constitutional amendment that would have eliminated the Electoral College, but he did obtain the next-best alternative: he persuaded the states to link their electoral votes to the popular vote. Under Jackson's reform, which is still in effect today, each party in a state has a separate slate of electors who gain the right to cast a state's electoral votes if their party's candidate places first in the state's popular voting. Thus, the popular vote for the candidates directly affects their electoral vote, and one candidate is likely to win both forms of the presidential vote. Since Jackson's time, only Rutherford B. Hayes (in 1876), Benjamin Harrison (in 1888), and

The White House contains, on the first floor, the president's Oval Office, other offices, and ceremonial rooms. The First Family's living quarters are on the second floor.

George W. Bush (in 2000) have won the presidency after having lost the popular vote.

Jackson also championed the national convention as a means of nominating the party's presidential candidate (before this time, nominations were made by party caucuses in Congress and in state legislatures). The parties' strength was at the grass roots, among the people, and Jackson saw the convention process as a means of bringing the citizenry and the presidency closer together. Since Jackson's time, presidential nominees have been formally chosen at national party conventions. Each state party sends delegates to the national convention, and these delegates select the party's nominee.

Jackson's system of presidential nomination remained fully intact until the early twentieth century, when the Progressives devised the primary election as a means of curbing the power of the party bosses (see Chapter 2). State party leaders had taken control of the nominating process by handpicking their states' convention delegates. The Progressives sought to give voters the power to select the delegates. Such a process is called an *indirect primary,* because the voters are not choosing the nominees directly (as they do in House and Senate races) but rather are choosing delegates who in turn select the nominees.

However, the Progressives were unable to persuade most states to adopt presidential primaries, which meant that party leaders continued to control enough of the delegates to pick the nominees. That arrangement held until 1968 when Democratic Party leaders ignored the strength of anti–Vietnam War sentiment in the primaries and nominated Vice President Hubert Humphrey, who had not entered a single primary and was closely identified with the Johnson administration's Vietnam policy. After Humphrey narrowly lost the 1968 general election to Richard Nixon, reform-minded Democrats forced changes in the nominating process. The new rules gave rank-and-file party voters more control by requiring states to choose their delegates through either primary elections or **open party caucuses** (meetings open to any registered party voter who wants to attend). Although the Democrats initiated the change, the Republicans also were affected by it. Most states that adopted a presidential primary in order to comply with the Democrats' new rules also required Republicans to select their convention delegates through a primary.

Today it is the voters in state primaries and open caucuses who play the decisive role in the selection of the Democratic and Republican presidential nominees.[15] A state's delegates are awarded to candidates in accordance with how well they do in the state's primary or caucus. Thus, to win the majority of national convention delegates necessary for nomination, a candidate must place first in a lot of states and do at least reasonably well in most of the rest. (About forty states choose their delegates through a primary election; the others use the caucus system.)

In sum, the presidential election system has changed from an elite-dominated process to one based on voter support. This arrangement has strengthened the presidency by providing the office with the reserve of power that popular election confers on democratic leadership.

The Primary Elections

The fact that voters pick the party nominees has opened the nominating races to any politician with the energy and resources to run a major national campaign. Nominating campaigns, except those in which an incumbent president is seeking reelection, typically attract a half-dozen contenders. The 2008 nominating races drew an even larger number—roughly ten candidates for each party.

Candidates have no choice but to start early and campaign hard. A key to success in the nominating campaign is **momentum**—a strong showing in the

open party caucuses
Meetings at which a party's candidates for nomination are voted on and that are open to all the party's rank-and-file voters who want to attend.

momentum (in campaigns)
A strong showing by a candidate in early presidential nominating contests, which leads to a buildup of public support for the candidate.

early contests that leads to a buildup of public support in subsequent ones. Nobody—not the press, not donors, not the voters—has an interest in candidates who are at the back of the pack. No candidate in recent decades has got off to a lousy start in the first few contests and then picked up enough steam to come anywhere near to winning the nomination. All the advantages rest with the fast starters. They get more attention from the press, more money from contributors, and more consideration by the voters. Not surprisingly, presidential contenders strive to do well in the early contests, particularly the first caucuses in Iowa and the first primary in New Hampshire. In 2008, Barack Obama's successful quest for the Democratic presidential nomination began with a victory in Iowa. John McCain lost there, but a win a few days later in New Hampshire's primary started the momentum that carried him to the Republican nomination.

Money, always a critical factor in elections, has become increasingly important in the past three decades because states have moved their primaries and caucuses to the early weeks of the nominating period in order to increase their influence on the outcome. Within the first month of the 2008 nominating period, more than half the states held their primary or caucus. To compete effectively in so many contests over such a short period, candidates need money—lots of it. A candidate can be in only one place at a time, so the campaign must be carried to other voters through costly televised political advertising. Observers estimate that it takes at least $40 million to run a strong nominating campaign, and possibly a lot more than that for a candidate who does not have substantial name recognition and public support before the campaign begins. In nearly every nominating race from 1984 to 2008, the winner was the candidate who had raised the most money before the start of the primaries.

Candidates in primary elections receive federal funding if they meet the eligibility criteria. The Federal Election Campaign Act of 1974 (as amended in 1979) provides for federal matching funds. Under the program, the government matches the first $250 of each private donation received by a primary election candidate, provided the candidate raises at least $5,000 in individual contributions of up to $250 in at least twenty states. This provision is designed to restrict matching funds to candidates who can show that they have a reasonable amount of public support. In addition, any candidate who receives matching funds must agree to limit expenditures for the nominating phase to a set amount overall (roughly $50 million in 2008) and in particular states (the 2008 limits in Iowa and New Hampshire, for example, were roughly $1.4 million and $800,000, respectively). The limits are adjusted upward each election year to account for inflation. Taxpayers fund the matching program by checking a box on their income-tax return allocating $3 of their taxes to it.

Until the 2000 election, when George Bush declined matching funds so that he could raise unrestricted amounts of money for his nominating campaign, candidates had routinely accepted matching funds, which meant they had to abide by the spending limits. In 2004, Bush again turned down matching funds, as did the two leading Democratic contenders, Howard Dean and John Kerry. In

John McCain campaigns on his way to winning the 2008 Republican presidential nomination. The modern presidential campaign is a marathon event that formally lasts nearly a year and speculatively is always under way. Two years before the 2008 election, about twenty presidential possibilities—half of them Republicans and half of them Democrats—were traveling the country in hopes of gathering enough support to make a successful run for their party's nomination.

2008, an even larger number of candidates declined public funds. Obama was easily the most successful of these candidates, raising in excess of $300 million for his nominating campaign—more than four times the amount he would have been allowed if he had accepted matching funds,

As candidates have increasingly declined public funding, there have been calls to raise the allowable spending limit under public financing, perhaps to as high as $100 million. Otherwise, observers say, the only candidates who will accept matching funds will be those with no chance of victory. This development would defeat the purpose of public funding, which is to free candidates from the obligations that come from accepting contributions from private groups and individuals.

The National Party Conventions

The summertime national party conventions mark the end of the nominating campaign. In an earlier era, the convention was where the nomination was actually decided. State party delegations would come together at their convention to bargain and choose among potential nominees. Since 1972, when the delegate selection process was changed, the leading candidate in every case has acquired enough delegates in the primaries to lock up the nomination before the convention begins. Nevertheless, the convention is a major event. It brings together the delegates elected in the state caucuses and primaries, who then approve a party platform and formally nominate the party's presidential and vice presidential candidates.

By tradition, the choice of the vice presidential nominee rests with the presidential nominee. In 2008, Obama selected Delaware senator Joe Biden, who had extensive foreign policy experience, to be his running mate. For his part, McCain picked little-known Alaska governor Sarah Palin, whose forceful acceptance speech at the Republican convention transformed her from a curiosity into a major force in the McCain campaign. She helped energize the party's supporters and drew huge crowds at campaign stops during the general election—a feat unprecedented in the recent annals of vice presidential nominees. (As Table 12-3 indicates, roughly a third of recent presidents reached that office serving first as vice president.)

The Campaign for Election

The winner in the November general election is certain to be either the Republican or the Democratic candidate. Two-thirds of the nation's voters identify with the Republican or Democratic Party, and most Independents lean toward one or the other of them. As a result, the major-party presidential nominees have a built-in source of votes. Even Democrat George McGovern, who had the lowest level of party support in the past half-century, was backed in 1972 by 60 percent of his party's identifiers.

Because the Democratic and Republican nominees have this huge advantage, a third-party candidate has no realistic hope of victory. Even Ross Perot, who in 1992 ran the most successful third-party campaign in nearly a century, was able to garner only a fifth of the vote. On the other hand, third-party candidates have sometimes caused problems for a major party by siphoning votes away from its nominee. In 2000, third-party candidate Ralph Nader drew 4 percent of the popular vote, most of it from voters who indicated that they otherwise would have backed Al Gore, the Democratic nominee. If Nader had not been in the race, Gore, rather than George W. Bush, would have won the 2000 presidential election.

TABLE 12-3 | The Path to the White House

President	Years in Office	Highest Previous Office	Second Highest Office
Theodore Roosevelt	1901–8	Vice president*	Governor
William Howard Taft	1909–12	Secretary of war	Federal judge
Woodrow Wilson	1913–20	Governor	None
Warren G. Harding	1921–24	U.S. senator	Lieutenant governor
Calvin Coolidge	1925–28	Vice president*	Governor
Herbert Hoover	1929–32	Secretary of commerce	War relief administrator
Franklin D. Roosevelt	1933–45	Governor	Assistant secretary of Navy
Harry S Truman	1945–52	Vice president*	U.S. senator
Dwight D. Eisenhower	1953–60	None (Army general)	None
John F. Kennedy	1961–63	U.S. senator	U.S. representative
Lyndon Johnson	1963–68	Vice president*	U.S. senator
Richard Nixon	1969–74	Vice president	U.S. senator
Gerald Ford	1974–76	Vice president*	U.S. representative
Jimmy Carter	1977–80	Governor	State senator
Ronald Reagan	1981–88	Governor	None
George H. W. Bush	1989–92	Vice president	Director, CIA
Bill Clinton	1993–2000	Governor	State attorney general
George W. Bush	2001–2008	Governor	None
Barack Obama	2009–	U.S. senator	State senator

*Became president on death or resignation of incumbent.

Election Strategy

The candidates' strategies in the general election are shaped by many considerations, including the constitutional provision that each state shall have electoral votes equal in number to its representation in Congress. Each state thus gets two electoral votes for its Senate representation and a varying number of electoral votes depending on its House representation. Altogether, there are 538 electoral votes (including 3 for the District of Columbia, even though it has no voting representatives in Congress). To win the presidency, a candidate must receive at least 270 votes, an electoral majority. (If no candidate receives a majority, the election is decided in the House of Representatives. No president since John Quincy Adams in 1824 has been elected in this way. The procedure is defined by the Constitution's Twelfth Amendment, which is reprinted in the appendixes.)

The importance of the electoral votes is magnified by the existence of the **unit rule:** all the states except Maine and Nebraska grant all their electoral votes as a unit to the candidate who wins the state's popular vote. For this reason, candidates are concerned with winning the most populous states, such as California (with 55 electoral votes), Texas (34), New York (31), Florida (27), Pennsylvania (21), Illinois (21), Ohio (20), Michigan (17), and Georgia, New Jersey, and North Carolina (15 each).

Even more so than a state's size, however, the closeness of the vote in a state dictates how much attention it will get from the candidates. Because of the unit rule, a state that is lopsidedly Democratic or Republican will be ignored. Its electoral votes are already locked up. Thus, the fall campaign becomes a fight over the toss-up states or, as they have come to be called, the battleground states. In 2008, only a third of the states were seen by the Obama and McCain campaigns

unit rule

The rule that grants all of a state's electoral votes to the candidate who receives the most popular votes in the state.

STATES IN THE NATION

ELECTORAL VOTE STRATEGY IN THE 2008 ELECTION

The Constitution of the United States specifies that the president is to be chosen by electoral votes. The candidate receiving a majority of the electoral vote, even if receiving fewer popular votes than the opponent, becomes president. The Constitution further specifies that states have authority to determine how their electors will be chosen. Today, all states except two (Maine and Nebraska, which give one electoral vote to the winner of each congressional district and two electoral votes to the statewide winner), give all of their electoral votes to the popular-vote winner in the state. This winner-take-all feature of the electoral vote system leads presidential candidates to focus on toss-up states—those that conceivably could be won by either party. These so-called battleground states are the only ones

where the candidates spend any appreciable amount of time and money. One-sided states—those that are strongly enough Republican or Democratic to be safely in one candidate's grasp—are more or less ignored during the fall campaign.

As the Obama and McCain campaigns began the 2008 general election, their strategists targeted the states where the popular vote might possibly go either way. The map below identifies these potential battleground states, as well as those that were conceded to the other party. As the campaign drew ever closer to the November election, the Obama and McCain campaigns further narrowed their strategies, pouring most of their resources into the half-dozen or so states where the race was closest.

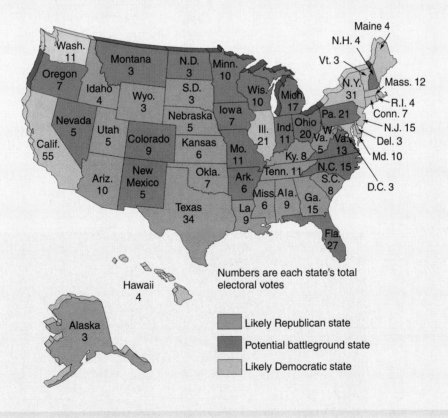

Numbers are each state's total electoral votes

■ Likely Republican state
■ Potential battleground state
■ Likely Democratic state

as states that realistically could be won by either candidate. The two candidates spent nearly all their money and time in the battleground states during the closing months of the campaign. Other states might just as well have been located in Canada for the attention they received from the candidates.

At campaign's end, electoral votes and not popular votes determine the winner (see "States in the Nation"). In 2000, George W. Bush was elected with 271 electoral votes, two more than required, even though he received 550,000 fewer popular votes than Al Gore. Bush was the first president since Benjamin Harrison in 1888 to win the presidency despite losing the popular vote.

Media and Money

The modern presidential campaign is a media campaign. At one time, candidates relied heavily on party organization and rallies to carry their messages to the voters, but now they rely on the media, particularly television. Candidates strive to produce the pithy ten-second sound bites that the television networks prefer to highlight on the evening newscasts. They also rely on the power of the "new media," making appearances on programs such as *Larry King Live* and *The Daily Show* and creating their own websites.

The television campaign includes political advertising. Televised commercials are by far the most expensive part of presidential campaigns, accounting for about half the candidates' general election expenditures. Most of this advertising is shown in the battleground states, with the result that Americans in these locations are bombarded with ads while those living elsewhere see relatively few. In most recent campaigns, televised ads have been the main vehicle by which candidates have attacked their opponents. Unlike the news coverage they receive, candidates fully control the content of their ads, enabling them to craft unflattering, one-sided portrayals of their opponent.[16]

Television is also the forum for the major confrontation of the fall campaign: the presidential debates. The first televised debates took place in 1960 between John Kennedy and Richard Nixon, and an estimated 100 million people watched at least one of their four debates. Televised debates resumed in 1976 and have become a fixture of presidential campaigns. Debates can influence voters' assessments of the candidates, though they have only occasionally had a large effect on the race. The 2008 Obama-McCain debates were typical in this respect. Most Americans judged Obama to have won all three debates. However, the polls indicated that the debates did not greatly affect the candidates' support, perhaps because voters were concerned with the widening financial crisis, which helped Obama's candidacy.

The highlight of the general election campaign is the televised debates between the Republican and Democratic nominees. Shown here is a scene from one of the McCain-Obama debates in 2008.

The Republican and Democratic nominees are each eligible for federal funding of their general election campaigns even if they did not accept it during the primaries. The amount for the general election was set at $20 million in 1975 and has been adjusted for inflation in succeeding elections. The figure for the major-party nominees in 2008 was roughly $85 million. The only string attached to this money is that candidates who accept it can spend no additional funds on their campaigns (although each party is allowed to spend some money—in 2008, roughly $5 million—on behalf of its nominee).

Candidates can choose not to accept public funds, in which case the amount they spend is limited only by their ability to raise money privately. However, all major-party nominees since 1976 had accepted federal funding in the general election until Barack Obama, after having promised to run on public funds, opted out in 2008. Other candidates for the presidency qualify for a proportional amount of federal funding if they receive at least 5 percent of the vote and do not spend more than $50,000 of their own money on the campaign.

The Winners

The Constitution specifies that the president must be at least thirty-five years old, be a natural-born U.S. citizen, and have been a U.S. resident for at least fourteen years. Yet the holding of high public office is nearly a prerequisite for gaining the presidency. Except for four army generals, all presidents to date have served previously as vice presidents, members of Congress, state governors, or top federal executives. Historians have developed rankings of the presidents (see Table 12-4), and if one thing is clear from these rankings, it is that there is no template for a successful presidency. The best presidents have differed considerably

TABLE 12-4

Ranking America's Presidents Historian Arthur Schlesinger, Sr., began the game of ranking U.S. presidents when he sought the opinions of leading historians in a 1948 article for *Life* magazine. Since then, a great many scholars and analysts, including historian Arthur Schlesinger, Jr., have tried their hand at it. Here is the list from a survey in 2000 of seventy-eight history, political science, and law professors that was conducted by the Federalist Society and the *Wall Street Journal*. Unlike many such lists, this list ranks Abraham Lincoln second rather than first.

Great
1 George Washington
2 Abraham Lincoln
3 Franklin Roosevelt

Near Great
4 Thomas Jefferson
5 Theodore Roosevelt
6 Andrew Jackson
7 Harry Truman
8 Ronald Reagan
9 Dwight Eisenhower
10 James Polk
11 Woodrow Wilson

Above Average
12 Grover Cleveland
13 John Adams
14 William McKinley
15 James Madison
16 James Monroe
17 Lyndon Johnson
18 John Kennedy

Average
19 William Taft
20 John Quincy Adams
21 George H. W. Bush
22 Rutherford Hayes
23 Martin Van Buren
24 William Clinton
25 Calvin Coolidge
26 Chester Arthur

Below Average
27 Benjamin Harrison
28 Gerald Ford
29 Herbert Hoover
30 Jimmy Carter
31 Zachary Taylor
32 Ulysses Grant
33 Richard Nixon
34 John Tyler
35 Millard Filmore

Failure
36 Andrew Johnson
37T Franklin Pierce
37T Warren Harding
39 James Buchanan

DEBATING THE ISSUES

SHOULD THE ELECTORAL COLLEGE BE ABOLISHED?

As the votes in the 2000 election were counted, the country was thrown into turmoil by the electoral vote system. The president is chosen by an indirect system of election. Voters cast ballots for candidates, but their votes choose only each state's electors, whose subsequent ballots result in the actual selection of the president. Electoral votes are apportioned by states based on their representation in Congress, which creates the possibility that the candidate who receives the most popular votes will not receive the most electoral votes and thus will not be elected president. The 2000 election was of this type. Although George W. Bush trailed Al Gore by 550,000 votes nationally, he won Florida by 537 votes, thereby getting the state's twenty-five electoral votes, which gave him a slim majority of the electoral vote. Bush's victory renewed the debate about retaining the electoral vote system. The following are two of the arguments that were heard, one by a Democratic House member, and one by a Republican House member, who himself ran for the presidency in 2008.

YES It's time to abolish the Electoral College and to count the votes of all Americans in presidential elections. . . . Two centuries ago the Constitutional Convention considered many ways to select the president of the emerging republic, from popular election to assigning the decision to the Congress. The Electoral College was a compromise that reflected a basic mistrust of the electorate—the same mistrust that denied the vote to women, African-Americans, and people who did not own property. The Electoral College may or may not have made sense in 1787. But through 21st-century eyes it is as anachronistic as the limitations on suffrage itself. Whether or not you like the results of a particular election . . . your vote should count. . . . If the Electoral College merely echoes the election results, then it is superfluous. If it contradicts the voting majority, then why tolerate it? It is a remarkable and enduring virtue of our political system that our elections are credible and decisive—and that power changes hands in a coherent and dignified manner. . . . Every other public official is chosen by majority vote. That's the way it's supposed to work in a democracy. For reasons both philosophical and practical, that's also how we should elect the president.

—*William D. Delahunt, U.S. representative (D-Mass.)*

NO The pundits will argue that it is not fair to deny the presidency to the man who received the most total votes. After all, to do so would be "undemocratic." This argument ignores the fundamental nature of our constitutional system. The Founding Fathers sought to create a loose confederacy of states, joined together by a federal government with very little power. They created a constitutionally limited republic, not a direct democracy. They did so to protect fundamental liberties against the whims of the masses. The Electoral College likewise was created in the Constitution to guard against majority tyranny in federal elections. The President was to be elected by the states rather than the citizenry as a whole, with votes apportioned to states according to their representation in Congress. The will of the people was to be tempered by the wisdom of the Electoral College. By contrast, election of the President by pure popular vote totals would damage statehood. Populated areas on both coasts would have increasing influence on national elections, to the detriment of less populated southern and western states. A candidate receiving a large percentage of the popular vote in California and New York could win a national election with very little support in dozens of other states! A popular vote system simply would intensify the populist pandering which already dominates national campaigns.

—*Ron Paul, U.S. representative (R-Tex.)*

in their backgrounds, as have the worst ones. Of the four army generals, for example, one of them (George Washington) is ranked as a "great" president while another (Dwight Eisenhower) is seen as "near great." The other two (Zachary Taylor and Ulysses S. Grant) are rated "below average" by historians.

Until Obama's election in 2008, all presidents had been white. No woman has won the presidency, though it is only a matter of time before the nation has its first woman president. Until the early 1950s, a majority of Americans polled said they would not consider voting for a woman for president. Today, fewer than 10 percent hold this view. A similar change of opinion preceded John Kennedy's election to the presidency in 1960. Kennedy was the nation's first Catholic president and only the second Catholic to receive a major party's nomination.

Staffing the Presidency

When Americans go to the polls on election day, they have in mind the choice between two individuals, the Democratic nominee and the Republican nominees. In effect, however, they are choosing a lot more than a single executive leader. They are also picking a secretary of state, the director of the FBI, the chair of the Federal Reserve Board, and a host of other executives. Each of these is a presidential appointee.

Presidential Appointees

A president's ability to make executive appointments is a significant source of power. For one thing, modern policymaking rests on a deep understanding of policy issues and also on knowledge of how to successfully guide proposals through policy channels. Many presidential appointees have these skills. Further, the president cannot be in a hundred places at once—but the president's appointees can be. They extend the president's influence into the huge federal bureaucracy by overseeing those agencies they are appointed to head. Not surprisingly, the president seeks to appoint individuals who are members of the same political party and are committed to the Administration's policy goals.

The Executive Office of the President

The key staff organization is the Executive Office of the President (EOP), created by Congress in 1939 to provide the president with the staff necessary to coordinate the activities of the executive branch.[17] The EOP has since become the command center of the presidency. Its exact configuration is determined by the president, but some of its organizational units have carried over from one president to the next. These include the White House Office (WHO), which consists of the president's closest personal advisers; the Office of Management and Budget (OMB), which consists of experts who formulate and administer the federal budget; and the National Security Council (NSC), which advises the president on foreign and military affairs.

The Vice President   The Constitution assigns all executive authority to the president, and none to the vice president. Earlier presidents typically refused to delegate significant duties to their vice presidents, which diminished the office's appeal. Nomination to the vice presidency was refused by many leading politicians, including Daniel Webster and Henry Clay. Said Webster, "I do not propose to be buried until I am really dead."[18] When he assumed the presidency in 1977, Jimmy Carter redefined the vice presidency, giving his vice president, Walter Mondale, an office in the West Wing of the White House and assigning him significant policy responsibilities. The vice president is now entrenched in the West Wing and is supported by an administrative staff (the Office of the Vice President) of a dozen people, including a domestic policy adviser and a national security policy adviser.

The change owes partly to the control that recent presidential nominees have had in selecting their running mate. They have tended to choose someone they trust or who fills a deficit in their background. Carter had never served in Washington, which was a reason he selected Mondale, an experienced and widely admired U.S. senator. Obama selected Joe Biden as his running mate in 2008 in part because of Biden's foreign policy expertise, an area in which Obama was weak. Biden's lengthy experience in the Senate was also counted on to be of help in getting Obama's legislative proposals through Congress.

The Constitution assigns no policy authority to the vice president, whose role is determined by the president. Recent vice presidents have been assigned major policy responsibilities. Earlier vice presidents played smaller roles. Vice President Dick Cheney, pictured here with President George W. Bush, was the most powerful vice president in history, having played a pivotal role in the decision, among others, to invade Iraq.

George W. Bush may have given his vice president, Dick Cheney, too large a role in his administration. Much of the policy advice and information that Bush received was channeled through Cheney, enabling him to cast it to fit his objectives.[19] Among other things, Cheney was a chief architect of the Iraq invasion and other policies that weakened Bush's presidency, including warrantless wiretapping and the harsh treatment of enemy detainees (see Chapter 4). Cheney successfully fought attempts by congressional investigative committees to secure memos and other material that might have revealed more fully his role in Bush administration policies.

The White House Office   Of the EOP's other organizational units, the White House Office serves the president most directly and personally. The units within the WHO include the Communications Office, the Office of the Press Secretary, the Office of the Counsel to the President, and the Office of Legislative Affairs. As these names suggest, the WHO consists of the president's personal assistants, including close personal advisers, press agents, legislative and group liaison aides, and special assistants for domestic and international policy. They work in the White House, and the president can hire and fire them at will. These personal assistants do much of the legwork for the president and serve as a main source of advice. Most of them are skilled at developing political strategy and communicating with the public, Congress, state and local governments, key groups, and the news media. Because of their proximity to the president, they are among the most powerful individuals in Washington.

Policy Experts   The president is also served by the policy experts in the EOP's other organizations. These include economists, legal analysts, national security specialists, and others. The president is advised on economic issues, for example, by the National Economic Council (NEC). The NEC gathers information to develop indicators of the economy's strength and applies economic theories to various policy alternatives. Modern policymaking cannot be conducted in the absence of such expert knowledge and advice.

The President's Cabinet

The heads of the fifteen executive departments, such as the Department of Defense and the Department of Agriculture, constitute the president's **cabinet.** They are appointed by the president, subject to confirmation by the Senate. Although the cabinet once served as the president's main advisory group, it has not played this role since Herbert Hoover's administration. As national issues have become increasingly complex, the cabinet has become outmoded as a policymaking forum: department heads are likely to be well informed only about issues in their particular area. Accordingly, cabinet meetings are no longer the scene of lengthy deliberations on how the president should respond to major policy issues. These discussions now take place between the president and top presidential advisers. Nevertheless, cabinet members, as individuals who head major departments, are important figures in any administration. The president chooses them for their prominence in politics, business, government, or the professions.[20] The office of secretary of state is generally regarded as the most prestigious cabinet post.

cabinet
A group consisting of the heads of the executive (cabinet) departments, who are appointed by the president, subject to confirmation by the Senate. The cabinet was once the main advisory body to the president, but it no longer plays this role.

Other Presidential Appointees

In addition to cabinet secretaries, the president appoints the heads and top deputies of federal agencies and commissions. Altogether, the president appoints a few thousand executive officials. However, most of these appointees are selected at the agency level or are part-time workers. This still leaves nearly seven hundred full-time appointees who serve the president more or less directly, a much larger number than are appointed by the chief executive of any other democracy.[21]

The Problem of Control

Although the president's appointees are a huge asset, they can also be a liability: because they are so numerous, the president has difficulty controlling all that they do. President Truman had a wall chart in the Oval Office listing more than one hundred officials who reported directly to him; he often told visitors, "I cannot even see all of these men, let alone actually study what they are doing."[22] Since Truman's time, the number of bureaucratic agencies has more than doubled, compounding the problem of presidential control over subordinates.[23]

The problem of presidential control is most severe in the case of appointees who work outside the White House, in the departments and agencies. The loyalty of agency heads and cabinet secretaries often is split between a desire to promote the president's goals and an interest in boosting themselves or the agencies they lead. In 2005, when Hurricane Katrina devastated New Orleans, FEMA director Michael Brown, a Bush appointee, took the lead even though he had no appreciable experience with disaster relief. Intent on taking full control, Brown ignored the chain of command, withholding information from his immediate superior, the Homeland Security secretary, thereby making a coordinated relief effort harder to accomplish. Brown's incompetence was initially obscured by the scale of the disaster. Two days into the relief effort, President Bush said publicly, "Brownie, you're doing a heck of a job." Several days later, however, Brown's missteps had become clear and were headline news, leading the White House to force him to resign.

Lower-level appointees within the departments and agencies pose a different type of problem. The president rarely, if ever, sees them, and they typically are political novices (most have fewer than two years of government experience) and are not very knowledgeable about policy. These appointees are often "captured" by the agency in which they work because they depend on the agency's career bureaucrats for advice. (Chapter 13 examines further the relationship between presidential appointees and career bureaucrats.)

In sum, the modern presidential office is a double-edged sword. Presidents today have greater responsibilities than their predecessors, and this increase in responsibilities expands their opportunities to exert power. At the same time, the range of these responsibilities is so broad that presidents must rely on staff who may or may not act in the president's best interests. The modern president's recurring problem is to find some way of making sure that appointees place the interests of the presidency ahead of all others. (The subject of presidential control of the executive branch is discussed further in Chapter 13.)

Factors in Presidential Leadership

The president operates within a system of separate institutions that share power (see "How the U.S. Compares"). Significant presidential action normally depends on the approval of Congress, the cooperation of the bureaucracy, and sometimes the acceptance of the judiciary. Because other officials have their own priorities, presidents do not always get their way. Congress in particular—more than the courts or the bureaucracy—holds the key to presidential success. Without congressional authorization and funding, most presidential proposals are nothing but ideas, empty of action.

Whether a president's initiatives succeed or fail depends substantially on several factors, including the force of circumstance, the stage of the president's term, the nature of the particular issue, the president's support in Congress, and

HOW THE U.S. COMPARES

SYSTEMS OF EXECUTIVE POLICY LEADERSHIP

The United States instituted a presidential system in 1789 as part of its constitutional checks and balances. This form of executive leadership was copied in Latin America but not in Europe. European democracies adopted parliamentary systems, in which executive leadership is provided by a prime minister, who is a member of the legislature. In recent years, some European prime ministers have campaigned and governed as if they were a singular authority rather than the head of a collective institution. France in the 1960s created a separate chief executive office but retained its parliamentary form of legislature.

The policy leadership of a president can differ substantially from that of a prime minister. As a singular head of an independent branch of government, a president does not have to share executive authority but nevertheless depends on the legislative branch for support. By comparison, a prime minister shares executive leadership with a cabinet, but once agreement within the cabinet is reached, he or she is almost assured of the legislative support necessary to carry out policy initiatives.

Presidential System	Presidential/ Parliamentary System	Parliamentary System
Mexico	Finland	Australia
United States	France	Belgium
Venezuela	Russia	Canada
		Germany
		Great Britain
		Israel
		Italy
		Japan
		Netherlands
		Sweden

the level of public support for the president's leadership. The remainder of this chapter examines each of these factors.

The Force of Circumstance

During his first months in office and in the midst of the Great Depression, Franklin D. Roosevelt accomplished the most sweeping changes in domestic policy in the nation's history. Congress moved quickly to pass nearly every New Deal initiative he proposed. In 1964 and 1965, Lyndon Johnson pushed landmark civil rights and social welfare legislation through Congress on the strength of the civil rights movement, the legacy of the assassinated President Kennedy, and large Democratic majorities in the House and Senate. When Ronald Reagan assumed the presidency in 1981, inflation and high unemployment had greatly weakened the national economy and created a mood for change, enabling Reagan to persuade Congress to support some of the most substantial taxing and spending changes in history.

From such presidencies has come the popular impression that presidents single-handedly decide national policy. However, each of these periods of presidential dominance was marked by a special set of circumstances: a decisive election victory that gave added force to the president's leadership, a compelling national problem that convinced Congress and the public that bold presidential action was needed, and a president who was mindful of what was expected and who vigorously advocated policies consistent with those expectations.

When conditions are favorable, the power of the presidency is remarkable. The problem for most presidents is that conditions normally are not conducive to strong leadership. Political scientist Erwin Hargrove suggests that presidential influence depends largely on circumstance.[24] Some presidents serve in periods when resources are scarce or when important problems are surfacing in American society but have not yet reached a critical point. Such situations, Hargrove contends, work against the president's efforts to accomplish significant policy change. In 1994, reflecting on the constraints of budget deficits and other factors beyond his control, President Clinton said he had no choice but "to play the hand that history had dealt" him. Stark reality also confronted Obama when he assumed the presidency in 2009. A large budget deficit stood in the way of his campaign promise to spend heavily on health care and education.

The Stage of the President's Term

If conditions conducive to great accomplishments occur infrequently, it is nonetheless the case that nearly every president has favorable moments. Such moments often come during the first months in office. Most newly elected presidents enjoy a **honeymoon period** during which Congress, the press, and the public anticipate initiatives from the Oval Office and are more predisposed than usual to support them. Not surprisingly, presidents have put forth more new programs in their first year in office than in any subsequent year. James Pfiffner uses the term *strategic presidency* to refer to a president's need to move quickly on priority items in order to take advantage of the policy momentum gained from the election.[25] Later in their terms, presidents tend to be less successful in presenting initiatives and getting them enacted. They may run out of good ideas, get caught up in scandal, or exhaust their political resources; further, the momentum of their election is gone, and sources of opposition have emerged. Even successful presidents like Johnson and Reagan had weak records in their final years. Franklin Roosevelt began his presidency with a remarkable period of achievement—

honeymoon period
The president's first months in office, a time when Congress, the press, and the public are more inclined than usual to support presidential initiatives.

Presidents rely on trusted advisers in making critical policy decisions. During the Cuban missile crisis in 1962, this group of advisers to President John F. Kennedy helped him decide on a naval blockade as a means of forcing the Soviet Union to withdraw its missiles from Cuba.

the celebrated "Hundred Days"—but during his last six years in office, few of his major domestic proposals were enacted.

An irony of the presidency, then, is that presidents are usually most powerful when they are least knowledgeable—during their first months in office. These months can, as a result, be times of risk as well as times of opportunity. An example is the Bay of Pigs fiasco during the first year of John Kennedy's presidency, in which a U.S.-backed invasion force of anticommunist Cubans was easily defeated by Fidel Castro's army.

The Nature of the Issue: Foreign or Domestic

In the 1960s, political scientist Aaron Wildavsky wrote that although the nation has only one president, it has two presidencies: one domestic and one foreign.[26] Wildavsky was referring to Congress's greater tendency to defer to presidential leadership on foreign policy issues than on domestic policy issues. He had in mind the broad leeway Congress had granted Truman, Eisenhower, Kennedy, and Johnson in their foreign policies. Wildavsky's thesis is now regarded as a somewhat time-bound conception of presidential influence. Today, many of the same factors that affect a president's domestic policy success, such as the partisan composition of Congress, also affect foreign policy success.

Nevertheless, presidents still have somewhat of an advantage when the issue is foreign policy, because they have more authority to act on their own and are more likely to receive support from Congress.[27] The clash between powerful interest groups that occurs over many domestic issues is less prevalent in the foreign policy area. Additionally, the president is recognized by other nations as America's voice in world affairs, and members of Congress sometimes will defer to the president in order to maintain America's credibility abroad. In some cases, presidents literally decide the direction of foreign policy. In their 2008 race, Obama and McCain took sharply opposing positions on the U.S. military presence in Iraq. Obama's victory meant a more substantial drawdown of U.S. troops than McCain had proposed.

Presidents also have leverage in foreign and defense policy because of their special relationship with the defense, diplomatic, and intelligence agencies, sometimes called "presidential agencies." Other agencies that are responsive to the president are sometimes even more receptive to Congress; the Department of Agriculture, for example, often is more concerned with having the support of farm-state senators and representatives than with having the president's backing. The defense, diplomatic, and intelligence agencies, however, are different in that their missions are closely tied to the president's constitutional authority as commander in chief and chief diplomat. In the buildup to the Iraq war, for example, the defense and intelligence agencies operated in ways that promoted President Bush's stand on the need to confront Saddam Hussein militarily. Only later did Congress discover that the intelligence information it had been provided, as well as the assessments it had been given by the Defense Department on the level of military force required to invade and pacify Iraq, had been tailored to suit Bush's plans.

Relations with Congress

Although the power of the presidency is not nearly as extensive as some Americans assume, presidents' ability to influence the agenda of national debate is unrivaled, reflecting their unique claim to represent the whole country. Whenever the president directs attention to a particular issue, members of Congress take notice. But will they take action? The answer is sometimes yes and sometimes no, depending in part on whether the president takes their concerns into account.

Seeking Cooperation from Congress

As the center of national attention, presidents can start to believe that their ideas should prevail over those of Congress. This reasoning invariably gets any president into trouble. Jimmy Carter had not held national office before he was elected president in 1976 and thus had no clear understanding of how Washington operates.[28] Soon after taking office, Carter deleted from his budget nineteen public works projects that he believed were a waste of taxpayers' money, ignoring the determination of members of Congress to obtain federally funded projects for their constituents. Carter's action set the tone for a conflict-ridden relationship with Congress.

In order to get the help of members of Congress, the president must respond to their interests as they respond to those of the president.[29] The most basic fact about presidential leadership is that it takes place in the context of a system of divided powers. Although the president gets most of the attention, Congress has most of the constitutional authority in the American system, and presidents must get the cooperation of Congress to achieve their legislative goals.

Even the president's most direct legislative tool, the veto, has limits. Congress can seldom muster the two-thirds majority in each chamber required to override a presidential veto, so the threat of a veto can make Congress bend to the president's demands. Yet, as presidential scholar Richard Neustadt argued, the veto is as much a sign of presidential weakness as it is a sign of strength, because it arises when Congress refuses to go along with the president's ideas.[30] An example is the first veto cast by George W. Bush. Until then, Bush was on track to join Thomas Jefferson as the only two-term president not to veto a bill. In 2006, however, Bush vetoed a bill that would have expanded federal support for embryonic-stem-cell research. He had announced his opposition to such research early in his presidency and was successful for a time in getting congressional Republicans to back him. As Bush's popularity plummeted in 2005, however, some congressional Republicans separated themselves from the president

President Lyndon Johnson addresses a joint session of Congress in 1965. Johnson had an extraordinary record of success with Congress, which adopted the great majority of his legislative proposals. Johnson had the good fortune of working with a Congress controlled—by a wide margin—by his own party.

out of concern for their reelection chances. Enough Republicans defected on the stem-cell bill to get it through Congress, setting the stage for Bush's veto. Bush was further weakened when his party lost control of the House and Senate in the 2006 midterm elections. He increasingly resorted to actual and threatened vetoes in dealing with Congress.

Congress is a constituency that all presidents must serve if they expect to have its support. Neustadt concluded that presidential power, at base, is "the power to persuade."[31] Like any singular notion of presidential power, Neustadt's has limitations. Presidents at times have the power to command and to threaten. They can also appeal directly to the American people as a means of pressuring Congress. But Congress can never be taken for granted. Theodore Roosevelt expressed the wish that he could "be the president and Congress, too," if only for a day, so that he would have the power to enact as well as to propose laws.

Benefiting from Partisan Support in Congress

For most presidents, the next best thing to being "Congress, too" is to have a Congress filled with members of their own party. The sources of division within Congress are many. Legislators from urban and rural areas, wealthier and poorer constituencies, and different regions of the country often have very different views of the national interest. To obtain majority support in Congress, the president must find ways to overcome these differences.

No source of unity is more important to presidential success than partisanship. Presidents are more likely to succeed when their own party controls Congress (see Figure 12-1). Between 1954 and 1992, each Republican president—Eisenhower, Nixon, Ford, Reagan, and Bush—had to contend with a Democratic majority in one or both houses of Congress. Congress passed a smaller percentage of the initiatives supported by each of these presidents than those supported by any Democratic president of the period: Kennedy, Johnson, or Carter. In his first two years in office, backed by Democratic majorities in the House and Senate, more than 85 percent of the bills Clinton supported were enacted into law. After Republicans took control of Congress in 1995, Clinton's legislative success rate sank below 40 percent. George W. Bush suffered a similar fate when control of Congress shifted from the Republicans to the Democrats in 2007. Bush had a legislative success rate of 81 percent in 2006, but it fell to 38 percent in 2007—a sharp illustration of how presidential power depends on which party controls Congress.

Colliding with Congress

On rare occasions, presidents have pursued their goals so zealously that Congress has been compelled to take steps to curb their use of power.

The ultimate sanction of Congress is its constitutional power to impeach and remove the president from office. The House of Representatives decides by majority vote whether the president should be impeached (placed on trial), and the Senate conducts the trial and then votes on the president's case, with a two-thirds vote required for removal from office. In 1868, Andrew Johnson came within one Senate vote of being removed from office for his opposition to Congress's harsh Reconstruction policies after the Civil War. In 1974, Richard Nixon's

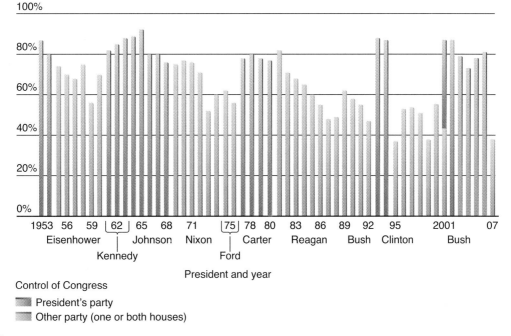

Percentage of bills on which Congress
supported president's position

Control of Congress
■ President's party
■ Other party (one or both houses)

FIGURE 12-1   **Percentage of Bills Passed by Congress on Which the President Announced a Position, 1953–2007**   In most years, presidents have been supported by Congress on a majority of policy issues on which they have taken a stand. Presidents fare better when their party controls Congress.
Source: *Congressional Quarterly Weekly Report,* various dates.

resignation halted congressional proceedings on the Watergate affair that almost certainly would have ended in his impeachment and removal from office.

The specter of impeachment arose again in 1998 when the House of Representatives by a vote of 258 to 176 authorized an investigation of President Clinton's conduct. He was accused of lying under oath about his relationship with intern Monica Lewinsky and of obstructing justice by trying to conceal the affair. The gravity of the allegations was leavened by the circumstances. The charges had grown out of an extramarital affair rather than a gross abuse of executive power, and though Americans disapproved of Clinton's behavior, most of them did not think it constituted "treason, bribery, or other high crimes and misdemeanors," the Constitution's basis for impeachment and removal from office. Not surprisingly, congressional Republicans and Democrats differed sharply on the impeachment issue. At all formal stages of the process—the House vote to authorize an inquiry, the House vote on the articles of impeachment, and the Senate vote on whether to remove the president—the vote was divided largely along party lines. In the end, Clinton was acquitted by the Senate, but his legacy will forever be tarnished by his impeachment by the House.

The gravity of an impeachment action makes it an unsuitable basis for curbing presidential power except in rare instances. More often, Congress has responded legislatively to what it sees as unwarranted assertions of executive power. An example is the Budget Impoundment and Control Act of 1974, which prohibits a president from indefinitely withholding funds that have been appropriated by Congress. The legislation was enacted in response to President Nixon's practice of withholding funds from programs he disliked. A similar controversy erupted in 2006 when it was revealed that President Bush had used so-called signing statements to challenge the constitutionality of more than seven hundred bills. These statements, appended to a bill when the president signs it, are meant to indicate that the president does not necessarily plan to abide by particular provisions of a law. Although Bush was not the first president to use this device, he had attached signing statements to more bills than all of his predecessors combined and had done so in secrecy. Even congressional Republicans expressed concern about the practice. At Senate Judiciary Committee hearings, Senator Arlen Specter (R-Penn.), chair of the committee, argued that presidents do not have the authority to pick and choose among legislative provisions, approving those they like and disregarding the rest. The president's choice is to accept or reject a bill in its entirety. Said Specter, "The president has the option under the Constitution to veto or not."[32]

Congress's most significant historical effort to curb presidential power is the War Powers Act. During the Vietnam War, Presidents Johnson and Nixon repeatedly misled Congress, supplying it with intelligence estimates that painted a falsely optimistic picture of the military situation. Believing the war was being won, Congress regularly voted to provide the money necessary to keep it going. However, congressional support changed abruptly in 1971 with publication in the *New York Times* of classified documents (the so-called Pentagon Papers) that revealed the Vietnam situation to be much worse than Johnson and Nixon had claimed.

To prevent future presidential wars, Congress in 1973 passed the War Powers Act. Nixon vetoed the measure, but Congress overrode his veto. The act does not prohibit the president from sending troops into combat, but it does require the president to notify Congress of the reason for committing combat troops within forty-eight hours of their deployment. The act also specifies that hostilities must end within sixty days unless Congress extends the period; gives the president an additional thirty days to withdraw the troops from hostile territory, although Congress can shorten this period; and requires the president to consult with Congress whenever feasible before sending troops into a hostile situation.

Every president since Nixon has claimed that the War Powers Act infringes on his constitutional power as commander in chief, and each has refused to accept it fully. The Supreme Court has not ruled on the constitutionality of the War Powers Act, leaving open the question of whether it is a substantial constraint on the president's war-making powers.

Thus, the effect of presidential efforts to circumvent congressional authority has been to heighten congressional opposition. Even if presidents gain in the short run by acting on their own, they undermine their capacity to lead in the long run if they fail to keep in mind that Congress is a coequal branch of the American governing system.

Public Support

Every recent president has had the public's confidence at the start of his term of office. When asked in polls whether they "approve or disapprove of how the president is doing his job," a majority of Americans have expressed approval during the first months of the president's term. Sooner or later, however, all **presidential approval ratings** have slipped below this high point, and several recent presidents have left office with a rating below 50 percent (see Table 12-5).

presidential approval ratings
A measure of the degree to which the public approves or disapproves of the president's performance in office.

Public support affects a president's ability to achieve policy goals. Presidential power rests in part on a claim to national leadership, and the legitimacy of that claim is roughly proportional to the president's public support. With public backing, the president's leadership cannot easily be dismissed by other Washington officials. When the president's public support sinks, officials are less inclined to accept presidential leadership. Congress's response to George W. Bush's leadership illustrates the pattern. In the early years of his presidency,

TABLE 12-5 | Percentage of Public Expressing Approval of President's Performance
Presidential approval ratings generally are higher at the beginning
of the term than at the end.

President	Years in Office	Average During Presidency	First-Year Average	Final-Year Average
Harry Truman	1945–52	41%	63%	35%
Dwight Eisenhower	1953–60	64	74	62
John Kennedy	1961–63	70	76	62
Lyndon Johnson	1963–68	55	78	40
Richard Nixon	1969–74	49	63	24
Gerald Ford	1974–76	46	75	48
Jimmy Carter	1977–80	47	68	46
Ronald Reagan	1981–88	53	58	57
George H. W. Bush	1989–92	61	65	40
Bill Clinton	1993–2000	57	50	60
George W. Bush	2001–8	51	68	33

Source: Averages compiled from Gallup polls.

Bush got from the Congress nearly everything he asked for, a reason that five years elapsed before he cast his first veto. As his popularity declined, however, congressional inaction on or opposition to his major proposals became nearly the rule. Among the casualties were Bush's social security and immigration reform proposals.

Events and Issues

The public's support for the president is affected by national and international conditions. Threats from abroad tend to produce a patriotic "rally 'round the flag" reaction that initially creates widespread support for the president. Every foreign policy crisis in the past four decades has followed this pattern. Americans were deeply divided in 2003 over the wisdom of war with Iraq, but when the fighting began, President Bush's approval rating rose. However, ongoing crises can erode a president's support if they are not resolved successfully or soon. Bush's approval rating jumped above 70 percent with the invasion of Iraq in 2003 but then fell steadily as U.S. casualties mounted. By 2006, his approval rating had fallen below 40 percent, and his party suffered heavy losses in that year's midterm election.

Historically, presidents' public support has rested mainly on the strength of the economy. Economic downturns invariably reduce the public's confidence in the president.[33] Ford, Carter, and the first President Bush lost their reelection bids when their popularity plummeted after the economy swooned. In contrast, Clinton's popularity rose in 1995 and 1996 as the economy strengthened, contributing to his reelection in 1996. The irony, of course, is that presidents do not actually have that much control over the economy. If they did, it would always be strong.

The Televised Presidency

A major advantage that presidents enjoy in their efforts to nurture public support is their access to the media, particularly television. Only the president can expect the networks to provide free air time on occasion, and in terms of the amount

White House reporters gather in the cramped space of the White House press room, where they receive daily briefings on the president's activities. Effective communication is an essential part of the modern presidency.

of news coverage, the president and top presidential advisers receive twice as much coverage as all members of Congress combined.

Political scientist Samuel Kernell calls it "going public" when the president bypasses inside bargaining with Congress and promotes "himself and his policies by appealing to the American public for support."[34] Such appeals are at least as old as Theodore Roosevelt's use of the presidency as a "bully pulpit," but they have increased substantially in recent years. As the president's role has moved from administrative leader to policy advocate and agenda setter, public support has become increasingly important to presidential success. Television has made it easier for presidents to go public with their programs, though the public's response depends partly on the president's rhetorical skill. Ronald Reagan was called "the Great Communicator" because of his skilled use of television to mobilize public support.

However, presidents cannot count on favorable press coverage. Journalists are adept at putting their own spin on what political leaders say and tend to play up adverse developments. For example, although presidents get some credit in the press when the economy is doing well, they get mounds of negative coverage when the economy is doing poorly. They also get hammered whenever there is a whiff of wrongdoing within the Administration. In 2004, for example, informed sources claimed that the Bush administration had targeted Iraq long before it ordered an invasion of that country. Secretary of Defense Donald Rumsfeld reportedly wanted to bomb Iraq immediately after the terrorist attacks of September 11, 2001, even though there was no evidence linking Iraq to the attacks. Rumsfeld was quoted by a White House insider as saying "There aren't any good targets in Afghanistan and there are lots of good targets in Iraq." The allegations were front-page news for days on end, putting the Bush administration on the defensive.

The Illusion of Presidential Government

Presidents have no choice but to try to counter negative press coverage with their own version of events. President George W. Bush did exactly that by scheduling blocks of interviews with journalists from local and regional news outlets to say that the real story of the Iraq effort—the success story of reopened schools, restored oil production, and renewed hope for the Iraqi people—was not being told by the Washington press corps. Bush accused national reporters of focusing only on the death and destruction in Iraq.

Such efforts can carry a president only so far, however. No president can fully control his communicated image, and national conditions ultimately have the largest impact on a president's public support. No amount of public relations can disguise adverse developments at home or abroad. Indeed, presidents run a risk by building up their images through public relations. By thrusting themselves into the limelight, presidents contribute to the public's belief that the president is in charge of the national government, a perception political scientist Hugh Heclo calls "the illusion of presidential government."[35] If they are as powerful as they project themselves to be, they will be held responsible for policy failures as well as policy successes.

Because the public expects so much from its presidents, they get too much credit when things go well and too much blame when things go badly. Therein lies an irony of the presidential office. More than from any constitutional grant, more than from any statute, and more than from any crisis, presidential power derives from the president's position as the sole official who can claim to represent the entire American public. Yet because presidential power rests on a popular base, it erodes when public support declines. The irony is that the presidential office typically grows weaker as problems mount. Just when the country most needs effective leadership, strong leadership often is hardest to achieve.[36]

Summary   Self-Test www.mhhe.com/pattersontad9e

The presidency has become a much stronger office than the Framers envisioned. The Constitution grants the president substantial military, diplomatic, legislative, and executive powers, and in each case the president's authority has increased measurably over the nation's history. Underlying this change is the president's position as the one leader chosen by the whole nation and as the sole head of the executive branch. These features of the office have enabled presidents to claim broad authority in response to the increased demands placed on the federal government by changing global and national conditions.

During the course of American history, the presidential selection process has been altered in ways intended to make it more responsive to the preferences of ordinary people. Today, the electorate has a vote not only in the general election but also in the selection of party nominees. To gain nomination, a presidential hopeful must gain the support of the electorate in state primaries and open caucuses. Once nominated, the candidates receive federal funds for their general election campaigns, which today are based on televised appeals.

Although the campaign tends to personalize the presidency, the responsibilities of the modern presidency far exceed any president's personal capacities. To meet their obligations, presidents have surrounded themselves with large staffs of advisers, policy experts, and managers. These staff members enable the president to extend control over the executive branch while at the same time providing the information necessary for policymaking. All recent presidents have discovered, however, that their control of staff resources is incomplete and that some things others do on their behalf can work against what they are trying to accomplish.

As sole chief executive and the nation's top elected leader, presidents can always expect that their policy and leadership efforts will receive attention. However, other institutions, particularly Congress, have the authority to make presidential leadership effective. No president has come close to winning approval of all the programs he has placed before Congress, and the presidents' records of success have varied considerably. The factors in a president's success include whether national conditions that require strong leadership from the White House are present and whether the president's party has a majority in Congress.

To hold onto an effective leadership position, the president depends on the backing of the American people. Recent presidents have made extensive use of the media to build support for their programs, yet they have had difficulty maintaining that support throughout their terms of office. A major reason is that the public expects far more from its presidents than they can deliver.

Study Corner

Key Terms

cabinet (*p. 325*)
honeymoon period (*p. 327*)
momentum (in campaigns)
(*p. 315*)
open party caucuses (*p. 315*)

presidential approval
ratings (*p. 332*)
stewardship theory (*p. 311*)
unit rule (*p. 318*)
Whig theory (*p. 311*)

Self-Test

1. Which two features of the presidency have enabled it to become more powerful than the Framers envisioned?
   a. power to disregard the Supreme Court and also Congress during national emergencies
   b. power to use presidential resources to defeat members of Congress and power to veto acts of Congress
   c. election by national vote and president's position as sole chief executive
   d. power to appoint federal judges and to appoint high-ranking executives

2. Key presidential appointees who are responsible for coordinating the activities of the executive branch are located in the:
   a. Office of the General Counsel.
   b. Attorney General's Office.
   c. General Accounting Office.
   d. Executive Office of the President.

3. A president is most successful passing legislative initiatives when Congress is:
   a. in recess.
   b. acting in an election year as opposed to a year when no federal election is scheduled to be held.
   c. controlled by the president's own party.
   d. concentrating on domestic policy issues as opposed to foreign policy issues.

4. Which of the following is **not** an important factor in the success that presidents have had in getting their policy proposals enacted into law?
   a. the force of circumstance, such as war or economic instability
   b. stage of the president's term
   c. level of public support for the president's leadership
   d. ability to raise campaign funds

5. Systems that have been used in the United States for presidential selection include all **except** which one of the following?
   a. congressional caucus
   b. national party convention
   c. direct election by popular vote

   d. combination of national convention and primary elections
   e. party primary and open party caucus

6. Advantages that newly elected presidents gain from their appointment powers include all **except** which one of the following?
   a. gain a source of information for policymaking
   b. can force Congress to confirm the appointment even of nominees Congress judges as unfit to hold executive office
   c. can extend the president's authority into the federal bureaucracy
   d. can make sure that some people in key positions share the president's political and policy goals

7. A candidate running for president has to accept federal campaign funding. (T/F)

8. Under the War Powers Act, the president must have the formal consent of Congress to send U.S. troops into combat. (T/F)

9. National conditions, such as the state of the economy, rarely affect the level of public confidence in the president. (T/F)

10. Big government after the Roosevelt era has favored the growth of legislative authority at the expense of executive authority. (T/F)

Critical Thinking

Why is presidential power "conditional"—that is, why is it affected so substantially by circumstance, the makeup of Congress, and popular support? (The separation of powers should be part of your answer.)

Suggested Readings

Campbell, James E. *The American Campaign: U.S. Presidential Campaigns and the National Vote.* College Station, Tex.: Texas A&M University Press, 2008. An analysis that reveals the predictability of presidential campaign outcomes.

Entman, Robert M. *Projections of Power: Framing News, Public Opinion, and U.S. Foreign Policy.* Chicago: University of Chicago Press, 2003. An assessment of the president's power to set the news agenda.

Jones, Charles O. *The Presidency in a Separated System.* Washington, D.C.: Brookings Institution Press, 2005. A careful analysis of president-Congress relations.

Milkis, Sidney, and Michael Nelson. *The American Presidency: Origins and Development, 1776–2002,* 5th ed. Washington, D.C.: Congressional Quarterly Press, 2007.

A thoughtful assessment of the factors and conditions that have molded the presidential office.

Neustadt, Richard E. *Presidential Power and the Modern Presidents: The Politics of Leadership from Roosevelt to Reagan.* New York: Free Press, 1990. The classic analysis of the limitations on presidential power.

Pika, Joseph A., and John Anthony Maltese. *The Politics of the Presidency,* 7th ed. Washington, D.C.: Congressional Quarterly Press, 2008. An insightful look at the leadership skills demanded of presidents.

Schlesinger, Arthur M., Jr. *The Imperial Presidency.* Boston: Mariner Books, 2004. An analysis of the modern presidency by a Pulitzer Prize–winning historian.

Skowronek, Stephen. *Presidential Leadership in Political Time: Reprise and Reappraisal.* Lawrence: University of Kansas Press, 2008. An assessment of how conditions of the time have affected presidents' role and power.

List of Websites

http://www.ibiblio.org/lia/president
A site with general information on specific presidents and links to the presidential libraries.

http://www.ipl.org/ref/POTUS
A site that profiles the nation's presidents, their cabinet officers, and key events during their time in office.

http://www.usa.gov/
A site that gives information on the presidency and the Executive Office of the President, as well as links to key executive agencies and organizations.

http://www.whitehouse.gov/
The White House's home page; has an email guest book and includes information on the president, the vice president, and current White House activities.

Participate!

Consider writing a letter or sending an email to the president or a top presidential appointee that expresses your opinion on an issue that is currently the object of executive action. You can inform yourself about the administration's policy or stance on the issue through the website of the White House (www.whitehouse.gov) or of the agency in question (for example, the State Department's site, www.state.gov).

Extra Credit

For up-to-the-minute *New York Times* articles, interactive simulations, graphics, study tools, and more links and quizzes, visit the text's online learning center at www.mhhe.com/pattersontad9e.

Self-Test Answers

1. c   2. d   3. c   4. d   5. c   6. b   7. F   8. F   9. F   10. F

BUSH'S LEGACY

"Worst. President. Ever."

That succinct judgment, received not long ago via e-mail from a political scientist, sums up a good deal of what conventional wisdom has to say about President Bush. In an unscientific online poll of 109 historians, more than 60 percent rated Bush's presidency as the worst in U.S. history. In his 2007 book, Second Chance: Three Presidents and the Crisis of American Superpower, former National Security Adviser Zbigniew Brzezinski titles his chapter on Bush "Catastrophic Leadership." "A calamity," Brzezinski wrote. "A historical failure."

> One hypothesis is at odds with the prevailing wisdom that **Bush, whatever you think of him,** has been a president of major consequence.

And he was referring to just the Iraq war. The litany of disasters and failures commonly attributed to Bush has grown familiar enough to summarize in checklist format: WMD; Guantanamo; Abu Ghraib; waterboarding; wiretapping; habeas corpus; "Osama bin Forgotten"; anti-Americanism; deficits; spending; Katrina; Rumsfeld; Cheney; Gonzales; Libby. In this view, George W. Bush is at least as destructive as was Richard Nixon, a president whose mistakes and malfeasances took decades to undo.

Though a smaller band, Bush's defenders parry that he will look to history more like Harry Truman, a president whose achievements took decades to appreciate. In this view, Bush will be remembered as the president who laid the strategic groundwork for an extended struggle against Islamist terrorism; who made democratization the center-

piece of foreign policy; who transformed the federal-state relationship in education; who showed that a candidate can touch the "third rail" of Social Security and still get elected (twice).

Notice what those two views assume in common: Bush has been a game-changing president. For better or worse, he has succeeded in his ambition of being a transformative figure rather than one who plays "small ball," in Bush's own disdainful phrase. Hasn't he?

Perhaps not. Bush may go down in history as a transitional and comparatively minor figure. His presidency, though politically traumatic, may leave only a modest policy footprint. In that sense—though by no means substantively or stylistically—Bush's historical profile may resemble Jimmy Carter's more than Truman's or Nixon's.

Odd as it may sound today, this president entered office as a proponent of bipartisanship. Bush brought off a bipartisan education reform, and after the September 11 terrorist attacks, he did what even his critics agreed was a masterful job of rallying the country. His public approval rose to a dizzying 90 percent.

The fruits of this early period of two-party government were considerable: a new campaign finance law, the USA PATRIOT Act's revisions to domestic-security law, the Sarbanes-Oxley corporate accountability law, the creation of the Homeland Security Department, and more. "Seventeen major legislative acts were passed in the first two years of the Bush presidency—the second-highest among first-term presidents in the post-World War II period," writes Charles O. Jones, a presidential historian.

But 2002 also marked the Bush administration's transition to a more rigidly partisan governing style. That January, Karl Rove, Bush's top political adviser, signaled that Republicans would "make the president's handling of the war on terrorism the centerpiece of their strategy to win back the Senate," as The Washington Post reported. This

represented a distinct change in tone: "Until now," The Post noted, "Bush has stressed that the fight against terrorism is a bipartisan and unifying issue for the country."

That year's midterm election, which gave Republicans control of the Senate and consolidated their margin in the House, vindicated their strategy but also trapped the party within it.

In firm control of both branches, Bush and congressional Republicans embarked on an experiment in one-party government. What followed was a period of substantive excess and stylistic harshness that came to define Bush's presidency in the public's mind, obliterating memories of the "compassionate conservative."

Profligate spending and a major Medicare expansion disgusted conservatives. Efforts to reform Social Security and immigration policy collapsed embarrassingly; Bush's sluggish response to Hurricane Katrina cratered Americans' faith in his competence. Abroad, Abu Ghraib, Guantanamo, waterboarding and extrajudicial detentions called the country's basic decency into question.

By 2006, the president's approval rating was in the 30 percent range and falling. The Democrats swept control of Congress in November. If Bush's presidency had ended in January 2007, his reputation as our era's Nixon might have been assured.

But Bush has used his last two years as, in effect, a third term, behaving as if he were his own successor.

"There was unquestionably a sharp change in their approach to the world and in their policies," says Kenneth Pollack, a senior fellow at the Brookings Institution. Frequently cited examples include the Iraq surge, patient but rigid dealings with Iran, a relaunch of Israeli-Palestinian peace talks, a denuclearization deal with North Korea, and a promise to halve greenhouse-gas emissions by 2050.

What changed? "I think we learned a bit," Stephen Hadley, Bush's national security adviser, told reporters in June.

But ever protective of Bush's trademark steadfastness, the White House takes issue with any talk of U-turns. "I think there's actually remarkable continuity," says Tony Fratto, the deputy press secretary. He asserts that reality has caught up with the administration rather than the other way around.

Whatever the explanation, Bush hands the next president a healing rather than a broken Iraq, diplomatic processes rather than deadlocks in the Middle East and the Korean Peninsula, and a position on global warming that is widely viewed as moving the United States past obstructionism.

"I think what you see here is a guy who has learned to be as effective as possible in reduced circumstances," says political scientist Steven Schier. Paradoxically, this chief executive who prided himself on assertive, even aggressive, leadership proved to be a weak strong president but a surprisingly strong weak one.

The harder question is where Bush will leave matters after eight years, not after just the past two. One hypothesis is odds with the prevailing wisdom that Bush, whatever you think of him, has been a president of major consequence. Consider, again, the five problems mentioned earlier. The situation in Iraq in January 2001 was unstable and dangerous but not critical, and the same is true today. With regards to Iran, the Israeli-Palestinian conflict, North Korea, and global warming, the country is in roughly the same place it was when Bill Clinton left office.

Two other areas, the war on terrorism and fiscal policy, deserve a closer look.

September 11, 2001, it is often said, "changed everything." It certainly changed Americans' attitudes, convincing the public that Al Qaeda and its affiliates are a threat rather than a nuisance, and that the United States must apply military as well as civilian tools to confront terrorism. September 11 thereby triggered a cascade of policy changes, ranging from the PATRIOT Act to the Iraq war.

The threat was pre-existing, however, as Bush's supporters tirelessly repeat (adding that the Clinton administration failed to deal with it). The question is whether Bush, like Truman, has set up a lasting strategic and institutional architecture for managing the conflict. "If we wait for threats to fully materialize, we will have waited too long," Bush said in June 2002. That statement, the core of the Bush Doctrine, is hardly controversial today.

Similarly, the Detainee Treatment Act, the Military Commissions Act, the PATRIOT Act, and the new Foreign Intelligence Surveillance Act have put in place mechanisms that subsequent presidents may revise but will not repudiate.

Bush's critics, meanwhile, argue that he trashed the country's finances. He cut taxes steeply, waged an expensive war without paying for it, engineered a costly expansion of Medicare (also without paying for it), and untethered federal spending, thus turning healthy surpluses into chronic deficits—all while failing to come to grips with an imminent crisis in entitlement programs.

"We're in much worse fiscal shape today than we were in 2001," says David Walker, who until recently headed the Government Accountability Office and is now president of the Peter G. Peterson Foundation.

As for Bush's tax cuts, viewed in historical perspective they were a blip, not a turning point. Overall, taxes went down early in this decade but then bobbed back up again, though not all the way.

Bush failed to deal with the long-term entitlement problem. He left the ledger in worse shape than he found it, and his botched effort to reform Social Security may have made entitlement reform more difficult politically. "I think we've lost a tremendous opportunity during the Bush period and, really, over the last part of the Clinton period," says Stuart Butler, an analyst at the Heritage Foundation.

Still, as Butler's comment implies, Bush's failure in this regard is not unique. His predecessors ducked the entitlement problem and his would-be successors are all but promising to do the same. Bush's fiscal failing, in short, arguably lies not in being exceptional but in being all too ordinary.

Indeed, what is most striking about the Bush presidency is not the new problems it has created (though Iraq may yet change that verdict) or the old problems it has solved (though Iraq may yet change that verdict, too). What is striking, rather, is that Bush will pass on to his successor all the major problems and preoccupations he inherited: Iraq, Iran, Israel and the Palestinians, North Korea, global warming, Islamist terrorism, nuclear proliferation, health care, entitlement costs, immigration. What is remarkable, in other words, is not how much Bush has done to reshape the agenda but how little.

Reagan removed inflation from the agenda; he and George H.W. Bush (still sadly underrated) removed the Cold War; Clinton removed welfare and the deficit. Bush, as of now, ends up more or less where he started—not exactly, of course (he resurrected the deficit, for example), but about as close as history's turbulence allows. The biggest surprise of the Bush presidency is its late-breaking bid to join the middling ranks of administrations that are judged not by their triumph or tragedy but by their opportunity cost: What might a greater or lesser president have done with Bush's eight years?

In his recent book The Bush Tragedy, Jacob Weisberg menions the he was "originally going to call this book The Bush Detour, thinking of the Bush presidency simply as lost time for the country." His original title may have been closer to the mark. If so, history's ironic judgment on this singularly ambitious president will be that his legacy was small ball, after all.

FOR DISCUSSION: Will the Bush legacy be a disaster, a detour, or a golden age?

How does the legacy of a president, such as Truman or Carter, affect us today?

Will the legacy of the Bush administration restrict what the next presidency can achieve?

NATIONAL PARK SERVICE

CRATER LAKE NATIONAL PARK

WEST ENTRANCE

U.S. DEPARTMENT OF INTERIOR

The Federal Bureaucracy
Administering the Government

Federal Administration: Form, Personnel, and Activities

The Structure of the Federal Bureaucracy
Federal Employment
The Federal Bureaucracy's Policy Responsibilities

Development of the Federal Bureaucracy: Politics and Administration

Small Government and the Patronage System
Growth in Government and the Merit System
Big Government and the Executive Leadership System

The Bureaucracy's Power Imperative

The Agency Point of View
Sources of Bureaucratic Power

Bureaucratic Accountability

Accountability Through the Presidency
Accountability Through Congress
Accountability Through the Courts
Accountability Within the Bureaucracy Itself

Reinventing Government?

> [No] industrial society could manage the daily operations of its public affairs without bureaucratic organizations in which officials play a major policymaking role. **Norman Thomas**[1]

Early on the morning of September 7, 1993, a truck pulled up to the south lawn of the White House and unloaded pallets stacked with federal regulations. The display was the backdrop for a presidential speech announcing the completion of the National Performance Review or, as it is commonly called, NPR. The federal regulations piled atop the pallets symbolized bureaucratic red tape, and the NPR was the Clinton administration's initiative to make government more responsive.

The origins of the NPR were plain enough. For years, the federal bureaucracy had been derided as being too big, too expensive, and too intrusive. These charges gained strength as federal budget deficits increased and the public became increasingly dissatisfied with the performance of the government in Washington. Reform attempts in the 1970s and 1980s had not stemmed the tide of federal deficits or markedly improved the bureaucracy's performance. Clinton campaigned on the issue of "reinventing government" and acted swiftly on the promise. Vice President–elect Al Gore was placed in charge of the NPR. He assembled more than two hundred career bureaucrats, who knew firsthand how the bureaucracy operated, and organized them into "reinventing teams." The NPR's report included 384 specific recommendations grouped into four broad imperatives: reducing red tape, putting customers first, empowering administrators, and cutting government back to basic services.[2]

The NPR was the most recent in a lengthy list of major efforts to remake the federal bureaucracy. The NPR was different in its particulars, but its claim to improve administration while saving money was consistent with the claims of earlier reform panels, including the Brownlow, Hoover, and Volcker commissions.[3] Like those efforts, the NPR addressed an enduring issue of American politics: the bureaucracy's efficiency, responsiveness, and accountability.

Modern government would be impossible without a large bureaucracy. It is the government's enormous administrative capacity

As one of thousands of services provided by the federal bureaucracy, the National Hurricane Service monitors hurricane activity and provides early warning to affected coastal areas.

that makes it possible for the United States to have ambitious programs such as space exploration, social security, interstate highways, and universal postal service. Yet the bureaucracy also poses special problems. Even those who work in federal agencies agree that the bureaucracy can be unresponsive, wasteful, and self-serving.

This chapter examines both the need for bureaucracy and the problems associated with it. The chapter describes the bureaucracy's responsibilities, organizational structure, and management practices. The chapter also explains the "politics" of the bureaucracy. Although the three constitutional branches of government impose a degree of accountability on the bureaucracy, its sheer size confounds their efforts to control it fully. The main points discussed in this chapter are these:

- *Bureaucracy is an inevitable consequence of complexity and scale.* Modern government could not function without a large bureaucracy. Through authority, specialization, and rules, bureaucracy provides a means of managing thousands of tasks and employees.

- *The bureaucracy is expected simultaneously to respond to the direction of partisan officials and to administer programs fairly and competently.* These conflicting demands are addressed through a combination of personnel management systems—the patronage, merit, and executive leadership systems.

- *Bureaucrats naturally take an "agency point of view," seeking to promote their agency's programs and power.* They do this through their expert knowledge, support from clientele groups, and backing by Congress or the president.

- *Although agencies are subject to oversight by the president, Congress, and the judiciary, bureaucrats exercise considerable power in their own right.*

Federal Administration: Form, Personnel, and Activities

For many Americans, the word *bureaucracy* brings to mind waste, mindless rules, and rigidity. This image is not unfounded, but it is one-sided. Bureaucracy is a highly effective form of organization. Although Americans tend to equate bureaucracy with the federal government, bureaucracy is found wherever there is a need to manage large numbers of people and tasks. All large-scale, task-oriented organizations—public and private—are bureaucratic in form.[4] General Motors is a bureaucracy, as is every university. The state governments are also every bit as "bureaucratic" as the federal government (see "States in the Nation").

In formal terms, **bureaucracy** is a system of organization and control that is based on three principles: hierarchical authority, job specialization, and formalized

bureaucracy

A system of organization and control based on the principles of hierarchical authority, job specialization, and formalized rules.

STATES IN THE NATION

THE SIZE OF STATE BUREAUCRACIES

Although the federal bureaucracy is often criticized as being "too big," it is actually smaller on a per capita basis than even the smallest state bureaucracy. There are 83 federal employees for every 1,000 Americans. Illinois, with 103 state employees for every 1,000 residents, has the smallest state bureaucracy on a per capita basis. Hawaii has the largest—428 state employees per 1,000 residents.

Q: What do the states with larger per capita bureaucracies have in common?

A: In general, the least populous states, especially those that are larger geographically, have larger bureaucracies on a per capita basis. This pattern reflects the fact that a state, whatever its population, has basic functions (such as highway maintenance and policing) that it must perform.

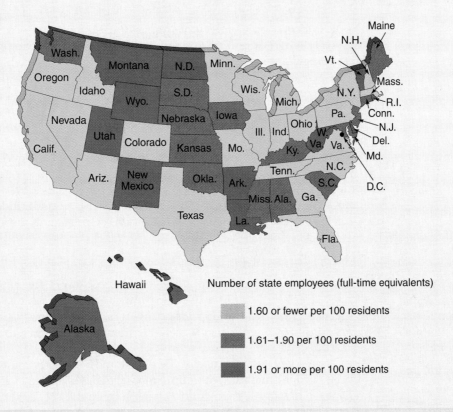

Number of state employees (full-time equivalents)

- 1.60 or fewer per 100 residents
- 1.61–1.90 per 100 residents
- 1.91 or more per 100 residents

Source: U.S. Bureau of the Census, 2008.

rules. These features are the reason bureaucracy, as a form of organization, is the most efficient means of getting people to work together on tasks of great magnitude. **Hierarchical authority** refers to a chain of command whereby the officials and units at the top of a bureaucracy have authority over those in the middle, who in turn control those at the bottom. Hierarchy speeds action by reducing conflict over the power to make decisions: those higher in the organization have authority over those below them. **Job specialization** refers to explicitly defined duties for each job position and to a precise division of labor within the organization. Specialization yields efficiency because each individual concentrates on a particular job and thereby becomes proficient at the tasks it involves. **Formalized rules** are the standardized procedures and established regulations by which a bureaucracy conducts its operations. Formalized rules enable workers to make quick and consistent judgments because decisions are based on preestablished rules rather than on elaborate case-by-case assessments.

hierarchical authority

A basic principle of bureaucracy that refers to the chain of command within an organization whereby officials and units have control over those below them.

job specialization

A basic principle of bureaucracy holding that the responsibilities of each job position should be explicitly defined and that a precise division of labor within the organization should be maintained.

formalized rules

A basic principle of bureaucracy that refers to the standardized procedures and established regulations by which a bureaucracy conducts its operations.

These same organizational characteristics are also the source of bureaucracy's pathologies. Administrators perform not as whole persons but as parts of an organizational entity. Their behavior is governed by position, specialty, and rule. At its worst, bureaucracy grinds on, heedless of the interests of its members or their clients. Fixed rules can become an end unto themselves, as anyone who has applied for a driver's license or a student loan knows all too well.

If bureaucracy is an indispensable condition of large-scale organization, gross bureaucratic inefficiency and unresponsiveness are not. At least that is the assumption underlying efforts to strengthen the administration of government, a topic examined later in this chapter.

The Structure of the Federal Bureaucracy

The U.S. federal bureaucracy has roughly 2.5 million employees, who have the responsibility for administering thousands of programs. The president and Congress get far more attention in the news, but the bureaucracy has the more immediate impact on Americans' everyday lives. The federal bureaucracy performs a wide range of functions; for example, it delivers the daily mail, maintains the national forests, administers social security, enforces environmental protection laws, develops the country's defense systems, provides foodstuffs for school lunch programs, and regulates the stock markets.

The U.S. federal bureaucracy is organized along policy lines. One agency handles veterans' affairs, another specializes in education, a third is responsible for agriculture, and so on. No two units are exactly alike. Nevertheless, most of them take one of five general forms: cabinet department, independent agency, regulatory agency, government corporation, or presidential commission.

Cabinet Departments

cabinet (executive) departments

The major administrative organizations within the federal executive bureaucracy, each of which is headed by a secretary or, in the case of Justice, the attorney general. Each department has responsibility for a major function of the federal government, such as defense, agriculture, or justice.

The major administrative units are the fifteen **cabinet (executive) departments** (see Figure 13-1). Except for the Department of Justice, which is led by the attorney general, the head of each department is its secretary (for example, the secretary of defense), who also serves as a member of the president's cabinet.

Cabinet departments vary greatly in their visibility, size, and importance. The Department of State, one of the oldest and most prestigious departments, is also one of the smallest, with approximately 25,000 employees. The Department of Defense has the largest workforce, with more than 600,000 civilian employees (apart from the more than 1.4 million uniformed active service members). The Department of Health and Human Services has the largest budget; its activities account for more than a fourth of all federal spending, much of it in the form of social security benefits. The Department of Homeland Security is the newest department, dating from 2002.

Each cabinet department has responsibility for a general policy area, such as defense or law enforcement. This responsibility is carried out within each department by semiautonomous operating units that typically carry the label "bureau," "agency," "division," or "service." The Department of Justice, for example, has thirteen such operating units, including the Federal Bureau of Investigation (FBI), the Civil Rights Division, the Tax Division, and the Drug Enforcement Administration (DEA).

Independent Agencies

independent agencies

Bureaucratic agencies that are similar to cabinet departments but usually have a narrower area of responsibility. Each such agency is headed by a presidential appointee who is not a cabinet member. An example is the National Aeronautics and Space Administration.

Independent agencies resemble the cabinet departments but typically have a narrower area of responsibility. They include organizations such as the Central

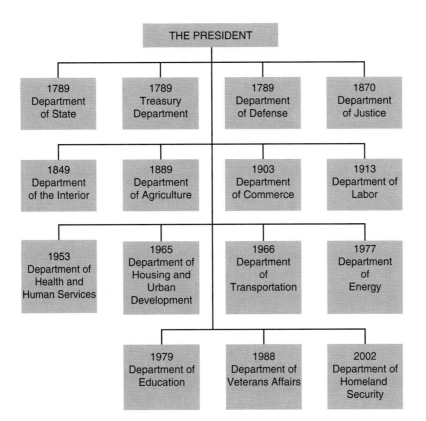

FIGURE 13-1 **Cabinet (Executive) Departments**
Each executive department is responsible for a general policy area and is headed by a secretary or, in the case of Justice, the attorney general, who serves as a member of the president's cabinet. Shown is each department's year of origin. (The Office of the Attorney General was created in 1789 and became the Justice Department in 1870.)

Intelligence Agency (CIA) and the National Aeronautics and Space Administration (NASA). The heads of these agencies are appointed by and report to the president but are not members of the cabinet. In general, the independent agencies exist apart from cabinet departments because their placement within a department would pose symbolic or practical policy problems. NASA, for example, could conceivably be located in the Department of Defense, but such positioning would suggest that the space program exists solely for military purposes and not also for civilian purposes such as space exploration and satellite communication.

Regulatory Agencies

Regulatory agencies are created when Congress recognizes the need for ongoing regulation of a particular economic activity. The Securities and Exchange Commission (SEC), which oversees the stock and bond markets, is a regulatory agency. So is the Environmental Protection Agency (EPA), which monitors and prevents industrial pollution. Table 13-1 lists some of the regulatory agencies and other noncabinet units of the federal bureaucracy.

Some regulatory agencies, particularly the older ones (such as the SEC), are headed by a commission of several members who are nominated by the president and confirmed by Congress but who are not subject to removal after they are appointed to office. Commissioners serve for a fixed number of years, a legal stipulation intended to make them "independent" of political pressure. However, the newer regulatory agencies (such as the EPA) lack this independence. They are headed by a single presidential appointee who can be removed at the president's discretion.

regulatory agencies

Administrative units, such as the Federal Communications Commission and the Environmental Protection Agency, that have responsibility for the monitoring and regulation of ongoing economic activities.

TABLE 13-1 | Selected U.S. Regulatory Agencies, Independent Agencies, Government Corporations, and Presidential Commissions

Central Intelligence Agency	National Labor Relations Board
Commission on Civil Rights	National Railroad Passenger Corporation (Amtrak)
Consumer Product Safety Commission	National Science Foundation
Environmental Protection Agency	
Equal Employment Opportunity Commission	National Transportation Safety Board
Export-Import Bank of the United States	Nuclear Regulatory Commission
Farm Credit Administration	Occupational Safety and Health Review Commission
Federal Communications Commission	Office of Personnel Management
Federal Deposit Insurance Corporation	Peace Corps
Federal Election Commission	Securities and Exchange Commission
Federal Maritime Commission	
Federal Reserve System, Board of Governors	Selective Service System
Federal Trade Commission	Small Business Administration
General Services Administration	U.S. Arms Control and Disarmament Agency
National Aeronautics and Space Administration	U.S. Information Agency
National Archives and Records Administration	U.S. International Trade Commission
National Foundation on the Arts and the Humanities	U.S. Postal Service

Source: *The U.S. Government Manual.*

Beyond their executive functions, regulatory agencies have legislative and judicial functions. They issue regulations and judge whether individuals or organizations have complied with them. The SEC, for example, can impose fines and other penalties on business firms that violate regulations pertaining to the trading of stocks and bonds.

Government Corporations

Government corporations are similar to private corporations in that they charge clients for their services and are governed by a board of directors. However, government corporations receive federal funding to help defray operating expenses, and their directors are appointed by the president with Senate approval. The largest government corporation is the U.S. Postal Service, with roughly 700,000 employees. Other government corporations include the Federal Deposit Insurance Corporation (FDIC), which insures savings accounts against bank failures, and the National Railroad Passenger Corporation (Amtrak), which provides passenger rail service.

Presidential Commissions

Presidential commissions provide advice to the president. Some of them are permanent bodies; examples include the Commission on Civil Rights and the Commission on Fine Arts. Other presidential commissions are temporary and disband after making recommendations on specific issues. An example is the President's Commission to Strengthen Social Security, which was created by President Bush in 2001 to study possible ways of reforming social security.

government corporations
Bodies, such as the U.S. Postal Service and Amtrak, that are similar to private corporations in that they charge for their services but differ in that they receive federal funding to help defray expenses. Their directors are appointed by the president with Senate approval.

presidential commissions
Advisory organizations within the bureaucracy that are headed by commissioners appointed by the president. An example is the Commission on Civil Rights.

Federal Employment

The roughly 2.5 million civilian employees of the federal government include professionals who bring their expertise to the problems involved in governing a large and complex society, service workers who perform such tasks as the typing of correspondence and the delivery of mail, and middle and top managers who supervise the work of the various federal agencies.

More than 90 percent of federal employees are hired by merit criteria, which include educational attainment (in the case, for example, of lawyers and engineers), employment experience, and performance on competitive tests (such as the civil service and foreign service examinations). The merit system is intended to protect the public from inept or biased administrative practices that could result if partisanship were the employment criterion.

Federal employees are underpaid in comparison with their counterparts in the private sector. The large majority of federal employees have a GS (Graded Service) job ranking. The regular civil service rankings range from GS-1 (the lowest rank) to GS-15 (the highest). College graduates who enter the federal service usually start at the GS-5 level, which provides an annual salary of roughly $27,000 for a beginning employee. With a master's degree, employees begin at level GS-9 with a salary of roughly $40,000 a year. Federal employees' salaries increase with rank and length of service. Public employees receive substantial fringe benefits, including full health insurance, secure retirement plans, and generous vacation time and sick leave.

The U.S. Postal Service is regarded by many as the best entity of its kind anywhere. It delivers more mail to more addresses than any other postal administration in the world, and it does so inexpensively and without undue delay. Yet, like many other government agencies, it is often criticized for its inefficiency and ineptness.

Public service has its drawbacks. Federal employees can form labor unions, but their unions by law have limited authority: the government maintains full control of job assignments, compensation, and promotion. Moreover, the Taft-Hartley Act of 1947 prohibits strikes by federal employees and permits the firing of striking workers. When federal air traffic controllers went on strike anyway in 1981, they were fired by President Reagan. There are also limits on the partisan activities of civil servants. The Hatch Act of 1939 prohibited them from holding key positions in election campaigns. In 1993, Congress relaxed this prohibition but retained it for certain high-ranking career bureaucrats.

Government employment is overseen by two independent agencies. The Office of Personnel Management supervises the hiring and job classification of federal employees. The Merit Service Protection Board handles appeals of career civil servants who have been fired or who face other disciplinary action.

The Federal Bureaucracy's Policy Responsibilities

The Constitution mentions executive departments but does not grant them any powers. Their authority derives from grants of power to the three constitutional branches: Congress, the president, and the courts. Nevertheless, the bureaucracy is far more than an administrative extension of the three branches. It exercises considerable power of its own.

Administrative agencies' main job is **policy implementation**—that is, the carrying out of decisions made by Congress, the president, and the courts. Although implementation has been described as "mere administration," it is in fact a creative activity. In the course of their work, administrators develop policy ideas that they then bring to the attention of the White House or Congress. Administrative agencies also make policy in the process of determining how to implement congressional, presidential, and judicial decisions. The Telecommunications Act of 1996, for example, had as its stated goal "to promote competition and reduce regulation in order to secure lower prices and higher quality services

policy implementation
The primary function of the bureaucracy; it refers to the process of carrying out the authoritative decisions of Congress, the president, and the courts.

for American telecommunication consumers and encourage the rapid deployment of new telecommunications technologies." Although the act included specific provisions, its implementation was left largely to the Federal Communications Commission (FCC) to determine. The FCC ruled, for example, that regional telephone companies (the Bell companies) had to open their networks to AT&T and other competitors at wholesale rates far below what they were charging their retail customers, which enabled these other carriers to compete with the Bell companies for local phone customers. Through this ruling, the FCC was responding to its legislative mandate "to promote competition." However, it was the FCC rather than Congress that determined the wholesale rates and competitors' access to Bell's customers. Such *rulemaking*—establishing how a law will work in practice—is the chief way administrative agencies exercise power over policy.[5]

Agencies also are charged with the delivery of services—carrying the mail, processing welfare applications, approving government loans, and the like. Such activities are governed by rules, and in most instances the rules determine what gets done. But some services give agency employees enough discretion that laws can be applied arbitrarily, a situation that Michael Lipsky describes as "street-level bureaucracy."[6] For example, FBI agents pursue organized crime more vigorously than they pursue white-collar crime, even though the laws do not say that white-collar crime should be treated more lightly.

In sum, administrators exercise discretion in carrying out their responsibilities. They initiate policy, develop it, evaluate it, apply it, and decide whether others are complying with it. The bureaucracy does not simply administer policy; it also *makes policy.*

Development of the Federal Bureaucracy: Politics and Administration

Agencies are responsible for programs that serve society, yet each agency was created and is maintained in response to partisan interests. Each agency thus confronts two simultaneous but incompatible demands: that it administer programs fairly and competently and that it respond to partisan demands.

Historically, this conflict has worked itself out in ways that have made the organization of the modern bureaucracy a blend of the political and the administrative. This dual line of development is reflected in the mix of management systems that characterizes the bureaucracy today—the patronage, merit, and executive leadership systems.

Small Government and the Patronage System

The federal bureaucracy originally was small (three thousand employees in 1800, for instance). The federal government's role was confined mainly to defense and foreign affairs, currency and interstate commerce, and the delivery of the mail. The nation's first six presidents, from George Washington through John Quincy Adams, believed that only distinguished men should be entrusted with the management of the national government. Nearly all top presidential appointees were men of education and political experience, and many of them were members of socially prominent families. They often remained in their positions year after year.

The nation's seventh president, Andrew Jackson, did not share his predecessors' admiration for the social elite. In Jackson's view, government would be more responsive to the public if it were administered by ordinary people of good sense.[7] Jackson also believed that top administrators should remain in office only

HISTORICAL
Background

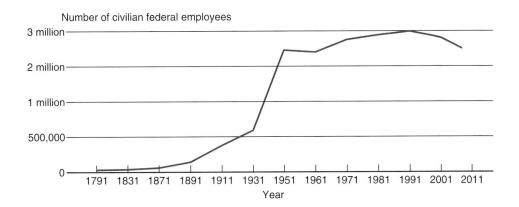

Number of civilian federal employees

FIGURE 13-2   **Number of Persons Employed Full-Time by the Federal Government**
The federal bureaucracy grew slowly until the 1930s, when an explosive growth began in the number of programs that required ongoing administration by the federal government.
Source: Historical Statistics of the United States and Statistical Abstract of the United States, 1986, 322; recent figures from U.S. Office of Personnel Management. Figure excludes military personnel.

for short periods to ensure a steady influx of fresh ideas that were consistent with the president's. Jackson's **patronage system** was popular with the general public but opposed by elites, who labeled it a **spoils system**—a device for giving government jobs to friends and party hacks. Although this depiction was not entirely accurate in the case of Jackson's appointees, it was true of those of several later presidents, who extended patronage to all levels of administration without much regard for its impact on governance.

Growth in Government and the Merit System

In the latter part of the 1800s, the federal government began to grow rapidly in size (see Figure 13-2), largely because rapid economic growth was placing new demands on it. Farmers were among the groups clamoring for help from government, and Congress in 1889 created the Department of Agriculture. Business and labor interests also pressed their claims, and in 1903, Congress established the Department of Commerce and Labor to "promote the mutual interest" of the nation's firms and workers. (The separate interests of business and labor proved stronger than their shared concerns, and thus in 1913, Commerce and Labor became separate departments.)

As government expanded, the need for a more skilled and experienced workforce became apparent. Movement away from the patronage system got a boost when Charles Guiteau, a disappointed officeseeker, assassinated President James A. Garfield in 1881. Two years later, Congress passed the Pendleton Act, which established a **merit (civil service) system** whereby certain federal employees were hired through competitive examinations or by virtue of having special qualifications, such as training in a particular field. The transition to a career civil service was gradual. Only 10 percent of federal positions in 1885 were filled on the basis of merit. But the pace accelerated when the Progressives championed the merit system as a way of eliminating partisan graft and corruption in the administration of government (see Chapter 2). By 1920, as the Progressive Era was concluding, more than 70 percent of federal employees were merit appointees. Since 1950, the proportion of merit employees has never dipped below 80 percent.[8]

The administrative objective of the merit system is **neutral competence.**[9] A merit-based bureaucracy is "competent" in the sense that employees are hired and retained on the basis of their skills, and it is "neutral" in the sense that employees are not partisan appointees and are expected to be of service to everyone, not just those who support the incumbent president. Although the merit system contributes to impartial and proficient administration, it has its own biases and inefficiencies. Career bureaucrats tend to place their agency's interests ahead of those of other agencies and typically oppose efforts to trim their agency's

patronage system
An approach to managing the bureaucracy whereby people are appointed to important government positions as a reward for political services they have rendered and because of their partisan loyalty.

spoils system
The practice of granting public office to individuals in return for political favors they have rendered.

merit (civil service) system
An approach to managing the bureaucracy whereby people are appointed to government positions on the basis of either competitive examinations or special qualifications, such as professional training.

neutral competence
The administrative objective of a merit-based bureaucracy. Such a bureaucracy should be "competent" in the sense that its employees are hired and retained on the basis of their expertise and "neutral" in the sense that it operates by objective standards rather than partisan ones.

The assassination of President James A. Garfield in 1881 by Charles Guiteau, a disappointed officeseeker, did much to end the spoils system of distributing government jobs.

executive leadership system

An approach to managing the bureaucracy that is based on presidential leadership and presidential management tools, such as the president's annual budget proposal.

programs. They are not partisans in a Democratic or Republican sense, but they are partisan in terms of protecting their own agencies, as will be explained more fully later in the chapter.

Big Government and the Executive Leadership System

As problems with the merit system surfaced after the early years of the twentieth century, reformers looked to a strengthened presidency—an **executive leadership system**—as a means of coordinating the bureaucracy's activities to increase its efficiency and responsiveness.[10] The president was to provide the general leadership that would overcome agency boundaries. As Chapter 12 describes, Congress in 1939 provided the president with some of the tools needed for improved coordination of the bureaucracy. The Office of Management and Budget (OMB) was created to give the president the authority to coordinate the annual budgetary process. Agencies were required to prepare their budget proposals under the direction of the president, who then submitted the overall budget to Congress for its approval and modification. The president was also authorized to develop the Executive Office of the President, which oversees the agencies' activities on the president's behalf.

Like the merit and patronage systems, the executive leadership system has brought problems as well as improvements to the administration of government. In practice, the executive leadership concept can give the president too much leverage over the bureaucracy and thereby weaken Congress's ability to act as a check on presidential power. A case in point is the intelligence estimates the Bush administration gave Congress while seeking a congressional resolution authorizing a military attack on Iraq. The Bush administration said that the CIA had discovered that Iraq had weapons of mass destruction (WMDs) and was prepared to use them to attack U.S. interests. In his 2003 State of the Union address, President Bush said, "The dictator of Iraq is not disarming. To the contrary, he is deceiving." In a speech to the United Nations, Secretary of State Colin Powell claimed, "The facts on Iraq's behavior demonstrate . . . that Saddam Hussein and his regime are concealing their efforts to produce more weapons of mass destruction."

Yet "the facts" proved otherwise. In testimony before Congress in 2004, the chief U.S. weapons inspector in Iraq, David Kay, said that his team had failed to uncover evidence of WMDs in Iraq. This and other revelations produced heated debate over who was to blame for the faulty claim. Did the blame rest largely with the intelligence agencies or with the White House, which had pressured the intelligence agencies to make a strong case for war with Iraq? Many observers blamed both, concluding that the White House had overstated the evidence and that the intelligence agencies had been too eager to tell the White House what it wanted to hear.

Thus, the executive leadership system, like the patronage and merit systems, is not foolproof. It can make bureaucratic agencies overly dependent on the presidency, thereby distorting their activities and reducing congressional checks on executive power. Nevertheless, the executive leadership system is a necessary

DEBATING THE ISSUES

THE CASE OF IRAQ'S WEAPONS OF MASS DESTRUCTION: DID THE CIA PLAY POLITICS?

The federal bureaucracy is a storehouse of knowledge that informs national policy. Though major policy decisions are made primarily by elected officials, these officials rely on agencies for policy-related information. Seldom has this relationship created more controversy than in the case of Iraq's weapons programs. The Bush administration justified its invasion of Iraq in 2003 by saying that intelligence agencies had confirmed Iraq's possession of large stockpiles of weapons of mass destruction and its willingness to use them. After U.S. military forces took over Iraq, investigators could not find evidence of an Iraqi weapons program on anywhere near the scale portrayed by the Administration. Suddenly, the intelligence agencies themselves were on the spot. Had they misread their intelligence or slanted it to fit the Bush administration's agenda? Or had they offered their best judgment based on the intelligence they had? There were sharply conflicting views on this issue, including those of Senator Carl Levin, a member of the Senate Select Committee on Intelligence, and George Tenet, the director of central intelligence.

YES
There is now confirmation from the administration's own leading weapons inspector that the intelligence community produced greatly flawed assessments about Iraq's weapons of mass destruction in the months leading up to the invasion of Iraq. It is my opinion that flawed intelligence and the administration's exaggerations concerning Iraq's weapons of mass destruction resulted from an effort to make the threat appear more imminent and the case for military action against Iraq appear more urgent than they were. . . . Director Tenet, after 12 months of indefensible stonewalling, recently relented and declassified the material that I requested, which makes clear that his public testimony before the Congress on the extent to which the United States shared intelligence with the United Nations on Iraq's weapons of mass destruction programs was false. . . . In other words, honest answers by Director Tenet might have undermined the false sense of urgency for proceeding to war and could have contributed to delay, neither of which fit the administration's policy goals. . . . We rely on our intelligence agencies to give us the facts, not to give us the spin on the facts. The accuracy and objectivity of intelligence should never be tainted or slanted to support a particular policy.

—*Carl Levin, U.S. senator (D-Mich.)*

NO
Much of the current controversy centers on our prewar intelligence on Iraq, summarized in the National Intelligence Estimate of October 2002. . . . This Estimate asked if Iraq had chemical, biological, and nuclear weapons and the means to deliver them. We concluded that in some of these categories, Iraq had weapons. And that in others—where it did not have them—it was trying to develop them. Let me be clear: analysts differed on several important aspects of these programs and those debates were spelled out in the Estimate. They never said there was an "imminent" threat. Rather, they painted an objective assessment for our policymakers of a brutal dictator who was continuing his efforts to deceive and build programs that might constantly surprise us and threaten our interests. No one told us what to say or how to say it. . . . Did these strands of information weave into a perfect picture—could they answer every question? No—far from it. But, taken together, this information provided a solid basis on which to *estimate* whether Iraq did or did not have weapons of mass destruction and the means to deliver them. It is important to underline the word *estimate*. Because not everything we analyze can be known to a standard of absolute proof.

—*George J. Tenet, director of central intelligence*

part of an overall strategy for the effective handling of the bureaucracy. At its best, the system imposes principles of effective management—such as eliminating wasteful duplication—on the work of government agencies.

The federal bureaucracy today embodies aspects of all three systems—patronage, merit, and executive leadership—a situation that reflects the tensions inherent in governmental administration. The bureaucracy is expected to carry out programs fairly and competently (the merit system), but it is also expected to respond to political forces (the patronage system) and to operate efficiently (the executive management system). Table 13-2 summarizes the strengths and weaknesses of each of these administrative systems.

TABLE 13-2 | Strengths and Weaknesses of Major Systems for Managing the Bureaucracy

System	Strengths	Weaknesses
Patronage	Makes the bureaucracy more responsive to election outcomes by allowing the president to appoint some executive officials.	Gives executive authority to individuals chosen for their partisan loyalty rather than for their administrative or policy expertise; can favor interests that supported the president's election.
Merit	Provides for *competent* administration in that employees are hired on the basis of ability and allowed to remain on the job and thereby become proficient, and provides for *neutral* administration in that civil servants are not partisan appointees and are expected to work in an evenhanded way.	Can result in fragmented, unresponsive administration because career bureaucrats are secure in their jobs and tend to place the interests of their particular agency ahead of those of other agencies or the nation's interests as a whole.
Executive leadership	Provides for presidential leadership of the bureaucracy in order to make it more responsive and to coordinate and direct it (left alone, the bureaucracy tends toward fragmentation).	Can upset the balance between executive and legislative power and can make the president's priorities, not fairness or effective management, the basis for administrative action.

The Bureaucracy's Power Imperative

A common misperception is that the president, as the chief executive, has the sole claim on the bureaucracy's loyalty. In fact, Congress also has reason to claim ownership because it is the source of the bureaucracy's programs and funding. One presidential appointee asked a congressional committee whether it had any problem with his plans to reduce one of his agency's programs. The committee chairman replied, "No, you have the problem, because if you touch that bureau I'll cut your job out of the budget."[11]

The U.S. system of separate institutions sharing power encourages each institution to guard its turf. In addition, the president and members of Congress differ in their constituencies and thus in the interests to which they are most responsive. For example, although the agricultural sector is just one of many concerns of the president, it is of vital interest to senators and representatives from farm states. Finally, because the president and Congress are elected separately, the White House and one or both houses of Congress may be in the hands of opposing parties. Since 1968, this source of executive-legislative conflict has been more the rule than the exception.

If agencies are to operate successfully in this system, they must seek support where they can find it—if not from the president, then from Congress. In other words, agencies have no choice but to play politics.[12] Any agency that sits by idly while other agencies seek support from the White House and Congress is certain to lose out.

The Agency Point of View

Administrators tend to look out for their agency's interests, a perspective that is called the **agency point of view.** This perspective comes naturally to most high-ranking civil servants. More than 80 percent of top bureaucrats reach their high-level positions by rising through the ranks of the same agency.[13] As one top administrator said when testifying before the House Appropriations Committee, "Mr. Chairman, you would not think it proper for me to be in charge of this work and not be enthusiastic about it . . . would you? I have been in it for thirty years, and I believe in it."[14] Studies confirm that bureaucrats believe in the

agency point of view

The tendency of bureaucrats to place the interests of their agency ahead of other interests and ahead of the priorities sought by the president or Congress.

importance of their agency's work. One study found, for example, that social welfare administrators are three times as likely as other civil servants to believe that social welfare programs should be a high policy priority.[15]

Professionalism also cements agency loyalties. High-level administrative positions have increasingly been filled by scientists, engineers, lawyers, educators, physicians, and other professionals. Most of them take jobs in an agency whose mission they support, as in the case of the aeronautical engineers who work for NASA or the doctors who work for the National Institutes of Health (NIH).

Sources of Bureaucratic Power

In promoting their agency's interests, bureaucrats rely on their specialized knowledge, the support of interests that benefit from the programs they run, and the backing of the president and Congress.

The Power of Expertise

Most of the policy problems that the federal government confronts do not lend themselves to simple solutions. Whether the issue is space travel or hunger in America, expert knowledge is essential to the development of effective public policy. Much of this expertise is held by bureaucrats. They spend their careers working in a particular policy area, and many of them have had scientific, technical, or other specialized training (see "How the U.S. Compares").[16]

HOW THE U.S. COMPARES

EDUCATIONAL BACKGROUNDS OF BUREAUCRATS

To staff its bureaucracy, the U.S. government tends to hire persons with specialized educations to hold specialized jobs. This approach heightens the tendency of bureaucrats to take the agency point of view. By comparison, Great Britain tends to recruit its bureaucrats from the arts and humanities, on the assumption that general aptitude is the best qualification for detached professionalism. The continental European democracies also emphasize detached professionalism, but in the context of the supposedly impartial application of rules. As a consequence, high-ranking civil servants in Europe tend to have legal educations. The college majors of senior civil servants in the United States and other democracies reflect these tendencies.

College Major of Senior Civil Servant	Norway	Germany	Great Britain	Italy	Belgium	United States
Natural science/ engineering	8%	8%	26%	10%	20%	32%
Social science/ humanities/business	38	18	52	37	40	50
Law	38	63	3	53	35	18
Other	16	11	19	—	5	—
	100%	100%	100%	100%	100%	100%

Source: Adapted from *The Politics of Bureaucracy*, 5th ed., by B. Guy Peters. Copyright © 2001 by Routledge. Printed by permission of Thomsen Publishing Services.

The popular children's program *Sesame Street* is produced through the Corporation for Public Broadcasting, a government agency that gains leverage in budgetary deliberations from its public support. Shown here in a photo of a display at the Smithsonian National Museum of American History is Oscar the Grouch, a *Sesame Street* puppet whose home is a garbage can.

clientele groups

Special interest groups that benefit directly from the activities of a particular bureaucratic agency and therefore are strong advocates of the agency.

By comparison, elected officials are generalists. To some degree, members of Congress do specialize through their committee work, but they rarely have the time or the inclination to acquire a commanding knowledge of a particular issue. The president's understanding of policy issues is even more general. Not surprisingly, the president and members of Congress rely on the bureaucracy for policy advice and guidance.

All agencies acquire some power through their careerists' expertise. No matter how simple a policy issue may appear at first, it invariably involves more complexity than meets the eye. A recognition that the United States has a trade deficit with China, for example, can be the premise for policy change, but this recognition does not begin to address basic issues such as the form the new policy might take, its probable cost and effectiveness, and its links to other issues, such as America's standing in Asia. Among the officials most likely to understand these issues are the career bureaucrats in the Commerce Department and the Federal Trade Commission.

The Power of Clientele Groups

Most agencies have **clientele groups**—special interests that benefit directly from an agency's programs. Clientele groups assist agencies by placing pressure on Congress and the president to support those programs from which they benefit.[17] For example, when House Speaker Newt Gingrich threatened in 1995 to "zero out" funding for the Corporation for Public Broadcasting, audience members and groups such as the Children's Television Workshop wrote, called, faxed, and cajoled members of Congress, saying that programs like *Sesame Street* and *All Things Considered* were irreplaceable. Within a few weeks, Gingrich had retreated from his position, saying that a complete cessation of funding was not what he had in mind.

In general, agencies both assist and are assisted by the clientele groups that depend on the programs they administer.[18] Many agencies were created for the purpose of promoting particular interests in society. For example, the Department of Agriculture's career bureaucrats are dependable allies of farm interests year after year. The same cannot be said of the president, Congress as a whole, or either political party, all of whom must balance farmers' demands against those of other interests.

The Power of Friends in High Places

Although members of Congress and the president sometimes appear to be at war with the bureaucracy, they need it as much as it needs them. An agency's resources—its programs, expertise, and group support—can assist elected officials in their efforts to achieve their goals. When President George W. Bush in 2001 announced plans for a war on terrorism, he needed the help of careerists in the CIA and the Department of Defense to make his efforts successful. At a time when other agencies were feeling the pinch of a tight federal budget, these agencies received new funding.

Bureaucrats also seek favorable relations with members of Congress. Congressional support is vital because agencies' funding and programs are established through legislation. Agencies that offer benefits to major constituency interests are particularly likely to have close ties to Congress. In some policy areas, more or less permanent alliances—iron triangles—form among agencies, clientele groups, and congressional subcommittees. In other policy areas, temporary issue networks form among bureaucrats, lobbyists, and members of Congress. As explained in Chapters 9 and 11, these alliances are a means by which an agency can gain support from key legislators and groups.

Bureaucratic Accountability

Even though most Americans say that they have a favorable impression of their most recent personal experience with the bureaucracy (as, say, when a senior citizen applies for social security), they have an unfavorable impression of the bureaucracy as a whole (see Figure 13-3). Along with citizens of other democracies, they see the programs of government bureaucracies as wasteful and inefficient. This view is overly harsh. In areas such as health care and retirement insurance, government bureaucracies are actually more efficient than private organizations. In other areas, efficiency is an inappropriate standard for government programs. The most efficient way to administer government loans to college students, for example, would be to give money to the first students who apply and then close down the program when the money runs out. However, college loan programs, like many other government programs, operate on the principles of fairness and need, which require that each application be judged on its merits.

Studies indicate that the U.S. bureaucracy compares favorably to government bureaucracies elsewhere. "Some national bureaucracies," writes Charles Goodsell, "may be roughly the same [as the U.S. bureaucracy] in quality of overall performance, but they are few in number."[19] Of course, not all U.S. agencies have strong performance records (see Figure 13-4). The Immigration and Naturalization Service (INS) is one agency that has been chronically mismanaged. Yet the performance of many U.S. agencies is superior to that of their counterparts in other industrialized democracies. The U.S. Postal Service, for example, has an on-time and low-cost record that few postal services can match.

Nevertheless, it is easy to see why most Americans hold a relatively unfavorable opinion of the federal bureaucracy. Americans have traditionally mistrusted political power, and the bureaucracy is the symbol of "big government." It is also a convenient target for politicians who claim that "Washington bureaucrats" are wasting taxpayer money. (The irony is that the bureaucracy has no

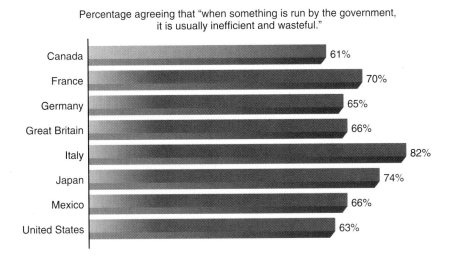

Percentage agreeing that "when something is run by the government, it is usually inefficient and wasteful."

Canada	61%
France	70%
Germany	65%
Great Britain	66%
Italy	82%
Japan	74%
Mexico	66%
United States	63%

FIGURE 13-3 Opinions on Bureaucratic Inefficiency and Waste Although Americans believe that government programs are inefficient and wasteful, they are not alone in their belief. Public opinion on this issue is remarkably consistent across democratic nations.

Source: Global Attitudes Survey, Pew Research Center on the People and the Press, 2002.

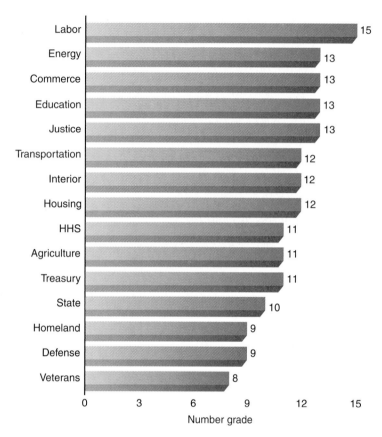

FIGURE 13-4 **Ranking the Cabinet Departments by Managerial Performance** Through its Executive Branch Management Scorecard, OMB evaluates federal agencies by five managerial reform criteria: human capital, competitive sourcing, financial management, e-government, and budget and performance integration. By these criteria, the Department of Labor ranks as the best-managed cabinet department and the Veterans Administration ranks as the worst.

Source: Office of Management and Budget, 2008. OMB has three levels of performance in each of its five categories. Author derived the scores in figure by assigning the numbers 3, 2, and 1 for an agency's score in each category, with a "3" representing the highest level of performance.

power to create programs or authorize spending; these decisions are made by Congress and the president.)

Adapting the requirements of the bureaucracy to those of democracy is challenging. Bureaucracy is the antithesis of democracy. Bureaucrats are unelected and hold office indefinitely, and they make decisions based on fixed rules rather than on debate and deliberation. This situation raises the question of **bureaucratic accountability**—the degree to which bureaucrats are held accountable for the power they exercise. Bureaucratic accountability occurs primarily through oversight by the president, Congress, and the courts.[20]

Accountability Through the Presidency

The president can only broadly influence, not directly control, the bureaucracy. "We can outlast any president" is a maxim of bureaucratic politics. Each agency has its clientele and its congressional supporters as well as statutory authority for its existence and activities. No president can unilaterally eliminate an agency or its funding or programs. Nor can the president be indifferent to the opinions of career civil servants—not without losing their support and expertise in developing and implementing presidential policy objectives.

To encourage the bureaucracy to act responsibly, the president can apply management tools that have developed out of the "executive leadership" concept discussed earlier in this chapter. These tools include reorganization, presidential appointments, and the executive budget.

bureaucratic accountability

The degree to which bureaucrats are held accountable for the power they exercise.

Reorganization

The bureaucracy's extreme fragmentation—its hundreds of separate agencies—makes presidential coordination of its activities difficult. Agencies pursue independent and even contradictory paths, resulting in an undetermined amount of waste and duplication of effort. For example, more than one hundred governmental units are responsible for different pieces of federal education policy.

All recent presidents have tried to streamline the bureaucracy and make it more accountable. Such changes seldom greatly improve things, but they can produce marginal gains.[21] For George W. Bush, the challenge came after the terrorist attacks on the World Trade Center and the Pentagon. Breakdowns in the FBI and CIA had undermined whatever chance there might have been to prevent the attacks. These agencies had neither shared nor vigorously pursued the intelligence information they had gathered. Bush decided, and Congress agreed, that a reorganization of the FBI and CIA, as well as the creation of the Department of Homeland Security (DHS), was necessary. Nevertheless, neither the White

House nor Congress was under the illusion that this reorganization would fully correct the coordination problems plaguing the agencies accountable for responding to external and internal threats to Americans' safety.[22]

Indeed, the DHS failed miserably in its first big test after the reorganization. That test came not from terrorists but from Hurricane Katrina, which slammed into the Gulf Coast in 2005, killing hundreds of Americans and displacing tens of thousands. One of DHS's agencies, the Federal Emergency Management Agency (FEMA), has responsibility for coordinating disaster response efforts, and its response by all accounts was disorganized and inadequate. At times, FEMA appeared to know less than the news media about what was happening in the Gulf area. Its communication and transportation systems broke down, resulting in long delays in providing relief assistance. FEMA's director, Michael Brown, did not even keep his boss, DHS secretary Michael Chertoff, informed of his actions, telling Congress months later that doing so would have been "a waste of time" because the DHS did not have the needed resources. Brown was fired two weeks into the relief effort, and some observers felt that Chertoff's job was saved only to avoid the appearance that the entire department was in disarray.

The Old Executive Office Building is adjacent to the West Wing of the White House. Its occupants are part of the Executive Office of the President (EOP) and serve as contacts between the president and agency bureaucrats.

Presidential Appointments

Although there is almost no direct confrontation with a bureaucrat that a president cannot win, the president does not have time to deal personally with every troublesome careerist or to ensure that the bureaucracy has complied with every presidential order. The president relies on political appointees in federal agencies to ensure that directives are followed.

The power of presidential appointees is greater in those agencies where wide latitude exists in the making of decisions. Although the Social Security Administration (SSA) has a huge budget and makes monthly payments to more than 40 million Americans, the eligibility of recipients is determined by fixed rules. The head of the SSA does not have the option, say, of granting a retiree an extra $100 a month because the retiree is facing financial hardship. In contrast, most regulatory agencies have discretion over regulatory policy, and the heads of these agencies have latitude in their decisions. For example, President Ronald Reagan's appointee to chair the Federal Trade Commission (FTC), James Miller III, was a strong-willed economist who shared Reagan's belief that consumer protection policy had gone too far and was adversely affecting business interests. In Miller's first year as head of the FTC, the commission dropped one-fourth of its pending cases against business firms.[23] Overall, enforcement actions declined by half during Miller's tenure compared with that of his predecessor.

However, as noted in Chapter 12, there are limits to what a president can accomplish through appointments. High-level presidential appointees number in the hundreds, and their turnover rate is high: the average appointee remains in the Administration for less than two years before moving on to other employment.[24] No president can keep track of all appointees, much less instruct them in

POLITICAL CULTURE

LIBERTY, EQUALITY, AND SELF-GOVERNMENT

The Bureaucracy

Americans are distrustful of bureaucracy, associating it with big government, which they historically have seen as a threat to liberty. This opinion may be based more on cultural bias than on personal experience, but it is not without foundation. Bureaucrats in agencies charged with law enforcement and national security, like bureaucrats in other agencies, can become insular in their thinking. A narrow-minded pursuit of their mission can override their dedication to the nation's governing principles. Abuses of individual rights, of intelligence gathering, and of the use of military force are a part of America's history, just as they are a part of the history of other democracies.

At times the power of the bureaucracy is also difficult to reconcile with the principle of self-government. Bureaucracy entails hierarchy, command, permanence of office, appointment to office, and fixed rules, whereas self-government involves equality, consent, rotation of office, election to office, and open decision making. At base, the conflict between bureaucracy and self-government centers on the degree of power held by officials who are not elected by vote of the people.

The answer to such dilemmas is not found in making the bureaucracy more efficient. Often, those bureaucratic decisions made in the name of efficiency are the very ones that run counter to the principles of self-government and liberty. When some U.S. soldiers and intelligence agents were charged with using interrogation techniques in Iraq and Afghanistan that are banned by the Geneva Conventions, they defended their actions by saying it was the quickest way to get the information they were seeking.

The United States, like any large-scale society, has no choice but to accept bureaucracy as a fact of life. Indeed, the United States could not possibly operate as a nation without its defense establishment, its education and welfare programs, the regulation of business, its transportation system, and the hundreds of other undertakings of the federal government.

The challenge, then, is to make the bureaucracy work in ways that are compatible with the principles of liberty, equality, and self-government. America's approach to this challenge has been to entrust oversight to Congress, the president, and the judiciary. Can you think of ways this oversight might be made more effective? Can you also think of ways of reorganizing the bureaucracy that would enhance accountability? For example, do you think the bureaucracy would be more accountable if civil servants rotated from one agency to another every few years, much as military personnel rotate in their assignments? What would be the disadvantages of such a personnel system?

detail on all intended policies. Moreover, many presidential appointees have little knowledge of the agencies they head, which makes it difficult for them to exercise control. FEMA's fired director, Michael Brown, was appointed to head the agency because of his political connections. He had little management experience and virtually no disaster relief experience before taking up his post at FEMA.

The Executive Budget

Faced with the difficulty of controlling the bureaucracy, presidents have come to rely heavily on their personal bureaucracy, the Executive Office of the President (EOP).

In terms of presidential management, the key unit within the EOP is the Office of Management and Budget (OMB). Funding, programs, and regulations are the mainstays of every agency, and the OMB has substantial influence on each of these areas. No agency can issue a major regulation without the OMB's verification that the regulation's benefits outweigh its costs, and no agency can propose legislation to Congress without the OMB's approval. However, the OMB's greatest influence over agencies derives from its budgetary role. At the start of the annual budget cycle, the OMB assigns each agency a budget limit in accord with the president's instructions. The agency then develops a proposed budget, which is reviewed and revised by the OMB before being included in the budget package that the president sends to Congress (see Table 13-3).

In most cases, an agency's overall budget does not change much from year to year, indicating that a significant portion of the bureaucracy's activities persist regardless of who sits in the White House or Congress. It must be noted,

TABLE 13-3   **The Budgetary Process**   Bureaucratic agencies are funded through a process that assigns significant roles to the president and Congress, as well as to the agencies themselves. The annual federal budget allocates the hundreds of billions of dollars that support federal agencies and programs. This table gives a simplified step-by-step summary of the process.

1. In the calendar year preceding enactment of the budget, the Office of Management and Budget (OMB) instructs each agency to prepare its budget request within guidelines established by the White House.

2. Agencies work out their budget proposals in line with White House guidelines and their own goals. Once completed, agency proposals are sent to the OMB for review and adjustment to fit the president's goals.

3. In January, the president submits the adjusted budget to Congress.

4. The president's budget is reviewed by the Congressional Budget Office (CBO) and is referred to the House and Senate Budget and Appropriations Committees. The Budget Committees in each chamber then set expenditure ceilings in particular areas, which are voted upon by the members of Congress. Once set (usually in April), the budget ceilings establish temporary limits within which the Appropriations Committees must act.

5. Through subcommittee hearings, the House and Senate Appropriations Committees meet with agency heads and adjust

the president's budgetary recommendations to fit congressional goals. Once the Appropriations Committees have completed their work, the proposals are submitted to the full House and Senate for a vote. Differences in the House and Senate versions are reconciled in conference committee.

6. The legislation is sent to the president for approval or veto. Before this point, the White House and Congress will have engaged in intense negotiations to resolve differences in their priorities. If the White House is satisfied with the outcome of the bargaining, the president can be expected to sign the legislation.

7. The new budget takes effect October 1, unless Congress has not completed its work by then or the president exercises the veto. If agreement has not been reached by this date, temporary funding (authorized by Congress and approved by the president) is required to keep the government in operation until a permanent budget can be enacted. If temporary funding is not provided, a shutdown of nonessential government services occurs.

however, that the bulk of federal spending is for programs such as social security that, although enacted in the past, enjoy the continuing support of the president, Congress, and the public.

Accountability Through Congress

Congress has powerful means of influencing the bureaucracy. All agencies depend on Congress for their existence, authority, programs, and funding.

The most substantial control that Congress exerts on the bureaucracy is through its power to authorize and fund programs. Without authorization and funding, a program simply does not exist, regardless of the priority an agency claims it deserves. Congress can also void an administrative decision through legislation that instructs the agency to follow a different course of action. However, Congress lacks the time and expertise to work out complex policies down to the last detail.[25] The government would grind to a halt if Congress tried to define fully how federal programs will be designed and run.

Congress also exerts some control through its oversight function, which involves monitoring the bureaucracy's work to ensure its compliance with legislative intent.[26] However, as noted in Chapter 11, oversight is a difficult and relatively unrewarding task, and members of Congress ordinarily place less emphasis on oversight than on their other major duties. Only when an agency has clearly stepped out of line is Congress likely to take decisive corrective action by holding hearings to ask tough questions and to warn of legislative punishment.

Because oversight is burdensome, Congress has shifted much of the responsibility to the Government Accountability Office (GAO). The GAO's primary function once was to keep track of the funds spent within the bureaucracy; it now also monitors whether policies are being implemented as Congress intended. The Congressional Budget Office (CBO) carries out oversight studies as well. When the GAO or CBO uncovers a major problem with an agency's handling of a program, it notifies Congress, which can then take corrective action.

Bureaucrats generally are kept in check by an awareness that misbehavior can trigger a response from Congress. Nevertheless, oversight cannot correct mistakes

HERBERT HOOVER
(1874–1964)

Herbert Hoover was president when the Wall Street Crash of 1929 propelled the United States into the Great Depression. Convinced that the free market would correct itself and bring a recovery, Hoover stood by as Americans lost their jobs and their homes until 1932 when they voted him out of office. For such reasons, Hoover is not ranked among the country's top presidents. However, he has been described as the finest bureaucrat America has ever produced. He was in China during the Boxer Rebellion and used the engineering skills he had been taught at Stanford to build barricades that protected his work crew from marauding gangs. He was in London when World War I broke out and was asked to head a relief effort to help 10 million food-starved Belgians. Although Belgium was sandwiched between the British and German armies, Hoover's organizing skills enabled him to dispatch the food, trucks, and ships to get the job done. When the United States entered the war in 1917, Hoover became U.S. Food Administrator, charged with supplying food to the U.S. military and its allies without starving the American public in the process. Hoover developed a campaign—"Food Will Win the War"—that asked Americans to eat less. "Meatless Mondays" was part of it. Domestic food consumption declined by a sixth, enabling the United States to triple its shipments abroad. After the war, Hoover headed the American Relief Organization that was the main supplier of food for more than 300 million people in nearly two dozen countries. Hoover's food packets were the origin of the CARE packages.

When Warren Harding was elected president in 1920, Hoover was appointed to head the Commerce Department, which took on the task of eliminating waste and duplication in industry—for example, by standardizing the size of nuts, bolts, and other parts. He brought statistical methods into the department, arguing that policy decisions should be based on precise analysis, not guesswork. In 1927, Hoover oversaw the nation's response to a devastating Mississippi River flood. A year later, Hoover was elected to the presidency. After his White House years, Hoover stayed active in public life. Presidents Roosevelt and Truman placed him in charge of food and famine relief efforts during and after World War II. In the 1950s, at the request of President Eisenhower, he chaired the first and second Hoover Commissions, which proposed ways to improve the bureaucracy.

or abuses that have already occurred. Recognizing this limit on oversight, Congress has devised ways to constrain the bureaucracy *before* it acts. The simplest method is to draft laws that contain very specific provisions that limit bureaucrats' options in implementing policy. Another restrictive device is the **sunset law,** which establishes a specific date when a law will expire unless it is reenacted by Congress. Advocates of sunset laws see them as a means to counter the bureaucracy's reluctance to give up programs that have outlived their usefulness. Because members of Congress usually want the programs they create to last far into the future, however, most legislation does not include a sunset provision.

Accountability Through the Courts

The bureaucracy is also overseen by the judiciary. Legally, the bureaucracy derives its authority from acts of Congress, and an injured party can bring suit against an agency on the grounds that it has failed to carry out a law properly. Judges can then order an agency to change its application of the law.[27]

However, the courts have tended to support administrators if their actions seem at all consistent with the laws they are administering. The Supreme Court has held that agencies can apply any reasonable interpretation of statutes unless Congress has specifically stated something to the contrary and that agencies in many instances have wide discretion in deciding whether to enforce statutes.[28] These positions reflect the need for flexibility in administration. The bureaucracy and the courts would both grind to a halt if judges regularly second-guessed bureaucrats' decisions. The judiciary promotes bureaucratic accountability primarily by encouraging administrators to act responsibly in their dealings with the public and by protecting individuals from the bureaucracy's worst abuses. In 1999, for example, a federal court approved a settlement in favor of African American farmers who demonstrated that the Department of Agriculture had systematically favored white farmers in granting federal farm loans.[29]

Accountability Within the Bureaucracy Itself

A recognition of the difficulty of ensuring adequate accountability of the bureaucracy through the presidency, Congress, and the courts has led to the development of mechanisms of accountability within the bureaucracy itself. Two measures—whistle-blowing and demographic representativeness—are particularly noteworthy.

Whistle-Blowing

Although the bureaucratic corruption that is rampant in some countries is relatively uncommon in the United States, a certain amount of waste, fraud, and abuse is inevitable in a bureaucracy as big as that of the federal government. **Whistle-blowing,** the act of reporting instances of official mismanagement, is a potentially effective internal check. To encourage whistle-blowers to come forward with their information, Congress enacted the Whistle Blower Protection Act to protect them against retaliation. Federal law also provides whistle-blowers with financial rewards in some cases.

Nevertheless, whistle-blowing is not for the faint-hearted. Many federal employees are reluctant to report instances of mismanagement because they fear retaliation. Their superiors might claim that they are malcontents or find subtle ways to punish them. Even their fellow employees are unlikely to think highly of "tattletales."

Accordingly, whistle-blowing sometimes does not occur until an employee has left an agency or quit government service entirely. A case in point is former CIA intelligence official John Kiriakou, who said in 2007 that the CIA had used waterboarding to interrogate Abu Zubaydah, a high-ranking leader of Al Qaeda. It was the first such admission by a CIA operative and prompted some CIA officials to demand an FBI investigation of Kiriakou. They withdrew the request upon realizing that an investigation would result in further disclosures that could embarrass the CIA or compromise its mission. (Waterboarding is an interrogation technique in which the person is strapped down with the head inclined downward. Water is then poured over the face, leading to inhalation and a sense of drowning and pending death. The technique was once considered a war crime by the U.S. government and violates the Geneva Conventions on the treatment of detainees.)

Demographic Representativeness

Although the bureaucracy is an unrepresentative institution in the sense that its officials are not elected by the people, it can be representative in the demographic sense. If bureaucrats were a demographic microcosm of the general public, they presumably would treat the various groups and interests in society more fairly.[30]

At present, the bureaucracy is not demographically representative at its top levels (see Table 13-4). About three in every five managerial and professional positions are held by white males. However, the employment status of women and, to a lesser extent, minorities has improved in recent decades, and top officials in the bureaucracy

Richard Clarke, arguably the most famous whistle-blower since the Watergate era, testifies about Bush administration antiterrorism policies in the months before the September 11, 2001, attacks on the World Trade Center and the Pentagon. In high-profile appearances before Congress and the 9/11 Commission, Clarke accused the Bush administration, in which he had served as the top terrorist adviser, of ignoring warnings of a possible large-scale terrorist attack on the United States. "I believe the Bush administration in the first eight months considered terrorism an important issue, but not an urgent issue," Clarke told the 9/11 Commission, a bipartisan commission formed by Congress to investigate the attacks. The White House countered with Vice President Dick Cheney's claim that Clarke "wasn't in the loop" and could not possibly have known what was going on in the Bush administration's inner circle. The White House slowed its attack on Clarke after documents surfaced supporting some of his allegations. In a pre-9/11 memo prepared for National Security Advisor Condoleezza Rice, Clarke had expressed alarm at the slow pace of the Administration's antiterrorism planning, saying "Imagine a day after hundreds of Americans lay dead at home or abroad after a terrorist attack."

TABLE 13-4 | Federal Job Rankings (GS) of Various Demographic Groups Women and minority-group members are underrepresented in the top jobs of the federal bureaucracy, but their representation has been increasing.

Grade Level*	WOMEN'S SHARE		BLACKS' SHARE		HISPANICS' SHARE	
	1982	2002	1982	2002	1982	2002
GS 13–15 (highest ranks)	5%	32%	5%	10%	2%	4%
GS 9–12	20	46	10	16	4	7
GS 5–8	60	67	19	26	4	9
GS 1–4 (lowest ranks)	78	69	23	28	5	8

*In general, the higher-numbered grades are managerial and professional positions, and the lower-numbered grades are clerical and manual labor positions.
Source: Office of Personnel Management, 2008.

demographic representativeness
The idea that the bureaucracy will be more responsive to the public if its employees at all levels are demographically representative of the population as a whole.

include a greater proportion of women and minorities than is found in Congress or the judiciary. Moreover, if all employees are considered, the federal bureaucracy comes reasonably close to being representative of the nation's population.

Demographic representativeness is only a partial answer to the problem of bureaucratic accountability. A fully representative civil service would still be required to play agency politics. The careerists in, say, defense agencies and welfare agencies are similar in their demographic backgrounds, but they differ markedly in their opinions about policy. Each group believes that the goals of its agency should take priority. The inevitability of an agency point of view is the most significant of all political facts about the U.S. federal bureaucracy.

Reinventing Government?

In *Reinventing Government*, David Osborne and Ted Gaebler argue that the bureaucracy of today was created in response to earlier problems, particularly those spawned by the Industrial Revolution and a rampant spoils system. They claim that the information age requires a different kind of administrative structure, one that is leaner and more responsive. Osborne and Gaebler assert that government should set program standards but should not necessarily take on all program responsibilities. If, for example, a private firm can furnish meals to soldiers at U.S. army posts at a lower cost than the military can provide them, it should be contracted to provide the meals. Osborne and Gaebler also say that administrative judgments should be made at the lowest bureaucratic level feasible. If, for example, Department of Agriculture field agents have the required knowledge to make a certain type of decision, they should be empowered to make it rather than being required to get permission from superiors. Finally, Osborne and Gaebler argue that the bureaucracy should focus on outputs (results) rather than inputs (dollars spent). Federal loans to college students, for example, should be judged by how many students stay in college as a result of these loans rather than by how much money is doled out.[31]

These ideas informed the Clinton administration's National Performance Review (described in this chapter's introduction). Even though the Bush administration decided not to continue the initiative, the NPR's impact is felt through laws and administrative practices established during its tenure. An example is a law that requires agencies to systematically measure their performance by standards such as efficiency, responsiveness, and outcomes.

Some analysts question whether government bureaucracy can or even should be reinvented. They have asked, for example, whether the principles of decentralized management and market-oriented programs are as sound as their advocates claim. A reason for hierarchy is to ensure that decisions made at the bottom of the bureaucracy are faithful to the laws enacted by Congress. Free to act on their own, lower-level administrators, as they did under the spoils system, might favor certain people and interests over others.[32] There is also the issue of the identity of the "customers" in a market-oriented administration.[33] Who are the Security and Exchange Commission's customers? Are they firms, brokerage houses, or shareholders? Won't some agencies inevitably favor their more powerful customers at the expense of their less powerful ones?

Furthermore, there are practical limits on how much the federal bureaucracy can be trimmed. While some activities can be delegated to states and localities and others can be privatized, most of Washington's programs cannot be reassigned. National defense, social security, and Medicare are but three examples, and they alone account for well over half of all federal spending. In addition, the outsourcing of tasks to private contractors does not necessarily result in smaller government or reduced waste. Many contracts are a better deal for the private firms awarded them than for taxpayers. In one case, the GAO found that a contractor was charging the government $86 per sheet for plywood that normally sold for $14 a sheet. Nor does outsourcing necessarily result in better performance. When the space shuttle *Columbia* disintegrated upon reentry in 2003, some analysts suggested that the tragedy was rooted in NASA's decision to assign many of the shuttle program's safety checks to private contractors in order to cut costs.

Thus, although the current debate over the functioning of the federal bureaucracy is unique in its specific elements, it involves long-standing issues. How can the federal government be made more efficient and yet accomplish all that Americans expect of it? How can it be made more responsive and yet act fairly? How can it be made more creative and yet be held accountable? As history makes clear, there are no easy or final answers to these questions.

Summary   Self-Test www.mhhe.com/pattersontad9e

Bureaucracy is a method of organizing people and work, based on the principles of hierarchical authority, job specialization, and formalized rules. As a form of organization, bureaucracy is the most efficient means of getting people to work together on tasks of great magnitude and complexity. It is also a form of organization that is prone to waste and rigidity, which is why efforts are always being made to "reinvent" it.

The United States could not be governed without a large federal bureaucracy. The day-to-day work of the federal government, from mail delivery to provision of social security to international diplomacy, is done by the bureaucracy. Federal employees work in roughly four hundred major agencies, including cabinet departments, independent agencies, regulatory agencies, government corporations, and presidential commissions. Yet the bureaucracy is more than simply an administrative giant. Administrators exercise considerable discretion in their policy decisions. In the process of implementing policy, they make important policy and political choices.

Each agency of the federal government was created in response to political demands on national officials. Because of its origins in political demands, the administration

of government is necessarily political. An inherent conflict results from two simultaneous but incompatible demands on the bureaucracy: that it respond to the preferences of partisan officials and that it administer programs fairly and competently. This tension is evident in the three concurrent personnel management systems under which the bureaucracy operates: patronage, merit, and executive leadership.

Administrators are actively engaged in politics and policymaking. The fragmentation of power and the pluralism of the American political system result in a contentious policy process, which leads government agencies to compete for the power required to administer their programs effectively. Accordingly, civil servants tend to have an agency point of view: they seek to advance their agency's programs and to repel attempts by others to weaken their position. In promoting their agency, civil servants rely on their policy expertise, the backing of their clientele groups, and the support of the president and Congress.

Administrators are not elected by the people they serve, yet they wield substantial independent power. Because of this, the bureaucracy's accountability is a central issue. The major checks on the bureaucracy are provided by the president,

Congress, and the courts. The president has some power to reorganize the bureaucracy and the authority to appoint the political head of each agency. The president also has management tools (such as the executive budget) that can be used to limit administrators' discretion. Congress has influence on bureaucratic agencies through its authorization and funding powers and through various devices (including sunset laws and oversight hearings) that hold administrators accountable for their actions. The judiciary's role in ensuring the bureaucracy's accountability is smaller than that of the elected branches, but the courts do have the authority to force

agencies to act in accordance with legislative intent, established procedures, and constitutionally guaranteed rights.

Nevertheless, administrators are not fully accountable. They exercise substantial independent power, a situation not easily reconciled with democratic values. Because of this, and also because of the desire to make the bureaucracy more efficient, there have been numerous efforts over time to reform the bureaucracy. The most recent such effort includes contracting out the work of government to private firms. Like all such efforts, this latest reinvention has solved some problems while creating new ones—an indication of the immensity of the challenge.

CHAPTER 13

Study Corner

Key Terms

agency point of view (p. 350)
bureaucracy (p. 340)
bureaucratic accountability (p. 354)
cabinet (executive) departments (p. 342)
clientele groups (p. 352)
demographic representativeness (p. 360)
executive leadership system (p. 348)
formalized rules (p. 341)
government corporations (p. 344)

hierarchical authority (p. 341)
independent agencies (p. 342)
job specialization (p. 341)
merit (civil service) system (p. 347)
neutral competence (p. 347)
patronage system (p. 347)
policy implementation (p. 345)
presidential commissions (p. 344)
regulatory agencies (p. 343)
spoils system (p. 347)
sunset law (p. 358)
whistle-blowing (p. 359)

Self-Test

1. America's governmental bureaucracy operates under which three personnel management systems?
   a. merit, patronage, civil service
   b. executive leadership, exchange theory, streamlined management
   c. patronage, merit, executive leadership
   d. executive agreements, civil service, merit

2. The strength of bureaucracy as a form of organization is that it:
   a. leads to flexibility in the completion of tasks.
   b. can be used only in the public sector.
   c. is the most efficient means of getting people to work together on tasks of great magnitude.
   d. allows individuals great latitude in making decisions.

3. Bureaucratic accountability through the presidency includes all of the following **except:**
   a. appointment of agency heads.
   b. budgetary oversight through the Office of Management and Budget.
   c. the power to fire at will any civil servant the president chooses to fire.
   d. the president's authority to recommend the reorganization of federal agencies.

4. Merit hiring has provided all **except** which one of the following advantages?
   a. a more competent work force through use of competitive exams
   b. ability to hire people with special qualifications
   c. greater responsiveness to presidential leadership
   d. employees who are likely to treat clients and customers the same whether they are Republicans or Democrats

5. Sources of bureaucratic power in the federal bureaucracy include all of the following **except:**
   a. power of broad public support and esteem.
   b. power of expertise.
   c. power of clientele groups.
   d. power of friends in Congress and the White House.

6. The primary function of America's federal bureaucracy is:
   a. oversight of the executive branch.
   b. developing laws for review by Congress.
   c. bringing cases for trial before the Supreme Court.
   d. policy implementation.

7. Bureaucracies are found only in the governmental sector of society and not in the private and corporate sectors. (T/F)

8. Regulatory agencies such as the Securities and Exchange Commission are permitted only to issue advisory opinions to the firms they regulate. Only the judiciary and Congress are allowed to take more decisive action if a firm disregards the law. (T/F)

9. Congress holds the bureaucracy accountable in part through its power to authorize and fund agency programs. (T/F)

10. Once they are in place, federal programs are often terminated at the request of their clientele groups. (T/F)

Critical Thinking

What are the major sources of bureaucrats' power? What mechanisms for controlling that power are available to the president and Congress?

Suggested Readings

Aberbach, Joel D., and Bert A. Rockman. *In the Web of Politics: Two Decades of the U.S. Federal Executive.* Washington, D.C.: Brookings Institution, 2000. An evaluation of the federal bureaucracy and its evolving nature.

Du Gay, Paul. *The Values of Bureaucracy.* New York: Oxford University Press, 2005. An insightful analysis of how bureaucracies work and the values they embody.

Huber, Gregory A. *The Craft of Bureaucratic Neutrality: Interests and Influence in Governmental Regulation of Occupational Safety.* New York: Cambridge University Press, 2007. An argument that claims political neutrality is the best political strategy, as well as the proper administrative approach, for agencies.

Ketti, Donald F. *System Under Stress: Homeland Security and American Politics.* Washington, D.C.: Congressional Quarterly Press, 2007. An award-winning study of executive reorganization that focuses on the Department of Homeland Security.

Meier, Kenneth J., and Laurence J. O'Toole, Jr. *Bureaucracy in a Democratic State.* Baltimore, Md.: Johns Hopkins University Press, 2006. A careful assessment of the relationship between bureaucracy and democracy.

Osborne, David, and Ted Gaebler. *Reinventing Government: How the Entrepreneurial Spirit Is Transforming the Public Sector.* New York: Addison-Wesley, 1992. The book that Washington policymakers in the 1990s regarded as the guide to transforming the bureaucracy.

Page, Edward C., and Bill Jenkins. *Policy Bureaucracy: Government with a Cast of Thousands.* New York: Oxford University Press, 2005. An assessment of the bureaucracy as a policymaking institution.

Sagini, Meshack M. *Organizational Behavior: The Challenges of the New Millennium.* Lanham, Md.: University Press of America, 2001. A comprehensive assessment of bureaucratic structures and behaviors.

List of Websites

http://www.census.gov/
The website of the Census Bureau, the best source of statistical information on Americans and the government agencies that administer programs affecting them.

http://www.whistleblower.org/
The Government Accountability Project's website; is designed to protect and encourage whistle-blowers by providing information and support to federal employees.

http://www.whitehouse.gov/government/cabinet.html
A website that lists the cabinet secretaries and provides links to each cabinet-level department.

Participate!

If you are considering a semester or summer internship, you might want to look into working for a federal, state, or local agency. Compared with legislative interns, executive interns are more likely to get paid and to be given significant duties. (Many legislative interns spend the bulk of their time answering phones or responding to mail.) Internship information can often be obtained through an agency's website. You should apply as early as possible; some agencies have application deadlines.

You might even consider a career in government. President John F. Kennedy said that government is "the highest calling." Although this view is not widely shared today, government service can be a satisfying career. A 2002 study by Harvard's Kennedy School of Government found that public-sector managers get more intrinsic satisfaction from their work, which focuses on improving public life, than do private-sector managers. For people who want to pursue a government career, a first step is often a master's degree program in public administration or public policy. Many of these programs require only a year of study after the bachelor's degree. For an entry-level employee with a master's degree rather than a bachelor's degree, the initial salary is 40 percent higher. Appointees with master's degrees enter the civil service at a higher rank (GS-9 rather than GS-5) and are placed in positions that entail greater responsibility than those assigned to newly hired appointees with bachelor's degrees. Those who enter the civil service at the higher rank also are more likely to advance to top positions as their careers develop.

Extra Credit

For up-to-the-minute *New York Times* articles, interactive simulations, graphics, study tools, and more links and quizzes, visit the text's Online Learning Center at www.mhhe.com/pattersontad9e.

Self-Test Answers

1. c 2. c 3. c 4. c 5. a 6. d 7. F 8. F 9. T 10. F

BIRTH OF A NUMBER

On March 11, the Centers for Disease Control and Prevention announced that one in four teenage girls has a sexually transmitted disease.

This eye-opening statistic landed like a dead rat on the doorsteps of America's 37 million households and 30 million teenagers. The *New York Times,* among other papers, put the news on the front page. CBS news anchor Katie Couric told her viewers that "at least one in four teenage girls in America has a sexually transmitted disease," and she ended by saying, "I know what I'll be talking about at the dinner table tonight."

The one-in-four number "really caught every parent in America's attention," said Cecile Richards, the president of the Planned Parenthood Federation of America, because it is so simple and "so stunning." Richards said that her 17-year-old daughter read it "and personalized it, and said, 'There are some girls I know who have an STI'"—shorthand for sexually transmitted infection. "It really brought it home."

Rival Washington advocates pounced on the CDC's startling statistic. One faction, led by Planned Parenthood and other groups that get federal grants, said the number shows that the Bush administration's abstinence-promotion programs don't work and that funding should be transferred to sex-education and condom-distribution programs. The rival faction, led by social conservatives, said that the one-in-four number demonstrates the failure of condoms and sex-education classes.

An April 23 hearing of the House Oversight and Government Reform Committee showcased this dispute. Chairman Henry Waxman opened the hearing by declaring: "A few weeks ago, the CDC released data showing that one in four teenage girls in the U.S. has a sexually transmitted infection. . . . We will hear today from multiple experts that after more than a decade of huge government spending, the weight of the evidence doesn't demonstrate abstinence-only programs to be effective."

But how useful or valid is that one-in-four number? Are 25 percent of America's teenage girls really in imminent danger from HIV/AIDS, gonorrhea, and the human papillomavirus (HPV) that leads to cervical cancer?

A close examination of the CDC's star statistic reveals several serious shortcomings that undermine its validity, as well as its usefulness to parents, legislators, health officials, and advocacy groups on the left and the right.

For instance, Couric's and Waxman's shorthand summaries were misleading. The CDC's study referred to "infections," but most biological infections never turn into diseases; the body suppresses them before symptoms appear. Most news accounts, including the first line of an Associated Press story that ran in many newspapers, likewise referred to "diseases" rather than infections. The CDC did little to correct this inflated interpretation.

Other problems were numerous. For instance, the infections referred to in the study are not the ones that leap to people's minds when they worry about sexually transmitted diseases. The data excluded the two most-feared diseases, HIV/AIDS and syphilis. The most common infection was from HPV, which can have serious consequences but in the vast majority of cases disappears on its own.

The focus on "teenagers," moreover, covers a broad age range, from those who are 14 (only 13 percent of whom have had sexual intercourse, according to other studies) to women of 18 and 19 (70 percent of whom have had sex before their 19th birthday). CDC officials declined to describe to *National Journal* the infection rates in each of the two-year age groupings, even though they have the data.

Perhaps most critical, the CDC's March 11 news conference, and the materials distributed there, failed to put the numbers into historical context. Other CDC research shows that infection rates for most serious sexual diseases, including syphilis, gonorrhea, and chancroid, are sharply below 1990 levels—syphilis reached a historic low in 2000. The CDC's tests showed that none of the 18- and 19-year-old women in the study were infected with HIV or syphilis, but officials did not mention this success in the press release. Teenagers' exposure to STDs has also dropped because their sexual activity declined from 1998 to 2002.

Some of **the CDC's statements fall neatly in line** with liberal stances on sex policy.

CDC officials say they acted appropriately when they prepared and released the one-in-four number. "The last thing we want is for people to believe that 25 percent of girls have something that will bring them serious harm," John Douglas, director of the CDC's STD prevention division, told the *Chicago Tribune* in April. Asked about the substitution of "disease" for "infection," CDC officials replied in an e-mailed statement: "We use STD because it is more widely understood than STI among both health professionals and the lay public."

CDC Director Julie Gerberding declined to be interviewed for this article. In a statement to *National Journal,* she said, "As the nation's health protection agency . . . we pride ourselves in following three core values—accountability, respect, and integrity. In all my years as director, I have never been pressured or asked to make any decisions which were not based on the sound scientific research that the world expects from CDC."

Officials at the CDC's Division of STD Prevention at the National Center for HIV/AIDS, Viral Hepatitis, STD, and TB Prevention arrived at the one-in-four number in 2007. Officials already knew the approximate STI rates among teenagers, but they sought to reframe the existing data on young women. Douglas told *NJ,* "They're the cutting edge of prevention."

To get the new number, CDC researcher Sara Forhan turned to a database—the CDC's National Health and Nutrition Examination Survey—that goes back to the 1960s. The CDC's Center for Health Statistics, which collects information on the health and nutritional status of Americans, sends a mobile laboratory to 15 counties every year to survey and give laboratory tests to approximately 5,000 randomly selected volunteers. Since the 1960s, officials have used the NHANES database to expose problems caused by iron deficiency, cholesterol, lead, and many other hazards. Its data served as the basis for children's growth charts, for guidelines to reduce exposure to lead, and for awareness of obesity as a public health hazard.

Forhan examined the 2003–04 database for the age groups covering 14 to 19. She found good records on 615 women, of whom 18.3 percent had HPV, 3.9 percent carried chlamydia, 2.5 percent had trichomoniasis, and 1.9 percent had HSV-2 (herpes simplex virus). The four mini-surveys were combined, and CDC officials determined that 25.7 percent of the 615 women had one or more of the four diseases, according to a CDC briefing chart.

CDC officials, including Douglas, announced the number in Chicago at the CDC's biannual National STD Prevention Conference, which is attended by many experts, state officials, and reporters. The subsequent media reports and editorials generally echoed the recommendations of CDC officials, and their advocacy allies, for greater government-funded testing and intervention.

The one-in-four figure immediately became fodder in the ongoing debate over whether the government should support comprehensive sex education or fund advocacy for sexual abstinence until marriage. Sex-education advocates were first out of the gate, announcing even before the press conference (in time for initial news reports) that funding should be transferred from "failed" abstinence-only programs to education that includes lessons on the use of contraceptives.

Proponents for abstinence and marriage programs countered that the CDC's number demonstrates just the opposite. "The half [of the adolescents] that weren't having sex did not have STIs," said the Family Research Council's Gaul. The CDC's one-in-four number "represents a failure of contraceptive-based education," Rep. Mark Souder, R-Ind., said at the Waxman hearing. The statistic "verifies that what we've been saying is true—the only safe sex is inside marriage." Souder announced that he's campaigning for a health warning on condom packages, akin to the warning on cigarette packs.

Boonstra, a comprehensive-education advocate at Guttmacher, responds that abstinence-until-marriage programs nearly always fail because, surveys show, 95 percent of people have sex before marriage.

Under the Bush administration, the federal government has spent about $180 million a year on classroom programs that promote abstinence until marriage (and don't train in condom use) to more than 2 million youths. The federal government also gives at least $300 million to federal agencies and states to fund comprehensive sex education, STI testing, and condom distribution. In the fiscal year ending June 2007, Planned Parenthood and its state affiliates received $337 million in government money, and the group's activities included spending $48 million on sexuality education programs, according to its annual report.

CDC officials try to stay clear of politics, Douglas said. They present scientific conclusions, he said, and "let the chips fall where they may politically." Yet some of the CDC's statements fall neatly in line with liberal stances on sex policy.

The March 11 study was, moreover, closely associated with the CDC's funding aspirations. On the day it was released, CDC officials used the study to tout their sexually transmitted disease programs. "Continued commitment to STD prevention is essential," Kevin Fenton, the director of the CDC's STD division and Douglas's boss, said at the beginning of the press conference. "CDC estimates that approximately 19 million new [sexually transmitted] infections occur every year in the United States, [and] our task is to maximize the use of these new tools—from vaccines to innovative STD screening and treatment."

Because of the study, "we got some really good press, and we've been able to get the [budget] discussion on the table," said Don Clark, the executive director of the National Coalition of STD Directors, which is pushing to increase the STD budget. The CDC's STD programs have been reduced since 2003, and they're now stuck at about $150 million, he said. Last year, the agency asked for $267 million a year.

Overall, the CDC's primary budget—excluding vaccine programs—has been cut 15 percent since 2005, says Karl Moeller, the executive director of the Campaign for Public Health, an industry-funded coalition formed in 2004 to boost the CDC's core budget from $6.3 billion in 2005 to $15 billion by 2012.

The CDC is a science agency, yet it is expected to advocate for policies that aid public health, said Jeffrey Koplan, the CDC's director from 1998 to 2002. Science demonstrates that seat belts and air bags reduce automobile deaths, so "it would be irresponsible for public health leaders not to advocate for them," said Koplan, who is now the executive director of Emory University's Global Health Institute. "Large parts of public health are political."

FOR DISCUSSION: Should we be troubled by political implications of the statistics released by federal agencies? Will we conclude from the CDC's statistic that abstinence-only or safe-sex programs are more effective in fighting the spread of sexually transmitted diseases? Does the case of the CDC statistic show that politicians, not agencies of government, play with objective facts to further political causes?

CHAPTER **14**

The Federal Judicial System
Applying the Law

The Federal Judicial System

The Supreme Court of the
United States
Other Federal Courts
The State Courts

Federal Court Appointees

The Selection of Supreme Court
Justices and Federal Judges
Justices and Judges as Political
Officials

**The Nature of Judicial Decision
Making**

The Constraints of the Facts
The Constraints of the Law

**Political Influences on Judicial
Decisions**

Outside Influences on Court
Decisions
Inside Influences: The Justices' Own
Political Beliefs

**Judicial Power and Democratic
Government**

The Limits of Judicial Power
Defining the Judiciary's Proper Role

It is emphatically the province and duty of the judicial department to say what the law is. Those who apply the rule to particular cases, must of necessity expound and interpret that rule. If two laws conflict with each other, the courts must decide on the operation of each. **John Marshall**[1]

Through its rulings in *Parents v. Seattle School District* (2007) and *Meredith v. Jefferson County Board of Education* (2007), the Supreme Court effectively ended the use of forced busing of schoolchildren as a means of integrating public schools. At issue were busing programs that the Seattle and Louisville school boards had adopted voluntarily (rather than in response to court order) as a means of creating racially diverse schools. The programs took race, neighborhood, and student preference into account in school placements. The large majority of students were placed in their school of choice, but some were assigned elsewhere, an arrangement challenged by white parents whose children did not get their school of choice.

The Supreme Court ruled in their favor, saying their children had been denied the equal protection guaranteed by the Fourteenth Amendment. In doing so, the Court reversed long-standing positions. Busing as a means of integrating public schools dated to the early 1970s, when the Supreme Court ruled that it was an acceptable means of overcoming the effects of past discrimination.[2] The Fourteenth Amendment's equal protection clause had a longer history, having been invoked for the first time in *Brown v. Board of Education* (1954), which outlawed state laws forcing black children to attend separate schools from whites.[3]

The Court's rulings in the Seattle and Louisville cases were decided by a 5-4 vote with the opposing justices taking starkly different positions. Writing for the majority, Chief Justice John Roberts said, "Before *Brown*, schoolchildren were told where they could and could not go to school based on the color of their skin. The school districts in these cases have not carried the heavy burden of demonstrating that we should allow this once again—even for very different reasons." Roberts concluded: "The way to stop discrimination on

The Supreme Court's Louisville and Seattle busing decisions in 2007 effectively ended the use of forced busing as a means of integrating public schools, an illustration of the power of the judiciary.

the basis of race is to stop discriminating on the basis of race." In his dissenting opinion, Justice John Paul Stevens said there was "a cruel irony" in the majority's use of the *Brown* decision as an argument against voluntary efforts to achieve school integration.[4]

The Court's rulings illustrate three key points about court decisions. First, the judiciary is an important policymaking body. Some of its rulings are as consequential as a law of Congress or an executive order of the president. Second, the judiciary has considerable discretion in its rulings. The Seattle and Louisville school rulings were not based on any literal reading of the law or else the justices would have been in full agreement on the proper ruling. Third, the judiciary is a political as well as legal institution. The busing rulings were a product of contending political forces, had political content, and were decided by political appointees.

This chapter describes the federal judiciary and the work of its judges and justices. Like the executive and legislative branches, the judiciary is an independent branch of the U.S. government, but unlike the two other branches, its top officials are not elected by the people. The judiciary is not a democratic institution, and its role is different from and, in some areas, more contentious than the roles of the executive and legislative branches. This chapter explores this issue in the process of discussing the following main points:

- *The federal judiciary includes the Supreme Court of the United States, which functions mainly as an appellate court; courts of appeals, which hear appeals; and district courts, which hold trials.* Each state has a court system of its own, which for the most part is independent of supervision by the federal courts.

- *Judicial decisions are constrained by applicable constitutional law, statutory and administrative law, and precedent.* Nevertheless, political factors have a major influence on judicial appointments and decisions; judges are political officials as well as legal ones.

- *The judiciary has become an increasingly powerful policymaking body in recent decades, raising the question of the judiciary's proper role in a democracy.* The philosophies of judicial restraint and judicial activism provide different answers to this question.

The Federal Judicial System

The Constitution establishes the judiciary as a separate and independent branch of the federal government. The Constitution provides for the Supreme Court of the United States but gives Congress the power to determine the number and types of lower federal courts.

Federal judges are nominated and appointed to office by the president, subject to confirmation by majority vote in the Senate. Unlike the office of president, senator, or representative, the Constitution places no age, residency, or citizenship requirements on the office of federal judge. Nor does the Constitution require judges to have legal training, though by tradition they do. Once seated on the bench, as specified in the Constitution, they "hold their offices during good behavior." This has meant, in effect, that federal judges serve until they die or voluntarily retire. No Supreme Court justice and only a handful of lower-court judges have been removed through impeachment and conviction by Congress, the method of early removal provided for by the Constitution.

The argument for life tenure for federal judges was forcefully made by Alexander Hamilton in *Federalist* No. 78. Responding to arguments by anti-Federalists that unelected, life-appointed judges would be a threat to the republic, Hamilton argued that the judicial branch would be the weakest of the three branches because it had no way to force the other two branches to comply with its rulings. Its authority would rest instead on "judgment"—the reasonableness and even-handedness of its decisions. The best way to ensure that judicial decisions met this standard, Hamilton claimed, was to grant life tenure to federal judges so that they would be free of immediate political pressure and owe allegiance only to the rule of law.

The Supreme Court of the United States

The Supreme Court of the United States is the nation's highest court. The chief justice of the United States presides over the Supreme Court and, like the eight associate justices, is nominated by the president and is subject to Senate confirmation.

Article III of the Constitution grants the Supreme Court both original and appellate jurisdiction. A court's **jurisdiction** is its authority to hear cases of a particular type. **Original jurisdiction** is the authority to be the first court to hear a case. The Supreme Court's original jurisdiction includes legal disputes involving foreign diplomats and cases in which the opposing parties are state governments. The Court in its history has convened as a court of original jurisdiction only a few hundred times and has rarely done so in recent decades.

The Supreme Court does its most important work as an appellate court. **Appellate jurisdiction** is the authority to review cases that have already been heard in lower courts and are appealed to a higher court by the losing party; these higher courts are called *appeals courts* or *appellate courts*. The Supreme Court's appellate jurisdiction extends to cases arising under the Constitution, federal law and regulations, and treaties. The Court also hears appeals involving legal controversies that cross state or national boundaries. Appellate courts, including the Supreme Court, do not retry cases; rather, they determine whether a trial court acted in accord with applicable law.

Selecting and Deciding Cases

The Supreme Court's power is most apparent when it declares another institution's action to be unconstitutional. This power, called **judicial review,** was first asserted

jurisdiction (of a court)
A given court's authority to hear cases of a particular kind. Jurisdiction may be original or appellate.

original jurisdiction
The authority of a given court to be the first court to hear a case.

appellate jurisdiction
The authority of a given court to review cases that have already been tried in lower courts and are appealed to it by the losing party; such a court is called an *appeals court* or *appellate court*.

judicial review
The power of courts to decide whether a governmental institution has acted within its constitutional powers and, if not, to declare its action null and void.

The Supreme Court building is located across from the Capitol in Washington, D.C. Sixteen marble columns support the pediment. Two bronze doors, each weighing more than six tons, lead into the building. The courtroom, the justices' offices, and the conference room are on the first floor. Administrative staff offices and the Court's records and reference materials occupy the other floors.

by the Supreme Court in *Marbury v. Madison* (1803), when the Court rebuked both the president and Congress (see Chapter 2). It is a power that the Supreme Court has used sparingly. During its history, it has invoked judicial review in roughly fifteen hundred cases.[5] About 90 percent of these cases have involved actions by state and local governments. Only about 10 percent of the cases have involved action by Congress or the president, an indication that the Supreme Court does not routinely seek confrontations with the other branches of the federal government.

Although judicial review is the most dramatic application of the Supreme Court's power, its primary responsibility is to establish legal precedents that will guide the decisions of lower courts. A **precedent** is a judicial decision that serves as a rule for settling subsequent cases of a similar nature. Lower courts are expected to follow precedent—that is, to resolve cases of a like nature in ways consistent with upper-court rulings.

The Supreme Court's ability to set legal precedent is strengthened by its control over the cases it will hear. Nearly all cases that reach the Supreme Court do so after the losing party in a lower-court case has requested a Supreme Court hearing, which occurs only if at least four of the nine justices agree to hear it. If they do so, a **writ of certiorari** is granted, whereby the lower court is asked to submit a transcript of the case for the Supreme Court to review. Each year roughly eight thousand parties apply for certiorari, but the Court grants certiorari to fewer than a hundred cases (see Figure 14-1).

The Supreme Court is most likely to grant certiorari when the U.S. government through the solicitor general (the high-ranking Justice Department official who serves as the government's lawyer in Supreme Court cases) requests it.[6] The solicitor general tracks cases in which the federal government is a party. When the government loses a case in a lower court, the solicitor general decides whether to appeal it to the Supreme Court. Such cases often make up half or more of the cases the Court hears in a term.

precedent

A judicial decision that serves as a rule for settling subsequent cases of a similar nature.

writ of certiorari

Permission granted by a higher court to allow a losing party in a legal case to bring the case before it for a ruling; when such a writ is requested of the U.S. Supreme Court, four of the Court's nine justices must agree to accept the case before it is granted certiorari.

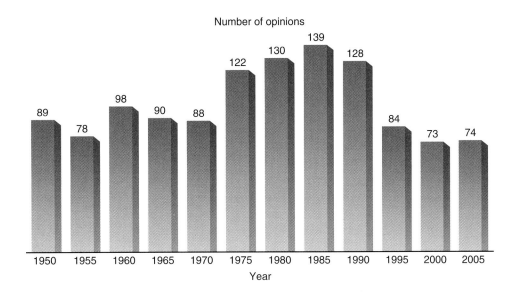

Number of opinions

89 78 98 90 88 122 130 139 128 84 73 74

1950 1955 1960 1965 1970 1975 1980 1985 1990 1995 2000 2005

Year

FIGURE 14-1 **Supreme Court Opinions, 1950–2005**
The number of signed Supreme Court opinions each term is relatively small. The Court has considerable control over the cases it selects. The cases that are heard by the Supreme Court tend to be ones that have legal significance beyond the particular case itself. The Court's term runs from October 1 to June 30; the year indicated is the closing year of the term.
Source: Supreme Court of the United States.

The Supreme Court seldom accepts a routine case, even if the justices believe that a lower court has made a mistake. The Court's job is not to correct the errors of other courts but to resolve substantial legal issues. This broad standard essentially means that a case must center on an issue of significance not merely to the parties involved but to the nation. As a result, most cases heard by the Court raise major constitutional issues, affect the lives of many Americans, address issues that are being decided inconsistently by the lower courts, or involve rulings that conflict with a previous Supreme Court decision. When the Court does accept a case, chances are that most of the justices disagree with the lower court's ruling. About three-fourths of the Supreme Court's decisions have reversed the judgments of lower courts.[7]

Once the Supreme Court accepts a case, it sets a date on which the attorneys for the two sides will present their oral arguments. Strict time limits, usually thirty minutes per side, are imposed on these presentations. Although the oral arguments are a time for the lawyers to highlight their key points and for the justices to raise questions,[8] these arguments are usually less decisive than the lengthy written **brief** each side submits, which contains its full argument.

The oral session is also less important than the **judicial conference** that follows, which is attended only by the nine justices and in which they discuss and vote on the case. The conference's proceedings are secret, which allows the justices to speak freely about a case and to change their minds as the discussion unfolds.[9]

Issuing Decisions and Opinions

After a case has been decided in conference, the Court prepares and issues its ruling, which consists of a decision and one or more opinions. The **decision** indicates which party the Court supports and by how large a margin. The **opinion** explains the reasons behind the decision. The opinion is the most important part of a Supreme Court ruling because it contains the justices' legal reasoning. For example, in the landmark *Brown* opinion, the Court held that government-sponsored school segregation was unconstitutional because it violated the Fourteenth Amendment provision that guarantees equal protection under the law to all citizens. This opinion became the legal basis by which communities throughout the southern states were ordered by lower courts to end their policy of segregating public school students by race.

brief
A written statement by a party in a court case that details its argument.

judicial conference
A closed meeting of the justices of the U.S. Supreme Court to discuss and vote on the cases before them; the justices are not supposed to discuss conference proceedings with outsiders.

decision
A vote of the Supreme Court in a particular case that indicates which party the justices side with and by how large a margin.

opinion (of a court)
A court's written explanation of its decision, which serves to inform others of the legal basis for the decision. Supreme Court opinions are expected to guide the decisions of other courts.

majority opinion

A court opinion that results when a majority of the justices are in agreement on the legal basis of the decision.

plurality opinion

A court opinion that results when a majority of justices agree on a decision in a case but do not agree on the legal basis for the decision. In this instance, the legal position held by most of the justices on the winning side is called a *plurality opinion.*

concurring opinion

A separate opinion written by one or more Supreme Court justices who vote with the majority in the decision on a case but who disagree with their reasoning.

dissenting opinion

The opinion of a justice in a Supreme Court case that explains his or her reasons for disagreeing with the majority's decision.

When a majority of the justices agree on the legal basis of a decision, the result is a **majority opinion.** In some cases there is no majority opinion because a majority of the justices agree on the decision but cannot agree on the legal basis for it. The result in such cases is a **plurality opinion,** which presents the view held by most of the justices who side with the winning party. Another type of opinion is a **concurring opinion,** a separate view written by a justice who votes with the majority but disagrees with its reasoning.

Justices on the losing side can write a **dissenting opinion** to explain their reasons for disagreeing with the majority position. Sometimes these dissenting arguments have later become the majority opinion. In a 1942 dissenting opinion, Justice Hugo Black wrote that defendants in state felony trials should have legal counsel even if they cannot afford to pay for it. Two decades later, in *Gideon v. Wainwright* (1963), the Court adopted Justice Black's position.[10]

When part of the majority, the chief justice decides which justice will write the majority opinion. Otherwise, the senior justice in the majority determines the author. Chief justices have often given themselves the task of writing the majority opinion in important cases. John Marshall did so often; *Marbury v. Madison* (1802) and *McCulloch v. Maryland* (1819) were among the opinions he wrote (see Chapters 2 and 3). The justice who writes the Court's majority opinion has the responsibility to express accurately the majority's reasoning. The vote on a case is not considered final until the opinion is written and agreed upon, so plenty of give-and-take can occur during the writing stage.[11] In rare cases, the writing stage has produced a change in the Court's decision. In *Lee v. Weisman* (1992), a case involving prayer at a public school graduation, Justice Anthony Kennedy originally sided with the four justices who said the prayer was allowable. While writing the 5-4 majority opinion, Kennedy found that he could not make a persuasive case for that position. He switched sides, resulting in a 5-4 majority the other way.

Other Federal Courts

There are more than one hundred federal courts but only one Supreme Court, and its position at the top of the judicial system gives the Supreme Court unparalleled importance. It is a mistake, however, to conclude that the Supreme Court is the only court that matters. Judge Jerome Frank once wrote of the "upper-court myth," which is the view that appellate courts, and in particular the Supreme Court, are the only truly significant judicial arena and that lower courts just dutifully follow the rulings handed down by courts at the appellate level.[12] The reality is very different, as the following discussion explains.

U.S. District Courts

The lowest federal courts are the district courts (see Figure 14-2). As noted above, there are nearly one hundred federal district courts altogether—at least one in every state and as many as four in some states. District court judges, who number about seven hundred in all, are appointed by the president with the consent of the Senate. Except for the small number of cases heard by the Supreme Court in its original jurisdiction, the federal district courts are the chief trial courts of the federal system. Nearly all criminal and civil cases arising under federal law are argued first in the district courts. They are the only courts in the federal system where the two sides present their case to a jury for a verdict. Cases at this level are typically presided over by a single judge.

Lower federal courts unquestionably rely on and follow Supreme Court decisions in their own rulings. The Supreme Court reiterated this requirement

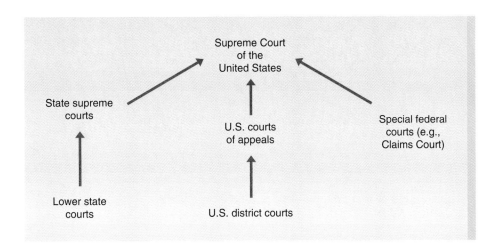

FIGURE 14-2   The Federal Judicial System   The simplified diagram shows the relationships among the various levels of federal courts and between state and federal courts. The losing party in a case can appeal a lower-court decision to the court at the next-highest level, as the arrows indicate. Decisions normally can be moved from state courts to federal courts only if they raise a constitutional question.

in a 1982 case, *Hutto v. Davis:* "Unless we wish anarchy to prevail within the federal judicial system, a precedent of this Court must be followed by the lower federal courts no matter how misguided the judges of those courts may think it to be."[13] However, the idea that lower courts are rigidly bound to Supreme Court rulings is part of the upper-court myth. District court judges might misunderstand the Supreme Court's position and deviate from it for that reason. In addition, the facts of a case before a district court are seldom identical to those of a case settled by the Supreme Court. The lower-court judge must decide whether a different legal judgment is appropriate. Finally, it is not unusual for the Supreme Court to issue a general ruling that is ambiguous enough to give lower courts some flexibility in deciding similar cases that come before them.

Most federal cases end with the district court's decision; the losing party does not appeal the decision to a higher court. This fact is another indication of the highly significant role of district court judges.

U.S. Courts of Appeals

When cases are appealed from district courts, they go to a federal court of appeals. These appellate courts are the second level of the federal court system. Courts of appeals do not use juries. Ordinarily, no new evidence is submitted in an appealed case; rather, appellate courts base their decisions on a review of lower-court records. Appellate judges act as supervisors in the legal system, reviewing trial court decisions and correcting what they consider to be legal errors. Facts (that is, the circumstances of a case) found by district courts are ordinarily presumed to be correct.

The United States has thirteen courts of appeals, each of which serves a "circuit" comprised of between three and nine states, except for the circuit that serves the District of Columbia only and the U.S. Court of Appeals for the Federal Circuit, which specializes in appeals involving patents and international trade (see Figure 14-3). Between four and twenty-six judges sit on each court of appeals, but each case usually is heard by a panel of three judges. On rare occasions, all the judges of a court of appeals sit as a body (*en banc*) in order to resolve difficult controversies, typically ones that have resulted in conflicting decisions within the same circuit. Each circuit is monitored by a Supreme Court justice, who normally takes the lead in reviewing appeals originating in that circuit. Conflict or inconsistency in how the different circuits are applying a law can lead the Supreme Court to review such cases.

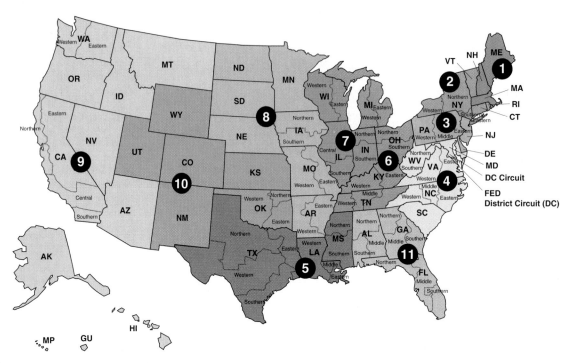

FIGURE 14-3 **Geographic Boundaries of U.S. Courts of Appeals** The United States has thirteen courts of appeals, each of which serves a "circuit." Eleven of these circuit courts serve anywhere from three to nine states, as the map shows. The other two are located in the District of Columbia: the Court of Appeals for the District of Columbia and the Court of Appeals for the Federal Circuit, which specializes in appeals involving patents and international trade. Within each circuit are federal trial courts, most of which are district courts. Each state has at least one district court within its boundaries. Larger states like California (which has four district courts, as can be seen on the map) have more than one.

Source: Administrative Office of the U.S. Courts.

Courts of appeals offer the only real hope of reversal for many appellants, because the Supreme Court hears so few cases. The Supreme Court reviews less than 1 percent of the cases heard by federal appeals courts.

Special U.S. Courts

In addition to the Supreme Court, the courts of appeals, and the district courts, the federal judiciary includes a few specialty courts. Among them are the U.S. Claims Court, which hears cases in which the U.S. government is being sued for damages; the U.S. Court of International Trade, which handles cases involving appeals of U.S. Customs Office rulings; and the U.S. Court of Military Appeals, which hears appeals of military courts-martial. Some federal agencies and commissions also have judicial powers (for example, the issuing of fines), and their decisions can be appealed to a federal court of appeals.

The State Courts

The American states are separate governments within the U.S. political system. The Tenth Amendment protects each state in its sovereignty, and each state has its own court system. Like the federal courts, state court systems have trial courts at the bottom level and appellate courts at the top.

Each state decides for itself the structure of its courts and the method of selecting judges. In some states judges are appointed by the governor, but in most states judgeships are *elective offices*. The most common form involves competitive elections

STATES IN THE NATION

PRINCIPAL METHODS OF SELECTING STATE JUDGES

The states use a variety of methods for selecting the judges on their highest court, including the merit plan, election, and political appointment. The states that appoint judges grant this power to the governor, except in Virginia, Connecticut, and South Carolina, where the legislature makes the choice.

Q: What might explain why several states in the middle of the nation use the merit plan for selecting judges?

A: The merit plan originated in the state of Missouri. Innovations in one state sometimes spread to adjacent states that have similar political cultures.

Political appointment

Partisan/nonpartisan election

Merit plan

Source: Council of State Governments.

of either a partisan or a nonpartisan nature. Other states use a mixed system called the *merit plan* (also called the "Missouri Plan" because Missouri was the first state to use it) under which the governor appoints a judge from a short list of acceptable candidates provided by a judicial selection commission. The judge selected must then periodically be reviewed by the voters, who, rather than choosing between the judge and an opponent, simply decide by a "yes" or "no" vote whether the judge should be allowed to stay in office (see "States in the Nation").

Besides the upper-court myth, there exists a "federal court myth," which holds that the federal judiciary is the most significant part of the judicial system and that state courts play a subordinate role. This view also is inaccurate. More than 95 percent of the nation's legal cases are decided in state courts. Most crimes (from shoplifting to murder) and most civil controversies (such as divorces and business disputes) are defined by state or local law. Moreover, nearly all cases that originate in state courts end there. The federal courts don't come into the picture because the case does not involve a federal issue.

Texas solicitor general Ted Cruz presents a case before the Supreme Court of Texas. It is one of two high courts in the state and has final say in civil and juvenile cases. The other high court in Texas is the Court of Criminal Appeals, which hears appeals of criminal cases. Each court has nine judges, elected to staggered six-year terms. More than 95 percent of the nation's legal cases are decided entirely by state courts, a refutation of the federal court myth, which wrongly holds that the federal courts are all that matter in the end. The United States has a federal system of government, and the division of power between the national and state governments affects the courts as well as other governing institutions.

In state criminal cases, after a person has been convicted and after all avenues of appeal in the state court system have been exhausted, the defendant can seek a writ of habeas corpus from a federal court on grounds that a state court made a decision that contravened a provision of the U.S Constitution—as, for example, in a claim that the suspect's Fifth Amendment right to remain silent was violated by state officials (see Chapter 4). If the federal court accepts such an appeal, it ordinarily confines itself to the federal aspects of the matter, such as whether the defendant's constitutional rights were in fact violated. In addition, the federal court accepts the facts determined by the state court unless such findings are clearly in error. Federal courts are also disinclined, when a provision of federal law does not clearly resolve a case, to substitute their own interpretation of a state's constitution for the interpretation provided by the state court. In short, legal and factual determinations of state courts can bind the federal courts—a clear contradiction of the federal court myth.

However, issues traditionally within the jurisdiction of the states can become federal issues through the rulings of federal courts. In its *Lawrence v. Texas* decision in 2003, for example, the Supreme Court invalidated state laws that made it illegal for consenting adults of the same sex to engage in private sexual relations.[14] Earlier, the Court had held that states had the authority to decide whether to prohibit such acts.[15] Lawrence had appealed his conviction in state court as a violation of the due process clause of the Fourteenth Amendment. The fact that he grounded his appeal in federal law allowed his case to be heard in federal court. And when the Supreme Court then decided in his favor on the basis of the Fourteenth Amendment, federal law became the governing authority in such cases.

Federal Court Appointees

The quiet dignity of the courtroom and the lack of fanfare with which a court delivers its decisions give the impression that the judiciary is as far removed from the world of politics as a governmental institution can possibly be. In reality, federal judges and justices are political officials who exercise the authority of a separate and powerful branch of government. All federal jurists bring their political views with them to the courtroom and have regular opportunities to promote their political beliefs through the cases they decide. Not surprisingly, the process by which federal judges are appointed is a partisan one.

The Selection of Supreme Court Justices and Federal Judges

The formal method for appointments to the Supreme Court and to the lower federal courts is the same: the president nominates, and the Senate confirms or rejects. Beyond that basic similarity, however, lie significant differences.

Supreme Court Nominees

A Supreme Court appointment is a real opportunity for a president.[16] Most justices retain their positions for many years, enabling presidents to influence judicial policy through their appointments long after they have left office. The careers of some Supreme Court justices provide dramatic testimony to the enduring nature of judicial appointments. For example, Franklin D. Roosevelt appointed William O. Douglas to the Supreme Court in 1939, and for thirty years after Roosevelt's death in 1945, Douglas remained a strong liberal influence on the Court.

Presidents invariably seek nominees who share their political philosophy, but they also must take into account a nominee's acceptability to others. Every nominee is closely scrutinized by the legal community, interested groups, and the media; must undergo an extensive background check by the FBI; and then must gain the approval of a Senate majority. Within the Senate, the key body is the Judiciary Committee, whose members have responsibility for conducting hearings on judicial nominees and recommending their confirmation or rejection by the full Senate.

The justices of the U.S. Supreme Court pose for a photo. From left, they are: Anthony Kennedy, Stephen Breyer, John Paul Stevens, Clarence Thomas, Chief Justice John Roberts, Ruth Bader Ginsburg, Antonin Scalia, Samuel Alito, David Souter.

Nearly 20 percent of presidential nominees to the Supreme Court have been rejected by the Senate on grounds of judicial qualification, political views, personal ethics, or partisanship. Most of these rejections occurred before 1900, and partisan politics was the main reason. Today a nominee with strong professional and ethical credentials is less likely to be blocked for partisan reasons alone. An exception was Robert Bork, whose 1987 nomination by President Reagan was rejected primarily because of intense opposition to his judicial philosophy from Senate Democrats. On the other hand, nominees can expect confirmation if they have personal integrity and a solid legal record and also show during Senate confirmation hearings the temperament and reasoning expected of a Supreme Court justice. The nomination of John Roberts in 2005 to be chief justice is a case in point. He faced tough questioning during Senate hearings, but nothing startlingly new or disturbing came out, and he was confirmed by a 78-22 vote. Senate hearings held a few months later on the nomination of Samuel Alito, whose past record raised more issues than did that of Roberts, went less smoothly, but he nonetheless was confirmed by a 58-42 vote.

Lower-Court Nominees

The president normally delegates to the deputy attorney general the task of identifying potential nominees for lower-court judgeships, a process that includes seeking recommendations from U.S. senators of the president's party, and sometimes House members as well. **Senatorial courtesy,** a tradition that dates back to the 1840s, holds that a senator from the state in which a vacancy has arisen should be consulted on the choice of the nominee if the senator is of the same party as the president.[17] If not consulted, the senator involved can request that confirmation be denied, and other senators will normally grant the request as a "courtesy" to their colleague.

Although the president does not become as personally involved in selecting lower-court nominees as in naming potential Supreme Court justices, lower-court appointments are collectively a significant factor in the impact of a president's administration. Recent presidents have appointed on average more than one hundred judges during a four-year term of office.

senatorial courtesy

The tradition that a U.S. senator from the state in which a federal judicial vacancy has arisen should have a say in the president's nomination of the new judge if the senator is of the same party as the president.

Justices and Judges as Political Officials

Presidents generally manage to appoint jurists who have a similar political philosophy. Although Supreme Court justices are free to make their own decisions, their legal positions can often be predicted from their background. A study by judicial scholar Robert Scigliano found that about three of every four appointees have behaved on the Supreme Court approximately as presidents could have expected.[18] Of course, a president has no guarantee that a nominee will fulfill his hopes. For example, Justices Earl Warren and William Brennan proved to be more liberal than President Dwight D. Eisenhower had anticipated. Asked whether he had made any mistakes as president, Eisenhower replied, "Yes, two, and they are both sitting on the Supreme Court."[19]

The Role of Partisanship

Presidents nearly always choose members of their own party as Supreme Court nominees. The same is true of lower-court judgeships. More than 90 percent of recent district and appeals court nominees have been members of the president's political party.[20]

This fact does not mean that federal judges and justices engage in blatant partisanship while on the bench. They are officers of a separate branch of government and prize their judicial independence. All Republican appointees do

TABLE 14-1 | Justices of the Supreme Court   Most recent appointees held an appellate court position before being nominated to the Supreme Court.

Justice	Year of Appointment	Nominating President	Position Before Appointment
John Paul Stevens	1975	Ford	Judge, U.S. Court of Appeals
Antonin Scalia	1986	Reagan	Judge, U.S. Court of Appeals
Anthony Kennedy	1988	Reagan	Judge, U.S. Court of Appeals
David Souter	1990	G. H. W. Bush	Judge, U.S. Court of Appeals
Clarence Thomas	1991	G. H. W. Bush	Judge, U.S. Court of Appeals
Ruth Bader Ginsburg	1993	Clinton	Judge, U.S. Court of Appeals
Stephen Breyer	1994	Clinton	Judge, U.S. Court of Appeals
John Roberts, Jr.*	2005	G. W. Bush	Judge, U.S. Court of Appeals
Samuel Alito, Jr.	2006	G. W. Bush	Judge, U.S. Court of Appeals

*Chief justice.

not vote the same way on cases, nor do all Democratic appointees. Nevertheless, partisanship influences judicial decisions. A study of the voting records of appellate court judges, for example, found that Democratic appointees were more likely than Republican appointees to side with parties that claimed their civil rights or civil liberties had been violated.[21]

Other Characteristics of Judicial Appointees

In recent years, increasing numbers of federal justices and judges have had prior judicial experience; the assumption is that such individuals are best qualified for appointment to the federal bench. Most recent appellate court appointees have been district or state judges or have worked in the office of the attorney general.[22] Elective office (particularly a seat in the U.S. Senate) was once a common route to the Supreme Court,[23] but recent justices have typically held an appellate court judgeship before their appointment (see Table 14-1).

White males are greatly overrepresented on the federal bench, just as they dominate in Congress and at the top levels of the executive branch. However, the number of women and minority-group members appointed to federal judgeships has increased significantly in recent decades. The number of such appointees has varied according to which party controls the presidency. Women and minority-group members are key constituencies of the Democratic Party; not surprisingly, Democratic presidents have appointed more judges from these groups than have Republican presidents (see Figure 14-4). Of President Bill Clinton's appointees, for example, roughly 30 percent were women and 25 percent were members of racial or ethnic minority groups, compared with 20 percent in each category for George W. Bush.

The Supreme Court is less demographically representative than are the lower courts. Of the nine current justices, only one (Ruth Bader Ginsburg) is a woman, and only one (Clarence Thomas) is a minority-group member. The historical pattern is even more one-sided. Until 1916, when Louis D. Brandeis was appointed to the Court, no Jewish justice had ever served. Prior to the twentieth century, only one Catholic, Roger Taney, had served on the Court. Thurgood Marshall in 1967 was the first black justice, and Sandra Day

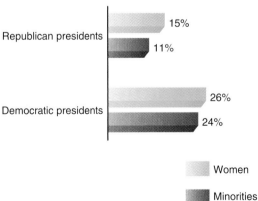

FIGURE 14-4   Political Parties, Presidents, and Women and Minority Judicial Appointees
Reflecting differences in their parties' coalitions, recent Republican and Democratic presidents have quite different records in terms of the percentage of their judicial appointees who have been women or minority-group members.
Source: Various sources. Data based on appointees of Presidents Carter, Reagan, G. H. W. Bush, Clinton, and G. W. Bush.

O'Connor in 1981 was the first woman justice. Antonin Scalia in 1986 was the Court's first justice of Italian descent. No person of Hispanic or Asian descent has been appointed to the Supreme Court. Of the Court's current members, five are Catholic, the first time ever that a majority of the justices have not been Protestants.

The Nature of Judicial Decision Making

Federal judges and justices are political officials: they constitute one of three co-equal branches of the national government. Yet, unlike members of Congress or the president, judges make their decisions within the context of a legal process. As a consequence, their discretionary power is less than that of elected officials. Article III of the Constitution bars a federal court from issuing a decision except in response to an actual case presented to it. As federal judge David Bazelon noted, a judge "can't wake up one morning and simply decide to give a helpful little push to a school system, a mental hospital, or the local housing agency."[24]

Judicial decisions are also restricted in scope. Technically, a court ruling is binding only on the parties involved. Its broader impact depends on the willingness of others to accept it. If a court were to decide, for example, that a school was bound by law to spend more on programs for the learning disabled, the ruling would extend to other schools in the same situation only if those schools voluntarily complied or were forced by subsequent court action to do so. By comparison, if Congress were to pass legislation granting funds for programs for the learning disabled, all eligible schools would receive the funding.

Another major restriction on the courts is the law itself. Although a president or Congress can make almost any decision that is politically acceptable, the judiciary must justify its decisions in terms of existing provisions of the law. When asked by a friend to "do justice," Justice Oliver Wendell Holmes Jr. said that the law, rather than his inclination, was his guide.[25] In applying the law, judges engage in a creative legal process that requires them to identify the facts of the case, determine and sometimes formulate the relevant legal principles or rules, and then apply these to the case at hand.

The Constraints of the Facts

facts (of a court case)

The relevant circumstances of a legal dispute or offense as determined by a trial court. The facts of a case are crucial because they help determine which law or laws are applicable in the case.

A basic distinction in any legal case is between "the facts" and "the laws." The **facts** of a case, as determined by trial courts, are the relevant circumstances of a legal dispute or offense. In the case of a person accused of murder, for example, key facts would include evidence about the murder and whether the rights of the accused were respected by police in the course of their investigation. The facts of a case are crucial because they determine which law or laws apply to the case. A murder case cannot be used as an occasion to pronounce judgment on freedom of religion, for example.

The Constraints of the Law

laws (of a court case)

The constitutional provisions, legislative statutes, or judicial precedents that apply to a court case.

In deciding cases, the judiciary is also constrained by existing **laws.** To use an obvious comparison, the laws that apply to a case of alleged murder differ from those that apply to a case of alleged shoplifting. A judge must treat a murder case as a murder case, applying to it the laws that define murder and the penalties that can be imposed when someone is found guilty of that crime.

civil law

Laws governing relations between private parties where no criminal act is alleged and where the parties are making conflicting claims or are seeking to establish a legal relationship.

Laws fall into three broad categories—civil, criminal, and procedural. **Civil law** governs relations with and between private parties. Marriage, divorce, business contracts, and property ownership are examples of relations covered by civil law. As an example, the civil law in nearly all states limits marriage to a man and a woman; same-sex couples in these states are prohibited by law from marrying. In this example, civil law defines the basis for a legally binding contract. Civil law also applies to disputes between private parties. The courts ordinarily do not get involved in such disputes unless the parties themselves cannot resolve their differences. For example, a dispute in which a homeowner alleges that an insurance company has failed to pay a policy claim could end up in court if they cannot settle it themselves. The losing party in a civil suit might be ordered to pay or otherwise compensate the other party but would not face jail unless he or she refuses to comply with a court order, which can be a punishable offense. Government can also be a party to a civil suit, as when the IRS sues a taxpayer in a dispute over how much the taxpayer owes the government.

Criminal law deals with acts that government defines as illegal and that can result in a fine, imprisonment, or other sanction. Murder, assault, shoplifting, and drunk driving are examples of acts that are covered by criminal law. The government is always a party to a criminal law case; the other party is the individual alleged to have broken the law. (Legal relationships between government and private parties, whether criminal or civil, are defined as *public law. Private law* refers to the legal rights and relationships between private parties.)

Procedural law refers to rules that govern the legal process. In some cases, these rules apply to government, as in the example of the obligation of police to inform suspects of their right to an attorney and to remain silent. In other cases, the rules apply to private parties. For example, in some states, a homeowner cannot take an insurance company to court over a policy claim without first having that claim heard, and possibly resolved, by an arbitration board.

There are three sources of law that constrain the courts: the Constitution, legislative statutes (and the administrative regulations derived from them), and precedents established by previous court rulings (see Table 14-2).

criminal law

Laws governing acts deemed illegal and punishable by government, such as robbery. Government is always a party to a criminal law case; the other party is the individual accused of breaking the law.

procedural law

Laws governing the legal process that define proper courses of action by government or private parties.

The Constitution and Its Interpretation

The Constitution of the United States is the nation's highest law, and judges and justices are sworn to uphold it. When a case raises a constitutional issue, a court has the duty to apply the Constitution to the case. For example, the Constitution prohibits the states from printing their own currency. If a state decided that it would do so anyway, a federal judge would be obligated to rule against the practice.

TABLE 14-2 | **Sources of Law That Constrain the Decisions of the Federal Judiciary**   Federal judges make their decisions in the context of law, which limits their discretion. The Constitution, statutes, and precedents are major constraints on the judiciary.

U.S. Constitution: The federal courts are bound by the provisions of the U.S. Constitution. The sparseness of its wording, however, requires the Constitution to be applied in the light of present circumstances. Thus, judges are accorded some degree of discretion in their constitutional judgments.

Statutory law: The federal courts are constrained by statutes and by administrative regulations derived from the provisions of statutes. Most laws, however, are somewhat vague in their provisions and often have unanticipated applications. As a result, judges have some freedom in deciding cases based on statutes.

Precedent: Federal courts tend to follow precedent (or stare decisis), which is a legal principle developed through earlier court decisions. Because times change and not all cases have a clear precedent, judges have some discretion in their evaluation of the way earlier cases apply to a current case.

Nevertheless, constitutional provisions are open to interpretation in some cases. For example, the Fourth Amendment of the Constitution protects individuals against "unreasonable searches and seizures," but the meaning of "unreasonable" is not specified. Judges must decide upon its meaning in particular situations. Take, for example, the question of whether wiretapping, which was not invented until 150 years after ratification of the Fourth Amendment, is included in the prohibition on unreasonable searches and seizures. Reasoning that the Fourth Amendment was intended to protect individuals from government snooping into their private lives, judges have ruled that indiscriminate wiretapping is unconstitutional.

Statutes and Administrative Laws, and Their Interpretation

The vast majority of cases that arise in courts involve issues of statutory and administrative law rather than constitutional law. *Statutory law* is legislative (statute) law. *Administrative law* is based on statutory law but is set by government agencies rather than by legislatures. Administrative law consists of the rules, regulations, and judgments that agencies make in the process of implementing and enforcing statutory law.

All federal courts are bound by federal statutory and administrative laws, as well as by treaties, and judges must work within the confines of these laws. A company that is charged with violating an air pollution law, for example, will be judged within the context of that law—what it permits and what it prohibits, and what penalties apply if the company is found to have broken the law. When hearing such a case, judges will often try to determine whether the meaning of the statute or regulation can be determined by common sense (the "plain meaning rule"). The question for the judge is what the law or regulation was intended to safeguard (such as clean air). The law or regulation in most cases is clear enough that when the facts of the case are considered, the decision is fairly predictable. Not all cases, however, are clear-cut in their facts or in the applicable law or laws. Where, for example, do college admissions programs that take race into account cross the line from legal to illegal by placing too much weight on race? In such instances, courts have no choice but to exercise their judgment.

Legal Precedents (Previous Rulings) and Their Interpretation

The U.S. legal system developed from the English common-law tradition, which includes the principle that a court's decision on a case should be consistent with previous judicial rulings. This principle, known as precedent, reflects the philosophy of stare decisis (Latin for "to stand by things that have been settled"). Precedent holds that principles of law, once established, should be applied in subsequent similar cases. Judges and justices often cite past rulings as justification for their decisions in the cases before them.

Precedent is important because it gives predictability to the application of law. Government has an obligation to make clear what its laws are and how they are being applied. If courts routinely ignored how similar cases had been decided in the past, they would create confusion and uncertainty about what is lawful and what is not. A business firm that is seeking to comply with environmental protection laws, for example, can develop company policies that will keep the company safely within the law if court decisions in this area are consistent. If courts routinely ignored precedent, a firm could unintentionally engage in an activity that a court might conclude was unlawful.

Political Influences on Judicial Decisions

Although judicial rulings are constrained by existing laws, judges nearly always have some degree of discretion in their decisions.[26] The Constitution is a sparsely worded document and must be adapted to new and changing situations. The judiciary also has no choice at times but to impose meaning on statutory law. Congress cannot always anticipate specific applications of a legislative act, and in these case it relies on general language to describe the act's purpose. The judiciary must decide what this language means in the context of a specific case arising under the act. Precedent is even less precise as a guide to decisions in that it is specific to particular cases. A new case may differ in important ways from its closest precedent or rest at the intersection of competing precedents.

The Supreme Court's ruling in *Faragher v. City of Boca Raton* (1998), involving sexual harassment in the workplace, illustrates the ambiguity that can exist in the law. The Court developed its ruling in the context of the antidiscrimination provisions of the Civil Rights Act of 1964. However, the act itself contains no description of, or even reference to, job-related sexual harassment. Nevertheless, the act does prohibit workplace discrimination, and the Court was unwilling to dismiss sexual harassment as an irrelevant form of job-related discrimination. In judging the case, the Court had to determine for itself which actions in the workplace are instances of harassment and which are not. In this sense, the Court was "making" law; it was deciding how legislation enacted by Congress applied to behavior that Congress had not specifically addressed when it wrote the legislation.[27]

In sum, judges have leeway in their decisions. As a consequence, their rulings reflect not only legal influences but political ones as well. Political influences can come from both outside and inside the judicial system.

HOW THE U.S. COMPARES

JUDICIAL POWER

U.S. courts are highly political compared to the courts of most other democracies. First, U.S. courts operate within a common-law tradition, in which judge-made law becomes (through precedent) a part of the legal code. Many democracies have a civil-law tradition, in which nearly all law is defined by legislative statutes. Second, because U.S. courts operate in a constitutional system of divided powers, they are required to rule on conflicts between state and nation or between the executive and the legislative branches, which thrusts the judiciary into the middle of political conflicts. Not surprisingly, then, federal judges and justices are appointed through an overtly political process in which partisan views and activities are major considerations. Many federal judges, particularly at the district level, have no significant prior judicial experience. In fact, the United States is one of the few countries that does not mandate formal training for judges.

The pattern is different in most European democracies, where judgeships tend to be career positions. Individuals are appointed to the judiciary at an early age and then work their way up the judicial ladder largely on the basis of seniority. Partisan politics does not play a large role in appointment and promotion. By tradition, European judges see their job as the strict interpretation of statutes, not the creative application of them.

The power of U.S. courts is nowhere more evident than in the exercise of judicial review—the voiding of a legislative or executive action on the grounds that it violates the Constitution. Judicial review had its origins in European experience and thought, but it was first formally applied in the United States when, in *Marbury v. Madison* (1803), the Supreme Court declared an act of Congress unconstitutional. Some democracies, including Great Britain, still do not allow broad-scale judicial review, but most democracies now provide for it.

In the so-called American system of judicial review, all judges can evaluate the applicability of constitutional law to particular cases and can declare ordinary law invalid when it conflicts with constitutional law. By comparison, the so-called Austrian system restricts judicial review to a special constitutional court. Judges in other courts cannot declare a law void on the grounds that it is unconstitutional; they must apply ordinary law as it is written. In the Austrian system, moreover, constitutional decisions can be made in response to requests for judicial review by elected officials when they are considering legislation. In the American case, judges can act only within the framework of actual legal cases; thus, their rulings are made only after laws have been enacted.

Outside Influences on Court Decisions

The courts can and do make unpopular choices, but in the long run, judicial decisions must be seen as fair if they are to be obeyed. In other words, the judiciary cannot ignore the expectations of the general public, interest groups, and elected representatives.

Public Opinion and Interest Groups

Judges are responsive to public opinion, although much less so than are elected officials. In some cases, for example, the Supreme Court has tailored its rulings in an effort to gain public support or reduce public resistance. In the *Brown* case, the justices, recognizing that school desegregation would be an explosive issue in the South, required only that desegregation take place "with all deliberate speed" rather than immediately or on a fixed timetable. The Supreme Court typically has stayed close enough to public opinion to avoid massive public resistance to its decisions.[28]

The courts also respond to interest groups, primarily through rulings in the lawsuits filed by them. Some groups rely on lawsuits as their primary political strategy because their issues are more likely to be decided favorably in a court than through an elected institution. An example is the American Civil Liberties Union (ACLU), which has filed hundreds of lawsuits over the years on issues of individual rights. In 2006, for example, the ACLU filed suit against the Bush administration over its wiretapping of individuals' phone and email messages without obtaining a court order, claiming such action to be a violation of the First and Fourth Amendments. A group can also try to influence the courts by filing an amicus curiae ("friend of the court") brief in which it presents its views on a case in which it is not one of the parties directly involved (see Chapter 9).[29] Groups' influence on the courts has increased in recent decades as a result of both a sharp rise in group activity and the use of more sophisticated judicial strategies. Groups carefully select the cases they pursue, choosing those with the greatest chance of success. They also carefully pick the courts in which they file, because some judges are more sympathetic than others to their particular issue.

Congress and the President

Groups and the general public also make an impact on the judiciary indirectly, through their elected representatives. Both Congress and the president have powerful means of influencing the federal judiciary.

Congress is constitutionally empowered to establish the Supreme Court's size and appellate jurisdiction and can rewrite legislation that it feels the judiciary has misinterpreted. Meanwhile, the president is responsible for enforcing court decisions and has some influence over the issues that come before the courts. Under President Ronald Reagan, for instance, the Justice Department pushed lawsuits that challenged the legality of affirmative action. Judicial appointments also provide the president and Congress with opportunities to influence the judiciary's direction. When Democrat Bill Clinton took office in 1993, more than a hundred federal judgeships were vacant. The first President Bush had expected to win reelection and had not moved quickly to fill vacancies as they arose. As it became apparent that he might lose the election, the Democrat-controlled Congress delayed action on his appointments. This enabled Clinton to fill many of the positions with loyal Democrats. The tables were turned in 2001. Senate Republicans had slowed action on Clinton nominees, enabling George W. Bush to appoint Republicans to existing vacancies when he took office.

In recent decades, the judicial appointment process has been unusually contentious, reflecting both the growing partisanship in Congress (see Chapter 11) and the widening range of issues (everything from abortion to the environment) being fought out in the courts. Nevertheless, the influence of elected officials on the judiciary is never total. Judges prize their independence. The fact that they hold their appointments indefinitely allows them to resist undue pressure from the elected branches of government. In 2004, for example, the Supreme Court, though it was filled with Republican appointees, rejected the Bush administration's claim that U.S. citizens charged with terrorism can be jailed indefinitely without a judicial hearing (see Chapter 4).

Inside Influences: The Justices' Own Political Beliefs

Although the judiciary symbolizes John Adams's characterization of the U.S. political system as "a government of laws, and not of men," judicial rulings are affected by the political beliefs of the men and women who sit on the courts.[30] Most Supreme Court justices do not change their views greatly during their tenure. As a result, major shifts in the Court's positions usually occur when its membership changes. The appointment of Samuel Alito to the Court in 2006 appears to have marked such a shift. Although the justice he replaced, Sandra Day O'Connor, usually voted with the Court's four most conservative justices, she did not invariably do so. She cast the deciding vote, for example, in the 2003 University of Michigan case that upheld affirmative action (see Chapter 5) and in a 2001 Nebraska case that upheld the use of partial-birth abortion when the mother's life is endangered. In contrast, Alito cast the deciding vote in the 2007 Seattle and Louisville school integration decisions and in the 2007 decision to uphold a congressional ban on the use of partial-birth abortion. These and other Alito decisions prompted liberal and conservative observers alike to say that the Court had swung solidly to the right. Even one of the Supreme Court justices admitted as much. "It is not often in the law," wrote Justice Stephen Breyer, "that so few have so quickly changed so much."[31]

Studies by Jeffrey Segal and Harold Spaeth show that justices generally vote in line with their political attitudes.[32] Nonunanimous decisions of the Supreme Court frequently divide along the same political lines. In most such recent decisions, for example, justices Antonin Scalia and Clarence Thomas, who are Republican

Demonstrators rally outside the U.S. Supreme Court building during hearings on the *Bush v. Gore* case that effectively brought the 2000 presidential election to an end. At times, the policy rulings of the judiciary are as significant as the decisions of the president or Congress.

appointees, have been opposed by justices Breyer and Ruth Bader Ginsburg, the Court's two Democratic appointees.[33] It is true, of course, that disputes that reach the Supreme Court are anything but clear-cut. If they were, they would have been settled in the lower federal courts. Nevertheless, Supreme Court decisions are a mix of law and politics.

Arguably, partisanship was never more evident than in the Supreme Court's *Bush v. Gore* (2000) decision that blocked a manual recount of the Florida presidential vote in 2000, thereby assuring the election of the Republican nominee, George W. Bush.[34] The five justices in the majority—Chief Justice William Rehnquist and associate justices Sandra Day O'Connor, Anthony Kennedy, Antonin Scalia, and Clarence Thomas—were all Republican appointees and were the same justices who in previous decisions had deferred to state authority and had opposed new applications of the Fourteenth Amendment's equal protection

DEBATING THE ISSUES

SHOULD ALL THE FLORIDA BALLOTS HAVE BEEN COUNTED?

In *Colegrove v. Green* (1946), Justice Felix Frankfurter warned the Supreme Court about getting involved in election politics, saying that it "ought not to enter this political thicket." In 2000, the Court thrust itself into the thorniest political thicket of all—a presidential campaign. In *Bush v. Gore,* the Court by a narrow majority blocked a statewide manual recount of uncounted ballots in Florida, thereby settling the election in favor of Republican George W. Bush. His Democratic opponent, Al Gore, had argued that all the Florida votes—not just those that could be read by machine—should count. Bush supporters retorted that a manual recount would be inherently subjective and open to mischief. These opposing views also existed within the Supreme Court, as the following opinions show.

YES Florida law holds that all ballots that reveal the intent of the voter constitute valid votes. . . . [The Florida Supreme Court] decided the case before it in light of the legislature's intent to leave no legally cast vote uncounted. In so doing, it relied on the sufficiency of the general "intent of the voter" standard articulated by the state legislature, coupled with a procedure for ultimate review by an impartial judge, to resolve the concern about disparate evaluations of contested ballots. If we assume—as I do—that the members of that court and the judges who would have carried out its mandate are impartial, its decision does not even raise a colorable federal question. . . . What must underlie petitioners' entire federal assault on the Florida election procedures is an unstated lack of confidence in the impartiality and capacity of the state judges who would make the critical decisions if the vote count were to proceed. Otherwise, their position is wholly without merit. . . . Although we may never know with complete certainty the identity of the winner of this year's Presidential election, the identity of the loser is perfectly clear. It is the Nation's confidence in the judge as an impartial guardian of the rule of law.

—*John Paul Stevens, associate justice of the Supreme Court*

NO The standards for accepting or rejecting contested ballots might vary not only from county to county but indeed within a single county from one recount team to another. . . . The question before the Court is not whether local entities, in the exercise of their expertise, may develop different systems for implementing elections. Instead, we are presented with a situation where a state court with the power to assure uniformity has ordered a statewide recount with minimal procedural safeguards. . . . It is obvious that the recount cannot be conducted in compliance with the requirements of equal protection and due process without substantial additional work. It would require not only the adoption (after opportunity for argument) of adequate statewide standards for determining what is a legal vote, and practicable procedures to implement them, but also orderly judicial review of any disputed matters that might arise. . . . The Supreme Court of Florida has said that the legislature intended the State's electors to "participat[e] fully in the federal electoral process." That statute, in turn, requires that any controversy or contest that is designed to lead to a conclusive selection of electors be completed by December 12. That date is upon us, and there is no recount procedure in place under the State Supreme Court's order that comports with minimal constitutional standards.

—*Supreme Court's majority opinion*

clause. Yet they rejected the authority of the Florida high court, which had ordered a statewide manual recount of the vote. They also employed a never-before-used application of the equal protection clause, ruling that the recount could not go forward because no uniform standard for counting the ballots existed. Justice John Paul Stevens, who thought the Florida high court had acted properly in ordering a recount, accused the Court's majority of devising a ruling based on their partisan desires rather than on the law. Stevens noted that different standards for casting and counting ballots are used throughout the country, even within the same state. Stevens argued that the Supreme Court's majority had ignored "the basic principle, inherent in our Constitution and our democracy, that every legal vote should be counted."[35] Some observers suggested that if Bush had been trailing in the Florida vote, the Court's majority would have come up with reasons why a recount was required.

Judicial Power and Democratic Government

The issue of judicial power is heightened by the fact that federal judges are not elected.[36] The principle of self-government asserts that lawmaking majorities have the power to decide society's policies. Because the United States has a constitutional system that places checks on the will of the majority, the judiciary clearly has a key role in the system. Nevertheless, there is a basic issue of **legitimacy**—the proper authority of the judiciary in a governing system based on the principle of majority rule.

legitimacy (of judicial power)
The issue of the proper limits of judicial authority in a political system based in part on the principle of majority rule.

The Limits of Judicial Power

The judiciary's power has been a source of controversy throughout the nation's history, but the controversies have seldom been livelier than during recent decades. The judiciary at times has acted almost legislatively by defining broad social policies, such as abortion, busing, affirmative action, church-state relations, and prison reform. During the 1990s, for example, the prison systems in forty-two states were operating under federal court orders that mandated improvements in health care or reductions in overcrowding. Through such actions the judiciary has restricted the policymaking authority of the states, has narrowed legislative discretion, and has made judicial action an effective political strategy for certain interests.[37]

The judiciary has become more extensively involved in policymaking for many of the same reasons that Congress and the president have been thrust into new policy areas and become more deeply involved in old ones. Social and economic changes have required government to play a larger role in society, and this development has generated a seemingly endless series of new legal controversies. Environmental pollution, for example, was not a major issue until the 1960s; since then, it has been the subject of numerous court cases.

Nevertheless, judges are not elected by the voters to make law. They are appointed and charged with applying the law. How far should judges go in asserting their interpretations of the law, as opposed to those put into effect by the people's elected representatives? There are competing schools of thought on this issue, none of which is definitive. The Constitution is silent on the question of how it should be interpreted, which has left the judiciary's proper role open to dispute. Nevertheless, it is instructive to review briefly some of the competing theories.

POLITICAL CULTURE

LIBERTY, EQUALITY, AND SELF-GOVERNMENT

The Judiciary

The French writer Alexis de Tocqueville observed that there is barely a political controversy in America that sooner or later does not become also a judicial issue. Abortion, age-related discrimination, and Internet content are but a few of the recent examples.

Americans know less about the judiciary than about the elected branches of their government—Congress and the presidency. Nevertheless, when it comes to the protection of their liberty, the judiciary is key. Its power to protect personal freedom is most evident when the Supreme Court strikes down actions taken by elected officials. In most cases, the target of Supreme Court action is not the Congress or the president, but state and local officials. The Supreme Court has struck down well over a thousand state laws and local

ordinances, most of which have involved issues of personal freedom, as in *Near v. Minnesota* (freedom of the press) and *Gideon v. Wainwright* (the right to an attorney, even if the defendant is too poor to hire one). That the actions of state and local governments would more often prompt judicial review is hardly surprising. There are fifty state governments and thousands of local governments, compared with a single federal government. Moreover, state and local governments have most of the responsibility for law enforcement and public order, which is where individual rights most frequently collide with authority.

Imagine, as was originally the case, that the Supreme Court had no authority to rule on Bill of Rights issues arising from state and local action. Do you think you would have less liberty in that situation? Why or why not?

Debating the Judiciary's Proper Role

judicial restraint

The doctrine that the judiciary should closely follow the wording of the law, be highly respectful of precedent, and defer to the judgment of legislatures. The doctrine claims that the job of judges is to work within the confines of laws set down by tradition and lawmaking majorities.

compliance

The issue of whether judicial decisions will be respected and obeyed.

judicial activism

The doctrine that the courts should develop new legal principles when judges see a compelling need, even if this action places them in conflict with precedent or the policy decisions of elected officials.

The doctrine of **judicial restraint** holds that judges should broadly defer to precedent and to decisions made by legislatures. The restraint doctrine holds that in nearly all cases public issues should be decided by elected lawmakers and not appointed judges. The role of judges is to apply the law rather than redefine it. According to the doctrine of judicial restraint, judges should refrain from declaring a law to be unconstitutional unless it clearly conflicts with the Constitution. Advocates of judicial restraint say that when judges substitute their views for those of elected representatives, they undermine the fundamental principle of self-government—the right of popular majorities, through their representatives, to decide the policies by which they will be governed.[38] Deference to Congress or a state legislature recognizes that legislation results from striking a balance between contending interests and that elected representatives, not judges, are in the best position to determine the proper balance. Advocates also claim that restraint serves to maintain public confidence in the judiciary, thereby increasing the likelihood of **compliance** with its decisions—that is, acceptance of and obedience to court rulings.[39]

In contrast, the doctrine of **judicial activism** holds that judges should actively interpret the Constitution, statutes, and precedents in light of established principles when elected representatives fail to act in clear accord with these principles. Although advocates of judicial activism acknowledge the importance of majority rule, they claim that the courts should not be subservient to the decisions of elected officials when core principles are at issue. Judges should not hesitate to override precedent or law when it conflicts with constitutional principles or fails to meet society's vital needs.

Over its history, the Supreme Court has had many proponents of each doctrine. Chief Justice John Marshall was an activist who used the Court to enlarge the judiciary's power and to promote the national government (see Chapters 2 and 3). Judicial review—the most substantial form of judicial power—is not explicitly granted by the Constitution but was claimed through Marshall's opinion in *Marbury v. Madison*. Associate Justice Oliver Wendell Holmes Jr. was Marshall's philosophical opposite, favoring judicial restraint. One of the nation's most influential jurists, Holmes wrote of the need for the judiciary to defer to the elected branches except when they blatantly overstep their authority.[40] Holmes wrote the opinion in *Schenck v. United States* (1919) that upheld a congressional restriction on free speech, despite the First Amendment admonition that Congress shall pass "no law . . . abridging the freedom of speech." Holmes argued that the law in question was aimed at "substantive evils that Congress has a right to prevent" (see Chapter 4).[41]

The Supreme Court as a whole has at times been activist and at other times been restrained. Although judicial activism is sometimes associated with liberal justices, history indicates that justices' partisanship is not a precise predictor of their judicial philosophy. The conservative-dominated Supreme Court in the period between the Civil War and the Great Depression was an activist judiciary, striking down most state and congressional legislation aimed at economic regulation (see Chapter 3). Similarly, the liberal-dominated Supreme Court in the period after World War II was an activist judiciary, striking down state legislative acts by the dozen in expanding the civil liberties of the criminally accused (see Chapter 4) and the civil rights of black Americans (see Chapter 5). The recent Supreme Court has also been an activist court. In the past dozen years, the Supreme Court has struck down more acts of Congress than were invalidated during the entire previous half-century.[42] Walter Dellinger, a former U.S. solicitor general, said of the Court: "[It] doesn't defer to government at any level. [It] is confident it can come up with the right decisions, and it believes it is constitutionally charged with doing so."[43]

Liberal and conservative justices can be distinguished more clearly by their views on how to interpret the Constitution. **Originalism theory,** a prominent philosophy of conservatives, holds that the Constitution should be interpreted in the way that a reasonable person would have viewed it at the time it was written.[44] Originalists emphasize the wording of the law, arguing that words of

originalism theory

A method of interpreting the Constitution that emphasizes the meaning of its words at the time they were written.

I was sentenced to the State Penitentiary by The Circuit Court of Bay County, State of Florida. The present proceeding was commenced on a petition for a Writ of Habeus Corpus To The Supreme Court of The State of Florida To vacate the sentence, on the grounds that I was made to stand Trial without the aid of counsel, and, at all times of my incarseretion. The said Court refused To appoint counsel and therefore deprived me of Due process of law, and violate my rights in The Bill of Rights and the constitution of The United States.
Clarence Earl Gideon
5th day of Jan 1962 Petitioner
Notary Public

Gideon's Letter to the Supreme Court
John F. Davis, Clerk, Supreme Court of the United States

The handwritten letter that Clarence Gideon (insert) sent to the Supreme Court in 1962. The letter led eventually to the *Gideon* decision, in which the Court held that states must provide poor defendants with legal counsel (see Chapter 4). Seen by many people at the time as judicial activism, the ruling is now fully accepted.

JOHN MARSHALL
(1755–1835)

John Marshall served thirty-four years as chief justice of the Supreme Court, the longest tenure in that position in U.S. history. Marshall had served for a time as John Adams's secretary of state and in the House of Representatives before being appointed chief justice by Adams. Prior to Marshall's tenure, the Supreme Court was perceived as a feeble branch of the federal government. Marshall changed that notion. An ardent nationalist who saw himself as a guardian of federal authority, Marshall steered the Court through a series of decisions that established it as a powerful institution and helped lay the foundation for a strong Union. The Supreme Court's ruling in *McCulloch v. Maryland* (1819) affirmed the claims that national law was supreme over conflicting state law and that the federal government's powers were not narrowly constrained by the Constitution.

Despite philosophical differences with the presidents who succeeded Adams, Marshall dominated the Court throughout his long tenure, persuading newly appointed justices to back him on key constitutional issues. Marshall saw himself as a Framer of the Constitution, acting as the ongoing architect of the work begun in Philadelphia during the summer of 1787. Although Marshall was a distant cousin of Thomas Jefferson, the two men were bitter opponents. Marshall's first landmark decision, *Marbury v. Madison* (1803), which established the principle of judicial review, was a rebuke to President Jefferson's executive authority. Their ongoing dispute peaked in 1807 at the trial of Aaron Burr, who was justly accused of treason by the Jefferson administration. Marshall presided over the trial and acquitted Burr, ruling that the word of a single eyewitness was insufficient grounds for conviction.

the Framers can be plainly understood whereas their intent is hard to determine. The judge's task then is to determine the original meaning of the Constitution's words and, once that is done, to apply that meaning to the case at hand. Current Supreme Court justice Antonin Scalia is an avowed originalist: "You figure out what [the Constitution] was understood to mean when it was adopted and that's the end of it." The difficult part, Scalia claims, comes in trying to figure out what the words meant to those who wrote and ratified them. "It requires immersing oneself in the political and intellectual atmosphere of the time—somehow placing out of mind knowledge that we have which an earlier age did not."[45]

An opposing theory, embraced more often by liberal justices than conservative ones, is the notion that the Constitution is a living document that should be interpreted in light of changing circumstances. Proponents of the **living constitution theory** claim that the Framers, by inserting essential principles and general propositions into the Constitution, intended it to be an adaptable instrument. They cite the preamble of the convention's Committee of Detail, which says the Constitution "ought to be accomodated to times and events." Current Supreme Court justice Stephen Breyer embraces this view, saying that the judiciary should be intent on promoting in today's world the kind of government the Constitution was meant to establish. "The Constitution," Breyer argues, "provides a framework for the creation of democratically determined solutions, which protect each individual's basic liberties and assures that individual equal respect by government, while securing a democratic form of government."[46]

living constitution theory

A method of interpreting the Constitution that emphasizes the principles it embodies and their application to changing circumstances and needs.

These disputes are philosophical ones. As indicated, the Constitution does not specify a method by which judges should arrive at their decisions. Nevertheless, the disputes are important because they address the question of the role that judges ought to play in a governing system based on the often-conflicting concepts of majority rule and individual rights. The United States is a constitutional democracy that recognizes both the power of the majority to rule and the claim of the minority to protection of its rights. The judiciary was not established as the nation's final authority on all things relating to the uses of political power. Yet the judiciary was established as a coequal branch of government charged with responsibility for protecting individual rights and constraining political authority. The issue of how far the courts should go in asserting their authority is an open one, but it is also an important one for students of American government to ponder.

Summary   Self-Test www.mhhe.com/pattersontad9e

At the lowest level of the federal judicial system are the district courts, where most federal cases begin. Above them are the federal courts of appeals, which review cases appealed from the lower courts. The U.S. Supreme Court is the nation's highest court. Each state has its own court system, consisting of trial courts at the bottom and one or two appellate levels at the top. Cases originating in state courts ordinarily cannot be appealed to the federal courts unless a federal issue is involved, and then the federal courts can choose to rule only on the federal aspects of the case. Federal judges at all levels are nominated by the president, and if confirmed by the Senate, they are appointed by the president to the office. Once on the federal bench, they serve until they die, retire, or are removed by impeachment and conviction.

The Supreme Court is unquestionably the most important court in the country. The legal principles it establishes are binding on lower courts, and its capacity to define the law is enhanced by the control it exercises over the cases it hears. However, it is inaccurate to assume that lower courts are inconsequential (the upper-court myth). Lower courts have considerable discretion, and the great majority of their decisions are not reviewed by a higher court. It is also inaccurate to assume that federal courts are far more significant than state courts (the federal court myth).

The courts have less discretionary authority than elected institutions do. The judiciary's positions are con-strained by the facts of a case and by the laws as defined through the Constitution, statutes and government regulations, and legal precedent. Yet existing legal guidelines are seldom so precise that judges have no choice in their decisions. As a result, political influences have a strong impact on the judiciary. It responds to national conditions, public opinion, interest groups, and elected officials, particularly the president and members of Congress. Another political influence on the judiciary is the personal beliefs of judges, who have individual preferences that are evident in the way they decide issues that come before the courts. Not surprisingly, partisan politics plays a significant role in judicial appointments.

In recent decades, the Supreme Court has issued broad rulings on individual rights, some of which have required governments to take positive action on behalf of minority interests. As the Court has crossed into areas traditionally left to lawmaking majorities, the legitimacy of its rulings has been questioned. Advocates of judicial restraint claim that the justices' personal values are inadequate justification for exceeding the proper judicial role; they argue that the Constitution entrusts broad issues of the public good to elective institutions and that judicial activism ultimately undermines public respect for the judiciary. Judicial activists counter that the courts were established as an independent branch and should not hesitate to promote new principles when they see a need, even if this action brings them into conflict with elected officials.

CHAPTER 14

Study Corner

Key Terms

appellate jurisdiction (p. 367)
brief (p. 369)
civil law (p. 378)
compliance (p. 386)
concurring opinion (p. 370)
criminal law (p. 379)
decision (p. 369)

dissenting opinion (p. 370)
facts (of a court case) (p. 378)
judicial activism (p. 386)
judicial conference (p. 369)
judicial restraint (p. 386)
judicial review (p. 367)

jurisdiction (of a court) (p. 367)
laws (of a court case) (p. 378)
legitimacy (of judicial power) (p. 385)
living constitution theory (p. 388)
majority opinion (p. 370)

opinion (of a court) (p. 369)
original jurisdiction (p. 367)
originalism theory (p. 387)
plurality opinion (p. 370)
precedent (p. 368)
procedural law (p.379)
senatorial courtesy (p. 376)
writ of certiorari (p. 368)

Self-Test

1. When nominating a justice to the U.S. Supreme Court, presidents:
   a. are required by law to consult with the American Bar Association.
   b. in accordance with senatorial courtesy have usually decided the choice by finding out who a majority of the senators in their party would like the nominee to be.
   c. tend to select a nominee who shares their political philosophy.
   d. get their nominee confirmed by the Senate only about half the time.

2. Judges in the U.S. judiciary:
   a. after issuing a ruling are personally responsible for seeing that the ruling is carried out by other officials.
   b. by law must attend public meetings from time to time and, while at these meetings, advise the public on judicial matters.
   c. are prohibited from issuing decisions except on actual cases that come to their court.
   d. have greater freedom than legislators or executives to choose the issues they will address.

3. The federal district courts are:
   a. courts of original jurisdiction.
   b. the only federal courts that regularly use juries to determine the outcome of cases.
   c. the courts that, in practice, make the final decision in most federal cases.
   d. the lowest level of federal courts.
   e. all of the above.

4. Most cases reach the U.S. Supreme Court through:
   a. appeal of cases that the court is bound by the Constitution or by act of Congress to hear even if it would prefer not to hear them.
   b. grant of a writ of certiorari.
   c. plea bargaining.
   d. its power of original jurisdiction.

5. Which constitutional power does Congress have in relation to the Supreme Court?
   a. Congress can change the number of justices on the Supreme Court.
   b. Congress can change the Supreme Court's original jurisdiction.
   c. By two-thirds vote of both chambers, Congress determines which justice will become Chief Justice when that office becomes vacant.
   d. Congress can refuse to implement Supreme Court decisions when it disagrees with those decisions.

6. A court exercising judicial activism would likely:
   a. totally disregard judicial precedent.
   b. totally disregard legislative and executive action.
   c. not hesitate to act when it thought an important constitutional principle was at issue, even if such action would bring the court into conflict with public opinion or the elected branches.
   d. none of the above.

7. State court systems in the United States are lower-level administrative units of the federal court system and not independent judicial units. (T/F)

8. The U.S. judiciary is not influenced by either public opinion or the actions of interest groups. (T/F)

9. The "federal court myth" implies that the federal courts are far more important than state courts. (T/F)

10. According to the text, social and economic changes have required the government, including the judiciary, to play a larger role in resolving societal problems and conflicts. (T/F)

Critical Thinking

Which philosophy—judicial restraint or judicial activism—comes closer to your own thinking about the proper role of the courts? Does your support for restraint or activism depend on whether a judicial decision conforms to your own preference on the issue in question?

Suggested Readings

Davis, Richard. *Electing Justices: Fixing the Supreme Court Nomination Process*. New York: Oxford University Press, 2005. An examination of the now-contentious process through which Supreme Court justices are nominated and confirmed.

Gillman, Howard. *Votes That Counted: How the Court Decided the 2000 Presidential Election*. Chicago: University of Chicago Press, 2001. An accounting of the *Bush v. Gore* ruling.

Hansford, Thomas G., and James F. Spriggs II. *The Politics of Precedent on the Supreme Court*. Princeton, N.J.: Princeton University Press, 2006. An examination of how the Court interprets precedent to suit new situations and goals.

Maltzman, Forest, Paul Wahlbeck, and James Spriggs. *The Collegial Game: Crafting Law on the U.S. Supreme Court*. New York: Cambridge University Press, 2000. A fascinating look at the strategic considerations that go into Supreme Court justices' interactions and decisions.

McGuire, Kevin T. *Understanding the Supreme Court: Cases and Controversies*. New York: McGraw-Hill, 2002. An overview of Supreme Court decisions and approaches to legal disputes.

O'Brien, David M. *Storm Center: The Supreme Court in American Politics*, 7th ed. New York: Norton, 2005. A thorough assessment of the Supreme Court.

Sandler, Ross, and David Schoenbord. *Democracy by Decree: What Happens When Courts Run Government*. New Haven, Conn.: Yale University Press, 2003. A critical evaluation of the courts' growing policy role.

Segal, Jeffrey A., and Harold J. Spaeth. *The Supreme Court and the Attitudinal Model Revisited*. New York: Cambridge University Press, 2002. A study of interjustice agreement on Supreme Court decisions that reveals the importance of political attitudes in the Court's rulings.

List of Websites

http://www.cnn.com/CRIME/
A website that allows you to take the facts of actual court cases, examine the law and the arguments, and then decide each case for yourself.

http://www.fjc.gov/
The home page of the Federal Judicial Center, an agency created by Congress to conduct research and provide education on the federal judicial system.

http://www.lib.umich.edu/govdocs/fedjudi.html
A University of Michigan web page that provides detailed information on the federal judicial system.

http://www.law.cornell.edu
The Cornell University Legal Information Institute's website; includes full-text versions of historic and recent Supreme Court decisions, as well as links to state constitutions and other subjects.

Participate!

The right to a jury trial is one of the oldest features—dating to the colonial period—of the American political experience. Jury trials also offer the average citizen a rare opportunity to be part of the governing structure. Yet Americans increasingly shirk jury duty. When summoned, many of them find all sorts of reasons why they should be excused from jury duty. In some areas of the country, the avoidance rate exceeds 50 percent. Some citizens even give up their right to vote be-cause they know that jurors in their area are selected from names on voter registration lists. There are reasons, however, to look upon jury duty as an opportunity as well as a responsibility. Studies indicate that citizens come away from the jury experience with a fuller appreciation of the justice system. Jurors acquire an understanding of the serious responsibility handed to them when asked to decide upon someone's guilt or innocence. The legal standard in American courts—"guilty beyond a reasonable doubt"—is a solemn one. The fairness of the jury system also requires full participation by the community. Studies show that jurors' life experiences can affect the decisions they reach. If everyone on a jury is from the same background and one that is different from the defendant's, the odds of a wrongful verdict increase. "A jury of one's peers" should mean just that—a jury of individuals who, collectively, represent the range of groups in the community. If you are called to serve on a jury, you should answer the call. You would want nothing less from others than if you or one of your family members or friends were the person on trial.

Extra Credit

For up-to-the-minute *New York Times* articles, interactive simulations, graphics, study tools, and more links and quizzes, visit the text's Online Learning Center at www.mhhe.com/pattersontad9e.

Self-Test Answers

1. c   2. c   3. e   4. b   5. a   6. c   7. F   8. F   9. T   10. T

National Journal

BRAINS IN THE DOCK

The MacArthur Foundation will spend at least $10 million over the next several years to infuse the legal system with high-tech research from brain scientists.

MacArthur's Law and Neuroscience Project, advocates say, will provide scientific, legal, and philosophical advice to judges now facing a wave of courtroom claims that are based on early, and often shaky, research into the workings of the human brain. Lawyers and academic advocates are citing brain research to validate witness statements, strengthen claims for injury and clemency, break contracts, bolster an Illinois curb on the sale of violent video games, and even shift the goal of sentencing away from retribution toward crime prevention.

The project began last October following a proposal from Stanford University neuroscientist Robert Sapolsky, said Jonathan Fanton, president of the John D. and Catherine T. MacArthur Foundation in Chicago, which annually gives more than $260 million to mostly liberal causes and is best known for its "genius grants" to individuals. The foundation had been looking for novel projects to fund, Fanton told National Journal, and Sapolsky's proposal held out the promise of fundamentally changing criminal law and the justice system.

Critics contend that the project may prove counterproductive. If people believe that behavior and beliefs are controlled by brain physiology and chemistry rather than by the traditional notions of mind, soul, and character, that could boost the view that people can't control their decisions and desires, said Yuval Levin. He is a fellow at the Ethics and Public Policy Center, a think tank dedicated to promoting traditional ethics in policy debates, and until last year served as a White House domestic policy adviser. "If you believe you can't control your behavior, you don't work at controlling your behavior," he said. That belief, he said, could increase crime and prompt judges to regard some citizens as patients best

treated by long-term confinement; it could even lead to more death-penalty sentences for people who have what are considered irredeemably damaged brains.

For decades, scientists have tried to peer inside the living brain. In recent years, they have developed technology that can detect the movement of oxygen-rich blood and track which parts of the brain are most active when a person is making a particular decision or reacting to a threat. Manufacturers and advocates of the technology are using these early results to sell lie-detection services, persuade juries, and sway politicians, even though the reliability and relevance of the devices are unproven.

The technology is most frequently used to show apparent damage to, or incomplete development of, a person's brain. Attorneys are employing these high-tech images of brain problems, whether caused by genes, wounds, age, or early-childhood deprivation, to argue that their clients were not fully responsible for their actions and thus deserve clemency. Some attorneys have contended that the criminal justice system should treat teenage defendants leniently because the brain's amygdala—which reacts strongly to perceived threats—is active in teenagers, but the frontal cortex—which is thought to restrain aggression—does not fully develop until ages 18 to 21.

These arguments fit uneasily with traditional standards of responsibility, which assume that young people gradually learn from their parents, community, and culture how to govern their behavior, and that when they are no longer children, they should be liable for their actions.

Yet the new views have won some arguments. Congress supplemented funding for early-childhood programs in the 1990s after hearing from Vice President Gore and others that brain scans show that the first few years of a child's life deeply shape later educational achievement. Similarly, in 2005,

the Supreme Court cited the new science in its 5-4 decision in Roper v. Simmons, which ruled that executing those convicted of committing murder before their 18th birthday is unconstitutional. During the oral argument, the justices focused 16 of their 20 questions to the condemned man's attorney on scientific evidence concerning juvenile development. MacArthur can claim some credit for the Roper decision, Fanton said, because the foundation helped to focus attention on the limited competence of juveniles.

The honorary chairwoman of the MacArthur project is Sandra Day O'Connor, a former Supreme Court justice who disagreed with the Roper decision. The six-year effort will include seminars for students, lawyers, judges, and politicians, and will also draft guideline for judges, Fanton said. "It is important to get the best neuroscience connected to the law," he said, "so this is properly used and not misused."

Eventually, the project will likely bring in politicians, said neuroscientist Michael Gazzaniga, director of the Sage Center for the Study of Mind at the University of California (Santa Barbara) and a co-director of the project. The 50 or so scientists, lawyers, judges, and academics working on the effort were chosen for the variety of their perspectives. The project has no agenda whatsoever, said Stephen Morse, a law professor at the University of Pennsylvania and a co-director of the project's panel on addiction and antisocial behavior.

So far, the new science is being cited in a tiny fraction of legal proceedings, mostly death-penalty cases and civil lawsuits, said Hank Greely, a Stanford law professor who is involved in the MacArthur project. But over the next 10 or 20 years, the use of the technology will broaden, he said. Brain-scanning equipment might be used to detect the early signs of Alzheimer's disease, Greely said, and the resulting information could impact the health insurance industry, spur states to cancel older peoples' driver's licenses, and guide investment by the nursing home industry. "The legal implications of this will be much broader than the courtroom," he said.

One likely early use for the technology in the legal system, according to Greely, could be to tailor treatments for drug-addicted criminals or to measure pain in people claiming injury or disability. Some evidence indicates that today's technology can detect brain patterns consistent with pain, and could help judges and juries to identify the "nontrivial chunk of those people [who] are exaggerating or flat-out lying," he said. Lawyers could someday also employ the technology in civil disputes to argue that their clients were unable to understand a complex contract or were not competent to sign a will.

Attorneys are already citing the technology in seeking to protect convicted defendants from execution. "Retribution is not proportional if the law's most severe penalty is imposed on one whose culpability or blameworthiness is diminished, to a substantial degree, by reason of youth and immaturity," the Supreme Court said in the Roper decision, which included four citations to a journal article about juveniles' developmental immaturity that was written by a MacArthur-funded psychologist.

The new science is also shaping cultural attitudes toward personal responsibility, Gazzaniga said. "Neuroscience is oozing into the public consciousness," especially through the universities, he said. The result, he argues, is that increasing numbers of people believe that free will is an illusion of brain mechanics, and that people can't be blamed for doing what their brain determined that

Increasing numbers of people believe that **free will is an illusion of brain mechanics,** and that people can't be blamed for doing what their brain determined that they would do.

they would do. "That idea is around in every college bull session and every defense attorney's 'Can we try that out?'" he said.

Some experts in the MacArthur project—including Sapolsky, who serves on the governing board—hold that view, according to Gazzaniga. Greely says, "A lot of philosophers and neuroscientists say this will be revolutionary." He added, "I'm skeptical because I don't think the neuroscientists have convinced us there is no free will."

"Everyone agrees that we should be locking up people that are dangerous to other people," said one of the determinists on the project, Joshua Greene, an assistant professor of psychology at Harvard University. If the technological advances persuade citizens and judges to embrace a new view of the brain, he said, they will be more likely to forgo their desire for retribution—inflicted in the form of long sentences in harsh prisons—and accept shorter sentences similar to those imposed in Europe.

The materialistic argument may lead to different results if it gains ground, said O. Carter Snead, an associate law professor

at the University of Notre Dame. Judges and citizens could discard traditional notions of mercy, in his view, and support severe penalties for murderers who can't show that their brain is damaged, as well as for criminals whose damaged brains make them more likely to commit crimes if they are released from prison.

Anthony Daniels, a former psychiatrist in British prisons, warned against any claim that people are wholly controlled by the biological workings of their brain. "If you take it seriously, it has the most illiberal consequences possible, at least as long as there is no cure [because each brain-damaged prisoner] needs to be locked up forever since he cannot control himself," said Daniels, who has cited his prison experiences in books and articles under the pen name Theodore Dalrymple.

Morse responds that the deterministic view of the brain can be made compatible with traditional notions of responsibility. This view holds that even if brains are soulless machines, people can still distinguish between right and wrong, and what is legal and illegal. Science needn't change the legal system, he argues. Plenty of room remains for advocates to persuade the public to accept or reject the contention that society could discard its claim to retribution for crimes, he said. "It's up for grabs."

And even if science eventually proves the determinists correct, the people and the politicians have the right and ability to reject scientists' prescriptions, Greely said. "My doctor, every time I see him, tells me to lose weight, but I'd rather have the cheeseburger than the apple."

FOR DISCUSSION: As in the Supreme Court decision Roper v. Simmons, should brain science define the culpability of defendants? How should judges incorporate this kind of science into your courtroom in order to balance the imperatives of justice and fairness? Will science, not commonly held values, settle the question of free will in the court room?

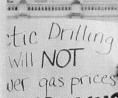

CONSERVE ENERGY
CONSERVE OUR REFUGE!
DRILLING FOR OIL!

Arctic Drilling
will NOT
lower gas prices

NO DRILLING

MAINE

Economic and Environmental Policy
Contributing to Prosperity

The Public Policy Process
  Problem Recognition
  Policy Formation
  Policy Implementation

**Government as Regulator
of the Economy**
  Efficiency Through Government
    Intervention
  Equity Through Government
    Intervention
  The Politics of Regulatory Policy

**Government as Protector
of the Environment**
  Conservationism: The Older Wave
  Environmentalism: The Newer Wave

**Government as Promoter
of Economic Interests**
  Promoting Business
  Promoting Labor
  Promoting Agriculture

**Fiscal Policy: Government
as Manager of the Economy, I**
  Taxing and Spending Policy and
    Politics
  The Budgetary Process

**Monetary Policy: Government
as Manager of the Economy, II**
  The Fed
  The Politics of the Fed

We the people of the United States, in order to . . . insure domestic tranquility . . .   **Preamble, U.S. Constitution**

The financial markets in 2008 were downright scary. The U.S. dollar, long the standard of international trade, was weakening dramatically due to excessive consumer and government spending. The stock market, too, was shaky. A few weeks into the year, it had shed all of the gains of the previous year, and then headed lower. The housing market was in turmoil. Home values were dropping at a record pace, as were foreclosures, as homeowners with subprime adjustable rate mortgages increasingly found it difficult to make their monthly payments. Some economists predicted that the United States was entering its steepest downturn since the Great Depression of the 1930s.

Few economists, however, predicted another Great Depression. The reason was simple enough. Back in the early 1930s, there were no government programs in place to stabilize and stimulate the economy. Moreover, the response to the 1929–31 drop in stock prices had worsened the situation. Businesses had cut back on production, investors had fled the stock market, depositors had withdrawn their bank savings, and consumers had slowed their spending—all of which had accelerated the downward spiral. In 2008, on the other hand, government programs were in place to protect depositors' savings, slow the drop in home and stock prices, and steady the economy through adjustments in interest rates and government spending. Among the government initiatives was an economic stimulus bill that gave tax rebates to more than 130 million American households in the expectation they would spend the money, thereby giving the economy a boost.

This chapter examines economic and environmental policy. As was discussed in the first chapter, public policy is a decision by government to follow a course of action designed to produce a particular result. In this vein, economic policy centers on the promotion and regulation of economic interests and, through fiscal and monetary actions, on economic growth and stability. Although the private decisions of firms and individuals are the main force in the American economic system, these decisions are influenced by government policy. Washington seeks to maintain high productivity, employment, and purchasing power; regulates business practices that otherwise would harm the environment or result in economic inefficiency and inequity; and promotes economic interests. The main ideas presented in this chapter are these:

■ *Through regulation, the U.S. government imposes restraints on business activity for the purpose of promoting economic efficiency and equity.* This regulation is often the cause of political conflict, which is both ideological and group-centered.

■ *Through regulatory and conservation policies, the U.S. government seeks to protect and preserve the environment from the actions of business firms and consumers.*

■ *Through promotion, the U.S. government helps private interests achieve their economic goals.* Business in particular benefits from the government's promotional efforts, including, for example, tax breaks and loans.

■ *Through its taxing and spending decisions (fiscal policy), the U.S. government seeks to maintain a level of economic supply and demand that will keep the economy prosperous.*

■ *Through its money supply decisions (monetary policy), the U.S. government—through the Fed—seeks to maintain a level of inflation consistent with sustained, controllable economic growth.*

The Public Policy Process

public policy process

The political interactions that lead to the emergence and resolution of public policy issues.

Government action in the economic sector is part of the **public policy process**—the political interactions that lead to the emergence and resolution of public policy issues. Before examining economic policy, it is helpful to describe the process through which it and other types of policy are developed.

Political scientists have identified three stages that together make up the policy process (see Figure 15-1). The first stage—problem recognition—refers to the emergence of issues. The second stage—policy formation—refers to the formulation and enactment of a policy response to the problem. The third stage—policy implementation—refers to the carrying out of policy.

Problem Recognition

Policy problems stem from conditions of society—the employment rate, the quality of the schools, the security of the nation, the safety of the streets, and so on. Yet only certain conditions will be seen as problems of a *public* nature. Even life-threatening conditions can worsen for years without people thinking of them as anything but a personal problem. Obesity is an example. Americans did not gain dozens of pounds overnight. Rather, over the course of several decades, they

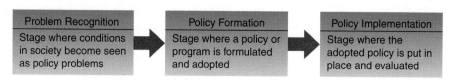

Problem Recognition	Policy Formation	Policy Implementation
Stage where conditions in society become seen as policy problems	Stage where a policy or program is formulated and adopted	Stage where the adopted policy is put in place and evaluated

FIGURE 15-1 **The Public Policy Process** The public policy process refers to the political interactions that lead to the emergence and resolution of public policy issues. The process includes three stages, although each stage can involve elements of the other two stages.

slowly got heavier to the point where obesity was a leading cause of poor health. Only recently, after research studies revealed the scope of the problem, have Americans begun to think of obesity as a public policy problem.

In some cases **problem recognition** happens suddenly, even shockingly, as in the case of the terrorist attacks of September 11, 2001, when hatred of the United States by extremist elements abroad—a condition—erupted into a threat to America's long-term security—a policy problem. Yet it ordinarily takes time for people to realize that they have a problem requiring attention. During World War II, Americans of all races fought together against Nazi Germany and its racist ideology. But when the war ended, white Americans initially acted as if nothing in their own society needed correcting. Black Americans knew better. They were still by law shuttled off to separate and inferior public schools and denied entry to white hospitals, restaurants, and theaters. The contradiction was simply too large to be ignored. Within a decade, America had begun to dismantle its system of government-imposed racial segregation.

Policy problems come to public attention in a variety of ways. Interest groups, members of Congress, political parties, and the news media are among the actors that set the policy agenda. By highlighting a problem day after day, for example, the news media can convince people that something needs to be done about it. No agenda setter, however, has a more direct influence than does the president. Even a single presidential pronouncement can trigger a policy response. The AIDS crisis in Africa was far from Americans' minds until January 28, 2003. That evening, in his State of the Union address, President George W. Bush declared that Africa's problem could no longer be ignored. Within months, Congress had appropriated $1.4 billion to fight AIDS in Africa.

Policy Formation

After a policy problem is recognized, the question of how to address it arises. What is the proper policy response? **Policy formation**—the development of a policy for dealing with the problem—is seldom easy.

For one thing, an array of actors are likely to want a say in what gets done. Such actors will include elected officials but could also include interest groups, citizens, and civic organizations. At times, a small set of actors is able to limit what the political scientist E. E. Schattschneider called the "scope of conflict,"[1] thereby effectively deciding among themselves what gets done. Iron triangles (see Chapter 9) are an arrangement of this type. More commonly, the scope of conflict widens, subjecting policymakers to a broader set of influences and forcing them to accommodate a variety of interests.

In addition, because society is complex, most policy problems are intertwined with other problems and issues, and thus cannot be resolved without also taking them into account. Consider, for example, the question of whether government price supports for corn should be increased as a way of easing the economic pressures on corn farmers. Although a subsidy would clearly help corn growers, there are other interests that may or may not be helped by it. How would a subsidy impact on consumers, on farmers' decisions about which crops to plant, on ethanol production, and on the federal deficit? How might such a subsidy affect even foreign policy? Other countries have corn growers who compete in the world market with America's farmers. If U.S. growers are provided a subsidy, they can sell their corn at a lower price, giving them an advantage over other sellers in the world market. Faced with that prospect, foreign governments might decide to subsidize their own corn growers, possibly triggering a trade war. As far-fetched as this example might seem, it approximates what happened in 2006 at the international round of trade talks. After five years of negotiation among

problem recognition
The stage of the policy process where conditions in society become recognized as a public policy problem.

policy formation
The stage of the policy process where a policy is formulated for dealing with a policy problem.

The policy process includes three stages: problem recognition, policy formulation, and policy implementation. Here, spectators look out at the former site of the World Trade Center, which was destroyed in the terrorist attacks of September 11, 2001. The attacks brought instant problem recognition: the United States was a target of international terrorism. In the ensuing weeks, policymakers formulated a policy response: a military attack on terrorist forces in Afghanistan. The implementation of that policy is still taking place; the United States has about 25,000 soldiers fighting in Afghanistan.

scores of countries, the talks collapsed, partly because the United States refused to reduce its hefty farm subsidies.

The complexity of modern policymaking has created an entire industry—that of the policy analyst. Thousands of scholars, consultants, and policy specialists are engaged in formulating solutions to policy problems. Most economic policy, for example, is designed by trained economists. Politicians also formulate policy. They lack the analytic tools of the policy specialists but have their own strength: they have a sense of what other politicians will support. When President Lyndon Johnson decided in 1965 to tackle the issue of public health, some of his advisers wanted him to propose to Congress a government-paid universal health care system like those of Europe. Knowing that congressional conservatives would block it, Johnson pursued a more limited objective that he believed Congress would accept. The result was Medicare and Medicaid, which offer government-provided health care to the elderly and poor, respectively.

Policy formation in the United States takes place through a system of divided powers. To become law, a bill must get majority support in the House and in the Senate and be signed by the president. Unless there is solid support at each stage for the bill, it is unlikely to pass. For this reason, most policies enacted by Congress are the product of considerable bargaining and compromise, and are typically modest in scope. As the political scientist Aaron Wildavsky noted, incremental policies—those that depart only somewhat from existing policy—are the characteristic output of the U.S. policy process.[2]

Policy Implementation

policy implementation

The stage of the policy process where a policy is put into effect and evaluated.

Once a policy is adopted, it has to be put into effect. This stage is the **policy implementation** phase. Responsibility for implementation rests mainly with bureaucrats, who are charged with carrying out the law (see Chapter 13).

It is often assumed that, once a policy has been formulated, the implementation of that policy is clear-cut. The assumption is sometimes warranted. When Congress in 2008 authorized rebates to taxpayers as a means of stimulating the economy, the implementation—getting the rebate checks into the hands of tax-payers—was time consuming but straightforward. The rebates were based on the income tax returns that had been filed earlier in the year; those taxpayers that met the eligibility criteria were identified by the Internal Revenue Service and received a rebate.

In most cases, however, policy implementation is an open-ended process. Bureaucratic agencies have to decide exactly how a policy will be put into action. In doing so, they may encounter resistance from interests that are adversely affected by the policy. Even interests that benefit from the policy are likely to want a say in how it is carried out. Agencies may also have to take into account local differences when implementing policy. Legislation aimed at improving local transportation poses different implementation problems in Manhattan than in rural Mississippi. And sometimes a bureaucratic agency lacks the resources to implement a policy in the way it was envisioned. When a prescription drug benefit was added to Medicare in 2006, for example, the eligibility rules established by Congress were so intricate that many retirees could not on their own determine how best to obtain the benefit. The bureaucrats in charge of the program were flooded with requests for assistance and lacked the manpower to meet the demand, resulting in delayed or improper responses to the benefit applications of hundreds of thousands of retirees.

Policy evaluation is part of the implementation stage. Sometimes the question of whether a policy is working can be answered in specific terms, such as whether the construction of a new stretch of federal highway is on time and within budget. Many policies, however, are hard to evaluate. An example is foreign economic aid. Economic development in poor countries is subject to so many factors that it is difficult to assess the impact of assistance grants. In such cases, policy evaluation usually centers on how well the program is being administered—for example, whether the money is being channeled to the right places or is finding its way into the pockets of corrupt officials.

In summary, the public policy process is a set of analytically distinct stages that problems go through on their way to some sort of resolution. The problem recognition stage is when conditions in society become seen as public policy problems; the policy formation stage is when a solution is settled upon in the form of a policy or program; and the policy implementation stage is when the adopted policy is put into place and its effectiveness assessed.

We turn now to a particular area of policy—the economy. The discussion will start with regulatory policy and conclude with an explanation of government's efforts to maintain a stable economy.

Government as Regulator of the Economy

An **economy** is a system of production and consumption of goods and services that are allocated through exchange. When a shopper buys food at a store, that transaction is one of the millions of economic exchanges that make up the economy.

In *The Wealth of Nations* (1776), Adam Smith advanced the doctrine of **laissez-faire economics,** which holds that private individuals and firms should be allowed to make their own production and distribution decisions. Smith reasoned that firms will supply a good when there is a demand for it (that is, when people are willing and able to buy it). Smith argued that the desire for profit is the "invisible hand" that guides supply decisions in a capitalist system. He acknowledged that the doctrine of laissez-faire capitalism has limits. Certain areas of the economy, such as roadways, are natural monopolies and are better run by government than by private firms. Government is also needed to impose

economy
A system for the exchange of goods and services between the producers of those goods and services and the consumers of them.

laissez-faire economics
A classic economic philosophy holding that owners of business should be allowed to make their own production and distribution decisions without government regulation or control.

order on private transactions by regulating banking, currency, and contracts. Otherwise, Smith argued, the economy should be left in private hands.

Communism is an alternative to capitalism. In *Das Kapital* (*Capital*, 1867), Karl Marx argued that a free-market system is exploitative because employees work for a wage below the value they add to the market price of the goods they produce. They do the work while the owners reap the profits from their labor. Marx proposed a collective economy in which the workers are also the owners. The former Soviet Union and its satellite countries attempted a variation of the model—firms were put under collective ownership, although ordinary workers had little say in their operation. The Soviet model collapsed because it proved to be an inefficient method for allocating capital and labor and for coordinating the supply of goods with the demand for them.

Today, free-market systems dominate the world economy, although they are mixed systems rather than the pure laissez-faire systems that Smith envisioned. They are called *mixed economies* because, though they center on private firms and transactions, they also assign a substantial role to government. The U.S. economy is no exception. The U.S. government owns some industry (for example, the Tennessee Valley Authority, which produces electricity) and provides some welfare services (for example, the Medicare program). However, in comparison, say, with the Scandinavian countries, where government provides health care to all citizens and controls a number of major industries, including the airlines, the U.S. economy relies more heavily on the free market to make its production, distribution, and consumption decisions.

One way the U.S. government participates in the economy is through the **regulation** of privately owned businesses.[3] U.S. firms are not free to act as they please but rather operate within the constraint of government regulation, which is designed to promote either economic *efficiency* or *equity* (see Table 15-1).

Efficiency Through Government Intervention

Economic efficiency results when firms fulfill as many of society's needs as possible while using as few of its resources as possible.[4] **Efficiency** refers to the relationship of inputs (the labor and material that go into making a product or service) to outputs (the product or service itself). The greater the output for a given input, the more efficient the production process.

Preventing Price Fixing

Adam Smith and other classical economists argued that the free market is the optimal means of achieving efficiency. Producers will try to use as few resources as possible in order to keep their prices low so that customers will buy their

regulation

A term that refers to government restrictions on the economic practices of private firms.

efficiency

An economic principle holding that firms should fulfill as many of society's needs as possible while using as few of its resources as possible. The greater the output (production) for a given input (for example, an hour of labor), the more efficient the process.

TABLE 15-1 | The Main Objectives of Regulatory Policy   The government intervenes in the economy to promote efficiency and equity.

Objective	Definition	Representative Actions by Government
Efficiency	Fulfillment of as many of society's needs as possible at the cost of as few of its resources as possible. The greater the output for a given input, the more efficient the process.	Preventing restraint of trade; requiring producers to pay the costs of damage to the environment; reducing restrictions on business that cannot be justified on a cost-benefit basis.
Equity	When the outcome of an economic transaction is fair to each party.	Requiring firms to bargain in good faith with labor; protecting consumers in their purchases; protecting workers' safety and health.

products. To compete, less efficient producers will have to find a way to cut their production costs or be forced out of business.

However, the assumption that efficiency is inherent in free markets is flawed. The same incentive—the profit motive—that drives producers to keep prices low can drive them to seek a monopoly on a good or to conspire with other producers to fix its price at an artificially high level. If they succeed in this effort, they do not have to be concerned with efficiency because consumers who want or need a good will have no choice but to buy it from them for the asking price.

Price fixing was prevalent in the United States in the late nineteenth century when large trusts came to dominate many areas of the economy, including the oil, steel, railroad, and sugar industries. Railroad companies, for example, had no competition on short routes and charged such high rates that many farmers went broke because they could not afford to ship their crops to markets. In 1887, Congress enacted the Interstate Commerce Act, which created the Interstate Commerce Commission (ICC) and charged it with regulating railroad practices and fares.

Business competition today is regulated by a wide range of federal agencies, including, for example, the Federal Trade Commission (FTC), the Food and Drug Administration (FDA), and the Antitrust Division of the Justice Department. The goal of regulatory activity is to protect consumers by preserving market competition. This does not mean in all cases that government will take action to increase the number of competitors in a particular sector of the economy. The government is inclined to accept concentrated ownership in the oil, automobile, and other industries where the capital costs are so high that it is difficult for small firms to operate, much less compete.[5] Government acceptance of corporate giants also reflects the realization that market competition is no longer simply an issue of domestic firms. For example, the major U.S. automakers—Chrysler, Ford, and General Motors—compete for customers not only with each other but with Asian and European auto manufacturers.

Making Business Pay for Indirect Costs

Economic inefficiencies also result when businesses or consumers fail to pay the full costs of resources used in production. Consider companies whose industrial wastes seep into nearby lakes and rivers. The price of these companies' products does not reflect the cost to society of the resulting water pollution. Economists label these unpaid costs **externalities.**

Until the 1960s, the federal government did not require firms to pay such costs. The impetus to begin doing so came not only from lawmakers but also from the scientific community and environmental groups. The Clean Air Act of 1963 and the Water Quality Act of 1965 required industry to install antipollution devices to keep the discharge of air and water pollutants within specified limits. In 1970, Congress created the Environmental Protection Agency (EPA) to monitor firms and ensure their compliance with federal regulations governing air and water quality and the disposal of toxic wastes. (Environmental policy is discussed more fully later in the chapter.)

externalities
Burdens that society incurs when firms fail to pay the full costs of production. An example of an externality is the pollution that results when corporations dump industrial wastes into lakes and rivers.

Deregulation

Although government regulation is intended to increase economic efficiency, it can have the opposite effect if it unnecessarily increases the cost of doing business.[6] Firms have to expend work hours to monitor and implement government regulations, which in some instances (for example, pollution control) also require companies to buy and install expensive equipment. These costs are efficient to

HOW THE U.S. COMPARES

GLOBAL ECONOMIC COMPETITIVENESS

The United States ranked first on the World Economic Forum's 2007–8 global economic competitiveness index. The World Economic Forum (WEF) is a private economic research organization that bases its rankings on factors such as a nation's corporate management, finance, institutional openness, government regulation, public infrastructure, science and technology, and labor. Its rankings also reflect the results of an annual survey of roughly ten thousand business executives from around the globe who are asked about their experiences in dealing with various countries and markets.

The United States has been at or near the top of the WEF's rankings for a number of years. It has consistently ranked higher than major economic rivals such as Germany and Japan, whose management, regulatory, and finance systems are more rigid, reducing their capacity to respond flexibly to the global marketplace. The United States ranks particularly high on the quality of its technology, management, and finance. A weakness is its labor practices. U.S. workers enjoy fewer protections and benefits (such as health care coverage) than do their counterparts in many other industrialized societies. The 2007–8 survey was conducted before U.S. financial markets declined due to the subprime mortgage crisis and other economic problems.

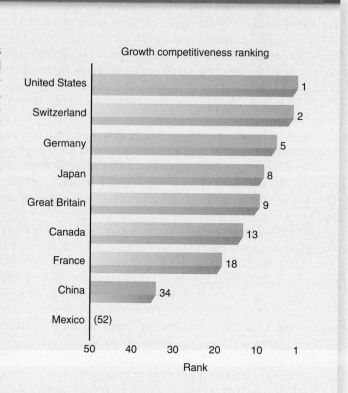

Growth competitiveness ranking

Country	Rank
United States	1
Switzerland	2
Germany	5
Japan	8
Great Britain	9
Canada	13
France	18
China	34
Mexico	(52)

Rank

deregulation

The rescinding of excessive government regulations for the purpose of improving economic efficiency.

the degree that they produce commensurate benefits. Yet if government places excessive regulatory burdens on firms, they waste resources in the process of complying. The result is higher-priced goods that are more expensive for consumers and less competitive in the domestic and global markets (see "How the U.S. Compares").

In response to this problem, Congress in 1995 enacted legislation that prohibits administrators in some instances from issuing a regulation unless they can demonstrate that its benefits will outweigh its costs. A more concerted response has been **deregulation**—the rescinding of regulations already in force for the purpose of improving efficiency. This process began in 1977 with passage of the Airlines Deregulation Act, which eliminated government-set airfares and the requirement that airlines provide service to smaller-sized cities. The change had the intended effect: airfares declined, and competition between airlines increased on routes between larger-sized cities. Congress followed airline deregulation with partial deregulation of the trucking, banking, energy, and communications industries, among others.

Reductions in regulation, however, can be carried too far.[7] Underregulation can result in harmful business practices. The profit motive can lead firms and their executives to act recklessly or illegally. Companies are more likely to engage in questionable practices when weak regulation leads them to believe they can get away with it. Such was the case with the subprime mortgage crisis that surfaced in 2007. Mortgage firms lured marginally qualified homebuyers with low interest rates and small down payments. When the price of homes then began to decline and home buyers were unable to keep up with their mortgage payments, many of them defaulted. The result was a crisis in the financial markets that required a government bailout. In 2008, the U.S. government felt compelled to provide banking and investment firms roughly $1 trillion in loans and buyouts to keep them afloat. Expressing a view held by many Democratic and Republican leaders, Barack Obama said that government had failed to regulate Wall Street closely enough. "The free market," said Obama, "was never meant to be a free license to take whatever you can get."

The subprime mortgage crisis demonstrates that the issue of business regulation is not a simple question of whether or not to regulate. On one hand, too much regulation can burden firms with bureaucratic red tape and costly implementation requirements. On the other hand, too little regulation can give firms the leeway to exploit the public unfairly or recklessly. Either too little or too much regulation can result in economic inefficiency. The challenge for policymakers is to strike the proper balance between regulatory measures and free-market mechanisms.

A meltdown in the subprime mortgage sector contributed to falling home prices and a rise in foreclosures. This development rippled through the economy and the financial markets, contributing to an economic downturn in 2008.

Equity Through Government Intervention

The government intervenes in the economy to bring equity as well as efficiency to the marketplace. **Equity** occurs when an economic transaction is fair to each party.[8] A transaction can be considered fair if each party enters into it freely and is not unknowingly at a disadvantage (for example, if the seller knows a product is defective, equity requires that the buyer also know of the defect).

An early equity initiative was the creation of the Food and Drug Administration (FDA) in 1907. Because consumers often cannot tell whether foods and drugs are safe to consume, the FDA works to keep adulterated foods and dangerous or ineffective drugs off the market. In the 1930s, financial reforms were among the equity measures enacted under the New Deal. The Securities and Exchange Act of 1934 and the Banking Act of 1934 were designed in part to protect investors and savers from dishonest or imprudent brokers and bankers. The New Deal also provided greater equity for organized labor, which previously had been in a weak position in its dealings with management. The Fair Labor Standards Act of 1938, for example, established a minimum wage and placed limits on the use of child labor.

The 1960s and 1970s produced the greatest number of equity reforms. Ten federal agencies, including the Consumer Product Safety Commission, were established to protect consumers, workers, and the public from harmful business activity. Among the products declared to be unsafe in the 1960s and 1970s were cigarettes, lead paint, and leaded gasoline. The benefits have been substantial. Lead, for example, can cause brain damage in children. In the period since lead paint and leaded gasoline have been banned, the average level of lead in children's blood has dropped by 75 percent.[9]

equity (in relation to economic policy)

The situation in which the outcome of an economic transaction is fair to each party. An outcome can usually be considered fair if each party enters into a transaction freely and is not unknowingly at a disadvantage.

The Politics of Regulatory Policy

Economic regulation has come in waves, as changes in national conditions have produced bursts of social awareness. The first wave came during the Progressive Era, when reformers sought to stop the unfair business practices of the new monopolies, such as the railroads. The second wave came during the Great Depression, when reformers sought to regulate financial and labor markets.

Although businesses fought the Progressive and New Deal reforms, their opposition was lessened in the long term by the fact that most of the resulting regulation applied to a particular industry rather than to firms of all types. This pattern makes it possible for a regulated industry to gain influence with those officials responsible for regulating it. By cultivating close ties to the FDA, for example, pharmaceutical companies have managed to obtain faster clearance to market new drugs, which are a main source of their profits.[10] In some cases, the FDA's fast-track approval process has been harmful to consumers. The anti-inflammatory drug Vioxx, for example, had to be withdrawn from the market in 2004 after it was found to increase the risk of heart attacks and strokes. Although not all industries have as much leverage as the drug firms with their regulators, it is generally true that industries have not been greatly hampered by the older form of regulation and in many cases have benefited from it.

The third wave of regulatory reform, in the 1960s and 1970s, differed from the Progressive and New Deal phases in both its form and its politics. This third wave has been called the era of "new social regulation" because of the broad social goals it addressed in three policy areas: environmental protection, consumer protection, and worker safety. Most of the regulatory agencies established during the third wave have larger mandates than those created earlier. They have responsibility not for a single industry but for firms of all types, and their policy scope covers a wide range of activities. The Environmental Protection Agency (EPA), for example, is charged with regulating environmental pollution of almost any kind by almost any firm.

Because newer agencies such as the EPA have a wide-ranging clientele, no one firm or industry can easily influence agency policy to a great extent. There is also strong group competition within some of the newer regulatory spheres. For example, business lobbies must compete with environmental groups such as the Sierra Club and Greenpeace for influence with the EPA.[11] The firms regulated by the older agencies, in contrast, typically face no powerful competition in their lobbying activities. Broadcasters, for example, are virtually unopposed in most of their efforts to influence the Federal Communication Commission (FCC). Although television viewers and radio listeners have a stake in FCC decisions, they are not well enough organized to lobby it effectively.

Unlike the older agencies that are run by a commission whose members serve for fixed terms and cannot be removed during their term of office, some of the newer agencies, including the EPA, are headed by a single director who is appointed by the president with Senate approval and is subject to immediate removal by the president. This arrangement also weakens the link between the regulatory agency and the firms it regulates. An agency head who gives favorable treatment to a firm risks removal if the president disapproves.

Government as Protector of the Environment

Few changes in public opinion and policy during recent decades have been as dramatic as those relating to the environment. Most Americans today recycle some of their garbage, and roughly two-thirds say they are either an active environmentalist or sympathetic to environmental concerns. In the 1960s, few Americans sorted their trash, and few could have answered a polling question that asked them whether they were an "environmentalist." The term was not commonly used, and most people would not have understood its meaning.

The publication in 1962 of Rachel Carson's *The Silent Spring* helped launch the environmental movement.[12] Written at a time when the author was dying of breast cancer, *Silent Spring* revealed the threat to birds and animals of pesticides such as DDT. Carson's appearance at a Senate hearing contributed to legislative action that produced the 1963 Clean Air Act and the 1965 Water Quality Act. They were the first major federal laws designed to protect the nation's air, water, and ground from pollution. Today, environmental protection extends to nearly two hundred harmful forms of emission.

Conservationism: The Older Wave

Although antipollution policy is relatively new, the government has been involved in land conservation for more than a century.[13] The first national park was created at Yellowstone in 1872 and, like the later ones, was established to preserve the nation's natural heritage for generations to come. The national park system serves more than 100 million visitors each year and includes a total of 80 million acres, an area larger than every state except Alaska, Texas, California, and Montana. The national parks are run by the National Park Service, an agency within the Department of Interior. Another agency, the U.S. Forest Service, located within the Department of Agriculture, manages the national forests, which cover an area more than twice the size of the national parks. They too have been preserved in part to protect America's natural heritage.

However, the nation's parks and forests are subject to a "dual use" policy. They are nature preserves and recreation areas, but they are also rich in natural resources—minerals, timber, and grazing lands. The federal government sells permits to ranchers, logging companies, and mining firms that give them the right to take some of these resources, a policy that can place their interests in conflict with those of conservationists. A case in point is Alaska's Arctic National Wildlife Refuge. The refuge is home to numerous species, including caribou and moose, but it also contains substantial oil and natural gas reserves. Oil companies have long wanted to drill in this wilderness area, while environmental groups have sought to prohibit drilling. Over the past few decades, the Arctic National Wildlife Refuge has periodically been the focus of intense political debate and lobbying. President Bill Clinton threatened to veto any bill that would open the area to drilling. President George W. Bush, in contrast, proposed to open the area to drilling as part of his program to increase the nation's energy supplies.

As the debate over Alaska's Arctic National Wildlife Refuge reveals, conservation is more than an issue of protecting nature's unspoiled beauty. Also

LEADERS

RACHEL CARSON
(1907–64)

Born on a farm near Pittsburgh, Rachel Carson had hoped to become a writer but switched to biology as an undergraduate and went on to earn a master's degree in zoology at Johns Hopkins University. She then started work on a doctorate, but the untimely death of her father and the need to take care of her mother ended this pursuit. In 1936, while working part-time at the U.S. Bureau of Fisheries (later the U.S. Fish and Wildlife Services), she learned of a full-time position that was opening up and decided to take the civil service exam, an uncommon ambition at the time for a woman. Carson outscored all the men who took the exam with her and was awarded the position.

In her job, Carson worked on scientific journals but sought a wider audience. She astonished even herself when *The Atlantic Monthly* accepted an article she had submitted. The article led to a book contract with Simon and Schuster, but the resulting book sold poorly. Undeterred, she continued to publish articles in popular magazines and won the 1952 National Book Award for her second book, *The Sea Around Us*. However, it was *The Silent Spring*, published in 1962, that brought her lasting fame. Even before the book was released, chemical companies were threatening lawsuits and seeking to undermine her argument by portraying her as mentally unstable and scientifically untrained. The Department of Agriculture also came out against her, labeling as false her charge that the insecticide DDT was a carcinogen and environmental threat. Despite the attacks, *The Silent Spring* became a huge best-seller and led to invitations for Carson to testify before Congress. Her book and congressional testimony contributed to passage of the first federal safe air and water legislation. Tragically, at the height of her fame, Carson was fatally stricken with breast cancer. In 1981, she was posthumously awarded the Presidential Medal of Freedom, the nation's highest civilian award.

The federal government's environmental efforts include programs designed to conserve nature through the protection of forests and other natural assets. Shown here is a scene from Yellowstone National Park.

involved is the protection of species that need their natural habitat to survive. Some species, such as the deer and the raccoon, adapt easily to human encroachment. Other species are threatened by it. These species are covered by the Endangered Species Act (ESA) of 1973; it directs federal agencies to protect threatened and endangered species and authorizes programs that will preserve natural habitats. Hundreds of mammals, birds, fishes, insects, and plants are currently on the ESA's protection list.

Disputes have arisen between ESA administrators and those individuals and firms that depend on natural resources for their jobs and profits. The northern spotted owl, which inhabits the forests of Oregon and Washington, was at the center of one of these controversies. The spotted owl nests in old-growth trees that are prized by the logging industry. Federal administrators, citing the ESA, banned logging in the owl's habitat. The ensuing legal battle ended with a compromise in which logging was permitted in some old-growth timber areas and prohibited in others. Although this outcome left neither side fully satisfied, it is typical of how most such disputes are settled. More recently, federal officials have emphasized cooperative relationships with private parties. They are eligible for grants if they act to protect threatened and endangered species. In 2006, for example, a Wyoming association received a $120,000 federal grant to dredge a creek that a rare species of trout travels to get to its traditional spawning area.

Environmentalism: The Newer Wave

The pivotal decade in the federal government's realization that Americans needed protection from the harmful effects of air, water, and ground pollutants was the 1960s. The period was capped by the first Earth Day. Held in the spring of 1970, it was the brainchild of Senator Gaylord Nelson (D-Wis.), who had devoted nearly ten years to finding ways to increase public interest in environmental issues. With Earth Day, Nelson succeeded to a degree not even he could have imagined: ten thousand grade schools and high schools, two thousand colleges, and one thousand communities participated in the event, which included public rallies and environmental cleanup efforts. Earth Day has been held every year since 1970 and is now a worldwide event.

Environmental Protection

The year 1970 also marked the creation of the Environmental Protection Agency. Within a few months, the EPA was issuing new regulations at such a rapid pace that business firms had difficulty keeping track of all the mandates, much less complying fully with them. Corporations eventually found an ally in President Gerald Ford, who in a 1975 speech claimed that business regulation was costing $150 billion annually, or $2,000 for every American family.[14] Although Ford's estimate exceeded that of economic analysts, his point was not lost on policymakers or the public. The economy was in a slump, and the costs of complying with the new regulations were slowing an economic recovery. Polls indicated a decline in public support for regulatory action.

Since then, environmental protection policy has not greatly expanded, but neither has it greatly contracted. The emphasis has been on the effective administration of laws put into effect in the 1960s and 1970s. The EPA particularly was granted a broad mandate from Congress to protect America's air and water. In a 2001 decision, for example, the Supreme Court ruled unanimously that public health is the only thing that the EPA should take into account in establishing air quality standards; the costs to industry are not to be considered.[15] The Court went further in 2007 by ordering the EPA to act on carbon emissions. The Bush administration claimed that the EPA could choose for itself which actions to take and not to take. By a 5-4 vote, the Supreme Court ruled that the EPA had to comply with its legislative mandate: "Under the clear terms of the Clean Air Act, EPA can avoid taking further action only if it determines that greenhouse gases do not contribute to climate change. . . ."[16]

Environmental regulation has led to dramatic improvements in air and water quality. Pollution levels today are far below their levels of the 1960s, when yellowish-gray fog ("smog") hung over cities like Los Angeles and New York and when bodies of water like the Potomac River and Lake Erie were open sewers. In the past four decades, toxic waste emissions have been cut by half, hundreds of polluted lakes and rivers have been revitalized, energy efficiency has increased, food supplies have been made safer, and urban air pollution has decreased by more than 60 percent.[17]

Progress has been slower in cleaning up badly contaminated toxic waste sites. These sites can contaminate local water supplies and become a health hazard. Abnormally high cancer rates have been found in the vicinity of some of these sites. In the 1980s, Congress established the so-called Superfund program to rid these sites of their contaminants. However, the cleanup process has been slow and contentious. Firms that caused the pollution are liable for some of the cleanup costs, but many of these firms are no longer in business, have since been purchased by other companies, or lack the money. Firms that could pay have often chosen instead to fight the issue in court, further delaying the cleanup. To date, only about half of the sites targeted by the Superfund program as posing serious hazards have been cleaned up.

Energy Policy and Global Warming

No environmental issue has received more attention recently than global warming. The scientific community has been warning for more than a decade that carbon emissions are creating a "greenhouse effect" (the trapping of heat in the

In 2007, Al Gore received the Nobel Prize for his efforts to awaken policymakers around the globe to the dangers of global warming. His documentary film on climate change, *An Inconvenient Truth*, received an Oscar. Gore was vice president during the Clinton administration, and though he received more popular votes in the 2000 presidential election, Gore lost the presidency when George W. Bush garnered a majority of the electoral vote.

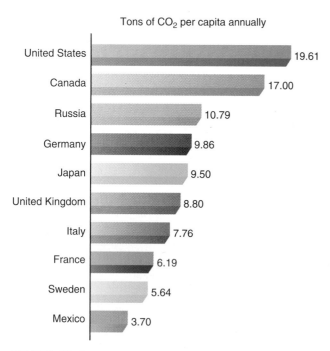

Tons of CO_2 per capita annually

United States	19.61
Canada	17.00
Russia	10.79
Germany	9.86
Japan	9.50
United Kingdom	8.80
Italy	7.76
France	6.19
Sweden	5.64
Mexico	3.70

FIGURE 15-2 **Per Capita Carbon Emissions** Americans emit more carbon dioxide into the atmosphere on a per capita basis than do the people of other countries. Carbon dioxide is the major cause of global warming and is a by-product of the burning of fossil fuels, such as coal and oil.
Source: OECD, 2008.

atmosphere). The result has been a rise in the earth's temperatures and in ocean levels, as a result of melting of the polar ice caps.

Until recently, some political leaders dismissed the evidence, saying repeatedly that "more research was needed." Today, few politicians openly question the existence of global warming. Political leaders disagree, however, on what should be done about it. Global warming can be retarded only by carbon emission reductions that in some cases require costly technological innovations and would slow economic growth. So far in the United States, the pro-growth side has had the upper hand. The United States is the single largest source of worldwide carbon emissions (see Figure 15-2), and U.S. policymakers have resisted demands at home and from abroad for substantial new restrictions on air pollution. In 2002, for example, President Bush declared that the United States would not participate in the Kyoto agreement, a multinational effort to reduce the emission of greenhouse gases.

Even critics of Bush's action acknowledged that the Kyoto agreement was problematic. It imposed light burdens on some countries and heavy burdens on others, including the United States. Nevertheless, support is growing among Republican and Democratic leaders alike for a substantial response to the problem of global warming. Energy conservation through a steep hike in the tax on gasoline would be a short-term answer, but it is unlikely that America's consumers would embrace it or that officeholders would risk their political careers by voting for it. The price of gasoline is already a hot issue because of the rise in the world price of oil. Instability in the Middle East, a weakening of the value of the dollar, and increased demand for oil in China and India helped push oil prices in 2008 above $140 a barrel—eight times the price of a few years earlier. And as the price of oil rose, so did the price of gasoline; in some places, it reached $4 a gallon, far more than Americans are accustomed to paying.

In addition to its impact on oil prices, worldwide economic growth is accelerating the rate at which carbon emissions are being spewed into the atmosphere, exacerbating the problem of global warming. The situation spurred passage in 2007 of the Energy Independence and Security Act, which had the backing of President Bush and large majorities in the Senate and House. The legislation mandated higher fuel-efficiency standards for vehicles for the first time in three decades, requires a fivefold increase over fifteen years in the production of renewable fuels such as ethanol, and set a goal of eliminating incandescent light bulbs within a decade. House Speaker Nancy Pelosi (D-Calif.) described the bill as "a moment of change." President Bush said the legislation was a "major step . . . toward confronting global climate change."

However, Congress and the White House were unable to reach agreement on subsidies for alternative energy sources such as wind, solar, and geothermal power, and provisions of the bill that would have provided tens of billions of dollars toward development of alternative sources were dropped from consideration. This deletion evoked criticism from environmental groups, who have pressured policymakers to move more quickly on alternative sources. In the 2008 presidential campaign, Barack Obama adopted that position, proposing initiatives designed to speed up the development of alternative energy sources. John McCain also advanced proposals that would provide federal funding and tax incentives for the development of such sources. However, McCain also proposed aggressive oil exploration, including opening up additional offshore areas to drilling. "We need to drill, drill, drill," said McCain, prompting protests from environmentalists. Obama subsequently endorsed offshore drilling, though on a more limited basis.

In the years ahead, Americans will increasingly have to make trade-offs between environmental protection, energy costs, and economic growth. To a degree, they are prepared to make them. Polls indicate that a majority of Americans would support further environmental regulation even if the result is slower economic growth. However, in part because of their greater resistance to government regulation and to taxes (including the gas tax), Americans are less willing to make the trade-offs than are Canadians, the Japanese, or most Western Europeans (see Figure 15-3).

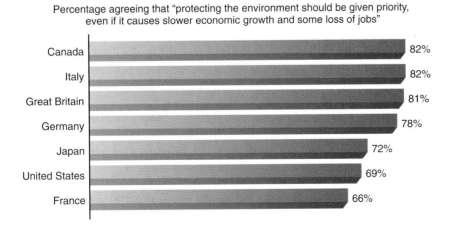

Percentage agreeing that "protecting the environment should be given priority, even if it causes slower economic growth and some loss of jobs"

Canada	82%
Italy	82%
Great Britain	81%
Germany	78%
Japan	72%
United States	69%
France	66%

FIGURE 15-3 Opinions on the Environment and Economic Growth Majorities in industrialized democracies support environmental protection, even if it means somewhat slower economic growth. However, Americans are somewhat less likely than citizens elsewhere to accept this trade-off.
Source: The Pew Research Center for the People and the Press, Global Attitudes Survey, 2002.

Government as Promoter of Economic Interests

The U.S. government has always made important contributions to the nation's economy. Congress in 1789 gave a boost to the nation's shipping industry by placing a tariff on goods brought into the United States on foreign ships, thereby encouraging importers to use American ships. Since that first favor, the U.S. government has provided thousands of direct benefits to economic interests. The following sections provide examples of a few of these benefits.

Promoting Business

American business is not opposed to government regulation as such. Corporations object only to regulatory policies that hurt their interests. At various times and in different ways, as in the case of the FCC and broadcasters, some regulatory agencies have promoted the interests of the very industries they are supposed to regulate in the public interest.

Providing loans and tax breaks is another way that government promotes business. Firms receive loan guarantees, direct loans, tax credits for capital investments, and tax deductions for capital depreciation. Over the past forty years, the burden of federal taxation has shifted dramatically from corporations to individuals. A few decades ago, the revenues raised from taxes on corporate income were roughly the same as the revenues raised from taxes on individual income. Today, individual taxpayers carry a much heavier burden. Some analysts do not regard the change as particularly significant, arguing that higher corporate taxes would be passed along to the public anyway in the form of higher prices for goods and services.

The most significant contribution that government makes to business is the traditional services it provides, such as education, transportation, and defense. Colleges and universities, which are funded primarily by governments, furnish business with most of its professional and technical workforce and with much of the basic research that goes into product development. The nation's roadways, waterways, and airports are other public-sector contributions without which business could not operate. In short, America's business has no bigger booster than government.

Striking janitors parade in Beverly Hills, California. Although the U.S. government promotes labor interests, it does so less substantially than it promotes business interests and less substantially than do other Western democracies.

Promoting Labor

Laissez-faire thinking dominated government's approach to labor well into the twentieth century. The governing principle, developed by the courts a century earlier, held that workers had limited rights of collective action. Union activity was regarded as interference with the natural supply of labor and the free setting of wages. Government's hostility toward labor was evident, for example, in the use of police and soldiers during the late 1800s to break up strikes.

The 1930s brought major changes. The key legislation was the National Labor Relations Act of 1935, which guaranteed workers the right to bargain collectively and prohibited business from discriminating against union employees and from unreasonably interfering with union activities. Government has also aided labor over the years by legislating minimum wages and maximum work hours, unemployment benefits, safer and more healthful working conditions, and nondiscriminatory hiring practices. Although government support for labor extends beyond these examples, it is not nearly as extensive as its assistance to business. America's culture of individualism has resulted in public policies that are less favorable to labor than are policies in European countries.

Promoting Agriculture

Until well into the twentieth century, most Americans still lived on farms and in small rural communities. Agriculture was America's dominant business and was assisted by the government's land policies. The Homestead Act of 1862, for example, opened government-owned lands to settlement, creating spectacular "land rushes" by offering 160 acres of government land free to each family that staked a claim, built a house, and farmed the land for five years.

Farm programs today provide assistance to both small farmers and large commercial enterprises (agribusinesses) and cost the federal government billions of dollars annually. A major goal of this spending is to eliminate some of the risks associated with farming. Weather, world markets, and other factors can radically affect crop and livestock prices, and federal programs are designed to protect farmers from adverse developments.

Experience has shown that the agricultural sector benefits from government intervention. In 1996, Congress passed legislation that trimmed long-standing crop subsidy and crop allocation programs. The goal was to let the free market largely determine the prices farmers would get for their crops and to let farmers themselves decide on the crops they would plant. The result was a depressed farm economy—prices fell sharply because of the surplus production of particular crops. In 2002, Congress abandoned the free-market approach. Crop subsidies were increased and expanded to include more crops. Then, in 2008, Congress overrode a presidential veto to enact a five-year, $300-billion farm bill that puts farmers in line for hefty government assistance in future years. At present, federal payments account for more than a fourth of net agricultural income, making America's farmers among the most heavily subsidized anywhere in the world.

Fiscal Policy: Government as Manager of the Economy, I

Until the 1930s, the U.S. government adhered to the prevailing free-market theory and made no attempt to regulate the economy as a whole. The economy, which was regarded as largely self-regulating, was fairly prosperous, but it collapsed periodically, resulting in widespread unemployment.

The greatest economic collapse in the nation's history—the Great Depression of the 1930s—finally brought an end to traditional economics. President Franklin D. Roosevelt's government spending and job programs, designed to stimulate the economy and put Americans back to work, heralded the change.[18] Although Roosevelt's use of government policy as an economic stimulus was highly controversial, today it is accepted practice. Government is expected to pursue policies that will foster economic growth and stability.

TABLE 15-2 | **Fiscal Policy: A Summary** Taxing and spending levels can be adjusted in order to affect economic conditions.

Problem	Fiscal Policy Actions
Low productivity and high unemployment	Demand side: increase spending Supply side: cut business taxes
Excess production and high inflation	Decrease spending Increase taxes

Taxing and Spending Policy and Politics

The government's efforts to maintain a thriving economy are made mainly through its taxing and spending decisions, which together are referred to as its **fiscal policy** (see Table 15-2).

The annual federal budget is the basis of fiscal policy. Thousands of pages in length, the budget allocates federal expenditures among government programs and identifies the revenues—taxes, social insurance receipts, and borrowed funds—that will be used to pay for these programs (see Figure 15-4). From one perspective, the budget is the national government's allocation of costs and benefits. Every federal program benefits some interest, whether it be farmers who get price supports, defense firms that obtain military contracts, or retirees who receive monthly social security checks. From another standpoint, that of fiscal policy, the budget is a device for stimulating or dampening economic growth. Through changes in overall levels of spending and taxing, government can help keep the economy running smoothly.

Fiscal policy has origins in the economic theories of John Maynard Keynes. In *The General Theory of Employment, Interest, and Money* (1936), Keynes noted that employers naturally become cautious during an economic downturn and cut back on production and the number of workers. Challenging the traditional idea that government should also cut back during a downturn, Keynes claimed that a downturn can be shortened only by increased government spending. Keynes said that government should engage in **deficit spending**—spending more than it gets from taxes—which can be accomplished through the borrowing and printing of money. By placing additional money in the hands of consumers, government can stimulate spending, which in turn will stimulate production and create jobs, thereby promoting an economic recovery.[19]

---

fiscal policy

A tool of economic management by which government attempts to maintain a stable economy through its taxing and spending policies.

---

deficit spending

The situation when the government spends more than it collects in taxes and other revenues.

FIGURE 15-4 **The Federal Budget Dollar, Fiscal Year 2009**
Source: Congressional Budget Office.

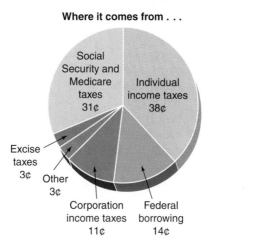

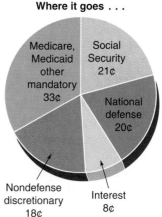

According to Keynesian theory, the level of the government's response should be commensurate with the severity of the problem. During an **economic depression**—an exceptionally steep and sustained downturn in the economy—the government should engage in massive new spending programs to hasten the recovery. During an **economic recession,** which is a less severe downturn, government spending should also be increased but by a smaller amount.

Demand-Side Stimulation

Keynes's theory focused on government's efforts to stimulate consumer spending. This **demand-side economics** emphasizes the consumer "demand" component of the supply–demand equation. When the economy is sluggish, the government by increasing its spending can place additional money in consumers' hands. With more money to spend, consumers buy more goods and services. This increase in demand stimulates businesses to produce more goods and hire more workers. In this way, government spending contributes to economic recovery. This rationale was the basis for the tax rebates that more than 100 million Americans received in 2008. The economy had slowed dramatically, and President Bush and Congress responded by sending checks totaling $150 billion to taxpayers, urging them to spend their rebate. Most of the money was in fact spent within a few months, giving the economy a much needed boost.

The tax rebates were not the government's only contribution in 2008 to reversing the economic downturn. Since the 1930s, federal spending has been at permanently high levels. Each month, for example, roughly 40 million Americans receive a social security check from the government. In turn, they spend it on food, clothing, housing, entertainment, and other goods and services. They pump billions of dollars each month into the U.S. economy, which creates jobs and income for millions of other Americans. And social security is only one—albeit the largest—of numerous federal spending programs. Each day, the federal government spends about $5 billion, more than the typical large corporation pumps into the economy during an entire year. The U.S. economy thus has a constant demand-side stimulus: government spending on an ongoing and massive scale.

Although increased spending is a tool that government can employ to alleviate a severe economic crisis, it is a tool that needs to be applied sensibly. Excessive spending results in a **budget deficit**—the situation where the federal government spends more in a year than it receives in tax and other revenues. The shortfall increases the **national debt,** which is the total cumulative amount that the U.S. government owes to creditors. At present, the national debt exceeds $9 trillion, which requires enormous expenditures just to pay the interest on it. Interest payments on the national debt are roughly the total of all federal income taxes paid by Americans living west of the Mississippi. Only rarely in recent decades has the U.S. government had a **balanced budget** (the situation where revenues are equal to government expenditures) or a **budget surplus** (the situation where the federal government receives more in tax and other revenues than it spends). The usual situation has been a budget deficit, which is also the outlook for the foreseeable future (see Figure 15-5).

Supply-Side Stimulation

A fiscal policy alternative to demand-side stimulation is **supply-side economics,** which emphasizes the business (supply) component of the supply-demand equation. Supply-side theory was a cornerstone of President Ronald Reagan's economic program. He believed that economic growth could occur as easily from

economic depression

A very severe and sustained economic downturn. Depressions are rare in the United States; the last one was in the 1930s.

economic recession

A moderate but sustained downturn in the economy. Recessions are part of the economy's normal cycle of ups and downs.

demand-side economics

A form of fiscal policy that emphasizes "demand" (consumer spending). Government can use increased spending or tax cuts to place more money in consumers' hands and thereby increase demand.

budget deficit

The situation when the government's expenditures exceed its tax and other revenues.

national debt

The total cumulative amount that the U.S. government owes to creditors.

balanced budget

The situation when the government's tax and other revenues for the year are roughly equal to its expenditures.

budget surplus

The situation when the government's tax and other revenues exceed its expenditures.

supply-side economics

A form of fiscal policy that emphasizes "supply" (production). An example of supply-side economics is a tax cut for business.

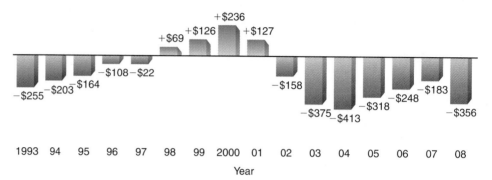

Annual federal budget deficit/surplus
(in billions of dollars)

FIGURE 15-5 **The Federal Budget Deficit/Surplus** The federal government ran a budget deficit until 1998, at which time a surplus that was expected to last for years emerged. In 2001, however, the surplus quickly disappeared as a result of an economic downturn, costs associated with the war on terrorism, and a cut in federal taxes.
Source: Office of Management and Budget, 2008. Figure for 2008 based on preliminary estimates.

stimulation of the business sector as from stimulation of consumer demand. "Reaganomics" included substantial tax breaks for businesses and upper-income individuals.[20] Supply-side theory was also the basis of President George W. Bush's economic initiatives, which included sharp cuts in the tax rate on individuals, with most of the gains going to high-income taxpayers, and a reduction in the **capital-gains tax,** the tax that individuals pay on gains in capital investments such as property and stocks. Under Bush, the capital-gains tax rate, which had been 28 percent, fell to 15 percent, and the highest marginal rate on individual income fell to 35 percent, down from 39 percent.

Supply-side measures are designed to encourage investment in business expansion and capital markets, creating economic growth that results in increases in employment and income. As jobs and wages increase, so does consumer spending, furthering the economic growth.

As with demand-side stimulation, supply-side policy can be taken too far. Both Reagan and Bush argued that the increased business activity resulting from their tax cuts would soon produce the additional revenues needed to offset the loss of revenue from the cuts. Although the Reagan and Bush tax cuts provided an economic boost, the loss of revenue in each case was greater than the gain in revenue from the resulting economic growth. As a consequence, the tax cuts contributed to increases in the budget deficit and the national debt.[21] In Bush's case, the tax cuts in combination with the costs of the Iraq war drove the U.S. budget deficit to record highs, threatening to cancel any long-term contribution the tax cuts might have made to economic growth.[22] During congressional testimony, outgoing Federal Reserve chairman Alan Greenspan warned that the budget deficits were "unsustainable" and a severe threat to the long-term health of the U.S. economy. (Bush's tax cuts are discussed further in Chapter 16.)

Controlling Inflation

High unemployment and low productivity are only two of the economic problems that government is called on to solve. Another is **inflation**—an increase in the average level of prices of goods and services. Before the late 1960s, inflation was a minor problem—a less than 4 percent annual rate. But inflation rose

capital-gains tax

The tax that individuals pay on money gained from the sale of a capital asset, such as property or stocks.

inflation

A general increase in the average level of prices of goods and services.

Inflation rate since 1979 (Consumer Price Index)

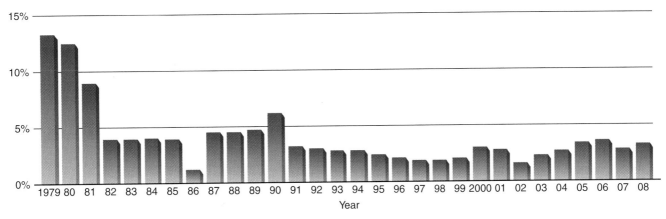

FIGURE 15-6 **The Annual Rate of Inflation, 1979–2008** Price increases have declined in the last decade compared to the late 1970s. *Source:* U.S. Department of Labor, 2008.

sharply during the last years of the Vietnam War and remained high throughout the 1970s, reaching a postwar record rate of 13 percent in 1979. The effects were substantial. Prices were rising but personal income was stagnant. Many Americans were forced to cut back on basics, such as food and medical care. Personal and business bankruptcies rose sharply as a result of rising costs and skyrocketing loan rates. The interest rates on business and home loans topped 15 percent—up from 5 percent a few years earlier.

Since the early 1980s, the annual inflation rate has been more manageable (see Figure 15-6), and public concern with inflation has receded. Nevertheless, recent developments, including sharp increases in consumer and government debt, have weakened the U.S. dollar, which could trigger another inflationary period in the near future. To fight inflation, government applies policies exactly the opposite of those used to fight unemployment and low productivity. By cutting spending or raising personal income taxes, government can take money from consumers, thus reducing demand and dampening prices. (The main policy tool for addressing inflation is monetary policy, which is discussed later in the chapter.)

Partisan Differences

Partisan politics is a component of fiscal policy. Working-class Americans are a significant part of the Democratic coalition and are usually the first and most deeply affected by rising unemployment. Accordingly, Democratic leaders have usually responded to a sluggish economy with increased government spending (demand-side fiscal policy), which offers direct help to the unemployed and stimulates consumption. Virtually every increase in federal unemployment benefits during the past fifty years, for example, has been initiated by Democratic officeholders.

Republican leaders are more likely to see an economic downturn through the eyes of business firms. Republicans in Washington typically have sought ways to stimulate business activity as a means of economic recovery. Thus, Republicans have usually resisted large increases in government spending (with the exception of defense spending) as a response to a sluggish economy. Such spending requires government to borrow money, which leads to upward pressure on interest rates. This pressure in turn raises business costs, because firms must pay higher interest rates for the money they borrow.

LIBERTY, EQUALITY, AND SELF-GOVERNMENT

Economic Policy

The U.S. economy is based on free-market principles. Producers and consumers are more or less free to act as they please, subject of course to their financial resources. Few Americans would trade their free-enterprise system for a socialist system that would put more constraints on their economic activity in return for greater economic security (see Chapter 1). In fact, Americans' notions of liberty and economic freedom are closely connected. Americans want the liberty that attends economic freedom, even if it means that in the end only some of them will do well economically.

Paradoxically, a minimum of economic security ordinarily is required for people to exercise their liberty. If people have to scrape to make a living, they will have neither the energy nor the financial means to enjoy fully the fruits of liberty. The Framers of the Constitution saw economic well-being as a precondition of liberty, which is why the Fifth (and later the Fourteenth) Amendment speaks at once of "life, liberty, or property." The Framers believed that America, in its abundance of land, offered a natural basis for the widespread prosperity that would bring meaningful liberty to all, as well as a greater measure of equality. Twenty-first-century America is a different kind of nation, vastly more affluent on one level but offering less economic opportunity on another. Studies show a widening gap between rich and poor in America, raising the issue of whether wealth in the United States is properly distributed across the society.

In your opinion, is wealth distributed widely enough to allow nearly all Americans to enjoy the type of liberty the economic marketplace can supply? Or do you believe that too many Americans lack the economic means to attain the full measure of their liberty?

graduated (progressive) personal income tax

A tax on personal income in which the tax rate increases as income increases; in other words, the tax rate is higher for higher income levels.

Tax policy also has partisan dimensions. Democratic policymakers have typically sought tax policies that help working-class and lower-middle-class Americans. Democrats have favored a **graduated** (or **progressive**) **personal income tax**, in which the tax rate increases significantly as income rises. Republicans have preferred to keep taxes on upper incomes at a relatively low level, contending that this policy encourages the savings and investment that foster economic growth (supply-side fiscal policy). These differences are evident, for example, in the battle over the Economic Growth and Tax Relief Reconciliation Act of 2001. Proposed by President Bush, the legislation contained a huge tax cut for upper-income taxpayers. In Congress, the bill had the support of 90 percent of Republicans and only 20 percent of Democrats.[23] Then, in the 2008 presidential campaign, Democratic nominee Barack Obama vowed to rescind the Bush tax cut and raise taxes in upper incomes, while Republican nominee John McCain promised to preserve the cut (Tax policy is discussed further in Chapter 16.)

The Budgetary Process

The president and Congress jointly determine fiscal policy, mainly through the annual budgetary process. The Constitution grants Congress the power to tax and spend, but the president, as chief executive, plays a major role in shaping the budget (see Chapter 12). In reality, the budgetary process involves give-and-take between Congress and the president as each tries to exert influence over the final budget.[24]

The budgetary process is an elaborate one, as might be expected when billions of dollars in federal spending are at issue. From beginning to end, the process lasts a year and a half (see Figure 15-7). The process begins in the executive branch when the president, in consultation with the Office of Management and Budget (OMB), establishes general budget guidelines. The OMB is part of the Executive Office of the President (see Chapter 12) and takes its directives from the president. Hundreds of agencies and thousands of programs are covered by the budget, and

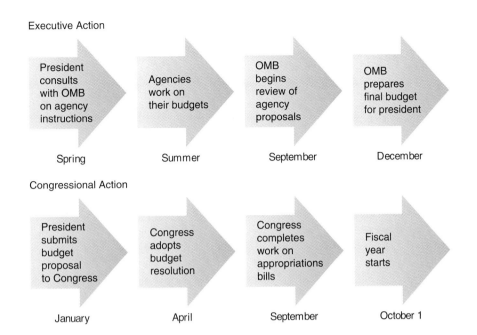

Executive Action

President consults with OMB on agency instructions — Spring

Agencies work on their budgets — Summer

OMB begins review of agency proposals — September

OMB prepares final budget for president — December

Congressional Action

President submits budget proposal to Congress — January

Congress adopts budget resolution — April

Congress completes work on appropriations bills — September

Fiscal year starts — October 1

FIGURE 15-7 Federal Budgetary Process The budget begins with the president's instructions to the agencies and ends when Congress enacts the budget. The entire process spans about eighteen months.

the OMB uses the president's directives to issue the instructions that will guide each agency's budget preparations. For example, each agency is assigned a budget ceiling within which it must work.

The agencies receive these instructions in the spring and then work through the summer to develop a detailed agency budget, taking into account their existing programs and any new proposals. These agency budgets then go to the OMB in September for a full review that invariably includes further consultation with each agency. The agency budgets are then finalized and combined into the full budget. Throughout, the OMB stays in touch with the White House to ensure that the budget items conform to the president's objectives.

The agencies naturally tend to want more money for their programs, whereas the OMB has the job of matching the budget to the president's priorities. In fact, however, the president does not have any real say over most of the budget, about two-thirds of which involves mandatory spending. This spending is authorized by current law, and the government must allocate and spend the money unless the law itself is rescinded, an unlikely occurrence. Examples are social security and Medicare, which provide benefits to the elderly. The president does not have the authority to suspend or reduce these programs. Interest on the national debt is also part of the budget, and here too the president has no real option. The federal government is obligated to pay interest on the money it has borrowed.

The OMB focuses on the one-third of the budget that involves discretionary spending, which includes areas such as defense, foreign aid, education, national parks, space exploration, public broadcasting, and highways. In reality, even a large part of this spending is not truly discretionary. No president would even consider slashing defense spending to almost nothing or closing the national parks, and even modest cuts in a discretionary program may encounter resistance in Congress.

The president, then, works on the margins of the budget, trying to push it in directions that are consistent with administration goals. The effort in many policy areas consists of a modest increase or decrease in spending compared with the previous year. There are always a few areas, however, where the president will attempt a more dramatic adjustment. In each of his budgets, for example, President Bush asked for large increases in defense spending to assist in the war on terrorism and to pay for the Iraq war and reconstruction.

In January, the president transmits the full budget to Congress. This budget is just a proposal, because Congress alone has the constitutional power to appropriate funds. During Congress's work on the budget, the president's recommendations undergo varying degrees of change. The priorities of a majority in Congress are never exactly those of the president, even when they are members of the same party. When they are members of opposite parties, their priorities may differ greatly.

Upon reaching Congress, the president's budget proposal goes first to the House and Senate budget committees. Their job is to establish overall spending and revenue levels. Once they have settled on these levels, the full House and Senate vote on them. Once approved, the levels are a blueprint for the rest of Congress's work on the budget.

The House and Senate Appropriations Committees take over at this point. They are the most important part of congressional deliberations on the budget. The House Appropriations Committee through its subcommittees has the primary task of reviewing the budget items, a review that includes hearings with each federal agency. There are ten such subcommittees, each of which has responsibility for a substantive area, such as defense or agriculture. Agency budgets invariably are changed at this stage. A subcommittee may cut an agency's budget because it believes that the agency's work is not a priority or that the agency has asked for more funds than it needs. Or the subcommittee may decide to increase an agency's budget beyond what the president has requested. The subcommittees' recommendations are then submitted to the House Appropriations Committee for final review and submission to the full House for a vote. The Senate Appropriations Committee and its subcommittees conduct a similar review, but the Senate is a smaller body, and its review of agency requests is normally less thorough. To some degree, the Senate committee and its subcommittees serve as a "court of appeals" for agencies that have had their budget requests reduced by the House.

Throughout this process, members of the House and Senate rely heavily on the Congressional Budget Office (CBO), which, as discussed in Chapter 11, is the congressional equivalent of the OMB. If the CBO believes that an agency has misjudged the amount of money needed to meet its legislatively required programs, it will make this information known. Similarly, if the CBO concludes that the OMB has miscalculated how much the government can be expected to receive in taxes and other revenues, members of Congress will be notified of the discrepancy.

After the work of the appropriations committees has been completed and is approved by the full House and Senate, differences in the Senate and House versions of the appropriations bill are reconciled in conference committee (see Chapter 11). The legislation is then sent to the president for approval or veto. The threat of a presidential veto can be enough to persuade Congress to accept many of the president's recommendations. In the end, the budget inevitably reflects both presidential and congressional priorities. Neither branch ever gets everything it wants, but each branch always gets some of what it wants.

Once the budget has been passed by both the House and the Senate and is signed by the president, it takes effect on October 1, the starting date of the federal government's fiscal year. If agreement on the budget has not been reached by October 1, temporary funding is required in order to maintain government operations. In late 1995, President Clinton and the Republican Congress deadlocked on budgetary issues to such an extent that they could not even agree on temporary funding. Their standoff twice forced a brief shutdown of nonessential government activities.

STATES IN THE NATION

FEDERAL TAXING AND SPENDING: WINNERS AND LOSERS

Fiscal policy (the federal government's taxing and spending policies) varies in its effect on the states. The residents of some states pay a lot more in federal taxes than they receive in benefits. The biggest loser is New Jersey, whose taxpayers get back in federal spending in their state only $0.61 for every dollar they pay in federal taxes. Nevada taxpayers ($0.65 for every dollar) are the next-biggest losers. In contrast, the residents of some states get back more from federal spending programs than they contribute in taxes. The biggest winners are New Mexico and Mississippi, whose taxpayers get back $2.03 and $2.02, respectively, in federal spending in their states for every dollar they pay in federal taxes.

Q: Why are most of the "losers" in the northeastern section of the country?

A: The federal taxes that originate in a state reflect its wealth, and the northeastern states are generally the wealthier ones. Because they are wealthier, they also get less federal assistance for programs designed to help lower-income people and areas. Finally, most federal lands and military installations—sources of federal money—lie outside the northeastern region.

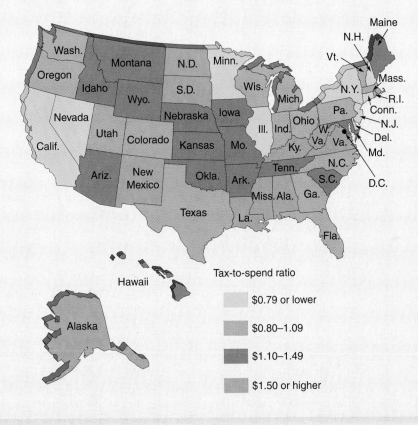

Tax-to-spend ratio

- $0.79 or lower
- $0.80–1.09
- $1.10–1.49
- $1.50 or higher

Source: Adapted from Tax Foundation Calculations, 2007.

Monetary Policy: Government as Manager of the Economy, II

Fiscal policy is not the only instrument of economic management available to government; another is **monetary policy,** which is based on adjustments in the amount of money in circulation (see Table 15-3). Monetarists, as economists who emphasize monetary policy are called, contend that the money supply is the key

monetary policy

A tool of economic management, available to government, based on manipulation of the amount of money in circulation.

TABLE 15-3 | Monetary Policy: A Summary of the Fed's Role   The money supply can be adjusted in order to affect economic conditions.

Problem	Monetary Policy Actions by Federal Reserve
Low productivity and high unemployment (requiring an increase in the money supply)	Decrease interest rate on loans to member banks
	Decrease cash reserve that member banks must deposit in Federal Reserve System
Excess productivity and high inflation (requiring a decrease in the money supply)	Increase interest rate on loans to member banks
	Increase cash reserve that member banks must deposit in Federal Reserve System

to sustaining a healthy economy. Their leading theorist, the American economist Milton Friedman, held that supply and demand are best controlled through the money supply.[25] Too much money in circulation contributes to inflation because too many dollars are chasing too few goods, which drives up prices. Too little money in circulation results in a slowing economy and rising unemployment, because consumers lack the ready cash and easy credit required to push up spending levels. Monetarists believe in increasing the money supply when the economy needs a boost and decreasing the supply when it needs to be slowed down.

The Fed

Control over the money supply rests not with the president or Congress but with the Federal Reserve Board System (known as "the Fed"). Created by the Federal Reserve Act of 1913, the Fed has a board of governors whose seven members serve for fourteen years, except for the chair and vice chair, who serve for four years. All members are appointed by the president, subject to Senate approval. The Fed regulates all national banks and those state banks that meet certain standards and choose to become members of the Federal Reserve System.

The Fed decides how much money to add to or subtract from the economy, seeking a balance that will permit steady growth without causing an unacceptable level of inflation. One way the Fed affects the money supply is by raising or lowering the cash reserve that member banks are required to deposit with the Federal Reserve. This reserve is a proportion of each member's total deposits. By increasing the reserve rate, the Fed takes money from member banks and thereby takes it out of circulation. When the Fed lowers the reserve rate, banks have more money available to loan to consumers and investors.

A second and more visible way the Fed affects the money supply is by lowering or raising the interest rate that member banks are charged when they borrow from the Federal Reserve. When the Fed raises the interest rate, banks also tend to raise the rate they charge for new loans, which discourages borrowing and thus reduces the amount of money entering the economy. Conversely, by lowering the interest rate, the Fed encourages firms and individuals to borrow from banks, which increases the money supply. The Fed's interest-rate adjustments are often front-page news because they are a signal of the strength of the economy and thus affect the decisions of consumers and firms. As the economy slowed down in 2008, for example, the Fed began a series of adjustments that dropped the interest rate by several percentage points, which enabled member banks to lower their rates, thereby making loans more affordable for firms and consumers.

DEBATING THE ISSUES

SHOULD THE FED BAIL OUT TROUBLED FINANCIAL INSTITUTIONS?

When the subprime mortgage crisis hit in 2008, a number of venerable financial institutions found themselves in trouble. One of these institutions was the investment bank Bear Stearns, which was established in 1923 and had survived the Great Depression, a time when many financial institutions went bankrupt. More recently, during the housing boom in the United States, Bear Stearns had made a fortune in mortgage-backed securities. However, it had overinvested in these securities and found itself in a liquidity crisis when those investments turned sour. As it was teetering on the edge of bankruptcy, the Federal Reserve stepped in with a huge loan guarantee that enabled J. P. Morgan, another financial institution, to buy Bear Stearns to keep it from folding. But should the Fed have done it? As an investment bank, Bear Stearns was not a member bank of the Federal Reserve and the firm had gotten itself in trouble by overinvesting in high-yield but risky securities. The federal government does not bail out small businesses or individuals who make bad financial decisions. Why should huge firms be an exception? Here are two opposing views on the subject. U.S. Treasury Secretary Henry Paulson argues that the Fed's decision was appropriate because it was designed to keep the broader financial markets from crashing. Paul Volcker, former chair of the Federal Reserve, questions whether the Fed should get into the business of underwriting bad investment decisions, while acknowledging that policymakers need to regulate the financial markets more closely. Which view comes closer to your own? Do you see any merit in the opposing view?

YES I appreciate the additional actions taken this evening by the Federal Reserve to enhance the stability, liquidity and orderliness of our markets.... [It] was not a difficult decision. It was the right decision.... When you go through a period like this, policymakers need to balance various consequences. . . . No one is debating the fact that this economy has slowed way down. We feel it, we know it, the American people know it.... We have to respond to the circumstances we're facing today, and my concern is to minimize the impact on the broader economy as we work our way through this situation, and again, the stability of our financial situation. . . . And I'm convinced that they're going to come out of this situation very strong.

—*Henry Paulson, U.S. Treasury secretary*

NO [This action was a] more extreme measure in some respects than any that have been taken in the past to deal with a financial crisis, which raises some real questions not only for the Federal Reserve and its authorities, but for the structure of the financial system.... The Federal Reserve ... has not, in the past, been conceived as a place where you put in bad assets, possibly bad assets. Lending institutions take risks. I'm not suggesting the assets are terrible, but they have collateral. But that is a new departure. And at some point, the government ought to—in my view, the government ought to be taking responsibility for that kind of action, not the Federal Reserve, which is an independent agency designed to provide an ample supply of liquidity to the economy but not too much, protect against inflation, not to protect particular sectors of the economy from bad loans. . . . If we can stabilize the financial market, we ought to come out of this [downturn in good shape]. Then we've got a lot of work to do about what we do with the regulatory system, the supervisory system, what the role of the Federal Reserve is, what the role of the Treasury and the government is, because this is a different financial market.

—*Paul Volcker, former chair, Federal Reserve*

Economists debate the relative effectiveness of monetary policy and fiscal policy, but monetary policy has one obvious advantage: it can be implemented more quickly than fiscal policy. The Fed can adjust interest and reserve rates on short notice, thus providing the economy with a psychological boost to go along with the financial effect of a change in the money supply. In contrast, changes in fiscal policy usually take months to implement. Congressional action is relatively slow, and new taxing and spending programs ordinarily require a preparation period before they can be put into effect. Five months elapsed, for example, before the tax rebate checks authorized by Congress in early 2008 actually reached the taxpayers.

The Politics of the Fed

The greater flexibility of monetary policy has positioned the Fed as the institution with primary policy responsibility for keeping the U.S. economy on a steady course. The Fed's power can easily be exaggerated. The U.S. economy is subject to a lot of influences, of which the money supply is only one. Nevertheless, the Fed is a vital component of U.S. economic policy.[26]

At the time the Fed was created in 1913, economists had not yet "invented" the theory of monetary policy, and the Fed had no role in the management of the nation's economy. It now plays a large role, which raises important questions about the power it wields. One question is the issue of representation: whose interests does the Fed serve, those of the public as a whole or those of the banking sector? The Fed is not a wholly impartial body. Although it makes decisions in the context of economic theories and projections, it is "the bankers' bank" and as such is protective of monied interests. In 2008, the Fed stepped in with loans to financial institutions to prevent them from bankruptcy as a result of their holdings in shaky mortgage-related securities. The Fed justified its intervention by saying that the financial markets might otherwise collapse, adversely affecting every American. What was immediately clear, however, was that taxpayers were being forced to subsidize the banks. A related question is the issue of accountability: should the Fed, an unelected body, have so much power? Though appointed by the president, members of the Federal Reserve Board are not subject to removal. They serve for fixed terms and are relatively insulated from political pressures, including the changes that take place through elections. Of course, the Fed, as a banking institution, has a vested interest in a healthy economy (too much inflation erodes banks' returns on loans; too much unemployment decreases demand for loans) and thus operates within its own system of checks and balances. Nevertheless, the restraints on the Fed are weaker than those on popularly elected institutions.

Regardless, the Fed is part of the new way of thinking about the federal government and the economy that emerged during the Great Depression of the 1930s. Prior to that time, the federal government's economic role was largely confined to the provision of a limited number of public services, such as the currency and mail delivery. Roosevelt's New Deal permanently changed the government's role. Through its economic management and regulatory activities, the government has assumed an ongoing role in the economy, contributing to its stability and efficiency. The results are impressive. In the roughly three-quarters of a century that the U.S. government has played a significant policy role, the American economy has progressed at a relatively steady pace. There have been recessions, but none of them has been remotely like the devastating depressions of earlier times, a testimony to the soundness of economic theory and of its application by policymakers. (The economic policies of the federal government in the areas of social welfare and national security are discussed in the next two chapters.)

Summary Self-Test www.mhhe.com/pattersontad9e

Although private enterprise is the main force in the American economic system, the federal government plays a significant role through its policies to regulate, promote, and stimulate the economy.

Regulatory policy is designed to achieve efficiency and equity, which require the government to intervene, for example, to maintain competitive trade practices (an efficiency goal) and to protect vulnerable parties in economic trans-

actions (an equity goal). Many of the regulatory decisions of the federal government, particularly those of older agencies (such as the Food and Drug Administration), are made largely in the context of group politics. Business lobbies have an especially strong influence on the regulatory policies that affect them. In general, newer regulatory agencies (such as the Environmental Protection Agency) have policy responsibilities that are broader in scope and apply to a larger number of firms than those of the older agencies. As a result, the policy decisions of newer agencies are more often made in the context of party politics. Republican administrations are less vigorous in their regulation of business than are Democratic administrations.

Business is the major beneficiary of the federal government's efforts to promote economic interests. A large number of programs, including those that provide loans and research grants, are designed to assist businesses, which are also protected from failure through measures such as tariffs and favorable tax laws. Labor, for its part, obtains government assistance through laws concerning matters such as worker safety, the minimum wage, and collective bargaining. Yet America's individualistic culture tends to put labor at a disadvantage, keeping it less powerful than business in its dealings with the government. Agriculture is another economic sector that depends substantially on government's help, particularly in the form of income stabilization programs such as those that provide crop subsidies.

The U.S. government pursues policies that are designed to protect and conserve the environment. A few decades ago, the environment was not a policy priority. Today, there are many programs in this area, and the public has become an active participant in efforts to conserve resources and prevent exploitation of the environment. The continuing challenge is finding a proper balance between the nation's natural environment, its economic growth, and its energy needs.

Through its fiscal and monetary policies, Washington attempts to maintain a strong and stable economy—one characterized by high productivity, high employment, and low inflation. Fiscal policy is based on government decisions in regard to spending and taxing, which are aimed at either stimulating a weak economy or dampening an overheated (inflationary) economy. Fiscal policy is worked out through Congress and the president and consequently is responsive to political pressures. However, because it is difficult to raise taxes or cut programs, the government's ability to apply fiscal policy as an economic remedy is limited. Monetary policy is based on the money supply and works through the Federal Reserve, which is headed by a board whose members hold office for fixed terms. The Fed is a relatively independent body, a fact that has given rise to questions as to whether it should play such a large role in influencing national economic policy.

CHAPTER 15

Study Corner

Key Terms

balanced budget (*p. 411*)
budget deficit (*p. 411*)
budget surplus (*p. 411*)
capital-gains tax (*p. 412*)
deficit spending (*p. 410*)
demand-side economics (*p. 411*)
deregulation (*p. 400*)
economic depression (*p. 411*)
economic recession (*p. 411*)
economy (*p. 397*)
efficiency (*p. 398*)
equity (in relation to economic policy) (*p. 401*)
externalities (*p. 399*)
fiscal policy (*p. 410*)

graduated personal income tax (*p. 414*)
inflation (*p. 412*)
laissez-faire economics (*p. 397*)
monetary policy (*p. 417*)
national debt (*p. 411*)
policy formation (*p. 395*)
policy implementation (*p. 396*)
problem recognition (*p. 395*)
public policy process (*p. 394*)
regulation (*p. 398*)
supply-side economics (*p. 411*)

Self-Test

1. Which of the following steps in the U.S. budget process is not in its proper sequential order?
   a. The Office of Management and Budget compiles the budget.
   b. The proposed budget is studied in the House and Senate Budget and Appropriations Committees.
   c. The president sends the budget proposal to Congress.
   d. The budget is approved by Congress and presented to the president to be signed.

2. The challenge for policymakers in devising and implementing regulatory and deregulatory policies is to:
   a. simply remove all regulations.
   b. not be concerned about economic inefficiency in protecting the public interest.
   c. favor equity at the expense of efficiency.
   d. strike a proper balance between regulatory measures and free-market mechanisms.

3. The institutions of the U.S. government involved in determining fiscal policy are:
   a. the executive and legislative branches.
   b. the Fed and the regulatory agencies.
   c. the judicial branch and the states.
   d. the legislative branch and the Fed.

4. The era of new social regulation in the 1960s and 1970s differed from that of previous eras in:
   a. narrowing the scope and range of activities regulated.
   b. concentrating on reforms of labor practices.
   c. expanding social goals to the areas of environment and consumer protection as well as worker safety.
   d. pioneering the idea of cost-benefit analysis as a regulatory standard.

5. Examples of services provided by government that aid business include:
   a. loan guarantees and direct loans to business.
   b. funding of public colleges and universities.
   c. subsidizing the building of roads, waterways, and airports.
   d. all of the above.

6. The Federal Reserve Board affects the economy by taking all **except** which one of the following actions?
   a. meeting periodically to evaluate the economy and to decide on a proper response
   b. lowering or raising interest charged on money borrowed by banks
   c. raising or lowering the cash reserve that member banks are required to deposit with regional Federal Reserve banks
   d. submitting monetary strategies to Congress for a vote

7. Early in the development of America's economy, there was hostility toward labor union activity. (T/F)

8. In times when the economy needs a quick fix, one would be better off to use fiscal policy than monetary policy because fiscal policy can be implemented within a faster time frame. (T/F)

9. Rachel Carson's *Silent Spring* encouraged the growth of the modern environmental movement. (T/F)

10. Fiscal policy has its origins in the economic theories of John Maynard Keynes. (T/F)

Critical Thinking

What are the tools of fiscal policy and monetary policy? What are the advantages and disadvantages of each of these two approaches to managing the economy?

Suggested Readings

Duncan, Richard. *The Dollar Crisis: Causes, Consequences, Cures*, rev. ed. New York: John Wiley, 2005. A look at the problem of budget and trade deficits.

Jones, Bryan D., and Walter Williams. *The Politics of Bad Ideas: The Great Tax-Cut Delusion and the Decline of Good Government in America*. New York: Longman, 2008. A critique of the idea that tax cuts are the key to economic prosperity.

Lindbloom, Charles E. *The Market System: What It Is, How It Works, and What to Make of It*. New Haven, Conn.: Yale University Press, 2001. A clear analysis of the advantages and disadvantages of the market system.

Mayer, Martin. *Fed: The Inside Story of How the World's Most Powerful Financial Institution Drives the Markets*. New York: Free Press, 2001. A look at the Fed's impact on the economy and politics.

McChesney, Robert. *The Problem of the Media*. New York: Monthly Review Press, 2004. A scathing critique of media regulation.

Rosenbaum, Walter A. *Environmental Politics and Policy*, 6th ed. Washington, D.C.: Congressional Quarterly Press, 2004. A comprehensive examination of the politics of environmental policy.

Schick, Allen. *The Federal Budget*, 3d ed. Washington, D.C.: The Brookings Insitution Press, 2007. An explanation of the federal budgetary process.

Sheingate, Adam D. *The Rise of the Agricultural Welfare State*. Princeton, N.J.: Princeton University Press, 2003. A penetrating analysis of farm policy in the United States, France, and Japan.

List of Websites

http://www.federalreserve.gov/default.htm
The Federal Reserve System website; describes the Fed, provides information about its current activities, and has links to some of the Fed's national and international information sources.

http://www.epa.gov/
The Environmental Protection Agency (EPA) website; provides information on environmental policy and regulations, EPA projects, and related subjects.

http://www.ftc.gov/
The website of the Federal Trade Commission, one of the older regulatory agencies; describes the range of the FTC's activities.

http://www.whitehouse.gov/OMB
The home page of the Office of Management and Budget; contains a summary of the annual federal budget and describes the OMB's operations and responsibilities.

Participate!

The environment is a policy area where individual citizens can make a difference by reducing waste and pollution. If you have a car, you will burn significantly less fuel if you accelerate and drive more slowly. Choosing a fuel-efficient car, keeping your car properly tuned, walking rather than driving short distances to stores, and living closer to work or school are other ways to cut gas consumption. In your residence, the simplest steps are to use lights sparingly and keep the thermostat lower during cold periods and higher during hot periods. Smaller but meaningful savings can be achieved through simple things such as using low-flow shower heads and replacing incandescent bulbs with fluorescent lights, which require less energy and last longer. Even a change in eating habits can make a difference. Frozen convenience foods are wasteful of energy. They are cooked, frozen, and then cooked again—not to mention the resources used up in packaging. Fresh foods are more nutritious and less wasteful. And if you prefer bottled water to tap water, consider using a water filter system instead. Nearly all of the cost of bottled water is due to the plastic container, which is a nonbiodegradable petroleum product. The recycling of paper, plastics, and bottles also conserves natural resources.

However, the recycling process itself requires the use of energy. By cutting back on your use of recyclables and by recycling those you do use, you will contribute twice over to a cleaner environment.

Extra Credit

For up-to-the-minute *New York Times* articles, interactive simulations, graphics, study tools, and more links and quizzes, visit the text's Online Learning Center at www.mhhe. com/pattersontad9e.

Self-Test Answers

1. c   2. d   3. a   4. c   5. d   6. d   7. T   8. F   9. T   10. T

As Congress looks for culprits in the collapse of the subprime mortgage market, some lawmakers have fingered the man who has been portrayed as an economic genius and the leading architect of American prosperity for the past 15 years: former Federal Reserve Board Chairman Alan Greenspan.

In March, Senate Banking Committee Chairman Christopher Dodd, D-Conn., criticized a 2004 speech in which Greenspan urged lenders to help more consumers become homeowners by coming up with alternatives to traditional fixed-rate mortgages. The Fed "seemed to encourage the development and use of adjustable-rate mortgages that today are defaulting and going into foreclosure at record rates," Dodd said.

That is just the latest entry in a growing rap sheet that critics are compiling to document the Federal Reserve's role in what looks to be the second major asset bubble in a decade. The first was a boom in high-tech and Internet-based stock prices during the late 1990s, which ended with the NASDAQ Composite Index losing 78 percent of its value between March 2000 and October 2002.

Although there's no hard-and-fast definition of an asset bubble, the term typically describes a rapid run-up in prices that is driven more by buyers' expectations that prices will keep rising than by any conventional measure of underlying value.

The Fed, some experts say, ignores bubbles when they're inflating and then overreacts when they burst, lowering interest rates to cushion the effects on the broader economy. Easy credit may indeed ease a fall, but it also can set the stage for another spike in asset prices.

The Federal Reserve risks becoming "something of a serial bubble creator," says economist Nouriel Roubini, part of a mounting chorus of economists begging to differ with Greenspan and his successor as Fed chairman, Ben Bernanke, in their view that central banks should consider only growth and inflation when setting interest rates.

In recent decades, the Federal Reserve's Open Market Committee has ignored major increases in asset prices (for financial instruments such as stocks, or real property such as houses) unless they spark inflation or an ensuing bust seems likely to drag down the rest of the economy.

The debate began as a somewhat academic affair in 1999, when Bernanke, then an economist at Princeton University, wrote a paper with fellow economist Mark Gertler that laid out the arguments against modifying Fed policy to try to lessen bubbles. At the time, some critics, including some members of the Federal Reserve Board, had been suggesting that the Fed should raise rates to dampen the Internet stock frenzy.

By the time Bernanke took his views public in a speech to business economists shortly after joining the Fed's Board of Governors in 2002, the matter was no longer academic: The price of tech stocks had already tumbled, the economy had gone into recession, and the shock of 9/11 had put the board on a course that would drop interest rates to a minuscule 1 percent.

The Fed cannot identify a bubble with certainty early enough to make a difference, Bernanke argued in 2002. Even if it could, raising interest rates to tamp down demand for an asset would be dangerous—a small rate increase would have no effect, and a large hike could jeopardize the economy. "In short, we cannot practice 'safe popping,' at least not with the blunt tool of monetary policy," Bernanke said.

Instead, he argued, the Fed would do better to use some of its more pointed tools, including its rule-making and supervisory oversight of some financial institutions, to prevent bubbles from forming in the first place.

Bernanke contended that a reinterpretation of the events leading to the Great Depression bolstered his case: Rather than the stock market crash causing the Depression, several scholars have concluded recently that the drop in stock prices was merely a response to a slowing economy—which was caused by the Fed's decision in 1928 to raise interest rates

to slow a giddy rise in the financial markets. Instead of repeating such missteps, Bernanke said, the Federal Reserve should stand ready to counter any damage that falling asset prices wreak on the broader economy. That is, in fact, the approach the Fed took in 2001.

By 2002, however, the academic debate was gathering steam. Nearly half a dozen economists weighed in with papers challenging Bernanke's arguments on theoretical grounds, and Bernanke occasionally fired back. The challengers argued that the Fed, even if it wasn't sure a bubble was forming, could produce a better outcome by factoring asset prices into its policy equation than by ignoring them.

Those who want the Federal Reserve to be more bubble-conscious aren't looking for radical changes. "No one is in favor of aggressively using monetary policy to prick bubbles," Roubini said. Some observers just want the Fed to take "a more nuanced view." Roubini and others agree that the Fed should start by using some of the more refined tools in its workshop: the power of the podium—since lenders and financial markets closely follow the Fed's pronouncements—and the power to curb credit, whether by limiting investors' ability to buy securities on margin, or by scrutinizing the lending standards of the mortgage lenders it oversees.

The Fed has failed to use either of these tools, the challengers say. Despite Greenspan's famous remark in 1996 about the "irrational exuberance" of the stock markets, many observers viewed him as a cheerleader for the idea of a "New Economy" that encouraged the mania for high-tech and Internet-based corporate stocks.

During the run-up in housing prices, Greenspan was likewise blithe—referring to some "froth" in the housing market only shortly before his retirement in early 2006. "He should have put the facts out, and said that these sorts of prices were not likely to be sustainable, and that people should realize that they are taking a big risk," said Dean Baker, co-director of the Center for

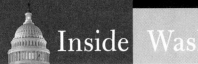

Economic and Policy Research. The markets, and homebuyers, would have given such cautions "lots of respect," Baker said.

The Fed likewise never used its power to restrain margin investing in the late 1990s, critics say, or to scrutinize mortgage-lending standards or the newfangled mortgage products being offered to higher-risk borrowers. "This was more than a failure of monetary policy; it was also failure of appropriate supervision," Roubini said. The regulators "were asleep at the wheel; they did nothing."

Many analysts note that the housing market is different than the stock market in key respects. For one, it is really made up of many different housing markets, which vary greatly by region. Moreover, houses are not merely an asset; they provide shelter for their owners. Faced with declining prices, would-be sellers will often choose to retain their homes—which protects against a downward price spiral.

In a 2005 study, researchers at the Federal Deposit Insurance Corp. noted that "the lion's share of home price booms have not ended in busts historically," but rather in price stagnation. The report noted, however, that "there are reasons to think that history might be an imperfect guide to the present situation" because changes in financial products, including subprime mortgages, are pushing these markets into "uncharted territory."

Even steeply falling housing prices might not chasten supporters of the Bernanke-Greenspan hands-off view. The key, for this camp, is whether a large price decline leads to broader economic woes, as people begin to feel poorer and cut back on spending.

"If you look back to the first bubble, to me what ratifies mopping up was how little damage the evaporation of $8 trillion did to the economy," says Princeton economist and former Fed board member Alan Blinder, referring to the loss of on-paper value of stocks from the dot-com bubble. A recession fol-

The Federal Reserve risks becoming something of a serial bubble creator.

lowed, he said, but it was extremely short-lived. "I call it a recessionette."

"If we look back and see the same reaction" to decline in house prices, Blinder says, he would consider that as "pretty much clinching the argument" for the current Fed policy of ignoring asset price run-ups. Although some asset-holders get hurt when bubbles pop, he acknowledges, "it may well be a requirement of exuberant capitalism—which is the kind we want—that it goes overboard now and then."

Although Bernanke has said that the Federal Reserve would pay attention to the impact of a housing boom on overall inflation, former New York Federal Reserve economist Stephen Cecchetti says that quirks in the way the government measures housing costs may have led the Fed to misread the economic cues both during the current boom and as prices decline. Government statisticians use "a fiction that homeowners rent from themselves, and treat renters and homeowners the same way," he says. Because rents tend to rise more slowly than home prices during a housing boom, the Consumer Price Index understates actual housing costs. With housing costs making up nearly 24 percent of the CPI, this measure thus understates inflation during a housing boom. And once home prices cool and rents rise, the CPI looks artificially high.

The lag could lead the Fed to keep rates unnecessarily low during a housing boom, thereby fueling the boom. During a housing bust, the Fed might keep interest rates high to fight phantom inflation, thereby exacerbating problems in the housing market.

Even if housing prices merely stagnate for 10 years, the costs for individuals could be severe, according to Baker. Baby Boomers who counted on rising home prices to finance their retirement could find themselves in straitened circumstances, he argues. That, in turn, could lead to lower consumer spending and a slower-growing economy—albeit too far down the road to be blamed on Greenspan and Bernanke.

As yet, the Federal Reserve Board hasn't officially embraced a change of heart on the wisdom of more-aggressive bubble management.

But Greenspan, now on the speaking circuit as a civilian, has darkened his views of the seriousness of a potential housing bust. "If prices go down from here, I think we're going to have problems that could spill over to other areas," he told the Futures Industry Association in mid-March. He has also suggested that a recession is possible later this year. But he blames subprime lenders rather than easy credit for the decline in prices.

Bernanke, whose job precludes much public doomsaying, has waved off Greenspan's suggestions of an impending recession and remained fairly quiet about the housing market. At a mid-March hearing of Congress's Joint Economic Committee, he said that slower economic growth reflected a "correction" in the housing sector. He blamed poor lending practices for the turmoil in the subprime market and said that the problems in the housing arena seemed unlikely to spread to the broader economy. The Fed was continuing to monitor the situation closely, he said.

If a bursting housing bubble does drag the economy down, will the Federal Reserve lower rates aggressively, potentially feeding yet another asset bubble? Bernanke hasn't had to face that question—yet.

FOR DISCUSSION: Who and what is to blame for the housing bubble?
How should the Fed and other government agencies work to control bubbles?
Should the Fed take an active hand or let the market work itself out?

Don't
rivatize

Don't
Privatize
Social Security

Welfare and Education Policy
Providing for Personal Security and Need

Poverty in America: The Nature of the Problem
 The Poor: Who and How Many?
 Living in Poverty: By Choice
  or Chance?

The Politics and Policies of Social Welfare
 Social Insurance Programs
 Public Assistance Programs
 Culture, Welfare, and Income

Education as Equality of Opportunity
 Public Education: Leveling Through
  the Schools
 Public School Issues
 The Federal Role in Education:
  Political Differences

The American Way of Promoting the General Welfare

We the people of the United States, in order to . . . promote the general welfare . . . Preamble, U.S. Constitution

As the Welfare Reform Act came up for renewal in 2002, there was cause for both hope and fear. The original legislation had been a stunning success. By the latter 1990s, the number of people on the welfare rolls had been cut almost in half. In only three states—Hawaii, Rhode Island, and New Mexico—was the drop less than 20 percent (see "States in the Nation"). The trend defied what had been called welfare policy's "reverse gravity" law: welfare rolls that went up but never came down. Two factors accounted for the change. One was the booming national economy. As more Americans got jobs, the demand for welfare decreased. The second factor was the 1996 Welfare Reform Act, which shortened the length of eligibility for welfare benefits and required that able-bodied recipients find work or risk loss of benefits.

The situation in 2002 was starkly different. Those welfare recipients who had found work were the ones easiest to place in jobs. Many of those still unemployed lacked the education, skill, or temperament to find and hold a job. Moreover, the economy had weakened, and welfare rolls were starting to rise even as government revenues were declining. "At the beginning of welfare reform, we had the happy circumstance of a booming economy, low unemployment, falling welfare caseloads, and the states having the money to give more help to the poor, especially the working poor," said Sharon Parrott of the Center on Budget and Policy Priorities. "Now, everything is going the other way. Caseloads are rising, the value of the federal block grant is down, and state budgets are in catastrophic shape."[1]

The 2002 debate in Congress reflected these new realities. Yet it also brought out old differences. Congressional Republicans wanted to increase pressure on the states to move more people off welfare and into work; they also argued for strict adherence to the eligibility rules, tight controls on federal spending, and increased work hours for welfare recipients. Congressional Democrats sought more funding for day care, education, and job-training programs; they also wanted to give the states more latitude in their administration of the welfare program.

STATES IN THE NATION

THE DECLINING NUMBER OF FAMILIES ON WELFARE

The welfare rolls in the United States peaked in March 1994. After that, the number of American families on welfare dropped precipitously, which analysts attributed to both the surge in the U.S. economy and the 1996 welfare reform bill that instituted new work rules. Between 1994 and 2002, welfare cases fell by 57 percent. The biggest drop (89 percent) was in Wisconsin. The smallest (7 percent) was in Hawaii. The decline in each state during this period is shown in the map below.

Q: What might explain the state-to-state variation in the decline in the welfare rolls?

A: States that had weaker economies in the early 1990s had bigger drops in their welfare rolls in the latter part of the 1990s. These states had more laid-off workers on welfare, and as the economy strengthened, many of these unemployed workers found jobs.

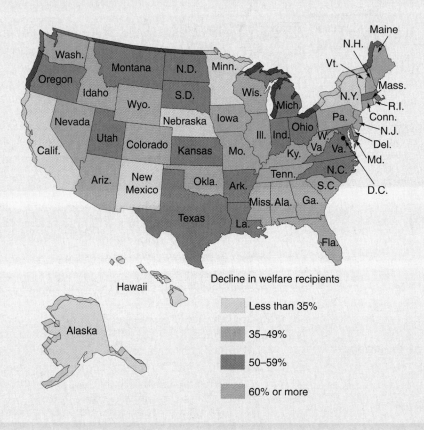

Decline in welfare recipients

- Less than 35%
- 35–49%
- 50–59%
- 60% or more

Source: U.S. Bureau of the Census, 2004.

The differences were substantial enough to create a months-long deadlock between the Republican-controlled House and the Democratic-controlled Senate. "By stalling on . . . welfare reform," said Bill Thomas (R-Calif.) of the House Committee on Ways and Means, "the Senate is shaping their legacy—inaction." Senate majority leader Tom Daschle (D-S. Dak.) was unbending, vowing to hold out until the Republicans agreed to "strong child care provisions."[2]

Social welfare policy is an area in which opposing philosophies of government collide. Some people, like Senator Daschle, hold that government should provide substantial assistance to those Americans who are less equipped to compete effectively in the marketplace. Others, like Representative Thomas, hold that welfare payments, except to those who are indisputably unfit to work, discourage personal effort and create welfare dependency.

America's federal system of government is also a source of conflict over welfare policy. Welfare was traditionally a responsibility of state and local governments. Only since the 1930s has the federal government played a major role by providing some of the funding and imposing restrictions on the use of the money. The strictness of federal guidelines and the amount that the federal government should contribute to welfare spending are contentious issues.

This chapter examines the social problems that federal welfare programs are designed to alleviate and describes how these programs operate. It also addresses public-education policies. This chapter seeks to provide an informed basis for understanding issues of social welfare and education and to show why disagreements in these areas are so substantial. These issues involve hard choices that inevitably require trade-offs between federal and state power and between the values of individual self-reliance and egalitarian compassion. The main points of the chapter are these:

■ *Poverty is a large and persistent problem in America, deeply affecting about one in seven Americans, including many of the country's most vulnerable—children, female-headed families, and minority-group members.* Social welfare programs have reduced the extent of poverty in the United States.

■ *Welfare policy has been a partisan issue, with Democrats taking the lead on government programs to alleviate economic insecurity and Republicans acting to slow down or reverse these initiatives.*

■ *Social welfare programs are designed to reward and foster self-reliance or, when this is not possible, to provide benefits only to those individuals who are truly in need.* U.S. welfare policy is not based on the assumption that every citizen has a right to material security.

■ *Americans favor social insurance programs (such as social security) over public assistance programs (such as food stamps).* As a result, most social welfare expenditures are not targeted toward the nation's neediest citizens.

■ *A prevailing principle in the United States is equality of opportunity, which in terms of policy is most evident in the area of public education.* America invests heavily in its public schools and colleges.

Poverty in America: The Nature of the Problem

In the broadest sense, social welfare policy includes any effort by government to improve social conditions. In a narrower sense, which is the way the term generally will be used in this chapter, social welfare policy refers to government programs that help individuals meet basic human needs, including food, clothing, and shelter.

The Poor: Who and How Many?

Americans' social welfare needs are substantial. Although Americans are far better off economically than most of the world's peoples, poverty is a significant and persistent problem in the United States. The government defines the **poverty line** as the annual cost of a thrifty food budget for an urban family of four, multiplied by three to include the cost of housing, clothes, and other necessities. Families whose incomes fall below that line are officially considered poor. In

poverty line

As defined by the federal government, the annual cost of a thrifty food budget for an urban family of four, multiplied by three to allow also for the cost of housing, clothes, and other expenses. Families below the poverty line are considered poor and are eligible for certain forms of public assistance.

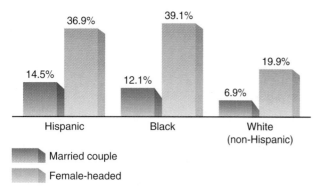

14.5% 36.9% 39.1% 12.1% 6.9% 19.9%

Hispanic   Black   White
                        (non-Hispanic)

Married couple

Female-headed

FIGURE 16-1 **Percentage of Families Living in Poverty, by Family Composition and Race/Ethnicity** Poverty is far more prevalent among female-headed households and African American and Hispanic households.

Source: U.S. Bureau of the Census, 2008.

2007, the poverty line was set at an annual income of roughly $20,000 for a family of four. One in eight Americans—roughly 35 million people, including more than 10 million children—live below the poverty line. If they could all join hands, they would form a line stretching from New York to Los Angeles and back again.

America's poor include individuals of all ages, races, religions, and regions, but poverty is concentrated among certain groups. Children are one of the largest groups of poor Americans. One in every five children lives in poverty. Most poor children live in families with a single parent, usually the mother. In fact, as can be seen from Figure 16-1, a high proportion of Americans residing in families headed by divorced, separated, or unmarried women live below the poverty line. These families are at a disadvantage because most women earn less than men for comparable work, especially in nonprofessional fields. Women without higher education or special skills often cannot find jobs that pay significantly more than the child-care expenses they incur if they work outside the home. Single-parent, female-headed families are roughly five times as likely as two-income families to fall below the poverty line, a situation referred to as "the feminization of poverty."[3]

Poverty is widespread among minority-group members. Compared with whites, twice as many African Americans and Hispanics live below the poverty line. Poverty is also geographically concentrated. Although poverty is often portrayed as an urban problem, it is somewhat more prevalent in rural areas. About one in seven rural residents—compared with one in nine urban residents—lives in a family with income below the poverty line. The urban figure is misleading, however, in that the level of poverty is very high in some inner-city areas. Suburbs are the safe haven from poverty. Because suburbanites are far removed from it, many of them have no sense of the impoverished condition of what Michael Harrington called "the other America."[4]

The "invisibility" of poverty in America is evident in polls showing that most Americans greatly underestimate the number of poor in their country. Nothing in the daily lives of many Americans or in what they see on television would lead them to think that poverty rates are uncommonly high. Yet the United States has the highest level of poverty among the advanced industrialized nations, and its rate of child poverty is more than twice the average rate of the other countries (see "How the U.S. Compares").

Living in Poverty: By Choice or Chance?

Many Americans hold to the idea that poverty is largely a matter of choice—that most low-income Americans are unwilling to make the effort to hold a responsible job and get ahead in life. In his book *Losing Ground*, Charles Murray argues that America has a permanent underclass of unproductive citizens who prefer to live on welfare and whose children receive little educational encouragement at home and grow up to be copies of their parents.[5] There are, indeed, many such people in America. They number in the millions. They are the toughest challenge for policymakers because almost nothing about their lives equips them to escape from poverty and its attendant ills.

Yet most poor Americans are in their situation as a result of circumstance rather than choice. After reviewing the extensive research on the causes of poverty and examining data that tracked individuals over periods of time, economists Signe-Mary McKernan and Caroline Ratcliffe concluded that most of the poor

HOW THE U.S. COMPARES

CHILDREN LIVING IN POVERTY

The United States has the highest child poverty rate among industrialized nations. One in five American children lives in poverty; in most other industrialized nations, the number is fewer than one in ten. These numbers are from the Office of Economic Development, which defines as being in poverty any household with an income less than half that of the median household.

The United States ranks at the top in part because its income is less evenly distributed. As a consequence, the United States has the highest percentage of both rich and poor children in the industrialized world. In addition, the United States spends less on government assistance for the poor. Without government help, for example, the child poverty rates in the United States and France would be about equal. Through its governmental programs, France has reduced the rate to just over 7 percent. Through its welfare programs, the United States reduces the rate only somewhat.

Child poverty in the United States is made worse by the relatively large number of single-parent families, although Sweden, which has a similarly large number of such families, has one of the world's lowest rates of child poverty.

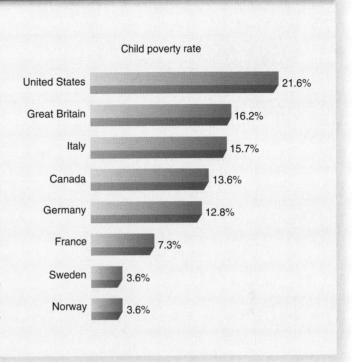

Child poverty rate

United States	21.6%
Great Britain	16.2%
Italy	15.7%
Canada	13.6%
Germany	12.8%
France	7.3%
Sweden	3.6%
Norway	3.6%

Source: OECD, 2008. Figures are from various years depending on the availability of country-level data.

are poor only for a while, and then for reasons largely beyond individual control—such as a job layoff or desertion by the father—rather than because they prefer not to work.[6] When the U.S. economy goes into a tailspin, the impact devastates many families. The U.S. Department of Labor estimated in early 2008 that the pending economic recession could eventually cause several million workers to lose their jobs. Moreover, a full-time job does not guarantee that a family will rise above the poverty line. A family of four with one employed adult who works forty hours a week at $7 an hour (roughly the minimum wage) has an annual income of about $14,000, which is $6,000 below the poverty line. Millions of Americans—mostly household workers, service workers, unskilled laborers, and farmworkers—are in this position. The U.S. Bureau of Labor Statistics estimates that roughly 10 percent of full-time workers do not earn enough to lift their family above the poverty line.[7]

The Politics and Policies of Social Welfare

At one time in the nation's history, the federal government was not involved in social welfare policy. Poverty and other welfare problems were deemed to fall within the powers reserved to the states by the Tenth Amendment and to be adequately addressed by them, even though they did not offer substantial welfare services. Individuals were expected to fend for themselves, and those unable to do so were usually supported by relatives and friends. This approach reflected the idea of **negative government,** which holds that government governs best by staying out of people's lives, giving them as much freedom as possible to determine their own pursuits and encouraging them to become self-reliant.

negative government

The philosophical belief that government governs best by staying out of people's lives, giving individuals as much freedom as possible to determine their own pursuits.

HISTORICAL
Background

LYNDON B. JOHNSON
(1908–1973)

Aside from Franklin D. Roosevelt, no American left a larger social welfare legacy than President Lyndon B. Johnson. LBJ's Great Society programs include Medicare and Medicaid, as well as increased federal spending in areas such as education, childhood nutrition, and poverty alleviation. A Democrat from Texas, Johnson served first in the House of Representatives and then in the Senate, where he quickly rose through the ranks to become Senate majority leader in the 1950s. In 1960, John F. Kennedy picked Johnson to be his running mate, hoping that Johnson could deliver Texas to the Democratic column. Texas did vote Democratic, which gave Kennedy a narrow victory in the Electoral College. Ascending to the presidency when Kennedy was assassinated in 1963, Johnson won a landslide election victory in 1964. Backed by huge Democratic majorities in Congress, he then won enactment of his Great Society programs. Johnson was also instrumental in passage of the 1964 Civil Rights Act and the 1965 Voting Rights Act. He had grown up in a poor area of Texas, which contributed to his desire to use government to help the disadvantaged. However, Johnson also presided over the escalation of the Vietnam War, which tarnished his legacy. He had intended to seek reelection in 1968, and likely would have won a narrow victory, but the war had created a deep split within the Democratic Party. In a nationally televised speech, Johnson announced he would not seek or accept his party's 1968 presidential nomination, saying he intended to devote the remainder of his presidency to ending the Vietnam War. The goal eluded him, and he returned to Texas, where he died of a heart attack shortly before his successor, Richard Nixon, concluded a truce ending U.S. involvement in Vietnam.

The Great Depression changed that outlook. The unemployment level reached 25 percent, and many of those with jobs were working for pennies. Americans looked to the federal government for help. Franklin D. Roosevelt's New Deal brought economic relief in the form of public jobs and assistance programs and changed opinions about the federal government's welfare role.[8] This new attitude reflected a faith in **positive government**—the idea that government intervention is necessary in order to enhance personal liberty and security when individuals are buffeted by economic and social forces beyond their control.

Not all Americans of the 1930s embraced the new philosophy. Most Republican leaders and loyalists clung to traditional ideas about self-reliance and free markets. Democrats spearheaded the change. The key vote in the House of Representatives on the Social Security Act of 1935, for example, had 85 percent of Democrats voting in favor of it and 99 percent of Republicans voting against it.[9]

Republicans gradually came to accept the idea that the federal government has a role in social welfare but argued that the role should be kept as small as practicable. Thus, in the 1960s, Republican opposition to President Lyndon Johnson's Great Society was substantial. His programs included federal initiatives in health care, education, public housing, nutrition, and other areas traditionally dominated by state and local governments. More than 70 percent of congressional Republicans voted against the 1965 Medicare and Medicaid programs, which provide government-paid medical assistance for the elderly and the poor.

In contrast, the 1996 Welfare Reform Act, which was designed to cut welfare rolls and costs, had the overwhelming support of congressional Republicans, while a majority of congressional Democrats voted against it. Republicans embraced it because it limited the time that recipients would be eligible to receive welfare benefits and because it gave the states greater control over the welfare program.

Although the Republican and Democratic parties have been at odds on social welfare issues, they have also had reason to work together. Millions of Americans depend on the federal government to provide benefits to ease the loss of income caused by retirement, disability, unemployment, and the like. Some social welfare spending, such as federal grants for health research, benefits society broadly. Other spending directly helps individuals. **Transfer payments** are government benefits given directly to individual recipients, such as the monthly social security checks that retirees receive. Most programs that support individuals are

---

positive government

The philosophical belief that government intervention is necessary in order to enhance personal liberty and security when individuals are buffeted by economic and social forces beyond their control.

transfer payments

Government benefits that are given directly to individuals, as in the case of social security payments to retirees.

Social security benefits make it possible for many elderly Americans to maintain a secure, independent retirement.

entitlement programs, meaning that any individual who meets the criteria for eligibility is entitled to the benefit. For example, upon reaching the legal retirement age, any senior citizen who has paid social security taxes for the required amount of time is entitled to receive social security benefits. In this sense, entitlement programs have the same force of law as taxes. Just as individuals are required by law to pay taxes on the income they earn, they are entitled by law to receive government benefits for which they qualify.

Individual-benefit programs fall into two broad groups: social insurance programs and public assistance programs. Social insurance programs enjoy broader public support, are more heavily funded, and provide benefits to individuals of all income levels. Public assistance programs have less public support, receive less funding, and are restricted to people of low income. The next two sections discuss these two types of programs.

entitlement programs

Any of a number of individual-benefit programs, such as social security, that require government to provide a designated benefit to any person who meets the legally defined criteria for eligibility.

Social Insurance Programs

More than 40 million Americans receive monthly benefits from social insurance programs—including social security, Medicare, unemployment insurance, and workers' compensation. The two major programs, social security and Medicare, cost the federal government more than $800 billion per year. Such programs are labeled **social insurance** because eligibility is restricted to individuals who paid special payroll taxes during their working years.

Social Security

The main social insurance program is social security for retirees. The program began with passage of the Social Security Act of 1935 and is funded through payroll taxes on employees and employers (currently set at 6.2 percent). Franklin D. Roosevelt emphasized that retiring workers would receive an insurance benefit that they had earned through their payroll taxes, not a handout from the government. In part because of this method of financing, the social security program has broad public support.[10] Opinion polls indicate that the large majority of Americans favor current or higher levels of social security benefits for the

social insurance

Social welfare programs based on the "insurance" concept, requiring that individuals pay into the program in order to be eligible to receive funds from it. An example is social security for retired people.

elderly. Social security is one of the few welfare programs run entirely by the federal government. Washington collects the payroll taxes that fund the program and sends monthly checks directly to the nearly 40 million social security recipients, who receive on average about $1,000 a month.

Although people qualify for social security by paying payroll taxes during their working years, the money they receive upon retirement is funded by payroll taxes on current workers' salaries. This arrangement poses a long-term threat to the viability of the social security program because people are living longer than they once did. Three decades from now, about one in five Americans will be over age sixty-five, at which time—unless changes are made in the social security program—there will not be enough workers to pay for retiree benefits.

In 2005, President George W. Bush proposed a partial privatization of social security as an answer to the long-term problem. Workers would have been allowed to place roughly a third of social security tax payments into private, individual stock market accounts. Bush claimed that individuals would get a greater return on their money through the stock market, thereby reducing what government would need to pay when workers retired. Bush's proposal was attacked by congressional Democrats and by powerful groups including the American Association of Retired Persons (AARP), who argued that Bush's proposal would expose retirees to the risks of the stock market. Critics also said that the Bush plan would make the solvency problem worse, not better. Payroll taxes that otherwise would have been used to offset payments to retirees would have been diverted into private accounts. Bush's plan failed to win congressional approval, but a need to overhaul social security remains. At some point, as happened in the 1980s, a bipartisan commission is likely to be formed to develop a compromise solution that will preserve America's commitment to its elderly retirees.

Unemployment Insurance

The 1935 Social Security Act provides for unemployment benefits for workers who lose their jobs involuntarily. Unemployment insurance is a joint federal-state program. The federal government collects the payroll taxes that fund unemployment benefits, but states have the option of deciding whether the taxes will be paid by both employees and employers or by employers only (most states use the latter option). Individual states also set the tax rate, conditions of eligibility, and benefit level, subject to minimum standards established by the federal government. Although unemployment benefits vary widely among states, they average $350 a week, somewhat more than a third of what an average worker makes while employed. The benefits in most cases are terminated after twenty-six to thirty-nine weeks.

The unemployment program does not have the broad public support that social security enjoys. This situation reflects the widespread assumption that the loss of a job, or the failure to find a new one right away, is often a personal failing. Unemployment statistics indicate otherwise. For example, U.S. Bureau of Labor statistics reveal that of those workers who lost their jobs in 2001, only 13 percent were fired or quit voluntarily. The rest became unemployed because of either a temporary layoff or the permanent elimination of a job position.

Medicare

After World War II, most European democracies created government-paid health care systems, and President Harry Truman, a Democrat, proposed a similar program for Americans. The American Medical Association (AMA) called Truman's plan "un-American" and vowed to mobilize local physicians to campaign against members of Congress who supported "socialized medicine." Truman's proposal never came to a vote in Congress. In 1961, President John F. Kennedy, also a Democrat, proposed a health care program restricted to social security recipients, but the AMA, the insurance industry, and congressional conservatives succeeded in blocking the plan.[11]

The 1964 elections swept a tide of liberal Democrats into Congress, and the result was Medicare. Enacted in 1965, the program provides medical assistance to retirees and is funded primarily through payroll taxes. Medicare is based on the insurance principle, and because of this, it has gained as much public support as social security. Medicare does not cover all hospital, nursing home, or physicians' fees, but enrollees in the program have the option of paying an insurance premium for fuller coverage of these fees. Enrollees who cannot afford the additional premium can apply to have the government pay it. In 2006, a prescription drug benefit was added to the Medicare program, though it has restrictions that limit the benefits primarily to retirees who either are too poor to afford prescription drugs or have very high prescription drug costs. Retirees not in these categories receive a small benefit from the program but are required to pay most of the cost of their prescription drugs.

At some point soon, Congress will have to overhaul the Medicare program. The rising cost of medical care and the growing number of elderly have combined to threaten the solvency of the program; it is projected to run out of money within a decade unless new revenues and cost-cutting measures are devised. Among the options under consideration are increased payroll taxes, more cost sharing by recipients, more use of managed-care options, and reductions in government payments to doctors and hospitals.

Public Assistance Programs

Unlike social insurance programs, **public assistance** programs are funded through general tax revenues and are available only to the financially needy. Eligibility for these programs is established by a **means test;** that is, applicants must prove that they are poor enough to qualify for the benefit. Once they have done so, they are entitled to the benefit, unless their personal situation changes or government legislates different eligibility criteria. These programs often are referred to as "welfare," and the recipients as "welfare cases."

Americans are far less supportive of public assistance programs than they are of social insurance programs. Americans tend to look upon social insurance benefits as having been "earned" by the recipient, while they see public assistance benefits as "handouts." Because of their individualistic culture, Americans are less inclined than Europeans to believe that government should provide substantial help to the poor (see Figure 16-2). Support for public assistance programs also is weakened by Americans' perception that the government is already spending vast amounts on welfare. A poll found that Americans believe public assistance programs to be the second costliest item in the federal budget. These programs actually rank much farther down the list. In fact, the federal government spends hundreds of billions of dollars more on its two major social insurance programs—social security and Medicare—than it does on all public assistance programs combined.

public assistance
A term that refers to social welfare programs funded through general tax revenues and available only to the financially needy. Eligibility for such a program is established by a means test.

means test
The requirement that applicants for public assistance must demonstrate that they are poor in order to be eligible for the assistance.

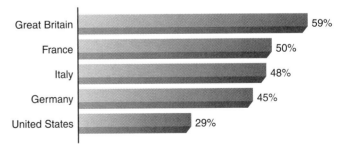

FIGURE 16-2 **Opinions on Government's Responsibility for the Poor** Compared to Europeans, Americans are much less likely to believe that government has a responsibility for the poor.
Source: The Pew Research Center for the People and the Press, Global Attitudes Survey, 2002.

Supplemental Security Income (SSI) is a combined federal-state program that provides public assistance to the disabled.

Supplemental Security Income

A major public assistance program is Supplemental Security Income (SSI), which originated as federal assistance to the blind and elderly poor as part of the Social Security Act of 1935. By the 1930s, most states had begun or were considering such programs. Although the federal legislation was designed to replace their efforts, the states have retained a measure of control over benefits and eligibility and are required to provide some of the funding. Because SSI recipients (who now include the disabled in addition to the blind and elderly poor) have obvious reasons for their inability to provide fully for themselves, this public assistance program is not widely criticized.

Temporary Assistance for Needy Families (TANF)

Before passage of the 1996 Welfare Reform Act (discussed in the chapter's introduction), needy American families had an open-ended guarantee of cash assistance. As long as their income was below a certain level, they were assured of government support. The program (Aid for Families with Dependent Children, or AFDC for short) was created in the 1930s as survivors' insurance to assist children whose fathers had died prematurely. Relatively small at the outset, the program became controversial as Americans increasingly linked it to welfare dependency and irresponsibility. AFDC was an entitlement program, which meant that any single parent (and in some states two parents) living in poverty could claim the benefit and keep it for as long as a dependent child was in the household. Some AFDC recipients were content to live on this assistance, and in some cases their children also grew up to become AFDC recipients, creating what was called "a vicious cycle of poverty." By 1995, AFDC was supporting 14 million Americans at an annual cost of more than $15 billion.

The 1996 Welfare Reform Act abolished AFDC, replacing it with the program titled Temporary Assistance for Needy Families (TANF). TANF's goal is to reduce long-term welfare dependency by limiting the length of time recipients can receive assistance and by giving the states an incentive to place welfare recipients into jobs. Each state is given an annual federal bloc grant that it uses to help poor families meet their subsistence needs and to develop programs that will help the parents find employment. The state programs operate within strict federal guidelines, including the following:

- Americans' eligibility for federal cash assistance is limited to no more than five years in their lifetime.
- Within two years, the head of most families on welfare must find work or risk the loss of benefits.
- Unmarried teenage mothers qualify for welfare benefits only if they remain in school and live with a parent or legal guardian.
- Single mothers lose a portion of their benefits if they refuse to cooperate in identifying for child support purposes the father of their children.

Although states can grant exceptions to some of the rules (for example, an unmarried teenage mother who faces sexual abuse at home is permitted to live elsewhere), the exceptions are limited. States can even choose to impose more restrictive rules in some areas. For example, states have the option of denying increased benefits to unwed mothers who give birth to another child.

So far, TANF has been relatively successful. The percentage of families on public assistance has declined significantly since passage of the 1996 Welfare Reform Act. The biggest challenge facing the states has been creating welfare-to-work programs that qualify people for jobs secure enough to free them from welfare dependency. Most welfare recipients who have found employment since 1996 had enough skills that they required little or no job training from the state. In contrast, most of those who have been unable to find long-term employment have limited education and few job-related skills.[12]

Food Stamps

The Food Stamps program, which took its present form in 1961, is fully funded by the federal government. The program provides an **in-kind benefit**—not cash, but food stamps that can be spent only on grocery items.

Food stamps are available only to people who qualify on the basis of low income. The program is intended to improve the nutrition of poor families by enabling them to purchase qualified items—mainly foodstuffs—with food stamps. Some critics say that food stamps stigmatize their users by making it obvious to onlookers in the checkout line that they are "welfare cases." More prevalent criticisms are that the program is too costly and that too many undeserving people receive food stamps.

in-kind benefit
A government benefit that is a cash equivalent, such as food stamps or rent vouchers. This form of benefit ensures that recipients will use public assistance in a specified way.

Subsidized Housing

Low-income persons are also eligible for subsidized housing. Most of the federal spending in this area is on rent vouchers, an in-kind benefit. The government gives the individual a monthly rent payment voucher, which the individual gives in lieu of cash to the landlord, who then hands the voucher over to the government in exchange for cash. About 5 million households annually receive a federal housing subsidy.

The U.S. government spends much less on public housing than it gives in tax breaks to homeowners, most of whom are middle- and upper-income Americans. Homeowners are allowed tax deductions for their mortgage interest payments and their local property tax payments. The total of these tax concessions is three times as much as is spent by the federal government on housing for low-income families.

Medicaid

When Medicare, the health care program for the elderly, was created in 1965, Congress also established Medicaid, which provides health care for poor people who are already on welfare. It is considered a public assistance program, rather than a social insurance program like Medicare, because it is based on need and funded by general tax revenues. Roughly 60 percent of Medicaid funding is provided by the federal government, and about 40 percent by the states. More than 20 million Americans receive Medicaid assistance.

Medicaid is controversial because of its costs. As health care costs have spiraled far ahead of the inflation rate, so have the costs of Medicaid. It absorbs roughly half of all public assistance dollars spent by the U.S. government and has forced state and local governments to cut other services to meet their share of the costs. "It's killing us" is how one local official described the impact of Medicaid on his community's budget.[13] As is true of other public assistance programs, Medicaid has been criticized for supposedly helping too many people who could take care of themselves if they tried harder. This belief is contradicted, ironically, by the situation faced by many working Americans. There are roughly 45 million Americans living in families with incomes that are too high to qualify them for Medicaid but too low to cover the cost of health insurance.[14]

Culture, Welfare, and Income

Surveys repeatedly show that most Americans are convinced that people on welfare could get along without it if they tried. As a consequence, there is constant political pressure to reduce welfare expenditures and to weed out undeserving recipients. The result is a welfare system that is both inefficient, in that much of the money spent on welfare never reaches the intended recipients, and inequitable, in that less than half of social welfare spending goes to the people who need it the most.[15]

Inefficiency and Inequity

The United States has the most inefficient welfare system in the Western world. Because of the unwritten principle that the individual must somehow earn or be in absolute need of assistance, the U.S. welfare system is heavily bureaucratic. For example, the 1996 Welfare Reform Act—which limits eligibility to families with incomes below a certain level and, in most instances, to families with a single parent living in the home—requires that the eligibility of each applicant be checked periodically by a caseworker. This procedure makes such programs doubly expensive; in addition to making payments to recipients, the programs must pay local caseworkers, supervisors, and support staffs (see Figure 16-3). These costs do not include the costs of the state and federal agencies that oversee the programs.

The bureaucratic costs of welfare are substantially lower in Europe because most European countries have unitary rather than federal systems, which eliminates a layer of government, and also because eligibility is more often universal, as in the case of government-paid health care. Caseworkers do not have to pore over records to determine who is and who is not eligible for medical treatment—everyone is.[16]

European welfare programs are also more equitable in the sense that the major beneficiaries are those individuals most in need, unlike the case in the United States. The federal government spends far more on social security and Medicare, which assist rich and poor alike, than it spends in total on all public assistance programs, which help only the needy. Of course, social insurance

FIGURE 16-3 The Cumbersome Administrative Process by Which Welfare Recipients Receive Their Benefits

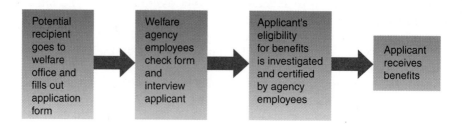

Potential recipient goes to welfare office and fills out application form → Welfare agency employees check form and interview applicant → Applicant's eligibility for benefits is investigated and certified by agency employees → Applicant receives benefits

programs do help many who are needy. Monthly social security checks keep millions of Americans, mostly widows, out of poverty; about one-fourth of America's elderly have no significant monthly income aside from what they receive from social security. Nevertheless, families in the top fifth of the income population receive more in federal social insurance benefits than is spent on TANF, food stamps, and housing subsidies combined.

Income and Tax Measures

The American political culture's emphasis on individualism is also evident in its tax and income policies. Economic redistribution—the shifting of money from the more affluent to the less affluent—is an aspect of these policies, but it is a relatively small component.

The United States has substantial income inequality (see Figure 16-4). Americans in the top fifth by income receive half of total U.S. income, while those in the bottom fifth get less than a twentieth. The imbalance is greater than that in any other industrialized democracy. One reason is that income taxes are not used for economic redistribution to the extent that they are in other democracies. In 2008, the top tax rate in the United States was 35 percent and applied to net income above $335,000. Income below that level is taxed at lower rates. Thus, a taxpayer with a net income of $500,000 pays the 35 percent rate on the amount above $335,000 and lower rates on the rest. In Europe, a top rate of 50 percent is not uncommon, and the top rate starts at a lower income level than in the United States.

The U.S. tax code also includes tax breaks for upper-income individuals, such as the deduction for mortgage interest on a vacation home. Moreover, the well-to-do escape social security taxes on a large part of their income. The social security tax is a flat rate of about 6 percent that begins with the first dollar earned and stops completely after roughly $100,000 in earnings. Thus, individuals earning less than $100,000 pay social security taxes on every dollar they make, while those earning more than $100,000 pay no social security taxes on the dollars they make over this amount.

The net result is that the **effective tax rate** (the actual percentage of a person's income spent to pay taxes) of high- and middle-income Americans is not greatly different. When all taxes (including personal income taxes, social security taxes, state sales taxes, and local property taxes) are combined, the average American family's effective tax rate is about three-fourths that of a family with an income over a million dollars. In Europe, where tax breaks for the well-to-do are few, the effective tax rate for high-income taxpayers is substantially greater than that for average taxpayers.[17] Of course, although well-to-do Americans pay relatively low taxes, the fact that they earn a lot of money means that they contribute the large share of tax revenues in absolute dollars. The top 10 percent of U.S. earners pay about half the personal income taxes received by the federal government. On the other hand, they keep much more of what they earn than do high-income taxpayers elsewhere.

In recent decades, taxes on the wealthy have been reduced considerably, a development that began during the Reagan administration and continued under George W. Bush. Arguing that high taxes on the wealthy stunted economic growth (see Chapter 15), Bush persuaded Congress to enact phased-in tax cuts

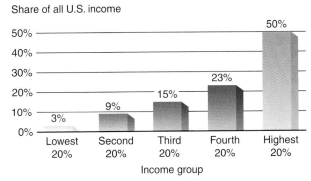

FIGURE 16-4 **Income Inequality in the United States**
The United States has the highest degree of income inequality of any industrialized democracy. Citizens in the top fifth by income get half of all income; those in the bottom fifth get less than a twentieth of all income.
Source: U.S. Bureau of the Census, 2006.

effective tax rate

The actual percentage of a person's income that is spent to pay taxes.

One of the many ironies of U.S. social welfare policy is that tax deductions for home mortgages for the middle and upper classes are government subsidies, just as are rent vouchers for the poor, but only the latter are stigmatized as a government "handout."

that sharply reduced taxes on high incomes. Capital-gains taxes were slashed, and marginal tax rates on personal income were reduced. The savings to Americans in the top 1 percent of income is $54,493 per year, compared with an average of $67 for those in the bottom 20 percent and $611 for those in the middle 20 percent. In terms of total dollars, less than 1 percent of the cuts are for those in the bottom fifth by income, while those in the middle fifth get 8 percent of the cuts and those in the top fifth receive 75 percent of the cuts.[18]

Portions of this tax cut are scheduled to be phased out in 2010 unless Congress decides to renew them, which made them an issue in the 2008 presidential campaign. Democratic nominee Barack Obama came out against renewal of the tax cuts, saying that they benefited the wealthy at the expense of the middle class. Republican nominee John McCain supported renewal, saying that continuation of the tax cuts would spur economic growth.

Although America's wealthiest individuals have been the major beneficiaries of recent tax policy, the nation's poorest working families have also received tax relief through the Earned Income Tax Credit (EITC). One of Democrat Bill Clinton's first acts as president was to expand EITC eligibility, and today, about 10 million low-income American families receive an EITC payment each year. The maximum yearly payment to any family is roughly $4,500, and eligibility is limited to families that include a wage earner. EITC payments occur when the wage earner files a personal income tax return. Those whose incomes are low enough receive an EITC payment, the amount of which depends on the level of their income and whether they have dependents. The EITC program is now the federal government's largest means-tested cash assistance program. According to U.S. Census Bureau calculations, the EITC lifts about a third of low-income Americans above the poverty line. Moreover, because EITC payments are based on income tax returns, the program does not require a costly bureaucracy of caseworkers. EITC payments are processed at the same time and in the same way as tax refunds for employees who have paid too much in withholding.

DEBATING THE ISSUES

ARE TAX CUTS FOR HIGH-INCOME TAXPAYERS GOOD FOR AMERICA?

Few issues spark more controversy than taxes. When a tax cut is at issue, the debate is usually over how the cut is to be divided. Supply-side economists have a unique answer to the question: those taxpayers who are personally least in need of tax relief are the ones who should get the largest share of the cut. Supply-side theory holds that high-income taxpayers will invest their extra income, thus boosting the economy and, along with the economy, the fortunes of everyone else. It is this argument that the Heritage Foundation's Daniel Mitchell makes below in support of President George W. Bush's supply-side tax initiatives, which substantially cut taxes for America's wealthier citizens. Among the critics of the Bush tax program was Warren Buffett, one of America's richest people. Buffett called Bush's tax program "voodoo economics"—a term he borrowed from debates over the same issue in the 1980s. In his argument below, Buffett rejects both the logic and the symbolism of supply-side economics.

YES Pro-growth tax cuts are an important part of fiscal discipline. They take money out of Washington, thereby removing the temptation to spend tax dollars on programs that are wasteful, duplicative, or counterproductive. . . . Any money the government gives to one person must first be taken from someone else. This Keynesian approach—attempting to boost the economy by giving people more money to spend—makes sense only if one assumes that the money distributed by the government for tax relief or new spending materializes out of thin air. The essential insight of supply-side economics is that the right kind of tax cuts will help an economy by increasing incentives to work, save, and invest. This relationship is the reason why President Reagan's across-the-board reductions in marginal tax rates resulted in nearly 20 years of above-average economic performance. President Bush's . . . tax cut package seeks to reduce the tax penalty on productive behavior, so there is every reason to think it would yield significant benefits as well. . . . People invest in the expectation of earning after-tax income. . . . The argument for supply-side tax policy is simple: Lowering tax rates on productive behavior will improve the incentives to work, save, and invest.

—*Daniel J. Mitchell, senior fellow, Heritage Foundation*

NO [These tax cuts] supply major aid to the rich in their pursuit of even greater wealth. . . . Administration officials say that the $310 million suddenly added to my wallet would stimulate the economy because I would invest it and thereby create jobs. But they conveniently forget that if Berkshire [Buffett's investment company] kept the money, it would invest that same amount, creating jobs as well. . . . Instead, give reductions to those who both need and will spend the money gained. Enact a Social Security tax "holiday" or give a flat-sum rebate to people with low incomes. Putting $1,000 in the pockets of 310,000 families with urgent needs is going to provide far more stimulus to the economy than putting the same $310 million in my pockets. When you listen to tax-cut rhetoric, remember that giving one class of taxpayer a "break" requires—now or down the line—that an equivalent burden be imposed on other parties. In other words, if I get a break, someone else pays. Government can't deliver a free lunch to the country as a whole. It can, however, determine who pays for lunch. And last week the [government] handed the bill to the wrong party.

—*Warren Buffett, chief executive officer, Berkshire Hathaway, Inc.*

Education as Equality of Opportunity

Although the Earned Income Tax Credit is subject to budgetary and political pressures, it enjoys more support than most assistance programs. The reason is simple: EITC is tied to employment. Only those who work are eligible to receive the payment. Polls that span more than a half century reveal that Americans have consistently favored work-based assistance to welfare payments as the answer to poverty. Work is believed to foster initiative and accountability; welfare "handouts" are believed to breed dependency and irresponsibility.

At the same time, Americans believe that people should have a fighting chance to succeed in the job market. Although few Americans would support economic equality for all, most Americans endorse the principle of **equality of opportunity**—the idea that people should have a reasonable chance to succeed

equality of opportunity

The idea that all individuals should be given an equal chance to succeed on their own.

if they make the effort. The concept includes a commitment to equality in the narrow sense that everyone should have a fair chance to get ahead. But it is a form of equality shaped by liberty because the outcome—personal success or personal failure—depends on what individuals do with that opportunity. The expectation is that people will end up differently—some will make a good living and some will be poor. It is sometimes said that equality of opportunity gives individuals an equal chance to become unequal.

Equality of opportunity is an ideal. Americans obviously do not start life on an equal footing. It was said of one successful American politician, whose father before him was a successful politician and a millionaire, that "he was born on third base and thought he hit a triple."[19] Some Americans are born into privilege, and others start life in such abject poverty that they realistically have no chance of escaping it. Nonetheless, equality of opportunity is more than a catchphrase. It is the philosophical basis for a number of government programs, none more so than public education.

Public Education: Leveling Through the Schools

During the nation's first century, the question of a free education for all children was a divisive issue. Wealthy interests feared that an educated public would challenge their power. Egalitarians, on the other hand, saw education as a means of enabling ordinary people to get ahead. The egalitarians won out. Public schools sprang up in nearly every community and were open free of charge to children who could attend.[20]

Today, as discussed in Chapter 1, the United States invests more heavily in public education at all levels than does any other country. The curriculum in American schools is also relatively standardized. Unlike those countries that divide children even at the grade school level into different tracks that lead ultimately to different occupations, the United States aims to educate all children in essentially the same way. Of course, public education is not a uniform experience for American children. The quality of education depends significantly on the wealth of the community in which a child resides. The Supreme Court has upheld this arrangement, saying that states are obliged to give all children an "adequate" education as opposed to an "equal" one across all communities.

The United States does have a federal education program, Head Start, dedicated to helping poor children. Established in the 1960s during the Johnson administration, it provides preschool education to low-income children in order to help them succeed when they begin kindergarten. At no time in its history, however, has the Head Start program been funded at a level that would allow all eligible children to participate. The low point was reached in the 1980s, when there was only enough money to allow the enrollment of one in ten of those eligible. Today, less than half of all eligible children get to participate.

Nevertheless, the United States through its public schools educates a broad segment of the population. Arguably, no country in the world has made an equivalent effort to give children, whatever their parents' background, an equal opportunity in life through education. Per-pupil spending on public elementary and secondary schools is

Shown here is a teacher with one of her students at a Head Start program in Athens, Georgia.

POLITICAL
CULTURE

LIBERTY, EQUALITY, AND SELF-GOVERNMENT

Public Education

Public education has never been a uniform experience for American children. Cities in the late nineteenth century neglected the education of many immigrant children, who were thereby placed at a permanent disadvantage. During the first half of the twentieth century, southern public schools for black children were designed to keep them down, not lift them up. Today, many children in poorer neighborhoods attend overcrowded, understaffed, and underfunded public schools. Nevertheless, the nation's public schools have been the primary means by which Americans of all nationalities, colors, creeds, and income levels have been brought together. At no time in most Americans' lives are they as thoroughly immersed in a socially diverse environment as when, as children and adolescents, they attend public schools.

America's broad-based system of public education stems from a melding of its egalitarian and individualistic traditions. Leon Sampson, a nineteenth-century socialist, noted the stark difference between the philosophy of public education in the United States and that in Europe. "The European ruling classes," he wrote, "were open in their contempt for the proletariat. But in the United States equality, and even classlessness, the creation of wealth for all and political liberty were extolled in the public schools." Sampson concluded that American schools embodied a unique conception of equality. Everyone was being trained in much the same way so that each person would have the opportunity to succeed. "It is," he said, "a socialist conception of capitalism."

The making of one people out of many is fostered by the general philosophy of public education in America, which holds that students should share a common curriculum. A system that would seek instead to enhance the education of top students would work to the disadvantage of poor students and others who, for reasons of language or life circumstances, are less prepared to do well when they enter school. An elite-centered school system of the type found in some European societies would serve to widen the gap between the country's richer and poorer groups and to slow the assimilation into American society of its newer arrivals.

Of course, other institutions also contribute to the integration of American society, but no institution does it as well or as thoroughly as the public schools. This is not to say that the schools are mirrors of America's diversity. A great deal of ethnic, racial, and class segregation still exists in the schools. For example, in some suburban schools, few of the children come from families earning less than $75,000 a year. And in some urban schools, few of the children come from families earning more than $25,000 a year. Yet, were it not for public schools, America would be a substantially more stratified society, in terms of both one's classmates while in school and one's prospects for success after leaving school. Public education in America was called "the great leveler" when it began in the early nineteenth century. Since then it has earned that label. Rarely has a public institution served so many so well for such a long period.

roughly twice as high in the United States as it is in the nations of Western Europe. America's commitment to broad-based education extends to college. The United States is far and away the world leader in terms of the proportion of adults receiving a college education.[21]

The nation's education system preserves both the myth and the reality of an equal-opportunity society. The belief that success can be had by anyone who works for it could not be sustained if the education system were tailored for a privileged elite. And educational attainment is related to personal success, at least as measured by annual incomes. In fact, the gap in income between those with and those without a college education is greater now than at any time in the country's history.

Public School Issues

Because America's public schools play such a key role in creating an equal-opportunity society, they are closely scrutinized. Parents of schoolchildren are not shy about saying what they think of their local schools. Interestingly, parents tend to rate their own children's schools more highly than they rate other schools. A national survey found that two-thirds of parents gave their children's schools a grade of A or B but only a fourth gave the nation's schools as a whole a grade that high.[22]

The issues facing public schools are far-ranging. Disorder in the schools is a major issue in some communities. So is student performance on standardized tests—U.S. students do not even score in the top ten internationally on tests in science or math. Few policy issues are more contentious, however, than proposals to reallocate money among schools. School choice is one such issue. Under this policy, the public schools compete for students, and schools that attract the most students are rewarded with the largest budgets. Advocates of the policy claim that it forces school administrators and teachers to do a better job and gives students the option of leaving a school that is performing poorly.[23] Parents favor such a policy by a wide margin, unless their children are harmed by it. Poor children in particular often have little choice but to attend the nearest school because their parents are unable to transport them to a better but more distant school.[24]

School vouchers are a related issue. A voucher system allows parents to use tax dollars to keep their children out of the public schools entirely. Parents receive a voucher from the government that they can give to a private or parochial school to cover part of the cost of their child's tuition. Proponents say that vouchers force failing public schools to improve their instructional programs or face a permanent loss of revenue. Opponents, however, argue that vouchers weaken the public schools by siphoning off revenue and say that vouchers subsidize many families that would have sent their children to private or parochial schools anyway. They note that vouchers are of little use to students from poor families because they lack the additional money required to pay the full tuition costs at a nonpublic school.

Although the courts have upheld the constitutionality of vouchers in some circumstances, polls indicate that Americans are divided over whether they would like to see a universal voucher system.[25] The question gets majority support when it is framed in the context of choice among public schools but is opposed by the majority when private and parochial schools are included among the choices. The issue of vouchers reflects the tensions inherent in the concept of equal opportunity. Vouchers expand opportunity by increasing the number of choices available to students. Yet not all students are able to take advantage of the choices, and not all taxpayers want their tax dollars used to support private and parochial schools. (Another public school issue—uniform testing of all schoolchildren—is discussed in the next section.)

The Federal Role in Education: Political Differences

Education has traditionally been a state and local responsibility. Most school policies—from length of the school year to teachers' qualifications—are set by state legislatures and local school boards. Over 90 percent of the funds spent on schools are provided through state and local tax revenues.

Federal intervention in school policy has often been resisted by states and localities, as exemplified by their response to desegregation and busing directives (see Chapter 5). State and local governments have been less hesitant when it comes to federal education grants, but it is difficult to get congressional support for grant programs targeted at those schools that are most in need. Few members of Congress are willing to support large appropriations for education that do not benefit their constituents, a situation that has reduced Washington's contribution to a goal—quality education for every American child—that nearly every official endorses, at least in principle.

Indeed, not until 1965, with passage of the Higher Education Act and the Elementary and Secondary Education Act (part of President Lyndon Johnson's Great Society initiatives), did the federal government become involved in public

The Supreme Court has held that American children are entitled to an "adequate" education but do not have a right to an "equal" education. America's public schools differ greatly in quality primarily as a result of differences in the wealth of the communities they serve. Some public schools are overcrowded and have few facilities and little equipment. Others are very well equipped, have spacious facilities, and offer small class sizes.

education in a comprehensive way.[26] Earlier federal efforts in the area of education had been either one-time or targeted interventions. In 1862, for example, Congress passed the Morrill Act, which provided states with free tracts of land if they used the land to establish colleges—the nation's great "land-grant" universities are the product of that legislation. Another one-time federal program was the G.I. Bill, enacted after World War II, giving financial assistance to enable military veterans to attend college or vocational school.

With passage of the 1965 legislation, the federal government assumed an ongoing role in public education. Federal grants to public schools and colleges became a regular part of their funding, though still a smaller part than that provided by state and local governments (see Chapters 3 and 18). The Higher Education Act became the foundation for Pell Grants, federal loans to college students, and federally subsidized college work-study programs. The Elementary and Secondary Education Act provides funding for items such as school construction, textbooks, special education, and teacher training. Federal funding is split almost evenly between support for colleges and support for elementary and secondary schools.

In recent years, education has increasingly become an issue of national debate, involving Washington officials ever more deeply in the issues.[27] President Bill Clinton rejected the idea of unrestricted school choice, arguing that it would weaken the nation's public schools and make them a repository of America's poorest children. Clinton persuaded Congress instead to appropriate billions in new funding to enable overcrowded schools to hire tens of thousands of new teachers. President George W. Bush brought a different education agenda to the White House, persuading Congress in 2001 to enact the No Child Left Behind Act. The legislation requires national testing in reading, math, and science and ties federal funding to the test results. Schools that show no improvement in students' test scores after two years receive an increased amount of federal aid. If these schools show no improvement by the end of the third year, however, their students become eligible to transfer elsewhere, and their school's federal assistance is reduced.

Few federal education policies have provoked as much controversy as No Child Left Behind.[28] The National Education Association (NEA) claims that the law has forced teachers to teach to the national tests and thus has interfered with real learning in the classroom. Congressional Democrats say that the program has failed to provide struggling schools with enough funds to improve the quality of classroom education and has encouraged the flight of students from public to private schools. For their part, congressional Republicans have applauded the law, saying that it holds teachers and schools accountable for their students' performance. Congressman John Boehner (R-Ohio) said, "Money alone is not the answer to the problems facing our children's schools. High standards and accountability for results—not just spending—are the key to erasing the achievement gap in education."[29]

Some states and localities have embraced No Child Left Behind as an answer to underperforming schools. Some schools have, in fact, improved in terms of their performance on the national tests. Other places have opposed the act, saying that the federal government has not provided the funds necessary to fully implement the testing program. In the 2008 presidential campaign, Barack Obama said he backed full funding of NCLB while John McCain proposed to strengthen NCLB by getting rid of ineffective teachers and allowing students greater choice among schools. Opinion polls show that Americans are split nearly 50-50 on NCLB, with Republicans more supportive of it and Democrats less supportive.[30]

Thus, many of the partisan and philosophical differences that affect federal welfare policy also affect federal education policy. Democrats are more inclined to find the answer to how to improve schools in increased federal spending on education, particularly in less affluent communities, while Republicans are more inclined to look to marketlike mechanisms such as school choice and achievement tests.

The American Way of Promoting the General Welfare

All democratic societies promote economic security, but they do so in different ways and to different degrees. Economic security has a higher priority in European democracies than in the United States. European democracies have instituted programs such as government-paid health care for all citizens, compensation for all unemployed workers, and retirement benefits for all elderly citizens. As this chapter shows, the United States provides these benefits only to some citizens in each category. On the other hand, the American system of public education dwarfs those in Europe.

The American way of welfare was on display in the 2008 presidential election campaign. More than 40 million Americans do not have health insurance and do not qualify for Medicaid. Although both Barack Obama and John McCain spoke of a need to extend health care insurance to more people, neither candidate proposed anything like a European-style system. They focused instead on expanding employer-provided health care. Even if fully implemented, this approach would leave at least 15 million Americans without health insurance. Anything more substantial would risk the public and congressional rejection that President Bill Clinton encountered when he sought a near-universal health care system in 1993.

The differences between the European and American approaches to welfare stem from historical and cultural differences. Democracy in Europe developed in reaction to centuries of aristocratic rule, which brought the issue of economic privilege to the forefront. When strong labor and socialist parties then emerged as a consequence of industrialization, European democracies initiated sweeping social welfare programs designed to bring about greater economic equality. Social inequality was harder to root out because it was thoroughly embedded in European society, shaping everything from social manners to education. Private schools and university training were the preserve of the elite, a tradition that, though now past, continues to affect how Europeans think about educational opportunity.

The American historical experience is a different one. Democracy in America grew out of a tradition of limited government that emphasized personal liberty, which included a belief in self-reliance. This belief contributed to Americans' strong support for public education and their weak support for public assistance. Unlike political equality, the idea of economic equality never captured Americans' imagination. Try as they might during America's Industrial Age, labor and socialist parties were unable to gain large and loyal followings. Even today, when Americans think of the plight of poorer people, they are as likely to make moral judgments as political ones. Political scientists Stanley Feldman and John Zaller found that Americans' support for public assistance programs rests more on compassion for the poor than on an ideological belief in economic sharing.[31] Or, as the political scientist Robert Lane expressed it, Americans have a preference for market justice, meaning that they prefer that society's material benefits be allocated through the economic marketplace rather than through government policies.[32]

Summary   Self-Test www.mhhe.com/pattersontad9e

The United States has a complex social welfare system of multiple programs addressing specific welfare needs. Each program applies only to those individuals who qualify for benefits by meeting the specific eligibility criteria. In general, these criteria are designed to encourage self-reliance or, when help is necessary, to ensure that laziness is not rewarded or fostered. This approach to social welfare reflects Americans' traditional belief in individualism.

Poverty is a large and persistent problem in the United States. About one in nine Americans falls below the government-defined poverty line, including a disproportionate number of children, female-headed families, minority-group members, and rural and inner-city dwellers. The ranks of the poor are increased by economic recessions and are reduced through government assistance programs.

Welfare policy has been a partisan issue, with Democrats taking the lead on government programs to alleviate economic insecurity and Republicans acting to slow down or decentralize these initiatives. Changes in social welfare have usually resulted from presidential leadership in the context of public support for the change. Welfare policy traditionally has involved programs to provide jobs and job training, education programs, income measures, and especially transfer payments through individual-benefit programs.

Individual-benefit programs fall into two broad categories: social insurance and public assistance. The former includes programs such as social security for retired workers and Medicare for the elderly. Social insurance programs are funded by payroll taxes paid by potential recipients, who thus, in a sense, earn the benefits they later receive. Because of this arrangement, social insurance programs have broad public support. Public assistance programs, in contrast, are funded by general tax revenues and are targeted toward needy individuals and families. These programs are not controversial in principle; most Americans believe that government should assist the truly needy. However, because of a widespread belief that most welfare recipients could get along without assistance if they tried, these programs do not have universal public support, are only modestly funded, and are politically vulnerable.

Social welfare is a contentious issue. In one view, social welfare is too costly and assists too many people who could help themselves; another view holds that social welfare is not broad enough and that too many disadvantaged Americans live in poverty. Because of these irreconcilable differences and because of federalism and the widely shared view that welfare programs should target specific problems, the existing system of multiple programs, despite its administrative complexity and inefficiency, has been the only politically feasible solution.

The balance between economic equality and individualism tilts more heavily toward individualism in the United States than in other advanced industrialized democracies. Other democracies, for example, have government-paid health care for all citizens whereas the United States does not. Compared to other democracies, however, the United States attempts to more equally educate its children, a policy consistent with its cultural emphasis on equality of opportunity. Like social welfare, however, education is a contentious issue involving disputes over the federal government's role, school choice, spending levels, and mandatory testing.

Study Corner

Key Terms

effective tax rate (*p. 437*)
entitlement programs
(*p. 431*)
equality of opportunity
(*p. 439*)
in-kind benefit (*p. 435*)
means test (*p. 433*)

negative government
(*p. 429*)
positive government (*p. 430*)
poverty line (*p. 427*)
public assistance (*p. 433*)
social insurance (*p. 431*)
transfer payments (*p. 430*)

Self-Test

1. The shape of the U.S. welfare policy system has been strongly influenced by:
   a. the cultural emphasis placed on economic equality.
   b. the fact that the United States has a federal system of government.
   c. the fact that the United States is the wealthiest nation on earth and thus can afford the most generous benefit system.
   d. a and b only.

2. The 1996 Welfare Reform Act that Congress passed provides:
   a. an end to the federal guarantee of cash assistance to needy families.
   b. a limitation of five years in most cases for a person to receive assistance.
   c. that states must train and help welfare recipients find employment.
   d. all of the above.

3. Which of the following programs is based on the social insurance principle?
   a. subsidized housing
   b. unemployment benefits
   c. Medicaid
   d. food stamps

4. Regarding American education, all **except** which one of the following statements are true?
   a. The U.S. invests more heavily in public education than any other nation.
   b. U.S. law requires states to spend roughly equal amounts on each public school student, regardless of whether that student is going to school in a city, suburb, or rural area.
   c. Free public education provides a way that more people can gain the foundation for economic advantage.
   d. The curriculum in U.S. schools is relatively standardized on the assumption that children should be given an equal opportunity to get ahead in life.

5. Administrative costs of welfare are substantially lower in Europe than in the United States because:
   a. European eligibility is universal for certain programs, such as health care, and thus money does not have to be spent on the paperwork necessary to determine eligibility, which is the case in the United States.
   b. European eligibility for most programs is restricted to providing services to only the poorest 5 percent of the population.
   c. Europe has primarily unitary governments, which means they have to administer only one set of rules, rather than fifty different sets as is the case in the United States because of state involvement in social welfare programs.
   d. both a and c.

6. Regarding unemployment:
   a. according to research, the loss of a job or failure to immediately find a new job is in most cases the fault of the individual.
   b. U.S. Bureau of Labor statistics indicate that of those who have lost jobs, the large majority made the decision on their own to stop working rather than being terminated as part of a larger job layoff.
   c. government unemployment payments enjoy high levels of public support.
   d. none of the above.

7. The United States has one of the lowest poverty rates of any Western democracy. (T/F)

8. The Republican Party has initiated nearly all major federal welfare programs. (T/F)

9. Social security and Medicare have widespread public support because they cost less than other welfare programs. (T/F)

10. There is a wide gap in income levels between the top and bottom fifth of the American population. (T/F)

Critical Thinking

How has U.S. policy on welfare and education been influenced by Americans' belief in individualism? By America's federal system of government?

Suggested Readings

Alesina, Alberto, and Edward Glaeser. *Fighting Poverty in the U.S. and Europe: A World of Difference.* New York: Oxford University Press, 2006. A comparison of poverty policies in the United States and Europe.

Howard, Christopher. *The Welfare State Nobody Knows: Debunking Myths About U.S. Social Policy.* Princeton, N.J.: Princeton University Press, 2006. A critical assessment of the U.S. social welfare system.

Kornbluh, Felicia Ann. *The Battle for Welfare Rights: Politics and Poverty in Modern America.* Philadelphia: University of Pennsylvania Press, 2007. An analysis of welfare rights and conditions, with particular attention to the feminization of poverty.

Patterson, James T. *America's Struggle Against Poverty in the Twentieth Century.* Cambridge, Mass.: Harvard University Press, 2000. A careful study of poverty and its history.

Quadagno, Jill. *One Nation, Uninsured: Why the United States Has No National Health Insurance.* New York: Oxford University Press, 2005. A look at the politics of U.S. health care policy.

Reed, Douglas S. *On Equal Terms: The Constitutional Politics of Educational Opportunity.* Princeton, N.J.: Princeton University Press, 2003. An insightful analysis of school reform issues.

Spring, Joel H. *The American School 1642–2004: From the Puritans to No Child Left Behind.* New York: McGraw-Hill, 2008. A history of U.S. public schools.

Van Dunk, Emily, and Anneliese M. Dickman. *School Choice and the Question of Accountability.* New Haven, Conn.: Yale University Press, 2003. A careful look at the voucher system as applied in the Milwaukee school system.

List of Websites

http://www.doleta.gov/
The U.S. Department of Labor's website on the status of the welfare-to-work program, including state-by-state assessments.

http://www.nea.org/
The home page of the National Education Association; provides information on the organization's membership and policy goals.

http://www.os.dhhs.gov/
The website of the Department of Health and Human Services—the agency responsible for most federal social welfare programs.

http://www.npc.umich.edu
The website of the University of Michigan's National Poverty Center, which seeks to stimulate interest in policy issues and to transmit research findings to policymakers.

Participate!

When it comes to partisan politics, poverty is a contentious issue. Republicans and Democrats disagree mightily on the question of how far government should go in helping the poor. On the other hand, virtually all Americans—on the right and on the left—support private efforts to help the poor. Numerous local religious, civic, social, and economic groups run programs for the poor, such as food kitchens and clothing drives. Also, many national organizations work locally to assist the poor. An example is Habitat for Humanity, which builds modest houses with volunteer labor and then makes them available to low-income families, which assist in the construction and receive low-interest or no-interest mortgages to pay for the cost of construction materials. Consider volunteering some of your time to a group that gives a helping hand to those in need—whether a church or a community group or a nonprofit organization like Habitat for Humanity. Habitat for Humanity has a website that makes it easy for you to volunteer.

Extra Credit

For up-to-the-minute *New York Times* articles, interactive simulations, graphics, study tools, and more links and quizzes, visit the text's Online Learning Center at www.mhhe.com/pattersontad9e.

Self-Test Answers

1. b   2. d   3. b   4. b   5. d   6. d   7. F   8. F   9. F   10. T

National Journal

GLOBAL WARMING: FROM LUKEWARM TO HOT

Reps. Rick Boucher, D-Va., and Edward Markey, D-Mass., are two key players in the global-warming debate who have significantly different policy views, political styles, and legislative roles. But they've voiced surprising agreement that major action on the issue is increasingly likely this year, despite the conventional wisdom about holding off until a new president is in the White House.

"I think this is achievable" in 2008, said the low-profile Boucher, a moderate subcommittee chairman who emphasizes the need for bipartisan, industry-supported global-warming legislation. "Some Democrats would rather wait until 2009. Among the key reasons to act now are that we can have a U.S. position sooner in international negotiations. And industry is waiting for the rules before they make financial investment. The sooner we do that, the sooner we have a green industry to export to the rest of the world."

Markey, an often-fervent liberal whom Speaker Nancy Pelosi, D-Calif., tapped to promote wide-ranging legislation to address climate change, echoed the case for immediacy. "It's preferable to give everything that you can when you have the opportunity," he said. "The issue is too urgent to treat as an item on the political agenda."

Markey even suggested that President Bush could become part of an international breakthrough on global warming, akin to the bold strides on nuclear weapons reduction that President Reagan discussed with Soviet President Mikhail Gorbachev in 1986. Although those talks foundered, the summit was eventually seen as helping pave the way for a major arms treaty the following year. "The experts were dumbfounded when the Berlin Wall came down two years later," Markey said.

Most environmental groups contend that global-warming legislation is needed now because scientific research has shown that the problem has become more urgent. And political momentum has mounted considerably as the public has become more acutely aware of the threat, they argue. "There is no time for delay," Fred Krupp, the president of Environmental Defense, told a Senate hearing in November.

Still, the odds that Bush and the Democratic-controlled Congress will agree on a plan to reduce greenhouse gases seem at least as long as when Reagan and Gorbachev were trying to thaw the Cold War. The global-warming debate is highly complex, and the solutions would impose major costs on the public and on businesses. Plus, expectations are low for Congress getting much of anything.

The House has barely begun its legislative work on climate change, although the Senate is further along, after the Environment and Public Works Committee in December approved a comprehensive, bipartisan bill. Sponsored by Sens. Joe Lieberman, ID-Conn., and John Warner, R-Va., the legislation would cap greenhouse-gas emissions, provide emission allowances to polluters, and set up government auctions for a small portion of the allowances.

Proponents of the Lieberman-Warner bill face widespread skepticism that they can garner the 60 votes needed on the Senate floor to overcome hard-line foes. Although some prominent Republicans—including Sen. John McCain of Arizona and California Gov. Arnold Schwarzenegger—support global-warming legislation, many others in their party are dubious. A House GOP leadership aide dismissed the Senate measure as "focusing more on message than on substance," and added, "Republicans can show that Democrats are hitting consumers in the pocketbook without tangible benefit."

Barack Obama has endorsed similarly sweeping reductions in greenhouse gases. "I don't believe that climate change is just an issue that's convenient to bring up during a campaign," Obama said in an Iowa speech. "I believe it's one of the greatest moral challenges of our generation."

Some Republicans, though, contend that Democrats are poised to force what could become a fruitless debate merely to score political points. Legislative deadlock on global warming—either at the hands of filibustering Senate Republicans or a veto-wielding Bush—could provide fodder for Democrats' campaign attacks. But Pelosi's chief of staff, John Lawrence, brushed aside such talk of disingenuousness.

"We will try our best to send a bill to the president," Lawrence said in an interview. "We want a bill, not an issue."

Those who advocate action this year point to the bipartisan success on energy legislation—including the first statutory increase in automobile fuel-efficiency standards since 1975—that Bush signed into law on December 19.

Just a year ago, the prospects for that measure were bleak. Its backers didn't achieve all of their initial goals, but the effort showed Democratic leaders' deep commitment to reducing the nation's oil consumption and confronting global warming.

Pelosi, in particular, has been actively involved in making the environmental challenge what she calls her "flagship issue." At a pre-holiday roundtable discussion in her office, she reminded reporters, "Many people said to me" that the energy bill could not be done, and she described the result as "a Christmas present to the American people."

It showed that "change is possible," she asserted, while conceding that the next steps on climate change will be complicated.

Pelosi has not set a timetable for global-warming action this year. Key lawmakers are aware of "the imperative of getting it done," Lawrence said, and added that the speaker will likely discuss details with members soon after the House returns to work on January 15.

Pelosi could once again find herself at odds with the venerable House Energy and Commerce Committee Chairman John Dingell, D-Mich., a longtime auto-industry champion

whom she successfully steered toward supporting the tougher fuel-efficiency standards last year. He emphasized the challenges facing the global-warming legislation in a year-end conference call with reporters.

"Working with the administration has been very difficult for me," Dingell said. "I truthfully and honestly don't know" about the chances for a bill. He also contended that the enactment of last year's energy legislation makes it unlikely that Congress can impose additional demands on his home state's auto manufacturers. "We have now squeezed the auto industry just about as hard as I think we can," he said. "We're going to try to see to it that everybody makes their proper contribution."

Dingell seemed more upbeat about the legislative prospects on global warming. "The chances of moving the bill are good," he said. "The country wants it. The legislation is needed. Members are supportive." Dingell acknowledged that the issues will be tough to address and that "a high level of bipartisanship" will be required.

Scientific experts generally agree that U.S. greenhouse-gas emissions should be reduced by 60 to 80 percent from current levels by 2050. The Senate committee's highly prescriptive global-warming bill would achieve a roughly 70 percent goal for U.S. emissions. In the most broadly co-sponsored House legislation on the issue—whose chief sponsor is Rep. Henry Waxman, D-Calif.—the explicit goal is an 80 percent cut, although the measure largely delegates to the Environmental Protection Agency the steps to achieve that objective. According to Markey, the energy bill signed by Bush will achieve about 25 percent of the required reduction in emissions by 2030.

The debate over the 2007 energy bill offers insight into the potential stumbling

The global-warming debate is highly complex, and **the solutions would impose major costs** on the public and on businesses.

blocks that lie ahead on global-warming legislation. The Senate, heeding objections from Southern-based utility companies, rejected a House-passed plan to require utilities to produce a larger share of electric power from renewable sources. Markey contended that removing that provision significantly lowered the potential to cut greenhouse gases. He vowed that the issue will come up again this year, "forcing the Senate to be accountable."

One of the leading foes of the renewable-fuels requirements for utilities was Boucher, who led the opposition to the House's 220–190 passage of that amendment during the August debate. "Wind and solar energy are less available in the South," said Boucher, who represents a rural western Virginia district where coal is king. "The proposal would require more taxes for our ratepayers and would not be a fair cost to impose." He noted that only 53 senators were willing to support the House-passed provision, seven votes short of what is needed to break a filibuster.

Boucher has focused on technologies to make coal cleaner and reduce pollution, and Pelosi and others have encouraged some of his proposals. He describes the looming climate-change measure as "the most complex legislation in the nation's history," in both substance and politics. He is seeking a consensus-driven approach and has conducted

extensive discussions with lawmakers and private-sector leaders. "I have spoken with everyone in the White House at every level of responsibility," Boucher added, but he would not disclose whether he had spoken with Bush.

Waxman, the No. 2 Democrat on Energy and Commerce who worked closely with Dingell in crafting the landmark 1990 Clean Air Act, is among those whom Boucher describes as an "essential" player on global warming. The two have had two lengthy meetings in Waxman's office on the prospective legislation. "I anticipate his support," Boucher said. "He and I have always had a very cordial relationship."

Waxman has a decidedly more liberal viewpoint in the global-warming debate, though he says he respects Boucher's work. "I have a very high regard for him," Waxman said in an interview. "He wants to develop a consensus proposal, though his goals are not as ambitious as mine. . . . My sense is that the American public is ready for strong legislation."

Waxman's history of contentious dealings with the Bush administration—including on energy issues—makes him somewhat more skeptical of chances for securing an agreement this year. "My view is that if we can get a strong bill, we should go for it," he said. He speculated, however, that some industry groups might prefer to resolve the issue with Bush in office this year, rather than face what likely would be more-rigorous demands from a Democratic president.

Should Congress actually get global-warming legislation near the finish line this fall, Boucher suggested that final action might require a lame-duck session after the election. If he and other proponents succeed in this campaign year, that would be an extraordinary result.

FOR DISCUSSION: Will a new generation of voters force Congress to pass comprehensive global-warming legislation? Should government compensate industries for complying with new global-warming regulations? Will comprehensive global-warming legislation prove too divisive to become law?

CHAPTER **17**

Foreign and Defense Policy
Protecting the American Way

The Roots of U.S. Foreign and Defense Policy

The Cold War Era
A New World Order
The War on Terrorism
The Iraq War

The Military Dimension of National Security Policy

Military Power, Uses, and Capabilities
The Politics of National Defense

The Economic Dimension of National Security Policy

Promoting Global Trade
Maintaining Access to Oil and Other Natural Resources
Assisting Developing Nations

A Challenging World

We the people of the United States, in order to . . . provide for the common defense . . . Preamble, U.S. Constitution

The leaders of eight of the world's most powerful nations met in Japan in 2008 for their annual G8 summit. The 2008 meeting, which was the final summit for President George W. Bush and the first for British Prime Minister Gordon Brown and Russian President Dmitry Medvedev, addressed a wide range of global issues. Climate change was on the agenda, as was the issue of sustainable energy supplies. A joint policy toward African economic development was also discussed, along with global trade and the protection of intellectual property rights. Iraq received only passing attention, although approaches to international terrorism and nuclear nonproliferation were areas of discussion.

As the G8 summit illustrates, national security is an issue of economic strength as well as of military power. The world's top leaders did not ignore the military threats existing in the world, but they concentrated on economic and related issues. The emphasis reflected a core reality: the goal of foreign policy includes the preservation of a nation's way of life as well as its physical security. In the case of the United States, this goal requires both a level of military readiness that will protect the United States and a level of marketplace vitality that will enable a society of 300 million people to thrive in an increasingly globalized economy.

National security, unlike other areas of government policy, rests on relations with actors outside rather than within the country. As a result, the chief instruments of national security policy differ substantially from those of domestic policy. One of these instruments is diplomacy—the process of negotiation between countries. The lead agency in U.S. diplomatic efforts is the Department of State, which is headed by the secretary of state and coordinates the efforts of U.S. embassies abroad, each of which is directed by a U.S. ambassador. American diplomacy also takes place through international organizations—such as the United Nations—to which the United States belongs. A second instrument of foreign policy is military power. The lead agency in military affairs is the Department of Defense, which is headed by the secretary of defense and oversees the three U.S. military branches—the Army, Navy, and Air Force. Here, too, the United States sometimes works through alliances, the most important of which is the North Atlantic Treaty Organization (NATO). NATO has nearly thirty member nations, including the United States, Canada, and most Western and Eastern European countries. A third instrument of world politics is intelligence gathering, or the process of monitoring other countries' activities. For many reasons, but primarily because all countries pursue their own self-interest, each nation keeps a watchful eye on other nations. In the United States, the task of intelligence gathering falls to specialized federal agencies including the Central Intelligence Agency (CIA) and the National Security Agency (NSA). Economic exchange, the fourth instrument of foreign affairs, involves both international trade and foreign aid. U.S. interests in this area are promoted by a range of U.S. agencies, such as the Agriculture, Commerce, Labor, and Treasury Departments, as well as specialty agencies such as the Federal Trade Commission. The United States also pursues its economic goals through international organizations of which it is a member, including the World Trade Organization (WTO), the World Bank, and the International Monetary Fund (IMF).

The national security policies of the United States include an extraordinary array of activities—so many, in fact, that they could not possibly be addressed adequately in an entire book, much less a single chapter. There are roughly two hundred countries in the world, and the United States has relations of one kind or another—military, diplomatic, economic—with all of them. This chapter narrows the subject by concentrating on a few main ideas:

■ *Since World War II, the United States has acted in the role of world leader, which has substantially affected its military, diplomatic, and economic policies.*

■ *The United States maintains a high degree of defense preparedness, which mandates a substantial level of defense spending and a worldwide deployment of U.S. conventional and strategic forces.*

■ *Changes in the international marketplace have led to increased economic interdependence among nations, which has had a marked influence on the U.S. economy and on America's security planning.*

The Roots of U.S. Foreign and Defense Policy

isolationist

The view that the country should deliberately avoid a large role in world affairs and instead concentrate on domestic concerns.

internationalist

The view that the country should involve itself deeply in world affairs.

HISTORICAL
Background

Prior to World War II, the United States was an **isolationist** country, deliberately avoiding a large role in world affairs. A different America emerged from the war. It had more land, sea, and air power than any other country in the world; a huge military-industrial base; and several hundred overseas military bases. The United States had become an **internationalist** country, deeply involved in the affairs of other nations.

It was also a nation not fully at peace. The United States was locked in a sprawling conflict with the Soviet Union, which had aided the takeover of power by communist parties in Eastern Europe. Poland, Hungary, Czechoslovakia, Hungary, and the other Eastern European nations were forced into the Soviet orbit, leading Britain's Winston Churchill to say that an "iron curtain" had fallen across Europe. Thereafter, U.S. security policy was designed to contain Soviet power. President Harry Truman and other American leaders regarded communist Russia as an implacable foe, a view that led to the formulation of the doctrine of containment—the idea that Soviet Union could be stopped from achieving its global ambitions only by the forceful use of American power.[1]

The Cold War Era

Developments in the late 1940s embroiled the United States in a **cold war** with the Soviet Union.[2] The term refers to the fact that the two countries were not directly engaged in actual combat (a "hot war") but were locked in deep-seated hostilities that lasted forty-five years. The structure of international power was **bipolar:** the United States against the Soviet Union. Each side was supreme in its sphere and was blocked from expanding its influence by the power of the other. For example, when the Soviet-backed North Koreans invaded South Korea in June 1950, President Truman sent troops into the conflict, which ended three years later in stalemate and resulted in the death of 35,000 U.S. soldiers.

A major turning point in U.S. foreign policy was the Vietnam War. Responding to the threat of a communist takeover, the United States became ever more deeply involved in the civil war in Vietnam. By the late 1960s, 550,000 Americans were stationed in South Vietnam. Although U.S. forces were technically superior in combat to the communist fighters, Vietnam was a guerrilla war, with no front lines and few set battles.[3] U.S. public opinion, most visibly among the young, gradually turned against the war, contributing to President Lyndon Johnson's decision not to seek reelection in 1968. Public opinion forced Richard Nixon, who became president in 1969, to aim not for victory but for a gradual disengagement. U.S. combat troops left Vietnam in 1973, and two years later North Vietnamese forces completed their takeover of the country. Vietnam was the most painful and costly application of the containment doctrine: 58,000 American soldiers lost their lives in the fighting.

America's defeat in Vietnam forced U.S. policymakers to reconsider the country's international role. The "lesson of Vietnam" was that there were limits to the country's ability to assert its will in the world. Nixon sought to reduce tensions with communist countries, asserting that the United States could no longer be the free world's "Lone Ranger." In 1972, Nixon visited the People's Republic of China, the first official contact with that country since the communists seized power in 1949. Nixon also initiated the Strategic Arms Limitation Talks (SALT), which resulted in reductions in the nuclear weapon arsenals of the United States and the Soviet Union. This spirit of cooperation lasted until the Soviet invasion of Afghanistan in 1979, which convinced U.S. leaders that the USSR was still bent on expansion and was a threat to Western interests in the oil-rich Middle East. Ronald Reagan, elected president in 1980, called for a renewed hard line toward the Soviet Union, which he described as the "evil empire."

Although U.S. policymakers did not know it at the time, the Soviet Union was collapsing under the weight of its heavy defense expenditures, its isolation from Western technology and markets, and its inefficient centralized economy. In 1985, the Soviet Union's newly chosen leader, Mikhail Gorbachev, ordered its troops to leave Afghanistan (which had become his country's Vietnam) and announced a plan to restructure Soviet society, an initiative known as *perestroika*. However, Gorbachev's reforms came too late to save the Soviet Union. In 1989, Soviet troops withdrew from Eastern Europe, freeing Poland, Austria, and other Eastern European countries from Soviet control and culminating in the dismantling of the Berlin Wall that separated communist East Germany from democratic West Germany. In late 1991, the leaders of the Russian, Belarus, and Ukrainian

Cold war propaganda, like this poster warning of the danger of communism, contributed to a climate of opinion in the United States that led to public support for efforts to contain Soviet power.

containment

A doctrine, developed after World War II, based on the assumption that the Soviet Union was an aggressor nation and that only a determined United States could block Soviet territorial ambitions.

cold war

The lengthy period after World War II when the United States and the Soviet Union were not engaged in actual combat (a "hot war") but were locked in a state of deep-seated hostility.

bipolar (power structure)

A power structure dominated by two powers only, as in the case of the United States and the Soviet Union during the cold war.

In the jungle warfare of Vietnam, American soldiers had difficulty finding the enemy and adapting to guerrilla tactics.

unipolar (power structure)

A power structure dominated by a single powerful actor, as in the case of the United States after the collapse of the Soviet Union.

multilateralism

The situation in which nations act together in response to problems and crises.

republics declared that the Soviet Union no longer existed. The bipolar power structure that had dominated world politics since the end of World War II had collapsed. The new structure was **unipolar**—the United States was now the world's unchallenged superpower.

A New World Order

The end of the cold war prompted the first President Bush in 1990 to call for a "new world order." George H. W. Bush advocated **multilateralism**—the idea that major nations should act together in response to problems and crises. Included in Bush's plan was a stronger role for multinational organizations such as the UN and NATO.

Multilateralism defined America's response to the Iraqi invasion of Kuwait in August 1990. President Bush obtained UN resolutions ordering Iraq to withdraw from Kuwait and authorizing the use of force if it did not. Five months later, a half million troops, mostly American but including contingents from nearly two dozen nations, attacked Iraq, first with an aerial bombardment and then with ground troops. Four days into the ground fighting, Iraqi units fled the battlefield, ending the war.

The Gulf operation was a military triumph, prompting President Bush to declare that the United States had "kicked the Vietnam syndrome [the legacy of America's defeat in Vietnam] once and for all." The Gulf War, however, was in another way less successful. Believing that an overthrow of Hussein's regime would destabilize Iraq, President Bush ordered a halt to the hostilities after Iraqi forces retreated. Hussein remained in power but was ordered by a UN resolution to dismantle his weapons programs, subject to UN inspections. However, Hussein repeatedly interfered with UN inspectors' attempts to verify the status of his weapons programs, raising concerns about his intentions.

Multilateralism carried over into the Clinton administration. Confronting Serb atrocities in Bosnia—where tens of thousands of Muslims and Croats were murdered, raped, and driven from their homes—President Bill Clinton pursued UN economic sanctions as a means of halting the slaughter. When sanctions failed, the United States and its NATO allies attacked Serb forces with air power.

The result was a U.S.-negotiated peace agreement (the Dayton Accords) that included the deployment to Bosnia of nearly 60,000 peacekeeping troops, including 20,000 Americans. War in the Balkans flared again in 1999 when the Serbs undertook a campaign of "ethnic cleansing" in the Serbian province of Kosovo, whose population was 90 percent Albanian. When attempts at a negotiated settlement failed, NATO planes, including U.S. aircraft, attacked Serbia.[4] After weeks of intensive bombing, Yugoslav president Slobodan Milosevic (who died in 2006 while on trial for war crimes) pulled his troops out of Kosovo. Ethnic Albanians moved back in and, despite the presence of UN peacekeeping troops, launched revenge attacks on some of the Serbs who remained. (In 2008, Kosovo became an independent state.)

As these examples indicate, multilateralism was only partly successful as a strategy for resolving international conflicts. With the deployment of enough resources, the world's major powers showed that they could act together with some success. However, these interventions offered no guarantee of long-term success. Regional and internal conflicts typically stem from enduring ethnic, religious, factional, or national hatreds or from chronic problems such as famine, overcrowding, or government corruption. Even if these hatreds or problems can be momentarily eased, they are often too deep-seated to be permanently resolved.

The War on Terrorism

Upon assuming the presidency in 2001, George W. Bush pointedly said that he would not follow his father's multilateral approach to world affairs. He declared that he would reduce America's military presence abroad, as well as its reliance on the United Nations. He also announced that the United States would not participate in either the Kyoto Accord (a global climate treaty) or the International Criminal Court (the ICC, a permanent tribunal with jurisdiction over war crimes). However, the terrorist attacks of September 11, 2001, on the World Trade Center and the Pentagon forced Bush to change course. Although he continued to oppose the ICC and the Kyoto Accord, Bush urged other nations to join the United States in a global "war on terrorism."

Unlike past wars, the war on terrorism targets not nations but groups engaged in terrorism that is aimed at U.S. interests at home and abroad. A war without sharply defined battlefronts, it is being waged through a wide variety of instruments, including military force, intelligence gathering, law enforcement, foreign aid, international cooperation, and immigration control. The tactics are also unusual. The rooting out of terrorist cells in the United States and Europe, for example, is entrusted to law enforcement agencies rather than to military units.

The war on terrorism resulted in the first major reorganization of the U.S. national security bureaucracy since the Department of Defense was created after World War II to combine the previously separate War and Navy Departments. This time, the new agency was the Department of Homeland Security (DHS), which was created in 2002 to coordinate domestic efforts to protect the United States against terrorist threats. The DHS's responsibilities include securing the nation's borders, enhancing defenses against biological attacks, preparing emergency personnel (police, firefighters, and rescue workers) for their roles in responding to terrorist attacks, and coordinating efforts to stop domestic terrorism.[5]

The first U.S. military action in the war on terrorism was an attack on Afghanistan. Its Taliban-led government had provided training sites and protection to the al Qaeda terrorists who carried out the September 11 attacks. Backed

POLITICAL CULTURE

LIBERTY, EQUALITY, AND SELF-GOVERNMENT

Defense Policy

During the 1950s, when the cold war was at a peak, President Dwight D. Eisenhower warned against actions that undermined the principles for which America stands. "The problem in defense," Eisenhower said, "is how far you can go without destroying from within what you are trying to defend from without." He worried that threats originating abroad would lead Americans to compromise the nation's ideals. Eisenhower believed that excessive government secrecy—justified in the name of national security—threatened liberty. He worried that a huge permanent military and the industrial firms that benefited from it would sap America of its resources and encourage the country to seek military solutions to international

problems. If America was to remain a beacon of freedom for the world, it had to remain steadfast in its ideals.

Similar concerns have been raised in the context of the war on terrorism. Nearly all Americans agree that the terrorist threat cannot be met without making some adjustments in how government operates. However, disagreement has arisen over specific policies, such as the prolonged detention of noncitizens, the preemptive invasion of Iraq, and the hundreds of billions being spent on the reconstruction of Iraq and Afghanistan. How much leeway do you think policymakers should have in their pursuit of the war on terrorism? If you disagree on what America's leaders have done, what are the alternatives, and how, if at all, are they more consistent with America's ideals?

by a UN resolution authorizing the use of force and supported by other NATO member countries, the United States toppled the Taliban government in early 2002; however, al Qaeda leader Osama bin Laden and most of his top lieutenants evaded capture.

In 2002, President Bush labeled Iraq, Iran, and North Korea an "axis of evil," thereby signaling a widening of the war on terrorism. Shortly thereafter, he announced a new national security doctrine: the **preemptive war doctrine.** Speaking at West Point, Bush said that the threat of international terrorism meant that the United States could not afford to wait until it was attacked by hostile nations. Bush declared that America was prepared to take "preemptive action."[6] This concept was not wholly new—U.S. officials had long maintained a right to strike first if faced with a direct and serious threat. What was new about the Bush doctrine was that it extended the option to include military action against less immediate threats.

preemptive war doctrine
The idea, espoused by President George W. Bush, that the United States could attack a potentially threatening nation even if the threat had not yet reached a serious and immediate level.

The Iraq War

In the summer of 2002, Bush targeted the regime of Iraq's Saddam Hussein, claiming that it had weapons of mass destruction (WMDs)—chemical and biological weapons, and possibly nuclear weapons. That October, Congress authorized the use of military force against Iraq if it did not voluntarily disarm. Facing the possibility of an unwanted war in Iraq, America's European allies urged that the disarmament of Iraq occur through the use of UN weapons inspectors. In late 2002, the United Nations passed a resolution requiring Iraq to accept weapons inspections. A two-track policy ensued. UN weapons inspectors entered Iraq in search of WMDs, while at the same time the United States deployed combat units to the Middle East.

Over strong objections from France, Germany, and Russia, and despite the UN's refusal to authorize a military attack, President Bush in March 2003 ordered U.S. forces to invade Iraq. Although British units were also involved, the assault was essentially an act of **unilateralism**—the situation in which one nation takes action against another state or states.[7] The Iraqi regime quickly

unilateralism
The situation in which one nation takes action against another state or states.

collapsed—Hussein was deposed after less than a month of fighting. However, the postcombat phase proved deadlier than the Bush administration had anticipated. Roadside mines and suicide bombers took a heavy toll on U.S. soldiers, and the cost of rebuilding Iraq soon exceeded $100 billion. Moreover, the WMDs that had been the justification for the war were not to be found. In early 2004, the chief U.S. weapons inspector, David Kay, testified before Congress that U.S. intelligence agencies had grossly exaggerated the extent of Iraq's weapons program.

The American public, which had backed the invasion of Iraq, came to question the war. Opinions elsewhere were harsher. For the first time since World War II, Western Europeans held that the United States should not be entrusted with world leadership. A year before the war, roughly 65 percent of Western Europeans had expressed a favorable opinion of the United States; fewer than 50 percent held that view after the invasion (see Figure 17-1). This attitude hampered America's ability to get European governments to contribute to the postwar reconstruction of Iraq. Although some assistance was provided, it was limited by public opposition to what was seen as "America's war." Postwar reconstruction was also hampered by instability in Iraq. Age-old animosities between Sunni, Shiite, and Kurdish groups within Iraq blocked political compromise and fueled violence. As the sectarian killings escalated, the animosities deepened. Foreign-born fighters compounded the problem. Iraq's lengthy border with Iran and Syria—countries antagonistic to the United States—allowed Islamic militants from other countries to join the fighting in Iraq.

During White House deliberations before the war, Secretary of State Colin Powell had invoked what he called "the Pottery Barn rule." Powell warned that officials who believed Iraqis would welcome U.S. troops with open arms were engaging in wishful thinking. Foreseeing a difficult postinvasion phase, Powell said, "If you break it, you own it." Indeed, the United States has largely gone it alone in the reconstruction of Iraq, at considerable cost in terms of American lives and dollars. Ninety percent of the casualties and the monetary costs have been borne by the United States.

In 2007, President Bush authorized a "surge" to afford the struggling Iraqi government an opportunity to govern more effectively. Thirty-thousand U.S. soldiers were added to the 130,000 troops already there, and military operations were launched to quell the sectarian violence. The surge contributed to a reduction in the violence, but the Iraqi government continued to have difficulty asserting its

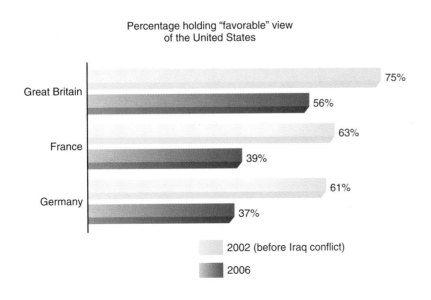

Percentage holding "favorable" view
of the United States

Great Britain — 75% (2002), 56% (2006)
France — 63% (2002), 39% (2006)
Germany — 61% (2002), 37% (2006)

2002 (before Iraq conflict)
2006

FIGURE 17-1   Impact of the Iraq Conflict on Europeans' Opinion of the United States
The Iraq conflict led to a sharp decline in Europeans' opinion of the United States.
Source: The Pew Research Center for the People and the Press surveys.

DEBATING THE ISSUES

SHOULD U.S. FORCES BE WITHDRAWN FROM IRAQ?

In 2003, at the order of President George W. Bush, U.S. forces invaded Iraq. Within a few weeks, the regime of Saddam Hussein had been toppled. The reconstruction phase, however, proved far more difficult than the White House had anticipated. Continuing attacks on U.S. forces and Iraqi civilians slowed the rebuilding of Iraq's infrastructure and the creation of an effective Iraqi government. Two years after the invasion, a majority of Americans had come to believe that it was a mistake and the percentage who held this opinion increased as the war continued beyond this point. Polls indicated, however, that Americans were divided on the issue of whether U.S. troops should be withdrawn from Iraq. Some Americans preferred a rapid withdrawal while others held that the United States needed to stay long enough to allow the Iraqi government to gain the strength it would need to pacify the country. These opposing views clashed head-on during the 2008 presidential campaign. Democratic nominee Barack Obama, who had opposed the Iraq invasion, promised a phased withdrawal of U.S. forces. Republican nominee John McCain promised to keep troops in Iraq until U.S. objectives there had been achieved. Which opinion is closer to your own?

YES When I am Commander-in-Chief, I will set a new goal on Day One: I will end this war. Not because politics compels it. Not because our troops cannot bear the burden—as heavy as it is. But because it is the right thing to do for our national security, and it will ultimately make us safer. In order to end this war responsibly, I will immediately begin to remove our troops from Iraq. We can responsibly remove 1 to 2 combat brigades each month. If we start with the number of brigades we have in Iraq today, we can remove all of them in 16 months. After this redeployment, we will leave enough troops in Iraq to guard our embassy and diplomats, and a counter-terrorism force to strike Al Qaeda if it forms a base that the Iraqis cannot destroy. What I propose is not—and never has been—a precipitous drawdown. It is instead a detailed and prudent plan that will end a war nearly seven years after it started. My plan to end this war will finally put pressure on Iraq's leaders to take responsibility for their future. Because we've learned that when we tell Iraq's leaders that we'll stay as long as it takes, they take as long as they want. We need to send a different message. We will help Iraq reach a meaningful accord on national reconciliation. We will engage with every country in the region—and the UN—to support the stability and territorial integrity of Iraq. And we will launch a major humanitarian initiative to support Iraq's refugees and people. But Iraqis must take responsibility for their country. It is precisely this kind of approach—an approach that puts the onus on the Iraqis, and that relies on more than just military power—that is needed to stabilize Iraq.

—*Barack Obama, 2008 Democratic presidential nominee*

NO We have the responsibility to finish the job—to place true sovereignty in the hands of the Iraqi people. . . . If we leave, violence will fill the vacuum as groups struggle for political power, and we risk all-out civil war. At the very least, scores will be settled, warlords will reign, and the violence we see today will pale in comparison to the bloodletting. . . . If we leave, we doom reform in the Arab world. Why should other Arabs embrace democracy and freedom when it cannot take root even after a wholesale regime change in Iraq? If we leave, we risk turning Iraq into a failed state, handing its neighbors—including leading terrorist sponsors Iran and Syria—a prime opportunity to expand their influence in the region, and creating a breeding ground for terrorism. But if we succeed in stabilizing the country, in building a new government to which we hand sovereignty, in establishing a political system based on freedom and democracy, what will we then have accomplished? . . . If we succeed, we send a message to every despot in the region that their day is done—that no people will tolerate forever leaders who deprive them of liberty. If we succeed, we help create in the center of the Middle East a representative and humane government that provides an example to the region. We help bring an end to the political repression and economic stagnation in which extremist roots grow. People in the region can then express their views within the political system, rather than being forced to its margins. They will have access to economic opportunity that will bring them hope, rather than despair.

—*John McCain, 2008 Republican presidential nominee*

authority and resolving contentious issues, such as how the oil revenues would be distributed among Iraq's regions. Against this backdrop, the 2008 presidential candidates differed sharply on the future course of Iraq policy, with Barack Obama promising to withdraw U.S. troops and John McCain promising to stay in Iraq until it had a stable government.

The difficulty of the Iraq reconstruction phase has limited America's ability to respond to other fronts in the war on terrorism. Since the Iraq invasion, North Korea has acquired nuclear weapons, Iran is developing the technology that could lead to the acquisition of such weapons, and Taliban forces in Afghanistan have regrouped and are expanding the fighting there. Thus, as was true of multilateralism, unilateralism has been shown to have limits. Even with the world's most powerful military, the United States has found it difficult to go it alone in Iraq. Wars like those in Iraq and Vietnam do not lend themselves to quick and tidy battlefield solutions. It is one thing to defeat a conventional army in open warfare and quite another to prevail in a conflict in which the fight is not so much a battle for territory as for people's loyalties, especially when the people involved distrust each other, as in the case of Iraq's Sunnis, Shiites, and Kurds.

The Military Dimension of National Security Policy

The launching of the war on terrorism brought about the first major increase—several hundred billion dollars—in U.S. defense spending since the 1980s. The United States for decades has spent far more on defense than any other country and, with the recent increase, now accounts for roughly half of all military spending worldwide (see "How the U.S. Compares"). U.S. defense spending is six times that of China and nearly ten times that of Russia.

Military Power, Uses, and Capabilities

U.S. military forces are trained or called on for different types of military action, ranging from nuclear conflict to guerrilla warfare.

HOW THE U.S. COMPARES

WORLDWIDE MILITARY SPENDING

The United States spends roughly half of all the money spent worldwide on the military. The U.S. military establishment is huge and is deployed all over the world, and American taxpayers spend more than half a trillion dollars each year to support it. China is second in military spending, but its expenditures are only a sixth those of the United States. Russia spends about a tenth of what the United States spends. Even on a per-capita basis, the United States ranks far ahead of other nations in military spending.

The United States has pressured its Western allies to carry a larger share of the defense burden, but some of these countries have resisted, contending that the cost would be too high and that their security would not be substantially improved. Of the Western European countries, Britain spends the most; its military spending on a per-capita basis is about a third that of the United States.

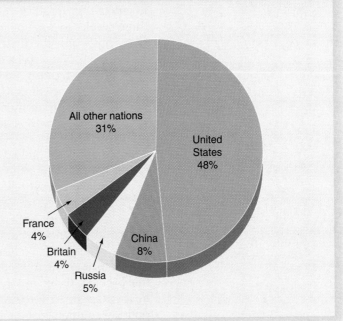

Source: Center for Arms Control and Non-Proliferation, 2008.

Nuclear War Capability

Although the possibility of all-out nuclear war with Russia declined dramatically with the end of the cold war, the United States retains a nuclear arsenal designed to prevent such a war from ever happening. **Deterrence policy** is based on the notion that any nation would be deterred from launching a full-scale nuclear attack on the United States by the knowledge that, even if it destroyed the country, it too would be obliterated. America's nuclear weapons are deployed in what is called the "nuclear triad." This term refers to the three ways nuclear weapons can be launched: by land-based missiles, by submarine-based missiles, and by bombers. The triad provides a second-strike capability—that is, the ability to absorb a first-strike nuclear attack and survive with enough nuclear punch for a massive retaliation (second strike). Since the end of the cold war, the United States and Russia have negotiated reductions in their nuclear arsenals and have created monitoring systems designed to reduce the possibility that either side could launch an effective surprise attack.

A greater fear today than nuclear war with Russia is the possibility that a terrorist group or rogue nation will smuggle a nuclear device into the United States and detonate it. The technology and materials necessary to build a nuclear weapon (or to buy one clandestinely) are more readily available than ever before. Accordingly, the United States, Russia, and other nations are cooperating to halt the spread of nuclear weapons. This effort has had some success, but not to the point where the nuclear threat has been eliminated.

Conventional and Guerrilla War Capability

Nuclear preparedness is just one part of America's combat readiness. A second is conventional-force preparedness. Not since World War II has the United States fought an all-out conventional war, nor at present does it have the capacity to fight one. That type of war would require a reinstatement of the military draft and full mobilization of the nation's industrial capacity. Instead, the United States today has an all-volunteer military force (see "States in the Nation") that is second to none in its destructive power. When U.S. forces invaded Iraq in 2003, they were outnumbered by three to one yet took only three weeks to seize control of Baghdad, at which point the remaining Iraqi army units quit the field.

The U.S. Navy has a dozen aircraft carriers, scores of attack submarines, and hundreds of fighting and supply ships. The U.S. Air Force has thousands of high-performance aircraft, ranging from fighter jets to jumbo supply planes. The U.S. Army has roughly 500,000 regular troops and more than 300,000 Reserve and National Guard soldiers, who are supplied with tanks, artillery pieces, armored personnel carriers, and attack helicopters. This armament is doubly lethal because it is linked to sophisticated surveillance, targeting, and communication systems. No other nation has anywhere near the advanced weapons systems that the United States possesses.

This capability, however, is not a large advantage in the type of war taking place in Iraq and Afghanistan—guerrilla actions featuring roadside explosive devices and suicide bombings. Such tactics are extremely difficult to defend against and virtually impossible to stop by conventional military means. To defeat such an enemy requires the full support of the local population. Without this backing, the enemy has the capacity to sustain operations over a long period in an attempt to force a withdrawal of U.S. forces. Such situations require a political solution, not a military one, and political solutions are never as decisive as battlefield encounters. They require compromise and concessions from both

---

deterrence policy

The idea that nuclear war can be discouraged if each side in a conflict has the capacity to destroy the other with nuclear weapons.

STATES IN THE NATION

THE ALL-VOLUNTEER MILITARY'S RECRUITS

Until 1973, the United States had an active military draft. Upon reaching age 18, males were required to register for the draft. Local draft boards would then pick the draftees based on quotas that varied with the size of the local population. Accordingly, each state contributed equally to the military's manpower needs relative to its population size. Today's military is an all-volunteer force, and the states' contributions vary significantly. The map below indicates the degree to which each state is over- and underrepresented in the military as indicated by the ratio of military recruits from a state to the number of males ages 18–34 in that state's population. Montana has the largest number of recruits relative to its population, followed in order by Alaska, Wyoming, and Maine. Utah, Rhode Island, and Massachusetts rank lowest, in that order.

Q: What might explain why military recruits come disproportionately from states like Montana, Alaska, Wyoming, and Maine as well as from the southern states?

A: According to Department of Defense data, recruits are more likely to come from rural areas, particularly areas where few well-paying jobs are available to young adults. The four states with the highest recruitment ratios have these characteristics. As for the South, higher recruitment levels there have been explained in terms of its stronger military tradition and its numerous military installations. Individuals from areas near these installations, as well as the sons and daughters of military personnel, are more likely to enlist in the military. (Mississippi and Tennessee, with the south's lowest recruitment rates, have relatively few military installations.)

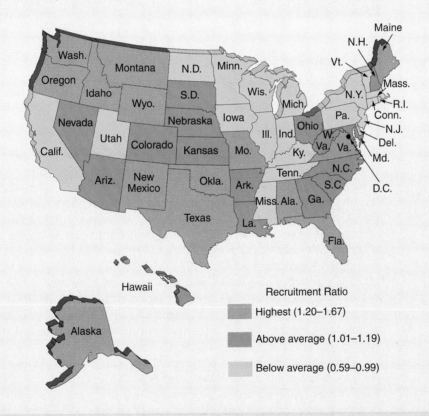

Source: Adapted from Tim Kane, "Who Bears the Burden? Demographic Characteristics of U.S. Military Recruits Before and After 9/11," Heritage Foundation, Center for Data Analysis Report #05-08, November 7, 2005.

sides. An occupying power, such as the United States, often is at a disadvantage in these negotiations because its interests include the withdrawal of its forces. If the occupier is dealing with a determined enemy that has the will and the capacity to continue the fight indefinitely, as was the case in Vietnam and could be the situation in Iraq, at some point it can be forced to accept an arrangement that is far less satisfying than the outcome that was anticipated upon entering into war.

In March 2003, by order of President George W. Bush, U.S. troops attacked Iraq. The intense combat phase was relatively short, ending in the defeat of Iraqi forces. However, the reconstruction phase that followed was marked by continuing violence and destruction. Seen here is a view of U.S. soldiers through a bullet hole in a window.

The Politics of National Defense

Policy elites, public opinion, and special interests all play significant roles in national defense policy. The U.S. public usually supports the judgments of its political leaders on the use of military force. In nearly all military initiatives of the past half-century, Americans have backed the action. When President Bush spoke of the need for an invasion and then ordered U.S. forces into Iraq in 2003,[8] two-thirds of Americans supported the decision. The other third were split between those who opposed the war and those who were unsure about whether it was the proper course of action. Public support for a war can persist, as was the case during the first six years of the Vietnam conflict. However, if the war seems endless and as the human and financial toll rises, public support erodes. A swing in public opinion against the Vietnam War forced U.S. policymakers to withdraw American troops in 1973. Public opinion on the Iraq War soured more quickly, partly because the official reason for the war—the threat of Iraq's weapons of mass destruction—proved erroneous. Research on the Korean and Vietnam wars indicates that, once Americans turn against a war, it is almost impossible to regain their support for it. If that pattern holds true for Iraq, U.S. policymakers have only limited options in trying to resolve that conflict.

Wars are only one area of national defense policy, however. In other areas, such as the recent decision to expand NATO to include Eastern European countries, public opinion plays only a small role.[9] The general public is not interested or informed enough about most national security issues to contribute to their resolution, particularly during the formative stage when critical first decisions are made. The American people ordinarily trust their leaders to make the right decisions in such cases and will back them unless the decisions turn out badly.

Although citizens may assume that national security policy is decided strictly on the basis of what is necessary to protect U.S. interest, the assumption is unwarranted. In his 1961 farewell address, President Dwight D. Eisenhower, who had commanded U.S. forces in Europe during World War II, warned Americans against "the unwarranted influence" and "misplaced power" of what he termed **"the military-industrial complex."** Eisenhower was referring to the fact that national defense is big business, involving the annual expenditure of hundreds

military-industrial complex

The three components (the military establishment, the industries that manufacture weapons, and the members of Congress from states and districts that depend heavily on the arms industry) that mutually benefit from a high level of defense spending.

of billions of dollars.[10] As Eisenhower described it, the military-industrial complex has three components: the military establishment, the arms industry, and the members of Congress from states and districts that depend heavily on the arms industry. All three benefit from a continuously high level of defense spending. A considerable proportion of U.S. defense spending reflects the self-interest of the military-industrial complex rather than what is required to keep America safe. The problem is that no one knows exactly what that proportion is.

The Economic Dimension of National Security Policy

Economic considerations are a vital component of national security policy. National security is more than an issue of military might. It is also a question of maintaining a position in the world that will enable the United States to remain an economically prosperous society.

In economic terms, the world today is tripolar—power is concentrated in three centers. One center is the United States, which produces roughly 20 percent of the world's goods and services. Another center is Japan and China, which account for more than 15 percent of the world's economy. The third and largest center, responsible for more than 25 percent of the world's economy, is the twenty-five-country European Union (EU). The EU is dominated by Germany, Britain, and France, which together account for roughly half its economy.

LEADERS

DWIGHT D. EISENHOWER
(1890–1969)

One of four army generals to be elected to the presidency, Dwight D. Eisenhower left his mark on war and peace. Born in Abilene, Texas, Eisenhower was an accomplished athlete and student, and in his senior year of high school, he received an appointment to West Point. During World War II, he commanded the Allied Forces that landed in North Africa and drove the German army back to the European mainland. He was Supreme Commander of the multinational force that on June 6, 1944 (D-Day), landed at Normandy, initiating the drive across Europe that eventually would force Germany to surrender. He declined an opportunity to run for the presidency in 1948 but accepted a Republican draft to run in 1952. Given his stature as the most popular figure in America, Eisenhower won easily.

Though trained in the art of war, Eisenhower sought throughout his presidency to reduce cold war tensions. He signed the truce that led to the end of the Korean conflict. Although he was unsuccessful in negotiating a thaw in the nuclear arms race with Soviet leaders, he convinced them that the United States was not seeking their country's destruction. In 1956, after Egypt nationalized the Suez Canal, a plan by the governments of Britain, France, and Israel to take it back by force was aborted when Eisenhower refused to support it, saying that Egypt had a right to self-determination and that the United Nations, not the force of arms, was the proper avenue for settling the dispute. As he was leaving the presidency, he used his farewell address to warn of the dangers of the military-industrial complex, arguing that sustained high levels of military expenditure and secrecy would only weaken America in the long run.

By some indicators, the United States is the weakest of the three economic centers. For example, it has the worst trade imbalance. Although the United States exports roughly $1 trillion annually in goods and services, it imports an even larger amount. The result is a trade deficit that is easily the world's largest. The United States has not had a trade surplus since 1975, and in recent years it has frequently had deficits exceeding $500 billion (see Figure 17-2). In other ways, however, the United States is the strongest of the three economic powers. For one thing, the American economy is the best balanced. Like the other economic powers, the United States has a strong industrial base, but it has a stronger agricultural sector and more abundant natural resources. Its vast fertile plains have made it the world's leading agricultural producer. The United States ranks among the top three countries worldwide in production of wheat, corn, potatoes, peanuts, cotton, eggs, cattle, and pigs. As for natural resources, the United States ranks among the top five nations in deposits of

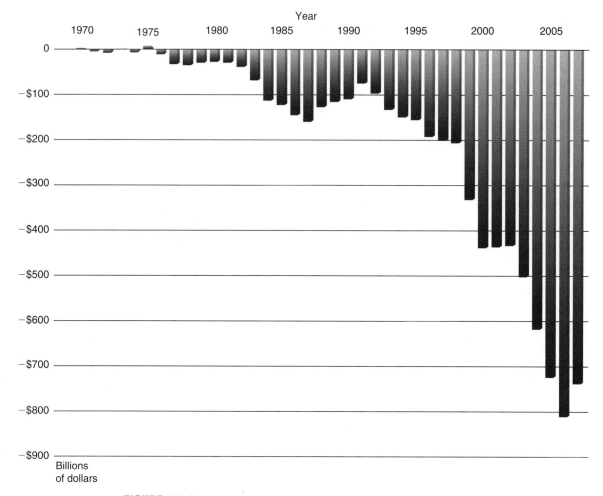

Year

FIGURE 17-2 **The U.S. Trade Deficit** Not since 1975 has the United States had a trade surplus; the deficit reached a record level in 2006.
Source: U.S. Bureau of Economic Analysis, 2008.

copper, uranium, lead, sulfur, zinc, coal, gold, iron ore, natural gas, silver, and magnesium.[11]

According to the Switzerland-based World Economic Forum, the United States also is more economically competitive than are its major trading rivals (see Chapter 15). The United States owes this position to factors such as its technological know-how.[12] This competitive advantage has been evident since the early 1990s. The slowdown in the U.S. economy that began in 2008 tempered the belief that technological know-how had unleashed unstoppable growth. Nevertheless, other countries have looked to the United States, particularly its technology sector, for policy and market innovations that can drive their own economic growth.

Nevertheless, the United States cannot "go it alone" economically. It depends on other countries for raw materials, finished goods, markets, and capital to meet Americans' production and consumption demands. Meeting this objective requires the United States to exert global economic influence. The broad goals of the United States in the world economy include the following:[13]

■ Sustaining a stable and open system of trade that will promote prosperity at home

- Maintaining access to energy and other natural resources vital to the strength of the U.S. economy
- Keeping the widening gap between the rich and poor countries from destabilizing the world economy

Promoting Global Trade

After World War II, the United States helped enact a global trading system centering on itself. The U.S. dollar had become the major currency in international trade, replacing the English pound, which had held that position for more than a century. The war had weakened Britain's economic position in the world and elevated that of the United States, which moved swiftly to solidify its dominance. A leading initiative was the European Recovery Plan, better known as the Marshall Plan, that provided unprecedented aid (more than $100 billion in today's dollars) for the postwar rebuilding of Europe. Apart from enabling the countries of Western Europe to better confront the perceived Soviet threat, the Marshall Plan served the economic needs of the United States. Wartime production had lifted the country out of the Great Depression, but the end of the war had brought a recession and renewed fears of hard time. A rejuvenated Western Europe furnished a market for American products. In effect, Western Europe became a junior partner within a system of global trade dominated by the United States.

Since then, major changes have taken place in the world economy. Germany is now a trading rival of the United States, as is Japan, which also received substantial postwar reconstruction assistance from the United States. More recently, China and the European Union have taken their place as trading giants, and Russia, propelled by its huge oil and gas reserves, is developing into one.

At the same time, the American economy depends more heavily on international commerce than in any period in the past. The domestic manufacturing sector that once was the source, directly or indirectly, of most U.S. jobs has shrunk, and many of the goods that Americans now buy, from their television sets to their automobiles, are produced by foreign firms. Indeed, nearly all large U.S. firms are themselves **multinational corporations,** with operations in more than one country. From a headquarters in New York City, a firm has no difficulty directing a production facility in Thailand that is filling orders for markets in Europe and South America. Money, goods, and services today flow freely and quickly across national borders, and large firms increasingly think about markets in global rather than national terms.

Economic globalization is a term that describes the increased interdependence of nations' economies. This development is both an opportunity for and a threat to U.S. economic interests. The opportunity rests with the possibility of increased demand abroad for U.S. products and lower prices to U.S. consumers as a result of inexpensive imports. The threat lies in the fact that foreign firms also compete in the global marketplace and may use their competitive advantages, such as cheaper labor, to outposition U.S. firms.

In general, international commerce works best when countries trade freely with one another. This situation keeps the prices of traded items, whether finished goods or raw materials, at their lowest level, resulting in economic efficiency (see Chapter 15). However, global trade is a political issue as well as an economic one, and different countries and interests have different views on how trade among nations should be conducted. **Free trade** describes the situation where barriers to trade between nations are kept to a minimum. Proponents of free trade claim that the long-term economic interests of all countries are advanced when tariffs and

HISTORICAL
Background

---

multinational corporations

Business firms with major operations in more than one country.

---

economic globalization

The increased interdependence of nations' economies. The change is a result of technological, transportation, and communication advances that have enabled firms to deploy their resources around the globe.

---

free trade

The condition where tariffs and other barriers to trade between nations are kept to a minimum.

Some U.S. firms are now as recognizable in other countries as they are in the United States. A Pepsi sign adorns the front of this small shop in Vietnam's Ho Chi Minh City (formerly Saigon).

protectionism

The placing of the immediate interests of domestic producers (through, for example, protective tariffs) above that of free trade between nations.

other trade barriers are kept to a minimum. Most free-trade advocates couple their advocacy with fair-trade demands, but they are committed, philosophically and practically, to the idea that free trade fuels economic growth, results in a net gain for business, and provides consumers with lower-priced goods.

As opposed to the free-trade argument, **protectionism** emphasizes the immediate interests of domestic producers and includes measures designed to enable them to compete with foreign competitors in the domestic market. For some protectionists, the issue is simply a matter of defending domestic firms against the actions of their foreign competitors. For others, the issue is one of fair trade; they are protectionists in those instances where foreign firms have an unfair competitive advantage—as, for example, when government subsidies allow them to market their goods at an artificially low price. Protectionist sentiment has usually come from Congress rather than the White House. Although most members of Congress say they support free trade and some are unabashed advocates of it, many of them act differently when their state or district is threatened by foreign competition. Then they often try to protect their constituents' interests through measures such as favorable treatment of U.S. goods or tariffs on the goods of foreign competitors.

During the past two decades, the free-trade position has usually prevailed in U.S. policy disputes. In 1993, for example, Congress ratified the North American Free Trade Agreement (NAFTA), which creates a mostly free market among the United States, Canada, and Mexico. Although NAFTA was opposed by most congressional Democrats and by environmental and labor groups that objected to its weak protection of their interests, proponents prevailed due to the backing of President Bill Clinton and most congressional Republicans. The final votes needed for passage were gained by promises of trade protection for Florida citrus and vegetable growers. Another example of support for free trade is U.S. membership in the World Trade Organization (WTO). The WTO, created in 1995, is the formal institution through which most nations negotiate general rules of international trade.[14] The WTO's mission is to promote a global free market through reductions in tariffs, protections for intellectual property (copyrights and patents), and similar policies. WTO members (roughly one hundred thirty in number) are committed to an open trade policy buttressed by regulations designed to ensure fair play among participating nations. Trade disputes among WTO members are settled by arbitration panels, which consist of representatives from the member nations. In 2003, for example, the WTO held that U.S. tariffs on imported steel, which were intended to protect U.S. steelmakers, were illegal under WTO trade rules and had to be rescinded.

Recently, protectionist sentiment has gained strength in the United States. The WTO, for example, has been criticized for placing trade ahead of environmental protection and human rights. Some countries have gained a trade advantage through production processes that degrade the environment and exploit workers, including child laborers. Loss of jobs has also been an issue. Employment in American textile factories, for example, has declined in the face of foreign competition. Even some high-tech jobs have been shipped abroad. Telephone-based technical services, for example, often can be provided at lower cost by hiring educated English-speaking technicians in India instead of their American counterparts.

The jobs issue did not receive much attention during the late 1990s, when the overall U.S. economy was growing at a rapid pace. More recently, as trade deficits mounted and U.S. manufacturing jobs continued to be lost, the question of whether America benefits from free-trade initiatives has become a heated political issue. Free-trade proposals have produced increasingly fierce debate in

"Do you think the fact that the American economy has become increasingly global is good because it has opened up new markets for American products and resulted in more jobs, or bad because it has subjected American companies and employees to unfair competition and cheap labor?"

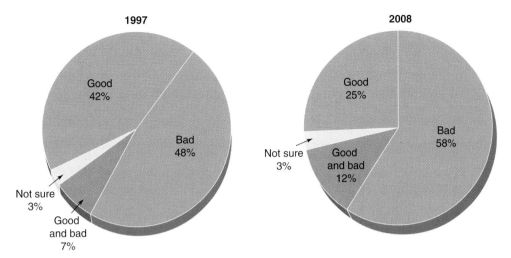

FIGURE 17-3   **Americans' Opinion of Free Trade**
In the late 1990s, Americans were as likely to think that free trade was good for the country as to think that it was bad for the country. Opinion has since shifted to a point where most Americans think free trade is a problem.
Source: Figure created from NBC/Wall Street Journal poll responses of June 1997 and March 2008.

Congress, and Barack Obama and John McCain split sharply on the issue in the 2008 presidential campaign. McCain said that protectionism was no substitute for retraining America's workers to adjust to global trade, while Obama promised protections for America's workers in trade agreements.

Public opinion on global trade has also shifted. Although the American people have not been as supportive of free trade as their leaders, they were about equally divided on its merits in polls taken during the late 1990s. In more recent years, a majority of Americans have come to believe that international trade is hurting the country. Twice as many Americans believe it hurts the nation as believe it serves the country's interest (see Figure 17-3).

U.S. officials have struggled to find an effective response to this development. Economists argue that the job losses are simply part of the "creative destruction" that occurs naturally in free markets. Firms have no choice but to adapt if they are to survive. Public officials, however, cannot so easily take such a long-range view, because they face immediate pressures from constituents who have lost jobs and from communities that have lost firms. In response to these pressures, U.S. officials have sought to preserve free trade by insisting that foreign governments improve their labor and environmental practices and end their protectionist policies. The stated goal is to make global trade work in ways that will allow U.S. goods to compete on an even playing field. However, other countries are not always convinced that the United States itself plays fair. In 2006, WTO trade talks collapsed in part because the United States refused to reduce its hefty farm subsidies, which enable U.S. agricultural producers to sell their products at a lower price thereby giving them an advantage in world commodity markets.

Trade with China in particular is an issue that looms ever larger with U.S. policymakers.[15] In the past decade, America's trade deficit with China has increased more than thirtyfold, surpassing $250 billion annually. The United States has provided China with a marketplace for its goods, which has helped fuel China's economic growth. China in turn has provided the United States with inexpensive goods, which has satisfied America's consumers and helped keep inflation in check. But Congress is increasingly concerned with the trade deficit. Many members of Congress have urged China to increase the value of its currency, which would raise the price of its goods and thereby dampen consumer demand in the United States. Such a step would make U.S. goods more competitive with those produced in China and offer some protection to U.S. firms and workers.

China is also a key to the future of the U.S. dollar as the dominant currency of international trade. As America's trade imbalance has grown, and as the United States has piled up increasing levels of government and consumer debt, the value of the dollar has been declining. Because of trade imbalances, China, Japan, and other countries have accumulated several trillion dollars in U.S. currency and securities, which decline in value with every drop in the dollar. About 65 percent of all international reserves are in dollars, but the proportion is slowly dropping, with the euro (the European dollar) as the leading alternative. Since 2000, the euro has climbed from less than 20 percent of reserves to 25 percent. Should the trend accelerate, the dollar could conceivably lose the benchmark status it has held since World War II, which would weaken it further.

Maintaining Access to Oil and Other Natural Resources

Although the United States is rich in natural resources, it is not self-sufficient. Oil is the main problem; domestic production provides only about half the nation's needs. Oil has been called "black gold," and even that description understates its significance. Oil is the engine of American society, powering the economy and providing fuel for automobiles and heat for homes and offices. For decades, the United States has used its economic and military power to protect its access to oil.

Outside the United States, most of the world's oil is found in the Middle East, Latin America, Africa, and Russia. Access to oil occurs through world markets. After World War II, the United States acquired a foothold in those markets when its leading oil companies, with their technical expertise and huge amounts of capital, acquired a stake in Middle Eastern oil fields. Since then, U.S. firms have been leaders in worldwide oil exploration and production. Underpinning their activities is the military might of the United States. For example, the U.S. Navy patrols the world's shipping routes to ensure that oil tankers reach their destinations safely.

Oil has a major influence on U.S. foreign policy. The 1991 Gulf War was driven by a concern with oil. Iraq's invasion of Kuwait threatened access not only to Kuwait's oil fields but also to those of its neighbors. Access to oil may also have contributed to President Bush's decision in 2003 to invade Iraq, which has oil reserves of more than 100 billion barrels, second only to those of Saudi Arabia. Oil has also restricted U.S. actions. When Iranian militants in 1979 overthrew their country's pro-Western ruler and seized U.S. embassy personnel as hostages, the United States refrained from a military response in part out of fear of disrupting the flow of Iranian oil. In 2008, when Russia invaded parts of neighboring Georgia, a U.S. ally, the restrained response of the United States and its European allies was a result in part of Europe's dependence on Russian oil and natural gas.

The issue of oil will grow in significance in coming years.[16] Oil production may be nearing peak capacity. New oil fields are still being developed, but the world's major oil reserves are being depleted. Meanwhile, the demand for oil is rising as a result of the rapid economic growth of China, India, and other emerging industrialized countries. Oil topped $140 a barrel for the first time in 2008. If a major disruption in the world's oil supply were to occur, oil prices would skyrocket, possibly causing a global recession.

Assisting Developing Nations

Although political instability in less developed countries can disrupt world markets, less developed countries also offer marketplace opportunities. In order to develop further, they need to acquire the goods and services that more industrialized countries can provide. To foster this demand, the United States and the other industrialized countries provide developmental assistance to poorer countries. Contributions include direct foreign aid and also indirect assistance through international organizations, such as the International Monetary Fund (IMF) and the World Bank. These two organizations were created by the United States and Great Britain at the Bretton Woods Conference near the end of World War II. The IMF makes short-term loans to prevent countries experiencing temporary problems from collapsing economically or resorting to destructive practices such as the unrestricted printing of paper money. The World Bank, on the other hand, makes long-term development loans to poor countries for capital investment projects such as dams, highways, and factories.

Since World War II, the United States has been the leading source of aid to developing countries. Although the United States still contributes the most in terms of total dollars, Canada, Japan, and the European countries spend more on a per-capita basis than does the United States (see Figure 17-4). The United States has narrowed the gap since the events of September 11, 2001, which awakened some policymakers to the fact that global poverty generates resentment of the United States.[17]

Public opinion is an obstacle to higher levels of spending on foreign aid. Polls show that most Americans believe the United States is already spending

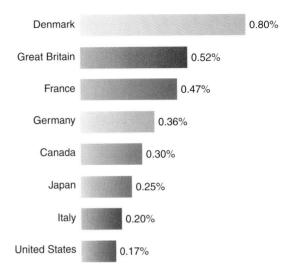

Foreign aid, as percentage of GNI

Denmark 0.80%
Great Britain 0.52%
France 0.47%
Germany 0.36%
Canada 0.30%
Japan 0.25%
Italy 0.20%
United States 0.17%

FIGURE 17-4 **Assistance to Developing Countries, as a Percentage of Gross National Income** The United States ranks highest in terms of total amount spent on foreign aid to developing countries but ranks lower in terms of percentage of gross national income (GNI). Data exclude Iraq reconstruction spending.
Source: OECD (Organization for Economic Cooperation and Development), 2008.

After Saddam Hussein's regime in Iraq was toppled, the United States began the task of reconstructing Iraqi oil operations, schools, hospitals, roads, and other facilities. The reconstruction costs were far higher than policymakers had anticipated and pushed total U.S. foreign assistance spending to new heights.

huge amounts on foreign aid. In a poll that asked Americans to name the largest federal programs, foreign aid topped the list, with 27 percent identifying it as the most expensive program.[18] In fact, foreign aid is far from the top. Nevertheless, Americans' perception makes foreign aid a potent political issue for politicians who would like to decrease it. Jesse Helms (R-N.C.), a past chair of the Senate Foreign Relations Committee, liked to say that foreign aid was nothing more than pouring billions of dollars "down foreign ratholes."[19]

Under President George W. Bush, following a precedent established a quarter-century earlier by President Jimmy Carter, the United States increasingly tied its foreign aid to developing countries' commitment to development, human rights, and democratization. This precondition does not apply to all foreign assistance. For decades, Israel has been at or near the top in terms of the amount of U.S. foreign aid received. After Egypt made peace with Israel in 1979, it also became a major foreign-aid recipient. More recently, assistance to the Palestinians was increased when their leadership agreed to work toward a peaceful solution to their conflict with the Israelis. These efforts reflect America's long-standing commitment to the preservation of the state of Israel. In the case of the poorer countries, Bush's Millennium Challenge Account program provided proportionately more money to those countries that were making progress in improving the lives of their people. Critics charged that the Bush administration never delivered as much money to these countries as had been promised and that money was not withheld from authoritarian regimes that were instrumental in its war on terrorism. Nevertheless, the program was applied in parts of Africa, South America, and Asia. The largest Millennium Challenge grant was $700 million to Tanzania to reduce poverty in that country through improvements in water, energy, and transportation.

A Challenging World

Seldom has the United States faced as bewildering an array of foreign and defense policy challenges as it faces today. "The world will never again be the same" was a common refrain after September 11, 2001, but few analysts foresaw just how much the world would change in a few short years, let above the difficulties the United States would have in adjusting to it.

The terrorist threat has expanded beyond all expectations. According to the National Intelligence Estimate that U.S. intelligence agencies compile yearly, global terrorism has worsened in the past few years, partly because the Iraq conflict mobilized and united Islamic extremists around the globe. What analysts disagree about is the duration of America's struggle with radical Islamists. Some analysts predict that the conflict will unwind within a decade or so. Others see it stretching across a far longer period, much like the religiously motivated Thirty Years' War that consumed the first half of the seventeenth century in Europe.

No less daunting is the challenge of the global economy. A decade or so ago, the U.S. economy was the envy of the world, but it is now wobbling as a result of developments at home and abroad. Even the U.S. dollar—long the symbol of America's preeminence in the world—has lost much of its luster. Some analysts predict that the United States will soon recapture its global momentum. Other analysts foresee a long-term decline, fueled by America's financial excesses and oil dependency and by surging economies elsewhere, particularly China's.

Summary
Self-Test www.mhhe.com/pattersontad9e

The chief instruments of national security policy are diplomacy, military force, economic exchange, and intelligence gathering. These are exercised through specialized agencies of the U.S. government, such as the Departments of State and Defense, that are largely responsive to presidential leadership. National security policy has also relied on international organizations, such as the United Nations and the World Trade Organization, that are responsive to the global concerns of major nations.

From 1945 to 1990, U.S. foreign and defense policies were dominated by a concern with the Soviet Union. During most of this period, the United States pursued a policy of containment based on the premise that the Soviet Union was an aggressor nation bent on global conquest. Containment policy led the United States to enter into wars in Korea and Vietnam and to maintain a large defense establishment. U.S. military forces are deployed around the globe, and the nation maintains a large nuclear arsenal. The end of the cold war, however, made some of this weaponry and strategic planning less relevant to America's national security.

A first response to the post–cold-war world was multilateralism—the idea that major nations could achieve common goals by working together, including using force as a means of restraining regional conflicts. The interventions in the Persian Gulf and the Balkans during the 1990s are examples. They demonstrated that major nations can intervene with some success in global hot spots but also showed that the ethnic, religious, and national conflicts that fuel these flashes are not easily resolved. The terrorist attacks on the World Trade Center and the Pentagon in 2001 led to broad changes in national security organization and strategy. Increased spending on defense and homeland security has been coupled with a partial reorganization of U.S. intelligence, law enforcement, and immigration agencies, as well as new laws affecting the scope of their activities. However, the defining moment of the post–September 11 period was America's invasion of Iraq in 2003, which was rooted in President George W. Bush's preemptive war doctrine and his willingness to commit the United States to unilateral action.

In recent decades, the United States has increasingly taken economic factors into account in its national security considerations, which has meant, for example, that trade has played a larger part in defining its relationships with other countries. The trading system that the United States helped erect after World War II has given way to one that is more global in scale and more competitive. Changes in communication, transportation, and computing have altered the way large corporations operate, and as businesses have changed their practices, nations have had to adapt. The changes include the emergence of regional and international economic structures, such as the European Union, NAFTA, and the WTO. Nevertheless, nations naturally compete for economic advantage, including access to natural resources; accordingly, trade is a source of conflict as well as a source of cooperation. In the coming years, oil is likely to be at the center of the conflict.

CHAPTER 17

Study Corner

Key Terms

bipolar (power structure) (*p. 451*)
cold war (*p. 451*)
containment (*p. 451*)
deterrence policy (*p. 458*)
economic globalization (*p. 463*)
free trade (*p. 463*)
internationalist (*p. 450*)
isolationist (*p. 450*)

military-industrial complex (*p. 460*)
multilateralism (*p. 452*)
multinational corporations (*p. 463*)
preemptive war doctrine (*p. 454*)
protectionism (*p. 464*)
unilateralism (*p. 454*)
unipolar (power structure) (*p. 452*)

Self-Test

1. Diplomacy is distinct from military power as a foreign policymaking instrument in that diplomacy:
   a. is effective only when used in conjunction with other instruments.
   b. requires a bilateral relationship; it cannot be employed unilaterally.
   c. is subject to direction by the president.
   d. is sometimes applied through an international intermediary, such as the United Nations.

2. Economic exchange primarily takes place through:
   a. entering into military alliances that then turn into trading alliances.

b. monitoring other countries' economic activities and enacting tariffs if necessary.

c. developing trade relations with nations that are premised on the assumption that these relations will benefit both sides.

d. military takeovers of countries that have raw materials of value.

3. Drawbacks to the pursuit of a policy of multilateralism include which of the following?

a. Multilateral interventions are almost always less successful than when the United States acts unilaterally.

b. Multilateral intervention does not guarantee long-term success in solving situations.

c. Multilateral interventions abroad almost always reduce the president's popularity at home.

d. All of the above.

4. The formal organization through which nations administer and negotiate the general rules governing international trade is:

a. the UN.

b. NATO.

c. the World Bank.

d. the WTO.

5. The lesson of Vietnam for the United States was that:

a. there are limits to America's ability to assert its will in the world alone.

b. America's military arsenal was obsolete and needed updating.

c. appeasement only encourages further aggression.

d. an isolationist foreign policy is the only safe direction for U.S. policy.

6. After World War II, the United States emerged as:

a. an economically impoverished country.

b. the major country with the least amount of domestic oil reserves.

c. an internationalist country.

d. the world's only superpower.

7. The main threat to the physical security of the United States since the attacks on the World Trade Center and the Pentagon is international terrorists who fight on behalf of causes. (T/F)

8. High levels of congressional support for an expensive weapons program are sometimes linked more to the jobs it creates than to its overall usefulness to the U.S. arsenal. (T/F)

9. The United States spends more on foreign aid as a percentage of its total national budget than do most Western democracies. (T/F)

10. U.S. military intervention both in the Persian Gulf and in Kosovo not only punished the aggressor party in each case but also settled the underlying dispute once and for all. (T/F)

Critical Thinking

What are the major objectives of U.S. foreign and defense policy? What are the mechanisms for pursuing those objectives?

Suggested Readings

Clarke, Richard A. *Against All Enemies: Inside America's War on Terror*. New York: Free Press, 2004. A best-selling book by the nation's former top-ranking presidential adviser on terrorism.

Fishman, Ted C. *China, Inc.: How the Rise of the Next Superpower Challenges America and the World*. New York: Scribner, 2005. A look at China's rapid economic growth and its implications.

Hixson, Walter L. *The Myth of American Diplomacy: National Identity and U.S. Foreign Policy*. New Haven, Conn.: Yale University Press, 2008. An analysis of the influence of America's cultural ideals on its foreign policy.

Nye, Joseph S. *Soft Power: The Means to Success in World Politics*. New York: PublicAffairs, 2004. An argument for making diplomacy, assistance, and other forms of "soft power" the basis of U.S. foreign policy.

Odom, William E. *Fixing Intelligence*. New Haven, Conn.: Yale University Press, 2003. A detailed critique of U.S. intelligence efforts by a former military intelligence officer.

Sobel, Richard. *The Impact of Public Opinion on U.S. Foreign Policy Since Vietnam*. New York: Oxford University Press, 2001. An account of public opinion's impact on foreign policy.

Stiglitz, Joseph E., and Linda J. Bilmes. *The Three Trillion Dollar War: The True Cost of the Iraq Conflict*. New York: W.W. Norton, 2008. An analysis of the current and future costs associated with the Iraq war, written by a Nobel Prize–winning economist and a former Commerce Department official.

Woodward, Bob. *Plan of Attack*. New York: Simon & Schuster, 2004. An inside look at the Bush administration's decision to go to war in Iraq.

List of Websites

http://www.defenselink.mil/

The U.S. Department of Defense website; provides information on each of the armed services, daily news from the American Forces Information Service, and other material.

http://www.cfr.org/

A website that includes reports and assessments of the Council of Foreign Relations and transcripts of speeches by U.S. and world political leaders on topics of international interest.

http://www.igc.org/igc

The website of the Institute for Global Communications (IGC); provides information and services to organizations and activists on a broad range of international issues, including human rights.

http://www.wto.org/

The World Trade Organization (WTO) website; contains information on the organization's activities and has links to related sites.

Participate!

In his 1961 inaugural address, President John F. Kennedy said, "Ask not what your country can do for you. Ask what you can do for your country." Kennedy called America's young people to service on behalf of their country. His call was not just a call to military service. One of Kennedy's early initiatives, the Peace Corps, offered Americans the opportunity to apply their skills to development projects in other countries. Under Kennedy's successor, President Lyndon Johnson, a domestic version of the Peace Corps—Volunteers in Service to America (VISTA)—was established. Before the military draft ended in 1973, male Americans expected to serve their country. Not all did so, but millions served in the Army, Navy, Air Force, or Marines. Since the end of the draft, Congress has from time to time considered establishing a National Service that would require every young American man and woman to serve the country in one way or another for a set period of time. However, you do not need an act of Congress if you want to serve your country. There are a range of alternatives including the all-volunteer military, the Peace Corps, and AmeriCorps (a network of local, state, and national service programs).

Extra Credit

For up-to-the-minute *New York Times* articles, interactive simulations, graphics, study tools, and more links and quizzes, visit the text's Online Learning Center at www.mhhe.com/pattersontad9e.

Self-Test Answers

1. b   2. c   3. b   4. d   5. a   6. c   7. T   8. T   9. F   10. F

National Journal

ENEMY OF MY ENEMY

On paper, the Mujahedeen-e Khalq sounds like the sort of group the United States government might like to cultivate: well-organized Iranian exiles concentrated in Europe and Iraq who share Washington's antipathy to the theocracy in Iran. The group—whose name translates as "warriors for the people of Iran"—has its own "parliament in exile," the National Council of Resistance of Iran, and says it supports a secular government, democracy, human rights, and women's rights in Iran.

In practice, however, the Iranian group has some major shortcomings in the ally department. For the past decade, the State Department has listed the MEK as a "foreign terrorist organization," and more recently has argued that the group displays "cult-like characteristics."

The MEK has been waging a spirited campaign to persuade the U.S. to drop the terrorist designation—which would require either the secretary of State's say-so or an act of Congress.

Although the group can't make its own case directly, in the past several years two prominent former U.S. government officials have been publicly touting the MEK's virtues and arguing that the United States should remove it from the terrorist list.

At the moment, the more high-profile and influential of these advocates is former House Majority Leader Dick Armey, R-Texas, a senior policy adviser at the global law and lobbying firm DLA Piper. Last year, Armey wrote two op-eds for Washington newspapers urging the State Department to drop the MEK's terrorist designation.

"Never has the old adage 'The enemy of my enemy is my friend' been more true than in the case of the MEK," he wrote in The Hill in July. And in The Washington Times in December, Armey wrote, "With a stroke of the pen, the secretary of State could, and should, remove the Mujahedeen-e-Khalq and the National Council of Resistance of Iran from the list of foreign terrorist organizations."

Another public advocate for the MEK is Raymond Tanter, who was a senior staff member at the National Security Council in the Reagan administration and is now an adjunct professor at Georgetown University. In 2005, Tanter co-founded the nonprofit Iran Policy Committee, which lists as directors or advisers a half-dozen former executive branch, military, and intelligence officials and describes its mission as promoting a "central role for the Iranian opposition" in bringing about "democratic change" in Iran. The committee's publications, conferences, and congressional briefings routinely urge the U.S. to take the MEK off its terrorist list, as well as to meet with and fund the group.

The MEK began as an anti-shah leftist group in the 1960s. It got on the wrong side of the United States when members assassinated several of the shah's American advisers in the 1970s. In the three decades since Iran became an Islamic regime, the State Department says, the MEK has waged violent attacks inside that country, and it maintains the "capacity and will to commit terrorist acts in Europe, the Middle East, the United States, Canada, and beyond."

A charismatic husband-and-wife team leads the group: Massoud Rajavi, whose whereabouts are unknown, is the military leader, and Maryam Rajavi heads the political wing from France. The MEK's size is also unknown, but the Council on Foreign Relations estimates that it could have as many as 10,000 members worldwide.

In 2005, Human Rights Watch issued a report detailing complaints from a dozen former MEK members that they suffered physical and psychological abuse while they were in the group. The State Department says that members undergo indoctrination and weekly "ideological cleansings," are separated from their young children, and must vow "eternal divorce"—that is, to remain unmarried or to divorce their spouse.

The U.S. invasion of Iraq in 2003 took a toll on the MEK, which had set up operations there after being driven out of Iran and, later, France in the 1980s. Because Saddam Hussein had been providing the bulk of its military and financial support, the State Department says, the MEK subsequently began to use "front organizations" to solicit contributions from expatriate Iranian communities.

The U.S. military disarmed the group's foot soldiers in Iraq and now holds some 3,500 of them as "protected persons" under the Geneva Conventions at an encampment there. "We are not embracing them, we just don't know how to [disperse] them" without putting their lives in danger, says Brookings Institution senior fellow Peter Rodman, who was an assistant Defense secretary through 2006.

MEK supporters argue that the group has renounced violence, poses no terrorist threat, and, in fact, presents a viable alternative to the theocracy in Tehran. The terrorist designation, they say, was a futile Washington sop to appease that regime. "The U.S. government at any moment can make that decision, and decide [that the designation] is unwarranted," says Alireza Jafarzadeh, the former representative in Washington for the NCRI, and now a self-described consultant and a commentator on Fox News. Jafarzadeh blames "politics" for Washington's failure to act and says that the MEK spends about 80 percent of its resources "to counter the consequences of the designation."

MEK supporters argue that the group provided vital intelligence about Iran's covert nuclear program in 2002, as well as about Iranian-sponsored attacks on U.S. soldiers in Iraq.

Although more than 220 members of Congress signed a letter in 1998 protesting the group's terrorist designation, the MEK's several legal challenges to the designation have failed, and legislative efforts to remove it have gone nowhere.

Despite the Bush administration's tough line on the Tehran regime, the MEK's political fortunes in the U.S. have declined in recent years. The NCRI was once allowed to maintain an office, hire lobbyists, hold press conferences, and generally operate openly in the United States. But in late 2003, the administration got tough and the Justice Department shut down the office. The group still has some congressional supporters.

Armey's history as an outspoken advocate for the MEK is murky. DLA Piper has received $860,000 in fees over the past four and a half years from Saeid Ghaemi, whom the firm identifies as an "Iranian-American businessman who works closely with the Iranian-American community in the U.S. to promote human rights and democracy in Iran." Public records identify Saeid Ghaemi as a used-car dealer in the Denver area, but an Internet search turned up no information about his political work with the Iranian-American community. When National Journal reached him by phone to ask about his hiring of Armey and DLA Piper, Ghaemi said he was busy and would return the call. He failed to return that or subsequent calls.

Last year, Armey and the other lobbyists also worked on Ghaemi's behalf for a House measure urging the secretary of State to designate the Quds Force of Iran's Islamic Revolutionary Guards Corps as a foreign terrorist organization. Shortly after a broader measure targeting Iran and the Quds Force overwhelmingly passed the House last fall, Secretary of State Condoleezza Rice designated the force a terrorist group.

DLA Piper also lobbied in the Senate for the Iran Human Rights Act of 2007 that would, among other things, expand U.S. support for Iranian opposition groups to include those outside Iran, and would establish a State Department envoy to reach out to such groups.

Tanter, like some other MEK defenders, says he supports the group because it is the only opposition organization that really worries the mullahs in Tehran. "I did an analysis of all the opposition groups and found that the [Islamic Iranian] regime paid attention to [the MEK] 350 percent more than all the others. I am not here to lobby on behalf of groups on the foreign terrorist organization list. I am

MEK supporters argue that the group has renounced violence, poses no terrorist threat, and, in fact, presents a viable alternative to the theocracy in Tehran. The terrorist designation, they say, was a futile Washington sop to appease that regime.

an American trying to preserve American national security abroad and save lives."

Tanter's tax-exempt Iran Policy Committee has raised a substantial amount of money in a short period of time. The law prohibits anyone in the United States or subject to its laws from providing "material support or resources" to a designated foreign terrorist organization. But these financial sanctions don't prohibit "U.S. citizens from expressing their views on economic sanctions matters—and that includes the designation of the MEK—to Congress or the Executive Branch" according to the Treasury Department, whose Office of Foreign Assets Control oversees the sanctions. Bill Livingstone, who worked with his brother Neil on the 2006 report, said that the authors made sure the report did not violate Treasury's rules.

"The First Amendment protects Dick Armey to make his opinions known, and protects the Iran Policy Committee's educational mission to find options to reinforce our diplomacy" toward Iran, Tanter said. He has hired an attorney who specializes in the arcane Treasury rules and contends that his group tries "to vet our money to make sure we're not getting any" from prohibited groups. Tanter also points out that several of his group's advisers and directors are retired military and intelligence officers with security clearances that they would do nothing to jeopardize.

The effect of Armey's and Tanter's efforts is unclear. So far, the MEK's efforts to shed its

terrorist designation have met with far more success in Europe than here. The group has won court decisions mandating that the European Union unfreeze the group's assets and that Great Britain remove it from that country's list of terrorist groups. The British government says it intends to appeal.

Although the State Department is required to review its designation of the MEK later this year, the group's supporters fear that the decision will reflect a political climate that has become less sympathetic to their cause. Administration hard-liners, who have lost ground to pragmatists, have been further undercut by the recent National Intelligence Estimate stating that Iran stopped its nuclear weapons program in 2003—a conclusion that the MEK disputes. "This so-called hard-line [Bush] administration is more interested in striking a grand bargain with Iran than the E.U. is," Tanter said. He and other MEK boosters also contend that if relations with Tehran worsen, the MEK's prospects could revive.

The neoconservative community, where the MEK has found support in the past, has become sharply divided, with critics becoming as vocal as supporters in conservative publications. "I don't think any administration is going to want to include them," said Rodman, who describes himself as a hard-line opponent of the Tehran regime. "Everyone has rejected [the MEK]. They're not the kind of people we want to work with."

FOR DISCUSSION: Should the MEK, and similar groups hostile to unfriendly nations, remain a terrorist organization? Should America regard the enemies of its enemies as friends, no matter how distasteful? Do the threats of some regimes, such as the theocracy in Iran, require you to compromise and make pragmatic concessions to militant groups trying to overthrow them?

State and Local Politics
Maintaining Our Differences

The Structure of State Government

    The State Constitutions
    Branches of Government
    Citizen Politics: Elections, Parties,
        and Interest Groups

The Structure of Local Government

    Types of Local Government
    Local Elections and Participation

State and Local Finance

    Sources of State Revenue
    Sources of Local Revenue

State and Local Policy

    Policy Priorities
    Public Policy Patterns

The Great Balancing Act: Localism in a Large Nation

The powers not delegated to the United States by the Constitution, nor prohibited by it to the States, are reserved for the States . . . Tenth Amendment

In late 2001, Attorney General John Ashcroft directed federal agents to take action that would stop Oregon physicians from prescribing federally controlled drugs to assist terminally ill patients in committing suicide. Ashcroft sought to void the Oregon law that permits physician assistance in cases where a patient, in the judgment of at least two doctors, has less than six months to live, is suffering painfully, and is mentally competent to decide whether to end his or her life. Ashcroft's action was not the first federal attempt to nullify the Oregon law. Congress had twice initiated action—in one instance, a bill passed in the House but failed to come up for a vote in the Senate.

Oregon's voters had approved the assisted-suicide law in a statewide referendum, becoming the first state (and, as of 2009, the only state) to do so. A majority of Oregon's voters had been persuaded by the argument that no public benefit derives from requiring the dying to accept prolonged suffering. Opponents had countered that society's interest in preserving life outweighs a patient's desire to die, that doctors and relatives in some instances might persuade terminally ill patients to accept death against their will, and that depressed patients who asked to die should be treated for their depression (after which they might choose to live). In filing suit against the Oregon law, the U.S. Department of Justice argued that "there are important medical, ethical and legal distinctions between intentionally causing a patient's death and providing sufficient dosages of pain medications to eliminate or alleviate pain."

In 2006, the U.S. Supreme Court decided the issue in Oregon's favor, ruling that its physicians could not be punished for prescribing the drugs in question. The Court held in *Gonzales v. Oregon* that federal law did not grant Ashcroft "the extraordinary authority" he had claimed in trying to regulate medical practice, which traditionally has been within the power of the states. The Supreme Court did

A supporter of Oregon's Death with Dignity law holds a sign outside the federal courthouse in Portland, Oregon, where a hearing on the U.S. Justice Department's challenge to the law is being held. This type of struggle between the power of the federal government and the power of a state government has been repeated countless times in American history, a reflection of the U.S. federal system that vests sovereignty in both the national and state governments. In this particular case, the state, Oregon, prevailed. The U.S. Supreme Court in 2006 ruled that Attorney General John Ashcroft had exceeded his authority in trying to invalidate the Oregon law.

not repudiate Congress's power to regulate drugs, but it did reject Ashcroft's claim that he had the authority to decide the issue in the case of physician-assisted suicide.[1]

The controversy surrounding Oregon's Death with Dignity Act reflects both the dynamic and the contentious nature of American federalism. The U.S. political system divides power between a national government and the separate states. Americans are governed by two sovereign entities, each of which has a claim to final authority over those who reside within its boundaries. Over time, as was described in detail in Chapter 3 and discussed elsewhere in this text, there has been a gradual expansion of national power and a corresponding reduction in the discretionary authority of state governments.

Yet the states and their creations, the local governments, continue to be vital centers of politics and policies. As the Oregon case illustrates, the federal government cannot simply impose its will on the states. Its actions must conform with the constraints on federal power provided for in the Constitution of the United States. Moreover, in terms of day-to-day impact on Americans' lives, states and localities are far more significant than the government in Washington. The roads Americans drive on, the schools they attend, the civil and criminal laws they obey, and much more are defined principally by state and local action rather than by federal action. In fact, contrary to what many Americans might believe, states and localities have vastly more employees—nearly six times the number—than the federal government has (see Figure 18-1).

The purpose of this chapter is to describe more fully the American states and the localities within them. The great number of state and local governments and the variety they exhibit hinder any easy summary of what they are all about. Yet there are some general patterns. The chapter includes a comparison of the states that will explain some

FIGURE 18-1 **Employees of the Federal, State, and Local Governments** The state and local governments have substantially more employees than does the federal government.
Source: U.S. Department of Labor, 2008.

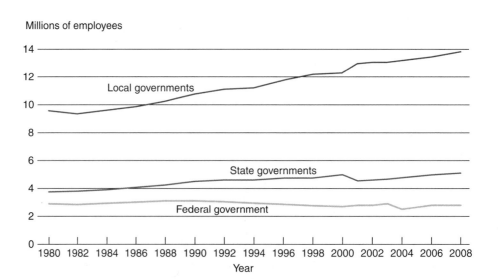

of the differences in their politics and policies. The main points of discussion in this chapter are these:

■ *All states apply the constitutional principle of separation of powers, but the states otherwise differ from one another—and from the federal government—in the way in which they structure their governments.* The use of elections as a means of choosing officials of all types, including judges and lesser executives (for example, state treasurer), is widespread.

■ *Local governments are not sovereign; they are chartered by their state government, which sets the limits of their power.* Of the units of local government (county, municipality, township, school district, and special district), the basic unit is the municipality. A municipality may be governed in one of four ways—the strong mayor–council, weak mayor–council, commission, or city manager system.

■ *States and localities have primary responsibility for most of the policies, such as public education, that directly touch Americans' daily lives.* The nature of these policies is affected by the wealth of the state or locality and also by its political culture, party system, and group system.

The Structure of State Government

The Constitution of the United States contains provisions that forbid the states from interfering with the lawful exercise of national authority, and the states are required by the Constitution to provide their residents with a "republican" (that is, a representative) form of government. In addition, the "supremacy clause" of the Constitution requires the states to comply with legitimate national laws, while the "full faith and credit" provision requires them to respect the laws of other states (for example, a legal contract issued by one state ordinarily is legally binding in other states).

Nevertheless, the Constitution was intended primarily to define national power and national institutions and does not say very much about the states or their powers. In fact, the Framers of the Constitution did not believe it was necessary to define the powers of the states. They held that the Constitution implied that the states held all legitimate governing powers not granted to the national government. This situation was unsettling to states'-rights advocates, who insisted on a constitutional amendment—the Tenth Amendment—which reserves for the states those powers not delegated to the national government. Although the Tenth Amendment has not given states the ironclad protection from federal encroachment that the Framers may have envisioned (see Chapter 3), the U.S. federal system gives the states broader authority than is typical of federal systems (see "How the U.S. Compares"). The American states are substantial centers of power by almost any applicable standard.

The State Constitutions

Each state's constitution establishes executive, legislative, and judicial branches and defines the lawful powers of each branch. The concept of checks and balances—the notion that each branch will act as a curb on the power of the others—is embedded in all state constitutions. All of them also include a bill of rights.

Although the state constitutions in these respects resemble the Constitution of the United States, they have distinctive features. On average they are roughly four times the length of the U.S. Constitution. Vermont is the only state whose

HOW THE U.S. COMPARES

STATE POWER IN A FEDERAL SYSTEM

Federalism involves the division of sovereign authority between a national government and area (state) governments. As discussed in Chapter 3, the first federal system of government in world history was established in the United States in 1787. The American states already existed, and the only realistic alternative for the Framers of the Constitution was a form of government that protected the states' integrity and authority. Other nations of the period had unitary systems (sovereignty invested solely in the national government), and most nations today still follow that system. However, the federal system has been adopted in some countries, including Canada and Germany.

Federal systems, however, are not the same everywhere. They differ primarily in the degree of autonomy granted to the subnational (state) governments. The United States allo-

cates an extraordinary level of authority to the state governments. They have more discretionary authority and more far-reaching power than is typically the case in a federal system, a reflection of the American tradition of local control and of Americans' long-standing suspicion of centralized power. The American states and their local units, for example, have a degree of control over education policy that is nearly unmatched. The federal government provides some of the funding for public schools and has imposed antidiscrimination requirements on these institutions. It has also established a national testing program that affects the amount of federal assistance a school is entitled to receive. However, the states and localities decide nearly all aspects of education policy: school calendar, course requirements, achievement standards, teacher qualifications, and so on.

---

constitution is shorter than the nation's. Louisiana's constitution, until it was replaced in 1974, was by far the longest and most detailed. At 250,000 words, it was more than thirty times the length of the U.S. Constitution. The longest state constitution still in effect today is Alabama's, which has more than 200,000 words and has been amended more than seven hundred times (compared with twenty-seven times for the U.S. Constitution).

The length of the state constitutions reflects the significant issues they address, such as the lawful powers and forms of local governments, the taxing authority of both the state and local governments, and the number and type of executive agencies of the state government. However, the state constitutions also contain many provisions that more properly belong in statutes than in a constitution. Alabama's constitution, for example, has amendments relating to catfish and beaver tails.

Most constitutional scholars believe that the length of state constitutions is a drawback. The U.S. Constitution is a sparsely worded document, which, as indicated in Chapter 2, has enabled succeeding generations to adapt it to their changing needs. Not so with many of the state constitutions, which often are so loaded down with narrow and detailed provisions that they deny policymakers the flexibility to respond effectively to new challenges.

The length of state constitutions reflects the relative ease with which they can be amended. Unlike the U.S. Constitution, for which amendments require a two-thirds majority in the House and Senate and then ratification by three-fourths of the state legislatures, a state constitution can be amended by legislative action combined with voter ratification. The typical process is a two-thirds vote of approval in each chamber of the state legislature and ratification by a simple majority of voters in the next election. Delaware is the only state where voter ratification is not required; however, two consecutive sessions of the Delaware legislature must approve an amendment for it to be ratified. More than forty states also provide for amendment by a **state constitutional convention,** and more than two hundred such conventions have been held. Finally, a third of the states permit amendment through a **constitutional initiative.** By obtaining the signatures of a specified number of registered voters, a citizen or group can petition to place

state constitutional convention

A state convention convened to amend the state constitution or draft a new one.

constitutional initiative

The process by which a citizen or group can petition to place a proposed amendment on the ballot at the next election by obtaining the signatures of a certain number of registered voters; if the amendment gets majority support, it becomes part of the constitution.

a proposed amendment on the ballot at the next election. If it gets majority support, it becomes part of the constitution. California leads the nation in terms of the number of constitutional initiatives proposed and enacted; its constitution has roughly five hundred amendments, many of which were added through the initiative process. Among the initiatives considered by California voters in the 2008 election, for example, were ones relating to high-speed rail transportation and limits on the power of eminent domain.

Branches of Government

All states make use of the principle of checks and balances that underpins the national government (see Chapter 2). There is nothing in the Constitution of the United States that would prohibit a state from adopting a parliamentary form of government, but no state has tried it. The executive, legislature, and judiciary in each state are separate branches that share power. Each branch thus serves as a check on the power of the others.

The Executive Branch

Most states wrote their first constitutions during periods when mistrust of executive authority was high. Consequently, they provided for relatively weak governors. The model still applies in some states, especially in the South and in New England. Political scientist Thad Boyle has systematically evaluated the institutional powers of the states' governors and has concluded that the office is "very strong" in nine states (including Ohio, Pennsylvania, and Tennessee), "strong" in twenty-one states (including Arizona, Kentucky, and Michigan), "moderate" in seventeen states (including California, Florida, and Texas), and "weak" in three states (Vermont, North Carolina, and South Carolina).[2] Regardless of formal powers, however, the governor is often the most visible and widely known politician in the state. The position provides a bully pulpit that allows the governor to assume a leadership role on policy issues.

Roughly half the states impose a two-term limit on their governors. Virginia, Mississippi, and Kentucky restrict the governor to a single term. In nearly all states, the governor's term of office is four years, but New Hampshire and Vermont limit it to two years. Most newly elected governors previously held other public office, such as state lieutenant governor, state attorney general, big-city mayor, or state legislator. An exception is Arnold Schwarzenegger, who was a Hollywood star before being elected California's governor in a 2003 recall election. Campaigns for governor, like those for the U.S. Senate, have become increasingly expensive. In a large state like New York or Texas, spending in the governor's campaign can easily top $20 million.

Although the governorship in most states is not a highly powerful office, governors have gained power in recent decades as a result of an increase in the size and complexity of government. The initiation of the state budget now resides with the governor rather than with the legislature in nearly every state, and every state now grants the governor the power to veto legislative acts. There was a time when a number of states denied their governors this power. North Carolina was

The U.S. Constitution, in its emphasis on a separation of executive, legislative, and judicial power, has been a model for state constitutions. The U.S. Capitol Building has also served as a model for the states. Shown here is the capitol building of the state of Texas, located in Austin.

STATES IN THE NATION

DIVIDED POWER IN THE EXECUTIVE

The president operates in a system of divided power in which joint action by Congress is often required for the president's programs to be adopted. The chief executives in the states are the governors, nearly all of whom must contend with a further division: a separation of power within the executive itself. Maine and New Jersey are the only states in which executive power is vested solely in a governor. In five additional states, the only other elected executive is a lieutenant governor. In most of the rest of the states, other major executive officials, such as the attorney general and the secretary of state, are also elected. Finally, there are twelve states in which even minor executive officials, such as the commissioner of education, are chosen by the voters. In the case of the federal government, these other major and minor officials are appointed by the president.

Q: Why is divided executive power particularly characteristic of southern states?

A: This structure is a legacy of former times when many southerners were philosophically opposed to concentrated political power, whether at the national or state level. It is noteworthy that the governor's powers in most southern states are weak in comparison to the governor's powers in most other states, even apart from the fact that southern governors are more likely to share executive power with other elected officials in their state.

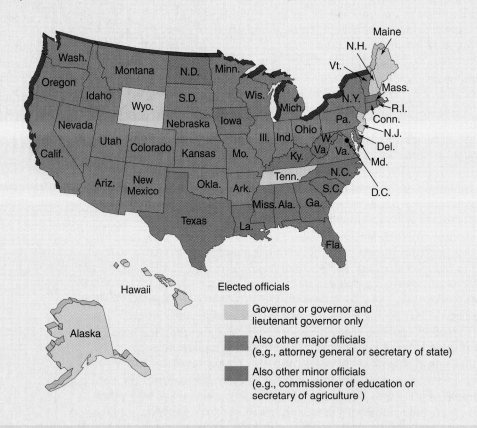

Elected officials

☐ Governor or governor and lieutenant governor only

☐ Also other major officials (e.g., attorney general or secretary of state)

☐ Also other minor officials (e.g., commissioner of education or secretary of agriculture)

Source: Compiled by author from various sources.

the last to change, amending its constitution in 1996 to give the governor veto power. In forty-three states, the governor also has a line-item veto, which permits the veto of part of an appropriations bill without voiding the whole act.

The governor is the state's chief executive but, in nearly every state, is not the sole elected executive official (see "States in the Nation"). In all but three states—Maine, New Hampshire, and New Jersey—the voters also directly choose one or more of the following executives: lieutenant governor, attorney general, secretary of state, state treasurer, education commissioner, agriculture commissioner, and public utilities commissioner. The governor shares executive power with these other officials, who are elected separately and who may belong to the opposition party. Except in the case where they are elected, the heads of state departments and agencies are appointed to office by the governor.

The direct election of multiple executive officials traces to early Americans' distrust of executive power and also to the Jacksonian and Progressive Eras, when accountability to the people through the vote was a prevailing philosophy. The multiple-executive system weakens the governor's control of the executive branch. At times, even the governor's control of his own office can be at risk. In California, for example, the lieutenant governor is elected separately from the governor and becomes acting governor when the governor travels outside the state's borders. When Jerry Brown was California's governor, the state's lieutenant governor, Mike Curb, was from the opposite party, and Brown would sometimes cancel, delay, or shorten a trip outside the state in order to prevent the lieutenant governor from taking action while he was away. On one of Brown's trips, Curb lifted the state's pollution control regulations. Upon his return, Brown issued an executive order reinstating them.[3]

Of the executive officials other than governor, the most powerful is the attorney general, who is elected to the post in forty-three states. The attorney general, as the state's chief legal officer, sets priorities for legal action. An attorney general might decide, for example, to concentrate the state's legal resources on environmental protection or investigations of alleged political corruption. The office of attorney general has often been a stepping-stone to a governorship or a seat in the U.S. Senate. Eliot Spitzer was elected New York's governor in 2006, largely on the basis of the reputation he made for investigating Wall Street fraud while serving as the state's attorney general. In 2008, Spitzer found himself on the other end of an investigation. The FBI discovered that he had been paying for the services of a prostitute, a revelation that led him to resign as New York's governor.

The Legislature

Like Congress, state legislatures have within their authority the most impressive array of constitutional powers a democracy can bestow. The legislatures make the laws, appropriate the money, oversee the operations of the other branches, and represent the people.

Despite their power, state legislatures are largely overlooked by the public, largely because most of them get almost no news coverage. News organizations concentrate on the geographical area defined by their "media market." For the television networks, this market is the nation as a whole. As a result, their news coverage concentrates on the activities of the national government. For local newspapers and local television affiliates, the media market is the local community. State governments are disadvantaged by these tendencies. In most cases, state boundaries do not coincide with media markets, which can even cut across state lines, as in the case of the St. Louis and Kansas City markets. Accordingly, reporters largely ignore the activities of state government, except for those of the governor.

State legislatures resemble Congress in their structure. With one exception, the state legislatures are **bicameral legislatures**—that is, they have two chambers. The upper house in every state is called the senate. State senates average about forty members, who serve four-year terms in most states. The lower house is always the larger one. Lower houses average about a hundred members, who are elected to two-year terms in most states. In nearly all states, the lower chamber is called either the house of representatives or the general assembly. Nebraska

bicameral legislatures

Legislatures having two chambers.

is the only state with a unicameral (one-house) legislature. It is called, simply enough, the Nebraska Unicameral Legislature.

The state legislatures' operations are also similar to those of Congress (see Chapter 11). Their leadership is provided by party leaders chosen by each chamber's members, but most of the legislative work and executive oversight is carried out in committees. Some states allow executive officials to introduce bills directly into the legislature. In Congress, only the members themselves have the power to submit bills, although the bills are sometimes drafted by the executive branch.

The locus of power within state legislatures varies widely. Some legislatures are extraordinarily democratic in the sense that power is widely disbursed and the job of the leaders is primarily to organize the members' work. In other states, power is concentrated in the top leadership, and other legislators—especially relative newcomers—are expected to follow their lead. In New York State, the annual budget is determined through bargaining among three top officials: the senate majority leader, the speaker of the assembly, and the governor. They negotiate until a final "deal" is reached, which the legislature as a whole is then expected to enact in its entirety.

Historically, most of the state legislatures were in session for only short periods each year, were deficient in staff and information resources, and were vulnerable to powerful lobbying groups. Beginning in the 1960s, however, they began to meet for longer periods and to expand their staffs. Legislators' pay also increased significantly at this time. The increase was substantial enough in a few states, such as New York and California, to create professional legislators—individuals whose chief occupation is an elective position within a state legislature. California's legislators are the highest paid, with an annual salary of roughly $115,000.

Shown here is the senate chamber of the New York legislature. Except for Nebraska, all the states have a two-chamber legislature.

Most analysts have welcomed the move toward more professional state leg-islatures. The Advisory Commission on Intergovernmental Relations, an agency established by Congress, noted in one of its reports: "Today's state legislatures are more functional, accountable, independent, and representative, and are equipped with greater information handling capacity than their predecessors."[4]

States that have resisted the movement toward professional legislators include New Hampshire, Alabama, Texas, and Wyoming, all of which pay their legislators $10,000 a year or less. New Mexico's legislators are the lowest paid, receiving no salary, though they do get $150 per day for expenses while the legislature is in session. Many states also severely restrict the time that the leg-islature can meet. The Texas legislature is in regular session for less than five months and meets only every other year. Term limits are a more systematic method for discouraging state legislators from staying in office indefinitely. Vot-ers in Oklahoma were the first to enact term limits, deciding by a two-to-one margin in 1990 to limit state legislators to twelve years of service. California and Colorado voters followed suit in the same year, and nearly half the states now have term limits for at least some offices.

The Courts

As a consequence of America's federal system, each state has its separate court system. These systems have trial courts at the bottom level and appellate courts at the top. About two-thirds of the states have two appellate levels, and the other third have only a single appellate court (the state's supreme court). Most of the less populated states have determined that they do not need a second appellate level. Those with a second appellate level have created it primarily to relieve the heavy caseload that would otherwise fall on the top court.

State courts are undeniably important. As indicated in Chapter 14, there is a federal court myth that holds that the federal courts are the more significant component of the American judicial system. In fact, upward of 95 percent of the nation's legal cases are decided in state courts (or local courts, which are agents of the states). Moreover, nearly all cases that originate in state courts also end there; the federal courts never enter the picture. Of course, one federal court—the U.S. Supreme Court—is a silent partner of the state and local courts, requiring them to act within the bounds of the U.S. Constitution (for example, in uphold-ing the rights of the accused).

The workload of the state court systems is considerable. State courts handle more than 100 million cases annually. Though many of these cases involve minor infractions, more than 10 million have potentially serious consequences for at least one party in the case, including imprisonment, financial deprivation, or personal loss (as in the case of a parent who loses a child custody dispute).

State courts differ in how they are organized and labeled. Most of the states have district courts and a supreme court, but the states also tend to give some lower courts specialized titles and jurisdictions. Family courts, for example, settle issues such as divorce and child custody disputes, and probate courts handle the disposition of the estates of people who have died. Below such specialized trial courts are less formal trial courts, such as magistrate courts and justice of the peace courts. These handle a variety of minor cases, such as traffic infractions, and usu-ally do not use a jury. Jury trial is not a constitutional requirement of the states, nor do they have to follow the federal tradition of a twelve-member jury or of a unanimous verdict when a jury is used.

States also vary in their methods of selecting judges. In about a fourth of the states, judges are appointed by the governor, but in most states judgeships are elective offices. Several states use the Missouri Plan (so called because Missouri was the first state to use it), under which a judicial selection commission provides a short list of acceptable candidates from which the governor selects one. After a trial period of a year or more, the judge selected must be approved by the electorate in a yes-no vote in order to serve a longer term.

The quality of justice in the state court systems is uneven. To say that the state courts are riddled with incompetence and favoritism would be unfair to the many skilled and conscientious jurists who work within them. But it is accurate to say that the state courts do not have enough resources to handle adequately the staggering load of cases thrust on them. Long delays are common, placing pressure on these systems to reduce the caseload through plea bargains and other mechanisms that increase the likelihood of arbitrary outcomes. Many judges, particularly those who operate in the lower courts, are poorly informed about the laws they are asked to apply. And a few are downright incompetent, having acquired their positions simply because they had the political connections or name recognition to win a judicial election.

Most states have made efforts in recent decades to raise the performance level of their court systems. Administrative and legal procedures have been changed, for example, to expedite the handling of cases. In the past, the pursuit of justice in many state courts was slow and arbitrary. Delays and procedural injustices still occur, but they are less prevalent today as a result of federally imposed standards and state-initiated reforms, such as those that require law enforcement officials to dismiss a case unless it is presented to a judge or grand jury within a specified period of time. States have also established disciplinary boards to identify and remove or reprimand incompetent judges.

Citizen Politics: Elections, Parties, and Interest Groups

When the Framers wrote the U.S. Constitution, they allowed for only minimal popular participation. The House of Representatives was the only popularly elected institution and the only one with a short term of office—two years. The democratic spirit of the Revolution of 1776 was more apparent at the state level. Every state but South Carolina held an annual legislative election, and several states chose their governors through annual election by the people.

Today, the states hold elections less frequently, but they have stayed ahead of the federal government in their emphasis on elections as a means of popular influence and control. As noted previously, most states elect their treasurer, attorney general, and secretary of state by popular ballot. Many states also choose their judges by direct election. No federal judges are chosen by this means.

State voters also have the opportunity to vote directly on issues of policy. In all states except Delaware, amendments to the state constitution require the approval of the electorate. In addition, more than a third of the states give popular majorities the power of the **initiative,** which allows citizens through signature petitions to place legislative measures on the ballot. If such a measure receives a majority vote, it becomes law, just as if it had been enacted by the state's legislature. A related measure is the **referendum,** which permits the legislature to submit proposals to the voters for approval or rejection. The initiative and referendum were introduced around 1900 as Progressive reforms. The Progressives also sought to protect the public from wayward state and local officials through the **recall,** in which citizens can petition for the removal from office of an elected official before the scheduled completion of his or her term. The state of California recalled its governor, Gray Davis, in the 2003 election that installed Arnold Schwarzenegger as the state's new chief executive.

initiative

The process by which citizens can place legislative measures on the ballot through signature petitions; if the measure receives a majority vote, it becomes law.

referendum

The process through which the legislature may submit proposals to the voters for approval or rejection.

recall

The process by which citizens can petition for the removal from office of an elected official before the scheduled completion of his or her term.

Of these mechanisms, the initiative has been the most important. Increasingly, it has become an instrument of group politics.[5] The average citizen does not have the time or money to organize a statewide petition drive. Many groups do, however, and they have increasingly used the initiative as an alternative to the traditional method of lobbying the state legislature. Not only are their chances of success often greater, but they also get the opportunity to decide exactly how the measure will be worded. Once the initiative is placed on the ballot, a group can use its financial resources to mount a statewide advertising campaign to urge its passage. An irony is that the initiative was devised by the Progressives to protect citizens against the hold that powerful groups had acquired over state legislatures. The initiative was to be a means by which citizens could bypass the legislature and thereby overcome the power of entrenched interests.

In 2003, Hollywood star Arnold Schwarzenegger was elected governor of California in a recall election that attracted scores of candidates. He was elected to a second term in 2006.

Election Participation

Some states, including Maine, Wisconsin, and Wyoming, have pioneered methods aimed at encouraging voting—such as election day registration. These states are among the leaders in voter turnout with participation rates that are more than 10 percentage points above the national average.

Although states have at times been electoral innovators, they have also at times tried to keep citizens from voting. The Fifteenth Amendment, ratified after the Civil War, prohibited states from denying suffrage on the basis of race. That prohibition did not stop southern states from inventing all sorts of devices, from whites-only primaries to poll taxes, to keep blacks away from the polls. The last of those barriers was outlawed by the Supreme Court in the 1960s, but the legacy of the earlier period remains. The South still has a lower voter turnout rate than do other regions.

Ballot manipulation did not end in the 1960s. Even today, there are state and local election officials who have few qualms about interfering with the right to vote if doing so will help their party. In 2000, Florida officials purged thousands of names from voter registration lists in some areas of the state, knowing that many of those on the lists were eligible to vote. On election day, these citizens were turned away from the polls on grounds that they had failed to register. In 2004, Ohio officials used an old trick to tilt the odds in their party's favor. They deliberately distributed too few voting machines to polling places that were in areas with large numbers of voters of the opposite party. When these voters went to the polls on election day, they had to wait in line for hours to cast their ballots, which discouraged some of them from doing so.

Another and more systematic device for holding down turnout is the voter identification card, which some observers say is a thinly veiled effort to keep lower-income voters away from the polls. As explained in Chapter 7, several state legislatures have recently enacted laws requiring citizens to have a government-issued photo ID card in order to register and vote. Such laws are claimed to reduce illegal voting by noncitizens, although research indicates that very little such voting occurs.[6] These laws penalize citizens who do not have a driver's license or passport—the two most commonly held forms of government-issued photo ID.

In general, voter participation has not been a high priority for state officials. There was a time when most statewide elections coincided with the presidential election, when turnout is highest. This scheduling helped whichever party ran strongest in the presidential race. In an effort to insulate their election races from this effect, states began in the 1930s to hold their gubernatorial elections in non-presidential years. Most states now have this schedule and two states, Virginia and New Jersey, elect their governors in odd-numbered years, thus insulating them from even the effect of the midterm congressional elections. Virginia and New Jersey rank near the bottom in terms of voter turnout level in gubernatorial elections.

Party Competition

The electorate's influence is not simply a matter of whether citizens are encouraged to vote, and make the effort to do so. The competitiveness of a state's party system also affects the public's influence. In states where party competition is weak, politics tends to be somewhat exclusive: a sizable share of the population, usually the poorest groups, are more or less ignored by government. The dominant party has gained control without the help of these groups, and the minority party could not gain control even with their help. In other words, neither party has a strong incentive to seek their vote. The classic case of a neglected public was the black community in the South in the period before the modern civil rights movement of the 1950s and 1960s. African Americans were politically powerless. Neither the white Democrats who ran the south nor the white Republicans who offered token opposition wanted black people in their coalition.

Where party competition is more intense, any sizable group in a state is likely to receive the attention of one party or the other and thus to be in a position to influence public policy. In the modern South, which is increasingly competitive between the parties, black voters are a growing force and have tipped the balance in some elections.

The state party systems have become more competitive by some indicators and less competitive by others. Compared with the 1960s, there are fewer states today in which one party controls the governor's seat and both chambers of the state legislature. However, the number of state legislative races in which the incumbent has no or only token opposition has increased.[7] Faced with a well-funded and popular incumbent, the opposing party increasingly has conceded the election. The professionalization of state legislatures has had an effect similar to that of the professionalization of Congress: legislators have used their positions to solidify public support and amass campaign contributions, thereby discouraging election challengers.

Group Competition

A state's interest-group system also affects the level of citizen influence.[8] In those states where interest groups are many in number and somewhat evenly balanced in their political resources, government tends to serve a broad range of interests. An example is the state of New York, which has many competing factions—including, for example, business and labor, the upstate and downstate areas, and environmentalists and developers. Significant legislation that makes it through the New York state legislature almost always requires negotiation among various groups.

In states where a particular group or interest is dominant, however, government tends to serve that group or interest above all others. A classic example was the Anaconda Copper Company in Montana, which, during the period when it accounted for nearly all the state's mining and manufacturing, virtually ran the state. A more recent example is the influence of the Church of Jesus Christ of Latter-day Saints in Utah. A majority of the state's residents are Mormons, and a policy alternative that is actively opposed by the church has little chance of becoming law. For example, the church for years opposed the sale of hard liquor in Utah, and such sales were prohibited by law. The law was modified in 1990, but only after Mormon leaders agreed not to oppose the change, which was

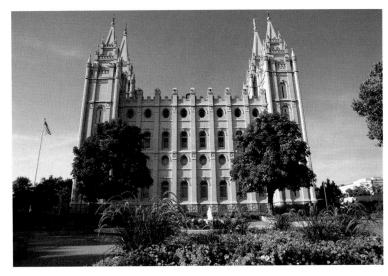

Utah is a state in which political alternatives are substantially shaped by a dominant interest. Policy proposals that are actively opposed by the Church of Jesus Christ of Latter-day Saints have little chance of becoming law. Shown here is the Mormon Temple in Salt Lake City.

prompted by the state's desire to improve its ability to attract tourists and conventions. The change enabled Utah to win its bid to host the 2002 Winter Olympics.

The Structure of Local Government

If the significance of a level of government were determined strictly on the basis of numbers, the local level would win handily. The United States has one national government and 50 state governments, but it has more than 80,000 local governments, including counties, municipalities, school districts, and special districts such as water, sewage, and conservation districts.

Local governments, however, do not have sovereignty—that is, they do not have final authority within their governing spheres. Their authority derives from that of the state within which they are located. The general principle that describes the relationship between state power and localities is called **Dillon's rule.** It holds that local governments are creatures of their state, which in theory even has the power to abolish them. The rule gets its name from Judge John F. Dillon, who propounded it in a nineteenth-century treatise on municipal governments. These governments, he wrote, possess only those powers that are "expressly granted" them by their state or are "implied in or incident to" these expressly granted powers.[9] The state's power extends even to the issue of whether a local unit of government will provide a particular service. The state of Wisconsin, for example, requires each of its cities to have a solid-waste disposal facility.

States differ markedly in the degree of freedom they grant their local units. The states that grant the highest degree of autonomy to local units, and those that grant the least, are found in all regions of the country. For example, Oregon, North Carolina, and Connecticut rank high on local autonomy, while Idaho, Mississippi, and Massachusetts rank low.

The chief instrument by which a state governs its local units is the **charter.** No local government can exist without a charter, which is issued by the state

HISTORICAL
Background

Dillon's rule

The term used to describe relations between state and local governments; it holds that local governments are creatures of the state, which in theory even has the power to abolish them.

---

charter

The chief instrument by which a state governs its local units; it spells out in detail what a local government can and cannot do.

and defines the limits within which a local unit must operate. By tradition, local charters are restrictive. They spell out in considerable detail what a local government can and cannot do. A typical charter, for example, specifies the types and limits of taxation that a local government may impose on its residents. The charters of some types of local government include a grant of lawmaking power. These governments can issue **ordinances,** or local laws. A locality might, for example, pass an ordinance requiring dog owners to leash their pets or an ordinance banning parking on certain streets.

There are practical limits to a state's ability to control its local units. A state government does not have the money or the staff to make all the decisions concerning its many local units, nor can a state expect the same restrictions to work equally well for all local units. A charter that is suited to a village of several hundred people would not work for a city of a million inhabitants. Accordingly, all states give their local units some discretionary authority and make allowances for differences among them. In most cases, the charters for cities are different from those for towns, which in turn differ from those for villages.

Home rule is a device designed to give local governments wide leeway in their policies. It developed out of a protest movement that sought to free local government from meddlesome interference by the states. Its guiding principle was the so-called **Cooley's rule,** articulated in an 1871 ruling by a Michigan judge, Thomas Cooley, who boldly declared that cities should be self-governing.[10] Home rule, first tried in 1875 in Missouri, allows a local government to design and amend its own charter, subject to the laws and constitution of the state and also subject to veto by the state. Home rule has grown in popularity over the years, a response to residents' demands for local control. It is also a practical solution to the states' inability to oversee the everyday decisions of their local governments.

Local government is the source of most public employment. While there are fewer than 3 million federal workers and 4 million state employees, more than 10 million people work in local government. Local government workers are one of the most heavily unionized groups in the country. Schoolteachers are represented through the American Federation of Teachers (AFT) and the National Education Association (NEA), and other local public employees are represented through unions such as the International Association of Fire Fighters (IAFF) and the American Federation of State, County, and Municipal Employees (AFSCME). These unions, with more than 3 million members, have been successful in negotiating better working conditions and job benefits for their members.

Types of Local Government

Local governments vary widely in their structure and responsibilities. The following sections highlight some of the variations.

County Government

The oldest form of local government in the United States is the county. It remains a top local governing unit in rural areas and in those few states, such as New York, where the county has broad responsibility for providing government services. The county is governed through an elected county commission (which, in some states, is called a county legislature or board of supervisors). Most states also have elected county sheriffs and county attorneys, and a few states have elected chief county executives.

Each state is divided into county units. The shape and number of these county units, however, varies markedly. Texas is divided into 254 counties;

---

ordinances

Laws issued by a local government under authority granted by the state government.

---

home rule

A device designed to give local governments more leeway in their policies; it allows a local government to design and amend its own charter, subject to the laws and constitution of the state and also subject to veto by the state.

Cooley's rule

The term used to describe the idea that cities should be self-governing, articulated in an 1871 ruling by Michigan judge Thomas Cooley.

Alaska, though larger in area, has only 16 county units. In most states, the county functions as an administrative subdivision of the state. The county's responsibility is to carry out programs, such as highway maintenance or welfare services, that are established by the state. Some analysts believe that the county will increase in importance in coming years because of the emergence of problems, such as waste disposal, that can be resolved more effectively at the county level than the community level.

County government illustrates the variation that exists in local governmental structures. Two states—Louisiana and Alaska—call their counties by another name (parishes in Louisiana, boroughs in Alaska). Moreover, the role of the county is not always the same even within a particular state. The county is typically a more visible unit of government in rural areas (where, for example, the county sheriff is often the most widely known public official) than in urban areas (where, for example, residents may not even know where their county offices are located). Also, counties vary greatly in population. They range from some urban counties with more than a million inhabitants to some rural counties with only a few thousand residents. The largest county is Los Angeles County in California, with a population of roughly 10 million.

Municipal Government

In most parts of the United States, the major unit of local government is the municipality, which can be a city, town, or village. While municipalities exist partly to carry out activities of the state government, they exist primarily to serve the needs of their residents. Most Americans depend on their municipal governments for law enforcement, water, and sanitation services.

Municipalities are legal entities that operate under a charter granted by the state. As indicated previously, a charter defines the limits within which a local governing unit must operate. Over the years, and consistent with the philosophy of local autonomy, municipal charters have become less restrictive. Moreover, rather than drafting separate charters for each municipality, states have developed more general charters that apply to all municipalities within a category (such as

Police and firefighters are among the most visible symbols of local government. Their courageous actions in New York City on September 11, 2001, cost hundreds of them their lives and serve as a tragic reminder of the indispensable role they play in America's communities.

TABLE 18-1 | Common Forms of Municipal Government

Strong mayor–council system: an elected mayor has veto power over an elected council and has substantial authority over the budget and other policies.

Weak mayor–council system: an elected mayor does not have veto power and generally is weak relative to the elected council.

Commission system: executive and legislative power is vested in an elected commission whose members each have a specified policy role, such as police commissioner.

City manager system: an appointed chief executive administers programs and can be fired by the elected council.

strong mayor–council system

The most common form of municipal government, consisting of the mayor as chief executive and the local council as the legislative body, in which the mayor has veto power and a prescribed responsibility for budgetary and other policy actions.

weak mayor–council system

The form of municipal government in which the mayor's policymaking powers are less substantial than the council's; the mayor has no power to veto the council's actions and often has no formal role in activities such as budget making.

commission system

The form of municipal government that invests executive and legislative authority in a commission, with each commissioner serving as a member of the local council but also having a specified executive role, such as police commissioner or public works commissioner.

city manager system

The form of municipal government that entrusts the executive role to a professionally trained manager, who is chosen—and can be fired—by the city council.

"small city" or "medium-size city," as defined by population). Of course, some municipalities are in a class by themselves and require a specific charter. New York City, for example, has taxing and other powers not granted to other cities in New York State.

The traditional and still most common form of municipal government is the mayor-council system, which includes the mayor as the chief executive and the local council as the legislative body (see Table 18-1). The mayor-council system takes one of two forms. The more common form is the **strong mayor–council system,** in which the mayor has veto power and direct responsibility for budgetary and other policy actions. The mayor, rather than the council, is the more powerful policymaker. The alternative form is the **weak mayor–council system,** in which the mayor's policymaking powers are less substantial than those of the council. The mayor has no power to veto the council's actions and often has no formal role in activities such as budget making.

A different type of municipal government entirely is the **commission system.** This form invests executive and legislative authority in a commission, with each commissioner serving as a member of the local council but also having a specified executive role, such as police commissioner or public works commissioner. The commission system has lost considerable favor in recent decades. Its major weakness is that it has no chief executive with the power and responsibility to set the local government's overall direction. Today, less than a hundred U.S. communities employ this governing system. Fargo, North Dakota, is one of the remaining cities in this group.

A final type of municipal government is the **city manager system,** which was pioneered in Ohio during the Progressive Era in reaction to inefficiency and partisan corruption in many of the nation's cities. The system entrusts the executive role to a professionally trained manager, who is chosen—and can be fired—by the city council. Most city managers have specialized university training in the operation of municipal government. The typical form of this education is the master of public administration (MPA), which includes courses in areas such as public finance, budgeting, and organization. However, city managers are usually "outsiders" who did not grow up in the community they administer and who typically lack the political support necessary to exert strong leadership. Most of the larger cities that installed the city manager system have since reverted to the mayor-council system, but the city manager form is the most common type of government in smaller cities. California is a state where the city manager system has been widely adopted. San Jose, Long Beach, Sacramento, and Anaheim are among the California cities with this form of local government.

A local chief executive, whether a mayor or a city manager, is, above all, an administrator whose main responsibility is to oversee the work of the component units of local government—the police, fire, sanitation, and other departments. Increasingly, local chief executives are also expected to provide economic leadership by fostering a business climate that will keep old firms in the community and attract new ones. In many cities, including Baltimore and Minneapolis, mayors have played key roles in the revitalization of downtown areas. Of course, not all chief executives accomplish much, or even get the opportunity. In smaller towns and villages particularly, the position of mayor is often more honorary than active; it is a part-time position held by a respected member of the community.

Towns and Townships

The word *town* is used in reference to a municipality that is smaller than a city and larger than a village. In New England, however, a town more often refers to a governing unit that functions as both a municipality and a county. In these areas, the county is often nothing more than a geographical entity—the town encompasses one or more communities and also the surrounding rural area. The town has responsibility for both community streets and rural roads, as well as other local services. The fabled town meetings that once governed New England towns still exist, but now few residents attend. The towns are governed by a town council of elected officials, who in the larger towns usually entrust day-to-day operations to a full-time town manager.

In several Midwestern states and a few states elsewhere, *townships* are an important governing unit. They are subdivisions of counties and, in rural areas particularly, have key policy responsibilities, including roadways and other public services. They resemble New England towns in that they were created as geographical units and vary widely in their population density. Thus, they are unlike municipalities where, for the most part, residents live close together. Townships also differ from municipalities in that, as subunits of the county, they do not have lawmaking power. They carry out county policy; they do not make policy of their own.

School Districts

The United States has a tradition of local public schools. Unlike Europe, where private schools and national educational standards have historically been more important, the United States has emphasized public education and local control. This control is exercised through local school boards. In a few places, the school board is subordinate to the municipal government, but elsewhere it is an independent body. School policy is established by the local school board rather than by the local mayor or council. The chief executive of the local public school system is a specially trained professional, the superintendent of schools. The superintendent is hired—and can be fired—by the local school board.

Some states have recently authorized charter schools as an alternative to traditional public schools. Such schools are granted a charter (much as local governments have a charter) within which they must operate. Charter schools have greater freedom than other public schools in selecting their admission, curriculum, and other policies.

Special Districts and Metropolitan Government

Another form of municipal government, and one of increasing importance, is the special district. These units deal with policy areas such as water supply, soil conservation, and waste disposal. Issues such as pollution control are not easily addressed within a single community. Special districts bring neighboring municipalities together. The typical form of governance of these districts is a board that includes a member from each municipality within the district's boundaries. The

POLITICAL CULTURE

LIBERTY, EQUALITY, AND SELF-GOVERNMENT

The American States

Americans share a common political heritage built around core values, including liberty, equality, and self-government. But do such values have the same meaning and priority throughout the country, or are there regional variations? That is the subject Daniel Elazar addressed years ago in his book *American Federalism*. Elazar posited that the United States has three cultural variants that reflect differences in ethnic settlement patterns, wealth, historical circumstances, and other regional influences. Although Elazar's thesis has not been carefully tested and is today somewhat dated because modern systems of communication and transportation have lessened regional differences, it is nonetheless worth pondering.

The northern tier of the United States—from New England to the Upper Midwest, then skipping to the West Coast—has what Elazar described as a moralistic subculture, reflecting the religious and communitarian values of the English, Germans, and Scandinavians who settled these regions. Self-government is more highly valued in this area than in other parts of the United States, as is social equality. Voter participation rates are high, and government is used extensively as an instrument of social purposes. For example, states in these regions spend more on public education than do states in other regions.

The middle part of the United States—from the Mid-Atlantic region through Kansas and into the Rocky Mountains—

is described by Elazar as having an individualistic subculture. This is the region where liberty—in the sense of freedom from government—is most pronounced. Government receives less attention here than in the moralistic tier, with lower voting rates and less public spending. On the other hand, individualism is more pronounced. Self-reliance weighs heavily in the thinking of residents in this subculture.

The third variant, a traditionalist subculture in Elazar's terms, typifies the states of the old Confederacy. This subculture reflects the stratified society out of which it grew. Government is a central institution but is often deployed to uphold traditional values and elites. The voting laws in the region, for example, historically were used to keep government in the hands of established interests. Ironically, the inequality that has typified southern society has made equality a driving force at times in the region's politics, not only for blacks but also for poor whites. Some legendary southern politicians, including Louisiana's Huey Long and Alabama's George Wallace, first rose to power on the resentment felt by lower-income whites as to their place in southern society.

Elazar's thesis is somewhat oversimplified and dated. Nevertheless, do you find in it ideas that are at least somewhat close to your own thinking about the region in which you live? Or do you think Elazar is off the mark in describing your part of the country? How would you describe the values of the political culture of your area?

---

day-to-day operation of these districts, however, is typically entrusted to trained administrators who often have specialized educations, such as the waste-management engineers who oversee municipal sewage systems.

Special districts ordinarily have responsibility for a specific policy activity, such as solid-waste management or soil conservation. In some urban areas, however, local governments have joined to create a **metropolitan government** that is given responsibility for a broader range of activities. An example is the Dade County (Florida) Metropolitan Government, which includes Miami and surrounding communities. Each community is represented on the Dade County Commission, which has responsibility for providing most local services. A metropolitan government is designed to reduce the waste and duplication that result when every locality in a densely populated area has its own sanitation department, its own planning board, and so on. Although metropolitan government saves money, the tradition of local control makes this option unappealing to most urban communities.

metropolitan government

The form of local government created when local governments join together and assign it responsibility for a range of activities, such as sanitation, so as to reduce the waste and duplication that result when every locality in a densely populated area provides its own services.

Local Elections and Participation

The principle of elective office dominates local government. In addition to an elected mayor, most communities have an elected town or city council. The office of county commissioner is also an elective office throughout the country. Except in a few states, most of them in the East, local officials are chosen in nonpartisan elections. No party labels appear on the ballot.

Perhaps no local institution symbolizes America's emphasis on the vote better than the public schools. School board members are elected, and in many communities the voters even have the opportunity to approve or reject school budgets and bond proposals. In contrast, school officials in European countries typically are appointed to their positions, and school budgets are set primarily by national governments.

Voting in local elections is subject to state registration laws. However, as noted in Chapter 7, many local governments have tried to weaken the link between their level of government and the state and national levels by scheduling local elections for odd-numbered years rather than the even-numbered years during which all federal and most state elections are held. A predictable effect of this scheduling is reduced voter participation. The turnout in most local elections in most states is very low—30 percent or less. However, local turnout can be high when a contentious issue is on the

Elections are a hallmark of American government at all levels. Over the course of an average year, citizens in many locations easily could vote in three or four different elections. In most states, citizens can also vote directly on issues of public policy through the referendum or initiative.

ballot. School bond issues, for example, often produce a high turnout and increasingly have pitted families with children in the public schools against the growing number of elderly Americans who, on the whole, are less supportive of school spending proposals.[11]

Local elections embody many of the conflicts that are found, in one form or another, throughout American politics. Many communities, for example, use at-large (community-wide) districts to elect members of the local council. At-large council members presumably will act on behalf of the whole community and not sections of it, as might be the case if they were elected from separate districts within the community. However, at-large districts tend to result in the election of council members who are demographically similar to the majority of voters. Minority groups have fared poorly in these systems, creating pressures to change at-large districts to separate-district systems.

It would be a mistake to conclude, however, that local officials are highly responsive to voting majorities. Studies have found that officials in some locations are primarily responsive to the wishes of the community's economic and social leaders. These citizens constitute a local power elite that, through their influence on elected officials, shape their community's policies.[12]

State and Local Finance

The federal government raises more tax revenues than do all fifty states and the thousands of local governments combined. The federal government is able to impose higher taxes than states and localities can because few citizens will migrate to a country that has lower taxes. The superior taxing power of the federal government is a prime reason why, in the second half of the twentieth century, federal revenue sharing became part of national policy (see Chapter 3). States and localities were faced with increased demand for public services but did not have the money to provide them. Federal grants-in-aid to states and localities became a means of getting the money they needed. Today, more than 15 percent of state revenue is provided by federal grants, which are targeted for specific programs or policy areas. Local governments get more than 10 percent of their revenue from the federal government. Some of it is in the form of direct grants, while the rest is channeled through the state government, which allocates it to localities based on its assessment of their needs.

States are in a competitive situation regarding taxes. People and businesses faced with high state taxes can move to another state where taxes are lower. Between the 1960s and the 1980s, many business firms moved from the Northeast and Midwest to the Southeast and Southwest, lured by cheaper labor and lower energy costs and also by lower state tax rates. Local governments are also in a relatively weak position to levy taxes. They compete with one another for the jobs and income that business firms represent. Every sizable city in the United States offers tax breaks or other incentives to lure companies to relocate there. The predatory nature of the competition makes it difficult for any locality to raise its tax rate substantially and virtually forces localities to give tax breaks to firms that could well afford to pay more. A community may even find that it has to pay a business to remain in that community. An obvious example, but not the only one, is the sports franchise that threatens to move its team unless the host city builds an expensive new stadium. Houston and Miami are among the cities that decided it was in the community's interest to comply with such a demand. Los Angeles is among those that refused the demand and lost a professional sports team as a result.

Compared with the federal government, states and localities also have a limited capacity to borrow money. Because the federal government prints the currency, investors are always willing to buy federal bonds, knowing that they will be repaid. States and localities are forbidden by the Constitution to print money, forcing them to be conservative in their borrowing practices. If their debt becomes too large, investors will not buy state and local bonds unless they carry a high enough interest rate to justify the risk, but high-interest bonds worsen a state's or locality's deficit problem in the long run. Accordingly, states and localities try to refrain from heavy borrowing. They also go through cycles of boom and bust depending on the overall health of the economy. When jobs are plentiful and income is rising, as was the case in the late 1990s, states and localities usually have budget surpluses. When the economy turns downward, as it did in 2008, their tax revenues decline and budgetary problems ensue.

Sources of State Revenue

States get most of their revenue from two sources: personal income taxes and sales taxes (see Figure 18-2). For all states combined, personal income and sales taxes each account for about a third of state revenue. However, the states vary in how much revenue they derive from each source. A few states, such as South Dakota, have no income tax. South Dakota also has no corporate income tax. Not surprisingly, South Dakota spends less on public services than nearly all other states. Its neighbor Minnesota spends about a third more per capita on public education and twice as much per capita on public health as does South Dakota.

The personal income tax is progressive in the sense that the effective tax rate increases as an individual's income rises, though no state has an income tax rate in excess of 10 percent (the top federal rate is 35 percent). In contrast, the sales tax is a regressive tax in that lower-income individuals are taxed on a larger percentage of their income than are higher-income individuals. Lower-income individuals spend mainly on items, such as food and clothing, that in most states are subject to the sales tax, while higher-income individuals put a larger share of their earnings toward things that are not subject to sales tax, such as bank savings and mortgage payments. States also levy a form of sales tax that goes by a different name—the excise tax. It is applied to selected items such as liquor and cigarettes. The excise tax has been called the "sin tax" because of the items it is levied on. State taxes on gasoline are also a form of sales tax in that the amount of the tax is based on the amount of gasoline purchased.

License and user fees are another important source of state revenue. The most important of these fees are the drivers' license and vehicle registration fees. There

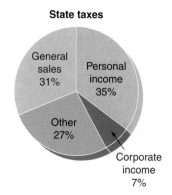

State taxes

FIGURE 18-2 State Government Taxes States rely on sales and personal income taxes for most of their revenue.

Source: U.S. Bureau of the Census, 2008.

SHOULD CONGRESS EXEMPT THE INTERNET FROM SALES TAXES?

Congress in 1998 enacted the Internet Tax Freedom Act (ITFA), which placed a temporary moratorium on state and local taxes on e-commerce. The states that had already enacted a sales tax on Internet purchases were exempted, but few states had done so. Congress has twice extended the moratorium, and each time there was substantial debate on whether the Internet ought to be a tax-free zone. Proponents of the exemption say that the Internet is still developing as a commercial medium and that its tax-free status is offset by the shipping costs and intense competition associated with Internet sales. Opponents say that a tax-free Internet is unfair to walk-in retailers whose goods and services are subject to sales taxes. They also note that state and local governments lose substantial amounts of revenue as a result of the sales-tax ban. What's your view? Which statement below comes closer to your opinion? Is there any room for compromise on this issue?

YES When the economic evidence [against a sales tax on Internet transactions] becomes too overwhelming to ignore, the Internet tax proponents usually turn to the "fairness" issue—even though it has been as thoroughly debunked as the economic argument. That's right, our selfless [public officials] are simply attempting to level the playing field for small "mom and pop" and "brickfront" stores that must collect sales taxes while Internet companies currently do not. This argument holds that small hardware stores across the nation will go under—thrusting their salt-of-the-earth proprietors into the cold—because the "Big Hardware" Internet site is not forced to collect taxes and therefore has an unfair competitive advantage. . . . This line of reasoning has been debunked numerous times, but for the sake of argument let's briefly review its more blatant fallacies. The same argument was made about catalogue sales with no such dire consequences for local merchants. . . . Shipping and handling costs often offset any price advantage enjoyed by Internet retailers thanks to the absence of sales taxes. . . . This is hardly an exhaustive list. . . . Suffice it to say, the case against Internet sales taxes is solid and well known.

—*National Taxpayers Union*

NO We must be sensitive to issues of basic competitive fairness and the negative effect our action or inaction can have on brick-and-mortar retailers. . . . I understand the importance of protecting and promoting the growth of Internet commerce because of its potential economic benefits. It is a valuable resource because it provides access on demand. In addition, it is estimated that the growth of online businesses will create millions of new jobs nationwide in the coming years. . . . I do, however, have concerns about using the Internet as a sales tax loophole. Sales taxes go directly to state and local governments, and I am very leery of any federal legislation that bypasses their traditional ability to raise revenue to perform needed services such as school funding, road repair and law enforcement. . . . While those who advocate a permanent loophole on the collection of a sales tax over the Internet claim to represent the principles of tax reduction, they are actually advocating a tax increase. Simply put, if . . . sales over the Internet go untaxed . . . revenues to state and local governments will fall and property taxes will have to be increased to offset lost revenue or states who do not have or believe in state income taxes will be forced to start one.

—*Mike Enzi, U.S. senator (R-Wyo.)*

are also license fees, for example, for restaurants and liquor stores. Doctors and lawyers are among the professionals who pay a license fee in order to practice in a state.

States also derive revenue from gambling, particularly from lotteries, which were banned by Congress as an illegal form of gambling until a few decades ago.[13] Today, most states run a lottery from which they keep about a third of the revenue. Many participants are lower-income individuals who cannot afford to play but dream of striking it rich. States play up this dream in their lottery advertising but do not mention that the odds of winning a huge jackpot are roughly the same as those of being hit—not once but twice—by lightning.

Finally, a few states derive substantial revenue from severance taxes, which are taxes on the extraction of natural resources. This tax is triggered by the act of taking a resource from the ground, as in the mining of coal or the pumping of oil. The logic of this tax is that once the resource has been removed, it is lost forever to the state.

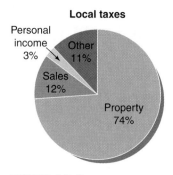

Local taxes

FIGURE 18-3
Local Government Taxes
Localities depend heavily on property taxes for their revenue.
Source: U.S. Bureau of the Census, 2008.

police power

A term that refers to the broad power of government to regulate the health, safety, and morals of the citizenry.

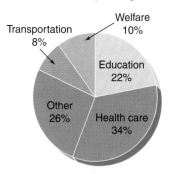

State spending

FIGURE 18-4   **Spending Priorities of State Governments**
Health care and education account for more than half of state government spending. Much of the health care spending is for Medicaid, which can also be regarded as welfare spending in that it is restricted to low-income persons.
Source: U.S. Bureau of the Census, 2008.

Sources of Local Revenue

As Figure 18-3 shows, local governments get most of their revenue from the property tax, which accounts for nearly three-fourths of all revenue they raise directly. However, the property tax has its drawbacks. It is paid in a lump sum, which heightens taxpayers' awareness of the tax and leads them to resist increases. Few actions are more likely to make local officeholders unpopular than a sharp rise in property taxes.[14]

In recent decades, localities have turned increasingly to the sales tax, which is collected with the state's permission in combination with the state sales tax. In Texas, for example, the state sales tax is 6.25 percent, with localities allowed to add up to 2 percent on top of that figure. A few cities—New York City among them—also raise revenues from the personal income tax. This tax, too, can be levied only with the state's permission. A local income tax enables a city to tax individuals who work in the community and use its services but have their residence elsewhere, usually in a nearby suburb.

State and Local Policy

Through the Tenth Amendment, the states possess what has been called the **police power,** a term that refers to the broad power of government to regulate the health, safety, and morals of the citizenry. Possession of this power has meant that the American states carry out many of the policy responsibilities that in other countries are dealt with at the national level. Although the policies enacted by Congress typically get more attention from the press, the acts of state legislatures have more influence on the day-to-day lives of most Americans. Law enforcement, public education, public health, and roads are among the policy areas that in America are determined largely by the state and local governments.

The economic wealth of a state has a substantial impact on its policies. Richer states are simply in a stronger position to provide more and better services than poorer states are. West Virginia, with a per-capita income only two-thirds that of Massachusetts, can hardly be expected to have schools, hospitals, roadways, and other facilities that match those of the Bay State. States' policies also vary with differences in the strength of their political parties and interest groups. For example, in states where Republicans are stronger, as in the mountain states, taxes and the level of public services tend to be lower. Where Democrats are stronger, as in the northeast, the reverse situation tends to hold.[15] These differences reflect the cumulative effect of the parties' opposing conceptions of government, as well as the cultural, economic, and social forces that tend to give one party or the other an advantage in a particular state or region.

Policy Priorities

One way to see how the states and localities use their power is to rank policy areas by level of spending. The top spending category for the states is health care, followed by public education, public welfare, and transportation (see Figure 18-4). These four areas are by far the most significant components of state spending.

The policy priorities of local governments are less easily described. Some local units, such as school boards, operate in only one policy area. Municipalities vary in size from the largest cities to the smallest villages, and their policies differ accordingly. Despite such differences, a few patterns are discernible in local spending. Far and away the biggest expense for local governments is public education, which accounts for roughly 40 percent of all spending at the local level (see Figure 18-5). Public safety (police, fire, corrections), health care, transportation, and welfare are next in line, in that order.

Public Policy Patterns

A brief description of some of the policy activities of state and local governments will provide a broader perspective on their role in the American system.

Education

Public education—including primary schools, secondary schools, and colleges and universities—accounts for the largest share of combined state and local spending, about a third of the total. Education spending by state and local governments dwarfs that by the federal government—more than 90 percent of the money for public schools is provided by states and localities. Higher education is also mainly a state and local responsibility. Thus, the greatest share of the country's investment in the technical research and personnel that underpin the economy is provided by subnational governments, which also make the major substantive policy decisions in the education area, from curriculum to performance standards to length of schooling.

Of the many issues affecting public education, two have stood out in recent years. One is the disparity in spending among school districts, which, in most instances, reflects differences in communities' wealth. Suburban schools typically are better funded and have better facilities than the inner-city schools in the same metropolitan area. Should such differences be allowed? In a 1973 case, the Supreme Court concluded that a state has no obligation to provide students with an *equal* education; rather, its obligation is "to provide an 'adequate' education for all children."[16] Nevertheless, state financial contributions to local schools typically are designed to help poorer districts more than wealthier ones. This tendency, however, does not begin to offset the disparity in the quality of schools between a state's poorest communities and its richest ones. In recent years, pressures have intensified to reduce disparities in school spending. In 1998, for example, New Jersey's highest court settled a battle over school funding by ordering the state to develop a plan to equalize spending in its public schools. Although New Jersey has not yet fully achieved that goal, it has made steady progress in implementing the court ruling.[17] Courts in about twenty other states have also ordered that spending on schools be more evenly balanced, but they have not gone as far as New Jersey's top court in requiring an equalization plan.

A second major education issue is the quality of American schools. U.S. students perform poorly on standardized tests in comparison to students of other advanced industrialized nations. American high school students are not even among the top ten in subjects such as science and math, where cross-national comparisons can reliably be made.[18] This situation has contributed to debates over merit pay for teachers, national tests for all U.S. students, and parent-student choice of schools. Some analysts claim that the schools are not the real problem, citing instead both the diversity of American society and the absence of a strong intellectual tradition as factors limiting the schools' ability to perform at a level equal to that of schools in other Western democracies. Other analysts claim

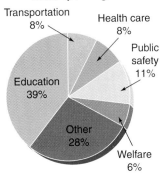

Local spending

FIGURE 18-5 Spending Priorities of Local Governments Education is by far the major spending category for local governments.
Source: U.S. Bureau of the Census, 2008.

America's tradition of local government is embodied in its public schools, which are governed by a school board, which in many locations is an elected body. Pictured here is Michael Rubin, a principal at Massachusetts' East Boston High.

that American public schools must be substantially changed if they are to provide high-quality education. The No Child Left Behind Act of 2001, discussed in Chapters 3 and 16, is an attempt by Congress to foster that kind of change.

Welfare Assistance

The most expensive social welfare program in the United States is entirely a national one—social security for retirees. However, the states are vitally involved in the provision of welfare services, particularly public assistance programs for the needy. Programs such as TANF (assistance for poor families) and food stamps operate within federal guidelines, but the states have discretionary authority over benefit and eligibility levels. These programs are funded jointly by the state and national governments but are administered primarily by the states. They have the local offices necessary for administering need-based welfare programs, which require regular contacts between caseworkers and welfare recipients. Welfare programs (excluding Medicaid) account for about a tenth of all state and local spending. This spending and the American tradition of self-reliance make welfare a contentious political issue.

LEADERS

SAM HOUSTON
(1793–1863)

Every state has had a distinguished governor. Only one individual, however, has served with distinction as the governor of two states. A Virginian by birth, Sam Houston fought in the War of 1812 and settled in Tennessee, where he was elected governor. A running feud with one of the state's leading politicians and the lure of the frontier eventually led Houston to leave for Texas, which was then part of Mexico. Houston became a leader in the movement for Texas's independence, arguing that a free Texas should join the United States rather than becoming a separate nation. Shortly before armed conflict with Mexico began, Houston was named commander-in-chief of the Texas Army. Following the loss of his forces at the Alamo, Houston defeated Mexican general Santa Ana's army in a surprise attack at San Jacinto, forcing Santa Ana to grant Texas its independence in 1836. Houston was twice elected president of Texas and then was elected to the U.S. Senate after Texas joined the Union. In the Senate he spoke against the rising sentiment in the South for secession, saying that it would result only in bloodshed and ruin. In 1859 he ran for governor of Texas as a Unionist and won the position, only to be evicted from his office after refusing to swear an oath to the Confederacy when Texas seceded in 1861. He also refused Abraham Lincoln's offer of command of an army of 50,000 soldiers to block Texas's secession. After leaving office, Houston retired to his home in Huntsville where he died in 1863, a year before the Civil War ended.

Health Care

More than 20 percent of state and local expenditures are in the health and hospitals policy area. All states and many localities operate public hospitals, and most of the laws and regulations affecting medical practices are established by state governments. In addition, states and localities offer public health programs such as immunization campaigns, mobile x-ray units, and health inspections of motels and restaurants.

Health care for the poor through the Medicaid program takes up an even larger share of the spending. States have devised various ways of holding down this spending. In response to the rapid increase in Medicaid costs, for example, the state of Oregon conducted a systematic study of medical procedures in order to eliminate Medicaid reimbursement for procedures that physicians apply electively, such as liposuction and surgery to remove benign skin lesions. Medicaid, however, is sure to remain a contentious issue. The rising cost of medical care has made Medicaid one of the two largest items (education is the other) in state budgets, and states are struggling to find new sources of money to pay for the program.

Highways

Until the 1950s, the roadways of America were built almost entirely with state and local funds. The interstate highway system, begun in the 1950s, was funded largely by the national government. Today, Washington provides about a third of the total spending on highways, and states and localities contribute the rest. State and local governments set most policies governing use of highways, including traffic infractions and shipping methods. Transportation spending accounts for about 8 percent of state and local expenditures.

Police and Prisons

While some democracies have a large national police force, the United States does not. Its law enforcement is entrusted almost entirely to local and state police forces. They enforce state laws and local ordinances, which collectively govern most aspects of crime and punishment. The state police include the highway patrol, game wardens, prison guards, and liquor control officers, and they are generally well trained and highly professional. Local police are less specialized, are more uneven in their training and professionalism, and are required to do most of the "dirty" work of law enforcement—crime control and the maintenance of public order. More than 5 percent of state and local spending is for public-safety activities.

States and localities in recent years have invested heavily in prisons and other correctional facilities. As indicated in Chapter 4, the United States on a per-capita basis is rivaled only by Russia in the number of its people who are imprisoned. The large prison population in the United States reflects a policy of lengthened and mandatory sentencing that developed in the past two decades largely around drug-related crime. Many prisoners are in jail for possession or purchase of relatively small quantities of illegal drugs. As the fiscal and human costs of this policy have increased, some state and local officials have sought alternatives, including giving judges greater discretion in the sentencing of nonviolent first-time offenders.

Homeland Security

A growing share of state and local budgets is devoted to homeland security. Prior to the events of September 11, 2001, homeland security was not even a part of the vocabulary of state and local officials. As the events of that day tragically revealed, however, states and localities are at the domestic forefront of the terrorist threat. Four hundred New York City firefighters and police officers lost their lives on September 11 as they rushed to assist people trapped in the twin towers of the World Trade Center.

State and local public employees are the "first providers" in the war on terrorism. Besides being the first on the scene in the event of a terrorist attack, they have responsibility for monitoring domestic sites that might be terrorist targets and for training citizens and public employees to respond to such attacks. The federal government assists state and local governments in funding activities related to the war on terrorism, but the federal funds have been insufficient to meet the costs. The U.S. Conference of Mayors has complained that cities have been saddled with an "unfunded local mandate." Some cities, including New York and Boston, have also complained that federal officials pay insufficient attention to risk when allocating homeland security funds, saying that too much of the funding goes to cities like Milwaukee and Memphis that are unlikely terrorist targets.

The Environment

The environment is a small part of state and local budgets, but money alone is not a reliable indicator of policy effort in the environmental area. Much of it involves regulatory activities that impose costs on firms and consumers.

Many environmental initiatives in the United States have originated with state and local governments. An obstacle to these efforts is the local attitude that environmentally friendly projects are desirable, as long as they are located somewhere else—Not In My Back Yard (NIMBY). This Greenpeace boat is mocking the opposition of Cape Cod residents to a proposed wind farm that would be located offshore but within sight of land.

Most states and localities were complacent about environmental protection until the federal government in the 1960s and 1970s greatly broadened the scope of its activities. Today, states and localities are also active participants. For example, they routinely require environmental impact statements for major development projects and have acted to protect their land and water resources from pollutants. In addition, conservation through the preservation of parks, natural resources, and wildlife has increasingly been a focus of state policy. New York, for example, has purchased and otherwise protected tens of thousands of acres of undeveloped land in its Adirondack Mountains.

Several states have also taken a leading role in addressing the problem of global warming. Concerned that the federal government was stalling on the issue, their governors, sometimes in combination with governors of nearby states, have recently devised state-level plans to restrict carbon emissions. California's plan is one of the most ambitious. It aims to reduce the state's greenhouse gas emissions by 25 percent by 2020. In California's case, the contribution could be a significant one. Because of its massive size, population, and economy, California is the twelfth largest carbon-emitting governing entity in the world.

At the local level, a leading environmental problem is sewage and garbage disposal. As environmental standards have been raised, it has become an increasingly costly activity, ranking behind only schools, roadways, and public safety as an expenditure item. It has also become increasingly contentious because most neighborhoods resist the nearby placement of a sewage treatment plant, garbage incinerator, or landfill. This opposition has acquired an acronym—NIMBY, for "Not In My Back Yard." Public opposition has forced many communities to undertake costly solutions, such as the shipping of garbage to distant landfills.

Civil Rights and Liberties

Civil rights and liberties also represent a small part of state and local budgets, but like the environment, they are of substantial importance. For a long period in U.S. history, the protections guaranteed in the Bill of Rights applied only to action by the national government. States were more or less free to decide for themselves the free-expression and fair-trial rights their residents would enjoy. During the twentieth century, however, federal courts, largely through the vehicle of the Fourteenth Amendment, assumed the power to compel states and localities to uphold certain individual rights (see Chapter 4). An example is the requirement that states and localities provide legal assistance to the criminally accused who are too poor to afford their own attorney.

Nevertheless, states retain discretionary authority in many areas of civil rights and liberties. Although discrimination on the basis of race, ethnicity, sex, or religion is not permitted, states can decide, for example, the age-discrimination standards that will apply to their own employees (see Chapter 5). No civil rights issue at the state and local levels has received more attention recently than the legal status of gays and lesbians. Although civil unions and same-sex marriages have received the most attention (see Chapter 5), other issues, including job and housing discrimination, have also come under scrutiny. A decade or two ago, almost no state or locality had a law that banned discrimination based on sexual orientation. Today, most Americans reside in a state or locality with such a law, although the scope of these laws varies greatly.[19] Only a few state and local governments, for example, require public and private employers to extend health benefits to the same-sex partner of employees if such benefits are provided to the opposite-sex spouse of employees.

The Great Balancing Act: Localism in a Large Nation

Every state in the American union has its special characteristics. California is no more like Mississippi than Mississippi is like Rhode Island. Yet, as this chapter has shown, the American states also have many things in common. The differences and similarities among the states are testimony to the enduring nature of the American governing experiment. The states are different enough to provide their residents with a special identity and a special political experience, yet they are alike enough to allow the triumph of the national union that the Framers so keenly envisioned over two centuries ago.

When the Constitution of the United States was written, 7 million Americans lived closer together and yet far apart. They were crowded along the eastern seaboard, but travel from Savannah in the South to Boston in the North could take weeks. Communication was equally slow; news traveled no faster than horses or ships could carry it. Today, the United States has nearly 300 million people spread across a continent, reaching even into Alaska and Hawaii. Yet communication is instantaneous, and an airplane can span the distance between Boston and Los Angeles in six hours.

The constitutional system that was created over two hundred years ago has endured because it has proved to be an adaptable one. As the nation's needs have changed, so has the relative balance among the three levels of government. The state-centered federalism of the early years of the United States gave way to a form of federalism in which the national government plays a larger role than previously. The Framers of the Constitution could not possibly have envisioned the particulars of this transformation. Theirs was a world of horse-drawn carriages, not that of the factories of the Industrial Age or the computers of today. But they did envision a governing system flexible enough to respond to changing needs during changing times.[20] The persistence of this system across more than two centuries is testimony to their vision and to the willingness of succeeding generations of Americans to find a combination of national, state, and local authority that could meet their governing needs.

Summary
Self-Test www.mhhe.com/pattersontad9e

Although developments in the twentieth and early twenty-first centuries have narrowed the differences among the American states, they—and the localities that govern under their authority—remain distinctive and vital systems of government.

All states apply the constitutional principle of separate branches sharing power, but the structure of the state governments differs in some respects from that of the federal government. An example is the more widespread use of elections at the state level. Most states elect by popular vote their judges and a number of executives, including an attorney general and treasurer in addition to a governor. Through the initiative or the referendum, nearly all states also allow their residents to vote directly on policy issues.

Local governments are chartered by the state. They are not sovereign governments, but most states have chosen to grant local units a considerable level of policymaking discretion. Local governments include counties, municipalities,

school districts, and special districts. Of these, the independent school district is the most distinctively American institution. The municipality is the primary governing unit. Municipalities are governed by one of four types of system: the strong mayor–council system, the weak mayor–council system, the commission system, or the city manager system.

The states and localities have primary responsibility for most of the public policies that directly touch Americans' daily lives. For example, the major share of legislation devoted to public education and more than 90 percent of the funding for it are provided by the states and localities. Public welfare, public health, roads, and police are other policy areas dominated by these subnational governments. They do not, however, have the amount of revenue that is available to the federal government. Competition between the states and localities holds down their taxing capacity. Their policies are also conditioned by the wealth of the state or locality and by the structure of its party and interest-group systems.

CHAPTER 18

Study Corner

Key Terms

bicameral legislatures
    (p. 479)
charter (p. 485)
city manager system
    (p. 488)
commission system (p. 488)
constitutional initiative
    (p. 476)
Cooley's rule (p. 486)
Dillon's rule (p. 485)
home rule (p. 486)
initiative (p. 482)

metropolitan government
    (p. 490)
ordinances (p. 486)
police power (p. 494)
recall (p. 482)
referendum (p. 482)
state constitutional
    convention (p. 476)
strong mayor–council
    system (p. 488)
weak mayor–council
    system (p. 488)

Self-Test

1. Which of the following statements about state governors is true?
    a. Nearly all power in state governments is vested in the office of governor.
    b. Only a few states give the governor a line-item veto.
    c. Most governors are mere figureheads; they have no significant political power.
    d. The large majority of governors share executive power with other elected executive officials.

2. The largest share of local government spending is for:
    a. police and fire protection.
    b. roadways.
    c. education.
    d. welfare.

3. The largest share of state government spending is for:
    a. police and fire protection.
    b. roadways.
    c. health care.
    d. state parks.

4. The two major sources of revenue for state governments are:
    a. personal income and general sales taxes.
    b. personal income and property taxes.
    c. property and general sales taxes.
    d. personal income and corporate income taxes.

5. About the relationship of local governments to their respective state government, it is accurate to say that:
   a. local governments are not sovereign; their power derives from that of the state.
   b. the long-term trend in most states has been to grant more autonomy to local governments.
   c. local governments depend on state government for some of their revenues.
   d. all of the above.
6. The type of municipal government that is now used by only a few localities is:
   a. the strong-mayor system.
   b. the weak-mayor system.
   c. the city manager system.
   d. the commission system.
7. The property tax is by far the most important revenue source for local governments. (T/F)
8. The condition of the national economy has almost no impact on state and local tax revenues. (T/F)
9. Most of the state constitutions are shorter and contain fewer amendments than the U.S. Constitution. (T/F)
10. In most states, judges are nominated for office by the governor. (T/F)

Critical Thinking

What are the general limits on the capacity of states and localities to raise the revenues they need in order to provide services to their residents through taxes? What is the impact of a state or locality's wealth on its revenue-raising capacity? What is the impact of economic growth? Of an economic downturn?

Suggested Readings

Beyle, Thad L. *State and Local Government*. Washington, D.C.: Congressional Quarterly Press, 2004. An edited volume of articles on recent developments in state and local government.

Broder, David. *Democracy Derailed*. San Diego: Harcourt, 2000. An analysis of how powerful groups have captured the initiative process.

Brunori, David. *Local Tax Policy: A Federalist Perspective*. Washington, D.C.: Urban Institute Press, 2007. A look at the revenue efforts of local governments.

Jewell, Malcolm E., and Sarah M. Morehouse. *Political Parties and Elections in American States*, 4th ed. Washington, D.C.: Congressional Quarterly Press, 2000. A state-by-state comparison of parties and elections.

Henig, Jeffrey R., and Wilbur C. Rich. *Mayors in the Middle*. Princeton, N.J.: Princeton University Press, 2004. An edited volume on mayoral takeovers of troubled schools.

Hero, Rodney. *Faces of Inequality*. New York: Oxford University Press, 2000. An assessment of how states' politics and policies are shaped by their racial and ethnic composition.

Smith, Kevin B., Alan Greenblat, and Michele Mariani. *Governing States and Localities*. Washington, D.C.: CQ Press, 2007. An up-to-date standard text on state and local government.

Tarr, G. Alan. *Understanding State Constitutions*. Princeton, N.J.: Princeton University Press, 1998. A thorough assessment of state constitutions and how they differ from the U.S. Constitution.

List of Websites

http://www.nga.org/
The website of the National Governors Association.

http://www.nyc.gov/
The website for New York City's government. Most cities and towns have their own website.

http://www.state.tx.us/
The website for the state of Texas. Every state government has a website.

http://www.usmayors.org/
The website for the U.S. Conference of Mayors.

Participate!

Local government offers many opportunities for participation and observation. Consider contacting a local official to arrange an internship in local government. If your time is limited, you might attend a local council meeting or school board meeting to see firsthand how government in your community is conducted. You might also choose to get involved in community affairs. Virtually every community has needs and also presents opportunities for involvement, from joining a civic-minded group to volunteering at a local hospital or school or helping with conservation or beautification projects. For more than thirty years, researchers at the University of California at Los Angeles have conducted annual surveys of college students. Their findings offer encouragement for anyone who might want to do volunteer work, as well as a cautionary note. Most college students volunteer time to worthy causes while in school—sometimes as part of a class, sometimes as part of a college-sponsored activity, and sometimes through a noncollege group such as a local church. The cautionary note is that students' participation declines over the course of the academic year. The lesson is that, if you do decide to do volunteer work, try to avoid getting totally wrapped up in the other opportunities that college provides.

Extra Credit

For up-to-the-minute *New York Times* articles, interactive simulations, graphics, study tools, and more links and quizzes, visit the text's Online Learning Center at www.mhhe.com/pattersontad9e.

Self-Test Answers

1. d 2. c 3. c 4. a 5. d 6. d 7. T 8. F 9. F 10. F

GENEROUS TO A FAULT

It's not that Vallejo doesn't need tough, experienced cops and seasoned firefighters. It's just that the midsize California city can't afford the jaw-dropping salaries it has been lavishing on them: Vallejo is broke.

Even within the pricey San Francisco Bay region, the city's generous payments to public safety workers stand apart: $306,000 a year in pay and benefits for a police captain (six times what the average schoolteacher in Vallejo earns); $171,000 for the average firefighter. Vallejo's city manager earns nearly $317,000, more than Vice President Cheney.

"All of our salaries are too high," says Mayor Osby Davis, a real estate and probate lawyer, whose part-time city job pays just $10,000 a year. The cure, he hopes, is to declare bankruptcy.

After nearly two years of contract talks and months of difficult debate, the mayor and council decided last month that it's worth the stigma of being the largest city in California history to seek bankruptcy protection if that gets Vallejo out from under its crushing financial commitments.

and greater demand for city services during hard times. But Vallejo's situation might turn out to be worse than most.

Bankruptcy lawyers are divided over whether Vallejo will become a trendsetter, especially during a rocky economic period. "It's anyone's guess," says Vallejo's bankruptcy adviser, Marc Levinson. "Whether other cities may be in such extremus, we don't know. The economy is what the economy is. Vallejo is not unique; it's just the first."

All California cities are in a special bind: They can't just jack up property taxes because their income isn't covering their bills. Proposition 13, which California voters passed in 1978, caps the taxes on residential property at 1 percent of the assessed value. And "assessed value" can rise only 2 percent a year until the property is sold.

"Proposition 13 is the third rail of politics in California," says Chris Hoene, director of policy and research for the National League of Cities. "You just don't touch it."

Hammered by the housing downturn, especially in the state's southern reaches,

survey of municipalities that it will release in July. "I don't think city finances are in the tank yet," Hoene said. "I don't know whether we'll see a round of bankruptcies in this case," he added, "but the circumstances will be similar around the country in terms of the revenue shortfalls that a lot of cities will be dealing with in the next few years."

Taking the temperature of city budgets can begin with a sweeping scan of state coffers. The Rockefeller Institute reports that nine states' tax revenues have plummeted compared with revenues for the first quarter of 2007. The states in trouble are Arizona, Florida, Georgia, Montana, North Carolina, Oklahoma, Rhode Island, South Carolina, and Utah.

Looking ahead to fiscal 2009, the Center on Budget and Policy Priorities examined projected shortfalls between what states need to maintain current services and the money they'll have on hand, plus the projected revenues they could tap. The center's analysts concluded that more than half the states will have to retrench to stay in the black.

"The problem started out with sales tax revenues being hit hard," said CBPP analyst Elizabeth McNichol. "People were not buying houses and not buying new materials for those houses, not consuming." Because the economy kept slowing and more people lost jobs, a more complete picture of the impact on states will emerge when the income-tax collection data from April are dissected. Many economists are anticipating dour news.

The responsibility for new schools, hospitals, and many social services rests largely with the states and cities, whose traditional sources of revenue are real estate and general sales taxes. In the last recession, Washington distributed more Medicaid money and other aid to the states to goose the economy and, as a result, helped localities avoid deeper cuts in health programs, McNichol added. That has not been the federal response this time, at least not yet.

The mayor and council decided last month that **it's worth the stigma of being the largest city in California history to seek bankruptcy protection** if that gets Vallejo out from under its crushing financial commitments.

Economists and budget-watchers who specialize in state and local governments say that although more than half the states are being squeezed, it's too early to know how much pain the economy's downturn will cause cities. Few are likely to escape unscathed, judging from the ominous mix of mounting costs for energy, food, and petroleum-based products (think asphalt); declining property-tax and sales tax revenues; rising pension and health care commitments to public workers;

California's state government is struggling to patch a $15 billion to $17 billion budget gap and is cutting programs in most areas, including education, welfare, and health care. Cities throughout the state are braced for the eventual effects.

Budget experts are waiting expectantly to get a better read on how cities are adjusting their balance sheets. The National League of Cities, for example, is gathering data about fiscal conditions as part of a large annual

Analysts believe that states will face added turmoil triggered by their long-range spending commitments for retiree health care and pensions—agreements reached in rosier times, when property values floated up like hot-air balloons. Cities are in the same situation.

Vallejo is not alone in its budget troubles. The National Conference of State Legislatures said that Georgia as a whole can weather the current downturn if it taps its reserve funds but that Atlanta might not be so fortunate. The city has flat or declining revenues and rising pension and health care costs that now swallow a quarter of its budget. For the fiscal year that begins on July 1, Atlanta officials anticipate a budget gap of about $140 million. Local news accounts describe the situation faced by Mayor Shirley Franklin as a "crisis."

Meanwhile, Alabama's Jefferson County informed banks late last winter that it would have trouble repaying debt for its sewer system and making payments on related interest-rate swaps. As credit markets faltered, Jefferson County was ensnared by financial products that became too rich for its dwindling budget.

In the Midwest, Detroit is in the fourth year of a structural deficit, now estimated at $58 million. "Detroit wasn't ever not struggling, but it's worse now," says Kim Rueben, an Urban Institute public finance economist.

On May 27, the Detroit City Council approved a $3 billion budget for fiscal 2009, opting to deficit-borrow its way out of the city's budget hole using $78 million in fiscal stabilization bonds to be sold late this year if officials fail to identify other revenue sources. The hope, however vague or overly optimistic, is that the revenue picture will somehow improve, justifying the decision to borrow rather than slash spending.

Cities with severe financial problems are nothing new, of course. More than 30 years ago, New York City memorably struggled with national economic stresses, dwindling revenue options, and urban upheaval. Local officials warned that with a $300 million shortfall and an inability to repay loans, the city risked insolvency and elimination of essential services if it did not get federal and state assistance. Bankruptcy was averted in 1975 with the grudging help of President Ford, the state Legislature, and other backers. But the city's obligations were spread out over years, and New York did not recover its preferred investment-grade ratings for two decades.

In 1991, Bridgeport, Conn., became the largest city ever to file for Chapter 9 bankruptcy protection. With 142,000 residents, Bridgeport faced a $12 million gap in a $304 million budget. The mayor and other city officials failed in their attempts to claw the $12 million out of the unions through contract concessions and saw bankruptcy protection as an alternative to what it anticipated would be an unwelcome state order to hike property taxes by as much as 18 percent. At the time, the city faced $220 million in general-obligation debt.

Although it never declared bankruptcy, San Diego weathered notorious budget problems. It went astray by repeatedly underfunding its pension obligations after being rocked by a recession in 1990 and losing much of its tax base when the defense industry shrank after the Persian Gulf War. With an approving wink from the unions, city officials survived the lean years by putting aside too little for future obligations, promising to add benefits to those contracts in the outyears. San Diego was like a condemned man who insists on tying his own noose.

By the summer of 2005, the city was in a crunch that residents could feel. Municipal workers were laid off. Swimming pools closed. Libraries cut their hours. And San Diego abandoned hopes for new construction and basic maintenance. The municipal pension fund was in arrears by $1.7 billion. Mismanagement and misdeeds triggered federal investigations, litigation, and expensive settlements, all of it capped by a voter revolt, recounts journalist Roger Lowenstein.

Vallejo Mayor Davis believes that California cities are in for rougher times. "I think it's a matter of time before an awful lot of cities in this state consider this same thing, and it's because we all have the same sort of contracts," he says. The relevant unions are opposing bankruptcy, arguing that the city doesn't qualify and has other fiscal options.

Two fire stations had to be closed. Workers were laid off. Residents must leave messages with an automated emergency number when they call for help.

As far back as 1993, Vallejo's leaders realized that the costs of negotiated contracts were rising so sharply that they would outpace the city's revenues by 2010, the mayor added. A citizen's committee had studied the data and created a chart to illustrate precisely when the city would run out of money. Nothing happened. The general fund drained away, and Vallejo is now awash in $17 million of red ink, according to the city's filing with the court. By the time Davis became mayor in December, he says, the city was desperate for change: "Crisis is the time to re-evaluate."

A fresh start is what he hopes bankruptcy will give Vallejo. "Within five years, we'll see something totally different," he gushed, describing the city's ambition to build an orthopedic college, a cancer research center, and a convention center near the interstate.

"Come to Vallejo!" the mayor urged. "We're right by the water. We're in the middle of everything!"

FOR DISCUSSION: Will California repeal Proposition 13 or look for means other than raising property taxes to balance the budget? Will bankruptcy offer an increasing number of cities an alternative to resolving their financial obligations? Should localities seek help from the state or federal government to manage their finances in a tough economy?

Appendixes

The Declaration of Independence

The Constitution of the United States of America

Federalist No. 10

Federalist No. 51

The Declaration of Independence

In Congress, July 4, 1776

The Unanimous Declaration of the Thirteen United States of America

When, in the course of human events, it becomes necessary for one people to dissolve the political bands which have connected them with another, and to assume, among the powers of the earth, the separate and equal station to which the laws of nature and of nature's God entitle them, a decent respect to the opinions of mankind requires that they should declare the causes which impel them to the separation.

We hold these truths to be self-evident, that all men are created equal; that they are endowed by their Creator with certain unalienable rights; that among these, are life, liberty, and the pursuit of happiness. That, to secure these rights, governments are instituted among men, deriving their just powers from the consent of the governed; that, whenever any form of government becomes destructive of these ends, it is the right of the people to alter or to abolish it, and to institute a new government, laying its foundation on such principles, and organizing its powers in such form, as to them shall seem most likely to effect their safety and happiness. Prudence, indeed, will dictate that governments long established, should not be changed for light and transient causes; and, accordingly, all experience hath shown, that mankind are more disposed to suffer, while evils are sufferable, than to right themselves by abolishing the forms to which they are accustomed. But, when a long train of abuses and usurpations, pursuing invariably the same object, evinces a design to reduce them under absolute despotism, it is their right, it is their duty, to throw off such government and to provide new guards for their future security. Such has been the patient sufferance of these colonies, and such is now the necessity which constrains them to alter their former systems of government. The history of the present King of Great Britain is a history of repeated injuries and usurpations, all having, in direct object, the establishment of an absolute tyranny over these States. To prove this, let facts be submitted to a candid world:

He has refused his assent to laws the most wholesome and necessary for the public good.

He has forbidden his governors to pass laws of immediate and pressing importance, unless suspended in their operation till his assent should be obtained; and, when so suspended, he has utterly neglected to attend to them.

He has refused to pass other laws for the accommodation of large districts of people, unless those people would relinquish the right of representation in the legislature; a right inestimable to them, and formidable to tyrants only.

He has called together legislative bodies at places unusual, uncomfortable, and distant from the depository of their public records, for the sole purpose of fatiguing them into compliance with his measures.

He has dissolved representative houses repeatedly for opposing, with manly firmness, his invasions on the rights of the people.

He has refused, for a long time after such dissolutions, to cause others to be elected; whereby the legislative powers, incapable of annihilation, have returned to the people at large for their exercise; the state remaining, in the meantime, exposed to all the danger of invasion from without, and convulsions within.

He has endeavored to prevent the population of these States; for that purpose, obstructing the laws for naturalization of foreigners, refusing to pass others to encourage their migration hither, and raising the conditions of new appropriations of lands.

He has obstructed the administration of justice, by refusing his assent to laws for establishing judiciary powers.

He has made judges dependent on his will alone, for the tenure of their offices, and the amount and payment of their salaries.

He has erected a multitude of new offices, and sent hither swarms of officers to harass our people, and eat out their substance.

He has kept among us, in time of peace, standing armies, without the consent of our legislatures.

He has affected to render the military independent of, and superior to, the civil power.

He has combined, with others, to subject us to a jurisdiction foreign to our Constitution, and unacknowledged by our laws; giving his assent to their acts of pretended legislation:

For quartering large bodies of armed troops among us:

For protecting them by a mock trial, from punishment, for any murders which they should commit on the inhabitants of these States:

For cutting off our trade with all parts of the world:

For imposing taxes on us without our consent:

For depriving us, in many cases, of the benefit of trial by jury:

For transporting us beyond seas to be tried for pretended offences:

For abolishing the free system of English laws in a neighboring province, establishing therein an arbitrary government, and enlarging its boundaries, so as to render it at once an example and fit instrument for introducing the same absolute rule into these colonies:

For taking away our charters, abolishing our most valuable laws, and altering, fundamentally, the powers of our governments:

For suspending our own legislatures, and declaring themselves invested with power to legislate for us in all cases whatsoever.

He has abdicated government here, by declaring us out of his protection, and waging war against us.

He has plundered our seas, ravaged our coasts, burnt our towns, and destroyed the lives of our people.

He is, at this time, transporting large armies of foreign mercenaries to complete the works of death, desolation, and tyranny, already begun, with circumstances of cruelty and perfidy scarcely paralleled in the most barbarous ages, and totally unworthy of the head of a civilized nation.

He has constrained our fellow citizens, taken captive on the high seas, to bear arms against their country, to become the executioners of their friends, and brethren, or to fall themselves by their hands.

He has excited domestic insurrections amongst us, and has endeavored to bring on the inhabitants of our frontiers, the merciless Indian savages, whose known rule of warfare is an undistinguished destruction of all ages, sexes, and conditions.

In every stage of these oppressions, we have petitioned for redress, in the most humble terms; our repeated petitions have been answered only by repeated injury. A prince, whose character is thus marked by every act which may define a tyrant, is unfit to be the ruler of a free people.

Nor have we been wanting in attention to our British brethren. We have warned them, from time to time, of attempts made by their legislature to extend an unwarrantable jurisdiction over us. We have reminded them of the circumstances of our emigration and settlement here. We have appealed to their native justice and magnanimity, and we have conjured them, by the ties of our common kindred, to disavow these usurpations, which would inevitably interrupt our connections and correspondence. They, too, have been deaf to the voice of justice and of consanguinity. We must, therefore, acquiesce in the necessity which denounces our separation, and hold them as we hold the rest of mankind, enemies in war, in peace, friends.

We, therefore, the representatives of the United States of America, in general Congress assembled, appealing to the Supreme Judge of the world for the rectitude of our intentions, do, in the name, and by the authority of the good people of these colonies, solemnly publish and declare, that these united colonies are, and of right ought to be, free and independent states: that they are absolved from all allegiance to the British Crown, and that all political connection between them and the state of Great Britain is, and ought to be, totally dissolved; and that, as free and independent states, they have full power to levy war, conclude peace, contract alliances, establish commerce, and to do all other acts and things which independent states may of right do. And, for the support of this declaration, with a firm reliance on the protection of Divine Providence, we mutually pledge to each other our lives, our fortunes, and our sacred honor.

The foregoing Declaration was, by order of Congress, engrossed, and signed by the following members:

John Hancock

New Hampshire
Josiah Bartlett
William Whipple
Matthew Thornton

Massachusetts Bay
Samuel Adams
John Adams
Robert Treat Paine
Elbridge Gerry

Rhode Island
Stephen Hopkins
William Ellery

Connecticut
Roger Sherman
Samuel Huntington
William Williams
Oliver Wolcott

New York
William Floyd
Philip Livingston
Francis Lewis
Lewis Morris

New Jersey
Richard Stockton
John Witherspoon
Francis Hopkinson
John Hart
Abraham Clark

Pennsylvania
Robert Morris
Benjamin Rush
Benjamin Franklin
John Morton
George Clymer
James Smith
George Taylor
James Wilson
George Ross

Delaware
Caesar Rodney
George Reed
Thomas M'Kean

Maryland
Samuel Chase
William Paca
Thomas Stone
Charles Carroll, of Carrollton

Virginia
George Wythe
Richard Henry Lee
Thomas Jefferson
Benjamin Harrison
Thomas Nelson, Jr.
Francis Lightfoot Lee
Carter Braxton

North Carolina
William Hooper
Joseph Hewes
John Penn

South Carolina
Edward Rutledge
Thomas Heyward, Jr.
Thomas Lynch, Jr.
Arthur Middleton

Georgia
Button Gwinnett
Lyman Hall
George Walton

Resolved, That copies of the Declaration be sent to the several assemblies, conventions, and committees, or councils of safety, and to the several commanding officers of the continental troops; that it be proclaimed in each of the United States, at the head of the army.

The Constitution of the United States of America[1]

We the People of the United States, in Order to form a more perfect Union, establish Justice, insure domestic Tranquility, provide for the common defence, promote the general Welfare, and secure the Blessings of Liberty to ourselves and our Posterity, do ordain and establish this CONSTITUTION for the United States of America.

Article I

Section 1

All legislative Powers herein granted shall be vested in a Congress of the United States, which shall consist of a Senate and House of Representatives.

Section 2

The House of Representatives shall be composed of Members chosen every second Year by the People of the several States, and the Electors in each State shall have the Qualifications requisite for Electors of the most numerous Branch of the State Legislature.

No Person shall be a Representative who shall not have attained to the Age of twenty-five Years, and been seven Years a Citizen of the United States, and who shall not, when elected, be an Inhabitant of that State in which he shall be chosen.

[Representatives and direct Taxes[2] shall be apportioned among the several States which may be included within this Union, according to their respective Numbers, which shall be determined by adding to the whole Number of free Persons, including those bound to Service for a Term of Years, and excluding Indians not taxed, three fifths of all other Persons.][3] The actual Enumeration shall be made within three Years after the first Meeting of the Congress of the United States, and within every subsequent Term of ten Years, in such Manner as they shall by Law direct. The Number of Representatives shall not exceed one for every thirty Thousand, but each State shall have at Least one Representative; and until such enumeration shall be made, the State of New Hampshire shall be entitled to chuse three, Massachusetts eight, Rhode-Island and Providence Plantations one, Connecticut five, New York six, New Jersey four, Pennsylvania eight, Delaware one, Maryland six, Virginia ten, North Carolina five, South Carolina five, and Georgia three.

When vacancies happen in the Representation from any State, the Executive Authority thereof shall issue Writs of Election to fill such Vacancies.

The House of Representatives shall chuse their Speaker and other Officers; and shall have the sole Power of Impeachment.

Section 3

The Senate of the United States shall be composed of two Senators from each State, chosen by the Legislature thereof, for six Years; and each Senator shall have one Vote.

Immediately after they shall be assembled in Consequence of the first Election, they shall be divided as equally as may be into three Classes. The Seats of the Senators of the first Class shall be vacated at the Expiration of the second Year, of the second Class at the Expiration of the fourth Year, and of the third Class at the Expiration of the sixth Year, so that one-third may be chosen every second Year; and if Vacancies happen by Resignation, or otherwise, during the Recess of the Legislature of any State, the Executive thereof may make temporary Appointments until the next Meeting of the Legislature, which shall then fill such Vacancies.

No Person shall be a Senator who shall not have attained to the Age of thirty Years, and been nine Years a Citizen of the United States, and who shall not, when

---

[1]This version, which follows the original Constitution in capitalization and spelling, was published by the United States Department of the Interior, Office of Education, in 1935.
[2]Altered by the Sixteenth Amendment.
[3]Negated by the Fourteenth Amendment.

No Person shall be a Senator who shall not have attained to the Age of thirty Years, and been nine Years a Citizen of the United States, and who shall not, when elected, be an Inhabitant of that State for which he shall be chosen.

The Vice President of the United States shall be President of the Senate, but shall have no vote, unless they be equally divided.

The Senate shall chuse their other Officers, and also a President pro tempore, in the absence of the Vice President, or when he shall exercise the Office of President of the United States.

The Senate shall have the sole Power to try all Impeachments. When sitting for that purpose they shall be on Oath or Affirmation. When the President of the United States is tried, the Chief Justice shall preside: And no person shall be convicted without the Concurrence of two thirds of the Members present.

Judgment in Cases of Impeachment shall not extend further than to removal from Office, and disqualification to hold and enjoy any Office of honor, Trust, or Profit under the United States: but the Party convicted shall nevertheless be liable and subject to Indictment, Trial, Judgment and Punishment, according to Law.

Section 4

The Times, Place and Manner of holding Elections for Senators and Representatives, shall be prescribed in each State by the Legislature thereof; but the Congress may at any time by Law make or alter such Regulations, except as to the Places of Chusing Senators.

The Congress shall assemble at least once in every Year, and such Meeting shall be on the first Monday in December, unless they shall by Law appoint a different Day.

Section 5

Each House shall be the Judge of the Elections, Returns and Qualifications of its own Members, and a Majority of each shall constitute a Quorum to do Business; but a smaller number may adjourn from day to day, and may be authorized to compel the Attendance of absent Members, in such Manner, and under such Penalties, as each House may provide.

Each House may determine the Rules of its Proceedings, punish its Members for disorderly Behaviour, and, with the Concurrence of two thirds, expel a Member.

Each House shall keep a Journal of its Proceedings, and from time to time publish the same, excepting such Parts as may in their Judgment require Secrecy; and the Yeas and Nays of the Members of either House

on any question shall, at the Desire of one fifth of those Present, be entered on the Journal.

Neither House, during the Session of Congress, shall, without the Consent of the other, adjourn for more than three days, nor to any other Place than that in which the two Houses shall be sitting.

Section 6

The Senators and Representatives shall receive a Compensation for their Services, to be ascertained by Law, and paid out of the Treasury of the United States. They shall in all Cases, except Treason, Felony, and Breach of the Peace, be privileged from Arrest during their Attendance at the Session of their respective Houses, and in going to and returning from the same; and for any Speech or Debate in either House, they shall not be questioned in any other Place.

No Senator or Representative shall, during the Time for which he was elected, be appointed to any civil Office under the Authority of the United States, which shall have been created, or the Emoluments whereof shall have been increased, during such time; and no Person holding any Office under the United States shall be a Member of either House during his continuance in Office.

Section 7

All Bills for raising Revenue shall originate in the House of Representatives; but the Senate may propose or concur with Amendments as on other bills.

Every Bill which shall have passed the House of Representatives and the Senate, shall, before it becomes a Law, be presented to the President of the United States; if he approve he shall sign it, but if not he shall return it, with his Objections, to that House in which it shall have originated, who shall enter the Objections at large on their Journal, and proceed to reconsider it. If after such Reconsideration two thirds of that House shall agree to pass the bill, it shall be sent, together with the objections, to the other House, by which it shall likewise be reconsidered, and if approved by two thirds of that House, it shall become a Law. But in all such Cases the Votes of both Houses shall be determined by Yeas and Nays, and the Names of the Persons voting for and against the Bill shall be entered on the Journal of each House respectively. If any Bill shall not be returned by the President within ten Days (Sundays excepted) after it shall have been presented to him, the Same shall be a Law, in like Manner as if he had signed it, unless the Congress by their Adjournment prevent its Return, in which Case it shall not be a Law.

Every Order, Resolution, or Vote to which the Concurrence of the Senate and House of Representatives may be necessary (except on a question of Adjournment) shall be presented to the President of the United States; and before the Same shall take Effect, shall be approved by him, or being disapproved by him, shall be repassed by two thirds of the Senate and House of Representatives, according to the Rules and Limitations prescribed in the Case of a Bill.

Section 8

The Congress shall have Power To lay and collect Taxes, Duties, Imposts and Excises, to pay the Debts and provide for the common Defence and general Welfare of the United States; but all Duties, Imposts and Excises shall be uniform throughout the United States;

To borrow money on the credit of the United States;

To regulate Commerce with foreign Nations, and among the several States, and with the Indian Tribes;

To establish a uniform rule of Naturalization, and uniform Laws on the subject of Bankruptcies throughout the United States;

To coin Money, regulate the Value thereof, and of foreign Coin, and fix the Standard of Weights and Measures;

To provide for the Punishment of counterfeiting the Securities and current Coin of the United States;

To establish Post Offices and post Roads;

To promote the Progress of Science and useful Arts, by securing for limited Times to Authors and Inventors the exclusive Right to their respective Writings and Discoveries;

To constitute Tribunals inferior to the Supreme Court;

To define and punish Piracies and Felonies committed on the high Seas, and Offenses against the Law of Nations;

To declare War, grant Letters of Marque and Reprisal, and make Rules concerning Captures on Land and Water;

To raise and support Armies, but no Appropriation of Money to that Use shall be for a longer Term than two Years;

To provide and maintain a Navy;

To make Rules for the Government and Regulation of the land and naval forces;

To provide for calling forth the Militia to execute the Laws of the Union, suppress Insurrections and repel Invasions;

To provide for organizing, arming, and disciplining the Militia, and for governing such Part of them as may be employed in the Service of the United States,

reserving to the States respectively, the Appointment of the Officers, and the Authority of training the Militia according to the discipline prescribed by Congress;

To exercise exclusive Legislation in all Cases whatsoever, over such District (not exceeding ten Miles square) as may, by Cession of particular States, and the acceptance of Congress, become the Seat of the Government of the United States, and to exercise like Authority over all Places purchased by the Consent of the Legislature of the State in which the Same shall be, for the Erection of Forts, Magazines, Arsenals, Dock-yards, and other needful Buildings;—And

To make all Laws which shall be necessary and proper for carrying into Execution the foregoing Powers, and all other Powers vested by this Constitution in the Government of the United States, or in any Department or Officer thereof.

Section 9

The Migration or Importation of such Persons as any of the States now existing shall think proper to admit, shall not be prohibited by the Congress prior The Constitution of the United States of America to the Year one thousand eight hundred and eight, but a tax or duty may be imposed on such Importation, not exceeding ten dollars for each Person.

The privilege of the Writ of Habeas Corpus shall not be suspended, unless when in Cases of Rebellion or Invasion the public Safety may require it.

No bill of Attainder or ex post facto Law shall be passed.

No capitation, or other direct, Tax shall be laid unless in Proportion to the Census or Enumeration herein before directed to be taken.

No Tax or Duty shall be laid on Articles exported from any State.

No Preference shall be given by any Regulation of Commerce or Revenue to the Ports of one State over those of another: nor shall Vessels bound to, or from, one State, be obliged to enter, clear, or pay Duties in another.

No Money shall be drawn from the Treasury, but in Consequence of Appropriations made by Law; and a regular Statement and Account of the Receipts and Expenditures of all public Money shall be published from time to time.

No Title of Nobility shall be granted by the United States: And no Person holding any Office of Profit or Trust under them, shall, without the Consent of the Congress, accept of any present, Emolument, Office, or Title, of any kind whatever, from any King, Prince, or foreign State.

Section 10

No State shall enter into any Treaty, Alliance, or Confederation; grant Letters of Marque and Reprisal; coin Money; emit Bills of Credit; make any Thing but gold and silver Coin a Tender in Payment of Debts; pass any Bill of Attainder, ex post facto Law, or Law impairing the Obligation of Contracts, or grant any Title of Nobility.

No State shall, without the Consent of the Congress, lay any Imposts or Duties on Imports or Exports, except what may be absolutely necessary for executing its inspection Laws; and the net Produce of all Duties and Imposts, laid by any State on Imports or Exports, shall be for the use of the Treasury of the United States; and all such Laws shall be subject to the Revision and Control of the Congress.

No state shall, without the Consent of Congress, lay any duty of Tonnage, keep Troops, or Ships of War in time of Peace, enter into any Agreement or Compact with another State, or with a foreign Power, or engage in War, unless actually invaded, or in such imminent Danger as will not admit of delay.

Article II

Section 1

The executive Power shall be vested in a President of the United States of America. He shall hold his Office during the Term of four years, and, together with the Vice President, chosen for the same Term, be elected, as follows:

Each State shall appoint, in such Manner as the Legislature thereof may direct, a Number of Electors, equal to the whole Number of Senators and Representatives to which the State may be entitled in the Congress: but no Senator or Representative, or Person holding an Office of Trust or Profit under the United States, shall be appointed an Elector.

[The Electors shall meet in their respective States, and vote by Ballot for two persons, of whom one at least shall not be an Inhabitant of the same State with themselves. And they shall make a List of all the Persons voted for, and of the Number of Votes for each; which List they shall sign and certify, and transmit sealed to the Seat of the Government of the United States, directed to the President of the Senate. The President of the Senate shall, in the Presence of the Senate and House of Representatives, open all the Certificates, and the Votes shall then be counted. The Person having the greatest Number of Votes shall be the President, if such Number be a Majority of the whole Number of Electors appointed; and if there be more than one

who have such Majority, and have an equal Number of Votes, then the House of Representatives shall immediately chuse by Ballot one of them for President; and if no Person have a Majority, then from the five highest on the List the said House shall in like Manner chuse the President. But in chusing the President, the Votes shall be taken by States, the Representation from each State having one Vote; a quorum for this Purpose shall consist of a Member or Members from two-thirds of the States, and a Majority of all the States shall be necessary to a Choice. In every Case, after the Choice of the President, the Person having the greatest Number of Votes of the Electors shall be the Vice President. But if there should remain two or more who have equal votes, the Senate shall chuse from them by Ballot the Vice President.][4]

The Congress may determine the Time of chusing the Electors, and the Day on which they shall give their Votes; which Day shall be the same throughout the United States.

No person except a natural-born Citizen, or a Citizen of the United States, at the time of the Adoption of this Constitution, shall be eligible to the Office of President; neither shall any Person be eligible to that Office who shall not have attained to the Age of thirty-five years, and been fourteen Years a Resident within the United States.

In Case of the Removal of the President from Office, or of his Death, Resignation, or Inability to discharge the Powers and Duties of the said Office, the same shall devolve on the Vice President, and the Congress may by Law provide for the Case of Removal, Death, Resignation, or Inability, both of the President and Vice President, declaring what Officer shall then act as President, and such Officer shall act accordingly, until the disability be removed, or a President shall be elected.

The President shall, at stated Times, receive for his Services a Compensation, which shall neither be increased nor diminished during the Period for which he shall have been elected, and he shall not receive within that Period any other Emolument from the United States, or any of them.

Before he enter on the execution of his Office, he shall take the following Oath or Affirmation:—"I do solemnly swear (or affirm) that I will faithfully execute the Office of President of the United States, and will, to the best of my Ability, preserve, protect, and defend the Constitution of the United States."

[4]Revised by the Twelfth Amendment.

Section 2

The President shall be Commander in Chief of the Army and Navy of the United States, and of the Militia of the several States, when called into the actual Service of the United States; he may require the Opinion, in writing, of the principal Officer in each of the executive Departments, upon any subject relating to the Duties of their respective Offices, and he shall have Power to Grant Reprieves and Pardons for Offenses against the United States, except in Cases of Impeachment.

He shall have Power, by and with the Advice and Consent of the Senate, to make Treaties, provided two-thirds of the Senators present concur; and he shall nominate, and by and with the Advice and Consent of the Senate, shall appoint Ambassadors, other public Ministers and Consuls, Judges of the supreme Court, and all other Officers of the United States, whose Appointments are not herein otherwise provided for, and which shall be established by Law: but the Congress may by Law vest the Appointment of such inferior Officers, as they think proper, in the President alone, in the Courts of Law, or in the Heads of Departments.

The President shall have Power to fill up all Vacancies that may happen during the Recess of the Senate, by granting Commissions which shall expire at the End of their next Session.

Section 3

He shall from time to time give to the Congress Information of the State of the Union, and recommend to their Consideration such Measures as he shall judge necessary and expedient; he may, on extraordinary occasions, convene both Houses, or either of them, and in Case of Disagreement between them, with respect to the Time of Adjournment, he may adjourn them to such Time as he shall think proper; he shall receive Ambassadors and other public Ministers; he shall take care that the Laws be faithfully executed, and shall Commission all the Officers of the United States.

Section 4

The President, Vice President and all civil Officers of the United States, shall be removed from Office on Impeachment for, and Conviction of, Treason, Bribery, or other high Crimes and Misdemeanors.

Article III

Section 1

The judicial Power of the United States, shall be vested in one supreme Court, and in such inferior Courts as the Congress may from time to time ordain and establish. The Judges, both of the supreme and inferior Courts, shall hold their Offices during good Behaviour, and shall, at stated Times, receive for their Services, a Compensation, which shall not be diminished during their Continuance in Office.

Section 2

The judicial Power shall extend to all Cases, in Law and Equity, arising under this Constitution, the Laws of the United States, and Treaties made, or which shall be made, under their Authority;—to all Cases affecting ambassadors, other public ministers and consuls;—to all cases of admiralty and maritime Jurisdiction;—to Controversies to which the United States shall be a Party;—to Controversies between two or more states;—between a State and Citizens of another State;[5] —between Citizens of different States—between Citizens of the same State claiming Lands under Grants of different States, and between a State, or the Citizens thereof, and foreign States, Citizens, or Subjects.

In all Cases affecting Ambassadors, other public Ministers and Consuls, and those in which a State shall be Party, the supreme Court shall have original Jurisdiction. In all the other Cases before mentioned, the supreme Court shall have appellate Jurisdiction, both as to Law and Fact, with such Exceptions, and under such Regulations as the Congress shall make.

The trial of all Crimes, except in Cases of Impeachment, shall be by Jury; and such Trial shall be held in the State where the said Crimes shall have been committed; but when not committed within any State, the Trial shall be at such Place or Places as the Congress may by Law have directed.

Section 3

Treason against the United States, shall consist only in levying War against them, or in adhering to their Enemies, giving them Aid and Comfort. No Person shall be convicted of Treason unless on the Testimony of two Witnesses to the same overt Act, or on Confession in open Court.

The Congress shall have power to declare the Punishment of Treason, but no Attainder of Treason shall work Corruption of Blood, or Forfeiture except during the Life of the Person attainted.

[5]Qualified by the Eleventh Amendment.

Article IV

Section 1

Full Faith and Credit shall be given in each State to the public Acts, Records, and judicial Proceedings of every other State. And the Congress may by general Laws prescribe the Manner in which such Acts, Records and Proceedings shall be proved, and the Effect thereof.

Section 2

The Citizens of each State shall be entitled to all Privileges and Immunities of Citizens in the several States.

A Person charged in any State with Treason, Felony, or other Crime, who shall flee from Justice, and be found in another State, shall on demand of the executive Authority of the State from which he fled, be delivered up, to be removed to the State having Jurisdiction of the crime.

No Person held to Service or Labour in one State, under the Laws thereof, escaping into another, shall, in Consequence of any Law or Regulation therein, be discharged from such Service or Labour, but shall be delivered up on Claim of the Party to whom such Service or Labour may be due.

Section 3

New States may be admitted by the Congress into this Union; but no new State shall be formed or erected within the Jurisdiction of any other State; nor any State be formed by the Junction of two or more States, or parts of States, without the Consent of the Legislatures of the States concerned as well as of the Congress.

The Congress shall have Power to dispose of and make all needful Rules and Regulations respecting the Territory or other Property belonging to the United States; and nothing in this Constitution shall be so construed as to Prejudice any Claims of the United States, or of any particular State.

Section 4

The United States shall guarantee to every State in this Union a Republican Form of Government, and shall protect each of them against Invasion; and on Application of the Legislature, or of the Executive (when the Legislature cannot be convened) against domestic Violence.

Article V

The Congress, whenever two-thirds of both Houses shall deem it necessary, shall propose Amendments to this Constitution, or, on the Application of the Legislatures of two-thirds of the several States, shall call a Convention for proposing Amendments, which, in either Case, shall be valid to all Intents and Purposes, as part of this Constitution, when ratified by the Legislatures of three-fourths of the several States, or by Conventions in three-fourths thereof, as the one or the other Mode of Ratification may be proposed by the Congress; Provided that no Amendment which may be made prior to the Year One thousand eight hundred and eight shall in any Manner affect the first and fourth Clauses in the Ninth Section of the first Article; and that no State, without its Consent, shall be deprived of its equal Suffrage in the Senate.

Article VI

All Debts contracted and Engagements entered into, before the Adoption of this Constitution, shall be as valid against the United States under this Constitution, as under the Confederation.

This Constitution, and the Laws of the United States which shall be made in Pursuance thereof; and all Treaties made, or which shall be made, under the Authority of the United States, shall be the supreme Law of the Land; and the Judges in every State shall be bound thereby, any Thing in the Constitution or Laws of any State to the Contrary notwithstanding.

The Senators and Representatives before mentioned, and the Members of the several State Legislatures, and all executive and judicial Officers, both of the United States and of the several States, shall be bound by Oath or Affirmation to support this Constitution; but no religious Tests shall ever be required as a qualification to any Office or public Trust under the United States.

Article VII

The Ratification of the Conventions of nine States shall be sufficient for the Establishment of this Constitution between the States so ratifying the same.

Done in Convention by the Unanimous Consent of the States present the Seventeenth Day of September in the Year of our Lord one thousand seven hundred and Eighty seven, and of the Independence of the United States of America the Twelfth. In Witness whereof We have hereunto subscribed our Names.[6]

---

[6]These are the full names of the signers, which in some cases are not the signatures on the document.

George Washington
*President and deputy from
Virginia*

New Hampshire
John Langdon
Nicholas Gilman

Massachusetts
Nathaniel Gorham
Rufus King

Connecticut
William Samuel Johnson
Roger Sherman

New York
Alexander Hamilton

New Jersey
William Livingston
David Brearley
William Paterson
Jonathan Dayton

Pennsylvania
Benjamin Franklin
Thomas Mifflin
Robert Morris
George Clymer
Thomas FitzSimmons
Jared Ingersoll
James Wilson
Gouverneur Morris

Delaware
George Read
Gunning Bedford, Jr.
John Dickinson
Richard Bassett
Jacob Broom

Maryland
James McHenry
Daniel of St. Thomas
  Jenifer
Daniel Carroll

Virginia
John Blair
James Madison, Jr.

North Carolina
William Blount
Richard Dobbs Spaight
Hugh Williamson

South Carolina
John Rutledge
Charles Cotesworth
  Pinckney
Charles Pinckney
Pierce Butler

Georgia
William Few
Abraham Baldwin

*Articles in Addition to, and Amendment of, the Constitution
of the United States of America, Proposed by Congress, and
Ratified by the Legislatures of the Several States, Pursuant to
the Fifth Article of the Original Constitution*[7]

Amendment I

Congress shall make no law respecting an establishment of religion, or prohibiting the free exercise thereof; or abridging the freedom of speech, or of the press; or the right of the people peaceably to assem-

---

[7]This heading appears only in the joint resolution submitting the first ten amendments, which are collectively known as the Bill of Rights. They were ratified on December 15, 1791.

ble, and to petition the Government for a redress of grievances.

Amendment II

A well regulated Militia, being necessary to the security of a free State, the right of the people to keep and bear Arms shall not be infringed.

Amendment III

No Soldier shall, in time of peace, be quartered in any house, without the consent of the Owner, nor in time of war, but in a manner to be prescribed by law.

Amendment IV

The right of the people to be secure in their persons, houses, papers, and effects, against unreasonable searches and seizures, shall not be violated, and no Warrants shall issue, but upon probable cause, supported by Oath or affirmation, and particularly describing the place to be searched, and the persons or things to be seized.

Amendment V

No person shall be held to answer for a capital or otherwise infamous crime, unless on a presentment or indictment of a Grand Jury, except in cases arising in the land or naval forces, or in the Militia, when in actual service in time of War or public danger; nor shall any person be subject for the same offence to be twice put in jeopardy of life or limb; nor shall be compelled in any criminal case to be a witness against himself, nor be deprived of life, liberty, or property, without due process of law; nor shall private property be taken for public use, without just compensation.

Amendment VI

In all criminal prosecutions, the accused shall enjoy the right to a speedy and public trial, by an impartial jury of the State and district wherein the crime shall have been committed, which district shall have been previously ascertained by law, and to be informed of the nature and cause of the accusation; to be confronted with the witnesses against him; to have compulsory process for obtaining witnesses in his favour, and to have the Assistance of Counsel for his defence.

Amendment VII

In suits at common law, where the value in controversy shall exceed twenty dollars, the right of trial by jury shall be preserved, and no fact tried by a jury, shall be otherwise reexamined in any Court of the United States, than according to the rules of the common law.

Amendment VIII

Excessive bail shall not be required, nor excessive fines imposed, nor cruel and unusual punishments inflicted.

Amendment IX

The enumeration of the Constitution, of certain rights, shall not be construed to deny or disparage others retained by the people.

Amendment X

The powers not delegated to the United States by the Constitution, nor prohibited by it to the States, are reserved to the States respectively, or to the people.

Amendment XI [1795]

The Judicial power of the United States shall not be construed to extend to any suit in law or equity, commenced or prosecuted against one of the United States by Citizens of another State, or by Citizens or Subjects of any Foreign State.

Amendment XII [1804]

The Electors shall meet in their respective States and vote by ballot for President and Vice-President, one of whom, at least, shall not be an inhabitant of the same State with themselves; they shall name in their ballots the person voted for as President, and in distinct ballots the person voted for as Vice-President, and they shall make distinct lists of all persons voted for as President, and of all persons voted for as Vice-President, and of the number of votes for each, which lists they shall sign and certify, and transmit sealed to the seat of the government of the United States, directed to the President of the Senate;—The President of the Senate shall, in the presence of the Senate and House of Representatives, open all the certificates and the votes shall then be counted;—The person having the greatest number of votes for President, shall be the President, if such number be a majority of the whole number of Electors appointed; and if no person have such majority, then from the persons having the highest numbers not exceeding three on the list of those voted for as President, the House of Representatives shall choose immediately, by ballot, the President. But in choosing the President, the votes shall be taken by states, the representation from each state having one vote; a quorum for this purpose shall consist of a member or members from two-thirds of the states, and a majority of all the states shall be necessary to a choice. And if the House of Representatives shall not choose a President whenever the right of choice shall devolve upon them, before the fourth day of March next following, then the Vice-President shall act as President, as in the case of the death or other constitutional disability of the President—The person having the greatest number of votes as Vice-President, shall be the Vice-President, if such number be a majority of the whole number of Electors appointed, and if no person have a majority, then from the two highest numbers on the list, the Senate shall choose the Vice-President; a quorum for the purpose shall consist of two-thirds of the whole number of Senators, and majority of the whole number shall be necessary to a choice. But no person constitutionally ineligible to the office of President shall be eligible to that of Vice-President of the United States.

Amendment XIII [1865]

Section 1

Neither slavery nor involuntary servitude, except as a punishment for crime whereof the party shall have been duly convicted, shall exist within the United States, or any place subject to their jurisdiction.

Section 2

Congress shall have power to enforce this article by appropriate legislation.

Amendment XIV [1868]

Section 1

All persons born or naturalized in the United States, and subject to the jurisdiction thereof, are citizens of the United States and of the State wherein they reside. No State shall abridge the privileges or immunities of citizens of the United States; nor shall any State deprive any person of life, liberty, or property, without due process of law; nor deny to any person within its jurisdiction the equal protection of the laws.

Section 2

Representatives shall be apportioned among the several States according to their respective numbers, counting the whole number of persons in each State, excluding Indians not taxed. But when the right to vote at any election for the choice of electors for President and Vice-President of the United States, Representatives in Congress, the Executive and Judicial officers of a State, or the members of the Legislature thereof, is denied to any of the male inhabitants of such State, being twenty-one years of age, and citizens of the United States, or in any way abridged, except for participation in rebellion, or other crime, the basis of representation therein shall be reduced in the proportion which the number of such male citizens shall bear to the whole number of male citizens twenty-one years of age in such State.

Section 3

No person shall be a Senator or Representative in Congress, or elector of President and Vice-President, or hold any office, civil or military, under the United States, or under any State, who, having previously taken an oath, as a member of Congress, or as an officer of the United States, or as a member of any State legislature, or as an executive or judicial officer of any State, to support the Constitution of the United States, shall have engaged in insurrection or rebellion against the same, or given aid or comfort to the enemies thereof. But Congress may by a vote of two-thirds of each House, remove such disability.

Section 4

The validity of the public debt of the United States, authorized by law, including debts incurred for payment of pensions and bounties for services in suppressing insurrection or rebellion, shall not be questioned. But neither the United States nor any State shall assume or pay any debts or obligation incurred in aid of insurrection or rebellion against the United States, or any claim for the loss or emancipation of any slave; but all such debts, obligations, and claims shall be held illegal and void.

Section 5

The Congress shall have the power to enforce, by appropriate legislation, the provisions of this article.

Amendment XV [1870]

Section 1

The right of citizens of the United States to vote shall not be denied or abridged by the United States or by any State on account of race, color, or previous condition of servitude.

Section 2

The Congress shall have power to enforce this article by appropriate legislation.

Amendment XVI [1913]

The Congress shall have power to lay and collect taxes on incomes, from whatever source derived, without apportionment among the several States, and without regard to any census or enumeration.

Amendment XVII [1913]

The Senate of the United States shall be composed of two Senators from each State, elected by the people thereof, for six years; and each Senator shall have one vote. The electors in each State shall have the qualifications requisite for electors of the most numerous branch of the State legislatures.

When vacancies happen in the representation of any State in the Senate, the executive authority of such State shall issue writs of election to fill such vacancies: Provided, That the legislature of any State may empower the executive thereof to make temporary appointments until the people fill the vacancies by election as the legislature may direct.

This amendment shall not be so construed as to affect the election or term of any Senator chosen before it becomes valid as part of the Constitution.

Amendment XVIII [1919]

Section 1

After one year from the ratification of this article the manufacture, sale, or transportation of intoxicating liquors within, the importation thereof into, or the exportation thereof from the United States and all territory subject to the jurisdiction thereof for beverage purposes is hereby prohibited.

Section 2

The Congress and the several States shall have concurrent power to enforce this article by appropriate legislation.

Section 3

This article shall be inoperative unless it shall have been ratified as an amendment to the Constitution by the legislatures of the several States, as provided in the Constitution, within seven years from the date of the submission hereof to the States by the Congress.

Amendment XIX [1920]

The right of citizens of the United States to vote shall not be denied or abridged by the United States or by any State on account of sex.

Congress shall have power to enforce this article by appropriate legislation.

Amendment XX [1933]

Section 1

The terms of the President and Vice-President shall end at noon on the 20th day of January, and the terms of Senators and Representatives at noon on the 3d day of January, of the years in which such terms would have ended if this article had not been ratified; and the terms of their successors shall then begin.

Section 2

The Congress shall assemble at least once in every year, and such meeting shall begin at noon on the 3d day of January, unless they shall by law appoint a different day.

Section 3

If, at the time fixed for the beginning of the term of the President, the President elect shall have died, the Vice-President elect shall become President. If a President shall not have been chosen before the time fixed for the beginning of his term or if the President elect shall have failed to qualify, then the Vice-President elect shall act as President until a President shall have qualified; and the Congress may by law provide for the case wherein neither a President elect nor a Vice-President elect shall have qualified, declaring who shall then act as President, or the manner in which one who is to act shall be selected, and such person shall act accordingly until a President or Vice-President shall have qualified.

Section 4

The Congress may by law provide for the case of the death of any of the persons from whom the House of Representatives may choose a President whenever the right of choice shall have devolved upon them, and for the case of the death of any of the persons from whom the Senate may choose a Vice-President whenever the right of choice shall have devolved upon them.

Section 5

Sections 1 and 2 shall take effect on the 15th day of October following the ratification of this article.

Section 6

This article shall be inoperative unless it shall have been ratified as an amendment to the Constitution by the legislatures of three-fourths of the several States within seven years from the date of its submission.

Amendment XXI [1933]

Section 1

The eighteenth article of amendment to the Constitution of the United States is hereby repealed.

Section 2

The transportation or importation into any State, Territory, or possession of the United States for delivery or use therein of intoxicating liquors, in violation of the laws thereof, is hereby prohibited.

Section 3

This article shall be inoperative unless it shall have been ratified as an amendment to the Constitution by conventions in the several States, as provided in the Constitution, within seven years from the date of the submission hereof to the States by the Congress.

Amendment XXII [1951]

No person shall be elected to the office of the President more than twice, and no person who has held the office of President, or acted as President, for more than two years of a term to which some other person was elected

President shall be elected to the office of the President more than once.

But this Article shall not apply to any person holding the office of President when this Article was proposed by the Congress, and shall not prevent any person who may be holding the office of President, or acting as President, during the term within which this Article becomes operative from holding the office of President or acting as President during the remainder of such term.

This article shall be inoperative unless it shall have been ratified as an amendment to the Constitution by the legislatures of three-fourths of the several states within seven years from the date of its submission to the states by the Congress.

Amendment XXIII [1961]

Section 1

The District constituting the seat of Government of the United States shall appoint in such manner as the Congress may direct:

A number of electors of President and Vice-President equal to the whole number of Senators and Representatives in Congress to which the District would be entitled if it were a State, but in no event more than the least populous State; they shall be in addition to those appointed by the States, but they shall be considered, for the purposes of the election of President and Vice-President, to be electors appointed by a State; and they shall meet in the District and perform such duties as provided by the twelfth article of amendment.

Section 2

The Congress shall have power to enforce this article by appropriate legislation.

Amendment XXIV [1964]

Section 1

The right of citizens of the United States to vote in any primary or other election for President or Vice President, for electors for President or Vice President, or for Senator or Representative in Congress, shall not be denied or abridged by the United States or any state by reason of failure to pay any poll tax or other tax.

Section 2

The Congress shall have the power to enforce this article by appropriate legislation.

Amendment XXV [1967]

Section 1

In case of the removal of the President from office or of his death or resignation, the Vice President shall become President.

Section 2

Whenever there is a vacancy in the office of the Vice President, the President shall nominate a Vice President who shall take office upon confirmation by a majority vote of both Houses of Congress.

Section 3

Whenever the President transmits to the President Pro Tempore of the Senate and the Speaker of the House of Representatives his written declaration that he is unable to discharge the powers and duties of his office, and until he transmits to them a written declaration to the contrary, such powers and duties shall be discharged by the Vice President as Acting President.

Section 4

Whenever the Vice President and a majority of either the principal officers of the executive departments or of such other body as Congress may by law provide, transmit to the President Pro Tempore of the Senate and the Speaker of the House of Representatives their written declaration that the President is unable to discharge the powers and duties of his office, the Vice President shall immediately assume the powers and duties of the office as Acting President.

Thereafter, when the President transmits to the President Pro Tempore of the Senate and the Speaker of the House of Representatives his written declaration that no inability exists, he shall resume the powers and duties of his office unless the Vice President and a majority of either the principal officers of the executive departments or of such other body as Congress may by law provide, transmit within four days to the President Pro Tempore of the Senate and the Speaker of the House of Representatives their written declaration that the President is unable to discharge the powers and duties of his office. Thereupon Congress shall decide the issue, assembling within forty-eight hours for that purpose if not in session. If the Congress, within twenty-one days after receipt of the latter written declaration, or, if Congress is not in session, within twenty-one days after Congress is required to assemble, determines by two-thirds vote of both Houses that the President is unable to discharge the powers and duties of his office, the Vice President shall continue to discharge the same as Acting President; otherwise, the President shall resume the powers and duties of his office.

Amendment XXVI [1971]

Section 1

The right of citizens of the United States, who are eighteen years of age or older, to vote shall not be denied or abridged by the United States or by any State on account of age.

Section 2

The Congress shall have the power to enforce this article by appropriate legislation.

Amendment XXVII [1992]

No law varying the compensation for the service of Senators and Representatives shall take effect until an election of Representatives shall have intervened.

Federalist No. 10 (James Madison)

Among the numerous advantages promised by a well-constructed union, none deserves to be more accurately developed than its tendency to break and control the violence of faction. The friend of popular governments never finds himself so much alarmed for their character and fate as when he contemplates their propensity to this dangerous vice. He will not fail, therefore, to set a due value on any plan which, without violating the principles to which he is attached, provides a proper cure for it. The instability, injustice, and confusion introduced into the public councils have, in truth, been the mortal diseases under which popular governments have everywhere perished, as they continue to be the favorite and fruitful topics from which the adversaries to liberty derive their most specious declamations. The valuable improvements made by the American constitutions on the popular models, both ancient and modern, cannot certainly be too much admired; but it would be an unwarrantable partiality to contend that they have as effectually obviated the danger on this side, as was wished and expected. Complaints are everywhere heard from our most considerate and virtuous citizens, equally the friends of public and private faith and of public and personal liberty, that our governments are too unstable, that the public good is disregarded in the conflicts of rival parties, and that measures are too often decided, not according to the rules of justice and the rights of the minor party, but by the superior force of an interested and overbearing majority. However anxiously we may wish that these complaints had no foundation, the evidence of known facts will not permit us to deny that they are in some degree true. It will be found, indeed, on a candid review of our situation, that some of the distresses under which we labor have been erroneously charged on the operation of our governments; but it will be found, at the same time, that other causes will not alone account for many of our heaviest misfortunes; and, particularly, for that prevailing and increasing distrust of public engagements and alarm for private rights which are echoed from one end of the confinent to the other. These must be chiefly, if not wholly, effects of the unsteadiness and injustice with which a factious spirit has tainted our public administration.

By a faction I understand a number of citizens, whether amounting to a majority or minority of the whole, who are united and actuated by some common impulse of passion, or of interest, adverse to the rights of other citizens, or to the permanent and aggregate interests of the community.

There are two methods of curing the mischiefs of faction: the one, by removing its causes; the other, by controlling its effects.

There are again two methods of removing the causes of faction: the one, by destroying the liberty which is essential to its existence; the other, by giving to every citizen the same opinions, the same passions, and the same interests.

It could never be more truly said than of the first remedy that it was worse than the disease. Liberty is to faction what air is to fire, an aliment without which it instantly expires. But it could not be a less folly to abolish liberty, which is essential to political life, because it nourishes faction than it would be to wish the annihilation of air, which is essential to animal life, because it imparts to fire its destructive agency.

The second expedient is as impracticable as the first would be unwise. As long as the reason of man continues fallible, and he is at liberty to exercise it, different opinions will be formed. As long as the connection subsists between his reason and his self-love, his opinions and his passions will have a reciprocal influence on each other; and the former will be objects to which the latter will attach themselves. The diversity in the faculties of men, from which the rights of property originate, is not less an insuperable obstacle to a uniformity of interest. The protection of these faculties is the first object of government. From the protection of different and unequal faculties of acquiring property, the possession of different degrees and kinds of property immediately results; and from the influence of these on the sentiments and views of the respective proprietors ensues a division of the society into different interests and parties.

The latent causes of faction are thus sown in the nature of man; and we see them everywhere brought into different degrees of activity, according to the different circumstances of civil society. A zeal for different opinions concerning religion, concerning government, and many other points, as well of speculation as of practice; an attachment to different leaders ambitiously contending for pre-eminence and power; or to persons of other descriptions whose fortunes have been interesting to the human passions, have, in turn, divided mankind into parties, inflamed them with mutual animosity, and rendered them much more disposed to vex and oppress each other than to co-operate for their common good. So strong is this propensity of mankind to fall into mutual animosities that where no substantial occasion presents itself the most frivolous and fanciful distinctions have been sufficient to kindle their unfriendly passions and excite their most violent conflicts. But the most common and durable source of factions has been the various and unequal distribution of property. Those who hold and those who are without property have ever formed distinct interests in society. Those who are creditors, and those who are debtors, fall under a like discrimination. A landed interest, a manufacturing interest, a mercantile interest, a moneyed interest, with many lesser interests, grow up of necessity in civilized nations, and divide them into different classes, actuated by different sentiments and views. The regulation of these various and interfering interests forms the principal task of modern legislation and involves the spirit of party and faction in the necessary and ordinary operations of government.

No man is allowed to be a judge in his own cause, because his interest would certainly bias his judgment, and, not improbably, corrupt his integrity. With equal, nay with greater reason, a body of men are unfit to be both judges and parties at the same time; yet what are many of the most important acts of legislation but so many judicial determinations, not indeed concerning the rights of single persons, but concerning the rights of large bodies of citizens? And what are the different classes of legislators but advocates and parties to the causes which they determine? Is a law proposed concerning private debts? It is a question to which the creditors are parties on one side and the debtors on the other. Justice ought to hold the balance between them. Yet the parties are, and must be, themselves the judges; and the most numerous party, or in other words, the most powerful faction must be expected to prevail. Shall domestic manufacturers be encouraged, and in what degree, by restrictions on foreign manufacturers? [These] are questions which would be differently decided by the landed and the manufacturing classes, and probably by neither with a sole regard to justice and the public good. The apportionment of taxes on the various descriptions of property is an act which seems to require the most exact impartiality; yet there is, perhaps, no legislative act in which greater opportunity and temptation are given to a predominant party

to trample on the rules of justice. Every shilling with which they overburden the inferior number is a shilling saved to their own pockets.

It is in vain to say that enlightened statesmen will be able to adjust these clashing interests and render them all subservient to the public good. Enlightened statesmen will not always be at the helm. Nor, in many cases, can such an adjustment be made at all without taking into view indirect and remote considerations, which will rarely prevail over the immediate interest which one party may find in disregarding the rights of another or the good of the whole.

The inference to which we are brought is that the *causes* of faction cannot be removed and that relief is only to be sought in the means of controlling its *effects*.

If a faction consists of less than a majority, relief is supplied by the republican principle, which enables the majority to defeat its sinister views by regular vote. It may clog the administration, it may convulse the society; but it will be unable to execute and mask its violence under the forms of the Constitution. When a majority is included in a faction, the form of popular government, on the other hand, enables it to sacrifice to its ruling passion or interest both the public good and the rights of other citizens. To secure the public good and private rights against the danger of such a faction, and at the same time to preserve the spirit and the form of popular government, is then the great object to which our inquiries are directed. Let me add that it is the great desideratum by which alone this form of government can be rescued from the opprobrium under which it has so long labored and be recommended to the esteem and adoption of mankind.

By what means is this object attainable? Evidently by one of two only. Either the existence of the same passion or interest in a majority at the same time must be prevented, or the majority, having such coexistent passion or interest, must be rendered, by their number and local situation, unable to concert and carry into effect schemes of oppression. If the impulse and the opportunity be suffered to coincide, we well know that neither moral nor religious motives can be relied on as an adequate control. They are not found to be such on the injustice and violence of individuals, and lose their efficacy in proportion to the number combined together, that is, in proportion as their efficacy becomes needful.

From this view of the subject it may be concluded that a pure democracy, by which I mean a society consisting of a small number of citizens, who assemble and administer the government in person, can admit of no cure for the mischiefs of faction. A common passion or interest will, in almost every case, be felt by a majority of the whole, a communication and concert result from the form of government itself; and there is nothing to check the inducements to sacrifice the weaker party or an obnoxious individual. Hence it is that such democracies have ever been spectacles of turbulence and contention; have ever been found incompatible with personal security or the rights of property; and have in general been as short in their lives as they have been violent in their deaths. Theoretic politicians, who have patronized this species of government, have erroneously supposed that by reducing mankind to a perfect equality in their political rights, they would at the same time be perfectly equalized and assimilated in their possessions, their opinions, and their passions.

A republic, by which I mean a government in which the scheme of representation takes place, opens a different prospect and promises the cure for which we are seeking. Let us examine the points in which it varies from pure democracy, and we shall comprehend both the nature of the cure and the efficacy which it must derive from the Union.

The two great points of difference between a democracy and a republic are: first, the delegation of the government, in the latter, to a small number of citizens elected by the rest; secondly, the greater number of citizens and greater sphere of country over which the latter may be extended.

The effect of the first difference is, on the one hand, to refine and enlarge the public views by passing them through the medium of a chosen body of citizens, whose wisdom may best discern the true interest of their country and whose patriotism and love of justice will be least likely to sacrifice it to temporary or partial considerations. Under such a regulation it may well happen that the public voice, pronounced by the representatives of the people, will be more consonant to the public good than if pronounced by the people themselves, convened for the purpose. On the other hand, the effect may be inverted. Men of factious tempers, of local prejudices, or of sinister designs, may, by intrigue, by corruption, or by other means, first obtain the suffrages, and then betray the interests of the people. The question resulting is, whether small or extensive republics are most favorable to the election of proper guardians of the public weal; and it is clearly decided in favor of the latter by two obvious considerations.

In the first place it is to be remarked that however small the republic may be the representatives must be raised to a certain number in order to guard against the cabals of a few; and that however large it may be they must be limited to a certain number in order to guard against the confusion of a multitude. Hence, the number of representatives in the two cases not being in proportion to that of the constituents, and being

proportionally greatest in the small republic, it follows that if the proportion of fit characters be not less in the large than in the small republic, the former will present a greater option, and consequently a greater probability of a fit choice.

In the next place, as each representative will be chosen by a greater number of citizens in the large than in the small republic, it will be more difficult for unworthy candidates to practice with success the vicious arts by which elections are too often carried; and the suffrages of the people being more free, will be more likely to center on men who possess the most attractive merit and the most diffusive and established characters.

It must be confessed that in this, as in most other cases, there is a mean, on both sides of which inconveniencies will be found to lie. By enlarging too much the number of electors, you render the representative too little acquainted with all their local circumstances and lesser interests; as by reducing it too much, you render him unduly attached to these, and too little fit to comprehend and pursue great and national objects. The federal Constitution forms a happy combination in this respect; the great and aggregate interests being referred to the national, the local and particular to the State legislatures.

The other point of difference is the greater number of citizens and extent of territory which may be brought within the compass of republican than of democratic government; and it is this circumstance principally which renders factious combinations less to be dreaded in the former than in the latter. The smaller the society, the fewer probably will be the distinct parties and interests composing it; the fewer the distinct parties and interests, the more frequently will a majority be found of the same party; and the smaller the number of individuals composing a majority, and the smaller the compass within which they are placed, the more easily will they concert and execute their plans of oppression. Extend the sphere and you take in a greater variety of parties and interests; you make it less probable that a majority of the whole will have a common motive to invade the rights of other citizens; or if such a common motive exists, it will be more difficult for all who feel it to discover their own strength and to act in unison with each other. Besides other impediments, it may be remarked that, where there is a consciousness of unjust or dishonorable purposes, communication is always checked by distrust in proportion to the number whose concurrence is necessary.

Hence, it clearly appears that the same advantage which a republic has over a democracy in controlling the effects of faction is enjoyed by a large over a small republic—is enjoyed by the Union over the States composing it. Does this advantage consist in the substitution of representatives whose enlightened views and virtuous sentiments render them superior to local prejudices and to schemes of injustice? It will not be denied that the representation of the Union will be most likely to possess these requisite endowments. Does it consist in the greater security afforded by a greater variety of parties, against the event of any one party being able to outnumber and oppress the rest? In an equal degree does the increased variety of parties comprised within the Union increase this security. Does it, in fine, consist in the greater obstacles opposed to the concert and accomplishment of the secret wishes of an unjust and interested majority? Here again the extent of the Union gives it the most palpable advantage.

The influence of factious leaders may kindle a flame within their particular States but will be unable to spread a general conflagration through the other States. A religious sect may degenerate into a political faction in a part of the Confederacy; but the variety of sects dispersed over the entire face of it must secure the national councils against any danger from that source. A rage for paper money, for an abolition of debts, for an equal division of property, or for any other improper or wicked project, will be less apt to pervade the whole body of the Union than a particular member of it, in the same proportion as such a malady is more likely to taint a particular county or district than an entire State.

In the extent and proper structure of the Union, therefore, we behold a republican remedy for the diseases most incident to republican government. And according to the degree of pleasure and pride we feel in being republicans ought to be our zeal in cherishing the spirit and supporting the character of Federalists.

Federalist No. 51 (James Madison)

To what expedient, then, shall we finally resort, for maintaining in practice the necessary partition of power among the several departments as laid down in the Constitution? The only answer that can be given is that as all these exterior provisions are found to be inadequate, the defect must be supplied, by so contriving the interior structure of the government as that its several constituent parts may, by their mutual relations, be the means of keeping each other in their proper places. Without presuming to undertake a full development of this important idea I will hazard a few general observations which may perhaps place it in a clearer light, and enable us to form a more correct judgment of the principles and structure of the government planned by the convention.

In order to lay a due foundation for that separate and distinct exercise of the different powers of government, which to a certain extent is admitted on all hands to be essential to the preservation of liberty, it is evident that each department should have a will of its own; and consequently should be so constituted that the members of each should have as little agency as possible in the appointment of the members of the others. Were this principle rigorously adhered to, it would require that all the appointments for the supreme executive, legislative, and judiciary magistracies should be drawn from the same fountain of authority, the people, through channels having no communication whatever with one another. Perhaps such a plan of constructing the several departments would be less difficult in practice than it may be in contemplation appear. Some difficulties, however, and some additional expense would attend the execution of it. Some deviations, therefore, from the principle must be admitted. In the constitution of the judiciary department in particular, it might be inexpedient to insist rigorously on the principle; first, because peculiar qualifications being essential in the members, the primary consideration ought to be to select that mode of choice which best secures these qualifications; second, because the permanent tenure by which the appointments are held in that department must soon destroy all sense of dependence on the authority conferring them.

It is equally evident that the members of each department should be as little dependent as possible on those of the others for the emoluments annexed to their offices. Were the executive magistrate, or the judges, not independent of the legislature in this particular, their independence in every other would be merely nominal.

But the great security against a gradual concentration of the several powers in the same department consists in giving to those who administer each department the necessary constitutional means and personal motives to resist encroachments of the others. The provision for defense must in this, as in all other cases, be made commensurate to the danger of attack. Ambition must be made to counteract ambition. The interest of the man must be connected with the constitutional rights of the place. It may be a reflection on human nature that such devices should be necessary to control the abuses of government. But what is government itself but the greatest of all reflections on human nature? If men were angels no government would be necessary. If angels were to govern men, neither external nor internal controls on government would be necessary. In framing a government which is to be administered by men over men, the great difficulty lies in this: you must first enable the government to control the governed; and in the next place oblige it to control itself. A dependence on the people is, no doubt, the primary control on the government; but experience has taught mankind the necessity of auxiliary precautions.

This policy of supplying, by opposite and rival interests, the defect of better motives, might be traced through the whole system of human affairs, private as well as public. We see it particularly displayed in all the subordinate distributions of power, where the constant aim is to divide and arrange the several offices in such a manner as that each may be a check on the other—that the private interest of every individual may be a sentinel over the public rights. These inventions of prudence cannot be less requisite in the distribution of the supreme powers of the State.

But it is not possible to give to each department an equal power of self-defense. In republican government, the legislative authority necessarily predominates. The remedy for this inconveniency is to divide the legislature into different branches; and to render them, by different modes of election and different principles of action, as little connected with each other as the nature of their common functions and their common dependence on the society will admit. It may even be necessary to guard against dangerous encroachments by still further precautions. As the weight of the legislative authority requires that it should be thus divided, the weakness of the executive may require, on the other hand, that it should be fortified. An absolute negative on the legislature appears, at first view, to be the natural defense with which the executive magistrate should be armed. But perhaps it would be neither altogether safe nor alone sufficient. On ordinary occasions it might not be exerted with the requisite firmness, and on extraordinary occasions it might be perfidiously abused. May not this defect of an absolute negative be supplied by some qualified connection between this weaker department and the weaker branch

of the stronger department, by which the latter may be led to support the constitutional rights of the former, without being too much detached from the rights of its own department?

If the principles on which these observations are founded be just, as I persuade myself they are, and they be applied as a criterion to the several State constitutions, and to the federal Constitution, it will be found that if the latter does not perfectly correspond with them, the former are infinitely less able to bear such a test.

There are, moreover, two considerations particularly applicable to the federal system of America, which place that system in a very interesting point of view.

First. In a single republic, all the power surrendered by the people is submitted to the administration of a single government; and the usurpations are guarded against by a division of the government into distinct and separate departments. In the compound republic of America, the power surrendered by the people is first divided between two distinct governments, and then the portion allotted to each subdivided among distinct and separate departments. Hence a double security arises to the rights of the people. The different governments will control each other, at the same time that each will be controlled by itself.

Second. It is of great importance in a republic not only to guard the society against the oppression of its rulers, but to guard one part of the society against the injustice of the other part. Different interests necessarily exist in different classes of citizens. If a majority be united by a common interest, the rights of the minority will be insecure. There are but two methods of providing against this evil: the one by creating a will in the community independent of the majority—that is, of the society itself; the other, by comprehending in the society so many separate descriptions of citizens as will render an unjust combination of a majority of the whole very improbable, if not impracticable. The first method prevails in all governments possessing an hereditary or self-appointed authority. This, at best, is but a precarious security; because a power independent of the society may as well espouse the unjust views of the major as the rightful interests of the minor party, and may possibly be turned against both parties. The second method will be exemplified in the federal republic of the United States. Whilst all authority in it will be derived from and dependent on the society, the society itself will be broken into so many parts, interests and classes of citizens, that the rights of individuals, or of the minority, will be in little danger from interested combinations of the majority. In a free government the security for civil rights must be the same as that for religious rights. It consists in the one case in the multiplicity of interests, and in the other in the multiplicity of sects. The degree of security in both cases will depend on the number of interests and sects; and this may be presumed to depend on the extent of country and number of people comprehended under the same government. This view of the subject must particularly recommend a proper federal system to all the sincere and considerate friends of republican government, since it shows that in exact proportion as the territory of the Union may be formed into more circumscribed Confederacies, or States, oppressive combinations of a majority will be facilitated; the best security, under the republican forms, for the rights of every class of citizen, will be diminished; and consequently the stability and independence of some member of the government, the only other security, must be proportionately increased. Justice is the end of government. It is the end of civil society. It ever has been and ever will be pursued until it be obtained, or until liberty be lost in the pursuit. In a society under the forms of which the stronger faction can readily unite and oppress the weaker, anarchy may as truly be said to reign as in a state of nature, where the weaker individual is not secured against the violence of the stronger; and as, in the latter state, even the stronger individuals are prompted, by the uncertainty of their condition, to submit to a government which may protect the weak as well as themselves; so, in the former state, will the more powerful factions or parties be gradually induced, by a like motive, to wish for a government which will protect all parties, the weaker as well as the more powerful. It can be little doubted that if the State of Rhode Island was separated from the Confederacy and left to itself, the insecurity of rights under the popular form of government within such narrow limits would be displayed by such reiterated oppressions of factious majorities that some power altogether independent of the people would soon be called for by the voice of the very factions whose misrule had proved the necessity of it. In the extended republic of the United States, and among the great variety of interests, parties, and sects which it embraces, a coalition of a majority of the whole society could seldom take place on any other principles than those of justice and the general good; whilst there being thus less danger to a minor from the will of a major party, there must be less pretext, also, to provide for the security of the former, by introducing into the government a will not dependent on the latter, or, in other words, a will independent of the society itself. It is no less certain than it is important, notwithstanding the contrary opinions which have been entertained, that the larger the society, provided it lie within a practicable sphere, the more duly capable it will be of self-government. And happily for the republican cause, the practicable sphere may be carried to a very great extent by a judicious modification and mixture of the federal principle.

Glossary

A

affirmative action A term that refers to programs designed to ensure that women, minorities, and other traditionally disadvantaged groups have full and equal opportunities in employment, education, and other areas of life.

agency point of view The tendency of bureaucrats to place the interests of their agency ahead of other interests and ahead of the priorities sought by the president or Congress.

agenda setting The power of the media through news coverage to focus the public's attention and concern on particular events, problems, issues, personalities, and so on.

agents of socialization Those agents, such as the family and the media, that have significant impact on citizens' political socialization.

air wars A term that refers to the fact that modern campaigns are often a battle of opposing televised advertising campaigns.

alienation A feeling of personal powerlessness that includes the notion that government does not care about the opinions of people like oneself.

Anti-Federalists A term used to describe opponents of the Constitution during the debate over ratification.

apathy A feeling of personal noninterest or unconcern with politics.

appellate jurisdiction The authority of a given court to review cases that have already been tried in lower courts and are appealed to it by the losing party; such a court is called an appeals court or appellate court. (See also **original jurisdiction.**)

authoritarian government A form of government in which leaders, though they admit to no limits on their powers, are effectively limited by other centers of power in the society.

authority The recognized right of an individual or institution to exercise power. (See also **power.**)

autocracy A form of government in which absolute control rests with a single person.

B

balanced budget When the government's tax revenues for the year are roughly equal to its expenditures.

bicameral legislatures Legislatures having two chambers.

bill A proposed law (legislative act) within Congress or another legislature. (See also **law.**)

Bill of Rights The first ten amendments to the Constitution. They include such rights as freedom of speech and trial by jury.

bipolar (power structure) A power structure dominated by two powers only, as in the case of the United States and the Soviet Union during the cold war.

block grants Federal grants-in-aid that permit state and local officials to decide how the money will be spent within a general area, such as education or health. (See also **categorical grants.**)

brief A written statement by a party in a court case that details its argument.

budget deficit When the government's expenditures exceed its tax revenues.

budget surplus When the government's tax and other revenues exceed its expenditures.

bureaucracy A system of organization and control based on the principles of hierarchical authority, job specialization, and formalized rules. (See also **formalized rules; hierarchical authority; job specialization.**)

bureaucratic accountability The degree to which bureaucrats are held accountable for the power they exercise.

bureaucratic rule The tendency of large-scale organizations to develop into the bureaucratic form, with the effect that administrators make key policy decisions.

C

cabinet A group consisting of the heads of the (cabinet) executive departments, who are appointed by the president, subject to confirmation by the Senate. The cabinet was once the main advisory body to the president but no longer plays this role. (See also **cabinet departments.**)

cabinet (executive) departments The major administrative organizations within the federal executive bureaucracy, each of which is headed by a secretary (cabinet officer) and has responsibility for a major function of the federal government, such as defense, agriculture, or justice. (See also **cabinet; independent agencies.**)

candidate-centered politics Election campaigns and other political processes in which candidates, not political parties, have most of the initiative and influence. (See also **party-centered politics.**)

capital-gains tax The tax that individuals pay on money gained from the sale of a capital asset, such as property or stocks.

capitalism An economic system based on the idea that government should interfere with economic transactions as little as possible. Free enterprise and self-reliance are the collective and individual principles that underpin capitalism.

categorical grants Federal grants-in-aid to states and localities that can be used only for designated projects. (See also **block grants.**)

charter The chief instrument by which a state governs its local units; it spells out in detail what a local government can and cannot do.

checks and balances The elaborate system of divided spheres of authority provided by the U.S. Constitution as a means of controlling the power of government. The separation of powers among the branches of the national government, federalism, and the different methods of selecting national officers are all part of this system.

citizens' (noneconomic) groups Organized interests formed by individuals drawn together by opportunities to promote a cause in which they believe but that does not provide them significant individual economic benefits. (See also **economic groups; interest group.**)

city manager system The form of municipal government that entrusts the executive role to a professionally trained manager, who is chosen, and can be fired, by the city council.

civic duty The belief of an individual that civic and political participation is a responsibility of citizenship.

civil law Laws governing relations with or between private parties where no criminal act is alleged and where the parties are making conflicting claims or are seeking to establish a legal relationship.

civil liberties The fundamental individual rights of a free society, such as freedom of speech and the right to a jury trial, which in the United States are protected by the Bill of Rights.

civil rights (equal rights) The right of every person to equal protection under the laws and equal access to society's opportunities and public facilities.

civil service system See **merit system.**

clear-and-present-danger test A test devised by the Supreme Court in 1919 to define the limits of free speech in the context of national security. According to the test, government cannot abridge political expression unless it presents a clear and present danger to the nation's security.

clientele groups Special interest groups that benefit directly from the activities of a particular bureaucratic agency and are therefore strong advocates of the agency.

cloture A parliamentary maneuver that, if a three-fifths majority votes for it, limits Senate debate to thirty hours and has the effect of defeating a filibuster. (See also **filibuster.**)

cold war The lengthy period after World War II when the United States and the USSR were not engaged in actual combat (a "hot war") but were nonetheless locked in a state of deep-seated hostility.

collective (public) goods Benefits that are offered by groups (usually citizens' groups) as an incentive for membership but that are nondivisible (such as a clean environment) and therefore are available to nonmembers as well as members of the particular group. (See also **free-rider problem; private goods.**)

commerce clause The clause of the Constitution (Article I, Section 8) that empowers the federal government to regulate commerce among the states and with other nations.

commission system The form of municipal government that invests executive and legislative authority in a commission, with each commissioner serving as a member of the local council but also having a specified executive role, such as police commissioner or public works commissioner.

common-carrier function The media's function as an open channel through which political leaders can communicate with the public. (See also **partisan function; signaling function; watchdog function.**)

communism An economic system in which government owns most or all major industries and also takes responsibility for overall management of the economy.

compliance The issue of whether a court's decisions will be respected and obeyed.

concurring opinion A separate opinion written by a Supreme Court justice who votes with the majority in the decision on a case but who disagrees with their reasoning. (See also **dissenting opinion; majority opinion; plurality opinion.**)

confederacy A governmental system in which sovereignty is vested entirely in subnational (state) governments. (See also **federalism; unitary system.**)

conference committees Temporary committees that are formed to bargain over the differences in the House and Senate versions of a bill. The committee's members are usually appointed from the House and Senate standing committees that originally worked on the bill.

constituency The individuals who live within the geographical area represented by an elected official. More narrowly, the body of citizens eligible to vote for a particular representative.

constitution The fundamental law that defines how a government will legitimately operate.

constitutional democracy A government that is democratic in its provisions for majority influence through elections and constitutional in its provisions for minority rights and rule by law.

constitutional initiative The process by which a citizen or group can petition to place a proposed amendment on the ballot at the next election by obtaining the signatures of a certain number of registered voters. If the amendment gets majority support, it becomes part of the constitution.

constitutionalism The idea that there are definable limits on the rightful power of a government over its citizens.

containment A doctrine, developed after World War II, based on the assumptions that the Soviet Union was an aggressor nation and that only a determined United States could block Soviet territorial ambitions.

Cooley's rule The term used to describe the idea that cities should be self-governing, articulated in an 1871 ruling by Michigan judge Thomas Cooley.

cooperative federalism The situation in which the national, state, and local levels work together to solve problems.

criminal law Laws governing acts deemed illegal and punishable by government, such as robbery. Government is always a party to a criminal law case; the other party is the individual accused of breaking the law.

D

de facto discrimination Discrimination on the basis of race, sex, religion, ethnicity, and the like that results from social, economic, and cultural biases and conditions. (See also **de jure discrimination.**)

de jure discrimination Discrimination on the basis of race, sex, religion, ethnicity, and the like that results from a law. (See also **de facto discrimination.**)

decision A vote of the Supreme Court in a particular case that indicates which party the justices side with and by how large a margin.

deficit spending When the government spends more than it collects in taxes and other revenues.

delegates Elected representatives whose obligation is to act in accordance with the expressed wishes of the people whom they represent. (See also **trustees.**)

demand-side economics A form of fiscal policy that emphasizes "demand" (consumer spending). Government can use increased spending or tax cuts to place more money in consumers' hands and thereby increase demand. (See also **fiscal policy; supply-side economics.**)

democracy A form of government in which the people govern, either directly or through elected representatives.

demographic representativeness The idea that the bureaucracy will be more responsive to the public if its employees at all levels are demographically representative of the population as a whole.

denials of power A constitutional means of limiting governmental action by listing those powers that government is expressly prohibited from using.

deregulation The rescinding of excessive government regulations for the purpose of improving economic efficiency.

détente A French word meaning "a relaxing" and used to refer to an era of improved relations between the United States and the Soviet Union that began in the early 1970s.

deterrence policy The idea that nuclear war can be discouraged if each side in a conflict has the capacity to destroy the other with nuclear weapons.

devolution The passing down of authority from the national government to states and localities.

Dillon's rule The term used to describe relations between state and local government; it holds that local governments are creatures of the state, which in theory even has the power to abolish them.

direct primary See **primary election.**

dissenting opinion The opinion of a justice in a Supreme Court case that explains his or her reasons for disagreeing with the majority's decision. (See also **concurring opinion; majority opinion; plurality opinion.**)

dual federalism A doctrine based on the idea that a precise separation of national power and state power is both possible and desirable.

due process clause (of the Fourteenth Amendment) The clause of the Constitution that has been used by the judiciary to apply the Bill of Rights to the actions of state governments.

E

economic conservatives Those who believe government tries to do too many things that should be left to firms and economic markets. (See also **economic liberals; libertarians; populists; social conservatives; social liberals.**)

economic depression A very severe and sustained economic downturn. Depressions are rare in the United States: the last one was in the 1930s.

economic globalization The increased interdependence of nations' economies. The change is a result of technological, transportation, and communication advances that have enabled firms to deploy their resources across the globe.

economic groups Interest groups that are organized primarily for economic reasons but that engage in political activity in order to seek favorable policies from government. (See also **citizens' groups; interest group.**)

economic liberals Those who believe government should do more to assist people who have difficulty meeting their economic needs on their own. (See also **economic conservatives; libertarians; populists; social conservatives; social liberals.**)

economic recession A moderate but sustained downturn in the economy.

Recessions are part of the economy's normal cycle of ups and downs.

economy A system of production and consumption of goods and services that are allocated through exchange among producers and consumers.

effective tax rate The actual percentage of a person's income that is spent to pay taxes.

efficiency An economic principle that holds that firms should fulfill as many of society's needs as possible while using as few of its resources as possible. The greater the output (production) for a given input (for example, an hour of labor), the more efficient the process.

elastic clause See **"necessary and proper" clause.**

Electoral College An unofficial term that refers to the electors who cast the states' electoral votes.

electoral votes The method of voting that is used to choose the U.S. president. Each state has the same number of electoral votes as it has members in Congress (House and Senate combined). By tradition, electoral voting is tied to a state's popular voting; thus, the presidential candidate with the most popular votes overall has usually also had the most electoral votes.

elitism The view that the United States is essentially run by a tiny elite (composed of wealthy or well-connected individuals) who control public policy through both direct and indirect means.

entitlement program Any of a number of individual benefit programs, such as social security, that require government to provide a designated benefit to any person who meets the legally defined criteria for eligibility.

enumerated (expressed) powers The seventeen powers granted to the national government under Article I, Section 8 of the Constitution. These powers include taxation and the regulation of commerce as well as the authority to provide for the national defense.

equal-protection clause A clause of the Fourteenth Amendment that forbids any state to deny equal protection of the laws to any individual within its jurisdiction.

equal rights See **civil rights.**

equality The notion that all individuals are equal in their moral worth and are thereby entitled to equal treatment under the law.

equality of opportunity The idea that all individuals should be given an equal chance to succeed on their own.

equality of result The objective of policies intended to reduce or eliminate the effects of discrimination so that members

of traditionally disadvantaged groups will have the same benefits of society as do members of advantaged groups.

equity (in relation to economic policy) The situation in which the outcome of an economic transaction is fair to each party. An outcome can usually be considered fair if each party enters into a transaction freely and is not knowingly at a disadvantage.

establishment clause The First Amendment provision that government may not favor one religion over another or favor religion over no religion, and that prohibits Congress from passing laws respecting the establishment of religion.

exclusionary rule The legal principle that government is prohibited from using in trials evidence that was obtained by unconstitutional means (for example, illegal search and seizure).

executive departments See **cabinet departments.**

executive leadership system An approach to managing the bureaucracy that is based on presidential leadership and presidential management tools, such as the president's annual budget proposal. (See also **merit system; patronage system.**)

expressed powers See **enumerated powers.**

externalities Burdens that society incurs when firms fail to pay the full cost of resources used in production. An example of an externality is the pollution that results when corporations dump industrial wastes into lakes and rivers.

F

factional (minor) party A minor party created when a faction within one of the major parties breaks away to form its own party.

facts (of a court case) The relevant circumstances of a legal dispute or offense as determined by a trial court. The facts of a case are crucial because they help determine which law or laws are applicable in the case.

federalism A governmental system in which authority is divided between two sovereign levels of government: national and regional. (See also **confederacy; unitary system.**)

Federalists A term used to describe supporters of the Constitution during the debate over ratification.

filibuster A procedural tactic in the U.S. Senate whereby a minority of legislators prevents a bill from coming to a vote by holding the floor and talking until the majority gives in and the bill is withdrawn from consideration. (See also **cloture.**)

fiscal federalism A term that refers to the expenditure of federal funds on programs run in part through states and localities.

fiscal policy A tool of economic management by which government attempts to maintain a stable economy through its taxing and spending decisions. (See also **demand-side economics; monetary policy; supply-side economics.**)

formalized rules A basic principle of bureaucracy that refers to the standardized procedures and established regulations by which a bureaucracy conducts its operations. (See also **bureaucracy.**)

framing The process of selecting certain aspects of reality and making them the most salient part of the communication, thereby conveying a particular interpretation of a situation.

free-exercise clause A First Amendment provision that prohibits the government from interfering with the practice of religion or prohibiting the free exercise of religion.

free-rider problem The situation in which the benefits offered by a group to its members are also available to nonmembers. The incentive to join the group and to promote its cause is reduced because nonmembers (free riders) receive the benefits (for example, a cleaner environment) without having to pay any of the group's costs. (See also **collective goods.**)

free-trade position The view that the long-term economic interests of all countries are advanced when tariffs and other trade barriers are kept to a minimum. (See also **protectionism.**)

freedom of expression Americans' freedom to communicate their views, the foundation of which is the First Amendment rights of freedom of conscience, speech, press, assembly, and petition.

G

gender gap The tendency of women and men to differ in their political attitudes and voting preferences.

gerrymandering The process by which the party in power draws election district boundaries in a way that advantages its candidates.

government corporations Bodies, such as the U.S. Postal Service and Amtrak, that are similar to private corporations in that they charge for their services, but different in that they receive federal funding to help defray expenses.

Their directors are appointed by the president with Senate approval.

graduated personal income tax A tax on personal income in which the tax rate increases as income increases; in other words, the tax rate is higher for higher income levels.

grants-in-aid Federal cash payments to states and localities for programs they administer.

grants of power The method of limiting the U.S. government by confining its scope of authority to those powers expressly granted in the Constitution.

grassroots lobbying A form of lobbying designed to persuade officials that a group's policy position has strong constituent support.

grassroots party A political party organized at the level of the voters and dependent on their support for its strength.

Great Compromise The agreement of the constitutional convention to create a two-chamber Congress with the House apportioned by population and the Senate apportioned equally by state.

H

hard money Campaign funds given directly to candidates to spend as they choose.

hierarchical authority A basic principle of bureaucracy that refers to the chain of command within an organization whereby officials and units have control over those below them. (See also **bureaucracy.**)

hired guns The professional consultants who run campaigns for high office.

home rule A device designed to give local governments more leeway in their policies; it allows a local government to design and amend its own charter, subject to the laws and constitution of the state and also subject to veto by the state.

honeymoon period The president's first months in office, a time when Congress, the press, and the public are more inclined than usual to support presidential initiatives.

I

ideological (minor) party A minor party characterized by its ideological commitment to a broad and noncentrist philosophical position.

ideology A consistent pattern of opinion on particular issues that stems from a core belief or set of beliefs.

imminent lawless action test A legal test that says government cannot lawfully

suppress advocacy that promotes lawless action unless such advocacy is aimed at producing, and is likely to produce, imminent lawless action.

implied powers The federal government's constitutional authority (through the "necessary and proper" clause) to take action that is not expressly authorized by the Constitution but that supports actions that are so authorized. (See also **"necessary and proper" clause.**)

in-kind benefit A government benefit that is a cash equivalent, such as food stamps or rent vouchers. This form of benefit ensures that recipients will use public assistance in a specified way.

inalienable (natural) rights Those rights that persons theoretically possessed in the state of nature, prior to the formation of governments. These rights, including those of life, liberty, and property, are considered inherent and as such are inalienable. Since government is established by people, government has the responsibility to preserve these rights.

independent agencies Bureaucratic agencies that are similar to cabinet departments but usually have a narrower area of responsibility. Each such agency is headed by a presidential appointee who is not a cabinet member. An example is the National Aeronautics and Space Administration. (See also **cabinet departments.**)

individual goods See **private goods.**

individualism The idea that people should take the initiative, be self-sufficient, and accumulate the material advantages necessary for their well-being.

inflation A general increase in the average level of prices of goods and services.

initiative The process by which citizens can place legislative measures on the ballot through signature petitions. If the measure receives a majority vote, it becomes law.

inside lobbying Direct communication between organized interests and policymakers, which is based on the assumed value of close ("inside") contacts with policymakers.

interest group A set of individuals who are organized to promote a shared political interest. (See also **citizens' groups; economic groups.**)

interest-group liberalism The tendency of public officials to support the policy demands of self-interested groups (as opposed to judging policy demands according to whether they serve a larger conception of "the public interest").

internationalist A person who holds the view that the country should involve itself deeply in world affairs. (See also **isolationist.**)

iron triangle A small and informal but relatively stable group of well-positioned legislators, executives, and lobbyists who seek to promote policies beneficial to a particular interest. (See also **issue network**.)

isolationist A person who holds the view that the country should deliberately avoid a large role in world affairs and, instead, concentrate on domestic concerns. (See also **internationalist**.)

issue network An informal network of public officials and lobbyists who have a common interest and expertise in a given area and who are brought together temporarily by a proposed policy in that area. (See also **iron triangle**.)

J

job specialization A basic principle of bureaucracy that holds that the responsibilities of each job position should be explicitly defined and that a precise division of labor within the organization should be maintained. (See also **bureaucracy**.)

judicial activism The doctrine that the courts should develop new legal principles when judges see a compelling need, even if this action places them in conflict with precedent or the policy decisions of elected officials. (See also **judicial restraint**.)

judicial conference A closed meeting of the justices of the U.S. Supreme Court to discuss and vote on the cases before them; the justices are not supposed to discuss conference proceedings with outsiders.

judicial restraint The doctrine that the judiciary should broadly defer to precedent and the judgment of legislatures. The doctrine claims that the job of judges is to work within the confines of laws set down by tradition and lawmaking majorities. (See also **judicial activism**.)

judicial review The power of courts to decide whether a governmental institution has acted within its constitutional powers and, if not, to declare its action null and void.

jurisdiction (of a congressional committee) The policy area in which a particular congressional committee is authorized to act.

jurisdiction (of a court) A given court's authority to hear cases of a particular kind. Jurisdiction may be original or appellate.

L

laissez-faire doctrine A classic economic philosophy that holds that owners of businesses should be allowed to make their own production and distribution decisions without government regulation or control.

large-state plan See **Virginia Plan**.

law (as enacted by Congress) A legislative proposal, or bill, that is passed by both the House and Senate and is either signed or not vetoed by the president. (See also **bill**.)

lawmaking function The authority (of a legislature) to make the laws necessary to carry out the government's powers. (See also **oversight function; representation function**.)

laws (of a court case) The constitutional provisions, legislative statutes, or judicial precedents that apply to a court case.

legitimacy (of judicial power) The issue of the proper limits of judicial authority in a political system based in part on the principle of majority rule.

libel Publication of material that falsely damages a person's reputation.

libertarians Those who believe government tries to do too many things that should be left to firms and individuals and who oppose government as an instrument of traditional values. (See also **economic conservatives; economic liberals; populists; social conservatives; social liberals**.)

liberty The principle that individuals should be free to act and think as they choose, provided they do not infringe unreasonably on the rights and freedoms of others.

limited government A government that is subject to strict limits on its lawful uses of powers and hence on its ability to deprive people of their liberty.

living constitution theory A method of interpreting the Constitution that emphasizes the principles it embodies and their application to changing circumstances and needs.

lobbying The process by which interest-group members or lobbyists attempt to influence public policy through contacts with public officials.

logrolling The trading of votes between legislators so that each gets what he or she most wants.

M

majoritarianism The idea that the majority prevails not only in elections but also in determining policy.

majority opinion A Supreme Court opinion that results when a majority of the justices is in agreement on the legal basis of the decision. (See also **concurring opinion; dissenting opinion; plurality opinion**.)

means test The requirement that applicants for public assistance must demonstrate they are poor in order to be eligible for the assistance. (See also **public assistance**.)

merit (civil service) system An approach to managing the bureaucracy whereby people are appointed to government positions on the basis of either competitive examinations or special qualifications, such as professional training. (See also **executive leadership system; patronage system**.)

metropolitan government The form of local government created when local governments join together and assign it responsibility for a range of activities, such as police and sanitation, so as to reduce the waste and duplication that results when every locality in a densely populated area provides its own services.

military-industrial complex The three components (the military establishment, the industries that manufacture weapons, and the members of Congress from states and districts that depend heavily on the arms industry) that mutually benefit from a high level of defense spending.

momentum (in campaigns) A strong showing by a candidate in early presidential nominating contests, which leads to a buildup of public support for the candidate.

monetary policy A tool of economic management, available to government, based on manipulation of the amount of money in circulation. (See also **fiscal policy**.)

money chase A term used to describe the fact that U.S. political campaigns are very expensive and that candidates must spend a great amount of time raising funds in order to compete successfully.

multilateralism The situation in which nations act together in response to problems and crises.

multinational corporations Business firms with major operations in more than one country.

multiparty system A system in which three or more political parties have the capacity to gain control of government separately or in coalition.

N

national debt The total cumulative amount that the U.S. government owes to creditors.

natural rights See **inalienable rights.**

"necessary and proper" clause (elastic clause) The authority granted Congress in Article I, Section 8 of the Constitution "to make all laws which shall be necessary and proper" for the implementation of its enumerated powers. (See also **implied powers.**)

negative government The philosophical belief that government governs best by staying out of people's lives, thus giving individuals as much freedom as possible to determine their own pursuits. (See also **positive government.**)

neutral competence The administrative objective of a merit-based bureaucracy. Such a bureaucracy should be "competent" in the sense that its employees are hired and retained on the basis of their expertise and "neutral" in the sense that it operates by objective standards rather than partisan ones.

New Jersey (small-state) Plan A constitutional proposal for a strengthened Congress but one in which each state would have a single vote, thus granting a small state the same legislative power as a larger state.

news The news media's version of reality, usually with an emphasis on timely, dramatic, and compelling events and developments.

news media See **press.**

nomination The designation of a particular individual to run as a political party's candidate (its "nominee") in the general election.

noneconomic groups See **citizens' groups.**

North-South Compromise The agreement over economic and slavery issues that enabled northern and southern states to settle differences that threatened to defeat the effort to draft a new constitution.

O

objective journalism A model of news reporting that is based on the communication of "facts" rather than opinions and that is "fair" in that it presents all sides of partisan debate. (See also **partisan press.**)

oligarchy Government in which control rests with a few persons.

open party caucuses Meetings at which a party's candidates for nomination are voted on and that are open to all the party's rank-and-file voters who want to attend.

open-seat election An election in which there is no incumbent in the race.

opinion (of a court) A court's written explanation of its decision, which serves to inform others of the legal basis for the decision. Supreme Court opinions are expected to guide the decisions of other courts. (See also **concurring opinion; dissenting opinion; majority opinion; plurality opinion.**)

ordinances Laws issued by a local government under authority granted by the state government.

original jurisdiction The authority of a given court to be the first court to hear a case. (See also **appellate jurisdiction.**)

originalism theory A method of interpreting the Constitution that emphasizes the meaning of its words at the time they were written.

outside lobbying A form of lobbying in which an interest group seeks to use public pressure as a means of influencing officials.

oversight function A supervisory activity of Congress that centers on its constitutional responsibility to see that the executive carries out the laws faithfully and spends appropriations properly. (See also **lawmaking function; representation function.**)

P

packaging (of a candidate) A term of modern campaigning that refers to the process of recasting a candidate's record into an appealing image.

partisan function (of the press) Efforts by media actors to influence public response to a particular party, leader, issue, or viewpoint.

partisan press Newspapers and other communication media that openly support a political party and whose news in significant part follows the party line. (See also **objective journalism.**)

party caucus A group that consists of a party's members in the House or Senate and that serves to elect the party's leadership, set policy goals, and determine party strategy.

party-centered politics Election campaigns and other political processes in which political parties, not individual candidates, hold most of the initiative and influence. (See also **candidate-centered politics.**)

party coalition The groups and interests that support a political party.

party competition A process in which conflict over society's goals is transformed by political parties into electoral competition in which the winner gains the power to govern.

party discipline The willingness of a party's House or Senate members to act together as a cohesive group and thus exert collective control over legislative action.

party identification The personal sense of loyalty that an individual may feel toward a particular political party. (See also **party realignment.**)

party leaders Members of the House and Senate who are chosen by the Democratic or Republican caucus in each chamber to represent the party's interests in that chamber and who give some central direction to the chamber's deliberations.

party organizations The party organizational units at national, state, and local levels; their influence has decreased over time because of many factors. (See also **candidate-centered politics; party-centered politics; primary election.**)

party realignment An election or set of elections in which the electorate responds strongly to an extraordinary issue that has disrupted the established political order. A realignment has a lasting impact on public policy, popular support for the parties, and the composition of the party coalitions. (See also **party identification.**)

patronage system An approach to managing the bureaucracy whereby people are appointed to important government positions as a reward for political services they have rendered and because of their partisan loyalty. (See also **executive leadership system; merit system; spoils system.**)

pluralism A theory of American politics that holds that society's interests are substantially represented through the activities of groups.

plurality opinion A court opinion that results when a majority of justices agree on a decision in a case but do not agree on the legal basis for the decision. In this instance, the legal position held by most of the justices on the winning side is called a plurality opinion. (See also **concurring opinion; dissenting opinion; majority opinion.**)

police power A term that refers to the broad power of government to regulate the health, safety, and morals of the citizenry.

policy Generally, any broad course of governmental action; more narrowly, a specific government program or initiative.

policy formation The stage of the policy process in which a policy is formulated for dealing with a policy problem.

policy implementation (in reference to bureaucracy) The primary function of the bureaucracy; it refers to the process of carrying out the authoritative decisions of Congress, the president, and the courts.

policy implementation (in reference to policy process) The stage of the policy process in which a policy is put into effect and evaluated.

political action committee (PAC) The organization through which an interest group raises and distributes funds for election purposes. By law, the funds must be raised through voluntary contributions.

political culture The characteristic and deep-seated beliefs of a particular people.

political movements See **social movements.**

political participation Involvement in activities intended to influence public policy and leadership, such as voting, joining political parties and interest groups, writing to elected officials, demonstrating for political causes, and giving money to political candidates.

political party An ongoing coalition of interests joined together to try to get their candidates for public office elected under a common label.

political socialization The learning process by which people acquire their political opinions, beliefs, and values.

political system The various components of American government. The parts are separate, but they connect with each other, affecting how each performs.

politics The process through which society settles its conflicts and decides the policies by which it will be governed.

population In a public opinion poll, the people (for example, the citizens of a nation) whose opinions are being estimated through interviews with a sample of these people.

populists Those who believe government should do more to solve the nation's problems and who look to it to uphold traditional values. (See also **economic conservatives; economic liberals; libertarians; social conservatives; social liberals.**)

pork-barrel projects Legislative acts whose tangible benefits are targeted at a particular legislator's constituency.

positive government The philosophical belief that government intervention is necessary in order to enhance personal liberty when individuals are buffeted by economic and social forces beyond their control. (See also **negative government.**)

poverty line As defined by the federal government, the annual cost of a thrifty food budget for an urban family of four, multiplied by three to allow also for the cost of housing, clothes, and other expenses. Families below the poverty line are considered poor and are eligible for certain forms of public assistance.

power The ability of persons or institutions to control policy. (See also **authority.**)

precedent A judicial decision in a given case that serves as a rule of thumb for settling subsequent cases of a similar nature; courts are generally expected to follow precedent.

preemptive war doctrine The idea, espoused by President George W. Bush, that the United States could attack a potentially threatening nation even if the threat had not yet reached a serious and immediate level.

presidential approval ratings A measure of the degree to which the public approves or disapproves of the president's performance in office.

presidential commissions Organizations within the bureaucracy that are headed by commissioners appointed by the president. An example is the Commission on Civil Rights.

press (news media) Those print and broadcast organizations that are in the news-reporting business.

primary election (direct primary) A form of election in which voters choose a party's nominees for public office. In most states, eligibility to vote in a primary election is limited to voters who designated themselves as party members when they registered to vote. A primary is direct when it results directly in the choice of a nominee; it is indirect (as in the case of presidential primaries) when it results in the selection of delegates who then choose the nominee.

prior restraint Government prohibition of speech or publication before the fact, which is presumed by the courts to be unconstitutional unless the justification for it is overwhelming.

private (individual) goods Benefits that a group (most often an economic group) can grant directly and exclusively to the individual members of the group. (See also **collective goods.**)

probability sample A sample for a poll in which each individual in the population has a known probability of being selected randomly for inclusion in the sample. (See also **public opinion poll.**)

problem recognition The stage of the policy process whereby conditions in society become recognized as a policy problem.

procedural due process The constitutional requirement that government must follow proper legal procedures before a person can be legitimately punished for an alleged offense.

procedural law Laws governing the legal process that define proper courses of action by government or private parties.

proportional representation A form of representation in which seats in the legislature are allocated proportionally according to each political party's share of the popular vote. This system enables smaller parties to compete successfully for seats. (See also **single-member districts.**)

prospective voting A form of electoral judgment in which voters choose the candidate whose policy promises most closely match their own preferences. (See also **retrospective voting.**)

protectionism The view that the immediate interests of domestic producers should have a higher priority (through, for example, protective tariffs) than free trade between nations. (See also **free-trade position.**)

public assistance A term that refers to social welfare programs funded through general tax revenues and available only to the financially needy. Eligibility for such a program is established by a means test. (See also **means test; social insurance.**)

public goods See **collective goods.**

public opinion The politically relevant opinions held by ordinary citizens that they express openly.

public opinion poll A device for measuring public opinion whereby a relatively small number of individuals (the sample) is interviewed for the purpose of estimating the opinions of a whole community (the population). (See also **probability sample.**)

public policy A decision of government to pursue a course of action designed to produce an intended outcome.

public policy process The political interactions that lead to the emergence and resolution of public policy issues.

purposive incentive An incentive to group participation based on the cause (purpose) that the group seeks to promote.

R

realignment See **party realignment.**

reapportionment The reallocation of House seats among states after each census as a result of population changes.

reasonable-basis test A test applied by courts to laws that treat individuals unequally. Such a law may be deemed constitutional if its purpose is held to be "reasonably" related to a legitimate government interest.

recall The process by which citizens can petition for the removal from office of an elected official before the scheduled completion of his or her term.

redistricting The process of altering election districts in order to make them as nearly equal in population as possible. Redistricting takes place every ten years, after each population census.

referendum The process through which the legislature may submit proposals to the voters for approval or rejection.

reform (minor) party A minor party that bases its appeal on the claim that the major parties are having a corrupting influence on government and policy.

registration The practice of placing citizens' names on an official list of voters before they are eligible to exercise their right to vote.

regulation Government restrictions on the economic practices of private firms.

regulatory agencies Administrative units, such as the Federal Communications Commission and the Environmental Protection Agency, that have responsibility for the monitoring and regulation of ongoing economic activities.

representation function The responsibility of a legislature to represent various interests in society. (See also **lawmaking function; oversight function.**)

representative democracy A system in which the people participate in the decision-making process of government not directly but indirectly, through the election of officials to represent their interests.

republic Historically, the form of government in which representative officials met to decide on policy issues. These representatives were expected to serve the public interest but were not subject to the people's immediate control. Today, the term *republic* is used interchangeably with *democracy.*

reserved powers The powers granted to the states under the Tenth Amendment to the Constitution.

retrospective voting A form of electoral judgment in which voters support the incumbent candidate or party when their policies are judged to have succeeded and oppose the candidate or party when their policies are judged to have failed. (See also **prospective voting.**)

rider An amendment to a bill that deals with an issue unrelated to the content of the bill. Riders are permitted in the Senate but not in the House.

right of privacy A right implied by the freedoms stated in the Bill of Rights that grants individuals a degree of personal privacy upon which government cannot lawfully intrude. The right gives individuals a level of free choice in areas such as reproduction and intimate relations.

S

sample In a public opinion poll, the relatively small number of individuals interviewed for the purpose of estimating the opinions of an entire population. (See also **public opinion poll.**)

sampling error A measure of the accuracy of a public opinion poll. It is mainly a function of sample size and is usually expressed in percentage terms. (See also **probability sample.**)

selective incorporation The process by which certain of the rights (for example, freedom of speech) contained in the Bill of Rights become applicable through the Fourteenth Amendment to actions by the state governments.

self-government The principle that the people are the ultimate source and proper beneficiary of governing authority; in practice, a government based on majority rule.

senatorial courtesy The tradition that a U.S. senator from the state in which a federal judicial vacancy has arisen should have a say in the president's nomination of the new judge if the senator is of the same party as the president.

seniority A member of Congress's consecutive years of service on a particular committee.

separated institutions sharing power The principle that, as a way to limit government, its powers should be divided among separate branches, each of which also shares in the power of the others as a means of checking and balancing them. The result is that no one branch can exercise power decisively without the support or acquiescence of the others.

separation of powers The division of the powers of government among separate institutions or branches.

service relationship The situation in which party organizations assist candidates for office but have no power to require them to accept or campaign on the party's main policy positions.

service strategy Use of personal staff by members of Congress to perform services for constituents in order to gain their support in future elections.

signaling (signaler) function The accepted responsibility of the media to alert the public to important developments as soon as possible after they happen or are discovered. (See also **common-carrier function; partisan function; watchdog function.**)

single-issue (minor) party A minor party formed around a single issue of overriding interest to its followers.

single-issue politics The situation in which separate groups are organized around nearly every conceivable policy issue and press their demands and influence to the utmost.

single-member districts The form of representation in which only the candidate who gets the most votes in a district wins office. (See also **proportional representation.**)

slander Spoken words that falsely damage a person's reputation.

small-state plan See **New Jersey Plan.**

social capital The sum of face-to-face interactions among citizens in a society.

social conservatives Those who believe government power should be used to uphold traditional values. (See also **economic conservatives; economic liberals; libertarians; populists; social liberals.**)

social contract A voluntary agreement by individuals to form a government, which is then obligated to work within the confines of that agreement.

social insurance Social welfare programs based on the "insurance" concept, so that individuals must pay into the program in order to be eligible to receive funds from it. An example is social security for retired people. (See also **public assistance.**)

social liberals Those who believe it is not government's role to buttress traditional values at the expense of unconventional or new values. (See also **economic conservatives; economic liberals; libertarians; populists; social conservatives.**)

social (political) movements Active and sustained efforts to achieve social and political change by groups of people who feel that government has not been properly responsive to their concerns.

socialism An economic system in which government owns and controls many of the major industries.

soft money Campaign contributions that are not subject to legal limits and are given to parties rather than directly to candidates.

solicitor general The high-ranking Justice Department official who serves as the government's lawyer in Supreme Court cases.

sovereignty The ultimate authority to govern within a certain geographical area.

split ticket The pattern of voting in which the individual voter in a given election casts a ballot for one or more candidates of each major party.

spoils system The practice of granting public office to individuals in return for political favors they have rendered. (See also **patronage system**.)

standing committees Permanent congressional committees with responsibility for a particular area of public policy. An example is the Senate Foreign Relations Committee.

state constitutional convention A state convention convened to amend the state constitution or draft a new one.

stewardship theory A theory that argues for a strong, assertive presidential role, with presidential authority limited only at points specifically prohibited by law. (See also **Whig theory**.)

strict-scrutiny test A test applied by courts to laws that attempt a racial or ethnic classification. In effect, the strict-scrutiny test eliminates race or ethnicity as legal classification when it places minority group members at a disadvantage. (See also **suspect classifications**.)

strong mayor–council system The most common form of municipal government, consisting of the mayor as chief executive and the local council as the legislative body, in which the mayor has veto power and a prescribed responsibility for budgetary and other policy actions.

suffrage The right to vote.

sunset law A law containing a provision that fixes a date on which a program will end unless the program's life is extended by Congress.

supply-side economics A form of fiscal policy that emphasizes "supply" (production). An example of supply-side economics would be a tax cut for business. (See also **demand-side economics; fiscal policy**.)

supremacy clause Article VI of the Constitution, which makes national law supreme over state law when the national government is acting within its constitutional limits.

suspect classifications Legal classifications, such as race and national origin, that have invidious discrimination as

their purpose and are therefore unconstitutional. (See also **strict-scrutiny test**.)

symbolic speech Action (for example, the waving or burning of a flag) for the purpose of expressing a political opinion.

T

totalitarian government A form of government in which the leaders claim complete dominance of all individuals and institutions.

transfer payment A government benefit that is given directly to an individual, as in the case of social security payments to a retiree.

trustees Elected representatives whose obligation is to act in accordance with their own consciences as to what policies are in the best interests of the public. (See also **delegates**.)

two-party system A system in which only two political parties have a real chance of acquiring control of the government.

tyranny of the majority The potential of a majority to monopolize power for its own gain and to the detriment of minority rights and interests.

U

unilateralism The situation in which one nation takes action against another state or states.

unipolar (power structure) A power structure dominated by a single powerful actor, as in the case of the United States after the collapse of the Soviet Union.

unitary system A governmental system in which the national government alone has sovereign (ultimate) authority. (See also **confederacy; federalism**.)

unit rule The rule that grants all of a state's electoral votes to the candidate who receives most of the popular votes in the state.

V

veto The president's rejection of a bill, thereby keeping it from becoming law unless Congress overrides the veto.

Virginia (large-state) Plan A constitutional proposal for a strong Congress with two chambers, both of which would be based on numerical representation, thus granting more power to the larger states.

voter turnout The proportion of persons of voting age who actually vote in a given election.

W

watchdog function The accepted responsibility of the media to protect the public from deceitful, careless, incompetent, and corrupt officials by standing ready to expose any official who violates accepted legal, ethical, or performance standards. (See also **common-carrier function; partisan function; signaling function**.)

weak mayor–council system The form of municipal government in which the mayor's policymaking powers are less substantial than the council's; the mayor has no power to veto the council's actions and often has no formal role in such activities as budget making.

Whig theory A theory that prevailed in the nineteenth century and held that the presidency was a limited or restrained office whose occupant was confined to expressly granted constitutional authority. (See also **stewardship theory**.)

whistle-blowing An internal check on the bureaucracy whereby individual bureaucrats report instances of mismanagement that they observe.

writ of certiorari Permission granted by a higher court to allow a losing party in a legal case to bring the case before it for a ruling; when such a writ is requested of the U.S. Supreme Court, four of the Court's nine justices must agree to accept the case before it is granted certiorari.

Notes

CHAPTER 1

[1] Alexis de Tocqueville, *Democracy in America (1835–1840)*, ed. J. P. Mayer and A. P. Kerr (Garden City, N.Y.: Doubleday/Anchor, 1969), 640.

[2] See John Harmon McElroy, *American Beliefs: What Keeps a Big Country and a Diverse People United* (Chicago: I. R. Dee, 1999); but see Michael B. Katz and Mark J. Stern, *One Nation Divisible: What America Was and What It's Becoming* (New York: Russell Sage Foundation, 2006).

[3] Clinton Rossiter, *Conservativism in America* (New York: Vintage, 1962), 67; see also Robert A. Ferguson, *Reading the Early Republic* (Cambridge, Mass.: Harvard University Press, 2004).

[4] Tocqueville, *Democracy in America*, 310.

[5] James Bryce, *The American Commonwealth*, vol. 2 (New York: Macmillan, 1960), 247–54. First published in 1900.

[6] See Michael Foley, *American Credo: The Place of Ideas in American Politics* (New York: Oxford University Press, 2007).

[7] Paul Gagnon, "Why Study History?" *Atlantic Monthly*, November 1988, 47.

[8] Robert Middlekauff, *The Glorious Cause: The American Revolution, 1763–1789* (New York: Oxford University Press, 2007).

[9] Louis Hartz, *The Liberal Tradition in America* (New York: Harcourt, Brace, 1953), 12; see also Jeffrey Stout, *Democracy and Tradition* (Princeton, N.J.: Princeton University Press, 2004).

[10] James Bryce, *The American Commonwealth*, vol. 2 (Indianapolis, Ind.: Liberty Fund, 1995), 1419.

[11] See Seymour Martin Lipset, *American Exceptionalism: A Double-Edged Sword* (New York: Norton, 1996); Claude Lévi-Strauss, *Structural Anthropology* (Chicago: University of Chicago Press, 1983); Clifford Geertz, *Myth, Symbol, and Culture* (New York: Norton, 1974).

[12] U.S. Census Bureau data, 2006.

[13] Quoted in Ralph Volney Harlow, *The Growth of the United States*, vol. 2 (New York: Henry Holt, 1943), 497.

[14] For a substantial look at Lincoln's positions on slavery, see George M. Fredrickson, *Big Enough to Be Inconsistent: Abraham Lincoln Confronts Slavery and Race* (Cambridge, Mass.: Harvard University Press, 2008).

[15] Theodore H. White, *America in Search of Itself: The Making of the President, 1956–1980* (New York: Harper & Row, 1982).

[16] Harold D. Lasswell, *Politics: Who Gets What, When, How* (New York: McGraw-Hill, 1938).

[17] See Charles H. McIlwain, *Constitutionalism: Ancient and Modern* (Ithaca, N.Y.: Cornell University Press, 1983).

[18] Russell Hardin, *Liberalism, Constitutionalism, and Democracy* (New York: Oxford University Press, 1999).

[19] Harold D. Lasswell and Abraham Kaplan, *Power and Society* (New Haven, Conn.: Yale University Press, 1950), 75–77.

[20] Benjamin I. Page and Robert Shapiro, "Effects of Public Opinion on Policy," *American Political Science Review* 77 (March 1983): 178; see also Lawrence R. Jacobs and Robert Shapiro, *Politicians Don't Pander* (Chicago: University of Chicago Press, 2000).

[21] See Robert Dahl, *On Democracy* (New Haven, Conn.: Yale University Press, 2000).

[22] C. Wright Mills, *The Power Elite* (New York: Oxford University Press, 1965).

[23] G. William Domhoff, *Who Rules America? Power and Politics*, 5th ed. (New York: McGraw-Hill, 2005).

[24] See, for example, Dahl, *On Democracy*.

[25] See H. H. Gerth and C. Wright Mills, eds., *From Max Weber: Essays in Sociology* (New York: Oxford University Press, 1958).

[26] Roberto Michels, *Political Parties* (New York: Collier Books, 1962). First published in 1911.

[27] David Easton, *The Political System* (New York: Knopf, 1965), 97.

[28] E. E. Schattschneider, *Two Hundred Million Americans in Search of a Government* (New York: Holt, Rinehart & Winston, 1969), 42.

CHAPTER 2

[1] Quoted in Charles S. Hyneman, "Republican Government in America," in George J. Graham Jr. and Scarlett G. Graham, eds., *Founding Principles of American Government*, rev. ed. (Chatham, N.J.: Chatham House, 1984), 19.

[2] See Russell Hardin, *Liberalism, Constitutionalism, and Democracy* (New York: Oxford University Press, 1999); A. John Simmons, *The Lockean Theory of Rights* (Princeton, N.J.: Princeton University Press, 1994).

[3] George Bancroft, *History of the Formation of the Constitution of the United States of America*, 3d ed., vol. 1 (New York: D. Appleton, 1883), 166.

[4] Quoted in "The Constitution and Slavery," Digital History Website, December 1, 2003.

[5] Gaillard Hunt, ed., *The Writings of James Madison* (New York: Putnam, 1904), 274; see also Garret Ward Sheldon, *The Political Philosophy of James Madison* (Baltimore: Johns Hopkins University Press, 2000).

[6] See Vincent Ostrom, *The Political Theory of a Compound Republic: Designing the American Experiment* (Lanham, Md.: Lexington Books, 2007).

[7] See *Federalist* Nos. 47 and 48.

[8] Richard Neustadt, *Presidential Power* (New York: Macmillan, 1986), 33.

[9] Henry J. Abraham, *The Judicial Process*, 6th ed. (New York: Oxford University Press, 1993), 320–22.

[10] *Marbury v. Madison*, 1 Cranch 137 (1803).

[11] Martin Diamond, *The Founding of the Democratic Republic* (Itasca, Ill.: Peacock, 1981), 62–71.

[12] *Federalist* No. 10.

[13] Leslie F. Goldstein, "Judicial Review and Democratic Theory: Guardian Democracy vs. Representative Democracy," *Western Political Quarterly* 40 (1987): 391–412.

[14] Benjamin Ginsberg, *The Consequences of Consent* (New York: Random House, 1982), 22.

[15] Robert Dahl, *Pluralist Democracy in the United States* (Chicago: Rand McNally, 1967), 92.

[16]This interpretation is taken from Walter Lippmann, *Public Opinion* (New York: Free Press, 1965), 178–79.

[17]Michael McGeer, *A Fierce Discontent: The Rise and Fall of the Progressive Movement in America, 1870–1920* (New York: Free Press, 2005).

[18]Charles S. Beard, *An Economic Interpretation of the Constitution* (New York: Macmillan, 1941). First published in 1913.

[19]See Randall G. Holcombe, *From Liberty to Democracy* (Ann Arbor: University of Michigan Press, 2002).

CHAPTER 3

[1]Woodrow Wilson, *Constitutional Government in the United States* (New York: Columbia University Press, 1908), 173.

[2]"NCSL Task Force on No Child Left Behind Report," National Conference of State Legislatures, Denver, Colorado, February 23, 2005; for a broader perspective, see Patrick J. Mcquinn, *No Child Left Behind and the Transformation of Federal Education Policy, 1965–2005* (Lawrence: University Press of Kansas, 2006).

[3]See Samuel Beer, *To Make a Nation: The Rediscovery of American Federalism* (Cambridge, Mass.: The Belknap Press of Harvard University, 1993).

[4]*Federalist* No. 2; for the Anti-Federalist view, see Saul Cornell, *The Other Founders* (Chapel Hill: University of North Carolina Press, 1999).

[5]*McCulloch v. Maryland,* 4 Wheaton 316 (1819).

[6]*Gibbons v. Ogden,* 22 Wheaton 1 (1824).

[7]Oliver Wendell Holmes Jr., *Collected Legal Papers* (New York: Harcourt, Brace, 1920), 295–96.

[8]See John C. Calhoun, *The Works of John C. Calhoun* (New York: Russell & Russell, 1968).

[9]*Dred Scott v. Sanford,* 19 Howard 393 (1857).

[10]*U.S. v. Cruikshank,* 92 U.S. 452 (1876).

[11]*Slaughter-House Cases,* 16 Wallace 36 (1873); *Civil Rights Cases,* 109 U.S. 3 (1883).

[12]*Plessy v. Ferguson,* 163 U.S. 537 (1896).

[13]*Santa Clara County v. Southern Pacific Railroad Co.,* 118 U.S. 394 (1886).

[14]*U.S. v. E. C. Knight Co.,* 156 U.S. 1 (1895).

[15]*Hammer v. Dagenhart,* 247 U.S. 251 (1918).

[16]*Lochner v. New York,* 198 U.S. 25 (1905).

[17]Alfred H. Kelly, Winifred A. Harbison, and Herman Belz, *The American Constitution,* 7th ed. (New York: Norton, 1991), 529; but also see Kimberley Johnson, *Governing the American State: Congress and the New Federalism, 1877–1929* (Princeton, N.J.: Princeton University Press, 2006).

[18]James E. Anderson, *The Emergence of the Modern Regulatory State* (Washington, D.C.: Public Affairs Press, 1962), 2–3.

[19]*Schechter Poultry Co. v. United States,* 295 U.S. 495 (1935).

[20]*NLRB v. Jones and Laughlin Steel,* 301 U.S. 1 (1937).

[21]*American Power and Light v. Securities and Exchange Commission,* 329 U.S. 90 (1946).

[22]Louis Fisher, *American Constitutional Law,* 6th ed. (Durham, N.C.: Carolina Academic Press, 2005), 390.

[23]*North American Company v. Securities and Exchange Commission,* 327 U.S. 686 (1946).

[24]*Brown v. Board of Education,* 347 U.S. 483 (1954).

[25]See Thomas Anton, *American Federalism and Public Policy* (Philadelphia: Temple University Press, 1989).

[26]Morton Grodzins, *The American System: A New View of Government in the United States* (Chicago: Rand McNally, 1966).

[27]Rosella Levaggi, *Fiscal Federalism and Grants-in-Aid* (Brookfield, Vt.: Avebury, 1991).

[28]Timothy J. Conlan, *From New Federalism to Devolution* (Washington, D.C.: Brookings Institution, 1998).

[29]*Garcia v. San Antonio Authority,* 469 U.S. 528 (1985).

[30]See Tinsley E. Yarbrough, *The Rehnquist Court and the Constitution* (New York: Oxford University Press, 2000); David L. Hudson, *The Rehnquist Court: Understanding Its Impact and Legacy* (Westport, Conn.: Praeger, 2006).

[31]*United States v. Lopez,* 514 U.S. 549 (1995).

[32]*Printz v. United States,* 521 U.S. 98 (1997).

[33]*Kimel v. Florida Board of Regents,* 528 U.S. 62 (2000).

[34]*Board of Trustees of the University of Alabama v. Garrett,* 531 U.S. 356 (2002).

[35]*Gonzales v. Raich,* No. 03-1454 (2005).

[36]Patrick M. Garry, *An Entrenched Legacy: How the New Deal Constitutional Revolution Continues to Shape the Role of the Supreme Court* (University Park: Pennsylvania State University Press, 2008).

[37]Andrew W. Dobelstein, *Politics, Economics, and Public Welfare* (Englewood Cliffs, N.J.: Prentice-Hall, 1980), 5.

[38]Lloyd A. Free and Hadley Cantril, *The Political Beliefs of Americans* (New York: Simon & Schuster, 1968), 21.

[39]Survey for the Times Mirror Center for the People and the Press by Princeton Survey Research Associates, July 12–27, 1994.

CHAPTER 4

[1]Julian P. Boyd, ed., *The Papers of Thomas Jefferson,* vol. 12 (Princeton, N.J.: Princeton University Press, 1955), 440.

[2]*Anderson v. Creighton,* 483 U.S. 635 (1987).

[3]*United States v. Carolene Products Co.,* 304 U.S. 144 (1938).

[4]*Schenck v. United States,* 249 U.S. 47 (1919).

[5]*Dennis v. United States,* 341 U.S. 494 (1951); for a broad look at the relationship between issues of national security and liberty, see Geoffrey Stone, *War and Liberty: An American Dilemma: 1790 to the Present* (New York: W. W. Norton, 2007).

[6]See, for example, *Yates v. United States,* 354 U.S. 298 (1957); *Noto v. United States,* 367 U.S. 290 (1961); *Scales v. United States,* 367 U.S. 203 (1961).

[7]*United States v. O'Brien,* 391 U.S. 367 (1968).

[8]*Texas v. Johnson,* 109 S. Ct. 2544 (1989).

[9]*New York Times Co. v. United States,* 403 U.S. 713 (1971).

[10]*Nebraska Press Assn. v. Stuart,* 427 U.S. 539 (1976).

[11]*Barron v. Baltimore,* 32 U.S. (7 Pet.) 243 (1833).

[12]*Gitlow v. New York,* 268 U.S. 652 (1925).

[13]*Fiske v. Kansas,* 274 U.S. 30 (1927); *Near v. Minnesota,* 283 U.S. 697 (1931); *Hamilton v. Regents, U. of California,* 293 U.S. 245 (1934); *DeJonge v. Oregon,* 299 U.S. 253 (1937).

[14]*Near v. Minnesota,* 283 U.S. 697 (1931).

[15]*Brandenburg v. Ohio,* 395 U.S. 444 (1969).

[16]*R.A.V. v. St. Paul,* No. 90-7675 (1992).

[17]*Wisconsin v. Mitchell,* No. 92-515 (1993).

[18]*National Socialist Party v. Skokie,* 432 U.S. 43 (1977).

[19]*Forsyth County v. Nationalist Movement,* No. 91-538 (1992).

[20]*Milkovich v. Lorain Journal,* 497 U.S. 1 (1990); see also *Masson v. The New Yorker,* No. 89-1799 (1991).

[21]*New York Times Co. v. Sullivan,* 376 U.S. 254 (1964).

[22]*Roth v. United States,* 354 U.S. 476 (1957).

[23]*Miller v. California,* 413 U.S. 15 (1973).

[24]*Barnes v. Glen Theatre,* No. 90-26 (1991).

[25]*Stanley v. Georgia,* 394 U.S. 557 (1969).

[26]*Osborne v. Ohio,* 495 U.S. 103 (1990); see also *Ashcroft v. Free Speech Coalition,* No. 00-795 (2002).

[27]*United States v. Williams,* No. 06-694 (2008).

[28]*Denver Area Consortium v. Federal Communications Commission,* No. 95-124 (1996); *Reno v. American Civil Liberties Union,* No. 96-511 (1997); *Ashcroft v. ACLU,* No. 03-0218 (2004).

[29]*Engel v. Vitale*, 370 U.S. 421 (1962).
[30]*Abington School District v. Schempp*, 374 U.S. 203 (1963).
[31]*Wallace v. Jaffree*, 472 U.S. 38 (1985).
[32]*Santa Fe Independent School District v. Does*, No. 99-62 (2000).
[33]*Van Orden v. Perry*, No. 03-1500 (2005).
[34]*McCreary County v. American Civil Liberties Union*, No. 03-1693 (2005).
[35]*Board of Regents v. Allen*, 392 U.S. 236 (1968).
[36]*Lemon v. Kurtzman*, 403 U.S. 602 (1971).
[37]Ibid.
[38]*Mitchell v. Helms*, No. 98-1648 (2000).
[39]*Zelman v. Simmons-Harris*, No. 00-1751 (2002); see also *Locke v. Davey*, No. 02-1315 (2004).
[40]*Locke v. Davey*, No. 02-1315 (2004).
[41]*Hein V. Freedom from Religion*, No. 06-157 (2007).
[42]*Wisconsin v. Yoder*, 406 U.S. 295 (1972); see also *Church of the Lukumi Babalu Aye v. City of Hialeah*, No. 91-948 (1993).
[43]*Edwards v. Aguillard*, 487 U.S. 578 (1987).
[44]*District of Columbia v. Heller*, No. 07-290 (2008).
[45]*Griswold v. Connecticut*, 381 U.S. 479 (1965); for an assessment of the Ninth Amendment, see Daniel A. Farber, *Retained by the People: The "Silent" Ninth Amendment and the Constitutional Rights Americans Don't Know They Have* (New York: Basic Books, 2007).
[46]*Vacco v. Quill*, 117 S.C. 36 (1996); *Washington v. Glucksberg*, No. 96-110 (1997); *Gonzalez v. Oregon*, No. 04-63 (2006).
[47]*Roe v. Wade*, 401 U.S. 113 (1973).
[48]*Gregg v. United States*, No. 00-939 (2001).
[49]*Webster v. Reproductive Health Services*, 492 U.S. 490 (1989); see also *Rust v. Sullivan*, No. 89-1391 (1991).
[50]*Planned Parenthood v. Casey*, No. 91-744 (1992).
[51]*Ayotte v. Planned Parenthood of Northern New England*, No. 04-1144 (2006).
[52]*Stenberg v. Carhart*, No. 99-830 (2000).
[53]*Gonzalez V. Carhart*, No. 05-380 (2007).
[54]*Bowers v. Hardwick*, 478 U.S. 186 (1986).
[55]*Lawrence v. Texas*, 539 U.S. 558 (2003).
[56]*McNabb v. United States*, 318 U.S. 332 (1943).
[57]*Powell v. Alabama*, 287 U.S. 45 (1932).
[58]*Palko v. Connecticut*, 302 U.S. 319 (1937).
[59]*Mapp v. Ohio*, 367 U.S. 643 (1961).
[60]*Gideon v. Wainwright*, 372 U.S. 335 (1963).
[61]*Malloy v. Hogan*, 378 U.S. 1 (1964).
[62]*Miranda v. Arizona*, 384 U.S. 436 (1966); see also *Escobedo v. Illinois*, 378 U.S. 478 (1964).
[63]*Pointer v. Texas*, 380 U.S. 400 (1965).
[64]*Klopfer v. North Carolina*, 386 U.S. 213 (1967).
[65]*Duncan v. Louisiana*, 391 U.S. 145 (1968).
[66]*Benton v. Maryland*, 395 U.S. 784 (1969).

[67]*Dickerson v. United States*, No. 99-5525 (2000).
[68]*Missouri v. Siebert*, 542 U.S. 600 (2004).
[69]*Michigan v. Sitz*, No. 88-1897 (1990).
[70]*Indianapolis v. Edmund*, No. 99-1030 (2001).
[71]*Kyllo v. United States*, No. 99-8508 (2001).
[72]*Ferguson v. Charleston*, No. 99-936 (2001).
[73]*Board of Education of Independent School District No. 92 of Pottawatomie County v. Earls*, No. 01-332 (2002).
[74]*Weeks v. United States*, 232 U.S. 383 (1914).
[75]*Nix v. Williams*, 467 U.S. 431 (1984); see also *United States v. Leon*, 468 U.S. 897 (1984).
[76]*Whren v. United States*, 517 U.S. 806 (1996).
[77]*Hudson v. Michigan*, No. 04-1360 (2006).
[78]*Townsend v. Sain*, 372 U.S. 293 (1963).
[79]*Keeney v. Tamaya-Reyes*, No. 90-1859 (1992); see also *Coleman v. Thompson*, No. 89-7662 (1991).
[80]*Bowles v. Russell*, No. 06-5306 (2007).
[81]*Felker v. Turpin*, No. 95-8836 (1996); but see *Stewart v. Martinez-Villareal*, No. 97-300 (1998).
[82]*Williams v. Taylor*, No. 99-6615 (2000).
[83]*Miller-El v. Cockrell*, No. 01-7662 (2003); *Wiggins v. Smith*, No. 02-311 (2003).
[84]Kurt Heine, "Philadelphia Cops Beat One of Their Own," *Syracuse Herald-American*, January 15, 1995, A13.
[85]Alejandro Del Carmen, *Racial Profiling in America* (Upper Saddle River, N.J.: Prentice-Hall, 2007).
[86]*Wilson v. Seiter*, No. 89-7376 (1991).
[87]*Harmelin v. Michigan*, No. 89-7272 (1991).
[88]*Lockyer v. Andrade*, No. 01-1127 (2003); see also *Ewing v. California*, No. 01-6978 (2003).
[89]*Atkins v. Virginia*, No. 01-8452 (2002); *Panetti v. Quarterman*, No. 06-6407 (2007).
[90]*Roper v. Simmons*, No. 03-633 (2005); *Kennedy v. Louisiana*, No. 07-343 (2008).
[91]*Baze v. Rees*, No. 07-5439 (2008); see also *Hill v. McDonough*, No. 05-8794 (2006).
[92]*Ring v. Arizona*, No. 01-488 (2002).
[93]*Blakely v. Washington*, No. 02-1632 (2004).
[94]"Justices: Judges Can Slash Crack Sentences," CNN.com, December 10, 2007.
[95]*Kimbrough v. United States*, No. 06-6330 (2007).
[96]*Korematsu v. United States*, 323 U.S. 214 (1944).
[97]Case cited in Charles Lane, "In Terror War, 2nd Track for Suspects," *Washington Post*, December 1, 2001, A1.
[98]*Rasul v. Bush*, No. 03-334 (2004); *al-Odah v. United States*, No. 03-343 (2004).

[99]*Hamdi v. Rumsfeld*, No. 03-6696 (2004); see also, *Rumsfeld v. Padilla*, No. 03-1027 (2004).
[100]*Hamdan v. Rumsfeld*, No. 05-184 (2006).
[101]*Boumediene et al. v. Bush*, No. 06-1195 (2008).
[102]Quoted in "Feds Get Wide Wiretap Authority," CBSNEWS.com, November 18, 2002.
[103]See Alpheus T. Mason, *The Supreme Court: Palladium of Freedom* (Ann Arbor: University of Michigan Press, 1962); see also Jeffrey Rosen, *The Most Democratic Branch: How the Courts Serve America* (New York: Oxford University Press, 2006).

CHAPTER 5

[1]Speech of Martin Luther King Jr. in Washington, D.C., August 2, 1963.
[2]*Washington Post* wire story, May 14, 1991.
[3]"African-American Health," amednews.com (online newspaper of the American Medical Association), May 1, 2000.
[4]Robert Nisbet, "Public Opinion Versus Popular Opinion," *Public Interest* 41 (1975): 171.
[5]See, for example, Gloria J. Browne-Marshall, *Race, Law, and American Society: 1607 to Present* (New York: Routledge, 2007).
[6]Douglas A. Blackmon, *Slavery by Another Name: The Re-Enslavement of Black Americans from the Civil War to World War II* (New York: Doubleday, 2008).
[7]*Plessy v. Ferguson*, 163 U.S. 537 (1896).
[8]Ada Lois Sipuel Fisher, Danney Gable, and Robert Henry, *A Matter of Black and White: The Autobiography of Ada Lois Sipuel Fisher* (Norman: University of Oklahoma Press, 1996).
[9]*Brown v. Board of Education of Topeka*, 347 U.S. 483 (1954).
[10]See, for example, Alejandro Del Carmen, *Racial Profiling in America* (Upper Saddle River, N.J.: Prentice-Hall, 2007).
[11]Data from National Office of Drug Control Policy, 1997.
[12]See Keith Reeves, *Voting Hopes or Fears?* (New York: Oxford University Press, 1997); Tali Mendelberg, *The Race Card* (Princeton, N.J.: Princeton University Press, 2001).
[13]See Kathleen S. Sullivan, *Women and Rights Discourse in Nineteenth-Century America* (Baltimore, Md.: Johns Hopkins University Press, 2007).
[14]*Tinker v. Colwell*, 193 U.S. 473 (1904).
[15]See Jane Mansbridge, *Why We Lost the ERA* (Chicago: University of Chicago Press, 1986).

[16]*Pennsylvania State Police v. Suder*, No. 03-95 (2004).

[17]*Burlington Northern and Santa Fe Railroad Company v. White*, No. 05-259 (2006).

[18]Jennifer L. Lawless and Richard L. Fox, *It Takes a Candidate: Why Women Don't Run for Office* (New York: Cambridge University Press, 2005).

[19]Lois Duke Whitaker, ed., *Voting the Gender Gap* (Urbana: University of Illinois Press, 2008).

[20]U.S. Department of Education, 2006.

[21]See Sara M. Evans and Barbara Nelson, *Wage Justice* (Chicago: University of Chicago Press, 1989).

[22]U.S. Census Bureau data, 2008; see also Daniel McCool, Susan M. Olson, and Jennifer L. Robinson, *Native Vote: American Indians, the Voting Rights Act, and the Right to Vote* (New York: Cambridge University Press, 2007).

[23]See David E. Wilkins, *American Indian Politics and the American Political System* (Lanham, Md.: Rowman & Littlefield, 2006).

[24]William Evans and Julie Topoleski, "The Social and Economic Impact of Native American Casinos," National Bureau of Economic Research, Working Paper No. 9198, September 2002, Cambridge, Massachusetts.

[25]Sean Page, "Gambling on the Future: US Native American Casinos," BNET web story, December 22, 1997.

[26]James G. Gimpel, "Latinos and the 2002 Election: Republicans Do Well When Latinos Stay Home," Center for Immigration Studies, University of Maryland, January 2003, web download; see also Jorge Ramos, *The Latino Wave: How Hispanics Are Transforming Politics in America* (New York: Harper Paperbacks, 2005); F. Chris Garcia and Gabriel Sanchez, *Hispanics and the U.S. Political System: Moving Into the Mainstream* (Upper Saddle River, N.J.: Prentice-Hall, 2007).

[27]James Truslow Adams, *The March of Democracy*, vol. 4 (New York: Scribner's, 1933), 284–85.

[28]*Lau v. Nichols*, 414 U.S. 563 (1974).

[29]See Gordon Chang, ed., *Asian Americans and Politics* (Stanford, Calif.: Stanford University Press, 2001).

[30]*Kimel v. Florida Board of Regents*, No. 98-791 (2000); but see *CBOCS West, Inc. v. Humphries*, No. 06-1431 (2008).

[31]*Board of Trustees of the University of Alabama v. Garrett*, No. 99-1240 (2002); *Tennessee v. Lane*, No. 02-1667 (2004).

[32]See William N. Eskridge Jr., *Dishonorable Passions: Sodomy Laws in America, 1861–2003* (New York: Viking 2008); Nancy D. Polikoff, *Beyond (Straight and Gay) Marriage: Valuing All Families under the Law* (Boston: Beacon Press, 2009); Craig A. Rimmerman and Clyde Wilcox, *The Politics of Same-Sex Marriage* (Chicago: University of Chicago Press, 2007).

[33]*Romer v. Evans*, 517 U.S. 620 (1996).

[34]*Lawrence v. Texas*, 539 U.S. 558 (2003).

[35]*Boy Scouts of America v. Dale*, No. 99-699 (2000).

[36]*Craig v. Boren*, 429 U.S. 190 (1976).

[37]*Rostker v. Goldberg*, 453 U.S. 57 (1980).

[38]*United States v. Virginia*, No. 94-1941 (1996).

[39]U.S. Conference of Mayors Report, 1998; see also Survey by Federal Financial Institutions Examination Council, 1998.

[40]V. O. Key Jr., *Southern Politics* (New York: Knopf, 1949), 495.

[41]*Smith v. Allwright*, 321 U.S. 649 (1944).

[42]*League of United Latin American Voters v. Perry*, No. 05-204 (2006).

[43]*Muller v. Johnson*, No. 94-631 (1995); *Bush v. Verg*, No. 94-805 (1996); *Shaw v. Hunt*, No. 94-923 (1996).

[44]*Easley v. Cromartie*, No. 99-1864 (2001).

[45]Terry H. Anderson, *The Pursuit of Happiness: A History of Affirmative Action* (New York: Oxford University Press, 2005).

[46]*University of California Regents v. Bakke*, 438 U.S. 265 (1978).

[47]*Steelworkers v. Weber*, 443 U.S. 193 (1979); *Fullilove v. Klutnick*, 448 U.S. 448 (1980).

[48]*Local No. 28, Sheet Metal Workers v. Equal Employment Opportunity Commission*, 478 U.S. 421 (1986); see also *Local No. 93, International Association of Firefighters v. Cleveland*, 478 U.S. 501 (1986); *Firefighters v. Stotts*, 459 U.S. 969 (1984); *Wygant v. Jackson*, 476 U.S. 238 (1986).

[49]*Adarand v. Pena*, No. 94-310 (1995).

[50]*Gratz v. Bollinger*, No. 02-516 (2003).

[51]*Grutter v. Bollinger*, No. 02-241 (2003).

[52]See J. Edward Kellough, *Understanding Affirmative Action: Politics, Discrimination, and the Search for Justice* (Washington, D.C.: Georgetown University Press, 2006).

[53]*Swann v. Charlotte-Mecklenburg County Board of Education*, 402 U.S. 1 (1971).

[54]Christopher Jencks and Meredith Phillips, eds., *The Black-White Test Score Gap* (Washington, D.C.: Brookings Institution Press, 1998).

[55]*Milliken v. Bradley*, 418 U.S. 717 (1974).

[56]*Board of Education of Oklahoma City v. Dowell*, 498 U.S. (1991).

[57]*Sheff v. O'Neill*, No. 95-2071 (1996).

[58]*Parents Involved in Community Schools v. Seattle*, No. 05-908 (2007); *Meredith, Custodial Parent and Next Friend of McDonald v. Jefferson County Board of Education*, No. 05-915 (2007).

[59]Gunnar Myrdal, *An American Dilemma: The Negro Problem and Modern Democracy* (New York: Harper, 1944).

CHAPTER 6

[1]V. O. Key Jr., *Public Opinion and American Democracy* (New York: Knopf, 1961), 8.

[2]See Brandice Canes-Wrone, *Who Leads Whom? Presidents, Policy, and the Public* (Chicago: University of Chicago Press, 2005).

[3]See Jeremy Bentham, *An Introduction to the Principles of Morals and Legislation* (Oxford, England: Clarendon Press, 1996; originally published in 1789).

[4]Vincent Hutchings, *Public Opinion and Democratic Accountability: How Citizens Learn about Politics* (Princeton, N.J.: Princeton University Press, 2005).

[5]Elisabeth Noelle-Neumann, *The Spiral of Silence*, 2d ed. (Chicago: University of Chicago Press, 1993), ch. 1.

[6]"Study Finds Widespread Misperceptions on Iraq Highly Related to Support for War," web release of the Program on International Policy Attitudes, School of Public Affairs, University of Maryland, October 2, 2003.

[7]Joshua Buntin III, "Start with Civics 101," *Miami Herald*, January 21, 2008, p. 25A.

[8]Survey of students of the eight Ivy League schools by Luntz & Weber Research and Strategic Services, for the University of Pennsylvania's Ivy League Study, November 13–December 1, 1992.

[9]See R. Michael Alvarez and John Brehm, *Hard Choices, Easy Answers* (Princeton, N.J.: Princeton University Press, 2002); see also Samuel L. Popkin, *The Reasoning Voter* (Chicago: University of Chicago Press, 1991).

[10]See Herbert Asher, *Polling and the Public*, 7th ed. (Washington, D.C.: CQ Press, 2007).

[11]Political Arithmetic, May 31, 2007, web release.

[12]M. Kent Jennings and Richard G. Niemi, *Generations and Politics* (Princeton, N.J.: Princeton University Press, 1981).

[13]See Orit Ichilov, *Political Socialization, Citizenship Education, and Democracy* (New York: Teachers College Press, 1990).

[14]Noelle-Neumann, *Spiral of Silence*.

[15]Jon Western, *Selling Intervention and War: The Presidency, the Media, and the American Public* (Baltimore, Md.: Johns Hopkins University Press, 2005); see also Wojtek Mackiewicz Wolfe, *Winning the War of Words: Selling the War on Terror from Afghanistan to Iraq* (Westport, Conn.: Praeger, 2008).

16See, however, Dietram A. Scheufele, Matthew C. Nisbet, and Dominique Brossard, "Pathways to Political Participation: Religion, Communication Contexts, and Mass Media," *International Journal of Public Opinion Research* 15 (Autumn 2003): 300–324.

17The classic study of citizen ideology is Philip Converse, "The Nature of Belief Systems in Mass Publics," in David Apter, ed., *Ideology and Discontent* (New York: Free Press, 1965), 206.

18 Kenneth D. Wald, *Religion and Politics in the United States* (Lanham, Md.: Rowman & Littlefield, 2003).

19CNN/USA Today Poll conducted by the Gallup Organization, 1997.

20Lois Duke Whitaker, ed., *Voting the Gender Gap* (Urbana: University of Illinois Press, 2008).

21Susan A. MacManus, *Young v. Old: Generational Combat in the Twenty-first Century* (Boulder, Colo.: Westview Press, 1996).

22See Angus Campbell, Philip Converse, Warren Miller, and Donald Stokes, *The American Voter* (New York: Wiley, 1960), chs. 3 and 4.

23Martin P. Wattenberg, *Where Have All the Voters Gone?* (Cambridge, Mass.: Harvard University Press, 2002).

24Donald Green, Bradley Palmquist, and Eric Schickler, *Partisan Hearts and Minds* (New Haven, Conn.: Yale University Press, 2002).

25See William Domhoff, *Who Rules America?* 5th ed. (New York: McGraw-Hill, 2005).

26Benjamin I. Page and Robert Y. Shapiro, "Effects of Public Opinion on Policy," *American Political Science Review* 77 (March 1983): 178; see also Richard Sobel, *The Impact of Public Opinion on U.S. Foreign Policy* (New York: Oxford University Press, 2001); James Stimson, *Tides of Consent: How Public Opinion Shapes American Politics* (New York: Cambridge University Press, 2004).

27Lawrence R. Jacobs and Robert Y. Shapiro, *Politicians Don't Pander* (Chicago: University of Chicago Press, 2000).

28Christopher J. Grill, *The Public Side of Representation: A Study of Citizens' View About Representatives and the Representative Process* (Albany: State University of New York Press, 2007).

CHAPTER 7

1Walter Lippmann, *Public Opinion* (New York: Free Press, 1965), 36.

2Quoted in Ralph Volney Harlow, *The Growth of the United States* (New York: Henry Holt, 1943), 312.

3Example from Gus Tyler, "One Cheer for the Democrats," *New Leader,* November 3, 1986, 6.

4Thomas E. Patterson, *The Vanishing Voter* (New York: Vintage, 2003), 10.

5Mark N. Franklin, *Voter Turnout and the Dynamics of Electoral Competition in Established Democracies Since 1945* (New York: Cambridge University Press, 2004).

6Patterson, *Vanishing Voter,* 134.

7Russell Dalton, "The Myth of the Disengaged American," web publication of the Comparative Study of Electoral Systems, October 2005, 2.

8Patterson, *Vanishing Voter,* 179–80.

9*Crawford et al. v. Marion County Election Board et al.,* No. 07-21 (2008).

10Ivor Crewe, "Electoral Participation," in David Butler, Howard R. Penniman, and Austin Ranney, eds., *Democracy at the Polls* (Washington, D.C.: American Enterprise Institute, 1981), 251–53.

11Richard Boyd, "Decline of U.S. Voter Turnout," *American Politics Quarterly* 9 (April 1981): 142.

12David Hill, *American Voter Turnout: An Institutional Perspective* (Boulder, Colo.: Westview Press, 2006).

13David C. Leege, Kenneth D. Wald, Brian S. Krueger, and Paul D. Mueller, *The Politics of Cultural Differences* (Princeton, N.J.: Princeton University Press, 2002).

14Larry Bartels, *Unequal Democracy: The Political Economy of the Gilded Age* (Princeton, N.J.: Princeton University Press, 2008).

15Patterson, *Vanishing Voter,* 135.

16See Bruce Bimber and Richard Davis, *Campaigning Online* (New York: Oxford University Press, 2003); Bruce Bimber, *Information and American Democracy* (New York: Cambridge University Press, 2003); Joe Trippi, *The Revolution Will Not Be Televised* (New York: HarperCollins, 2004).

17Dalton, "Myth of the Disengaged American," 2.

18Robert Putnam, *Bowling Alone* (New York: Simon & Schuster, 2000); but see Cliff Zukin et al., *A New Engagement: Political Participation, Civic Life, and the Changing American Citizen* (New York: Oxford University Press, 2006).

19See Benjamin Ginsberg, *The Consequences of Consent* (New York: Random House, 1982), ch. 2.

20See, for example, Charles J. Stewart, Craig Allen Smith, and Robert E. Denton, Jr., *Persuasion and Social Movements,* 5th ed. (Long Grove, Ill.: Waveland Press, 2007).

21ABC News/Washington Post poll, March 23, 2003.

22Dalton, *Citizen Politics,* 38.

23Gallup poll, January 2003.

24William Watts and Lloyd A. Free, eds., *The State of the Nation* (New York: University Books, Potomac Associates, 1967), 97.

25Robert E. Lane, "Market Justice, Political Justice," *American Political Science Review* 80 (1986): 383; see also Jennifer Nedelsky, *Private Property and the Limits of American Constitutionalism* (New York: Oxford University Press, 1990).

26Sidney Verba and Norman Nie, *Participation in America* (New York: Harper & Row, 1972), 131.

27Robert Kaplan, "Was Democracy Just a Moment?" *Atlantic Monthly,* December 1997. Located on Atlantic Monthly website.

28Daniel Pope, ed., *American Radicalism* (New York: Blackwell, 2001).

29Bartels, *Unequal Democracy.*

CHAPTER 8

1E. E. Schattschneider, *Party Government* (New York: Rinehart, 1942), 1.

2See John Aldrich, *Why Parties? The Origin and Transformation of Political Parties in America* (Chicago: University of Chicago Press, 1995); L. Sandy Maisel, *American Political Parties and Elections* (New York: Oxford University Press, 2007).

3E. E. Schattschneider, *The Semisovereign People: A Realist's View of Democracy in America* (New York: Holt, Rinehart & Winston, 1961), 140.

4Thomas E. Patterson, *The Vanishing Voter* (New York: Knopf, 2002), ch. 2.

5See Richard P. McCormick, *The Second American Party System: Party Formation in the Jacksonian Era* (Chapel Hill: University of North Carolina Press, 1966).

6Alexis de Tocqueville, *Democracy in America (1835–1840),* ed. J. P. Mayer and A. P. Kerr (Garden City, N.Y.: Doubleday/Anchor, 1969), 60.

7Aldrich, *Why Parties?* 151.

8See Kristi Andersen, *The Creation of a Democratic Majority, 1928–1936* (Chicago: University of Chicago Press, 1979).

9See Kevin Phillips, *The Emerging Republican Majority* (New Rochelle, N.Y.: Arlington House, 1969).

10See Arthur C. Paulson, *Electoral Realignment and the Outlook for American Democracy* (Boston: Northeastern University Press, 2006).

[11]Gallup Organization, 2008.

[12]Lewis L. Gould, *Grand Old Party* (New York: Random House, 2003); but also see Jacob S. Hacker and Paul Pierson, *Off-Center: The Republican Revolution and the Erosion of American Democracy* (New Haven, Conn.: Yale University Press, 2006).

[13]See John B. Judis and Ruy Teixeira, *The Emerging Democratic Majority* (New York: Scribner, 2002).

[14]See, for example, Everett Carll Ladd, "The Brittle Mandate: Electoral Dealignment and the 1980 Presidential Election," *Political Science Quarterly* 96, No. 1 (Spring 1981): 1–25.

[15]Clinton Rossiter, *Parties and Politics in America* (Ithaca, N.Y.: Cornell University Press, 1960), 11; see also James H. Fowler and Oleg Smirnov, *Mandates, Parties, and Voters: How Elections Shape the Future* (Philadelphia: Temple University Press, 2007).

[16]Nancy Gibbs and Michael Duffy, "Fall of the House of Newt," *Time*, November 16, 1998, 47.

[17]Jeffrey M. Stonecash, *Political Parties Matter: Realignment and the Return of Partisan Voting* (Boulder, Colo.: Lynne Rienner Publishers, 2005).

[18]John Green, Mark Rozell, and William Clyde Wilcox, eds., *The Christian Right in American Politics* (Washington, D.C.: Georgetown University Press, 2003).

[19]Micah L. Sifrey, *Spoiling for a Fight: Third-Party Politics in America* (New York: Routledge, 2003).

[20]Daniel A. Mazmanian, *Third Parties in Presidential Elections* (Washington, D.C.: Brookings Institution, 1984), 143–44.

[21]See Lawrence Goodwyn, *The Populist Movement* (New York: Oxford University Press, 1978).

[22]Lewis L. Gould, *Four Hats in the Ring: The 1912 Election and the Birth of Modern American Politics* (Lawrence: University Press of Kansas, 2008).

[23]See Anthony King, *Running Scared* (New York: Free Press, 1997); but see James E. Campbell, *The American Campaign: U.S. Presidential Campaigns and the National Vote* (College Station: Texas A&M Press, 2008).

[24]See Paul S. Herrnson and John C. Green, eds., *Responsible Partisanship* (Lawrence: University Press of Kansas, 2003).

[25]See Marjorie Randon Hershey, *Party Politics in America*, 13th ed. (New York: Longman, 2009).

[26]David Adamany, "Political Parties in the 1980s," in Michael J. Malbin, ed., *Money and Politics in the United States* (Chatham, N.J.: Chatham House, 1984), 114.

[27]*Senator Mitch McConnell et al. v. Federal Election Commission et al.*, No. 02-1674 (2003).

[28]Michael J. Malbin, *The Election After Reform: Money, Politics, and the Bipartisan Campaign Reform Act* (Lanham, Md.: Rowman & Littlefield, 2006).

[29]Joseph Napolitan, *The Election Game and How to Win It* (New York: Doubleday, 1972); for a contemporary look at the campaigning process, see D. Sunshine Hillygus and Todd G. Shields, *The Persuadable Voter: Wedge Issues in Presidential Campaigns* (Princeton, N.J.: Princeton University Press, 2008).

[30]Federal Elections Commission data, 2008.

[31]David B. Magelby, J. Quin Monson, and Kelly D. Patterson, eds., *Dancing Without Partners: How Candidates, Parties and Interest Groups Interact in the New Campaign Finance Environment* (Provo, Utah: Brigham Young University Press, 2005).

[32]David Chagall, *The New King-Makers* (New York: Harcourt Brace Jovanovich, 1981).

[33]Lawrence R. Jacobs and Robert Y. Shapiro, *Politicians Don't Pander: Political Manipulation and the Loss of Democratic Responsiveness* (Chicago: University of Chicago Press, 2000).

[34]Emmett H. Buell Jr. and Lee Sigelman, *Attack Politics: Negativity in Presidential Campaigns Since 1960* (Lawrence: University Press of Kansas, 2008). For opposing views on the effect of negative advertising, see Stephen Ansolabehere and Shanto Iyengar, *Going Negative* (New York: Free Press, 1995), and John Geer, *In Defense of Negativity* (Chicago: University of Chicago Press, 2006).

[35]Darrell M. West, *Air Wars: Television Advertising in Election Campaigns,1952–2004*, 4th ed. (Washington, D.C.: CQ Press, 2005), 140–46.

[36]Ibid, 12.

[37]Peter J. Peterson, *Running on Empty: How the Democratic and Republican Parties Are Bankrupting Our Future and What Americans Can Do About It* (New York: Farrar, Straus, and Giroux, 2005).

CHAPTER 9

[1]E. E. Schattschneider, *The Semisovereign People: A Realist's View of Democracy in America* (New York: Holt, Rinehart & Winston, 1960), 35.

[2]See Matthew J. Burbank, Ronald J. Hrebenar, and Robert C. Benedict, *Parties, Interest Groups, and Political Campaigns* (Boulder, Colo.: Paradigm Publishers, 2008).

[3]Alexis de Tocqueville, *Democracy in America (1835–1840)*, ed. J. P. Mayer and A. P. Kerr (Garden City, N.Y.: Doubleday/Anchor, 1969), bk. 2, ch. 4.

[4]Mancur Olson, *The Logic of Collective Action*, rev. ed. (Cambridge, Mass.: Harvard University Press, 1971), 147; see also Theda Skocpol, *Diminished Democracy* (Norman: University of Oklahoma Press, 2003).

[5]See Jack L. Walker, *Mobilizing Interest Groups in America* (Ann Arbor: University of Michigan Press, 1991).

[6]Olson, *Logic of Collective Action*, 64.

[7]Christopher J. Bosso, "The Color of Money: Environmental Groups and the Pathologies of Fund Raising," in Allan J. Cigler and Burdett Loomis, eds., *Interest Group Politics*, 4th ed. (Washington, D.C.: CQ Press, 1995), 101–3.

[8]Kay Lehman Schlozman and John T. Tierney, *Organized Interests and American Democracy* (New York: Harper & Row, 1986), 54; see also Jeffrey M. Berry and Clyde Wilcox, *The Interest Group Society*, 5th ed. (New York: Longman, 2008).

[9]Norman J. Ornstein and Shirley Elder, *Interest Groups, Lobbying, and Policymaking* (Washington, D.C.: CQ Press, 1978), 82–86.

[10]See John Mark Hansen, *Gaining Access* (Chicago: Chicago University Press, 1991); Bruce Wolpe and Bertram Levine, *Lobbying Congress* (Washington, D.C.: CQ Press, 1996).

[11]See Paul S. Herrnson, Ronald G. Shaiko, and Clyde Wilcox, *The Interest Group Connection: Electioneering, Lobbying, and Policymaking in Washington*, 2d ed. (Washington, D.C.: CQ Press, 2004).

[12]Quoted in Ornstein and Elder, *Interest Groups, Lobbying, and Policymaking*, 77.

[13]Steve Reinberg, "Debate Builds Over Drug Companies' Fees to FDA," *Washington Post*, April 13, 2007, web copy.

[14]Paul J. Quirk, *Industry Influence in Federal Regulatory Agencies* (Princeton, N.J.: Princeton University Press, 1981); John E. Chubb, *Interest Groups and the Bureaucracy: The Politics of Energy* (Stanford, Calif.: Stanford University Press, 1983), 200–201.

[15]Lee Epstein and C. K. Rowland, "Interest Groups in the Courts," *American Political Science Review* 85 (1991): 205–17.

[16]Richard Davis, *Electing Justice: Fixing the Supreme Court Nomination Process.* (New York: Oxford University Press, 2005).

[17]Hugh Heclo, "Issue Networks and the Executive Establishment," in Anthony King, ed., *The New American Political System* (Washington, D.C.: American Enterprise Institute, 1978), 87–124.

[18]Ornstein and Elder, *Interest Groups, Lobbying, and Policymaking*, 88–93.

[19]Quoted in Mark Green, "Political PAC-Man," *The New Republic*, December 13, 1982, 20; see also Richard Skinner, *More than Money: Interest Group Action in Congressional Elections* (Lanham, Md.: Rowman & Littlefield, 2006); Mark J. Rozell, Clyde Wilcox, and David Madland, *Interest Groups in American Campaigns*, 2d ed. (Washington, D.C.: CQ Press, 2005).

[20]Quoted in Larry Sabato, *PAC Power: Inside the World of Political Action Committees* (New York: Norton, 1984), 72.

[21]Federal Elections Commission data, 2008.

[22]See Thomas L. Gatz, *Improper Influence* (Ann Arbor: University of Michigan Press, 1996); Gene M. Grossman and Elhanan Helpman, *Interest Groups and Trade Policy* (Princeton, N.J.: Princeton University Press, 2002); Harry L. Wilson, *Guns, Gun Control, and Elections: The Politics and Policy of Firearms* (Lanham, Md.: Rowman & Littlefield, 2006).

[23]Walker, *Mobilizing Interest Groups in America*, 112.

[24]Theodore J. Lowi, *The End of Liberalism: The Second Republic of the United States* (New York: Norton, 1979).

[25]Larry Bartels, *Unequal Democracy: The Political Economy of the New Gilded Age* (Princeton, N.J.: Princeton University Press, 2008).

CHAPTER 10

[1]Theodore H. White, *The Making of the President, 1972* (New York: Bantam Books, 1973), 327.

[2]See Bill Kovach and Tom Rosenstiel, *The Elements of Journalism* (New York: Three Rivers Press, 2001).

[3]See Rodger Streitmatter, *Mightier than the Sword: How the News Media Have Shaped American History* (Westport, Conn.: Praeger Publishers, 2008).

[4]Frank Luther Mott, *American Journalism, a History: 1690–1960* (New York: Macmillan, 1962), 114–15; see also Si Sheppard, *The Partisan Press: A History of Media Bias in the United States* (Jefferson, N.C.: McFarland, 2007).

[5]Mott, *American Journalism*, 122–23, 220–27.

[6]Edwin Emery, *The Press and America: An Interpretive History of the Mass Media* (Englewood Cliffs, N.J.: Prentice-Hall, 1977), 350.

[7]Quoted in Mott, *American Journalism*, 529.

[8]Quoted in David Halberstam, *The Powers That Be* (New York: Knopf, 1979), 208–9.

[9]Donald Shaw and Maxwell McCombs, *The Emergence of American Political Issues: The Agenda-Setting Function of the Press* (St. Paul, Minn.: West Publishing, 1977).

[10]Bernard C. Cohen, *The Press and Foreign Policy* (Princeton, N.J.: Princeton University Press, 1963), 13.

[11]Thomas E. Patterson, *The American Democracy*, 5th ed. (New York: McGraw-Hill, 2001), 309–10.

[12]Kathleen Hall Jamieson and Karlyn Kohrs Campbell, *The Interplay of Influence*, rev. ed. (Boston: Wadsworth, 2005), 4.

[13]Michael Schudson, *Discovering the News* (New York: Basic Books, 1981).

[14]Michael Schudson, "What Time Means in a News Story," Occasional Paper No. 4, p. 8 (New York: Gannett Center for Media Studies, 1986).

[15]Comment at the annual meeting of the American Association of Political Consultants, Washington, D.C., 1977.

[16]Project for Excellence in Journalism, "Character and the Primaries of 2008," web release, May 29, 2008.

[17]Michael X. Delli Carpini and Scott Keeter, *What Americans Know About Politics and Why It Matters* (New Haven, Conn.: Yale University Press, 1997).

[18]Times Mirror Center for the People and the Press survey, 1994

[19]W. Lance Bennett, Regina G. Lawrence, and Steven Livingston, *When the Press Fails: Political Power and the News Media from Iraq to Katrina* (Chicago: University of Chicago Press, 2008).

[20]Quoted in David Shaw, "Beyond Skepticism: Have the Media Crossed the Line Into Cynicism?" *Los Angeles Times*, April 17, 1996, p. A1.

[21]Clark Hoyt, "What That McCain Article Didn't Say," *New York Times*, web release, February 24, 2008.

[22]See Scott McClellan, *What Happened: Inside the Bush White House and Washington's Culture of Deception* (New York: PublicAffairs, 2008).

[23]Stephen J. Farnsworth and S. Robert Lichter, *The Mediated Presidency: Television News and Presidential Governance* (Lantham, Md.: Rowman & Littlefield, 2006).

[24]Kiku Adatto, "Sound Bite Democracy," Joan Shorenstein Center on the Press, Politics, and Public Policy, Research Paper R-2, Harvard University, Cambridge, Mass., June 1990.

[25]Center for Media and Public Affairs data, 2008.

[26]Thomas Patterson, *Out of Order* (New York: Knopf, 1993), ch. 2.

[27]Robert Entman, "Framing: Towards Clarification of a Fractured Paradigm," in Denis McQuail, ed., *McQuail's Reader in Mass Communication Theory* (London: Sage Publications, 2002): 391–92.

[28]Michael Levy, "Disdaining the News," *Journal of Communication* (1981): 24–31.

[29]Thomas E. Patterson, *The Vanishing Voter* (New York: Knopf, 2002), 59.

[30]Walter Lippmann, *Public Opinion* (New York: Free Press, 1965), 214. First published in 1922.

[31]Greg Mitchell, "E&P/TIPP Poll: Bird in the Hand for Bush?" *Editor & Publisher*, November 6, 2000.

[32]*Editor & Publisher*, online edition, November 1, 2004.

[33]Bernard Goldberg, *Bias: A CBS Insider Exposes How the Media Distort News* (New York: Harper Paperbacks, 2003).

[34]David H. Weaver, Randal A. Beam, Bonnie J. Brownlee, Paul S. Voakes, G. Cleveland Wilhoit, *The American Journalist in the 21st Century* (Mahwah, N.J.: LEA, 2006).

[35]Center for Media and Public Affairs, *Media Monitor*, various dates.

[36]Michael Robinson, "Public Affairs Television and the Growth of Political Malaise," *American Political Science Review* 70 (1976): 409–32.

[37]Center for Media and Public Affairs, *Media Monitor*, various dates.

[38]Ibid.

[39]Mark Rozell, "Press Coverage of Congress," in Thomas Mann and Norman Ornstein, eds., *Congress, the Press, and the Public* (Washington, D.C.: American Enterprise Institute and Brookings Institution, 1994), 109.

[40]Robinson, "Public Affairs Television and the Growth of Political Malaise."

[41]The press's negativity and sensationalism have had another effect as well; they have damaged the press's credibility. According to a 2007 survey conducted by Center for Public Leadership at Harvard University's John F. Kennedy School of Government, the press has the lowest public confidence rating of any major U.S. institution.

[42]Joseph N. Cappella and Kathleen Hall Jamieson, *Spiral of Cynicism* (New York: Oxford University Press, 1997), 159.

[43]Quoted in Doreen Carvajal, "For News Media, Some Introspection," *New York Times*, April 5, 1998, 28.

[44]Project for Excellence in Journalism, "The Debate Effect," web release, October 27, 2004.

[45]William Cole, ed., *The Most of A. J. Liebling* (New York: Simon, 1963), 7.

[46]See Bruce A. Bimber and Richard Davis, *Campaigning Online: The Internet in*

U.S. Elections (New York: Oxford University Press, 2003).

[47] Robinson, "Public Affairs Television and the Growth of Political Malaise."

[48] Donald F. Roberts, Uila G. Foehr, Victoria J. Rideout, and Mollyann Brodie, "Kids and Media at the New Millennium," A Kaiser Family Foundation Report, November 1999, p. 19.

[49] See David T. Z. Mindich, *Tuned Out: Why Americans Under 40 Don't Follow the News* (New York: Oxford University Press, 2005).

[50] Thomas E. Patterson, "Young People and News," report of the Joan Shorenstein Center on the Press, Politics, and Public Policy, John F. Kennedy School of Government, Harvard University, June 2007.

[51] Martin P. Wattenberg, *Is Voting for Young People?* (New York: Pearson Longman, 2008), 32.

[52] Ibid., 75–80.

CHAPTER 11

[1] Roger H. Davidson and Walter J. Oleszek, *Congress and Its Members,* 10th ed. (Washington, D.C.: CQ Press, 2008), 4.

[2] See Paul S. Herrnson, *Congressional Elections: Campaigning at Home and in Washington,* 5th ed. (Washington, D.C.: CQ Press, 2008).

[3] See Gary C. Jacobson, *The Politics of Congressional Elections,* 5th ed. (New York: Longman, 2001).

[4] Bruce Cain, John Ferejohn, and Morris P. Fiorina, *The Personal Vote* (Cambridge, Mass.: Harvard University Press, 1987).

[5] Information provided by Clerk of the House.

[6] U.S. Code Online, 2006.

[7] Edward Sidlow, *Challenging the Incumbent: An Underdog's Undertaking* (Washington, D.C.: CQ Press, 2003); David C. W. Parker, *The Power of Money in Congressional Campaigns, 1880–2006* (Norman: University of Oklahoma Press, 2008).

[8] Quoted in Jennifer Babson and Kelly St. John, "Momentum Helps GOP Collect Record Amounts from PACs," *Congressional Quarterly Weekly Report,* December 3, 1994, 3456.

[9] Quoted in "A Tale of Myths and Measures: Who Is Truly Vulnerable?" *Congressional Quarterly Weekly Report,* December 4, 1993, 7; see also Dennis F. Thompson, *Ethics in Congress* (Washington, D.C.: Brookings Institution Press, 1995).

[10] James E. Campbell, *The Presidential Pulse of Congressional Elections* (Lexington: University Press of Kentucky, 1993).

[11] Robert Erikson, "The Puzzle of Midterm Losses," *Journal of Politics* 50 (November 1988): 1011–29.

[12] Linda L. Fowler and Robert D. McClure, *Political Ambition* (New Haven, Conn.: Yale University Press, 1989).

[13] Keith R. Poole and Howard Rosenthal, "Patterns of Congressional Voting," *American Journal of Political Science* 35 (February 1991): 228.

[14] *Congressional Quarterly Weekly Report,* various dates.

[15] Linda Witt, Karen M. Paget, and Glenna Matthews, *Running as a Woman: Gender and Power in American Politics* (New York: Free Press, 1993); Sue Thomas, *How Women Legislate* (New York: Oxford University Press, 1994); Tali Mendelberg, *The Race Card* (Princeton, N.J.: Princeton University Press, 2001).

[16] Steven Smith, *Party Influence in Congress* (New York: Cambridge University Press, 2007); Barbara Sinclair, *Party Wars: Polarization and the Politics of National Policy Making* (Norman: University of Oklahoma Press, 2006).

[17] Randall Strahan, *Leading Representatives: The Agency of Leaders in the Politics of the U.S. House* (Baltimore, Md.: Johns Hopkins University Press, 2007); David King, *Turf Wars* (Chicago: University of Chicago Press, 1997).

[18] See Stephen E. Frantzich and Steven E. Schier, *Congress: Games and Strategies* (Dubuque, Iowa: Brown & Benchmark, 1995), 127.

[19] See Gerald S. Strom, *The Logic of Lawmaking* (Baltimore, Md.: Johns Hopkins University Press, 1990).

[20] See Barbara Sinclair, *Unorthodox Lawmaking: New Legislative Processes in the U.S. Congress,* 3d ed. (Washington, D.C.: CQ Press, 2007).

[21] See Jon R. Bond and Richard Fleisher, eds., *Polarized Politics: Congress and the President in a Partisan Era* (Washington, D.C.: CQ Press, 2000).

[22] See Gary Orfield, *Congressional Power: Congress and Social Change* (New York: Harcourt Brace Jovanovich, 1975).

[23] James L. Sundquist, "Congress and the President: Enemies or Partners?" in Lawrence C. Dodd and Bruce I. Oppenheimer, eds., *Congress Reconsidered* (New York: Praeger, 1977), 240.

[24] Barry C. Burden, *Personal Roots of Representation* (Princeton, NJ: Princeton University Press, 2007).

[25] Keith Krehbiel, "Are Congressional Committees Composed of Preference Outliers?" *American Political Science Review* 84 (1990): 149–64; Richard L. Hall and Bernard Grofman, "The Committee Assignment Process and the Conditional Nature of Committee

Bias," *American Political Science Review* 84 (1990): 1149–66.

[26] Jason Mycoff, *Confrontation and Compromise: Presidential and Congressional Leadership, 2001–2006* (Lanham, Md.: Rowman & Littlefield, 2007).

[27] Joel A. Aberbach and Mark A. Peterson, eds., *The Executive Branch* (New York: Oxford University Press, 2005), 534–35.

[28] Davidson and Oleszek, *Congress and Its Members,* 7.

CHAPTER 12

[1] Woodrow Wilson, *Constitutional Government in the United States* (New York: Columbia University Press, 1908), 67.

[2] Sidney Milkis and Michael Nelson, *The American Presidency: Origins and Development, 1790–2007,* 5th ed. (Washington, D.C.: CQ Press, 2007).

[3] James W. Davis, *The American Presidency* (New York: Harper & Row, 1987), 13; see also Bruce Ackerman, *The Failure of the Founding Fathers* (Cambridge, Mass.: Belknap Press of Harvard University Press, 2005).

[4] See Barry M. Blechman and Stephen S. Kaplan, *Force Without War* (Washington, D.C.: Brookings Institution, 1978); Arthur M. Schlesinger Jr., *War and the American Presidency* (New York: W. W. Norton, 2004).

[5] *United States v. Belmont,* 57 U.S. 758 (1937).

[6] Robert DiClerico, *The American President,* 5th ed. (Englewood Cliffs, N.J.: Prentice-Hall, 1999), 47.

[7] Quoted in Wilfred E. Binkley, *President and Congress,* 3d ed. (New York: Vintage, 1962), 142.

[8] Theodore Roosevelt, *An Autobiography* (New York: Scribner's, 1931), 383.

[9] See Richard M. Pious, *The American Presidency* (New York: Basic Books, 1979), 83.

[10] Harry S Truman, *Years of Trial and Hope* (New York: Signet, 1956), 535.

[11] See Thomas S. Langston, *The Cold War Presidency: A Documentary History* (Washington, D.C.: CQ Press, 2006).

[12] James Bryce, *The American Commonwealth* (New York: Commonwealth Edition, 1908), 230.

[13] Erwin C. Hargrove, *The Effective Presidency: Lessons on Leadership from John F. Kennedy to George W. Bush* (Boulder, Colo.: Paradigm, 2007).

[14] James W. Ceaser, *Presidential Selection: Theory and Development* (Princeton, N.J.: Princeton University Press, 1979).

[15] John S. Jackson and William J. Crotty, *The Politics of Presidential Selection* (New York: Longman, 2001).

16See John G. Geer, *In Defense of Negativity* (Chicago: University of Chicago Press, 2006).

17John P. Burke, *The Institutionalized Presidency* (Baltimore, Md.: Johns Hopkins University Press, 1992); Charles E. Walcott and Karen M. Hult, *Governing the White House* (Lawrence: University Press of Kansas, 1995).

18Quoted in Stephen J. Wayne, *Road to the White House, 1992* (New York: St. Martin's Press, 1992), 143; but see Jody C. Baumgartner, *The American Vice Presidency Reconsidered* (Westport, Conn.: Praeger, 2006).

19See Barton Gellman and Jo Becker, "Angler: The Cheney Vice Presidency," *Washington Post*, June 24–27, 2007, a four-part series of articles.

20See Jeffrey E. Cohen, *The Politics of the United States Cabinet* (Pittsburgh: University of Pittsburgh Press, 1988); Shirley Anne Warshaw, *Powersharing: White House–Cabinet Relations in the Modern Presidency* (Albany: State University of New York Press, 1995).

21James Pfiffner, *The Modern Presidency* (New York: St. Martin's Press, 1994), 123.

22Quoted in James MacGregor Burns, "Our Super-Government—Can We Control It?" *New York Times*, April 24, 1949, 32.

23See Paul C. Light, *Thickening Government: Federal Hierarchy and theDiffusion of Accountability* (Washington, D.C.: Brookings Institution, 1995).

24Erwin Hargrove, *The Power of the Modern Presidency* (New York: Knopf, 1974); see also John H. Kessel, *Presidents, the Presidency, and the PoliticalEnvironment* (Washington, D.C.: CQ Press, 2001); Stephen Skowronek, *Presidential Leadership in Political Time: Reprise and Reappraisal* (Lawrence: University Press of Kansas, 2008).

25James P. Pfiffner, *The Strategic Presidency: Hitting the Ground Running*, 2d ed. (Chicago: Dorsey Press, 1996).

26Aaron Wildavsky, "The Two Presidencies," *Trans-Action*, December 1966, 7.

27Pfiffner, *Modern Presidency*, ch. 6.

28Thomas P. (Tip) O'Neill, with William Novak, *Man of the House: The Life and Political Memoirs of Speaker Tip O'Neill* (New York: Random House, 1987), 297.

29Charles O. Jones, *The Presidency in a Separated System* (Washington, D.C.: Brookings Institution Press, 2005).

30Richard E. Neustadt, *Presidential Power and the Modern Presidents* (New York: Free Press, 1990), 71–72.

31Ibid., 33.

32Charlie Savage, "Senator Considers Suit Over Bush Law Challenge," *Boston Globe*, June 28, 2006, Internet copy.

33John E. Mueller, "Presidential Popularity from Truman to Johnson," *American Political Science Review* 64 (March 1970): 18–34; Kathleen Frankovic, "Public Opinion in the 1992 Campaign," in Gerald M. Pomper, ed., *The Election of 1992* (Chatham, N.J.: Chatham House, 1993); Chris J. Dolan, *The Presidency and Economic Policy* (Lanham, Md.: Rowman & Littlefield, 2007).

34Samuel Kernell, *Going Public: New Strategies of Presidential Leadership*, 3d ed. (Washington, D.C.: CQ Press, 1997), 1; see also Robert M. Eisinger, *The Evolution of Presidential Polling* (New York: Cambridge University Press, 2003); Stephen J. Farnsworth and S. Robert Lichter, *Mediated Presidency: Television News & Presidential Governance* (Lanham, Md.: Rowman & Littlefield, 2005).

35Hugh Heclo, "Introduction: The Presidential Illusion," in Hugh Heclo and Lester M. Salamon, eds., *The Illusion of Presidential Government* (Boulder, Colo.: Westview Press, 1981), 2.

36Theodore J. Lowi, *The "Personal" Presidency: Power Invested, Promise Unfulfilled* (Ithaca, N.Y.: Cornell University Press, 1985).

CHAPTER 13

1Norman Thomas, *Rule 9: Politics, Administration, and Civil Rights* (New York: Random House, 1966), 6.

2James P. Pfiffner, "The National Performance Review in Perspective," working paper 94-4, Institute of Public Policy, George Mason University, 1994, 2.

3Ibid., 12.

4Max Weber, *Economy and Society*, trans. Guenther Roth and Claus Wittich (New York: Bedminster Press, 1968), 23; see also Paul Du Gay, *The Values of Bureaucracy* (New York: Oxford University Press, 2005).

5See Cornelius M. Kerwin, *Rulemaking*, 3d ed. (Washington, D.C.: CQ Press, 2003); Daniel E. Hall, *Administrative Law: Bureaucracy in a Democracy* (Upper Saddle River, N.J.: Prentice-Hall, 2005).

6Michael Lipsky, *Street-Level Bureaucracy* (New York: Russell Sage Foundation, 1980); see also George Serra, "Citizen-Initiated Contact and Satisfaction with Bureaucracy," *Journal of Public Administration* 5 (April 1995): 175–88.

7Paul Van Riper, *History of the United States Civil Service* (Evanston, Ill.: Peterson, 1958), 36.

8David H. Rosenbloom, *Federal Service and the Constitution* (Ithaca, N.Y.: Cornell University Press, 1971), 83.

9Gregory A. Huber, *The Craft of Bureaucratic Neutrality: Interests and Influence in Governmental Regulation of Occupational Safety* (New York: Cambridge University Press, 2007); Herbert Kaufman, "Emerging Conflicts in the Doctrine of Public Administration," *American Political Science Review* 50 (December 1956): 1060.

10Kaufman, "Emerging Conflicts," 1062.

11Quoted in Hugh Heclo, *A Government of Strangers* (Washington, D.C.: Brookings Institution, 1977), 225.

12Norton E. Long, "Power and Administration," *Public Administration Review* 10 (Autumn 1949): 269; Joel D. Aberbach and Bert A. Rockman, *In the Web of Politics* (Washington, D.C.: Brookings Institution Press, 2000).

13See Heclo, *Government of Strangers*, 117–18.

14Quoted in Aaron Wildavsky, *The Politics of the Budgetary Process*, 4th ed. (Boston: Little, Brown, 1984), 19; see also Dennis D. Riley, *Bureaucracy and the Policy Process: Keeping the Promises* (Lanham, Md.: Rowman & Littlefield, 2005).

15Joel D. Aberbach and Bert A. Rockman, "Clashing Beliefs Within the Executive Branch," *American Political Science Review* 70 (June 1976): 461.

16See B. Dan Wood and Richard W. Waterman, *Bureaucratic Dynamics* (Boulder, Colo.: Westview Press, 1994); Edward C. Page and Bill Jenkins, *Policy Bureaucracy: Government with a Cast of Thousands* (New York: Oxford University Press, 2005).

17See John Brehm and Scott Gates, *Working, Shirking, and Sabotage* (Ann Arbor: University of Michigan Press, 1996).

18Long, "Power and Administration," 269; see also John Mark Hansen, *Gaining Access* (Chicago: University of Chicago Press, 1991).

19Charles T. Goodsell, *The Case for Bureaucracy*, 2d ed. (Chatham, N.J.: Chatham House, 1985), 55–60, see also B. Guy Peters, *The Politics of Bureaucracy*, 5th ed. (New York: Routledge, 2001).

20William T. Gormley Jr. and Steven J. Balla, *Bureaucracy and Democracy* (Washington, D.C.: CQ Press, 2003); Kevin B. Smith, *Public Administration: Power and Politics in the Fourth Branch of Government* (New York: Oxford University Press, 2006).

21See Paul Light, *Thickening Government* (Washington, D.C.: Brookings Institution, 1995); James G. March and Johan P. Olson, "Organizing Political Life: What Administrative Reorganization Tells Us About Government," *American Political Science Review* 77 (June 1983): 281–96.

22Donald F. Ketti, *System Under Stress: Homeland Security and American Politics* (Washington, D.C.: CQ Press, 2007).

[23]Kenneth J. Meier, *Regulation* (New York: St. Martin's Press, 1985), 110–11.

[24]See Heclo, *Government of Strangers*.

[25]See Donald Kettl, *Deficit Politics* (New York: Macmillan, 1992).

[26]See Joel D. Aberbach, *Keeping a Watchful Eye* (Washington, D.C.: Brookings Institution, 1990).

[27]David Rosenbloom, "The Evolution of the Administrative State, and Transformations of Administrative Law," in David Rosenbloom and Richard Schwartz, eds., *Handbook of Regulation and Administrative Law* (New York: Marcel Dekker, 1994), 3–36.

[28]See *Vermont Yankee Nuclear Power Corp. v. National Resources Defense Council, Inc.,* 435 U.S. 519 (1978); *Chevron v. National Resources Defense Council,* 467 U.S. 837 (1984); *Heckler v. Chaney,* 470 U.S. 821 (1985); but see *FDA v. Brown & Williamson Tobacco Co.* (2000).

[29]*Pigeford v. Veneman,* U.S. District Court for the District of Columbia, Civil Action No. 97-1978 (1999).

[30]See Brian J. Cook, *Bureaucracy and Self-Government* (Baltimore, Md.: Johns Hopkins University Press, 1996).

[31]David Osborne and Ted Gaebler, *Reinventing Government: How the Entrepreneurial Spirit Is Transforming the Public Sector* (New York: Addison-Wesley, 1992); see also Elaine Ciulla Kamarck, *End of Government … as We Know It: Making Public Policy Work* (Boulder, Colo.: Lynne Rienner, 2007).

[32]Pfiffner, "National Performance Review in Perspective," 7; see also David G. Frederickson and H. George Frederickson, *Measuring the Performance of the Hollow State* (Washington, D.C.: Georgetown University Press, 2006).

[33]Ronald C. Moe, "The 'Reinventing Government' Exercise: Misinterpreting the Problem, Misjudging the Results," *Public Administration Review,* March/April 1994, 125–36.

CHAPTER 14

[1]*Marbury v. Madison,* 5 U.S. 137 (1803).

[2]*Swann v. Charlotte-Mecklenburg County Board of Education,* 402 U.S. 1 (1971).

[3]*Brown v. Board of Education of Topeka,* 347 U.S. 483 (1954).

[4]*Parents Involved in Community Schools v. Seattle,* No. 05-908 (2007) *Meredith, Custodial Parent and Next Friend of McDonald v. Jefferson County Board of Education,* No. 05-915 (2007).

[5]Linda Camp Keith, "The United States Supreme Court and Judicial Review of Congress, 1803–2001," *Judicature* 9(2007): 166.

[6]Rebecca Mae Salokar, *The Solicitor General: The Politics of Law* (Philadelphia:

Temple University Press, 1992); see also Cornell W. Clayton, *The Politics of Justice: The Attorney General and the Making of Legal Policy* (Armonk, N.Y.: Sharpe, 1992).

[7]Henry Glick, *Courts, Politics, and Justice,* 3d ed. (New York: McGraw-Hill, 1993), 120.

[8]Timothy R. Johnson, Paul Wahlbeck, and James Spriggs, "The Influence of Oral Arguments on the U.S. Supreme Court," *American Political Science Review,* 100 (2006): 99–113.

[9]Lawrence Baum, *The Supreme Court,* 8th ed. (Washington, D.C.: CQ Press, 2003), 120.

[10]*Gideon v. Wainwright,* 372 U.S. 335 (1963).

[11]See Forest Maltzman, Paul Wahlbeck, and James Spriggs, *The Collegial Game: Crafting Law on the U.S. Supreme Court* (New York: Cambridge University Press, 2000).

[12]From a letter to the author by Frank Schwartz of Beaver College; this section reflects substantially Professor Schwartz's recommendations to the author, as does the later section that addresses the federal court myth.

[13]*Hutto v. Davis,* 370 U.S. 256 (1982).

[14]*Lawrence v. Texas,* No. 02-102 (2003).

[15]*Bowers v. Hardwick,* 478 U.S. 186 (1986).

[16]See Richard Davis, *Electing Justices* (New York: Oxford University Press, 2005).

[17]See Lee Epstein and Jeffrey Segal, *Advice and Consent: The Politics of Judicial Appointments* (New York: Oxford University Press, 2005).

[18]Robert Scigliano, *The Supreme Court and the Presidency* (New York: Free Press, 1971), 146; see also Lee Epstein and Jack Knight, *The Choices Justices Make* (Washington, D.C.: CQ Press, 1998).

[19]Quoted in Baum, *Supreme Court,* 37.

[20]See Virginia A. Hettinger et al., *Judging on a Collegial Court: Influences on Federal Appellate Decision Making* (Charlottesville: University of Virginia Press, 2006).

[21]John Gottschall, "Reagan's Appointments to the U.S. Courts of Appeals," *Judicature* 48 (1986): 54.

[22]See Robert A. Carp and Ronald Stidham, *The Federal Courts,* 4th ed. (Washington, D.C.: CQ Press, 2001).

[23]Joseph B. Harris, *The Advice and Consent of the Senate* (Berkeley: University of California Press, 1953), 313.

[24]Quoted in Louis Fisher, *American Constitutional Law* (New York: McGraw-Hill, 1990), 5.

[25]Quoted in Charles P. Curtis, *Law and Large as Life* (New York: Simon & Schuster, 1959), 156–57.

[26]See Lee Epstein and Jack Knight, *The Choices Justices Make* (New York: Long-

man, 1995); Thomas G. Hansford and James F. Spriggs II, *The Politics of Precedent on the Supreme Court* (Princeton, N.J.: Princeton University Press, 2006).

[27]*Faragher v. City of Boca Raton,* No. 97-282 (1998).

[28]Stephen L. Wasby, *The Supreme Court in the Federal Judicial System,* 4th ed. (Chicago: Nelson-Hall, 1993), 53.

[29]For a helpful explanation of amicus curiae briefs, see Bradley Best, "Amicus Curiae," in David Schultz and John P. Vile, eds., *The Encyclopedia of Civil Liberties in America,* Vol. 1 (Armonk, N.Y.: M. E. Sharpe, 2005), 33–35.

[30]John Schmidhauser, *The Supreme Court* (New York: Holt, Rinehart & Winston, 1964), 6.

[31]Linda Greenhouse, "In Steps Big and Small, Supreme Court Moved Right," *New York Times,* July 1, 2007, web copy.

[32]Jeffrey A. Segal and Harold J. Spaeth, *The Supreme Court and the Attitudinal Model Revisited* (New York: Cambridge University Press, 2002).

[33]Linda Greenhouse, "In a Momentous Term, Justices Remake the Law, and the Court," *New York Times,* July 1, 2003, A1.

[34]*Bush v. Gore,* No. 00-949 (2000).

[35]See, however, James L. Gibson, Gregory A. Caldeira, and Lester Kenyatta Spence, "The Supreme Court and the U.S. Presidential Election of 2000," *British Journal of Political Science* 33 (2003): 535–56.

[36]David M. O'Brien, *Storm Center: The Supreme Court in American Politics,* 7th ed. (New York: Norton, 2005), 14–15.

[37]Ross Sandler and David Schoenbrod, *Democracy by Decree* (New Haven, Conn.: Yale University Press, 2003).

[38]Henry J. Abraham, "The Judicial Function Under the Constitution," *News for Teachers of Political Science* 41 (Spring 1984): 14.

[39]Alexander M. Bickel, *The Supreme Court and the Idea of Progress* (New Haven, Conn.: Yale University Press, 1978), 173–81.

[40]Frederic R. Kellogg, *Oliver Wendell Holmes, Jr.: Legal Theory and Judicial Restraint* (New York: Cambridge University Press, 2006).

[41]*Schenck v. United States,* 249 U.S. 47 (1919).

[42]Frank H. Easterbrook, "Do Liberals and Conservatives Differ in Judicial Activism?" *University of Colorado Law Review* 73 (2002): 1401.

[43]Quoted in Linda Greenhouse, "The Justices Decide Who's in Charge," *New York Times,* June 27, 1999, sect. 4, p. 1.

[44]See Antonin Scalia, *A Matter of Interpretation: Federal Courts and the Law* (Princeton, N.J.: Princeton University Press, 1997).

[45]Remarks by Antonin Scalia at the University of Delaware, April 30, 2007. Reported on the Web by *University of Delaware Daily.*

[46]Stephen Breyer, "Our Democratic Constitution," James Madison Lecture, New York University Law School, New York, New York, October 22, 2001.

CHAPTER 15

[1]E. E. Schattschneider, *The Semisovereign People* (New York: Holt, Rinehart & Winston, 1960).

[2]Aaron Wildausky, *The Politics of the Budgetary Process,* 4th ed. (Glenview, Ill.: Scott Foresman & Co., 1984).

[3]Marc Allen Eisner, Jeffrey Worsham, and Evan J. Rinquist, *Contemporary Regulatory Policy* (Boulder, Colo.: Lynne Rienner, 2006).

[4]The section titled "Efficiency Through Government Intervention" relies substantially on Alan Stone, *Regulation and Its Alternatives* (Washington, D.C.: CQ Press, 1982).

[5]See Marc Allen Eisner, *Regulatory Politics in Transition,* 2d ed. (Baltimore, Md.: Johns Hopkins University Press, 1999).

[6]See Richard A. Harris and Sidney M. Milkis, *The Politics of Regulatory Change* (New York: Oxford University Press, 1996).

[7]Lawrence E. Mitchell, *Corporate Irresponsibility* (New Haven, Conn.: Yale University Press, 2003).

[8]H. Peyton Young, *Equity: In Theory and Practice* (Princeton, N.J.: Princeton University Press, 1995).

[9]"Hill Foes of New Clean Air Rules Unite Behind Moratorium Bill," *Congressional Quarterly Weekly Report,* Spring 1998 (Washington, D.C.: CQ Press, 1998), 61.

[10]Board on Population Health and Public Health Practice, *The Future of Drug Safety: Promoting and Protecting the Health of the Public* (Washington, D.C.: National Academies Press, 2007).

[11]See Thomas Streeter, *Selling the Air* (Chicago: University of Chicago Press, 1996); Robert McChesney, *The Problem of the Media* (New York: Monthly Review Press, 2004); Christopher J. Bosso, *Environment, Inc.: From Grassroots to Beltway* (Lawrence: University Press of Kansas, 2005).

[12]Rachel Carson, *The Silent Spring* (Boston: Houghton Mifflin, 1962); see also Lester R. Brown, *Plan B2.0: Rescuing a Planet Under Stress and a Civilization in Trouble* (New York: W. W. Norton, 2006).

[13]Robert B. Keiter, *Keeping Faith with Nature* (New Haven, Conn.: Yale University Press, 2003).

[14]*U.S. News & World Report,* June 30, 1975, 25.

[15]*Whitman v. American Trucking Association,* No. 99-1257 (2001).

[16]*Massachusetts v. EPA,* No. 05-1120 (2007).

[17]See Walter A. Rosenbaum, *Environmental Politics and Policy,* 6th ed. (Washington, D.C.: CQ Press, 2004); Norman J. Vig and Michael E. Kraft, eds., *Environmental Policy: New Directions for the Twenty-First Century* (Washington, D.C.: CQ Press, 2003).

[18]Elliot A. Rosen, *Roosevelt, the Great Depression, and the Economics of Recovery* (Charlottesville: University of Virginia Press, 2007).

[19]See Robert Lekachman, *The Age of Keynes* (New York: Random House, 1966); see also Richard Kopke, Geoffrey M. B. Tootell, and Robert K. Trist, eds., *The Macroeconomics of Fiscal Policy* (Cambridge, Mass.: MIT Press, 2006).

[20]See Bruce Bartlett, *Reaganomics: Supply-Side Economics* (Westport, Conn.: Arlington House, 1981).

[21]For opposing views on the success of the tax-cutting strategy, see Gene W. Heck, *Building Prosperity: Why Ronald Reagan and the Founding Fathers Were Right on the Economy* (Lanham, Md.: Rowman & Littlefield, 2007), and Bryan D. Jones and Walter Williams, *The Politics of Bad Ideas: The Great Tax-Cut Delusion and the Decline of Good Government in America* (New York: Longman, 2008).

[22] See Richard Duncan, *The Dollar Crisis: Causes, Consequences, Cures,* rev. ed. (New York: John Wiley & Sons, 2005).

[23]U.S. Senate clerk, 2002.

[24]See Allen Schick, *The Federal Budget,* 3rd ed. (Washington, D.C.: Brookings Institution Press, 2007).

[25]Alan O. Ebenstein, *Milton Friedman: A Biography* (New York: Palgrave Macmillan, 2007).

[26]Martin Mayer, *FED: The Inside Story of How the World's Most Powerful Financial Institution Drives the Markets* (New York: Free Press, 2001).

CHAPTER 16

[1]Quoted in E. J. Dionne Jr., "Reflecting on 'Reform,'" *Washington Post,* web download, February 15, 2004.

[2]Press releases of House Committee on Ways and Means and National Conference of State Legislatures, September 19 and June 26, 2002, respectively.

[3]See Felicia Ann Kornbluh, *The Battle for Welfare Rights: Politics and Poverty in Modern America* (Philadelphia: University of Pennsylvania Press, 2007).

[4]Michael Harrington, *The Other America: Poverty in the United States* (New York: Macmillan, 1962); see also James T. Patterson, *America's Struggle Against Poverty in the Twentieth Century* (Cambridge, Mass.: Harvard University Press, 2000).

[5]Charles Murray, *Losing Ground: American Social Policy, 1950–1980* (New York: Basic Books, 1984).

[6]Signe-Mary McKernan and Caroline Ratcliffe, "Events That Trigger Poverty Entries and Exits," *Social Science Quarterly* 86 (2005): 1146–69.

[7]See Katherine S. Newman, *No Shame in My Game* (New York: Alfred A. Knopf and Russell Sage Foundation, 1999), 41.

[8]V. O. Key Jr., *The Responsible Electorate* (Cambridge, Mass.: Belknap Press of Harvard University, 1966), 43.

[9]Everett Carll Ladd, *American Political Parties* (New York: Norton, 1970), 205.

[10]Institute on Taxation and Economic Policy poll, 2002.

[11]For a general overview of 1950s and 1960s policy disputes, see James Sundquist, *Politics and Policy* (Washington, D.C.: Brookings Institution, 1968).

[12]See Jason DeParle, *American Dream: Three Women, Ten Kids, and a Nation's Drive to End Welfare* (New York: Penguin, 2005).

[13]Quoted in Malcolm Gladwell, "The Medicaid Muddle," *The Washington Post National Weekly Edition,* January 16–22, 1995, 31.

[14]Jill Quadagno, *One Nation, Uninsured: Why the United States Has No National Health Insurance* (New York: Oxford University Press, 2005).

[15]See Christopher Howard, *The Welfare State Nobody Knows* (Princeton, N.J.: Princeton University Press, 2006).

[16]Alberto Alesina and Edward Glaeser, *Fighting Poverty in the U.S. and Europe* (New York: Oxford University Press, 2006).

[17]Robert D. Ebel, Tuan Minh Le, and Zicheng Li Swift, "National Tax Levels and the Rich vs. the Poor," publication of the Tax Policy Center, Washington, D.C., June 6, 2005.

[18]Paul Krugman, "Hey, Lucky Duckies," *New York Times,* December 3, 2002, A31.

[19]Said of George H. W. Bush at the 1988 Democratic Convention. The quote is variously attributed to Ann Richards or Jim Hightower.

[20]For a history of public education, see Joel H. Spring, *The American School 1642–2004* (New York: McGraw-Hill, 2008).

[21]Based on Organization for Economic Cooperation and Development (OECD) data, 2006; see Douglas S. Reed, *On Equal Terms: The Constitutional Politics of Educational Opportunity*

(Princeton, N.J.: Princeton University Press, 2003).

[22]Kaiser Family Foundation/Washington Post/Kennedy School of Government poll, September 1999.

[23]See John E. Chubb and Terry M. Moe, *Politics, Markets, and America's Schools* (Washington, D.C.: Brookings Institution, 1990); Tony Wagner and Thomas Vander Ark, *Making the Grade* (New York: Routledge, 2001).

[24]See Jeffrey R. Henig, *Rethinking School Choice* (Princeton, N.J.: Princeton University Press, 1995).

[25] Phi Delta Kappa/Gallup poll, 2002.

[26]See Lee Anderson, *Congress in the Classroom* (University Park: Pennsylvania State University Press, 2007).

[27]See Neal McCluskey, *Feds in the Classroom* (Lanham, Md.: Rowman & Littlefield, 2007).

[28]See, for example, David Hursh, *High Stakes Testing and the Decline of Teaching and Learning* (Lanham, Md.: Rowman & Littlefield, 2008.)

[29]Press release, Congressman John Boehner, January 4, 2003.

[30]Phi Delta Kappa/Gallup poll, 2005.

[31]Stanley Feldman and John Zaller, "The Political Culture of Ambivalence: Ideological Responses to the Welfare State," *American Journal of Political Science* 36, no. 1 (1992): 268–307.

[32]Robert E. Lane, "Market Justice, Political Justice," *American Political Science Review* 80 (1986): 383.

CHAPTER 17

[1]See Mr. X. (George Kennan), "The Sources of Soviet Conduct," *Foreign Affairs* 25 (July 1947): 566–82.

[2]See Wilson Miscamble, *From Roosevelt to Truman: Potsdam, Hiroshima, and the Cold War* (New York: Cambridge University Press, 2008).

[3]David M. Barrett, *Uncertain Warriors: Lyndon Johnson and His Vietnam Advisors* (Lawrence: University Press of Kansas, 1993); see also Stanley Karnow, *Vietnam: A History* (New York: Penguin, 1983).

[4]See Dag Henriksen, *NATO's Gamble* (Annapolis, Md.: Naval Institute Press, 2007).

[5]See Mark Sauter and James Carafano, *Homeland Security* (New York: McGraw-Hill, 2005).

[6]West Point speech, June 1, 2002; for an opposing view, see Gary Hart, *The Shield and the Cloak: The Security of the Commons* (New York: Oxford University Press, 2006).

[7]Nick Ritchie, *The Political Road to War with Iraq: Bush, 9/11 and the Drive to Overthrow Saddam* (New York: Routledge, 2007).

[8]See Ofira Seliktar, *The Politics of Intelligence and American Wars with Iraq* (New York: Palgrave Macmillan, 2008).

[9]See Ole Holsti, *Public Opinion and American Foreign Policy* (Ann Arbor: University of Michigan Press, 1996); Richard Sobel, *The Impact of Public Opinion on U.S. Foreign Policy Since Vietnam* (New York: Oxford University Press, 2001).

[10]George C. Wilson, *This War Really Matters: Inside the Fight for Defense Dollars* (Washington, D.C.: CQ Press, 2000).

[11]U.S. government data, various agencies, 2008.

[12]*The World Competitiveness Yearbook* (Lausanne, Switzerland: International Institute for Management Development, 2008).

[13]American Assembly Report (co-sponsored by the Council on Foreign Relations), *Rethinking America's Security* (New York: Harriman, 1991), 9.

[14]Robert Z. Lawrence, *The United States and the WTO Dispute Settlement System* (New York: Council on Foreign Relations, 2007).

[15]Ted C. Fishman, *China, Inc.: How the Rise of the Next Superpower Challenges America and the World* (New York: Scribner, 2005).

[16]John Duffield, *Over a Barrel: The Costs of U.S. Foreign Oil Dependence* (Stanford, Calif.: Stanford Law and Politics, 2007).

[17]See Joseph S. Nye, *Soft Power: The Means to Success in World Politics* (New York: PublicAffairs, 2003); Michael Lind, *The American Way of Strategy* (New York: Oxford University Press, 2006).

[18]Hobart Rowen, "The Budget: Fact and Fiction," *The Washington Post National Weekly Edition*, January 16–22, 1995, 5.

[19]Tom Masland, "Going Down the Aid 'Rathole'?" *Newsweek*, December 5, 1994, 39.

CHAPTER 18

[1]*Gonzales, Attorney General, et al. v. Oregon, et al.*, No. 04-623 (2006).

[2]Thad Beyle, "Governors: The Middlemen and Women in Our Political System," in Virginia Gray and Herbert Jacobs, eds., *Politics in the American States: A Comparative Analysis* (Washington, D.C.: CQ Press, 1996), 237; see also Sarah McCally Morehouse, *The Governor as Party Leader* (Ann Arbor: University of Michigan Press, 1998).

[3]Amy Pyle, "California and the West," *Los Angeles Times*, October 24, 1999, A30.

[4]Advisory Commission on Intergovernmental Relations (ACIR), *The Question of State Government Capability* (Washington, D.C.: ACIR, 1985), 123; see also Marjorie Sarbaugh Thompson, Lyke Thompson, Charles D. Elder, John Strate, and Richard Elling, *The Political and Institutional Effects of Term Limits* (New York: Palgrave Macmillan, 2005).

[5]David Broder, *Democracy Derailed* (San Diego: Harcourt, 2000).

[6]Thomas E. Patterson, *The Vanishing Voter* (New York: Vintage, 2003), 179–80.

[7]Thomas R. Dye, *Politics in States and Communities*, 8th ed. (Englewood Cliffs, N.J.: Prentice-Hall, 1994), 162.

[8]Alan Rosenthal, *The Third House: Lobbyists and Lobbying in the States*, 2d ed. (Washington, D.C.: CQ Press, 2001).

[9]John F. Dillon, *Commentaries on the Law of Municipal Corporations*, 5th ed. (Boston: Little, Brown, 1911), vol. 1, sec. 237.

[10]*People v. Hurlbut*, 24 Michigan 44 (1871).

[11]Susan MacManus, *Young v. Old: Generational Combat in the Twenty-first Century* (Boulder, Colo.: Westview Press, 1996).

[12]See, for example, G. William Domhoff, *Who Rules America?* 5th ed. (New York: McGraw-Hill, 2005).

[13]See Michael Nelson and John Lyman Mason, *How the South Joined the Gambling Union* (Baton Rouge: Louisiana University Press, 2007).

[14]David Brunori, *Local Tax Policy: A Federalist Perspective* (Washington, D.C.: Urban Institute Press, 2007).

[15]See Malcolm E. Jewell and Sarah M. Morehouse, *Political Parties and Elections in American States*, 4th ed. (Washington, D.C.: CQ Press, 2000).

[16]*San Antonio Independent School District v. Rodriquez*, 411 U.S. 1 (1973).

[17]"Public School Funding in New Jersey," report of the Joint [New Jersey] Legislative Committee on Public School Funding Reform, August 10, 2006.

[18]Greg Tuppo, "U.S. Teens Have Weak Practical Math Skills," *USA Today*, December 7, 2004, 7D.

[19]Gay and Lesbian Task Force data, 2003.

[20]See articles in Thad Beyle, ed., *State and Local Government 2004–2005* (Washington, D.C.: CQ Press, 2004).

Credits

Chapter 1
Opener: © Daryl Benson/Digital Vision/Getty Images; p. 4 © Justin Sullivan/Getty Images; p. 5: © Damian Dovarganes/Pool/Reuters/Corbis; p. 8: Library of Congress, Prints & Photographs Division [LC-USZC4-2474]; p. 12: © Ernest C. Withers, Courtesy, Panopticon Gallery, Waltham, MA; p. 14: © AP Images; p. 16: USHMM, courtesy of National Archives; p. 20: © Bob Daemmrich/Image Works; p. 22: © Spencer Platt/Getty Images

Chapter 2
Opener: © Joseph Sohm/Visions of America/Corbis; p. 28: © Jim Wells; p. 29: © The Granger Collection; p. 31: Library of Congress, Prints & Photographs Division; p. 32: © The Granger Collection; p. 34: © Bettmann/Corbis; p. 37: ©Archivo Iconografico, S.A./Corbis; p. 40: © The Granger Collection; p. 46: © The Granger Collection; p. 49: © Bettmann/Corbis; p. 50: © Architect of the Capitol

Chapter 3
Opener: © The Granger Collection; p. 58: ©Jim West/Image Works; p. 59: © The Granger Collection; p. 62: © Bettmann/Corbis; p. 65: © The Granger Collection; p. 66: Library of Congress, Prints & Photographs Division [LC-B811-560]; p.67:©TheGrangerCollection;p.68:©Bettmann/Corbis; p. 70: Library of Congress, Prints & Photographs Division; p. 71: © Scherl/Sueddeutsche Zeitung Photo/Image Works; p. 73: © Lenny Ignelzi/AP Images; p. 77: © Doug Pensinger/Getty Images

Chapter 4
Opener: © Jim West/Alamy; p. 87: © AP Images; p. 89: © AP Images; p. 92: © Paul Conklin/PhotoEdit; p. 97: © AP Images; p. 100: © Greg Gibson/AP Images; p. 105: © Jeff Greenberg/age fotostock; p. 107: Library of Congress, Prints & Photographs Division; p. 112: © Paul Conklin/PhotoEdit

Chapter 5
Opener: ©Jim West/Image Works;p.119:©Charles Moore/Black Star; p. 122: © Scott Olson/Getty Images; p. 127: © Adele Starr/AP Images; p. 128: © Nati Harnik/AP Images; p. 130: © The Art Archive/Culver Pictures; p. 135: © Manish Swarup/AP Images; p. 140:© Danny Moloshok/AP Images

Chapter 6
Opener: © Eyewire/Photodisc/PunchStock; p. 149: ©UniversityCollegeLondon;p.150:©JoelStettenheim/Corbis; p. 153: © Bettmann/Corbis; p. 156: © Charles Gupton; p. 157: © Najlah Feanny/Corbis; p. 160: Library of Congress, Prints & Photographs Division [LC-USZ62-117121]; p. 161: © Digital Vision Ltd.; p. 165: Courtesy, Obama for America/wwwbarackobama.com

Chapter 7
Opener: © Bob Daemmrich/Image Works; p. 172: © Culver Pictures; p. 175: © Jonathon Nourok/Stone/Getty Images; p. 179: © The Granger Collection; p. 180: © The Charlotte Observer/AP Images; p. 183: © Frederic Larson/Corbis; p. 185: © AP Images

Chapter 8
Opener: © JupiterImages/Comstock Image/Alamy; p. 192: © LM Otero/AP Images; p. 195 (top): Library of Congress, Prints and Photographs Division [LC-USZ62-13016]; p. 195 (bottom): © Bettmann/Corbis; p. 200: © I.P.O.L., NYC; p. 201: © Mark Wilson/Getty Images; p. 203: © The Granger Collection; p. 208: © Alex Wong/Getty Images; p. 213: © Allan Tannenbaum; p. 216: © Toby Jorrin/AP Images

Chapter 9
Opener: © Bob Daemmrich/Image Works; p. 222: www.aarp.orgReprintedwithPermission;p.225: © Burstein Collection/Corbis; p. 226: © Mark Duncan/AP Images; p. 227: Library of Congress, Prints & Photographs Division; p. 229: © Chuck Burton/AP Images; p. 231: © AP Images; p. 235: © Jonathan Blair/Corbis; p. 236: © Gerald Herbert/AP Images; p. 241: © Chip Somodevilla/Getty Images

Chapter 10
Opener: © Gary Gershoff/Getty Images; p. 248: © Timothy A. Clary/Getty Images; p. 250: © Stock Montage; p. 251: © Michael Smith/Getty Images; p. 257: © Underwood & Underwood/Corbis; p. 258: © AP Images; p. 264: © David Duprey/AP Images; p. 265: © Jason DeCrow/AP Images; p. 269: © Patrick Olear/PhotoEdit

Chapter 11
Opener: © Chip Somodevilla/Getty Images; p. 276: © Vanessa Vick/Photo Researchers; p. 280: © Bettmann/Corbis; p. 282: © Dennis Cook/AP Images; p. 290: © Douglas Graham/Roll Call/Corbis; p. 295: Library of Congress, Prints & PhotographsDivision[LC-USZ62-37502];p.298: © Bob Daemmrich/Corbis; p. 300: Courtesy, Office of the Speaker, Washington, DC

Chapter 12
Opener: © Doug Mills/AP Images; p. 310: © Christie's Images/Corbis; p. 312: © UPI/Bettmann/Corbis; p. 314: © Punchstock/Brand X Pictures; p. 316: © Charlie Neibergall/AP Images; p. 320: © Win McNamee/Getty Images; p. 324: © Eric Draper/AP Images; p. 328: © UPI/Bettmann/Corbis; p. 330: © Rene Burri/Magnum Photos; p. 334: © Pablo Martinez Monsivais/AP Images

Chapter 13
Opener: © JupiterImages/Thinkstock/Alamy; p. 340: © AP Images; p. 345: All Rights Reserved in Photographs © United States Postal Service. Used with Permission; p. 348: © Bettmann/Corbis; p. 352: © Marc Bryan-Brown/WireImage/Getty Images; p. 355: © Getty Images; p. 358: © White House Historical Association/White House Collection [No. 22]; p. 359: ©Mark Wilson/Getty Images

Chapter 14
Opener: © Royalty-Free/Corbis; p. 366: © Michael Conroy/AP Images; p. 368: © Collection of the Supreme Court of the United States; p. 374: © Harry Cabluck/AP Images; p. 375: © Collection, The Supreme Court Historical Society. Photo by Steve Petteway, Supreme Court; p. 383: © Breck Smither/AP Images; p. 387 (left): © AP Images; p. 387 (right): © AP Images; p. 388: Library of Congress, Prints & Photographs Division [LC-USZ62-54940]

Chapter 15
Opener: © Win McNamee/Getty Images; p. 396: © Spencer Platt/Getty Images; p. 401: © Ryan McVay/Getty Images; p. 403: © Alfred Eisenstaedt/Time Life Pictures/Getty Images; p. 404: © John M. Roberts/Corbis; p. 406: © Lawrence Bender Prods./The Kobal Collection/Lee, Eric; p. 408: © Damian Dovarganes/AP Images

Chapter 16
Opener: © Jim West/Image Works; p. 430: Library of Congress, Prints & Photographs Division [LC-USZ62-13036]; p. 431: © William Johnson/Stock Boston; p. 434: © Dana Fineman; p. 438 (left): © Sally Weigand/Index Stock Imagery/Photolibrary; p. 438 (right): © Glenn Kulbako/Index Stock Imagery/Photolibrary; p. 440: © Jim West/Image Works; p. 443: © Bob Daemmrich/The Image Work

Chapter 17
Opener: DoD photo by Cpl. Brian M. Henner, U.S. Marine Corps; p. 451: © The Michael Barson Collection; p. 452: © Bettmann/Corbis; p. 460: © Nicolas Asfouri/AFP/Getty Images; p. 461: © Ed Clark/Life Magazine/Time & Life Pictures/Getty Images; p. 464: © Wolfgang Kaehler/Corbis; p. 467: Photo Courtesy of U.S. Army

Chapter 18
Opener: © Danilo Donadoni/age fotostock; p. 474: © Don Ryan/AP Images; p. 477: © Bob Daemmrich/Image Works; p. 480: © Andy Olenick/Fotowerks Ltd.; p. 483: © Stephan Savoia/AP Images; p. 485: © Royalty-Free/Corbis; p. 487: © Matthew McDermott/Corbis; p. 491: © John Elderfield; p. 495: © Melody Ko/Tufts University Photography © 2007 Trustees of Tufts College; p. 496: Library of Congress, Prints & Photographs Division; p. 498: © Todd Warshaw/Greenpeace.

Index

A

AARP. *See* American Association of Retired Persons (AARP)
ABC, 254, 262
abolitionism, 10, 121, 179
abortion rights, 16, 100–101, 113, 160, 161
Abramoff, Jack, 236–237
absolute monarchs, 14
Abu Ghraib prison, Iraq, 111
Act of Toleration, 95
Adamany, David, 209
Adams, John, 8, 37, 44, 49, 88, 193, 383
Adams, John Quincy, 318, 346
Adarand v. Pena, 139
administrative agencies, 345–346
administrative law, 380
advanced weapons systems, 458
Advisory Commission on Intergovernmental Relations, 481
affirmative action policy, 118, 240, 382
    and de facto inequality, 137
    in the law, 139–140
    more strongly supported by African Americans than white Americans, 161
    narrowed focus of, 143
    as part of national education policy, 140
    public opinion on, 138
Afghanistan, 111, 157, 307, 312, 451, 453
AFL-CIO, 225, 232
African Americans
    alignment with Democratic Party, 201
    as crack-cocaine defendants, 109
    discrimination against, 9, 119
    discrimination against as job applicants, 117
    discrimination against in criminal justice system, 120
    discrimination by Department of Agriculture in farm loans, 358
    as elected officials, 120
    family income, 137
    and government-imposed racial segregation, 395
    growing electoral force in modern South, 484
    health care, 118
    infant mortality rates, 142
    northward migration, 255
    as a percentage of state population, 1790, 35
    politically powerless in pre–civil rights South, 484
    and poverty, 428
    representation in state legislatures, 121
    and right to vote, 136, 172

separate and unequal treatment of, 119
    in state public policies, 80
    struggle for equality, 118–124
    support for affirmative action, 161
age
    and attention to news, 268–269
    and political opinions, 162
    and voter turnout, 180
Age Discrimination Act of 1975, 130
Age Discrimination in Employment Act of 1967, 130
age-discrimination standards, 499
"agency capture," 232
agency heads, 325
"agency point of view," 340, 350–351, 361
agenda setting, 252–255
Agnew, Spiro, 263
agricultural groups, 226–227, 234
agriculture
    government intervention, 409
    income stabilization programs, 421
    strength of sector in U.S., 461
agriculture committees of Congress, 233
Aid for Families with Dependent Children (AFDC), 434
Ailes, Roger, 212, 251, 263, 264
airline passengers, screening of, 77
Airlines Deregulation Act, 400
air pollution, 399, 405
air quality standards, 405
air wars, 214–215
Alaska Natives, 125
Albanians, 453
alienation, 179, 180
Alito, Samuel, 101, 375, 376, 383
All Things Considered, 352
all-volunteer military, 458, 459
al Qaeda, 45, 149, 157, 359, 453, 454
alternative energy sources, 407
American Association of Retired Persons (AARP), 162, 182, 221, 222, 236, 432
American Association of University Professors (AAUP), 227
American Bar Association (ABA), 227
American Civil Liberties Union (ACLU), 107, 112, 233, 382
American Conservative Union (ACU), 230
An American Dilemma (Myrdal), 142
American Farm Bureau Federation, 226
American Federalism (Elazar), 490
American Federation of State, County, and Municipal Employees (AFSCME), 226, 486
American Federation of Teachers (AFT), 486
American Hospital Association (AHA), 232

American Independent Party, 204
American Medical Association (AMA), 227, 432–433
American Nazi Party, 92
American Petroleum Institute, 225, 231–232
American political culture, core principles of, 4–5, 16
American Revolution, 5, 8, 15, 30
Americans
    core values, 5–12, 155
    distinction between personal lives and public life, 172
    lack of access to adequate health care, 186
    power and limits of ideals, 8
    preferences in teaching children about the nation's history, 10
    See also public opinion; United States
Americans for Democratic Action (ADA), 230
American Soybean Association, 226
Americans with Disabilities Act, 131
Ames, Fisher, 27
amicus curiae ("friend of the court"), 382
Amish, 98
Amnesty International, 110
Amtrak (National Railroad Passenger Corporation), 344
Anaconda Copper Company, and Montana politics, 485
Anderson, Desiree, 279
Anderson, Russell, 85
An Economic Interpretation of the Constitution (Beard), 50
Anglicanism, 96
Anthony, Susan B., 3, 172, 179
antiabortion groups, 92, 101, 229, 233
Antietam, battle of, 66
Anti-Federalists, 36, 61, 64, 69
"antiparties," 203
antipollution policy, 403
antislavery movement, 67
Antitrust Division of the Justice Department, 399
antiwar demonstrations, 16, 185
apathy, 179
appellate courts, 367, 481
appellate judges, 371
appellate jurisdiction, 367
Arab Americans, 111, 112, 113
Arctic National Wildlife Refuge, 403
arms industry, 461
Articles of Confederation, 30–32, 58, 59, 62, 80
Ashcroft, John, 112, 473, 474
Asian Americans
    discrimination against, 129
    emphasis on academic achievement, 130
    family income, 137

Associated Milk Producers, 226, 233
Associated Press (AP), 253–254
Association of Wheat Growers, 222, 226, 233
asylum seekers, 110
Atkins v. Virginia, 107–108
at-large (community-wide) election
    districts, 491
attack politics, 213
attorney general, 342
authoritarian government, 17
authority, 19, 24
autocracy, 15
automakers, 399
automatic voter registration, 175, 187

B

"backbenchers," 292
Baker, James, 178
Bakke, Alan, 139
Bakke decision *(Regents of the University of
    California v. Bakke),* 140
balanced budget, 411
Balkans War, 469
Ballor, Jordon J., 152
ballot manipulation, 483–484
Banking Act of 1934, 401
banking industry, 71
banking practices, effect on housing
    segregation, 136
Bank of the United States, *65*
Barr, Bob, 204
Bartels, Larry, 187
battleground states, 318, 319, 320
Bay of Pigs invasion, 328
Bazelon, David, 378
BBC, 256
BCRA. *See* Bipartisan Campaign Reform
    Act (BCRA)
Beard, Charles S., 50
Bear Stearns, 419
Beck, Glenn, 265
Beeson, Ann, 112
Bentham, Jeremy, 148, 149
Bentley, Clyde, 269
Benton v. Maryland, 103
Bentsen, Lloyd, 298
Berlin Wall, 451
bicameral (two-chamber) legislatures, 287, 479
Biden, Joe, 191, 317, 323
Big Three U.S. automakers, 225
bilingual education programs, 127, 130
bill, process of becoming law, 292–295
    committee hearings and decisions, 292–294
    from committee to the floor, 294
    conference committees and the
        president, 295
    leadership and floor action, 294–295
Bill of Rights, 28, 37, 43–44, 53, 85, 86, 87,
    90–91, 113, 498–499
bin Laden, Osama, 213, 454
Bipartisan Campaign Reform Act (BCRA),
    209, 211
bipolar (power structure), 451
Birch, William, 29
Birmingham, Alabama demonstrations,
    119, 120

Black, Hugo, 370
Blair, Tony, 216
Blakley v. Washington, 109
blanket primary, 205
block grants, 75–76, 76
blogs, 251, 252, 266, 271
"blue states," 161
*Board of Education of Independent School
    District No. 92 of Pottawatomie
    County v. Earls,* 105
*Board of Trustees of the University of Alabama
    v. Garrett,* 79
Boehner, John, 444
Boing Boing, 251
Bork, Robert, 376
born-again Christians, 160
boroughs, 487
Bosnia, 452, 453
Boss Tweed, 205
Boston Tea Party, 30
Bowers v. Hardwick, 101
Bowles v. Russell, 106
Bowling Alone (Putnam), 184
Boyle, Thad, 477
Boy Scouts, 131
Bradenburg, Clarence, 92
Braille, 131
Brandeis, Louis D., 377
Brandenburg v. Ohio, 92
The Brass Check (Steffens), 257
Breckinridge, John C., 194
Brennan, William, 376
Bretton Woods Conference, 467
Breyer, Stephen, 106, 141, 375, 383, 384, 388
bribes, 231
"the bridge to nowhere," 275
brief, 369
Britain
    military spending, 457
    parliamentary system, 42
    relations with American colonists, 29–30
British Conservative Party, 216, 283
British House of Commons, 42
British House of Lords, 42
British Labour Party, 216, 283
British Parliament, 29, 287
British prime minister, 313
broadcast networks, 248
broadcast news
    claim of neutrality, 262
    preference for the negative, 262–263
    tone of, and Americans' confidence in polit-
        ical leaders and institutions, 263
    See also cable television; news media;
        television news
broadcast news journalists, tendency
    toward Democratic in personal
    beliefs, 262
Broder, David S., 238
Brown, Gordon, 449
Brown, Jerry, 479
Brown, Linda Carol, 119
Brown, Michael, 325, 355, 356
Brownback, Sam, 94
Brown v. Board of Education, 72, 119–120,
    134, 140, 143, 365, 366, 369, 382
Bryan, William Jennings, 262
Bryce, James, 4, 7, 37, 313

Buchanan, James, 311
Buchanan, Pat, 203
Budget and Accounting Act, 313
budgetary process, 357, 414–417, 415
budget deficit, 411, 412
Budget Impoundment and Control Act of
    1974, 298, 331
budget surplus, 411
Buffett, Warren, 439
Bull Moose Party, 204
Bundesrat, 287
Bundestag, 200
bureaucracy
    antithesis of democracy, 354
    defined, 340–341
    formalized rules, 341
    hierarchical authority, 341
    job specialization, 341
    strengths and weaknesses of major
        systems for managing, 350
    vs. self-government, 356
bureaucratic accountability, 354
bureaucratic inefficiency and waste,
    opinions on, 353
bureaucratic rule, 4, 19, 21
Bureau of Indian Affairs, 125
Burke, Edmund, 47
Burr, Aaron, 37, 388
Bush, George H. W., 197, 198, 308, 452
Bush, George W., 264, 266, 311
    and AIDS crisis in Africa, 395
    and Arctic National Wildlife Refuge, 403
    authorization of "surge," 455
    Congressional response to, 332–333
    decline in legislative success rate, 330
    defense spending, 415
    detention and treatment of enemy
        combatants, 111–112, 324
    economic initiatives, 412
    2000 election, 215, 322
    endorsement by more daily papers than
        Al Gore, 262
    federal education policies, 443
    first veto cast by, 329–330
    G8 summit, 449
    and immigration reform bill, 127, 166
    increased approval ratings after 9/11, 307
    and intelligence estimates about Iraq, 348
    and Iraq War, 147, 163, 185, 197, 281,
        454, 460
    judicial appointees, 377
    linking of foreign aid to human rights, 468
    and matching funds for nominating
        campaign, 316
    Millennium Challenge Account
        program, 468
    and negative press coverage, 334–335
    No Child Left Behind Act, 57–58, 77
    oil, and decision to invade Iraq, 466
    preemptive war doctrine, 454, 469
    proposed temporary worker program, 13
    reduction of taxes on wealthy, 437
    2004 reelection, 201, 204
    refusal to sign Kyoto agreement, 406
    reorganization of FBI and CIA, 354
    response to 9/11 attacks, 157, 312
    and role of vice president, 324
    secret military tribunals, 111–112

Bush, George W., (*continued*)
and social security, 432
2005 State of the Union address, 221
supply-side tax initiatives, 439
use of signing statements, 331–332
veto of bill to reduce American presence
   in Iraq, 297
war on terrorism, 352, 359, 453
warrantless wiretaps, 8, 45, 112–113, 258,
   259, 302, 324, 382
and weakened economy, 198
"weapons of mass destruction" argument, 349
White House Office of Faith-Based and
   Community Initiatives, 97
won presidency after losing popular
   vote, 49, 315, 319
Bush v. Gore, 383, 384
business groups, 225
business interests, judicial protection of, 69–70
business lobbies, influence on regulatory
   policies, 420
business regulation, 195
busing, 16, 137, 140–142, 143, 161, 365, 442

C

cabinet, outmoded as a policymaking
   forum, 325
cabinet departments, 343
   ranking by managerial performance, 354
   semiautonomous operating units, 342
cabinet secretaries, 325
cable television, 248, 251, 263
   and decline in broadcast news
      audience, 267
   news viewers, by party identification, 264
   talk shows, 271
Calhoun, John C., 50, 66, 295
California
   ballot initiative to ban same-sex
      marriage, 133
   food boycotts, 127
   number of constitutional initiatives, 477
   Proposition 227, 130
   widely adopted city manager
      systems, 488
CALPIRG (California), 229
campaign finance laws, 210
campaign fund-raising
   Congressional incumbents, 278–279
   through the Internet, 183
campaigns
   candidate-centered, 211–217
   dirty-tricks, 27
   election campaigns, 317–322
   federal funds for, 335
   greater activity in United States than in
      Europe, 182
   hired guns, 211–213
   media campaigns, 214–215
   nominating campaigns, 315–316
   party-centered, 217
   platforms tailored to those who vote, 187
   presidential, 308, 318–321
Campbell, Ben Nighthorse, 126
Canada, aid to developing countries, 467

candidate-centered campaigns
   advantages, 215–216
   campaign funds, 211–215
   disadvantages, 216–217
   organization and strategy, 211–215
   voter contacts, 214–217
candidate-centered politics, 192
candidate recruitment, in party-centered
   systems, 215
Cantwell, Maria, 282–283
capital-gains tax, 412, 438
capitalist (free-market) system, 4, 17, 24
Cappella, Joseph, 263
capture theory, 232, 233
carbon emissions, 405, 406
carbon emissions, state-level plans to
   restrict, 498
career bureaucrats, 347–348
Carson, Rachel, 402–403, 403
Carter, Jimmy, 178, 216, 308, 311, 323, 329, 468
Carville, James, 212
Casey, Bob, 281
Castro, Fidel, 328
categorical grants, 75–76
Catholics, 9, 13
Cayuga, 29
CBS, 254, 262
CBS Evening News, 266
CBS News/New York Times poll, 154
Center for Media and Public Affairs, 262
Center for Voting and Democracy, 281
Center on Budget and Policy Priorities, 425
Central Intelligence Agency (CIA), 342–343,
   348, 352, 354, 359, 450
Chagall, David, 212
charters, 485–486, 487
charter schools, 489
Chavez, Cesar Estrada, 127
checks and balances, 23, 29, 38, 41–43, 45, 242
Cheney, Dick, 264, 324, 359
Cherokee, 125
Chertoff, Michael, 355
Chesterton, G. K., 7
Chicago Tribune, 254
chief diplomat, 309
chief executive, 309
chief justice of the United States, 367, 370
child labor, 70, 401, 464
Child Online Protection Act, 95
child pornography, 95
Children's Television Workshop, 352
China. *See* People's Republic of China
Chinese immigration, 9
Chinese workers, in the late 1800s, 130
Chippewa, 125
Christian Broadcasting Network, 251
Christian Coalition of America, 230
Christian Moral Government Fund, 182, 237
Christian right, 165
Chrysler, 225, 399
church-affiliated schools, public funding
   of, 96–97
church and state, separation of, 7, 96
churches, as socializing agents, 157
Churchill, Winston, 312, 450
Church of Jesus Christ of Latter-Day Saints,
   and Utah politics, 485
CIA. *See* Central Intelligence Agency (CIA)

cigarettes, 401
Citadel, 135
citizen politics
   election participation, 483–484
   group competition, 484–485
   party competition, 484
citizens' groups, 243
   advantages and disadvantages held
      by, 229
   dependence on voluntary contributions,
      226
   free-rider problem, 228
   ideological groups, 230
   offer collective (public) goods as an
      incentive for membership, 227
   public-interest groups, 228–229
   single-issue groups, 229
   types of, 228–230
citizens' participation rates, 224
Citizens Party, 204
city manager system, of municipal government, 475, 488, 500
civic attitudes, and voter turnout, 179–180
civic duty, 179
"civic literacy," 149
civil law, 378–379, 381
civil liberties, 23, 43, 86, 87
civil rights, 23, 143
Civil Rights Act of 1964, 120, 126, 129,
   135–136, 138, 143, 185, 381, 430
   Title VII, 122
Civil Rights Act of 1968, 136
civil rights and liberties, state and local
   expenditure on, 498–499
civil rights movement, 10, 103, 119, 120,
   129, 327, 484
civil service careerists, 360
Civil War, 9, 10, 66, 80, 119, 194, 195, 225, 311
Clarke, Richard, 359
class, and political opinions, 160–161
class-based political organizations, 187
class segregation, in public schools, 441
Clay, Henry, 50, 295, 323
Clean Air Act of 1963, 399, 403, 405
clear-and-present-danger test, 88
Cleland, Max, 213
Cleveland, Grover, 195
clientele groups, 352
Clinton, Bill, 265, 281, 300, 301, 310, 382
   and Arctic National Wildlife Refuge,
      403
   backed by Democratic majorities in
      House and Senate, 330
   and Balkan conflict, 163
   1996 campaign, 209
   deadlock on budgetary issues, 416
   defeat of George Bush, 197
   and EITC eligibility, 438
   health care reform proposal, 166, 187
   investigation of, 331
   judicial appointees, 377
   Lewinsky scandal, 258
   multilateralism, 452
   and NAFTA, 464
   negative press coverage, 262
   reelection, 198, 308
   and "reinventing government," 339
   rejection of unrestricted school choice, 443

and unfunded mandates, 76
and universal health care, 444
Clinton, Hillary, 122, 153, 171, 213, 216, 228, 255, 270, 465
Clinton administration, National Performance Review, 339, 360
closed primaries, 205
"closed rule," 294
cloture, 294, 297
CNN, 251, 254, 264, 265
CNN.com, 266
Cobb, David, 204
Coca-Cola PAC, 237
Cohen, Bernard, 252
The Colbert Report, 265
Cold War, 257, 451–452, 461, 469
Colegrove v. Green, 384
collective bargaining, 421
collective interest, 240
collective (public) goods, 227
college admission programs, affirmative action in, 140
college degree, by state, percentage of adults with, 11
college work-study programs, 443
colonial America, 7
colonial charters, 29
Columbia, 361
Columbia University, 250
Comedy Central, 265
commander in chief, 309
commerce clause, 66, 69
Commerce Department, 352
commerce powers, 71, 77
Commission on Civil Rights, 344
Commission on Fine Arts, 344
commission system, of municipal government, 475, 488, 500
committee system of Congress, 277, 288–292, 302
    committee chairs, 291
    committee jurisdiction, 289–290
    committee membership, 290–291
    committees and parties, 291–292
    joint committees, 289
    jurisdiction, 290
    select committees, 289
    standing committees, 288, 289, 303
    subcommittees, 288, 291, 303
Committee to Re-elect the President, 27
common-carrier function, 248, 260–261
Common Cause, 182
common good, 240
common-law tradition, 381
Common Sense (Paine), 172, 266
Communications Act, 250
Communications Office, 324
Communications Workers of America, 225
communism, 17, 398, 451
community activities, 184
comparable worth, 124
compelling news, 248
competing interests, 23
competitive parties, number of, 199
compliance, with judicial decisions, 386
Compromise of 1850, 295
computer-assisted direct mail, 228
concurrent powers, 60

concurring opinion, 370
confederacy, 59, 60
conference committee, 289, 295, 416
confronting witnesses, right of, 102, 104
Congress
    and accountability, 217
    agency oversight function, 357
    careerist members of, 302
    constitutional power to impeach the president, 330–332
    deference to president on foreign policy vs. domestic policy issues, 328
    difficulty taking lead on broad issues of national policy, 297
    disproportionately white and male, 284
    dual nature of, 275–276
    fragmentation, 298–299, 303
    influence of lobbies on, 232, 302
    influence on judicial systems, 382–383
    investigative power, 302
    key to presidential success, 326
    lawmaking function, 296–299, 303
    majoritarian impulse, 303
    members of from districts that depend on arms industry, 461
    oversight function, 296, 301–302, 304
    party leadership in, 285–288
    percentage of bills passed on which the president announced a position, 1953-2007, 331
    pluralism, 302–303
    policymaking role, 277, 296–303
    powers of, 63
    representation function, 296, 299–301, 304
    and self-government, 302
    See also committee system of Congress
Congressional Budget Office (CBO), 298, 357, 416
Congressional campaign expenditures, by decade, 279
Congressional elections, 276, 277–285
    midterm, 174, 282
    winners in, 283–285
    See also incumbency, Congressional; incumbents, Congressional
Congressional Research Service (CRS), 298
Connecticut, legal rights for same-sex couples, 133
Connor, Eugene "Bull," 120
conscientious objectors, 40
conservation, 498
conservationism, 403–404
conservative, 159
constituency, 278
Constitutional Convention of 1787, 33, 35, 36, 37–38, 313
constitutional democracy, 52
constitutional framework, 23
constitutional initiative, 476–477
constitutionalism, 4, 16–17, 24
constitutional law, 366
constitutional system, 499
Constitution of the United States, 3
    altering, 48–51
    amendment process, 39–40
    Article II, 309
    Article III, 367, 378
    checks and balances, 16

defined, 38
establishment clause, 96–97, 98
and federal courts, 379
full faith and credit clause, 133
grants and denials of power, 39–40
model for state constitutions, 477
opening words, 8
and popular influence on government, 48
Preamble, 6, 393, 425, 449
prohibitions on states, 63
provisions for limited government, 39
ratification debate, 36
supremacy clause, 475
Constitution of the United States, Amendments, 3
    First Amendment, 6, 7, 16, 86, 88, 113
    Second Amendment, 98, 99
    Fourth Amendment, 45, 85, 86, 102, 104–105, 380
    Fifth Amendment, 86, 102
    Sixth Amendment, 86, 102, 109
    Eighth Amendment, 86, 102, 107–109
    Ninth Amendment, 99
    Tenth Amendment, 58, 64, 70, 77, 80, 372, 429, 473, 475
    Eleventh Amendment, 79
    Twelfth Amendment, 318
    Fifteenth Amendment, 121, 136, 172, 483
    Seventeenth Amendment, 50, 210
    Eighteenth Amendment, 203
    Nineteenth Amendment, 121, 122, 172
    Twenty-first Amendment, 39
    Twenty-second Amendment, 310
    Twenty-fourth Amendment, 136, 172
    Twenty-sixth Amendment, 173
    See also Fourteenth Amendment
constraints of law
    constitution and its interpretation, 379–380
    legal precedents and their interpretation, 380
    statutes and administrative laws and their interpretation, 380
Consumer Product Safety Commission, 401
consumer protection, 402
containment, doctrine of, 450, 469
Continental Army, 310
contraception, 99, 101
Controlled Substances Act (CSA), 78
conventional war capability, 458–459
Conyers, John Jr., 178
Cooley, Thomas, 486
Cooley's rule, 486
Coolidge, Calvin, 9
cooperative federalism, 72–73, 81
corporate lobbyists, 231
corporate PACs, 237
Corporation for Public Broadcasting, 352
corporations, 243
correctional facilities, state and local investment in, 497
cost-benefit analysis, 400
Council of State Governments, 230
country attorneys, 486
county government, 486–487, 500
county sheriffs, 486, 487
court review, 134

courts
and a free society, 113
and issues of individual rights, 16
See also federal judicial system
crack-cocaine offenses vs. powder-cocaine
offenses, sentencing disparities,
109–110
Craig v. Boren, 135
creationism, 98
Creek Iroquois, 125
Creighton, Robert, 85
Creighton, Sarisse, 85
criminal justice system
discrimination against African
Americans, 9, 120
sentencing and incarceration policies, 110
criminal law, 379
criminal punishment, 107–110
crop subsidy programs, 409
crosscutting cleavages, 162
cruel and unusual punishment, 102,
107–108
Cruz, Ted, 374
C-SPAN, 297
Cuban Americans, 129
Cuban missle crisis, 328
cultural analysis, 23
cultural beliefs, 8, 158
cultural ideals, 23
Curb, Mike, 479
Cureton, Adrienne, 107

D

Dade County Commission, 490
Dade County Metropolitan
Government, 490
Dahl, Robert, 20
Daily Kos, 183, 251
The Daily Show, 265, 320
Daschle, Tom, 426
Das Kapital (Marx), 398
Davidson, Roger, 275, 303
Davis, Gray, 482
Dayton Accords, 453
DDT, 403
dealignment, 198
Dean, Howard, 183, 208, 316
death penalty, 103, 107–108, 153
for the mentally retarded, 109
number of executions by state,
1976-2006, 108
debates, 214–215
decision (of a court), 369
Declaration of Independence, 3, 5, 6, 7, 8,
30, 49
de facto discrimination, 137
de facto equality, 118
defendants' rights, limits on, 104–107
defense, 67
Defense of Marriage Act, 133
defense policy. *See* foreign and defense
policy; national security policy
deficit spending, 410
DeJonge v. Oregon, 91
de jure discrimination, 137
Delahunt, William D., 322

Delaware, first state to ratify the
Constitution, 37
DeLay, Tom, 236, 237, 282
delegates, 49
Dellinger, Walter, 387
demand-side fiscal policy, 411, 413
democracy, 15–16, 24
versus bureaucracy, 354
constitutional, 52
direct, 51
Jacksonian, 49
Jeffersonian, 48–49
representative, 47
versus republic, 46–47
Democratic coalition, 201
Democratic Congressional Campaign
Committee (DCCC), 209
Democratic National Committee (DNC), 208
Democratic Party, 165, 179, 193, 194
and behind social welfare and workers'
rights policies, 163
disappearance of conservative wing, 287
division over Vietnam War, 196
fiscal policy, 413
1968 nominating process, 315
recent gains among women, 202
sectional split in, 67
support for government involvement, 201
tax policy, 414
Democratic presidential nominating race,
2008, 171, 270
democratic procedures, 4
Democratic Republicans, 193
Democratic Senatorial Campaign
Committee (DSCC), 209, 216
demographic representativeness, 360
denials of power, 39
Department of Agriculture, 233, 325, 329,
347, 352, 358, 403
Department of Commerce and Labor, 347
Department of Defense, 325, 342, 343, 352,
450, 453, 469
Department of Education, 79
Department of Health and Human
Services, 79, 342
Department of Homeland Security, 77, 79,
213, 325, 342, 354–355, 453
Department of Housing and Urban
Development, 79
Department of Interior, 403
Department of Justice, 342, 343
Department of State, 342, 449, 469
Department of Transportation, 79
deregulation, 399–401
desegregation, of schools, 140–142, 442
deterrence policy, 458
developing nations, assistance to as
percentage of gross national
income, 467
devolution, 72, 76–79, 81
Dewey, Thomas, 153
Dickerson v. United States, 104
Dillon, John F., 485
Dillon's rule, 485
diplomacy, 449, 469
direct democracy, 51
direct election of senators, 53
dirty-tricks campaign, 27

disadvantaged groups, struggle for equal
rights, 118
discrimination
against African American job
applicants, 117
against African Americans, 9, 107, 119
against African Americans in criminal
justice system, 9, 120
against African Americans in farm loan
program, 9
against Chinese and other Asians, 9
government-imposed racial
segregation, 395
persistence of, 142
dissenting opinion, 370
district court judges, 370, 371
district courts, 366
District of Columbia, 318
District of Columbia v. Heller, 98–99
diversity, 24
Dixon, Robert G. Jr., 281
Dobbs, Lou, 265
dollar, declining value, 466, 468
domestic manufacturing sector, 463
"don't ask, don't tell" policy, 132
double jeopardy, 102
Douglas, Frederick, 67
Douglas, Stephen A., 194
Douglas, William O., 375
Dred Scott decision, 66–67
drivers' license fees, 492–493
Drudge Report, 251, 257
Drug Enforcement Administration (DEA), 342
dual federalism, 67, 70, 72
"dual use" policy," 403
due process of law, 43, 87, 102, 114
Duncan v. Louisiana, 103
DWB—"driving while black," 107

E

Earned Income Tax Credit (EITC), 438, 439
Earth Day, 404–405
Earthwise Legal Defense Fund, 233
Easley v. Cromartie, 137
Easton, David, 22
economic conservatism, 158, 159
economic depression, 411
economic efficiency, 398
economic equality, 445
economic exchange, 450, 469
economic groups, 224–227, 243
access to financial resources, 227
advantages and disadvantages held
by, 229
agricultural groups, 226–227
business groups, 225
labor groups, 225–226
professional groups, 227
economic growth, opinions on, 407
Economic Growth and Tax Relief
Reconciliation Act of 2001, 414
economic interdependence, 71
economic interest groups, 223–230
economic interests, government as
promoter of, 408–409
economic liberals, 158

economic policy, 414
economic recession, 411
economic redistribution, 437
economic security, 444
economy
    defined, 397
    government as regulator of, 397–402
    industrial, 71
    world, 462–463
editorializing, 251
education
    American preferences for teaching
        children about the nation's
        history, 10
    church-affiliated schools, 96–97
    as equality of opportunity, 11, 439–444
    political differences about federal role
        in, 442–444
    and political socialization, 155
    public opinion on assistance to, 161
    traditional domain of state and local
        governments, 57
    See also federal education policy; higher
        education; public education
Education Amendment of 1972, Title IX, 122
Education for All Handicapped Children
    Act of 1975, 131
effective tax rate, 437
efficiency, 398, 399
Egypt, 461, 468
Eisenhower, Dwight D., 195, 257, 322, 376,
    454, 460–461
Elazar, Daniel, 490
elected officials, 352
2004 election, Florida ballots, 384
2008 election, electoral vote strategy in, 319
election activity, as outside lobbying, 236–239
election day registration, 483
election-day registration policy, 178
"the election game," 211
elections
    as basic form of self-government in
        modern democracies, 15
    free, 15
    local, 174
    national, 310
    popular, 52
    primary, 12, 28, 50, 52, 177, 205, 217,
        315–319
    recall, 50
    of senators, 50, 53
    single-member-district system of,
        199–200, 217
    state, 212
    virtual participation in, 182–184
    See also presidential selection
electoral and party systems, 199–211
Electoral College, 36, 48, 53, 314, 322
electoral vote system, 15–16, 48
    linked to the popular vote, 314
    votes equal in number to state's repre-
        sentation in Congress, 318
    winner-take all feature, 319
Elementary and Secondary Education Act,
    442, 443
elitism, 19, 20–21
elitist rule, 4
email, 215

Emancipation Proclamation, 195
"embedded" correspondents, 258
embryonic-stem-cell research, 329
en banc, 371
Endangered Species Act (ESA) of 1973, 404
enemy combatants, detention of, 114
energy efficiency, 405
Energy Independence and Security Act, 407
energy policy, and global warming,
    405–407
Engel v. Vitale, 96
England. See Britain
English common law, 120, 380
Enlightenment period, 5
entitlement programs, 431, 434
enumerated (expressed) powers, 63
environment
    government as protector of, 402–407
    opinions on, 407
environment, state and local expenditure
    on, 497–498
Environmental Defense Fund, 229, 233
environmental groups, 229
environmental impact statements, 498
environmentalism, 235, 402, 404–407
Environmental Protection Agency (EPA),
    343, 399, 402, 405, 420
Enzi, Mike, 493
equal access
    accommodations and jobs, 135–136
    housing, 136
Equal Credit Act of 1974, 122
equality, 4, 6–7, 24, 159
    Americans' commitment to, 10–12
    defined, 6
    under the law, 118, 134–137
    not an American birthright, 9
    of opportunity, 439–440
    of result, 137–142
equality, struggle for
    African Americans, 118–124
    Asian Americans, 129–130
    disabled Americans, 131
    gays and lesbians, 131–134
    Hispanic Americans, 126–129
    Native Americans, 124–126
    older Americans, 130–131
    women, 120–124
Equal Pay Act of 1963, 122
equal protection clause, 134, 385
Equal Rights Amendment (ERA), 122
equal rights (or civil rights), 118
equity (in relation to economic policy), 401
Era of Good Feeling, 193
Espionage Act of 1917, 88
establishment clause, 96–97, 98
ethanol, 407
ethnic cleansing, 453
ethnic profiling, 107, 111, 112
euro, 466
Europe
    aid to developing countries, 467
    effective tax rate, 437
    judges, 381
    news systems, 253
    parliamentary systems, 53, 326
    parties, 201
    policies that redistribute wealth, 18

revolutions, 18
    welfare programs, 436, 444–445
European Recovery Plan, 463
European Union (EU), 461, 463, 469
excessive bail or fines, 102
excise tax, 492
exclusionary rule, 105–106, 114
executive agreements, 309–310
executive branch, 16
executive budget, 313
executive bureaucratic management, 354–355
executive leadership system, 348–349, 349,
    350, 361
Executive Office of the President (EOP),
    323, 348, 355, 356, 414
executive policy leadership, systems of, 326
executive power, unwarranted assertions
    of, 331
executive privilege, 302
"exigent circumstances," 85
expert knowledge, 351–352
ex post facto laws, 39
expressed powers, doctrine of, 43
externalities, 399

F

factional (minor) party, 204
factions, 40, 242
facts (of a court case), 378
Fair Labor Standards Act of 1938, 401
Fairness Doctrine, 250, 251, 263
fair trade, 464
fair-trial rights, 114
faith-based initiatives, 97
families, as agents of political
    socialization, 155
Family and Medical Leave Act of 1993, 124
family courts, 481
family income, by race and ethnicity, 137
Faragher v. City of Boca Raton, 381
Fargo, North Dakota, commission system
    of municipal government, 488
farm organizations, 226, 233, 243
farm subsidies, 20, 395–396, 465
farmworkers' strikes, 126
FBI. See Federal Bureau of Investigation (FBI)
federal accountability, 361–362
federal administration, 340–346
federal air traffic controllers, 345
federal budget deficit, 339
federal budget dollar, fiscal year 2009, 410
federal bureaucracy, 339–340
    agencies, 357
    big government and the executive
        leadership system, 348–349
    blend of the political and the adminis-
        trative, 346
    cabinet departments, 342
    consequence of complexity and
        scale, 340
    development of, 346–349
    government corporations, 344
    growth in government and the merit
        system, 347–348
    implementing of policy, 361
    independent agencies, 342–343

federal bureaucracy (*continued*)
  personnel management systems, 361
  policy responsibilities, 345–346
  presidential commissions, 344
  regulatory agencies, 343–344
  small government and the patronage
    system, 346
  structure of, 342–344
federal bureaucratic accountability, 353–360
  within the bureaucracy itself, 359–360
  demographic representatives, 359–360
  and executive budget, 356–357
  presidential appointments, 355–356
  through Congress, 357–358
  through the courts, 358
  through the presidency, 354–357
  whistle-blowing, 359
federal bureaucratic power, sources of,
    350–353
  power of clientele groups, 352
  power of expertise, 351–352
  power of friends in high places,
    352–353
federal bureaucrats, educational back-
    grounds of, 351
Federal Bureau of Investigation (FBI),
    342, 354
Federal Communications Commission
    (FCC), 250, 251, 346
federal contracts, preference to minority-
    owned firms, 139–140
"federal court myth," 373, 374, 389
Federal Deposit Insurance Corporation
    (FDIC), 71, 344
federal education policy
  and affirmative action, 140
  Bush policies, 443
  federal education grants, 442
Federal Election Campaign Act of 1974, 316
Federal Election Commission (FEC), 211
Federal Emergency Management Agency
    (FEMA), 355
federal employment
  GS (Graded Service) job ranking, 345
  job ranks (GS) of various demographic
    groups, 360
  merit system, 345
  number of employees, 347, 474
  salaries, 345
federal grants-in-aid to states and localities,
    74, 75, 491
federalism, 38, 58–64, 80, 224
  argument for, 60–63
  contemporary, 72–80
  defined, 59
  division of responsibilities, 60
  division of sovereign authority between
    national government and area or
    state governments, 476
  dynamic nature of, 474
  era of dual federalism and laissez-faire
    capitalism (1865-1937), 67–71
  era of indestructible union (1789-1865),
    64–67
  examples of national, state, and concur-
    rent powers, 60
  in historical perspective, 64–72
  and localism, 499

  moderating the power of government,
    61–62
  national authority, 70–71
  powers of the nation, 63
  powers of the states, 64
  protection of liberty, 61
  states'-rights view, 66–67
  strengthening the union, 62–63
  system of divided powers, 60
Federalist No. 10, 8, 22, 40, 52, 62, 224, 225, 242
Federalist No. 28, 61
Federalist No. 47, 37
Federalist No. 48, 37
Federalist No. 49, 37
Federalist No. 50, 37
Federalist No. 51, 27, 37
Federalist No. 69, 309
Federalist No. 76, 310
Federalist No. 78, 367
Federalist Papers, 37
Federalist Party, 193
Federalists, 36–37
federal jobs program, 71
federal judges, life tenure, 367
federal judges, selection of, 374–378
  lower-court nominees, 376
  nominated and appointed to office by
    president, 48, 367, 389
  Supreme Court nominees, 375–376
  See also judicial appointees; judicial
    appointment process
federal judicial system, 366, 371, 389
  sources of law that constrain the
    decisions of, 379
  special U.S. courts, 372
  Supreme Court of the United States,
    367–370
  U.S. courts of appeals, 371–372, 389
  U.S. district courts, 367, 370–371, 389
  See also judiciary
federal minimum wage standards, 77
Federal Reserve Act of 1913, 418
Federal Reserve Board ("the Fed"), 21,
    418–420
federal revenue sharing, 491
federal social programs, 80
federal-state power, public's influence
    in setting the boundaries of,
    79–80
federal system, 58
federal tax policy, 63, 74, 410–414, 417, 491
  capital-gains tax, 412, 438
  partisanship and, 414
  shift of taxation from corporations to
    individuals, 408
  wealthiest individuals as major benefici-
    aries of, 437, 438, 439
  See also tax rates
Federal Trade Commission (FTC), 352, 355,
    399, 450
federal versus unitary governments, 61
Federline, Kevin, 255
Feingold, Russell, 94
Feldman, Stanley, 445
Felker v. Turpin, 106
FEMA, 325, 356
"the feminization of poverty," 428
Fenno, John, 249

Ferguson v. Charleston, 105
Ferraro, Geraldine, 122
Ferris, J. L., 49
filibuster, 294
financial crisis of 2008, 21, 225, 401, 420
firefighters, 487
First Bank of the United States, 37, 65
First Continental Congress, 30
first-strike nuclear attack, 458
fiscal federalism, 74–75
fiscal policy, 37, 394, 409–417, 421
  budgetary process, 414–417
  demand-side, 411, 413
  and partisan differences, 413–414
  summary of, 410
  supply-side, 411–412, 439
  taxing and spending policy and politics,
    410–414, 417
Fishe v. Kansas, 91
527 groups, 210
flag burning, 89, 93, 94
focus groups, 212
Foley, Mark, 282
Food and Drug Administration (FDA),
    232–233, 399, 401, 402, 420
food stamp program, 496
Food Stamps program, 435
Ford, Gerald, 308, 405
Ford Motor Company, 225, 399
Ford Motor Company Civic Action Fund, 237
foreign aid, 450, 467–468
foreign and defense policy
  Cold War era, 451–452
  instruments of, 449–450
  and Iraq War, 454–457
  roots of, 450–457
  war on terrorism, 453–454
  See also national security policy
foreign government lobbying, 230
Foreign Intelligence Surveillance Act
    (FISA), 45, 113
formalized rules, 340, 341, 342, 361
Fourteenth Amendment, 113, 499
  age and disability not protected by, 79
  due process clause, 90–91, 102, 103, 374
  equal protection clause, 86, 87, 134–136,
    143, 365, 369
  and state discretion, 68–69, 70
Fox News, 251, 254, 264
Foxwoods, 126
frames of reference, and political
    socialization, 157–166
framing, 261
France
  chief executive office, 326
  child poverty rate, 429
  unitary government, 61
"frank," 278
Frank, Jerome, 370
Franken, Bob, 263
Frankfurter, Felix, 102, 384
Franklin, Benjamin, 29, 33, 35, 49
Free, Lloyd, 18, 186
freedom of expression, 87–95
  limits on, 113
  limits on authority of states to restrict,
    91–93
  in modern period, 88–90

and state governments, 90–93
    uncertain status of in early period, 88
freedom of religion, 95–99
free elections, 15
free-enterprise, 414
free-exercise clause, 97–98
free-market principle, 17, 24, 398, 409, 465
free-rider problem, 228, 243
Free Soil Party, 203
free speech, 16, 20, 43, 87, 89–90
free states, 66
free television time, 214
free trade, 463–464, 465
French and Indian War, 29, 310
Freneau, Philip, 249
Friedman, Milton, 418
fuel-efficient vehicles, 225
"full faith and credit" provision, 475
Fullilove v. Klutznick, 139
Fundamentalist Protestants, 160, 202
fund-raising specialists, 212

G

Gaebler, Ted, 360
Gallup polls, 80, 151, 153, 154, 164
gambling revenues, state, 493
game wardens, 497
Garcia v. San Antonio Authority, 77
Garfield, James A., 347, 348
Garry, Joan, 132
gasoline, price of, 407
gasoline, state taxes on, 492
gays and lesbians
    "don't ask-don't tell" policy of military, 131
    legal status of at state and local levels, 499
    opinions on in U.S. and western
        European countries, 133
Gazette of the United States, 249
G8 summit, 449
gender
    as intermediate category for Supreme
        Court, 135
    and political opinions, 161–162
gender bias
    toward women's role in the home, 125
    in U.S. vs. Europe, 124
gender gap, 202
    in opinions and votes, 122–123
    in salaries and wages, 124
general election campaigns, federal funds
    for, 335
General Motors, 225, 399
*The General Theory of Employment, Interest,
    and Money* (Keynes), 410
general welfare, American way of promot-
    ing, 444–445
Geneva Conventions, 111, 114, 359
George III, 30, 31
German Green Party, 200
Germany
    Bundesrat, 287
    electoral system, 200
    federal system, 61
    trading rival of U.S., 463
    Weimar Republic, 52
Gerry, Elbridge, 280

gerrymandering, 280, 281
get-out-the-vote drives, 207, 209, 212, 215
Gettysburg Address, 7, 195
G.I. Bill, 443
Gibbons v. Ogden, 65–66
Gideon, Clarence, 104, 387
Gideon v. Wainwright, 103, 104, 370, 386, 387
Gingrich, Newt, 76, 200, 352
Ginsburg, Ruth Bader, 101, 375, 377, 384
Gitlow, Benjamin, 90
Gitlow v. New York, 90–91
glass ceiling, 124
global economic competitiveness, 400, 463, 468
global terrorism, 468
global trade, promotion of, 463–466
global warming, 405–407, 498
Glorious (Bloodless) Revolution of 1689, 95
Goldberg, Bernard, 262
Goldwater, Barry, 200
Gonzales v. Carhart, 101
Gonzales v. Raich, 78, 79
Gonzalez, Alberto, 45
Goodsell, Charles, 353
Google News, 266
GOP ("Grand Old Party"). *See* Republican
    Party
Gorbachev, Mikhail, 451
Gordon, Anne, 259
Gore, Al, 204, 215, 317, 322, 339, 384, 406
Gorton, Slade, 282
governing authority, division of, 16
government, as promoter of economic
        interests
    promotion of agriculture, 409
    promotion of business, 408
    promotion of labor, 408
Government Accountability Office (GAO),
        298, 357, 361
government corporations, 344, 345
government intervention
    and business payment for indirect
        costs, 399
    deregulation, 399–401
    efficiency through, 398–401
    equity through, 401
    preventing price fixing, 398–399
government-issued photo identification
        card, 177, 178
government revenues, and intergovern-
        mental relations, 73–76
graduated (or progressive) personal income
        tax, 414
Grant, Ulysses S., 322
granted powers, 39, 53
grants-in-aid, 74, 79, 81
grassroots lobbying, 223, 236
grassroots party, 194, 206
Gratz v. Bollinger, 139, 140
Gravina Island, 275
graying of America, 162
Great Britain. *See* Britain
Great Compromise, 33, 37
Great Depression, 12, 70, 71, 79, 154, 167,
        311, 313, 358, 393, 401, 409, 430
Great Society, 72, 79, 430, 442
"Great Triumvirate," 295
Greek city-states, 60
Greenback Party, 203

Greenfield, Meg, 258
"greenhouse effect," 405–406
Green Party, 204
Greenpeace, 182, 402, 498
Greenpeace U.S.A., 229
Greenspan, Alan, 412
Griswold v. Connecticut, 99, 101
Gross Domestic Product (GDP), 18
group orientations, 167
group system, 239–243
group thinking, 159–162
Grutter v. Bollinger, 139, 140
Guantanamo Bay, 111
guerrilla war capability, 457, 458–459
guest worker program, 127, 128
Guiteau, Charles, 347, 348
Gulf War, 452, 466
gun control, 18, 99

H

habeas corpus appeals, 106–107
Hamdan v. Rumsfeld, 112
Hamdi v. Rumsfeld, 111
Hamilton, Alexander, 7, 35, 37, 61, 64–65,
        80, 193, 249, 302, 309, 310, 367
Hamilton v. Regents, University of California, 91
Hammer v. Dagenhart, 70
handgun control laws, 236
Handgun Violence Prevention Act (the
        so-called Brady bill), 77
Hannity, Sean, 264
Hanseatic League, 60
"hard events," 255
Harding, Warren, 358
hard money, 209
Hargrove, Erwin, 327
Harlan, John Marshall, 68
Harrington, Michael, 428
Harrison, Benjamin, 49, 314, 319
Harry, Prince, 257
Hartz, Louis, 6
Hastert, Dennis, 200, 285
Hatch, Orrin, 290
Hatch Act of 1939, 345
hate crimes, 92
hate speech, 92
Hayes, Rutherford B., 49, 314
HBO, 265
Head Start program, 440
health care, 17
    state and local spending on, 494, 496
Hearst, William Randolph, 249, 250
Heclo, Hugh, 335
Hein v. Freedom from Religion, 97
Helms, Jesse, 468
Henry, Patrick, 59
Heritage Foundation, 439
"a heroic presidency," 308
Hibbing, John, 282
hierarchical authority, 340, 341, 361
higher education
    and equality of opportunity, 11
    mainly a state and local responsibility, 495
Higher Education Act, 442, 443
highway patrol, 497
highways, state and local spending on,
        496–497

hired guns, 211–213
Hispanic Americans
    civil rights movement, 126–127
    family income, 137
    growing political power, 128–129
    legal and political action, 126–128
    nation's largest racial or ethnic minority
        group, 126
    party identification, *129*
    and poverty, 428
    representation in state legislatures, 121
Hispanic immigration, 9
historical reasoning, 23
The History of the Standard Oil Company
    (Tarbell), 257
Hitler, Adolf, 16, 17, 52
Hobbes, Thomas, 14, 15
Holmes, Oliver Wendell, 66, 88, 378, 387
homeland security, state and local
        provision for, 497
home mortgages, tax deductions for, 438
home rule, 486
Homestead Act of 1862, 409
homosexual acts among consenting adults,
        101–102
Honest Leadership and Open Government
        Act of 2007, 231
honeymoon period, 327
Hoover, Herbert, 195, 311, 325, 358
Hoover Commissions, 339, 358
House Interior Committee, 299
House of Commons, 287
House of Lords, 287
House of Representatives, 28, 61, 276
    age and citizenship requirements, 283
    Agriculture Committee, 299
    Appropriations Committee, 357, 416
    direct popular election of, 47
    Foreign Affairs subcommittees, 288
    incumbents, 283
    incumbents, and redistricting, 279–280
    leadership, 285–286
    majority leader, 286
    majority whip, 286
    minority leader, 286
    minority whip, 286
    number of Democrats and Republicans
        in, 1999-2010, 285
    in original constitution, 482
    and reapportionment, 280
    Rules Committee, 285, 291, 294
    Speaker of the House, 277, 285–286, 303
    standing committees, 288
    Ways and Means Committee, 291
housing discrimination, 136
how a bill becomes law, 292–295
Hudson, Booker, 106
Hudson v. Michigan, 106
Huffington, Arianna, 266
Huffington Post, 266
Humphrey, Hubert, 52, 315
Hurricane Katrina, 275, 325, 355
Hussein, Saddam, 147, 213, 329, 348, 452,
        454, 455, 456, 467
Hutchison, Kay Bailey, 298
Hutto v. Davis, 371
hydrogen fuel cells, 407
Hyot, Clark, 260

I

ideological groups, 230
ideological (minor) party, 204
ideological thinking, 158
ideology, 158, 159, 167
illegal immigrants, 127, 128
illegally obtained evidence, 105, 114
immigration, 9, 10, 13, 66, 240
Immigration and Naturalization Service
        (INS), 353
imminent lawless action test, 88, 92
impeachment, 43, 330–331
"the imperial presidency," 307, 308
implied powers, 63, 65
inalienable (natural) rights, 30
incandescent light bulbs, 407
incarceration rates by county, 110
income
    and tax policies, 437–438
    and voter turnout, 181
income inequality in the U.S., 437
Inconvenient Truth (Gore), 406
incremental policies, 396
incumbency, Congressional
    advantages, 303
    disadvantages, 303
    pitfalls of, 280–283
    use of to stay in Congress, 277–283
incumbents, Congressional, 276, 283
    campaign fund-raising, 211, 278–279
    and disruptive issues, 280–281
    personal misconduct, 282
    and redistricting, 279–280
    reelection rates, 277
    service strategy, 278
    strong challengers to, 282–283
    and turnout variation, 282
independent agencies, 342, 344
independents, 198
India, demand for oil, 407
Indianapolis v. Edmund, 104–105
Indian Bill of Rights, 126
indirect primary, 315
individual-benefit programs, 445
individualism, 6, 8, 24, 167, 445, 490
individual rights, 12, 16, 23, 87
industrial economy, must be subject to
        national regulation, 71
Industrial Revolution, 67, 360
infant mortality, of whites and African
        Americans, 142
inflation
    annual rate, 1979-2008, 413
    controlling, 412–413
information age, 360
information gap, 249, 270
initiative process, 50, 51, 238, 477, 482, 483
in-kind benefit, 435
inputs, 22, 23, 398
inside lobbying, 231–235, 236, 243
Instapundit, 251
institutional analysis, 23
institutionalized racism, 69
integration, 161
intelligence gathering, 450, 469
intelligence-gathering wiretaps, 112–113
intelligent design, 98

Intercollegiate Studies Institute, 149
interdependence, 72, 73, 80
interest groups, 221–223, 242
    characteristics, 222
    citizens' groups, 227
    economic interest groups, 223–230
    focus on issues of direct concern to
        members, 223
    governments, 230
    and group's interest versus public
        interest, 223
    influence on judicial decisions, 382
    and initiative process, 238, 483
    and issues neglected by political
        parties, 240
    liberalism, 240–241
    in the policy process, 233–235
    and public or collective goods, 223
interest rate, 418
intergovernmental lobbying, 230
intergovernmental relations, 72
intermediate scrutiny, 134
International Association of Fire Fighters
        (IAFF), 486
International Association of Machinists, 226
International Brotherhood of Electrical
        Workers, 225
International Brotherhood of Teamsters, 226
International Criminal Court (ICC), 453
internationalism, 450
International Monetary Fund (IMF), 450, 467
international trade, 450
Internet
    blogs, 251, 252, 266, 271
    and citizens' groups, 228, 229
    exemption from sales tax, 493
    as instrument of mass political
        participation, 183
    medium of election politics, 215
    mostly liberal, 265–266
    news, 251, 266, 268–269
    new venue for political participation, 182
    sites, 248
Internet Tax Freedom Act (ITFA), 493
interstate commerce, 64, 67, 69
Interstate Commerce Act, 399
Interstate Commerce Commission (ICC), 399
interstate highway system, 496–497
intrastate commerce, 64, 67
"invisible hand," 397
Iran, 455, 456
Iran-Contra scandal, 258, 308
Iraq, 111, 163
    allegations of abuse in U.S. military
        prisons, 258
    invasion of Kuwait, 452, 466
    U.S. invasion of, 149, 258, 469
Iraq War, 89, 197, 459
    buildup to, 329
    and Bush's approval rating, 333
    and Bush's "war on terrorism," 307
    and foreign and defense policy, 454–457
    and global terrorism, 468
    impact on European opinion of U.S., 455
    issue of withdrawal, 456
    protests against, 16, 186
    public opinion of, 147, 460
    reconstruction phase, 456–457, 460, 467

and Republican loss of favor, 197
  spending for, 415
"iron curtain," 450
"iron law of oligarchy," 21
iron triangles, 233–234, 235, 242, 353, 395
Iroquois Confederacy, 29
isolationism, 312, 450
Israel, U.S. foreign aid to, 468
issue advocacy, 211
issue networks, 234–235
issue voting, 206
Is Voting for Young People?
  (Wattenberg), 268
Izaak Walton League, 229

J

J. P. Morgan, 419
Jackson, Andrew, 296
  and Battle of New Orleans, 225
  as "champion of the people,"
    193, 213, 311
  and "doctrine of nullification," 66
  and electoral college, 49
  and grassroots parties, 194
  patronage system, 346–347
  and system of presidential nomination,
    314–315
Jacksonian democracy, 49, 479
Jacksonian Democrats, 206
Jackson State University, 186
Jacobs, Lawrence, 165
Jamieson, Kathleen Hall, 263
Japan
  aid to developing countries, 467
  trading rival of U.S., 463
Japanese Americans, forced relocation of,
    110–111
Jay, John, 37
Jefferson, Thomas
  and Adams' judicial appointees, 44
  and Bill of Rights, 43, 85
  and Democratic Party, 225
  and Hamilton, 37
  handwritten draft of Declaration of
    Independence, 31
  and Iroquois Confederacy, 29
  Jeffersonian democracy, 48–49
  and John Marshall, 388
  and *National Gazette*, 249
  opposition to federal bank, 65
  principal author of Declaration of
    Independence, 6–7, 8, 30
  rumors about sex life, 213
  on the Sedition Act, 88
  supporter of states' rights, 193
Jeffersonian democracy, 48–49
Jeffords, James, 307
Jews, 9, 13
Jim Crow, 9, 12, 176
job discrimination, 117, 135, 360
job specialization, 340, 341, 361
Johnson, Andrew, 330, 332
Johnson, Gregory Lee, 89
Johnson, Lyndon B., 200, 315, 430
  civil rights and social welfare
    legislation, 327

decision not to seek reelection in
    1968, 451
  Great Society program, 72, 80, 430, 442
  and issue of public health, 396
  and stronger role for government, 76
  success with Congress, 330
  and Vietnam War, 307
  and Voting Rights Act, 120, 143, 430
Joint Committee on the Library, 289
joint committees, 289
journalism schools, 250
judicial activism, doctrine of, 386, 389
judicial appointees
  characteristics of, 377–378
  overwhelming white men, 377
  as political officials, 376–378
  women and minority-group
    members, 377
judicial appointment process, 382
  and partisan politics, 376–377, 389
judicial branch, 16
judicial conference, 369
judicial decisions
  constraints on, 378–380
  and justices' political beliefs, 383–385
  outside influences on, 382–383
  political influences on, 381–385
  restricted in scope, 378
judicial lobbying, 233
judicial power, 381
  and democratic government, 385–388
  limits of, 385
judicial restraint, doctrine of, 386, 389
judicial review, 28, 42, 44, 367–368, 381,
    386–387, 388
judicial selection commission, 373
judicial supremacy, in economic sphere, 70
judiciary
  debates on proper role, 386–388
  as policymaking body, 366
  as political as well as legal institution,
    366
  See also federal judicial system
jurisdiction, 367
jury trial, right to, 109
justice of the peace courts, 481

K

Kaiser Family Foundation, 267
Kaplan, Robert, 187
Kay, David, 348, 455
Kennedy, Anthony, 101, 112, 370, 375, 384
Kennedy, John F., 320, 322, 327, 328, 433
Kennedy, Robert F., 127
Kent State University, 186
Kernell, Samuel, 334
Kerry, John, 211, 262, 264, 316
Key, V. O., Jr., 147
Keynes, John Maynard, 410, 411
Kimel v. Florida Board of Regents, 79
King, Martin Luther, Jr., 3, 46, 107, 117,
    120, 127
Kiriakou, John, 359
Klaas, Polly, 253
Klobuchar, Amy, 290–291
Klopfer v. North Carolina, 103

"knock-and-announce" rule, 106
Kohut, Andy, 153
Korean War, 451, 469
Kosovo, 163
K Street, 231
Ku Klux Klan, 92
Kurds, 457
Kuwait, 452, 466
Kyoto agreement, 406, 453

L

labor-management disputes, 71
labor parties, 177
labor practices, 400
labor unions, 215, 226, 227, 237, 243
laissez-faire economics, 69, 80, 397, 398
land conservation, 403
Länder, 287
land-grant universities, 443
land mines, international treaty banning, 266
Lane, Robert, 186, 445
large government, favors executive author-
    ity at expense of legislative
    authority, 313
large-state plan, 33
Larry King Live, 320
Lasswell, Harold, 12
Latinos. *See* Hispanic Americans
Lau v. Nichols, 129–130
law (as enacted by Congress), 295
law enforcement, state and local, 497
lawmaking function, fragmentation as a
    limit on Congress, 296
law (of a court case), 378
Lawrence v. Texas, 102, 131, 374
leaded gasoline, 401
lead paint, 401
League of Nations, 312
*League of United Latin American Voters v.
    Perry*, 137
League of Women Voters, 229
Leahy, Patrick, 8, 45–46, 290
Lee v. Weisman, 370
legal action, 233
legal analysis, 23
legal counsel, right to, 102, 104
legislative branch, 16
legislative leadership and authority,
    287, 309
legislative referendum, 51
Legislative Reorganization Act of 1946, 289
Legislative Reorganization Act of 1970,
    301
legitimacy (of judicial power), 385
"lesson of Vietnam," 451
lethal injections, 109
Letter to the Sheriffs of Bristol (Burke), 47
Leviathan (Hobbes), 14
Levin, Carl, 349
Lewinsky, Monica, 258, 308, 331
libel, 93, 257
liberal, 159
libertarian, 159
Libertarian Party, 204
liberty, 4, 6, 7, 8, 12, 24, 30, 159
Library of Congress, 96, 289

license and user fees, levied by states, 492–493
Liebling, A. J., 265
lieutenant governor, 478
life, inalienable right, 30
lifestyle liberals, 165
Limbaugh, Rush, 263, 265
limited government, 23, 28, 29, 38–46, 53
limited popular rule, 47–48
Lincoln, Abraham, 3, 7, 11, 67, 142, 194, 195, 213, 295, 296
Lippmann, Walter, 171, 270
liquor control officers, 497
literacy rates, 267
literacy tests, 136
living constitution theory, 388
lobbying, 240, 243
    of Congress, 232, 302
    of courts, 233
    of executive agencies, 232–233
    grassroots, 223, 236
    groups, 182, 241, 300
    influence through official contacts, 230–235
    inside, 231–235, 236, 243
    intergovernmental, 230
    outside, 231, 235–239, 243
    strategies, 231, 232
Lobbying Disclosure Act of 1995, 231
local elections, 490–491
    at-large (community-wide) districts, 491
    voter turnout, 174, 491
local government
    charters, 485–486
    employees of, 474, 486
    lack of sovereignty, 475
    local elections and participation, 490–491
    ordinances, 486
    policy priorities, 494
    public education expense, 494
    public safety expense, 494
    sewage and garbage disposal, 498
    source of most public employment, 486
    spending priorities of, 495
    structure of, 485–491
    tax breaks or incentives to lure businesses, 492
    taxes, 494
    weak tax levying position, 492
local government, types of
    county government, 486–487
    municipal government, 487–489
    school districts, 489, 500
    special districts and metropolitan government, 489–490
    towns and townships, 489
localism, in a large nation, 499
local party organizations, 207, 217
local police forces, 107–110, 487, 494, 497
local public employees, "first providers" in war on terrorism, 497
local representation, occurs through committee system, 299
local revenue, sources of, 494
local sales tax, 494
local school boards, 489
local television stations, national news coverage, 254
Lochner v. New York, 70

Locke, John, 7, 15, 30, 61, 95
Locke v. Davey, 97
logging industry, 404
logrolling, 299
Long, Huey, 490
Los Angeles County, 487
Los Angeles Times, 254
Losing Ground (Murray), 428
Lott, Trent, 252, 287
Louisiana Territory, 8
Lowi, Theodore, 240
Lumbee, 125
lynching, 9

M

MacManus, Susan: Young v. Old, 162
Maddow, Rachel, 264
Madison, James, 310
    and Adams' judicial appointees, 44
    and Bill of Rights, 43
    and Constitutional Convention, 33
    on economic self-interest, 224
    "father of the Constitution," 225
    on federal and state powers, 80
    on federalism, 69
    Federalist No. 10, 8–9, 22, 40, 52, 62
    Federalist No. 51, 27
    and Federalist Papers, 37
    misgivings about parties, 193
    on protection of liberty, 38
    and public opinion, 152
    on self-interest, 80, 242
magistrate courts, 481
Maine, 250
majoritarianism, 19–20
majority, tyranny of, 46
majority opinion, 370
majority rule, 4, 8, 15, 16, 28
Malloy v. Hogan, 103
mandatory retirement ages, 131
Mapp, Dollree, 103
Mapp v. Ohio, 103, 105
Marbury, William, 44
Marbury v. Madison, 44, 53, 368, 370, 381, 387, 388
March on Washington for Jobs and Freedom, 120
marginal tax rates, 438
Marshall, John, 44, 65, 66, 365, 370, 386, 387, 388
Marshall, Thurgood, 377
Marshall Plan, 312, 463
Martin, Luther, 35
Marx, Karl, 398
Mashantunket Pequots, 126
Mason, George, 35, 59
Massachusetts
    redistricting, 280
    and same-sex marriage, 132, 133
master of public administration (MPA), 488
matching funds, 74
Matthews, Chris, 264–265
mayor-council system, of municipal government, 488
mayors, 488–489
McCain, John, 3, 216, 266
    agreement with Bush tax cuts, 438

    allegations against in press, 260
    and "battleground" states, 318
    debates with Obama, 320
    health care insurance plan, 444
    and New Hampshire primary, 316
    position on U.S. military presence in Iraq, 328
    2008 presidential campaign, 192, 197, 216, 316, 319, 320
    2008 Republican nominee, 191
    running mate, 317
    on withdrawal from Iraq, 456
McCarthy, Joseph, 257
McClure's, 257
McCreary County v. American Civil Liberties Union, 96
McCulloch, Edwin, 65
McCulloch v. Maryland, 64–65, 370, 388
McGavick, Mike, 283
McGovern, George, 200, 317
McInturff, Bill, 152
McKernan, Signe-Mary, 428
McKinney, Cynthia, 204
McNabb v. United States, 102
means test, 433
media
    as common carrier, 271
    four basic functions, 271
    freedom from libel judgments, 257
    "no prior restraint," 257
    and partisanship, 270, 271
    and the public in Internet age, 269–270
    as socializing agents, 156
    traditional, 249, 262–263, 270, 271
    watchdog function, 271
    See also news media
media campaign, 214–215
    See also television
media consultants, 212
"media reality," 252
Medicaid, 72–73, 80, 396, 430, 435–436, 494, 496
medical marijuana, 78, 79
Medicare, 80, 396, 398, 415, 430, 432–433, 445
Medvedev, Dmitry, 449
melting pot, 9
Merck, 233
Meredith v. Jefferson County Board of Education, 365
merit (civil service) system, 206, 347, 349, 350
merit plan (Missouri Plan), 373
Merit Service Protection Board, 345
merit system, 361
metropolitan government, 490
Mexicans, illegal entry into U.S., 13
Michels, Roberto, 21
Middle Eastern immigration, 9
Middle Eastern oil fields, 466
midterm congressional elections, 174, 282
migrant workers, labor rights for, 127
military coups, 17
military courts-martial, 372
military draft, 458, 459
military establishment, 461
military force, 469
military-industrial complex, 460–461
military power, uses, and capabilities
    conventional and guerrilla war capability, 458–459
    nuclear war capability, 458

military spending, worldwide, 457
Mill, John Stuart, 184
Millennium Challenge Account program, 468
Miller, James III, 355
Miller v. California, 95
Mills, C. Wright, 21
Milosevic, Slobodan, 453
minimum wage, 401, 409, 421
minority-group members
    in at-large districts, 491
    disproportionately harsh prison sentences, 109
    judicial appointees, 377
    in poverty, 428
    underrepresentation in top jobs of federal bureaucracy, 360
    See also African Americans; Asian Americans; Hispanic Americans
minor (third) parties, 202–204
Minow, Newton, 256
Miranda, Ernesto, 104
Miranda v. Arizona, 103, 104
"Miranda warning," 104
Missouri Compromise, 66, 67
Missouri Plan, 373, 481–482
Missouri v. Siebert, 104
Mitchell, Daniel, 439
Mitchell, John, 258
mixed economies, 398
Mohawk, 29
Molinari, Susan, 178
momentum (in campaigns), 315–316
Mondale, Walter, 323
monetarists, 417–418
monetary policy, 21, 394, 413, 417–420, 421
money chase, 211
monopoly, 69, 399
Monroe, James, 193
Montesquieu, Charles-Louis de Secondat, Baron de, 40, 61
moralistic subculture, 490
Mormon Temple, Salt Lake City, 485
Morrill Act, 443
Morris, Dick, 212
"motor voter" law, 176
Mott, Lucretia, 121
MoveOn, 183, 211, 228, 229, 230
MSNBC, 254, 264
MSNBC.com, 266
Muckrakers, 257
mud-slinging, 216
multilateralism, 452, 453, 469
multinational corporations, 463
multiparty systems, 199, 200, 201
multiple balloting, 175
municipal charters, 487–488
municipal government, 487–489
    city manager system, 475, 488
    commission system, 475, 488
    common forms of, 486
    strong mayor-council system, 475, 488
    weak mayor-council system, 475, 488
municipalities, 475, 500
Murdoch, Rupert, 251, 263, 264
Murray, Charles, 428
Murrow, Edward R., 257
Myrdal, Gunnar, 142
mythic ideas, 8

N

Nader, Ralph, 204, 317
Napoleon, 8
Napolitan, Joe, 211
National Aeronautics and Space Administration (NASA), 343, 351
National Association for the Advancement of Colored People (NAACP), 230
National Association of Automobile Dealers, 240
National Association of Counties, 230
National Association of Manufacturers, 229
National Association of Realtors, 237
National Audubon Society, 229
national authority, long-term expansion of, 72
National citizenship, 72
National Conference of State Legislators, 57
National Conservative Political Action Committee (NCPAC), 182, 237
national debt, 217, 411, 412, 415
national defense, politics of, 460–461
National Economic Council (NEC), 324–325
National Education Association (NEA), 226, 443, 486
national election, 310
National Election Studies (NES) survey, 268
National Farmers Organization, 226
National Farmers Union, 226
National Gazette, 249
National Governors Conference, 230
National Grange, 226, 227
National Hurricane Service, 340
national identity, 4
National Industry Recovery Act (NIRA), 71
National Institutes of Health (NIH), 351
National Labor Relations Act of 1935, 71, 408
national leaders, methods of choosing, 47
National League of Cities, 230
National Organization for Women (NOW), 222, 230
National Park Service, 403
national parties
    conventions, 315, 317
    money and, 209–211
    organizations, 208–211, 217
    structure of, 208–209
National Performance Review (NPR), 339
national powers, 60
national pride index, *155*
National Public Radio (NPR), 228, 255, 256, 265, 360
National Railroad Passenger Corporation (Amtrak), 344
National Republican Congressional Committee (NRCC), 209
National Republican Senatorial Committee (NRSC), 209, 216
National Rifle Association (NRA), 18, 222, 229, 236
National Security Agency (NSA), 45, 112, 258, 450
national security bureaucracy, 453
National Security Council (NSC), 323
national security policy, economic dimension of, 461–468
    assisting developing nations, 467–468

    maintaining access to oil and other natural resources, 466
    promotion of global trade, 463–466
national security policy, military dimension of
    military power, uses, and capabilities, 457–459
    politics of national defense, 460–461
National Taxpayers Union, 493
"a nation of joiners," 224
Native Americans, 124–126
    activism, 125
    gaming casinos on reservation land, 126
    governments, 29
    languages, 125, 126
Nativists, 13
natural monopolies, 397
natural (or inalienable) rights, 15
natural resources, 403, 461–462, 466
    taxes on extraction of, 493
Navajo, 125
Nazi Germany, 16, 17, 395
NBC, 254, 262
NBC News, 254, 257
Near, Jay, 91
Near v. Minnesota, 91, 386
Nebraska Unicameral Legislature, 480
"necessary and proper" clause, 63, 64, 66, 80
negative campaigning, 213
negative government, 429
negative television ads, 213
Nelson, Gaylord, 404
Neustadt, Richard, 41, 329, 330
neutral competence, 347
New Deal, 70, 71, 154, 159, 200, 311, 313, 401, 402, 420
"new federalism," 76
New Jersey Plan, 33
"new" media, 249, 270, 271, 320
New Orleans residents, and Hurricane Katrina, 14
news
    attention to, 267–269
    audience, 249
    dramatic, 248
    Internet, 251, 266, 268–269
    politics of, 252–266
    round-the-clock, 267
    shrinking audience for, 267–268
    timely, 248
    widening age gap in consumption, 268
news magazines, 248
news media
    agenda setting, 252–255
    attracting an audience, 255–256
    common-carrier function, 260–261, 271
    focus on political leaders in Washington, 260
    focus on political strategy and infighting, 261
    functions, 248–249
    as gatekeepers, 252
    historical development, 249–252
    need for novelty, 255
    norm of neutrality, 253, 260
    objective-journalism era, 250
    partisan function, 261–267
    refracted version of reality, 248

news media (*continued*)
    and rise of "new" news, 251
    role in American political system, 248
    sensationalism, 250
    signaling function, 252–256
    tilt national policy leadership toward the president, 297
    watchdog function, 256–260
    See also broadcast news; cable television; newspapers; television news
"new social regulation," 402
newspapers, 248, 251, 262, 267, 268
newsprint, 249
Newsweek, 258
New York City media market, 214
New York Journal, 249, 250
New York legislature, senate chamber, 480
New York Sun, 249
New York Times, 250, 254, 258, 259
New York Times Co. v. Sullivan, 93
New York Times Co. v. United States, 90
nytimes.com 266
New York World, 249
NIMBY ("Not In My Back Yard"), 498
9/11 Commission, 359
Nixon, Richard M., 315
    and Congress, 332
    "new federalism," 76
    1972 reelection campaign, 210
    resignation, 330
    televised debates with Kennedy, 320
    and Vietnam War, 307, 451
    and Watergate cover-up, 27, 196–197, 258
    withholding of funds from programs he disliked, 331
No Child Left Behind (NCLB) Act, 57–58, 443–444
Noelle-Neumann, Elisabeth: *The Spiral of Silence,* 156
nominating campaigns, 315–316
nomination, 205
nondiscriminatory hiring practices, 409
"nonopinions," 152
nonviolent protest, 127
nonvoting, more prevalent in United States than in other democracies, 174
normative theory, 23
North American Free Trade Agreement (NAFTA), 232, 464, 469
North Atlantic Treaty Organization (NATO), 450, 452, 460
Northern Ireland, 162
northern spotted owl, 404
North Korea, 17, 457
North-South Compromise, 34–35
not-for-profit political groups, 210–211
nuclear arms race, 461
nuclear conflict, 457
nuclear power, 16, 407
"nuclear triad," 458
nuclear weapons, 451, 457
NYPIRG (New York), 229

O

Obama, Barack, 3, 4, 120, 260
    and "battleground" states, 318, 319

debates with McCain, 320
2008 Democratic nominee, 191
health care insurance plan, 444
Internet fund-raising, 183, 228, 266
and NAFTA, 465
2008 nominating campaign, 153, 171, 211, 255, 270
opposition to Bush tax cuts, 438
position on U.S. military presence in Iraq, 328, 456
2008 presidential campaign, 165, 197, 198
quick rise from obscurity, 215–216
refusal of federal campaign funding, 317, 321
running mate, 317, 323
Senate race in Illinois, 211
as "the candidate of change," 213
victory in Iowa, 316
and Wall Street regulation, 401
website, 215
obesity, as a public problem, 394–395
objective journalism, 253, 256, 257, 262, 271
objective press, 248
O'Brien, Conan, 247
obscenity, 93–95
Ochs, Adolph, 250
O'Connor, Sandra Day, 78, 101, 122, 140, 377–378, 383, 384
Office of Faith-Based and Community Initiatives, 97
Office of Legislative Affairs, 324
Office of Management and Budget (OMB), 323, 348, 356, 357, 414–415
    Executive Branch Management Scorecard, 354
Office of Personnel Management, 345
Office of the Attorney General, 343
Office of the Counsel to the President, 324
Office of the Press Secretary, 324
oil, maintaining access to, 466
oil reserves, depletion of, 466
Olbermann, Keith, 264
older Americans, 130–131
Old Executive Office Building, 355
Old Senate Chamber, 50
Oleszek, Walter, 275, 303
oligarchy, 15
Olson, Mancur, 225, 228
Olson, Theodore, 111
Oneida, 29
O'Neill, Thomas P. "Tip," 297
"Open Door" policy, 312
open party caucuses, 315, 335
open primaries, 205
"open rule," 294
open-seat races, 279, 284
opinionated journalism, 248
opinion (of a court), 369
Oregon
    assisted-suicide law, 473
    Death with Dignity Act, 474
O'Reilly, Bill, 251, 264
organizational theory, 23
Organization for Economic Cooperation and Development (OECD), 18
organized labor, 225–226, 401
originalism theory, 387–388

original jurisdiction, 367
Osborne, David, 360
Oscar the Grouch, 352
"the other America," 428
outputs, 22, 23, 398
outside lobbying, 231, 235–239, 243
outsourcing, 361
Oval Office, 314
oversight function, of Congress, 301–302
oversight hearings, 362

P

packaging, 213
Page, Benjamin, 19–20
Pahlavi, Mohammad Reza, 466
Paine, Thomas, 172, 266
Palestinians, receipt of U.S. foreign aid, 468
Palin, Sarah, 122, 191, 216, 317
pamphleteers, 265–266
Panetti v. Quarterman, 109
Parents v. Seattle School District, 365
parishes, 487
parliamentary system, 42, 326
Parrott, Sharon, 425
Partial-Birth Abortion Ban Act, 101
partisan neutrality, as journalism norm, 253
partisan press, 248, 249, 262–263
partisanship, 162, 167
    in Congress, 303
    and fiscal policy, 413–414
    influence on president's relationship with Congress, 301
    and issue opinions, 163
    and judicial appointments, 376–377, 389
    media and, 270, 271
    and tax policy, 414
partisan talk shows, 251, 263–265
party bosses, 315
party caucuses, 277, 285, 286, 295, 303, 315
party-centered campaigns, 217
party-centered politics, 191–192
party-centered television ads, 209
party coalitions, 201–202
party competition, and majority rule, 192–199
party discipline, 295, 297
party identification, 162–163, 196–197
party leaders, 285, 286–288, 303
party loyalties, in the states, 164
party machines, 51, 175, 205, 207
party organizations, 204–211
    local, 207
    national, 208–211
    state, 208
    structure and role of, 206–211
    weakening of, 205–206
party realignment, 194–195
party systems, 199
Paterson, William, 33
Patrick, Duval, 153
patronage system, 205–206, 346–347, 349, 350, 361
Paul, Ron, 322
Paulson, Henry, 419
Pearl Harbor, Japanese attack on, 110, 160
peers, as socializing agents, 156
Pell Grants, 443

Pelosi, Nancy, 201, 285, 300, 407
Pendleton Act, 347
Pentagon, 9, 453, 469
Pentagon Papers, 90, 258, 332
People for the American Way, 237
People's Republic of China, 451
    demand for oil, 407
    global trade, 463
    key to future of U.S. dollar as dominant
        currency of international trade, 466
    military spending, 457
perestroika, 451
Perot, Ross, 203, 317
Persian Gulf War, 251, 469
Peterson, Peter, 217
Pew Research Center, 153, 268
Pfiffner, James, 327
Philadelphia, 29
Phillips, Wendell, 172
"photo-ops," 212
physician-assisted suicide, 99, 473
"plain meaning rule," 380
Plame, Valerie, 259
Planned Parenthood v. Casey, 101
plea bargains, 482
Pledge of Allegiance, 156
Plessy, Homer Adolph, 68
Plessy v. Ferguson, 68–69, 119
pluralism, 4, 19, 20, 240
pluralist rule, 4
pluralist theory, 222, 239, 302
plurality opinion, 370
plurality voting, 199
pocket veto, 295
Pointer v. Texas, 103
police practices, 107–110
policy analyst, 396
policy evaluation, 397
policy experts, 324–325
policy formation, 395–396
policy implementation, 345, 396–397
political action committees (PACs), 182, 223,
        237, 238, 239, 243, 278–279, 303
political activism, 171, 186, 188
political and economic spheres, separation
        of, 23
political campaigns. *See* campaigns
political center, 200
political conflict, two primary sources of, 12
political culture, 4–5, 16
political economy, 23
political institutions, 22, 23
political interest groups, 243
political leaders and institutions, as social-
        izing agents, 157
political opinions, 148, 252
political participation, 171
    conventional forms of other than voting,
        181–186
    and the potential for influence, 186–191
    related to economic status in U.S., 188
    unconventional activism, 184
political parties, 206
    competition, 192–199
    defined, 191
    formal organization, 207
    graphic history of America's major
        parties, 193

grassroots parties, 194
loose associations of national, state, and
        local organizations, 207
    minor (third) parties, 202–204
    national parties, 208–211
    party machines, 51, 175, 205, 207
    party organizations, 204–211
    single-issue parties, 203
    and the vote, 197–198
political perceptions, derived from
        media, 252
political power, 18–22
political psychology, 23
political science, 23
political socialization, 148, 154–166
political sociology, 23
political systems, 22–23
politics
    of attack, 213
    candidate-centered, 192
    class bias in, 186
    competition for power among many
        interests, 21
    defined, 12
    major patterns, 4
    party-centered, 191–192
    as resolution of conflict, 12–22
    rules of, 14, 15–18
Polk, James K., 295
polls, 212
poll taxes, 136, 172, 178, 483
pollution control, 489
popular consent, 38
popular election, 52
popular government, 28, 52
popular referendum, 50, 51
popular sovereignty, 15, 52, 240
population, in a public opinion poll,
        150, 151
populist, 159
Populist Party, 204
pork-barrel projects, 275, 278, 303
positive government, 430
Postman, Neil, 256
"the Pottery Barn rule," 455
poverty, 161, 445
    among minority-group members, 428
    characteristics of the poor, 427–428
    children in, 428, 429
    "invisibility in America," 428
    percentage of families living in, by
        family composition and race/
        ethnicity, 428
    result of circumstances rather than
        choice, 428–429
    single-parent, female-headed families
        im, 428
poverty line, 427–428, 445
Powell, Colin, 348, 455
power, 4, 24
    defined, 18
    of ideals, 8
    theories of, 19–22
power-driven presses, 249
prayer in public school, 96
precedent, 366, 368, 379, 380, 381, 386
preemptive war doctrine, 454, 469
preferential treatment, 138, 139

presidency
    foundations of modern, 309–313
    not an inherently powerful office, 308
    staffing, 323–326
    strategic, 327
president
    access to the media, 333–334
    administrative authority, 310
    appointive capacity, 310
    assertion of claim to national leader-
        ship, 311
    benefiting from partisan support in
        Congress, 330
    better suited than Congress to provide
        leadership on major national
        issues, 297
    conditional power, 308, 335
    constitutional authority for roles, 309
    domestic policy leadership, 313
    executive power, 310
    foreign policy leadership, 312
    "going public," 334
    gradually became principal architect of
        U.S. foreign policy, 309
    "Hundred Days," 328
    influence on judicial systems, 382–383
    legislative authority, 310
    orders for war, 309
    path to White House, 321–322
    public support, 332–335
    ranking of America's, 321
    relations with Congress, 329–332
    requirements, 321
    shares legislative effort with Congress,
        296
    singular head of an independent branch
        of government, 326
    source of contention, 36
    variable influence on national policy, 308
"presidential agencies," 329
presidential appointees, 323–325, 346
presidential approval ratings, 332
presidential campaigns, 308
    federal funding of general election
        campaigns, 321, 335
    media and money, 320–321
    strategy, 318–319
    televised debates, 320
presidential commissions, 344, 345
presidential elections
    vote of selected demographic groups, 202
    voter turnout, 173, 176
presidential government, illusion of, 334–335
presidential leadership
    and Congress, 331, 335
    factors in, 326–335
    and force of circumstance, 327
    and nature of the issue, 328
    need for activist government, 311
    and stage of president's term, 327–328
presidential/parliamentary system, 326
presidential primary, 315
presidential selection, 48, 313–322, 335
    campaign for election, 317–322
    debates, 320
    four systems of, 314
    national party conventions, 315, 317
    primary elections, 315–317

presidential system, 326
presidential veto, 329
president's cabinet, 325
President's Commission to Strengthen
        Social Security, 344
press freedom. *See* news media
price fixing, 398–399
primary election (direct primary), 12, 28,
        50, 52, 177, 205, 217, 315–319
prime minister, 326
Primetime Live, 117
print media, 250
Printz v. United States, 77
Prior, Markus: *Post-Broadcast Democracy*, 270
prior restraint, 90
prison guards, 497
prison reform, 385
private (individual) good, 227
private law, 379
private property rights, 17
private retirement accounts, 222
probability sampling, 150
"probable cause," 85, 105, 106
probate courts, 481
problem recognition, 395
procedural due process, 102, 105
procedural law, 379
procedural rights, selective incorporation
        of, 103
professional associations, 243
professional groups, 227
profit motive, 399
Progressive Era, 49–52, 257, 401, 479, 488
Progressive Party, 203
Progressive reforms, 402, 482
Progressive Republicans, 204
Progressives, 205, 238, 315, 347, 483
progressive tax, 492
Prohibition Party, 203
property, 30
property tax, 494
proportional representation systems, 199,
        200
prospective voting, 198
protectionism, 464, 465
protest activity, 16, 87, 127, 185–186, 188
Protestant sects, 7
public assembly, regulation of time, place,
        and conditions of, 93
public assistance programs, 427, 431,
        433–436, 445
    Food Stamps program, 435
    Medicaid, 435–436
    subsidized housing, 435
    Supplemental Security Income (SSI), 434
    Temporary Assistance for Needy
        Families (TANF), 76–77,
        434–435, 496
public broadcasting, 256
public education, 440–441
    class segregation, 441
    disparity in spending among districts,
        495
    largest share of state and local
        spending, 495
    public school issues, 96, 441–442
    racial segregation, 119–120, 140–142,
        143, 441, 442

school bond issues, 491
school choice, 442, 443
school districts, 489, 500
school quality issues, 12, 495–496
and school vouchers, 97, 442
public health programs, 496
public hospitals, 496
public-interest groups, 228–229
Public Interest Research Groups (PIRGs),
        229
public law, 379
public opinion
    and approval of president's perform-
        ance, 333
    contradictory elements, 150, 158
    defined, 148, 167
    and free trade, 465
    influence on federal power, 79–80
    influence on government, 148, 164–166
    influence on judicial decisions, 382
    and Iraq War, 147, 186
    and lack of information, 148–149
    measurement of, 150–154
    nature of, 148–149
    on obligations of citizens, 173
    as obstacle to higher levels of foreign
        aid, 467–468
    and taxing and spending, 149
    weak support for public assistance
        programs, 433, 439, 445
public opinion polls, 150–151, 166, 167
    effects of question wording, 153
    problems with, 151–154
    role in specific policy decisions, 152
public policy process, 18
    policy formation, 395–396
    policy implementation, 396–397
    problem recognition, 394–397
public safety, 77, 497
public support, for president, 332–335
public utilities commissioner, 479
Publius, 37
Pueblo, 125
Pulitzer, Joseph, 249
Puritans, 157
Putnam, Robert, 184, 224

Q

Quakers, 40
quotas, 139

R

race and ethnicity, and political opinions,
        161
racial discrimination, 9, 69, 117, 120, 129,
        142, 358
racial equality, 161
racial profiling, 107, 111, 112
racial segregation, 9, 12, 69
    government-imposed, 395
    in public schools, 119–120, 140–142, 143,
        441, 442
racism, 119
radio broadcasting, 250

radio news, 267
radio talk shows, 251, 271
"rally 'round the flag" reaction, 333
random drug testing, 105
random selection, 150–151
rapid response, 214
Ratcliffe, Caroline, 428
Rather, Dan, 266
rational choice theory, 23
Reagan, Ronald, 3, 165, 200, 355
    appointment of first woman to Supreme
        Court, 122
    assessment of presidency, 308
    and challenges to affirmative action,
        382
    and federal air traffic controllers, 345
    "the Great Communicator," 334
    and Iran-Contra affair, 258
    "new federalism," 76
    reduction of taxes on wealthy, 437
    and Soviet Union, 451
    supply-side theory, 411–412
    taxing and spending changes, 327
    use of executive power, 310
RealNetworks, 282
Real Time with Bill Maher, 265
reapportionment, 280
reasonable-basis test, 134
recall election, 50, 482
Reconstruction, 68
recycling, 402
redistricting, 137, 279–280, 280
redlining, 136
"red states," 161
referendum, 50, 51, 482
reform (minor) party, 203
*Regents of the University of California v.
        Bakke*, 140
region, and political opinions, 161
regressive tax, 492
regulation, of privately owned businesses,
        398
regulatory agencies, 343–344
regulatory policy, 79, 420
    main objectives of, 398
    politics of, 401–402
Rehnquist, William, 384
Reid, Harry, 221
Reinventing Government (Osborne and
        Gaebler), 360–361
religion
    and political opinions, 160
    as socializing force, 157
religious freedom, 7, 8, 95–99
religious right, 160
religious symbolism, in public buildings,
        96
Remington, Frederic, 250
rent vouchers, 435, 438
reporters, and revealing of sources, 259
representation function, of Congress,
        299–301
representative democracy, 47
representative government, 23, 46
representatives
    as delegates, 49
    as trustees, 49
republic, 47

Republican coalition
  mainly white middle-class Americans, 202
  supportive of traditional values, 202
Republican-Democratic party system, 195
Republican National Committee (RNC), 208
Republican Party, 37, 165, 179, 194
  conservative wing, 287
  decline of moderate wing, 196
  devolution, 76
  dominance in South, 196
  fiscal policy, 413
  formation of, 193
  probusiness policies, 163
  tax policy, 163, 414
  traditional ideas, 430
Republican revolution, 76–77
Republicans and Democrats, differing
    perspectives on national issues, 300–301
Republic National Committee (RNC), 209
reservations, Native American, U.S. policy
    toward, 125
Reserve and National Guard, 458
reserved powers, 64
reserve rate, 418
retrospective voting, 198
reverse discrimination, 117
Revolutionary War, 29, 310
Revolution of 1776, 482
"Revolution of 1800," 49
Rhode Island, 36, 46
Rice, Condoleezza, 265, 359
riders, 294
Rifkin, Joel, 252–253
Rigby, Paul, 174
right of privacy, 99–102, 113
  abortion rights, 100–101
  sexual relations among consenting
      adults, 101–102
rights of the accused, 102–110
right to a fair trial, 43
right to bear arms, 98–99
right-to-life groups, 203, 229, 233
Riker, William, 69
Ring v. Arizona, 109
Rios, Maria Len, 269
risk assessment, 400
Roberts, John, 141, 365–366, 375, 376
Roberts, Owen, 71
Robertson, Pat, 251
Robinson, Michael, 262
Robinson v. California, 103
Rockefeller, John D., 257
Rock the Vote, 269
Roe v. Wade, 100–101
roll-call votes, 287, 288
Roman Catholicism, 7, 160
Romer v. Evans, 131
Roosevelt, Franklin D., 3, 165, 200, 307
  appointment of Douglas to Supreme
      Court, 375
  fireside chats, 160
  forced relocation of Japanese Americans, 110
  on "freedom from want," 12
  government spending and job programs, 409

New Deal, 70, 71, 79, 154, 313, 327, 430
  stewardship theory, 311
  and stronger role for government, 76
  third term, 310
  unprecedented business regulation and
      social welfare, 195
Roosevelt, Theodore, 160, 203, 204, 430
  "bully pulpit," 334
  "Open Door" policy, 312
  stewardship theory, 311
Rosenberg, Chuck, 259
Rossiter, Clinton, 4, 200
Rostker v. Goldberg, 135
rotary press, 249
Roth v. United States, 94
round-the-clock news, 267
Rousseau, Jean-Jacques, 7, 15
Rozell, Mark, 263
RPAC (National Association of
    Realtors), 237
Rubin, Michael, 495
Rudman, Warren, 210
"rugged individualism," 6
rule by law, 42
rulemaking, 346
rules
  formalized, 340, 341, 342, 361
  of politics, 14, 15–18
Rumsfeld, Donald, 258, 334
rural residents, and poverty, 428
Russia, 457, 458
Rutledge, John, 35

S

safe incumbency, and representation, 283
sales tax, 492
same-sex couples, 143
  civil unions, 132, 133
  marriage, 132
sample, in a public opinion poll, 150, 151
sampling error, 151
Sampson, Leon, 441
Santorum, Rick, 281
Saudi Arabia, 466
Scalia, Antonin, 95, 99, 112, 210, 375, 378,
    383, 384, 388
Scandinavian countries, 398
scarcity, 12
Schattschneider, E. E., 23, 191, 221, 242,
    395
Schecter v. United States, 71
Schenck v. United States, 88, 387
Schlesinger, Arthur Jr., 321
Schlesinger, Arthur Sr., 321
school board members, 491
school integration, 140–142, 442
school lunch programs, 75
schools. See public education
school vouchers, 97, 442
Schwarzenegger, Arnold, 50, 477, 482
scientific polls, 150–151
Scigliano, Robert, 376
"scope of conflict," 395
Scotland, 61
Scott, Dred, 67
The Sea Around Us (Carson), 403

search-and-seizure protection, 85, 102, 103,
    104–105, 114
Second Bank of the United States, 65
second-strike capability, 458
Second Treatise on Civil Government
    (Locke), 15
secretary of defense, 450
secretary of state, 325, 449
Securities and Exchange Act of 1934, 401
Securities and Exchange Commission
    (SEC), 343
Sedition Act of 1798, 88
Segal, Jeffrey, 383
select committees, 289
selective incorporation, 91, 113
self-government, 4, 6, 7–8, 12, 24, 28, 38,
    46–51, 52, 171, 490
self-reliance, 6, 490
Senate, 276
  age and citizenship requirements, 283
  apportioned strictly by geography, 287
  as federal institution, 61
  leadership, 286
  nicknamed the "Millionaires" Club," 50
  number of Democrats and Republicans
      in, 1999-2010, 285
  senatorial courtesy, 376
  standing committees, 288
  tradition of unlimited debate, 286
  wealthy challengers, 282
Senate Agriculture Committee, 290, 299, 301
Senate Appropriations Committee, 357, 416
Senate Foreign Relations Committee, 291
Senate Interior Committee, 299
Senate Judiciary Committee, 28, 375
Senate majority leader, 277, 286, 294, 303
Senate majority whip, 286
Senate minority leader, 286
Senate minority whip, 286
Senate president pro tempore, 286
Senate Select Committee on Intelligence, 289
senators
  direct election of, 50, 53
  selection of in original Constitution, 47–48
Seneca, 29
senior-citizen groups, 221
seniority, 291
separation of powers, 40–41, 42, 53, 224
September 11, 2001 attacks, 468
  and American attitudes about Middle
      Eastern immigration, 9
  and American attitudes toward Arab
      Americans, 113
  and American opinions about military
      retaliation, 157, 161
  Bush response to, 312
  and Bush's approval ratings, 307
  and 9/11 commission, 359
  and expansion of federal authority, 77, 111
  and news media, 257–258
  and opportunities for Bush, 201
  police and firefighter roles, 487, 497
  and problem recognition, 395
  and reorganization of security
      agencies, 354
  and U.S. invasion of Iraq, 149
  and "war on terrorism," 453
  and warrantless wiretapping, 8, 45

Sepuel, Ada, 119
Serbs, 452
Service Employees International, 226
service relationship, 211
service strategy, 278, 303
Sesame Street, 352
The 700 Club, 251
severance taxes, 493
sexual harassment, 122
Shapiro, Robert, 19–20, 165
shared executive powers, 43
shared judicial powers, 43
shared legislative powers, 42
Shays, Daniel, 32
Shays's Rebellion, 32–33
Sheet Metal Workers, 225
Sherman Anti-Trust Act, 69, 257
Shiites, 457
"shrinking sound bite," 260
Sierra Club, 229, 241, 402
signaling function, 248, 252–256
signing statements, 331–332
Silent Spring (Carson), 402–403
Sinclair, Upton, 257
single-issue interest groups, 203, 229, 230
single-issue parties, 203
single-issue politics, 222
single-member-district system of election, 199–200, 217
singular authority, 310
"sin tax," 492
"the size factor," 225
Skokie, Illinois, 92
slander, 93
slaveholders, 7
slavery, 7, 9, 34, 35, 66, 118
slave trade, 34
small-state plan, 33
Smith, Adam, 397–398, 398
Smith, Howard, 291
"smog," 405
social capital, 184
social conservatives, 158, 159
Social Contract (Rousseau), 15
social contract theory, 14–15
social democratic parties, 177
social equality, 490
social insurance programs, 427, 436–437, 445
   Medicare, 432–433
   social security, 431–432
   unemployment insurance, 432
socialism, 17
Socialist Workers Party, 204
social liberals, 158
social (political) movements, 184–185
Social Security Act of 1935, 430, 434
Social Security Administration (SSA), 355
social security benefits, 430, 431, 437, 445
social security program, 80, 221, 411, 415, 431–432, 432
social security taxes, 437
social welfare, 195, 445
   culture, welfare, and income, 436–438
   politics and policies of, 72, 429–439
   public assistance programs, 433–436
   social insurance programs, 431–433
sodomy laws, 102
soft money, 209–210
solicitor general, 368

solid-waste management districts, 490
Souter, David, 97, 177, 375
South
   dominance of Republican Party in, 196
   lower voter turnout rate than other regions, 483
   states'-rights sentiment in, 225
South Carolina, "doctrine of nullification," 66
sovereignty, 59
Soviet Union
   collapse of, 452
   economic model, 398
   invasion of Afghanistan, 451
   totalitarianism, 17
   and U.S. containment policy, 450, 469
Spaeth, Harold, 383
Spanish-American War, 249
Speaker of the House, 277, 285–286, 303
Spears, Britney, 255
special districts, 489–490, 500
special-interest groups, 216, 242
special U.S. courts, 372
Specter, Arlen, 332
speedy trial, right to, 102, 104
Spellings, Margaret, 57
Spitzer, Eliot, 247, 248, 479
split-ticket voting, 198
spoils system, 347, 360, 361
sports franchises, 492
Stalin, Josef, 17
Stamp Act, 30
stamp tax, 30
Standard Oil of New Jersey, 257
standing committees, 288, 289, 303
Stanton, Elizabeth Cady, 121, 179
stare decisis, 380
"Star-Spangled Banner," 6
state agriculture commissioner, 479
state and local finance, 491–494
state and local public policy patterns, 494–499
   civil rights and liberties, 498–499
   education, 495–496
   environment, 497–498
   health care, 496
   highways, 496–497
   Homeland Security, 497
   police and prisons, 497
   welfare assistance, 495
state attorney general, 478, 479
state central committees, 208
state constitutional conventions, 476
state constitutions
   amendments to, 482
   bill of rights, 475–477
   checks and balances, 475
   ease of amendment, 476
   length of, 475–476
state courts, 372–374, 389, 481–482
   appellate courts, 481
   district courts, 481
   family courts, 481
   justice of the peace courts, 481
   magistrate courts, 481
   probate courts, 481
   quality of justice in, 482
   supreme court, 481
   trial courts, 481
state education commissioner, 479
state elections, 212, 482, 500

state executive branch, 477–479
state general assembly, 479
state governments, 59
   discretion, 68
   election of executive officials, 478–479
   employees of, 474
   multiple-executive system, 479
   powers, 60
   size of bureaucracies, 341
   sources of revenue, 492–493
   spending priorities of, 494
state governments, structure of, 475
   branches of government, 477–482
   citizen politics, 482–485
   courts, 481–481
   legislature, 479–481
   separation of powers, 475
   state constitutions, 475–477
state governors
   campaigns, 477
   initiation of state budget, 477
   power to veto legislative acts, 477–478
   and separation of powers, 478
   two-term limit on most, 477
state house of representatives, 479
state interest-group systems, 484–485
state judges, 372–373, 481–482
state legislators, 47, 480, 481
state legislatures, 479–481
   African American and Hispanic American representation in, 121
   women in, 284
state lotteries, 493
state militias, 98
State of the Nation (Watts and Free), 18
state parks, 498
state party leaders, 315
state party organizations, 208, 217, 484
state personal income tax, 492
state police forces, 497
state power, in a federal system, 476
state primaries, 335
state religion, 96
state secretary of state, 479
state senates, 479
states' rights, 8, 225
states'-rights advocates, 475
States' Rights Party, 204
state supreme courts, 481
state treasurer, 479
state welfare assistance, 496
statewide petition drives, 483
Statue of Liberty, 6
statutory law, 366, 379, 380, 381
Steffens, Lincoln, 257
Stenberg v. Carhart, 101
Stevens, John Paul, 78, 85, 97, 99, 177, 366, 375, 384, 385
stewardship theory, 311
Stewart, Jon, 265
Stone, Harlan Eiske, 87
Strategic Arms Limitation Talks (SALT), 451
strategic presidency, 327
strict-scrutiny test, 134
strong mayor-council system, of municipal government, 475, 488, 500
subcommittees, 288, 291, 303
subjective journalism, 250
subprime mortgage crisis, 225, 400, 401, 419

subsidized housing, 435
Suez Canal, 461
suffrage, 10, 172, 179, 483
Sundquist, James, 299
Sunnis, 457
Sun Oil Company Political Action
    Committee (Sunpac), 237
sunset laws, 358, 362
Superfund program, 405
superintendent of schools, 489
Supplemental Security Income (SSI), 434
supply-side economics, 411–412, 439
supremacy clause, 63, 64, 65, 473
Supreme Court, 366, 389
    approach to religious controversies, 96
    authority, 44
    and constitutional basis for unrestricted
        economic power, 69–70
    decisions and opinions, 369–370
    and forced busing, 365–366
    Gonzales v. Oregon, 473–474
    granting of authority to Congress to
        enact policies affecting state and
        local governments, 77
    justices, 375, 377
    and obscenity, 95
    protections for the accused, 103
    rejection of indefinite incarceration of
        U.S. citizens charged with ter-
        rorism, 383
    Republican-appointed conservatives, 77
    requirement for "adequate" education
        versus "equal" education, 443, 495
    requirement that lower federal courts
        follow Supreme Court decisions,
        370–371
    ruling on executive agreements, 309
    rulings tailored to gain public support
        or reduce public resistance, 382
    selection of and decisions on cases,
        367–369
    "separate but equal" ruling, 68
    setting of legal precedent, 368
    silent partner of state and local courts, 481
    striking down of laws and local ordi-
        nances, 386
    and symbolic speech, 89
Supreme Court building, 368
Supreme Court nominees, 375
Supreme Court of Texas, 374
suspect classifications, 134, 135
Swann v. Charlotte-Mecklenburg County
    Board of Education, 141
Sweden, 17, 429
Swift Boat Veterans for Truth, 211
swing voters, 215, 217
symbolic speech, 89
Syria, 455

T

Taft, William Howard, 204
Taft-Hartley Act of 1947, 345
Taliban, 157, 312, 453, 454, 456
talk shows
    cable television, 271
    conservative, 263–265
    radio, 251, 271

Tancredo, Tom, 13
Taney, Roger, 66, 67, 377
Tanzania, 468
Tarbell, Ida, 257
tariffs, 34
Tax Division, 342
taxes
    capital-gains tax, 412, 438
    excise tax, 492
    local taxes, 494
    sales tax, 492
    severance taxes, 493
    social security taxes, 437
    state personal income tax, 492
tax rates
    effective, 437
    marginal, 438
    in the U.S. compared to Canada and
        Europe, 18
tax rebates, 411, 419
tax revenues, federal, state, and local shares
    of, 74
Taylor, Zachary, 322
Teamsters, 225
Tech-Crunch, 266
Telecommunications Act of 1996, 345–346
telegraph, 249
telephone-based technical services, 464
telephone surveys, 151–152
televised presidency, 333–334
television
    and Fairness Doctrine, 250
    in modern political campaigns, 209, 213,
        214–215, 320
television news, 260, 267. *See also* broadcast
    news; cable television; news media
temperance movement, 179
Temporary Assistance for Needy Families
    (TANF), 76–77, 434–435, 496
temporary worker program, 13
Tenet, George, 349
Tennessee Valley Authority, 398
Texas capitol building, 477
Texas Court of Criminal Appeals, 374
Texas v. Johnson, 94
TexPIRG (Texas), 229
third-party candidates, 317
Thirty Years' War, 468
Thomas, Bill, 426
Thomas, Clarence, 375, 377, 383, 384
Thomas, Norman, 339
Three-Fifths Compromise, 34–35
"three strikes and you're out" law, 108
timely news, 248
Tinsdale, Elkanah, 280
Title IX of the Education Amendment of
    1972, 122
Tocqueville, Alexis de, 3, 4, 6, 194, 224, 386
totalitarian government, 17
towns, 489
Townshend Act, 30
townships, 489
toxic waste disposal, 16, 399, 405
toxic waste emissions, 405
trade associations, 243
trade deficit, 461, 462, 464
    with China, 465–466
traditionalist subculture, 490
traditional media, 249, 262–263, 270, 271

transfer payments, 430, 445
treaties, 380
trial by jury, right of, 29, 102
trial courts, state, 481
tripolar economic power, 461
Truman, Harry S, 151, 153, 307, 311, 312,
    432–433, 450
trustees, 47
trusts, 399
Turner, Ted, 251
two-party system, 199, 200–202, 217
tyranny of the majority, 46

U

underregulation, pitfalls of, 400–401
unemployment benefits, 409, 413
unemployment insurance, 432
Unequal Democracy (Bartels), 187
"unfunded local mandate," 497
Unfunded Mandates Reform Act of 1995, 76
Uniform Code of Military Justice, 111
unilateralism, 454, 457
union lobbyists, 231
unipolar (power structure), 452
unitary system, 59, 60
unitary systems, 476
United Auto Workers (UAW), 226
United Brotherhood of Carpenters &
    Joiners, 226
United Farm Workers of America, 127
United Food and Commercial Workers
    International, 226
United Kingdom. *See* Britain
United Mine Workers, 225
United Nations, 449, 452, 461, 469
United States
    absence of a major labor or socialist
        party, 174, 181
    agricultural sector, 461
    aid to developing countries, 467
    citizens' participation rates, 224
    economic competitiveness, 462
    high level of authority granted to state
        governments, 476
    income inequality, 437
    individualistic subculture, 490
    industrial base, 461
    military spending, 457
    natural resources, 461–462
    shrinking domestic manufacturing
        sector, 463
    technology sector, 462
    trade deficit, 461, 462, 464, 465–466
    trade imbalance, 461
    in world economy, 462–463
United States v. Lopez, 77
United States v. Virginia, 135
unit rule, 318
unity, 24
University of California Regents v. Bakke, 139
University of Michigan, 140
University of Missouri, 250
University of Virginia, 8
"upper-court myth," 370, 371, 373, 389
Urban Institute, 117
urbanization, 267
U.S. Air Force, 458
U.S. ambassadors, 449

U.S. Army, 458
U.S. Capitol, 276
U.S. Capitol Building, model for the
    states, 477
U.S. Chamber of Commerce, 225
U.S. Claims Court, 372
U.S. Conference of Catholic Bishops, 132
U.S. Conference of Mayors, 230, 497
U.S. Court of Appeals for the Federal
    Circuit, 371, 372
U.S. Court of International Trade, 372
U.S. Court of Military Appeals, 372
U.S. Customs Office, 372
U.S. embassies, 449
U.S. Forest Service, 235, 403
U.S. Navy, 458
U.S. Postal Service, 344, 353
USA Patriot Act, 112, 113, 294

V

values, core American, 5–12, 155
Van Buren, Martin, 203
Van Orden v. Perry, 96
vehicle registration fees, 492–493
veterans' benefits, 299
veto, 295, 329
veto override, 295
vice presidential nominee, choice of, 317
vice president of the United States, 286,
    323–324
Vieth v. Jubelirer, 281
Vietnam war, 89, 258, 262, 451, 452, 459,
    460, 469
Villaraigosa, Antonio, 5
Vioxx, 233, 402
Virginia, 8, 37
Virginia Military Institute (VMI), 135
Virginia Plan, 33
virtual participation, in elections, 182–184
Volcker commission, 339
Volker, Paul, 419
"voodoo economics," 439
vote fraud, 177
voter contacts, in candidate-centered cam-
    paigns, 214–217
voter eligibility, 175
voter identification cards, 177, 483–484
voter participation rates, 490
voter registration, 181, 187
    laws, 176
    requirements, 175–177
voter registration drives, 207, 209, 212, 215
voter turnout, 172
    among working-class whites, 180
    among younger voters, 180
    factors in, 173–179
    lower in U.S. than in other democratic
        nations, 187
    obstacles to, 178
    party differences in, 177, 179
    in presidential elections, 173, 176
    reasons for low, 179–181
    in U.S. elections, 171
    in world's democracies, 174
voter turnout efforts, 215
Voting Rights Act of 1965, 120, 136–137,
    143, 173, 185, 465

W

Walker, Jack, 240
Wallace, George, 204, 490
Wall Street Crash of 1929, 358
Wall Street Journal, 254
War of 1812, 225
war on terrorism, 307, 312, 415, 453–454
    Bush and, 352, 359, 453
    and civil liberties, 110–113, 114, 383
War Powers Act, 332
warrantless domestic surveillance,
    45–46, 114
warrantless searches, 85
warrantless wiretaps, 8, 45, 112–113, 258,
    259, 302, 324, 382
Warren, Earl, 376
Washington, George, 3, 31, 33, 37, 40, 193,
    310, 322, 346
Washington Post, 254, 258
waste disposal, 487, 489
watchdog function, 249, 256–260
waterboarding, 359
Watergate break-in, 27, 197, 198, 209, 258,
    262, 308, 331
water pollution, 399
Water Quality Act of 1965, 399, 403
Waters, M. Dane, 238
Wattenberg, Martin, 268
Watts, William, 18, 186
weak mayor-council system, of municipal
    government, 475, 488, 500
The Wealth of Nations (Smith), 397–398
weapons of mass destruction (WMDs), 157,
    348, 349, 454, 455, 460
Weaver, James B., 204
Weber, Max, 21
websites, 215, 251, 320
Webster, Daniel, 50, 295, 323
*Webster v. Reproductive Health
    Services*, 101
Weigel, Lori, 152
welfare benefits, 76
welfare policy, 445
    as partisan issue, 427
    "reverse gravity" law, 425
welfare reform, 2002 debate in Congress,
    425–426
Welfare Reform Act of 1996, 19, 76, 77, 80,
    298–299, 425, 430, 434, 435
welfare system, 16
    administrative process, 436
    declining number of families in, 426
    inefficiency and inequity, 436–437
welfare-to-work programs, 435
West, Darrell, 214
Western Europe, and global trade, 463
West Virginia, proportion of college
    graduates, 11–12
westward expansion, 66, 125
Whigs, 194, 311
Whistle Blower Protection Act, 359
White, Theodore H., 12, 247
white flight, 141, 142
White House, 314
White House Office (WHO), 323, 324
White House press room, 334
whites

family income, 137
    and Republican Party, 202
    voter turnout among working-class,
        180
whites-only primaries, 136, 178, 483
Whren v. United States, 105
Wickard v. Filburn, 78
Wildavsky, Aaron, 328, 396
Wilder, Doug, 153
Wilderness Society, 229
Will, George, 255
Williams, Jody, 266
Williams, Roger, 7
Williams, Stanley, 89
Wilson, Woodrow, 57, 150, 195, 201, 204,
    307, 311, 312
wind-powered generators, 407
wiretapping, 112–113, 380
women
    disproportionately Democrats, 202
    job-related issues, 124
    judicial appointees by Democratic
        presidents, 377
    legal and political gains, 122
    opinions on role in marriage, 125
    representation in national
        legislatures, 123
    and right to vote, 172, 179
    struggle for equality, 120–124
    underrepresented in top federal
        jobs, 360
    in the U.S. military, 135
women's rights convention, Seneca Falls,
    New York, 121
worker safety, 402, 421
working-class whites, voter turnout
    among, 180
working conditions, 409
World Bank, 450, 467
World Economic Forum, 462
    2007–2008 global economic competitive-
        ness index, 400
World Trade Center, 9, 453, 469, 497
World Trade Organization (WHO), 450,
    464, 465, 469
World War I, 312
World War II, 312
worldwide military spending, 457
World Wildlife Fund, 222
Wounded Knee, 125
writ of ceritorari, 368
writ of habeas corpus, 39, 102
writ of mandamus, 44

Y

"yellow journalism," 249–250
Yellowstone National Park, 403, 404
Young, Don, 275

Z

Zaller, John, 445
Zelman v. Simmons-Harris, 97
Zubaydah, Abu, 359
Zuniga, Markos Moulitsas, 183